Constituencies 1885

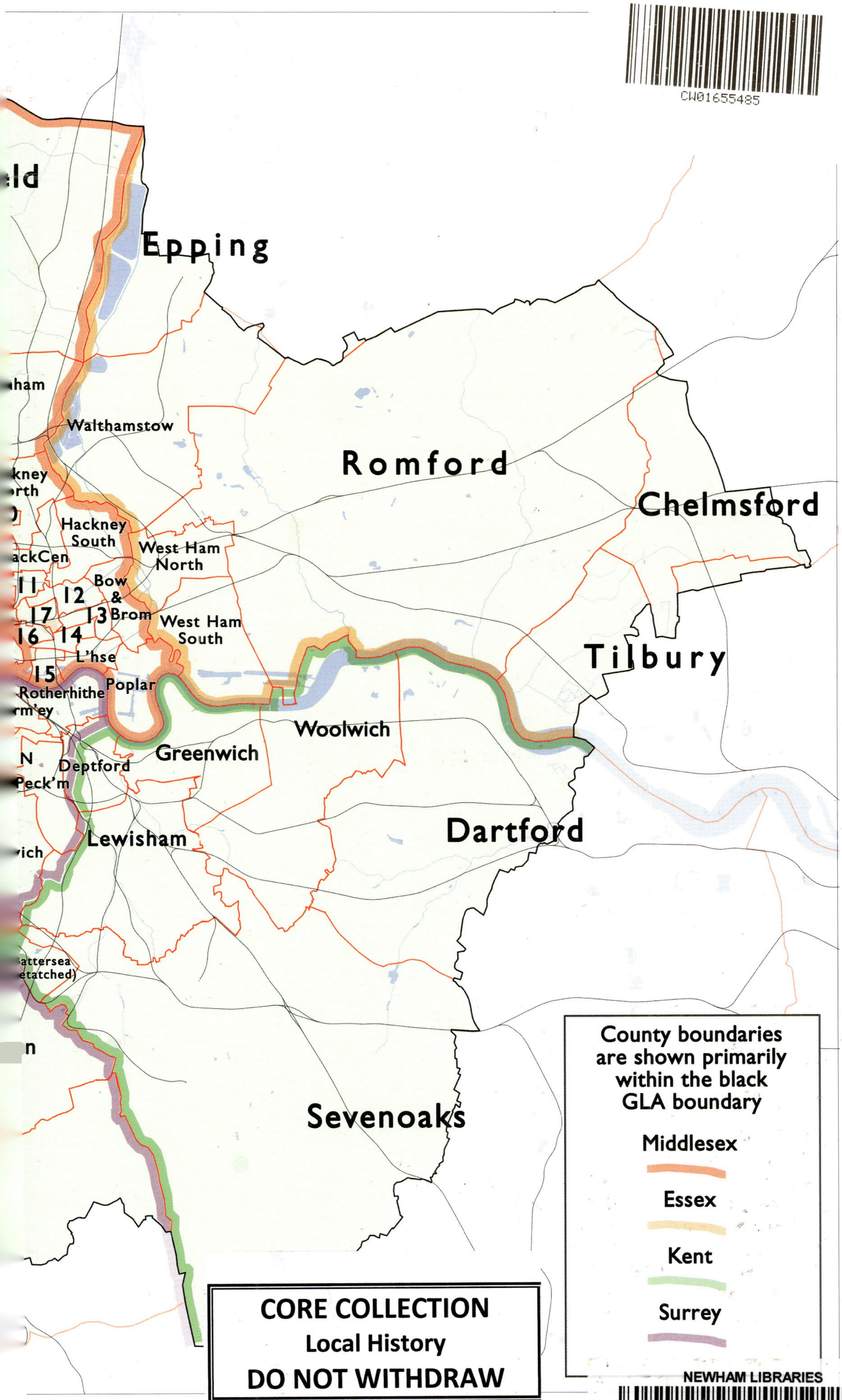

Voters' Limits

The Evolution of London's Parliamentary Constituencies

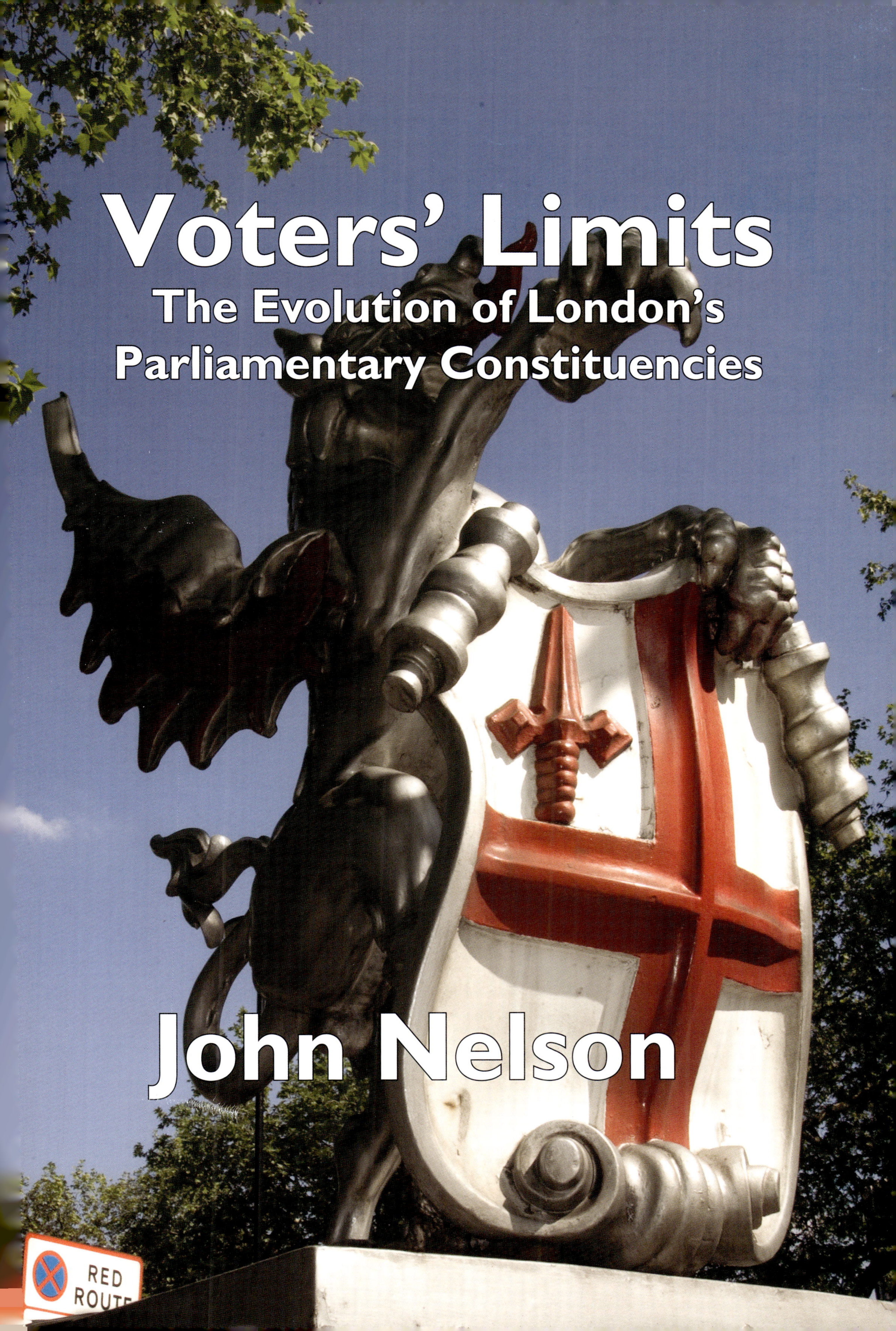

John Nelson

First Published 2015

ISBN 978-0-9571456-2-7

This book is published as a 'not for profit' project. Any surplus will be donated to **The Railway Benefit Fund** charity.

Author: John Nelson
Maps created by : Gordon Rushton
Book design by : Gordon Rushton.

Published by the **Adlestrop Press,** and an imprint of Rushton Video Rail Ltd, 15 Rycroft, MK4 1AH.

Printed by **Amadeus Press**, Cleckheaton, W. Yorkshire

Copyright

Contents

Foreword

The Parliamentarians

Frank Dobson MP

John Nelson's book is all about the boundaries of parliamentary constituencies. That is very welcome because up to now our parliamentary system has been based on a sense of place. MPs don't just represent voters. We represent the places where voters live and work, bring up families, make up local communities and look after their neighbours. My constituency of Holborn and St. Pancras has the largest population and the sixth most voters in the whole country. It ranges from Holborn and Covent Garden in the south, through King's Cross, Camden Town, Kentish Town as far as Highgate in the north. It includes places called Chalk Farm, Primrose Hill, Oak Village, Elm Village, Jockey's Fields, Hatton Garden and Saffron Hill. But don't be fooled it's really very urban, despite taking in most of Hampstead Heath and a slice of Regent's Park.

Although Holborn and St. Pancras is just one constituency the area it now covers used to be four constituencies and even in my own time as an MP it used to be two. So we have seen a lot of boundary changes. In the last but one boundary change I lost Gospel Oak Ward to Hampstead constituency represented by my good friend and world famous film star Glenda Jackson. Then in 2010 Gospel Oak came back to me. So I was canvassing there in the general election. A man came to the door and said he couldn't vote for me. When I asked him why, he gave the immortal reply "cos you haven't got two Oscars". Glenda had comprehensively outclassed me.

Most MPs believe there is something special about the place they represent. I certainly do. What an honour to represent Covent Garden where the Beggar's Opera was set or Holborn and Camden Town where Dickens lived amongst the downtrodden and the lawyers, and other villains who people his books. Great Ormond Street and the University College Hospitals represent all that's best in the NHS and I in turn try to represent them and the people who work there. The area now contains the greatest concentration of bio-medical research in Europe including my old friend John O'Keefe who has just got the Nobel Prize for Medicine. All that would have pleased Charles Darwin who lived here. John Betjeman, grew up in Highgate and Alan Bennett the greatest living Yorkshire man lives in Primrose Hill.

The Working Men's College and Birkbeck pioneered further education for people who had lost out. Bedford College and the Royal Free Hospital medical school pioneered higher education for women. Political figures as diverse as Karl Marx and Benjamin Disraeli lived here. The British Anti-Apartheid Movement was founded in my constituency. Jennie Lee who founded the Open University and her husband, Nye Bevan who founded the NHS lived here. What a place to try to represent – full of a huge variety of people who get along with one another despite their differences of race, religion, jobs, incomes, homes and interests.

So I welcome John Nelson's book with its emphasis on place, especially when the Tories wanted to push through changes in which equal numbers of electors were the only thing that mattered. They wanted anonymous agglomerations of electors – no sense of neighbourhood – no pride of place.

Sir George Young MP

The February 1974 General Election was my first and I was challenging the incumbent MP for Acton, Nigel Spearing. With a boundary change that included parts of Ealing, it became a Tory marginal rather than a Labour marginal. The background to that election was Ted Heath's question "Who runs the country?" - to which the answer was no one, as we ended up with a hung parliament.

The miners' strike and power shortages had led to a difficult winter, made more difficult by threats from the IRA to disrupt the election. (After the election was over, the police delivered a large parcel to my constituency headquarters, declaring the contents to be harmless. And so they were - 20,000 leaflets explaining why folk should vote for my Party!) I scraped home, and Nigel Spearing was returned weeks later for a by-election in Newham. We remained firm friends, united by a commitment to cycling.

Ealing Acton was an uncomfortable merger between Acton and Ealing. When the London Borough of Ealing was formed, Acton lost its Town Hall and the centre of gravity moved west from W3 to W5. There was resentment about this, and a belief that too much ratepayers money was spent in Ealing and not enough in Acton. This was followed by the loss of the Acton Gazette, absorbed into the Ealing Gazette, and the closure of the cottage hospital.

But it was a marvellous constituency to represent - multi-cultural, rich in voluntary organisations, compact and therefore easy to move around, and only seven miles from Westminster, with opportunities to look after it during the week as well as at weekends. The majority grew from three figures to five.

Boundary changes helped me win the seat, but boundary changes removed it. I survived the 1983 boundary changes, when a last minute decision gave me some good wards in Ealing, instead of a much more difficult redistribution. But in 1997 the seat was in effect abolished. It was divided into three, and each bit tacked on to seats occupied by my parliamentary neighbours. Although I was very sad at the time, it turned out to be a blessing in disguise. Had the seat survived, I would have lost in the Labour landslide on 1997; as it was I moved to North West Hampshire.

You could not find two Tory seats more different. North West Hampshire is mono-cultural, rural with a Conservative majority of 18500, with low unemployment and good housing. But Ealing Acton was a good grounding and, despite the majority, I still look after it as if I had that 808 majority in October 1974.

Preface

by the Author

Interest and absorption in a subject doesn't come in a rush. It is something that you discover about yourself, or perhaps you find out about from candid remarks from your friends. As a child of a headmaster, my tendency may not have been obligatory, but it was encouraged. I loved to read and learn of the Kings and Queens of England. This evolved to a discovery of places, their industries, the football teams, the people. Naturally, parliamentary representation came into focus with MPs and constituencies. The day after the 1959 General Election, I came down to breakfast and asked who had won. My father replied, "When Acton went Conservative, I went to bed."

This didn't answer the question, but it did indicate his party affiliation.

From that day, elections, the machinery, the struggle between partiality and fairness, and the state of our democracy, have all exercised a fascination rather than just a passing interest. I have forecasted outcomes with zeal, but generally with only moderate success. I study form, I pore over the results of by-elections, local and General Elections, and of course the stately progress of the Boundaries Commission, who's outcomes are two-edged indeed. The interest acquired the status of a hobby, and two events in my life accentuated that process. In 1995 I bought a computer and acquired the skills to use it, and shortly afterwards I entered the world of self-employment by courtesy of railway privatisation. The latter was the inspiration, the former the means, to begin the process that has matured over twenty years to become this work.

The computer enabled me to organise a database and to connect it with a narrative. Retirement from the responsibility of full-time work allowed me to indulge in its creation. It took two years of pleasurable writing to amass and enter every election result in every Parliamentary constituency that had existed since 1832. The way forward for this burgeoning interest became clear. I decided to justify the time I was spending on my hobby by writing a history of Parliamentary constituencies in Britain. These are our imaginings - of course a task like that would stretch beyond a sustainable lifetime. Yet it was such a fascinating thought that I opted to begin with a history of London's constituencies, to see if this could be published as a practical outcome.

The amount of data are so vast that diligence alone will not suffice, and forensic analysis must be tamed by compromise or nothing will emerge in any reasonable timescale. Every effort has been made to make the data both accurate, and consistent, but the important need for readability means that facts are not always catalogued as an academic might prefer. So this book does not assume the rigour of an academic work, although it might be read as one.

It may be the prism through which I see things as a railwayman – and one who has been responsible for the whole of its London network for a period in my life – but there is a striking interaction that exists between the transport system and much of the substance of the changes that are described in this book. Railways, surface and underground, buses, trolley buses, tram systems, new bridges, and new roads, have all sustained cities by enabling populations to spread and migrate. Their physical presence has often been such that they have themselves also become key features of constituency boundaries. It is therefore an additional pleasure that "transportation" emerges as having an almost symbiotic relationship with the development of London's constituencies; so as a transport professional I have justifiably woven this into the story.

When examining the fabric and context of the story one cannot fail to be struck by the continuity of administrative boundaries as they have affected the creation of local government units, and thereby constituencies. From the ancient Hundreds and Liberties of the counties that came to form London, to the parishes that begat boroughs, and the succession of boroughs, municipalities, rural and urban districts that have in turn begat the Greater London that we know today, all of these have shaped the constituency maps throughout the period of this study.

One of my aims has been to provide a sense of place and history, and I have thoroughly enjoyed my tour of local history websites that now abound on the Internet. Much of my data comes from these as well as from the local history sections of libraries across London that I visited in search of information relevant to this study. The City of London's Guildhall Library was an especially valuable source. That such a wealth of information is placed at the public's disposal is a remarkable philanthropy. It has enriched the undertaking, offering information in depth at the fingertips, and this has allowed the history of constituency evolution to be described more clearly.

The unexpected outcome of this work is the slow but accurate insight that has formed over the stately struggle between philanthropy, the exercise of privilege, the dark forces of party gain, and the shining light of democracy. It seems that good triumphs, but sometimes the margins are rather narrow. Even as the book is released for publication the issues of voter registration and fairness in the distribution of seats seem to be almost as contentious as they were nearly two centuries ago.

It seemed whilst writing that to make the complex series of interleaved events clearer as they unfold, a series of photographs was needed. It was impossible to gain full meaning from the involved written descriptions of changes in boundary, and so maps seemed the only way to do this. Photographs were easy to take with today's technology, and much pleasurable footwork was expended in collecting what was needed. Contemporary, historic images were available, and the various agencies, with only one notable exception, were helpful in providing us with material that lets us see the conditions people lived in and some of the grand men (and later women) that represented the people.

Maps were a problem. Those that existed were variable, and no two maps for comparison seemed to agree. Although there was no intention to commission cartography at the start of this project, specially drawn maps were the only answer available to open the door for the reader to have access to what it all 'means'. My erstwhile colleague and friend Gordon Rushton led me into the long adventure of creating common ground to illustrate all the changes, by using his computer skills to make the maps, for which the student will look in vain elsewhere. He also designed the book, so whilst all may now look homogenous, its origins certainly were not!

Finally I am conscious that I have spent too much time tucked away at the computer at many times of the day and night, and I am grateful for the extraordinary patience of my wife Pauline who has tolerated my eccentricities to a degree that many partners would not.

John Nelson,
York
January 2015

The clock tower of the Palace of Westminster, with Big Ben - powerful symbol of the Mother of Parliaments.
Gordon Rushton

Chapter 1 - Evolution

London's Parliamentary Constituencies from 1265 to the present Day

This book traces the evolution, electoral geography and politics of Parliamentary constituencies in London's Greater Metropolitan area. It does so by examining in detail the changes that have occurred, especially to constituency boundaries in the last two hundred years. It considers these in relation to the economic, demographic and social factors that brought them about as well as the political consequences. It also provides summary biographies of all London MPs since 1832. This overview provides the context in which the ancient counties of Middlesex, Essex, Kent and Surrey are individually considered in later chapters.

The Geographical Context

The study considers the Greater London Council area (**map shown above**) that was established by the London Government Act of 1963. This map shows the former counties and local councils within them that formed the GLC. Parts of Hertfordshire were included in it too; and through the book these are described with Middlesex. The Staines, Sunbury and Potters Bar districts of Middlesex however are excluded from the study except where in times past they were associated with Parliamentary constituencies that also covered districts within the GLC. Parts of Essex, Kent and Surrey beyond the GLC are also considered where they too were linked with districts that form part of the GLC.

Although today's conurbation would be unrecognisable to past generations, as early as 1840 maps were describing the area within a fourteen-mile radius of Charing Cross as the 'environs' of the metropolis and over the next Century most of it grew to become what we now call Greater London. Over the years this hinterland may have varied in size and shape but inter-dependence between the so-called Home Counties and London always existed. For centuries Hertfordshire, Essex, Kent, Middlesex and Surrey were producers of agricultural products consumed by Londoners. Key highways like the Great North Road[1] and Watling Street passed through many of their towns, whilst others led to important ports of embarkation in Essex and Kent. For several centuries wealthy Londoners had country homes within striking distance of the capital.

As London expanded not only on the back of its status as the world's greatest trading port but also as the capital city of Britain and its global Empire, so the Home Counties were brought increasingly within its orbit. When canals initially and then, more significantly in the case of London than other towns and cities, the railways arrived; they did much to stimulate the expansion of the metropolis. Modern communications – whether of road, rail or air – continue to play their part as the main stimuli to economic, industrial and residential growth. Their impact on London's electoral arrangements and its politics has been immense.

At various times in its history the local Government arrangements for London have been adjusted to recognize the physical and social realities of the metropolis. The historical and essentially Roman boundaries of the ancient walled City were what defined London until English monarchs made Westminster their home. Not only was there a physical separation of the City from nearby communities like Tower Hamlets, Westminster and Southwark, but that separation was also social and political. When Westminster developed it was as the seat of Government, separate from the City of London, which remained the centre of trade and commerce. The two were close but maintained a healthy distance; each was slightly wary of the other. Yet the City's importance to England's monarchs was never in doubt because therein lay much of the economic wealth and therefore the source of taxation.

This view from Lambeth Palace of the new Palace of Westminster with the Victoria Tower under construction was painted by an unknown artist . The new construction was necessary following a fire in 1834. The Houses of Parliament that we know today were built between 1843 and 1860.

© Palace of Westminster Collection www.parliament.uk/art

East of the City, the Tower Hamlets – literally the hamlets in the shadow of the Tower of London - owed their existence to the same commerce, but their populations toiled as the servants and labourers who sustained the trades that wealthy merchants owned. In every other important respect – socially, economically and politically - they were kept at a distance; and when London's commercial and industrial success led to the social classes coming within close proximity of one another, the wealthier ones moved away. Aided first by toll roads, then by the railways, this process has been going on ever since. It continues today.

Although the River Thames was the main trading artery that brought about London's great wealth it also acted as a physical barrier between the City and Southwark, which was nevertheless strategically important. It was the point on the old Roman road from Kent to Colchester where the river could first be crossed. It was itself an important trade and military route to the Cinque Ports as well as for Christian pilgrimage between London and Canterbury. Yet despite these advantages Southwark did not prosper in the same way as the City, being a place to which wealthier people might resort for pleasure, both legal and illicit, but for little else. It was surrounded by marshlands which made building difficult and was much more vulnerable to attack from the South. London therefore grew up north of the River Thames and to this day the metropolis is of greater mass there than it is in the south.

1 Originally Ermine Street, the road from London to Lincoln.

The Historical and Legislative Context

Over the Centuries from Simon de Montfort's 1265 Parliament or the 'model' Parliament convened by Edward I in 1295; it is possible to trace the emergence of politically significant groups and places from the way in which Parliamentary representation developed. Initially Parliamentarians were selected from particular interest groups such as the Knights of the Shire Counties or the burgesses and freemen of the boroughs and ports. They remained as such over many centuries but after June 1832, when the Representation of the People Act (sometimes called the First Reform Act) was passed, leading to a General Election based on new constituencies and a new franchise; the representative nature of the House of Commons began to change. This was hastened in 1867 and 1884 by Acts that extended the franchise and re-distributed Parliamentary seats.

Two other important pieces of Victorian legislation had an impact on elections. The Ballot Act (1872) introduced secret voting for the first time so that electors no longer needed to be quite so concerned about the influence of their landlord or employer. The General Election of 1874 was the first after the passing of this Act. Also significant was the 1883 Corrupt and Illegal Practices Prevention Act, which sought to eliminate bribery and corruption at election times by limiting the amount any candidate could spend on a campaign. This was first applied, together with the Representation of the Peoples Act 1884, in the General Election of 1885.

The First Reform Bill was given Royal Assent by King William IV, pictured here in a formal portrait by Samuel Lane dated between 1832 and 1834. **© Palace of Westminster Collection www.parliament.uk/art**

The 1918 Representation of the People Act made a greater impact still on the electoral process by abolishing the residency qualification for voting and enfranchising women over the age of thirty; though voting rights equal to those of men were not achieved until after the Equal Franchise Act of 1928. Until 1918 the property interests and residency qualifications of most electors remained the principal criteria by which male adults qualified to vote. From 1832 the notion of 'place' in representation (what we now term the Parliamentary constituency) began to change too. Although the nature of borough and county representation remained fundamentally the same as it had before, regard was paid to the realities of a changing society in the vanguard of the Industrial Revolution and global trade. So the list of borough constituencies was significantly changed to accommodate the interests of places like the northern industrial towns, though many of the older by now smaller boroughs remained. The Counties too were subject to a degree of redistribution with several being divided on a geographical basis. In the London area this applied to Essex, Kent and Surrey but not Middlesex which, although the most populous county next to Yorkshire, was the smallest geographically apart from Rutland.

Further small changes were made to the county divisions in Essex, Kent and Surrey in 1867, but after 1884 there was a much more fundamental change to the nature of Parliamentary constituencies. Greater equalization of electorates irrespective of borough or county status was initiated, although anomalies remained as boundary changes failed to keep up with the enormous population expansion and distribution that occurred; particularly between 1885 and the end of the First World War in 1918. Change has continued ever since reflecting the ebb and flow of populations as they have been shaped by economic and social factors as well as World events, such as the impact of bombing that so badly scarred and damaged many parts of the capital, both physically and economically, in the Second World War. Franchise extensions have also been a factor, though in a sense not significantly affecting the drawing of boundaries since these have generally affected all constituencies in similar proportions. The most significant were the extension to all women over the age of 21 (given in 1928), and to all eligible people over the age of 18 (given in 1969).

The creation of the Boundary Commission for England was the next major development in the history of London's representation. This, together with sister bodies covering other parts of the UK, was established by Act of Parliament in 1944[2]. These basically set the ground rules by which constituencies were established and the timescales within which reviews should be undertaken. Subsequent legislation modified some of these rules and to the extent that they were significant in London, reference is made to them where appropriate. Recommendations were always subject to ratification by Parliament. Such ratification has not always been timely.

The most recent legislation governing the drawing of constituencies was passed with amendment in January 2013. The amendment was significant because it meant that the number and shape of all Parliamentary constituencies would be unchanged at the next general election. This has to take place on 7th May 2015 unless a two thirds majority of MPs votes for an earlier dissolution. The amendment was contrary to the Government's original intention to reduce the number of seats in the House of Commons from 650 to 600 at that election. However, the Labour Opposition's amendment postponing the review was carried with the support of the Liberal Democrat partners in the Coalition and was therefore incorporated in the Electoral Registration and Administration Act that was passed on 31st January 2013. The Boundaries Commission for England had already undertaken a review which proposed a reduction of 4 seats to provide a total of 68 for Greater London. This would have maintained its share of English seats at 13.5%, and slightly increased its share of the total to 11.3%. These changes were effectively stalled, and even if the number of seats in future Parliaments were reduced to 600, the Boundary Commission would need to re-commence its review of individual constituencies on the basis of electoral registration as at 1st December 2015. Its report on the new statutory rules would not be produced until 2018.

Early Representation in Greater London (1265-1832)

Parliaments	*Essex*	*Middlesex*	*Surrey*	*Kent*	*Total Equivalent*	*% of all English MPs*	*% of all MPs*
1295-1355	*0*	*4*	*0*	*0*	*4*	*1.3%*	*1.3%*
1355-1386	*0*	*6*	*0*	*0*	*6*	2.4%	2.4%
1386-1542 a	*0*	*6*	2	*0*	*8*	2.7%	2.7%
1542-1545	*0*	*6*	2	*0*	*8*	2.7%	2.4%
1545-1571 b	*0*	*8*	2	*0*	*10*	2.5%	2.2%
1571-1708	*0*	*8*	2	*0*	*10*	2.2%	2.0%
1708-1801	*0*	*8*	2	*0*	*10*	2.2%	*1.8%*
1801-1832	*0*	*8*	2	*0*	*10*	2.2%	*1.5%*

a 1386-1542[1] b 1545-1571[2] **(Source: "The House of Commons, 700 Years of British Tradition")**

1 In 1543 Henry VIII gave representation to Wales, which had been conquered in 1284.
2 Several market towns were enfranchised during this period.

The **City of London** was the only borough that was required to send elected MPs to De Montfort's Parliament in 1265[3]. Then, like other boroughs, it sent two burgesses to Parliament but in 1355 this number was increased to four; early evidence of the City's exceptional importance. The timing may not have been without significance for, under Edward III, England was engaged in War with France and taxes were needed to fund it.

Southwark's significance relative to other areas of London is shown by its inclusion as a Parliamentary borough from 1386 in the reign of Richard II (1295 according to Boundaries Commission), but **Westminster** was not enfranchised until 1547, in Henry VIII's time. No other part of London was specifically represented except the **County of Middlesex,** which, in common with most other English Counties, returned two MPs from 1265 onwards.

Measured as a proportion of all MPs London's representation was not significant. Despite its economic importance and large population its representation languished at little more than two percent for around 350 years until the Act of Union with Scotland in 1707 ; when as the number of seats north of the border was increased London's proportion declined. Over the years the creation of new boroughs, some of them 'rotten'[4], and Welsh, Irish as well as Scottish Union with England, diluted London's influence. There was even a period in the Sixteenth Century when the French boroughs of Calais and Tournai sent MPs to Parliament. When Ireland was embraced within the House of Commons in 1801, London's representation fell proportionately to about 1.5%, its lowest levels since the days of Edward III.

2 The House of Commons (Redistribution of Seats) Act
3 Simon de Montfort summoned the first proper Parliament in the year 1265 sending out representatives to each county and to a select list of boroughs asking each to send two representatives. This was not the first Parliament in England but was the first in which the representatives were elected. (Source - David Boothroyd 'United Kingdom Election Results')
4 Rotten boroughs had few if any voters and one person or family 'owned 'the constituency. Elections rarely took place, with the owner choosing the MP.

A sketch of the first reformed House of Commons, painted by George Hayter in 1833. Although London's representation increased from 10 to 24 MPs it still comprised only 3.7% of the total. This gradually increased to reach a high point of 119 in 1945, which was 18.6% of the total.

Representation since 1832

London's position improved only marginally after the First and Second Reform Acts: and despite a significant uplift in 1885 it was not until after the First World War that a truer reflection of London's importance was seen. The Capital reached its maximum political potency in terms of its representation in 1945 when nearly one fifth of all seats in the Commons and a quarter of those in England were in London. Since the War there has been a steady reduction in the number of MPs representing London, and as a proportion of the House as a whole. By 2010 the number of MPs was below the absolute levels created after the Third Reform Act, and in proportional terms was significantly lower than the 1945 peak.

Parliaments	*Essex*	*Middlesex*	*Surrey*	*Kent*	*Total Equivalent*	*% of all English MPs*	*% of all MPs*
1832-1868	2	14	6	2	24	5.2%	3.7%
1868-1885	2	18	6	4	30	7.0%	4.9%
1885-1910	5	48	19	6	78	16.9%	11.4%
1918-1945	13	53	28	9	103	21.0%	14.4%
1945	18	61	29	12	119	22.9%	18.6%
1950-1955	15	52	25	13	105	20.8%	16.8%
1955-1974	15	52	26	13	106	20.9%	17.0%
1974-1983	14	43	22	13	92	18.0%	14.6%
1983-1997	14	37	20	13	84	16.3%	13.1%
1997-2010	12	34	17	11	74	14.2%	11.4%
2010-date	11	33	17	11	72	13.8%	11.1%

Source: Own research.
Notes: 1. Spelthorne is included in Middlesex totals before 1955, and Barnet from 1945.
2. The last election in which the whole of Ireland was represented in the House of Commons was 1918.

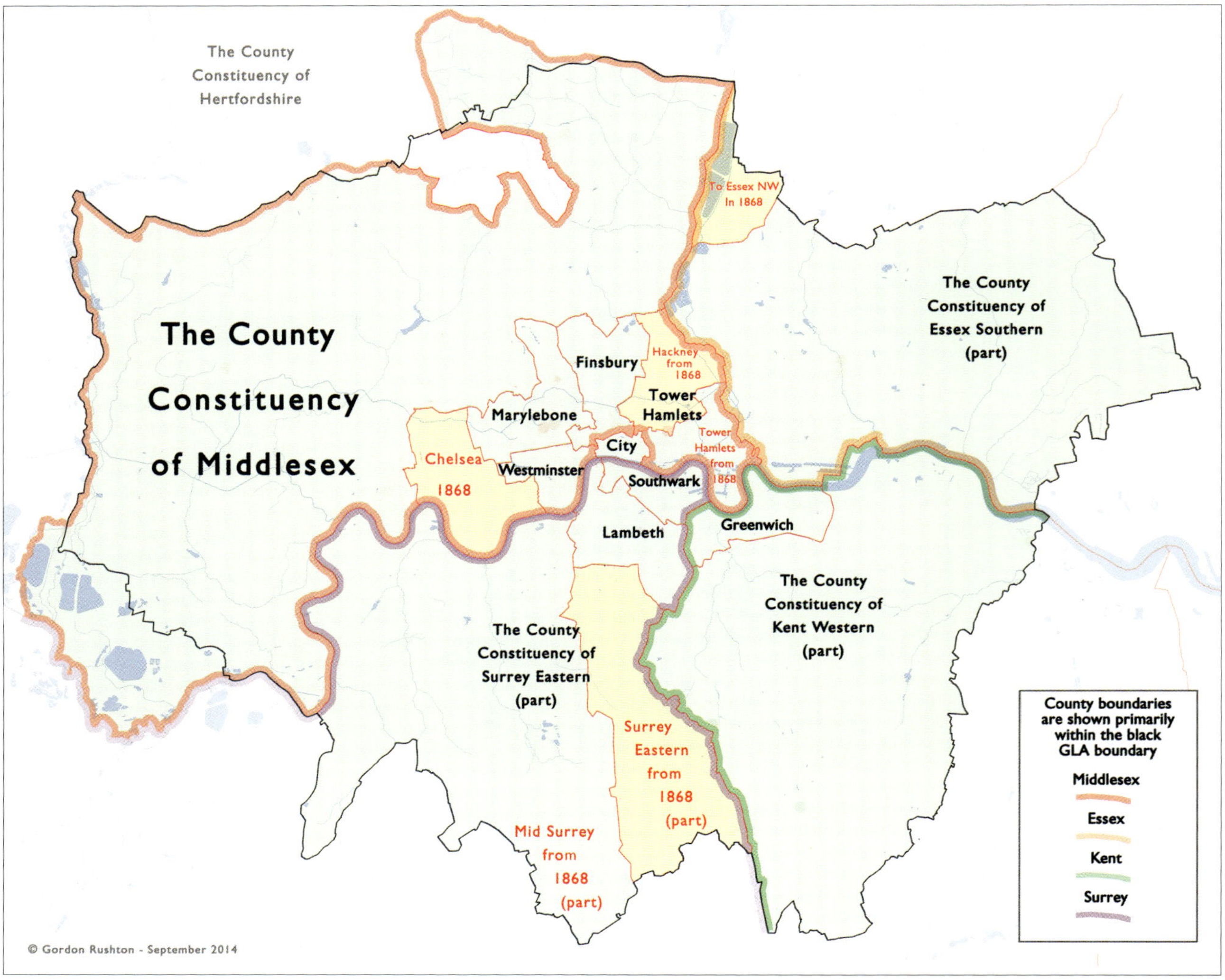

The map shows the constituencies within the present day GLA area as they were in 1832 before the great reforms to come. The effects of London's burgeoning population can already be seen in the larger number of central area borough constituencies. Chelsea and Hackney were added in 1868 and a Surrey Mid County seat also appeared. In Essex Chingford transferred to Essex North Western. Larger scale county maps appear in Chapters 2-6

Representation from 1832 to 1868

The map shows very clearly the preponderance of constituencies in Middlesex and the cluster of borough seats around the central core on both sides of the Thames together with the expanses beyond that were still represented by County constituencies. Note the complete absence of borough seats in Essex. Note too the small area to the North that was in Hertfordshire. This was the Barnet Valley. The area of South Middlesex beyond the GLC boundary is Spelthorne and Sunbury, which are today in Surrey. In the first election conducted after the franchise qualifications were changed; the number of electors on the various registers in the area covered by what is now 'Greater London' is estimated to have been only 92,702 adult males. As a point of comparison the population of the same area in the census of 1831 was an estimated 3,347,501. So London's electorate then was probably fewer than 2.8% of its total population. This was significantly worse than the proportion for the rest of England, which was an estimated 3.7%. In national terms London's electorate was an estimated 14.7% of the total for England, which compared with its population share of 18.9%, meant that it was well below par in terms of enfranchisement as well. [5]

Representation from 1868 to 1885

Changes in the representation of Greater London occurred when the 1867 Act established two new borough constituencies, one at Chelsea, and the other at Hackney. Both had become part of the London conurbation and contained electorates that were influential: Chelsea owing an affinity to Westminster, the Royal Court and Parliament

5 Source: F.H. McCalmont's Parliamentary Poll Book of British Election Results, 1832-1918

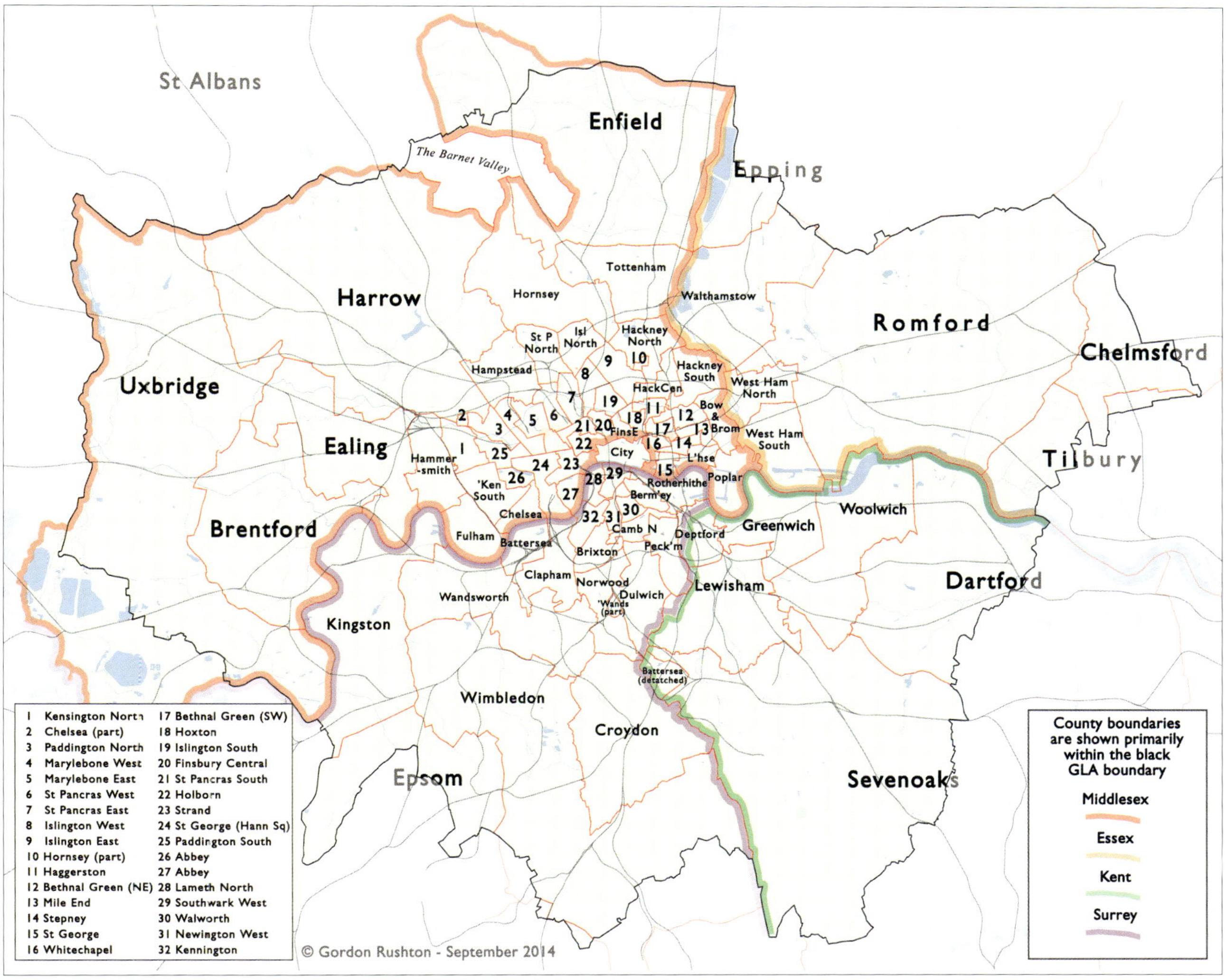

The map shows the constituencies within the present day GLA area as they were after the reforms of 1885. Note the radical increase in the number of constituencies after that reform. The map rested unchanged after this reorganisation until 1918. Larger scale county maps appear in Chapters 3-6.

itself; Hackney more to City trades and commerce. South of the Thames a new Mid Surrey constituency extending north to south from Battersea to Reigate was created out of the former Eastern Division, which remained in a contracted form running south from Dulwich to Lingfield. The creation of a new Mid Kent county constituency in the same year meant that Kent Western became more concentrated on that part of the County now in South East London, where the population was increasing at the faster rate, stimulated by the opening of the railways. Between 1831 and 1861 the population of the Western Kent Division doubled to 487,000. Similar changes brought Essex Southern into the metropolitan area; though by contrast its population in 1861 was less than half that of Kent Western.[6]

The overall impact of the 1868 changes brought the total of London's MPs to 32. With 7% of English MPs London still had less than half the equivalent percentage for its share of the electorate at that time.

Representation from 1885 to 1918

The 1884 Act had a huge impact. The General Election of 1885 was fought on the basis of radically changed constituency boundaries and a much-expanded male electorate. For the first time the vast majority of Parliamentary constituencies were configured along lines that we recognise today: that is borough and county divisions centred on defined communities and based at least to some extent on electoral numbers that were themselves more representative and balanced. These factors brought about a large increase in the numbers of constituencies and MPs in London. North of the Thames fifty-one MPs were returned from fifty constituencies with a further twenty-five coming from single-member constituencies south of the river.

The map illustrates the constituencies that were contested in general elections between 1885 and December 1910 inclusive. With seventy-six seats in a House of Commons that in each of the elections totalled 670 MPs, London's

6 The population of Essex Southern was only 214,000,

share rose to 11.3%, and to nearly 17% of all English seats, though still smaller than the 22% its population would have indicated. Its electorates were also slightly below par at around 20%.

The principal innovation at this time was the creation of a number of Parliamentary Boroughs that would five years later become the basis of much of London's local government, with the creation of the London County Council (or LCC) in 1889. County constituencies were only to be found at the outer margins of the growing metropolis. The number of MPs returned from borough and county seats in Middlesex increased from 18 to 47, the largest enfranchisement of any area in Britain. The City of London was reduced from 4 to 2 seats but was, despite a diminishing population, the only London constituency to retain multi-member representation. Essex was also beginning to experience population growth near London, the county increasing from fewer than 320,000 in 1834 to nearly 1,100,000 by 1901. This massive growth saw the emergence of large urban boroughs close to London such as East and West Ham; each heavily dependent on dock and related trades for employment. In total 4 new London based Essex constituencies were created in 1885.

South of the Thames Kent and Surrey also saw an expansion in their representation; though not on the same scale as North of the River. Of the two counties, Surrey initially developed faster, with Croydon, Kingston and Wimbledon constituencies appearing for the first time, coupled with a substantial increase in the number of borough constituencies in and around Southwark, Lambeth, and Wandsworth. 11 additional constituencies were created in these boroughs, and in all Surrey returned 19 MPs within the Greater London area, whilst Kent increased its London area representation to 6. Two single-member divisions replaced the former Greenwich, two-member borough constituency, whilst Deptford and Lewisham boroughs (both in Lewisham today) each provided one MP. In the more scattered suburbs even further away from London in what had at one time been the Western division of Kent, two new constituencies incorporated communities contained within today's London boroughs of Bromley and Bexley. These were Sevenoaks and Dartford.

The map shows the constituencies within the present day GLA area as they were between the Wars. Continuing suburban development saw an expansion, mainly of county constituencies. Had it not been for the outbreak of WW2, it is likely that further changes would have taken place before 1945, given the substantial growth of suburbia in the 1930s. Larger scale county maps appear in Chapters 7-10.

Representation from 1918 to 1945

The Boundary review of Parliamentary constituencies that started in May 1917 reported in September and, with legislation being passed on February 6th 1918; the 'Homes fit for Heroes' General Election was fought on new boundaries on December 14th. London was greatly affected by these revisions. There had been major population changes over the thirty-three years since the new constituency based system had been introduced, and demographic factors affected London's representation in Parliament arguably more than any other part of Britain.

The impact of surface railways and the London Underground had stimulated the construction of housing estates in new suburbs on a huge scale while the inner London boroughs had begun to lose population, as the middle classes and working class people increasingly too, migrated to new suburbs. Consequently the core inner London districts that had developed when the metropolis initially expanded lost representation. A substantial amount of new affordable housing, coupled with enforced cheap train fares, brought about a migration of a different kind to suburbs like Tottenham, Leyton Willesden and Lewisham. In addition industrial trends such as larger shipping requiring new dockyards further down the Thames, were causing workers to move elsewhere, while companies making consumer goods needed by the new homeowners were attracted on a vast scale to industrial estates in various parts of London. The population grew to seven and a half million in 1921.

103 Parliamentary constituencies covered the metropolis in 1918 and became the basis of London's representation until 1945. The increase was 27 seats and the total was over one fifth of English seats in the House of Commons. The map opposite illustrates the expansion of seats that occurred in 1918. The substantial number of new seats spreading outwards in all directions from the central core can be readily seen.

As a proportion of all MPs London's share increased further after the creation of the Irish Free State in an Act of Parliament of March 1922 after which the number of MPs in the House fell from 707 to 615, London's share rising successively from 11.4% pre-War to 14.6% in 1918 and16.7% in 1922 for the United Kingdom.

In total Middlesex accounted for 53 seats in 1918 compared with 47 in the previous Parliament while Essex recorded a significant increase from 4 to 13 in the metropolitan area reflecting the growth of the East London Docks and of the railway generated suburbs. The suburbs were also spreading outwards along the railway lines south of the Thames and metropolitan Surrey and Kent saw the number of its seats increased by 15, to reach 37 in total. Some of this expansion arose from new LCC council housing schemes with large estates being built to accommodate people from slum areas of central London.

Post War Changes in 1945

The Boundary Commission was created in 1944. This was and remains the body independent of government that recommends electoral boundary changes within the parameters that Parliament lays down from time to time. Prior to the post-War General Election in 1945 it undertook a special review of 20 English constituencies that had grown exceptionally large since 1918. Most of these were in London where 16 additional seats were created in the outer suburbs. Of these 13 were north of the Thames.

The map on page 18, overleaf, illustrates in yellow the new suburban constituencies that were specially established in 1945. The proportion of English MPs representing Greater London rose to 22.9%, numbering 119 out of a total of 510 MPs, an historical peak. In the Middlesex suburbs eight new constituencies were created. The extension of the Central Line to Ealing Broadway and another branch to West Ruislip, completed in the 1920s and 30s, together with the building of new trunk roads sponsored by the Ministry of Transport in the early 1920s, had a major impact on west Middlesex, especially around Ealing and Hounslow. Elsewhere the building by the Metropolitan Railway Company of two new lines, one towards Uxbridge/Watford and Amersham in 1925, the other to Stanmore in 1932, also brought about substantial property development, with the Metropolitan Country Estates Company Limited acting as a housing developer in places around Pinner and Harrow including Wembley. The building of an extension to the Northern Line of the Underground from Hampstead to Hendon in 1923 and then to Edgware and High Barnet also stimulated a suburban expansion there. The former St. Albans constituency in Hertfordshire was reduced in size, with Hatfield and the southern portion including Borehamwood, Radlett, Potters Bar and Elstree transferring to Barnet.

In Essex the development of new council estates in response to slum clearance in the East End, coupled with the building of a huge car factory by Fords at Dagenham, meant that populations increased rapidly. The growth of suburban and council estates also continued around the Central and District Line stations of the London Underground. In total five new seats were created, Romford spawning three of them. Kent and Surrey acquired three more in total.

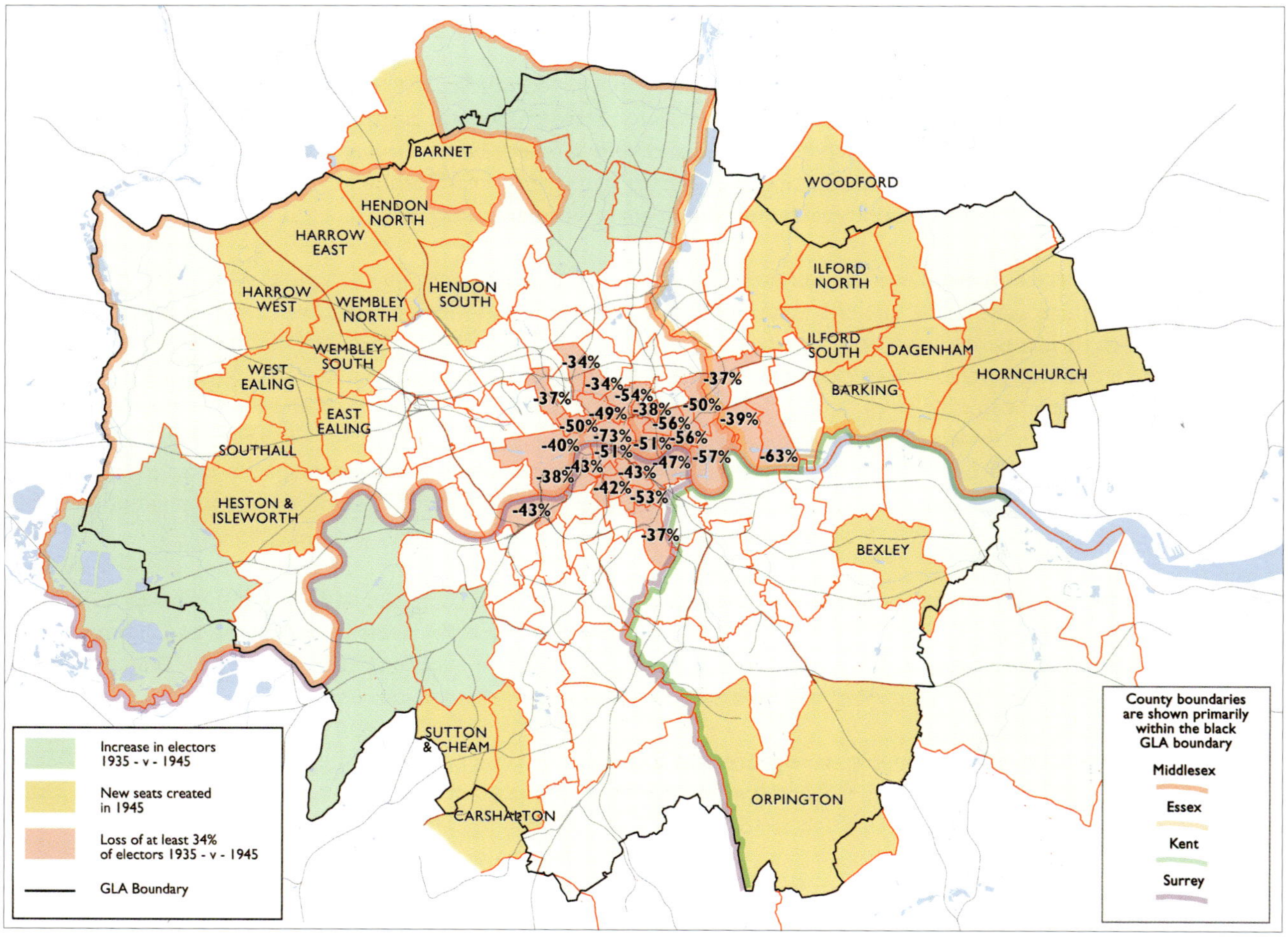

London reached its zenith in terms of Parliamentary representation in 1945. The seats shaded yellow were specially created to cater for exceptional population growth . No other constituencies were altered compared with 1918. A few outer suburbs (shaded green) increased their electorates without increasing representation but throughout the rest of the metropolis, electorates declined everywhere, and in the central, bombed out constituencies (shaded red) the effect was dramatic, as shown by the figures on the map, with electorates falling by as much as 63% in dockland areas.

The 1945 changes were something of a stop-gap measure, necessary to ensure a general election could be called as soon after the end of the War as possible. It was actually only partially effective because there were many other places, especially in the LCC area that had become over represented. So despite the special changes made in 1945 there were still major disparities between electorates. Whilst the number of seats in Greater London increased to its highest ever level, the electorate actually fell by 11% compared with 1935. Much of this was due to the ravages of the war. The combined electorates of equivalent seats in 1935 totalled over 5.8 million but in 1945 the figure was nearly 650,000 fewer. This was in contrast to England as a whole where the electorate increased by 5.6%. The major impact was in the inner London LCC area where electorates fell 30% from 2.9 million to roundly 2 million over a ten-year period. Even the outer suburban electorates increased only marginally, rising 7% from a little fewer than 3 million in 1935 to 3.2 million at the end of the War. These changes meant that whilst 61% of Greater London's electorate lived in outer suburban seats the proportion of seats there, even after the increase that occurred in 1945, was only 47%. In fact the outer suburban electorate had grown to be larger than that in the LCC area by 1935, and after the War it was clear that something further would need to be done to rectify a serious imbalance.

Apart from those constituencies that were split in 1945 to generate new seats only seven increased their electorates compared with 1935, indicating that, even as redistribution was beginning to occur, populations were either stagnating or in decline for the first time. Seats that bucked the trend were Enfield (+45%), Kingston-on-Thames (+20%), Edmonton (+14%), Wimbledon (+11%), Wood Green (+7%), Spelthorne (+1%) and Richmond (+0.3%).

Docklands constituencies and others nearby that had been badly bombed in the Blitz experienced massive reductions in electorates. Of the seats that lost more than a third of their electors most had the rivers Thames or Lea between Vauxhall Bridge and the Royal Docks as part of their boundaries. In fact all LCC constituencies lost electors and only four lost less than 10% from the register. The best of these was Woolwich West, which lost 4%, whilst Putney lost 8%, Lewisham East 9% and Hammersmith North slightly more.

The First Report of the Boundaries Commission (1950)

The Commission commenced its first fully comprehensive report on Parliamentary Boundaries in January 1946. Its Initial Report was published on 24th October 1947 and an Act of Parliament was passed on July 30th 1948 containing the new Parliamentary constituencies for England. The 1950 and 1951 General Elections were fought on the new boundaries and just about every constituency in the country was affected. In London the impact was significant and resulted in a net loss of 15 since 1945 although the total was still one more than the pre-War figure.

In Middlesex an overall reduction of 9 seats occurred and the opportunity was taken to give Westminster and the City of London the representation to which their populations were democratically entitled rather than that bestowed upon them by history and status. The new combined seat was re-named The City of London & Westminster. Metropolitan Essex was reduced from 18 to 15 constituencies and in Surrey there was an overall loss of 5 metropolitan constituencies despite the addition of two in the outer suburbs. Metropolitan Kent was the only area to gain from the redistribution, acquiring two new seats.

The average electorate of the constituencies covering Greater London in 1950 was 57,953 compared with 44,435 in 1945, but was much closer to the 1935 figure of 56,775. The closest to the 1950 average were St. Marylebone and Ealing North but there were strong variations, the largest being Leyton, where the 78,491electorate was 35% greater. Neighbouring Walthamstow retained two constituencies, the combined electorates of which were only around 10,000 greater than Leyton's single seat. The East division was 20% below and West 26% below the London average. Battersea South had the smallest electorate and was symptomatic of a general pattern that gave the largest electorates to outer London seats and the smallest to the inner city. This primarily arose from a requirement to allocate constituencies within local authority boundaries whilst aiming to equalise electorates. Generally the larger electorates were in Tory voting constituencies, and the smallest tended to be Labour. A number were subsequently split to spawn additional constituencies in 1955. In the case of the smallest constituencies, the majority were Labour, and two were withdrawn in 1955 to the Party's disadvantage

1955 Changes: The Boundary Commission's Second Report

Further changes were heralded by the Boundary Commission's next Report. Started in July 1953, the First Periodic Review was completed in November 1954; boundary changes were enacted in early 1955 and implemented at the General Election that took place in May of that year. By then the London metropolis was protected by a so-called 'Green Belt'; countryside on which further wholesale housing development was not permitted. Despite there being by then far fewer places on which houses could be sited; some had nevertheless been built and these spawned what were effectively the last outer suburban constituencies to be created within Greater London. The overall impact was numerically neutral.

North of the Thames a new Feltham seat was formed out of the former Spelthorne, which was modified to embrace only areas that are outside Greater London today, and which for the purposes of this study is not included as a London seat after that date. Elsewhere the four former Hammersmith and Fulham constituencies were merged to form three. Barnet was reduced in geographical size losing Hatfield to Hertford and so became even more centred on its metropolitan electorates. A similar exercise in Essex saw Romford, which since 1945 had extended between Collier Row to Brentwood, lose the latter town, which was instead placed in the new Billericay constituency. Romford thus became an entirely metropolitan constituency.

South of the river a new seat was created in Surrey at Surbiton, on the northern fringes of the County's commuter belt. Otherwise there were no other significant revisions in metropolitan Surrey, but in Kent major revisions to the former Dartford constituency affected the shape of things in the outer suburbs. Erith and Crayford was created a constituency separate from Dartford as London overspill continued down the south side of the Thames estuary, a mirror image of what was taking place on the north side in Essex. Dartford itself became a borough seat outside London. Chislehurst and Orpington were also reduced to their core districts as rural hinterlands were transferred to Dartford, which then fell outside the Greater London boundary.

Note: The maps in this chapter become increasingly complex as constituency names changed, and some disappeared. If the constituency was superseded, this is shown by a red line enveloping the name, The new name is then shown in red. When there is no room for names, then numbers are used, with an appropriate key. Colours show the new constituency boundary and territory transferred from adjacent constituencies. When more than one colour is chosen, it is only to avoid confusion and has no other significance. Constituency changes have the same format throughout.

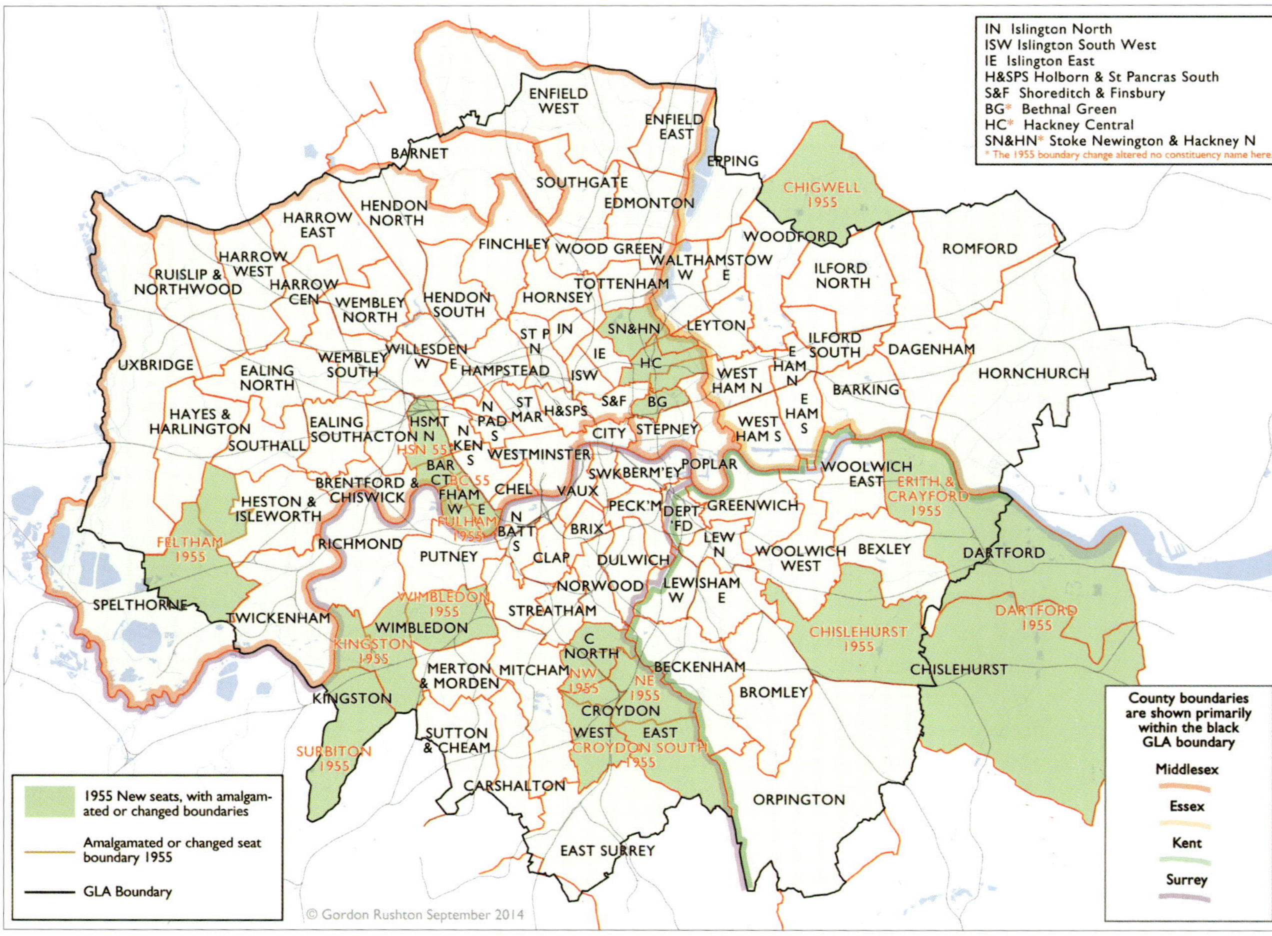

The map depicts London's constituencies created in 1950 and those that were modified in 1955. Comparing 1950 with the 1945 map on page 18 reveals the nature of the changes as primarily reducing the number of seats in Inner London whilst new seats in the outer suburbs emerged. The areas shaded green beyond the GLA boundary were transferred out of London in 1955 as constituencies within the metropolis, either contracted in area or created additionally. Heston & Isleworth contracted with Spelthorne to enable the creation of Feltham whilst Wimbledon and Kingston were altered to permit the creation of Surbiton. In Kent the semi rural districts of Chislehurst were absorbed by Dartford which in turn yielded a new Erith & Crayford. In Essex, Woodford contracted to lose northern commuter villages to Chigwell and Romford lost Brentwood to Billericay. Fulham and Hammersmith meanwhile were reduced from 4 to 3 in total. Croydon's 3 seats were simply re-orientated as were the 3 seats covering Hackney and Bethnal Green. Larger scale county maps appear in Chapters 11-15.

Greater London Authority Boundaries Fully Reflected, 1974-83

Whilst the 1954 review was marginal the same could not be said of the next changes heralded by the Boundary Commission's Second Periodic Review which commenced on 16th February 1965. Not completed until 1969 its implementation was delayed until the February 1974 General Election. Despite the recommendations having been received by the Wilson Labour Government in April 1969; they were not acted upon until after its defeat in the General Election of June 1970. The Heath Conservative Government accepted the proposals, which were enacted less than six months later. The changes took into account population movements and the new local authority boundaries established in 1965. It was a requirement that the Commission should establish London constituencies wholly within these borough boundaries and, with the exception of the City of London no seat was permitted to straddle two boroughs.

12 seats were eliminated and the total wholly within the metropolitan area fell to 92, lower than at any time since before the 1918 General Election. With 516 English MPs in total in the Commons, London's share fell to 17.8%. The biggest reduction occurred in the former LCC Middlesex boroughs where the number of constituencies fell by 8 to 43, the lowest total since before 1885.

In summary the new Middlesex based boroughs, together with the former boroughs they absorbed, were as follows:

Greater London Borough	Former Principal Local Government Areas
Westminster	Westminster, Marylebone and Paddington
Kensington & Chelsea	Chelsea and Kensington
Hammersmith & Fulham	Fulham and Hammersmith
Ealing	Acton, Ealing and Southall
Harrow	Harrow
Hillingdon	Hayes, Harlington, Ruislip and Uxbridge
Hounslow	Brentford, Isleworth, Feltham and Heston
Brent	Wembley and Willesden
Barnet	Barnet, Hendon and Finchley
Camden	Hampstead, Holborn and St. Pancras
Islington	Finsbury and Islington
Haringey	Hornsey, Tottenham and Wood Green
Enfield	Edmonton, Enfield and Southgate
Tower Hamlets	Stepney, Bethnal Green and Poplar
Hackney	Hackney, Shoreditch and Stoke Newington

The Corporation of the City of London remained an autonomous local government unit. Twickenham was allocated to Richmond (Surrey)but for the purposes of this analysis is accounted for in the Middlesex totals.

In metropolitan Essex there was a loss of one seat resulting in 14 embraced by new Greater London Boroughs as follows:

Greater London Borough	Former Principal Local Government Areas
Newham	East Ham and West Ham
Waltham Forest	Leyton, Walthamstow and Chingford
Redbridge	Ilford, Woodford and Wanstead
Barking & Dagenham	Barking and Dagenham
Havering	Romford and Hornchurch

In metropolitan Kent 13 seats were maintained following the Boundary Review; the loss of a seat in Lewisham being offset by the creation of a new one in Bexley. The new Boroughs were as follows:

Greater London Borough	Former Principal Local Government Areas
Lewisham	Deptford and Lewisham
Greenwich	Greenwich and Woolwich
Bexley	Bexley, Sidcup (formerly with Chislehurst), Erith and Crayford
Bromley	Bromley, Chislehurst (without Sidcup), Beckenham, Orpington and Penge

In metropolitan Surrey there was a reduction of four seats to 22. The new Boroughs were as follows:

Greater London Borough	Former Principal Local Government Areas
Southwark	Bermondsey, Southwark and Camberwell
Lambeth	Lambeth,Streatham and some districts of Clapham
Wandsworth	Battersea, including most of Clapham, and Wandsworth
Merton	Mitcham, Wimbledon , Morden & Morden and Malden & Coombe
Richmond	Barnes, Richmond and Twickenham
Kingston	Kingston and Surbiton
Sutton	Sutton, Cheam, Beddington & Wallington, and Carshalton (formerly with Banstead)
Croydon	Croydon, and Coulsdon & Purley

London's 1974 constituencies were allocated in the boundaries of the new boroughs created alongside the GLC, which by then had been in existence for a decade. When further changes were made in 1983, these too were confined within boroughs. Reductions occurred, mostly in Inner London where several 3 seat boroughs were reduced to 2. Harrow was an exception in the suburbs. Elsewhere the combination of the former Middlesex borough of Twickenham with Richmond borough from Surrey resulted in the allocation of the St. Margarets area of the former to the Surrey constituency. In Bromley Borough the Biggin Hill ward switched from Orpington to Ravensbourne. Larger scale county maps appear in Chapters 11-15.

The Third Periodic Review (1983 – 97)

The third review of the Boundary Commission started on 17th February 1976 and reported seven years later; by which time there had been a change of Government from Labour to Conservative in 1979. There might have been a report earlier than 1983 had the Labour Party not sought to question the basis of the review in the courts. Demographic changes in the South East of England once again affected the number of London seats adversely. With relative population drift to the Home Counties it was inevitable that the Commission would reduce the number of London seats; the total of which fell to 84, which accounted for only 16.0% of English seats. Once again there was a reduction of mainly Labour held constituencies. In total between the Elections of 1979 and 1983 London lost 8 seats bringing the number of Parliamentary constituencies lost since 1945 to 36, a decline of 29%. Most losses were in Middlesex where the number of seats fell to 37while in Surrey two seats were lost .There were no boundary revisions in Essex based London Boroughs and there were boundary changes but no reduction in seats in metropolitan Kent.

The Fourth Periodic Review (Implemented in 1997)

The Boundary Commissions Act of 1992 changed the interval between reports to not less than eight or more than twelve years, and the 4th Review, which started in February 1991, reported in February 1995. This time the Commission was allowed to consider constituencies that crossed borough boundaries. Its recommendations were enacted on April 11th 1995 and the General Election of 1997 was the first to be fought on the basis of the new boundaries. It considered every constituency in England and again the impact was to reduce the number of London MPs, this time from 84 to 74seats, a loss of 10 and the lowest total since 1868. This was not so much a reflection of London's absolute decline, but arose from a growth in populations in the South East of England according them greater representation. In terms of the national position, London's MPs accounted for just 14% of the total for England as a whole. Boundary changes affected all parts of the metropolis, and for the first time the reduction south of the Thames was equal to that than north of the river.

Changes in Middlesex brought about a reduction of four seats there, from 37 to 33. Westminster and Kensington & Chelsea were paired and the number of constituencies there reduced from four to three. More fundamental changes affected west London. Ealing and Hammersmith & Fulham were paired and one seat was lost. There were only minor changes in most other parts of West Middlesex. In Barnet the new electoral quotas brought about a reduction of one and in Tower Hamlets only one seat was left wholly within the borough's boundaries bringing its representation to its lowest ever level. A second seat included districts of Newham, the first time in history that the River Lea did not separate Essex seats from those in Middlesex. Wholly Essex based constituencies were reduced by one following the pairing of Redbridge and Waltham Forest Boroughs. In Surrey three constituencies were lost; one through the pairing of Southwark and Lambeth boroughs; and two in the outer Boroughs. In Kent too there was a loss of two seats, one in Greenwich, and another in the outer boroughs.

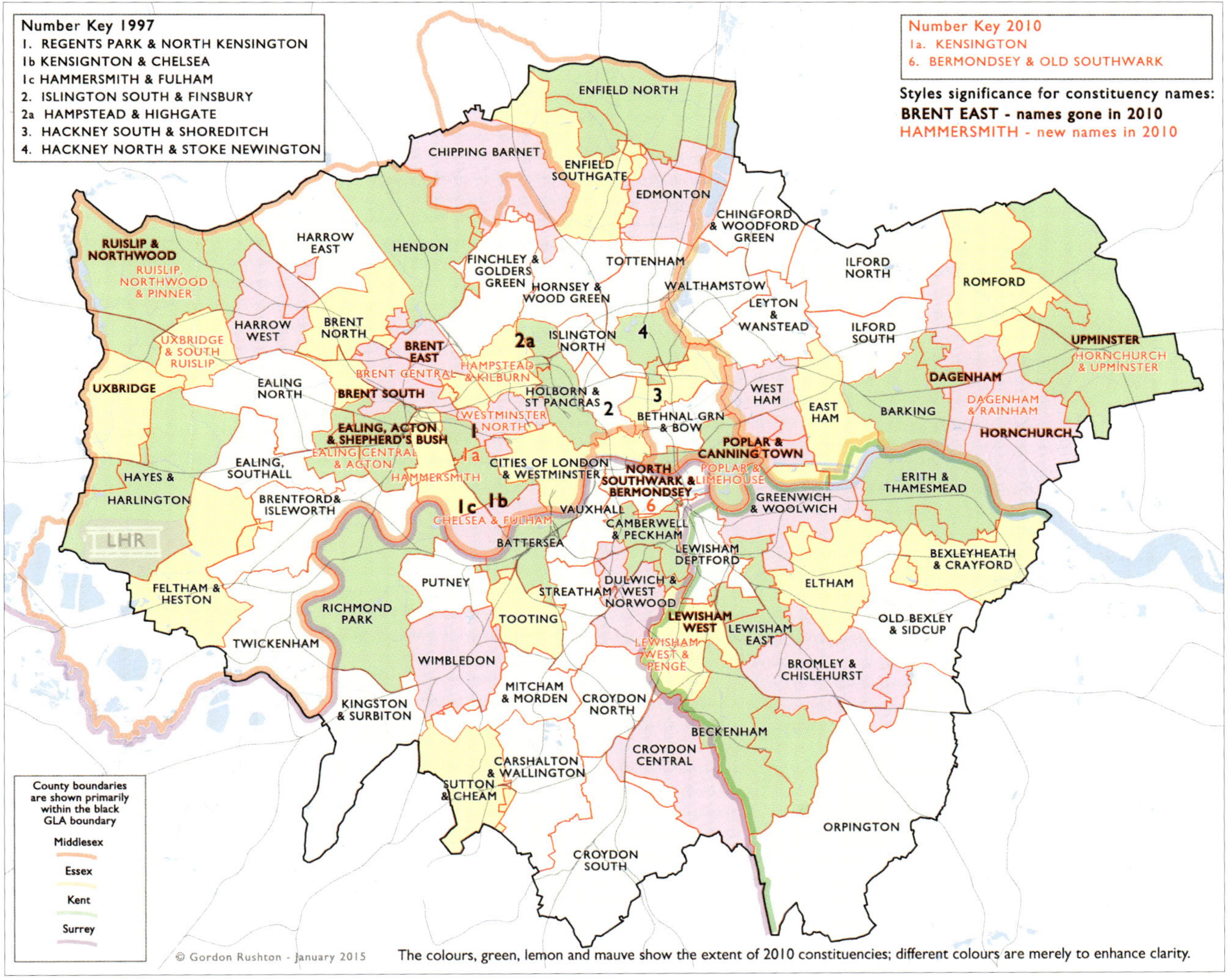

The map shows London's constituencies in 1997 when many individual constituencies were redrawn across more than one borough. The process was continued when the map was redrawn again in time for the 2010 General Election. Many of the changes were very minor taking account of small ward boundary alterations, which nevertheless are shown on the map. The illustration shows how 1997 constituencies were reorientated to produce the 2010 outcome of one seat fewer. The biggest changes affected Central, North London and West Middlesex; the East End, docklands and the old Essex Thameside boroughs, although there were some also south of the Thames. The changes are described in the text and can be cross referenced to the map to be better understood. Larger scale county maps appear in Chapters 15-18.

The Fifth Periodic Review (Implemented in 2010)

The Boundary Commission published its recommendations during the course of 2001, after the General Election of that year had been held. Further alterations were recommended in order to balance electorates within London as much as within the country as a whole. On this occasion there was renewed consideration of boundaries straddling boroughs and the overall effect was to reduce the number of seats by one to a total of 73. This reduction occurred in Essex where the pairing of Barking & Dagenham with Havering brought about a reduction in the number of seats in the two Boroughs from five to four. Other boroughs that were combined to determine constituencies were: Brent with Camden; Hammersmith & Fulham with Kensington & Chelsea; Harrow with Hillingdon; Redbridge with Waltham Forest; Greenwich with Bexley; Bromley with Lewisham; Southwark with Lambeth, and Richmond with Kingston. Those that were assessed separately were Barnet, Ealing, Enfield, Hackney, Haringey, Hounslow, Islington, Tower Hamlets, Westminster, Newham, Wandsworth, Merton, Croydon and Sutton.

The Sixth Review (Initial Proposals 2011)

The General Election of 2010 resulted in no one party having a majority. A Coalition was formed by the Conservatives and Liberal Democrats and the new government's programme was based on an agreement struck after the Election. This comprised two commitments that, if implemented, would significantly affect not only constituency boundaries but also the method of electing MPs. The Parliamentary Voting System and Constituencies Act was passed in 2011. Single member constituencies would be retained but the number of them would be reduced from a total of 650 to 600. Elections would continue to be held on the 'first past the post' system; unless through a referendum (subsequently held in May 2011) a new form of voting known as 'The Alternative Vote', was adopted. In the event the Referendum result favoured 'first past the post' but the government proceeded with the proposal to reduce the number of constituencies.

Within the total of 600 two were reserved for the Isle of Wight, and one each for the remote and scattered Scottish island constituencies covering the Outer Hebrides and Orkney & Shetland. The remaining 596 constituencies were proposed to be equivalent in size of electorate with no one part of the United Kingdom favoured over another. Individual constituency electorates could be no more than 5% greater or smaller than the average of the entire electorate (except the Island seats mentioned) divided by 596. This signalled a disproportionate reduction in the number of seats in Wales and Scotland.

Within English constituencies the Boundaries Commission gave early notice that it would allocate seats within the nine regions of the country that were applicable to European Elections. London and its 32 boroughs comprised one such region. The Commission subsequently allocated 68 seats to London out of a total for England of 502. This equated to 13.5% of English seats and 11.3% of the UK total. In the event and as explained earlier in this chapter; the Boundary Commission's proposals were not implemented. In passing it may be noted that had its original proposals been implemented there would effectively have been a reduction of 2 seats in Middlesex and 2 in Kent, but Essex and Surrey would have maintained their totals.

General Election Results Since 1832

The table opposite shows the results of general elections for London and the United Kingdom as a whole in terms of seats won by the parties. Since universal adult suffrage was introduced in time for the 1929 election London has generally voted the same way as the country as a whole. There have been only two exceptions (1970[7] and 2010) when Labour took more London seats than the Tories, who went on to form the government after those general elections. The Conservatives have never held most London seats under a Labour government

Before universal suffrage, however and especially in the years following the passing of the first three Reform Acts, there were often occasions when the Party winning the general election ended up with a minority of London seats. This was most marked between the 1832 and 1867 Acts when the Liberals out-polled the Conservatives in all eight elections in London, despite the Tories forming Governments on three occasions. The narrowness of the franchise and the tendency towards Liberalism amongst small borough electorates would be the most likely explanations for this variation.

After 1867 the variation was strongly in the opposite direction and the beginning of what may be fairly described as a Conservative and Unionist hegemony can clearly be seen. This lasted for practically the entire period from 1874 to the end of the Second World War. Only in 1906 did the Liberals win more London seats than the Tories, despite forming governments after six elections. Neither was this principally a result of the rise of the Labour Party and the decline of the Liberals in the period after the First World War; although this was obviously a key factor in the general elections of 1918, 1922, 1923, and 1924. The Liberals seem to have been adversely affected by several factors. The widening of the franchise coupled with the redrawing of boundaries during a period when massive suburban development was taking

7 In 1970 the Conservative and Labour Parties each polled 47.5% of the votes cast in London. In total 1,800,722 votes were cast for the two parties and the Conservatives polled 309 more than Labour – Source 'British Electoral Facts 1832-1999' by Rallings and Thrasher

London	Con	Lib	Lab	Other	Total	National Government	Con	Lib	Lab	Other
1832-1865										
1832	2	24	0	0	26	Liberal	175	441	0	42
1835	4	22	0	0	26	Liberal	273	385	0	0
1837	6	20	0	0	26	Liberal	314	344	0	0
1841	9	17	0	0	26	Conservative	367	271	0	20
1847	3	23	0	0	26	Conservative	325	292	0	39
1852	6	20	0	0	26	Conservative	330	324	0	0
1857	2	24	0	0	26	Liberal	298	356	0	0
1865	4	22	0	0	26	Liberal	289	369	0	0
Sub Total	36	172	0	0	208					
1868-1880										
1868	7	25	0	0	32	Liberal	271	387	0	0
1874	20	12	0	0	32	Conservative	350	242	0	60
1880	18	14	0	0	32	Liberal	237	352	0	63
Sub Total	45	51	0	0	96					
1885-1910										
1885	51	25	0	0	76	Liberal	249	319	0	102
1886	65	11	0	0	76	Conservative	393	192	0	85
1892	52	23	1	0	76	Conservative	313	272	3	82
1895	68	8	0	0	76	Conservative	411	177	0	82
1900	68	8	0	0	76	Conservative	402	183	2	83
1906	27	46	3	0	76	Liberal	156	399	31	84
1910 Jan	45	29	2	0	76	Liberal	272	274	40	84
1910 Dec	41	29	5	1	76	Liberal	271	272	42	85
Sub Total	417	179	11	1	608					
1918-1935										
1918	77	18	5	3	103	Coalition	523	36	58	90
1922	82	3	16	2	103	Conservative	397	62	142	14
1923	53	13	36	1	103	Conservative	258	158	191	8
1924	72	4	36	1	103	Conservative	412	40	151	12
1929	47	2	54	0	103	Labour	260	59	287	9
1931	90	3	9	1	103	National	522	32	52	5
1935	68	1	34	0	103	National	429	21	154	11
Sub Total	489	44	190	8	721					
1945-1970										
1945	27	0	89	3	119	Labour	200	12	393	23
1950	51	0	53	0	104	Labour	298	9	315	3
1951	53	0	51	0	104	Conservative	321	6	295	3
1955	55	0	49	0	104	Conservative	345	6	277	2
1959	61	0	43	0	104	Conservative	365	6	258	1
1964	49	1	54	0	104	Labour	304	9	317	0
1966	37	1	66	0	104	Labour	253	12	364	1
1970	49	0	55	0	104	Conservative	336	6	288	6
Sub Total	382	2	470	3	847					
1974-1979										
1974 Feb	42	0	50	0	92	Labour	297	14	301	23
1974 Oct	41	0	51	0	92	Labour	277	13	319	14
1979	50	0	42	0	92	Conservative	339	11	269	4
1983	56	2	26	0	84	Conservative	397	23	209	21
1987	58	3	23	0	84	Conservative	376	22	229	23
1992	48	1	35	0	84	Conservative	336	20	271	24
1997	11	6	57	0	74	Labour	165	46	418	30
2001	13	6	55	0	74	Labour	166	52	413	28
2005	21	8	44	1	74	Labour	197	62	355	31
2010	28	7	38	0	73	Coalition	307	57	258	28
Sub Total	368	33	421	1	823					
Grand Total	1737	481	1092	13	3303					
Percentage	52.50	14.50	33.00	0.00						

place, substantially changed the class composition and voting preferences of the electorate. The Conservatives were the major beneficiaries of these changes in London whilst Liberals tended to be elected in the less middle class, mainly industrialised parts of the metropolis. In the end the rise of the Labour Party to represent working class interests did for them there as well.

The rise of the Labour Party in the 1920s, and especially after the Second World War, coincided with a much more even balance of the two major parties as between London and the country as a whole. It is clear from the table that since 1945 Labour has overall enjoyed the better of it in London. The exceptions were the mid 1950s and the Thatcher period between 1979 and 1992.

A feature of more recent elections has been the strengthening of the Labour vote in parts of London which, from their inception as constituencies in their own right, could historically be relied upon to return Conservative MPs. These constituencies generally coincide with areas where ethnic minorities (often middle class) have provided significant numbers of electors. Harrow and Wembley are good examples. In both areas the proportion of white British has fallen to no more than about 40%. In Ealing and Redbridge the proportion is around 50%. Ethnic minorities have had a tendency to vote Labour in larger numbers than for other parties. However, parts of this electorate have occasionally swung against Labour when a particular issue (such as opposition to the Iraq War) has resonated with the minority communities who have voted to eject Labour MPs. Examples of this were Bethnal Green & Bow and Brent South in the 2005 General Election. In the first case George Galloway won the seat for the Respect Party and in the latter a Liberal Democrat did so having previously gained it at a by-election two years earlier at the height of the War.

Over the entire period covered by this book it can be seen that the Conservatives have returned slightly over half of all MPs at all general elections. However, if we choose to describe the Liberal and Labour Parties as 'progressive' in contradistinction to the Tories, the overall position has actually been very close.

Finally, there have been only three general elections when the results in London might have affected the national outcome. These have all been in recent times. In 1964 Labour won the general election by an overall majority of 4 seats, precisely the same as its advantage over other parties in London. In February 1974 Labour emerged from the election as the largest single party in terms of seats. Its advantage over the Conservatives was 4. In London its advantage was 8 seats. Most recently, in 2010 the Conservatives failed by 8 seats to secure the same number of seats as the Labour and Liberal Democrat Parties combined. In London their deficit was 17 seats, sufficient to affect not only the outcome of the election as a whole but of the subsequent Parliamentary vote on changing electoral boundaries in which Labour and the Liberal Democrats combined to defeat the Conservatives.

The Future

In the immediate future the results of the Coalition Government's plans to reduce the number of seats in the House of Commons have stalled and it is not clear how proposals to reduce the number of seats will materialise. For the foreseeable future the methods of voting and the concept of the single member constituency will survive. Nevertheless in taking stock of the past it is clear that a number of factors will come into play that are likely to affect the future distribution of seats and the extent to which they change hands, particularly as a result of demography.

The forecast growth in the metropolitan populations of London does seem likely to enhance its representation relative to other parts of the country, though possibly not in relation to its South East hinterland. According to the Office of National Statistics future population growth in London is forecast to increase at a slightly higher rate than for the UK as a whole (9.6% against 8.6%); but at 11.2% the inner boroughs will significantly outstrip the outer boroughs which will rise at a much lower rate (8.5%). These changes will play their part in determining the number and distribution of seats in London.

Another issue that could have an effect on the number of seats and their distribution (and thereby possibly the electoral outcome) is voter registration. The evidence from the Nineteenth Century is that restricting the size of the electorate tended to produce outcomes that we would today regard as either perverse or 'undemocratic'. The over representation of some groups has at various points in time worked to the advantage of all parties on certain occasions, and to their disadvantage on others. For example, the earlier chapters of this book identify electorates in relation to populations during the Nineteenth Century and it is very clear that these resulted in outcomes that were unrepresentative of the populations if not the electorates. In several chapters in this book the extent to which boundary changes failed to match population trends is also very clear, in some instances quite dramatically. The 1945 Post War election in London was clearly fought on constituencies that were considerably out of date, but it was not the only general election fought in such circumstances.

The progression to universal suffrage may in hindsight be seen as inexorable but in truth it took over a century to achieve and the amount of struggle involved was considerable. Despite this it is a fact that today there remain significant disparities between populations and voter registration. Because constituencies are determined on the basis of the numbers of people who register to vote it is a fact that some populations are under-represented. There has always been a problem of keeping electoral rolls up to date, and in certain places populations are itinerant if not nomadic. London is one of those places. The changes in economic migration, including within the UK and London in particular, seem likely to increase the difficulties of keeping electoral rolls as up to date as might be considered desirable. The number of eligible people who register to vote is actually the key determinant of constituency boundaries in the modern era. Population is, therefore, only one indicator of what could happen.

The registration of voters already varies significantly between London Boroughs. Data produced by the London Elections Centre indicated that in 2010 across London as a whole 89.7% of the population aged 18 and over registered to vote. The spread of registrations, however, was very wide. The lowest registration proportions were in the Inner London boroughs of Camden (70.1%); Westminster (70%); The City of London (75.8%); and Kensington & Chelsea (76.2%). The factors underlying these variations are likely to include substantial numbers of foreign residents who are ineligible to vote; as well as some who may have two residences and who choose not to register in central London; or where factors such as mobility and short term tenancies give rise to an inability to register. The highest registration proportions were either in the outer boroughs with the most stable populations; or in those where the population had increased rapidly through immigration and where registrations had appeared to exceed the population benchmark. So Bexley and Havering effectively had 100% registration, whilst in Newham where the population had been growing more rapidly than anywhere else, the electorate appeared to exceed the eligible population age groups by 8.7%.

Data from the 2011 census provides some clues as to future representation. In 2011 the Boundary Commission for England recommended that on current electoral registration data London was entitled to 13.5% of English seats. This accorded pretty well with the 2011 census data which showed that Greater London represented 13.2% of the English population. However, data underlying the census suggested that a different profile would probably emerge over the next 20 years. For example, the proportion of the English population under the age of 18 living in London in 2011 was 15.8%. Although some of this was no doubt accounted for by transitory immigration from European countries, for example; part too was explained by the higher birth rate in London, most of which was associated with the more settled non-white ethnic groups. In 2011 these accounted for 40.2% of London's total population.

If these data were to be suggestive of future electoral trends they would indicate two things. The first would be an expectation that, all other things being equal; the proportion of seats in London would rise. If the current under 18 populations were any indication then the number of seats in a future 600 member House of Commons London could rise from 68 to as many as 81. There are of course likely to be countervailing demographic factors, but the historical decline that London has experienced since the Second World War does seem set to change.

The second factor is the ethnicity of the electorate. Historically non white electorates have tended to favour Labour over other parties. Whilst past voting patterns might not guarantee future outcomes; it does at this point in time seem likely that an increase in these groups as a proportion of the population could favour Labour over the Conservatives. This factor is also relevant in considering the possible impact of future demography on the outcome of elections in different parts of London. For instance, the census shows that whilst the non White populations represent a greater proportion of the population in Inner London boroughs; there are nonetheless certain outer boroughs where the non Whites represent very substantial electorates. In Brent, for example, the non white population in 2011 was 63.5%. The equivalent figure in Harrow was 57.7%; in Redbridge 57.4%; and in Ealing 51.8%. In many boroughs the proportions are already more or less equal; and even in Havering where the proportion is lowest, it still represents one eighth of the population.

The expansion of the non-white populations coupled with the higher birth rates suggests that these will affect both the distribution of seats towards the outer boroughs, and in the short term at least, the outcome of elections, not only within them, but to some extent in all boroughs.

The outcomes of future elections are of course unknowable. What this book does show at least as far as its study area is concerned, is that whilst boundary changes can have a marginal impact on election outcomes, these are as nothing compared to the swings of opinion that occur within the electorate. Whilst the outcome of elections is not pre-ordained, what is essential is that the parties that contest them appeal to the electorates they seek to represent. Parties may not have to change their basic principles to get elected but what they must do is present them in such a way as to garner votes.

Notable London MPs

Throughout this book where MPs' biographies are to be found, there are many human stories that inspire. Even when not inspirational, MPs rarely cease to provide interest and surprises. From the days of the Corn Laws to the Expenses furore of more recent times London has provided a fund of human interest stories, many of historical significance. So in the pages of this book will be found biographies of no fewer than nine British Prime Ministers, each of whom served for a London constituency at one time or another: Lord John Russell (City of London) was also a Foreign Secretary and Home Secretary; William Ewart Gladstone (Greenwich), served also as a Chancellor of the Exchequer and Home Secretary; Arthur Balfour (City of London), also as Foreign Secretary; Andrew Bonar Law (Dulwich), also as a Chancellor of the Exchequer; Winston Churchill (Epping and Woodford), also at the Exchequer and Home Office; Clement Attlee (Limehouse and Walthamstow); Harold Macmillan (Bromley), also an occupant of 11 Downing Street, and a Foreign

Secretary ; Edward Heath (Bexley), and Margaret Thatcher (Finchley).

Party Leaders who never achieved Prime Ministerial status also represented London constituencies, though not necessarily at the time they held that position. Kier Hardie (West Ham) and George Lansbury (Bow & Bromley), were amongst Labour's earliest leaders in that category, whilst the Conservatives' Ian Duncan Smith (Chingford), the SDP's Roy Jenkins (Southwark Central) and Respect's George Galloway (Bethnal Green & Bow) shared the same distinction.

Chancellors of the Exchequer who did not attain the Prime Ministerial rank numbered 10 - George Goshen (City of London), Charles Ritchie (Tower Hamlets, and Croydon), Randolph Churchill (Paddington South), John Simon (Walthamstow, who also served as Foreign Secretary), Kingsley Wood (Woolwich West), Hugh Dalton (Peckham), Reginald Maudling (Barnet), Ian MacLeod (Enfield West), Roy Jenkins (Southwark Central) and Norman Lamont (Kingston).

Foreign Secretaries who did not become Prime Minister number 6 - Samuel Hoare (Chelsea), Ernest Bevin (Wandsworth Central and Woolwich East), Michael Stewart (Fulham East), Patrick Gordon Walker (Leyton) and Malcolm Rifkind (Kensington). Notable Home Secretaries who did not serve in other senior Cabinet roles included William Joynson – Hicks (Brentford, and Twickenham), George Cave (Kingston), Herbert Morrison (Hackney South, Lewisham East, and Lewisham South), Henry Brooke (Lewisham West, and Hampstead), Chuter Ede (Mitcham), Kenneth Baker (Acton, and St. Marylebone), and Robert Carr (Mitcham, and Carshalton).

Independent MPs from Horatio Bottomley (Hackney South) to George Galloway (Bethnal Green & Bow) make their appearance. Communists Shapurji Saklatvala (Battersea North 1922) and Philip Piratin (Mile End) are featured, and even elected politicians turned unelected Fascists, Oswald Mosley (Harrow) and John Beckett (Peckham).

Amongst all of London's MPs emerge rogues as well as heroes. There has been a tendency in recent times for critics of parliamentarians to focus on issues such as expenses scandals but the seamier side of life has been evident over a long period of time showing us that London's MPs are sometimes as flawed as the rest of us. A dozen or so honourable members were arrested and imprisoned for a variety of offences, many of them involving fraud. Others have been drawn into scandal, shame or disgrace of one sort or another, often offending the mores of the time. Some of these, especially those of a sexual nature, would be unlikely to be viewed as crimes or even resignation matters today.

Amongst London's MPs there are several notable 'firsts'. The first Jewish MP, (Lionel de Rothschild, City of London 1847), the first ethnic Indian MP (Nadabhai Naroji, Finsbury Central 1892), the first openly gay MP (Chris Smith, Islington South & Finsbury 1983), the first black male (Bernie Grant, Tottenham 1987) and female (Diane Abbot, Hackney North & Stoke Newington 1987) MPs, and the first Muslim to attend the Cabinet (Sadiq Khan, elected at Tooting in 2005). Even the first by-election in the reformed Commons took place, in the City of London, following the death of Richard Waithman MP who died within weeks of his election in December 1832.

In addition to British Prime Ministers, a number held the office of premier in various colonial jurisdictions including: Sir George Houston Reid (a Prime Minister of Australia), Sir Newton James Moore (Prime Minister of Western Australia); Joe Martin (Prime Minister of British Columbia), and Sir Richard Temple (Prime Minister of India). Others were politicians in British colonies before becoming MPs. These included Dr Frederick Harris (MP in South Africa), William and Henry Keswick (members of the Hong Kong Legislature).

Many others distinguished themselves in various walks of life outside politics before becoming MPs. Apart from the myriad lawyers, businessmen, financiers, industrialists, lecturers, journalists and trade unionists who entered the Commons, London has seen the election of 17 medical practitioners, 11 notable sportsmen including an English Rugby Captain and the Captain of the British Walker Cup Team.

Occasionally an MP has suffered mortal injuries. Sir Anthony Berry, Southgate's MP, was murdered, blown up by an IRA bomb whilst attending the Conservative Party Conference at Brighton in 1984. Norman Tebbit (Chingford) was injured in the same atrocity and his wife seriously so. One or two died in military service, notably Charles Mills the MP for Uxbridge, who was killed at the Battle of Loos in 1915. Others have been the victims of serious crime. Stephen Timms MP for East Ham was stabbed by a constituent in his constituency office in 2010.

The book includes hundreds of biographical pieces with interest attached to them all.

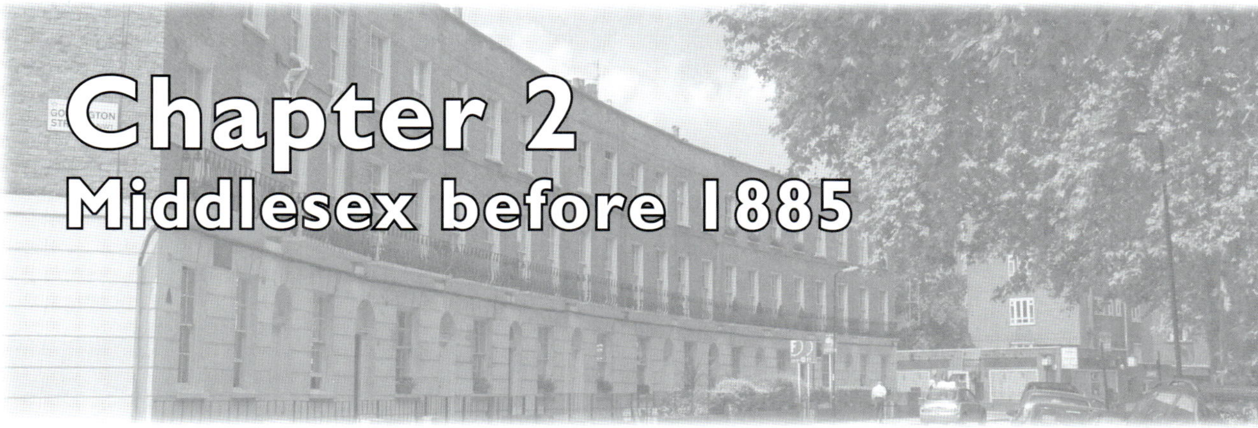

Chapter 2
Middlesex before 1885

Early History

Middlesex, the home of the 'Middle Saxons', contained both Roman London and the later Saxon settlements around Aldwych. It was the nucleus from which the metropolis we know today grew. London's initial significance was as a river crossing between Kent (Cantium) and the city of Colchester (Camulodonum), which was originally the centre of Roman power in Britain, but after the sacking of the town and garrison there by Bouddicca, London rapidly became the radial point for other Roman Roads. With its protected waters and access to Europe by sea, it developed as a major trading station and the new centre of Roman England. By the year 250 AD, with 30,000 inhabitants, it was the biggest city in Britain, and the fifth most populous north of the Alps. It developed almost exclusively on the north bank of the river Thames, opposite present-day Southwark to which it was connected by London Bridge. The river Fleet bounded it in the west, the Thames to the south, and a wall was constructed round the city for its protection to the north and east. The original Roman walls more or less still demarcate the core of the City of London as it is today. However, following the departure of the Romans from Britain in 410 AD, it probably fell into disuse until the Anglo Saxons came. They started to populate areas further up river in the sixth Century, and established a Christian mission in 604 AD, leading to the construction of the cathedral church of St. Pauls.

The gradual establishment of the Kingdom of England over the next two hundred and sixty years, and the predominance of Wessex within it, meant that the first capital was at Winchester, the seat of government under Alfred the Great from 871 AD. Commerce returned, and in 1016 AD the Danish King Cnut moved the court there. There were changes to the centres of power within London itself, and during the reign of Edward the Confessor (1042 – 1066) the court moved from the old City Wardrobe Palace near St.Pauls to Westminster. Thus began a rivalry between the Cities of London and Westminster that to some extent still exists today. The City was to continue as the principal commercial centre whilst Westminster became the centre of monarchy and Government.

With its roots in medieval times, the Corporation of London is the oldest local authority in England. It is said that the Parliament at Westminster is based on the Corporation's Court of Common Council. The right of the City to run its own affairs was gradually won as concessions were gained from the Crown, and London's importance as a centre of trade, population and wealth secured it rights and liberties earlier than other towns and cities. A Charter was granted by William the Conqueror in 1067, in which he promised to recognise the rights, privileges, and laws that the City had enjoyed since the time of Edward the Confessor. Since 1384 the wards of the City have elected the Common Council.

In the heart of the modern Barbican Estate remnants of the original Roman fortification are still visible.

Westminster Hall in Parliament Square as it is today, still acting as the focus of the Palace of Westminster, as it has since the 11th century. **Both Photographs John Nelson.**

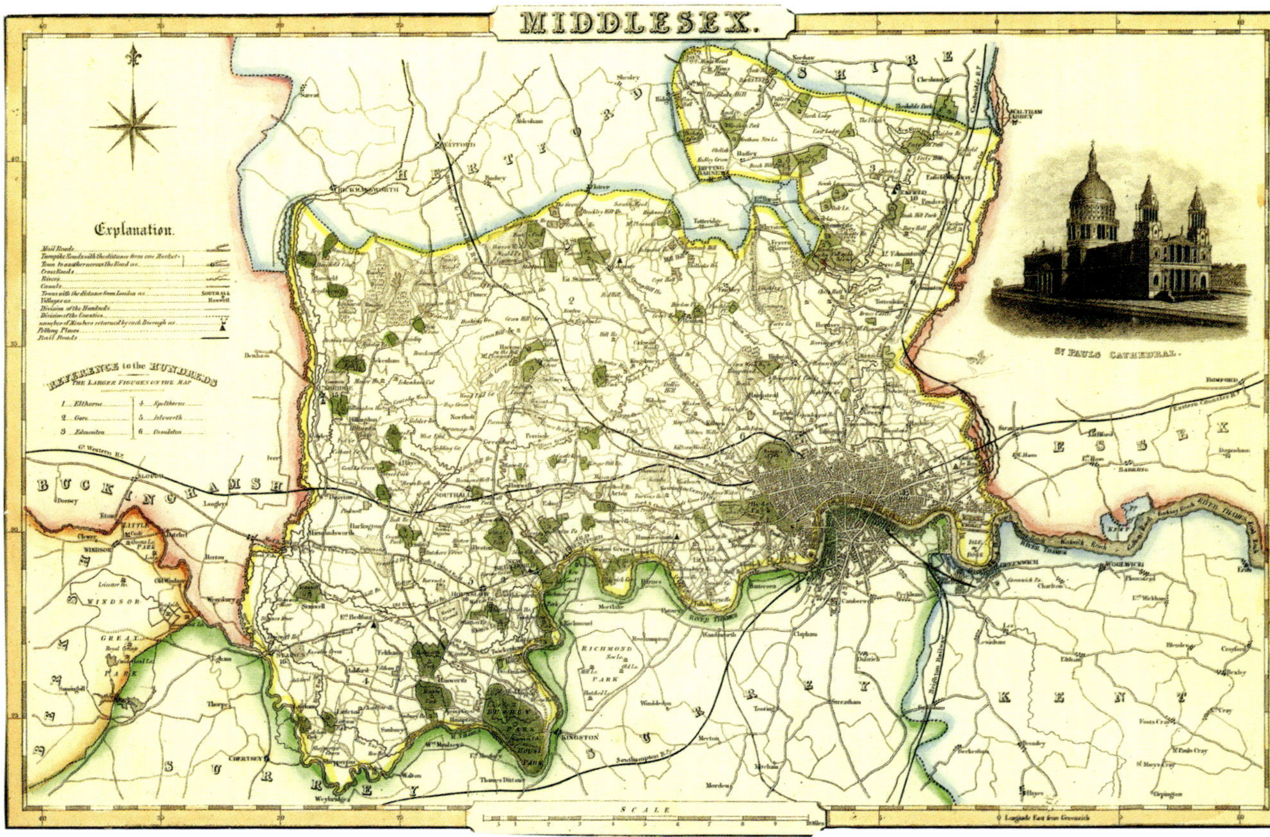

The County of Middlesex is shown here in a Pigot map of around 1840. The first railways from London begin from the perimeter of the built up area of the time. These arteries of communication would soon provide the means of sustenance that allowed the population to grow rapidly and steadily, to provide the story-line for this book. The largest constituency (from 1832) is called Middlesex; it takes all the land outside the built up area. That, as can be seen from the map on page 38, is divided into Tower Hamlets, Finsbury, Marylebone, Westminster and the City of London. Middlesex is bounded on the north side by Hertfordshire. The County's southern boundary was the north bank of the River Thames. It extended in the east as far as (and including) the Isle of Dogs. Broadly the eastern Middlesex County boundary (bounding Essex) followed the River Lea North to Waltham Abbey, where it turned west, and apart from an Hertfordshire inclusion of Barnet and Totteridge, this boundary continued west to the River Colne, then (bounding Buckinghamshire) following it south directly to the Thames.

Elections are held every year in wards that return between four and twelve members depending on the size of the electorate. Common Council members are known as Commoners. All these features are to be found in the way our modern electoral structures were established.

The AD 975 place name 'Westmynster' meant 'West Monastery', that is it was the monastery to the West of the City of London. King Offa founded it on Thorney Island (Isle of Brambles), formed by the forking of the river Tyburn near the present St James's Park Underground station. It fell into ruin after the Danes sacked it, but under Edward the Confessor it revived with the building of Westminster Abbey and Westminster Hall, to which 'Palace' he moved the Court[1]. Henry VIII decreed Westminster Abbey a cathedral in 1540, and so the town became a city. When after only ten years the cathedral was changed into a royal collegiate church, Westminster retained the title of a city, an unusual one because it had neither a mayor nor a council, being run instead by the Dean of Westminster Abbey and his manor court.

Despite these developments there was little population growth until the reign of Queen Elizabeth I. A map of 1560 indicates that only limited building had taken place on the roads connecting the City of London with the Palace of Westminster. However, the Strand and Holborn were beginning to develop and under Elizabeth, Westminster began to do so rapidly. Due to the dissolution of the monasteries ordered by her father, land that had formerly been in the ownership of religious orders became available for development. By 1579 the Inns of Court were under construction, between the Cities of London and Westminster, and there was an increase in the size of the Court and administration. With England also becoming a colonial power it was not long before major population growth occurred.

In 1586, the Government agreed that Westminster could have a town council in the form of the Court of Burgesses. With a new Act of Parliament twelve wards were created in the city, and for each of them there was one burgess and an assistant burgess. However, because the monarch wanted to keep control, the burgesses could not choose their own mayor. The chairman of the Court of Burgesses had to be the High Steward of Westminster Abbey. He was normally

1 The Palace remained a Royal residence until Tudor times.

a great officer of state, and therefore the position of chairman was held by a succession of famous men including many prime ministers. This system prevailed until 1900, when councillors were permitted to elect their own mayor for the first time. The last High Steward of Westminster to preside over the council was Robert Cecil, the Third Marquis of Salisbury, Prime Minster and a direct descendant of William Cecil, the first High Steward. The first mayor to be elected was the Duke of Norfolk.

Westminster continued to grow massively, so that by 1746 the London conurbation extended continuously from the City boundary northwards to Lambs Conduit Fields (half way to St Pancras), and westward to Hyde Park. Westminster Bridge was built in 1750 by which time development was moving west towards Chelsea. Between 1700 and 1750 it is estimated that the population of London (mostly comprising Westminster and the City) grew from 575,000 to 675,000 people, probably making it the largest City in the world at that time. The population of Middlesex as a whole was estimated to be 624,200 in 1700, and according to the first census this grew to 818,000 a century later[2]. Within the space of the next thirty years its population rose further to 1,358,541 at a time when that of the entire London metropolis, including Southwark, was measured at 1,474,069[3].

Middlesex was by far the most populous of the Home Counties. By the time of the Representation of the People Act in 1832 it was second to Yorkshire in Britain, though in geographical size only Rutland was smaller, giving an indication of just how densely populated it was even then. Although the largest centres of population within the County were the Cities of London and Westminster, a further 75,000 lived outside, with Marylebone, Islington, Hackney and Tower Hamlets all burgeoning. Middlesex contained most of London's centres of manufacturing industry, including: silk textiles, wire, pins, needles, iron making, soap, rope, paper, pottery, and chemical manufacture. Other industries included brewing, distilling, bleaching, dying, tanning, and shipping. There were around five-thousand coal barges operating on the Thames, while a further four-thousand ships were involved in import and export trades of all kinds. Three-thousand barges were additionally involved with inland trading, via the rivers and canals, all of which were flourishing at that time. The Port of London handled fifteen-thousand cargoes annually. Yet despite the strength of the manufacturing sector, based as it was on London's position as a huge population centre as well as its trading status with mainland Europe, agriculture was also strong, especially in the cultivation of fruit and vegetables. Hay making was prominent in servicing dairy-farming, whilst the meat markets at Smithfield and elsewhere were also on Middlesex soil.

Historically the County was divided for administrative purposes into six 'Hundreds'[4]. The largest geographically was Ossulstone which covered most of the metropolitan area between the rivers Brent, Thames and Lea. Within it were the four sub-divisions of Finsbury, Tower, Holborn and Kensington. Ossulston(e) Street today may be found between St. Pancras and Euston stations, next to the British Library. Edmonton Hundred extended from South Mimms and Enfield to the borders of Hackney, including places like Tottenham mainly to the east of the 'New River', a water course built

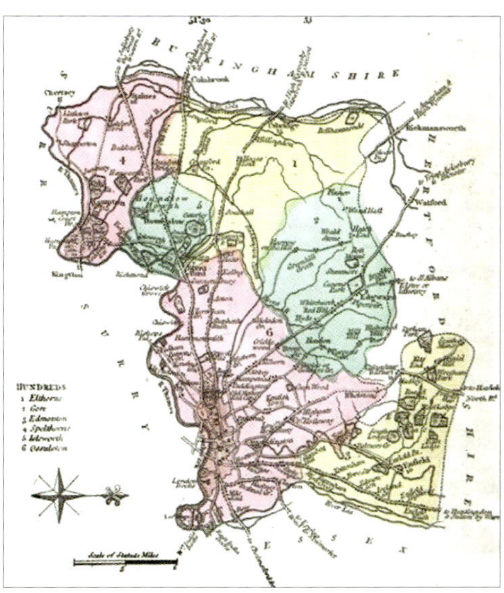

This copy of a rotated map of the Middlesex Hundreds dating from the Middle Ages, shows the entire built up area of London in 1832 was in the Ossulstone Hundred. The British Library at Ossulston Street, offers a reminder of this aspect of London's history. In 1832 this part of Somers Town was a heavily built up slum area in the Marylebone Constituency. Few inhabitants would have had a vote. **Photograph: John Nelson.**

2 1801

3 1831 census

4 Hundreds were first mentioned in the Laws of Edgar in 970, and by the time of King Ethelred the term referred to an area of one hundred hides for the purpose of taxation. For many centuries after this the Hundreds were used as a fiscal, judicial and sometimes a military district. The Hundred courts levied taxes, dealt with law and order matters, and tried some civil and criminal offences.

to supply London with Hertfordshire water. Gore Hundred covered the area of today's boroughs of Brent and Harrow whilst Elthorne embraced Hillingdon and Southall. Further south lay the Isleworth Hundred, the smallest, comprising Hounslow including Brentford, whilst on the borders with Surrey and Buckinghamshire, Spelthorne Hundred included Staines, Twickenham, and Feltham.

Parliamentary Representation

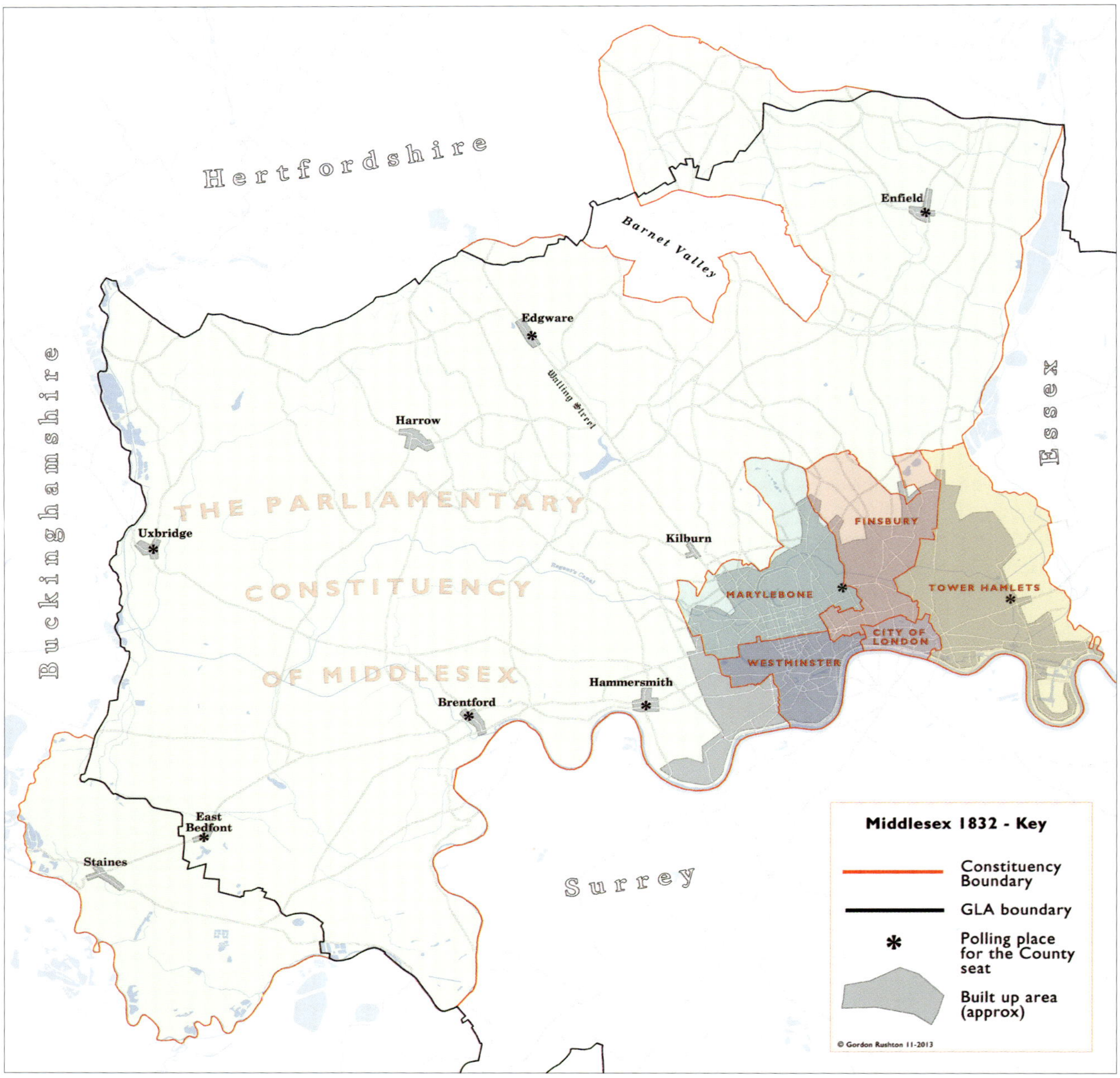

The map shows the Middlesex County and Borough constituencies created by the First Reform Act, and which were contested in 1832. The rural character of Middlesex outside the London built-up area accounts for the large size of the County Constituency.

The importance of Middlesex in the economic and political life of the nation was not reflected in its early Parliamentary representation. **The City of London** was the only Middlesex borough summoned by the King to send MPs to the House of Commons in 1295. The City has been represented by a constituency that includes its name in every Parliament since. In 1295, just like any other English Parliamentary borough, it sent two burgesses, though in London's case this number was increased to four in 1355, an indication of the importance that the City then had in the eyes of the monarchy. The timing was not without its significance. Under Edward III England was engaged in War with France and taxes were needed to fund it. The fact that the City's MPs numbered four until as late as the Parliament of 1880-85, after which it was reduced again to two, is indicative of its on-going actual as well as perceived importance. **Westminster** did not send MPs to the House of Commons until 1545, in Henry VIII's time, and no other part of London north of the Thames was specifically represented, except the County of Middlesex, which in common with most other English

Counties returned two MPs from 1295 onwards.

It was not until 1832 that other borough seats emerged, based on Tower Hamlets, Finsbury and Marylebone, so that Middlesex returned fourteen MPs, a near doubling of its previous representation. The **Middlesex County** constituency returned two MPs, with voters polling at Brentford (where the election result was also declared), Enfield, Hammersmith, Bedfont, Edgware, Mile End, Uxbridge and Kings Cross, or 'within half a mile thereof' as decreed by the legislation. At the 1832 General Election there were only 6,939 registered voters in the County constituency, making it the smallest by size of electorate compared with the Middlesex boroughs. In 1831 there were estimated to be 208,000 people living in the districts of Middlesex not covered by the borough constituencies. Areas of what we now call 'inner London' included in the Middlesex County constituency in 1832 were: Barons Court, Brompton, Chelsea, Earls Court, Fulham, Hammersmith, Holland Park, Kensal Green, Kensington, Ladbroke Grove, Notting Hill, Shepherds Bush and Wormwood Scrubs.

Westminster, with the City, formed a growing conurbation extending into Marylebone, Finsbury and Tower Hamlets. The main electorates were registered there, and the new borough constituencies of **Finsbury, Tower Hamlets, Marylebone** and **Westminster** returned two MPs each. **The City of London** kept four, retaining its position as the best represented constituency in terms of the number of MPs, if not relative to its population. Although it had the largest electorate, numbering 18,584 in 1832, of all the boroughs it had the smallest population (122,799 in 1831), evidence that the Act did not herald anything like the arrival of a democratic system. This was also indicated by the fact that Tower Hamlets, with a population of 359,864, had only 9,906 voters, 700 fewer than Westminster, which had a generally more affluent population of about 200,000. Even middle class Marylebone, with a population about 40,000 larger than Westminster, had 2,500 fewer electors. Finsbury was a shade more affluent, and with a population only slightly smaller than Marylebone's, had 1,500 more registered voters.

Westminster extended from Temple Bar, at the junction of Fleet St and the Strand, to Kensington Gore and Knightsbridge, and included: Belgravia, Buckingham Palace, Charing Cross, Covent Garden, Hyde Park, Mayfair, Millbank, Pimlico, St. James', Victoria, and Whitehall.

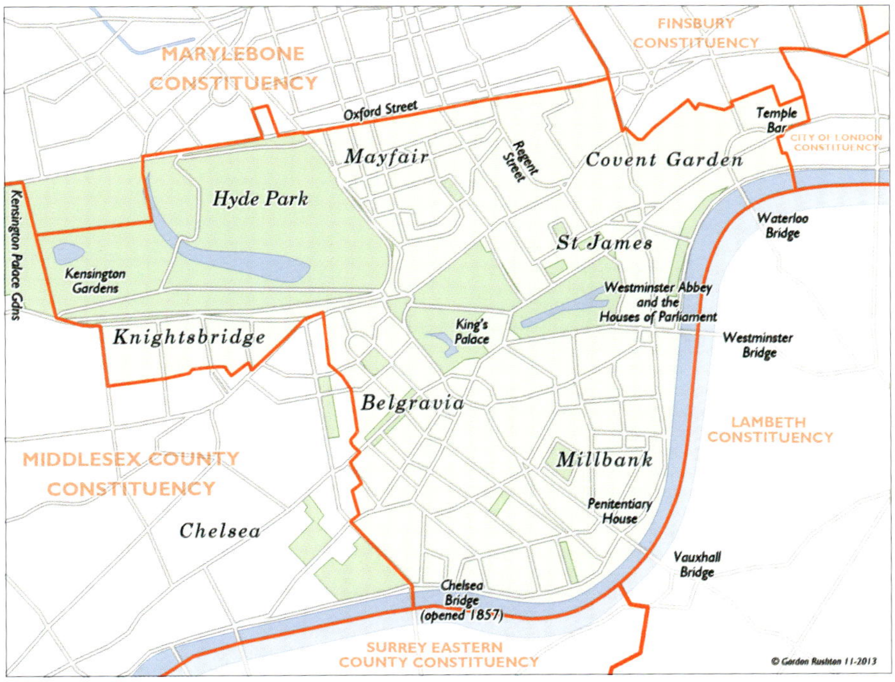

The Westminster Borough Constituency in 1832. At the time the whole area was already built up, with the exception of the green spaces that still exist today. By the time the constituency was restructured in 1885, Victoria and Charing Cross Stations had both been opened.

Finsbury was one of the first places outside the City of London to become an important borough in its own right. In 1832 the division's population was 224,839 with 10,309 registered voters, but the shape of the constituency was much larger than the immediate area. In addition to Bunhill, Finsbury and Clerkenwell, it included: Bloomsbury, Holborn, Farringdon, Pentonville, Islington, Holloway, Shacklewell, Dalston, and Stoke Newington. By 1868 it contained 31,759 voters and a population of 387,278. Named after the Fiennes family who owned land immediately north of the City, their Manor House of Finsbury was built beyond the Moorgate entrance to London. Much of the area was marshland and the 'moor' itself was drained in 1527, leading to further building. Finsbury Fields were used for archery practice in the 16th century, and at the time of the Fire of London in 1666 homeless Londoners camped there. In 1665 Bunhill Fields Cemetery was opened for nonconformists on a prehistoric burial site that became known as Bone Hill. Many famous people were buried there, including the authors John Bunyan and Daniel Defoe. The preacher and founder of Methodism, John Wesley, lived opposite the fields, on City Road. Finsbury Square was constructed nearby in 1777.

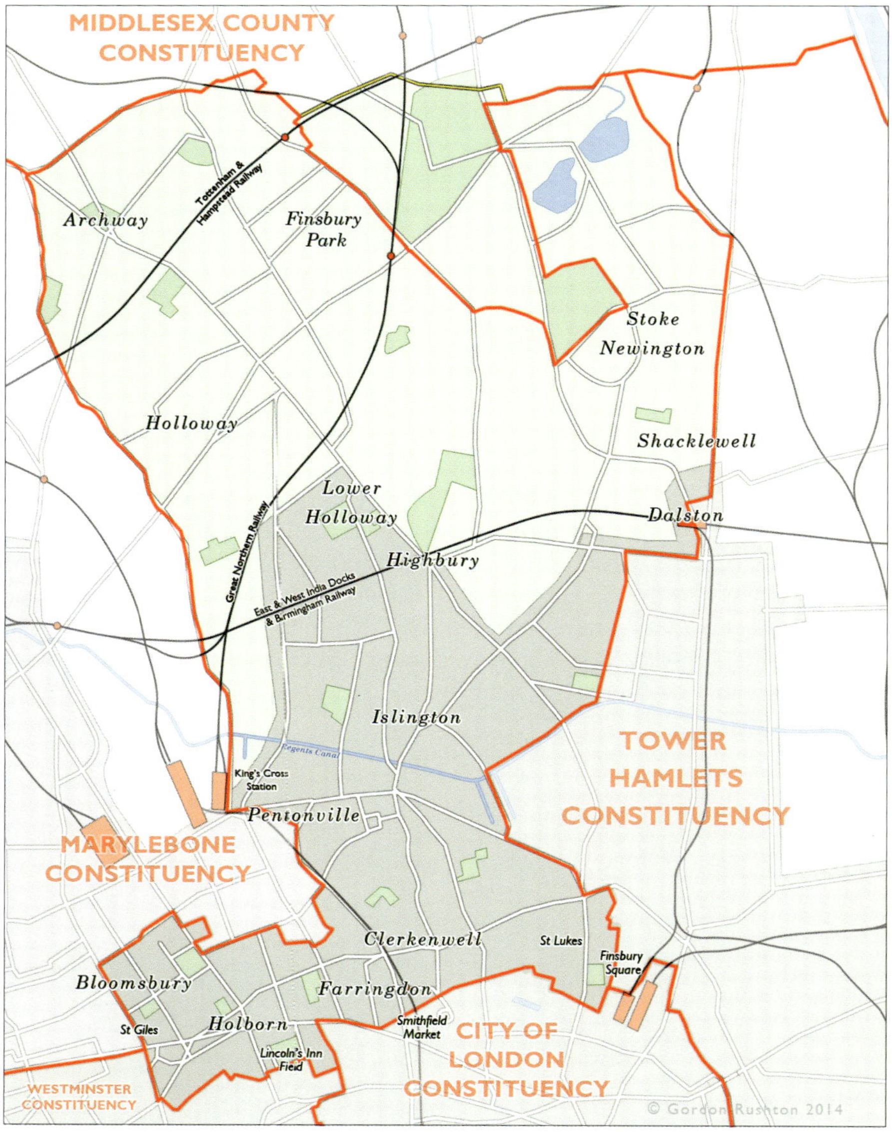

The Finsbury Borough Constituency in 1832 & 1868 showing the railways that had been built between 1837 and 1867. The grey shading marks the limit of the built up area in 1832. The Yellow boundary shows the Constituency expansion in the Finsbury Park area in 1868

Clerkenwell, which was the core district in central Finsbury, took its name from the Clerk's Well at Farringdon Lane meaning, 'spring or well frequented by students'. It had strong monastic traditions: the Monastic Order of the Knights Hospitallers of St John of Jerusalem, founded to give medical assistance during the crusades, had its English Headquarters here. 'Clerk's Well' stood next to the nunnery and priory of St John of Jerusalem, founded in 1140, and Carthusian Monks lived at the Charter House, near the boundary with the City, which later became a school and almshouse. Its proximity to the City and local waters meant that it became attractive to wealthy men, especially after the Great Plague[5] and the Fire. The Duke of Newcastle, head of the most powerful Whig family in the Land moved there. In the 18th Century its Green became especially fashionable with City merchants, but it was also an area in which the City located less attractive institutions. Bridewell Prison was built there in 1615 and remained operational until 1804. A new House of Detention was opened there in 1845 that lasted until 1877.

Before Clerkenwell became built up, it was famous as a resort of spas, tea gardens and theatres, of which Sadler's Wells survives. However, Clerkenwell was changed by the Industrial Revolution, becoming a centre for printing, jewellery, clock and watch making. The quality of water attracted the establishment of brewing and distilleries. Both Gordons and Booths had gin distilleries in Clerkenwell. It also became a place where radical politicians gathered. The Green was a place not unlike Hyde Park Corner where speakers addressed large crowds. The late eighteenth century Middlesex MP John Wilkes spoke there against his expulsion from the unreformed House of Commons.

St Luke's parish was separated from the City Parish of St Giles, Cripplegate in the eighteenth century, and as early as 1746 housing development occurred north of the City of London boundary reaching half way to Islington. By 1835 the whole of present-day Clerkenwell and Finsbury were built up between their boundaries with the City, Holborn, St. Pancras, the City Road, and Pentonville, and its population was about 100,000, a suburb for clerks and minor professionals. Agriculture remained into the early nineteenth century, and the great grandfather of Cecil Rhodes[6] farmed there. With industry thriving, the population rose to a little under 113,000 in 1841, twice that of neighbouring Islington. City merchants moved there in even greater numbers when the Lloyd Baker and Metropolitan Board estates were laid out between Clerkenwell and the Pentonville Road. Its population peaked in 1861 at 129,073, and by then Islington had outgrown it; development there was accelerated by the building of the railways. This did not impact significantly on Finsbury, which was south of the main line stations that had been constructed along the Euston Road. (see opposite)

5 1665 and the Great Fire was in 1666.

6 The founder of Rhodesia, now Zimbabwe.

When the parliamentary borough of **St Marylebone** was created in 1832 it was Finsbury's western neighbour. Separated from Westminster by Oxford Street, it included the parishes of Paddington, St Marylebone and St Pancras, extending as far North as Highgate. The Regents Canal had been completed between Limehouse Basin and Paddington twelve years earlier, and an extensive built-up area developed west of Marylebone: from Paddington Basin and the Uxbridge Road opposite Hyde Park (now the Bayswater Road) to Lords Cricket Ground in the North, it was matched in the east by development from Camden Town south towards Holborn. In 1831 the population of the constituency was already a massive 240,294 of who half lived in St Pancras, mostly around Kings Cross, in Somerstown and Camden Town. Yet in 1832 there were only 8,901 electors. Its population was then the eleventh highest, and its electorate thirteenth of all the English constituencies, but by 1861 it was second largest by population and seventh by number of registered electors.

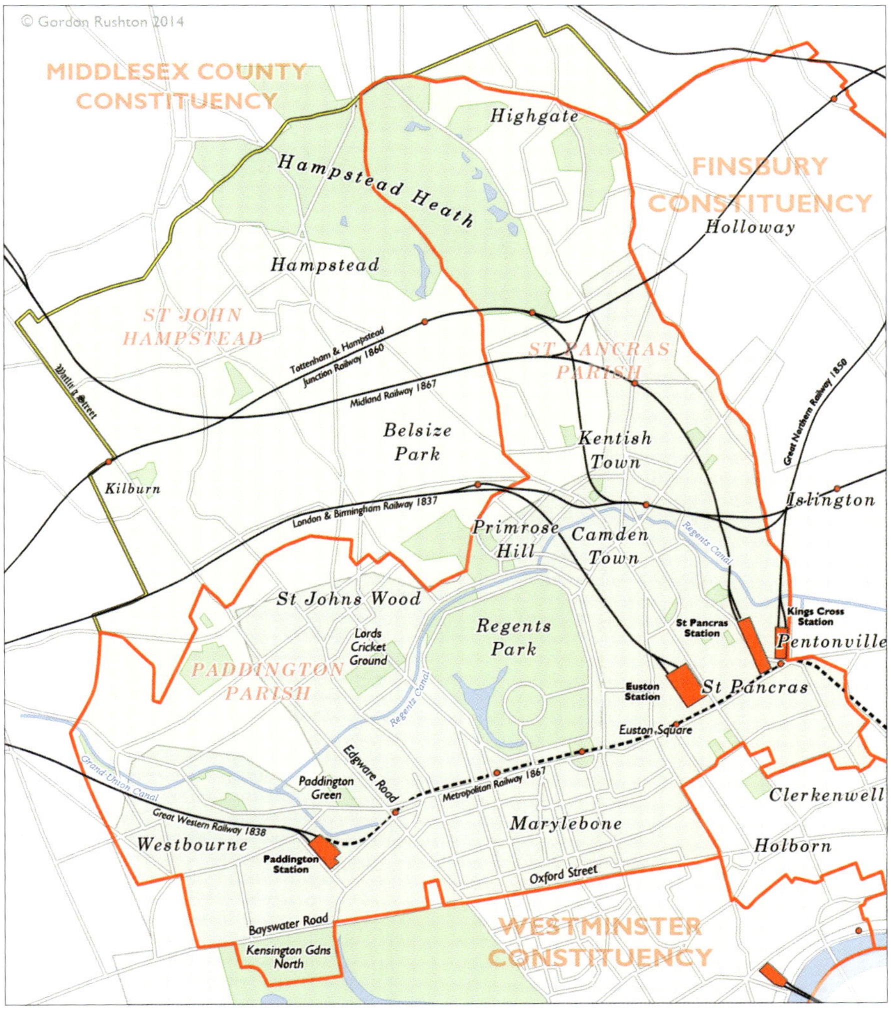

The Marylebone Borough Constituency in 1832 & 1868 showing the railways that had been built between 1837 and 1867. The grey shading marks the limit of the built up area in 1832. The Yellow boundary shows the Constituency expansion in 1868

'Maryburne', meaning 'place by St Mary's stream', dates from 1453 when a church was dedicated there. It dates from the seventeenth century when it was a small village beyond Westminster and a short distance from two others, Lissing (later to become Lisson), and Paddington. Around 1700, three farms, together with a private estate at Tottenham Court, occupied the land, which today lies between Oxford Street, Marylebone Road, the Edgware and Tottenham Court Roads. Some of the roads in the area had national significance. The Edgware Road was formerly part of the Roman Watling Street, which ran northwest to Wroxeter and Holyhead. At today's Marble Arch it intersected Oxford Street, another Roman road, built initially between London and Notting Hill. This became much used as a drover's trail, taking cattle and sheep to market as well as for the transport of people.

After Westminster became the seat of national government and of the Royal Court it was inevitable that sooner or later it would spill over into Marylebone. By 1745 houses had been built on the north side of Oxford Street, initially west of Tottenham Court and around Cavendish Square, but the major stimulus was the building of the so-called New Road, which was completed in 1757. Now the Marylebone Road, it was constructed to by-pass the congested streets of Westminster so that traffic, including cattle and sheep destined for the meat market at Smithfield could pass more freely. By 1795 the area between the New Road and Oxford Street had been developed, apart from the small corner occupied today by Bryanston Square, east of the Edgware Road. Baker Street was built in 1795, and further development occurred with the laying out of Regents Park and surrounding mansions in the 1820s. North of the New Road lay Crown Estate lands, then known as Marylebone Park, designed by George, Prince Regent (later George IV) as Regents Park. Regent's Street and Portland Place (on the eastern boundary of Marylebone parish) were part of the same development. Lands north of the Marylebone Road, and especially west of the Park, were built on when the property leases expired in 1811. Pastures and market gardens serving London became residential areas for the wealthy. In 1821 Sir Edward Baker bought land in Lisson Green, and the whole area became built-up very quickly. Baker Street is named after him. Between 1827

Left: *Marble Arch was originally located outside the King's Palace (now Buckingham Palace) in 1827, but was moved to its present location at the junction of Oxford Street and Edgware Road in 1833. Edgware Road was in the Marylebone constituency and Oxford Street separated Marylebone from Westminster. Both Oxford Street and Edgware Road have separated constituencies many times since.*

Gordon Rushton

Below: *Cumberland Gardens WC1, in the Lloyd Baker Estate, which was laid out between the 1820s and the 1840s at about the time that the Finsbury Constituency was created. The architectural concept was to recall the classic outlines of the Parthenon in Athens, which had at that time come to notice.* **John Nelson**

Below: *Cornwall Terrace (now a Grade 1 listed building), facing Regent's Park, was constructed between 1821 and 1823 in the Corinthian order, with Venetian style windows and cast iron balconies, as part of a scheme sponsored by the Prince of Wales (Prince Regent) to develop splendid housing around the Regent's Park. It was in the 1832 St Marylebone Constituency, and was a magnificent setting to its enfranchised inhabitants. Today the properties are within the Crown Estate development at Regent's Park.*

John Nelson

Right: *Westminster, Queen Anne's Gate, parallel with Birdcage Walk, contains fine houses from the 18th century in the unique architectural style of the period. Situated in the Petty France district, they are within easy walking distance of Parliament and Whitehall. They provided London homes to wealthy electors in 1832. Most people living in the upper rooms would have been unfranchised servants*

Below: *Temple Bar was constructed at the join of Fleet Street and The Strand, in 1672, marking the historical boundaries between the cities of London and Westminster. Commissioned by Charles II, it was designed by Sir Christopher Wren. In its position on such a busy thoroughfare it was a block to traffic, and thus was removed in 1878. It was re-erected by Henry Meux in Theobalds Park, but brought back to the City in 2004 to form the gateway to Paternoster Square.* **All photos: John Nelson**

Below: *This map of the City of London Constituency is set in about 1832, just before the coming of the railways. At that time the Thames was still in use by myriad barges and sailing ships that clustered along the banks at quays (such as Custom House Quay). All this would soon change as steamships arrived, growing in size and necessitating docks. Three Thames bridges serve the City, Blackfriars, Southwark and London Bridge. More would be added in the Victorian era to come. At this time there were four MPs for the City of London, all of them Liberal. The City streets were thronged with people and vehicles. Indeed congestion continued to grow, so that with all the horses, the carts, and the omnibuses it became gradually unworkable, thus use of the City was becoming difficult. In 1832 sweeping transport improvements had yet to be made. The Act for the London and Blackwall Railway was passed in 1836, and Fenchurch St Station was built in 1841. Across London Bridge there already was London's first station - for Greenwich - opened in 1836; change was coming.*

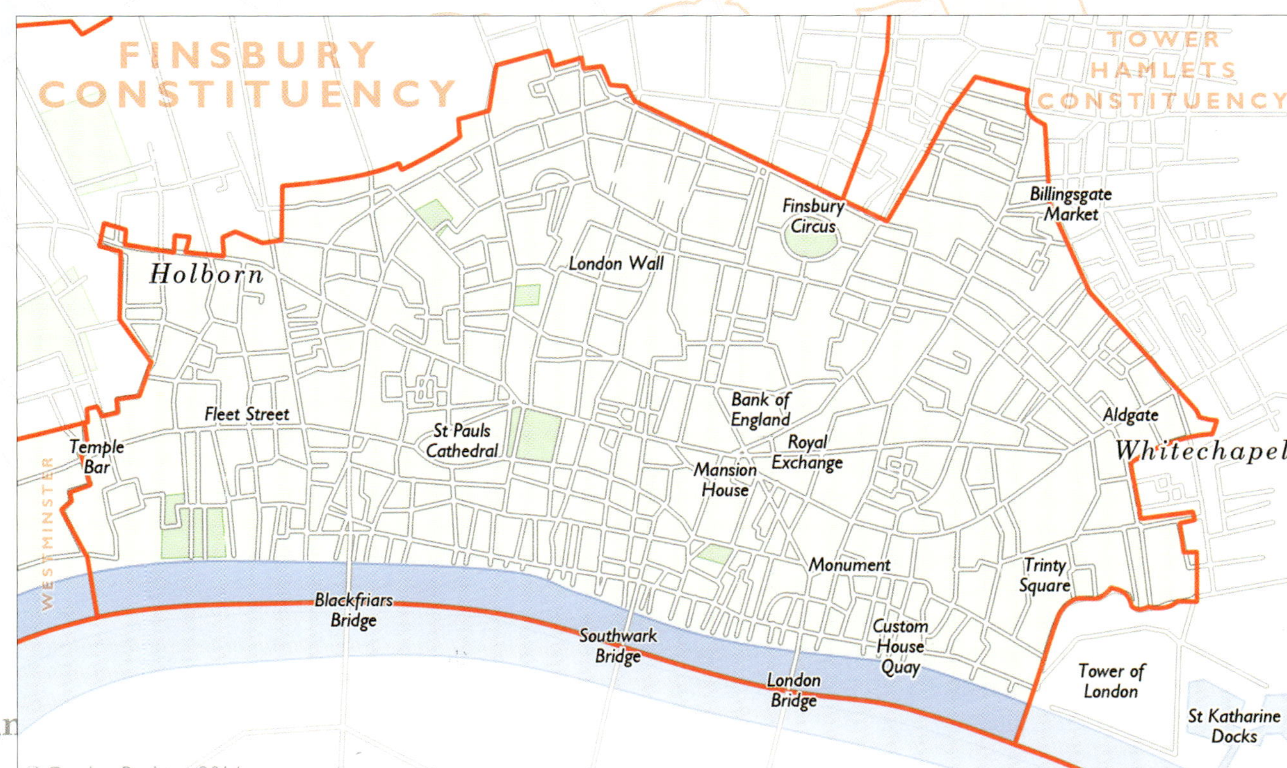

Shoredith High Street in 1868, a year after it was transferred to the new Hackney Constituency. **©TfL from the London Transport Museum Collection**

Dockside houses and offices at Wapping, Tower Hamlets Constituency created in 1832. The houses are still standing today, though the area has now become residential and dormitory, as the docks have moved away. **Gordon Rushton**

and 1850, the area west of the Park and as far north as the Marylebone Cricket Club at Lords had been developed. Apart from Marylebone the constituency comprised: Bayswater, Lisson Grove, Fitzrovia, Maida Vale, St Johns Wood, Regents Park, Primrose Hill, Queens Park, Camden Town, Kentish Town, Gospel Oak, and Waterlow Park.

Tower Hamlets, London's 'East End', comprised 359,864 inhabitants in 1831, and was not only the most populous in London but of all the then English borough constituencies. Its name originated in the eighteenth century meaning 'hamlets under the jurisdiction of the Tower of London', and in 1832 sent two members to Parliament. The Tower itself dates from the reign of William the Conqueror when the area was known as the Tower Liberties in the County of Middlesex.

At least three Roman trading routes pass through the borough to this day: Roman Road itself, Bethnal Green Road, and The Highway. The Saxons gained control after the Romans left and gave the inhabited area the name that later appears in the Doomsday book - Stibenhede, or Stebba's landing place. This became the Manor of Stepney, which the Bishops of London held for more than five hundred years until the Reformation. Their manor house was in what became Bethnal Green, near the present London Chest Hospital. The population of Tower Hamlets was about 900 at the time of the Doomsday Survey, and in the medieval period was still only 2,500 according to a survey in 1377.

As the City grew, certain trades such as metalworking, brick making, tanning and brewing, that were not allowed there because of danger, noise, or smell, came to be located in adjoining Spitalfields and Whitechapel. The riverside hamlets also grew, after banking was constructed to stop the Thames flooding. Blackwall, Poplar, Ratcliffe, Shadwell, and Wapping developed as centres of shipbuilding and repair, while limekilns to make mortar for the building industry were established, giving their name to Limehouse. The construction of Bow Bridge over the River Lea in Henry I's reign improved access to the tide mills on the east bank. A trading site for over nine hundred years, Three Mills was the country's largest ever tidal mill complex. Bromley and Bow (so named after the shape of the bridge), grew into important industrial centres.

The maritime character of Tower Hamlets changed during the nineteenth century with the building of huge warehouses behind the docks. West India, East India, London and St. Katharine Docks were all established. Shipbuilding spread along the riverside and became concentrated on the Isle of Dogs. Brunel's Great Eastern was launched in 1858 and laid the first telegraphic cables across the Atlantic. In 1825 its builder, Isambard Kingdom Brunel had, with his father Marc, also designed the Thames Tunnel, which linked Wapping with Rotherhithe on the Surrey side of the Thames. The tunnel was the first in the world to be built under a navigable river.

By 1835 the Tower Hamlets were already well developed. Warehouses and residential accommodation extended continuously, east from Limehouse to St Katharine Docks, and north to the Whitechapel Road, whilst beyond it Spitalfields, Hoxton, and Bethnal Green had already taken shape. Stepney, Mile End, and Globe Town were half-way to completing the urbanisation of East London between the Thames and the Regents Canal. Only the area between the Canal and the river Lea was largely undeveloped, although linear building had started in Poplar along the East India

Dock Road, and at Bow on the road towards Stratford. This area was to become built-up over the following decades. Victoria Park in Bow was first laid out in 1844, brought about by the demand of local people for a recreational area in an increasingly urban environment. Communities contained within the 1832 constituency were: Aldgate, Bethnal Green, Bow, Bromley by Bow, Limehouse, Mile End, Old Ford, Poplar, Ratcliffe, Shadwell, Spitalfields, Stepney, the Tower of London, Wapping, Whitechapel, Shoreditch, Hoxton, Haggerston, Hackney, Upper Clapton, and Stamford Hill - the northernmost point in the constituency.

The Hackney and Tower Hamlets Borough Constituencies in 1868.
Prior to 1868, the whole area was in the 1832 Tower Hamlets Constituency.
The grey shading marks the limit of the built up area in 1832.

Continuing population growth in mid century was reflected in the shape of the constituencies after the 1867 Representation of the People Act. As wealthy residences extended westward, so industry and associated workers' dwellings trended eastward, and two new, two-member borough divisions either side of the City of Westminster core were created, one centred on Chelsea, the other on Hackney. These also brought about significant boundary changes to most of the existing Middlesex constituencies, and added four MPs to the County's total. The Hackney constituency, for example, took most of its electorate from the former **Tower Hamlets** division, which reduced its geographical size so that it covered only: Bromley-by-Bow, Mile End, Poplar, Limehouse, Stepney, Wapping, and Whitechapel. Despite these significant boundary changes, the population of the constituency only fell from 360,000 in 1831 to 317,900. It still had the sixth-largest population of any of the English borough constituencies. Also, extensions to the franchise meant that the electorate increased to 32,547 in 1868, over three times what it had been in 1832 in the bigger area, still making it the eighth largest borough, compared with a ranking of sixth thirty years earlier. Despite hardship and poverty through much of Ratcliffe, Shadwell and Wapping, economic and riverside development continued to spread eastwards. Master builder William Cubit, twice Lord Mayor of London, developed the eastern half of the Isle of Dogs, and by the end of the nineteenth century, the bank from Limehouse to Blackwall was crowded with factories and warehouses. The local population continued to grow, and by 1881 had risen to 438,910, making Tower Hamlets the fifth largest borough constituency in England by population, with an electorate in 1884 of 41,586 (ninth in the same rankings).

The new **Hackney** borough constituency covered an extensive built-up area that also included: Bethnal Green, Cambridge Heath, Clapton, Dalston, Haggerston, Homerton, Hoxton, Kingsland, Moorfields, Shacklewell, and Shoreditch. Unlike today, it did not include Stoke Newington, which was then still incorporated within Finsbury, but it did include Stamford Hill. When the constituency was created, its population as measured by the 1861 census was 329,945, containing an electorate of 40,613 in 1868. By 1881 the population had increased to 417,191 (making it the sixth largest of the English boroughs); by 1884 the electorate was 48,076 (also sixth largest and second in London only to Lambeth).

Hackney's name is thought to derive from an island in the River Lea - 'Hacon's Eyot' – and was first recorded in 1198, though nearby Shoreditch was earlier (in 1148). For another four-hundred years they were farming communities in the Middlesex countryside. Each was a church parish, one was centred on St Leonard's, Shoreditch, the other on St Augustine's Tower in Mare Street, Hackney, which contained several other hamlets such as Homerton, Clapton, Dalston, and Shacklewell. Development was heavily influenced by the growth of London. Aristocrats and government officials who

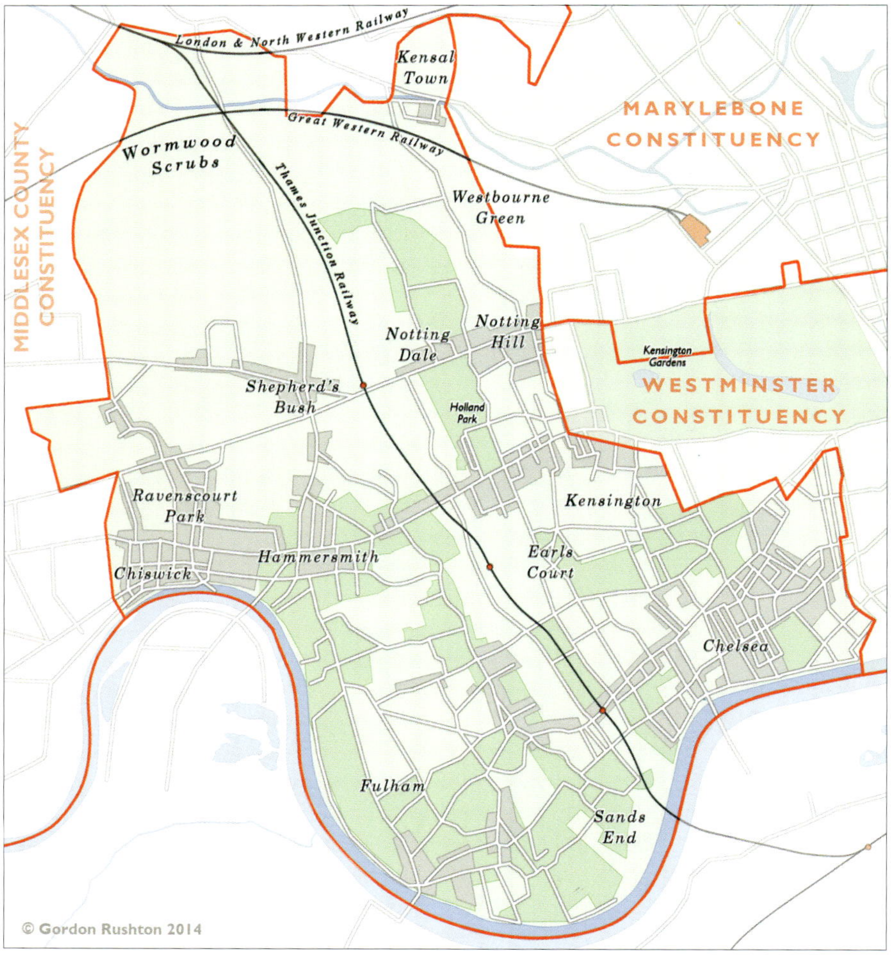

The new Chelsea Borough Constituency in 1868.
The grey shading marks the limit of the built up area in 1868.

wanted to be close to the City and Westminster had country houses at Hoxton and Homerton. After south Shoreditch became increasingly built up in the late seventeenth century, the aristocrats moved away, and several big houses were turned into schools or private lunatic asylums. However, developments such as Charles Square, and Hoxton Square were built for prosperous people who were active in the City. Hackney was also a centre of nonconformist worship and radical politics. People from many parts of Europe came to work in the furniture industry in Shoreditch in the nineteenth century, and Jews have lived in Hackney since 1684.

When the first modern constituencies were set up in 1832, although Hoxton and Shoreditch were well built up, Hackney and Kingsland were merely ribbon developments of large houses north of the Regents Canal still separated mostly by fields. Rich businessmen still had big houses in Hackney and Stoke Newington until the middle of the nineteenth century, but the middle classes started to move to more fashionable, less populated areas after the railways arrived in 1850. Then it became possible for the less well off to commute daily from Hackney to the City and the Victorian villas and terraces that still feature today were built. About the time that the Hackney constituency was established in 1867, the journalist George Rose Emerson wrote in the early 1860s that Hackney, Clapton and Dalston comprised 'one of the handsomest suburbs in London', and the creation of nearby Victoria Park enhanced the value of the houses.

Chelsea, the second new constituency created in 1867, lay beyond Westminster, extending both west and northwards to Chiswick, Fulham, Hammersmith, Kensington, and Kensal Town, incorporating communities formerly in the Middlesex county division. The constituency comprised today's London boroughs of Kensington & Chelsea and Hammersmith & Fulham combined, together with the easternmost parts of Hounslow. These places were expanding rapidly in the second half of the nineteenth century, so much so that the constituency population of 174,000 rose to 366,516 in 1881, with the electorate increasing when the seat was created in 1868 from 17,408 to 36,151 in 1884, the year before it was redistributed for a second time. The constituency included: Chiswick, Barons Court, Earls Court, Fulham, Hammersmith, Hans Town, Holland Park, Kensal Town, Kensington, Ladbroke Grove, Maida Vale, Notting Hill, Parsons Green, Queens Park, Ravenscourt Park, Shepherds Bush, and Wormwood Scrubs.

Chelsea was a Saxon settlement, but the origins of its name are uncertain. One theory is that it comes from an old Anglo-Saxon word for gravel bank, as it lies on gravel deposits by the Thames. In the eighth century Chelsea Manor was owned by Edward of Salisbury, but Henry VIII acquired it in 1536, and James I founded a theological college on a site later to be occupied by The Royal Hospital. Founded by Charles II for the care of permanently disabled soldiers, the Hospital is home to the Chelsea Pensioners. Chelsea was then a busy and thriving community on the River Thames, making it easily accessible from London. Many notables built or rented houses there. A 1694 account by the Rector of Chelsea, noted that 'the number of houses is mightily increased of late years, for there are 350 houses in the Parish'. Despite this neither Chelsea nor adjacent Kensington was particularly large, with probably not more than two to three thousand inhabitants in each. Both were predominantly rural villages with gardeners supplying London with fruit and vegetables.

Chelsea was increasingly considered to be a healthy area, free of London's smog and smells, and with so many large houses available; it became a natural location for private schools and asylums, just as had occurred in Hackney to the east. As London grew there was an increasing demand for building land. Knightsbridge was among the first to be affected. In 1777 Henry Holland began the Hans Town development, on land leased from the Cadogan family. Sloane Street, Square, and Hans Place, Street and Crescent, were built and became popular with wealthy Londoners. By the 1830s Chelsea had become part of the metropolis, with a population of 32,371. Neighbouring Kensington had a slightly smaller but still significant population of 20,902, but this was given a massive boost following the Great Exhibition of 1851, such that by 1871, just after the new constituency had been established, the population reached 120,299, a growth of nearly 80,000 in twenty years[7].

Meanwhile demographic changes were taking place in other constituencies. **Finsbury's** increased from 250,000 in 1831 to nearly 390,000 thirty years later, mostly in Islington, while **Marylebone's** population, enlarged by the growth of Paddington and the addition of Hampstead to the seat, increased by nearly 200,000 to top 436,000 - only slightly less than Liverpool, then the most populous English borough constituency. Marylebone's electorate nearly quadrupled between 1832 and 1868. Finsbury's rose threefold, largely due to the suburban development of Islington, and was slightly enhanced by the transfer from Middlesex of Finsbury Park including Stroud Green. Over the next twenty years the upward trends continued. In 1881 Finsbury's population reached 525,000, whilst Marylebone's was only 1,700 short of half a million, making them respectively the second and fourth largest Parliamentary boroughs by population in England. They were ranked seventh and eleventh in the same category by size of electorate. Finsbury's reached 47,560 in 1884, whilst Marylebone's was 41,023.

By contrast the **City of London** was affected by even more dramatic social and demographic changes that saw its 1831 population of 123,000 fall to 112,000 in 1861, and to a little over 50,000 in 1881. Despite this its electorate increased throughout the same period, from 18,584 in 1832 (when it had the biggest in the country), to 20,185 in 1868 (when it had the thirteenth largest borough electorate in England), to 26,783 in 1884. Despite its huge population decline, it fell only one place in terms of the size of its borough electorate. In addition, and despite the demographic changes that had occurred, the City was unique in retaining four MPs.

The population of **Westminster** was relatively stable. It remained in the range between 202,000 (in 1831) and 255,000 (in 1861), falling back to 229,000 in 1881, reflecting the rising tide of inner London's population during the first half of the nineteenth century, followed by an ebbing flow as it dispersed with the opening of the suburban railways. The electorate continued to grow throughout the period, due to the extensions of the franchise that took place; by 1884 it had more than doubled to 24,990 compared with 1832. The constituency boundaries were unaltered, extending from Aldwych to Kensington Gore and Knightsbridge, and including: Belgravia, Buckingham Palace, Charing Cross, Covent Garden, Hyde Park, Mayfair, Millbank, Pimlico, St. James', Victoria, and Whitehall.

Population changes affected the **Middlesex County** constituency too. In 1831 the number of people resident in Middlesex not also living in one or other of the boroughs totalled 208,285. According to the 1861 census this fell to a little over 194,000 when Chelsea was created and Marylebone expanded in 1868, yet twenty years later it had increased to 394,000, a reflection of the housing development that took place after the opening of the railways. During the same period the electorate also changed. In 1832 it was only 6,939 rising to 23,085 by 1868, and to 41,299 in 1884 when it was the tenth largest in England and the biggest of all the county constituencies.

The first half-century of modern Parliamentary representative politics in Middlesex was a period of population increase so great, that even as new constituencies were created, they were overtaken by the expansion that was taking place. The period after 1885 was to see a continuation of population growth, and a further increase in the number of constituencies as economic prosperity and the opening of the railways stimulated the dispersal of large numbers of people to new London suburbs that were to change the character of London politics fundamentally. These developments are described in Chapter 3.

7 The 1851 population of Kensington was 44,053

The Politics of Middlesex between 1832 and 1885

Overall the period from 1832 to 1885 was one of enormous Liberal advantage in Middlesex. At General Elections the Party won 151 seats as compared with only 29 Conservatives and at by-elections during the same period Liberals won 19 and Tories only four. It is likely that these outcomes reflected the urban nature of Middlesex, because even the County constituency returned mainly Liberals, although following the extension of the franchise in 1868 the Conservatives fared notably better. The most heavily Liberal parts of Middlesex during this period were the boroughs of Finsbury, Tower Hamlets, Hackney and Marylebone. The County seat, the City of London, Westminster and Chelsea were more mixed, and after the second Reform Act ,Tory representation predominated. Changes to the franchise and the creation of new constituencies in 1884 were to alter this early pattern even more fundamentally.

MPs for the City of London

From	*at*	*To*	*Surname*	*First Names*	*Party Affiliation*
1832	*G*	*1833*	*Waithman*	*Robert*	*Liberal*
1832	*G*	*1835*	*Key*	*Sir John*	*Liberal*
1832	*G*	*1837*	*Grote*	*George*	*Liberal*
1832	*G*	*1843*	*Wood*	*Sir Matthew*	*Liberal*
1833	*B*	*1835*	*Lyall*	*George*	*Conservative*
1833	*B*	*1841*	*Crawford*	*William*	*Liberal*
1835	*G*	*1841*	*Pattison*	*James*	*Liberal*
1841	*G*	*1847*	*Lyall*	*George*	*Conservative*
1841	*G*	*1857*	*Masterman*	*John*	*Conservative*
1841	*G*	*1861*	*Russell*	*Lord John*	*Liberal*
1843	*B*	*1849*	*Pattison*	*James*	*Liberal*
1847	*G*	*1868*	*De Rothschild*	*Baron Lionel*	*Liberal*
1849	*B*	*1865*	*Duke*	*Sir James*	*Liberal*
1861	*B*	*1863*	*Wood*	*Western*	*Liberal*
1863	*B*	*1880*	*Goschen*	*George Joachim*	*Liberal*
1865	*G*	*1874*	*Lawrence*	*William (Alderman)*	*Liberal*
1868	*G*	*1874*	*Bell*	*Charles*	*Liberal*
1869	*B*	*1874*	*De Rothschild*	*Baron Lionel*	*Liberal*
1874	*G*	*1880*	*Twells*	*Philip*	*Conservative*
1874	*G*	*1885*	*Cotton*	*William*	*Conservative*
1880	*G*	*1887*	*Hubbard*	*John*	*Conservative*
1880	*G*	*1891*	*Fowler*	*Sir Robert (Alderman)*	*Conservative*

NOTE First returned at a B = By-election; G =General Election

The City of London was predominantly Liberal, though there were isolated Tory successes in the early years of the constituency's existence, but after 1874, all of its MPs were Conservatives. Overall eleven Tories were returned compared with 37 Liberals. Furthermore, Tories did top the poll on an equal number of occasions, and from 1868 did so consistently. The Liberals additionally won six seats at by-elections compared with only one for the Tories. There was also an historic event that occurred on 27th February 1833, being the first recorded by-election in House of Commons history since the First Reform Act, in which the defending Party was defeated. The tendency for Government held seats lost at by-elections to swing back at the subsequent General Election was also in evidence there in 1835, when all four MPs returned were Liberals.

Between 1832 and 1885, nineteen individuals were elected to represent the City of London four-member constituency. Generally the City's MPs were mainstream Liberals who favoured free trade and electoral reform. However, even City Conservatives tended to favour free trade, a reflection of the overriding commercial interests of the world's most important trading centre at that time. Most City of London MPs were merchants, bankers, and merchant bankers. A few had military pedigrees and a couple were lawyers. Five were Lords Mayor of the City of London, including **Sir Matthew Wood,** who served two consecutive terms in that position, two more were Directors of the Bank of England including one Governor, **James Pattison**. Four were Directors, Proprietors, or officials of the Honourable East India Company (**Grote, Crawford, Lyall and Masterman**). The first two of these were Liberals, and the second pair were Conservatives; they served together as MPs for the period 1841-7, Lyall being the Company's Chairman.

Nepotism may not have been as rife in London, as in rural seats at that time, but there were nonetheless certain family traditions in the City. **Western Wood** MP (1861-3) was the son of **Sir Matthew Wood**, MP (1832-43). Both men were Liberals.

Lord John Russell MP in 1816
Wikipedia

The longest serving and by far the most distinguished MP was **Lord John Russell** (Liberal), who retained his City seat for 20 years from 1841. However, this understates his House of Commons career, which actually began in 1813 as MP for the family seat of Tavistock (Devon) and lasted for no less than 24 years before he even became an MP for the City. His tenure was not unbroken though because there was a four-year period between 1826 and 1830 when he did not serve as an MP. After Tavistock, which he represented until 1819, he was successively MP for Huntingdonshire (1820-26), Bandon Bridge (Ireland, 1830), Devon (1831), Devonshire South (1832-5), and Stroud, Gloucestershire (1835-41). He was elevated to the peerage as Earl Russell in 1861, and served in the House of Lords until his death in 1878. Of his 86 years, no less than 61 were spent in Parliament. During this period the great Whig statesman and architect of the First Reform Act held many senior positions in Government, including all of the major offices of State, with the exception of Chancellor of the Exchequer, which in those days was perceived as less important than the posts he did occupy. Despite his reformist credentials, Russell seems to have used the patronage he exercised over this seat to elect several Liberals who also appear later in this chapter as Middlesex MPs.

His first ministerial office came in 1830, when he was appointed Paymaster of the Forces, which post he held until 1834. It was during this period that he was active in promoting the idea of Parliamentary Reform, and it was he who steered the First Reform Bill for England and Wales through the House of Commons, where it was defeated in Committee in March 1831. This led directly to the dissolution of Parliament, and a General Election in which the Whig Reformers were in a majority. The newly elected Commons passed the Second Reform Bill in September 1831, but its defeat in the Lords on 8th October sparked civil unrest. Russell introduced a Third Bill in December, and when it came to the Lords in April 1832 it was passed with an amendment to retain the 'pocket boroughs'[8]. This led to a constitutional crisis in which the Whig Prime Minister, Earl Grey threatened to create enough new peers to force through the original Bill through Parliament. It was passed without this happening and the General Election of 1832 was fought on the basis of new constituencies. Grey's Government, of which Russell remained a member, had a majority of 300 out of a Commons of 658 MPs.

After 1835 he held the office of Home Secretary, becoming Colonial Secretary in 1839. With the defeat of the Liberals in 1841 he was out of Government until the Tories split over the repeal of the Corn Laws, when on 5th July 1846 he succeeded Sir Robert Peel as Prime Minister, or First Lord of the Treasury, a position he held for 6 years. He resigned on 21st February 1852, after a Commons defeat in which the Tories combined with supporters of Lord Palmerston. Russell had dismissed him from the post of Foreign Secretary after he had sent his personal congratulations to Louis Napoleon of France following a coup d'etat. As it turned out Russell was out of Government only briefly, because Lord Derby, who was made Prime Minister, did not command a Commons majority, and failed to obtain one when a General Election was called in July. The Earl of Aberdeen became Prime Minister of a Whig-Peelite coalition in which Russell was appointed Foreign Secretary, Gladstone Chancellor of the Exchequer, and Palmerston Home Secretary. Russell held this post for about a year, but became embroiled in an argument with Palmerston over further Parliamentary Reform. During this period Russell remained without office in the Cabinet and introduced another Reform Bill in February 1854, but the outbreak of War with Russia in the Crimea caused this to be withdrawn. He was appointed President of the Council in 1854, and in 1855 was once again made Secretary of State for the Colonies. This occurred when Palmerston became Prime Minister after the defeat of Lord Aberdeen's Government at the end of a debate concerning the condition of the Army before the battle of Sebastopol. Russell was sent to Vienna in March to explore the possibilities for making peace. However, his attempts were abandoned after five weeks, and it was Lord Clarendon who eventually negotiated the treaty that brought the Crimea War to an end in 1856. Meanwhile Russell's most significant act as Colonial Secretary was to accord responsible Government, in July 1855, to all but one of the Australian Colonies - the exception being Western Australia.

Out of Government after the General Election of 1857, Russell returned as Foreign Secretary under Palmerston two years later. In 1861 he announced that Britain would remain neutral in the American Civil War. Russell continued to hold this post both as MP for the City of London, and then as Earl Russell between 1861 and 1865. Following the re-election of the Liberal Government in 1865, Palmerston died, and Russell was himself appointed Prime Minister for the second

8 **'Pocket borough' was a term applied to constituencies with tiny electorates that were in the control of any individual or family.**

time, assuming that office on 29th October. Once more he promoted a Reform Bill, which was introduced to Parliament by Gladstone on March 12th 1866, but it provoked opposition from some Liberals, 48 of who supported the Tories in a debate held on June 19th. Russell resigned, and the Earl of Derby formed a minority Conservative Government with Disraeli as Leader of the House of Commons. Reform was the overriding issue at the time, and Disraeli remained in power at the head of a minority administration for long enough to promote the passage of the Representation of the People Act (often known as the Second Reform Act) on 15th August 1867. The General Election that ensued in 1868 saw the return of the Liberals, but on this occasion Gladstone was appointed Prime Minister to head his first Government, and Russell's illustrious career came to an end. He died in 1878 at the age of 85.

Baron de Rothschild MP
Wikipedia

The next longest serving MP for the City of London was **Baron Lionel Nathan De Rothschild** (Liberal), who was elected in successive General Elections between 1847 and 1868, his Parliamentary career finally coming to an end in 1874. He was the London-born son of Sir Nathaniel de Rothschild, founder of the famous Merchant Bank and a Jew who had emigrated from Frankfurt-am-Main in 1800. Because the taking of the Parliamentary oath in those days required affirmation of the Christian faith, he was debarred from taking his seat until 1858 despite having been returned by the electors.

Rothschild introduced in the House of Commons in 1858
Wikipedia - The Rothschild Archive.

George Goschen MP
© National Portrait Gallery

Throughout the fifty-three year period of Parliamentary history after 1832, only one City MP other than Russell attained Ministerial rank of any kind, an indication perhaps of the commercial orientation of most of the City of London members. He was **George Joachim Goschen** (Liberal), who was elected in 1863 and served until 1880 when he transferred to Ripon (Yorkshire West Riding), thence to Edinburgh East in 1885, and following defeat there in 1886, to St. George's Hanover Square (Westminster), which he won at a by-election in 1887, and held until 1900, when he retired. Goschen forged his career in the Liberal Party, becoming a Minister within two years of first being elected in 1863. He held the positions of Vice-President of the Board of Trade, and Paymaster-General from 1865-6, and was then successively, Chancellor of the Duchy of Lancaster (1866 -1868), and President of the Poor Law Board (1868-74), which post he held whilst also First Lord of the Admiralty (1871-4). Following the defeat of the Liberals at the 1874 Election he went into Opposition, but found himself on the Unionist side of the Party on the question of Irish Home Rule, and left the Party. He won Edinburgh East as an Independent Liberal in 1885, but lost in 1886 when he became a Liberal Unionist. However, he successfully fought a by-election at St. George's, Hanover Square in 1887, returning in that same year to Lord Salisbury's Conservative Cabinet as Chancellor of the Exchequer, which post he held until 1892, when the Conservatives and Unionists were defeated by a combination of Liberals and Irish Nationalists. Returned to power with the Conservatives in 1895, Goshen, still a Liberal Unionist, was once more made First Lord a post he held for the duration of that Government until 1900. Following his retirement from the Commons he was ennobled and died in 1907.

The City of London MP with the briefest term was **Robert Waithman** (Liberal), elected in December 1832 he died within weeks, precipitating the first contested by-election of the Reformed Parliament, which took place on 27th February 1833. He was born in 1864.

MPs for Westminster

The Tories did better in Westminster than in other parts of Middlesex, although they still only managed to secure a total of six MPs elected at a dozen General Elections during the period, compared with eighteen Liberals. However, after the passing of the 1867 Act the Tories topped the poll in all three General Elections that followed it, and actually won both seats in 1874 and 1880. By-elections resulted in more mixed outcomes; Liberals and Tories won two each.

Sir John Hobhouse had already been an MP for Westminster for twelve years before his re-election alongside Sir Francis Burdett in 1832. Burdett too had been an MP, initially for Boroughbridge in Yorkshire from 1796 to 1807 when he was also returned for Westminster. However, he was subsequently defeated, and although he stood several times for the County of Middlesex Constituency, it was not until 1832 that he returned to the Commons.

Sir John Cam Hobhouse (Liberal), who married the daughter of the 7th Marquis of Tweedsdale, was a man of

MPs for Westminster					
From	**at**	**To**	**Surname**	**First Names**	**Party Affiliation**
1832	G	1833	Hobhouse	Sir John	Liberal
1832	G	1837	Burdett	Sir Francis	Liberal
1837	B	1837	Burdett	Sir Francis	Conservative
1833	B	1841	Evans	De Lacy (Col)	Liberal
1837	G	1847	Leader	John Temple	Liberal
1841	G	1846	Rous	Henry John (Capt)	Conservative
1846	B	1865	Evans	Sir de Lacy (Col)	Liberal
1847	G	1852	Lushington	Charles	Liberal
1852	G	1865	Shelley	Sir John	Liberal
1865	G	1868	Mill	John Stuart	Liberal
1865	G	1874	Grosvenor	Robert Wellesley	Liberal
1874	G	1882	Russell	Sir Charles	Conservative
1874	G	1891	Smith	William Henry	Conservative
1882	B	1887	Percy	Lord Algernon	Conservative
NOTE First returned at a B = By-election; G =General Election					

business, being a partner in the Whitbread Brewing firm[9]. He travelled in Greece with the romantic poet Lord Byron, and had a somewhat exotic political career as a Whig reformer. At one time the House of Commons imprisoned him in 1819, for his support of the reformist agenda but he was released on the death of King George III. In 1832 he was appointed War Secretary, and a year later First Secretary for Ireland, but he resigned from the Government in 1833, and fought a by-election over the retention of window and house taxes. He lost to de Lacy Evans, but was out of Parliament for only about two years during which period he unsuccessfully contested Bristol in 1835. He was returned for Nottingham at a by-election shortly afterwards, and held his seat until 1847, resuming his career in Government as President of the Board of Control between 1835 and 1841, and from 1846 to 1847. He lost his Nottingham seat but was returned in 1848 for Harwich, which he represented until 1851 when he was made Baron Broughton. He died in 1869.

Francis Burdett MP
© National Portrait Gallery
Sir Martin Archer-Shee MP

Sir Francis Burdett (Liberal), initially held his Westminster seat in the pre-reform House of Commons from 1807 and then for five years more until 1837. He had first entered the Commons at Boroughbridge (Yorkshire) in 1796, then subsequently for Middlesex between 1802 and 1804, and 1805 and 1806. He was a banker and married the daughter of Thomas Coutts[10]. However, this traditional image belied the fact that the Government of George III had imprisoned him for advocating reform, and that he was actually held in the Tower of London and by the Kings Bench for his beliefs, which included advocating universal male suffrage, secret ballots and equal constituencies. In 1837 he resigned his seat on changing parties, and won the by-election as a Tory, but transferred to Wiltshire North at the General Election later that year. He held that seat until his death at the age of seventy-four in 1844.

Sir (George) de Lacy Evans (Liberal) was an Irishman, born in 1787 at Moig. He was a distinguished soldier who fought under Wellington at Waterloo in 1815, and became Commander of the British Auxiliary Force in Spain in 1835. Whilst fighting there he was appointed a Lieutenant-General in the Spanish Army. In 1853 he was promoted to Colonel in the 21st Fusiliers and fought in the Crimea. Despite being invalided out he received the thanks of Parliament for his heroism. He was also admitted to the Grand Office of the Legion of Honour in France in 1856. He was promoted to General of the British Army in 1861. During this period he was in and out of the House at various times. In pre-Reform Parliaments (1830 and again in 1831), he was elected MP for Rye in East Sussex. However, in 1832 he failed to secure election at either Rye or Westminster, though he stood for both, and it was at the 1833 by-election, occasioned by Hobson's resignation that he was returned. He was absent following defeat in 1841 until 1846, when he was once again returned at Westminster, holding the seat until his retirement in 1865. He died in 1870.

de Lacy Evans MP in 1855
© National Portrait Gallery
Roger Fenton

John Temple Leader (Liberal), formerly MP for Bridgwater (1835-7), was a Westminster

9 In 1750 Samuel Whitbread moved his brewing operations to premises in Chiswell Street on the eastern rim of Georgian London, establishing the first purpose-built mass-production brewery in Britain. It is now a five star hotel.

10 Coutts Bank was established in the Strand in London in 1755. It is now owned by the Royal Bank of Scotland.

A Punch cartoon showing John Stuart Mill MP advocating female suffrage in 1867.
Wikipedia

MP from 1837 to 1847. Born in 1810, the son of a former Winchelsea MP, this Charterhouse educated man was an unremarkable Parliamentarian. He died in 1903.

For most of his term he was partnered by **Captain Henry John Rous** (Conservative), who sat from 1841 until 1846. Rous was brother of the Earl of Stradbroke, and pursued a naval career becoming a Commander. He was appointed First Lord of the Admiralty in 1846, but lost to de Lacy in the by-election necessary to endorse his position. He resumed a successful naval career and was made Admiral in 1863. He was also a keen 'man of the turf' and published, '*The Laws and Practice of Horse Racing*' in 1850. He died in 1877, aged 82.

Charles Lushington (Liberal) who was born in 1785, was the younger brother of Stephen, the MP for Tower Hamlets from 1832 to 1841. The two men both sat together as MPs for a while because Charles first entered the House as MP for Ashburton in Devon in 1835 and served six years before being returned at Westminster in 1841. He was an administrator like his brother but opted for the Indian Civil service rather than the Church, though he did publish a book on the subject of Religious Dissenters. His principal appointment was Chief Secretary to the Government of Bengal. He held his seat until 1852 and died in 1866.

Sir John Villiers Shelley (Liberal), a landowner who retained the seat until 1865, succeeded Lushington in 1852. Born in 1808, he first entered the House in 1830 for the rotten borough of Gatton (Surrey), which in 1831 had only seven registered voters. At the 1831 election (at which Parliamentary reform was the major issue), Shelley was returned at Great Grimsby (Lincolnshire). Despite having represented one of the most notorious rotten boroughs, Shelley stood on a reformist platform. However, he did not contest the 1832 General Election, and it was not for another nine years that he did so, unsuccessfully, for the county constituency of East Sussex in 1841. In 1865 he contested Bridgwater (Somerset) but lost. He died two years later.

The 1865 Election saw the return of two new candidates, and was the last occasion in Parliamentary history that a Liberal topped the poll in a Westminster constituency. The writer and philosopher John Stuart Mill was one of the pair, and the aristocrat Robert Grosvenor was the other. Mill lasted only one term, and Grosvenor two, making him the last Liberal MP to sit for a Westminster constituency.

John Stuart Mill (Liberal), who was born in London in 1806, became an administrator with the East India Company for which he worked in its Home Service from 1823 until 1858. He was a renowned author of many historical and philosophical works including the *History of British India*, and more famously of *Principles of Economy* and *Considerations on Representational Government*. As early as 1824 he was advocating equal voting rights for women. He promoted advanced Liberal reformism through his acquisition of the *Westminster Review,* and became an advocate of proportional representation. In the year of his election to the Commons he was also made a Doctor of Philosophy at Vienna and Rector of St. Andrews University. Already approaching 60 when elected, he only served in one Parliament, being defeated by the Conservative W.H.Smith in 1868. When he won his seat in 1865 the *Times* commented: 'The very circumstances that this eminent writer declared his most controverted opinions in his address, and in his subsequent speeches, makes his return the more significant. Hundreds who voted for Mr Mill probably disagreed with him philosophically, and a still greater number politically. But it is creditable to the electors, and a hopeful sign for the metropolitan boroughs, that Westminster people will rather have a man who thinks for himself, even though his conclusions may be different from their own.' [11]He died in 1873.

John Stuart Mill MP
© National Portrait Gallery
John Watkins

11 Quote is from 'Spartacus Educational'

Robert Wellesley Grosvenor (Liberal), who was the eldest son of Lord Ebury, an MP for Middlesex between 1847 and 1857, was educated at Harrow School and Kings College London. He entered the Life Guards[12] in 1853 at the age of 19 and became a captain six years later. He was otherwise undistinguished and probably owed his political preferment to his membership of the family of the Duke of Westminster. He was defeated in 1874 when the Tories took both seats. In 1893 he succeeded as the second Baron and died in 1918.

The Conservative MPs elected in 1868 and 1874 respectively were two very contrasting men. WH Smith, first elected in 1868, was a successful newsagent who founded the company that became a High Street name throughout England and Wales, whilst Sir Charles Russell, first returned in 1874, was a soldier. **William Henry Smith** (Conservative) took his name from his father and was born in Duke Street off Grosvenor Square in 1825. After entering Parliament he embarked on a successful Ministerial career, being appointed Financial Secretary to the Treasury by Disraeli in 1874, and then First Lord of the Admiralty, which post he occupied from 1877 until 1880 when the Tories lost office. After the return of the Conservative Party in 1885, when he became MP for the new Strand division of Westminster, Smith was firstly War Secretary, and then First Secretary for Ireland in 1886. However, following the resignation from the Cabinet of the Chancellor of the Exchequer, Lord Randolph Churchill, there was a reshuffle, and Smith occupied his Irish post for only a few days before being made First Lord of the Treasury and Leader of the House of Commons (effectively head of the Government in the Lower House) by the Prime Minister, the Third Marquis of Salisbury. He was also made Lord Warden of the Cinque Ports and died in 1891.

W. H. Smith MP
© National Portrait Gallery

Sir Charles Russell VC (Conservative), second son of Sir Henry, was born at Swallowfield, Berkshire in 1826. From Eton he entered the Army in 1843 and within 15 years had attained the rank of Captain and Lieutenant in the Grenadier Guards. In the Crimean War he served as Deputy Assistant Adjutant, was awarded the Victoria Cross and made a Knight of the Legion of Honour. He had served previously in the 1865 Parliament as one of three MPs for his home county of Berkshire but lost his seat in 1868. He retired in 1882 and died in 1883.

The by-election triggered by his retirement was won by **Lord Algernon Malcolm Arthur Percy** (Conservative), the second son of the Duke of Northumberland, born in 1851. Following a University education at Christ Church College, Oxford, he entered the Grenadier Guards, and in 1881 was made a Major in the Royal Berkshire Regiment. After the 1885 redistribution he became MP for the St George Hanover Square division of Westminster. He broke Army service to enter the Commons, but he resigned his seat in 1887 shortly after his appointment as Major in the 3rd Battalion of the Northumberland Fusiliers. After he left Parliament he was Aide de Camp to the King between 1902 and 1920. He died in 1933. He was also known as the 1st Earl Beverley.

MPs for St Marylebone

Liberals also dominated in Marylebone where the Tories won only once at a General Election, when their candidate came second in 1874. Overall, Liberals won 21 seats at General elections and five by-elections as compared with only two Tory successes including a by-election. A slightly unusual event precipitated this solitary Tory by-election gain. The election of Samuel Whalley, one of two Liberals elected in 1837, was challenged and declared void forcing the by-election, which took place on 3rd March 1838. The Conservative was elected although at the 1841 General Election Marylebone reverted to type.

It is no coincidence that Portman Square and Portman Street lay within the former Parliamentary Borough of Marylebone. One of its first two MPs in 1832 was **Edward Berkley Portman** (Liberal), born in 1799 the son of William an MP for Shaftesbury in Dorset, and a landowner with many connections with that County. Indeed several Marylebone streets and squares still bear the names of Dorset towns and villages. Portman himself gave as his two principal addresses the Square that bears his name, and the town of Blandford in his home County. He had previously been an MP for the County of Dorset (1823-32) but was only a Marylebone MP for a year. In 1837 he was elevated to the House of Lords as The Baron Portman, devoting most of his life to rural affairs. He was President of the Royal Agricultural Society on no fewer than three occasions. He was made Viscount in 1873 and died in 1888.

Sir William Horne (Liberal), a lawyer, was Portman's companion MP, also elected in 1832, although he had briefly represented two 'rotten boroughs', Bletchingley (Surrey) and Newtown (Isle of Wight), each for only a few months in 1831. He was Solicitor General in 1830, and Attorney General in 1832, but stood down in 1835. He lived locally in

12 The Life Guards are the senior regiment of the British Army formed by Charles II in 1660 into three Troops of Horse Guards. The Regiment first saw action at the Battle of Sedgemoor (the Monmouth Rebellion) in 1665.

MPs for St Marylebone					
From	***at***	***To***	***Surname***	***First Names***	***Party Affiliation***
1832	*G*	*1833*	*Portman*	*E. Berkley*	*Liberal*
1832	*G*	*1835*	*Horne*	*Sir William*	*Liberal*
1833	*B*	*1838*	*Whalley*	*Sir Samuel*	*Liberal*
1835	*G*	*1837*	*Bulwer*	*Sir Henry Lytton*	*Liberal*
1837	*G*	*1838*	*Hall*	*Sir Benjamin*	*Liberal*
1838	*B*	*1841*	*Teignmouth*	*Lord John*	*Conservative*
1841	*G*	*1847*	*Napier*	*Sir Charles*	*Liberal*
1841	*G*	*1859*	*Hall*	*Sir Benjamin*	*Liberal*
1847	*G*	*1854*	*Stuart*	*Lord Dudley*	*Liberal*
1854	*B*	*1859*	*Ebrington*	*Viscount*	*Liberal*
1859	*G*	*1861*	*James*	*Edwin*	*Liberal*
1859	*B*	*1865*	*Fermoy*	*Lord*	*Liberal Conservative*
1861	*B*	*1874*	*Lewis*	*John Harvey*	*Liberal*
1865	*G*	*1885*	*Chambers*	*Thomas*	*Liberal*
1874	*G*	*1880*	*Forsyth*	*William*	*Conservative*
1880	*G*	*1885*	*Grant*	*Daniel*	*Liberal*
NOTE First returned at a B = By-election, G =General Election					

Upper Harley Street and died in 1860 when in his late 70s. He was first returned to Parliament in 1812 for Helston (Cornwall), and sat as a Whig until 1832.

Portman's successor at the March by-election, following his elevation in 1833, was **Sir Samuel St Swithin Burden Whalley** (Liberal), a reformer who lived in the constituency in St. Johns Wood Road, but who was compelled to step down when, following the 1837 Election, he was unable to prove his qualification as he had an 'insufficient estate'. Born in 1800, he died in 1883.

Lord John Teignmouth (Conservative), who had been born John Charles Shore in 1796, won the 1838 by-election that followed this disqualification. He was son of the first Baron who had been Governor-General of India. Born in 1796, he was an Irish peer and lived at York Terrace, Regents Park. He had contested Marylebone unsuccessfully in 1837, but after his election in 1838 only served three years before he retired. He died in 1885; Sir Charles Napier replaced him.

A former MP for Coventry (1832-5), and unsuccessful candidate at Hertford (1826), **Sir Henry Lytton Earle Bulwer** (Liberal), was returned with Whalley in 1835, but he too served only until 1837. The son of a General, he was born in 1804 and became a diplomat. Prior to becoming an MP he served in the British Embassies in Berlin, Vienna and The Hague, and after leaving the House continued in the diplomatic service, working in Paris, Constantinople, Brussels, Madrid, and Washington. His career reached its peak in 1858 when he was appointed the Ambassador to Constantinople, where he served for seven years. He returned to England, and was elected at Tamworth in 1868, where he served only 3 years before being elevated to the House of Lords as Baron Dalling and Bulwer. He died in 1872, aged 68.

Sir Benjamin Hall (Liberal), was elected in 1837 in succession to Bulwer. A Welshman born in Abergavenny in 1802, Hall's father was an MP for the County of Glamorgan, and he himself first stood unsuccessfully for Parliament at nearby Monmouth in 1831. He was elected the following year, and served as Monmouth's MP until 1837, when he transferred to Marylebone. Between 1854 and 1855 he was President of the Board of Health and was appointed the First Commissioner of Public Buildings and Works, which post he held until 1858, overseeing the completion of the rebuilding of the Houses of Parliament, and establishing the Metropolitan Board of Works. He was appointed Baron Llanover in 1859 when after 27 years service he left the Commons triggering a by-election. He died in 1867.

Sir Charles John Napier (Liberal), was a Marylebone MP between 1841 and 1847. He was born in Falkirk, Scotland in 1786, and entered the Royal Navy in which he pursued a gloriously successful career. In 1833 he became an Admiral in the Portuguese Navy of Don Pedro, and was made Admiral Cape St. Vincent by Donna Maria. In 1835 he contested the naval constituency of Portsmouth, but was defeated, and in 1837 was similarly unsuccessful at Greenwich, another naval seat. Two years later he was made Commander of the British Navy's Syrian squadron, but took his Marylebone seat in 1841. He left the House six years later to become Commander of the Fleet at the Tagus (Portugal), and in 1850 unsuccessfully contested the Parliamentary constituency of Lambeth, followed by Great Yarmouth in 1852, before

Sir Charles John Napier MP as Commodore, in the year of his election
© **National Portrait Gallery**
John Porter

taking another Naval command, this time in the Baltic in 1854, blockading Russian ports during the Crimean War. The next year he was returned for the Southwark constituency and remained an MP there until his death in 1860.

Lord Dudley Coutts Stuart (Liberal), was the son of the First Marquis of Bute, and lived at Stratford Place. Born in 1803, he went to University at Christ's College Cambridge, was a Deputy Lieutenant of Buteshire, and was first elected to Parliament as MP for Arundel (West Sussex), which he held from 1830 until 1837. He was a Reformist Liberal.

He was succeeded in 1854 by another aristocrat, the **Viscount Ebrington** (Liberal), otherwise known as Hugh Fortescue, and from 1861 as the Third Earl Fortescue. Born in 1818 and Harrow educated, Ebrington was the author of several books, first entering Parliament in 1841 at Plymouth, where he was an MP until 1852. During his time in the Commons he secured various low category ministerial offices, including that of Secretary to the Poor Law Board. He was a Deputy-Lieutenant of Devonshire and lived in Upper Brook Street. He was elevated to the House of Lords in 1859.

Edmond Roche MP
© **National Portrait Gallery**

Edmond Burke Roche ('Liberal' Conservative), an Irish aristocrat, was returned in 1859. Formerly a member of an Irish Party favouring Repeal of the Corn Laws, he was Lord Lieutenant of County Cork and sat as an MP until 1865. He was born Edmond Burke Roche, and had previously been MP for the Irish County constituency of Cork (1837-55). He was made the First Baron Fermoy in 1865 and died in 1874.

Elected with him in 1859 was **Edwin John James** (Liberal), who was the son of John, a Solicitor and Secondary of the City of London. He too was a lawyer, and became a QC at Lincoln's Inn 17 years after being called to the bar in 1835. Four years before his election to the House he was appointed Recorder of Brighton, but his political career was cut short in 1861 when he was disbarred, having run up debts of over £100,000: a fortune then. He went to New York almost immediately, and though he returned 11 years later, he never resumed a political career. He died in 1882.

John Harvey Lewis (Liberal), replaced him at a by-election held in 1861, and held the seat until 1874. Another lawyer, he was a Dubliner born in 1814, who practised at the Irish Bar between 1838 and 1850. He became a magistrate in Westminster and a Deputy Lieutenant of Middlesex and Tower Hamlets, but in 1857 was made High Sheriff of County Kildare. He contested Bodmin (Cornwall) in the General Election held the same year, also unsuccessfully. He failed again two years later at the General Election, and then at a by-election held in Hull. He favoured disestablishment of the Irish Church. He died in 1888.

Sir Thomas Chambers (Liberal), was born in Hertford and after Clare College Cambridge he became a lawyer. Called to the bar at Middle Temple in 1840, he entered politics as MP for his home town in 1852, but retired in 1857 and was appointed Common Serjeant of London. He became a QC in 1861, and was returned for Marylebone in 1865. While still a local MP he served as Recorder of London from 1878, and was a Commissioner of Lieutenancy there. He retired in 1885 and died six years later aged 77.

William Forsyth (Conservative), was the only Tory elected for Marylebone at a General Election before 1885, taking his seat in succession to John Harvey Lewis in 1874. Born at Greenock in 1812, he too became a lawyer being called to the Bar at the Inner Temple in 1839. Educated at Trinity College Cambridge, he became a Commissary to the University, a QC in 1857, and 2 years later Counsel to the Secretary of State for India, which post he occupied until 1872. He was also a Middlesex magistrate and author of several works on the Law. He was first elected an MP for Cambridge in 1865, but was disqualified on a legal technicality. He unsuccessfully contested a by-election at Bath in 1873 before being returned at Marylebone the following year. He died in 1899.

Daniel Grant (Liberal), the son of a master mariner from Caithness in Scotland, was 54 when elected at Marylebone in 1880. Born at South Shields, he was educated at the Upper School at Greenwich Hospital and went into business as a partner in the firm of Grant, engravers and designers. The author of a book entitled 'Home Politics', he lost his first two elections at Marylebone in 1868 and 1874 before being returned in 1880, succeeding Forsyth. Following re-distribution in 1885 he was unsuccessful as the Liberal candidate for Marylebone East and never returned to Parliament.

MPs for Chelsea					
From	at	To	Surname	First Names	Party Affiliation
1868	G	1874	Hoare	Sir Henry	Liberal
1868	G	1886	Dilke	Sir Charles	Liberal
1874	G	1880	Gordon	William	Conservative
1880	G	1885	Firth	Joseph	Liberal
NOTE First returned at a G =General Election					

Though Chelsea did manage to return a Tory in top spot in 1874, Liberals took the seat at the other three general elections. Altogether seven Liberals and one Conservative were elected at general elections. With the exception of Dilke, Chelsea MPs during the period 1868-1885 were unremarkable. Three were lawyers, the exception being **Sir Henry Hoare** (Liberal) who was a landowner and patron of eight 'livings' in Somerset where he was Deputy Lieutenant of the County. He was previously an MP for Windsor between 1865 and 1866 when one of its two seats was abolished.

Sir Charles Dilke MP
Wikipedia

None of Chelsea's MPs attained high office, although **Sir Charles Wentworth Dilke** (Liberal), the son of Prince Albert's Commissioner of Exhibitions[13], at one time seemed destined to do so. He was an Under-Secretary at the Foreign Office between 1880 and 1882, and served as President of the Local Government Board from then until 1885. Whilst occupying this post Gladstone entrusted him with the important task of drafting the legislation associated with the 1884 Representation of the People Act (sometimes known as the Third Reform Act). Ironically in view of his father's position: he was a republican who in 1872 called for an official inquiry into Queen Victoria's expenditure. A radical Liberal, Dilke was appointed Chairman of a Royal Commission set up in 1884 to consider issues surrounding the 'Housing of the Working Classes', but two years later his reputation was discredited when he was cited as co-respondent in a celebrated divorce case involving the wife of another MP. After his defeat at Chelsea in 1886, he finally found a seat as a Liberal at the Forest of Dean in Gloucestershire, which constituency he represented from 1892 until his death in 1911 aged 67, but he never resumed a ministerial career.

William Gordon (Conservative), the only Tory elected, was a London Solicitor who was strongly in favour of the Established Church, whilst his successor, **Joseph Firth Bottomley Firth** (Liberal), was a barrister at the Middle Temple who was born in Huddersfield, became President of the Municipal Reform League[14], and who after his spell as a Chelsea MP, re-appeared in the Commons in 1888 as MP for Dundee before his death the following year at the age of 57.

MPs for Finsbury

Finsbury returned only 1 Tory compared with 23 Liberals at General Elections in the period. Liberals also won by-elections in 1834 and 1861. Altogether between 1832 and 1885 the two-member constituency returned 10 individual MPs. Despite their varied backgrounds and interesting careers, none of Finsbury's MPs ever held significant public office at national level, although two did so in India. In addition to Grant's appointment in Bombay, Spankie was Advocate-General for India. The longest serving MP during the period was **Thomas Duncombe** (Liberal), who served for 27 years after winning a by-election in 1834. He died in 1861 whilst still an MP. There were two other long serving MPs: Alderman Sir Andrew Lusk, and William Torrens; both held seats for the same continuous period from 1865 until 1885, when neither of them contested the newly created Central and East divisions of the borough.

Before the election in 1865, **William Torrens** (Liberal), had been an MP elsewhere, firstly for the Irish constituency of Dundalk, which he won on petition in 1848 a year after the General Election and held until 1852, and secondly for the borough of Great Yarmouth, which he represented between 1857 and 1859. His combined Commons service was only one year less than Duncombe's overall

During this period all Finsbury's MPs were Reform-minded, mostly radical Liberals. The exception was **Robert**

13 The Great Exhibition was held in Hyde Park in 1851

14 Since the 1860s a campaign led by the London Municipal Reform League had urged the case for a single central elected authority, a demand opposed by the City of London and the vestries who sought greater municipal dignities for themselves.

MPs for Finsbury					
From	*at*	*To*	*Surname*	*First Names*	*Party Affiliation*
1832	*G*	*1834*	*Grant*	*Robert*	*Liberal*
1832	*G*	*1835*	*Spankie*	*Robert*	*Conservative*
1834	*B*	*1861*	*Duncombe*	*Thomas*	*Liberal*
1835	*G*	*1852*	*Wakley*	*Thomas*	*Liberal*
1852	*G*	*1857*	*Challis*	*Thomas (Alderman)*	*Liberal*
1857	*G*	*1859*	*Cox*	*William*	*Liberal*
1859	*G*	*1865*	*Peto*	*Sir Samuel Morton*	*Liberal*
1861	*B*	*1865*	*Cox*	*William*	*Liberal*
1865	*G*	*1885*	*Lusk*	*Sir Andrew (Alderman)*	*Liberal*
1865	*G*	*1885*	*Torrens*	*Wm.Thos.McCullagh*	*Liberal*
Notes: First returned at: **B** By-election, **G** General Election					

Spankie (Conservative), who made a fortune as legal counsel to the East India Company, and who was elected in 1832 along with the Liberal, Grant. Spankie, though a Tory, was also reform-minded, but such was the overwhelming position of Liberalism in Finsbury during this period that he served only one Parliament and was replaced in 1835.

Robert Grant (Liberal), served for the briefest period, being appointed Governor of Bombay in 1834, and was succeeded at a by-election by Duncombe, the longest serving. Not that Grant in 1832 was a stranger to the House of Commons benches, which he had occupied in previous Parliaments as one of the members for Norwich between 1830 and 1832, and before that in the pre-Reform Act constituencies for Elgin Burghs (1818-1820), and for the Inverness District of Burghs in Scotland (1826-30).

William Cox (Liberal), was defeated in one poll but secured re-election at another, the only Finsbury MP to do so. He was beaten by fellow Liberal Morton Peto at the 1859 General Election, but Duncombe's death in 1861 triggered a by-election at which he got back to the Commons, serving with Peto until 1865, after which both men were replaced, by Sir Andrew Lusk and Torrens.

Finsbury's MPs in this period were a fairly mixed bunch in terms of their professional backgrounds. Of the seven whose occupations are known, three were lawyers (Grant, Spankie and Torrens), one, **Thomas Wakley** (Liberal), was a surgeon who became Editor of the famous medical journal 'The Lancet', and another three were in businesses reflecting the nature of local trades at that time.

Thomas Challis (Liberal), was a skin broker, who sold hides at Leadenhall and Bermondsey markets. He rose through the City of London guilds to become successively, an Alderman, Sheriff, and ultimately Lord Mayor, which post he held during his first two years as MP.

Sir Andrew Lusk (Liberal), held similar City positions, and was also Lord Mayor (1873/4) about half way through his tenure as MP. He ran his own firm of merchants based at Fenchurch Street in the City and at Wapping docks. He originated from Barr in Ayrshire, where he was born in 1812, leaving home at a young age with only a few shillings to his name[15].

Sir Samuel Morton Peto (Liberal), was a well-known businessman in the firm of Peto and Betts, public buildings and works contractors, who built several railways in East Anglia, and built the Crimea Railway for no profit during the War in 1855. He was returned as MP for Finsbury in 1859, but in 1865 moved to represent Bristol, which he held until 1868, when he stood down after his business failed, though both Disraeli and Gladstone publicly eulogized his personal character[16].

15 Ayrshire roots website 2004

16 Born in 1809 Peto entered into partnership with Edward Ladd Betts and between 1846 and 1872 carried out many large railway contracts at home and abroad, notably the more important portions of the South-Eastern and of the London Chatham & Dover lines, and, in conjunction with Thomas Brassey, the Grand Trunk railway of Canada, and the London, Tilbury & Southend railway. In 1854-1855 Peto and Brassey constructed a railway in the Crimea between Balaklava and the British entrenchments before Sebastopol, charging the British government only the actual out-of-pocket expenses, and for his services in this matter Peto was in 1855 made a baronet. Peto entered parliament as a Liberal in 1847, and, with a few years interval, continued there till 1868, when, his firm having been compelled to suspend payment in the financial crisis of 1866, he was forced to resign his seat.' He died in1889. (Encyclopaedia Britannica 13th Edition)

MPs for Tower Hamlets					
From	at	To	Surname	First Names	Party Affiliation
1832	G	1841	Lushington	Stephen (Dr.)	Liberal
1832	G	1857	Clay	Sir William	Liberal
1841	G	1847	Fox	Charles Richard (Gen)	Liberal
1847	G	1852	Thompson	George	Liberal
1852	G	1868	Butler	Charles	Liberal
1857	G	1874	Ayrton	Acton	Liberal
1868	G	1880	Samuda	Joseph D'Aguiler	Liberal
1874	G	1885	Ritchie	Charles Thomson	Conservative
1880	G	1885	Bryce	James (Professor)	Liberal

NOTE First returned at a B = By-election; G =General Election

Stephen Lushington MP 1862 by Holman Hunt
© National Portrait Gallery (fragment)

The Tories fared no better in Tower Hamlets than in Finsbury and Marylebone. They failed to win a seat until 1874 when they topped the poll for the first time, repeating the performance again in 1880. Altogether there were 7 Liberals who won a total of 22 seats and only 1 Tory elected twice at General Elections during the whole period.

Stephen Lushington (Liberal), who worked for the Church, and became Judge of the Consistory Court[17] and Chancellor to the Diocese of both London and Rochester, was elected in 1832, having previously been the MP for Winchelsea (1830-2) and before that Tregony, Ilchester and several other boroughs. He was a strong advocate for the abolition of slavery and of capital punishment. He stood down in 1841, and went on to become the Commissioner for Building Churches and the Dean of Arches[18]. He was born in 1782, and died in 1873. His younger brother was MP for Westminster from 1847-52.

Sir William Clay (Liberal), was elected with him in 1832, and served until 1857 when he was defeated, not by Tories, but by fellow-Liberals Charles Butler and Acton Ayrton. Born in 1791, Clay was the son of a ship owner who lived at Fulwell Lodge at Twickenham and was himself the author of a work on joint stock banking. Between 1838 and 1841 he was Secretary to the Board of Control. He died in 1869.

Lushington was succeeded in 1841 by **General Charles Richard Fox** (Liberal). The illegitimate son of the third Earl Holland, he lived in Addison Road, Kensington, near Holland Park, which bore the family name. Born in 1796 he joined the Army and in June 1824 married Lady Mary Fitz-Clarence, a daughter of King William IV. He became Surveyor-General of the Ordnance in 1846. Renowned for having the finest collection of Greek coins in the world, Fox entered politics in the 1820s as MP successively for seats at Horsham, Calne, and Tavistock, before being elected in the immediate pre-Reform Parliament for Stroud in Gloucestershire. He served again as Tavistock's MP in the 1832 House, and was once again returned for Stroud in 1835, but applied for the Chiltern Hundreds in the same year. He sought to return at a by-election in Sandwich (Kent) in 1841, and though unsuccessful on that occasion, was returned for Tower Hamlets at the General Election held later that year. He retired in 1847 and died in 1873.

George DonisthorpeThompson (Liberal), was elected with Clay in 1847. Born in Liverpool in 1804, he was a proprietor of the East India Company and the accredited representative of the emperor of Delhi. He wrote 'Lectures in favour of the Amelioration of the Government of India' and was something of a radical reformer favouring free trade, the ballot, and short Parliaments, whilst opposing ecclesiastical endowments. A Congregationalist, he was also an important advocate of the abolition of slavery. He was unsuccessful in contesting Southampton in 1842, and the following year became a student at Grays Inn. Following his return at Tower Hamlets in 1847 he served as an MP until 1852 when he was defeated. He died in 1878.

Charles Salisbury Butler (Liberal), lived in Upper Clapton, and was MP for Tower Hamlets for sixteen years following his election in 1852. He was Chairman of the Westminster Quarter Sessions, a Middlesex JP, and chaired the divisional bench. An unexceptional politician, he fought Hackney unsuccessfully when it was first made a constituency in 1868, and died 2 years later.

17 Historically clergymen, laymen and women were brought before the court to answer a range of charges including adultery and the fathering of illegitimate children. The court also oversaw the proving of wills, and matrimonial, divorce and tithe cases. The consistory court of the bishop of Rochester met at Holy Trinity church in Dartford at least six times a year.

18 The Judge who sits at the ecclesiastical court of the Archbishop of Canterbury.

Acton Smee Ayrton (Liberal), served as a Tower Hamlets MP for seventeen years from 1857 until 1874. Born in 1816 he became a barrister at the Middle Temple in 1853, having failed to secure election at Tower Hamlets in 1852. Following his return in 1857 he pursued a moderately successful career being appointed a Parliamentary Secretary to the Treasury in 1868, and Chief Commissioner of Buildings and Works a year later. He was defeated in 1874, and never regained a Commons seat despite seeking election at Mile End in 1885. He died the following year.

Joseph D'Aguiler Samuda (Liberal) was elected to succeed Charles Butler in 1868. Born the son of a Finsbury merchant in 1813, Samuda qualified as a Civil Engineer in 1832 and became Vice President of the Institution of Naval Architects. He established a company that manufactured marine engines, and also advanced the theory for using atmospheric pressure as a means of propulsion for railways, providing engineering and equipment for a new railway between Croydon and Epsom, and working with Brunel on the South Devon Railway. The technology was unreliable, and failed. He lived in Trinity Square and from 1860 until 1865 was Chairman of the Metropolitan Board of Works. He was also active in Tower Hamlets as a Deputy Lieutenant and as Lieutenant Colonel of the local Volunteer force. He was MP for Tavistock in Devon for 3 years before his transfer to Tower Hamlets. He died in 1885.

Charles Thomson Ritchie (Conservative) was the first Tory to be elected for Tower Hamlets, defeating Ayrton in 1874. Born in Dundee in 1838, he came to live in Gerrards Cross, Buckinghamshire, and was a Middlesex JP, in addition to serving as Honorary Colonel in a Battalion of the West Surrey Volunteers. He was Secretary to the Admiralty between 1885 and 1886, when he became President of the Local Government Board. During his tenure of office in 1888 he introduced the Bill to create County Councils. After his tenure at Tower Hamlets he was elected MP for St. George's Whitechapel in 1885, but lost his seat in 1892, and after a failed attempt to get back to the House at a by-election in Walsall the next year, he became a member of the London County Council. However, he resigned in 1895 when, after the return of another Conservative Government, he secured election to the Commons for Croydon, and was appointed President of the Board of Trade which post he held until 1900 when Salisbury made him Home Secretary. He was briefly Chancellor of the Exchequer between 1902 and 1903, and afterwards Rector of Aberdeen University. In 1905 he was created Baron Ritchie of Dundee, but died the next year.

James Bryce MP
© National Portrait Gallery
William Holman Hunt

Professor James Bryce (Liberal) took Samuda's place in the House in 1880. Born of Scottish parents in Belfast in 1838, Bryce embarked on an academic career following his education at Glasgow High School and University, as well as Trinity College Oxford. His academic career was distinguished, and between 1870 and 1893 he was Regis Professor of Civil Law at Oxford. He unsuccessfully contested Wick (Caithness) in Scotland in 1874, but was returned for Tower Hamlets six years later though, following the redistribution of seats in 1885, he secured election at Aberdeen where he served as an MP until his retirement in 1907. He was appointed a Parliamentary Under-Secretary for Foreign Affairs in 1886, and in 1892 entered the Cabinet as Chancellor of the Duchy of Lancaster. From 1894 to 1895 he was President of the Board of Trade, and when the Liberals returned to office in 1905, he became Chief Secretary for Ireland, which post he held for two years. In 1907 he was appointed Ambassador to the USA, remaining in Washington until 1913. He was made Viscount Bryce in 1914 and died in 1922 aged 84.

MPs for Hackney

From	at	To	Surname	First Names	Party Affiliation
1868	G	1874	Reed	Sir Charles	Liberal
1868	G	1885	Holms	John	Liberal
1874	B	1884	Fawcett	Henry	Liberal
1884	B	1885	Stuart	James (Professor)	Liberal

NOTE First returned at a B = By-election; G =General Election

After its creation Hackney was a clean sweep for the Liberals. Four men were returned on nine occasions, including a double by-election victory on 24th April 1874 after the General Election outcome had been declared void, and a single by-election victory on 19th November 1884. One man held his seat throughout the period.

Sir Charles Reed MP
Wikipedia

Only one MP, **Sir Charles Reed** (Liberal), was a local man. Born there in 1819, and educated at the Grammar School before going to London University, he was the son of the Reverend Andrew Reed who established several asylums for London's orphans. Charles himself was a merchant and 'type founder' in London, who's other claims to fame were as an author of a book about his father's philanthropic works, and as a Conservator of the River Thames[19]. Reed's father was a Scot, as were two of Hackney's other MPs during this period. Holms was born in Paisley and Stuart at Markinch in Fife.

John Holms (Liberal), who was born in 1830, was a textile spinner and a partner in the family firm that was based in Glasgow. He was a magistrate, not only in Lanarkshire but also in Middlesex and Westminster, and a Deputy Lieutenant for Tower Hamlets. The author of several books about the British Army, Holms reached junior ministerial office late in his Parliamentary career. In 1880 he was appointed a Lord of the Treasury, and in 1882 was Parliamentary Secretary at the Board of Trade. He served continuously as a Hackney MP throughout the period, and died in 1891, six years after his retirement.

Henry Fawcett (Liberal), was the only one of Hackney's MPs during this period to attain full Ministerial Office. In 1880 he was appointed Postmaster-General, the pinnacle of a Parliamentary career that began in 1865 when he was first elected as an MP for Brighton, serving there until 1874 when he transferred to Hackney. At this time in its history, the Post Office was an important and relatively new force in Victorian life, and Fawcett launched two new services, savings stamps, and the parcels post. His attainment of political office was significant for another reason. He was blind, having sustained injuries at the age of 25 in a shooting accident. Born in 1833, he died in 1884.

James Stuart (Liberal) who won the by-election that followed his death was a contemporary Fellow of Fawcett at Trinity Hall College, Cambridge in 1856. Born in 1833, he had been educated in Fife at the Madras School and at the University of St. Andrews before moving south to Cambridge. Both men were Professors there, Fawcett of Political Economy from 1863, and Stuart of Mechanism and Applied Mechanics between 1875 and 1889, a post he held whilst still a Hackney MP. The similarities also extended to their being appointed Rectors of Scottish Universities, Fawcett at Glasgow in 1880, and Stuart at St. Andrews between 1899 and 1901. Following the creation of new constituencies in 1885 Stuart transferred to the neighbouring Hoxton division of Shoreditch, where he served until defeated in 1900 when he went in search of another seat. He returned to the Commons in 1906 as an MP for Sunderland (a ship-building town where his particular academic qualifications would have been well regarded) but lost his seat there in 1910 and retired from politics. He died in 1913.

MPs for Middlesex County

From	at	To	Surname	First Names	Party Affiliation
1832	G	1837	Hume	Joseph	Liberal
1832	G	1847	Byng	George	Liberal
1837	G	1847	Wood	Thomas	Conservative
1847	B	1857	Grosvenor	Lord Robert	Liberal
1847	G	1857	Osborne	Ralph	Liberal
1857	G	1867	Hanbury	Robert	Liberal
1857	B	1874	Byng	George Henry Charles	Liberal
1867	B	1868	Labouchere	Henry	Liberal
1868	G	1906	Hamilton	Lord George	Conservative
1874	G	1886	Coope	Octavius	Conservative

NOTE First returned at a B = By-election; G =General Election

Unusually for a County constituency Middlesex was predominantly Liberal during this period, reflecting the more urban nature of the area compared with most of the Shires. It returned seventeen Liberals as against only seven Tories, although Conservatives did top the poll in five of twelve General Elections including all three that followed the passing of the 1867 Act. In 1874 and 1880 they also won the second seat. Notwithstanding its comparatively urban nature several of its MPs came from landowning aristocratic families.

The first, **George Byng** (Liberal) was grandson of the infamous Admiral Lord Byng[20] and the Viscount Torrington, and was also the longest serving Middlesex County MP, although most of his 57 years were between 1790 and 1832. He was 26 when first returned, and died in 1847 at the age of 83. He was the younger brother of the First Earl Strafford and was therefore related to another MP bearing the Byng family name.

19 Until the mid 18th century London Bridge or boats were the only means by which to cross the River Thames. Because of the potential difficulties this posed, the Corporation of London was appointed Conservator of the Thames in 1193, its duties including the licensing of boat operators on the river.

20 Following a disastrous naval action in the Mediterranean in which he was accused of abandoning a fort he was sent to relieve, Byng was tried by court-martial, condemned to death and shot at Portsmouth in 1757.

George Henry Charles Byng (Liberal), son of the Third Earl of Strafford, was elected as Viscount Enfield. He was himself elevated to the House of Lords as Lord Enfield in 1874, and eventually succeeded to the Earldom in 1898. Byng had served previously as an MP for Chester between 1826 and 1847, and at Tavistock from 1852 to 1857 when he transferred to Middlesex. He was Under Secretary of State at the Foreign Office for the last three years of his political career.

Two more were from great aristocratic families. **Lord Robert Grosvenor** (Liberal), was third son of the First Earl of Westminster, whilst Hamilton was third son of the Duke of Abercorn, and grandson of the sixth Duke of Bedford. Even Osborne was from the Irish minor aristocracy, and Labouchere was the nephew of Lord Taunton, a sometime Secretary of State for the Colonies.

Four were Army men - Hamilton, George H Byng, Osborne and **Thomas Wood** (Conservative) - and Labouchere was a diplomat, whilst Grosvenor indulged his spare time as an author and founder in 1854 of the Prayer Book Revision Society. Three years later he was elevated to the House of Lords as the First Baron Ebury. His son became MP for Westminster eight years after he left the Commons. (See Robert Grosvenor 1865-74).

Of the rest, **Hume** was a surgeon, whilst both **Robert Hanbury** (Liberal), and Coope were brewers. One was a partner in the Company Truman-Hanbury, whilst the other was with Inde Coope. Hanbury's business partner, Charles Buxton, was also a Liberal MP during this period, sitting for Surrey East from 1865 to 1871(See Chapter 6).

The tenure of **Joseph Hume** (Liberal), in Middlesex may have been fairly short, but he held other seats in the Commons both prior to and after his two terms there. He was first returned in 1812 for the Dorset port of Weymouth, and between 1818 and 1830 represented the Scottish port of Montrose. Following his Middlesex defeat by Wood in 1837 he transferred to Kilkenny in Ireland, which he represented until being defeated again in 1841. He returned at a by-election the following year in his former constituency of Montrose, which he held until his death in 1855 at the age of 78. Despite his long career he never held Ministerial office of any kind.

Ralph Bernal Osborne (Liberal), was something of a nomad. Born in County Tipperary in 1811, and subsequently a magistrate and Deputy-Lieutenant of County Waterford, he pursued an Army career until he was elected an MP at Wycombe (Buckinghamshire) in 1841, transferring to Middlesex in 1847. Following his defeat there ten years later, he was returned in 1859 at Liskeard (Cornwall), which he lost in 1865, before being returned at a by-election in 1866 at Nottingham. However, he lost that too at the 1868 General Election, and was next returned two years later at a by-election in Waterford, which City he served until 1874. He died in 1882.

The tenure of **Henry Du Pre Labouchere** (Liberal) was the shortest, the MP serving only one year, when by-election success in 1867 was changed to defeat in 1868. He had previously served very briefly for Windsor (Berkshire) between 1865 and 1866, but did later serve a much longer period as MP for Northampton, from 1880 until 1906. He proposed an amendment to the Criminal Law Amendment Act of 1885 which made 'gross indecency' a crime. This was subsequently mainly applied to homosexual acts. Oscar Wilde was famously imprisoned on this basis. Labouchere was born in 1831 and died in 1912.

Lord George Hamilton (Conservative), was the second longest serving MP for Middlesex, which he represented for 38 years between 1868 and 1906. He was the younger brother of another Tory MP, Lord Claude Hamilton who represented various seats between 1865 and 1918, including nearby Kensington North. George was born in 1845 two years after Claude, and like him was also educated at Harrow School before embarking on a military career in the Army, followed by one in politics. Whereas his brother had joined the Grenadier Guards, George joined the Rifle Brigade as an Ensign in 1864, transferring to the Coldstream Guards as a Lieutenant in 1868. After his election to Parliament he was a much more successful politician than his brother, becoming Under-Secretary for India from 1874 to 1878, First Lord of the Admiralty between 1885 and 1886, and Secretary of State for India from 1895 until 1903. After 1885 he was MP for Ealing until 1906 when he retired. He was subsequently a Board director of the Underground Electric Railways Company and its chairman from 1915 to 1919. He died in 1927.

Octavius Edward Coope (Conservative), was a partner in the famous brewing Company of Ind Coope. Born in the 1820s at Leyspring, Essex, (modern Leytonstone), he became a magistrate and Deputy Lieutenant for his home county, where he was also an honorary Colonel of the Rifle Volunteers. He was first elected to the Commons as MP for Great Yarmouth in 1847, but was removed a year later when the borough was disfranchised for wholesale irregularities and corruption. Coope was then out of Parliament until 1874, when he was returned as one of Middlesex County's two MPs and subsequently for Brentford in 1885. He died in 1886.

The Coming of the Railways 1: Camden Town, The London and Birmingham Railway 1837*. The artist, J.C. Bourne captured this disruptive scene, where the new railway has cut a trench through the residential area of Camden Town on its way out of the new Euston Station, built on the New Road. The changes in the social fabric to follow were a major influence on the political scene, as suddenly electors became mobile.*

The Coming of the Railways 2: The Uxbridge Road, Hanwell 1846. *J.C. Bourne has captured the scene in Hanwell, on the Uxbridge Road, where citizens are about their business, and one of the new trains runs overhead on Brunel's Great Western Railway. The allegory is lost to us today. The wonder then was to come across this massive engineering work in the middle of rural Middlesex. All was about to change.*

Chapter 3
Middlesex 1885 - 1918

Introduction

The 1884 Representation of the People Act had a huge impact in Middlesex. The former County and Borough constituencies were abolished and replaced by a total of 47, the largest enfranchisement of any area in Britain, and an increase of 29 MPs, each of whom represented a single geographically defined area, except for the City of London, which was represented by a pair. The constituencies were contested for the first time in 1885, when the impact on the political balance in the House of Commons was substantial. Not only did the number of MPs increase significantly, but the re-drawing of boundaries, especially in suburban areas where the right to vote was proportionately high due to the residency property qualifications, was beneficial to the Conservative Party, which staked out its ground as the defender of the rights and interests of such people. Nowhere in Britain was the scale of suburban expansion greater than in Middlesex. The table below shows the impact in terms of the numbers of Middlesex MPs returned to Parliament for each of the parties at General Elections between 1832 and 1910. Before the Second Reform Act the Liberals dominated; after it the Tories improved their representation, but after the Third Act they decisively supplanted the Liberals as the major Party. Despite the return of Liberal led Governments in five of the eight General Elections held after 1880, the Liberal Party only had a majority of seats in Middlesex once, in 1906. Its relative decline after 1880 is clear to see.

Election	***After 1st Reform Act***	***After 2nd Reform Act***			***After 3rd Reform Act***							
Party	***1832-1865****	***1868***	***1874***	***1880***	***1885***	***1886***	***1892***	***1895***	***1900***	***1906***	***1910J***	***1910D***
C-LU	*1*	*3*	*10*	*8*	*31*	*38*	*33*	*42*	*43*	*17*	*28*	*28*
L	*13*	*15*	*8*	*10*	*16*	*9*	*14*	*5*	*4*	*30*	*19*	*17*
Lab	*0*	*0*	*0*	*0*	*0*	*0*	*0*	*0*	*0*	*0*	*0*	*2*
L/C-LU majority	*12*	*12*	*-2*	*2*	*-15*	*-29*	*-19*	*-37*	*-39*	*13*	*-9*	*-11*
Seats	*14*	*18*	*18*	*18*	*47*	*47*	*47*	*47*	*47*	*47*	*47*	*47*

*** These numbers are averages for all General Elections between 1832 and 1865 inclusive.**
Key: C = Conservative; L= Liberal; LU = Liberal Unionist; Lab = Labour; J = January, D= December

Central London

Central London districts of the former county of Middlesex are defined as the City of London, Westminster, Marylebone and Paddington, all of which fall today within the boundaries of the City of London and the London Borough of Westminster. Before 1885 the number of MPs was eight, and this increased to nine following the Third Reform Act. **The City of London** (2 MPs) boundaries were officially described as containing the space within the boundaries of the City of London and the Inner and Middle Temple. Stretching along the Thames from the boundary with The Strand, east of the Royal Courts of Justice to Tower Hill, the City extended north to Charterhouse Street, which formed the boundary with Finsbury Central, and to Ropemaker Street in the vicinity of Finsbury Circus. Embraced within its ancient boundaries were all the famous City institutions including the Bank of England, the Stock Exchange, Lloyds, The Mansion House, Guildhall, St Paul's Cathedral, The Old Bailey, St Bartholomew's Hospital, Leadenhall and Smithfield Markets.

In 1885 the City was at the centre of global finance, banking, insurance and commerce, but was then also a residential

Top Right: *Horseferry Road in the 1885 Abbey Constituency remains one of Westminster's thoroughfares. This scene reminds us of its importance as a busy commercial centre for the community in the period.* **John Nelson**

Below, Left: *Whitehall at Horse Guards in 1895. The boundary between Westminster Strand and Abbey Constituencies, crossed Whitehall at this point.* **©TfL from the London Transport Museum Collection**

Above Right: *The Strand in 1889, four years after Westminster, Strand Constituency was created. The busy street is of course populated entirely with horse-drawn vehicles. The output from so many horses was causing difficulty.* **©TfL from the London Transport Museum Collection**

Left: *The City of London's Guildhall has stood as its centre of administration since 1411. However, it is thought that a Guildhall existed on this site in the early Twelfth Century. Original Roman remains of an amphitheatre exist today beneath the Guildhall Yard and can be viewed in the basement of the adjacent Art Gallery. It is claimed that the system of government served as a model for the House of Commons.* **John Nelson**

Right: *A present-day view of palatial town houses for the 'well to do' in the Paddington South Constituency, created in 1885. Such houses were multi-storeyed to provide accommodation for servants above. Servants were not enfranchised even in 1885, unless they were male householders. Housing being built in the North Constituency was on a large scale, but the dwellings were much more modest. Over time this naturally created different political representation between different parts of the Borough of Paddington (now Westminster).* **John Nelson**

area despite many of its former inhabitants having moved away to surrounding suburbs. During the 1860s and 70s the City was refurbished with new infrastructure, including a modern sewage system that occasioned a drop in the resident population, whilst new suburbs like St Johns Wood became attractive to City merchants, and bankers, and the displaced working class moved to other areas such as Lisson Grove. The coming of the railways enabled people who worked in the City or who owned businesses there to commute longer distances, initially from places like Hampstead and later from further afield. As a consequence the population of the City of London declined from 112,000 in 1861 to only about 50,000 twenty years later, just before the new electoral arrangements for the area were made. Despite its declining population, the constituency retained its previous boundaries, but its representation was halved to two MPs. The City's population continued to decline, and six years after the two-member constituency was first contested in 1885 its population had fallen further to 37,705. By 1901 it was barely 27,000, and in 1911 it was below 20,000. This steep decline had little impact on voter registration, as the City had electors who, owning both businesses and second homes in the constituency, were entitled to vote there as well as in constituencies where they maintained their main homes.

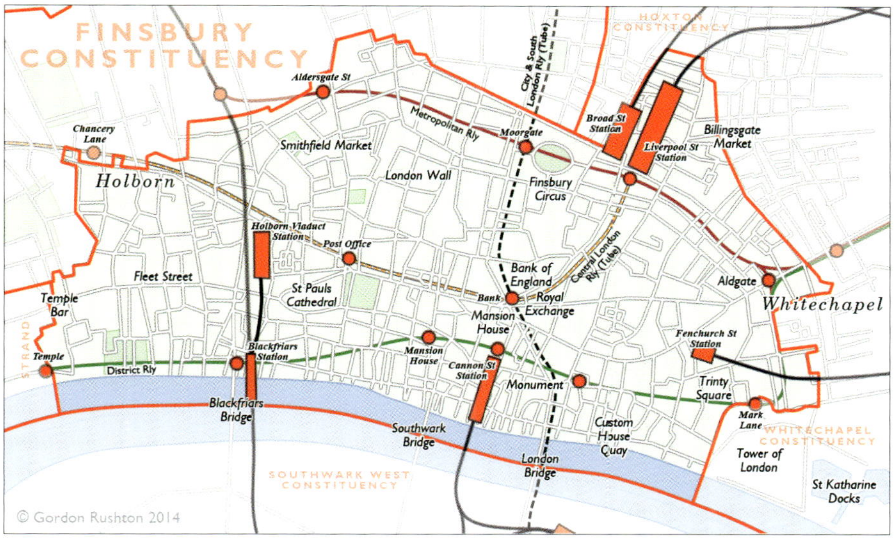

The City of London Constituency in 1918 has now been the subject of massive railway building. Although the chaos of construction of the main line stations and the 'cut and cover' Metropolitan and District Lines was extreme, it swept away many slums, and the relief to the City streets was great. The subsequent tube lines, deep beneath the streets, did not disturb the surface much. These railways were made possible by the development of the electric train. In addition trams also appeared. All offered affordable travel and resulted in the decline in the City's population.

The population electoral disparity was in strong evidence elsewhere. Neighbouring Westminster was divided into three new constituencies with a combined population of 198,000, nearly 31,000 fewer than had lived in the former two-member division ten years earlier. By 1901 the number had fallen still further, to a little over 181,000 and ten years later was under 158,000. However, electorates increased initially as a result of franchise extensions. The combined electorates in 1906 were 28,731 compared with 24,990 in 1884, but declining populations eventually had an effect. At 28,173 the 1910 electorate was smaller than in 1906, though by proportionately much less than population decline would have caused. It is likely that the business vote had an impact similar to that in the City of London. These trends were a clear reflection of the suburban growth that occurred following the building of London's surface and underground rail networks. There was also some population dispersal to the adjacent boroughs of Marylebone and Paddington despite which Westminster justified its additional seat on the basis of its relative population, indicating that it had been under-represented before 1885.

The **Westminster Abbey** constituency comprised the Abbey and St Margarets, the adjacent parish church in Parliament Square, together with the parish south of it known as St George's, Westminster. Officially it was described as comprising the Westminster District, and the Close Collegiate Church of Peter. This meant that the districts within the new constituency's boundaries were: Whitehall south of Horse Guards, the Palace of Westminster, the south side of St James's Park, the area between Birdcage Walk and Vauxhall Bridge, plus a small encroachment a little further west towards Pimlico. The main roads that dissected the constituency were Victoria Street, and Horse Ferry Road, whilst Millbank and the River Thames opposite Lambeth provided its eastern border. An unusual feature was that the parish of St Margaret's, Westminster comprised two separated sections. A detached portion that was part of the constituency lay further west covering Knightsbridge, Kensington Gore, and a part of Kensington Gardens, the rest of which was in the South Paddington division.

Between the two separated parts of Westminster was **St George Hanover Square,** based on the single parish of that name. The northern boundary was Oxford Street close to Hanover Square, but short of Regents Street in the east, the constituency extended south to the Thames at Chelsea Bridge, then downstream to the border with Westminster Abbey. In between were Hyde Park, Mayfair, Belgravia, and Pimlico. It contained the London residences of many of the wealthiest people in the Land. The third seat was **The Strand,** which comprised principally the parishes of St James, St

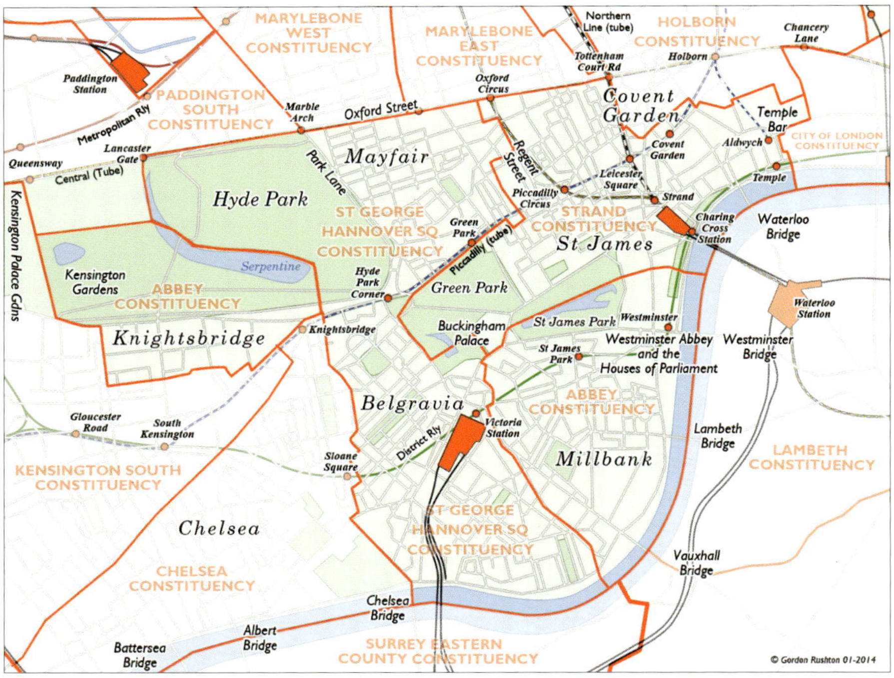

Westminster in 1918, just before the 1885 constituency boundaries changed. The main railways have been built. The nascent 'cut and cover' underground lines have expanded rapidly, bringing transport for those who could afford it. The tube lines are spreading in response, reducing the overcrowding in the streets, and supporting the growth of the suburbs; Westminster's population is already falling.

Anne, Soho, and St Martin-in-the-Fields, together with the smaller parishes of St Clement Danes, St Paul Covent Garden, St Mary-le-Strand, plus the Liberty of The Rolls[1] and the Precinct of the Savoy[2]. The main residential areas in the constituency were Piccadilly, Regents Street, St James's, the Embankment, Covent Garden and Soho, also containing many famous national institutions and monuments such as: The Royal Courts of Justice, the West End Theatres, The Royal Society of Arts, Somerset House, Trafalgar Square, Piccadilly Circus, Pall Mall, The Royal Academy, The National Gallery, St James's Palace, Clarence House, Buckingham Palace, Green Park, Charing Cross Station, the Admiralty and War Office, and the Victoria Embankment between Horse Guards Avenue and the Inner Temple.

Marylebone Parliamentary Borough retained two MPs, but was this time split geographically and shorn of its links with Hampstead, Paddington, and St Pancras, where huge expansion had occurred in the 1860s and 70s. The new borough comprised the whole of the parish of St Marylebone, the western and southern boundaries of which were respectively, the Edgware Road, and Oxford Street. The eastern boundary ran slightly west of the Tottenham Court Road towards Regents Park, which it traversed in a northwest direction to reach Primrose Hill, from where it ran west across the Finchley Road south of Swiss Cottage, to meet the Edgware Road at Kilburn Abbey. The boundary between the two constituencies ran north from Oxford Street, up Marylebone Lane and High Street, to the Euston Road, thence west to Lisson Grove, and north to St John's Wood Road, where it ran east past the gates of Lords Cricket Ground to Wellington Road, thence north to the Finchley Road, and the northern boundary with Hampstead. **Marylebone East** officially comprised: the St John's Wood Terrace, Dorset Square, Regent's Park Crescent, Langham, and Cavendish wards. It contained most of Regents Park, except the eastern portion belonging to St Pancras, Primrose Hill, and the eastern part of St John's Wood, Great Portland Street, Portland Place, Harley Street, Wigmore Street, Fitzrovia, and Cavendish Square. The boundary with the neighbouring Holborn and St Pancras boroughs included Cleveland Street, which was home to the Middlesex Hospital. The constituency contained an electorate that generally lived in very high quality housing.

Marylebone West extended from Marble Arch to well-to-do St John's Wood, between the Finchley Road and Maida Vale, and officially comprised the Hamilton Terrace, Church Street, Bryanston Square, and Portman wards. It too included expensive housing in the wealthy mansion-style terraces around Gloucester Place and Baker Street, but also the more down at heel Church Street and Lisson Grove areas, parts of which were cleared to build Marylebone Station in the 1890s. Lords Cricket Ground was also within its boundaries.

A new Paddington Borough, which generated two new seats, had been generally very rural until well into the 19th century, having been occupied by the Paddington Estate of the Bishops of London, after whom the Bishops Bridge Road, located east of the river Tyburn was named. Farms existed at: Kilburn Bridge, where at Manor House the Bays Water rivulet provided the parish boundary with Willesden (incorporating land between Paddington Village Green and Paddington Wood); Parsonage Farm, and Bell Farm, which occupied lands including Tyburn Field, standing opposite Hyde Park,

1 "Rolls Liberty, an extra parochial place in the Holborn division of Ossulstone Hundred, half a mile west of St Paul's, London containing the Rolls Court, with chapel, and a large block of building forming one side of the Record Repository." The first record of a building on the site was in 1232. In 1377 it became the Rolls Estate. In 1895 the original building was demolished and a chapel built within the new Public Record Office.

2 The Precinct of the Savoy was the location of Henry VII's Savoy Hospital on the Strand, on the site of John of Gaunt's palace.

The Paddington and Marylebone Constituencies in 1918. The grand houses remained, but as in adjoining Westminster, resident populations in Marylebone were already beginning to fall.

and infamously a place for public executions. In the early part of the 19th century, London's West End began to spread beyond Marble Arch and the Edgware Road, towards the area then known as Tyburnia, now as Paddington. Public executions ended at Tyburn in 1783, and the cutting of the Grand Junction Canal that reached Paddington Basin just west of the Edgware Road in 1801 energized the area.

The Harrow Road, which formed the western boundary of Paddington, had been a main route to the northwest long before the Romans built Watling Street, and in 1834 had been upgraded as an important Turnpike, bringing further development to the area. The Bishop of London embarked on a high-class building scheme on part of the six hundred acre Church estates. By the 1830s Sussex Gardens were completed, and within a decade Paddington had become a fashionable residential colony, Bayswater being the grandest of these smart neighbourhoods. Building began modestly in the 1840s around Westbourne Park before larger houses followed in the 1850s, in Lancaster Gate, and Kensington Gardens.

In 1838 Paddington Station was opened as the London terminus of the Great Western Railway, and added to the area's attractiveness. Soon there were long terraces linking Westbourne Grove and the Bayswater Road. The area was especially attractive to military families returning from India and other colonies, and became a symbol of Imperial London. Just as neighbouring Marylebone developed outwards into St John's Wood, so Paddington extended in parallel to include districts west of Maida Vale and Kilburn, both lying east of the Tyburn River. Kilburn began to develop, initially around 1840, and within the next 60 years the whole of Maida Vale had been built up. The building of the Metropolitan Railway between Paddington and Farringdon (for the City of London) in 1863 was a further stimulus to growth. It was an immediate success, and in the first six months of operations carried nearly 27,000 people daily. Paddington Basin became a major trading post. Goods and produce from west of London could be exported to the City and beyond, and coals and other materials were traded in the opposite direction. The Basin became a major centre for the collection and disposal of rubbish, with dustcarts bringing refuse on a constant basis to be shipped eastwards to brickfields on the Thames Estuary beyond Limehouse.

The areas west and north of the Tyburn River were amongst the last to be developed, and were generally much more socially mixed than the developments closest to Hyde Park. Although the Westbourne district and South Kensal Town had become built up by mid-century, it was not until the last quarter that Queens Park and West Kilburn became so. Kensal Town was an exceedingly poor district south of the canal, hemmed in by the GWR's tracks approaching Paddington. However, the land between the canal and the boundary with Willesden Parish became an area of much better quality housing, purpose-built for the working classes. In 1867 "The Artisans, Labourers and General Dwellings Company" was set up to build small houses for working people. In 1872 it acquired land at Queens Park owned by All Souls College, Oxford. By a historical quirk the land was not in Paddington Parish but a detached part of Chelsea. The new estate was built entirely to fit this enclave of land and to this day retains the fossilized shape of "Chelsea Removed". The new borough comprised several small parishes that lay west of the Edgware Road between Bayswater Road in the south, and the London and North Western Railway line in the north. The exceptions were West Kilburn, which was in Willesden parish, parts of two parishes south of the Brompton Road containing a small part of Kensington Gardens between Notting Hill and Hyde Park, and a detached area of Chelsea, comprising Kensal Town. **Paddington North** officially comprised the Harrow Road, Maida Vale and Church wards including Little Venice and Westbourne Green, west of the Edgware Road, whilst **Paddington South** officially comprised the Westbourne, Lancaster Gate (East and West) and Hyde Park wards. These incorporated the south side of Westbourne Park, the wealthier districts of Bayswater and Lancaster Gate on the northern edge of Kensington Gardens, and Hyde Park, extending up the Edgware Road as far as the Euston Road. The South constituency was built up in its modern form, but a few parts of North Paddington were yet to be developed, notably Maida Vale, and the area south of Queens Park.

Constituency Populations and Electorates

Within the area that since 1965 has formed the London Borough of Westminster and the City of London, the eight constituencies that existed between 1885 and 1918 had the following profiles.

Constituency	1891 pop	1901 pop	1911 pop	1910 electors	1910 electors as % of 1911 pop	% pop change 1891 to 1911	1891pop ratio of average 55092	1911 pop ratio of average 46875
City of London	37,705	26,923	19,657	30,010	152.7%	-48	0.68	0.42
Strand	64,733	53,297	40,894	8,019	19.6%	-37	1.17	0.87
St.George, Hanover Square	78,364	76,734	69,641	8,954	12.9%	-11	1.42	1.49
Westminster Abbey	54,776	51,204	47,379	11,200	23.6%	-14	0.99	1.01
Marylebone East	66,690	58,677	49,906	6,759	13.5%	-25	1.21	1.06
Marylebone West	75,714	73,618	67,278	8,576	15.0%	-11	1.37	1.44
Paddington North	64,668	72,214	72,939	10,945	15.0%	+13	1.17	1.56
Paddington South	53,178	55,114	54,180	6,415	11.8%	+2	0.97	1.16
Overall	495,828	467,781	421,874	90,878	21.5%	-15	1.00	1.00

NOTE: Ratios are calculated by dividing Constituency populations by the number of MPs and comparing the result to the overall average for Central London.

The most striking feature of all but the Paddington constituencies, was how they started to decline so soon after their creation. The impact of the class structure on the size of each constituency's electorate can also be assessed. The proportion of voters in relation to population was higher in those constituencies where the inhabitants were wealthy, and which had a substantial business vote, and lower where there were larger numbers of working class people such as railway workers and domestic servants, who were generally not enfranchised. The City of London was a particular anachronism. With less than one-in-twenty of the central area's population in 1911, it maintained one third of the electorate, and elected two MPs. Strikingly, its electorate was higher than its population even though this was falling fast. Westminster and the Strand were not as stark, but they too maintained electorates that were proportionately high in relation to their populations.

Politics in Central London

The political impact of the expansion of the franchise and the number of seats in the area was a huge benefit to the Conservatives. In total the Tories and their allies won 55 out of 56 seats at General Elections in the period, with a single Liberal victory coming at Paddington North in 1906. In addition, Tories and their allies won all eleven by-elections held. The following table shows the winning Party, together with the percentage margin of victory over the opposition for each election between 1885 and December 1910.

General Election Results 1885-1910 by % majority

Constituency	1885	1886	1892	1895	1900	1906	1910 Jan	1910 Dec
City of London	2xC21	2xC100++	2xC26	2xC100	2xC100+	2xC25	2xC33	2xC100
Strand	C32	C54++	C100	C100	C100	C36	C50	C57
St. George's, Hanover Square	C35	C100	LU100	C100	C50	C32	LU52	LU57++
Westminster Abbey	C39	C100	C30	C100	C72	C21	C38	C47
Marylebone East	C18	C31+	C15	C29	C37	C13	C21	C36
Marylebone West	C27	C61	C54	LU62+	C39	C11	C29	C34
Paddington North	C16	C25+	C6	C21	C38	L20	C10	C7
Paddington South	C42	C54	C100+	C100	C100	C32	C44	C43
C and LU	9	9++++++	9+	9+	9+	8	9	9++
L	0	0	0	0	0	1	0	0

Key: Numbers indicate percentage majority of the votes cast in the election. 100 = unopposed; C = Conservative; L = Liberal; LU = Liberal Unionist (in alliance with the Conservatives) + indicates seats retained at by-elections.

MPs for the City of London					
From	*at*	*To*	*Surname*	*First Names*	*Party Affiliation*
1885	*G*	*1887*	*Hubbard*	*John*	*Conservative*
1885	*G*	*1891*	*Fowler*	*Sir Robert (Alderman)*	*Conservative*
1887	*B*	*1891*	*Baring*	*Thomas Charles*	*Conservative*
1891	*B*	*1900*	*Hanson*	*Sir Reginald*	*Conservative*
1891	*B*	*1906*	*Gibbs*	*Alban George Henry*	*Conservative*
1900	*G*	*1906*	*Dimsdale*	*Sir Joseph Cockfield*	*Conservative*
1906	*G*	*1906*	*Clarke*	*Sir Edward George*	*Conservative*
1906	*B*	*1918*	*Balfour*	*Sir Arthur James*	*Conservative Unionist*
1906	*B*	*1918*	*Banbury*	*Sir Frederick George*	*Conservative Unionist*
NOTE First returned at a B = by-election; G = General Election					

Of the nine MPs elected during the pre-war period several held the office of Lord Mayor and most were high profile businessmen in the Square Mile. All were Tories in contrast to the period until 1880 when most were Liberals.

Hubbard and Fowler, who had both been elected in 1880, were returned again in 1885 and 1886. However, Hubbard was created Lord Aldington in 1887 and Fowler died in 1891 giving rise to two by-elections. **John Hubbard** (Conservative) was born at Stratford (Essex) in 1805 and became a merchant banker. He became a Director of the Bank of England, and from 1853 until 1874 was Chairman of the Public Loan Commission[3]. He published several works on the subjects of currency and income tax. Earlier in his political career he was MP for Buckingham between 1859 and 1868. He was elevated to the Lords in 1887 but died two years later.

Sir Robert Fowler (Conservative) also had banking connections, and followed his father into the family firm of Dimsdale and Fowler. Born and educated in Tottenham he went to University College London, and pursued a classic City career. He was a Middlesex, as well as a Wiltshire magistrate, and (like Hubbard) a Commissioner of Lieutenancy for London. He was a Sheriff of London and Middlesex in 1880/1 and Lord Mayor of London in 1883/4. He was also a member of the Senate of London University. His early political career was unsuccessful. He was defeated in the City of London in 1865, and subsequently also lost at Penryn and Falmouth before being elected there in 1868 and serving until 1874. Once returned for the City in 1880 he held his seat until he died in 1891 triggering a by-election.

Sir Reginald Hanson JP (Conservative) was elected. Son of a City Grocer and born in 1840, he was educated at Rugby School and Trinity College Cambridge. He joined the family firm of Hanson Son and Barter in 1861, and became a City common councillor in 1873. Elected an Alderman in 1880, he was Sheriff a year later and Lord Mayor in 1886/7, during which period he was also Chairman of the London Chamber of Commerce. He served on the LCC from 1889 to 1892, and was a member of the London School Board from 1882 to 1895. He retired in 1900.

There was a second by-election caused by death in 1891. Hubbard's successor in 1887, **Thomas Charles Baring** (Conservative) died that year. He too was a banker, in the firm that was to crash so spectacularly about a century later following the activities of the so-called Rogue Trader, Nick Leeson. Son of a Bishop of Durham, Baring was born in Oxfordshire in 1831 and educated at Harrow School, Wadham and Brasenose Colleges in Oxford. He became a banker in New York and a partner in Baring Brothers of London and Liverpool. He was a magistrate for Essex, Westminster, and Middlesex, was Deputy Lieutenant of Essex, and sat on the Commission for Lieutenancy for London. He was first elected MP for Essex South in 1874, and held the seat until 1885 when the county divisions were re-organised. He was unsuccessful at Essex South West, and was out of Parliament until returned at the City by-election in 1887.

Hanson retired in 1900, and was succeeded by **Sir Joseph Cockfield Dimsdale** (Conservative). Born at Cornhill in the City in 1849; he pursued a typical career in the Square Mile, becoming an Alderman in 1891, Lord Mayor in 1900/2, and Lord Chamberlain immediately afterwards. A Grand Treasurer of the Freemasons, he also retired after the 1906 General Election.

Alban Gibbs (Conservative), was returned at the 1891 by-election triggered by Baring's death. A partner in the Bishopsgate firm of Anthony Gibbs, he was a Tory loyalist who married a granddaughter of the Marquis of Salisbury. An unexceptional politician, Gibbs resigned following the 1906 General Election, to accommodate Arthur Balfour, Leader of the Conservative and Unionist Party who had lost his seat in the Liberal landslide.

Note: 3 The Public Works Loan Board was set up to administer Government loans to local authorities.

Sir Arthur Balfour MP
© Palace of Westminster Collection www.parliament.uk/art

Sir Arthur Balfour (Conservative), the outgoing Prime Minister in 1905, was one of the most distinguished and important politicians to represent a London constituency, which he only did as a result of the 1906 debacle. Arthur James was born in Haddington (now East Lothian) in Scotland in 1848, son of James Balfour and his wife, a daughter of the second Marquis of Salisbury. Educated at Eton and Trinity College Cambridge, Arthur entered politics in 1874 at the age of 26, taking the Borough of Hertford, near the Salisbury family's country seat. Such nepotism played a key role in shaping his political career, and after only four years in the House, he became Private Secretary to his uncle, the Third Marquis, James David Cecil, when he succeeded the Earl of Derby as Foreign Secretary. Balfour was appointed President of the Local Government Board in 1885, after the resignation of Gladstone, when Irish Nationalist MPs helped defeat the Budget and Salisbury was made Prime Minister. However, the Liberals won the ensuing General Election and he went into Opposition again, this time as MP for the newly created Manchester East, where he was encouraged by his uncle to seek nomination in order to demonstrate independence from the Salisbury family's patronage.

With the Tories back in power and the Liberals in disarray over the question of Irish Home Rule, Balfour's career took off in 1886. Salisbury became Prime Minister, and Balfour entered the Cabinet as Secretary of State for Scotland, but transferred to Chief Secretary for Ireland in 1887, a post he held until 1891. This was a period when Irish nationalism dominated the political agenda, and he imposed a tough policy of coercion in the face of a rising tide of militancy. Despite strong resistance in the House of Commons he suspended trial by jury as part of the Irish Crimes Bill, and handed strong powers to resident magistrates instead. Yet at the same time he introduced reformist legislation in the shape of the Irish Lands Act, which gave the courts powers to revise unjust rents, a source of grievance to many ordinary people, and legislation three years later was aimed at easing congested housing conditions. In 1891 he was made First Lord of the Treasury and Leader of the House of Commons – effectively head of the Government there. The Conservative Party fought the 1892 General Election campaign on the principles of Empire abroad and Unionism at home, and although Balfour found himself the leader of the largest Party in the Commons, the Irish Party and Liberals defeated the Government and Gladstone became Prime Minister at the age of 82. His Liberal Government survived for three years, but was defeated in the Commons in 1895 and the Tories returned to power after a General Election campaign in which the Liberals split over Home Rule. Balfour was once again appointed Leader of the House, a position he held until Salisbury's resignation in 1902.

Then on July 12th Balfour became Prime Minister, a position he occupied until December 1905 when a Party split over tariff reform caused him to resign. The Tories were heavily defeated at the January 1906 General Election, with Balfour losing East Manchester to the Liberals on a swing of nearly 23 per cent, comfortably overturning his 27 percent majority. He remained as Leader of the Opposition for nearly 7 years. Despite the Tories having clawed back their support, so that only two seats separated them from the Liberals in both 1910 General Elections, the Irish and newly formed Labour Party held the balance of power, and kept the Liberals in Government. Balfour resigned the leadership of the Conservative and Unionists in favour of Andrew Bonar Law in November 1911, but after the outbreak of the First World War a Coalition Government was formed in May 1915, and he accepted a post in Herbert Asquith's Cabinet as First Lord of the Admiralty in succession to Winston Churchill, then a Liberal. In this role Balfour oversaw further landings at Gallipoli and the subsequent evacuation. Although this was generally regarded as one of the more ignominious episodes during the War, Churchill took the blame, whilst Balfour's reputation was enhanced by a Naval victory at the Battle of Jutland in May 1916 when British supremacy in the North Sea was confirmed.

With his reputation intact, Balfour was promoted to Foreign Secretary when Lloyd-George succeeded Asquith as Prime Minister in December 1916. In this role he saw the successful conclusion of the War and was a co-signatory with Lloyd George of the Peace Treaty at Versailles, which brought the War to an end in June 1919 with humiliating terms for Germany. He was succeeded by Lord Curzon as Foreign Secretary in October 1919, but continued to serve in Lloyd-George's Cabinet as Lord President of the Council, attending the Washington Peace Conference in 1921. By then the Conservatives were split over whether or not to continue in coalition with the Lloyd George Liberals, and Balfour was one of a minority who supported the alliance. The majority vote to abandon the coalition led to the fall of the Government, and Balfour retired from the Commons at the ensuing 1922 General Election, when he was created an Earl. He did not serve in Bonar Law's Government between 1922 and 1923, but did return to the Cabinet as Lord President in 1925 under Stanley Baldwin, until Labour defeated the Tories in 1929, when he retired. He died the following year.

Sir Edward George Clarke (Conservative), who succeeded Dimsdale in 1906, was born in 1841 and, following

The population and electoral registers in the table show the substantial changes that took place in West London and West Middlesex at the turn of the century. Populations increased in all constituencies except Chelsea and Kensington South. Overall, there was a massive increase of 55% in the 20 year period after 1891, with by far the largest growth taking place in Harrow, Ealing, Brentford, and Fulham. Harrow's was the most remarkable, rising from less than 100,000 in 1891 to nearly a quarter of a million in 1911. The contrast between West London, where the population had peaked, and West Middlesex, where it was burgeoning, could not be more starkly illustrated.

Electorates also displayed some interesting variations. Overall, they equated to 14% of the population, but in furthermost Uxbridge the electorate was over 17%, and in Ealing and Brentford it exceeded 15%. The proportionately smaller voter numbers in Kensington and Chelsea may have been depressed because of a large, live-in working class, that did not have the vote, involved in domestic service. Apart from Hammersmith, the electorates in all the newer suburbs were larger than in Chelsea and Kensington. Hammersmith's was proportionately smaller, reflecting its more working class characteristics. Beyond the new boroughs the changes were seismic. The mainly middle class nature of the new owner-occupier populations in the four county constituencies is clear from the table. Their electorates were higher than those in West London, and even Harrow, which included the massively expanding working class area of Willesden, had a proportionately larger electorate than Fulham, the largest of the more urbanized constituencies.

Politics in West London between 1885 and 1918

The impact of all these electoral changes transformed the political landscape. The total number of Conservatives returned at all elections, including by-elections, was 69 as against only seven Liberals, and all but one of those were elected in 1906.

General Election Results 1885-1910 - by % majority

Constituency	*1885*	*1886*	*1892*	*1895*	*1900*	*1906*	*1910 Jan*	*1910 Dec*
Chelsea	*L2*	*C2*	*C6*	*C21*	*C17*	*L7*	*C16*	*C21*
Kensington North	*C9*	*C16*	*L3*	*C14*	*C13*	*L14*	*C6*	*C9*
Kensington South	*C37*	*C61*	*C100*	*C100+*	*C10*	*C50*	*C63*	*C66*
Fulham	*C1*	*C6*	*C2*	*C16*	*C21*	*L4*	*C11*	*C12*
Hammersmith	*C16*	*C26*	*C8*	*C22*	*C43*	*C5*	*C9*	*C11*
Brentford	*C22*	*C37+*	*C25*	*C100*	*C100*	*L4*	*C22*	*C20*
Ealing	*C24*	*C100*	*C25*	*C100*	*C100*	*C8*	*C22*	*C100*
Uxbridge	*C32*	*C100*	*C44*	*C100*	*C100*	*C1*	*C30*	*C36*
Harrow	*C13*	*C100*	*C28*	*C100++*	*C100*	*L2*	*C11*	*C100*
C	*8*	*9+*	*8*	*9+++*	*9*	*4*	*9*	*9*
L	*1*	*0*	*1*	*0*	*0*	*5*	*0*	*0*

Key: Numbers indicate percentage majority of the votes cast in the election. 100 = unopposed; C = Conservative; L = Liberal; LU = Liberal Unionist (in alliance with the Conservatives) + Seats retained at By-elections

From being a two-member constituency that mainly returned Liberals between 1868 and 1880, Chelsea spawned five constituencies that were all overwhelmingly Conservative. In these Liberals were successful on only five occasions, at General Elections between 1885 and December 1910, as compared with 35 when the Conservatives enjoyed success. The Liberals never won in Kensington South or Hammersmith (a lower middle class suburb which also contained many "respectable" working class voters of the type that the Tories sought to attract), and secured only a solitary victory in Fulham, in the 1906 Liberal landslide. They edged the Tories out only twice in Chelsea (1885 and 1906), and in Kensington North (1892 and 1906). Tory majorities were substantial in Kensington South, and were generally comfortable elsewhere, although never such as to appear invulnerable. The Tories' prime seat of Kensington South also went unchallenged at a by-election on 28th November 1895. In the four West Middlesex county constituencies the number of Tories returned at General Elections was 33 as compared with only two Liberals. Tories also won a by-election at Brentford on 23rd December 1886, and two more at Harrow, one on 30th November 1896, and another in April 1899. Ealing and Uxbridge were Conservative throughout the period in question, and Brentford and Harrow each elected a Liberal only once at a General Election: in 1906, by the slender margin of four per cent in Brentford and two per cent in Harrow.

MPs for Chelsea

From	at	To	Surname	First Names	Party
1885	G	1886	Dilke	Sir Charles	Liberal
1886	G	1906	Whitmore	Charles Algernon	Conservative
1906	G	1910(Jan)	Horniman	Emslie John	Liberal
1910(Jan)	G	1918	Hoare	Sir Samuel J.G.	Conservative Unionist

NOTE First returned at a B = By-election; G = General Election.

Sir Charles Dilke (Liberal), who had been in the House since 1865, survived as Chelsea's MP after the election of 1885, but was defeated the following year (See Chapter 2 for biographical details).

He was succeeded by **Charles Algernon Whitmore** (Conservative), the 35 year old son of the Recorder of Gloucester. Educated at Eton and Balliol, he also became a Fellow of All Souls and a lawyer who was called to the bar at the Inner Temple in 1876. After his election at Chelsea he was Assistant Private Secretary to the Home Secretary until 1892, but his career never really took off. He was made an Alderman of the LCC in 1895 and a Church Estates Commissioner.

In 1906 Chelsea swung away from the Conservatives for the first time in twenty years, and **Emslie John Horniman** (Liberal), was elected, though he served only one term before being defeated. Son of the MP for Falmouth (Cornwall), Emslie was born at Forest Hill in Surrey and became the Chairman of Horniman's Tea[9]. Also a member of the LCC from 1898 until 1907, and of Chelsea Borough Council between 1900 and 1906, after his defeat at Chelsea in the January 1910 General Election, he was unsuccessful in seeking a return to the Commons, being beaten at Walthamstow West in 1918.

Sir Samuel Hoare
Wikipedia

His successor, **Sir Samuel Hoare** (Conservative), went on to serve as Chelsea's MP until he was created Viscount Templewood in 1944. He enjoyed a distinguished ministerial career attaining the top posts of Foreign Secretary (in 1935 for six months, when he gave way to Anthony Eden), First Lord of the Admiralty (1936-7), and Home Secretary (1937-9), serving also in Chamberlain's War Cabinet as Air Minister (1939-40), though he did not do so under Churchill who sent him to Madrid as Ambassador to Franco's Spain. His first top rank Cabinet position had come in 1922 when he was Secretary for Air, which post he occupied again from 1924 to 1929. He was subsequently also Secretary of State for India, between 1931 and 1935, in the National Government led by Ramsey MacDonald. Born in 1880 and educated at Harrow and New College Oxford, Hoare started his career on the LCC, and was Chairman of the London Fire Brigade between 1907 and his election to Parliament. He had been unsuccessful at the 1906 Election when he contested Ipswich. He died in 1959.

MPs for Fulham

From	at	To	Surname	First Names	Party
1885	G	1906	Fisher	William Hayes	Conservative
1906	G	1910(Jan)	Davies	Timothy	Liberal
1910(Jan)	G	1918	Fisher	William Hayes	Conservative

NOTE First returned at a G = General Election.

William Hayes Fisher (Conservative), was born at Downham Priory Isle of Ely in 1853, and was subsequently educated at Haileybury College and University College Oxford, after which he went into the Law. He was called to the bar at the Inner Temple in 1879, and entered politics six years later when he was first elected at Fulham. Once in the House he went on to become a Conservative Whip in 1895, and was Financial Secretary to the Treasury between 1902 and 1903. In Lloyd-George's Coalition Government he served as Chancellor of the Duchy of Lancaster, albeit briefly, between November 1918 and 1919.

Hayes Fisher MP
© National Portrait Gallery

He left the Commons in 1918 and was made Baron Downham. In 1906 he was defeated by **Timothy Davies** (Liberal) who served in only one Parliament before Fisher was re-elected in January 1910. Born in Wales at Pant y Fedwen (Carmarthenshire), Davies was

9 Horniman's Tea was founded in 1826 by John Horniman and was probably the first tea to be sold in packets. It was a famous household name in Victorian times and considerably later. In 1918 J.Lyons bought out the company.

the son of a corn merchant and became a draper in Fulham in 1885. He entered local borough politics and served on the council becoming Mayor in 1901. He entered the LCC in 1901, and served there until 1907, a year after his return as Fulham's MP. He was also a local JP and a Commissioner for Income Tax who at the January 1910 General Election went in search of another seat. He was unsuccessful at Louth (Lincolnshire), but in December 1910 was returned there and served as MP until 1918.

MPs for Kensington

From	at	To	Surname	First Names	Constituency	Party
1885	*G*	*1892*	*Lethbridge*	*Sir Roper*	*Kensington North*	*Conservative*
1892	*G*	*1895*	*Frye*	*Frederick Charlwood*		*Liberal*
1895	*G*	*1906*	*Sharpe*	*William Edward Thompson*		*Conservative*
1906	*G*	*1910(Jan)*	*Stanger*	*Henry Yorke*		*Liberal*
1910(Jan)	*G*	*1918*	*Burgoyne*	*Sir Alan Hughes (Lt-Col)*		*Conservative**
1885	*G*	*1895*	*Borthwick*	*Sir Algernon*	*Kensington South*	*Conservative*
1895	*B*	*1909*	*Percy*	*Henry Algernon (Lord Warkworth)*		*Conservative*
1910(Jan)	*G*	*1918*	*Hamilton*	*Lord Claude*		*Conservative Unionist*

NOTE First returned at a B = By-election; G = General Election.
*** Supported the National Party between 1917-18 during the First World War.**

Kensington North

Sir Roper Lethbridge (Conservative), was elected in 1885. Born in Plymouth in 1840, he was educated at Exeter College Oxford and became an academic. He was appointed Professor of Political Economy at the University of Calcutta in 1868, and six years later became Principal of Krishnaghur College, Bengal. In 1878 he was appointed Press Commissioner of India, but returned to England in 1880 and was called to the bar of the Inner Temple. A Progressive Conservative, he was Vice-President of the Tariff Reform League and also wrote a "History of India".

In 1892 the seat was lost to **Frederick Charlwood Frye** (Liberal), a Buckinghamshire JP, although he only held it for three years. He was the son of a Professor of Music from Saffron Walden in Essex, where he was born and educated at the local Grammar School. He became a grocer's merchant and entered the wine and spirit trade in the Company of Leverett and Frye, which had establishments in forty places throughout Britain and Ireland. He was a left-leaning Liberal who became a vestryman in Kensington as early as 1877, and was Church Warden at St Mary Abbots between 1888 and 1891. He served on the LCC between 1889 and 1892 when he was elected an MP, a Public Library Commissioner, and also served on the Metropolitan Board of Works from 1888.

He retired in 1895 when **William Edward Thompson Sharpe** (Conservative) took the seat. Born in 1834 the son of Christopher from Birr in the then Irish King's County[10], he was educated at Trinity College Dublin before becoming a civil servant in Ceylon in 1857. He became Commissioner of the North West province of that island colony, a barrister in 1880, and retired from the diplomatic service in 1889. He was MP from 1895 to 1906, and died in 1909.

Henry Yorke Stanger (Liberal) who regained the seat for his Party, was born at Nottingham in 1849, received a private education and became a lawyer. A First Class Student, he was called to the bar at Lincolns Inn in 1874 and joined the Midland Circuit, becoming a revising barrister in Warwickshire in 1892, a QC in 1895, and a bencher three years later. In 1900 he contested his first election at Newark in his native county, but lost, and then suffered defeat in a by-election at Nottingham South in October of the same year. He went on to be a member of the Bar Council between 1902 and 1905, and then MP for Kensington North between 1906 January 1910 when, after his defeat, he became a High Court Judge, a position he held until 1922.

He lost the seat to **Lieutenant-Colonel Sir Alan Hughes Burgoyne** (Conservative), who was the son of Peter who owned a Colonial Merchants Company and lived in Ascot, Berkshire. Educated at Kelly College, Liege, Montpellier, and Queens College Oxford, he entered the family business as a partner, and contested his first Parliamentary seat at Kings Lynn (Norfolk) in 1906, before he succeeded at Kensington North. At the outbreak of War in 1914 he enlisted and served in the Army in France, Palestine, and the Indian North West Frontier until 1918, when he was appointed to a minor post at the Ministry of Munitions, holding the job for a year. He was also Secretary of the Parliamentary Air

10 County Offaly in the Irish Republic

Commission between 1918 and 1920. The founder and editor of the Navy League Annual, he supported the National Party[11] between 1917 and 1918, but after the War continued to represent Kensington North as a Tory until his defeat in 1922, when he turned his attentions to Aylesbury. He was unsuccessful there in 1923, but won it in 1924, and died in 1929.

Kensington South

Sir Algernon Borthwick (Conservative), who represented the seat for ten years from 1885, was the son of Peter who was for many years an MP for Evesham in Worcestershire, a seat he contested himself in 1880, though unsuccessfully. Educated in Paris and at Kings College London, Borthwick became the owner of The Morning Post newspaper[12] and President of the Newspaper Press Fund[13].

In 1895 he went to the House of Lords as Baron Glenesk, precipitating a by-election which **Henry Algernon Percy** (Conservative) won as Lord Warkworth, holding the seat until his death in 1909 shortly before the general election of January 1910. In 1899 he became Earl Percy. A member of the family of the Duke of Northumberland, he had unsuccessfully contested Berwick-upon-Tweed at a by-election in July 1895. As well as his aristocratic connections he had accomplishments to his name. He was a First Class student at Christ Church College Oxford, which he attended after Eton, and where he received the Newdigate Prize for poetry, and was for a while a Trustee of the National Portrait Gallery. He was an Under-Secretary for India between 1902 and 1903 and for Foreign Affairs from 1903 until 1905.

The prestigious Great Eastern Railway, Claude Hamilton Class express locomotive.

Percy was succeeded by another aristocrat, **Lord Claude Hamilton** (Conservative), whose father was the first Duke of Abercorn and mother the daughter of the 6th Duke of Bedford. Born at Stanmore Priory in Middlesex in 1843, he was educated at Harrow and joined the Grenadier Guards in 1862, going on to become Honorary Colonel of the 5th Battalion of the Royal Iniskillin Fusiliers, and an Aid de Camp to the Queen in 1887. He was initially elected MP for Londonderry City in 1865, and following his defeat in 1868, unsuccessfully contested Brecon at a by-election the following year. Later in 1869 he was returned for Kings Lynn, which he represented until 1880 when he became a Liverpool MP. Following redistribution in 1885 he was elected for the West Derby division of the city, but retired within only a few weeks, and it was fifteen years before he resumed his career, at Kensington South. He never held anything other than the most junior Ministerial post, but outside Parliament was Chairman of the Great Eastern Railway Company, and High Steward of Great Yarmouth in Norfolk. He retired in 1918.

MPs for Hammersmith

From	at	To	Surname	First Names	Party
1885	*G*	*1900*	*Goldsworthy*	*Walter (Maj-Gen)*	*Conservative*
1900	*G*	*1918*	*Bull*	*Sir William James*	*Conservative*

NOTE First returned at G = General Election

Major-General Walter Goldsworthy (Conservative) was born at Purbrook, Hampshire in 1837, but spent his early life in Calcutta, where he was educated, and joined the Army after serving as a volunteer at Oude during an Indian mutiny against British rule. He was subsequently commissioned as Cornet in the 8th Hussars, and served in Abyssinia before leaving the service in 1885 to enter politics. He retired after 15 years undistinguished service as a backbencher.

In 1900 the seat was won by **Sir William James Bull** (Conservative), the son of a solicitor whose practice he

11 A small group of dissident Conservatives led by H. Page Croft (MP for Christchurch) formed in 1917 with a programme of xenophobic imperialism. Most of its members drifted back to the Conservatives in 1918 and the National Party was disbanded in 1921. Only Croft and Sir Richard Cooper (MP for Walsall) sat as National members after 1918. (Source: British Political Facts).
12 The Morning Post was founded in 1772 and by 1855 was one of ten newspapers published in London and had the next highest circulation to The Times. In 1937 the Morning Post was purchased by the owner of the Daily Telegraph with which it was merged.
13 The fund was set up as a charity in 1838 to help journalists and their dependants

entered after an education at St Mary's College. He became head of the family firm of Bull and Bull of Lincolns Inn, and went on to become Honorary Solicitor to the Royal Life Saving Society[14] and the Chairman of Siemens,[15] as well as being the Governor of the Latymer charities[16]. He was first elected to represent Hammersmith on the LCC in 1892, but retired in 1901 following his election as MP. He was Chairman of the London Group of Unionist MPs and for eighteen years from 1903 was Secretary to Walter Long, a Cabinet Minister. When Hammersmith was split into two divisions in 1918, Bull was elected for the South constituency, which he represented until 1929. He was created the first Freeman of Hammersmith in 1930 and died the following year.

MPs for Brentford

From	*at*	*To*	*Surname*	*First Names*	*Party*
1885	*G*	*1886*	*Coope*	*Octavius*	*Conservative*
1886	*B*	*1906*	*Bigwood*	*James*	*Conservative*
1906	*G*	*1910(Jan)*	*Rutherford*	*Vickerman*	*Liberal*
1910(Jan)	*G*	*1911*	*Compton*	*Lord Alwyne*	*Conservative*
1911	*B*	*1918*	*Joynson-Hicks*	*Sir William*	*Conservative*

NOTE First returned at B = By-election; G = General Election.

Octavius Coope (Conservative) was one of Middlesex County's two MPs prior to 1885, and his election at Brentford then was consistent with his established position. His principal biographical details may be found in Chapter 2. Coupe held Brentford until his death after the General Election in 1886.

His place was taken by **James Bigwood** (Conservative), son of a businessman from Bristol where he was born and educated before going on to St Johns College Cambridge. After University he joined the firm of Champion and Company in the City Road, and entered civic life in Middlesex where he was an Alderman and magistrate, being also the Chairman of the Parliamentary Committee of London Justices. He was first elected at Finsbury East in 1885 but lost his seat to a Liberal in 1886 and transferred to Brentford at the by-election. He died in 1919.

Lord Alwyne Compton

Vickerman Rutherford (Liberal), son of a Newcastle Doctor, and himself a physician specialising in skin diseases, won in 1906. Educated at Edinburgh Royal High School and Sidney Sussex College Cambridge, he became Assistant Physician at St John's Hospital near Lewisham in South East London. He was an advanced radical who subsequently joined the Labour Party and fought Sunderland unsuccessfully in their colours at a by-election held in 1920, and then again at the 1922 General Election. He died in 1934.

The Tories resumed control at Brentford in January 1910 when **Lord Alwyne Compton** (Conservative), won the seat. He was the son of the fourth Earl of Northampton and was born in 1855. Educated at Eton, he went from there into the Army serving initially in the Grenadier Guards in 1874 and five years later joined the 19th Hussars. He married the daughter of an aristocratic family from Newby Hall in Yorkshire and became Aide de Camp to the Marquis of Ripon, a Viceroy of India from 1882 until 1884, and then fought in the Sudan, retiring from the Army in 1887. He became a Deputy Lieutenant of Argyllshire in Scotland, a Lieutenant Colonel in the Bedfordshire Yeomanry, and in 1895 was elected MP for

14 Founded in 1891 to save lives from drowning
15 Founded in Germany and England at about the same time in 1850 and named after William Siemens, a 19-year-old engineer and entrepreneur from Hamburg, who arrived in England in 1843 with a patent for a revolutionary electroplating process. Amongst other things he built the Landore Steel works in South Wales and the company pioneered many technological innovations including the first automatic dial telegraph in 1847, and in the same year, the first alarm bell system to warn railway workers of approaching trains. In 1873 it laid the first undersea cable linking Britain and the US. Siemens introduced the first devices for measuring voltage and resistance in 1860, and its founder's measurement system for resistance – the Ohm – was adopted as the standard in 1884. The company's discovery of the electro-dynamic principle in 1886 was the starting point for electrical power engineering, giving us power generation and electric motors. Siemens built the world's first electric train for Bush Mills, Northern Ireland, in 1879. In 1883 the first public railway designed by Siemens was opened on Brighton seafront and still runs today - Volks Railway. A principal pioneer of the UK's electricity industry, Siemens installed the world's first commercial power station, and in 1881, its first electric street lighting in Godalming, Surrey. (Source Siemens' Company website)
16 Associated with Latymer School, Hammersmith

Bedfordshire Northern, which he represented until 1906 when he was defeated. He resigned his Brentford seat in 1911 and died soon afterwards.

William Joynson-Hicks MP
© National Portrait Gallery
Bassano Ltd 1917

In the ensuing by-election **William Joynson-Hicks** (Conservative), was elected. Born at Highbury in 1865 and educated at Merchant Taylors School, Hicks was a solicitor and motor enthusiast who combined his professional and leisure pursuits in a successful career. He was Chairman of both the Automobile Association and the British and Irish Motor Union from 1908 until 1923, during which time he served on various committees reviewing aspects of transport. He first entered politics in the Tory cause in 1900 when he unsuccessfully contested Manchester North West; a seat he failed to win again in 1906. However, he did win it at a by-election in 1908, only to go down to defeat at the January 1910 General Election. Before he was elected at Brentford he lost at Sunderland in the December 1910 General Election. Once in the House, he became a Principal Private Secretary in three departments, and after the redrawing of boundaries in 1918 was adopted for the new (and then) safe Tory seat of Twickenham from when his ministerial career took off. His first appointment was as Minister of Health under Bonar Law in 1923, but his term was cut short by the fall of the minority Government and the election of the first led by Labour. This was also a short-lived minority administration, and when the Tories returned to Government in 1924, Joynson-Hicks was made Home Secretary by Baldwin; a post he held until 1929 when Labour won power again. He never returned to office and died in 1932.

MPs for Ealing

From	at	To	Surname	First Names	Party
1885	G	1906	Hamilton	Lord George	Conservative
1906	G	1918	Nield	Sir Herbert	Conservative

NOTE First returned at G = General Election

Lord George Hamilton (Conservative) was MP for Middlesex from 1868 until 1885 when he was adopted and elected at Ealing, then a new county seat. His principal biographical details may be found in Chapter 2.

Sir Herbert Nield (Conservative), who succeeded him in 1906, was a distinguished lawyer. He became a Solicitor in 1885 and barrister 10 years later at the Inner Temple. He was also a Deputy-Lieutenant and Alderman for Middlesex who was made Chairman of the Quarter Sessions in 1909. Eight years later he was appointed Recorder of York but maintained his Parliamentary seat throughout the period, eventually retiring in 1931, having served for the Ealing county seat until 1918 and the borough constituency thereafter. He held many internal positions within the Conservative Party but none in Government. He died in 1932.

MPs for Harrow

From	at	To	Surname	First Names	Party
1885	G	1899	Ambrose	William	Conservative
1899	B	1906	Cox	Irwin Edward Bainbridge	Conservative
1906	G	1910(Jan)	Gibb	James	Liberal
1910(Jan)	G	1918	Mallaby-Deeley	Sir Harry	Conservative Unionist

NOTE First returned at a B = By-election; G = General Election.

William Ambrose (Conservative), was born in Chester in 1832, the year the Great Reform Act was passed, and became Harrow's first MP in 1885. A lawyer, he was called to the bar in 1859 at Lincoln's Inn, became a QC in 1874, and a bencher at the Middle Temple in 1881. Three years after his election at Harrow he became an Alderman of the County of Middlesex, and was appointed the Attorney General for the Duchy of Lancaster in 1895, winning a by-election in 1896 held to confirm his position. Four years later he was appointed Master of Lunacy,[17] and resigned his seat forcing a by-election. He died in 1908.

17 Master of Lunacy was a position in the Court of Protection with responsibilities to oversee asylums and the welfare of people who were mentally ill.

The 1908 by-election was won by **Irwin Edward Bainbridge Cox** (Conservative), who served until the Liberal landslide of 1906. Born at Taunton in Somerset, where his father had been the local MP, Cox was educated at Magdalen College Cambridge, and initially became a lawyer at the Middle Temple in 1864 when he was 26. However, his interests lay in field sports and publishing and he became famous as the proprietor of *Field* and *Queen* Magazines,[18] and of the *Law Times*. He was a Deputy Lieutenant and High Sheriff of Middlesex, a County Councillor, Alderman, and a keen supporter of Arthur Balfour. He died in 1922.

Sir Harry Mallaby-Deeley MP
Wikipedia

James Gibb (Liberal), who took the seat in 1906 was born in London in 1844 and educated privately. He became a Lloyds Underwriter and Insurance Broker, and in political terms was a National Liberal.

His term as Harrow's MP lasted for only one Parliament, and he was defeated in January 1910 by **Sir Harry Mallaby-Deeley** (Conservative), who held it until 1918 when he was elected to serve for the new constituency of Willesden East, which he represented until 1922. Born in 1863, and educated at Shrewsbury School and Trinity College Cambridge, Deeley was a wealthy landowner who became a lawyer, practising as a barrister at the Middle Temple, and was a Director of the Norwich Union. He was a Governor of the Royal Agricultural Society, and Chairman of the Conservators of Mitcham Common in Surrey where he was also a JP. He died in 1937.

MPs for Uxbridge

From	at	To	Surname	First Names	Party
1885	G	1909	Dixon-Hartland	Sir Frederick	Conservative
1910(Jan)	G	1915	Mills	Charles Thomas	Conservative
1915	B	1918	Mills	Arthur Robert	Conservative

NOTE First returned at B = By-election; G = General Election

Sir Frederick Dixon-Hartland (Conservative), was the son of Sir Nathaniel Hartland of Gloucestershire and was born in 1832. Educated at Evesham and Cheltenham College, he became an author and was also a magistrate in five counties – his native Gloucestershire, Worcestershire, Sussex (where he was a Governor of Christ's Hospital), Middlesex, and London. He was a County Alderman in Middlesex, and Chairman of the Thames Conservancy Board. He had been MP for Evesham between 1880 and 1885 and was an extreme patriot who co-founded the Primrose League[19]. He died in 1909, and the seat was vacant on dissolution for the General Election of January 1910.

Charles Thomas Mills MP
Wikipedia

The seat was won by **Charles Thomas Mills** (Conservative), whose father and grandfather had both been Tory MPs in West Kent (See Chapter 5 for biographical details). He was the Eton-educated son of Lord Hillingdon, and a banker in the firm of Glyn Mills[20] in which he was also a partner. At the time of his election he was the youngest MP, but he only served until 6th October 1915, when at the age of 27 he was tragically killed[21] at the Battle of Loos.

At the by-election occasioned by his death in 1915, he was succeeded by his brother **Anthony Robert Mills** (Conservative), Lord Hillingdon's third son. Born in 1891, four years after his eldest brother, he attended the same school and University (Magdalen College Oxford), after which he became an Insurance broker. During the War, whilst still an MP, he was a Lieutenant in the West Kent Yeomanry, but afterwards stood down to concentrate on business. He became the Chairman of the Marine Insurance Company and died in 1952.

---

18 Upmarket style and fashion magazines. *Field* was founded in 1853 to portray country life.

19 Formed at the Carlton Club in London on the 17th November 1883 the 'Primrose Tory League' (the Tory part of the title was soon to be dropped) was launched by Lord Randolph Churchill (father of Sir Winston Churchill), Mr. (later Sir) John Gorst, Sir H. Drummond Wolff, Mr. Percy Mitford, Colonel Fred Burnaby, Sir Alfred Slade and others, who constituted themselves the Grand Council of the Primrose League. Their aim was to rectify 'the failure of Conservative and Constitutional Associations to suit the popular taste or to succeed in joining all classes together for political objects'. (Source: Primrose League website)

20 The bank opened for business at 70 Lombard Street in 1753, trading as Vere, Glyn & Hallifax. It developed a large business as London agent for many of the growing provincial banks, providing banking facilities for more than 200 of the new railway companies. In 1887 Glyn, Mills become the first private bank to publish a half yearly balance sheet. In 1939 it was acquired by The Royal Bank of Scotland

21 The First World War took a sad toll on elected representatives. Some 22 MPs died through enemy action during World War I, all of them officers. Five of these were Lieutenant Colonels, so the senior ranks perished as well as the junior.

North London

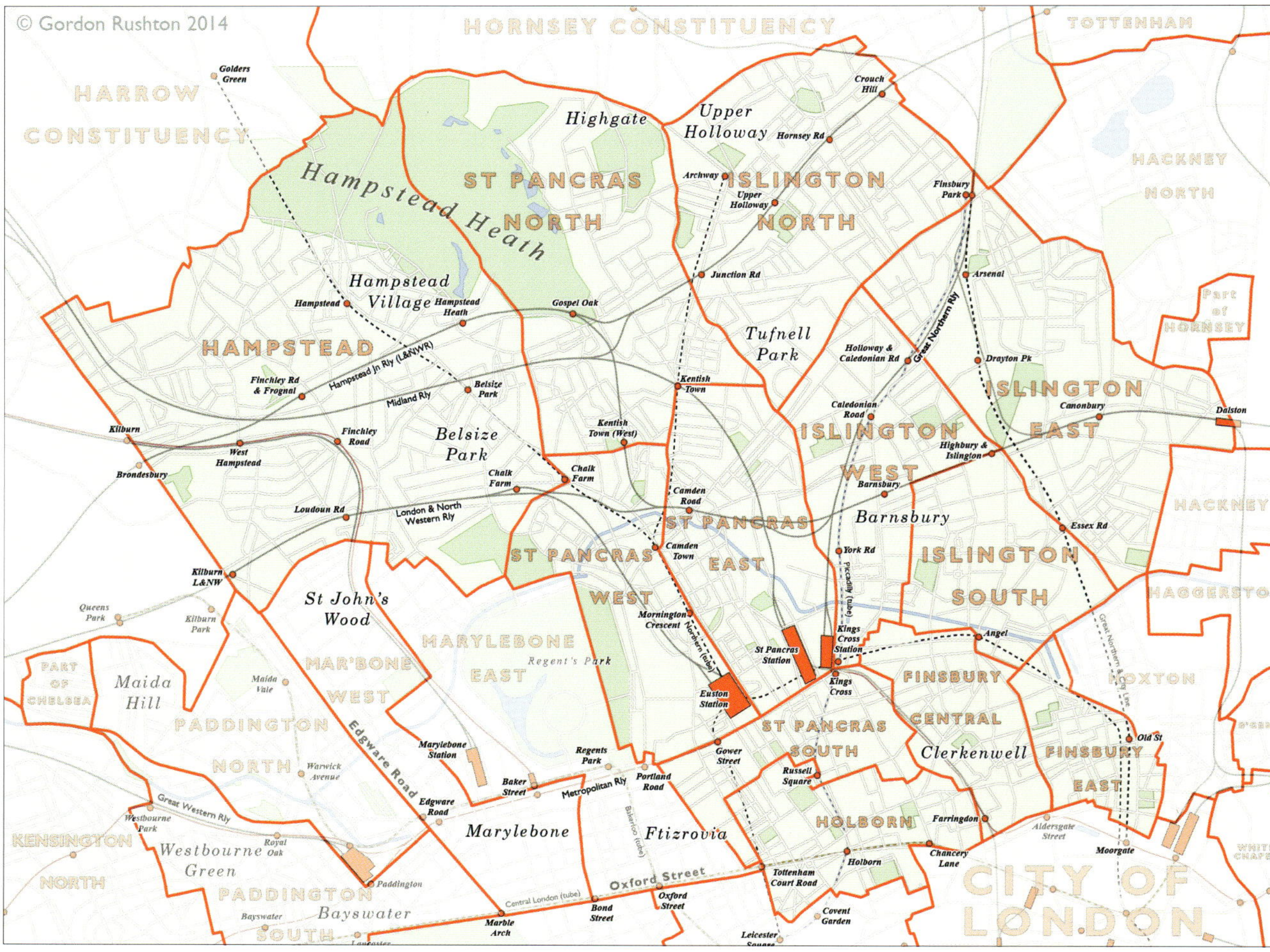

This map of the constituencies created in 1885 illustrates the suburban expansion taking place beyond the central London core. All were previously contained within either Finsbury or Marylebone. The spaciousness of the outer seats contrasts with those concentrated closest to the City.

The breakup of Finsbury and Marylebone resulted in 12 constituencies arising from the redistribution.

Holborn (1 seat)

The new Holborn borough was a very tight-knit and generally wealthy district, with a few pockets of severe poverty, carved from the former Finsbury division. Officially it comprised eight small parishes, including St Giles in the Fields, St George's Bloomsbury, St George the Martyr, St Andrew Holborn above the bars, Saffron Hill, Hatton Garden, Ely Place, and Ely rents, together with various parishes of the Inns of Court, including Gray's, Lincoln's, Furnival's, and Staple's. The main residential districts, apart from the Inns of Court, were around the south end of the Tottenham Court Road, St Giles Circus, Seven Dials, Holborn, Bloomsbury, and Hatton Garden. The constituency contained Bedford Square, the London University Senate House (though not the bulk of the University, which was in St Pancras South), the British Museum, Russell Square, Brunswick Square, and Great Ormond Street Hospital.

Holborn lies between the City of London and Westminster and gets its name from a reach of the River Fleet, known as the "Hole – Bourne", although this disappeared from view when it was culverted in 1733. The Romans built the road, known today as High Holborn, from the "New Gate" (of prison fame) of "Londinium" to the West. It owes its later development to its location, and became England's prime centre for the practice of law and medicine. London's academia also flourished within its boundaries. The prison and courts provided the stimulus for the legal profession to develop in the area. Grays Inn and Lincoln's Inn were both established in the 14th century, the former initially to provide students with education and lodgings combined; the latter was founded on land owned by the Earl of Lincoln. Bloomsbury was then undeveloped, having been a fortified manor (William "Blemond's-bury") since the 13th century. Holborn began to find favour in Tudor times. Sir Christopher Hatton, who was Queen Elizabeth I's Lord Chancellor (the country's principal Law Officer), built a residence in the area, which was to become the jewelry and diamond centre of England in the early 1800s. In 1680 a number of fine residences were built in Hatton Street (now Garden), described then as having rural views all the way to the hilly slopes of Pentonville. Southampton (later Bloomsbury) was London's first residential Square, built on land owned by the Fourth Earl of Southampton in the 1660s, and Red Lion Square soon followed.

Yet Holborn was something of a mixed community. Many impoverished people lived cheek-by-jowl with the wealthy lawyers in Seven Dials, a grossly overcrowded area of St Giles overwhelmed by crime and violence. To the west, along the Tottenham Court, lived and worked skilled artisans engaged in cabinet making and furniture manufacture, industries that were to gain sustenance from the building of many more fine houses over the next two hundred years. Further north, on the former Lambe's Conduit fields (an early London water course), a Captain Thomas Coram built the Foundling Hospital in 1742, an indication of the terrible social problems that existed in the area then.

It was in the 18th century that Holborn started to be laid out in the form recognised today. The Earls and Dukes of Bedford had acquired the Manor of Bloomsbury through marriage, and it was they who decided to develop the area. They owned most of the lands east of the Tottenham Court Road, and began to build a series of splendid Georgian Squares. Bedford Square was the first, between 1775 and 1780, and others followed in the early 19th century, including Wooburn, Gordon, Russell, and Tavistock Squares. Brunswick Square, opened in 1802, was named in honour of Princess Caroline, the wife whom the Prince Regent despised. New Oxford Street was built as a by-pass for the overcrowded St Giles High Street in 1847, by which time small hotels and boarding houses were also opening up to service the large number of visitors to the City, Westminster, and the law courts.

Next came a series of hospitals: London's Homeopathic Hospital in 1849; Great Ormond Street Hospital for Sick Children in 1851, and the Alexandra Hospital for Poor Children with Hip Disease opened in 1867. The British Museum and London University also arrived in the 19th century, providing the area with more service-based employment and a continued need for short-let flats, in which the area still abounds. Major road infrastructure improvements continued to be made, including the opening of Holborn Viaduct across the Fleet valley in 1869; Kingsway and the Aldwych followed in 1905.

In 1900, the year Holborn became a London borough, the first section of the Central Line Railway was opened from the Bank of England to Shepherds Bush, with stations at Holborn, and Chancery Lane. This improved access to the area, together with the opening of suburban railways serving nearby Waterloo and Charing Cross, as well as the termini for the north along the Euston Road. For the first time a convenient movement of the middle class population away from Holborn was enabled. Working class housing remained poor, but was helped by various charitable or low rent housing developers, including the London Housing Society, St Pancras Housing Association, and the Peabody Trust.

Finsbury (2 seats)

Two constituencies covered different parts of the borough. St Lukes, St Sepulchre (Charterhouse), and St Botolph parishes officially formed **Finsbury East,** whilst **Finsbury Central** included mainly the parishes of St James, and St John, Clerkenwell together with the tiny parishes of Charterhouse, Glass House Yard, and St Bartholomew the Great. The Goswell Road and the northernmost tip of Aldersgate Street separated the two where, in the vicinity of Fann Street, the southern boundaries of both divisions met the City of London, very close to what is now the Barbican Estate. From there the East division's southern boundary line with the City ran to a point just north of Finsbury Circus, northwards along Paul Street, which divided Finsbury and Shoreditch boroughs, to the junction of Old Street and Great Eastern Street, thence back to the junction with City Road, which it followed to a point where the St Lukes and Islington parishes met, a couple of hundred yards short of the Angel (Islington). Within East Finsbury were Finsbury Pavement and Square, the densely populated area of Bunhill Fields, Golden Lane, Old Street, and the communities living between there and City Road. Finsbury Central extended between Smithfield Market and Kings Cross station, and had its northern boundary with Islington, on a roughly east to west alignment, between the point at which Liverpool Road meets Upper Street at Islington, to the Caledonian Road just east of Kings Cross station. The constituency was bounded on the western flank by St Pancras South and Holborn, and faced the City of London along Charterhouse Street and Long Lane, near Smithfield Market. Its principal residential areas were Pentonville, Finsbury, Clerkenwell, and Farringdon.

St Pancras (4 seats)

Between Finsbury Central and Marylebone East lay the newly created borough of St Pancras, an area that expanded hugely in this period. During the 4th century, Romano-British inhabitants established premises that endure today as

Above (left): *High Holborn, near Chancery Lane, pictured at the time the Holborn Constituency was created in 1885.*
©TfL from the London Transport Museum Collection

Above (right): *St Luke, Old St, built in 1733, designed by John James, with tower and obelisk spire by Nicolas Hawksmoor. It closed in 1964 and was refitted to be the rehearsing, recording and concert hall for the London Symphony Orchestra in 2004. St Luke's Parish was the core of the Finsbury East Constituency in 1885.*
Gordon Rushton

Above: *Taken from the forecourt of Kings Cross station, this photograph shows the three-way junction of York Way, Pentonville Rd, and Grays Inn Rd, which was the boundary point of no less than four constituencies between 1885 and 1918. In clockwise order from and including Kings Cross Station they were: St Pancras East, Islington West, Finsbury Central, and St. Pancras South.*
©TfL from the London Transport Museum Collection

Right*: The splendour of this neo-gothic Victorian Station, in the St Pancras E Constituency, was designed for the Midland Railway by George Gilbert Scott as a cathedral to the new age of the train. In the 1860s it swept away some of the slum quality houses in its vicinity that had made the area disreputable.*
Gordon Rushton

Below: *The St John's Gate, Clerkenwell, home to the Order of St John, and in the 1885 Finsbury Central Constituency.*
©TfL from the London Transport Museum Collection

St Pancras old church, and the area remained largely agricultural for many centuries, serving as a market garden for London, but the 18th and 19th centuries saw the arrival of canals and then railways, many of which had their London termini there. These transformed Kings Cross and St Pancras into an urban area of slums and workmen's lodgings, one of London's poorest districts.

Between Holborn and the Euston Road was **St Pancras South**, which officially comprised borough wards numbers seven and eight, areas of high population density, mainly lower quality housing facing London's Northern railway termini. The constituency included the main part of London University and Coram's Fields but the Kings Cross district (so named when a cross was erected in honour of King George IV) formed its main component, the railways providing huge employment in addition to that already available to local people in the City and nearby Holborn. The streets either side of the Euston Road (as the former New Road had become) housed thousands of essential London workers and their families. The Duke of Bedford considered the housing so bad that he erected gates and other barriers on the south side of Euston Road to protect his own estates from their disreputable effects. The London Housing Society built many flats, tenements and terraces, especially south of Kings Cross around the turn of the century.

St Pancras West comprised borough wards numbers two, four and five covering the area between Euston station and Primrose Hill (both inclusive) including Mornington Crescent, Chalk Farm and the eastern fringes of Regents Park, while **St Pancras East** comprised wards three and six running northwest from Kings Cross and St Pancras stations towards Camden Town (incorporating its southern districts) and included St Pancras itself with Somers Town, infamous for its massive poverty and overcrowded conditions. It was also the area in which three of London's major railway termini were built in the 19th century on land that in 1697 had been the London residence of the Lord Chancellor, Baron Somers of Evesham, a descendant of a Court Jester to Henry VIII. After the New Road from Marylebone was constructed as a by-pass from the West to the City of London avoiding the congestion of Oxford Street and Holborn, Somers Town was developed for leased housing. However, the staged building of the railways represented a major opportunity for the landowners who had no compunction in evicting those who were in the way. Euston Station was built in 1837, Kings Cross in 1852 and St Pancras in 1868/9. It was the Midland Railway that caused most of the upheaval as its construction came after the housing had been built. Thousands of people were displaced and went to live in similarly overcrowded conditions in places like Islington. Another wave of dispossessions came in 1875 when more land was acquired to build the Somers Town Goods station. East of Regents Park on the estates of the Earl of Southampton some of London's worst housing developed in Somers Town and Agar Town. In a publication of Charles Dickens in 1851 this area was described as "a disgrace to the metropolis". Fortunately this shanty town was demolished in 1861 to make way for St Pancras Station. By the canal side at Somers Town arose the vast Imperial Company Gasworks, built in 1822. The canal and railways brought in timber and the construction trades had many centres of manufacture and distribution in later years, all giving employment to a hard pressed working class housed in slums and tenements. The terraces around Chalton and Ossulston Streets were so bad that they were demolished under the Housing of Working Classes Act of 1890. Matters started to be put to rights when some of the streets between Euston and St Pancras stations were built with new, high density, three storey houses. Somers Town gradually developed as a pleasant domicile for people working nearby. Many of the houses survive today, despite the battering they received during WW2.

St Pancras North comprised ward one and covered northern districts of Camden Town and the area beyond including Kentish Town, which developed in the mid-19th century surrounding the lands occupied by the North London, Tottenham & Hampstead Junction, and Midland Railways, violating the fields around the old village. The journalist Emerson wrote at the time that Gospel Oak, which was also in the constituency, was becoming "covered with terraces and crescents; and Kentish Town is throwing out lines of bricks and mortar to meet its neighbours, Hampstead and Downshire Hill." In 1866 the sanitary reformer James Hole commenting on Kentish Town, said: "The inhabitant whose memory can carry him back thirty years recalls pictures of rural beauty, suburban mansions and farmsteads, green fields, waving trees and clear streams where fish could live – where now can be seen only streets, factories and workshops, and a river or brook black as ink." Camden Town had developed rapidly from about 1820 when the Regents Canal attracted industry and coal wharves. Dickens, who lived there for a while, captured its unfinished state in "Dombey and Son" in which he wrote "there were frowzy fields and cow houses, and dung hills, and dust heaps, and ditches, and gardens, and summer houses, and carpet-beating grounds....and backs of mean houses, and patches of wretched vegetation."

Hampstead (1 seat)

Hampstead, north of Marylebone and between St Pancras North and Hornsey beyond, was created a separate borough based on the parish of St John. The new constituency incorporated Belsize Park, Dartmouth Park, Finchley Road, Hampstead Village, Kenwood, Kilburn Grange Park, Swiss Cottage, West Hampstead and Waterlow Park. An ancient village with a distinctive history it is thought that Hampstead lands there were granted by King Ethelred ("The

Top Left: *Prince of Wales Road at Kentish Town West Station was the boundary between the St. Pancras North and West Constituencies in 1885.* **John Nelson**

Top Right: *John Cobden's statue opposite Mornington Crescent Tube Station. Camden High St and Eversholt St to the south formed the boundary between the East and West St Pancras constituencies.*

Left: *Langland Gdns, Frognal, Hampstead Constituency 1885-1918 within 2 mins walk of the N. London Railway.* **John Nelson**

Above: *From the 1840s onwards Goldington Street and Goldington Crescent, in the 1885 St Pancras East Constituency, were laid out with three-storey terraced houses, some of which have survived subsequent redevelopment and Second World War bombing. Although considered to be high-density housing at the time of construction the neighbourhood offered domicile for working people close to where jobs were. As the need for housing rose steadily, the area filled with more and more residences.*

Left: *St Pancras, Euston Road (new) Parish Church in St Pancras South, was built between 1819-22, and designed by Henry and William Inwood in the Greek Revival style. If spiritual refreshment was required both this and the old parish churches were on hand to serve the close-packed residents.*

Photos by: Gordon Rushton, except as otherwise shown

Map background © Google Maps

Unready") to the Abbot of Westminster in AD 986. Some of these were sold in the 12th century and, when released for modern housing 700 years later, the phasing of the land sales shaped the way Hampstead was developed. Lands not retained by the Abbots were sold in four lots. Kilburn Priory acquired the land between today's Kilburn High Road and Swiss Cottage. From Swiss Cottage to Chalk Farm and south to Primrose Hill the Eton College Estate owned the land. South East of the Edgware Road (Watling Street) at Cricklewood (itself in Willesden Parish), the land was acquired by the Shoot-up Hill estate; and the area south of Hampstead village between the present Finchley Road and as far east as Gospel Oak was sold to the Belsize Park estate. Eventually Belsize Manor and Hampstead together were to form the new borough.

In the Middle Ages, Hampstead was a small agricultural village which in 1312 comprised only forty one dwellings. In the 16th and 17th centuries, however, it had become a rural retreat for wealthy City merchants, lawyers and Court functionaries, especially after the Court became less peripatetic and settled for longer periods at Westminster. Both Hampstead and Highgate were affected by this trend as a somewhat exclusive society began to take hold. Although agriculture remained the main activity, Hampstead became a tourist attraction as one of the first generation of London spas, Hampstead Wells being developed from about 1689 nearly 30 years after the first at Streatham. In 1701 a pump room was built to tap the chalybeate spring water and fashionable London society flocked in; a racecourse was built together with a bowling green, a concert hall and teashops. Although this fashion soon diminished, by 1750 Hampstead had assumed an arty, intellectual air with poets like Keats and writers lodging in the village. Although the spa had gone by 1800, Hampstead retained its attractiveness as a place to visit and Belsize House opened its grounds to visitors shortly afterwards. Yet well into the 19th century local people were holding off the development of new roads and housing. West End remained a tiny hamlet and in 1813 there was massive resistance to the plans of one local landowner, Colonel Eyre, to access his estates near St John's Wood by constructing a road to Finchley.

His proposals for a Turnpike Road were eventually agreed by Parliament and the Finchley Road was built opening up Hampstead for development. Chalk Farm was sold in the 1830s when, in the aftermath of the opening of Regents Park, it was thought that house building would be encouraged beyond its northern boundaries. In the 1850s Haverstock Hill and the area around the Swiss Cottage were developed and a railway station followed at the Roundhouse in 1837. Then, after the London to Birmingham Railway opened a station there in 1851, Primrose Hill was developed. Belsize and Rosslyn Parks followed from 1853. It was also in the 1850s that the East India and West India Docks and Birmingham Junction Railway opened. Though initially a freight route the running of passenger trains proved so popular with Hampstead residents travelling to the City of London that a new extension to Broad Street was opened from Dalston in about 1865. This was not only a further spur to Hampstead's growth but also to the middle class composition of its population. The old landed estates were mainly broken up in the third-quarter of the century after Parliament agreed to an extension of the Metropolitan and St Johns Wood Railway in the 1860s. A station was built at Swiss Cottage in 1868 leading to massive development of that area in the 1870s whilst The Midland Railway's arrival, also in 1868, stimulated house building on the western side of the borough. However, unlike adjoining Camden Town, Gospel Oak and Kentish Town, Hampstead avoided the desolation wrought by the construction of railway lines and freight yards, which, unusually for London, tended to follow rather than stimulate development in the area. Hampstead was incorporated as part of the London County Council in 1889 and as a borough in 1900.

Islington (4 seats)

When it was established as a Parliamentary borough in its own right in 1885, late Victorian Islington was so big it was divided into four parts, all sandwiched between St Pancras to the west and Hackney to the east. **Islington North** comprised three wards – Tufnell, Holloway and Tollington - a then partially developed outer London suburb south of Hornsey village adjoining open fields at the bottom of Highgate Hill near Archway. Bisected by the Holloway Road, the constituency incorporated Upper Holloway and Tufnell Park, and was bounded southwest to northeast at Finsbury Park by Camden Road and the Seven Sisters Road. Although much of the latter still comprised fields these would be built on within only a few more years. Holloway Road also formed the western boundary of **Islington East** for the whole of its length between Islington North and the border with Shoreditch. Its two borough wards were Canonbury and Highbury. Extending south from Finsbury Park Gates to a point beyond the Essex Road, the main areas of population were Canonbury and Mildmay although Highbury and Drayton Park were also beginning to develop. The area surrounding what became the Arsenal Football Highbury Stadium was still emerging, although the Club itself had yet to move from Woolwich in South East London.

Islington South comprised three wards – Barnsbury, St Mary's and St Peter's – and was separated from the East division by the Canonbury Road, an extension of Holloway Road running from Highbury Corner through central parts of Islington itself to the boundary with Finsbury. Its northern and western boundaries were with **Islington West**, and

Above & Below: *Archway Bridge is seen shortly after it was built in 1897 and Tuffnell Park Underground Station (below) opened ten years later. They were both in the St Pancras North Constituency which in 1885 was on the suburban fringe. The infrastructure enhancements triggered a population expansion before the First World War. By 1918 the area was on its way to becoming an Inner London Constituency!* **©TfL from the London Transport Museum Collection**

Bottom Left: *Hemmingford Road, Barnsbury separated the Islington West and South Constituencies. The terraced houses and public house pictured here were in Islington West Constituency.*

Below Right *Leafy Canonbury was an early suburb created for the middle classes, with excellent, well founded little villas, sited within convenient reach of railway station and City. The district was in the Islington East Constituency.*

John Nelson

Below Right: *An End of Terrace villa on the corner of Lofting Road and Barnsbury Terrace. The area is close to Caledonian Road and Barnsbury Station, afforded easy access between domicile and the City of London, via Broad Street Station. This part of Barnsbury was in the Islington South Constituency.*

Photos by: John Nelson, except as otherwise shown

were formed west of Highbury Corner by the North London Railway as far as the station at Barnsbury. Here the border turned south to meet the Finsbury borough boundary, north of Chapel Street, Pentonville. The Angel, Central Islington (Upper Street) and Barnsbury were the main residential areas. Islington West comprised the Lower Holloway and Thornhill wards and though mainly focused on the former extended north from Kings Cross station in a narrow strip along the Caledonian Road including Pentonville Prison.

Islington is mentioned both in an Anglo-Saxon charter and "Hill of Gisla" (a Saxon leader) is thought to be the origin of its name. A village was formed in the vicinity of Islington Green after the forests were cleared from lands then belonging to St Pauls cathedral and which were reached across fields that extended north from the City walls. Next to Islington were the manors of Barnsbury, Canonbury and Highbury. The first of these was named after Ralph de Berners whilst Canonbury belonged to the Priory of St Bartholomew at Smithfield, itself on the northern edge of the City bordering Finsbury. Highbury belonged to the Knights of St John of Jerusalem who had their headquarters in Finsbury. According to one early writer the area was a savage place, a forest "full of the lairs of wild beasts", where bears and wild bulls roamed while on the edges of the forest there was a pasture for hogs. In the Middle Ages most land belonged to religious institutions but, after the dissolution of the monasteries, much of it was given to aristocratic families, often friends of Tudor monarchs. The land north of London towards Islington, Highbury, Hornsey and Hampstead was at one time a Royal hunting ground but after the reign of Henry VIII it gradually became a place to which ordinary Londoners would resort for recreation. Wrestling, archery and games of all sorts were played there for centuries but following the Great Fire of London in 1666 these fields were put to a very different use. Over 200,000 people were displaced and lived there outdoors. Islington grew slowly from a hamlet to a village, spreading along Upper Street and Lower Road, which later became Essex Road. In time it became famous for dairy herds, supplying London with butter, cream and milk. As London grew, terraced housing began to consume the agricultural land and local farmers turned to manufacturing bricks and developing property. In the 18th and early 19h centuries Islington, like Hampstead, became a tourist area with many tea gardens and gaming houses to entertain visitors. It also became an area of popular resort for political purposes. Copenhagen Fields were the scene of radical gatherings, notably in support of the French Revolution and against the deportation of the Tolpuddle Martyrs.

It was the first London suburb to become truly built up. On high ground commanding a magnificent panorama over London its water well was credited with health giving properties and Islington developed a respectable but conservative reputation. Both the High Street and Upper Street were house lined by 1735 and building proceeded rapidly from 1760 when modern Islington began to develop, peaking after the Battle of Waterloo, when the New River Company built a water canal from Hertfordshire to Islington and Georgian streets and squares proliferated. Chapel Street was built in 1790 followed by the London Fever Hospital in 1802 on land at Battles Bridge (now Kings Cross) as the area began to accommodate both the overspill of London's middle class and facilities needed by the metropolis. In 1801 the local population was recorded as 10,212 but this increased by leaps and bounds throughout the 19th century. The opening of the Regents Canal in 1820 encouraged its development and the population more than doubled between 1801 and 1821 to 22,417. It did so again by 1841 when it reached 55,690 yet within another twenty years it had trebled, to 155,341 in 1861. Between 1801 and 1901 the numbers increased thirty fold.

Canonbury developed around 1800 and Cloudsley Square was built in 1820 followed in the 1840s by Gibson and Milner Squares. Pentonville Prison was opened in 1840 and the Fever Hospital moved to a new site in Liverpool Road in 1849. Holloway Prison for women opened during the same period and in 1855 the Caledonian Market and slaughterhouses for cattle were built to allow the central meat market to be developed at Smithfield. By then streets of houses were voraciously consuming the open spaces. The Islington Empire opened in 1860 as the Philharmonic Hall followed by other theatres, including Collins Music Hall, which started in a public house facing Islington Green in 1862. The Agricultural Hall was started in 1861 pre-dating Earls Court and Olympia as London's principal exhibition centre. The Smithfield Society called its annual livestock show there from 1862 and in 1899 the first Motor Show was held. Trains arrived in the shape of the North London Railway Company, which built a line with several imposing stations serving the City to carry wealthy middle class commuters from Highbury, Canonbury and Mildmay. Then the advent of Underground Railways before the First World War brought even greater access by train. The Great Northern & City and the Piccadilly Lines both served Finsbury Park, the first operating to Moorgate, the latter via Caledonian Road. The Northern Line also opened before the end of the 19th century and linked the Angel (close to old Islington's centre) with the Bank of England. The years after the arrival of the railways saw a further explosion in the population, which peaked at 335,000 in 1901. Part of the stimulus to growth was the displacement of many thousands from nearby Somers Town allowing the building of Euston and St Pancras Stations. Battles Bridge in the southwest corner of Islington next to St Pancras was transformed by the building of the Great Northern Railway's main London terminus at Kings Cross. Despite the employment opportunities provided by the railways, many people were displaced from their homes and moved to Islington bringing about a decline in its genteel character.

Dickens observed that in parts of Holloway "tiles and bricks were burnt, bones were boiled, carpets were beat, rubbish was shot, dogs were fought, and dust was heaped by contractors". These became abandoned areas for a time but they too were eventually built on with housing, not for the middle classes but the workers. By 1885 the only part of Islington that was not built on was Highbury Fields, which were saved as an open space. A movement of middle class people from Finsbury to Islington also occurred, as the adjacent inner London borough became increasingly working class in its character from the 1880s onwards but the 1883 Cheap Trains Act encouraged the building of affordable housing for the working man in suburbs further afield than Islington and eventually its population began to decline.

Constituency Populations and Electorates

Constituency	1891 pop	1901 pop	1911 pop	1910 electors	1910 electors as % of 1911 pop	% Pop change 1891 to 1911	1891 pop ratio of average 67032*	1911 pop ratio of average 64576*
Holborn	70,911	61,904	51,350	8,608	16.8	-28	1.06	0.8
St.Pancras E	60,666	60,276	57,402	9,487	15.6	-5	0.91	0.88
St.Pancras N	59,223	59,375	58,026	9,977	17.2	-2	0.88	0.9
St.Pancras S	53,776	55,495	45,598	5,536	12.1	-15	0.8	0.71
St.Pancras W	60,704	59,766	57,582	8,589	14.9	-5	0.91	0.89
Finsbury C	66,216	64,077	58,774	8,094	13.8	-11	0.99	0.91
Finsbury E	45,327	39,827	32,790	4,855	14.8	-28	0.68	0.51
Islington E	83,558	89,349	86,605	11,118	12.8	4	1.25	1.34
Islington N	90,235	99,895	101,251	12,677	12.5	12	1.35	1.57
Islington S	71,188	71,823	69,300	8,268	11.9	-3	1.06	1.07
Islington W	74,162	74,171	70,332	8,544	12.1	-5	1.11	1.09
Hampstead	68,416	82,329	85,907	12,050	14	26	1.02	1.33
Summary	804,382	818,287	774,917	107,803	13.9	-4	1	1

* **Note: population per MP, as a ratio of the average for the whole area.**

The table above is revealing of the population changes taking place at the time and of the social composition of the electorates. Overall the population of this part of North London fell by about 4% in the twenty years from 1891 to 1911, although for the first half of this period it had increased. However, there were substantial variations between constituencies ranging from a 28% reduction in two of them (Holborn and Finsbury East) and a 26% increase in Hampstead. Finsbury Central and St Pancras South also experienced large reductions whilst only Islington North showed a corresponding growth. These trends were all reflective of the suburbanisation of Middlesex with populations declining in all but the three outer suburban seats.

The table also shows that when these seats were created there was already some imbalance in the distribution of populations between them. In 1891 the average constituency population in the area was 67,032 but Finsbury East (33% below) and Islington North (35% above) stand out as varying substantially from the average, though St Pancras South (20% below) and Islington East (25% above) were also out of line. All of the others were within 12% of the average. Yet within 20 years half of them were at least 20% outside the average for the area, which was by then 64,576. The population changes in the intervening years accentuated the variations such that by 1911 Finsbury East and Islington North were 49% below and 57% above average respectively. Only the Islington South and West constituencies maintained equilibrium over the period as a whole.

Less than 14% of the population of north London had the vote in 1910. Only three constituencies – the then suburban divisions of Hampstead, St Pancras East and North - had electorates amounting to over 15% of the population, whilst the heavily working class constituencies were below one in eight of the population. The business vote in Holborn was probably a factor in maintaining a relatively high electorate there.

Politics in North London between 1885 and 1918

North London as a whole elected rather more Tories than Liberals during this period but its political representation would probably have been fairly evenly balanced had it not been for the split in the Liberal Party that gave rise to the Liberal Unionists. 49 Conservatives, 10 Liberal Unionists, 1 Labour and 36 Liberals were elected MPs at General Elections between 1885 and 1910. In addition there were six Tory by-election successes, one for the Liberal Unionists and 2 for the Liberals. Furthermore, the narrowness of the Liberal Party's winning majorities in so many seats was an indication of the fragility that underlay its national position. With the rise of the Labour Party it was in areas like these that the Liberal Party began to lose its hold on the constituencies it needed to maintain an effective power base. MPs elected during this period were as follows:

General Election Results 1885-1910 - by % majority

Constituency	*1885*	*1886*	*1892*	*1895*	*1900*	*1906*	*1910 Jan*	*1910 Dec*
Holborn	C24	C30+	C33	C100+	C100	C18	C36	C46
St Pancras East	L5	C12	C9	C6+	C18	L29	Llab9	Lab12
St Pancras North	L11	C7-	L1	C4	C13	L22	L16	L15
St Pancras South	LU5	LU36	LU10	LU33+	LU34	L1	LU18	LU16
St Pancras West	L9	L1	C0.8	C15	C35	L12	L0.2	C0.2
Finsbury Central	L11	C0.2+	L0.0	C13	C6	Llab11	C6	C9
Finsbury East	C0.4	Llab2	Llab6	C6	C9-	L16	L2	L3
Islington East	L0.6	C23	C6	C16	C24	L9	L3	L1
Islington North	C9	C27	C10	C16	C31	L9	L0.2	C4
Islington South	L10	C11	C5	C21	C40	L25	L10	L11
Islington West	LU21	LU30	LU2	L7	L0.2	L6	L3	L4
Hampstead	C19	C48+	C26	C100	C100++	C5	C22	C28
C and LU	6	10+++ –	9	11++	11++	2	4	6
L	6	1	2	1	1	9	7	5
Llab and Lab	0	1	1	0	0	1	1	1

Key: Numbers indicate percentage majority of the votes cast in the election. 100 = unopposed; C = Conservative; L = Liberal; Llab = Liberal with Labour support; Lab = Labour; LU = Liberal Unionist (in alliance with the Conservatives) + = Seats retained at By-elections; -- = Party that won seat at General Election lost by-election to main opposition Party in same Parliament.

MPs for Holborn

From	at	To	Surname	First Names	Party
1885	G	1888	Duncan	Francis (Col)	Conservative
1888	B	1892	Bruce	Sir Gainsford	Conservative
1892	B	1900	Hall	Sir Charles	Conservative
1900	B	1918	Remnant	Sir James Farquharson	Conservative and Unionist

NOTE First returned at a B = By-election; G = General Election

Holborn was solidly Conservative at all eight General Elections between 1885 and December 1910. The Party also won three by-elections (in 1888, August 1892 and March 1900). It was not just Tory politics that the MPs had in common. Most were also lawyers, not entirely surprising given the substantial influence of the Inns of Court in Holborn. In those days a substantial numbers of lawyers lived as well as worked there and this had a big impact on local politics.

Francis Duncan (Conservative) was the son of an Aberdeen man and was born there in 1836. He was educated at Universities in Aberdeen, Durham and Canada before entering the Royal Artillery in 1855, rising within 30 years to the rank of Colonel, after commanding the Egyptian Artillery between 1883 and 1885. He wrote a regimental history of the Royal Artillery and several books about Canada including one entitled "Our Empire in the West". Prior to his election at Holborn he unsuccessfully contested several seats in the Conservative cause including Morpeth (1874) City of Durham (1874 By-election) and Finsbury (1880).

He died in 1888 and the by-election was won by **Sir Gainsford Bruce** (Conservative), the son of the Reverend Collingwood Bruce of Newcastle-upon-Tyne, in which city Gainsford was born in 1834. Educated at Glasgow University, he entered the law; was called to the bar in 1853; became a QC in 1883 and a bencher two years later. He wrote several legal works on the subject of shipping and in 1877 became Recorder of Bradford (West Riding) moving back to County Durham in 1879 as its Solicitor-General. During this period in the Northeast he stood unsuccessfully for Gateshead at the 1880 General election; for Newcastle-upon-Tyne in an 1883 by-election; and for Northumberland South in 1885. In 1886 he unsuccessfully contested Barrow-in-Furness at a by-election, was promoted to Attorney-General of County Durham and a year later to the superior post of Chancellor. Once elected in 1888 his Parliamentary career was brief. He resigned in 1892 on his appointment as a High Court Judge, which post he held until retirement in 1904. He died in 1912.

Sir Charles Hall (Conservative) was the son of a University Vice-Chancellor. Born in London in 1843, he was educated at Harrow and Trinity College Cambridge after which he became a lawyer at Lincoln's Inn in 1866 serving until appointed a bencher at the Middle Temple in 1884. Between 1877 and 1892 he was Attorney General to the Prince of Wales and embarked on a political career. In 1885 he was elected MP for the Cambridgeshire constituency of Chesterton and after his defeat there in 1892 entered the House again at the Holborn by-election brought about by Bruce's resignation. The same year Hall was appointed Recorder of London.

He died in 1900 and **Sir James Farquharson Remnant** (Conservative) replaced him at a by-election. Son of a Suffolk magistrate from the coastal town of Southwold, Remnant was born in 1863, educated at Harrow School and at Magdalen College, Oxford. Between 1884 and 1888 he also held a commission in the Third Royal Sussex Regiment and it was during this period, in 1886, that he became a barrister at Lincoln's Inn. From 1892 until 1901 he sat as the LCC member for Holborn and was a Whip between 1895 and 1898. He also served on the Thames Conservancy from 1897-1901. After his election as MP for Holborn in 1900 he stood down from local politics but never achieved ministerial office. He was a member of the Royal Commission into Canals and Waterways that was established in 1906 and during the Great War was a Lieutenant Colonel in the Royal Army Service Corps. Afterwards he continued as Holborn's MP for another ten years until he was created Baron Remnant, moving to the Lords in 1928. He died five years later.

MPs for St Pancras

Although 12 Liberals were returned at elections in St Pancras compared with only seven Tories, it was the latter who enjoyed most success as they served for a longer period of 56 years compared with 46. Two of the 12 Liberals changed parties, one remaining in the House for a further seven years as a Labour MP whilst another sat as a Unionist for a further five. The negative impact of Party splits on Liberal fortunes is further evidenced by the fact that two other men sat as Liberal Unionists for 18 years. Because they sat with the Tories the balance of advantage during the period as a whole clearly lay with the Conservatives. This constituency returned a Liberal in 1885 but Conservatives at all four subsequent General Elections and at a by-election on 12th July 1899. The tide turned when a Liberal was elected in 1906 and the Party retained the seat in January 1910 with Labour support but in December the seat became the first in the borough to return a Labour MP. There was a large unionised railway workforce in the constituency which might have explained the extent of Labour support at that time.

St Pancras East

Thomas Eccleston Gibb (Liberal) was a Liverpudlian, born in 1838 and educated at Liverpool College prior to attending Kings College, London. Initially a journalist on the Mercury newspaper in his home City he subsequently became an administrator as clerk to the parish and vestry of St Pancras. He wrote pamphlets on the subject of the Poor Law and local Government and first stood for Parliament in 1885 when he won the newly created constituency. Defeated there in 1886 he went into local politics and, when the LCC was established in 1889, he was made an Alderman. He served in this capacity until 1892 when he failed again to secure election to the Commons for his former constituency and Tories held the division for the next 20 years. He died in 1894.

In 1886 Gibb was beaten by **Robert Grant Webster** (Conservative) who held the seat until his retirement in 1899. He was the son of an Edinburgh man but was himself born at Marylebone in 1845. Educated at St Peter's Radley and at Trinity College Cambridge, he became a lawyer, though he also served for several years in the Third Battalion of the South Lancashire Regiment. It is possible that an interest in canals was generated by his association with Lancashire as he wrote a work entitled "The Law relating to Canals". He first entered politics as the unsuccessful Conservative candidate at Cockermouth (Cumberland) in 1880 and was next defeated at St Pancras East by Gibb in 1885 before turning the tables the following year. He died in 1921.

MPs for St Pancras						
From	**at**	**To**	**Name**	**First Names**	**Constituency**	**Party**
1885	G	1886	Gibb	Thomas Eccleston	St. Pancras East	Liberal
1886	G	1899	Webster	Robert Grant		Conservative
1899	B	1906	Wrightson	Sir Thomas		Conservative
1906	G	1910(Jan)	Lea	Hugh Cecil		Liberal
1910(Jan)	G	1910(Dec)	Martin	Joseph		Liberal
1910(Dec)	G	1918	Martin	Joseph		Labour
1885	G	1886	Bolton	Thomas Henry	St. Pancras North	Liberal
1886	G	1890	Cochrane-Baillie	Charles Wallace		Conservative
1890	B	1895	Bolton	Thomas Henry		Liberal/Unionist
1895	G	1906	Moon	Edward Robert Pacy		Conservative
1906	G	1918	Dickinson	Sir Willoughby Hyett		Liberal
1885	G	1896	Goldsmid	Sir Julian	St. Pancras South	Liberal / Unionist
1896	B	1906	Jessel	Sir Herbert Merton (Col)		Liberal Unionist
1906	G	1910(Jan)	Wilson	Philip Whitwell		Liberal
1910(Jan)	G	1918	Jessel	Sir Herbert Merton (Col)		Liberal Unionist
1885	G	1892	Lawson	Harry	St. Pancras West	Liberal
1892	G	1906	Graham	Harry Robert		Conservative
1906	G	1910(Dec)	Collins	Sir William Job		Liberal
1910(Dec)	G	1916	Cassel	Felix		Conservative
1916	B	1918	Barrett	Sir Richard Whieldon		Conservative
NOTE First returned at a B = By-election; G = General Election						

He had an undistinguished career and retired in 1899 causing a by-election which **Sir Thomas Wrightson** (Conservative) won in July. He held the seat until 1906. Heir to the Neasham Hall estate in Darlington, Wrightson was born in 1839 and became an engineer in his native County Durham. He was a Director of a Stockton-on-Tees firm of bridge builders (Head, Wrightson and Company) and also of the Cramlington Colliery in Northumberland. He became a Deputy-Lieutenant and JP for County Durham and initially went into politics at Stockton where he fought and lost on three occasions (1885, 1886 and a by-election in 1888) before being returned there in 1892. He was defeated again in 1895 and was out of Parliament until his election at St Pancras East four years later. As an MP he promoted legislation for housing the working classes. He died in 1921.

He lost in 1906 and from then until 1918 St Pancras East resumed its original political loyalty. **Hugh Cecil Lea** (Liberal) was elected in the radical landslide of 1906. Born in London in 1869, he was educated abroad and later became a newspaper owner. He served in both the American and British Armies and after his retirement as MP in 1910 remained in politics for a further three years as a member of the LCC. His successor was a Canadian, Joseph Martin (Liberal) who was born in Milton (Ontario) in 1852 and educated at local schools there and in Michigan prior to attending the University of Toronto.

Joseph Martin MP

Following graduation 'Fightin' **Joe Martin**, as he was known, (Liberal, later Labour) entered the law as a barrister at the Canadian bar in Manitoba, where he was initially a member of the Legislative Assembly, representing Portage La Prairie between 1883 and 1889 serving as Attorney-General from 1891 to 1893. He served as MP for Winnipeg between 1893 and 1896 when he moved to Vancouver, where he was appointed Attorney-General for British Columbia[22], then briefly its Prime Minister in 1900. In that year he was also elected to the Canadian House of Commons but subsequently came to Britain and stood unsuccessfully at a by-election held in 1909 at Stratford-upon-Avon. With Labour support he was returned at St Pancras East in January 1910 and at the December General election held in the same year he stood as the official Labour candidate becoming the Party's first in St Pancras. He retired in 1918 and died in1923.

22 **British Columbia became the sixth province in 1871, four years after the Canadian Dominion was established.**

St Pancras North

St Pancras North was a mostly Conservative and Unionist constituency during the period although its first and last MPs were not Tories. **Thomas Henry Bolton** (Liberal) was elected in 1885 but lost a year later. Born in 1841 at Clerkenwell, the son of a Canonbury man, he became a solicitor in the firm of Bolton and Mote of Grays Inn Square in 1869. He practised for about 20 years before entering politics by which time he had become involved in a number of local activities in Islington and St Pancras. He was also Vice Chairman of the Hailsham Guardians in Sussex. Despite voting for it at Third Reading he broke with his Party over the Irish Home Rule Bill and joined the breakaway Liberal Unionist Party led by Jospeh Chamberlain. He stood as such in 1886 and although he was defeated, was subsequently re-elected at a by-election in 1890, serving until 1895 when he retired. He died in 1916.

C.W. Cochrane Baillee MP
Wikipedia

Charles Wallace Cochrane-Baillee (Conservative) was the Tory who beat Bolton in 1886 and whose elevation to the peerage provided the opportunity for his return . Son of the Scottish Lord Lamington, Baillee was born in 1860 and educated at Eton and Christ Church Oxford after which he embarked on an Army career, initially as a Lieutenant in the Yorkshire Yeomanry Cavalry, then in the Third Battalion of the Leicester Regiment. In 1885 he was briefly the Marquis of Salisbury's private secretary and unsuccessfully sought election at St Pancras. After his return in 1886 his political career did not take off despite Salisbury becoming Prime Minister and in 1890 he succeeded his father as Lord Lamington forcing him to retire and causing a by-election that was won by Bolton. In 1895, five years after he left the Commons, he was appointed Governor of Queensland [23] where he remained until 1901. Two years later he was appointed Governor of Bombay, serving there until 1907. He died in 1940.

Edward Robert Pacy Moon (Conservative) succeeded Bolton in 1895. Son of a QC, Moon was born in London in 1858 and educated at Winchester and New College, Oxford. Like his father he became a lawyer and practised as a barrister at the Chancery Bar. He was a keen traveller in the Far and Middle East and active in the London Chamber of Commerce. He first contested St Pancras North in 1892 but lost to Bolton. He eventually served 11 years as the MP but after he was defeated in 1906 went into local politics. In 1907 he became a Poor Law Guardian for Kensington, which post he held until 1919 and from 1913 to 1931 was a councillor in the same borough. He died in 1949, in his nineties.

Sir Willoughby Hyett Dickinson (Liberal) was the son of Sebastian Dickinson, the MP for Stroud from 1868 until 1874 and the grandson of WH Hyett, MP for the same town between 1832 and 1835. Willoughby was born in the Gloucestershire town in 1859 and became a lawyer after attending Eton and Trinity College, Cambridge. He was called to the bar in 1884 but entered politics soon afterwards. From 1889 to 1907 he was a member of the LCC, serving as deputy Chairman from 1892 to 1896 and as Chairman in 1900. He was Chairman of the London Liberal Federation and sat on the Board of Control for the Care of the Mentally Defective. Before his election in 1906, he stood unsuccessfully twice; at Stepney in 1895 and St Pancras North in 1900 when he was defeated by Moon. After leaving Parliament in 1918, Dickinson tried again at St Pancras North in 1922 and retired from politics. The following year he was appointed a substitute British delegate to the League of Nations becoming a Vice-President in 1924. He joined the Labour Party in 1930 and was appointed the First Baron Dickinson. However, with the creation of the National Government a year later he sided with Ramsey MacDonald and National Labour. He died in 1943.

Julian Goldsmid 1861
© National Portrait Gallery

St Pancras South

This was a constituency in which Liberal Unionism flourished but where no Conservative was ever elected during the period. Its first MP, **Sir Julian Goldsmid** (Liberal but a Unionist after 1886), a grandson of Sir Isaac, was born in 1838 and attended London University after which he became a lawyer; he was called to the bar at Lincolns Inn in 1864. A magistrate in Kent, London and Middlesex, he was also Deputy-Lieutenant of three counties, Berkshire, Kent and Sussex, where he owned a large estate. He first entered politics in an 1864 by-election when he contested Brighton. In the General Election held the following year he failed again, this time at Chichester, another Sussex borough but in 1866 he was successful at

23 Established as a new colony when Queensland was separated from New South Wales on June 6 1859, about thirty years after a penal colony had been set up at Brisbane. Just over four decades of autonomy elapsed before Federation, on 1 January 1901, created the union of the Commonwealth of Australia. The majority of Queenslanders voted 'yes' to a referendum asking whether Queensland should join the Federation. Once this referendum was passed, Queensland lost its colonial status and became a State.

Honiton (Devon), in a by-election although 2 years later the constituency was disfranchised for corrupt practices and Goldsmid found himself outside the Commons again. At the 1868 General Election he unsuccessfully contested Mid Surrey and it was not until an 1870 by-election at Rochester in Kent that he returned, remaining its MP for 10 years until 1880 when a Conservative took his seat. After his election at St Pancras South in 1885 he held the seat until his death in 1896 when he left an estate worth over one million pounds, an enormous fortune in those days.

Goldsmid was followed at an 1896 by-election by **Colonel Sir Herbert Merton Jessel** (Liberal Unionist), son of the Master of the Rolls[24], Sir George Jessel. Born at Brighton in 1866, and educated at Rugby School he attended New College Oxford, following which he entered the Army and became a Captain in both the 17th Lancers and the Berkshire Yeomanry. He served in India from 1887 to 1890 but retired from the Army in 1896 to contest the by-election. After being returned he became an Honorary Colonel in the Royal London Fusiliers and remained MP until his defeat at the hand of the Liberals in 1906. In the meantime he also entered local Government as an Alderman in Westminster of which new borough he was elected mayor in 1903, the same year he became Chairman of the Municipal Society, a post he held until 1915. He lost his Commons seat to a Liberal in 1906 but won it back in January 1910 serving until he retired in 1918. He came out of retirement to unsuccessfully contest the Westminster St George's by-election in 1921 and three years later was made the first Baron Jessel. He died in 1950.

Philip Whitwell Wilson (Liberal) was the interloper who served for only four years as MP between 1906 and January 1910. Born in Kendal (Westmorland) in 1870, he was the grandson of a man who published Bibles. Educated in his hometown and at Clare College Cambridge, Wilson became a journalist and eventually parliamentary correspondent of the Daily News[25] and was a member of the Press Gallery for twelve years before he went to Washington as the paper's American correspondent. He wrote a book entitled "Why we believe in Liberty and Religion" and after his defeat in 1910 unsuccessfully contested the Westmoreland county division of Appleby in December. He never returned to the Commons and died in 1956.

St Pancras West

St Pancras West was shared between the two major Parties with the Conservatives holding the advantage. Liberals won there in 1885 and 1886 and again in 1906 and January 1910. However, the Tories won in elections between 1892 and 1900 and took the seat from the Liberals in December 1910 when few seats changed hands. **Harry Lawson** (Liberal) was MP from 1885 until 1892. The son of Lord Burnham, he was born in London in 1862. Educated at Eton and Balliol, he initially entered the law as a barrister at the Inner Temple in 1891 when he was only twenty seven. After his 1892 defeat he unsuccessfully contested Gloucestershire East but was returned there at a by-election the following year remaining its MP only until 1895. A magistrate and Deputy-Lieutenant for his home county Buckinghamshire, Lawson was later elected to the LCC in 1897 and remained a member until 1904. In the meantime he unsuccessfully contested Bethnal Green North East in 1900 and Bury (Lancashire) in 1902 when he switched to Unionism. He became Managing Proprietor of the Daily Telegraph[26] in 1903 and won Mile End as a Unionist at a 1905 by-election. After he lost it in the following year's General Election he remained with the Telegraph for many years, relinquishing his position in 1928. Meanwhile he was Mayor of Stepney from 1907 to 1909 and was re-elected as Mile End's MP in January 1910 sitting for another 6 years until he became Lord Burnham. Made a Viscount in 1917, he was elected Chairman of the Newspaper Proprietors Association[27] and of the Institute of Journalists[28]. In 1920 he chaired a Government Committee set up to review pay scales for teachers. The so-called Burnham Scales have applied as a reference point ever since, an achievement that may have secured his reputation as a conciliator because he was appointed chairman of no less than three International Labour Conferences held in Geneva; in 1921, 1922 and 1926. He died in 1933.

Harry Robert Graham (Conservative) took the seat in 1892 and held it until 1906. Born at St Leonard's, Sussex in 1866 he attended Essex College Oxford and became something of a world traveller, visiting each of Britain's colonies during three global tours. He first entered politics by contesting the Staffordshire division of Handsworth (now in Birmingham) in 1885, St Pancras West in 1886 and St Pancras North in 1890. He died in 1952.

Doctor **Sir William Job Collins** (Liberal) who defeated Graham was born in 1859 and after attending the University College School in London, St Bartholomew's Hospital and London University qualified as an eye surgeon. After becoming a teacher in anatomy at St Bartholomew's and an oculist at the Royal Eye and London Temperance Hospitals he enjoyed

24 English judge who is the president of the civil division of the Court of Appeal, besides being responsible for Chancery records and for the admission of solicitors.
25 A daily newspaper established in 1846. It continued under various titles until taken over by the News Chronicle in 1931.
26 Established as the Daily Telegraph and Courier in 1855.
27 Founded in 1906
28 Founded in 1894 and given a Royal Charter in 1890, the Institute is the oldest organisation for journalists in the World.

a very distinguished medical career publishing many works and serving on Royal Commissions charged with providing advice to the Government on Vaccination and Vivisection. He was made a Life Governor of University College, London and became both a Fellow and a Senator at London University at which academic institution he was subsequently Vice Chancellor from 1907 to 1909, during his period as MP for St Pancras West, which he won in 1906 but lost in December 1910. Prior to this he had served continuously on the LCC from 1892 until 1907, being its Chairman in 1897/8, and had unsuccessfully contested the St Pancras West constituency in 1895 and the London University seat in 1900. After his defeat in 1910 he was once again elected Vice Chancellor of London University (1911-12) and then attended various International Opium Conferences that took place over a two-year period between 1912 and 1914. In 1916 he was returned as an MP for Derby at a by-election but retired in 1918. In the middle year of his final term he agreed to serve as Chairman of the Conciliation and Arbitration Board of Government Employees. He died in 1946.

Felix Cassel (Conservative) was the grandson of the Earl of Verulam (St Albans) and was born in 1869. Educated at Harrow and Corpus Christi (Oxford), Cassel became a lawyer being called to the bar of Lincoln's Inn in 1894. He entered politics initially via the LCC, which he joined in 1907, retiring in 1910 to contest Hackney Central in the January General Election. He was unsuccessful but did become MP for St Pancras West at the December 1910 election. During the Great War he was a Captain in the 19th Battalion of the London Regiment but in 1916 was appointed Judge Advocate-General[29], which posting required him to resign his seat in Parliament. He subsequently became High Sheriff of Hertfordshire and was also the Chairman of several family sponsored charities including a Hospital for Nervous Diseases at Ham (Surrey) and the Cassel Educational Trust. He died in 1953.

Elected at the 1916 by-election following Cassel's resignation, **Sir Richard Whieldon Barnett** (Conservative) was the son of a Doctor from County Down where he was born in 1863. Educated at Wadham College, Oxford, Barnett became a lawyer and barrister at the Middle Temple in 1889, the year he was made a Captain of Musketry, instructing in that martial art for the next eight years. He successfully contested St Pancras South West following boundary changes in 1918 and remained MP until 1929. During this period he was President of British Controlled Oilfields Limited and was also Chairman of the British Chess Federation[30]. He died in 1930.

MPs for Finsbury

From	at	To	Name	First Names	Constituency	Party
1885	G	1886	Spensley	Howard	Finsbury Central	Liberal
1886	G	1892	Penton	Frederick Thomas (Capt)		Conservative
1892	G	1895	Naoroji	Dadabhai		Liberal
1895	G	1906	Massey-Mainwaring	William Fredk. Barton		Conservative
1906	G	1910(Jan)	Steadman	William Charles		Labour
1910(Jan)	G	1918	Archer-Shee	Sir Martin (Major)		Conservative and Unionist
1885	G	1886	Bigwood	James	Finsbury East	Conservative
1886	G	1895	Rowlands	James		Liberal
1895	G	1905	Richards	Henry Charles		Conservative
1905	B	1918	Baker	Joseph Allen		Liberal
1918	B	1918	Cotton	Harry Evan Auguste		Liberal

NOTE First returned at a B = By-election; G = General Election

The two Finsbury constituencies did something to maintain the Liberal tradition of the former Parliamentary borough, although at General Elections during the period the spoils were shared. The East division was generally Liberal whilst Central marginally favoured the Conservatives. Liberals won the East seat on five occasions, twice with Labour support (in 1886 and 1892). On 29th June 1905 the Liberals also won it from the Conservatives at a by-election. On the other hand Liberals only won Central Finsbury twice; in 1885 and 1892 though in 1906 Labour came top. In 1892 the Liberal margin of victory was miniscule and generally Central was a Tory seat.

29 The office of the Judge Advocate General was created in 1666. The main duties are to appoint judge advocates to conduct proceedings at Service Courts and judicial officers to hear custody applications and applications for search warrants.
30 Founded in 1904

Finsbury Central

Howard Spensley (Liberal) who represented Finsbury Central from 1885 until 1886 was a Londoner whose family moved to Australia. Born in 1834 he was educated in Melbourne where he was called to the bar in 1864 and subsequently became the Solicitor-General in the Victoria Government[31] of Sir Charles Gavan Duffy[32]. In 1873 he came to London to represent the Victoria Colony at an Exhibition and remained in Britain. He was called to the Middle Temple Bar in 1876 and continued to represent Victoria at various European exhibitions held in the early 1880s. Finsbury Central was the first seat that he contested but after his defeat in 1886 he tried only once more to secure election, losing at Dudley in 1892.

He was succeeded by **Frederick Penton** (Conservative), who was the son of Sir Henry after whom the Pentonville area of Finsbury was named. Born in Boulougne, France in 1851, Penton was educated at Harrow School and at Christ Church College Oxford from where he entered the Army, joining the 4th Dragoon Guards in 1873. He saw active service in Egypt, attained the rank of Captain and was decorated prior to his retirement in 1884. For a short period he looked after his property in Pentonville and became not only a Deputy Lieutenant and magistrate for Middlesex but also an Honorary Colonel in the 21st Kings Royal (Finsbury) Rifle Corps. He served as MP for only one Parliament having won in 1886 by only five votes and going down to defeat himself by five votes in 1892 after which he did not resume a political career but was appointed High Sheriff of Buckinghamshire in 1896. He died in 1929.

Dadabhai Naoroji MP
© Palace of Westminster Collection www.parliament.uk/art

Penton's successor was **Dadabhai Naoroji** (Liberal), who was the son of a poor Indian Parsee priest and became the first ever Indian or South Asian Member of the British Parliament at a time when the British Empire was at its zenith. Born in Bombay in 1825, Naoroji was well educated at the Elphinstone Institute in the city and became Head Native teacher at the same college in 1845. Ten years later he was appointed Professor of Mathematics and Natural History at Elphinstone in which capacity he served for 26 years. All other professors at the time were British. In 1855 he sailed for England to join the first Indian business firm of the mercantile Cama family and four years later established his own company. During his time in England, he endeavoured to educate the British people about their responsibilities as rulers of India delivering speeches and publishing articles to support his opposition to what he saw as the unjust and oppressive regime of the British Raj. In 1867 he helped to establish the East India Association of which he became the Honorary Secretary. The purpose of the Association was to keep Britain well informed of India's plight and needs and to secure fair treatment for India's people. He advanced the "Drain Theory", illustrating systematic bleeding of the wealth and resources of India and his ideas were put into a volume called "Poverty and Un-British rule in India". He asked for and secured a Royal Commission to look into the charges, and was one of its members. He also took part in the inauguration of the Indian National Congress that was held in Bombay in 1865, and was three times elected its President. During this period he entered Government service in Bombay, and in 1874 was Prime Minister to the Dewan of Baroda State. Two years later he became a member of the Bombay Corporation, and from 1885 until 1888 sat on the Legislative Council. He served as President of the India National Congress on three separate occasions – in 1886, 1893 and 1906- and returned to England in 1886 with the idea of getting into the British Parliament to enable him to fight from within the system, and further the cause of India. He first entered British politics as the unsuccessful Liberal candidate at Holborn in 1886, but was subsequently elected at Finsbury Central in 1892, serving during 1895 as a member of a Royal Commission established to review Government expenditure in India. He served only one term as an MP and was defeated in 1895, although he sought election at Lambeth North in 1906, this time as an Independent Liberal but was defeated. He died in 1917.

William Frederick Barton Massey-Mainwaring (Conservative) was the somewhat grandly named MP between 1895 and his Party's debacle in 1906. Born plain Massey in 1845, he was in fact the son of the Third Baron Clarina of Ireland and after a scientific education at Trinity College in Dublin he went into the law being called to the Inner Temple bar in 1868 adding his wife's name to his own on getting married. He became the Director of several companies and was also somewhat curiously made a Deputy Lieutenant of Lincolnshire. He first contested a Parliamentary seat in 1880 at Norwich and, after his election at Finsbury Central, was a strong Unionist.

31 The State of Victoria was officially established as separate from New South Wales on 1st July 1851. A Legislative Council and Assembly were established in 1855 based on a very limited land ownership franchise.

32 Duffy was an Irish Nationalist and former MP for New Ross (1852) who emigrated to Australia in 1855 writing in the Irish Nation "there seems to be no more hope for the Irish Cause than for the corpse on the dissecting-table'. He was Prime Minister of Victoria in 1871but returned to Britain in 1880 to agitate for Irish and Australian Government. He died on 9th January 1901, eight days after the creation of the Commonwealth of Australia.

He died in 1907, a year after his defeat by **William Charles Steadman** (Labour) who was one of the first Labour members to be elected and in 1900, though still a Liberal, was chairman of the first meeting of the Labour Representation Committee. Born in Poplar in 1851, Steadman was educated locally at the National School and also at evening classes in Battersea. He became an apprenticed barge builder in 1866, and Secretary to the River Thames Barge Builders Union. He initially entered politics as the Liberal candidate for Mid Kent in 1892 becoming a member of Stepney Borough Council in the same year, remaining so until 1907. He was unsuccessful in the Liberal cause at Hammersmith in 1895 but in 1898 was elected MP for Stepney in a by-election. He was defeated in 1900 and shortly afterwards joined the Labour Party. He was elected Secretary to the Parliamentary Committee of the Trades Union Congress (1905-1910) and became MP for Finsbury Central in 1906 but was defeated in January 1910 and died the following year.

Major Sir Martin Archer-Shee (Conservative and Unionist) took the seat retaining it until 1918 when he was elected for the new Finsbury seat, which he held until 1923. He was born in 1873 and following a school education at the London Oratory, joined the Royal Navy as a midshipman at the age of 15 but left two years later for Sandhurst to train as an Army officer. He joined the 19th Hussars in 1893 and saw active service in South Africa in 1899/1900. He was at the siege of Ladysmith and was awarded DSO before becoming a Major in 1902 though he resigned three years later and joined the Reserves in 1906. He entered politics as MP for Finsbury Central in January 1910 but at the outbreak of War in 1914 he was placed in Command of the Gloucester Regiment becoming a Lieutenant Colonel in 1915. Though a Roman Catholic, he was a strong opponent of Irish Home Rule and withdrew his support from the Lloyd-George Coalition over the issue in 1921. Following his defeat at Finsbury in 1923 he sought a return to the Commons at Peckham in 1924 but was unsuccessful and left active politics. He died in 1935.

Finsbury East

James Bigwood (Conservative) shared a short tenure with Howard Spensley, Central's MP. Elected in 1885 he too was defeated in 1886, though this was unusual for an incumbent Conservative in that particular contest which saw the Tories return to Government. His principal biographical details may be found earlier in this Chapter under Brentford.

He was succeeded in 1886 by **James Rowlands** (Liberal) who held the seat until 1895 as a Lib-Lab member. Born locally in 1851, he was educated at the Great Ormond Street Working Men's College[33] after which he was initially apprenticed as a watch case maker. He pursued a successful career in his chosen trade and became active in the Goldsmith's Company[34] of which he was made a Freeman. He was made a member of the London School Board and became the Honorary Secretary of the Land Reform Association. He first contested Finsbury East unsuccessfully in 1885 but was returned in 1886 serving until 1895 when he was defeated. He returned to Parliament in 1906 as Liberal MP for Dartford (Kent), which he represented until his death in 1920 apart from the short period between the two General Elections of 1910 after he was defeated in the January contest. He died in 1920.

Henry Charles Richards (Conservative) defeated Rowlands in 1895 and held the seat until his death in 1905. Born at Hackney in 1851, Richards was educated at the Proprietary School, Gravesend (Kent) and at the City of London School for Boys. He was called to the bar in 1879 when he was the Bacon Scholar and practised at Grays Inn from 1881 becoming a QC and a bencher there in 1898. He specialised in laws governing public institutions and was for many years the Senior Counsel for the Post Office at the Central Criminal Court. He was also the author of several works covering subjects as diverse as parish councils, railway rates, election law and licensing. He first contested a Parliamentary seat in a 1884 by-election when he was defeated at Northampton, an experience he was to repeat twice - at the 1885 General Election and in 1886 at a second by-election. He regarded himself as a "Social Democrat".

Links with Biography on P101

Evan Cotton MP
© National Portrait Gallery
Bassano Ltd

After his death in 1905 **Joseph Allen Baker** (Liberal) took the seat which he held until 1918. A Canadian, born in 1852 at Trenton Ontario where he was educated at the local High School, he came to Britain, became an engineer and established the firm of J. Baker and Sons of Willesden, manufacturers of bakery equipment[35]. He was an active Quaker and member of the temperance movement. He was a member of the LCC for Finsbury East in 1895, unsuccessfully contesting the Parliamentary constituency in the same year, and remained a councillor until 1907, two years after his election as MP for the area. During this period he was Chairman of the Highways Committee, a Middlesex magistrate and Chairman of the Adult School Union.

33 Founded in 1854 by a Christian Socialist, the Rev.F.D. Maurice (Source – Internet)
34 One of the City of London's twelve companies, set up in 1300 to be responsible for hallmarking.
35 In 1919 the company merged with Perkins Engineers and in 1923 became Baker Perkins

Baker died in 1918 and the by-election was won by **(Harry) Evan (Auguste) Cotton** (Liberal) who held the seat for only a few months until the general election when the seat was abolished and he failed to win the new combined seat of Finsbury at the post war general election. This was one of the shortest 'modern' tenures. Cotton was born in India and became a barrister, Indian historian and writer. He practised at the Calcutta High Court and was a member of the Calcutta Municipal Corporation. He returned to India in the 1920s and was a member of the Bengal Legislative committee between 1922 and 1925.

Taken together Islington's four constituencies were politically finely balanced in the period from 1885 to 1918. Liberals

MPs for Islington

From	at	To	Name	First Names	Constituency	Party
1885	G	1886	Ince	Henry Bret	Islington East	Liberal
1886	G	1892	Lambert	Isaac Cowley		Conservative
1892	G	1906	Cohen	Sir Benjamin Louis		Conservative
1906	G	1917	Radford	Sir George Heynes		Liberal
1917	B	1918	Smallwood	Edward		Liberal
1885	G	1906	Bartley	Sir George	Islington North	Conservative
1906	G	1910 (Dec)	Waterlow	David Sydney		Liberal
1910(Dec)	G	1918	Touche	Sir George Alexander		Conservative
1885	G	1886	Spicer	Henry	Islington South	Liberal
1886	G	1906	Rollit	Sir Albert		Conservative
1906	G	1918	Wiles	Thomas		Liberal
1885	G	1892	Chamberlain	Richard	Islington West	Liberal Unionist
1892	G	1918	Lough	Rt. Hon Thomas		Liberal

NOTE First returned at a B = By-election; G =General Election

won 15 times, the Conservatives 14 and Liberal Unionists (in alliance with the Conservatives) on three occasions, all in Islington West between 1885 and 1892. Had it not been for the Irish question causing a rift in Gladstone's Liberal Party it seems likely that the Party would have won Islington West at every Election because it did so in the five consecutive General Elections between 1895 and December 1910. Islington East and South constituencies returned four MPs of each Party whilst Islington North preferred the Conservatives by six to two.

Islington East

Henry Bret Ince (Liberal) served only briefly as MP. A QC and bencher who had been called to the bar at Lincoln's Inn in 1857, he was born in London in 1830 and graduated from London University. A strong supporter of Gladstone, Ince first entered politics as MP for Hastings at a by-election in 1883 but transferred to Islington in 1885. He was defeated in 1886 and died three years later.

Ince was beaten by **Isaac Cowley Lambert** (Conservative), who was born at Stockwell (Surrey) in 1850 and subsequently educated at Harrow School and Trinity College Cambridge after which, like his predecessor MP, he entered the legal profession. Called to the bar at the Middle Temple in 1874, Lambert, a member of the Royal Geographical Society, had been defeated by Ince in 1885 but served as the MP from 1886 until 1892 when he retired. He died in 1918.

Sir Benjamin Louis Cohen (Conservative) was a prominent Jewish MP who succeeded Lambert and served until 1906 when the Liberals regained the seat. Born in South Street, Finsbury in 1844, he followed his father into the family firm of stockbrokers but also participated in public life as a member of the LCC, a London Deputy Lieutenant and magistrate as well as being a JP in Kent.

He died in 1909, three years after losing his seat to **Sir George Haynes Radford** (Liberal) who remained the MP until his death in 1917 at the age of 66. Born in Plymouth he was educated at Amersham Hall and University College London after which he practised as a solicitor from 1872. He first entered political life as a member for the Islington West ward on the LCC and was for a while Chairman of the National Liberal Club Buildings Committee. Also a Surrey magistrate, Radford's career as an MP was unremarkable.

The by-election following his death was won by **Edward Smallwood** (Liberal). Born in Birchwood, Lancashire in

1861, he was educated at Doncaster Grammar School, moved to London and became a coal merchant. Appointed a London magistrate in 1908, he was a Radical Liberal member of the LCC for East Islington but after his return for the same Parliamentary constituency in 1917 he served for only a relatively short period of time. He was re-elected in 1918 but was defeated four years later when he went in search of another seat. He was unsuccessful at East Ham South in 1922 and 1923 and never resumed a Commons career. He was active in the coal trade being from 1918 until 1921 the first President of the Coal Merchants' Federation fulfilling a similar role in London in 1934. He was President of the London Brotherhood Movement[36] in 1925/6 and National President three years later. He died in 1939.

Islington North

Sir George Bartley (Conservative) was an MP from 1885 until 1906. The son of Robert Bartley of Rectory House in Hackney, where he was born in 1842, George was educated at Clapton and University College Schools in London before becoming a civil servant. He was especially interested in promoting the education and thrift of the working classes and amongst other things founded the National Penny Bank in 1875, five years before he took his first step towards becoming an MP when he was defeated at Hackney in the 1880 General Election. After his tenure at Islington North came to an end he sought an early return to the Commons but was defeated in a by-election at Hull West in 1907 and never resumed his political career. He died in 1910.

He was beaten in 1906 by **David Sydney Waterlow** (Liberal),the son of Sir Sidney who lived at Highgate and after whom Waterlow Park is named. Born there in 1857, David was educated at Northampton and in Switzerland, afterwards going into the family printing business as a Director. He was also a Director and founder of the Improved Industrial Dwellings Company, a Governor of the Great Northern Hospital and Chairman of the Governors of Westminster School. He became a member of the LCC in 1898 but only served as Islington North's MP from 1906 until December 1910 when he was defeated, never to resume a political career. He became Chairman of Waterlow and Sons (Printers)[37] in 1922 but died two years later.

Sir George Alexander Touche (Conservative) was elected in December 1910 and served until 1918. He was born "Touch" in 1861 in Edinburgh, where he was brought up and educated to degree level and qualified as a Chartered Accountant. He added the "e" in 1906 when he tired of the English mispronunciation of his Scottish surname. He had moved to London in 1883 to seek his fortune, formed his own company of GA Touche and Company in 1899, and with his partner Niven, established branches in the USA, Canada and South America. He was also Chairman of the Industrial and General Trust as well as the Trustees Corporation. Active in the City of London, where he was a Lieutenant, he was an Alderman from 1915 and Sheriff in 1915/16. Also a Governor of the Royal Hospital he first contested a Parliamentary election in 1904 when he was defeated in a by-election at North East Lanarkshire, in his native Scotland. He contested Islington North for the first time in January 1910 but was not successful until the December contest of the same year. He retired in 1918 and died in 1935. Deloitte Touche Tohmatsu International is today one of the largest accounting firms in the world.

Sir George Touche MP
Deloitte-Touche

George Touche was a man of uncommon breadth of interests and accomplishments even for a Victorian. He was particularly noted for his skills as a lucid and effective speaker . On one occasion, after he had addressed an open-air political meeting in Hyde Park, one member of the crowd was heard to remark that he "liked the sandy-whiskered old devil the best"!

Islington South

Henry Spicer (Liberal) was only an MP briefly. Elected in 1885, he was born at Barnsbury 48 years earlier, son of the founder of a firm of Stationers. Educated at Mill Hill and St Johns Wood Schools, Henry attended London University and entered the family business. A strong supporter of Gladstone, he pursued a career of public service and amongst other roles was a member of the School Board (from 1879), a Middlesex JP, a member of the Fishmongers' Company[38],

36 The Brotherhood Movement was an organization in the Socialist tradition of the Free Churches, aimed at the reform of society on Christian lines. The basic premise of the Brotherhood was that "... *Christianity is chiefly concerned with man's brotherly relation to man, and with the redemption through human effort of every sphere of man's activity on Earth*"

37 The firm was established in 1810 and became one of the first to print stamps. It was acquired by De La Rue in 1960.

38 The Fishmongers' Company, established in 1272, is one of the oldest City livery companies. In 1381, Lord Mayor William Walworth, a member of the Fishmongers' Company, stabbed Wat Tyler, leader of the Peasants' Revolt, in the back. Although Tyler was taken to St Bartholomew's Hospital, he was dragged out and beheaded by the King's men.

and a Fellow of both the Geographical and the Zoological Societies. Defeated in 1886, he never resumed politics and died in 1915.

Sir Albert Rollitt (Conservative) took the seat in 1886 and held it for 20 years. A Yorkshireman born in Hull in 1842, Rollitt came to the capital and was educated at Kings College and London University where he gained several First Class degrees. He practised as a solicitor in London and Hull but became a ship owner in both cities and in Newcastle. He was Vice President of the Law Society for a time, President of the Association of Chambers of Commerce and of the Mutual Corporations Association and served as Sheriff of Hull in 1875/6 before being elected Lord Mayor for the period 1883/5. He was also active in civic life in London where he was a magistrate and Deputy Lieutenant though his activities were schizophrenically divided between the capital and Yorkshire where he was also Deputy Lieutenant of the West Riding. He was made a freeman of both Huddersfield, his father's home town, and of the City of Hull where he was chairman of the Botanical Garden. Rollitt initially entered politics as the unsuccessful Tory candidate for Hull West at the 1885 General Election before he secured Islington South in 1886. He was committed to women,' suffrage and Free Trade and gradually drifted away from his Party eventually resigning the Whip. He fought Islington South in 1906 as a Free Trader and subsequently joined the Liberal Party in whose colours he unsuccessfully contested Epsom (Surrey) in January 1910. He died in 1922.

Thomas Wiles (Liberal) sat from 1906 until 1918. Born at St Albans in 1861, Wiles died 90 years later. He was educated at Amersham Hall School and entered his father's mercantile firm of Joseph Wiles and Son in Mark Lane becoming a member of both the Baltic and Corn Exchanges. He was active in the London Liberal Federation and a member of the LCC for Bethnal Green southwest from 1900 to 1907. Elected to the House in 1906 he became Parliamentary Private Secretary to Mr. McKinnon Wood (Financial Secretary to the Treasury) but was generally much more successful in business. He became Chairman of the Anglo-Portuguese Colonial Bank and, after leaving politics, a member of the Port of London Authority[39] of which he was Chairman between 1941 and 1946. He failed to gain re-election at Islington in 1918 and was subsequently also unsuccessful at Eastbourne in 1922.

Islington West

Richard Chamberlain (Liberal and later Liberal Unionist) was MP for Islington West from 1885 to 1892 and with his older brother Joseph left the Liberals to establish the new Party. He was born in 1840 in London and educated at University College School. He went into the family businesses as a brass founder in Birmingham and was subsequently on the Board of several Companies including Chairman of the Hamstead Colliery (Staffordshire), Director of the Ebbw Vale Steel and Iron Company, and of the Union Rolling Stock Company. Twice mayor of Birmingham (1880/1) and a City Alderman he was a magistrate there and also in Warwickshire. He was Chairman of the Liberal Unionists for a period of time. He died in 1899.

In 1892 he was succeeded by **Thomas Lough** (Liberal) who was born in 1850 at Cavan (Ireland), where he was educated at the Royal School before attending Wesley College Dublin. He took a considerable interest in Irish affairs and once wrote a book entitled "England's Wealth, Ireland's Poverty". A tea wholesaler, he was also a member of the Statistical Society and of the Archaeological Society of Ireland. He entered politics initially unsuccessfully as the candidate for Truro (Cornwall) in 1886 but served for 26 years as MP for Islington West until 1918. During that period he was Parliamentary Secretary to the Board of Education (1905 to 1908) and after 1907 was His Majesty's Lord Lieutenant for County Cavan. He died in 1922.

MPs for Hampstead

Sir Henry Thurston Holland MP

Sir Henry Thurston Holland (Conservative) was elected in 1885 and served until 1888 when he succeeded as Baron Knutsford. He served as Secretary of State for the Colonies from 1887 until 1892 in the second government of Lord Salisbury. However, he was first elected to the Commons representing the Sussex borough of Midhurst in September 1874 and in Salisbury's first administration had been Chief Secretary to the Treasury and then Vice President of the Committee of Council on Education. Midhurst was abolished in 1885 when he transferred to the newly created Hampstead constituency. In 1895 he was elevated to become Viscount Sir Henry Thurston Holland MP (Hampstead) 1885-1888

He was succeeded by **Edward Brodie-Hoare** (Conservative), a banker, who served only until

39 The Port of London Authority is a public trust established by Act of Parliament in 1908 to 'administer, preserve and improve the Port of London'.

MPs for Hampstead

From	at	To	Surname	First Names	Party
1885	G	1888	Holland	Henry Thurston	Conservative
1888	B	1901	Brodie-Hoare	Edward	Conservative
1901	B	1905	Milvain	Thomas	Conservative
1905	B	1918	Fletcher	John Samuel	Conservative

NOTE First returned at a B = By-election; G = General Election

1901. He was born in 1842 and died in 1911.

Hoare was succeeded by **Thomas Milvain** (Conservative) , born in 1844 who was a Durham Grammar School and Trinity College Cambridge educated lawyer. He became a Middle Temple Barrister in 1869, was first elected as MP for Durham in 1885 but lost his seat in 1892 at which point he sought a return to the Commons, initially unsuccessfully at Maidstone in 1901 but subsequently successfully at Hampstead in 1902. He resigned his seat on being appointed Judge Advocate General in 1905, a post he occupied until 1915. He died the following year and was succeeded as Judge Advocate General by Sir Felix Cassel, MP for nearby St Pancras South (see above).

Sir John Fletcher (Conservative) succeeded Milvain at the 1905 by-election necessitated by the latter's appointment as a Judge. Also a barrister, he was the son of a Manchester merchant who was educated at Harrow School and Christ Church College Oxford where he graduated BA in 1864 and MA five years later. He was called to the Bar at Lincoln's Inn in 1868. He retired from Parliament in 1918 and was created a Baronet in Herefordshire. Born in 1841 he died in 1924.
The former Hackney and Tower Hamlets constituencies which represented the East End were substantially amended

The East End

in 1885 generating 10 additional seats in four new Parliamentary boroughs, namely Bethnal Green, Hackney (which included Stoke Newington transferred from Finsbury), Shoreditch and Tower Hamlets. Thus in total 14 single member constituencies replaced two two-member seats. (See map opposite)

Bethnal Green (2 seats)

Closest to Hackney and flanked by the Central constituency of that borough to the north and by Shoreditch (Haggerston) to the west, was the new Borough of Bethnal Green, based on the parish of St Matthew, created in 1743. Then it had a population of only about 15,000, mainly packed into the western end beyond Spitalfields but, like adjacent Stepney, developed rapidly after the Napoleonic Wars as a place dominated by small weavers' houses with attic workrooms. By 1851 Bethnal Green was a burgeoning slum area with a population of 85,000. It remained unremittingly poor despite re-housing efforts made by commercial philanthropists like Angela Burdett-Coutts, the millionairess granddaughter of the founder of the famous Bank who, in the early 1860s, built four Gothic blocks at Bethnal Green with a resident superintendent policing a community of 600 people. A contemporary description of late Victorian Bethnal Green was provided by the banker and philanthropist William Cotton who wrote: "Its courts and alleys are almost countless, and overwhelming with men, women, boys, dogs, cats, pigeons and birds. Its children are ragged, brought up to hard living. Its men are mainly poor dock labourers, poor costermongers, poor silk weavers, clinging hopelessly to a withering craft; the lowest kind of thieves, with a sprinkling of toy makers, shoe makers and cheap cabinet makers. Its women are mainly hawkers, seamstresses, the coarsest order of prostitutes, and aged stall keepers."

The new Parliamentary borough was divided into two parts. **Bethnal Green South West** covered the cramped tenements north of Liverpool Street station and Spitalfields. Sandwiched between Shoreditch and Cambridge Heath Road it extended towards the Hackney Road on the west side covering the so-called "Weavers" district with its northeast corner being in the vicinity of today's York Hall. Today's Tower Hamlets Borough retains a Weavers ward for council elections. **Bethnal Green North East** circled the northern part of the South West constituency west of Cambridge Heath Road and south of Hackney Road, which formed the boundary with Hackney Central but also extended east of Cambridge Heath Road as far as Victoria Park (most of which was in Hackney South), either side of the Bethnal Green and Roman Roads. Its eastern boundary was on a north/south alignment through Victoria Park in the vicinity of the Lido whilst the Great Eastern Railway broadly delineated its southern boundary. Its principal electorates lived in Cambridge Heath and Bethnal Green.

The East End: Between 1885 and 1918 there were major changes taking place here, as once the railways came, the dock activity leapt ahead. Great manufactories expanded, as did the population. The change didn't stop, and it continues today. Few if any thought then that containerisation would sweep away the ships, and the once humming dock area would be reborn as a world finance centre.

Top Left: *The Town Hall at Bethnal Green was opened in 1910 and was designed by Percy Robinson and William Alban Jones. Cambridge Heath Road, in front of the building was the boundary between the Borough's Southwest and Northeast Constituencies.*

Top Right: *The Old Hackney Town Hall was built in 1802, and stands in front of the 13th century St Augustine's Church Tower. Elections would have been declared here for Hackney's constituencies until replaced by the new Hackney Town Hall, completed in 1937.*

Centre Right: *Typical middle-class Hackney villas in Dalston Lane, Hackney Central Constituency. They were built close to Hackney Central and Downs stations, and were convenient for Mare St shops.*

Photos by: Gordon Rushton, except as otherwise shown

Above: *Haggerston Station in 1886, serving Broad Street on the North London Railway, in the Shoreditch, Haggerston Constituency created a year earlier.* **© Closed Stations**

Left: *Owned by the Quakers since 1893, Hoxton Hall first opened as a Music Hall in 1863 and has been at the centre of community activity ever since.* **John Nelson**

Hackney (3 seats)

Shorn of Bethnal Green, the now smaller Hackney Parliamentary Borough included Stoke Newington transferred from Finsbury. Development in the area was heavily influenced by the growth of the City of London whose richer businessmen had big houses in both parishes until the middle of the 19th century. They eventually moved away to more fashionable and less populated areas, especially after the railway came to Hackney in 1850 when it became possible for less affluent City workers to commute daily. Victorian villas and terraces were built which remain features of Hackney today. Industry also arrived in Victorian times. The Lewis Berger paint factory opened in Homerton and chemical plants owned by Carless Capel & Leonard opened at Hackney Wick. 'Petrol' was a brand name they created in Hackney. By the late 19th century much of the housing of industrial workers was recognised as unsatisfactory. Programmes of slum clearance were implemented and the local authorities of the day undertook a number of projects to re-house people in better conditions. These included the Bannister House estate in Homerton and Lordship South in Stoke Newington. Even then Hackney was a community of diverse ethnicity with different political and religious beliefs. In the 17th and 18th centuries, Stoke Newington and Hackney had been centres of nonconformist worship and radical politics and European migrants came to work in the furniture industry in the 19th century. Jewish people had lived in Hackney since 1684 and there has been a Black presence since at least 1630. Asian nurses of British children, visiting Britain with their employers, stayed in Hackney from 1900.

Although by 1885 Hackney with Stoke Newington were together large enough to justify the provision of three Parliamentary constituencies, there were still substantial areas that remained undeveloped, notably north of Stoke Newington church including Clissold Park and around the water reservoirs between Lordship Park Manor and Seven Sisters Road. Upper Clapton was still a village and Stamford Hill had not yet been much built upon although the two main roads from each of them heading towards Tottenham were both attracting housing development by the late 1880s. On the eastern side of the borough most of Lea Bridge and Clapton Park had been built up but there was still room for the further infill development that was to take place over the next decade or so.

Hackney Central was the smallest constituency geographically but the most densely populated. The principal districts within the constituency were officially De Beavoir Town , Kingsland, Dalston , London Fields, Hackney Downs and Lower Clapton. It formed the shape of a left facing boot extending east from Southgate Road (the boundary with Islington East), south of the Balls Pond Road and Dalston Lane, with Shoreditch (Haggerston) on its southern flank. It extended as far as Clapton Park Road and south to north from London Fields to Everingham Road, which connects Clapton and Rectory Road Stations, neither of which was in the constituency. Its western boundary with Hackney North was the railway line that runs south from Rectory Road to Hackney Downs. **Hackney South** was bounded on the east by the Lea and extended south from the river bridge to the border with Bethnal Green and Bow. The principal districts officially within the constituency were South Hackney, Victoria Park, Homerton, Hackney Wick, Clapton Park and Lea Bridge, although around half the area actually comprised the Hackney Marshes and Mill Fields south of Lea Bridge. Its western side was demarcated by the Lower Clapton Road as far as Homerton High Street where the boundary became less distinct, swinging south and west through South Hackney itself on the Bethnal Green side of London Fields. Occupying the remainder of the Parliamentary borough was **Hackney North**, then very much an outer suburban community on the fringes of open countryside. Its main centre of population was Stoke Newington parish which, together with Shacklewell (west ward), formed a relatively dense residential area in the south of the constituency. Rectory Road, Clissold Park and Lordship Park Manor were included as were the East and West Reservoirs, separated by Lordship Road. Other electorates in Stamford Hill and Upper Clapton were more scattered. Another populous district lying between Albion Road and Stoke Newington Road in Shacklewell was a detached part of Hornsey parish and in 1885 was included in Hornsey constituency rather than Hackney.

Shoreditch (2 seats)

Shoreditch was first recorded in 1148 and for 400 years was a farming community. Centred on its parish church of St Leonard's (rebuilt in 1740), Shoreditch became a popular residential area for aristocrats and government officials who wanted to be close to the City and Westminster. Many built country houses between Hoxton and Homerton but as south Shoreditch became increasingly built up after about 1660, the aristocrats moved away. In the 18th century the area became heavily urbanised when the development of the timber and furniture industry south of the Regents Canal provoked the emigration of the middle classes to Hackney and Islington. The Victorian period saw the development of industry in Shoreditch, particularly around Curtain Road, which became the centre of London's furniture manufacturing. The population grew faster than any other London parish in the first half of the 19th century and reached nearly 130,000 inhabitants in 1851. However, after that some of its largely working class inhabitants were in their turn levered out, firstly by the construction of the railway between Dalston and Broad Street in the 1860s and then by overspill offices from the

*1. **Top Left:** Whitechapel Rd homes of more affluent electors, of the Mile End Constituency next to the Anchor Brewery. The first MP was brewer Spencer Charrington.*

*2. **Top Right:** Artillery Passage was typical of the densely packed alleyways in the Spitalfields district of the Whitechapel constituency.*

*3. **Left:** Limehouse Town Hall on Commercial Road, once the civic centre of a vibrant docklands community all around it. Limehouse Constituency 1885.*

*4. **Above:** This Georgian terrace still looks well cared for in this contemporary view of housing in Stepney Green (1885 Stepney Constituency). The property was well placed, as there is a station within 150 yards. The area built up rapidly in the 1880s, leading to the establishment of the new constituency. It was subsequently badly bombed in the WW2, but has revived in the 21st century.*

*5. **Left:** The New Globe public house dating from the 1820s once served the busy trade from the Regents Canal behind it, and stood right on the boundary between the Stepney and Mile End Constituencies. It has survived through the WW2 bombing as a busy establishment in a prime location, and it is still next to a constituency boundary. Globe Town was in the Mile End Constituency in 1885.*

1 & 4 John Nelson; 2,3 & 5 Gordon Rushton

City of London. Even so in the 1891 census following the creation of the two seats the population of Haggerston was over 67,000 whilst Hoxton's was only about 10,000 fewer. The overwhelming aspect of the area was its deprivation. In 1865 170 people died in London's last cholera outbreak and a journalist writing in the 1870s described Hoxton Street's market as "motley, struggling and poverty-stricken". Many inhabitants were living in impossibly overcrowded and airless conditions, but the authorities could do little about it because initially they had nowhere to go.

The parish that formed the new Borough was divided into two constituencies, each comprising four wards. Somewhat confusingly **Shoreditch, Haggerston** covered the Whitmore and Kingsland wards of Hoxton south of the Regents Canal which separated it from Hackney (Central) on the west side of the Kingsland Road and the whole of the area east and south of it as far as the junction with the Hackney Road (the Acton and Haggerston wards), which, as it extended eastwards, formed another boundary with neighbouring Bethnal Green (South West), and Hackney (Central and South). **Shoreditch, Hoxton** abutted the City of London just north of Finsbury Circus (Moorfields ward) forming a wedge shape northwards between Finsbury East and the west side of Liverpool Street station at which point it broadened to take in the length of Great Eastern Street from its junction with Commercial Street (Church ward) and north up Shoreditch High Street and the west side of Kingsland Road (Hoxton ward), thence west and northwest to the boundary with Islington (Wenlock ward).

Tower Hamlets (7 seats)

The new Tower Hamlets Parliamentary Borough incorporated Bow, Bromley, Poplar, the Isle of Dogs, Stepney, Limehouse, Mile End, Wapping, Shadwell and Whitechapel. In 1885 these were growing residential and industrial areas, the latter being home to the East and West India Docks, which were then still expanding their trade.

Bow & Bromley comprised the entire parish of St Mary, Stratford-le-Bow and the northern and central parts of Bromley St Leonard. This was then an expanding suburban area separated from Essex by the River Lea and on the western side by a border that ran in a more or less parallel direction northwest to southeast on the Lea side of Burdett Road through Tower Hamlets Cemetery, down Bow Common Road, across Limehouse Cut to a point on the Poplar Dock railway north of East India Dock Road, thence back to meet the River Lea where it starts to form Bow Creek. Its main electorates were to be found between Victoria Park and the river Lea opposite Temple Mills and the new railway lands at Stratford; in Old Ford, Bow, Bromley-By-Bow, Bow Common and the streets around the small Langdon Park. **Poplar** comprised the parish of All Saints and the southeast segment of Bromley St Leonard which covered the area between East India Dock and Bow Creek (the south ward). It was bounded by Bow to the north, the rivers Lea and Thames on its east, south and west sides together with a short boundary with Limehouse on the east side of the Cut between Bow Common Road and Limehouse Hole Stairs on the Thames. Its main electorates lived in South Bromley, All Saints, Poplar, Westferry, the Isle of Dogs, Millwall, Blackwall and Cubitt Town, then all thriving on the developing Royal Docks. **Limehouse** embraced a small, compact docklands area between Wapping and the West India Dock at Poplar (both exclusive) and reached its peak population at about the time of its creation. The constituency incorporated the Thames-side parish of Shadwell and the so-called hamlet of Ratcliffe as well as Limehouse Basin including Stepney East and the area north of Commercial Road between Stepney Green and Bow Common that fell within Limehouse parish.

Mile End and Stepney were allocated four wards each of what was then described as the Hamlet of Mile End Old Town to generate two constituencies. Stepney had the west and central wards whilst Mile End held the north and east. **Stepney** was a wedge shaped division lying broadly north of the Commercial Road, west of Limehouse and extending to the Mile End Road in the vicinity of the junction with Burdett Road in the east and to the junction with Whitechapel Road opposite what is today the Aldgate East Underground Station. Stepney was itself enveloped to the north by **Mile End** constituency, which included Globe Town between Bethnal Green and the Mile End Road at its junction with Cambridge Heath Road, but also extended southwards to the east of Stepney down Burdett Road to the boundaries with Limehouse and Poplar.

St George lay west of the Limehouse constituency at Shadwell Basin but east of St Katherine Docks between the north side of Commercial Road and the Thames. It comprised the parishes of St George-in-the-East and Wapping, which was its main residential area. This incorporated the northern part of Shadwell in the vicinity of Watney Market, which lies between the London to Tilbury and Southend railway line and the Commercial Road. The constituency was dominated by the London and Eastern Docks including several Wharves along the Thames and the Tobacco Dock off Wapping Lane, which was connected to the river by canal. The area between Commercial Road and The Highway was a densely packed residential area bisected on an east west axis by Cable Street which several decades later in the 1930s was the scene of rioting when the Fascist Movement tried to organise demonstrations against the Jewish people, many of who lived in the area in question. **Whitechapel** was closest to the City of London and lay between there and St George's (on its southeastern flank) and Stepney (on its north eastern side). Bounded to the north by Bethnal Green Southwest, it ran south from Spitalfields to the Thames at St Katherine Docks and the Tower of London, all of which were in a constituency that also included Aldgate and the Whitechapel Road area around The Royal London Hospital and as far east as the junction with Cambridge Heath Road where the Mile End Road takes over.

Constituency Populations and Electorates

Constituency	1891 pop	1901 pop	1911 pop	1910 electorate	1910 electorate as % of 1911 population*	% Population change 1891 to 1911*
Shoreditch, Haggerston	67,651	62,429	53,865	8,530	15.8	-20
Shoreditch, Hoxton	56,358	55,277	56,999	7,936	13.9	+1
Hackney Central	64,760	67,726	67,594	9,343	13.8	+4
Hackney North	77,181	84,221	84,683	11,789	13.9	+10
Hackney South	87,601	101,344	102,655	14,128	13.8	+17
Bethnal Green North East	62,397	64,873	62,764	7,554	12.0	+1
Bethnal Green South West	66,735	64,854	65,518	7,103	10.8	-2
Bow & Bromley	88,418	90,554	86,930	10,330	11.9	-2
Poplar	73,330	78,332	75,677	8,857	11.7	+3
Limehouse	55,253	55,987	52,329	6,405	12.2	-5
Mile End	48.846	48,867	47,880	5,464	11.4	-2
St. George's	47,918	51,103	48,666	3,133	6.4	+2
Stepney	58,746	63,698	63,194	4,653	7.4	+8
Whitechapel	74,420	78,634	67,526	3,986	5.9	+9

Note: population per MP, as a ratio of the average for the whole area.

The population size of the East End in 1885 was enormous but by the turn of the century there were already signs that it had peaked as suburban development gathered pace. Significantly, electorates were also beginning to fall in some constituencies, though this may have been only in part a reflection of falling populations. It is probable that in some docklands constituencies another reason was the demographic characteristics of the resident population in relation to the franchise qualifications. Generally electorates in East End constituencies represented a lower proportion of the population than elsewhere in Middlesex, indicative of the restrictions on voter franchise in working class areas. In Bethnal Green, for example, it was estimated[40] that voter exclusions of one sort or another meant that in 1900 only 40% of males had the vote as compared with, say Oxford, where the proportion was three quarters.

The table illustrates the different characteristics of the East London constituencies from 1885 to 1910. Some of the statistical trends were significant in electoral terms. The total population in the East End was relatively stable, rising by only about 1% to around 940,000 between 1891 and 1911. Within the working class docklands constituencies there was a very slight decline of 3,000 to 443,000 during this period reflecting both a relatively stable local economy and the lack of opportunity for poor families to move to other areas unless compelled to do so. The areas furthest from the City on the other hand grew in population, especially in Hackney although there was a major reduction in Haggerston's population reflecting both slum clearance and the movement of some families to less crowded suburbs. The class base of each of the constituencies was also reflected in the size of electorate. The poorest riverside dock communities had small electorates with Whitechapel recording the lowest at less than 6% of the population. Hackney was more than double this figure and even Bethnal Green, Limehouse and Hoxton recorded bigger totals. The biggest was Haggerston, which appears to have been in the throes of a major transition in its social composition during the period. In fact by comparison with the East End seats they were substantially under strength even at the time they were established. On a straight population comparison with Tower Hamlets average electorate, East Middlesex would have had one additional seat in 1891 and by 1911 would have had five more.

40 "Parliamentary Reform 1790-1918" by Eric Evans

General Election Results 1885-1910 - by % majority

Constituency	1885	1886	1892	1895	1900	1906	1910 Jan	1910 Dec
Bethnal Green North East	Llab25	Llab9	Llab11	C3	C7	L32	L22	L22
Bethnal Green South West	L17	L12	L19	L6	C6	L26	L17	L14-
Bow & Bromley	L11	C11	L5	C15+	L27	L7	C8	Lab11-
Hackney Central	C3	C22	C4	C5	C25	L8	L7	L7
Hackney North	C7	C29+	C19	C32	C35	L2	C8	C12
Hackney South	L15	L2	L15+	C4	C4	L30	L26	IndL18
Haggerston	Llab37	Llab10	Llab22	C0.8	Llab0.6	Llab8-	L7	L7
Hoxton	L20	L6	L24	L2	C5	C12	L5	L11
Limehouse	C21	C22	L4	C12	C12	L20	L8	L9
Mile End	C16	C24	C7	C22	C31+ (LU)	L3	LU1	LU0.2
Poplar	L32	L1	L25	L12	L17	L34	L14	L30
St.George's	C19	C18	L14	C0.4	C11	L23	L16	L16
Stepney	L2	C13	C2	C11-	C24	C15	C6	L3
Whitechapel	L19	L16	L13	L0.8	L2	L10	L17	L18
C/LU	5	7+	4	10	10+	2	4	2
L/Llab/IndL	9	7	10+	4	4	12	10	11-
Lab	0	0	0	0	0	0	0	1-

Key: Numbers indicate percentage majority of the votes cast in the election. 100 = unopposed; C = Conservative; IndL = Independent Liberal; L = Liberal; Llab = Liberal with Labour support; Lab = Labour; LU = Liberal Unionist (in alliance with the Conservatives) + = Seats retained at By-elections; -- = Party that won seat at General Election lost by-election to main opposition Party in same Parliament.

As the table above shows from the General Election results, the East End played a significant part in returning Governments of both colours during the period, the victorious Party gaining a majority of the seats in this part of London at each Election. The same was true for North East Middlesex, as noted later.

MPs for Bethnal Green

From	at	To	Surname	First Names	Constituency	Party
1885	G	1895	Howell	George	Bethnal Green North East	Liberal
1895	G	1906	Bhownaggree	Sir Mancherjee Merwanjee		Conservative
1906	G	1918	Cornwall	Sir Edwin Andrew		Liberal
1885	G	1900	Pickersgill	Edward Hare	Bethnal Green South West	Liberal
1900	G	1906	Ridley	Samuel Forde		Conservative
1906	G	1911	Pickersgill	Edward Hare		Liberal
1911	B	1914	Masterman	Charles Frederick Gurney		Liberal
1914	B	1918	Wilson	Sir Matthew Richard		Conservative

NOTE First returned at a B = By-election; G =General Election, (1) = General Election January 1910; (2) = General Election December 1910

Bethnal Green North East

This was generally a Liberal seat in this period although a Conservative held sway between 1895 and 1906. The first MP, **George Howell** (Liberal), was born in 1833 in humble circumstances in Somerset and became a bricklayer. He moved to London at the age of 21 and, after becoming a member of the Bricklayers' Society, rose to prominence as Secretary to the London Trades Council. He served as Parliamentary Secretary to the Trade Union Congress between 1871 and 1874 and was the author of several radical political works. He contested Aylesbury unsuccessfully in both 1868 and 1874 and failed to win a by-election at Stafford in 1881. Eventually returned for Bethnal Green in 1885 he held the seat for 10 years as a Liberal with Labour support. He died in 1910.

Sir Mancherjee Bhownaggree MP
© National Portrait Gallery
Walter Stoneman 1931

He was succeeded in 1895 by **Sir Mancherjee Merwanjee Bhownaggree** (Conservative & Unionist), an Indian born lawyer and journalist, the son of a Bombay Parsee who was Head of the State Agency for Bhavnagar where he too became a

Judicial Councillor before emigrating to Britain. Educated at the Elphinstone Institute in Bombay he came to England at the age of thirty-one in 1882 and took up law being called to the bar at Lincoln's Inn in 1885. Unlike Naoroji, the first ethnic Indian to be a British MP and who had represented Finsbury Central as a Liberal between 1892 and 95, Bhownaggree was a strong supporter of British rule in India, though he was Secretary of the Rukhmibai Committee that upheld the rights of Indian women. He became a distinguished figure in London society and was both a member of the Council of the Society of Arts and a Life Fellow of the Imperial Institute. He held his seat until 1906 and died in 1933.

Sir Edwin Andrew Cornwall (Liberal), a local Bethnal Green councillor for the LCC since 1892, won the 1906 Election and retained the seat until 1922. Prior to his return as MP he had served in local Government as Mayor of Fulham (1900) and Chairman (1905-6) and Vice Chairman (from 1903) of the LCC. He remained a member of the Thames Conservancy Board until 1909 shortly after he had also become a member of the Port of London Authority on which he served until 1919. In 1916 he was made Insurance Minister and from 1919-22 served as Deputy Chairman of Ways and Means[41].

Bethnal Green South West

This was a predominantly Liberal seat although the Tories won it on two occasions. **Edward Hare Pickersgill** (Liberal) was MP twice, between 1885 and 1900 and from 1906 until resigning to become a Metropolitan Police Magistrate in 1911, the year he died at the age of 61. A York born lawyer, Pickersgill was educated at St Peter's School in his home city and attended University College London.

He was defeated in 1900 by **Samuel Forde Ridley** (Conservative), an officer in the Third Middlesex Artillery Volunteers, who was born in London in 1864 and educated at Clifton College and Trinity Cambridge. When Pickersgill defeated him in 1906 he went in search of another seat and was adopted at Rochester, which he won in January 1910. Unfortunately for him this was one of the seats that swung back to the Liberals at the December election so he only remained its MP for a matter of months. He retired from politics but lived a long life into his 80s.

Charles Gurney Masterman (Liberal) won the 1911 by-election that followed Pickersgill's death. At a subsequent by-election held in 1914 to confirm his position as Chancellor of the Duchy of Lancaster in Asquith's cabinet, he was defeated. His biography can be found in Chapter 4 (West Ham South, where he was formerly the MP).

Sir Mathew Richard Wilson (Conservative) served as MP from 1914 to 1922. Grandson of the fourth Baron Ribblesdale, he was born in 1875 and went to Harrow School. From there he went to Sandhurst and pursued an Army career in the 10th Hussars in South Africa from 1899 until 1902 when he was made a Captain. He served as an instructor at Sandhurst from 1907 to 1909 and was meanwhile promoted to the rank of Major going to India as Military Secretary to the Commander-in-Chief of the Imperial forces. He retired from politics in 1918 but died forty years later.

The middle class affluence of the borough at that time was reflected in its political complexion. With the exception of the South constituency, Hackney was predominantly Conservative voting during the period. The Central and North constituencies were strongly Conservative whilst even Hackney South elected a Tory in 1895 and 1900. Liberals took the seat 9 times (including a by-election on 7th May 1894) but only won in Hackney North once, in 1906. Otherwise this was a strong Tory seat that the Party won at 7 General Elections and at a by-election on 11th May 1892. However, Hackney Central moved in a Liberal direction in 1906 and remained faithful in the two 1910 Elections as well.

MPs for Hackney

Hackney Central

Though some were men of distinction not one of Hackney Central's MPs served as a minister in any capacity or enjoyed a notable Parliamentary career. **Sir William Guyer Hunter** (Conservative) was appointed Bombay's Surgeon General in 1877 and Vice Chancellor of its University two years later. He qualified following a medical education at Charing Cross Hospital and the Universities of Aberdeen, Edinburgh and London, and started his Indian career in 1854. He returned to London in 1880 to take up the post of Surgeon to Queen Victoria but retired from medicine in 1885 when he was elected, serving until his retirement in 1892. He died in 1902.

He was succeeded by **Sir Andrew Scoble** (Conservative) who was also prominent in India having served as

41 There are two Deputy Chairmen of Ways and Means who take turns in presiding over the business of the House of Commons when both the Speaker and the Chairman of Ways and Means (Deputy Speaker) are absent.

MPs for Hackney						
From	*at*	*To*	*Surname*	*First Names*	*Constituency*	*Party*
1885	*G*	*1892*	*Hunter*	*Sir William*	*Hackney Central*	*Conservative*
1892	*G*	*1900*	*Scoble*	*Sir Andrew*		*Conservative*
1900	*G*	*1906*	*Alhusen*	*Augustus Henry Eden.*		*Conservative*
1906	*G*	*1918*	*Spicer*	*Sir Albert*		*Liberal*
1885	*G*	*1892*	*Pelly*	*Sir Lewis*	*Hackney North*	*Conservative*
1892	*B*	*1906*	*Bousfield*	*William R.*		*Conservative*
1906	*G*	*1910(Jan)*	*Hart-Davies*	*Thomas*		*Liberal*
1910(Jan)	*G*	*1918*	*Greene*	*Sir Walter Raymond*		*Conservative*
1885	*G*	*1894*	*Russell*	*Sir Charles*	*Hackney South*	*Liberal*
1894	*B*	*1895*	*Moulton*	*Sir John Fletcher*		*Liberal*
1895	*G*	*1906*	*Robertson*	*Thomas Herbert*		*Conservative*
1906	*G*	*1912*	*Bottomley*	*Horatio*		*Liberal*
1912	*B*	*1918*	*Morison*	*Hector*		*Liberal*

NOTE First returned at a B = By-election; G = General Election

Advocate-General of Bombay[42] between 1872 and 1877. He was a member of the Advisory Council to the Governor-General of India between 1886 and 1891 when he returned to England a year before his election. His experience qualified him to sit as a member of the Judicial Committee of the Privy Council in 1901 shortly after he retired.

Augustus Henry Eden Alhusen (Conservative) took the seat in 1900. Though Gateshead born in 1864, he was the son of a wealthy man who owned Stoke Court near Slough. Educated at Cheltenham College and Trinity Cambridge, he was a career politician whose base was Buckinghamshire where he was a magistrate, a Deputy Lieutenant and also a Lieutenant in the Hussars. From 1897 to 1900 he was MP for Salisbury but transferred to Hackney in 1900, losing the seat in 1906. Seven years after his defeat he was made High Sheriff of Buckinghamshire. He died in 1925.

The seat was taken in 1906 by **Sir Albert Spicer** (Liberal) who sat until 1918. The son of a Woodford JP and Deputy Lieutenant of Essex, Spicer was born in Brixton in 1847 and educated at Mill Hill School, then in Germany after which he entered his father's paper business of which he would eventually become Chairman, serving 60 years on the Board. A prominent City businessman, he was Chairman of the London Chamber of Commerce[43] from 1907 to 1910 whilst serving as an MP and Chairman both of the London Missionary Society[44] and of the Congregational Union[45]. In fact he was the first lay Chairman of the latter and, despite his many involvements, also managed to fulfil the duties of an Essex magistrate. Indeed it was there that he first entered politics, unsuccessfully contesting Walthamstow in 1886. Thereafter he looked further afield and was adopted to fight the seat of Monmouth Boroughs in 1892, holding the seat until 1900 when he was defeated. A by-election arose in the same seat the following year but his attempt to make a quick return to the House failed and it was not until 1906 at Hackney Central that he succeeded. He died in 1934.

Hackney North

Sir Lewis Pelly (Conservative) served from 1885 until 1892 when he died. Born in 1825 at Hyde House, Minchinhampton, Gloucestershire, Pelly was the Rugby educated son of a Civil Servant in India who entered the diplomatic corps and rose to the rank of Lieutenant Colonel in the Indian Political Service. The author of many works, including several about India, he was ironically appointed a General on the day he died.

His successor was **William Bousfield** (Conservative), born in Bedford in 1854 and educated at the town's modern school before going to Caius College, Cambridge. He started his working life as an Engineer at the Sir Joseph Whitworth[46] Works in Openshawe, Manchester before moving to Bristol University as a Lecturer in Engineering and Mathematics. He got involved in politics and contested Mid Lanark in Scotland in 1885 and again at a by-election in 1888. He was unsuccessful at that stage and decided to change the direction of his career moving into the law to become a QC at the

42 In the Governments of India, Madras and Bombay the principal law officers were the Advocate General, the Government Solicitor and the Administrator General. The Advocate General was a barrister and led Government prosecutions.
43 The London Chamber of Commerce was established at Mansion House with 130 members on 25 July 1881.
44 Established in 1795.
45 Established in England and Wales in 1831 by a gathering of representatives of Independent churches.
46 Born in 1803, Whitworth made his reputation in developing finely tuned measurement systems for application in the textile trade and the manufacture of rifles.

Inner Temple in 1891 and a bencher six years later. Returned as MP for Hackney North in the 1892 by-election Bousfield retained the seat until his defeat in 1906. However, he never gained political office of any kind, and did not resume his career. He died in 1943.

Thomas Hart-Davies (Liberal) was an advocate of female suffrage and held the seat for a single Parliament only, between 1906 and January 1910 when the Tories won it back. Nottingham – born in 1849, Hart – Davies was the son of an Archdeacon and became a Civil Servant after his education at Marlborough School and Lincoln College Oxford. In 1869 he entered the Indian Civil Service in which he served all his working life. He unsuccessfully contested Rotherhithe in 1900 and, after his Hackney defeat, did not resume a political career. He died in 1920.

His successor as MP was **Sir Walter Raymond Greene** (Conservative) who sat from January 1910, though he had earlier represented the Chesterton division of Cambridgeshire between 1885 and 1906, when he was defeated. Born at Bury St Edmunds in 1869, Walter was the son of that borough's MP but initially pursued a career in the Army, which he joined following his education at Eton and Oriel College Oxford. He became a Lieutenant in the Loyal Suffolk Hussars and served in South Africa. Returning from the Boer War he was a magistrate in his home county but in 1907 was elected to the LCC as a councillor for North Hackney and chaired a Committee that investigated the housing conditions of the working classes. Elected to Parliament for the same area in 1910 he returned to the Army when the First World War broke out in 1914 and was a member of the British Expeditionary Force until 1915 as a Captain in the 9th Lancers. He was awarded the DSO in 1915 and made Lieutenant Colonel of the Second and Third County of London Yeomanry. Re-elected in 1918, he served until defeated in 1923. He died in 1947.

Hackney South

Sir Charles Arthur Russell (Liberal), represented Hackney South from 1885 until 1894, when he was appointed a Lord of Appeal and Chief Justice of England[47]. An Irishman, born at Newry in Armagh in 1833, Russell was educated at Castle Knock College and Trinity College Dublin where he studied law. He was called to the Bar in 1854 at Lincoln's Inn and was made a QC in 1872. During this period he became involved in politics and contested Dundalk (Ireland) in the General Elections that took place in 1868 and 1874. Though unsuccessful on both occasions he did take the seat at the third time of asking, and was the town's MP from 1880 until 1885, when he transferred to Hackney. He was briefly Attorney General in 1886 and again between 1892 and 1894. He died in 1900.

When he resigned his seat to go to the Lords, he was succeeded by **Sir John Fletcher Moulton** (Liberal), also a lawyer, but he lost a year later at the General Election. Educated at Kingswood College Bath and St John's Cambridge, where he was President of the Union, he was initially a lecturer at Jesus and Christ's College, where he was also a Fellow. Called to the Bar at the Middle Temple in 1874, he obtained a very large legal practice and took silk in 1885. In the same year he was elected MP for Clapham, but lost the seat in 1886. He continued to practice law whilst seeking a way back into the Commons, but a seat eluded him until the 1892 Election when he was defeated again, this time at Nottingham South. Moulton was eventually elected for the Launceston division of Cornwall in 1898, and in the same year became a member of the Senate of London University. He was made a Judge in 1906, and six years later Lord of Appeal in Ordinary[48], in which post he served until he died aged 77 in 1921. Created Baron Moulton in 1912, he was a Fellow of the Royal Society, and an officer of the Legion of Honour[49] for research (electrical science). He was a Liberal reformer who wrote several books.

Thomas Herbert Robertson (Conservative) defeated Moulton in 1895. The son of a Clapham Doctor, Robertson was born in 1849 and educated at Magdalen College Oxford. He too was a lawyer who was called to the bar at Lincoln's Inn, in 1873. Although London born his mother was Irish and he became a JP in her home county of Carlow (as well as in London) and in 1899 became High Sheriff of the County. Prior to his election at Hackney in 1895 he had unsuccessfully contested the seat against Russell in 1892 and Moulton in 1894. He died in 1916.

He remained MP until 1906 when **Horatio Bottomley** (Liberal) won the seat. Born in Bethnal Green in 1860, Bottomley lost his father at the age of three, then his mother six years later. He spent the next five years at Sir Josiah Mason's orphanage in Birmingham. From this unpromising start, he left for London to work in a solicitor's office. Although only 14 years of age, Bottomley quickly picked up knowledge of legal matters which would serve him time and

47 Lord Chief Justice is the name given to the judge who presides over the Queen's Bench Division of the High Court, which deals with all civil matters that do not fall within the jurisdiction of the other divisions. These include civil actions arising out of common-law liability, mainly actions in contract and tort, for example negligence, nuisance and defamation.

48 The phrase Law Lords is the more common term used for the Lords of Appeal in Ordinary, who are the judicial members of the House of Lords, the Highest Court in the Land.

49 The Légion d'honneur is one of the highest decorations awarded by France.

Horatio Bottomley MP
Eliott & Fry - via Library of Congress

time again in future years. He spent his early years working as a court shorthand writer, whetting his appetite for journalism. He founded a number of publications, most of which folded before making a profit. Between 1901 and 1905, he had 67 writs and petitions for bankruptcy served against him. He founded the *Financial Journal* and was also proprietor of *The Sun* (not to be confused with the modern daily newspaper) but became famous as the founder, editor and proprietor of the magazine *John Bull.* His interests also extended to two other publications, *The Sunday Illustrated,* and *The Sunday Evening Telegram*. He entered politics as the Liberal candidate in an 1887 by-election at Hornsey, and contested Hackney South in 1900 when he lost to Robertson. A larger than life character he was declared bankrupt in 1912, which meant that he had to resign his seat. The Liberal Party withdrew support from him a year before his enforced resignation. However, when he became a discharged bankrupt he resumed his political career and, standing in 1918 as an Independent, was elected MP for Hackney South once more, serving until 1922 when he was again mired in controversy. In August of that year he was charged with fraudulent conversion and expelled from the Commons. Found guilty and sentenced to 7 years penal servitude, he was released after 5 and died in 1933.

Hector Morison (Liberal) succeeded Bottomley at the by-election in 1912. Born in Dunbartonshire in1850, the son of a calico printer, he was educated at Glasgow Academy and University before becoming a stockbroker and member of the London Stock Exchange. Also a Surrey magistrate, he entered politics when he unsuccessfully contested Lewes at the 1906 General Election. In the two electoral contests of 1910 he contested Eastbourne but failed to gain election until the Hackney South by-election in 1912. He died in 1939.

MPs for Shoreditch

From	*at*	*To*	*Surname*	*First Names*	*Constituency*	*Party*
1885	*G*	*1895*	*Cremer*	*William Randal*	*Shoreditch-Haggerston*	*Liberal-Labour*
1895	*G*	*1900*	*Lowles*	*John*		*Conservative*
1900	*G*	*1908*	*Cremer*	*William Randal*		*Liberal-Labour*
1908	*B*	*1910(Jan)*	*Guinness*	*Rupert Edward Cecil Lee*		*Conservative*
1910(Jan)	*G*	*1918*	*Chancellor*	*Henry George*		*Liberal*
1885	*G*	*1900*	*Stuart*	*James (Prof)*	*Shoreditch-Hoxton*	*Liberal*
1900	*G*	*1910(Jan)*	*Hay*	*Claude Geo. Drummond*		*Conservative*
1910(Jan)	*G*	*1918*	*Addison*	*Dr Christopher*		*Liberal*

NOTE First returned at a B = By-election; G = General Election

Shoreditch was a generally radical borough. There were only 3 Tory successes throughout the pre-War period whereas Liberals scored 13, of which 5 were sustained with Labour support in Haggerston. However, on 1st August 1908, two years into the new Liberal Government, the Tories took the division at a by-election despite the Liberals, in association with Labour, having won by a margin of 8% in 1906. The seat returned to the Liberals in both Elections in 1910, on each occasion by a margin of 7%.

Shoreditch - Haggerston

Sir William Randal Cremer (Liberal) who sat with Labour support, was a man of many parts and considerable reputation. Born in 1838 in Fareham (Hampshire) and deserted by his father when he was a child, he was educated at the National School and later in his life became the Editor and Publisher of The Arbitrator, a peace journal, and Secretary to the International Arbitration League. He also founded a Trade Union, the Amalgamated Society of Carpenters and Joiners, in 1860, and the International Parliamentary Union, which argued for international boards of arbitration to adjudicate disputes among nations. He was awarded the Cross of the French Legion of Honour by the country's President and in 1903 gained the Gold Medal and Nobel Peace Prize, donating the substantial prize money of £8,000 to the International Arbitration League, a forerunner of the League of Nations. He had first entered politics in 1868 when he

Sir William Cremer MP
Wikipedia

was defeated at Warwick, trying his luck there, again without success, in 1874. He was elected at Haggerston in 1885 and, though defeated in 1895, was re-elected in 1900 and remained the MP until his death in 1908.

John Lowles (Conservative) was the man who interrupted Cremer's spell as MP. Born in London in 1850, the son of a man from Frant in Sussex, Lowles was especially interested in the British colonies. In 1896 he was appointed the United Empire Trade League's Commissioner to Australia and became an ardent Imperial Federalist[50]. As an MP he pursued the colonial interest through his backing of state-aided emigration, and was a strong Unionist who favoured legislation to improve the social conditions of the working classes at the time. He served on the LCC from 1889 to 1892. he died in 1903.

Rupert Edward Cecil Lee Guinness MP
Vanity Fair

Rupert Edward Cecil Lee Guinness (Conservative), later the Viscount Elvedon, succeed Cremer at the by-election that followed his death. A member of the Guinness brewing family[51], he was born in London in 1874 the son of Edward Guinness, the Earl of Iveagh, who made the family business a public company in 1886. Rupert's father gave him £5 million when he married the daughter of the 4th Earl of Onslow following an education at Eton and Trinity Cambridge, then fought in South Africa in 1900 after which he returned to London and was a member of the LCC between 1904 and 1910, sitting on the London School Board for a while.

He first contested Haggerston in 1906, when he was defeated, and at the first General Election after his 1908 by-election success he lost, a result that was repeated in December 1910. Two years later he was elected at a by-election in South East Essex and remained its MP until 1918 when he transferred to the new constituency of Southend-on-Sea. He became Viscount Elvedon in 1919 when his father inherited the Earldom and was returned at every subsequent election until he succeeded his father as Earl of Iveagh in 1927. From the time of his succession he remained Chairman of Arthur Guinness and Son until 1962 and for the whole of that period was also Chancellor of Dublin University, retiring from that post in 1963. A Deputy Lieutenant of Suffolk and Surrey as well as a Lieutenant of London, he died in 1967.

Henry George Chancellor (Liberal) was born in Bridgewater (Somerset) in 1863 but he was educated at Elmfield College in York before going into the paint manufacturing business. Like Cremer, he was also active in the International Arbitration League, of which he became the Honorary Secretary in 1938. He was elected President of the English League for the Taxation of Land Values in 1910 and again in 1920. He retired from politics in 1918 and died in 1945.

Shoreditch - Hoxton

The first MP was the former Hackney incumbent, elected in 1884, **Professor James Stuart** (Liberal). His biographical details are provided in Chapter 2. He was MP in Hoxton for fifteen years.

In 1900 he was succeeded by **Claude George Drummond Hay** (Conservative). Son of the 11th Earl of Kinnoull, he was educated at Radley College, then abroad and became Assistant Secretary of Lloyds of London. He was the first Secretary of the Primrose League, an organisation aimed at encouraging grass roots activity for the Conservative cause, and contested Hoxton twice (in 1892 and 1895) before he was elected. Defeated in January1910, he was made a temporary Army Captain in 1915. He died in 1920.

Hay was succeeded by **Dr. Christopher Addison** (Liberal), one of the most accomplished East End MPs in Parliamentary history. The son of a Lincolnshire man and born in 1869, Addison was educated at Trinity College, a school in Harrogate, and at St Bartholomew's Hospital in London. There he became an MB, BS and FRCS, before becoming Lecturer in Anatomy at the same institution. Such was his eminence as a surgeon that he was also Hunterian Professor and Examiner in Anatomy to the Universities of both Cambridge and London. He was Chairman of the Board of International Medical Studies at the University of London, Secretary of the Anatomical Society and editor of the Quarterly Medical Journal. Elected in January 1910, he became Parliamentary Secretary to the Board of Education in 1914, and then filled the same role at Munitions (when Lloyd-George was Minister) between 1915 and 1916. When his former boss became Prime Minister in that year, Addison was made Munitions Minister himself and served as Minister for Reconstruction between 1917 and 1919 when he was made President of the Local Government Board. Later the same

50 The League was established in 1891 to promote Imperial trade.
51 The Company was established by Arthur Guinness in Dublin in 1759.

Dr Christopher Addison MP
© National Portrait Gallery
Walter Stoneman 1917

year he was appointed First Minister of Health and in 1921 became Minister without Portfolio. After redistribution in 1918 he was MP for Shoreditch until his defeat in 1922 and afterwards joined the Labour Party contesting Hammersmith South in their colours, though unsuccessfully, in 1924. He went in search of a more comfortable seat and was finally elected at Swindon in 1929 becoming initially Parliamentary Secretary and then Minister of Agriculture in 1930. His tenure was short-lived, losing his seat in 1931, though he regained it temporarily at Swindon in a by-election held in 1934, before losing again at the General Election a year later. In 1937 he was made Baron Addison and from 1940 to 1951 was Leader of the Labour Party in the House of Lords. Following the return of the Attlee Government in 1945 he was elevated to Viscount and became Leader of the House which post he held until 1947 when he was made the very first Secretary of State for Commonwealth Relations, an important role in post Imperial Britain. His hold on this office was short because, later the same year, he was made Lord Privy Seal in the reshuffle brought about by the resignation of Hugh Dalton, Chancellor of the Exchequer. He held his new post until 1951 and was also briefly Paymaster-General from 1948 to 1949. In 1951 he became Lord President of the Council in the reshuffle that followed the death of Ernest Bevin, and held the post until Labour's defeat at the General Election. He died later that year.

MPs for Tower Hamlets

The Liberals were marginally the most successful Party at winning elections in Tower Hamlets during the period, winning 32 (including two by-elections) compared with 27 Conservatives (including four by-elections) plus two Liberal Unionists who won Mile End in both 1910 Elections. Labour secured a solitary success with the election of George Lansbury at Bow and Bromley in December 1910. The political complexion of the constituencies was surprisingly mixed given the demographic characteristics of the Borough but restrictions on the franchise meant that even in heavily working class areas the Conservative Party sometimes did well while the expansion of owner occupied housing also helped their cause. Although they never won in Poplar or Whitechapel, they were the most popular Party in Mile End and Stepney. They took both Bow & Bromley and St George's four times, equalling the record of the radicals in general elections, and they took Bromley twice in by-elections too.

Bow and Bromley

The most illustrious of Bow and Bromley's MPs during this period was **Sir William Robson** (Liberal), born and educated privately in Newcastle-on-Tyne, who became the division's first MP at the age of 33. However, he only held the seat for a year losing in 1886 to the Tories following the Liberal split over Irish Home Rule. After one unsuccessful attempt to return as a Liberal MP for Middlesbrough in 1892, he was subsequently elected for South Shields, a seat in his home area, in 1895, and held it until created Lord Robson in 1910. When elected for Bow and Bromley he had been at the bar for five years and after his defeat became a QC in 1892 and pursued a distinguished career in the Law. He was Solicitor-General and later Attorney General in Liberal Governments between 1906 and 1910 and as Lord Robson served as Lord of Appeal until 1912. He died in 1918.

Sir William Robson MP
Wikipedia

He was defeated by **Sir John Charles Ready Colomb** (Conservative), the son of an Irish-born General who pursued a military career himself, retiring in 1869 as a Captain in the Royal Marine Artillery. Pending his political career he lived in his native County Kerry where he was a Deputy-Lieutenant and magistrate. He wrote a book on the "Defence of Great and Greater Britain" and took a major interest in colonial affairs. Politically he was best described as an Imperialist and served as MP at Bow from 1886 until 1892 when he was defeated. He was elected at Great Yarmouth in 1895 and remained in the Commons until the 1906 Liberal landslide. Born in 1838, Colomb died in 1909.

John Archibald Murray MacDonald (Liberal), the son of a Minister from Argyll, was educated at Glasgow High School and the Universities of both Glasgow and Edinburgh. Standing as a supporter of Gladstone he defeated Colomb in 1895 but was himself beaten only three years later. He was outside the House until 1906 when he was elected at Falkirk Burghs where he had been unsuccessful in 1900, and remained MP there until 1922, continuing after 1918 as MP for the

MPs for Tower Hamlets

From	at	To	Surname	First Names	Constituency	Party
1885	G	1886	Robson	Sir William	Bow and Bromley	Liberal
1886	G	1892	Colomb	Sir John Charles Ready		Conservative
1892	G	1895	Macdonald	John Archibald Murray		Liberal
1895	G	1899	Holland	Lionel Raleigh		Conservative
1899	B	1906	Guthrie	Walter Murray		Conservative
1906	G	1910(Jan)	Brooke	Stopford William Wentworth		Liberal
1910(Jan)	G	1910(Dec)	Du Cros	Alfred Philip		Conservative Unionist
1910(Dec)	G	1912	Lansbury	George		Labour
1912	B	1918	Blair	Sir Reginald		Conservative
1885	G	1892	Norris	Edward Samuel	Limehouse	Conservative
1892	G	1895	Wallace	John Stewart		Liberal
1895	G	1906	Samuel	Sir Harry Simon		Conservative
1906	G	1918	Pearce	Sir William		Liberal
1885	G	1905	Charrington	Spencer	Mile End	Conservative
1905	B	1906	Levy-Lawson	Harry Lawson Webster		Conservative
1906	G	1910(Jan)	Strauss	Bertram Stuart		Liberal
1910(Jan)	G	1916	Levy-Lawson	Harry Lawson Webster		Conservative
1916	B	1918	Brookes	Warwick		Conservative
1885	G	1886	Green	Henry	Poplar	Liberal
1886	G	1914	Buxton	Sydney		Liberal
1914	B	1918	Yeo	Sir Alfred William		Liberal
1885	G	1892	Ritchie	Charles Thomson	St George	Conservative
1892	G	1895	Benn	John Williams		Liberal
1895	G	1900	Marks	Harry Hananel		Conservative
1900	G	1906	Dewar	Sir Thomas Robert		Conservative
1906	G	1918	Benn	William Wedgwood		Liberal
1885	G	1886	Durant	John Charles	Stepney	Liberal
1886	G	1898	Isaacson	Fredk. Wootton		Conservative
1898	B	1900	Steadman	William Charles		Liberal
1900	G	1907	Evans-Gordon	Sir Wm Eden		Conservative
1907	B	1910(Dec)	Harris	Frederick L.		Conservative Unionist
1910(Dec)	G	1918	Glyn-Jones	Sir William Samuel		Liberal
1885	G	1900	Montagu	Sir Samuel	Whitechapel	Liberal
1900	G	1916	Samuel	Sir Stuart M		Liberal
1916	B	1918	Kiley	John Daniel		Liberal

NOTE First returned at a B = By-election; G =General Election

newly drawn combined Stirling and Falkirk Burghs constituency. He died in 1939.

His successor at Bow was **Lionel Raleigh Holland** (Conservative), son of Viscount Knutsford. Though a Tory he was a social reformer who resigned in 1899 to join the Liberals. He sought election under his new colours at Romford in 1900 and then at Edgbaston (Birmingham) in 1906 but failed to gain another berth in Parliament. He died in 1936, aged 71.

William Murray Guthrie (Conservative) retained the seat at the 1899 by-election that followed Holland's defection. Born in London only 30 years earlier he had been educated at Eton and Trinity Cambridge. A typical "City" type, Guthrie became both a Director of the Commercial Union[52] and of the National Discount Company, a discount bank[53]. He was a City Alderman and a Merchant Taylor[54]. He died in 1911, at the age of only 41.

52 Following a fire that destroyed a London hemp warehouse in 1861 a committee decided to form a new company, the Commercial Union Fire Insurance Company. On 28 September its constitution was established and the Commercial Union Assurance Company started business.

53 Established 1856.

54 The Merchant Taylors' Company is one of the Great Twelve Livery Companies of the City of London and was founded in the

Defeated in 1906, Guthrie was succeeded by **Stopford William Brooke** (Liberal), a man whose maternal grandfather had also been an MP. Brooke himself was a Minister of the Unitarian Church based in Boston USA and served just one Parliament before the Tories regained the seat in January 1910. Brooke fought the December 1910 General Election at Bassetlaw in Nottinghamshire but failed to secure a return to Parliament. He died in 1938 in his late 70s.

Alfred du Cros MP
Parliamentary Archive

Alfred Du Cros (Conservative) was only an MP for a few months. Victorious in January 1910, he did not repeat that success in December and went in search of another seat which he found in a by-election at Hastings in 1908 transferring to Wandsworth, Clapham from 1918 to 1922 when he stood down. Du Cros was one of seven Irish brothers who were well known competition cyclists in the early days of that sport in the 1880s. Their father Harvey bought Dunlop's patent rights to the pneumatic tyre establishing in Belfast the first factory for the commercial production of air tyres. Alfred was born in Dublin in 1868 and became a director of several companies in the motor and cycle trades. In 1901 he established the Dunlop Tyre factory in Birmingham (later known as Fort Dunlop). He died in 1955 but in the intervening period was embroiled in several unsavoury financial dealings which brought the company close to bankruptcy. This may have accounted for his retirement from politics and his divorce the following year.

George Lansbury MP
Peoples' History Museum Manchester

George Lansbury (Labour) won the seat in December 1910 and went on to become an historically significant figure in his Party. Born the son of a cart contractor in Suffolk in 1859, Lansbury was educated at an Elementary School and became a political activist in Poplar where he was initially an agent for the Liberal Party before joining the Social Democratic Federation in 1892. He fought two elections unsuccessfully for the Federation, the first in the Walworth division of Newington (now Southwark) in 1895 and the second at Bow & Bromley in 1900. Despite these early setbacks he was elected to Poplar Borough Council in 1903 and served continuously until his death in 1940. He was a left-wing journalist with pacifist views who did not join the Labour Party when it was formed preferring to stand as an Independent Socialist at Middlesbrough in 1906. He subsequently did join the Labour Party and first fought Bow & Bromley in January 1910 when his intervention seems to have contributed to the Liberal losing the seat to Du Cros. Lansbury's winning margin in December was 11% but, ever the principled politician; he resigned the seat to fight a by-election in 1912 on the subject of female suffrage and, failing to secure the endorsement of the Labour Party, lost the seat to the Tories who held it until 1922 when Lansbury was re-elected. Whilst out of Parliament he became Editor of the left-wing *Daily Herald* Newspaper and, when he resumed his career, rose to become Leader of the Labour Party and of the Opposition after the split with Ramsay MacDonald in 1931. He remained Leader of the Party until 1935 when his pacifist views seemed less in keeping with the spirit of the times, and Clement Attlee replaced him. However, Lansbury remained MP for Bow & Bromley until his death in 1940.

George Lansbury MP in 1921 at the time when he was arrested with other Poplar councillors and imprisoned for refusing to levy 'unfair' rates. **Peoples' History Museum Manchester**

Sir Reginald Blair (Conservative) defeated Lansbury at the 1912 by-election by a margin of more than 10% and held the seat for 10 years. Born in Glasgow in 1881, Blair was educated at Kelvinside Academy and the University of Glasgow and became an accountant, being a member of the Institution of Accountants and Actuaries in Scotland for several years. However, he had diverse interests and was sometime Chairman of both the Race Course Control Board, and much later in life of the Race Course Betting Control Board in 1962. During the First World War he served as Field Cashier, with the rank of an Army Captain, in France and the Middle East between 1914 and 1916. After the War he was Chairman of the Municipal Society from 1919 until 1929. He stood down at Bromley & Bow in 1922, but contested Kennington unsuccessfully in 1923. Despite this setback, he re-secured his place in the Commons when in 1935 he was

13th century as a religious and social fraternity

elected MP for Hendon, a seat he held until 1945 when he retired from politics. He died in 1962.

Limehouse

Edward Samuel Norris (Conservative) was the MP between 1885 and 1892. Born in London in 1832, he was educated privately in London and joined the family mercantile company, which involved him in a lifetime associated with shipping and dock enterprises. A progressive Tory, Norris pursued several roles in the wider community in East London including Treasurer of the Merchant Seamen's Orphan Asylum at Snaresbrook (Essex) and Treasurer of the East London Children's Hospital. In his public life he was also a Middlesex magistrate at the Tower of London and Deputy Lieutenant of Tower Hamlets. In business he rose to become Deputy Chairman of the Southampton Docks Company[55] and was also Captain Commandant of the Sussex Volunteer Artillery. Following his period as MP for Limehouse he stood unsuccessfully as the Tory candidate for Colchester in 1895. He died in 1908.

John Stewart Wallace (Liberal) took Limehouse in 1892 but held it for only three years. Despite being an Ulsterman, born in Belfast in 1840, he was a supporter of Gladstone's Home Rule policy. Educated in the city he, like his predecessor as MP, was a merchant, specialising in timber but was also an inventor. He was a member of the London Chamber of Commerce who took a special interest in British colonial affairs including gold mining but domestically his principal concern was Ireland where he was Vice President of the Home Rule Association formed in 1870 by Isaac Butt and led in Parliament from 1880 by Charles Stewart Parnell until his death the year before Wallace was elected.

Elected in 1895, **Sir Harry Simon Samuel** (Conservative) was the son of Horatio and Henrietta Samuel, his mother being the niece of Sir Moses Montefiore[56]. Born at Gloucester Place, London in 1853 he came from a moneyed Jewish family and was educated at Eastbourne College and St John's Cambridge. He first contested Limehouse in 1892 and after his defeat there in 1906 was returned for Norwood, which he represented from 1910 until 1922. He died in 1934.

The seat was taken by **Sir William Pearce** (Liberal) who represented Limehouse from 1906 to 1922. Born in 1853 in Poplar he was educated at the Royal College of Science after which he went into business becoming a Director of a Chemical Company called Spencer, Chapman and Measel Limited. His business career saw him become Vice President of the Federation of British Industries founded in 1916 on the initiative of the Midlands industrialist, Dudley Docker who obtained pledges of £1,000 from each of 124 firms to launch a new representative organisation for industry. It absorbed other smaller organisations, which strengthened its regional and overseas work, and in 1923 was incorporated by Royal Charter[57]. Politically Pearce was a London County councillor from 1892 to 1901, a year after he had first contested Limehouse in a General Election. In 1920 he was Chairman of a Committee that was established to investigate War Wealth. Also a London magistrate, he died in 1932.

Mile End

The first MP was the locally born but Eton educated **Spencer Charrington** (Conservative), partner in the family brewing company of the same name whose Anchor brewery was a major local employer. He was MP for 20 years from the age of 67 until his death in 1904.

Modern use of the Anchor Brewery site as a retail park **John Nelson**

The 1905 by-election that followed his death was won by **Harry Webster Lawson** (Conservative), a son of Lord Burnham. He held the seat until 1906 and then again, having won by just two votes, from January 1910 until January 1916 when he succeeded to the peerage. Initially a Liberal, he was first elected to Parliament as MP for St Pancras West (1885-92), and his principal biographical details are found earlier in this chapter (North London – MPs for St Pancras).

Following his defeat in 1906, Lawson was succeeded by **Bertram Stuart Strauss** (Liberal) who was the MP until January 1910. Born at Prestwich, Lancashire in 1868, Strauss was the son of a Vice Consul of the Netherlands who, after an education

55 Established in 1843 and acquired by the London and South Western Railway Company in 1892.
56 Sir Moses Montefiore (1784-1885) made his fortune on the London Stock Exchange and by the age of forty had retired to devote himself to philanthropy and to counter oppression faced by Jewish communities overseas. He was Sheriff of London 1837-1838, made a baronet in 1846, and was a leader of the British Jewish community.
57 It was easily the biggest of the CBI's predecessors, having a membership of over 9,000 individual firms and 272 trade associations by 1964. It merged with the British Employers' Confederation and the National Association of British Manufacturers in 1965 to form the Confederation of British Industry.

at Harrow School, became a colonial broker and partner in the firm of Hale and Son of Mincing Lane. He stood unsuccessfully for Marylebone West in the General Election of 1895 and in 1898 joined the LCC as councillor for Mile End, which he represented until 1907. During that period he contested Whitechapel at the 1900 election and was the candidate Lawson defeated when he was first returned for Mile End at the 1905 by-election. He was also President of the League of Mercy[58] in the district and a London magistrate. An advocate of the universal franchise, he withdrew from politics after failing to secure re-election at Mile End in December 1910. He died in 1933.

Following Lawson's elevation in 1916 the resultant wartime by-election was won by **Warwick Brookes** (Conservative) who defeated an Independent candidate. A Mancunian born in 1875 he became a prominent businessman with an involvement in several companies. He was an Ironfounder in the firm of Booth Brookes based at Burnham-on-Crouch in Essex; Managing Director of the Junior Army and Navy Stores[59] in Regent Street, a Director of the Civil Service Co-operative Society, and of T.T. Nethercoat Limited. Prior to contesting Mile End he had been unsuccessful at Newington West in January and December 1910. He retired in 1918, and died in 1935.

Poplar

The first MP was a local ship owner, born at Blackwall in 1838. **Henry Green** (Liberal) was educated at Cheam School and Bonn University and became a partner in the family business at the age of 18. He was a Director of the East and West India Dock Company, which constructed the London Docks on the Isle of Dogs during this period. His maritime connections were strong and he even served on a Royal Commission Inquiry into loss of life and property at sea. He died in 1900.

In 1886 he stood down after only a year as MP to be succeeded by **Sydney Buxton** (Liberal) who was politically involved early. He was born in London in 1853 and educated at Clifton College and Trinity College Cambridge. Whilst serving as a Member of the London School Board from 1876 he contested his first Parliamentary election in 1880 when he was defeated at Boston (Lincolnshire). He left the Board in 1882 and the following year was returned as MP for Peterborough in a by-election. During this period he was also Honorary Secretary to the Irish Emigration Fund but lost Peterborough in 1885 and went on to lose a by-election at Croydon in January 1886 before being elected at Poplar in the General Election later that year. Author of several political works, including some on the Liberal leader Gladstone, he pursued a successful Ministerial career. In 1892 he was appointed by Lord Rosebury to be Under-Secretary for the Colonies, a post he held until the Tories returned to Government in 1895. After the Liberal landslide in 1906 he was made Postmaster-General, then President of the Board of Trade in 1910, which Cabinet post he retained until 1914 when he was appointed Governor-General of South Africa and made a Viscount. He resigned his seat to take up this posting, which he held until 1920 when he was made the first Earl Buxton. He died in 1934.

Sir Alfred William Yeo MP
By permission of the Yeo Family.

Sir Alfred William Yeo (Liberal) succeeded him at the by-election and remained a Poplar MP for eight years. Born in 1863, the son of a Devonshire man, he was educated at Marner Street and High Street Schools in Bromley-by-Bow. He worked initially in an iron foundry but for 30 years was in the music trade. He served on Poplar Borough Council for 25 years, was Mayor in 1903/4 and was also on the LCC for 9 years. A brass band enthusiast, Yeo was Chairman of the Poplar Board of Guardians for 6 years and a member for 10. He was left leaning politically and after the First World War represented Poplar South. He died in 1928.

St George

Charles Thomson Ritchie (Conservative) was an MP for the former Tower Hamlets division from 1874 until he was elected as the St George's MP for a further seven years after 1885. It was during this latter period that he served prominently in the Governments of the Marquis of Salisbury and his biographical details are in Chapter 2.

In 1892 St George's changed hands when **Sir John Williams Benn** (Liberal) was elected. The son of a Congregational Minister from Blackheath, Benn was born in Hyde (Cheshire) in 1850 and became a journalist, writing many articles about the social problems of the time. He joined the LCC in 1889 and served as MP for St George's between 1892 and 1895 when he was defeated. He was made LCC Vice Chairman in 1895, and

58 The Salvation Army's League of Mercy was established to help sick people and prisoners.
59 Army and Navy Stores were established in the late 19th century as a kind of co-operative of shareholders restricted to certain ranks in the Armed Services and some civil servants.

St George's Vestry Hall by Andrew Wilson was built in 1860, and became the town hall after the 1899 London Government Act. On Sunday 4th October 1936 the Battle of Cable St took place, when a march by Moseley's British Union of Fascists was forced to be abandoned by anti-fascists. The defeat for the fascists is commemorated on the end of the old St George's Town Hall building in Cable St, E1 (St George's constituency in 1885). The passing of the Public Order Act in 1936 was in part prompted by this incident. **Gordon Rushton**

unsuccessfully fought a Parliamentary by-election at Deptford in 1897 and the General Election of 1900 at Bermondsey. He was made Chairman of the LCC in 1904 but the same year won a Parliamentary by-election at Devonport, a seat he held until January 1910, when he retired. He was additionally a magistrate and Deputy Lieutenant for London. John Benn died in 1922 but was the first of a remarkable family dynasty of radical politicians and Cabinet ministers who have sat in the Commons since 1892. His son William, whose maternal grandfather was also a Liberal MP, later sat for St George's (see below), whilst his grandson Tony sat for Bristol and then Chesterfield constituencies for fifty years until 2001. His great grandson, Hilary Benn was elected a Labour MP for Leeds in a by-election in the 1997-2001 Parliament and entered the Cabinet in 2003.

Harry Hananel Marks (Conservative) was the son of the Reverend Professor Marks and was born in London in 1855. Educated at University College, London and in Brussels he became a financial journalist founding and editing the Financial News. As well as the East End he had connections with Kent where he was a magistrate and Officer Commanding of the East Kent Regiment. He was a member of the LCC from 1889 until 1898 and first contested a Parliamentary seat in 1892 at Bethnal Green. He was elected at St George's Whitechapel in 1895 but retired in 1900 after which he transferred his attentions to Kent winning a by-election at Thanet in 1904 and serving as MP until his final retirement in January 1910. A right wing imperialist Tory he died in 1916.

Sir Thomas Robert Dewar (Conservative) was the son of John Dewar, the Whiskey Distiller, and was born in Perth Scotland in 1864. Educated there and in Edinburgh he entered the family business but pursued other interests including travel round the world, publishing articles about his experiences and wrote a book against the principles of Prohibition. He was a Lieutenant of the City of London and later the Sheriff in 1897/8 but was also a magistrate in Kent. He was a member of the LCC representing Marylebone West for three years from 1892 and first stood for Parliament at a by-election in February 1897 when he was defeated at Essex South West. He won St George's in 1900 but after he was defeated in 1906 did not resume a Commons career. He was elevated to the House of Lords as the first Baron Dewar in 1919 and died in 1930.

He was succeeded in 1906 by **William Wedgwood Benn** (Liberal) who was the son of Sir John Benn (above) and the grandson of a former MP for Govan in Lanarkshire, Daniel Holmes. Born in 1877 William was the father of the famous Labour Cabinet Member and left wing radical, Tony Benn, and grandfather of Hilary, a Cabinet Minister in the Blair and Brown Governments. William was educated in Paris at the Lycée Condorcet and at University College London.

He entered politics before he was 30 and in 1910 Herbert Asquith appointed him as a Junior Lord of the Treasury and Government Whip, a post he held until 1915. At the outbreak of the First World War he saw active service in Egypt, Gallipoli, Italy and in the Mediterranean for which he was awarded the DSO in 1916. Following boundary changes in 1918 he ceased to be St George's MP, and was adopted instead to fight the Scottish burgh seat of Leith, which he won as a Liberal, but resigned to join the Labour Party in 1927 triggering a by-election, which he lost. The following year he was returned at another Scottish by-election as MP for Aberdeen North and when Labour emerged following the 1929 General Election as the largest Party he served in Ramsay MacDonald's Cabinet as Secretary of State for India. After the collapse of that Government in 1931 Benn broke with MacDonald and lost his seat at the General Election. He sought a return at Dudley in 1935 and was defeated once more but was eventually successful at a by-election held in the Gorton division of Manchester in 1937. In the Second World War he joined the RAF and was awarded several major military honours including a DFC, the Croix de Guerre, the Legion d'Honneur, the Italian Military Cross and Medal for Valour. In 1942 he was elevated to the House of Lords as the first Viscount Stansgate, a title that his son Tony was to revoke 20 years later. From 1943 to 1944 he was Vice President of the Allied Control Commission for Italy and following the return of the first majority Labour Government in 1945 he was Secretary of State for Air until 1946. He died in 1960.

Stepney

Stepney's first MP was a Radical Christian Socialist called **John Durant** (Liberal), an uneducated man from Fordingbridge in Hampshire, who came to London as apprentice to a printer before setting up his own businesses in 1874 at Hatton Garden and in the Strand. He was a founder of the Land Nationalization Society in 1881but had a very short political career, losing his seat in 1886.

He was succeeded by **Frederick Wootton Issacson** (Conservative), another man from the shires. Born in Suffolk he became a magistrate and Deputy-Lieutenant for Tower Hamlets and was also a JP in Monmouthshire. He entered politics in 1880 when he was defeated at Wednesbury (Staffordshire) and lost to Durant at Stepney in 1885 before taking the seat, which he held for 12 years.

William Charles Steadman (Liberal) was Stepney's MP for only two years (1898-1900) but subsequently changed Parties and was Labour MP for Finsbury Central between 1906 and 1910. His biographical details are contained earlier in this Chapter.

He lost in 1900 when **Sir William Eden Evans Gordon** (Conservative) was elected. William was the son of General Charles Gordon (of Khartoum fame) and was born at Chatham in 1857. He too had an Army career following an education at Cheltenham College and overseas. Having joined the Army in 1876 he served in India until he retired with the rank of Major twenty years later and went into politics, unsuccessfully contesting Stepney against Steadman in 1898. Appropriately for someone who represented an East End constituency he was a Tory who favoured measures to relieve the conditions of the working classes. He retired in 1907 and died six years later.

Frederick Leverton Harris (Conservative and Unionist) won the 1907 by-election and remained Stepney's MP until December 1910 when he was defeated. Born in 1864, Harris was educated at Winchester and Cauis College Cambridge. He entered politics as MP for Tynemouth in 1900 and in that Parliament served as PPS to Arnold Foster the War Minister in 1904. In the same year he was appointed to the Tariff Reform Commission, which was the issue that caused a rift in the Tory Party and was a contributory factor in the Liberal landslide of 1906. Harris lost Tynemouth but was returned at Stepney soon afterwards and also served on the LCC between 1907 and 1910. He held his Parliamentary seat in January 1910 with a majority of 6% but lost it in December by the margin of 3%. At the start of the First World War he became an adviser on trade and supplies and from 1916 to 1919 was the Parliamentary Secretary to the Ministry of Blockade. In 1918 he returned to Parliament after a by-election at Worcestershire East but only held the seat until the General Election that followed the ending of the War when the seat was abolished and re-drawn. He died in 1926.

Sir William Samuel Glyn-Jones (Liberal) took Stepney in December 1910 and remained the MP until 1918. Born in 1869 in Worcester he was a pharmacist who had been educated at Merthyr Tydfil Grammar School. He was also a lawyer called to the bar of the Middle Temple and practised in Merthyr from 1904. The author of "The Law of Poisons and Pharmacy" he was a Middlesex magistrate and Chairman of the Council of the Canadian Proprietary Articles Trade Association. He was appointed PPS to Christopher Addison (MP for the nearby constituency of Shoreditch, Hoxton – see above) when he was Minister of Munitions in 1916 and of Reconstruction in 1917.

Whitechapel

Whitechapel's first MP was **Sir Samuel Montagu** (Liberal), the famous financier and Jewish benefactor of many synagogues and benevolent institutions who formed his Bank in 1853. Born in Liverpool 21 years earlier, the son of a watchmaker and educated at the City Institute, Montagu married the wife of Louis Cohen, a London Stockbroker and himself the father of two MPs, both contemporaries of Samuel, but unlike him, Tories (See MPs for Paddington earlier in this chapter). He was elected in 1885 and changed his name to Montagu Samuel-Montagu in 1894. He stood aside in 1900 and contested Leeds Central but never returned to the Commons. He was made Baron Swaythling in 1907 and died four years later.

Sir Samuel Montagu MP
© National Portrait Gallery
Sir Benjamin Stone 1898

When he stood down in 1900 it was in favour of his cousin, **Sir Stuart Montagu Samuel** (Liberal), also Liverpool-born and a banker in the family firm. He too was educated at the Liverpool Institute, but also attended University College London. He held no Parliamentary office, but in 1913 was accused of holding a commercial contract with the Secretary of State for India, and resigned to fight a by-election in which he successfully defended his honour. He remained MP for Whitechapel until 1916 when he retired from politics. He died in 1926.

James Daniel Kiley (Liberal) who won the 1916 by-election, was born in 1865, became a London magistrate and member of Stepney Council where he was an alderman, and sat as Mayor in 1915. During this period he was a member of the Metropolitan Water Board, but was also Chairman of Messers Whyte, Ridsdale and Company, warehousemen of Houndsditch, and of the Fancy Goods Section of the London Chamber of Commerce. He also chaired the British Toy Manufacturers and Wholesalers Association, and was a director of several other firms. He was Whitechapel's MP from 1916 to 1918 when he was elected for the new constituency of Whitechapel and St George's, which he represented until 1922. He was defeated in 1922 and tried again in 1923 but without success. He died in 1953.

North East Middlesex

Beyond these very densely packed areas of East London the outer suburbs were beginning to develop and three new county constituencies were established based on Hornsey, Tottenham and Enfield.

Tottenham (1 seat)

In ancient times the area we now call the London Borough of Haringey was made up of two large manors, Hornsey and Tottenham, which became parishes with firm boundaries in 1300. Wood Green, originally part of Tottenham Parish, became a separate district in 1888. However, when Tottenham was first created a constituency in 1885 it included both these parishes together with the southern part of the Southgate parish around Bowes Park, the northern part being incorporated in Enfield (see below). The Tottenham constituency therefore included Bounds Green, Bowes Park, Bruce Grove, Harringay, Noel Park, Northumberland Park, Seven Sisters, Turnpike Lane, White Hart Lane and Wood Green. (See the map overleaf.)

According to local archives it was originally called "Toteham", meaning "homestead or village of a man called Totta". Bounded by the River Lea to the east and later by the New River to the west, the town was then strung out along the road between London and Hertford and Muswell brook divided the parish into north and south yet despite its origins has few significant historical links. The manor originally belonged to the Dukes of Northumberland but it passed to the Kings of Scotland through marriage. The father of Robert the Bruce of Scotland built Bruce Castle on the site of the original manor house and the district of Bruce Grove gets its name from this association. Tottenham was already developing as a sizable town in the mid-Victorian period and in 1871 was recorded as having 22,809 people living there of who 7,356 inhabited the central district of High Cross. Although the town extended continuously along the Hertford road without a break between Stamford Hill and Upper Edmonton it still had a rural aspect. The ward of Seven Sisters gets its name from seven Elm trees that stood by the roadside at Page Green whilst cattle grazed on the marshlands of the River Lea and flowers were grown for London's markets. 3,487 souls lived at the north end of the town in St Pauls

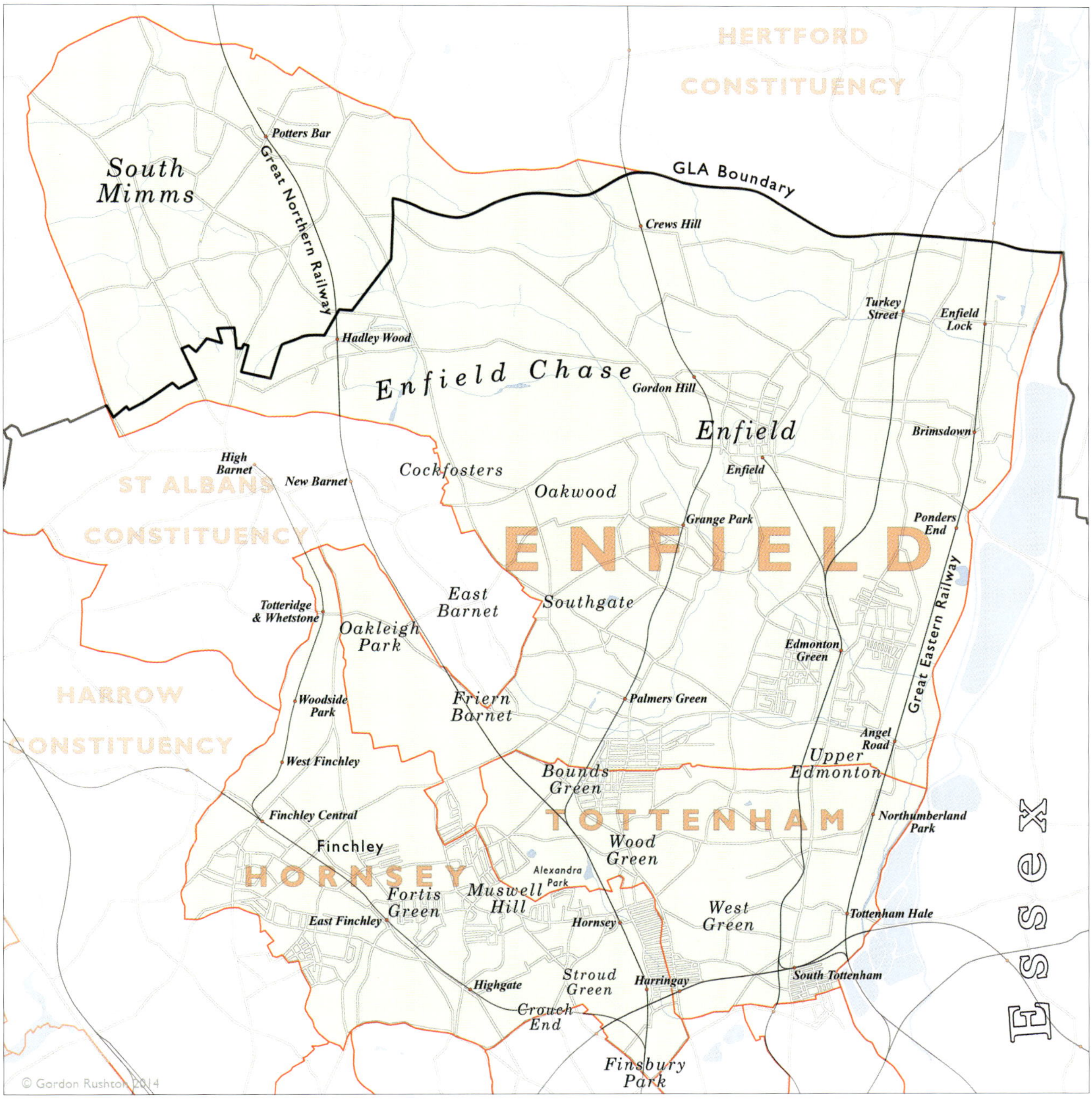

and 4,724 in the south area of St Anne's Road. Neighbouring Wood Green had a population of 5,011 in the same year but rapid population expansion followed the construction of the railways. Tottenham's growth was amongst the fastest anywhere in the country between 1881 and 1911. It was created an Urban District in 1894 and in 1905 Henrietta Barnett described a place of "small villas side by side…the monotony of mediocrity unbroken by fine public buildings or large open spaces". Wood Green was granted UDC status in 1894. Tottenham Town Hall was opened in 1905.

Hornsey (1 seat)

In 1201 the place was known as "Haringeie" and by 1243 was called "Haringesheye" meaning, either "enclosure in the grey wood", or "enclosure of a man called Haering". Nearby Harringay is a different derivation of the same name. According to the University of London & History of Parliament Trust, the main feature of Hornsey's history before 1850 was the expansion of farmland involving clearance of woods and commons, which covered half of the total area at the end of the 14th century and a third by the mid 17th. The predominant role of grassland rather than arable from 1550 kept the parish thinly populated, with settlement mainly confined to Hornsey village, Crouch End, and, from the mid 14th century, Highgate. It also included Fortis Green and Finsbury Park. The 1885 Hornsey constituency comprised the local parish (made an Urban District in 1894 and a municipal borough in 1903), together with Finchley, now in Barnet borough but itself created an Urban District in 1895. The seat also embraced all parts of Finchley, Muswell Hill, Oakley

Top Left and Right: *River View (L) and Holly Walk (R) Enfield, placed within minutes of |Enfield Town and Chase Stations, which generated a Victorian urban expansion.*

Left: *Hillfield Avenue, Hornsey was built towards the end of the 1890s. It typifies the middle class housing that was being developed in the latter part of the Victorian period, close to Hornsey's High Street and its station.*

Above: *Winchelsea Road in Tottenham is typical of the terraced housing stock built in the Borough in the late 19th century during the period of rapid growth of the Urban District created in 1894 and where local employment was substantial. Tottenham was a relatively self-sufficient suburb but the railway connection was available at nearby stations including Seven Sisters, Bruce Grove and Tottenham Hale.*

Left: *Tottenham Town Hall at Tottenham Green dates from the Edwardian era, and was constructed in the mid-life of the Tottenham Constituency that existed between 1885 and 1918. In modern times it has been sold off and developed as a community business enterprise space.*

All photos John Nelson

Park and Woodside Park together with the densely populated district of Stoke Newington near Shacklewell known as South Hornsey and referred to above in Hackney South.[60] (See also East End map, Page 110)

Enfield (1 seat)

The parish of Enfield (meaning Forest Clearing of a man called Eana, or "Enefelde" in 1086) was one of the largest centres of population in the orbit of the Capital City. Although it covered an extensive area from the East Barnet Valley, Cockfosters (a secluded hamlet in those days) and South Mimms across to the River Lea, the majority of the population was concentrated in the east around the London to Hertford Road on a north to south axis between Enfield Wash/Lock and Ponders End, including Edmonton. The new Enfield county division was centred on the parish of St Andrew, Enfield Market Place but including also those of Edmonton, Hadley, Monk Hadley, South Mimms and South Mimms Urban. It also included most of Southgate (southern parts were in Tottenham) but did not include the East Barnet valley or Chipping Barnet, which were then in Hertfordshire. Its main Middlesex communities and features were Alexandra Palace (opened in 1873 as a centre of recreation known as "The People's Palace"), Bowes, Brimsdown, Bush Hill Park (where the Great Eastern Railways 1849 - built station encouraged suburban development), Edmonton, all districts of Enfield, Forty Hill (where the Brigden Hall Estate had been sold for building in 1868), Hadley Wood, Ponders End, Potters Bar, South Mimms, Southgate and Trent Park, a part of Enfield Chase that had been enclosed in 1777. High Barnet, Monken Hadley and Brunswick Park were then left in Hertfordshire.

There were originally eight manors in Enfield and Enfield Chase had once been part of Middlesex Forest but was acquired by the Crown as a Royal hunting ground by King John and subsequently became a property of the Duchy of Lancaster. However, by the mid Victorian period the town itself had become a centre of industry notably as the home of the Royal Small Arms Factory, opened at Enfield Lock in 1857. This had the capacity to manufacture up to 3,300 (Enfield) rifles per week.

The story of the 19th century was one of continuous growth and development during which the quiet country towns of Enfield and Edmonton began to assume their present aspect. Enfield alone saw its population grow from 5,881 in 1801 to 42,738 by the close of the century and even greater increases were recorded at Edmonton and Southgate. Despite this the Ordnance Map of 1866 still showed far more open country than built-up areas. Lower Edmonton and Enfield were small towns separated by open country. Upper Edmonton, Ponders End, Enfield Wash and Winchmore Hill were growing villages but of Brimsdown and Bush Hill Park there was no trace. Two miles of open fields and farmland divided Southgate from Edmonton or Enfield with Palmers Green, an isolated hamlet amid the meadows. Roads were not numerous but the rail routes were beginning to take shape. The Great Northern Railway had been built through the area in 1850 with a station serving Southgate whilst the Cambridge line of the Eastern Counties Railway from Stratford had been built along the Lea Valley in 1840 with stations at Angel Road and Enfield Wash. Nine years later a branch was built from Angel Road to Enfield Town with a station at Edmonton Green.

St Albans

Mention should be made of this Hertfordshire county seat included parts of today's Greater London Borough of Barnet. These were Arkley, Chipping Barnet, East Barnet, Totteridge and Whetstone. This constituency is not included in the summary of London seats for 1885 as the great majority of the electorate were in or around St Albans, Hertford and Hemel Hempstead.

Constituency Populations and Electorates

Constituency	1891 pop	1901 pop	1911 pop	1906 electorate	1910 electorate	1915 electorate	1910 electorate as % of 1911 population
Enfield	84,414	125,291	180,096	23,386	28,571	34,276	15.9
Hornsey	77,744	109,752	138,944	19,651	23,450	28,036	16.9
Tottenham	97,174	136,774	186,619	23,409	29,260	34,816	15.7

The proportions of the population who were electors were similar in each of the new constituencies suggesting that the owner-occupier factor was relatively strong, in contrast to most of the older East End seats amongst which only Haggerston compared. These figures were comparable to those in West Middlesex but what may have been different

60 The area lay approximately between Clissold Park, Abery Park Cemetery and Stoke Newington High Street. It was transferred to Stoke Newington Borough in 1899 and incorporated in a constituency of that name in 1918.

in the county seats was the nature of owner occupation, which changed as new developments succeeded earlier ones. Tottenham and Edmonton in particular provided homes for the working classes.

The latter half of the century saw a marked acceleration in the urbanisation of all three of the present Enfield borough's constituent parts. The continuing growth of the railway system had a great deal to do with this expansion, the Hertford North branch through Enfield Chase being opened in 1870 and the line from Edmonton to Cheshunt following in 1872. In 1850 a Board of Health was set up to handle local affairs and from 1871 onwards there were extensive building developments in Bush Hill Park, Chase Side and Lancaster Road. Later Bycullah Park, the scene in previous years of the Easter week races, was to share the same fate. In 1894 Enfield became an Urban District and elected its first School Board, followed by the building of new elementary schools. The Board continued to function until the responsibility for primary education was accepted by the Urban District Council under the Education Act of 1902.

At Edmonton too, development was rapid. In the first half of the century it became a noted educational centre and in 1840 had no less than eleven boarding schools as well as several day schools. The population rose from 5,000 (including Southgate) in 1801 to 47,000 (excluding Southgate) at the century's end. In 1850 local government at Edmonton passed from the Old Vestry to the first local Board of Health and the Urban District Council in turn replaced this in 1894. Southgate was slower to develop and did not become a separate ecclesiastical parish until 1858. The 20th century saw the continued urbanisation of the area and was ushered in at Enfield by a ceremony with only one parallel in local history. In 1901 the accession of King Edward VII was proclaimed in Enfield Market Place and recalled the announcement in Elsynge Hall to Edward VI of his succession to the throne.

All three new North East Middlesex constituencies contained large populations when they were first established but by 1901 they had each increased by fifty percent to become amongst the biggest in the country. Electorates were rising with each successive year. The table indicates how they grew substantially between the General Elections of 1906 and January 1910. By comparison with the East End, North East Middlesex became seriously under-represented soon after the redistribution of 1885 had taken place.

General Election Results 1885-1910 - by % majority

Constituency	*1885*	*1886*	*1892*	*1895*	*1900*	*1906*	*1910 Jan*	*1910 Dec*
Enfield	*C15*	*C51+*	*C20*	*C100*	*C31*	*L06*	*C05*	*C04*
Hornsey	*C17*	*C100+*	*C36*	*C100*	*C100*	*C10*	*C16*	*C18*
Tottenham	*C9*	*C31*	*C17*	*C25*	*C25*	*L17*	*L02*	*L05*
C	*3*	*3++*	*3*	*3*	*3*	*1*	*2*	*2*
L	*0*	*0*	*0*	*0*	*0*	*2*	*1*	*1*

Key: Numbers indicate percentage majority of the votes cast in the election. 100 = unopposed; C = Conservative; L = Liberal; LU = Liberal Unionist (in alliance with the Conservatives) + Seats retained at By-elections.

Politics in North East Middlesex

As places like Tottenham and Edmonton became popular with working class owner-occupiers voting patterns started to be affected. After 1906 the Tory majorities in these seats were not as strong as they had been previously though they were by far the stronger of the two parties winning a total of 20 seats at General Elections as compared with only 4 for the Liberals, all elected in 1906 and 1910. The Tories also won by-elections at Hornsey and Enfield, on 19th July 1887 and 30th March 1889 respectively.

MPs for North East Middlesex

Enfield

Enfield was a Tory seat where the majority was only breached in 1906. Its first MP, born in 1841, was **Viscount Folkestone** (Conservative), the son of the 4th Earl of Radnor. He lived at Highworth near Swindon in Wiltshire, a county in which he held office as a magistrate and Deputy Lieutenant and served as MP for Wiltshire South between 1874 and 1885 when the seat was abolished. After transferring to Enfield he was appointed Treasurer of the Household, a post he held until 1892. Meanwhile he succeeded to the Earldom in 1889 triggering a by-election. He died in 1900.

Sir Henry Ferryman Bowles (Conservative) held the seat for his Party at the by-election and went on to serve until 1906. A lawyer by profession, he was born in 1858 and educated at Harrow School and Jesus College. In addition

MPs for North East Middlesex						
From	*at*	*To*	*Surname*	*First Names*	*Constituency*	*Party*
1885	*G*	*1889*	*Folkestone*	*Viscount William*	*Enfield*	*Conservative*
1889	*B*	*1906*	*Bowles*	*Sir Henry Ferryman*		*Conservative*
1906	*G*	*1910 (Jan)*	*Branch*	*James*		*Liberal*
1910(Jan)	*G*	*1918*	*Newman*	*John Robert Pretyman (Lt.Col)*		*Conservative*
1885	*G*	*1897*	*McGarel-Hogg*	*Sir James*	*Hornsey*	*Conservative*
1887	*B*	*1900*	*Stephens*	*Henry Charles*		*Conservative*
1900	*G*	*1907*	*Balfour*	*Charles Barrington*		*Conservative (Unionist)*
1907	*B*	*1916*	*Ronaldshay*	*Earl of (Lawrence Dundas)*		*Conservative*
1916	*B*	*1918*	*Jones*	*William Kennedy*		*Conservative*
1885	*G*	*1906*	*Howard*	*Joseph*	*Tottenham*	*Conservative*
1906	*G*	*1918*	*Alden*	*Sir Percy*		*Liberal*

NOTE: First returned at a B = By-election; G = General Election

to being a Barrister at the Inner Temple (1883) he was Chairman of the Edmonton Petty Sessions, a councillor and subsequently alderman of Middlesex. He was also a Deputy Lieutenant of the County and in 1926, after he retired from politics, its High Sheriff. In 1904 he was appointed Honorary Colonel of the 7th Battalion of the Middlesex Regiment. He lost his seat in 1906 and was out of the Commons until 1918 when he recaptured it, after major boundary changes made Enfield a borough constituency in 1918. He held it until 1922. He died in 1943.

James Branch JP (Liberal) was MP between 1906 and January 1910. Born at Bethnal Green in 1845, he was a boot maker with factories in Bethnal Green and Northampton. He was also a councillor on the LCC from 1889 until 1907 and was appointed a member of the Metropolitan Water Board in 1906. After his defeat he stood again in the General Election of December 1910 but lost and retired from Parliamentary politics. He died in 1918.

Lieutenant-Colonel John Robert Pretyman Newman (Conservative), an Irishman, took the seat from Branch in January 1910 and retained it until 1918 when he stood for nearby Finchley where he was the MP until 1923. Son of a landowner from County Cork where he was born in 1871 at Newbury Manor, the family home, he married firstly the daughter of the Archbishop of Dublin but she died in 1896. His second wife also died and he married for a third time in 1945, two years before his own death. He was educated at Charterhouse School and Trinity College, Cambridge following which he went into the Army, becoming a Captain in the 5th Battalion, the Royal Munster Fusiliers and subsequently a Major in the 17th Battalion of the Middlesex Regiment. He was a magistrate in Ireland and a Deputy-Lieutenant of Cork during a period of enormous tension in that country and was the County's High Sheriff in 1898. He was strongly in favour of Imperial Preference and first contested a Parliamentary seat in 1906, when he was defeated at South Eastern Essex. Although a Tory he supported a reformed House of Lords. He died in 1947.

Hornsey

Hornsey was a Tory stronghold throughout this period. The first MP was **Sir James McGarel-Hogg** (Conservative) who served until his elevation as the First Baron Magheramorne in 1887. Although he was only Hornsey's MP briefly he had served for many years in previous Parliaments as MP for Bath from 1865 to 1868 and for Truro in Cornwall from 1871 to 1885. Born in 1823 his father was Sir James Weir, himself a former MP for Beverley (East Riding), and for Honiton (Devon). Weir had Indian interests and James was born in Calcutta, though he was educated in England, at Eton and Christ's Church Oxford. He entered the Army and served in the First Life Guards from 1843 until 1859 by which time he had attained the rank of Lieutenant Colonel. After losing his seat at Bath he was appointed Chairman of the Metropolitan Board of Works before resuming his Parliamentary career at Truro. He died in 1890.

Henry Charles Stephens (Conservative) succeeded McGarel-Hogg at the 1887 by-election caused by his elevation. Educated at University College London, Stephens was the owner of an ink manufacturing business in Aldersgate Street and was 46 at the time of his election. He entered the political arena as an Alderman of Middlesex County where he was also a magistrate. He took an interest in local Government and wrote a book entitled "Parochial Self-Government in Rural Districts". He was a strong supporter of the British Empire and of the Union of Church and State. He retired in 1900 when the seat was won by Charles Barrington Balfour (Conservative), born in 1862 at Kelso in the Scottish

Borders. Educated at Eton and Sandhurst, he entered the Scots Guards in 1881, serving in Egypt where he was decorated, and in 1900 was promoted to the rank of Captain in the Royal Guards Regiment. His family and political roots remained in Scotland where he was a Roxburghshire magistrate, a Berwickshire Deputy-Lieutenant and County Councillor. He contested the Parliamentary constituency of Roxburghshire in 1885 and Berwickshire in 1892, 1894 and 1895 and between 1894/5 was President of the National Union of Conservative Associations in Scotland. He came south in 1899 to contest Southport before finally securing election at Hornsey, which he held until his retirement in 1907. He died in 1918.

His successor at the by-election following his resignation was **Lawrence John Lumley Dundas**, the Earl of Ronaldshay, (Conservative), born in 1876 the son of the Marquis of Zetland. This Harrow and Trinity – educated aristocrat was a Captain in the First North Riding Volunteer Artillery and served as aide de camp to the Earl of Curzon when he was Viceroy of India. He became Chairman of the Central Asian Society[61] and wrote several books about colonial life in the Far East. He was active in the Tory Party in the country being both a member of the Grand Council of the Primrose League and of the National Union of Conservative Associations. He first stood for Parliament unsuccessfully at Richmond (Yorkshire) in 1906 but was returned for Hornsey the following year. On being appointed Governor of Bengal in 1916 he resigned his seat returning to Britain in 1922 when he entered a non-active phase in his political life. He wrote two biographies, the first of Lord Curzon in 1928 and the second in 1932 of Lord Cromer and in the meantime succeeded to the title of the Second Marquis of Zetland in 1929. From 1928 to 1931 he was a Steward of the Jockey Club and in 1930 became President of the Society for the Study of Religions, a role he fulfilled until 1951; in 1930 he also became Chairman of the National Trust, serving until 1945. Meanwhile, in 1935 he was appointed Secretary of State for India by Stanley Baldwin and held the post until the resignation of the next Prime Minister, Neville Chamberlain, in 1940. He died in 1961.

William Kennedy Jones (Conservative) won the 1916 by-election created by Ronaldshay's move to Bombay. Jones was the son of a Northern Irishman from Newry County Down but was himself born in 1865 in Glasgow where he was also educated at the High School. From there he went into journalism, initially on the local "Glasgow News" transferring in time to Birmingham where he worked for the Mail, the Sun and the local Evening News of which he was News Editor from 1894 until 1900. He subsequently went into business establishing a publication called Fleet Street and Downing Street and in 1912 became Chairman of Waring and Gillow, furniture manufacturers. During the First World War he served as Director-General for Food Economy from 1917 to 1919 and was, with Lord Northcliffe, a co-founder of the Daily Mail. He first entered active politics at a by-election held at Wimbledon in 1916 when he stood as an Independent with the support of the Union of Attested Married Men[62] but was elected for Hornsey later the same year. he died in 1921.

Tottenham

When first created, Tottenham was a Tory seat but after the 1906 General election, the balance swung towards the Liberals who held the seat until the end of the First World War. Its first MP was **Joseph Howard** (Conservative) who was the son of a surgeon whose mother came from a banking family whilst he himself studied law at University College London and became a barrister. He took silk in 1856 but also had links with the Iron Tube trade. He was a Middlesex magistrate and a Lieutenant of the City of London. He died in 1923, aged 88.

Sir Percy Alden MP
© National Portrait Gallery
Walter Stoneman 1916

Sir Percy Alden (Liberal) won the seat in 1906 and held it until 1918 when he stood for the new North division losing it to the Conservatives. He subsequently joined the Labour Party in whose cause he won Tottenham South in 1923, until the Tories were returned again in 1924. Born in Oxford in 1865, Alden was educated at Balliol College and became a journalist, in 1891 founding the non-conformist Mansfield House University Settlement, a charity set up to further the educational needs of the poor in Bethnal Green. He was Warden for a decade with main concerns for the social and economic conditions of the poor. He wrote about the problem of unemployment. He was Honorary Secretary of the British Institute of Social Science[63] and of the Council of International Relations. He died in 1944, killed by a flying bomb.

61 Established in 1901 for those with an interest in Central Asia
62 Set up in 1916 to support the conscription of married men to the Army during the War.
63 Amongst other things it administered the Institute of Sociology, established in 1930 "to promote the study of Sociology and the sociological study of human communities; to encourage the use of such studies in education; and to advance the application of such studies to urban and rural development."

Chapter 4
Metropolitan Essex 1832 - 1918

Early History

The Roman Emperor Claudius staged a successful invasion of Britain in 43 AD when most of Essex was part of the territory of the Catuvellauni, an Iron Age tribe who had their capital at Camulodunum (Colchester). In 60 AD Boudicca, Queen of the Iceni tribe, led a revolt against the Romans. Colchester was burnt to the ground and the inhabitants massacred. This was followed by a march on London which she sacked before heading north along Watling Street to confront the Roman northern legions. After the revolt had been suppressed, in 61 AD, Colchester was rebuilt as a showpiece town, named Colonia Victricensis or City of the Victorious, this time with substantial walls as defences. The London road to Colchester passed through Essex. Many of the present day communities within what is now Greater London were established along it, including Stratford, West Ham, Ilford and Romford.

As the Romans withdrew their troops from the 4th century onwards, there was an increasing influence of Germanic peoples on aspects of life. Waves of Angles, Saxons, and Jutes settled, and Essex initially became the Kingdom of the "East Saxons". A unified East Saxon Kingdom probably emerged in the late 6th century (500-600 AD) out of a series of smaller territories such as the Rodings and Dengie. In the seventh century the kingdom probably extended as far as Middlesex and Surrey but around 700, Middlesex, Surrey and London were lost to the neighbouring kingdom of Mercia, and though Essex remained an independent kingdom, around 820 it was incorporated into Wessex. The kingdom was administered through a series of royal villas with a correlation with major Roman sites, and it is likely that some of the communications network represented by the Roman roads survived.

Following the Viking invasions of the Ninth Century Essex gradually fell under the influence of Dane Law and following the death of king Ethelred, Canute defeated King Edward II (Ironside) at Rochford to take control of the area in about 1020. The years following the Norman conquest saw the imposition of castles, as at Rayleigh and Castle Hedingham, and the 11th and 12th centuries saw the foundation of new towns, such as Braintree and Chelmsford founded by the Bishop of London in 1199 to capitalise on his manors' positions on communication nodal points.

Essex was then thickly wooded. The Royal Forest (remnants of which remain as Epping Forest) was not at all easy to penetrate. Communications were poor, and trade routes remained concentrated around the Roman road and the area's waterways. However, after the signing of Magna Carta by King John, he was also forced to sign a Charter of Forests paving the way for clearances, which created an altogether more agricultural landscape and economy. Deforestation resulted in Essex becoming the largest connected open space of level ground in Britain, with many water courses feeding the largely arable lands supplying London's markets. Nevertheless, the County's southern areas along the Thames estuary and the Lea mouth, which formed the county boundary with Middlesex, remained marshy and unhealthy. Essex was strategically important to London, and when it became necessary to defend it from the North Sea a Fort was built at Tilbury. In 1588 Queen Elizabeth I reviewed an Army assembled there to repel the Spanish Armada.

For administrative purposes the County historically was divided into twenty "Hundreds", of which four covered parts that are now within the Greater London Authority. These were: Becontree, based on present day Ilford; Chafford, centred on Upminster; Waltham Abbey, north of Chingford, and the Liberty of Havering-Atte-Bower, centred on Romford.

By the year 1700 it is estimated that the population of Essex was a little over 159,000 but a century later had risen to a quarter of a million and in 1831, just before the First Reform Act, the county's population was recorded as 317,233.

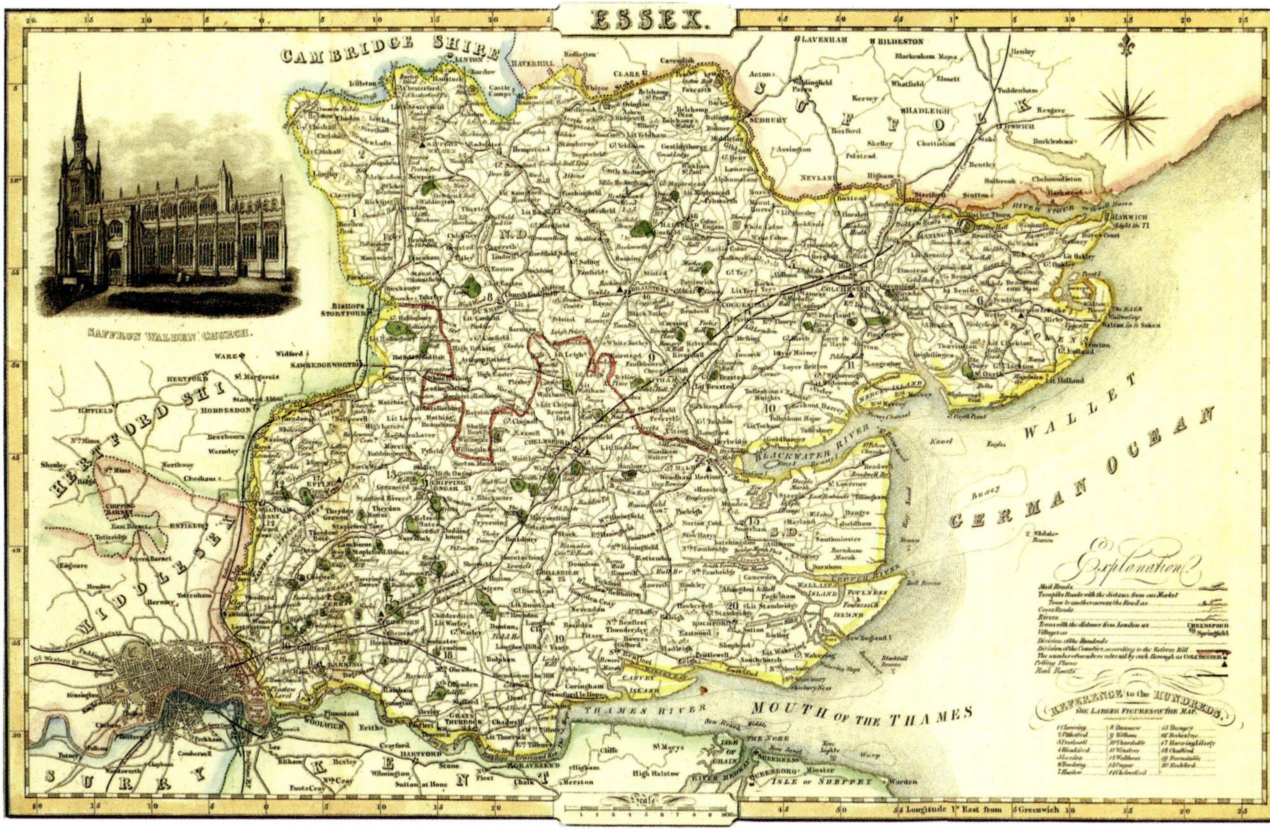

Pigot's map of 1840 shows the division of the County into two constituencies. Essex Southern is below the red line. It illustrates the county in relation to the developing metropolis to the west, and shows the first railway lines that would stimulate the growth of Metropolitan Essex within a few decades. At this early stage most development was taking place around Stratford and the Thames at Canning Town and Custom House.

Parliamentary Representation 1832-1885

Before 1832 Essex sent two MPs to the House of Commons, representing the whole County together, with three pairs of borough MPs representing: Colchester(from 1295); Maldon (from 1332), and Harwich (from 1640). None was within what we now define as the metropolitan area.

Essex Southern

At the time of the First Reform Act in 1832, the part of Essex that today comprises five London Boroughs was still a largely rural and agricultural area, but the County's representation was expanded by the creation of two separate geographical divisions. Greater London's electorates were contained within the new two-member county seat of Essex Southern, which then also included the area around Chelmsford, the Thames Estuary, and the North Sea coast as far as the Blackwater River near Maldon. Election results were declared at Chelmsford, but Romford, Billericay, Epping, Rochford and Maldon were also polling places. The fact that only one of these (Romford) was within what we today call London, indicates how sparse was the population of that part of Essex as recently as the 1830s. At the first General Election, after the passing of the First Reform Act, there were only 4,488 registered voters in the constituency, which contained a population of just over 150,000. This was some 17,000 fewer than lived in Essex Northern, which had 5,163 electors. However, by 1861 the population of the Southern constituency had increased to nearly 214,000, and the 1868 electorate was 7,127. Essex Northern was divided into rural North East and North West constituencies following the Second Reform Act (1867), whilst Southern Essex began to develop both industrial and suburban characteristics. The place of election also changed from Chelmsford to Brentwood, reflecting the new demographic profile of the area. There was an oddity. North Woolwich on the north bank of the Thames, a detached part of the Kent parish of Woolwich, remained in the Greenwich constituency. The redrawing of boundaries affected Essex Southern very little, the main change being the transfer of Epping and Harlow areas to the North West division, which included the village of Chingford.

The construction of docks, refineries, and sewer outfalls along the Thames Estuary east of the River Lea coupled with the building of strong flood defences, meant that marshland areas were reclaimed and urban development flourished. Further north, railway lines were constructed, the first of which was the Great Eastern, connecting London to Colchester, Ipswich, and Norwich. Stations were built in the London area at Stratford, Ilford, and Romford, where the development of the Essex suburbs began. By the 1880s, the population had increased further so that in the 1881 census, the constituency's was only 4,000 short of 300,000, with an electorate that had risen to nearly 18,000.

Essex Southern was a predominantly Conservative constituency throughout the period from 1832 to 1880 during which time there were twelve General Elections. Liberals were returned at only four. In 1868 the constituency's two MPs were both Liberals and in 1832, 1847, and 1857, the Party returned one but during the whole period twenty Tories were elected (including a June 1836 by-election).

MPs for Essex Southern 1832 - 1885

Parlia-ments	*at*	*Surname*	*First Names*	*Party*
1832-1837	*G*	*Dare*	*Robert Westley Hall*	*Conservative*
1832-1835	*G*	*Lennard*	*Sir Thomas Barrett*	*Liberal*
1835-1865	*G*	*Bramston*	*Thomas William*	*Conservative*
1837-1847	*B*	*Palmer*	*George*	*Conservative*
1847-1852	*G*	*Buxton*	*Sir Edward North*	*Liberal*
1852-1857	*G*	*Bowyer-Smijth*	*Sir William*	*Conservative*
1857-1859	*G*	*Wingfield*	*Richard Baker*	*Liberal*
1859-1865	*G*	*Watlington*	*John Watlington Perry*	*Conservative*
1865-1868	*G*	*Selwin-Ibbetson*	*Sir Henry John*	*Conservative*
1865-1868	*G*	*Gascoyne-Cecil*	*Lord Eustace Brownlow Henry*	*Conservative*
1868-1874	*G*	*Baker*	*Richard Baker Wingfield*	*Liberal*
1868-1874	*G*	*Johnston*	*Andrew*	*Liberal*
1874-1885	*G*	*Baring*	*Thomas Charles*	*Conservative*
1874-1885	*G*	*Makins*	*Colonel William Thomas*	*Conservative*

Notes: first returned at: B By-election, G General Election

The first two MPs for Essex South were **Robert Westley Hall Dare** (Conservative) and **Sir Thomas Barrett Lennard** (Liberal), both of whom were returned for the first time in 1832 but neither of who served for long. Lennard stood down at the 1835 election and although Dare once again topped the poll he died in 1837.

Dare who lived at Cranbrook, Ilford, was born Robert Hall , the son of a proprietor of the West India Company, established in the seventeenth century to develop and protect British colonial trade to what became known as the West Indies. He assumed the additional name of Dare upon his marriage to a woman of that name. In politics he was opposed to free trade and taxation of most kinds. By contrast Lennard was a radical who favoured the abolition of slavery, though he was a wealthy man too, the son of Lord Dacre, a Tithe owner with large estates in the Irish County of Monaghan. He remained MP for Essex Southern until his death in 1837.

At the 1835 election the Liberal candidate nominated to succeed Lennard was defeated by **Thomas William Bramston** (Conservative), albeit that he described himself as a Liberal Conservative, giving his support on critical motions to the government led by Lord Palmerston. He was born in 1796 and educated at All Souls College, Oxford where he obtained a BA in 1819, and an MA four years later. He lived at Skreens, west of Chelmsford, was a patron of two livings, and a Deputy-Lieutenant of Essex. Dare remained MP for thirty years, and retired in 1865.

Following Dare's death, **George Palmer** (Conservative), an East India trader, was elected at a by-election in 1836 and held his seat until 1847, when he retired. He had unsuccessfully contested the Durham borough seat of South Shields in 1832. A brother of a Governor of the Bank of England, he commanded a Corps of the Yeomanry, which he himself had raised. Politically his main interest was agricultural protection, and he was also actively involved in the founding of the National Lifeboat Institution, formed in 1824. He lived at Nazeing Park near Epping, and died in 1853.

Sir Edward North Buxton (Liberal) was elected in 1847 but served only one term being defeated in 1852. From

Cromer in Norfolk, he was born nearby at Earlham in 1812, and as a politician described himself as a "moderate Liberal". Following his defeat he sought another seat and, although absent in Nice at the time, was returned for Norfolk East in 1857 but died the following year. One of his sons was returned as an MP for Walthamstow (Essex South West) when it was created in 1885.

Sir William Bowyer–Smijth (Conservative) was the man who defeated Buxton in 1852, though he too went down to defeat five years later. Born in 1814, he was the son of the Reverend Sir Edward, and the owner of four livings including the manor of Theydon in Essex. Educated at Eton and Trinity College, Cambridge, he was a protectionist who first contested Essex South in 1847. He was MP for only one Parliament and died many years later, in 1883.

The man who defeated Smijth in 1857 was MP for Essex Southern for two periods.

As **Richard Wingfield** (Liberal) he served first only briefly until 1859, when he was defeated, and having in the same year assumed the additional name of Baker, he was returned as Wingfield – Baker in 1868, to be defeated again in 1874. The son of William of Orsett Hall near Grays, a former MP for Bodmin in 1813, he was educated at Rugby and Christ Church Oxford, where he gained a BA in 1827. He was Secretary to the Lord Chancellor (Lord Cottenham) but was also a JP and Deputy-Lieutenant for Essex. He favoured direct taxation but not income tax and in 1869 voted to disestablish the Irish Church. He died in 1880.

Orsett Hall near Grays in Essex was the home of Richard Wingfield MP. It burned down in 2007, but was rebuilt entirely in the style of the original.

© Rjm at sleepers at en.wikipedia

John Watlington Perry Watlington (Conservative) was born John Perry in London in 1823 and married a vicar's daughter. Educated at Harrow and Trinity College, Cambridge, he assumed the additional name of Watlington on his marriage. He was appointed a Deputy-Lieutenant of Essex in 1859, the year of his election and the following year he became a Major in the West Essex Yeomanry, whilst at the same time acquiring the manor of High Laver, a village in Epping Forest, for the sum of £12,050. He retired at the 1865 election when two new Tories were returned. The Church was his passion, however, and he paid for the restoration of local chapels in the area. He also established a reformatory school for young people and was the benefactor of a number of almshouses in Essex. He is believed to have lived until about 1884 when the manor was sold.

Sir Henry John Selwin-Ibbetson (Conservative) was born in 1826 as Ibbetson-Selwin and lived in Harlow. He assumed the reverse order of names as his father had done when he acquired the manor farm estate of Rookwood in 1817, interestingly from a man named William Perry, possibly John Perry's father. Rookwood was formerly part of the manorial estates of the Abbess of Roding, and was only a mile or so from High Laver where his predecessor was Lord of the manor. However, the Abbess manors appear to have been broken up in the eighteenth century, when Rookwood became a farm of about 250 acres. Before his election, Henry had previously but unsuccessfully contested Ipswich, in 1857 and 1859, and only sat for Essex South between 1865 and 1868, when he transferred to the newly created Essex North West constituency. He continued to represent Essex North West until 1885 when he sat for Epping, a seat he held until he was created Baron Rookwood in 1892. From 1874-8 he was Under Secretary at the Home Office, and then Financial Secretary to the Treasury until 1880. From 1885-92 he was the Second Church Commissioner, and he died in 1902.

Lord Eustace Brownlow Henry Gascoyne-Cecil (Conservative) was the second surviving son of the second Marquis of Salisbury who also owned lands in Abbotts Roding. Eustace was born in London in 1834, educated at Harrow and the Royal Military College at Sandhurst, becoming an Ensign in the 43rd Light Infantry in 1851, but retiring from the Army in 1863 as Captain and Lieutenant-Colonel in the Coldstream Guards. He was MP for Essex South from 1865 to 1868 when, along with Selwin-Ibbetson, he transferred to the newly created Essex North West, which he too represented until the next re-distribution in 1885, when he retired from politics. The owner of property in Lytchett

Matravers, Dorset, and in Eaton Square, London. He died in 1921.

Andrew Johnston (Liberal) was elected with Richard Wingfield – Baker in 1868 and served until 1874 when both men were defeated. Born in London in 1835 when his father was an MP for the Scottish Burgh constituency of St. Andrews, he was educated at Rugby School and University College, Oxford. He became a partner in Morewoods, an iron manufacturing company

Thomas Charles Baring (Conservative) lived at Loughton, Essex but was the son of the Bishop of Durham and a nephew of Lord Northmonk. Born in Oxford in 1831, he was educated at Harrow and Wadham College Oxford and was later a Fellow at Brasenose College. He took his BA in 1852 and MA in 1855. He became a banker in New York, where he married an American woman, and was a founding partner of Baring Brothers, Bankers of London and Liverpool. This was the firm that crashed so spectacularly about a century later, following the activities of the so-called rogue trader Nick Leeson. Baring was a JP in Essex, Middlesex and London and between 1885 and 1887 sat on the Royal Commission on Loss of Life at Sea, appointed under the chairmanship of the Earl of Aberdeen to 'inquire into the extent and causes of the loss of life at sea' following on from the Commission on Unseaworthy Ships that had reported in 1874. He was MP for Essex Southern from 1874 to 1885 when he unsuccessfully contested the new Walthamstow (South Western Essex) constituency. However, in 1887 he was elected MP for the City of London where he sat until his death in 1891. (See Middlesex Chapter Three).

Colonel William Thomas Makins (Conservative) was returned in 1874 alongside Baring and remained the MP until 1885 when redistribution occurred and he was elected for South East Essex. However, in 1886 he transferred to Walthamstow (South West Essex) which he represented until his retirement in 1892. Earlier he had contested Kidderminster (Worcestershire) unsuccessfully in 1868. Born in 1840 at Woodhouse, a district of Leeds, he was educated at Harrow and Trinity College, Cambridge where he gained his BA in 1861 and MA four years later. Meanwhile, in 1862 he was admitted to the bar of the Middle Temple and also became a JP in both Essex and Middlesex. Later he was a Deputy Lieutenant of Essex and sat on the Court of Lieutenancy for the City of London. In 1874 he was made Honorary Colonel Commanding of the Royal Artillery's 2nd Volunteer (Essex) Brigade's East Division and also enjoyed a career in business. He was a Governor of the Gas Light and Coke Company and a Director of the Great Eastern Railway Company of which he was for a while Deputy Chairman. He was knighted in 1902 and died in 1906.

Parliamentary Representation 1885-1918

When the 1884 Representation of the People Act was passed it had a significant impact on the representation of Southwest Essex. New constituencies were established and contested for the first time at the 1885 General Election. These primarily comprised two industrial and dockland communities in West Ham and two more that were suburban and rural in character, one based on Romford and another on Walthamstow. In addition the county divisions of Epping, Chelmsford and Essex South Eastern (or Tilbury as it was also called) incorporated some districts that are part of London today. There was also the continuing oddity in that North Woolwich, on the north bank of the Thames just east of Silvertown remained a detached part of Woolwich in Kent.

Chelmsford

Primarily focused on the county town of Essex, this county division included Ardleigh Green, Corbet's Tey, Cranham, Emerson Park, Squirrel's Heath and Upminster.

Epping

The county division of Epping included Chingford parish.

Essex South Eastern

Covering the Thames Estuary from Southend westward. This county seat included Rainham, Wennington and Ockendon. It was alternatively named the Tilbury division of Essex.

West Ham (2 seats – North and South)

Despite its late Nineteenth Century importance as the main London Docks, West Ham's origins were deeply embedded in English history. The name "Hamme" was first found in the area in 958 AD. Its Saxon name had many

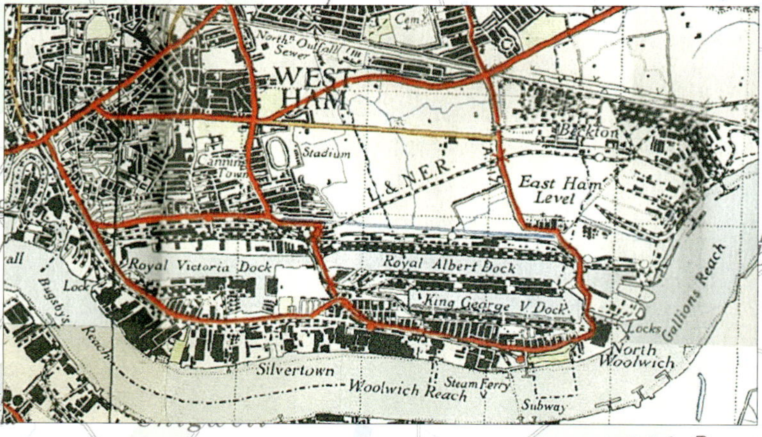

Left: *The river facilitated the dockland, which was served by ships to all parts of the world. Railways grew in profusion to serve the docks, the industries nearby, and to meet the needs of the people who needed to travel to and from their work in them. All around the population increased greatly during the period described in this chapter. This section of the One Inch Ordnance Survey map dates from just after 1921, and shows the extent of the docks and industry at Silvertown - West Ham South Constituency.*

Ordnance Survey Crown Copyright

Below: *Plashet Rd in Upton, was the boundary between the North and the South Constituencies of West Ham in 1885.* **John Nelson**

Below: *Mr & Mrs Sainsbury founded their famous grocery firm in 1869, and it has grown steadily since then to become a household name. This view of 1905 shows the branch in Romford, already one of many. It opened for business in 1902. There is still a store in Romford today.*

© Sainsbury Archive Museum in Docklands

Above: *This picture shows the typical standard of housing that was built in the Walthamstow Constituency between 1885 and 1918. Those depicted here are in Ruckholt Road, Leyton and were built primarily to serve the workforce in these parts, much of which was enfranchised at this time. The similarity with housing in Upton (above) is marked.* **Gordon Rushton**

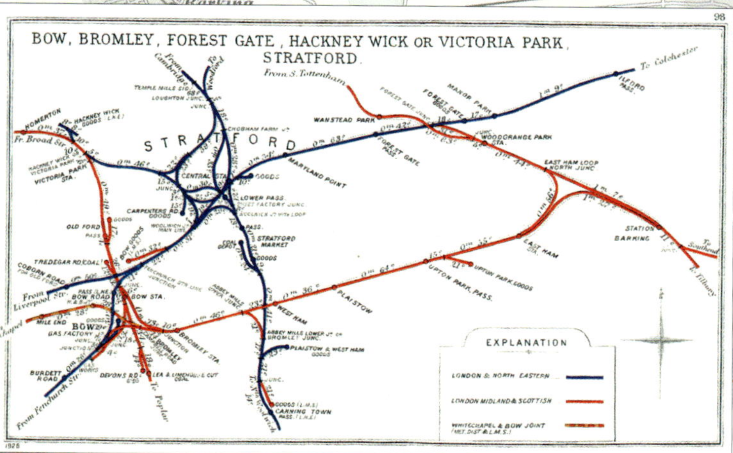

Left: *The railway network around Bow and Stratford became very dense. Much of the freight traffic to and from the docks used these tracks, and there had to be access to lines leading in all directions on to the network. There are many passenger stations shown on this map, as the railways were also used extensively by people travelling to and from their employment. The map was issued by the Railway Clearing House, to allow accurate charging of distances for goods.*

Constituency boundaries are shown in red. The grey shading represents the rapid eastward spread of the built up area, shown here in this map representing the period from 1885 to 1918. For comparison, the yellow tint indicates the extent of urbanisation today. On the map most of the railways have been built. The Tube and Underground extensions have yet to be made, as the electric railway is in this period a new concept. As elsewhere, mobility of population now becomes established and the demand for transport gradually predicates its provision. Before this period, the opposite was the case. Note the plentiful presence of green spaces in Essex, aside from the open spaces used for agriculture. Even when suburbia spread far further east , the green spaces have been preserved. As the grey shading expands to meet today's boundaries, representation required to be increased to keep pace, and as the book unfolds this process will be described further.

meanings, including "enclosure; land hemmed in by water; land in a river bend, or land on higher ground". "Westhamma" first appeared in 1186. By the Nineteenth Century "West Ham" was a large parish that extended from the boundaries with Leyton and Wanstead in the north as far south as the River Thames between the River Lea and East Ham, which was separate. In 1871 the parish had a population of 62,919 but the largest concentration was in Stratford. Only 7,928 lived in West Ham itself, which had never been a place of much consequence recording only 700 dwellings as recently as 1762. Despite this it seems to have been a prosperous area. Two thirds of its houses were described as mansions and one third as cottages suggesting a merchant population with probable business interests in the City of London.

Separated by the river Lea from the Middlesex parishes of Poplar, Bromley, Bow and Hackney, the West Ham of 1885 was a collection of former villages that, even then, were only just being developed. The building of railways had stimulated residential and industrial development whilst the new Victoria and Albert Docks in the south of the parish also had an impact. The most built-up districts were Stratford, Maryland and Forest Gate, each of them in the grip of a building boom brought on by the opening of railway stations on the Great Eastern Railway close to the Romford Road. Stratford was then the largest town in Essex and the population of its Langthorne ward was three times that of West Ham itself, a far cry from the Stratford of old when, in 1135, Cistercian Monks had established an Abbey where the road from London divided in the directions of Leyton and Romford. Close to the River Lea with a crossing to adjoining Bow and only five miles or so from the City of London it was a prime site in the Nineteenth Century to construct a massive complex of new railway lines, designed then to convey freight traffic. Stratford quickly became a large heavy industrial site housing all manner of trades and manufacture necessary to sustain London. Stratford New Town was actually built by the GER Company and was originally known as Hudson Town after the Railway King himself, George Hudson, who was also closely associated with the North Eastern Railway and was both a Lord Mayor of York and an MP for Sunderland.

The areas adjoining the railway provided the principal electorates in a **West Ham North** constituency that extended broadly on a northeast to southwest axis from Manor Park Cemetery to Mill Meads by the River Lea. Its northern boundary with a new Romford constituency was mainly with Wanstead parish although at its western end it adjoined Leyton parish in the Walthamstow division where Temple Mill Lane (just north of Stratford Marsh, the site for the 2012 Olympics) formed the boundary. Apart from a heavily built-up area along the West Ham Road to Stratford there was little residential development between Plashet Road (which formed the boundary with West Ham South) and Romford Road, which today contains the districts around West Ham Park, including North Upton. Nevertheless, West Ham proper was also developing an industrial character in which chemical, tar, soap, gas, candles and leather manufacture became prominent, as did distilling. At the time a commentator described it as very industrial and "pleasing to none of the senses". Despite West Ham's grimy characteristics the "pretty rural hamlet of Upton", as it was being described as recently as 1871, was on its doorstep just one mile up the road in the direction of Romford. In fact in 1874 the Corporation of the City of London secured Upton Park for the "crowded poor" of West Ham. A famous Victorian much concerned with prison reform, Elizabeth Fry, lived at a house in Upton Lane and just to its north east was Forest Gate, so called because it provided one entrance to the southern end of Epping Forest. This hamlet was included when the North constituency was created in 1885.

In the **West Ham South** constituency was Plaistow, another ward in West Ham parish. Lying just to the south of both West Ham and Stratford it had a population of 6,699 in 1871. The area between Plaistow and the River Thames began to develop significantly at this period, with the construction of the Victoria Docks and Canning Town, and a new food processing complex built on what had formerly been marshland where the Lea joined the River Thames. It was also the site at which the Great Metropolitan Sewer entered the Thames. In 1871 the population of Canning Town was 7,874, bigger than Plaistow itself and West Ham proper. It was an area transformed from rural to industrial almost overnight with a huge influx of labourers who lived in the mean tenements that constituted the housing put up for them. Despite these developments, most of the constituency initially comprised of fields, even though the Royal Docks consumed large tracts of land near the Thames as far east as Silvertown. The principal electorates in 1885 were Plaistow and Canning Town, which was an isolated but concentrated community, sandwiched between Custom House and the Barking Road connecting it to Plaistow. The area south of Upton Park was largely undeveloped as was the area north of the Docks, which today represents most of Custom House. The area between the Lea and Plaistow village was mostly agricultural.

West Ham's population growth in the late nineteenth Century was very rapid indeed. By 1901 the new County Borough had grown to 267,358 (over four times bigger than it had been in 1871) and its allocation of only two Parliamentary seats quickly fell below what was justified, although it was not until 1918 that this was remedied. The population of West Ham North rose in the decade after 1891 from 92,123 to 105,791 whilst West Ham South grew from 112,780 to 161,639. The electorates in 1906 were 15,101 and 22,753 respectively.

Romford (1 seat)

East Ham Borough had a recorded population of 96,018 in 1901 but no separate representation, it having been included in the new Romford constituency of which it formed the largest part. Romford was an old Essex market town at the centre of the former Hundred of Havering, the name of which derives from the Royal Liberty of Havering - Atte - Bower, to which Edward IV granted a charter in 1465. The Liberty was a very important unit of administration with its own High Steward and the control of local Justices. Prior to 1272 when it was called "Hauering" the Normans knew the area as "Haueringas" meaning, "Settlement of the family or followers of a man called "Haefer". Less than a hundred years ago Havering was still a scattered group of small towns and villages, strung across a landscape of open fields set in the heart of the countryside, with Romford at its centre.

The constituency officially comprised part of the Sessional Division of Becontree and the Liberty of Havering-atte-Bower, holding within its boundaries the area covered by present-day East Ham (except North Woolwich) and the London boroughs of Barking & Dagenham, together with most of Redbridge (though not Woodford which was placed in Walthamstow) and Havering (except those communities that were incuded in Chelmsford, and Tilbury see above). It therefore including Ilford, Wanstead, Barkingside, Hornchurch and Harold Hill. The fact that East Ham was the Romford constituency's largest centre of population demonstrates how most of this area of present day London was even then largely rural and undeveloped.

Romford, though was historic. Once the Roman staging post of Durolitum on the road between London and Colchester, major transport routes had always governed its economy. The Middle Ages saw the growth of this hamlet to a market town. In 1187 it was known as "Romfort", which meant "wide or spacious ford". The leather industry, which originated in nearby Hornchurch, found a ready market in the number of travellers using the old Roman road and in 1247 Henry III gave instructions to the Sheriff of Essex to hold a market every Wednesday, and this market still exists today.

After 1850 Romford's growth was rapid, spurred by the arrival of the Eastern Counties Railway in 1839. Originally designed with freight traffic in mind, this line soon saw an increase in passenger trains and the age of the commuter dawned. In 1871 Romford was a compact town with a population of 6,355 in a parish that was home to 8,239 whilst to the south, Hornchurch, known locally as "the Village", had a population of 2,476. As late as the 1870s Romford was still a centre for agricultural industries.

The population of neighbouring Great Ilford (a ford of the River Roding) was 3,689 in 1871 whilst Wanstead with Snaresbrook had a population of 5,119. To the southwest Barking had a population of 5,766 but the wider parish recorded 12,523. The Bishop of London had established an Abbey for nuns there as early as 670 AD. On the east bank of the Roding estuary (known as Barking Creek), the town became a small fishing port and harboured barges plying their horticultural trade between Essex and the London markets. Around the 1870s a huge outfall for the Northern Main Drain was constructed at Barking.

Dagenham with Becontree had a population of 2,879 in 1871. The area was prone to flooding of the Thames and over the centuries there had been occasions when the waters breached the sea defences causing catastrophic damage. The marshes closest to the Thames were eventually drained successfully in the 1700s although a lake known as Dagenham Breach remained. In 1864 a company was formed to convert the lake into a new dock that would take the world's largest shipping. The money ran out in 1866 but in the following Century the project was realised as part of the construction of the Ford Motor Plant on the reclaimed land. This was to become the major employer in this area of East London and sparked a massive development of workers' housing in Dagenham.

East Ham parish extended from Little Ilford in the north to North Woolwich (exclusive) on the River Thames but included some elements of both Forest Gate hamlet and Victoria Docks. In 1871 the parish had a population of only 4,334 of who 2,233 lived in East Ham itself. It was still a mostly agricultural area of market gardens growing produce such as onions and potatoes, which were sent by Thames barges from Barking Creek to London. Within thirty years population had risen to over 96,000. Signs of industry began to appear in the last third of the nineteenth Century as evidenced by the construction in 1869 at the Barking Parish village of Beckton (a recipient of sea-born coal from North East England) of the Chartered Gas Company, which supplied gas to the City of London and the West End. Close by were the hamlets of Plashet and Greenstreet.

After its creation in 1885 its population continued to grow. By 1901 the combined population of the Romford Urban and Rural Districts was over 32,000 having risen from less than 7,000 in 1834. The Parliamentary constituency, however, was much bigger. In the same year it was 217,085, which meant that since 1891 it had grown by a massive 114,539 people, mostly in East Ham. In 1891 Romford was eleventh in terms of its population size amongst English constituencies despite its 103,546 population being nearly 83,000 fewer than Newcastle-upon-Tyne borough, which was, then the largest. Also bigger were northern industrial boroughs including Oldham, Blackburn, Bolton, Preston and Sunderland as well as the south coast resort of Brighton. Neighbouring West Ham South was also just ahead but by 1901 Romford was the most populous Parliamentary constituency in Britain, larger by nearly 2,000 than Newcastle, which was a two-member division. Romford also had the largest electorate of any constituency in the country. In 1906 it was 45,579, some 8,670 greater than second placed Newcastle. By 1910 Romford's had grown even higher to reach 53,000, nearly 14,500 higher than Newcastle's.

Walthamstow (1 seat)

By then another Essex constituency established in 1885 was catching Romford up. Walthamstow in the south west of the old County of Essex became a constituency for the first time, officially comprising the parishes of Leyton, Walthamstow and Woodford. Its name derives from the Norman place name "Wilcumestow" meaning a "place where guests are welcome" or "holy place of a woman called Wilcume". Ralph de Toni, Walthamstow's first Norman Lord, inherited the Manor through his wife Alice, descendent of Waltheof, who held it at the time of Edward the Confessor. The Tonis held the manor called Walthamstow-Toni until 1309. The manor passed to the Earls of Warwick, until it was forfeited in 1471 by the death of Richard, Earl of Warwick at the Battle of Barnet.

Leyton, a town that by 1901 had a recorded population of just over 95,000 comprised most of the electorate. Yet only 30 years earlier Walthamstow parish and Leyton were of a similar, though smaller size. Then the town area had a population of only 5,717 and adjacent St James (between Leyton and Walthamstow) housed another 2,323. St John's was home to 1,915 more and St Peter's to 1,137. In the intervening years the railway lines in the area stimulated substantial housing and industrial development that led to a massive increase in the population. This occurred initially at Leyton, the nearer point to London. From the 1870s the local railway stations became surrounded by endless fields of regimented, plain, two- and three-storey terraces, whose occupants were typically skilled artisans, policemen and firemen, railway engineers or gaffers in the gas works; men who had the security and income to allow them to rent or even to buy a place of their own an half-hour's train ride from work.

In the 1880s these towns, which included Leytonstone, were among the top four fastest growing in the country though Woodford with a population of only 4,609 was much smaller. Woodford Manor had been given to the Abbey of Waltham Holy Cross by King Harold and by 1871 still only comprised four separate clusters of housing; Church End (the town proper), Woodford Green, Woodford Wells and Woodford Bridge (over the River Roding). Overall between 1891 and 1901 the constituency's population increased from 101,236 to 185,549 with most of the growth occurring in and around Walthamstow. The seat rose in rank from fourteenth to fifth in population size whilst its electorate reached 35,321 in 1906 and by 1910 grew further to 39,117 making it second in England only to Romford.

Constituency Populations and Electorates

In summary Essex Southern, which had started with a population of 150,000 when it was created as a much larger county constituency in 1832 had developed by 1885 into essentially four divisions covering the area that is today mostly within Greater London and which in 1891 had a combined population of 410,000, rising to 670,000 by 1901. By this time three of the four constituencies were in the top eight by size of population in England although of these West Ham South was only sixteenth in terms of its electorate, an indication of the more working class nature of its population compared with Romford and Walthamstow, the other two. West Ham North was smaller on both counts but was still amongst the largest. It ranked thirty-sixth in population but interestingly only at number one hundred in terms of its electorate, another indication of the working class nature of the borough's population. A summary of the populations and electorates of the four seats, together with a comparison with the Essex Southern county seat that preceded them, is as follows:

Constituency	1881 pop	1891 pop	1901 pop	1884 electorate	1906 electorate	1910 electorate	1906 electorate as % of pop
Romford		103,546	217,085		45,579	52,984	21
Walthamstow		101,236	185,236		35,321	39,117	19
West Ham N		92,123	105,719		15,101	15,661	14.3
West Ham S		112,780	161,639		22.753	26,682	14.1
Total	296,290	409,685	669,992	17,859	118,754	134,444	17.7
Essex Southern	296,290			17,859			6 (1884)
Electorate as % of equivalent population				6	17.7		17.7

Table source: F.H. McCalmont's Parliamentary Poll Book of British Election Results, 1832-1918, and author's calculations.

Whilst this table is most revealing of the population changes taking place at the time it also indicates something of the social composition of the electorates. It shows that at the time of the creation of these seats there was a reasonable balance in the distribution of populations between them and that each grew in the decade or so afterwards. However, the growth was extremely variable, with Romford growing the most. The social characteristics were also different. Romford had a far higher electorate as a percentage of its total population than did either of the West Ham seats reflecting its more middle class society. Walthamstow fell somewhere in between reflecting the mix of lower middle and skilled working class new housing that was then to be found in Leyton. Nevertheless there was a growing working class in all of them as industrial development took hold on London's eastern flank.

The Politics of Metropolitan Essex Between 1885 and 1918

The political impact of the expansion of the franchise and the number of seats in the area proved to be a benefit initially to the Liberals who in 1885 won all four seats. However, in 1886 they changed hands dramatically and mostly remained with the Conservatives until 1906 when a national swing occurred against them. Generally the seats with the most suburban characteristics (Romford, Walthamstow and West Ham North) swung between the two major Parties of that time depending on the national mood. West Ham South was an exception, developing working class-based radicalism from the moment that it was established. Nonetheless the Conservatives still managed to win the seat on three occasions but it was the new Labour Party, rather than the old Liberals, which gained a stranglehold from 1906 onwards. The Labour Party's majorities were substantial and their 34% margin of victory there in 1906 was the largest for any Party at any Parliamentary Election in an Essex-based London constituency during this period.

The table below shows the winning Party together with the percentage margin of victory over the opposition for each general election between 1885 and December 1910.

General Election Results 1885 to December 1910 - by % majority

Constituency	*1885*	*1886*	*1892*	*1895*	*1900*	*1906*	*1910 Jan*	*1910 Dec*
Romford	L 0.8	C 33	C 10+	C 12+	C 17	L 26	L 4	L 8
Walthamstow	L 2	C 26	C 10	C 20-	C 14	L 15	L 7+	L 9
West Ham N	L 9	C 10	L 0.4	C 7	C 23	L 15	L 7	L 7+
West Ham S	L 16	C 6	IndLab 13	C 9	C 12	Lab 34	Lab 26	Lab 33
C and LU	0	4	2+	4-	4	0	0	0
L	4	0	1	0	0	3	3+	3+
Lab	0	0	1	0+	0	1	1	1

Key: 100 - unopposed; C - Conservative; L - Liberal; LU Liberal Unionist (allied with Con); Lab - Labour
+ by-election won; - lost by defending party.

In total the Tories and their allies won sixteen seats, (two by-elections at Romford, once in April 1894 and then again on 1st February 1897) whilst the Liberals won seventeen (including a Lib-Lab by-election gain at Walthamstow in 1897; a win at West Ham North in 1911 and a win in the last by-election of the Parliament held at Walthamstow in 1910); whilst Labour won four (including the Independent Labour Party).

MPs for Metropolitan Essex, 1885 -1918

Romford (Essex South)

John Westlake QC (Liberal) was Romford's first MP in 1885 but was defeated a year later when he came third standing as a Liberal Unionist. Born at Lostwithiel (Cornwall) in 1828, he was educated privately and then at Trinity College, Cambridge, subsequently becoming a Fellow there. In 1854 he was admitted to the bar at Lincoln's Inn and took silk twenty years later, becoming a bencher in 1875. He retired from practice in 1882 but wrote several legal treatises including one on "Private International Law" and became a co-founder and editor of the "Revue de Droit International" (Brussels) as well as Vice President of the Institute of International Law. He was a radical who favoured MPs not having to swear an oath or affirmation and also strongly opposed the principle of heredity in the House of Lords. However, his entry into politics coincided with a period in which his Party was not very successful and after his defeat in 1886 he also lost at the subsequent election at Mid Cornwall, his home constituency. Nevertheless his legal career flourished and in 1888 he was appointed Professor of International Law at Cambridge University, a post he held until 1908. He died in 1913.

In 1886 Westlake and the official Liberal Party candidate were both defeated by **James Theobald** (Conservative) who refused to stand down in the face of Westlake's defection and who held Romford until his death in 1894. Living at Havering – atte – Bower at the time of his election, Theobald was born at Winchester in 1829 and educated at Trinity College, Oxford. He was an owner of large estates at Grays Thurrock in Essex where he was Lord of the Manor and was also a Deputy Lieutenant of the County. He had contested Romford unsuccessfully in 1885.

MPs for Metropolitan Essex, 1885 -1918

Parliaments	at	Surname	First Names	Constituency	Party
1886-1886	G	Westlake	John	Romford (Essex S)	Liberal
1886-1894	G	Theobald	James		Conservative
1894-1897	B	Wigram	Alfred Money		Conservative
1897-1906	B	Sinclair	Louis		Conservative
1906-1918	G	Bethell	Sir John Henry		Liberal
1885-1886	G	Buxton	Sir Edward North	Walthamstow (Essex SW)	Liberal
1886-1892	G	Makins	Colonel William Thomas		Conservative
1892-1897	G	Byrne	Edmund Widdrington		Conservative
1897-1900	B	Woods	Samuel		Liberal
1900-1906	G	Morgan	David John		Conservative
1906-1918	G	Simon	Major Sir John Allsebrook		Liberal
1885-1886	G	Cook	Edward Rider	West Ham North	Liberal
1886-1892	G	Fulton	James Forrest		Conservative
1892-1895	G	Grove	Thomas Newcomen Archibald		Liberal
1897-1906	G	Gray	Sir Ernest		Conservative
1906-1911	G	Masterman	Charles Frederick Gurney		Liberal
1911-1918	B	De Forest	LtCdr Maurice Arnold (Baron)		Liberal
1885-1886	G	Leicester	Joseph Lynn	West Ham South	Liberal
1886-1892	G	Banes	Major George Edward		Conservative
1892-1895	G	Hardie	(James) Keir		Independent Labour
1895-1906	G	Banes	Major George Edward		Conservative
1906-1918	G	Thorn(e)	William James (Will)		Labour

Notes: First returned at a: **B** By-election, **G** General Election

Alfred Money Wigram (Conservative) won the 1894 by-election caused by Theobald's death although his was a fairly short tenure as he resigned in 1897. He too lived at Havering - atte – Bower and was educated at Winchester. Born in 1856 he became Chairman of Reid's Brewery of Liquorpond Street, Gray's Inn Lane. He died in 1899.

Louis Sinclair (Conservative) won the 1897 by-election occasioned by Wigram's resignation and remained the MP until he was defeated in the landslide election of 1906.

Sir John Henry Bethell (Liberal) was MP between 1906 and 1918 having unsuccessfully contested the seat previously in 1894 and 1895. He was also unsuccessful at West Ham North in 1900. Born in 1861 he became a surveyor and was a director of Barclays Bank, the Warwick Estates Company and of the Royal Exchange Assurance Corporation. He was also Chairman of the British Land Company and of Frederick Hotels. A local Essex JP, he was twice Mayor of East Ham and of West Ham and lived at Wanstead. From 1918 to 1922 he was MP for East Ham North when he was made Baron Bethell. He died in 1945.

Walthamstow (Essex South West)

Sir Edward North Buxton (Liberal) was Walthamstow's first MP although he served only a year, retiring in 1886. He had previously contested Essex Southern unsuccessfully in 1880 and when he transferred to Suffolk North Western in 1886 he was defeated there too. Born in 1840 at Upton (West Ham), he was the third son of the former MP for Essex South (1847-52), also Sir Edward North Buxton, and was a member of the Company, Truman, Hanbury and Buxton. He was also a member of the London School Board, which he chaired from 1881 to 1885; was a "verderer" of Epping Forest concerning which he was author of an illustrated work. He was also the patron of the living of All Saints in Woodford, although this ownership of estates was held jointly with the Bishop of St. Albans. He was chairman of the Essex Quarter Sessions and an Alderman of Essex County Council. He died in 1924.

Colonel William Thomas Makins (Conservative), formerly the MP for Essex Southern between 1874 and 1885, was returned at Walthamstow in 1886, remaining MP until he retired in 1892. His full biographical details are covered earlier in this chapter (See Essex Southern 1832-85).

Edmund Widdrington Byrne (Conservative) won the seat again for the Tories in 1892 and held it until 1897 when he was made a High Court Judge at the Court of Chancery and had to resign the seat. Born at Islington in 1844, Byrne was the son of a Solicitor and was called to the Bar in 1887, becoming a QC the following year and also a bencher at Lincolns Inn. He was a founder member of the Bar Committee and subsequently of the General Council of the Bar. He died in 1904.

Samuel Woods (Liberal) who won the 1897 by-election as a Lib-Lab candidate when Byrne was made a High Court Judge sat for only three years when he was defeated. Born in 1846 in St. Helens, Lancashire, both his parents were coal miners and he too went down the pit but managed to obtain an education by attending a Night School run by a Baptist Minister. In 1878 he established the Lancashire Miners Federation of which he was the first President, also becoming Vice President of the Miners National Federation. He held the job until 1895 a year after he was elected Secretary to the Parliamentary Committee of the TUC, a post he held until 1905. In 1892 he was one of the first Labour MPs to be returned with Liberal support at Ince-in-Makerfield (Lancashire) and in 1895 he was also elected as a representative of Labour to the Ashton-in-Makerfield District Council. He was a radical politician who advocated an eight-hour working day for miners, Home Rule for Ireland and salaries for MPs. After his defeat at Walthamstow in 1900 he never resumed a Parliamentary career and died in 1915.

David John Morgan (Conservative) took the seat in 1900 and held it until 1906. An Essex man born in 1844 at Leytonstone, he later lived at Brentwood. He was educated at the Forest School in Walthamstow and at Vervey, Switzerland. He was in business as a Russian merchant and was chairman of the Surrey Commercial Docks as well as a Northampton Brewery. An Essex JP, County Council Alderman and verderer of Epping Forest, he was also a Deputy Lieutenant of the City of London and Chairman of the City of London Club. He died in 1918.

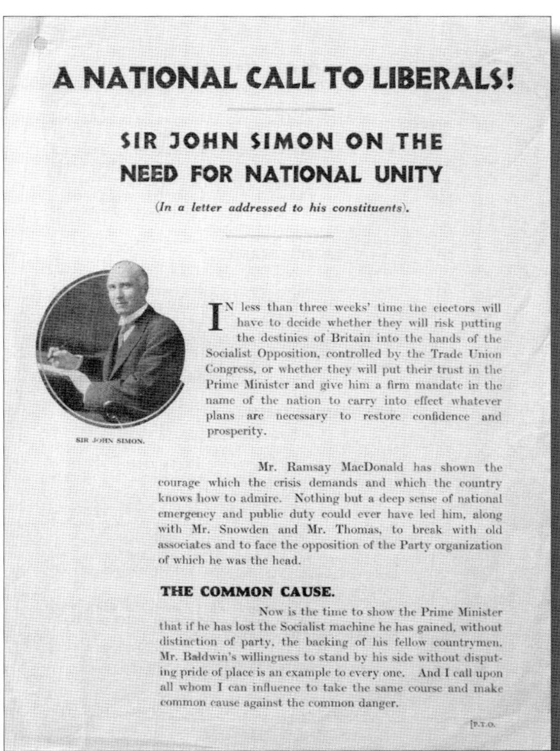

A NATIONAL CALL TO LIBERALS!

SIR JOHN SIMON ON THE NEED FOR NATIONAL UNITY

(In a letter addressed to his constituents).

SIR JOHN SIMON.

IN less than three weeks' time the electors will have to decide whether they will risk putting the destinies of Britain into the hands of the Socialist Opposition, controlled by the Trade Union Congress, or whether they will put their trust in the Prime Minister and give him a firm mandate in the name of the nation to carry into effect whatever plans are necessary to restore confidence and prosperity.

Mr. Ramsay MacDonald has shown the courage which the crisis demands and which the country knows how to admire. Nothing but a deep sense of national emergency and public duty could ever have led him, along with Mr. Snowden and Mr. Thomas, to break with old associates and to face the opposition of the Party organization of which he was the head.

THE COMMON CAUSE.

Now is the time to show the Prime Minister that if he has lost the Socialist machine he has gained, without distinction of party, the backing of his fellow countrymen. Mr. Baldwin's willingness to stand by his side without disputing pride of place is an example to every one. And I call upon all whom I can influence to take the same course and make common cause against the common danger.

[P.T.O.

Sir John Simon's 1931 election address.
People's History Museum, Manchester

Sir John Allesbrook Simon (Liberal) was the only son of a Congregational Minister and was born in 1873 at Manchester. He was educated at Fettes College in Edinburgh and at Wadham College becoming President of the Oxford University Union in 1896. In 1897 he became a Fellow of All Souls (Oxford) and married two years later, the same year he was called to the bar at both the Middle and Inner Temples. His wife died in 1902 and he pursued a legal career that included being a Counsel to an Arbitration Board set up to establish the boundary between Canada and Alaska. He first entered politics when he was elected at Walthamstow in 1906, became a barrister in 1908 and a Bencher two years later. He was Solicitor – General between 1910 and 1913 when he joined Asquith's Cabinet as Attorney – General, a post he held until 1915 when he became Home Secretary. He resigned when conscription was introduced in 1916, a factor which possibly contributed to his defeat in the 1918 General Election when he sought re-election at Walthamstow East. He was again unsuccessful at a by-election in the Spen Valley (West Riding of Yorkshire) in 1919. Although he was returned there in 1922, by then the Liberal Party was in general decline and he found himself opposing the first Labour Government and then the Conservatives. However, he started to move towards the Conservatives and during the General Strike in 1926 made several speeches in favour of the Government's position. From 1927-30 he chaired the Commission advising on a new Indian Constitution and in 1930-1 also chaired one set up to investigate the R101 airship disaster.

In 1931 he resigned from the Parliamentary Liberal Party because he disagreed with Lloyd-George's policy of co-operation with Labour and became a founder member and chairman of the Liberal National Organisation set up to support the MacDonald Government in measures to deal with the national economic crisis. He founded the Liberal National Party and in 1931 was re-elected at Spen Valley. In November Ramsey MacDonald appointed him Foreign Secretary. In Baldwin's Government he served as Home Secretary and Deputy Prime Minister from 1935 to 1937 and then as Chancellor of the Exchequer until May 1940 when he was one of the key ministers who persuaded Neville Chamberlain to resign as Prime Minister. He was elevated to the House of Lords to become Lord Chancellor in Churchill's Government, a post he retained until the Conservatives' defeat in 1945. He died in 1954.

West Ham North

Edward Rider Cook (Liberal) was the first MP for West Ham North though he sat only from 1885 to 1886. Born in London in 1836 and from a family that lived at Hatfield Peverel near Chelmsford, he was educated at the City of London School and University College, London where he obtained a silver medal in various aspects of chemistry. He became head of Edward Cook and Company, soap makers of Bow, and was also a director of the Annual Charcoal Company from 1883 to 1893 and of the London Fish Market Company between 1886 and 1898. A Fellow of the Chemistry Society he was made a member of the Metropolitan Board of Works in 1865 and was a conservator of the River Lea. A JP in Essex, Middlesex and London, he died in 1898.

Fulton James Forrest (Conservative), who failed to win the seat in 1885, was its MP from 1886 until 1892 when he was defeated. Born in 1846 in Ostend, Belgium, he was educated at Norwich Grammar School and London University where he obtained a BA in 1867 and LLB in 1873, the year after he was called to the bar at the Middle Temple. Author of a manual describing the constitution of the Hertfordshire Mint, he took silk the year he lost at West Ham and from 1900 to 1922 was Recorder for London. He was also a Lieutenant of the City of London. He died in 1925.

Thomas Newcomen Archibald Grove (Liberal), who contested Winchester unsuccessfully in 1886 won West Ham North in 1892 but lost it three years later although he subsequently returned to the Commons as MP for Northamptonshire South in 1906, having lost there in 1900. Following defeat in January 1910 he retired from politics. Born in 1855, he was educated privately and at Oriel College, Oxford, where he was awarded double honours. He studied law and was called to the bar at the Inner Temple but went on to found, own and edit the "New Review", a critical periodical whose contributors included the poet Tennyson. He lived at Chalfont St Giles in Buckinghamshire where he was also a magistrate, as he was in Essex. He died in 1920.

Sir Ernest Gray (Conservative) took the seat from Grove in 1895. Born in 1857, he was educated at St. John's College, Battersea, and became a teacher. He was active in the National Union of Teachers being its Education Secretary and in 1894 was President. He was also a Major in the Sixth Essex Regiment and from 1907 to 1925 was a member of the London County Council, of which he was Vice Chairman in 1915-16. He remained MP for West Ham North until 1906 when he was defeated and, having repeated the experience in January 1910, was adopted at the December election as the Tory candidate for Accrington. He was initially unsuccessful but at the 1918 election was returned there, remaining the Lancashire town's MP until 1922 when he lost yet again. He died in 1932.

Charles Gurney Masterman (Liberal), who was elected in 1906, was born in 1873, the son of a Sussex man and was educated at Weymouth College and Christ Church Cambridge where he was a Fellow and President of the Union in 1896. He became a writer for "The Daily News", the "Nation" and "Athenaeum" and was the author of several serious works. In 1903 he contested Dulwich unsuccessfully at a by-election but was returned for West Ham North in 1906, though he was unseated on petition in 1911 and later that year was returned at a by-election in Bethnal Green South West. From 1908 to 1909 he was Parliamentary Secretary to the Local Government Board and then an Under-Secretary at the Home Department until 1912 when he was appointed Financial Secretary to the Treasury, a post he held until 1914 when he was made Chancellor of the Duchy of Lancaster. However, at the by-election necessary to confirm his appointment he was defeated and after another failed attempt, at Ipswich later in the year, abandoned his Ministerial post in 1915. He subsequently contested the Stratford division of West Ham in 1918 but was unsuccessful and tried again in 1922 when he lost at Clay Cross (a Derbyshire mining constituency). He was finally re-elected in 1923 for the Rusholme division of Manchester, but there was another General Election the following year and he lost the seat, the defeat finally putting paid to his career. It may be fairly said that the electors of Bethnal Green destroyed a man who, had it not been for the necessity to seek re-election following a ministerial appointment, would probably have had a rather more distinguished political career. He was also overtaken by the decline of the Liberals and the rise of the Labour Party.

Lieutenant-Commander Maurice Arnold, Baron De Forest (Liberal), later Count Bendern, was the adopted son of Baron Hirsch. He was born in 1879 and received his education at Eton and Christ Church College, Oxford. In 1900 he was granted British citizenship. He unsuccessfully contested the Southport division of Lancashire in January 1910 but was returned at a by-election in 1911 following the disqualification of his predecessor. He enjoyed a military career in the Norfolk Artillery, the Prince of Wales Own Militia and the Staffordshire Yeomanry and was also a Lieutenant Commander in the Royal Naval Reserve. Heir to a banking fortune, he was the holder of the land speed record from 1903 to 1905 and a friend of Winston Churchill. He did not serve as an MP after 1918. He died in 1968.

West Ham South

Joseph Lynn Leicester (Liberal) was from 1885 to 1886 the first MP for West Ham South and was elected as a representative of Labour with Liberal support. He was born in 1825, the son of a Warrington glass blower, an occupation he himself took up aged ten. He had only an elementary education and later became Secretary of the Glassblowers' Friendly Society. He was also prominent in the temperance movement. He died in 1903.

Leicester was beaten in 1886 by **Major George Edward Banes** (Conservative) who was MP for the constituency for two periods, 1886-1892 and 1895-1906. He was born in 1829 at Chatham where his father was Surveyor of Iron Building at the Admiralty, and was also educated in the town and at Rochester High School. He became a wharfinger and bonded warehouseman trading as Banes, Noel and Company and as Colonial Wharves, Wapping. He founded the Third Essex Artillery Voluntary Corps in 1859 and retired as major in 1876. He was a West Ham magistrate and member of the West Ham School Board between 1874 and 1901. Although a Tory, he was in favour of free trade (unsurprising given his business interests) and was also unusual in favouring devolved self-government for the four home countries within the framework of a United Parliament. He retired as an MP in 1906 and died the following year.

(James) Keir Hardie (Independent Labour) who won West Ham South in 1892 was the founder of the modern Labour Party. Born in 1856, the illegitimate son of Mary Keir, a servant from Legbrannock in Lanarkshire who later married David Hardie and moved to Glasgow, he was brought up in poverty in the Scottish city and became a baker's boy, and was the only breadwinner in his family. He lost his job because he stayed at home to tend his dying brother and the family moved back to Lanarkshire where he went down the coalmines at the age of eleven. He was illiterate; having never attended school but nevertheless learned to read and write by the time he was seventeen and started to take an interest in wider affairs. He read about trade unionism and set one up at the pit at which he worked in 1879, leading a strike in 1880. He was blacklisted as a result of the strike and moved to Cumnock in Ayrshire where he became a journalist in 1882. A convert to Christianity, he began to combine an interest in radical politics with his religious beliefs. In 1886 he became the leader of the Ayrshire Miners' Union and later the Scottish Miners' Federation, editing a newspaper called "The Miner "which he established in 1887. Originally a Liberal, he became disillusioned with Gladstone's Government as a vehicle for serious reform for the working classes and became a Socialist. He stood for Mid Lanark in 1888 and although he came last, thus began a political career that was to become mould breaking in its outcome for British politics. His manifesto in the West Ham election of 1892 was for graduated income tax, pensions, equal rights for women, free schooling and the abolition of the House of Lords, all but one of which aims were subsequently achieved. He formed the Independent Labour Party in 1893, meaning that it was "independent" of the Liberal Party.

James Keir Hardie MP
Wikipedia

Hardie made an attack on the Royal Family in 1894 when he called on Parliament to send Royal condolences to the victims of a Welsh mining disaster as part of a message of congratulations on the birth of the Prince of Wales – the future Edward VIII – but this made him unpopular and he lost his seat in 1895. He unsuccessfully contested Bradford East and Preston in by-elections held in 1896 and 1900 respectively. He devoted his efforts to mobilising support for Socialism and in 1900, with others, he convened the Labour Representation Committee in London, the aim of which was to send Labour candidates to Parliament. He was himself elected at Merthyr Tydfil, a Welsh mining seat, at the 1900 general election and held it until his death in 1915. The LRC became the Labour Party in 1906 and at the election held that year it secured the election of 29 MPs. Hardie resigned the leadership of the Labour Party in favour of Arthur Henderson in 1908 and campaigned for women's rights and Indian independence in the last seven years of his life.

This house in Lawrence Rd, West Ham, was where Will Thorne lived when he was MP - right among his constituents in housing typical of the area. The building now carries a Blue Plaque in his memory. John Nelson

William James (Will) Thorne (Labour), who added the "e" to his surname in later life, was one of the first Labour MPs and instrumental in founding the Party. He took the seat in 1906 when Banes was defeated at the end of his second spell as the MP. Born in Birmingham, the son of a brickfield worker in 1857 he started work at the age of six for a rope and twine spinner and when his father died the following year, Thorne became the main breadwinner in the family, also working in the brick yards. In 1875 his mother married an alcoholic and William decided to leave home and go "on the tramp" working as a navvy. However, he returned to Birmingham to work at the Saltley Gas Works, met his wife and in 1882 moved to London to work at the Beckton Gas Works. He joined the Canning Town branch of the Social Democratic Federation and became its Secretary which necessitated his learning to read and write. He was taught to do so by Eleanor Marx, the youngest daughter of Karl Marx, the author of the Communist Manifesto. In 1889 he helped to set up the new Gasworkers and General Labourers Union and subsequently defeated Ben Tillet to become General Secretary. Tillet led a London Dock Strike in the same year and Thorne was active in supporting the strikers and raising money. After five weeks the dockers secured their demands. He became further embroiled in a series of industrial actions in the Gas industry and became a nationally known figure securing election to the Trade Union Congress in 1894. He remained a member of its Parliamentary Committee until 1934, the year he retired as General Secretary of his Union, and in 1912 was TUC President. He campaigned to get Keir Hardie elected at West Ham South in 1892 and after his defeat there in 1895 became the Party's candidate himself standing in 1900. He was elected to West Ham Borough Council in 1890 and was deputy mayor in 1899-1900 before being elected as MP. He remained a member of the Council as long as he was an MP and was mayor in 1917. Unlike several of his colleagues he supported the Great War, in which he lost his son and he himself joined the West Ham Volunteer Force with the rank of Lieutenant Colonel. In 1918 he was elected for the Plaistow division of West Ham, which he represented until 1945. He died in 1946.

People's History Museum, Manchester

Chapter 5
Metropolitan Kent 1832 - 1918

Early History

Kent's history is heavily influenced by its proximity to London on the one hand and mainland Europe on the other. It was settled well before most other parts of England and has the oldest recorded place name in the British Isles. The Romans who landed at Ritchborough, Pegwell Bay in 54BC, called it 'Cantium'; and the Saxons,'Cant-guar-lantd', which signified 'the country of the inhabitants of Kent'. Some have said that the name derives from the word 'Cainc', being descriptive of a 'country abounding in open downs', which is a general characteristic of Kent. In the Domesday Book the place was written as 'Chenth', and the modern name and pronunciation came into common usage thereafter.

Many of Kent's coastal towns were significant either as commercial ports or in the defence of the realm. Dover, Hythe, New Romney and Sandwich were four of the original 'Cinque Ports' and ease of access by water to London led to the development of Chatham and Sheerness as dockland towns as early as 1488. In the 18th Century the growth of Margate and Ramsgate as seaside resorts was also encouraged by water transport even before the arrival of the railways cemented their importance. The River Thames was London's vital artery and, forming as it did the northernmost boundary of Kent, the local economy in that part of the county owed much to the strategic importance of London in terms of its trade as well as militarily. This was especially true of Deptford, which grew as a naval shipbuilding town and Woolwich, established as a naval base by Henry VIII in 1510; these towns, together with intermediate Greenwich, all had Royal connections.

Travelling from London to Kent the first habitation of any consequence beyond Southwark was the village of Deptford, which grew up at the point where the River Ravensbourne enters the Thames. The ancient parish of Deptford St Nicholas extended into Surrey in which county lay the district of Hatcham. In 1730 this was included in a new Deptford parish of St Pauls and with the coming of the railways became better known as New Cross. In 1845 Hatcham parish was separately created but with New Cross still straddling the Kent-Surrey border and it was not until the creation of the Parliamentary borough of Deptford in 1885 that the whole of the area came to be within metropolitan Kent. The village's name meant literally, 'deep ford', and was recorded first in 1293. The River was the basis of the local economy but the pilgrims' route between the capital and the cathedral at Canterbury, now called the Old Kent Road, also skirted the southern edge of Deptford and a town developed between these two arteries. Deptford Creek separated the town from Greenwich which, dating from 964 AD, meant literally 'green port or harbour'. Together with nearby Blackheath dating from AD 1166, (meaning 'dark-coloured open heath lands') both developed because of their locations near the river. The whole area became quite fashionable, as it was easily accessible by boat. In AD 1086 the King built a Palace at Eltham, or 'Elteham', meaning 'a river meadow frequented by swans', south of the Old Kent Road and close to Blackheath.

Suburban development in London was initially based on riverboat transport for city dwellers looking for country calm close to the town. Henry VIII built Greenwich Palace, where his daughter, the future Queen Elizabeth I was born, and, later in his reign, the Royal Naval Hospital was located there too. Charles II initiated this as a riverside Palace in the 1660s, a building that is now part of the Naval History Museum. Yet Kent had no single natural urban centre but several towns of medium size. Many of them developed as important river crossings, like Tonbridge and Maidstone, for example, where the Medway was bridged, and trade routes developed to other towns and ports of importance such as the Sussex Cinque Ports of Rye, Winchelsea and Hastings. After Tunbridge Wells was founded as a spa resort in 1606 this too began to attract visitors from London. Travellers' routes cut through parts of Kent close to London, such as Lewisham and Bromley, and as a result these began to develop viable economies themselves. Nevertheless the area now enclosed within the London Boroughs of Lewisham, Greenwich, Bexley and Bromley, did not really begin to develop significantly until well into the 19th Century.

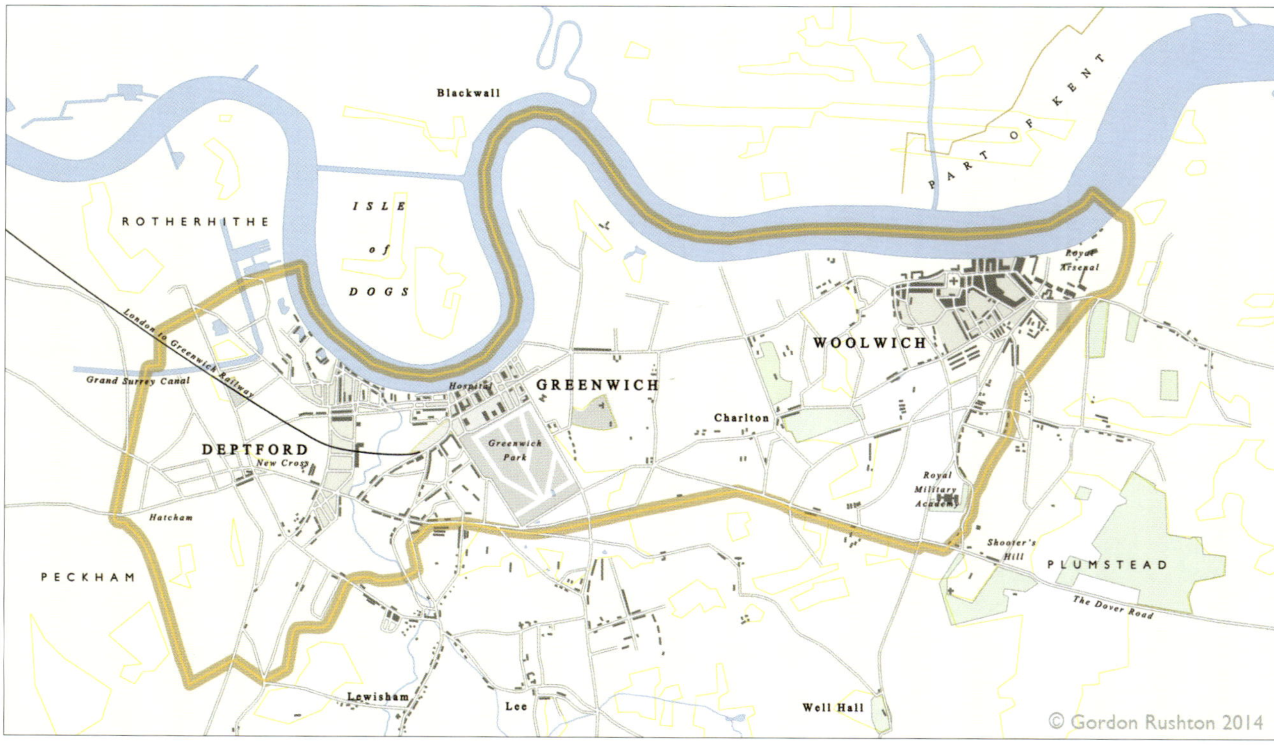

The Greenwich Constituency boundary in 1835, showing the newly arrived railway from London Bridge Station. The whole area was open, except where marked on the map. The yellow tint indicates the extent of today's built up area, with the parks and commons left white. The ease of communications led to rapid growth within the area, and the joining of the three communities marked of Deptford, Greenwich and Woolwich. The rest of metropolitan Kent, including Lewisham, Lee, Eltham and Plumstead depicted here, was in the Western Division of the County which extended beyond the Medway and as far as Romney Marsh. North Woolwich (now in Metropolitan Essex) was also in Western Kent.

Parliamentary Representation 1832-1885

1835 maps of London showed three relatively free-standing communities all of which were included in the new two member Parliamentary Borough of **Greenwich** which, with a total population close to 66,000, covered a wide band of Kent along the riverside from the Surrey boundary with Rotherhithe as far east as the canal separating the Royal Arsenal from Plumstead Marshes, taking in Deptford, the eastern part of New Cross, St Johns and Woolwich. However, it stopped short of Lewisham, Blackheath and Eltham, all of which were allocated to the Western Division of Kent. Neither did it include the western part of New Cross, or Hatcham as it was historically known, which were in the Surrey borough constituency of Lambeth. Woolwich itself was something of an oddity in that parts of two of its parishes (St Mary and St John the Evangelist) were on the north side of the Thames. They remained in Kent until 1899, when they were transferred to London, but stayed part of Woolwich borough until 1965. Despite the sizable population of the Greenwich constituency its electorate was a mere 2,714, although it has been estimated that a majority of the electorate were artisans, or working class voters, though this proportion may have decreased over the period after 1832 as pre-existing voters who enjoyed ancient voting rights that were protected by the Reform Act gradually diminished as a proportion of the total electoral population.

The first community downstream from Rotherhithe in the new constituency was Deptford, with the density of its housing greatest between the river Thames and the line of the new London to Greenwich Railway which was then being constructed and which opened the following year. There too were the established Royal Dock Yards, mast pond and 'Victualling' Office of the Royal Navy and all the factors that were to lead to a massive increase in the economic development of the whole area were in place. The Surrey Docks, already opened at Rotherhithe on the Surrey side of the border from Deptford, together with the Surrey Canal, cutting under the Deptford Lower Road and linking close by to the Croydon canal; these, together with the new railway, provided the essential infrastructure that led to the development of modern Deptford, and which in 1889 was to be created a London borough in its own right. Its population in the 1841 census was 23,165.

Greenwich itself was the base for the Billingsgate Fishing Fleet, famous for its whitebait and other catches, and was also developing strongly. By 1832 Greenwich Park together with the Royal Observatory, Hospital and Naval Asylum were well established and residential development was taking place towards Deptford, Woolwich and Blackheath. By early mid century Greenwich was well towards being absorbed into London's built-up area. The 1841 population of the town was 29,755, greater than Deptford's and 4,000 larger than Woolwich. In 1861 (a quarter of a century or more

'Pigot's 1840 map of Kent. The red line separates the Eastern and Western Parliamentary divisions, with today's metropolitan area in the far north west. Then it was barely attached to the growing metropolis.'

after the opening of the London and Greenwich Railway) the constituency's population had risen to 139,436 and the electorate to 15,509 (in 1868). Twenty years later the equivalent figures in 1881 and 1884 were 206,651 and 22,863 respectively, indicating the massive development that occurred in this area of South East London. By the time that the original Greenwich constituency gave way to its successor seats in 1885 it covered three large built-up areas, based on its three towns.

Historically local administration in the County of Kent had been divided into two units; the East was home to the Men of Kent and was run from Canterbury; the West was home to the Kentish Men and was run from Maidstone. Local government was originally administered through six 'lathes', or districts of Kent that themselves embraced a number of further divisions, or Hundreds. Western Kent comprised the 'lathes' of Aylesford and Sutton-at-Hone, and the Lower Division of the 'lathe' of Scray. All districts that are now part of London fell within four Hundreds of the lathe of Sutton-at-Hone, which overall extended south from the Thames to the Sussex border near Edenbridge and southeast to Swanscombe, which lies between Dartford and Gravesend. In 1814 the two separate geographical administrations of Kent were merged and Maidstone became the County town but when the first Parliamentary divisions of the County were established in 1832 they were still based on pre-1814 boundaries. In the 19th Century the Hundreds that constituted the area we now know as metropolitan Kent were Blackheath – comprising: Deptford, Greenwich, Woolwich, Lewisham, Beckenham, and Bromley; Little and Lessness – comprising: Plumstead, Erith and Crayford; and Ruxley – comprising: Bexley, Orpington, Chislehurst, West Wycombe, and Hayes.

The **Western Kent** county constituency was geographically large. It extended from the boundary with Greenwich at Plumstead marshes down the Thames estuary and beyond the Medway as far as Gillingham and south to the Sussex border including the Weald and Isle of Oxney. Its main centres of population were the Medway towns, Maidstone, Tunbridge Wells, Sevenoaks, Erith, Dartford, Gravesend, Bromley and Lewisham. The election was held at Maidstone but there were six polling places, two of which were in what is the London area today; one at Bromley and another at Blackheath. The population of Western Kent, excluding Greenwich, was 178,000 in 1831, with an electorate registered in the following year's General Election numbering 6,678. Yet within the next 30 years the population had increased to 348,000, despite the creation of a new Mid-Kent constituency that had reduced the geographical size of the Western Division, and made it much more aligned with the southeast London suburbs as we know them today. Despite its increased population, the electorate in 1868 had only risen to 8,828, evidence perhaps that the new residents were largely from the yet to be enfranchised labouring classes.

MPs for Metropolitan Kent 1832 - 1885

From	at	To	Surname	First Names	Constituency	Party
1832	G	1835	Dundas	John Whitley Deans, RN	Greenwich	Liberal
1832	G	1851	Barnard	Edward George		Liberal
1835	G	1837	Angerstein	John		Liberal
1837	G	1841	Attwood	Matthew Wolverley		Conservative
1841	G	1852	Dundas	John Whitley Deans, RN		Liberal
1851	B	1852	Salomons	David (Alderman)		Liberal
1852	G	1857	Rolt	Peter		Conservative
1852	G	1857	Chambers	Montague		Liberal
1857	G	1859	Codrington	Sir William John (LtGen)		Liberal
1857	G	1859	Townsend	John		Liberal
1859	B	1873	Salomons	David (Alderman)		Liberal
1859	G	1865	Angerstein	William		Liberal
1865	G	1868	Bright	Sir Charles Tilston		Liberal
1868	G	1880	Gladstone	William Ewart		Liberal
1873	B	1885	Boord	Thomas William		Conservative
1880	G	1885	De Worms	Baron Henry		Conservative
1832	G	1841	Hodges	Thomas Law	Kent West	Liberal
1832	G	1835	Rider	Thomas		Liberal
1835	G	1838	Geary	Sir William Richard Powlett		Conservative
1838	B	1857	Filmer	Sir Edmund		Conservative
1841	G	1845	Marsham	Viscount		Conservative
1845	B	1847	Austen	Thomas (Col)		Protectionist
1847	G	1852	Hodges	Thomas Law		Liberal
1852	G	1857	Smith	William Masters		Conservative
1857	B	1859	Martin	Charles Wykeham		Liberal
1857	G	1859	Whatman	James		Liberal
1859	G	1868	Holmesdale	Viscount		Conservative
1859	G	1865	Filmer	Sir Edmund		Conservative
1865	G	1868	Dyke	Sir William Hart		Conservative
1868	G	1885	Mills	Sir Charles Henry		Conservative
1868	G	1878	Talbot	John Gilbert		Conservative
1878	B	1885	Lewisham	Viscount (William Heneage Legg)		Conservative

NOTE First returned at a B = By-election; G = General Election

The Politics of Metropolitan Kent between 1832 and 1885

The general pattern of politics nationally after the 1832 Act was for the boroughs to elect mainly Liberals and the Counties to return Tories and this is precisely what occurred in this part of Kent until the Second Act. Overall the Liberals performed much better than the Tories. In the 9 General Elections that were held in Greenwich from 1832 until 1865 the Liberals won both borough seats on 8 occasions. The Tories won only once, in 1837, when they also topped the poll but even then a Liberal was elected in second place. Overall in Greenwich 17 Liberals were returned and only one Conservative. Neither was there much excitement in the contested by-elections that were held during that period. Liberals won these at Greenwich in 1851, 1852, 1857 and 1859. By contrast, the Tories won both seats in the Western Kent division on four occasions, and topped the poll on three more, winning eleven MPs in all to seven for the Liberals. They topped the poll only twice, first in 1832, and again in 1857. On this second occasion the Liberal's election was confirmation of what had previously taken place at a by-election. Shortly before the 1857 General Election one of two Tories returned at the previous poll in 1854 resigned, and on 16th February 1857 the Liberal candidate captured the seat, a result that was confirmed in April's General Election when two Liberals were returned.

After the Second Reform Act the franchise was further extended and the Conservatives did much better in this part of Kent. In the three General Elections that took place before the Third Reform Act, Western Kent returned two Tories on every occasion and Greenwich too became much more closely contested between the Parties. In 1868 the Liberals were returned for both seats but evidence of a pro-Tory mood emerged at a by-election which was held there on 2nd August 1873 following the death of one of the two Liberal MPs. The Tories gained the seat and retained it at the 1874 General Election when one Liberal was also elected but in the General Election after that, held in 1880, the Conservatives actually won both seats.

The Western Kent constituency maintained its Tory traditions throughout including a by-election on 15th May 1878 which was uncontested by the Liberals following the resignation of one of a pair of sitting Tories. Two Conservatives were returned at the 1880 poll as well.

MPs for Greenwich

Sir John Dundas MP
Wikipedia

Captain John Whitley Deans Dundas RN (Liberal), later a Lord of the Admiralty, was one of the first two MPs elected for the naval constituency of Greenwich in 1832. He served twice as the MP, firstly until 1835 and then between 1841 and his retirement in 1852 to become commander of the British fleet in the Mediterranean. Born in 1785, he was the son of Dr. James Deans of Calcutta and assumed the names Whitley and Dundas on his first marriage, acquiring his wife's family names. He rose to become Rear Admiral of the Red, Clerk of the Ordinance, and in 1846 a Lord of the Admiralty, a promotion that necessitated him fighting a by-election, which he did successfully. A patron of one living, he was a Deputy-Lieutenant of Berkshire and started out his political career as a Whig. In the pre-Reform General Election of 1831 he contested Queensborough unsuccessfully and after his first spell as Greenwich's MP he contested Devizes unsuccessfully in 1835 before succeeding there at a by-election the following year. He sat until 1838 when he resigned to resume his naval career three years before being elected once again at Greenwich. He died in 1862.

Edward George Barnard (Liberal) sat with Dundas for most of his period as a Greenwich MP. He was elected with him in 1832 and only ceased to be an MP when he died in 1851. A ship builder, he was also the patron of one living and lived at Deptford Green. He was a political radical believing in the ballot and triennial Parliaments.

Whilst Dundas was absent from the Greenwich Hustings, his place was taken by **John Angerstein** (Liberal), son of the celebrated Underwriter and founder of the Gallery that bore his name. John, who lived in St James Square, but who also had homes in Norfolk and Kent where he was the patron of two livings had, before the Reform Act was passed, paid for nomination as a Parliamentary candidate, though without success. In later years he was to become a supporter of reforms that abolished such privileges. He had contested Greenwich unsuccessfully at the 1832 election and, following his retirement from the same seat in 1837, he lost at Surrey East, a constituency to which he transferred his candidacy. He was never elected again and died in 1858.

Angerstein was succeeded at Greenwich by **Matthias Wolverley Attwood** (Conservative) who took the seat at the 1837 General Election but only held it for one term, until 1841. Attwood's father (also Matthias) was the MP for Whitehaven between 1832 and 1847 and so sat in the House with his son for fours years. Attwood senior had also previously sat as an MP in unreformed Parliaments for Callington (Cornwall) and Boroughbridge (West Riding of Yorkshire). The younger Attwood, who lived in Lombard Street, had contested Greenwich initially but unsuccessfully in 1835, and at the time of his defeat there in 1841 also sought election in three other constituencies at the same contest: at the City of London; Kinsale(Ireland); and at Sunderland (County Durham); all of them unsuccessful. He died in 1865.

Alderman David Salomons (Liberal) succeeded Edward Barnard at a by-election after he died in 1851, but was quickly defeated at the subsequent General Election in 1852. However, he regained a seat at a by-election in 1859, following the resignation of John Townsend (elected in 1857). Salomons retained the seat until his death in 1873. Born in 1797, he lived near Hyde Park in London and also had a home at Broom Hill, Tunbridge Wells. He was the son of a City merchant and Underwriter and he too became a merchant though he was also admitted to the bar of the Middle Temple. From 1835-6 he was Sheriff of London; then from 1839-40 was High Sheriff of Kent. He was elected an Alderman of the City of London in 1847 and Lord Mayor in 1855 whilst serving also as a magistrate in Middlesex, Kent and Sussex. He was also a Commissioner of Lieutenancy for the City but had interests beyond the purely ceremonial, being the author of several books on a variety of subjects including the Corn Laws, Banking and Railways.

When Salomons was defeated in 1852, he was replaced by **Peter Rolt** (Conservative), who retained the seat until 1857. He was born at Deptford in 1798, where he was the son of the clerk to the Surrey Dockyard Company,

The Commercial Dock in Rotherhithe in 1827, a bustling and important centre close to where Peter Rolt MP was born in 1797. **Wikipedia**

and subsequently married a daughter of the managing director of the General Steam Navigation Company. He became a timber merchant and contractor in his grandfather's firm of Brocklebank & Rolt. He then lived at Rotherhithe but also had a home in Cornhill. In 1854 he was made a Deputy Lieutenant of Middlesex and whilst in the House opposed the Maynooth grant. He chose to resign in 1857 when his firm accepted a government contract. He died in 1882.

Sitting alongside Rolt was **Montague Chambers QC** (Liberal) who was also elected in 1852 and defeated in 1857. Born in Huntingdonshire, he was the grandson of Lord Rodney. Educated at Eton, Sandhurst and Christ's College Cambridge, he entered the Grenadier Guards but in 1828 was called to the bar at Lincoln's Inn and took silk in 1845 working on the Home Circuit. He was a conservative Liberal who favoured containing public spending except where this adversely affected military and naval establishments. The extent to which he held these apparently opposed principles is not recorded but it may have had something to do with his associations with Greenwich. Chambers unsuccessfully contested the Greenwich by-election in 1852 but was returned at the general election. Defeats followed in the same seat in both 1857 and 1859 and he also lost at Bedford in 1865 before being returned at a by-election for the naval port of Devonport in 1866. He sat there until 1874 and died in 1885.

Gen. Sir William Codrington MP **Wikipedia**

Lieutenant – General Sir William John Codrington (Liberal) was elected at a by-election held in 1857 following Rolt's resignation and was re-elected at the general election held the same year. He was born in 1804 and at the time of his election was the eldest surviving son of Admiral Sir Edward Codrington. He joined the Army in 1821 rising through the ranks to command a brigade of the Light Infantry and then a Division. In 1855 he was appointed Commander in Chief of the Eastern Army, a post he retained until the evacuation of the Crimea. In 1886 he was promoted to Lieutenant - General of the 54th Foot and Light Infantry. He was awarded several military honours including the Legion d'Honneur and the Grand Cross of the Order of Savoy. He remained an MP only for a short period of time because in 1859 he was appointed Governor of Gibraltar, a post he held until 1865. He made two failed attempts to gain re-election to the Commons, once at Westminster in 1874 and secondly at Lewes in 1880. He died in 1884.

Elected alongside Codrington at the 1857 general election was **John Townsend** (Liberal), the son of a Greenwich auctioneer. He was educated at Deptford and at Fairford, Gloucestershire, and afterwards became an auctioneer himself, continuing to live locally in Nelson Street. He set up in business on his own account in 1843 and claimed, in his own words, to have entered politics 'to rescue the borough from the control of jobbery of an individual', by which he possibly meant Chambers whom he defeated in 1857. Once elected he was a political radical supporting such causes as the secret ballot, an extended franchise and the admission of Jews to Parliament. Despite this apparent enthusiasm for a cause he emigrated to Canada in 1859 precipitating a by-election. Once in his new surroundings he became quite a well-known actor and died in 1892. Salomons (see above) succeeded him at the 1859 by-election.

Having been unsuccessful at the by-election held in February 1859, **William Angerstein** (Liberal), son of the former Greenwich MP from 1835-7, John, was returned alongside Salomons at the May 1859 general election. He only served until 1865 when he chose instead to fight Kent Western. He was defeated there and again in 1868. He was born locally in 1811 and educated at Harrow School and Christ Church Oxford. In 1860 he became a Deputy Lieutenant of Kent and in 1872 was made High Sheriff of Norfolk, a post he still held when he contested a by-election at Greenwich in 1873. However, he was defeated and never resumed a political career. He died in 1892. He favoured a more equitable distribution of seats in the House of Commons and an extended franchise.

King Charles' Court in the Old Royal Naval College, Greenwich. In 1869 the Royal Naval College moved to Greenwich from Portsmouth whilst William Gladstone was the MP. This essentially naval constituency included the Arsenal and Dockyard at Woolwich, the Royal Naval College and the Dockyard at Deptford and naval activity was at its height from the British foreign policy feature of gunboat diplomacy. In 1882 Gladstone's government ordered the naval bombardment of Alexandria. After the occupation of Egypt, Gladstone sold at a profit his Egyptian Government Stocks which were estimated at the time as 37% of his personal capital [Philip Mansel - writing in the Spectator 28.01.2012]. **Gordon Rushton**

The man who succeeded Angerstein at Greenwich in 1865 was **Sir Charles Tilston Bright** (Liberal), who lived at Lancaster Gate and also had a home in Victoria Street, Westminster. However, long before he inhabited these affluent addresses he was born in West Ham in 1832. He sat until 1868 when he retired and was a somewhat less radical Liberal than many of his colleagues. Whilst favouring an extended franchise he opposed the secret ballot. In 1860-1 he was Captain of the Surrey Volunteers. He died in 1888.

The most famous MP to sit for Greenwich was **William Ewart Gladstone** (Liberal), the three times Prime Minister of Victoria's Britain. His tenure as a local MP from 1868 to 1880 included a substantial period of his premiership from 1868 to 1874, and the subsequent six years when he was Leader of the Opposition. Gladstone was born in Liverpool in 1809 where his father, Sir John, was a wealthy merchant. His maternal grandfather was the Provost of Dingwall in Scotland and he was a devout Christian as well as a politician. He was educated at Eton College and Christ Church Oxford where he attained a Double First in 1831 and his MA three years later. In 1848 he was made Honorary DCL. A Deputy-Lieutenant of Wiltshire, he married the eldest daughter of Sir Stephen Glynne who owned the Harwarden Castle estate in Flintshire where Gladstone was to spend much of his life. He entered politics in 1832 at the first election following the First Reform Act but although he represented the Nottinghamshire town of Newark, this was still effectively a 'nomination borough' in the gift of the Duke of Newcastle. In those days Gladstone's politics could be best described as anti - reform Tory and it was as such that he served as one of the town's MPs until 1845. As was sometimes the custom in those days, he also contested Manchester in 1837, but unsuccessfully. He was appointed to his first Government post in 1834 when he was made a Lord of the Treasury (a whip) by Sir Robert Peel, two months after the Houses of Parliament burnt down and a month after King William IV dismissed Lord Melbourne's Liberal Government when it had proposed reforms to the Church with which he disagreed. A year later Peel appointed him Under Secretary for the Colonies, though he held the post only between January and April when Peel was forced to resign in favour of Melbourne in the face of a Commons majority opposed to the Tories. Following the 1841 General Election Melbourne resigned in favour of Peel and Gladstone once more returned to office, this time as Vice President of the Board of Trade a post he held until promoted to be President in 1843. He also held the post of Master of the Mint and remained in

William Ewart Gladstone MP
Photographed by Mayall in 1861 when he was Chancellor of the Exchequer and MP for Oxford University. **Wikipedia**

William Ewart Gladstone MP
Painted by Sir John Everett Millais
© **Palace of Westminster Collection www.parliament.uk/art**

both jobs until he resigned in February 1845. He was a strong supporter of Peel's approach to free trade and supported his Repeal of the Corn Laws, a measure that completely split the Tory Party. Although the split initially forced Peel to resign he was able to resume as Prime Minister within a matter of weeks when in December the Liberals and free trade Tories combined to form a Commons majority. Outraged by this turn of events, the Duke of Newcastle withdrew his support from Gladstone who, though no longer an MP, was nevertheless still appointed Secretary of State for the Colonies, a post he held between December 1845 and July 1846 when the Government resigned in the light of a Commons defeat on the Irish Coercion Bill, which was opposed by Irish Nationalists and Tories in a somewhat unholy alliance.

In 1847 Gladstone sought another seat and was this time elected Conservative MP for Oxford University remaining out of office until 1852 when, following a General Election, a coalition of Liberals, Peelites and Irish Nationalists was formed under the leadership of the Earl of Aberdeen. Gladstone was appointed Chancellor of the Exchequer; a position he continued to hold after Aberdeen's Government fell in 1855 over a Commons defeat on a motion critical of 'the condition of the Army before the battle of Sebastopol'. Palmerston re-appointed him and he held the post until the Government lost the 1857 general election. Gladstone next resumed a ministerial career after the 1859 election, the year he was first elected as Rector of Edinburgh University, when he was once again appointed Chancellor of the Exchequer, this time by Lord Palmerston. This move essentially saw Gladstone move from the Tories to become a Liberal, a situation cemented when he allied himself for the first time to the question of electoral reform. He held the post until 1866 and for a year after the 1865 election, following which Earl Russell became Prime Minister, he was also Leader of the Commons. However, his switch of parties caused him to lose support in his University constituency and in 1865 he sought election for the county constituency of South Lancashire, which seat he held for three years. The Government fell in June 1866 when the Liberals split over electoral reform and a minority Tory Government took power under the Earl of Derby with Disraeli assuming the offices of State relinquished by Gladstone. However, the Tory Government did not survive the 1868 General Election that followed the passing of its own Reform Act and this time Gladstone became Prime Minister for the first time, coinciding with his election as a Greenwich MP.

Gladstone's first Administration was one of the great reforming Governments in modern British history, amongst other things passing the first Education Act enabling all children to receive a basic state education; the Ballot Act (introducing secret voting for the first time and thus going a long way to eliminate intimidation of voters); competitive examinations for entry into the civil service; the introduction of short-service enlistment into the Armed Forces and the abolition of the ability to purchase commissions; the Married Women's Property Act acknowledging the principle that women may have property rights of their own; the University Test Act removing the requirement of religious tests for applicants to Oxford and Cambridge Universities; a Trade Union Act legalizing unions and recognising them for the first time as 'friendly societies'; and the Licensing Acts regulating the opening hours of public houses. The latter caused riots in the Midlands during the 1874 general election which the Liberals lost heavily in the face of a resurgent Conservative Party under the leadership of Disraeli who famously described Gladstone's Government in 1873 as being like a 'range of exhausted volcanoes'.

In Opposition Gladstone turned his attentions to academia becoming Professor of Ancient History at the Royal Academy in 1876, Rector of Glasgow University in 1877 and completing a major work on the poet Homer. He also wrote a pamphlet entitled 'Bulgarian Horrors and the Question of the East' which was a denunciation of Turkey's rule in the area. He resigned the leadership of the Liberals in 1875 but was prevailed upon to return in 1880 when his Party was once again returned at a general election and Gladstone resumed the Prime Ministership. This time he relinquished his Greenwich seat, which must have eased the role of Prime Minister enormously, to fight two seats, one in Leeds and the other in Mid Lothian, or Edinburghshire as it was then known. He was returned in both but chose to sit for the Scottish seat, which he retained until his retirement in 1895, though in 1886 he also contested the Scottish Burgh seat of Leith. Unusually he was also Chancellor of the Exchequer from 1880 to 1882. This time, however, though the administration was still a reforming one in terms of domestic policy, he decided to make Irish Home Rule the major issue and the consequence of this was that it split his Party. Following his re-election in 1885 the unionist faction, led by Joseph Chamberlain, split to form an alliance with the Conservatives. This brought about a Liberal defeat in 1886 but when his Party was returned in 1892 it seemed that there was some prospect of the Home Rule Bill being passed with the additional support of the Irish MPs. The Bill did indeed survive the Commons but was defeated in the Lords provoking a constitutional crisis. Gladstone, by now past his mid Eighties, resigned as Prime Minister in 1894. He died in 1898, in his 90th year.

In Gladstone's early tenure as a Greenwich MP the fellow Liberal Salomons accompanied him until 1873, but thereafter he was paired with a Tory.

Thomas William Boord (Conservative), who went on to sit for the borough until 1895, was born in 1838 and educated at Harrow and in Germany. A Sussex JP whose London home was in Berkley Square, Boord was a partner in a distilling company, Boord and Son. He died in 1912.

Boord was succeeded by **Baron Henry de Worms** (Conservative), son of the first baron, a hereditary baron of the Austrian Empire but was born in London in 1840 where he later took a degree at Kings College, becoming a fellow in 1868. He was called to the bar at the Inner Temple in 1863, afterwards joining the South East Circuit. A fellow of the Royal Society, he was a magistrate and Deputy-Lieutenant in Middlesex and also a commissioner of the Patriotic Fund and from 1872 to 1886 President of the Anglo-Jewish Association. He first contested a Parliamentary seat in 1868 when he was defeated at Sandwich (Kent) but did not resume a career in politics until after his return at Greenwich. Following redistribution of seats in 1885 he transferred to the Toxteth division of Liverpool, which he represented until 1895. During this latter period he held only minor ministerial office, initially as PPS to the President of the Board of Trade (1885-8); then as Parliamentary Under Secretary at the Colonial Office until 1892. During this period he chaired an international conference on sugar bounties. In 1892 he was elevated to the House of Lords with a British peerage, Lord Pirbright. He died in 1903.

MPs for Kent Western

Thomas Law Hodges (Liberal), who gave his London address as 12 Suffolk Street, Pall Mall, was elected at the top of the first poll that occurred in the new West Kent constituency following the passing of the Reform Act. He had previously represented the county of Kent in the pre Reform Parliament from 1830 and sat for Western Kent initially from 1832 to 1841 and after a six-year retirement, returned to represent the seat from 1847 to 1852. His son Thomas also sat as a Kent MP during this period, representing the borough of Rochester from 1835 to 1837 and from 1847 to 1852 when he emigrated to Australia. Thomas Law Hodges was born in 1776, the eldest son of a man from Hemsted, Kent of which County he became a Deputy- Lieutenant and magistrate, a role he also fulfilled in neighbouring Sussex. He was a Major in the West Kent Militia but was comparatively radical politically, favouring the ballot and short Parliaments. He died in 1857.

Thomas Rider (Liberal) was elected in second place to Hodges in 1832 but unlike his colleague was not re-elected after his first term. Whether by coincidence or design, he too gave his London address as Suffolk Street, living four doors away at number 16 and, like Hodges, he too was a Kentish man whose county home was at Monchelsea. He had the distinction of displacing the other previous incumbent MP at the time of the 1832 election, Sir Edward Knatchbull, who had voted against the 1831 Reform Bill and appears to have suffered the electoral consequences. However, Rider lost in 1835 and at the subsequent general election in 1837 contested the neighbouring County seat of Kent Eastern where he was again unsuccessful and retired from politics.

Sir William Richard Powlett Geary (Conservative) who was beaten by Rider in 1832, returned not only to defeat him in1835 but also to top the poll. He was born in 1810 and lived at Oxon Hoath, Kent but owned considerable property in Wexford, Ireland. Nevertheless, his family roots were firmly in Kent where his father had also been a county MP in the Parliaments of 1796, 1802 and 1812. Geary retired in 1838 at the age of only 28 and died forty years later in 1877.

Sir Edmund Filmer (Conservative), who was the patron of one living, succeeded him at a by-election held in 1838. Born in 1809 he lived at East Sutton in Kent and was the son of a Captain and nephew of the Reverend Sir John Filmer whom he succeeded in the baronetcy in 1834. Married to a Canadian he became a Deputy – Lieutenant of Kent in 1849. He was politically conservative and was especially hostile to concessions being made to Catholics. He held the seat until 1857 when he died shortly before the general election.

Viscount Marsham (Conservative) was elected in 1841. He too lived in Kent (at Boxley Park) and was the eldest son of the Earl of Romney. Born in 1808, he married the fourth daughter of the Duke of Buccleugh and himself succeeded as third Earl Romney in 1845, when he left the Commons for the Lords. He died in 1874.

Colonel Thomas Austen (Conservative) won the by-election caused by Marsham's elevation unopposed but only held the seat until 1847 when he was defeated at the general election. He lived at Kippington in Kent where he was also a magistrate and Deputy – Lieutenant of the County. He was an ardent protectionist and as President of the West Kent Agricultural Protection Society believed in the extension of the Corn Laws, not their repeal. He died in 1859.

William Masters Smith (Conservative) was elected in 1852 and served until defeated in 1857. Whilst in London he lived at 16 Suffolk Street, the address occupied by Rider and Hodges twenty years earlier. Smith was born in 1802 and lived at Cramer near Gravesend where he married the daughter of Major – General Sir Howard Elphinstone. Educated at Harrow School and Edinburgh, he was a Kent magistrate and Deputy – Lieutenant who was appointed High Sheriff of the County in 1848. Fiercely anti-Catholic he died in 1861.

Charles Wykeham Martin (Liberal) won the be-election caused by Filmer's death in 1857 but only held the seat for two years before he was defeated. The son of Fiennes Wykeham Martin, Charles lived at Leeds Castle near Maidstone in Kent and arguably the finest home in southeast England. Born in 1801 he was Eton and Balliol (Oxford) educated and a Deputy – Lieutenant of Hampshire. He was the senior Major in the 3rd Battalion of the Kent Volunteers and patron of one living. Despite his so-called liberalism he was opposed to the ballot and had contested several elections before he became MP for Kent Western. He first contested Newport in 1837 before being elected there in 1841, serving until defeated in 1852. The following year he contested a by-election in the local Maidstone constituency but lost once more. Following his defeat at Kent Western in 1859 he was returned at Newport Isle of Wight in 1865, serving until his death in 1870.

James Whatman (Liberal) was elected behind Martin in 1857 and was also defeated with him two years later. Born in 1813, he was the grandson of a former Kent Sheriff (1767) and of Richard Ganssen, an MP in pre- Reform Parliaments. James, who lived at Vintners near Maidstone was educated at Eton and Christ Church College Oxford where he only managed to secure a 4th class degree in Classics in 1834. His poor results did not prevent him from going on to secure his MA four years later. He was a Kent magistrate and Deputy – Lieutenant and served in the County militia from 1838. He favoured the franchise extension and the admission of Jews to Parliament and prior to his return at Kent Western had been MP for Maidstone since 1852. He died in 1887.

Viscount Holmesdale (Conservative) lived at Linton Park, Staplehurst and was the eldest son of Earl Amherst and a grandson of the Bishop of Carlisle. Born in 1836, he entered the Army in 1854 and became a Lieutenant and then Captain in the Coldstream Guards serving more or less immediately in the Crimea. He saw action at Balaklava, Inkerman and Sebastopol being wounded severely and was decorated for his pains. He retired from the Army in 1862, three years after his election for Kent West and was also a Deputy – Lieutenant of the County. In 1868 he transferred to the newly created Mid Kent division, which he represented until 1880 when he was appointed Baron Amhurst, becoming the third Earl six years later. He died in 1910.

Sir Edmund Filmer (Conservative), was the son of his namesake who had represented the same constituency between 1838 and 1857. Filmer Junior was returned in 1859 alongside Holmesdale having spent a short time in the Grenadier Guards. He had no great claims to fame but nevertheless served as a Captain in the West Kent militia and in 1870 was appointed High Sheriff of Kent. Meanwhile he had retired from the House in 1865 but made a return in 1880 when he was elected for Mid Kent, though he retired in 1884 and died two years later.

Sir William Hart Dyke (Conservative) lived at Lullington Castle, Dartford and also had family connections with Bickley Park. Altogether his estate was estimated at 9,000 acres. Born in 1837 he married the eldest daughter of the Earl of Sandwich having been educated at Harrow and Christ Church Oxford where he obtained an MA in 1834. Following his election at West Kent in 1865 he went on to serve continuously for this and two other successor constituencies until 1906 when he was defeated. He transferred to Mid Kent in 1868 and then to the newly created Dartford seat in 1885. From 1868 to 1874 he was a Tory Whip and then Chief Whip (Patronage Secretary to the Treasury) in Disraeli's 1874-1880 Government. He was briefly (1885-6) Chief Secretary for Ireland, then from 1887 to 1892 served as Vice

President of the Central Committee in Education. A strong Unionist he was a magistrate and Deputy – Lieutenant for Kent and Deputy Chairman of the London, Chatham and Dover Railway Company. He died in 1931.

Sir Charles Henry Mills (Conservative) was returned in 1868 when a new Western Kent constituency was formed. Living at Wildernesse, Sevenoaks, he was the son of Sir Charles Mills of Uxbridge, a partner in the banking firm of Glyn Mills. Born in 1830 he was educated at Eton and Christ Church Oxford and later married the eldest daughter of the 3rd Earl of Harewood. A magistrate and Deputy – Lieutenant of Kent, he was a Commissioner of Metropolis Roads and had previously been MP for Northallerton (Yorkshire North Riding) from 1865 to 1866 when he was unseated on petition. He retired from the Commons in 1885 and was made the first Baron Hillingdon. He died in 1898. His son and two grandsons followed him into the Commons, the former being MP for Sevenoaks (1885-1892) and the latter two for Uxbridge (1910-1915 and 1915-1918 respectively – see Chapter 3, Uxbridge).

John Gilbert Talbot (Conservative) was elected in 1868 and served until 1878 when he retired via the Chiltern Hundreds in order to secure election at Oxford University which he represented until he died in 1910. Born in 1835 he was educated at Charterhouse School and Christ Church Oxford where he obtained an MA in 1860. He married the eldest daughter of the 4th Baron Lyttelton and sought election to Parliament. He was initially unsuccessful at Kidderminster (Worcestershire) in 1862, then at Malmesbury (Wiltshire) in 1865 and despite his subsequent long Parliamentary tenure had a totally undistinguished career. He was made Hon D.C.L in 1878, the same year that he achieved his one and only ministerial post, that of Parliamentary Secretary to the Board of Trade, which he relinquished following the Tories' election defeat in 1880. A low profile Commons career was matched by a local political career that saw him elected to the County Council in 1889 and become an alderman in 1904. He served also as an Ecclesiastical Commissioner and was appointed chairman of the West Kent Quarter Sessions in 1868.

John Gilbert Talbot MP
Illustration from 1897 Vanity Fair
Wikipedia

Viscount William Heneage Legge Lewisham (Conservative) won the by-election created by Talbot's resignation in 1878 and went on to serve continuously as a Kent MP until 1891. He was born in 1851, the eldest son of the Earl of Dartmouth and a grandson on his mother's side of the 5th Earl of Aylesford. The aristocratic connections were completed with his marriage to the youngest daughter of the Earl of Leicester. Educated at Eton and Christ Church College, Oxford he entered the House at the age of 27 and in 1885 was appointed a Vice Chamberlain of Her Majesty's Household, seeking re-election at a by-election held to confirm his appointment. Elected as MP for Lewisham in 1885 he remained its MP until he succeeded to the Earldom in 1891, the year he also became Lord Lieutenant of Staffordshire, a role he held until 1927. As Earl he owned around 20,000 acres of estates. He died in 1936.

Viscount William Lewisham MP
Wikipedia

Metropolitan Kent had its greatest concentration of population in the London area. The dark shading shows approximately the built up areas in 1880, and the yellow wash, for comparison, shows the extent of the urban sprawl today. In the period of this chapter the railways had already reached their maximum extent, and although the London area has seen more recent growth of Underground and similar, it was the spread of the main lines that facilitated the urban sprawl, and the presence of so many electors that required the increase in the number of constituencies. The red lines show the constituencies as they were from 1881 until 1910. The black boundary line progressing diagonally from SW to NE represents the GLA area (formed much later).

Constituency	1881 pop	1891 pop	1901 pop	1911 pop	1884 electors and % 1881 pop	1906 electors	1910 electors	1910 electors as % of 1911 pop
Dartford		79,853	109,889	124,671		19,741	21,398	17.2
Deptford		101,286	100,122	109,444		15,397	15,159	13.9
Greenwich	206,651	78,167	95,578	95,825	22,863	13,049	13,153	13.7
Lewisham		88,653	128,346	160,963		22,243	25,021	15.5
Sevenoaks		80,063	94,789	111,919		17,256	19,035	17.0
Woolwich		98,966	117,170	121,381		17,870	18,536	15.3
Western Kent	208,260				18,183			
Totals	414,911	526,988	645,894	724,203	41,046 = 9.9%	105,556	112,302	16.4

Parliamentary Representation 1885 – 1918

When the 1884 Representation of the People Act was passed it had a significant impact on the representation of northwest Kent. New constituencies were established and contested for the first time at the 1885 General Election. In total six Parliamentary constituencies were created to cover the area of the Sutton-at-Hone 'lathe' of Kent and each of them included some part of what we now recognise as Greater London. The Western Kent and Greenwich seats were divided to form new single – member constituencies with only Greenwich being retained whilst new ones were established at Dartford, Deptford, Lewisham, Sevenoaks and Woolwich. Dartford and Sevenoaks were county divisions otherwise known as North West and Kent Western respectively, whilst the remaining four, which were established as new boroughs within the London County Council in 1889, were also set up as self-contained Parliamentary seats.

By the latter part of the Nineteenth Century London was beginning to mushroom in all directions and the riverside communities of Deptford, Greenwich and Woolwich burgeoned, the latter around the Naval Dockyard and Royal Arsenal, the Royal Academy and Royal Artillery Barracks. Behind Deptford and Greenwich the new middle class suburbs of Blackheath and Lewisham also started to develop as by then the building of huge residential areas was becoming well established in the wake of the expansion of the railways.

The changes reflected population expansion and the extension to the franchise. The overall population of the area had increased from 415,000 in 1881 to 527,000 by 1891 and rose further to 646,000 by 1901. The electorate as a percentage of the population before the 1884 Reform Act was only about 10% but this proportion just about doubled afterwards. A summary of the populations and electorates of the six new seats compared with the two old ones is as follows:

The **Greenwich** constituency, formerly the largest now became the smallest in both population and electorate, comprising the parishes of St Nicholas, Deptford, a small dockside area west of Deptford Creek; Greenwich St Alphege, Kidbrooke and Charlton. It incorporated the riverside settlements around the town itself and extended to include the smaller but rapidly developing outer suburbs surrounding Charlton Park, Blackheath (exclusive) and Woolwich Common. These included Maze Hill and Westcombe Park. The Royal Observatory and Naval College were both within its boundaries, which remained unaltered until the 1997 General Election when they were extended eastwards along the Thames for the first time since before 1885 to include central Woolwich including the Arsenal. The population of the Greenwich constituency in 1891 was over 78,000 yet within ten years it had grown to nearly 96,000, which figure contained an electorate of a little over 13,000 registered voters. However, its electorate was at 13.7%, proportionately the smallest of the new Kent seats relative to its population.

The adjacent 1885 **Woolwich** constituency had a larger population but covered a much wider area extending east from the border with Greenwich (more or less at the point where the Thames Barrier is now located), via the Royal Arsenal and along the Thames estuary but stopping short of Erith marshes. Within its boundaries were the parishes of Plumstead and Eltham including the emerging suburb of Well Hall. Its communities included Abbey Wood, Eltham, New Eltham and Shooters Hill. Until 1997 the Parliamentary Borough boundaries of the Woolwich and Greenwich constituencies established in 1885 remained intact with the only alterations taking place internally when an additional seat was created in Woolwich in 1918, and North Woolwich was transferred to Newham in 1974. Known in Saxon England in 918 AD as 'Uuluuich' – 'port where the wool is shipped' - its principal features were to become the Royal Dockyard where wooden galleons were built from the early 16th Century and the Arsenal, established in 1716. The constituency population in 1891 was roundly 99,000 and by 1901 it had increased to over 117,000, stimulated by the growth of suburbs in the south of the borough. The constituency's electorate was around 18,000 in the early 20th Century, which at 15.3% was proportionately higher than in neighbouring Greenwich but lower than in some other seats. This reflected the mix of working class docklands and middle class suburbia represented by the new Thames – side borough. In those days the constituency also incorporated parts of the parish of Woolwich that were in Essex on the north bank of the Thames. The area still known as North Woolwich included small settlements in the vicinity of Barking Creek.

Deptford (literally 'deep ford' or 'deop ford') was smaller in area than the present day constituency and did not include the parish of Deptford St Nicholas which was in Greenwich. In 1885 it comprised the parishes of St Paul's, Deptford and Hatcham (Surrey) extending from the Surrey Docks south of Rotherhithe via Deptford itself to New Cross Gate, New Cross and St Johns. The constituency's southernmost centre of population was Brockley. It was geographically smaller than any of the neighbouring Kent constituencies yet initially it had the largest population. In 1891 the census recorded over 101,000 people living in the borough. Thereafter the population steadied as wealthier people moved to the more spacious surroundings of the suburbs developing around Lewisham. Nevertheless it was, like Woolwich, a constituency that had a mix of both middle and working class voters.

Left: *The ragged Victorian building profile still persists in Deptford High Street, as evidence of its rapid rate of growth, sandwiched between the Royal Naval Dockyard and the London to Greenwich Railway line that was built in 1834. It had grown enough by 1885 to have its own constituency and was made a Metropolitan Borough in 1900.* **Gordon Rushton**

Below: *Even today with the Cutty Sark in the background, the maritime flavour of Greenwich remains. The 1832 Constituency was reduced in area in 1885 to accommodate the general expansion of population that led to the creation of the neighbouring Deptford and Woolwich constituencies.* **Gordon Rushton**

Below: *In 1868, employees of the Royal Arsenal created a co-operative society which prospered and grew, ultimately attaining 500k members. The HQ shown here in Woolwich was rebuilt in 1903. The Society affiliated directly to the Labour Party, and sponsored the election of Will Crooks as the Constituency's first Labour MP at a by election in 1903.* **Gordon Rushton**

Above: *In 1849 the South Eastern Railway built its line to Dartford, and at Slade Green, to the south of Erith, it provided houses for its workers, next to the railway in Oak Road. Such housing in the Dartford Constituency at the time was a valuable 'perk' for railway staff, and in time the area became built up, around the cottages.*

Both images John Nelson

Left: *Victorian terraced 'villas' at Leahurst Road, Hither Green in the Lewisham Constituency. Moments away from the railway station, these houses were built by speculative builders in huge numbers across Metropolitan Kent. It was practical and easy for people who lived in them to travel to jobs in London. At this time both commuting and the suburbs were created in London, the world's largest city at the time.*

Lewisham (Saxon 'Liofshema' in 862, meaning 'village of a man called Leofsa') was a much more affluent suburb in 1885 than its nearest northern neighbours. Comprising the parishes of Lewisham and Lee, several of its modern components, like Catford, Bellingham and Grove Park, were still villages that were yet to witness the construction of large housing estates, but Hither Green in the east of the constituency was beginning to grow around the railway junction there and Forest Hill was developing quickly in the west of the borough near stations such as Honour Oak Park, on the line connecting London Bridge with Croydon. At that time the core residential population lived south of New Cross and St Johns in Ladywell and Crofton Park; west of Blackheath (inclusive) and in Lee; east of Brockley and south towards Catford. Other scattered communities included Beckenham Hill, Downham, Grove Park, Rushey Green, Lower and Upper Sydneham but during the relatively short period between 1885 and the First World War, Lewisham was undergoing rapid social change. The borough's population increased by nearly a half between 1891 and 1901, going up from under 89,000 to over 128,000 in the space of ten years. Its electorate also rose to exceed 25,000 in1910. The proportion of voters to population was 17.3%, reflecting the more affluent owner-occupier profile of Lewisham at that time.

East of Woolwich a new **Dartford** constituency was first established in 1885 comprising the Petty Sessional District of Dartford and part of the Petty Sessional Division of Bromley. This was far from being the industrial borough of later years. The Thames estuary town was the oldest established centre of population in the North West Kent county constituency (as it was alternatively known) but it also included developing southeast London commuter suburbs such as Bexley, Bexleyheath and Sidcup together with more industrial places like Erith and Crayford. Villages such as Swanley in the Darent Valley, which was part of the Dartford Rural District, were also included, but this was mainly a suburban constituency with a strong middle class, reflected in a proportion of voters (numbering nearly 20,000) that represented 18% of a population that grew rapidly during this period. In 1891 it stood at a little below 80,000 but by 1891 had increased to 110,000, a rise of 38%, reflecting the suburbanisation of much of the area. Other scattered communities included in the then semi rural constituency were Barnehurst, Belvedere, Bexleyheath, Blackfen, Danson, Lamorbey, Longlands, North Cray, Northumberland Heath, Slade Green, Thamesmead and West Heath.

Dartford derives its name from its location and means 'ford over the river Darent(h)', or 'Tarentefort' in Norman times (1086). It owes its significance to the fact that it lay on the main road between London and Dover and was originally a fishing village at the point where the river Darent enters the Thames. Wat Tyler lived in Dartford and in 1355 Edward III established a Priory there for Augustinian Nuns. Henry VIII later converted it into a Royal Palace for himself and subsequently granted it to Anne of Cleeves. James I exchanged it for other lands with Sir Robert Cecil (the Salisbury family) who also owned nearby Lullingstone Castle.

West of Dartford and south of Lewisham lay the then freestanding towns of Beckenham and Bromley with villages surrounding them that included Orpington, West Wickham and Hayes. These were not yet greatly affected by the building of the railways (that was to happen in the Twentieth Century) and in 1885 these were part of a new **Sevenoaks** (Western Kent) constituency that also included Westerham, Hildenborough and, further south, the town itself, none of which have ever been part of London. Other communities which today are in London and which were then part of the Sevenoaks constituency were Bickley, Biggin Hill, Bromley Park, Chelsfield, Chislehurst, Coney Hall, East Wickham, Eden Park, Elmers End, Elmstead Woods, Falconwood, Farnborough, Foots Cray, Green Street Green, Kelsey Park, Keston, Mottingham, Petts Wood, Plaistow, Pratts Bottom, Shortlands, St Mary Cray, St Pauls Cray, Sundridge Park, Welling and Widmore. Population was increasing there too, though at a slightly lesser rate than in either neighbouring Lewisham or Dartford. The 1891 constituency population was 80,000, which rose to 95,000 by 1901, an increase of nearly 19%. With an electorate in 1906 of 17,256 the voter to population ratio was similar to the adjoining Dartford division but at 18.2% was the highest in this part of Kent. Sevenoaks ('Seouenacca' circa 1100) has a literal name, deriving from the oak trees on the ridge around which its original houses clustered.

Politics in Metropolitan Kent between 1885 and 1918

For the first two decades after the 3rd Reform Act politics in Northwest Kent took a distinctly Conservative turn although the General Election of 1906 heralded a more radical outcome with Labour emerging as the Left-leaning Party favoured by the electorate. Nevertheless in total 44 Tory MPs were elected for these constituencies at all General and by-elections held between 1885 and December 1910 in comparison with 6 for Labour, 2 Liberal MPs with Labour support, and only one pure Liberal. In fact the absence of a Liberal tradition of any sustainable kind is a notable feature of politics in this area. A summary of the results by constituency is shown in the table overleaf.

Each of the four borough constituencies in the LCC area returned a Conservative MP at every General Election until 1906 when, in the face of a Liberal landslide nationally, all but Lewisham were lost and it was significant that Labour

General Election Results, Metropolitan Kent 1885-1910 - by % majority								
Constituency	**1885**	**1886**	**1892**	**1895**	**1900**	**1906**	**1910 Jan**	**1910 Dec**
Deptford	C5	C9+	C3	C12	C24	Lab11	Lab4	Lab3
Greenwich	C6	C12	C4	C15	C22	L12	C11	C16
Woolwich	C14	C25	C19	C27	C10+-	Lab13	C2	Lab1
Lewisham	C17	C39	C29	C100	C100+	C10	C17	C24
Dartford	C6	C17	C6	C11	C100	LLab17	C4	LLab1
Sevenoaks	C8	C100	C21	C100	C57	C3	C24	C100
C and LU	6	6+	6	6	6+	2	5	3
L	0	0	0	0	0	2	0	1
Lab	0	0	0	0	0+	2	1	2
Total	6	6+	6	6	6+++	6	6	6

Key: 100 - unopposed; C - Conservative; L - Liberal; LU Liberal Unionist (allied with Con); Lab - Labour
+ by-election won by defending party; - lost by defending party.

performed better than the official Liberals despite the overall results in the country as a whole. A similar trend was evident in the two county seats. At Dartford a Liberal candidate with Labour support was returned whilst the Tory majority at Sevenoaks was reduced to only 3% of the votes cast. The Tory MP for Sevenoaks (1900 majority 57%) was a Minister and on his appointment to office in 1902 he had comfortably retained the seat at the statutory by-election held on 21st August to confirm his position.

The success of the fledgling Labour Party which took both Deptford and Woolwich for the first time at a General Election in 1906 was the most significant development. In fact the result at Deptford was a defining moment for the Party, which went on to win that constituency in every subsequent General Election except one, in 1931. Yet prior to 1906 Deptford had been a reasonably safe Tory seat. Their smallest majority was in 1892 when it fell to only 3% in the first General Election following an 1888 by-election in which the Party had again retained the seat. In 1895 the Party had a General Election majority of 12% and the Party retained the seat at yet another by-election held on 15th November 1897 following the MP's resignation. The Party increased its majority to 24% in 1900 and it was, therefore, a major turnaround when Labour took Deptford by a margin of 11% in 1906.

The Woolwich result also confirmed a breakthrough for Labour. The Conservative Party had been returned unopposed there in 1900 and it was again in a by-election declared on 25th April 1902 following the MPs resignation. However, the successful candidate himself resigned soon afterwards precipitating a second by-election. This was held on 11th March 1903 when Labour won its first Parliamentary seat south of the Thames. In the 1906 General Election the Party retained the seat with a majority of 13%. At the same Election the Liberals regained Greenwich topping the poll for the first time since 1868, leaving the Conservatives in possession of only two seats, Lewisham and Sevenoaks.

1906 proved to be a high water mark for the radical parties because, although Labour won Woolwich and Dartford went to the Liberal-Labour candidate again in December 1910 (though not at the earlier General Election held in January), the period from 1885 to the December 1910 Election, which was the last to be held before the Great War, was one of significant Conservative Party success in northwest Kent. No doubt the rise of the Labour Party at the expense of many Liberal votes was partly the cause of this domination but the social composition of the electorates is likely to have helped too. Lewisham exemplified how the Conservative Party had established itself amongst the suburban middle classes. Even in the Party's worst election of the period (1906) it scored a 10% margin of victory in winning the seat and its largest majority was a stunning 39% in 1886. Indeed apart from a by-election there in December 1903, after the General Election of 1892 no other Party bothered to contest Lewisham until 1906, so safe had it become for the Tories.

On the other hand the first political impact of social and demographic change can be detected taking place in Woolwich. There the riverside communities around the dockyard and the Arsenal were becoming essentially working class, whilst the southern parts of the borough, based on Eltham, were burgeoning new middle class suburbs. So although Labour won the seat fairly comfortably from the Tories for the first time in 1906 with a majority of 13%, the Conservatives regained it in January 1910, but by only 2%, before Labour got it back in the December Election by 1%. The movement of votes that was beginning to occur from Liberal to Labour amongst the working class electorate probably affected the fluidity of these results as between Labour and Tory candidates.

Voting features similar to those observed within the LCC boroughs were also seen in the county constituencies of

Dartford and Sevenoaks. The latter may be seen as an outer suburban equivalent of Lewisham, containing many new middle class communities and fewer of the working class, returning Tories with sometimes large majorities throughout the period. In the General Election of 1900 the Tory majority was a massive 57%. At neighbouring Dartford, however, which contained working class communities along the industrial riverside at both Dartford and Erith, the majorities, whichever Party won, were generally marginal. When Liberal-Labour regained the seat in December 1910 it was by a wafer-thin majority of 1%, replicating almost exactly the result in next-door Woolwich. In these early results after the establishment of new Parliamentary constituencies a pattern can be discerned that has generally repeated itself ever since. The riverside constituencies attracted the industry, which attracted workers in large numbers, who generally voted for the radical parties. The inland areas on the other hand became home to the middle class suburbs, which have generally supported the Conservative Party.

MPs for Metropolitan Kent 1885 – 1918

From	at	To	Surname	First Names	Constituency	Party
1885	G	1906	Hart Dyke	Sir William	Dartford	Conservative
1906	G	1910(Jan)	Rowlands	James		Liberal-Labour
1910(Jan)	G	1910(Dec)	Mitchell	William Foot		Conservative
1910(Dec)	G	1918	Rowlands	James		Liberal-Labour
1885	G	1888	Evelyn	William John	Deptford	Conservative
1888	B	1897	Darling	Sir Charles John		Conservative
1897	B	1906	Morton	Arthur Henry Aylmer		Conservative
1906	G	1918	Bowerman	Charles William		Labour
1885	G	1895	Boord	Thomas William	Greenwich	Conservative
1895	G	1906	Gascoyne-Cecil	Lord Hugh Richard Heathcote		Conservative
1906	G	1910(Jan)	Jackson	Richard Stephen		Liberal
1910(Jan)	G	1918	Benn	Sir Ion Hamilton		Conservative
1885	G	1891	Lewisham	Viscount (William Heneage Legg)	Lewisham	Conservative
1891	B	1903	Penn	John		Conservative
1903	B	1918	Coates	Sir Edward Feetham (Major)		Conservative
1885	G	1892	Mills	Charles William	Sevenoaks	Conservative
1892	G	1918	Forster	Henry William		Conservative
1885	G	1902	Hughes	Edwin (Col)	Woolwich	Conservative
1902	B	1903	Beresford	Lord Charles		Conservative
1903	B	1910 (Jan)	Crooks	William		Labour
1910(Jan)	G	1918	Adams	William Augustus (Major)		Conservative

Notes: First returned at: **B** By-election, **G** General Election

MPs for Dartford

Sir William Hart Dyke MP
Wikipedia

Sir William Hart Dyke (Conservative), who had been the MP for Kent Western between 1865 and 1868, returned to successfully contest Dartford in 1885. He remained the MP there until the radical landslide of 1906. His principal biographical details are contained earlier in this chapter.

However, in 1906 **James Rowlands** (Liberal) was elected with Labour support and was one of three metropolitan Kent MPs - half of the area's total - to be returned for the Party at the election. He held the seat until January 1910 when he lost to a Conservative but was elected again in December 1910 serving until 1918 when he was re-elected but died in 1920. Born in 1851 at Finsbury, where he was apprenticed as a watchmaker, he first entered politics when he contested Finsbury East in 1885, being elected there in 1886 and serving until 1895. His principal biographical details may be found in Chapter 3 (Middlesex – North London).

William Foot Mitchell (Conservative) served for less than a year having the distinction of being one of only a handful of MPs who gained a seat at the January election only to lose it again at the December contest later in 1910.

MPs for Deptford

The four MPs who represented Deptford in the House of Commons between 1885 and 1918 were unusual as a group in that they all lived to a ripe old age, the youngest attaining the age of 77 whilst the oldest lived to within three years of his centenary.

William John Evelyn MP
Wikipedia

William John Evelyn (Conservative) was no stranger to the House when elected at Deptford in 1885. He was first elected as MP for Surrey West in 1849 though he retired in 1857 and remained out of Parliament for nearly 30 years, though he did contest Guildford unsuccessfully in 1858. He was born in 1822 at Wotton near Dorking, Surrey where he married the daughter of the local rector in 1873 at the somewhat advanced age of 51. He was educated at Rugby School and attained a BA at Balliol College Oxford in 1848, a year before he entered politics. He was a member of the same family as the well known diarist and author of 'Sylvia'. One of Deptford's local council wards bears the family name. William was a Surrey magistrate and Deputy – Lieutenant, a Captain in the first Surrey Militia and in 1860 was High Sheriff of the County. He served only three years as Deptford's MP retiring (via the Chiltern Hundreds) in 1888. He died in 1908.

He was succeeded at an 1888 by-election by **Sir Charles John Darling QC** (Conservative) who was born at Colchester in 1849. Educated privately he was called to the Bar at the Inner Temple in 1874 going on to work on the Oxford Circuit in 1885. Seven years later he became a bencher at the Inner Temple and in 1896 was appointed Royal Commissioner of Assize for the Oxford Circuit. He contested Hackney South in 1885 and 1886 and after his election at Deptford sat until 1897 when he resigned to become a Judge. Appointed a Privy Councillor in 1917, he retired in 1923 and the following year was made Baron Darling. He died in 1936.

Arthur Henry Aylmer Morton (Conservative) won the 1897 by-election created by Judge Darling's resignation and went on to hold the seat until he was defeated in the 1906 landslide. He was born in 1836 and married the daughter of Sir W.H. Wilson – Todd, who himself became a Tory MP sitting in the Commons between 1892 and 1906. Educated at Eton and Kings College, Cambridge, Morton became a Fellow there and later its Senior Dean and Bursar. He was something of a champion of the interests of the industrial working class and his first attempts to gain election to the Commons were made in northern city seats, at Leeds East in 1892 and Manchester North in 1895, though he was unsuccessful. He was elected a London County Councillor in 1895 and became a Vice Chairman of the Housing of the Working Classes Committee. In 1904 he was appointed an Ecclesiastical Commissioner and died in 1913.

C W Bowerman MP
Wikipedia

The first non- Tory MP for Deptford was **Charles William Bowerman** (Labour) who was born in 1851 and lived until 1947. He was apprenticed as a Compositor going on to be an active trade unionist creating a platform from which he was able to launch a political career. He was firstly the General Secretary and later Parliamentary Secretary of the London Society of Compositors. In 1901, the year in which the Labour Party was formed, he was President of the Trades Union Congress and between 1901 and 1906 sat as an alderman on the LCC. After his election at Deptford he became Secretary of the TUC in 1911, serving until 1923. He was also elected President of the National Printing and Kindred Trades Employees' Federation. He was a Junior Whip in 1916 but held no other Parliamentary office despite a long career that ended in defeat at the 1931 Election. He was meanwhile a member of the Board of Trade Arbitration Court and in 1919 was appointed a London County magistrate.

MPs for Greenwich

Thomas William Boord (Conservative), elected in 1873, retained his Greenwich seat when it became a single member borough constituency in 1885. He held it until 1895 when he retired. His principal biographical details may be found earlier in this chapter.

Lord Hugh Richard Heathcote Cecil
Wikipedia

He was succeeded by **Lord Hugh Richard Heathcote Cecil** (Conservative), son of the third Marquis of Salisbury. Born in 1869, Cecil was educated at Eton and University College Oxford where he attained his MA in 1894 three years after gaining a DCL whilst a Fellow at Hertford College. He also gained LL.Ds at both Edinburgh and Cambridge Universities. His life of privilege continued following his election at Greenwich when he was appointed PPS to his own father when he held the office of Foreign Secretary. Unusually for a Conservative during this period he was a supporter of free trade but this did not prevent his defeat in 1906 after which he was out of the House until 1910 when he was elected as an MP for Oxford University, a seat he retained until 1937 when he became Provost of Eton College. During the First World War he was a Lieutenant in the Royal Flying Corps in 1915 and the following year served as a member of the Mesopotamia Commission. He was made Baron Quickswood in 1941, retired from Eton three years later and died in 1956.

Cecil was defeated in 1906 by **Richard Stephen Jackson** (Liberal) who sat for one term only. Born in 1850 at Newington, Kent, he was educated at the Elm House School, Sittingbourne and was admitted to legal practice as a solicitor in 1872, working in London and Greenwich where he entered local politics serving as a councillor on the LCC between 1889-95 and 1898-1907. He was Mayor of Greenwich in 1900 and contested the Parliamentary Borough unsuccessfully in the general election held the same year. He sat until January 1910 and died in 1938.

In January 1910 Jackson was defeated by **Captain Sir Ion Hamilton Benn** (Conservative), the son of the Reverend Benn of Douglas, County Cork in Southern Ireland, where he was born in 1863. He went into business as a Director of the London based Price and Pierce Limited and of the Price Brothers Company in Montreal, Quebec, Canada, where he met his second wife having been previously widowed. He was active both in local politics and business, becoming Mayor of Greenwich in 1901-02 and a member of the Metropolitan Water Board from 1903-06. He served on the LCC between 1907 and 1910 but was most noted for an extremely long tenure as a Director of the Port of London Authority on the Board of which he served from 1909 until his death in 1961, two years short of his centenary. From 1937 to 1946 he was a member of the Thames Conservancy Board. In his middle years he was active in the voluntary services being an Honorary Colonel of the 20th Battalion of the London Regiment; a temporary Lieutenant-Commander in the RNR in 1914 and in the RNVR in 1915. He was mentioned in despatches several times during the War and in 1917 was awarded the DSO following the naval bombardment of Zeebrugge and Ostende. He was made an Acting Captain in 1918. He first contested Greenwich in 1906. He was MP for Greenwich until 1922.

MPs for Lewisham

William Heneage Legg, Viscount Lewisham (Conservative) was elected in 1885 having previously sat for Kent Western. He remained MP until 1891 when he succeeded to the peerage. His principal biographical details can be found on page 163.

John Penn (Conservative) won the by-election occasioned by his predecessor's elevation to the Lords in 1891 and held it until he died in 1903. He was the son of a marine engineer who established a company of the same name. A keen golfer he owned a golf course at North Berwick, Scotland.

Maj Sir E Feetham Coates MP
Epsom & Ewell History Explorer

Major Sir Edward Feetham Coates (Conservative) won the 1903 by-election and held the seat until 1918. Born in 1853, Coates was the eldest son of a Deputy – Lieutenant of North Yorkshire from Helperby Hall near Thirsk. He was educated at Marlborough and became a stockbroker. He held several grace and favour public appointments himself including a Lieutenancy of the City for London, a Deputy-Lieutenancy of Surrey, where he was also a magistrate and county alderman; and he too became a Deputy-Lieutenant of North Yorkshire where he was also a magistrate. From 1905 to 1909 he was chairman of the Surrey County Council. He was a Committee member of the Surrey Territorial Force Association and a trustee of Crystal Palace. The patron of one living he was a major in the third Battalion of the West Yorkshire Regiment. It was in that county that he first contested a Parliamentary election, in 1900 at Elland, where he was defeated. He eventually served as an MP from 1903 until his death in 1921.

MPs for Sevenoaks

Charles William Mills (Conservative) whose father was Kent Western's MP between 1868 and 1880 was returned for Sevenoaks in 1885 and sat until 1892. He was born in 1855 and followed his father into the family banking firm of Glyn Mills. Educated at Eton he inherited his father's title in 1898 when he became the second Baron Hillingdon and entered the House of Lords. He died in 1919.

Henry William Forster (Conservative) won the seat in 1892 and held it until 1918 when he transferred to a new Bromley seat until 1919. Born at Southend Hall, Kent in 1866 he was Eton and New College, Oxford educated, and married the daughter of the 1st Lord Montagu of Beaulieu. He went into politics at an early age but achieved as Junior Lord of the Treasury (i.e. a Government Whip) from 1902-5 and an Opposition Whip from 1905 – 1911. During the First World War he was appointed Financial Secretary at the War Office in 1915 and served until 1919. A year later he was appointed Governor – General of Australia, a posting that lasted for five years. He died in 1936.

MPs for Woolwich

The first MP for Woolwich was **Colonel Sir Edwin Hughes** (Conservative) who was born at Droitwich, Worcestershire in 1832 and educated in Birmingham at King Edward VI's Grammar School. He was admitted to legal practice as a solicitor in 1860 and later became a Conservative Agent in the City of London, Kent and Greenwich. He was a member of the LCC and the Technical Education Board and of the London School Board. He was additionally an Honorary Colonel in the Second Kent Artillery Volunteers and was Mayor of Woolwich in 1900. He retired from the House via the Chiltern Hundreds in 1902 and died two years later.

Hughes was succeeded at a by-election by **Lord Charles Beresford** (Conservative) but he too took the Chiltern Hundreds route to exit the Commons quickly in 1903. He had formerly sat for Marylebone East and his principal biographical details are contained in Chapter 3 (Middlesex – Central London).

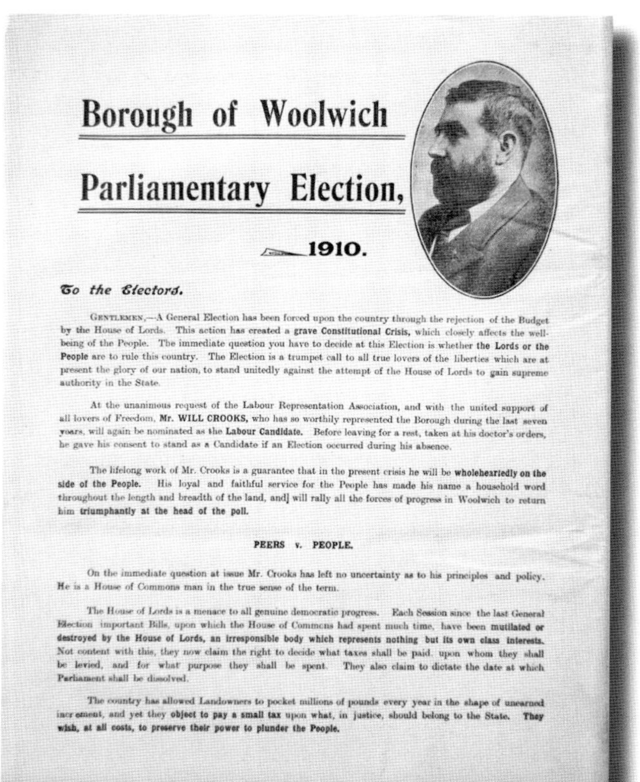
Borough of Woolwich

Parliamentary Election,

1910.

To the Electors.

Gentlemen,—A General Election has been forced upon the country through the rejection of the Budget by the House of Lords. This action has created a **grave Constitutional Crisis,** which closely affects the well-being of the People. The immediate question you have to decide at this Election is whether **the Lords or the People** are to rule this country. The Election is a trumpet call to all true lovers of the liberties which are at present the glory of our nation, to stand unitedly against the attempt of the House of Lords to gain supreme authority in the State.

At the unanimous request of the Labour Representation Association, and with the united support of all lovers of Freedom, **Mr. WILL CROOKS,** who has so worthily represented the Borough during the last seven years, will again be nominated as the **Labour Candidate.** Before leaving for a rest, taken at his doctor's orders, he gave his consent to stand as a Candidate if an Election occurred during his absence.

The lifelong work of Mr. Crooks is a guarantee that in the present crisis he will be **wholeheartedly on the side of the People.** His loyal and faithful service for the People has made his name a household word throughout the length and breadth of the land, and] will rally all the forces of progress in Woolwich to return him **triumphantly at the head of the poll.**

PEERS v. PEOPLE.

On the immediate question at issue Mr. Crooks has left no uncertainty as to his principles and policy. He is a House of Commons man in the true sense of the term.

The House of Lords is a menace to all genuine democratic progress. Each Session since the last General Election important Bills, upon which the House of Commons had spent much time, have been **mutilated or destroyed by the House of Lords, an irresponsible body which represents nothing but its own class interests.** Not content with this, they now claim the right to decide what taxes shall be paid, upon whom they shall be levied, and for what purpose they shall be spent. They also claim to dictate the date at which Parliament shall be dissolved.

The country has allowed Landowners to pocket millions of pounds every year in the shape of unearned incr ement, and yet they **object to pay a small tax** upon what, in justice, should belong to the State. **They wish, at all costs, to preserve their power to plunder the People.**

Will Crooks MP for Woolwich, for many years was a Labour Hero, as the first MP to be elected for the new party. He was defeated at the 1910 January General Election by Adams, a Conservative, but Asquith presided over a hung parliament, and so there was a second General election in December 1910. Crooks was re-elected at this election in December 1910. He was gradually joined by more and more Labour MPs, as the then leader Arthur Henderson saw seats rise from 29 to 40. **People's History Museum Manchester**

The by-election created by his retirement was held in 1903 and was sensationally won by **William Crooks** (Labour), one of the first to be elected following the Party's creation only two years earlier. Crooks was born in Poplar in 1852 and educated at the George Green School and partly at the Poplar Poor Law School. However, he started work at the age of nine and later on became apprenticed to a cooper in 1866. He served on the Borough Council between 1892 and 1910 and was Mayor of Poplar in 1901. He was a member of the LCC, sat on the Metropolitan Asylum Board, and was Chairman of the Poplar Board of Guardians from 1898 to 1906. He was defeated at Woolwich at the January 1910 election but regained the seat in December, going on to hold it until 1918, when it was subdivided. Thereafter he sat for Woolwich East until he resigned in 1921, dying a few months later.

The person who unseated Crooks briefly was **Major William Augustus Adams** (Conservative), the son of a rector from Bantry, County Kerry in Southern Ireland. He was born at Dublin in 1865 and went to Harrow School, returning to his home city to attend the University where he achieved a First Class Honours Degree in Classics and a Masters in Modern History before entering the Royal Military College, Sandhurst. He joined the 5th Royal Irish Lancers in 1887, was made a Lieutenant two years later and a Captain in 1893. Following service in South Africa (1988-1902), and Japan (1903-05) he was promoted to the rank of Major in 1905 and served on the General Staff at Army HQ between 1909 and his election at Woolwich in January 1910. He died in 1940.

Chapter 6
Metropolitan Surrey 1832 - 1918

Early History

Surrey gets its name from Anglo-Saxon words that meant 'the land south of the river'. Originally called 'Suth-Rea' it was part of a kingdom that included Sussex, belonging to the South Saxons. Certain Surrey towns and settlements have been of historical significance for many centuries past. Southwark was probably the most important and it may be fairly claimed that London owes its own position to the natural features of Southwark's early landscape. The first London Bridge was probably built in the First Century AD connecting it with the City and being the first crossing place of the Thames, Roman Southwark grew rapidly. In Anglo Saxon times in the 10th Century it came to be known as 'Suthriganawoerc' meaning 'fort of the men of Surrey' and became the greatest traffic and trading centre in the country, known in Norman times as 'Sudwerca' meaning, 'southern defensive work, or fort'.

Other settlements had significant historical roots including Lambeth, now very much part of central London, but which in 1188 when the Archbishop of Canterbury built a Palace there, was a place cut off from London by the river and accessible mainly by boat or barge. Westminster, on the opposite bank, had yet to become the home of the Royal Court, let alone of the Houses of Parliament. Another upstream Thames settlement at Runnymede will be forever etched in the annals of English constitutional history as it was there that King John and the Barons signed the so-called Magna Carta, which some argue began the process of circumscribing the power and authority of the sovereign that was in time to lead to the rise of Parliamentary government in this country.

Nearly three centuries after the monarchy had established the Court at Westminster opposite Lambeth, the Tudor King Henry VII established a Palace upstream at Sheen, which he renamed Richmond after the town of which he was fond in Yorkshire, and whose name he had taken when a Prince. The Palace occasionally accommodated the whole Royal Court, most notably during an outbreak of the Plague in 1603, and subsequently in 1625 also.

Southwark was traditionally the place with the largest population in Surrey with industries that attracted labour from far and wide. By the 15th century it had one of London's largest immigrant populations. German, Dutch and Flemish craftspeople, excluded by the City of London on the basis that they were not members of a trade guild, settled in Southwark where their skills were put to good use in the leather industry. Southwark's proximity to the river Thames led to strong links across the world. Emigration as well as immigration flourished. A local man captained the 'Mayflower', which carried the Pilgrim Fathers to America in 1620. As Southwark's importance as a trading centre grew, ships carrying imports of tea from China, dairy produce from New Zealand and foods from British colonies were regular visitors to the Thames wharves. From the 16th to the 18th centuries as a result of immigration, its population tripled from ten to thirty thousand and there was plenty of activity going on in the borough. A bullring and bear pit as well as theatres and other amusements were to be found close to the riverside. By 1746 the river frontage between Bankside and Rotherhithe was pretty much fully built up and Southwark extended southwards to the Old Kent Road and included much of present-day Bermondsey. Southwark was by then the second largest urban area in England. The riverfront became increasingly important as overseas and domestic trade expanded. Landing places near the City were at a premium and new wharves and warehouses were built to accommodate the growing trade. Although Southwark was not powerful enough in the medieval period to achieve full Borough status, or in later years to repel the administrative control of the City of London; it nevertheless provided many of the elements for London that were crucial to its existence.

In 1700 the population of Surrey was estimated to be about 150,000 with perhaps over 20% living in Southwark but just over a century later the county had grown to 278,000 due mainly to the growth of the borough and of Lambeth. It was during the industrial revolution that Southwark first developed as a great manufacturing centre. The area witnessed enormous diversification to encompass engineering, glass, leather, hat making, paper, gas, brewing, vinegar and even steam powered corn mills. Its development as a place for trade and manufacture was such that by 1831 it had grown to have approximately 100,000 inhabitants. The poor in overwhelming numbers, immigrants, criminals, prisons and popular entertainment were all important features of Southwark life. Their presence brought advances in social welfare, pioneering new forms of transport, leading edge manufacturing inventions and the vitality arising from a rich social and ethnic mix.

Surrey's population growth rate continued to accelerate and within the first thirty years of the Nineteenth Century rose by over 200,000 as London's metropolis began to expand south of the Thames within the county, especially west of Southwark in Lambeth and Battersea. As the railways developed Surrey became more important as a county where wealthy people could live and travel to work in London. In fact the increasing urbanization of London stimulated a huge increase in Surrey's population. Although initially this growth occurred in the boroughs of Southwark, Bermondsey, Camberwell, Lambeth, Battersea and Wandsworth, all of which became part of the London County Council when it was established in 1889. After the First World War most growth occurred within the area of the County that was transferred in 1965 to the Greater London Boroughs of Merton, Croydon, Sutton, Kingston and Richmond. It even began to spill over into the more rural areas and, despite the Green Belt restrictions imposed on house building around London after the Second World War, suburbia has moved outwards ever since.

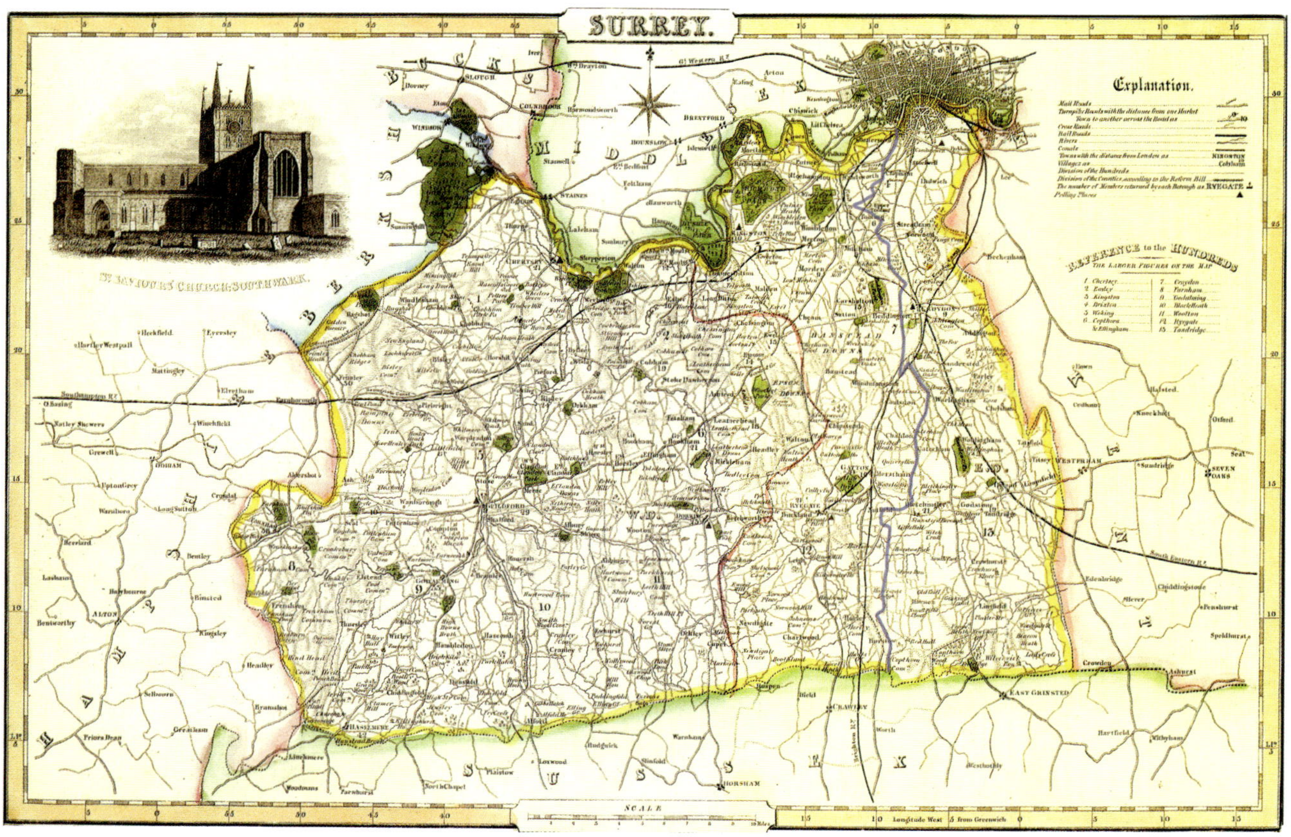

Pigot's map of 1840 shows the very small part of the County that has the bulk of the population. The Surrey bank of the Thames grew rapidly as part of London, and it was this area that developed many constituencies, whereas the 'country' areas of Surrey grew at a slower pace. In 1832 the county was divided into Eastern and Western parts indicated by the red line. In 1868 the Eastern Constituency was itself divided. The new Mid-Surrey Constituency is marked on its eastern border by the blue line.

Before the arrival of 19th Century local government, Surrey was divided into twelve Hundreds for administrative purposes. Five constituted eastern Surrey. Of the remainder, the western part, no element contained any slice of what we now describe as the London metropolitan area. The two most southeasterly ones of Reigate and Tandridge also fell outside it. However, the Brixton, Kingston and Wallington Hundreds covered an area virtually identical to that which is today contained within the London Boroughs of Southwark, Lambeth, Wandsworth, Croydon, Sutton, Merton and Kingston-on-Thames.

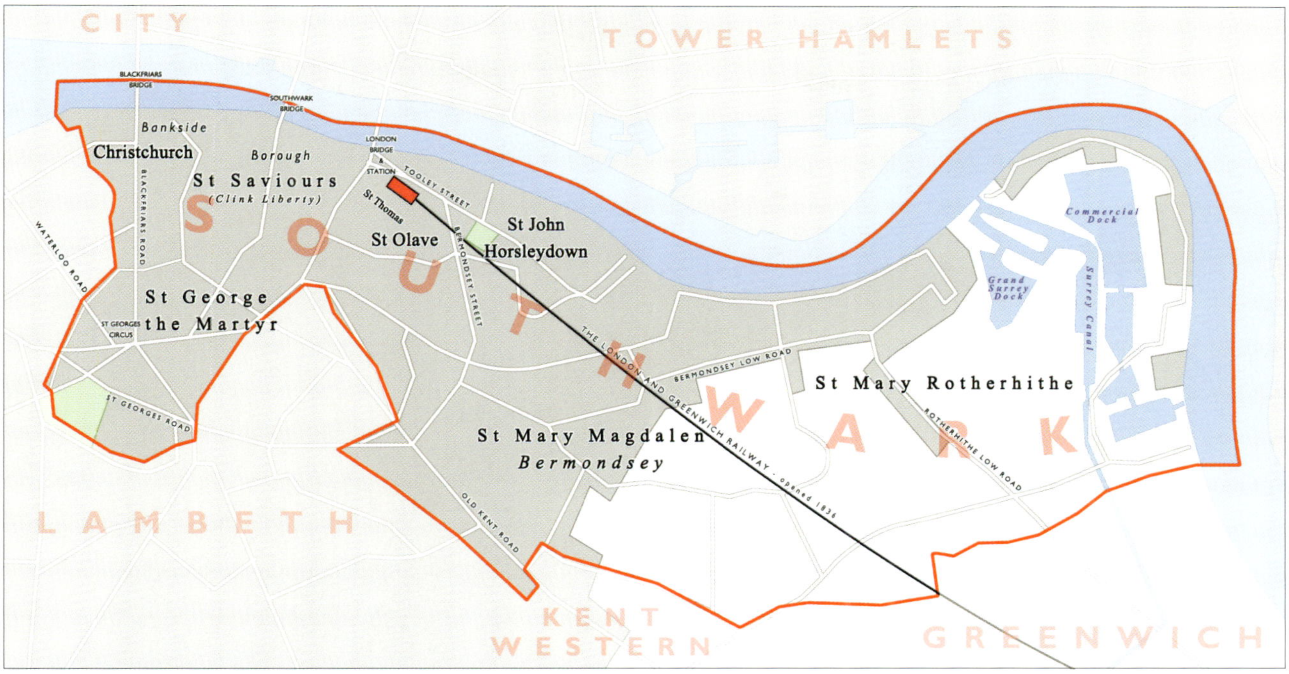

In 1832 the northern part of the County, near to London, held a large population. The arrival of the London & Greenwich Railway - London's first railway line - heralded a more rapid spread of population. In 1832 the effect has not yet been felt. The Southwark & Lambeth Constituencies together had more than twice the number of electors than in the rest of Surrey, but in 30 years time all would have changed.

Parliamentary Representation

According to 'The House of Commons, 700 Years of British Tradition', **Southwark** was first made a Parliamentary borough in the reign of Richard II in 1386, though the Boundaries Commission states that this occurred as early as 1295. It is certain, however, that the 1832 Representation of the People Act reconfirmed its status as a two-member Parliamentary borough constituency. The 1832 constituency boundaries contained a population of 134,117 and an electorate of 4,775. The original Parliamentary Borough was nothing like the shape of the present-day version. In those days the boundaries covered only Southwark, the Borough, Bermondsey and Rotherhithe. Neither Walworth nor Newington nor the Elephant & Castle were within the constituency's boundaries. Camberwell, Peckham, and Dulwich were well beyond it.

The King's Bench, Southwark depicted in 1830. This prison took its name from the King's Bench court of law and was one of a number of penal institutions in Southwark at the time. **Wikipedia**

Until the early 19th Century Southwark (The Borough), and the river developments towards Deptford (in Kent), were the only significant places in South London, but an influx of immigrants from Ireland fled the potato famine of the 1840s to work on the new London and Greenwich Railway, and this started to open up the whole area. A map of 1835 shows the line of the new railway as 'intended'. It opened between Bricklayers' Arms and Deptford in 1836 and was London's first. By then the Southwark borough already took up the entire riverside from Bankside towards Rotherhithe where the Surrey Docks had also recently been cut. The built-up area spread southwards through Newington to the New Kent Road, beyond which there was a substantial amount of Walworth already completed, with Camberwell just about included in its orbit. Still to develop was the area to the southeast of Bermondsey and Rotherhithe towards Peckham.

Cross's New Plan of London of 1835 also shows that housing south of the river already extended along the Thames westward through Lambeth to the parish boundary with St Mary's Battersea where, just beyond a small riverside settlement at Nine Elms, a New Town was being laid out along the Road to Wandsworth. Although Waterloo station was not yet built, the area of North Lambeth between Waterloo Bridge and Kennington Lane was already comprehensively

Top Left: *The Church of St Saviour, standing at the southern end of London bridge became Southwark Cathedral in 1905. The building dates from 1220.*

Top Right: *Opened in 1868 the Hop Exchange in Southwark Street received tons of hops from Kent, as this was a centre for the brewing industry during this period.*

Left: *The original Lambeth suspension bridge was opened in 1860 and led to the rapid development of Lambeth in the mid 19th century. The old bridge was replaced in 1932.*

Above: *Kingston Bridge was opened by the Duchess of Clarence four years before the Surrey Eastern Constituency was created in 1832. It was commissioned by the Kingston Corporation, and linked Surrey with Middlesex. It replaced an earlier medieval timber bridge. Election results were announced at Kingston Guildhall for the Eastern Surrey Constituency from 1832, and for Mid-Surrey after 1867. The Thames was the boundary between the Surrey and Middlesex County Constituencies.*

John Nelson

Left: *Lambeth Palace is the London residence of the Archbishop of Canterbury, and in 1832, it was placed in the new Lambeth Constituency. Standing facing the river Thames with the Palace of Westminster opposite at this time it was on the fringe of the built up area; by 1885 it had become surrounded by new buildings as Lambeth expanded southwards.*

All images Gordon Rushton, except where marked

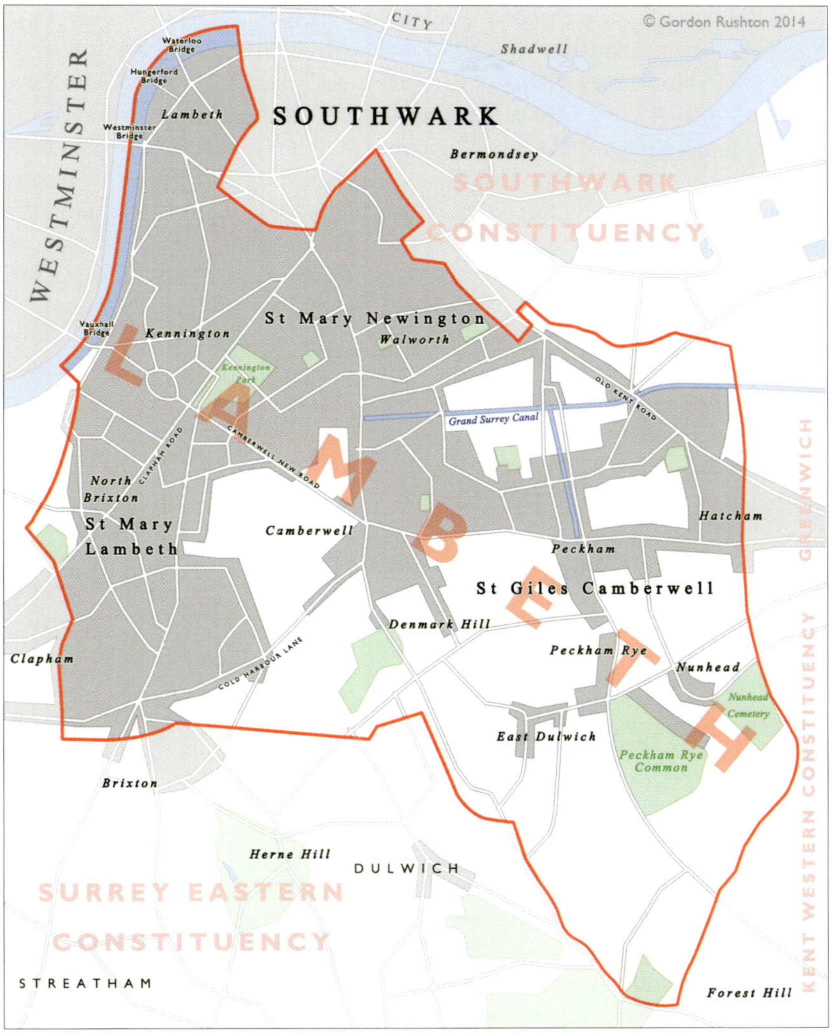

Lambeth Constituency in 1832 on the cusp of massive expansion, but still the largest constituency in population and electorate in Surrey. The Grand Surrey Canal moves the goods into and out of the Surrey Docks, but soon all this will change, with the coming of the railway.

developed and building in South Lambeth beyond the Oval (The home of Surrey County Cricket Club) was also under way towards Stockwell and Brixton.

Growth was such that a new **Lambeth** borough constituency was established for the first time on a two-member basis in 1832. By this time it had a population of 154,613, which was bigger than Southwark's although its electorate of 4,768 was virtually the same, indicating a less middle class socio-demographic profile. Lambeth was the 5th largest borough constituency in England and Southwark was the 7th. Lambeth extended south from Waterloo Bridge towards Brixton, which was not included, and east from Westminster Bridge as far as Peckham and Honor Oak, also taking in Kennington, Stockwell, Newington, Walworth, New Cross Gate (but not New Cross), Camberwell and East Dulwich.

The burning of the Houses of Parliament in 1834 as viewed from Lambeth
© Palace of Westminster Collection www.parliament.uk/art

'Lamhytha' meant a 'landing place for lambs' and somehow encapsulates Lambeth's role as one of London's 'provider' boroughs. It owed its development to the growing needs of the administrative, business and manufacturing Leviathan that London had become by the turn of the 18th Century. Although neighbouring Southwark outstripped it initially, when other river bridges were opened these stimulated rapid growth in Lambeth. The borough had no such connection until 1750 when Westminster Bridge was opened and until that time had been a resort for Londoners at play. Between Lambeth and Southwark were pleasure gardens, bear pits and bullrings. Amongst the most famous were the Vauxhall Pleasure Gardens in Kennington Lane close to what is now Vauxhall Bridge. The construction first of Westminster, then Vauxhall (in 1816) and Waterloo (in 1817) bridges, brought population development and, with the building there of the South Western Railways London Waterloo Terminus; future growth and development were assured. The Railway was opened between Nine Elms and Waterloo in 1848.

The only other Parliamentary constituency in this part of the metropolitan area in 1832 was **Surrey Eastern,** a county seat that had a population of 110,869 not included within the two borough constituencies. At this stage places like Battersea were still villages and all but 86,000 of the total population of Surrey lived in its two London borough constituencies and the Hundreds of the Eastern county division. Within the latter the election was held at Croydon, which was also a polling place. The others were at Camberwell (for the Brixton Hundred which contained most of the voters) and Kingston.

The 1867 Representation of the People Act did not alter the shape of the borough constituencies in metropolitan Surrey but Surrey Eastern was divided into two. Kingston hundred was placed in **Mid Surrey**. Apart from the town itself this included the parishes of Chessington, Ham, Hook, Kew, Malden, Richmond and Petersham; all of which are in the present-day metropolitan area together with Esher, Long Ditton, Thames Ditton, which are not. However, the constituency also extended as far south as Reigate and included Battersea, Wandsworth, Putney, Wimbledon, Mitcham, Beddington, Wallington, Carshalton, Coulsdon, Cheam and Sutton. Election results were announced at Kingston. **Surrey Eastern** was reduced in size and covered from Dulwich in the north to Lingfield near the Sussex border in the south. Its principal electorates were in Clapham, south Brixton, Streatham, Norwood, south Camberwell, Dulwich and Croydon, which was also where the election results were announced. The map of Surrey on page 174 shows the detail.

Populations & Electorates

The franchise extension, coupled with the massive population expansion that occurred throughout the area meant that by the 1880s the existing constituencies seriously under-represented the local populations; not that this appeared to be a major concern for many politicians at the time. The following table illustrates the changes that took place between the three Reform Acts, as measured by the national census taken in 1831, 1861 and 1881, and by their electorates:

Constituency	*1831 pop*	*1832 electorate*	*1861 pop*	*1868 electorate*	*1881 pop*	*1884 electorate*	*Pop change 31-81*	*Electorate change 32-84*
Lambeth	*154613*	*4768*	*294883*	*33377*	*498697*	*55558*	*223%*	*1065%*
Southwark	*134117*	*4775*	*193593*	*17703*	*221886*	*24817*	*65%*	*420%*
Surrey Eastern	*110869*	*3150*	*93490*	*9986*	*227208*	*25216*	*105%*	*701%*
Surrey Mid			*121586*	*10565*	*308134*	*26776*		

Lambeth was the dominant constituency throughout this period and grew such that both its population and electorate dwarfed the other two metropolitan constituencies in Surrey. This reflects the fact that Southwark was already a fairly built up constituency in the earlier parts of the century and was also encircled on its southern side by Lambeth, which was the constituency that had room to grow within its 1832 boundaries. Thus between 1832 and 1884 the growth of Kennington, Brixton, Newington, Camberwell and Peckham all took place within the Lambeth constituency. Surrey Eastern also grew strongly – especially allowing for the fact that Mid Surrey was created in 1868. Even after this is taken into account the constituency population grew by over 700% and by 1881 exceeded that of Southwark, which itself doubled in population in the period, making one of the most densely packed urban areas in the country. Mid Surrey became the second most populous constituency by the 1880s, reflecting the massive development of towns prompted by the opening of railway stations.

During the fifty year period in question Lambeth grew from 7th placed to become England's 3rd largest borough constituency by population (behind Liverpool and Finsbury), though Southwark dropped from 9th to 13th. The electorates in 1884 were 24,817 and 55,558 respectively, both a little over 11% of their populations. Lambeth's was 3rd behind Birmingham and Finsbury while Southwark had the 18th largest borough electorate. After the 1868 boundary changes in the county divisions Eastern Surrey contained a population of 227,208 by the 1880s and became the 12th largest county division in England, with an electorate of 25,216, representing a proportion of just over 11%. Mid Surrey was the 5th largest county constituency measured by population.

The Politics of Metropolitan Surrey between 1832 and 1885

Overall between 1832 and 1880 there were 62 Liberal successes at General Elections and only 10 for the Conservatives although the by-election outcomes were evenly matched at half a dozen each. Liberals won Lambeth at every General election between 1832 and 1880 and were also successful at three by-elections, in 1850, 1862 and 1865. However, this did not prevent MPs being defeated by fellow radicals, a strange phenomenon of the period but especially pronounced in Lambeth where elections were more often contested by other Liberals than by Conservatives. Liberals defeated other Liberals at general elections in 1847, 1852, 1857 and 1865 and at by-elections in 1850 and 1862. During the same period the Tories captured Southwark only once at a General Election, when they topped the poll in 1874 following a by-election success there in 1870. The Liberals won 3 other by-elections at Southwark, in 1840, 1845 and 1860. Again Liberal defeated other Liberals at four general elections (1852, 1857, 1859 and 1874) as well as at an 1845 by-election. In addition when Conservatives won by-elections in 1870 and 1880 they topped the poll against two Liberal candidates. In Eastern Surrey, where the same phenomenon was not in evidence, the Liberals outnumbered Tories by 15-9 and won both seats in 7 out of 12 General Elections, including six consecutively between 1847 and 1868. The Tories topped the poll five times, three consecutively between 1835 and 1847, winning both seats in the last two. They won them again, after the franchise was extended, in 1874 and 1880. The Tories also won two by-elections, one in 1841 during the earlier period of their success in the constituency, and again in 1871 when they took the seat from the Liberals.

MPs for Metropolitan Surrey, 1832 - 1885

From	at	To	Surname	First Names	Constituency	Party
1832	G	1852	Tennyson – D'Eyncourt	Charles	Lambeth	Liberal
1832	G	1847	Hawes (junior)	Sir Benjamin		Liberal
1847	G	1850	Pearson	Charles		Liberal
1850	B	1865	Williams	William		Liberal
1852	G	1857	Wilkinson	William Arthur		Liberal
1857	G	1862	Roupell	William		Liberal
1862	B	1868	Doulton	Frederick		Liberal
1865 (May)	B	1865 (Jul)	Lawrence	Sir James Clarke		Liberal
1865	G	1868	Hughes	Thomas		Liberal
1868	G	1885	Lawrence	James Clarke		Liberal
1868	G	1885	McArthur	Sir William		Liberal
1832	G	1835	Brougham	William	Southwark	Liberal
1832	G	1852	Humphery	John		Liberal
1835	G	1840	Harvey	Daniel Whittle		Liberal
1840	B	1845	Wood	Benjamin		Liberal
1845	B	1855	Molesworth	Sir William		Liberal
1852	G	1857	Pellatt	Apsley		Liberal
1855	B	1860	Napier	Admiral Sir Charles		Liberal
1857	G	1880	Locke	John		Liberal
1860	B	1870	Layard	Austen Henry		Liberal
1870	B	1880	Beresford	Marcus (Lieut-Col)		Conservative
1880 (Feb)	B	1880 (Apr)	Clarke	Sir Edward George		Conservative
1880	G	1885	Cohen	Arthur		Liberal
1880	G	1885	Rogers	James Edwin Thorold		Liberal
1832	G	1835	Ivatt - Briscoe	Sir John	Surrey Eastern	Liberal
1832	G	1837	Beauclerk	Aubrey William (Major)		Liberal
1835	G	1841	Alsager	Richard (Captain)		Conservative
1837	G	1847	Kemble	Henry		Liberal
1841	B	1847	Antrobus	Sir Edmund		Conservative
1847	G	1874	King	Peter John Locke		Liberal
1847	G	1865	Alcock	Thomas		Liberal
1865	G	1871	Buxton	Charles		Liberal
1871	B	1885	Watney	James		Conservative
1874	G	1885	Grantham	Sir William		Conservative
1868	G	1884	Peek	Sir Henry	Surrey Mid	Conservative
1868	G	1870	Brodrick	William		Conservative
1870	B	1875	Baggallay	Richard		Conservative
1875	B	1885	Lawrence	Sir James John Trevor		Conservative
1884	B	1885	Ellis	Sir John Whittaker		Conservative

Notes: First returned at: **B** By-election, **G** General Election

Lambeth

The first to be elected and topping the poll was **Charles Tennyson D'Eyncourt** (Liberal). A Lincolnshire man who was the patron of two livings and later became a magistrate and Deputy-Lieutenant, he was also High Steward of the town of Louth. However, he had connections with France, where he had a home at Aincourt en Vexin, a name he assumed as

D'Eyncourt in 1835 when he changed his name by Royal decree. He was therefore elected simply as Tennyson in 1832. Born sometime around 1780, he achieved an MA at St John's College, Cambridge and joined the Inner Temple where he was called to the bar in 1806. He entered the House as MP for the Lincolnshire port town of Great Grimsby in 1818 where he was re-elected in 1820. Then in the general elections of 1826 and 1830 he was returned for the 'rotten' Surrey borough of Bletchingley. As was allowed in those days he also contested Stamford in 1830, though unsuccessfully but in the immediate pre-reform Parliament of 1831 he was elected to serve as MP for the Lincolnshire market town in a contest that was so bitter between him and his rival, Lord Thomas Cecil, that the two of them fought a duel. In 1832 he was elected at Lambeth and went on to hold the seat until 1852 when he was defeated by fellow Liberals, Williams and Wilkinson. D'Eyncourt promoted an 1827 Act of Parliament that prohibited the use of spring guns in shooting game and in the years 1827 – 1830 conducted a Bill aimed at transferring the franchise from the Nottinghamshire Borough of East Retford to the City of Birmingham. In the years 1833, 1834 and 1837 he failed in introducing Bills to shorten the length of Parliaments but in 1849 did manage to secure a First Reading, though it progressed no further.

Sir Benjamin Hawes (Liberal) was also elected in 1832 and sat until 1847. Born in 1797, he became a soap maker and was the brother-in-law of the famous Victorian engineer, Isambard Kingdom Brunel. He was active in the pursuit of medical reform and introduced (unsuccessfully) a Bill in 1841 to regulate the qualifications of medical practitioners. He was appointed Under Secretary of State for the Colonies in 1846 but lost his seat in 1847 when D'Eyncourt and Charles Pearson, fellow Liberals, forced him into third place. He was later returned for the Irish constituency of Kinsale, which he represented from 1848 until he resigned in 1851. From 1852 until his death in 1862 he was Under Secretary for War.

One of his successors at Lambeth, **Charles Pearson** (Liberal) lived at Old Jewry, Clapham Common and was born in 1794. Educated at Eastbourne College, he became a Solicitor, being admitted in 1816. He made a modestly successful career being elected as the City of London's Solicitor in 1839 but was also variously solicitor to the Irish Society and an attorney of the Lord Mayor's Court. A radical who favoured reformatory treatment for juvenile offenders and opposed capital punishment, his principal claim to fame was as the original promoter of the Metropolitan Underground Railway in 1859. He only sat as Lambeth's MP from 1847 to 1850 when he resigned. He died in 1862.

William Williams (Liberal) was a merchant who lived in Park Square, Regents Park and although he was a *laissez faire* Liberal who was opposed to public spending and income tax, in matters affecting the franchise he was a radical. Prior to his tenure at Lambeth (1850-1865) he represented Coventry from 1835 to 1847. He died on April 18th 1865.

His partner MP was **William Arthur Wilkinson** (Liberal). Elected when he defeated fellow Liberal (D'Eyncourt) in 1852, he ironically suffered the same fate himself in 1857. Born in 1795 he was the son of a Peckham surgeon and at the time of his election lived at Shortlands, near Beckenham, Kent. He was educated at the Merchant Taylor's School and became a member of the Stock Exchange in 1816. Twice widowed, he was a Surrey magistrate who chaired the Croydon Railway Company from 1839 until its amalgamation with the Brighton Railway to form the London, Brighton and South Coast Company in 1846. The following year he contested Sunderland unsuccessfully in two elections (July and December) when his opponent was the Conservative entrepreneur, George Hudson, known as 'the railway king'. After his defeat at Lambeth in 1857 he tried unsuccessfully to re-enter Parliament on three occasions at Reigate – twice in 1859 and once more in 1863. He died on 13th April 1865, by coincidence only a week before William Williams.

Roupell Street, Waterloo (Lambeth constituency 1832), named after the Roupell family one of whom, William, a Liberal represented the constituency between 1857 and 1862 until he fled the country, subsequently returning to serve a 14 year sentence for having forged his father's will. **Gordon Rushton**

William Roupell (Liberal) was one of four illegitimate children of Richard Palmer Roupell, a Lambeth and Southwark lead smelter and wealthy landowner who developed Roupell Street, SE1 and Christchurch and Palace Roads, Streatham Hill, in the mid 1800s. William was born in Lambeth in 1831 and became an MP in 1857 when he defeated Wilkinson. He lived in Aspen House, a mansion on Brixton Hill, and his first election campaign has been described as one of the most corrupt in London's history[1].

1 **'The Roupells of Lambeth - Politics, Property and Peculation in Victorian London' by Judy Harris. London: Streatham Society,**

By 1862 he was on the verge of bankruptcy, having squandered a vast sum and lost most of the land it had taken his father and grandfather 50 years to acquire. At trials in 1862 and 1863 he confessed to destroying his father's will at his death-bed and forging a new one and was sent to prison for 14 years. He was a Major Commandant of the 19th Surrey Rifle Volunteers and politically was an Advanced Liberal. He was called to the Bar of the Inner Temple in 1861 the year before the fraud case. He resigned his seat in 1862 and went to Spain but returned to face the charges for which he was convicted.

He was succeeded at a by-election in 1862 by **Frederick Doullton** (Liberal), another man born locally in Lambeth in 1824, the son of John Doulton who with John Watts set up Doulton & Watts in Lambeth in 1815 producing salt glazed stoneware. Frederick's uncle, Henry, had a separate company producing drainpipes and when Watts retired in 1853, John and Henry joined forces to become Doulton & Co. The production of art pottery started at the end of the 1860s and grew massively during the next two decades. Although he favoured extending the franchise, Doulton opposed Russell's 1866 Bill, which was defeated, opening the way for Disraeli's legislation the following year. He was a member of the Metropolitan Water Board when it was first formed and initially sought entry to the Commons at Reigate in an 1858 by-election in which he was defeated. He retired in 1868 and died in 1872. Six years after his death Doultons bought a pottery works in Burslem, Staffordshire, to make pots for decoration at the Lambeth works and in 1901 they became Royal Doulton Ltd.

When William Williams died in 1865 the May by-election was won by **Sir James Clarke Lawrence** (Liberal) who initially held the seat for only two months, going down to defeat to fellow Liberals, Hughes and Doulton, at the July General Election. However, he was elected three years later and went on to represent Lambeth until 1885 when he was defeated contesting the new constituency of Lambeth North. The son of a former Sheriff of London and Middlesex, he was born in 1820 in London and became a partner in his father's business. He was active in City of London affairs where he was an alderman from 1860, Sheriff in 1862/3 and Lord Mayor in 1868/9. He was also a magistrate in Middlesex and Westminster and served as President of the Bridewell and Bethlehem Hospitals. A free trader, he died in 1897.

Thomas Hughes (Liberal) who held the seat between Lawrence's two terms as MP was born in Uffington, Berkshire in 1823 and married the daughter of the prebendary of Exeter. He was educated at Rugby School before going to Oriel College, Oxford after which he was called to the Bar at the Inner Temple in 1848. He was a novelist and author of many popular works including, famously, 'Tom Brown's Schooldays', based on his time at Rugby, but he also wrote a book about the famous prehistoric chalk White Horse near his Berkshire home. In 1868 he transferred to Frome, which he represented until 1874 when he retired from politics, though not from the Law, being appointed a County Court Judge in 1882. He died in 1896.

Sir William McArthur (Liberal) was elected alongside Lawrence in 1868 and also served until 1885. Living in Holland Park at the time of his election, he was born in Londonderry where he was an administrator and businessman, moving his company to London in 1857 to concentrate on the colonial trade with Australia and New Zealand. He had homes in Sidney, Melbourne and Auckland and rose to prominence in the City of London where he was Sheriff (with Middlesex) in 1867/8, an alderman in 1872 and Lord Mayor in 1880/1. He was also a commissioner of Lieutenancy for London and a Surrey magistrate. His business career spread to include Chairmanship of the Star Assurance Society and a Directorship of City Bank, He contested the Yorkshire borough of Pontefract in 1865 but was unsuccessful and in 1885 following redistribution was defeated as an Independent Liberal when he was deselected as the official candidate at the new Surrey seat of Newington West. He retired from politics.

Southwark

William Brougham (Liberal) topped the poll in Southwark's first election following the the 1832 Reform Act, which had been passed through the House of Lords largely as a result of the efforts of his brother Henry, the Lord Chancellor in Grey's Government. Theirs was a radical Whig family from Edinburgh, which was tireless in its efforts to advance the human rights of ordinary people. Henry had been especially active in such causes. Apart from the Reform Act he was also instrumental in the passing of the Anti-Slavery Act in 1833 and subsequently the Matrimonial Causes Act of 1857 promoting the rights of married women. Ironically the family's radicalism made it difficult for them to obtain election to the House of Commons other than through the patronage of radical Whig aristocrats who controlled various borough seats and it was by this route that Henry, and another brother, James, became MPs. Henry, who had run the Whigs press campaign in the election of 1807, was nominated by the Duke of Bedford in 1810 as the MP for Camelford in Cornwall and he became the radicals' most prominent speaker in the Commons. The Duke was forced to sell the seat in 1812 and Henry was out of the House until 1816 when Lord Darlington nominated him for the pocket borough

---

2001.

of Winchelsea, which he represented until 1830 when he was given a peerage (Lord Brougham and Vaux) to become Lord Chancellor. Meanwhile his brother James sat successively for three pocket boroughs - Tregony (1826), Downton (1830) and finally Winchelsea where he succeeded his brother as MP in 1831. In the same year William was elected at Southwark so all three brothers were in Parliament at the time of the passing of the Great Reform Act. Brougham, himself a Master in Chancery, sat for Southwark until 1835 during which time he was a strong advocate of the abolition of flogging in the Army. When he transferred to the Yorkshire City of Leeds in 1835 he was defeated and never resumed a House of Commons seat. Following Henry's death in 1868 he succeeded him as Second Baron and died in 1886.

John Humphery (Liberal) was elected with Brougham at the 1832 election and sat until he retired 20 years later. Born in 1794, he was a Southwark Wharfinger and merchant at Hibernia Wharf in Tooley Street, which runs alongside the southeastern railways lines at London Bridge station, built during this period following an Act of Parliament passed in 1833. His home was at Clapham Common and in 1842-3 he was Lord Mayor of London, where he was also a Deputy-Lieutenant. He died in 1863, the same year his son was returned as a Conservative MP for Andover, which he represented for four years.

Daniel Whittle Harvey (Liberal) succeeded Brougham in 1835 and sat until 1840 when he resigned after accepting appointment as Commissioner of the Metropolitan Police. Born in Essex in 1786, his father was a Witham man whilst his mother was brought up at nearby Feering House. He became a solicitor after the benchers of the Inner Temple refused to call him to the bar on account of adverse character references which he contested, ending up with a House of Commons Committee ruling in his favour in 1834. Having been elected MP for Colchester in 1818, he used his position to lobby for the appeal committee and at the 1835 election transferred to Southwark. He was known principally as a newspaper owner, having started the *'Sunday Times'*, the *'True Sun'* and the *'Weekly True Sun'* publications. He died in 1863.

Harvey was succeeded at an 1840 by-election by **Benjamin Wood** (Liberal), a local Hop Merchant, who lived at Eltham Lodge, Kent. Born at Tiverton in 1787, he contested that Devon borough constituency unsuccessfully in 1832, followed by a failed attempt at Hull in 1837. He survived only five years as MP for Southwark and died in 1845

Sir William Molesworth (Liberal) won the 1845 by-election that followed Wood's death and held the seat for ten years. Born in 1810 he attended Trinity College but was expelled on offering to fight a duel with his tutor, and continued his University education at Glasgow. Although born at Upper Brook Street in London, he lived at Pencarrow in Cornwall where he was the owner of four livings and it was there that he embarked on his political career. He was MP for East Cornwall from 1832-7 during which period he also founded the *'London Review'* and then became an MP for Leeds until 1841. He was a Deputy Lieutenant for Cornwall and its High Sheriff in 1842. In 1852 he was appointed Commissioner of Works and Buildings, successfully winning a by-election at Southwark in that year, and in July 1855 was appointed a Secretary of State for the Colonies, but died three months later.

Vice-Admiral Sir Charles Napier (Liberal), a national hero, was returned at the 1855 by-election that followed Molesworth's death and remained the MP until 1860 when he died. A former MP for Marylebone (1841-7) his principal biographical details can be found in Chapter II (Middlesex).

Apsley Pellatt (Liberal) succeeded Humphery in 1852. He too was a local merchant, living in Blackfriars Road, son of a Southwark Glass Manufacturer. Born in 1791, he was educated privately at Camberwell and eventually headed the family Company. He was active in the City where he was a member of the Court of Common Council and carried a bill to admit Jews to its affairs. He contested Bristol in 1847 and sat for Southwark from 1852 to 1857 when he was defeated by a fellow Liberal, contesting the same seat unsuccessfully again in 1859. He wrote 'Curiosities of Glass Making and Ancient Glass' and died in 1863.

John Locke (Liberal) represented Southwark from 1857, when he took the place of Pellatt, until January 1880 when he died. He too was the son of a Southwark trader; was born in London in 1805 and educated at Dulwich College and Trinity College Cambridge, where he obtained a BA in 1829 and then his MA. He was called to the bar at the Inner Temple in 1833, became a Bencher and worked on the Home, or South East circuit. From 1845-57 he was one of the Common Pleaders of the City of London and took silk in his last year. In 1861 he was appointed Recorder of Brighton and successfully contested a by-election in Southwark to confirm his appointment. Earlier he contested Hastings in 1852.

Austen Henry Layard (Liberal) won the by-election caused by Napier's death in 1860 and held the seat until shortly after he was appointed Ambassador to Madrid in 1869. Born in Paris in 1817 he was the son of a famous Egyptologist and Middle Eastern archaeologist, who specialised in the study of the ancient city of Nineveh. This itinerant lifestyle appears to have got into Austen's blood as he too became well travelled. He joined the diplomatic corps and

Austen Henry Layard MP
© **National Portrait Gallery**
Maull Polyblank

was initially appointed an attaché to the British embassy in Constantinople. Awarded a DCL at Oxford in 1848, he entered the House as MP for Aylesbury (Buckinghamshire) four years later and was immediately appointed an Under Secretary for Foreign Affairs, though this was only for a matter of weeks, and in 1857 he lost his seat to a Conservative. Meanwhile he had served as Lord Rector of Aberdeen University in 1855 and 1856. He contested York unsuccessfully in 1859 but soon after his return at Southwark, he was again appointed to the post of Under-Secretary, Foreign Affairs, a job he fulfilled for 5 years. In 1868 he was made Chief Commissioner of Works and Buildings, winning the by-election necessary to confirm his status but the following year resumed his diplomatic career. He was Ambassador to Madrid from 1869 to 1877 and then to the Sultan of Turkey between 1877 and 1880. He died in 1894

Lieutenant-Colonel Marcus Beresford (Conservative) was the first Tory to represent Southwark, winning the by-election following Layard's resignation in 1870. He held the seat until 1880. He was the son and grandson of Rectors and a member of a family that had owned a substantial countryseat in Staffordshire since 1087. He was born in 1818 at Aylestone (Leicestershire) and educated at Kings College, London. From 1836 to 1844 he served in the American Militia and became a commander in the 7th Surrey Rifles with the rank of Colonel. He was appointed a Surrey magistrate in 1859.

Sir Edward Clarke MP
Wikipedia

Sir Edward George Clarke (Conservative), was the shortest serving of Southwark's MPs. Elected at the February 1880 by-election that followed Locke's death, he was defeated at the April general election but was subsequently elected for Plymouth (Devon) and later made a brief return to the Commons as an MP for the City of London in January 1906 but resigned in June the same year. His principal biographical details can be found in Chapter 3 (Middlesex – City of London).

Arthur Cohen (Liberal) was elected in 1880 and served until 1885 when his seat was re-organised when he was returned for Southwark West, continuing in the House until 1888 when he retired. Born in 1829, he was the son of a London merchant but was educated at the Gymnasium in Frankfurt-am-Main, Germany before becoming a student at University College London after which he became a lawyer at the Inner Temple being called to the bar in 1857. He subsequently took his MA at Magdalen College, Cambridge in 1863 whilst a bencher at the Inner Temple and working as a barrister on the southeastern circuit. He took silk in 1874 and the same year was appointed a Judge of the Cinque Ports contesting the general election of that year in the Sussex borough of Lewes, where he was defeated. In 1876 he was elected as standing counsel at the University of Cambridge and after his retirement from politics in 1888 was appointed Counsel to the Secretary of State for India in 1893. In 1914, the year of his death, he was once again appointed Judge of the Cinque Ports.

Cohen's partner as a Southwark MP from 1880 to 1885 was **James Edwin Thorold Rogers** (Liberal) when he was returned at Bermondsey though he held the seat for only one term and was defeated there in 1886 as a Gladstonian Liberal. He was born at Westmeon (Hampshire) in 1823 and received a University education initially at Kings College, London graduating with a First in Classics in 1846; and later at Magdalen Hall, Oxford where he obtained his MA three years later. In 1853 he was appointed Master of the Schools at Oxford University and was a Classical Examiner there in1857-8. The following year he was appointed to the post of Tooke Professor of Economic Science at Kings College, London, then from 1862-68 was Professor of Political Economy at Oxford. He was in addition a clergyman in the Church of England but relinquished Holy Orders to become an MP, though after his defeat in 1886 he returned to academia. He was the author of several Political and Economic works and in 1888 was re-appointed to his former Professorship at Oxford but died two years later.

Surrey Eastern

Sir John Ivatt- Briscoe (Liberal) was one of Surrey Eastern's first two MPs but served for only three years being defeated in 1835. He had previously sat in the unreformed Parliament as MP for Surrey Western between 1830 and 1832. After his 1835 defeat he fought and won Westbury at the 1837 contest and sat there until 1847. Later, between 1857 and 1870 he sat once again for Surrey Western but died whilst still in the House. Briscoe was born in 1791 and was educated at University College, Oxford where he gained a BA in Classics in 1812 and an MA three years later.

Foxhills, Ottershaw, Surrey. Once home to Briscoe, now a top golfing resort.
© Foxhills

He was a student at Lincolns Inn but was not called to the bar though he did become a magistrate in both Surrey and Middlesex. He did not want for money after marrying the heiress to Sir Joseph Mawbay and commissioned the building of Foxhills Manor House, Ottershaw, Surrey, so named as it was on land originally owned by the radical Whig MP Charles James Fox. Today this is one of the top Golfing Resorts in Britain. As an MP himself, Briscoe was concerned mainly with local issues helping to found Chertsey Agricultural Association but his only significant national initiative was to campaign to outlaw the Treadmill as a form of punishment.[2]

Briscoe's companion MP in 1832 was **Major Aubrey William Beauclerk** (Liberal) who sat for five years. Born in 1801 he was the grandson of the Dowager Duchess of Leinster and a cousin of the Duke of St Albans, a descendant of the illicit union of King Charles II and Nell Gwynne. He had a career in the Army and died in 1854.

Henry Kemble (Liberal), who lived in Camberwell, succeeded Beauclerk in 1837and remained a Surrey East MP for ten years. Born in 1787, he was active in the Corporation of London and in 1833 was made a Director of Equitable Assurance[3]. He died in 1857.

Briscoe's successor in 1835 was **Captain Richard Alsager** (Conservative), a Tooting man and like Beauclerk also a soldier, who was the first Tory to be returned by a metropolitan Surrey constituency. He died in 1841 whilst still in the House.

Sir Edmund Antrobus (Conservative) succeeded Alsager at the 1841 by-election precipitated by his death. Born in Westminster in 1818, Antrobus, who described himself as a Liberal-Conservative, was educated at St Johns College, Cambridge and was the grand nephew of a man who made a fortune in the Lancashire cotton trade and purchased the historic estate of Amesbury near Stonehenge in Wiltshire in 1824. Sir Edmund's father succeeded him as baronet two years later restoring the Abbey as the manor house during the period. After his defeat in 1847 the West Country became more prominent in Antrobus's life. He became a Captain in the Wiltshire Yeoman Cavalry in 1851 and from 1855 to 1877, when he retired from politics, he was MP for nearby Wilton and three years later became Sheriff of Wiltshire. He succeeded his father as baronet on his death in 1870 and died himself in 1899.

Peter John Locke King MP
© National Portrait Gallery
John & Charles Watkins

In 1847 Antrobus was succeeded by **Peter John Locke King** (Liberal), whose family owned the Brooklands estate outside Weybridge, Surrey. Peter was the second son of the 7th Lord King and grandson on his mother's side of the 1st Earl Fortescue, brother of the 1st Earl Lovelace. Born at Ockham, Surrey in 1811 he was educated at Harrow and Trinity College Cambridge graduating MA in 1833. He married the niece of the 1st Earl of Gainsborough, and made his first attempt to enter the House at Surrey Eastern in 1837 when he was defeated. He promoted a failed Reform Bill in 1851; was made a Vice-Lieutenant of Surrey in 1871 and after his defeat at the 1874 election never resumed a political career. His grandson, Hugh built the Brooklands racetrack on the Weybridge estate in 1907. Peter died in 1885.

Thomas Alcock (Liberal) was elected with King in 1847 and remained MP until 1865, when he retired. Born at Epsom in 1801, he was the grandson of a Rear Admiral and was educated at Harrow School. A Surrey magistrate and the patron of two livings, he had earlier been MP for Newton (Lancashire) in the pre-reformed House between 1826 and 1830 and later contested Ludlow, unsuccessfully in 1837 but two years later as the victor. However, he was unseated on petition and was defeated at his first attempt to secure election at Surrey Eastern in 1841. After his retirement in 1865 he died the following year.

Charles Buxton (Liberal) took Alcock's place but died three years after his re-election in 1868 . By then living in Cobham, Surrey, he had been born at Cromer in Norfolk in 1823 and graduated from Trinity College, Cambridge as a Doctor of Education. However, he went into business and became a partner in the brewing firm of Truman, Hanbury and

2 Foxhills, a potted history on the web

3 The Equitable was established in 1762, the first mutual life assurance company run for its members and continues to run as the oldest mutual life assurance company in the UK, though following an exceptionally difficult period including a House of Lords ruling against it in 2000, the company closed to new business on 8 December 2000.

Company. His fellow partner, Robert Hanbury, was also a Liberal MP at the same time, sitting as one of the Middlesex County members from 1857 to 1867 (see Chapter 2). Buxton was a magistrate in both Norfolk and Surrey and a Lieutenant – Colonel in the 1st Battalion of the Tower Hamlets Rifle Volunteers. He entered politics as MP for Newport in 1857, transferring to Maidstone two years later but retiring from there to become a Surrey MP in 1865.

He was succeeded after his death by another brewer, **James Watney** (Conservative), who was born at Wandsworth in 1832 and educated at Clapham Grammar School. Watney who's Stag Brewery was in Pimlico, sat for Surrey Eastern until he retired in 1885 but had no notable political achievements to his name. He was appointed a Deputy Lieutenant of Middlesex in 1882 and died in 1886, the year after he left Parliament.

He was joined by fellow-Tory **Sir William Grantham** (Conservative) in 1874 when he gained the seat previously held by King. Born in 1835, he was educated at Kings College London and called to the bar of the Inner Temple in 1863. He practised on the Home Circuit becoming a Queens Councillor in 1877. He was made a bencher at the Inner Temple in 1880 and remained Surrey Eastern's MP until 1885 when, following re-distribution he was elected for the new constituency of Croydon. He retired from the House in 1886 when he was made a Judge of the Queen's Bench Division, a post he held until his death in 1911.

Surrey Mid

Sir Henry Peek (Conservative), a tea importer and subsequently Baron Peek of Rousdon, Devon, was MP for the new 1868 seat until his resignation in 1884. He had previously been an unsuccessful candidate in Surrey Eastern in 1865.

Peek's fellow Tory partner in 1868 was **William Broderick** (Conservative) but he only served until 1870 as he then succeeded as the eighth Viscount Middleton.At the 1870 by-election caused by Broderick's accession to the peerage .

Sir Richard Baggallay MP
© National Portrait Gallery
Lock & Whitfield

He was succeeded by **Sir Richard Baggallay** (Conservative) , the son of a Stockwell family which owned warehouses in the City of London. However, he pursued a legal career being called to the bar at Lincoln's Inn in 1843 at the age of 27. He first contested a general election in 1865 when he was elected at Hereford but after losing his seat in 1868, sought a seat closer to home. During 1868 he served briefly as Solicitor General and then again in 1874 when he became Attorney General in Disraeli's Government, resigning his seat a year later on being appointed a Judge at the Court of Appeal, a position he held until his death in 1888.

Sir James John Trevor Lawrence (Conservative) won the 1875 by-election and served until 1885 after which he represented Reigate until 1892 when he retired from politics. Born in 1831, the son of a woman who owned a Mayfair haberdashery business, he was educated at Winchester College following which he qualified as a Doctor at St Bartholomew's Hospital. He pursued a career in the Indian medical service. He first entered politics unsuccessfully as Tory candidate for Gloucester in 1874. His chief interest was horticulture and for a very long period from 1885 until his death in 1913 was President of the Royal Horticultural Society. He had inherited a love of orchids from his mother and created his own garden at a country house near Dorking. After his retirement from politics he served as Treasurer of Barts Hospital, a position he occupied until 1904.

Byfleet Fire Station - funded by Sir John Whittaker Ellis MP
Wikipedia

Sir John Whittaker Ellis (Conservative) was born in 1829 the son of the owner of the Star and Garter Hotel in Richmond, where he acquired land for the Town Hall. He lived at Petersham House, and following a fire there also funded fire station at Byfleet. In 1885 he transferred to the new Kingston constituency, which he represented until 1892. He was elected an alderman of the City, Broad Street Ward in 1872, was Sheriff of London and Middlesex in 1874-5, and Lord Mayor in 1881-2. He entered the Commons in 1884 at the by-election following the resignation of Sir Henry Peek. He was a member of the Merchant Taylors Company, a Commissioner of Lieutenancy for the City, a Governor of the Irish Society, a Londonderry JP, and High Sheriff of Surrey in 1899-1900. He died in 1912.

Parliamentary Representation 1885 – 1918

The 1885 General Election was fought on entirely new boundaries with borough and county seats alike covering defined individual constituency boundaries with electorates that were more evenly distributed than before. In total Surrey returned 19 MPs within the Greater London area, an increase of eleven since 1868. Most of the new constituencies were contained within the boundaries of the London boroughs that were formed in 1889 when the London County council was created. These were Bermondsey, Southwark, Camberwell, Lambeth, Battersea and Wandsworth. Of the new constituencies three – Southwark West, Bermondsey and Rotherhithe – were wholly carved out of the former Southwark Parliamentary borough. Parts of Newington West and Walworth had also formerly been in Southwark, but most of the area covered by them had formerly been in Lambeth Parliamentary borough from which another two were also wholly created – Lambeth North and Kennington. Another four had previously been mainly in Lambeth – Camberwell North, Brixton, Norwood and Peckham.

Five seats were created mainly out of the former two-member Eastern Surrey constituency. These were Dulwich, northern parts of which (around Denmark Hill) had previously been in Lambeth; Clapham, Brixton, Norwood, and Croydon. Mid Surrey spawned two, notably Kingston-upon-Thames and Epsom whilst three more (Battersea, Wandsworth and Wimbledon) were created from communities that had been formerly parts of both Eastern and Mid Surrey seats.

Populations and Electorates

Constituency	*1881 pop*	*1891 pop*	*1901 pop*	*1911 pop*	*1884 electors and % 1881 pop*	*1906 electors*	*1910 electors*	*1910 electors as % of 1911 pop*
Southwark West		*66785*	*62687*	*55,541*		*7066*	*8060*	*14.5*
Bermondsey		*82849*	*82150*	*79902*		*10619*	*12115*	*15.2*
Rotherhithe		*73915*	*70284*	*66037*		*8700*	*9990*	*15.1*
Newington West		*56623*	*61279*	*58636*		*8995*	*9635*	*16.4*
Newington, Walworth		*59181*	*60893*	*58463*		*7147*	*8521*	*14.5*
Camberwell North		*88916*	*93073*	*90476*		*12519*	*11918*	*13.2*
Peckham		*83483*	*91448*	*89925*		*12401*	*12341*	*13.7*
Dulwich		*83320*	*97369*	*101731*		*15286*	*16478*	*16.2*
Lambeth North		*63586*	*59542*	*53054*		*6802*	*6440*	*12.1*
Kennington		*73850*	*78313*	*72688*		*10382*	*10088*	*13.9*
Brixton		*70356*	*75366*	*75957*		*11010*	*11442*	*15.1*
Norwood		*68411*	*85730*	*93219*		*12867*	*13908*	*14.9*
Battersea		*98235*	*102469*	*101170*		*15369*	*18927*	*18.7*
Clapham		*96021*	*120761*	*128569*		*19180*	*22611*	*17.6*
Wandsworth		*113244*	*179877*	*253759*		*31398*	*38523*	*15.2*
Kingston-on-Thames		*85367*	*103034*	*126790*		*17270*	*19647*	*15.5*
Croydon		*102695*	*133895*	*169551*		*23858*	*27350*	*16.1*
Wimbledon		*69000*	*99112*	*160289*		*21899*	*27810*	*17.3*
Epsom		*70103*	*86799*	*116341*		*15933*	*18821*	*16.2*
Totals	*1255925*	*1505940*	*17444081*	*1952098*	*132367 =10.5%*	*268701*	*304625*	*15.6*

The populations of these suburban seats all rose massively after they were created such that they became seriously under represented, especially in relation to some of those more established Surrey constituencies where populations began to decline. Whilst the population as a whole increased throughout the period, the seats closest to the centre of London peaked in 1891. Those in the next closest radius did so in 1901. The next removed – places like Battersea,

Brixton and Dulwich - were beginning to plateau just before the First World War. The open spaces beyond were being swallowed up by suburban developments that saw most places increase their populations by a half in the years between 1891 and 1911; Wimbledon's increased by 132% and Wandsworth's by 124%. All the outer suburban seats increased by over 50%. As a proportion of the population electorates did not vary greatly from one seat to another – a function of the still rather limited franchise – although the more working class areas had lower electorates. Lambeth North's was the smallest (12.1%) and Battersea's the largest (18.7%), though this is a little surprising considering the heavily working class nature of some of its districts. There were well-to-do areas as well, of course, especially those around the Park and the Thames Bridges and these may well have compensated for the poor.

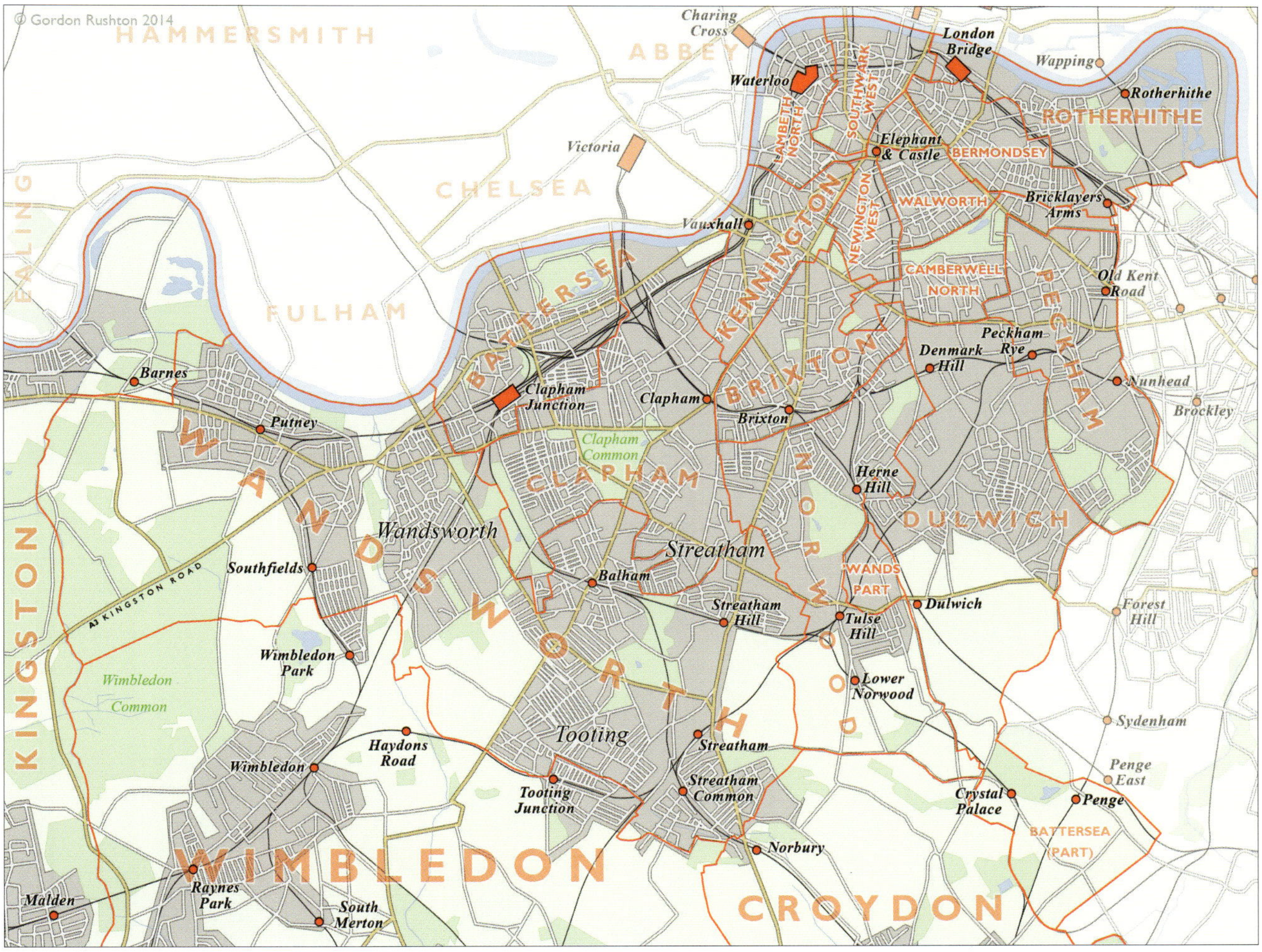

Metropolitan Surrey continued to expand, with the map showing in grey the spread of concentrated housing. Constituencies have proliferated to match the rise in population, and the railways are enabling the expansion to continue, though the current limits of the spread of the housing are clear.

Southwark, Bermondsey and Newington (5 seats)

Stretching along the Thames between London Bridge and Waterloo (exclusive) just west of Blackfriars Bridge Road was the constituency of **Southwark West,** essentially the ancient borough of Southwark within the boundaries of which were Southwark Cathedral and The Borough. Its constituent parts were officially the St Saviour's District, Christchurch (Surrey) and the St Michael's and St Jude's wards of St George the Martyr's parish (Southwark). Yet even as this constituency was created the signs of its subsequent decline were becoming evident. Its middle classes were already beginning to migrate from the central districts, which became increasingly poor in composition with up to 70% of its 1891 population estimated to live in poverty, the worst in London.

Downstream from Southwark were successively two new constituencies, both within the London Borough of Bermondsey, also established as part of the London County Council. These constituencies had busy and bustling dockland economies that sustained large populations, though as with Southwark itself, they also peaked at about the time that the 1885 constituencies were established. In fact the populations of all three riverside seats started to decline soon afterwards.

Top Left: *The corner of Toulmin Street and Lant Street, off Borough High Street, early 1900s, Southwark West Constituency, 1885-1918.*

Top Left/Left **©TfL from the London Transport Museum Collection**

Top Right: *St Mary's at Rotherhithe an oasis of calm and affluence in the bustling Rotherhithe Constituency containing Surrey Docks.* **Gordon Rushton**

Left: *The Elephant and Castle in 1895 – the intersection was at the boundary of three seats – Newington West, Newington Walworth and Southwark West.*

Above: *The Old Kent Road, pictured in 1890 was a boundary between Bermondsey and Newington, Walworth Constituencies. Shown are carts transporting in the vital needs of the burgeoning city and the stately progress of a horse tram on the Greenwich - Blackfriars route.*

©TfL from the London Transport Museum Collection

Bermondsey, including the area between the Tower Bridge Road and Bricklayers Arms, had previously been part of Southwark. It officially comprised the St George's ward of the parish of St George the Martyr (Southwark) and of the Bermondsey wards numbers 1-3. Bermondsey is almost certainly very old. It is believed that a Benedictine Monastery was based there during Saxon times and evidence has been found of Roman occupation. The place name derives from the Saxon, 'Vermundesei' dating from AD712, meaning either 'island' or 'dry ground in a marsh' belonging to 'Beornmund'. At that time the river Thames was much broader and shallower and a series of small islands formed between the low lying marshes around Southwark and Bermondsey, enabling the first London Bridge to be constructed at that point to the walled City on the North bank. However, a Millennium later it was a very different picture. By 1800 Bermondsey was already dominated by a tangle of works, warehouses, and slums. In 1835 the Spa Road to Deptford railway opened and was soon extended to London Bridge and Greenwich. This opened up Bermondsey to industry but with it came poverty and overcrowding. In 1801 the population was 27,465; in 1851 it was 65,932 and by 1891 it had reached 136,660. Open sewers and poor quality housing were common. Well over 50% of the population in the riverside districts were estimated to be living in poverty at that time; although inland the proportions were a lot less, but still over 30%. Cholera hit the area in the 19th century, especially the areas near open tidal sewers. Jacob's Island, whose residents took drinking water out of the Thames, was especially affected and featured in 'Oliver Twist', the novel by Charles Dickens. By the end of the century the whole borough was built over apart from Southwark Park. One of the main industries in the area was the food business and it became known as 'London's Larder.' By 1900 the living conditions were awful and the local council began to act. There were known examples of 9 people living in one room and one tap serving 25 houses with no sanitation.

The **Rotherhithe** constituency officially comprised the parishes of St Olave's and St Thomas's, St John's, St Mary (Rotherhithe) and St Mary Magdalen (Rotherhithe), including the Surrey Docks. It had a less stable population than Bermondsey, reducing in the decade after 1891when between 40 and 49% of its population lived in poverty. The old village of Rotherhithe had a close relationship with the sea. Its original name was 'Rederheia' meaning, 'landing-place for cattle' and dates from around 1105. Throughout history it was a favourite home for many seafarers and had a fine tradition of shipbuilding. Some of the first steamships were built in Rotherhithe and the first iron ship, the Aaron Manby, was constructed in the local shipyards. Rotherhithe was also home to many associated industries, for example iron works and gunpowder manufacturers. It was the major whaling base in London until the trade died in the 1840s, after which it was used for the importation of timber. As the sea-faring era drew to a close the improving transport saw the population of Rotherhithe rise. In 1801 it housed 10,296, a century later it was home to 38,424 a growth that was stimulated by the Surrey Commercial Dock Company, which chose Rotherhithe for its site and began building there in 1809.

South of Southwark West was **Newington West** (meaning in the Middle Ages,' the new homestead or farm'), which lay between the heavily populated Elephant and Castle district and Kennington. It officially comprised three wards – St Mary's, Trinity, and St Paul's. This area, which in the Middle Ages was an archery practise site (hence Newington Butts) was still expanding at the turn of the Century and becoming increasingly congested. In 1891 its population was 10,000 fewer than Southwark West's but by 1901 it was within 2,000 and by 1911 had overtaken it.

Further down the Old Kent Road was **Newington, Walworth** occupying principally the area between Kennington Park Road to the west and the Old Kent Road to the east, apart from a strip in Bermondsey that straddled the road to Kent. It officially comprised two wards – St Peter's and St John's. The name derives from 'Wealawyrth' dating from 1001 meaning, 'enclosure of the Britons'. Its 19th Century High Street was the Walworth Road which formed the boundary between Newington's two constituencies. In 1891 Walworth had a population of about 59,000, a figure that only grew by a couple of thousand during the following decade. It had similar characteristics to the Southwark area as a whole and, although there were districts where middle class people lived, in general it was poor the proportion living in poverty being 30%. Factories, warehouses and railways had replaced many houses in the centre of London, which meant that London's overflowing population spread out to places like Walworth. There was also a substantial amount of demolition to make way for the South Western Railway terminus at Waterloo, constructed during the 1840s. As a result, Walworth changed from a small community into a highly populated area. In 1801 there had been only 14,800 people living there but by 1901 the number had risen to 122,200, , indicating just how cramped conditions must have been. It is unsurprising that poverty increased and that the two 1885 constituencies held a small number of voters in proportion to the population of the district.

Camberwell (3 seats)

The Borough of Camberwell south of Bermondsey and Newington comprised three constituencies. It is mentioned in the Domesday Book as being owned by Haimo, half brother to King William I and is described as 'large and well inhabited'. The origins of the actual place-name are obscure, except that 'wella' meant 'spring or stream' and it was known in Old English as 'Cambrewelle'. It remained a farming village surrounded by woods and fields until about 1800 with the village surrounding its High Street, now called Denmark Hill in honour of Prince George of Denmark, the husband of Queen Anne, who had a residence there. The 19th Century saw a number of affluent people moving to Camberwell as the construction of Westminster Bridge, (1750), Blackfriars Bridge, (1769), Vauxhall Bridge, (1816), Waterloo Bridge, (1817) and Southwark Bridge, (1819) made it easier for them to commute to work in Central London. By the time Victoria came to the throne in 1837 Camberwell was essentially part of Greater London containing a fair percentage of prosperous residents and fine houses. 188 Camberwell Grove was the birthplace of the statesman Joseph Chamberlain in 1832. As with much of South London the coming of trains led to a dramatic change in the landscape. The first arrived in 1862, and for the next 6 years a plethora of tracks was laid. Trains offered a new, cheap way to travel meaning more people could afford to live in the suburbs. In 1801 the population of Camberwell was 7,059; one hundred years later the new borough's was 259,425. During the building boom some slums were created and parts of the borough were very poor and remain so to this day.

Camberwell North ran east-west roughly from South Bermondsey to Myatt's Fields (both exclusive) and included the major part of Camberwell. It officially comprised the St George's, East and West wards ; and Camden. As Southwark's population declined, so Camberwell's increased. Between 1891 and 1901 that of its northern constituency rose by a little over 4,000 to 93,000 but its population started to decline soon afterwards as did its electorate which actually fell in 1910 compared with 1906; evidence perhaps of the difficulties of voter registration in areas where qualification was highly dependent upon the length of time property had been occupied. At 13.2% of the population the electorate in working class Camberwell was amongst the smallest in Surrey. Despite this, it could not be described as 'grindingly poor'

Top Left: Camberwell Green was in the Camberwell North Constituency and formed the border with Dulwich in 1885.

Top Right: Peckham Rye Station, in the Peckham Constituency was designed sumptuously by Charles Henry Driver and opened in 1865 to become a key interchange for trains all over South London.

Left: Tranquil Nutfield Rd in East Dulwich was home to clerks when houses were built there in the late 1800s. Close to the station and shops in Lordship Lane, this was a relatively affluent area in the Dulwich Constituency.

Gordon Rushton 'Top Left' and 'Top Right'; John Nelson 'Left'

for those days as, although in the northern districts near Walworth the proportion of the population classified as living in poverty was over 30%, in Denmark Hill the proportion was less than 10%.

Peckham was a small constituency on a north/south axis running from north of Queens Road via Nunhead and the Rye to the borders with East Dulwich. It officially comprised two wards – North and South Peckham. 'Peac-ham' meant, 'village by a hill' and was a hamlet owned by the Norman Bishop Lisieux at the time of the Domesday survey. Valued at 30 shillings, Peckham was later owned by King Henry I who gave it to his son Robert, Earl of Gloucester, who later married the heiress to Camberwell thus uniting the two properties under royal ownership. It grew in favour as a residential area and in the 16th century became home to some quite well to do people. By the 18th century it had developed into a more commercialised area, market gardening in particular being very important. With the lack of refrigeration, food had to be grown close to its final market and Peckham was well situated to exploit the large London market on its doorstep. The adjacent parish of Nunhead was also regarded as being a London hamlet but both were recognised as villages by the mid 18 Century.

There were few roads in and around Peckham; one running west to Camberwell; another east towards New Cross; and a third running southeast to the open countryside. Peckham was the last grazing post for cattle being brought from Kent to London for slaughter and a public house was named 'The Kentish Drovers' in recognition of its role. Even in the 19th century it was a 'small, quiet, retired village surrounded by fields' although London Stagecoaches travelled with an armed guard to give protection from highwaymen on the Peckham road. In the early 19th Century came the first signs of the development that was to overwhelm Peckham. Schools and Asylums were followed by the opening of the Surrey Canal just north of the village in 1826. One of London's main Gas Works was constructed on the canal in 1833. Nunhead Cemetery was started in 1840 (created by Act of Parliament to facilitate the burial of London's dead) and shortly afterwards the so-called Peckham New Town was begun.

Horse-drawn coaches were introduced by Thomas Tillling between Rye Lane and Oxford Circus in 1851 to enable people to travel to the Great Exhibition in Hyde Park and between 1865 and 1871 the railways arrived. As the transport system improved more people were able to move to the suburbs and the last of the market gardens and fields vanished under housing developments of varying quality. To preserve some greenery Peckham Rye was bought in 1868 and maintained as common land, but by 1870 Peckham had become a poor neighbourhood as industries arrived to give employment to largely unskilled, labouring classes. Brock's Fireworks factory provided employment in Nunhead and during the Franco-Prussian War in 1870, production was given over to making two-million cartridge tubes for the French side. The South Metropolitan Gas Works and timber works along the banks of the canal provided employment in Peckham. Others – men and women – worked in laundries and basket manufacture on the Old Kent Road; brewing, cabinet making, safe manufacture, the making of floor cloths, and some were employed at a lacquer works. There was massive employment in the building trades as houses, sewers, roads and shops were built in London, the population of which rose from 865,000 in 1801 to around 4 million a century later. The 1883 Cheap Trains Act encouraged working class commuters and housing. Amongst other things this had the effect of stabilising the population of the area. By 1891 the population of Peckham constituency was just over 83,000 compared with only 12,653 half a century earlier and this rose to nearly 91,500 in 1901 when it peaked. The electorate was below average at about 13.7% of the total population and similar to adjacent working class districts. The proportion of the population living in poverty in 1891 was estimated at between 40 and 49%, higher than Camberwell and Rotherhithe and substantially greater than in Dulwich.

The semi-rural **Dulwich** constituency extended southwards from Camberwell and East Dulwich via Dulwich Village to Crystal Palace Hill. It officially comprised the Camberwell and Dulwich ward and the hamlet of Penge. Dulwich was a wealthy constituency with less than 10% of its population estimated to be living in poverty. It included Denmark Hill where the Maudsley Hospital had been built; all parts of Dulwich and Herne Hill. Meaning 'meadow where dill grows', the Manor of Dulwich originally comprised lands granted to Aelfheah by the Saxon King Eadgar in the year 967. It was separated from the adjacent manor (or lordship) of East Dulwich (sometimes called Peckham Rye) by what is today the main thoroughfare that connects Camberwell and Dulwich, namely Lordship Lane. In 1127 King Henry I gave Dulwich to Bermondsey Abbey but in 1538 Henry VIII seized control and sold the rights to a London goldsmith, Thomas Carlton, for the sum of £609.18s.2d. In 1605 his grandson sold to Edward Alleyn, a famous Elizabethan actor. He built a college to help educate 12 poor children, and made provision for 12 elderly people. Dulwich College is now world famous. Significantly Alleyn gave the manorial rights and freehold of his land to the College who in later years were able to block development. In 1739 a spa was discovered and Dulwich became popular with visitors. Then in the late 1700s and early 1800s rich London merchants began to build grand houses and Dulwich quickly outgrew its hamlet status. House building was encouraged by the enclosure of Dulwich Common in 1805 and the village flourished south east of Herne Hill and between it, the School and Park. Several prominent people built houses including Lord Thurlow, the Lord Chancellor, whose mansion was established in 1795 and after whom Thurlow Park Road is named.

Above: *The Lambeth North Constituency was generally much less affluent than its neighbouring borough seats. Belvedere Road was typical. To see what became of the road, look at the replacement buildings on page 209.* **©TfL from the London Transport Museum Collection**

Top Right: *Lambeth Town Hall, on Brixton Hill at the Junction of Acre Lane, the boundary between the Brixton and Norwood Constituencies.* **All images Gordon Rushton**

Top Left: *The view of Norwood from Herne Hill Station shows the suburban development that took place around the railway, at this time the boundary with Dulwich.*

Left: *Luxury mansion flats at Rushcroft Road, Brixton, which was in the Norwood Constituency. Norwood and Brixton were prosperous, Conservative voting London suburbs.*

Despite being served by stagecoaches operating between Sevenoaks and Piccadilly as well as another service running to Gracechurch Street in the City of London, Dulwich retained its market garden character until the coming of the railways in the middle of the 19th Century. In 1854 they came to Crystal Palace when the glass buildings that had housed the Great Exhibition in Hyde Park were moved to Sydenham Hill just south of Dulwich and within 14 years half a dozen other stations were built encouraging housing development on a grand scale. The Brighton and South Coast Railway Company opened stations at Crystal Palace and Herne Hill in 1856, at West Dulwich and Sydenham Hill in 1863, and at East and North Dulwich in 1868. Trains began operating as far as the Elephant and Castle in 1862 and soon afterwards to Holborn Viaduct in the City. Fields were taken over by streets and Dulwich became a middle class suburb of London which became part of the new London County in 1889. Two years later the constituency's population was in excess of 88,000, which by 1901 had grown to over 97,000, and in 1911 had reached 101,731. Its electorate was 16.2% of the population making it the most middle class of the constituencies in the Southwark area before the First World War.

Lambeth (4 seats)

Lambeth's population also expanded massively during the mid 19th Century and four new constituencies were created there. The riverside seat of **Lambeth North,** which extended from the Thames southwest of Waterloo towards Vauxhall Bridge (exclusive), included the densely populated area around the railway lines emanating from Waterloo. Lambeth Palace, residence of the Archbishop of Canterbury, was also within its boundaries, which officially comprised the borough's Marsh and Bishop's wards. As in neighbouring Southwark West, the population was already beginning to fall at the end of the Century. Its population was in continuous decline after 1891 and at 12.1% of the total the electorate was proportionately amongst the smallest, reflecting the strong working class identity of the area.

Kennington extended around the back of North Lambeth via The Oval cricket ground (home of the Surrey County Cricket Club) to South Lambeth, comprising the Prince's and Vauxhall wards. The name derives from 'Chenintune' meaning, 'farm associated with a man called Cena' and the area only became developed after about 1800 when the Vauxhall area of North Lambeth had become totally urbanised after the building of the Thames Bridges connecting the area to Westminster. There were similarities with neighbouring Camberwell from which it was separated by Kennington Park Road, and its 1901 population of 78,313 was 4,500 greater than in had been ten years earlier when up to 39% of its population was estimated to be living in poverty. Thereafter population and voter numbers declined and as a proportion of population the electorate was below average at 13.9%.

Brixton, a constituency south of Kennington that included Stockwell by the Thames and extended east towards Herne Hill, officially comprised Brixton and Stockwell wards. 'Brixges stan' was the name of one of the original Hundreds of Surrey and probably meant the 'stone of a man called Beorhtsige', where the elders of the Hundred met. Brixton had emerged after 1800 as an eligible middle class suburb between Camberwell and Clapham. Angell Town was especially favoured and businessmen set up in villas on the slopes of the Denmark and Herne Hills overlooking Camberwell. Its population increased from about 70,000 to 75,000 in the decade after 1891, when less than 20% of the population was estimated to be living in poverty. The population stabilised after 1901 and the electorate rose in consequence to 11,400 in 1910, representing about 15.1% of the population.

Norwood (literally North wood) extended south from Denmark Hill and Herne Hill via Brockwell Park to Tulse Hill, further west and then south to West Norwood and the eastern parts of Streatham, although the latter was then in the Wandsworth constituency. It official comprised three wards - Herne Hill, Tulse Hill and West Norwood. At the turn of the century Norwood was expanding rapidly and was relatively affluent with less than 10% of people living in poverty in its eastern districts bordering Dulwich although the proportion in Tulse Hill was probably twice that figure. Its electorate represented 14.9% of the population.

Battersea, Clapham and Wandsworth (3 seats)

West of Lambeth two new Parliamentary boroughs were created - Battersea and Clapham and, further west, Wandsworth, which also adjoined Battersea's southern flank.

Battersea ran southwest on the south bank of the Thames from Battersea Bridge to Clapham. Officially it comprised six Battersea wards –Park (2), Latchmere (3), Shaftesbury (4), Church (5) Winstanley (6) and St John (7) which at that time also included a detached part in Penge. Battersea was the site of a Saxon settlement ('Batrices - Ege') and the manor once belonged to the Abbey of Westminster. It was a market garden for London with successive draining of the marshland producing fine farmland taking place over many years until the coming of the railways when extensive tracks were laid throughout the area. The railways brought industrialisation. Yet less than half a century earlier it had still been

__Top Left:__ Wealthy Crescent Grove near Clapham Common was at the northern end of the Clapham Park estate which formed the heart of the 1885 constituency.

__Top Right:__ These distinctive villas on the Shaftesbury Estate were built for working class tenants many of who would have been enfranchised in the 1885 Battersea constituency.

__Left:__ Cowick Road, Upper Tooting typifies the terraced villa style of housing in the Wandsworth Constituency in 1885

__Above:__ The former Battersea Town Hall, on Lavender Hill - the boundary between the Battersea and Clapham Constituencies.

__Left:__ The Arding and Hobbs Department Store on the corner of Elspeth Road and Lavender Hill, Clapham Junction was in the Clapham Constituency at the boundary with Battersea, and served the burgeoning population of the area.

All images John Nelson

a relatively small community with a population in 1841 of 6,887 living mainly around Battersea Bridge (opened in 1772) and Nine Elms. Thereafter it began to develop quite significantly as a working class area supplying London with many of its essential services. The stretch of river towards Wandsworth gradually became dominated by factories with a Power Station opening in 1833 at Nine Elms (always the most industrialized district of Battersea on the borders with Vauxhall) followed by Price's Candle Works (1843), the Gas Works (1846), a gas mantle factory in Garratt Lane, the Orlando Starch factory (1848), and later in 1880 a steam laundry opened at Battersea Park. When the London to Southampton Railway opened for business in 1838 its London terminus was at Nine Elms and the London to Richmond/Windsor line followed in 1846. Other railways arrived soon after with Clapham Junction opening in 1863. The population mushroomed. In 1861 it was 19,600 with the majority living between the River Thames and the newly built railways and around the newly established Battersea. Within ten years the population was 54,016 with development having moved south of the railway lines as far as Clapham Common. By 1891 the constituency population was over 98,000. In 1867 'The Artisans, Labourers and General Dwellings Company' was set up to build small houses for working people. In 1872 it acquired 40 acres in Battersea and established the Shaftesbury Estate north of Lavender Hill, the first such development in London. The Prime Minister, Lord Shaftesbury, after whom it was named, opened it. Battersea was never a wealthy area. Even in 1891 somewhere between 30 and 49% of the entire population lived in poverty, the industrial area close to the river at Nine Elms being the worst part. Nevertheless there were over 15,000 electors in 1906, rising to over 18,000 by 1910 when they represented nearly 19% of the population, the highest proportion in metropolitan Surrey.

The **Clapham** constituency ('Clopp-ham', meaning 'enclosure near a hill') covered the areas around Battersea Park, Clapham and Wandsworth Commons. It comprised officially the three Battersea wards of Nine Elms (no. 1), Bolingbroke (8) and Broomwood (9) as well as the Clapham North and South wards of Wandsworth. Famous mainly for its Junction station - reputedly the busiest station in Europe - even before the railways arrived Clapham was a country crossroads and favourite stop for the gentry travelling between London and their Home Counties estates. As early as 1690 a stagecoach service had been established to the City and handsome houses were built during the reign of Queen Anne. In 1760 Clapham Marsh was drained to form Clapham Common, which began to develop as a classy suburb at an early stage. About this time the Clapham Sect, a group of evangelical Christians centred on the church of John Venn, rector of Clapham, was prominent in the campaign for the abolition of slavery and for promoting missionary work at home and abroad. Much credit for the abolition of slavery and the slave trade in Britain was given to Venn and his compatriots. The department store Arding and Hobbs which with the station dominates Clapham Junction, has been there since 1885 when the constituency was established and the population started increasing at a massive rate. In 1891 it was already 96,000 but within a decade had increased to nearly 121,000, or 26%, very similar to adjacent Norwood. Clapham was more prosperous than many other areas and in 1891 less than 20% of the population were estimated to be living in poverty. The 1910 electorate was 18% higher than in 1906, numbering 22,611 and represented nearly 18% of the population.

Wandsworth covered from Putney to Streatham and officially comprised 7 wards – Putney (ward no. 3), Streatham (4), Balham (5), Tooting (6), Springfield (7), Fairfield (8) and Southfield (9). The population was fairly scattered in 1885, Wandsworth itself being the main centre. It is thought that it got its name from a Saxon tribal leader known as 'Wendel' – 'Wendelsworth' meaning the place of Wendel. The river Wandle played the vital role in the development of Wandsworth town where the High Street has always been part of an important coaching route from the City of London to Southampton and Portsmouth. By 1805 the river was the busiest in England with over 40 water mills on its banks and as the 19th Century beckoned, the corn mills were producing enough flour for the whole of London. Brewing too has long been established there. In 1803 the world's first public railway, The Surrey Iron Railway, was established operating horse-drawn freight vehicles between Croydon and Wandsworth via Mitcham, Merton and Tooting. On arrival at the Thames, goods were transferred to barges for shipping to London.

Wandsworth Prison (originally named the Surrey House of Correction) was built in 1851 and Wandsworth Bridge over the Thames opened in 1873. The town's growth in the latter decades of the 19th Century was so great that its 1885 constituency boundaries were quickly out-of-date. Despite this they were not revised until after the First World War and in consequence the constituency became seriously under-represented. In 1891 its population was already greater than 113,000 and within ten years had risen to 180,000 and by 1911 reached a phenomenal 253,759, almost five times that of Lambeth North. In 1891 no part of the constituency was estimated to have a proportion of its population living in poverty of greater than 39%, and that was the immediate central district of the town. Streatham and Balham were less than 20% whilst Putney and Tooting were below 30%. The electorate increased between 1906 and 1910 by a further 7,000 as places like Balham, Tooting, Streatham and Putney expanded around the area's many railway lines. The electorate of 38,523 was by far the largest in Surrey and represented 15.2% of the population.

The outer Metropolitan Boroughs also expanded, with the map showing in grey the spread of concentrated housing. The wide stretches of countryside filled with people more slowly but the railways continued to enable growth to continue. The yellow wash indicates the limit of spread of the concentrated housing today.

Outer Metropolitan Surrey (5 seats)

Kingston-upon-Thames, formerly in Mid Surrey, ran north to south from Barnes with the Thames as its western boundary via Kew, Mortlake, Richmond, Ham and Surbiton to Hook. Officially it comprised principally the Sessional Division of Richmond, the Municipal Borough of Kingston-upon-Thames and the parish of Hatch and Ham. The Royal Borough is the oldest of only four such in England and Wales having been awarded the title because it was the place where seven Anglo-Saxon kings were crowned and the name, derived from 'Cyningestun', means 'royal estate or palace'. The stone used in coronation ceremonies can be seen outside its Guildhall: a silver penny from the reign of each Saxon king being set into the stone's plinth. After the Norman Conquest, the town became a Royal Manor. In 1086 records show that it owned five mills and three salmon fisheries. Eight hundred years later in 1891, six years after its first General Election, the constituency's population numbered 85,367 and within 20 years this had increased by about half to 126,790. Its electorate rose to 19,647 in 1910 and as a proportion of the population the electorate was about 15.5%.

To Kingston's east and south of Wandsworth was **Wimbledon,** formerly in Mid Surrey and alternatively known as North-Eastern Surrey in 1885. The new constituency also covered Mitcham (formerly in Surrey Eastern), Merton, Morden, Sutton and Carshalton but was officially described as comprising principally the Sessional Division of Croydon excluding the borough of Croydon; and the parishes of Merton, Wimbledon, Caterham, Chelsham, Farley, and Warlingham, the last four of which are not classified as being in the metropolitan area and which are today in East Surrey. The population of the 1885 constituency was around 69,000 rising to 99,000 in 1901 and 160,289 by 1911, an increase

Top Right: *Wimbledon Hill Road and Worple Road were in the commercial heart of the new suburb of Wimbledon in 1885 and only yards from the town's station. Development was enhanced by the coming of several railway lines in the mid 19th Century and by the arrival of the Metropolitan District Railway that opened in 1889. The suburb's population grew rapidly within a large constituency that was subsequently divided in 1918.* **©TfL from the London Transport Museum Collection**

Above: *Kingston upon Thames was the county town of Surrey with a market place that was home to several ancient buildings. Some Saxon Kings were crowned there. Then at the boundary of the Kingdoms of Wessex and Mercia, it has retained significance as a place of administration ever since.* **Kingston Museum Collection**

Right: *Croydon was already a free-standing town of significance in 1885. Its development enhanced by the Victorian railway expansion, the borough expansion was accelerated by the arrival of tramways, which opened up suburbs of the town. The tram pictured here c1901 is bound for Addiscombe, and is seen making its way through Croydon town centre.* **©TfL from the London Transport Museum Collection**

since its creation of 132%. The number of electors increased from a little over 15,000 to nearly 28,000 represented 17.3% of the population.

The village of Wimbledon, the name probably deriving from 'Wunnemannedune' in about AD950 and meaning,' hill of a man called Wynnmann, is not mentioned in the Domesday survey of 1086. It was not until the 16th Century that the merits of the place were recognised by Thomas Cecil, later the Earl of Exeter, who was responsible for the improvement of the road to London and built Wimbledon Manor House. In 1613 Robert Bell of the East India Company built a house from which he used to commute to London on horseback. Other large houses were built and during the 19th Century a number of them were redeveloped as suburban homes for London businessmen. To provide for this affluent community, a number of shops were established along the High Street, the first opening as early as 1670. The adjacent Common was the scene of many duels but as the 19th Century progressed it was used for less dangerous sports, becoming the home of the All England Croquet Club which became the All England Croquet and Lawn Tennis Club. After visits by the Prince of Wales in 1907 attendance sand the standard of play improved and the Club came to run the major Lawn Tennis Championships in the World. The coming of the railways and its reasonable proximity to London meant that Wimbledon developed rapidly as a commuting suburb. Its old estates were broken up and developed into smaller houses and the population grew exponentially.

East of Wimbledon but South of Norwood and Dulwich was **Croydon,** comprising a newly created Municipal Borough that in 1885 included the developing south London suburbs around Norwood and Thornton Heath plus the villages of Addiscombe, Monks Orchard and Lower Shirley, outside and just east of the municipality adjoining the Kent border near Elmers End and West Wickham. The 1891 population of the constituency was already over 103,000; by 1901 this number had increased to nearly 134,000 and further to 169,551, or about two thirds since its creation. By 1910 the electorate had increased to 27,350, or 16.1% of the population. Croydon is situated 10 miles south of London at the head of the River Wandle, just to the north of a significant gap in the North Downs. Its name is of Saxon origin, and is thought to mean either 'crooked valley' or 'saffron valley'. By the later Saxon period, it was at the heart of a huge estate belonging to the Archbishops of Canterbury who built palaces there. Croydon had always been a significant halt on the road south of London, and its role as a coaching town increased after Brighton became a fashionable resort in the 1780s. Soon afterwards, Croydon became the terminus of two important new commercial transport links, stretching southwards from the Thames. The first, opened in 1803, was the horse-drawn Surrey Iron Railway from Wandsworth (extended to Merstham, as the Croydon, Merstham and Godstone Railway, in 1805); and the second, opened in 1809, was the Croydon Canal, which came from Deptford. Neither was a great success: the canal closed in 1836, and the railway in 1846. However, the route of the canal was taken over by the steam-powered London & Croydon Railway, which opened between London Bridge and West Croydon in 1839. Croydon's subsequent suburban development stems from its railway connections. The town was already expanding, and the improvement in communications accelerated the process. It became especially popular with the middle classes, who could commute to work in the City. In 1889 Croydon became a County Borough.

The only other Surrey constituency that in 1885 incorporated any significant part of the present-day Greater London metropolis was **Epsom,** a county seat, which inherited the alternative designation of Mid Surrey. It covered an area that included Maldon, Cheam and Sutton, which are all now within London, together with several places beyond it including Banstead, Effingham, Walton-on-Thames, Thames Ditton, Leatherhead and Esher. Just like neighbouring Croydon, its 1891 population of 70,103 rose by two thirds to reach 116,341 within 20 years, due mainly to the development of housing estates in parts of the constituency that lie within London. The electorate represented about 16.2% of the population in 1910. **Reigate** included Purley and Coulsdon but was essentially a shire constituency beyond the London metropolis. Reigate results and MPs are not included in this study.

General Election Results 1885-1910 (Dec) - by % majority

Constituency	*1885*	*1886*	*1892*	*1895*	*1900*	*1906*	*1910 Jan*	*1910 Dec*
Southwark West	L4	L2+	L21	L2	L2	L8	C2	L0.2
Bermondsey	L1	C6	L8	C4	C4	L23-	L10	L14
Rotherhithe	C9	C20	C18	C29	C25	L20	L11	L14
Newington West	C13	C8	L19	L8	L19	L25	L5	L7
Walworth	C48	C6	L6-	C10	C16	L14	L3	L4
Camberwell North	L3	C7	L11	C9	L16	L29	L11	L11
Peckham	C6	C12	C2	C13	C19	L25	C0.8	L0.4
Dulwich	C24	C100	C26	C41	C14	C3	C17	C17
Battersea	L9	L3	IndL16	L2	L2	L12	L3	L9
Wandsworth	C15	C100	C23	C33	C100	C2	C14	C18
Clapham	L4	C7	C7	C21	C42	C1	C10	C11
Lambeth North	C3	C8	L3	LU8	C20	L5	C10	C7
Kennington	C6	C7-	L9	C14	C29	L21	L5	L0.7
Brixton	C11	C27+	C13	C31++	C100	L3	C10	C13
Norwood	C15	C35	C23	C100	C100	C8	C15	C19
Wimbledon	C25	C100	C48	C100	C100	C12	C24	C100
Kingston	C21	C100	C8	C23	C100	C7	C31	C100
Croydon	C12	C100	C15	C19	C100	LU3	C4	C7
Epsom	C32	C100	C31	C100	C100	C8	C35	C100
C and LU	14	17+	11+	16++	15	7+	12	10
L	5	2+	8	3	4	12	7	9
Lab	0	0	0	0	0	0	0	0
Total	19	19++	19+	19++	19	19+	19	19

Key: 100 - unopposed; C - Conservative; L - Liberal; LU Liberal Unionist (allied with Con); Lab - Labour; IndL - independent Labour + by-election won by defending party; - lost by defending party.

Politics in Metropolitan Surrey

Prior to 1885 politics here were dominated by the overwhelmingly Liberal preferences of the borough electorates in Lambeth and Southwark and to a slightly lesser extent in the Eastern county division. The extension of the franchise and re-distribution of seats transformed the political landscape when a large number of middle class suburbs formed the basis of many additional seats that were first contested in 1885. Overall, between 1885 and 1910, the Conservatives won 77 seats (including six at by-elections) in the LCC area and a further 34 in the outer metropolitan districts (including two by-elections), a total of 111. The Liberals won a total of 52 (including three by-elections), none of which was in the outer area and six were in Battersea, running either as an Independent or with Labour support. Although Labour won no seats in its own right, during a period when the Conservatives established a very dominant position, their increasing electoral support was starting to undermine the Liberals, and it was not long before Labour made the breakthrough as the main opposition to the Conservatives. The table opposite summarises the results:

The three newly created constituencies wholly within the outer metropolitan area – Croydon, Wimbledon and Kingston – returned a Conservative at every General Election between 1885 and December 1910; 24 MPs in total. Only Reigate, which included Purley and Coulsdon, returned a Liberal and that was on a single occasion, in 1906, and by a majority of only 2%. In addition Tories comfortably won all General Elections at Epsom, and by-elections at Croydon, in 1886 and 1895.

Within the area that became part of the London County Council in 1889 the Tories also became the majority Party in most places, except in the central areas of Southwark. Liberals only won elections in the latter part of the period in those constituencies that became more working class in their electoral composition. In the first election after re-distribution the Liberals won only 5 seats (Southwark West, Bermondsey, Camberwell North, Battersea and Clapham), none by a majority greater than 9%. The Tories by comparison won 10, seven of them with a majority of 9% or greater. Their biggest success was at Walworth where they carried a majority of 48%. Thereafter it began to get worse for the Liberals who, following the split over Irish Home Rule, won only 2 seats in 1886, securing Southwark West and Battersea by slim majorities. Even in the Liberal landslide victory of 1906 the Tories won Wandsworth, Clapham, Dulwich and Norwood. By 1910, when the Liberals were still in Government, although they were managing to win seats in Southwark and Camberwell, they only did so by small majorities.

The Tories best seats in the LCC area were Dulwich, Norwood and Wandsworth, which they won at every General Election. In addition they won Dulwich at by-elections in 1886 and 1893. The Party also did well in other seats, losing them to the Liberals only rarely. Clapham returned a Liberal only once, in 1885, and then by a slim majority of 4% whilst neighbouring Brixton was Tory every time except in the landslide year of 1906, when the Liberal majority was only 3%. Tories also won in by-elections; one was held in 1887, another in 1896. Newington West, Peckham and adjoining Rotherhithe were strong for the Tories initially but gradually they lost their grip. Newington West changed to the Liberals in 1892 and remained in their grasp throughout the rest of the period whilst the other two swung strongly to the Liberals in 1906 who retained them both until the War (barring Peckham which the Tories won at a by-election in 1908 and retained by less than 1% in January 1910). Socially these were heavily working class seats and it is possible that Liberal social welfare policies had some influence on the voters.

Lambeth North was also a predominantly Conservative-held seat during the period. It returned Liberals only in 1892 and 1906, although a Liberal Unionist was successful there in 1895. Kennington and its neighbour Walworth were the most marginal seats during the period, swinging between the two Parties, both seats being won together by the same Party at each of four Elections. There was a similar pattern in by-elections. The Liberals captured Kennington from the Tories at a by-election in 1889 whilst the reverse occurred in Walworth three years later in 1892, soon after the General Election.

Other seats were predominantly Liberal. The Party's best seat was Battersea, which they won at every election (including an 1886 by-election), although after 1895 they were dependent on wider radical support. It was an Independent Liberal who won in 1892 and thereafter the winning candidate always had Labour support. Southwark West returned a Liberal in every election except January 1910, including a by-election in 1887, though its 21% majority on that occasion was unusually comfortable. Camberwell North returned a Liberal in every election except 1886 and 1895. Bermondsey was also generally Liberal; though even there the Tories were successful in the contests held in 1886, 1895 and 1900. The Liberals did lose a by-election on 28th October 1909 but won it back in 1910.

MPs for Metropolitan Surrey 1885-1918

Southwark West

Arthur Cohen (Liberal) was elected in 1880 and represented Southwark until 1885 when he was returned for the equivalent new constituency of Southwark West. His principal biographical details can be found earlier in this chapter under Southwark.

Following his retirement in 1888 the seat was taken at a by-election by **Richard Knight Causton** (Liberal), born

MPs for Southwark, Bermondsey, Newington, and Camberwell						
From	at	To	Surname	First Names	Constituency	Party
1885	G	1888	Cohen	Arthur	Southwark West	Liberal
1888	B	1910	Causton	Richard Knight		Liberal
1910(Jan)	G	1910(Dec)	Dunn	Sir William Henry		Conservative
1910(Dec)	G	1918	Strauss	Edward Anthony		Liberal
1885	G	1886	Rogers	Thorold	Bermondsey	Liberal
1886	G	1892	Lafone	Alfred		Conservative
1892	G	1895	Barrow	Sir Reuben Vincent		Liberal
1895	G	1900	Lafone	Alfred		Conservative
1900	G	1906	Cust	Henry John Cockayne		Conservative
1906	G	1909	Cooper	Dr. George Joseph		Liberal
1909	B	1910	Dumphreys	John Molesworth Thomas		Conservative
1910	G	1918	Glanville	Harold James		Liberal
1885	G	1892	Hamilton	Sir Charles Edward	Rotherhithe	Conservative
1892	G	1906	Macdona	John Cumming		Conservative
1906	G	1918	Carr-Gomm	Hubert William Culling (Captain)		Liberal
1885	G	1892	Cooke	Charles Wallwyn Radcliffe	Newington West	Conservative
1892	G	1916	Norton	Cecil William (Captain)		Liberal
1916	B	1918	Gilbert	James Daniel		Liberal
1885	G	1892	Isaacs	Lewis Henry	Newington Walworth	Conservative
1892	G	1895	Saunders	William		Liberal
1895	B	1906	Bailey	Sir James		Conservative
1906	G	1910	O'Donnell	Charles James O'Cahan		Liberal
1910	G	1918	Dawes	James Arthur		Liberal
1885	G	1886	Strong	Richard	Camberwell North	Liberal
1886	G	1892	Kelly	John Richards		Conservative
1892	G	1895	Bayley	Edward Thomas		Liberal
1895	G	1900	Dalbiac	Philip Hugh (Colonel)		Conservative
1900	G	1918	Macnamara	Thomas		Liberal
1885	G	1892	Baumann	Arthur Anthony	Peckham	Conservative
1892	G	1906	Banbury	Sir Frederick George		Conservative
1906	G	1908	Clarke	Charles Goddard		Liberal
1908	B	1910(Dec)	Gooch	Henry Cubitt		Conservative
1910(Dec)	G	1918	Richardson	Sir Albion Henry Herbert		Liberal
1885	G	1887	Howard	John Morgan	Dulwich	Conservative
1887	B	1903	Maple	Sir John Blundell		Conservative
1903	B	1906	Harris	Dr. Frederick Rutherfoord		Conservative
1906	B	1910(Dec)	Law	Andrew Bonar		Conservative
1916	B	1918	Gilbert	James Daniel		Liberal

Notes: First returned at: B By-election, G General Election

in London in 1843, who was the son of a former Sheriff of the City of London and Middlesex (1868-70) and the son-in-law of Judge Chambers who had been an MP for Hertford (1852-7) and Marylebone (1865-85, see Chapter 2). He was a director in his father's company, a director of the Skinner's Company (1877-8), President of the London Chamber of Commerce and a Commissioner of Lieutenancy for the City of London. Between 1892 and 1895 he was a Lord of the Treasury (a Government whip); then an Opposition whip until 1905; and Paymaster-General from 1905 until 1910.

He had earlier contested Colchester in 1874 when he was defeated, but he was became Member for Colchester in

1880, serving until he lost in 1885. He was unsuccessful when he tried again in 1886. Following his defeat at Southwark West in 1910 he was elevated to the Lords as Baron Southwark. He died in 1929.

Richard Causton MP
Wikipedia

Sir William Henry Dunn (Conservative) took Southwark West in January 1910 but only held it until the December election of the same year when he was defeated. Dunn was born in 1856, and educated privately, after which he became a land agent and surveyor. From 1909-28 he was an Alderman of the City of London, where he was Sheriff in 1906/7, and a Lieutenant sitting also as a magistrate for London County. He was Lord Mayor of the City in 1916-17 and Honorary Colonel of the 1st London Transport and Supply Column. He was given a number of foreign honours including the *Dannebrog* (Denmark), the Legion of Honour (France) and the Order of the Crown (Germany), and he was made a Knight of St Olaf (Norway) and of the Rising Sun (Japan).

Edward Anthony Strauss (Liberal) won the seat in December 1910 and held it until 1918. Born in 1862, he came from Highbury and was educated at Kings College, London afterwards entering his father's business as a merchant. He was a magistrate for the counties of both London and Berkshire, where from 1906 to January 1910 he was the MP for Abingdon. In 1918 he transferred to the Southwark North constituency, which he represented until 1923 when he lost to Labour but regained it at a by-election in 1927. He was defeated in 1929 but emerged victorious once more in 1931 standing as a National Liberal in support of Ramsey McDonald. He was re-elected in 1935 but died four years later.

Bermondsey

James Edwin Thorold Rogers (Liberal) had been an MP for Southwark since 1880 and at the 1885 election was returned for the new Bermondsey seat. His details can be found earlier in this chapter.

He only held it until 1886 when **Alfred Lafone** (Conservative) won the seat, which he held twice; initially until he was defeated in 1892; then subsequently from 1895 until he retired in 1900. He was a Liverpudlian, born there in 1821, and lived at Park Lodge, Toxteth Park. Educated privately he was a Middlesex magistrate who sat on two School Boards in Southwark. He died in 1911.

Sir Reubens Barrow MP
Croydon On Line

Sir Reubens Vincent Barrow (Liberal) recaptured the seat for his Party in 1892 but only managed to hold it for one term. He was born at Exeter in 1838 and was educated by the British and Foreign Schools Society in the Borough Road after which he got a job in the leather trade at the age of sixteen. He was especially active in the Croydon area where he became an alderman on the newly formed Borough Council in 1885 and was the town's first Mayor. He was a magistrate in the borough and also a governor of the Whitgift's Foundation.

Henry John Cockayne Cust (Conservative) who was previously MP for Stamford (Lincolnshire) between 1890 and 1895, succeeded Lafone in 1900 and held the seat until 1906.Originally from Lincolnshire where he was a magistrate, Deputy County Lieutenant and Lord of the Manor of Cockayne - Hatley, Cust lived at Belton House which was then owned together with the Ashridge estate (today's management college in Hertfordhsire) by his cousin Earl Brownlow. Belton House was just outside Grantham where Cust's father was an MP between 1874 and 1880. Born in 1861 and Eton educated, Henry was a University graduate of Trinity College, Cambridge and initially studied law in London and Paris. Despite his landed background he had many other attributes being a member of the French bar and from 1893-6 and 1902-06, editor of the *Pall Mall Gazette*. This was a London evening newspaper that had originally been established as a Conservative supporting journal in 1865 but which changed in 1880 to become a radical organ specialising in exposing major social issues of the times. Cust moved the paper back towards a more independent conservative position. During the First World War he was active in promoting government propaganda and in its aftermath, devising employment schemes. He died in 1917 six years before the *Gazette* was incorporated into the *Evening Standard*, which survives to this day.

Dr. George Joseph Cooper (Liberal) captured Bermondsey in 1906 but only held it for three years until his death. Born in 1844, he was educated at Leeds Grammar School and became a doctor of medicine, practising in Bermondsey.

He was a member of the LCC between 1889 and 1906 and chaired its Public Health Committee.

Also a London magistrate, he died in 1909 when **John Molesworth Dumphreys** (Conservative) won the by-election to succeed him though he only held the seat until the January 1910 general election when he was defeated. He was, like his predecessor, born in 1844 and was very unusual in those days for being a working class Tory. He was a leather dresser in Bermondsey and became Secretary of Pearks Ltd [4], representing Deptford on the LCC. He was also a mayor of Bermondsey. He contested Birmingham West in 1885 as a working man's Conservative and Fair Trader and after his brief spell as Bermondsey's MP, stood again in December 1910, but was unsuccessful and his political career never resumed. He died in 1925.

Harold James Glanville (Liberal) took the seat in January 1910 and continued to represent it until 1918 when he was adopted for Bermondsey West, sitting until he retired in 1922. By then resident in Lewisham, he was educated at Deptford Grammar School and became a merchant. He was a member of the Bermondsey Vestry Committee and sat on the LCC from 1898 to 1910 being also a member of the Metropolitan Water Board and a magistrate for the County of London. He contested Rotherhithe unsuccessfully in 1892. He died in 1930.

Rotherhithe

Sir Charles Edward Hamilton (Conservative) was Rotherthithe's MP from 1985 to 1892. He was born in Liverpool in 1845 and was educated privately in his home city and then in Brussels. He joined the 80th Lancashire Rifle Volunteers in which he became a Lieutenant - Colonel. He was a magistrate in Lancashire and Liverpool, where he was also a city councillor, and died in 1928.

John Cumming Macdona (Conservative) won the seat in 1892 and held it until 1906. Born in 1836, he was educated at Trinity College, Dublin and at Oxford University going on to become a Queens Councillor. Originally from the North West of England in Cheshire, he was rector of Cheadle from 1874 until 1882. He first contested an election at Chesterfield in 1885, though he was unsuccessful on that occasion. As Rotherhithe's MP he introduced the Lancashire Electric Power Supply Bill, which preceded all other bills of a similar nature, and also introduced and passed the Floating Derelict Bill, a measure of some relevance it may be imagined in a riverside community such as the one he represented in Parliament. In 1895 he was appointed Parliamentary Secretary to the Treasury. He died in 1907.

Captain Hubert William Culling Carr-Gomm (Liberal) won the seat in 1906 and retained it until 1918 when he was defeated, suffering the same fate in the same seat four years later and at Paddington South in 1923. Born in India in 1877, he was educated at Eton and Oriel College, Oxford where he obtained his MA. He became an active worker for the Liberal Party and was Hon. Secretary of the Party's London Association before he became an Assistant Private Secretary to the Prime Minister, Sir Henry Campbell-Bannerman in 1905/6. He was a Captain in the 2/22 Battalion of the London Regiment (the Queen's Own) during the War serving in France (1916) and Salonika (1917) and was thereafter in the Territorial Reserve Force. He was also a Buckinghamshire magistrate and died in 1939.

Newington West

Charles Wallwyn Radcliffe Cooke (Conservative) sat from 1885 until 1892, partly because of a split in the Liberal vote at the 1885 election when the former MP for Lambeth, Sir William McArthur, stood as an Independent against the official candidate after he was deselected. Born in 1841, Cooke was educated at Emanuel College, Cambridge where he gained the Le Bas and Burney University prizes on two occasions. He was called to the bar at Lincolns Inn in 1872 and married the daughter of Rev. Broome, the Vicar of Houghton, the Norfolk estate[5] of the Marquis of Cholmondeley. He was a barrister on the Oxford Circuit, a magistrate and Deputy – Lieutenant of Herefordshire where he lived in the village of Much Marcle. He was President of the County's Committee of Agriculture, chairman of the Ledbury Highway Board and founding President of the National Association of English Cider makers, a major Herefordshire industry. He also founded the Constitutional Union. He was MP for Hereford between 1893 and 1900 after his defeat at Newington. He died in 1911.

Captain Cecil William Norton (Liberal) was returned in 1892 and sat until 1916 having previously contested Great Yarmouth unsuccessfully in the elections of 1885 and 1886. Born in 1850, he was the son of the Rector of Baltinglass, Ireland and was educated first at Trinity College, Dublin, where he was a double prize-winner; then secondly at the Royal Military and Staff Colleges. He joined the 5th Royal Irish Lancers later becoming a Brigade Major of Cavalry

4 A firm of this name is listed in Dickens' Dictionary of London with its offices at 44 Bond Street

5 By coincidence the place where the Author was christened!

at Aldershot. His second wife's father was Sir C.P. Huntingdon, who was elected the MP for Darwen, Lancashire in the same year as Norton was returned for Newington, though his in-law did not survive beyond the election of 1895. Norton was a junior Lord of the Treasury (a Government Whip) from 1905-10 and assistant Postmaster General from 1910 to 1915 when the Wartime Coalition was formed. In January 1916 he was elevated to the House of Lords as Lord Rathcreedan and after the War was made Additional Parliamentary Secretary to the Ministry of Munitions and Supply, serving in that capacity from 1919 to 1921. He died in 1930.

Following his elevation he was succeeded at a by-election in 1916 by **James Daniel Gilbert** (Liberal), a Newington man, born there in 1864. He was a local magistrate and county councillor on the LCC, a member of the Thames Conservancy and of the Port of London Authority. He chaired the LCC Fire Brigade Committee in 1900-2; its Rivers Committee in 1903-6; and the General Purposes Committee in 1906-7. He was elected in 1918 when he transferred to Southwark Central as a National Liberal but was defeated in 1924 and his political career came to an end.

Newington Walworth

Lewis Henry Isaacs (Conservative) represented Walworth from 1885 until 1892. He was a Mancunian, born in 1830, the son of Isaac Isaacs, who described himself as a 'gentleman'. His maternal grandfather was a Liverpool Merchant, Lewis Henry. He was educated at the Royal Lancaster Grammar School and University College London where he qualified as an architect, later becoming Surveyor to the Holborn Board of Works and the Gray's Inn Society (1868-99). He was the architect of Holborn Town Hall (See Chapter 3, North London), the Northumberland Avenue Hotel, and other major buildings in the capital. From 1902-04 was the Mayor of Kensington and wrote 'A Treatise on Sewerage and Drainage'. He died in 1908.

William Saunders (Liberal) took the seat in 1892 but only represented it for three years. Born in Wiltshire in 1823, Saunders was educated at Devizes Grammar School and became a journalist. He established the *Western* and *Eastern Morning News* papers, and the Central News Agency. From 1885-6 he was briefly MP for Hull East. Latterly he lived in Streatham and was a member of the LCC. He died in 1895, before the General Election held later that year.

Sir James Bailey (Conservative) took the seat at a by-election retaining it until 1906. He was born at Mattishall, Norfolk in 1840 and was educated at a private school in the small market town of East Dereham. He was a Deputy Lieutenant of Norfolk and an Essex magistrate and died in 1910.

Bailey was succeeded by **Charles James O'Cahan O'Donnell** (Liberal), the son of an Irish captain who retired from the House in January 1910. He was born in Port Louis, Mauritius in 1850 but was educated at St Ignatius College and Queens University, Belfast. He married the niece of E.R.Langworthy, who was briefly the MP for Salford in 1857, and embarked on a career in the Indian Civil Service between 1872 and 1900. He wrote several books on British policy in India and died in 1934.

James Arthur Dawes (Liberal) succeeded O'Donnell in January 1910 and retained the seat until 1918 when he was re-elected for the new Southwark South East constituency, which he represented until 1921, the year he died. Born at Blackheath in 1866, he lived later in his life at a house in Kennington Park Road, close to his Walworth constituency, and in Devonshire. He was educated at Harrow School and University College Oxford where he attained a MA before becoming a solicitor in 1891. He was active politically in local government, both on Southwark Borough Council where he was mayor three times (1900, 1913 and 1914), and on the LCC, where he was a member from 1906-09. He was appointed to the Metropolitan Water Board in 1900; he was a magistrate for the county of London, and chairman of the London Insurance Committee between 1912 and 1914. During the war, in 1918, he was an Acting Commander of the RNVR. In the year of his death he was Mayor of Dartmouth, Devon.

Camberwell North

Richard Strong (Liberal) was only briefly an MP, sitting from 1885 until 1886. He was born in Birmingham in 1833 and educated privately before coming to live in Denmark Hill. He was a Surrey magistrate and chairman of the Board of Guardians in Camberwell at a time when there were two workhouses (in Havil Road and Gordon Roads) with another planned at Constance Road, Dulwich. He sat also on the Board of Managers of the South Metropolitan District Schools while being a Governor of the Dulwich College estates. He was President of the Lambeth Liberal Association and a member of the LCC of which he was vice-chairman. He died in 1915.

John Richards Kelly (Conservative) took the seat in 1886 and held it until 1892 when he was defeated. Born in

London in 1844, he was the son of a senior Post Office official (a one-time Inspector-General of letter carriers), who appears to have been a man of means as the young John received an Eton schooling before going on to Trinity Hall, Cambridge and a career in the law. He was a member of the Inner Temple where he was called to the bar in 1879. A strong Unionist and 'fair-trader', he favoured reform of the House of Lords. He died in 1922.

The man who defeated Kelly at the 1892 election was **Edward Thomas Bayley** (Liberal) who lived at Southfields, near Wimbledon, and who was the son and grandson of ministers of the Church. He was born at Accrington (Lancashire) in 1841 and educated privately, including schools in France and Germany, and became chairman of the West Metropolitan Tramways Company. Active in the Masonic movement, he first contested the seat in 1886, but only held it himself from 1892 to 1895. He died in 1938.

He was succeeded by **Colonel Philip Hugh Dalbiac** (Conservative) who was born in Hyde Park Square, London in 1856, and came from a family that had a major involvement in Parliamentary politics on his mother's side and a military one on his father's. The political tradition was mostly Liberal and Philip's Toryism was exceptional. His grandfather was Sir Charles Seely, , who represented Nottingham (1869-74 and 1880-85) and Nottingham West (1885-6 and 1892-5), retiring from the political scene the year that Philip was elected. Sir Charles' father also sat in the House as a Midlands Liberal MP sitting for Lincoln from 1847-8 and again from 1861-85. Philip's cousin Sir Charles Hilton Seely (a Liberal Unionist) was returned for Lincoln in the same election as Philip and sat there until defeated in 1906 reappearing briefly at Mansfield where he was elected in a wartime by-election standing as a Coalition candidate in 1916. He retired in 1918. Another cousin, Major-General John Edward Bernard Seely, was also an MP. Initially sitting as a Conservative for the Isle of Wight from 1900 to 1904, when he joined the Liberals, in 1906 he transferred to the Abercromby division of Liverpool, which he represented until January 1910 when he was defeated. He popped up again in a March 1910 by-election as the MP for Ilkeston, which he held until defeated in 1922. He transferred to the Isle of Wight, which he won by the tiny margin of 0.3%, only to lose it the following year - becoming the last Liberal to be elected on the Isle of Wight for over another fifty years. Philip himself was educated at Winchester School and joined the Army in 1875 rising initially to become a Captain and served as Adjutant in the 1st Nottinghamshire Rifle Volunteers between 1885 and 1890. He was Colonel Commanding of the 18th Middlesex Rifle Volunteers but also enjoyed a business career. He was a partner in the publishing firm of Swan Sonnenschein and after he retired from the House in 1900 became a Director of George Allen and Unwin in 1914, three years after it was acquired by Swans. This firm had been established in 1871 as the publisher of John Ruskin. During the First World War he served in France and Salonika between 1916 and 1917 and died ten years later.

Thomas Macnamara (Liberal) who had contested Deptford unsuccessfully in 1895 won Camberwell North in 1900, an election in which the Tories suffered only nine net losses nationally compared with 1895. Macnamara went on to hold the seat until 1918 and then sat for Camberwell North West until 1924 when he was defeated. This brought the end to his Parliamentary career because, although he contested two more elections, at Walsall (Staffordshire) in 1925 and 1929, he was never re-elected and died in 1931. He was born in Montreal, Canada in 1861, the son of a regimental Sergeant and was educated at St Thomas's School, Exeter and the Borough Road Teachers Training College before becoming a journalist. From 1892 to 1907 he was editor of the '*Schoolmaster*' and, in 1896, President of the National Union of Teachers. As an MP he was Parliamentary Secretary to the Local Government Board between 1907 and 1908, then Parliamentary and Financial Secretary to the Admiralty until 1920. In the Coalition Government he was Minister of Labour under Lloyd-George from 1920-22 when the Tories withdrew their support. He was awarded honorary degrees at St Andrews (1898) and Oxford (1907) Universities.

Peckham

Arthur Anthony Baumann (Conservative) was Peckham's MP from 1885 until 1892 when he transferred to Salford North, where he was defeated. He was born in Glasgow in 1856, the son of a merchant, and was educated at Wellington College and Balliol College, Oxford. Called to the bar at the Inner Temple in 1880, he practised at the Parliamentary Bar until 1895 when he went into the City. He contested Kirkcaldy unsuccessfully in January 1910 and retired from politics. He died in 1936.

Baumann was succeeded in 1892 by **Sir Frederick George Banbury** (Conservative) who held the seat until he was beaten in 1906. Shortly afterwards he secured a by-election win in the City of London, which he served until 1918. His principal biographical details can be found in Chapter 3 (Central London - Middlesex)

In 1906 Banbury was beaten by **Charles Goddard Clarke** (Liberal) but he died two years later. Clarke was born in London in 1849 but was educated in Liverpool, thereafter joining the family firm of wholesale 'druggists', Potter and

Clarke. He was a London magistrate, a member of the LCC from 1898 and also of Camberwell Borough Council of which he was Mayor in 1902-3. He first contested Dulwich in 1895 and Mile End in 1900, both times unsuccessfully.

Henry Cubitt Gooch (Conservative) won the 1908 by-election caused by Gooch's death and held the seat until the election of December 1910. Born in London in 1871, Gooch was the grandson of a vicar who married the daughter of another one. He was educated at Eton and Trinity College, Cambridge and was called to the bar in 1894, becoming a member of the London Schools Board in 1897, serving until 1904. Between 1907-10 and 1914-34 he was a member of the LCC, where he was a Vice-Chairman of education, a Vice Chairman (1922-3) and Chairman (1923-4) of the Council. He was a Vice President of Kings College, Hospital in the constituency and President of Cambridge House, Camberwell, which still exists today as a project to help and motivate young people from the area. He died in 1959.

Sir Albion Henry Herbert Richardson (Liberal) took Peckham in December 1910, having contested it unsuccessfully at the January poll, and held it until 1922. He was born in 1874, educated at Herne House School as well as privately in France and Germany after which became a solicitor, being admitted in 1899. In 1904 he was elected Chairman of the United Law Society and first contested Peckham in January 1910 when Gooch defeated him. When he won Peckham in December 1910 it was one of only a handful of seats that changed hands compared with the January contest earlier that year. In 1912 he was called to the bar as a member of Grays Inn and eight years after he left the House he took silk being appointed Recorder of Warwick a year later in 1931. He fulfilled this role until 1936 when he was made Recorder of Nottingham, which post he occupied until his death in 1950. Meanwhile in 1944 he had been appointed Treasurer of Grays Inn.

Dulwich

John Howard MP
Wikipedia

John Morgan Howard (Conservative) sat from 1885 until he was made a County Court Judge in 1887, though he died only four years later. He was born in 1837 and after his formal education was called to the bar of the Middle Temple in 1858, taking silk in 1874 and becoming a bencher three years later. He was appointed Recorder of Guildford but in 1875 was Her Majesty's Chief Commissioner into the conduct and result of the 1874 General Eelction in Norwich. A magistrate for Middlesex and for Westminster, he contested Lambeth unsuccessfully on three occasions (1988, 1874 and 1880) before he was finally returned at Dulwich.

Sir John Blundell Maple (Conservative) succeeded at the 1887 by-election and held it until his own death in 1903. He had entered London politics initially at St Pancras South in 1885 but was not successful. He was also returned to the LCC in 1895, serving for six years. He was born in 1845 and educated at Cranford College, Maidenhead and Kings College, London. His father, John Maple (d 1900), had a small furniture shop in Tottenham Court Road, London, and his business began to develop about the time that his son entered it. The practical management soon devolved on the younger Maple, under whom it attained colossal dimensions. The firm became a limited liability company with capital of £2 million in 1890, with Maple as chairman. He was the owner of a large stud of racehorses, and from 1885 onwards won many important races, appearing at first under the name of 'Mr Childwick'. His public benefactions included a hospital and a recreation ground to the city of St Albans, near which his residence Childwickbury was situated, and the rebuilding, at a cost of more than £150 000, of University College Hospital, London, which was very close to his Store, and which was rebuilt again in 2004.

Dr. Frederick Rutherford Harris (Conservative) won the 1903 by-election that followed Maple's death. He was the son of a Judge in the Supreme Court of Madras, India and was born in 1856. He was educated at Leatherhead Grammar School, Surrey, then at Edinburgh University after which he went to the diamond centre of Kimberley in South Africa and set up in medical practice. There he met Cecil Rhodes for whom he became Confidential Secretary and was also First Secretary to the British Chartered Company, established initially to occupy the territory for trading and mining purposes as far as the Zambezi, and bring the whole under the protection of Great Britain. This initiated a further colonial expansion throughout Southern Africa leading to a number of territorial disputes, not least with the Dutch settlers in South Africa. In 1884 Harris was elected to the Cape Parliament as MP for Kimberley and was thus closely involved in all of the events associated with Rhodes during that period but returned to Britain around the time of the Boer War and was elected MP for Monmouth Boroughs in 1900. He was unseated on petition in 1901 but was soon successful at the Dulwich by-election. However, in 1906 he decided to stand down in order to 'travel abroad'. He died in 1920.

Andrew Bonar Law MP

Harris' resignation created the opportunity for the return to the House of a very senior Tory, **Andrew Bonar Law** (Conservative) who had been defeated in the general election earlier that year at the Glasgow Blackfriars constituency, which he had represented since 1900. Bonar Law was born in Rexton, New Brunswick, Canada in 1858, the son of an Ulster Protestant minister. Educated in Canada, he moved to Glasgow, his mother's home at the age of sixteen after she died and started work for the family's Iron Merchants business. Following his election as an MP he made a favourable impression on the Party's leader, the Prime Minister Arthur Balfour who appointed him as a PPS at the Board of Trade in 1902, which post he occupied until the Government resigned in 1905. Returned at Dulwich the following year he went into Opposition. In December 1910 he decided to stand down at Dulwich and contest the less favourable seat of Manchester North West, which he lost and was out of the House until winning a by-election at Bootle a year later. On his return to front line politics Balfour stood down as leader of the Party and Bonar Law was appointed Unionist leader, a position he retained until 1921 and then again in 1922-3. When Asquith formed a Wartime Coalition Government in 1915 Bonar Law was appointed Secretary of State for the Colonies but he faced some criticism at the time from opponents as his Iron Company had exported substantial supplies to Germany in the military build-up to the War. When Lloyd-George became Prime Minister in 1916, Bonar Law was made Chancellor of the Exchequer, a key post in Wartime, but also held the post of Leader of the House. He remained in the Cabinet throughout the War and afterwards led his Party into a peacetime Coalition under Lloyd George, even though at the 1918 General Election the Conservatives had been returned as by far the largest Party. At that poll he once again changed seats and became MP for Glasgow Central. In 1919 he attended the Versailles Peace Conference and was made Lord Privy Seal, remaining as Leader of the House. By the early 1920s he was in poor health, suffering from cancer and resigned as leader of his Party in 1921. However, the following year the Conservatives voted to abandon Lloyd-George and, although Bonar Law himself disagreed with this decision, he accepted the outcome and become Prime Minister. Unfortunately he died the following year. His principal contribution to British politics, apart from his sustaining Lloyd George and the Liberals long after they were a spent force, was his total solidarity with the Ulster Protestants, and he may reasonably be said to have been the man who above all others succeeded in preventing the 'six counties' from becoming part of the Irish Free State, when it was established in 1922, shortly after Lloyd George's resignation.

Lieutenant-Colonel Sir Frederick Hall (Conservative) was elected in December 1910 and remained as the MP until his death in 1932. Born in 1864, he became an industrialist, serving on the Boards of many companies. These included Garner, Mountain and Co., the County of London Electricity Supply Company, the South London Electricity Supply Corporation, the South Metropolitan Electricity Supply Company and the Mercantile Marine Finance Corporation of which he was Chairman and Managing Director. Harry Greer, a Peckham MP in 1918, was also a managing director of this company. Hall was a member of the LCC from 1907 to 1913 and of the Territorials Association. He was awarded the DSO in 1918

MPs for Battersea, Wandsworth, and Lambeth

Battersea

Octavius Vaughan Morgan (Liberal) represented Battersea from 1885 until 1892 when he transferred to Ashton-under-Lyne where he was defeated. He was born in 1837 in Monmouthshire where he was educated at Abergavenny. At the age of 21 he became a partner in the family firms of Morgan Brothers (of which there were 6), merchants and bankers of Cannon Street, London and of the Crucible Company, formed in 1855 by William Vaughan Morgan who acquired a Battersea-based merchant and druggist business which by 1857 was able to display a range of crucibles at the Crystal Palace Exhibition. The company was soon supplying customers throughout Africa, South East Asia, the Americas and Europe where it was awarded a Gold medal at the 1868 Paris Exhibition. Towards the end of the 1800s, the business began trading as The Morgan Crucible Company. It remains in business today. Octavius was an extensive foreign traveller, a founder of the *European Mail* and member of the Imperial Federal League. He favoured an elected House of Lords and was a member of the Municipal Reform League. He died in 1896.

John Elliott Burns (Liberal) succeeded him in 1892 and remained as the MP until his retirement in 1918. Although he migrated to the Liberals, he was in fact a Socialist, born into a working class family in London in 1858, later becoming a trade unionist and Government minister. He was educated at National Schools in his native Battersea and

MPs for Battersea, Wandsworth, and Lambeth

From	at	To	Surname	First Names	Constituency	Party
1885	G	1892	Morgan	Octavius Vaughan	Battersea	Liberal
1892	G	1918	Burns	John Elliott		Liberal
1885	G	1913	Kimber	Sir Henry	Wandsworth	Conservative
1913	B	1918	Samuel	Samuel		Conservative
1885	G	1886	Moulton	Sir John Fletcher	Clapham	Conservative
1886	G	1892	Gilliat	John Saunders		Conservative
1892	G	1910	Thornton	Percy Melville		Conservative
1910	G	1918	Faber	George Denison		Conservative
1918 (May)	B	1918 (Dec)	Greer	Harry		Conservative
1885	G	1892	Fraser	Sir Charles Crawfurd (Lieutenant-General)	Lambeth North	Conservative
1892	G	1895	Coldwells	Francis Moses		Liberal
1895	G	1900	Stanley	Sir Henry Morton		Liberal Unionist
1900	G	1906	Horner	Frederick William		Conservative
1906	G	1910	Myer	Horatio		Liberal
1910	G	1918	Gastrell	Sir William Henry Houghton (Lt-Col)		Conservative
1885	G	1889	Gent-Davis	Robert	Kennington	Conservative
1889	B	1895	Beaufoy	Mark Hanbury		Liberal
1895	G	1906	Cook	Sir Frederick Lucas		Conservative
1906	G	1918	Collins	Sir Stephen		Liberal
1885	G	1887	Bagallay	Ernest	Brixton	Conservative
1887	B	1895	Carmarthen	George Godolphin Osborne (Marquis of)		Conservative
1896	B	1900	Hubbard	Evelyn		Conservative
1900	B	1906	Mowbray	Sir Robert Gray Cornish		Conservative
1906	G	1910	Seaverns	Joel Herbert		Liberal
1910	G	1918	Dalziel	Sir Davison Alexander		Conservative
1885	G	1892	Bristowe	Thomas Lynn	Norwood	Conservative
1892	G	1906	Tritton	Sir Charles Ernest		Conservative
1906	G	1910	Bowles	George Frederic Stewart		Conservative
1910	G	1918	Samuel	Sir Harry Simon		Conservative

Notes: First returned at: B By-election, G General Election

John Burns MP
© National Portrait Gallery
Reginald Hains

became apprenticed as a mechanical engineer at the Millbank factory of Hoe's Printing Machine Works. He joined the Amalgamated Society of Engineers after completing his apprenticeship in 1879 but then went to work in West Africa where his experiences of the conditions of African and Chinese labourers confirmed his socialism. He joined the Social Democratic Federation (SDF) in 1885, but decided that the best way to achieve improvements in the lot of working people was to work with a wide range of radical forces, including left wing Liberals, to press for practical changes in legislation. He became estranged from the SDF, which he regarded as too narrowly focused, but retained the loyalty of the Battersea branch (which he had founded), and this helped him win a seat on the LCC in 1889, retaining it until 1907. He took a particular interest in the pay and conditions of workers in the employment of contractors to the Council (insisting on union rates), and helped to found the direct works department.

In 1889 he took an important role in the Dock Strike, leading marchers and giving speeches. On the success of the strike his reputation was very high and in 1890 he was elected to the Parliamentary Committee of the Trades Union Council (TUC), and became a Parliamentary candidate supported by the Battersea Labour League and the Battersea Liberal and Radical Association who sponsored his election in 1892 as Socialist-Labour. Burns sat in the House with Keir Hardie but he diverged from the ILP in tactics and having poor personal relations with Hardie was drawn towards the Liberal mainstream. During the Boer War he engaged in active opposition on humanitarian as well as traditional liberal economic and political grounds. In 1906 he became a minister, appointed as the President of the Local Government Board where he stayed until 1914 when he was appointed briefly President of the Board of Trade. However, he resigned on 2nd August 1914, objecting to the country's involvement in the First World War. He never returned to politics after his resignation but in 1919 was left an annuity of £1000 by Andrew Carnegie, which left him materially secure for the rest of his life and enabled him to develop his expertise on London history. He was an avid book collector who created a considerable personal collection, part of which is now lodged in the Senate House Library. He was awarded honorary degrees at Liverpool, Birmingham and Aberdeen Universities and died in 1943.

Wandsworth

Sir Henry Kimber (Conservative) was elected in 1885 and served a very long spell as MP until he retired in 1913. He was born in 1834 and became a solicitor in 1958 after taking first prize of the Incorporating Law Society and a second-class degree in Law at University College, Cambridge. He married the daughter of General George Dixon (Royal Engineers) and retired from the law in 1890, five years after he was first elected to the Commons. His political career itself was negligible despite his 28 years as an MP, preferring to concentrate on other areas of interest. He was Chairman of the South India Railway Company and a director of the Capital and Counties Bank. He favoured imperial federation and was a member of the Royal Colonial Institute. He died in 1923.

He was succeeded by a fellow Director of the Capital and Counties Bank, **Samuel Samuel** (Conservative), who won the by-election necessitated by his retirement. He was born in 1855 and educated in London after which he entered the family form to become senior partner of M.Samuel, Transport and Trading, as well as becoming a director of Lloyds Bank when it took over Counties and Consolidated in 1918.He was a lieutenant of the City of London and first contested a Parliamentary seat at Leeds West in 1906 when he was unsuccessful, repeating the performance in January 1910. He also went down to defeat at Sunderland in December 1910 before securing his place at Wandsworth. Following re-distribution in 1918 he was returned for Putney and remained its MP until his death in 1934.

Clapham

Clapham's first MP was **Sir John Fletcher Moulton** (Liberal) who served only briefly from 1885 until 1886 when he was defeated. He was later MP for Hackney South and his principal biographical details can be found in Chapter 3(East and London, Middlesex).

In 1886 **John Saunders Gilliatt** (Conservative) took the seat from Moulton. He was born in 1829 at Clapham Common, the son of the head of a US firm of bankers and merchants, John Kirton, who was his father. He was Harrow and University College, Oxford educated, attaining his BA in 1851 and an MA four years later after which he became head of the family business in the following year. He was a Director of the Bank of England in 1862 and became a Governor in 1883. He was also a Lieutenant for the City of London and a magistrate in Hertfordshire. He lost his Clapham seat at the 1892 general election but was returned at a by-election held at Widnes (South West Lancashire) later that year, serving until his retirement in 1900. He died in 1912.

Percy Thornton MP
© National Portrait Gallery
Benjamin Stone 1898

Gilliatt was defeated by **Percy Meville Thornton** (Conservative) who stood as a free trader. Born in 1841, the son of Rear Admiral Samuel Thornton, he was the grandson of a vicar and attended Harrow School after which he was awarded his LLB at Jesus College, Cambridge in 1864. He wrote several historical books and retired in January 1910. He died in 1918.

George Denison Faber (Conservative) succeeded Thornton in January 1910 and remained Clapham's MP until June 1918 when he was elevated to the House of Lords as Baron Wittenham. He was born in 1852, the son of a Deputy-Lieutenant of Hertfordshire and following an education at Marlborough College and University College Oxford, married the daughter of the Duke of Somerset. He was called to the bar in 1879 as a member of Lincolns Inn and became a partner in the firm of Beckett and Company, bankers of Leeds. From 1887 to 96 he was Registrar to the Privy Council and was also a magistrate and Deputy-Lieutenant for the West Riding of Yorkshire. He won a by-election in the 1906 Parliament and was MP for York between February 1900 and January 1910 when he lost the seat.

Harry Greer (Coalition Unionist) won the June 1918 by-election caused by Faber's elevation. However, at the December general election he transferred to the Somerset seat of Wells which he represented until he retired in 1922. He was a major City figure, being Managing Director of the Mercantile Marine Finance Corporation and a director of

Baird Television Limited as well as chairman of Lord Roberts Memorial Workshop. He died in 1947. A fellow MD at Mercantile was a fellow Tory MP, Sir Albion Richardson, sitting for Peckham between 1910 and 1932 (See below).

Lambeth North

Lieutenant-General Sir Charles Crawfurd Fraser (Conservative) won Lambeth North in 1885 and held it until he retired in 1892. A descendant of the first Lord Lovat, Chief of the Highland Fraser Clan of Lovat, Inverness-shire, he was born in Dublin in 1829, and educated at Eton, after which he entered the 7th Hussars, becoming a Captain seven years later, and serving in India during the mutiny of 1857-8. At that time not only was he severely wounded but he was also awarded the Victoria Cross for saving men and officers from drowning, and was later further rewarded by being put in command of the 11th Hussars (Prince Albert's Own) in 1865-7. He served in the Abyssinian Expedition in 1868, and was later appointed Commander of the Curragh, the British Army's base in Ireland. In 1886, whilst he was an MP, he was appointed Colonel of the 8th Hussars, and retired from the Army four years later. He died in 1895.

Francis Moses Coldwells (Liberal) won the seat in 1892 but committed suicide three years later. He was born in Stoke Newington in 1832 and educated locally at the British School before becoming a tailor and outfitter. He was especially active in Croydon where he lived and was an alderman and magistrate. He was one of five directors of the Liberator Building Society who were charged with fraud in April 1895. He was bailed but committed suicide in a Bournemouth Summer House in July.

Sir Henry Morton Stanley MP
Wikipedia

At the general election held the following month the contest was won by **Sir Henry Morton Stanley** (Liberal Unionist), by then a world famous journalist and explorer but who was actually born the illegitimate son of John Rowlands in 1841 and raised in a workhouse until the age of 15 when he emigrated to New Orleans. Once there he was befriended by Henry Stanley, a merchant, who adopted him. This was the time of the American Civil War and he fought for the Confederacy until he was captured and became a prisoner of War. Later he served in both the Army and Navy of the Federal Government and in 1867 became a special correspondent reporting for the *New York Herald* on the war campaigns of Generals Hancock and Sherman. He did the same during the Abyssinian campaigns and was then sent on a foreign tour through Spain, Crete, Turkey, Egypt and Persia. In 1871 he commenced the search for the Scottish missionary David Livingstone of whom little had been heard since he left Britain in 1867 to find the source of the River Nile. Stanley reached Zanzibar in January 1871 and proceeded to Lake Tanganyika, Livingstone's last known location. There he found the sick explorer, greeting him with the famous words 'Dr Livingstone, I presume?' Stanley published his famous book entitled *How I Found Livingstone* and when he died in 1873, Stanley resolved to take up his search for the source of the Nile himself.

In the same year he reported on the Ashanti War, and began the first of many journeys through central Africa. Leaving Zanzibar in November 1874, he circumnavigated Lake Victoria, and explored Lake Tanganyika, before pressing on to the Lualaba River. There he fought his way first to Stanley Pool and then down to the waterfalls he named Livingstone Falls. He reached the sea in August 1877, after an epic journey that he later described in *Through the Dark Continent* (1878). Failing to gain British support to develop the Congo region, Stanley took up with King Leopold II of Belgium, who wanted its riches for himself. With Stanley's help, Leopold succeeded in subjugating the indigenous people within ten years, using brutal means that included the widespread use of forced labour. From 1879 to 1884, Stanley was in the Congo basin, building a road from the lower Congo up to Stanley Pool, and launching steamers on the upper river. His work paved the way for the creation of the Congo Free State, but the means by which control was established earned for Leopold the scorn of much of Europe, and he was eventually forced to relinquish his personal rule. In 1885 Stanley represented the Government of the USA at the Berlin Conference on African affairs and his last expedition was to relieve Mehmed Emin Pasha, governor of Equatoria - at that time a province of Egyptian Sudan. He had been cut off by the Mahdist revolt of 1882 near Lake Albert. In April 1889, some 1,500 people set out from Lake Albert for the east coast, arriving in December. On the way, they found the Ruwenzori Range and proved that the Semliki River linked Lakes Edward and Albert, clearing up the last mysteries of the Nile sources. Stanley returned to Britain and decided to enter politics. He contested Lambeth North unsuccessfully in 1892 but was elected in 1895, serving until he retired in 1900. He died in 1904.

Frederick William Horner (Conservative) succeeded Stanley in 1900 and represented the seat until 1906. Born in 1854 and educated privately he was the proprietor of the *Whitehall Review*. He was an executive and finance committee member of the National Union of Conservative Associations (Metropolitan Division); chairman of the Works and Lighting Committees of St Martins in the Field Church; and chaired the Strand Labour Exchange. A novelist, he contested Southwark West in 1895. When he was finally elected he ran into trouble with his local Party Association who refused to re-adopt him pending bankruptcy proceedings, which were subsequently proved against him. He stood at the 1906 election as an Independent Conservative but was defeated.

In 1906 **Horatio Myer** (Liberal) was elected. He sat for just one Parliament losing in January 1910. He was born at Hereford in 1850 but became famous as the founder (in 1876) of Myers Beds and Iron founders manufacturing iron bedsteads and mattresses of woven wire from a factory at Vauxhall within sight of the Houses of Parliament on the opposite side of the River Thames. The firm survives today but is now based at Huntingdon. He represented Kennington on the LCC from 1889 to 1904 and was also a local magistrate. He died in 1916.

Colonel Sir William Henry Houghton Gastrell (Conservative) who contested the seat in 1906 as the official candidate of his Party, was eventually elected in January 1910 and remained the MP until he was defeated in 1918. He was born at Tetbury, Gloucestershire and educated at Cheltenham College before entering the Army. He rose to become a Major in the Imperial Yeomanry Division of the Cambridgeshire Hussars and raised and commanded the Lambeth Battalion of the National Reserve in 1912 later serving on the Western Front from 1914 to 1917 whilst still an MP. Latterly he became Colonel Commanding of the Woolwich District Service Corps. He entered politics initially with the LCC, representing St Pancras South from 1903-6, serving as a magistrate for the County and on the Finance and General Purposes Committee. He was a Board member of the Royal Free Hospital at Hampstead and a Governor of the Royal Eye Hospital in addition to his Party activities, which included Council membership of the National Union of Conservative Associations and of the Primrose League. He was also an Executive Committee member of the London Municipal Society as well as a Vice President of the Tariff Reform League, both mainstream organisations attached to the Tory Party. He died in 1935.

Kennington

Robert Gent – Davis (Conservative) sat from 1885 until 1889 when he was forced to resign his seat. He was born in 1857 and following a private education joined his uncle's firm of Sparkes, White and Company, who were distillers' chemists. He was only 21 yet within two years he became head of the firm. Initially things went well and before long he was a Governor and Auditor of St Bartholomew's Hospital but his life took a disastrous turn when he was arrested for 'non-compliance with an order directing him to pay into Court money that had come into his hands as a Receiver of the Court.' He served a year-long prison sentence in 1888-9, an event that destroyed his political aspirations.

Mark Hanbury Beaufoy (Liberal) won the 1889 by-election triggered by these events and sat for Kennington until 1895. He was born in 1854 at a house in the South Lambeth Road where his father was a Vinegar and Wine merchant. Educated at Eton and Trinity Hall Cambridge he became head of the family business himself and was in addition an alderman of the LCC and magistrate in Surrey and Wiltshire. He was a vestryman in Lambeth, President of Brixton Liberal Club and of the Kennington Liberals and Radicals. He had previously contested Kennington in 1886 but did not resume a political career following his spell as the local MP. He died in 1922.

Sir Frederick Lucas Cook (Conservative) won the seat in 1895 and remained the MP until the 1906 Liberal landslide. He was born to a Portuguese mother in 1844 but his father was a wealthy warehouseman, owning premises in St Pauls Churchyard and who gave the boy an education at Harrow School. Cook did not distinguish himself in politics though his maternal connection may have explained why in 1901 he became a baronet as Viscount Monserratte in the Peerage of Portugal. He was a Commissioner of Lieutenancy for London and died in 1920.

Cook's seat was taken in 1906 by **Sir Stephen Collins** (Liberal) who retained it until he retired in 1918. He was born at Swanage (Dorset) in 1847 and was educated locally before moving to the London area. He was a stonemason and set up his own business in Vauxhall becoming active in local affairs. He was a member of the Wandsworth Vestry and District Board until its abolition when he became a Lambeth borough alderman and sat for six years on the LCC representing Kennington where he was for a time President of the Liberal Association. A London magistrate, he was for two years the President of the Dorset Men in London.

Brixton

Ernest Baggalay (Conservative) was MP from 1885 until 1887 when he was appointed the Police magistrate for West Ham, when he resigned his seat. He was the son of a onetime Justice of Appeal and was born in 1850 at an address in Russell Square. Educated at Marlborough College and Caius College, Cambridge, he also entered the law, being called to the bar at Lincolns Inn in 1873, afterwards joining the South East circuit. He married the daughter of W.W. Burnell, the Tory MP for Shoreham since 1876 and who sat in the House with Baggalay until 1886. The year before he took up his post in West Ham he was appointed senior legal counsel to the Post Office and when he finished his role in the Essex borough he was made Metropolitan Police magistrate in 1901, serving until 1914. He died in 1931.

When Baggalay resigned his seat, **George Godolphin Osborne,** the Marquis of Carmarthen (Conservative), son of the Duke of Leeds, replaced him at a by-election in 1887. He was born in London in 1862 and married the daughter of the Earl of Durham following his education at Eton and Cambridge. He contested Cambridgeshire Eastern unsuccessfully in 1886 and after his return at Brixton in 1887 was appointed assistant private secretary to Sir Henry Holland, Secretary of State for the Colonies. He succeeded as Duke of Leeds in December 1895 and was Treasurer of the Household from then until 1901. A member of the LCC from 1898, he was the owner of 24,000 acres of estates and died in 1927.

Evelyn Hubbard (Conservative) succeeded the Marquis at a by-election held in 1896. He had previously contested North Buckinghamshire unsuccessfully in 1889 and 1991, and the City of Plymouth in 1895. He was the son of Lord Addington, who as John Hubbard had been MP for Buckingham and for the City of London between 1880 and 1887. Born in 1852, he was educated at Radley College and at Christ's College, Oxford, where he obtained his MA in 1878. He was a partner in the family firm of John Hubbard (Russian merchants of London) and of Eberton Hubbard of St Petersburg. He was active in City affairs being a Lieutenant and a Director of the Bank of England (1890-1909); a Commissioner of Public Works Loans and Chairman of the Guardian Assurance Company (1900-30). He resigned his seat on taking up this latter appointment in 1900 and died in 1934.

Sir Robert Gray Cornish Mowbray (Conservative), who was MP from the by-election that followed Hubbard's resignation until defeated in 1906, was the son of Sir J.R. Mowbray who had been an MP for Durham (1853-68) and Oxford University (1868-99), when he died having been 'Father of the House' for a year. Robert sat in the House with him from 1886 to 1895 when he was MP for Prestwich in Lancashire. He had previously unsuccessfully contested Whitby (Yorkshire) in 1880 and Prestwich in 1885. He was born in London in 1850 and was educated at Eton and Balliol College, Oxford where he gained a First Class Classics degree in 1872, becoming a Fellow of All Souls the following year. He was called to the bar at the Inner Temple in 1876 joining the Oxford circuit whilst serving also as a magistrate and Deputy-Lieutenant of Berkshire, where he chaired the County Quarter Sessions. In 1876-6 he was secretary to a Royal Commission set up to look into the Stock Exchange and ten years later was appointed PPS to the Chancellor of the Exchequer, J.G. Goschen (See Chapter 2, City of London). From 1893-4 he sat on another Royal Commission, this time investigating the Opium Trade and from 1896-1900 went on an expedition to India. He died in 1913.

Joel Herbert Seaverns (Liberal) was the only non-Tory to sit for Brixton between 1885 and 1918 and one of only two to do so in the 60 years before 1945. He was born in 1860 at Boston, Massachusetts and was educated at Harvard University. He was a member of the firm of Henry W. Peabody, Colonial merchants of London. After his defeat at Brixton in January 1910 he fought the seat in December but was defeated a second time. He made a final attempt to return to the Commons in 1922 but lost at Gainsborough (Lincolnshire) and died the following year.

Sir Davison Alexander Dalziel (Conservative) defeated Seaverns in 1910 and held the seat until 1923 regaining it in 1924. He was made Baron Dalziel of Wooler in 1927, though he died the following year. He entered politics in 1906 when he contested Brixton for the first time but was more influential outside than inside Parliament. He was born in 1852 and married the daughter of the Chairman of the Pullman Car Company who was also Chairman of the Management Committee of the International Sleeping Car Company. He succeeded to both positions himself and was the first person to introduce motor cabs into London (in 1907). He purchased the London *Evening Standard* in 1910 but sold it again five years later. He also owned the *Pall Mall Gazette*, which was amalgamated with the *Standard* in 1923. During the War he was awarded the Legion of Honour and the Commander of the Crown of Italy. He died in 1928.

Norwood

Thomas Lynn Bristoe (Conservative) was the first MP for Norwood and represented it from 1885 until 1892 when he died. He was born in Camberwell in 1833 and was a member of Bristoe Brothers and the London Stock Exchange from 1868 to 1885. A captain in the Number 1 Surrey Rifles, he was chairman of the Herne Hill and Brixton Conservative Association when it was founded in 1880.

Sir Charles Ernest Tritton (Conservative) succeeded Bristoe at the 1892 election and remained the MP until 1906 when he stood down. He was born in Battersea in 1844 and educated at Rugby and Trinity Hall, Cambridge where he was awarded a BA in 1868 after which he emerged as a partner in a firm of boll brokers in 1869. He was a member of the London Chamber of Commerce, Treasurer of the Church of England Temperance Society and a member of the London City Mission Committee. He died in 1918

He was succeeded in 1906 by **George Frederic Stewart Bowles** (Conservative) who contested the seat as a free trader, a minority section of the Party at that time. He was born in 1877 and was educated privately and at Trinity College, Cambridge where he graduated with an MA before entering the Navy. He married the daughter of the MP for Lewisham (1891-1903), John Penn (see Chapter 4, Kent), though he was later divorced and re-married. He was called to the bar at the Inner Temple in 1901 but never practised. In January 1910 he transferred to the Lancashire seat of Blackburn, more appropriate to his free trade beliefs, but was defeated and retired from politics. He died in1955.

Sir Harry Simon Samuel (Conservative) won the Norwood seat in January 1910 having previously sat for the Limehouse division of Stepney between 1895 and 1906. He represented Norwood until 1922. His principal biographical details can be found in Chapter 3 (East London, Middlesex).

MPs for Outer Suburban Surrey

From	at	To	Surname	First Names	Constituency	Party
1885	G	1900	Bonsor	Henry Cosmo Orme	Wimbledon (North East Surrey)	Conservative
1900	G	1907	Hambro	Charles Eric		Conservative
1907	B	1916	Chaplin	Henry		Conservative
1906	B	1918	Coats	Sir Stuart Auchincloss		Conservative
1885	G	1892	Ellis	Sir John Whittaker	Kingston	Conservative
1892	G	1895	Temple	Sir Richard		Conservative
1895	G	1906	Skewes-Cox	Sir Thomas		Conservative
1906	G	1918	Cave	Sir George		Conservative
1885	G	1886	Grantham	Sir William	Croydon	Conservative
1886	B	1894	Herbert	Sidney		Conservative
1895 May	B	1906	Ritchie	Charles Thomson		Conservative
1906	G	1909	Arnold-Foster	Hugh Oakley		Conservative
1909	B	1910 Dec	Hermon-Hodge	Sir Robert Trotter		Conservative
1910 Dec	G	1918	Malcolm	Ian Zachary		Conservative
1885	G	1892	Cubitt	George	Epsom (Mid Surrey)	Conservative
1892	G	1899	Bucknell	Sir Thomas Townsend		Conservative
1899	B	1912	Keswick	William		Conservative
1912	B	1918	Keswick	Henry		Conservative

Notes: First returned at: B By-election, G General Election

Wimbledon (North East Surrey)

Henry Cosmo Orme Bonsor (Conservative) who lived at Epsom at the time of his election in 1885 was born at Polesden in 1848 and after an Eton education went into business. He was chairman of the brewing company of Watney Coombe, Reid and of the South Eastern Railway as well as being a director of the Bank of England. Patron of one living, he had many other interests including being the Treasurer of Guy's Hospital, a Commissioner of Income Tax for the City

Henry Cosmo Orme Bonsor MP
Wikipedia

of London, a magistrate and a Deputy-Lieutenant for Surrey. He retired from the House in 1900 and died in 1929.

He was succeeded in 1900 by **Charles Eric Hambro** (Conservative), an Eton-educated banker and partner in the family firm of C J Hambro and Son, established in 1779 by a Danish immigrant and sold out of the family's control in 1998. Charles was born at Roehampton in 1872 and married the third daughter of Martin Smith, another banker. He retired from the House in 1907 and died in 1947.

Henry Chaplin MP
© National Portrait Gallery
Walter Stoneman

Henry Chaplin (Conservative) succeeded Hambro at the 1907 by-election created by his resignation. Born in 1840, he was the son of a vicar who married the third daughter of the Duke of Sutherland. Harrow- educated, he attended Christ's College Oxford where he qualified as LL.D and entered politics in 1868 when he was elected to represent Mid Lincolnshire, which he held until 1885 at which point he was returned for the successor constituency of Sleaford where he was MP until somewhat surprisingly defeated in the Liberal landslide of 1906. However, he was returned at the 1907 by-election in Wimbledon and continued to represent the constituency until 1916 when he was elevated to the peerage as Viscount Chaplin having been in the Commons for a total of forty-seven years since his Parliamentary career began. He died in 1923 so his total career in both Houses spanned a period of fifty-four years. Despite the longevity of his political career he never really enjoyed glittering success though he was Chancellor of the Duchy of Lancaster briefly in 1885, and President of the Local Government Board for slightly longer, between 1895 and 1900. He was a Lincolnshire magistrate, and Deputy-Lieutenant for the County. 'No one,' according to Lord Willoughby of Broke[6], 'was half such a country gentleman as Henry Chaplin looked.' Although energetic in the landed interest as an MP, Chaplin's primary enthusiasm was for horse racing and fox hunting. He won a celebrated Derby victory with *Hermit* in 1867 but, in later years, his fortune was impaired by his lavish hospitality and the upkeep of stables and kennels.

Sir Stuart Auchinloss Coats (Conservative) represented Wimbledon from 1916 to 1918 and then East Surrey until he retired in 1922. He had previously contested Morpeth in 1906 and Deptford, in the two elections of 1910 all unsuccessfully. He was born in Paisley, Scotland in 1868 where he was a member of a family that founded silk weaving in the town. James Coats (1774-1857),[7] a weaver had set up the company in 1802. He and a partner, Humphrey Fulton, were successful in producing Canton Crape in such quantities as to virtually corner the market. The company continued expanding by acquiring controlling interests in several other textile companies including Patons & Baldwins, the Pasolds group, which included 'Ladybird' children's wear, Dynacast Precision Engineering and Jaeger fashions. It amalgamated with Vantona Viyella to form Coats Viyella plc,, which became Coats plc in 2001. Stuart was educated in the USA. A devout Roman Catholic, he was the Privy Chamberlain of Sword and Cape[8] to four successive Popes from 1905 and a Commander of the Order of the Crown of Italy. He was a partner in the firm of J and P Coats, President and Director of the Canada Thread Company and of three others in the same trade as well as of the Spool Cotton Company. He was Chairman of the Committee of Management of the Italian Hospital. He died in 1959.

Kingston

Sir John Whittaker Ellis (Conservative) represented the seat from 1885 until he retired in 1892 having sat for Mid Surrey since 1884. His principal biographical details are to be found earlier in the chapter under Mid-Surrey.

Elected in 1892 was **Sir Richard Temple** (Conservative), formerly the MP for Evesham (1885-92) in his native Worcestershire where he had contested the Eastern county division in 1880, though unsuccessfully. He was born there in 1826 but by the time of his election at Kingston was living in Hampstead. He was educated at Rugby and Haileybury College and entered the Indian Civil service in Bengal in 1847 becoming successively Chief Commissioner of the Central Provinces of India, Foreign Secretary and Prime Minister of India (1868-73); Lieutenant-Governor of Bengal (1974-7); and Governor of Bombay (1877-80). He was a Vice-Chairman of the London School Board and a Worcestershire magistrate. Despite his education having finished at school he was later awarded degrees at three Universities – Cambridge, Oxford and Montreal. He wrote several books on a variety of subjects including India and Palestine and became a fellow of the Royal Society in 1896, a year after his retirement as Kingston's MP. He died in 1902.

6 National Portrait Gallery Website 2004

7 Records of Coats Vyella

8 Privy Chamberlains assist with Papal audiences, and the role dates from 1555.They are recruited from the upper classes of all Christian countries for special service to the Holy See. (*Catholic Forum website*)

Sir Thomas Skewes-Cox (Conservative), a Richmond man, was elected in 1895 and retired in 1906. He was born in 1849 with the surname Cox but acquired the additional name of Skewes in 1874, seven years before he set up in practice as a solicitor in the firm of Skewes-Cox and Nash. He was a Richmond magistrate, councillor and mayor (1892) and also sat on the Surrey County Council. He died in 1913.

Sir George Cave KC MP
Wikipedia

Sir George Cave KC (Conservative) succeeded as MP in 1906 and continued to represent the seat until he retired in 1918 and was made the 1st Viscount Cave. He lived in Richmond and was born the son of Thomas Cave, the Liberal MP for Barnstaple from 1865-85. He was educated at the Merchant Taylors School and at St John's College, Cambridge where he obtained a 1st Class degree in the final classical school in 1878. He became a barrister being called to the bar at the Inner Temple and taking silk in 1904. He was a Surrey magistrate, a Deputy and Vice-Lieutenant and from 1894-1911, Chairman of the Quarter Sessions. In 1915 he was appointed Solicitor General in Asquith's Coalition Government and then Home Secretary under Lloyd-George. As Viscount Cave (he was enobled in 1918) he served as Lord Chancellor under Bonar Law in 1922 and again under Baldwin in 1924., a post he held until his death in 1928. He defeated Asquith to become Chancellor of Oxford University in 1925.

Croydon

William Grantham (Conservative), who had previously been MP for Surrey Eastern, was elected at Croydon in 1885 and held the seat until 1886, on his appointment as a Judge. His principal biographical details can be found earlier in this Chapter.

He was succeeded by **Sidney Herbert** (Conservative), the second son of Baron Herbert Lea and held the seat until 1895 when he went to the House of Lords. He was born in 1853 and was raised to the rank of an Earl's son by Royal decree in 1862 when his brother succeeded to the Earldom of Pembroke. He was educated at Eton and Oxford taking his BA there in 1875. Two years later he married the daughter of the Earl of Durham. He entered politics in 1877 when he was elected at Wilton, a seat he represented until 1885 when he fought but lost the successor seat of Wiltshire South. He resigned the Croydon seat in 1895 when he succeeded to the Earldom on the death of his brother and was Lord Steward until 1905. He died in 1913.

Herbert was succeeded in 1895 by **Charles Thomson Ritchie** (Conservative) who had been defeated at the 1892 General election in Whitechapel, St George's. His principal biographical details can be found in Chapter 2 (Middlesex, Tower Hamlets). He was MP for Croydon from 1895 to 1906 when he retired.

He was succeeded by **Hugh Oakley Arnold – Foster** (Conservative) who had previously represented Belfast South since 1892 and who remained Croydon's MP until his death in 1909. He was the son of the Director of Public Instruction in the Punjab (India), was born in Dawlish, Devon in 1855, and attended Rugby School and University College, London. He became a barrister, called to the bar at Lincolns Inn. He married the daughter of Professor Story-Maskelyne, who was MP for Cricklade and North Wiltshire between 1880 and 1892. Hugh was appointed Secretary to the Admiralty in 1900 and three years later was made Secretary of State for War, serving until the end of the Balfour administration in 1905.

The winner of the 1909 by-election following Foster's death was **Colonel Sir Robert Trotter Hermon Hodge** (Conservative) who was born with the surname Hodge at Newcastle-on-Tyne in 1851. He was educated at Clifton College and Worcester College, Oxford University where he obtained an MA. He married the heiress to the fortune of Edward Hermon, a cotton magnate and MP for Preston between 1868 and 1881 when he died. Robert was the Officer Commanding of the Oxfordshire Hussars, an Oxfordshire County alderman, a magistrate and active mason. He contested the Accrington seat unsuccessfully in 1885 but was that Lancashire town's MP from 1886 to 1892 when he moved the 'loyal address'. However, he lost in 1892, and once more at a by-election in 1893, before transferring to Henley. He was the MP from 1895 to 1906, until he was defeated, popping up at Croydon at the 1909 by-election. Meanwhile in 1904 he had acquired the additional surname of Hermon from his wife. He retired from the House at the December 1910 election, only to be re-elected for Henley in a Wartime by-election held in 1917. He retired for a second time in 1918 and died in 1937.

Ian Zachary Malcolm (Conservative) sat for Croydon from December 1910 until 1918. He was born in 1868 in Quebec, Canada and educated at Eton and New College, Oxford before entering the diplomatic service. He married the daughter of Lily Langtry, a famous and beautiful actress of the Victorian era who was the mistress of the Prince of Wales, later Edward VII. He was elected in 1895 as MP for Stowmarket, or North West Suffolk, which he represented until 1906 when he retired in order to take up the role of Secretary of the Union Defence League. He sought re-election at Salford North in January 1910 but was not successful and transferred to Croydon in December. He was made an Assistant Private Secretary for Foreign Affairs between 1895 and 1898 and to the Secretary of State for Ireland (George Wyndham) from 1900 to 1901. When Arthur Balfour accepted the post of Foreign Secretary in Lloyd-George's War Coalition in 1916 Malcolm was made his Parliamentary Private Secretary. His home was in Argyllshire, Scotland where he was also a magistrate. He was elected for Croydon South in 1918 but after attending the Versailles Peace Conference resigned in 1919 to be the British Director on the Board of the Suez Canal Company, which he served until 1939. He died in 1944.

Ian Zachary Malcolm MP **Wikipedia**

Epsom (Mid Surrey)

George Cubitt (Conservative) was Epsom's first MP and was a local Surrey man born at Clapham Common in 1828. He was educated at Trinity College, Cambridge where he obtained his MA in 1854. Married to the daughter of the vicar of Dorking, he was a Surrey Western MP between 1860 and 1865. He retired in 1892 and became Baron Ashcombe. He was a Church Estates Commissioner between 1874 and 1879 and died in 1917. His son Henry represented the neighbouring constituency of Reigate from 1892 to 1906.

Sir Thomas Townsend Bucknell (Conservative) succeeded Cubitt when he retired in 1892 and sat until created a High Court Judge in 1899. Born in 1845, he was the son of an eminent surgeon and lived locally at Hylands House. He was educated at Westminster School and in Geneva, Switzerland after which he was called to the bar at the inner Temple in 1868. He took silk in 1885, the year he was appointed Recorder of Exeter and was a bencher in 1891. He was a Surrey County councillor and alderman between 1889 and 1892 and sat as a High Court Judge from 1899 until 1914. He died the following year. He edited the last edition of '*Abbot on Shipping*'.

William Keswick (Conservative) lived at Ewick Park Leatherhead and was MP for Epsom from 1899 until his death in 1912. He was a member of a company of merchants trading in China called Jardine and Company and a director of the Indo-China Steam Navigation Company. For a period he was also a member of the Hong Kong colony's Legislative Council. He was a Deputy-Lieutenant of Surrey, a county magistrate and, in 1898, its High Sheriff.

Henry Keswick (Conservative) succeeded his father at the 1912 by-election held after his death. He was born in Shanghai where his father was in business in 1870 but was educated at Eton and Trinity College, Cambridge where he obtained a BA. He followed his father as a member of Jardine, Matheson and Company and as a member of the Hong Kong legislature but was also a member of the Shanghai municipal council. He served in South Africa in 1900 and was a member of the Royal Company of Scottish Archers, part of the King's Body Guard. He retired to Scotland in 1918 where he became President of the Dunfermline Unionist Association and contested Dumfriesshire, unsuccessfully, at the 1922 General Election. He died in 1928.

County Hall, South Bank - Belvedere Road **Gordon Rushton**

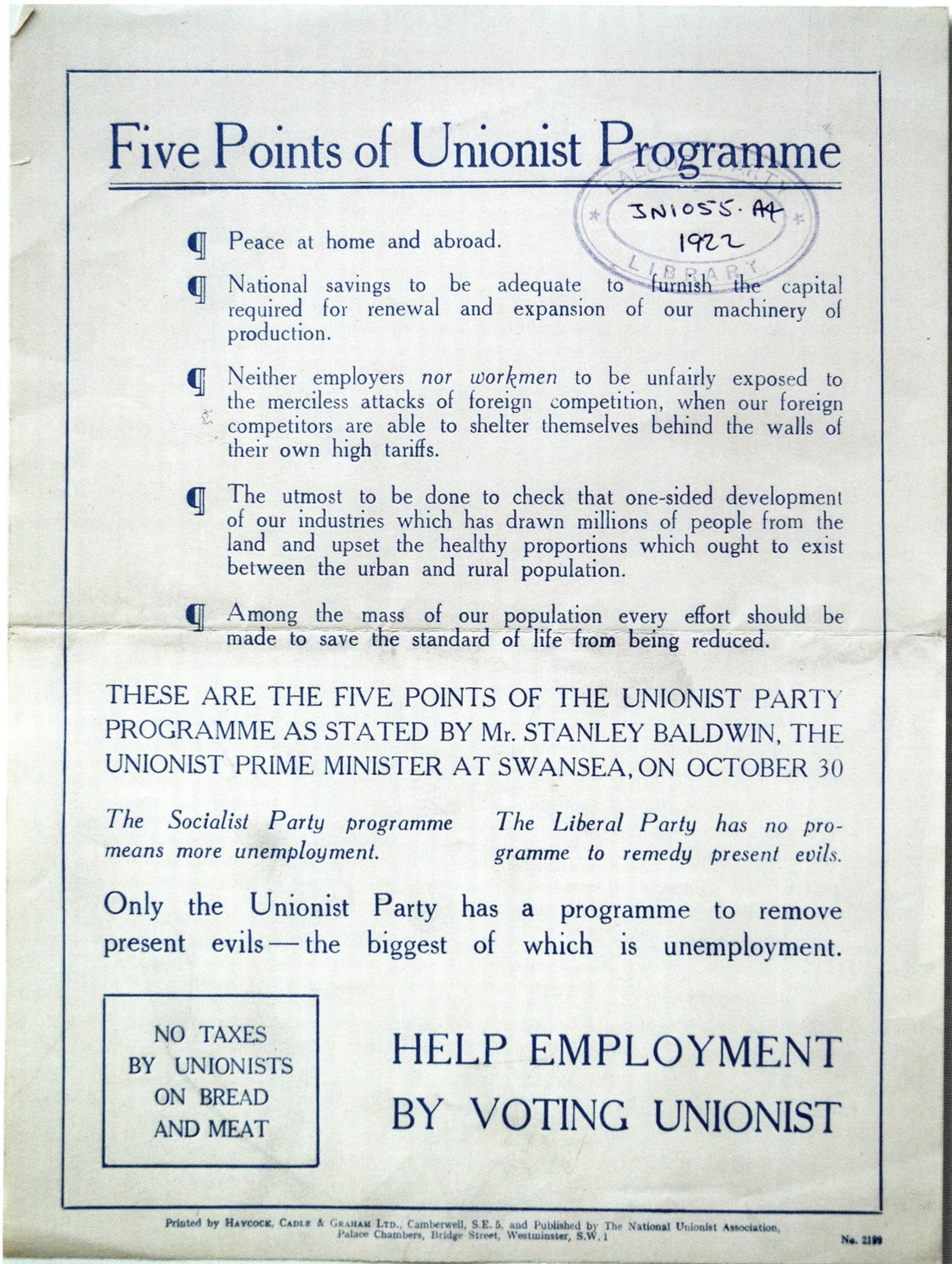

Five Points of Unionist Programme

- Peace at home and abroad.
- National savings to be adequate to furnish the capital required for renewal and expansion of our machinery of production.
- Neither employers *nor workmen* to be unfairly exposed to the merciless attacks of foreign competition, when our foreign competitors are able to shelter themselves behind the walls of their own high tariffs.
- The utmost to be done to check that one-sided development of our industries which has drawn millions of people from the land and upset the healthy proportions which ought to exist between the urban and rural population.
- Among the mass of our population every effort should be made to save the standard of life from being reduced.

THESE ARE THE FIVE POINTS OF THE UNIONIST PARTY PROGRAMME AS STATED BY Mr. STANLEY BALDWIN, THE UNIONIST PRIME MINISTER AT SWANSEA, ON OCTOBER 30

The Socialist Party programme means more unemployment.

The Liberal Party has no programme to remedy present evils.

Only the Unionist Party has a programme to remove present evils — the biggest of which is unemployment.

NO TAXES BY UNIONISTS ON BREAD AND MEAT

HELP EMPLOYMENT BY VOTING UNIONIST

Printed by HAYCOCK, CADLE & GRAHAM LTD., Camberwell, S.E. 5, and Published by The National Unionist Association, Palace Chambers, Bridge Street, Westminster, S.W. 1

No. 2199

The end of the First World War heralded a number of significant political changes. Women got the vote for the first time, and the pre-War political balance altered. Lloyd George's coalition collapsed in 1922, and a three-party system emerged that would operate during the inter-war period. This 1922 Conservative election leaflet attempts to distinguish the party from its opponents on one of the big issues of the day. The ephemeral flier has come down to us from the library of the People's History Museum in Manchester to offer insight to the arguments of the time.

Chapter 7
Middlesex 1918-1945

The Impact of the Boundary Review of 1917-18

Middlesex was greatly affected by revisions that took account of the major population changes that had occurred since 1885. Railways, including the London Underground, had encouraged the construction of housing estates on a scale that caused the inner London boroughs to lose population as the middle classes migrated to the new suburbs. There was a consequential reduction in the number of seats in Finsbury, Marylebone, Shoreditch and Tower Hamlets whilst the county areas gained seats. There were in total 53 seats in Middlesex, an increase of 5.

The Inter-War period saw the Conservatives dominate Middlesex at five of the seven general elections held. Only in 1929 did they not hold a majority of all the seats contested, when Labour staged its best result winning almost half of the seats and going on to form a minority Government, as the largest Party in the House of Commons for the first time in history. The decline of the Liberal Party occurred immediately after the Great War when the number of seats they occupied was halved, compared with their pre-War average, and although they enjoyed a brief recovery at the 1923 Election, when they won seven seats, this proved to be a false dawn and by 1935 they were left with a solitary MP. Labour first established itself as a party at least equal to the Liberals in 1922, and thereafter secured at least 13 Middlesex MPs in every subsequent general election except 1931, when the Party suffered a debacle and was reduced to only three seats, the same as the Liberals.

Party	*Pre 1918 average*	*1918*	*1922*	*1923*	*1924*	*1929*	*1931*	*1935*
C and allies	*32/36*	*46*	*44**	*27*	*38*	*25*	*47*	*35*
L	*12/15*	*6*	*2*	*7*	*2*	*2*	*3*	*1*
Lab	*0*	*0*	*6*	*19*	*13*	*26*	*3*	*17*
Ind	*0*	*1*	*1*	*0*	*0*	*0*	*0*	*0*
C majority	*17/24*	*39*	*35*	*1*	*23*	*-3*	*41*	*17*
Total	*48*	*53*	*53*	*53*	*53*	*53*	*53*	*53*

Key: C = Conservative; L = Liberal; Lab = Labour; I = Independent *included 2 National Liberals

Central London

City of London, Westminster, St Marylebone and Paddington (7 seats)

Westminster and Marylebone each lost one of their 1885 divisions. The **City of London** was unchanged but in Westminster the former Strand division was sacrificed. A new **Westminster, Abbey** constituency extended from the border with the City in the east from Aldwych to Whitehall and via Soho and the West End to Oxford Circus. Officially the constituency comprised the wards of Charing Cross, Covent Garden, Great Marlborough, Pall Mall, Regent, St Anne, St John, St Margaret and Strand. Between Regents Street and the area just south of Knightsbridge lay **Westminster, St George's** including Victoria and the Palace of Westminster itself. Its named wards were Conduit, Grosvenor, the Hamlet of Knightsbridge, Knightsbridge St George's and Victoria. These contained Belgravia, Hyde Park, Kensington Gore, Knightsbridge, Mayfair, Millbank, Pimlico, Victoria and Westminster itself. **Marylebone** now comprised the whole borough with the amalgamation of the former East and West divisions. Queens Park, north of the Harrow Road, was transferred to **Paddington North** and **Paddington South** was slightly adjusted compared with 1885.

The changes disadvantaged the Conservatives who had held all five seats at every General Election since 1885. Although they continued to win with large majorities after 1918 they did in effect suffer a reduction of two MPs through

Top Left: *Leadenhall Market in the City of London was originally a game and poultry market dating back to the 14th century. The current market, pictured here, was designed by Sir Horace Jones in 1881. The market is a reminder that the City was once a very different place, but at the time of the chapter, it was in transition to become the financial centre we know today. Jones also designed Billingsgate and Smithfield Markets.* **Gordon Rushton.**

Top Right: *The Abbey Constituency was centred on the St Margaret's Parish Church in Parliament Square, situated between the Palace of Westminster and Westminster Abbey.* **John Nelson**

Above: Marylebone Town Hall was built between 1914 and 1920 and stands in the Marylebone Road. It was designed by Sir Edwin Cooper. **John Nelson**

Left: *The Queen's Park Estate, including Oliphant Street (The illustration is of No.97, the home of the Author's Great Grandparents) was transferred from Chelsea to the Paddington North Constituency in 1918. It comprised mainly rented housing for the 'respectable' working classes. Isaac Merrifield, who lived in the house throughout the period of this chapter, was a typical resident of these dwellings. He worked for the Great Western Railway at the Bishop's Bridge Road Goods depot nearby. The Queen's Park Estate was built by the Artisans Labourers and General Dwellings Company in the last quarter of the 19th Century. Build in a Gothic Revival style, it included 2000 small houses, and was the estate where the first Queen's Park Rangers footballers are said to have had their homes.*
John Nelson

Right: Gerald Laing designed the striking dragon panels in Bank Underground Station, in 1994-5. The dragon is the symbol of the City of London and examples are found at all principal boundaries of the City.
Gordon Rushton

The population of London's central districts started to decline in the early part of the 20th century, partly as improving transport enabled people to travel in and out. This affected the Parliamentary representation of the area. Westminster lost one of its 1885 constituencies, and Marylebone's were combined. Paddington retained two constituencies, but in the process acquired the Queen's Park estate, north of the Harrow Road from Chelsea. The same population trends occurred in the City of London, despite which it kept its two MPs and its traditional boundaries, which is why no separate map is shown. The relevant City constituency map is in Chapter 3, page 59.

Election Results in the Inter-war Period - by % majority

Constituency	Pre 1918	1918	1922	1923	1924	1929	1931	1935
City of London	2xC	2xC100+	2xC100	2xC100	2xC100+	2xC31	2xC100	2xC29++
Wesminster St. Georges	1xC	C80-	Ind C18	C100	C100	C56+	C100	C69
Westminster Abbey	1xC	C100+	C62	C100+	C61	C48	C100	C55+
St.Marylebone	2xC	C100	C100	C33	C47+	C36	C3+	C59
Paddington North	C	C10	C25	C8	C13	C2	C43	C25
Paddington South	C	C100	C34	C43	C100	C100-	C71	C58
C	8	7+	6	7+	7++	7+	7+	7+++
L	0	0	0	0	0	0	0	0
Other	0	0+	1	0	0	0+	0	0

100 = unopposed **Key:** C = Conservative; L = Liberal; Lab = Labour; + = Party that won seat at General Election held by-election in same Parliament; - = Party that won seat at General Election lost by-election to main opposition Party in same Parliament.

the changes that were made. Both Paddington seats had also been predominantly Tory before 1918 and they remained so afterwards, although Labour came within 2% of taking Paddington North in 1929.

MPs for City of London 1918-1945

From		To	Surname	First Names	Constituency	Party
1918	G	1924	Banbury	Sir Frederick George	City of London	Conservative Unionist
1924	B	1938	Bowater	Sir Thomas Vansittart		Conservative
1938	B	1945	Broadridge	Sir George Thomas		Conservative
1918	G	1922	Balfour	Sir Arthur James		Conservative Unionist
1922	B	1935	Grenfell	Edward Charles		Conservative
1935	B	1940	Anderson	Sir Alan Garrett		Conservative
1940	B	1945	Duncan	Sir Andrew Rae		National

Notes: First returned at: B By-election, G General Election

Sir Frederick Banbury (Conservative Unionist) was elected MP for the City in 1906 and his biographical details are in Chapter 3. In 1924 he was made Baron Banbury of Southam.

Sir Thomas Vansittart Bowater MP
© National Portrait Gallery
Bassano Ltd 1922

At the by-election necessary to fill his place **Sir Thomas Vansittart Bowater** (Conservative), a paper magnate was elected and he held the seat until his death in 1938. Born in 1862, and educated in Manchester and Stourbridge, he was Chairman of the Bowater's company until 1927. A notable City businessman, he was Sheriff of London in 1905, and Lord Mayor in 1913-14. He initially stood as an Independent Conservative in the City in 1922, but was finally elected as an official candidate in 1924.

After his death in 1938 he was succeeded by **Sir George Thomas Broadridge** (Conservative), born in 1869, and himself a former Lord Mayor in 1936-7, the year before his election as MP. He held the seat until he was elevated to the Lords shortly after the 1945 General Election.

Arthur Balfour (Conservative), the former Conservative Prime Minister and Cabinet Minister in Lloyd-George's Coalition, had first been elected at the City in 1906 and he retained his seat until his elevation to the Lords as an Earl in 1922. His biographical details are in Chapter 3.

At the 1922 by-election created by his elevation, his place in the Commons was taken by **Edward Charles Grenfell** (Conservative), who sat until 1935 when he too was elevated to the peerage as Lord St Just. Born in 1870 and educated at Harrow and Trinity Cambridge, both his father and grandfather were MPs before him. He was a partner in the City firm of merchant bankers, Morgan Grenfell, (established in 1838 and in 1922 still a family concern) and was a Director of the Bank of England for 35 years after 1905. He died in 1941.

Grenfell's place was taken by another City notable, **Sir Alan Garrett Anderson** (Conservative), the son of Dr. Elizabeth, the founder of the first women's hospital in London. Born in 1877 and educated at Elstree, Eton and Trinity Oxford, he was a Director of the family firm of Anderson, Green and Company who owned the Orient shipping Line[1]. He immersed himself in business activities and was variously a Director of the Bank of England, the London Midland and Scottish Railway, and the Suez Canal. A Lieutenant of the City of London, he was awarded officer status in the French Legion of Honour, and after the First War was High Sheriff of the London County area, re-entering business life as President of the Chamber of Shipping in 1924/5. He never actually contested an election, being unopposed both at the by-election that brought him to the Commons in 1935, and at the General Election later that year. He resigned in 1940, and in 1941 took up the vitally important post of Controller of Railways at the Ministry of War Transport, a post he held until 1945. He died in 1952.

1945 Election Poster
The People's History Museum

The 1940 wartime by-election caused by Anderson's resignation was fought by **Sir Andrew Rae Duncan** (National Party[2]), an erstwhile Conservative. Born in 1884, he too was a distinguished City businessman though he had a legal background and was educated at Irvine Academy and Glasgow University, as well as at Dalhousie in Canada. He made his name after the First World War as Coal Controller (1919-29), and then as Chairman of an Advisory Committee on Mines until 1927. He became a Director of Imperial Chemical Industries, the Dunlop Rubber Company, the North British Locomotive Company, and of Royal Exchange Assurance. He first tried his hand at politics standing as a Coalition Liberal at Glasgow, Cathcart in 1922, but was defeated. Between 1929 and 1940, when he entered Parliament, he was a Director of the Bank of England, and from 1935 was Executive Chairman of the Iron and Steel Federation[3], a position he resumed in 1945. From 1927 to 1935 he was also Chairman of the Central Electricity Board, remaining a member until 1940[4]. During the War he entered Government, initially as President of the Board of Trade (1940-1), and then served as Minister of Supply until 1945. He was High Sheriff of London in the year before his election to the House, and remained MP for the City until 1950 when he retired. He died two years later.

MPs for Westminster 1918-1945

From		To	Surname	First Names	Constituency	Party
1918	G	1921	Burdett-Coutts	William L A-B	Westminster Abbey	Conservative
1921	B	1924	Nicholson	John Sanctuary		Anti Waste-Conservative
1924	B	1939	Nicholson	Otho William		Conservative
1939	B	1945	Webbe	Sir Harold CBE		Conservative
1918	G	1921	Long	Walter Hume	Westminster St George's	Conservative
1921	B	1929	Erskine	James Malcolm Montieth		Anti Waste-Conservative
1929	G	1931	Worthington-Evans	Sir Laming		Conservative
1931	B	1945	Cooper	Alfred Duff		Conservative

Notes: First returned at: B By-election, G General Election

1 So named after the three - masted vessels and steam packets that operated initially to Australia, New Zealand and South Africa from 1868. After World War I their competitor P & O acquired 51% of the company though they did not acquire the whole until 1965.
2 He chose the National designation as he was brought into the House specifically as a businessman to assist with the war effort
3 The National Federation of Iron and Steel Manufacturers was formed in 1918 and in 1934, as a condition of substantial tariff protection for the British industry, the government caused the industry to form a stronger central association, the British Iron and Steel Federation (BISF).
4 The Electricity (Supply) Act 1926 created the Central Electricity Board to establish a 'gridiron' transmission system, linking the biggest and most efficient power stations throughout the country. Its successor body, the Central Electricity Generating Board, was wound up in 2001 following privatisation of the industry a few years earlier.

Westminster Abbey

William Burdett-Coutts (Conservative), was the MP for the former Westminster division from 1885 to 1918, and was adopted for the new Abbey constituency after the War. He held the seat until his death in 1921 and his main biographical details are in Chapter 3.

The resultant by-election was won by **Brigadier-General John Sanctuary Nicholson** (Conservative), who held the seat until he died. Son of the former MP for Petersfield in his native Hampshire, John Nicholson was born in 1863 and educated at Harrow School from where he went to Sandhurst Military Staff College, afterwards joining the 7th Hussars in 1884. From 1898 to 1900 he was Commandant-General of the South Africa Police, and became the Inspector-General of the same force three years later, ending his tour of duty in 1905. He contested the county division of Dorset Eastern in January 1910, and at a by-election later the same year, but was unsuccessful on both occasions. He also failed to secure election at Stafford in the December 1910 General Election. In the Great War he served in France, and in August 1921 contested the Westminster, Abbey constituency as an Anti Waste[5] Conservative. He was re-elected in 1922 and 1923, but died before the General Election held in 1924.

The ensuing by-election proved to be one of the most dramatic and controversial of the inter-War years. Winston Churchill had recently resigned from the Liberal Party and sought the Tory nomination, but was rebuffed and the nomination went to the deceased member's nephew, **Otho William Nicholson** (Conservative), a distiller who had been a member of the LCC for three years and Mayor of Finsbury in 1923/4. Born in 1891, educated at Harrow and at Magdalene College Cambridge, he was a Lieutenant in the Rifle Brigade during the First World War. Churchill decided to fight anyway, and did so as an Independent Conservative. When the result was declared Nicholson had defeated him by a mere 43 votes, 0.1% of those cast. The turnout of 67% was the highest for any inter-War by-election and Nicholson held the seat until his resignation in 1939 when another by-election was held. He died in 1978.

Sir Harold Webbe CBE (Conservative), was MP from 1939 until 1950 when he was adopted as Tory candidate for the new constituency of the Cities of London and Westminster, which he represented until his retirement in 1959. Born in 1885, Webbe was educated at King Edward's School Birmingham and Queen's College Cambridge, after which he became a teacher at Oundle and St Pauls, both well-known Public Schools. From 1910 to 1914 he was a Schools Inspector, and from 1916 to 1918 Deputy Director of the Ministry of Munitions' Stores. In 1925 he was elected to the LCC, serving continuously until 1949, and was a member of both the Education and General Purposes Committees. From 1934 to 1945 he was the Leader of the Municipal Reform Party (effectively the Conservatives) on the LCC, a Deputy Lieutenant of London County and a director of several companies.

Westminster St Georges

Walter Hume Long (Conservative), was a distinguished and long-serving Westminster MP before his adoption for the new Westminster St George's constituency in 1918. His main biographical details are contained in Chapter 3 (Strand). In 1921 he was elevated to the peerage as Viscount Long of Wraxall, and the by-election that followed in 1921 was a strange affair.

James Malcolm Monteith Erskine MP
© National Portrait Gallery

It was won by a right wing candidate, **James Malcolm Monteith Erskine** (Anti-Waste League), who stood with the support of a substantial element of the local Conservative Association, whose official candidate, Sir Herbert Jessel, was defeated, arguably on the basis of anti-Semitic feeling in the constituency. At the 1922 General Election the Tories put up as their official candidate Leslie Wilson, a former Chief Whip, and when he too was defeated by the incumbent (standing this time as an Independent Conservative), the Party pragmatically accepted the inevitable. Erskine was subsequently adopted as the official candidate and was unopposed at the following two General Elections, in 1923 and 1924. Born in 1863, he was the son of Captain Daniel Erskine, a former Consul of Madeira, and was educated at Wellington College. He died in 1944. In 1929 the failing health of the then Secretary of State for War brought about a request for Erskine to stand down so that the Minister (the MP for Colchester since 1910) could occupy a seat that was close to Parliament.

5 The Anti Waste League was founded in 1921 by Lord Rothermere, owner of the Daily Mail, but was abandoned later the same year.

Sir Laming Worthington-Evans MP
Wikipedia

Sir Laming Worthington-Evans (Conservative), was adopted but the Tories were defeated nationally, and so he became an MP in Opposition. Worse still, he died within 20 months, and another by-election was held. Evans was a Solicitor who during the First World War was Parliamentary Secretary at the Ministry of Munitions from 1916 to 1917 and the following year was made Minister of Blockade[6] with the status of a Parliamentary Under-Secretary. He continued to serve in the Lloyd-George / Bonar Law Coalition Cabinet after the War initially as Pensions Minister from 1919 to 1921 and then as Secretary for War until the Coalition broke up in 1922. Following the Conservatives' Election victory in 1922 he served as Post Master General for a year until the resignation of Baldwin and the formation of the first Labour Government in 1923. When that Government fell, Worthington-Evans was once again appointed War Secretary after the 1924 General Election. The by-election that took place at Westminster St George's in 1931 was also notable. Conservative politics at the time were marked by dissention amongst many on the right of the Party about Baldwin's attitude towards the Empire, especially the status of India, and imperial trade. Lords Beaverbrook and Rothermere, owners of the Express and Mail Newspaper Groups respectively, allied themselves to the so-called Empire Free Trade Crusade, and sponsored a number of by-election candidates who were not the officially adopted Tory nominees. In February 1931 the result of the intervention of an Empire Crusader at a by-election in Islington East was that the official Tory candidate was forced into third place handing the seat to Labour.

Sir Alfred and Lady Diana Duff Cooper on their wedding day in 1919.
Wikpedia

The press barons persuaded Sir Ernest Petter, an industrialist, to stand at St George's as an Independent Conservative in the cause of Imperial Free Trade, whilst the official candidate was **Sir Alfred Duff Cooper** (Conservative). After a high profile and bitter campaign he was comfortably returned at the by-election in October 1931, and served until his retirement in 1945. His first Ministerial appointment came in 1934, when he was appointed by Ramsey MacDonald to the post of First Secretary to the Treasury, and in 1935 was made War Minister by Stanley Baldwin. When Neville Chamberlain took over in 1937 he was appointed a Cabinet Minister for the first time, and became First Lord of the Admiralty, a crucial appointment in the years before the outbreak of the Second World War. However, Duff Cooper resigned in protest at the Munich Agreement in 1938, and became one of a minority of Tories along with Churchill who opposed the Government's policy of appeasement towards Hitler. With the fall of the Chamberlain Government in 1940 he was made Minister of Information by Churchill, attending the War Cabinet, and in 1941 was made Chancellor of the Duchy of Lancaster, which office he occupied until November 1943. He died in 1954.

MPs for St Marylebone 1918-1945

From		*To*	*Surname*	*First Names*	*Constituency*	*Party*
1918	*G*	*1922*	*Scott*	*Sir Samuel Edward*	*St. Marylebone*	*Conservative Unionist*
1922	*G*	*1928*	*Hogg*	*Sir Douglas McGarel*	"	*Conservative*
1928	*B*	*1932*	*Rodd*	*Sir Rennell*	"	*Conservative*
1932	*B*	*1945*	*Cunningham-Reid*	*Alec Stratford (Captain)*	"	*Conservative/ Independent Conservative*

Notes: First returned at: B By-election, G General Election

Prior to 1918 **Sir Samuel Edward Scott** (Conservative), had been the MP for the former Marylebone West division. He held the new St Marylebone seat until 1922 when he retired. His main biographical details are in Chapter 3.

He was succeeded at the 1922 General Election by **Sir Douglas McGarel Hogg** (Conservative), the son of Quintin Hogg, founder of the Regent Street Polytechnic. Douglas was appointed Attorney General in Bonar Law's Government, resuming the appointment after the collapse of the 1923 Labour Government and the 1924 General Election. He became Lord Chancellor in 1928 when he was elevated to the peerage as Viscount Hailsham. He served until the fall of the Government in 1929, but when the National Government was formed two years later he did not resume a Cabinet ranked position, though he was made Leader of the Conservatives in the Lords in 1930 and remained so until 1935. His

6 In 1916 the Contraband Department of the Foreign Office was renamed Ministry of Blockade. It provided a service of economic intelligence about enemy countries and enforced the policy of blockade.

Doiuglas McGarel Hogg MP
© National Portrait Gallery
George Beresford 1930

former post of Lord Chancellor was given to Lord Sankey, a Labour turned National Labour politician. He was appointed to the War Office, which post he also held until 1935 when, following Baldwin's re-appointment as Prime Minister, Hailsham once again resumed service as Lord Chancellor. He survived the change of Prime Minister from Baldwin to Chamberlain, and in March 1938 was made Lord Privy Seal. However, he resigned from the Government in October 1938 in protest over the appeasement policy and the Munich Agreement. He died in 1950.

Hogg's election in 1922 began a remarkable family association with the Conservative Party, the Marylebone constituency, the peerage, and the office of Lord Chancellor. Douglas Hogg's son, Quintin was himself to play a high profile role in later 20th Century politics. He became MP for St Marylebone himself and also succeeded as Viscount Hailsham, though on one occasion he renounced that title in order to advance his chances of becoming the Leader of his Party and Prime Minister in succession to Harold Macmillan, only to fail in the quest. He resumed the title and he too was appointed Lord Chancellor, by Margaret Thatcher in 1979. Douglas Hogg's grandson, who shares his first name, also became an MP and a Minister in John Major's Conservative Government of the 1990s, though unlike his forbears was never an MP for Marylebone[7]. Douglas senior was born in 1863 the son of Quentin. Educated at Cheam School and Eton College he became a barrister, practising at Lincoln's Inn after 1902 when he returned from the South Africa War, becoming a bencher in 1920. In that year he was appointed Attorney-General to the Prince of Wales, the future Edward VIII, holding that post until his entry into Government in 1922. In 1934 Hogg was President of the MCC[8], the Lords Headquarters of which were within his own Parliamentary constituency.

The by-election created by Hogg's elevation was won by **Sir Rennell Rodd** (Conservative), who served as MP for St Marylebone from 1928 until his death in 1932. A career diplomat, Rodd first entered the service in 1883, becoming Minister to Sweden in 1904, following which he was sent as Ambassador to Rome in 1908, remaining in that post for eleven years. In 1920 he was appointed to join a mission to Egypt and entered politics late in his life.

In 1932 Rodd was succeeded at a by-election by **Captain Alec Stratford Cunningham-Reid** (Conservative), who, though standing as the Party's official candidate, soon caused divisions within the constituency association, some members of which backed an Independent Conservative candidate at the by-election. Cunningham-Reid won but by a margin of less than 5%. In 1935 he lost official Party backing and so stood as an Independent Conservative in which capacity he was elected. Although he was given the Tory Whip this was withdrawn in 1942, when he sought to create a new political movement, and a year later Central Office disaffiliated the St Marylebone Conservative Association[9]. Normal service was resumed with a new candidate who defeated Cunningham-Reid in 1945. Born the son of the Reverend Arthur Cunningham-Reid in 1895, he was educated at Edinburgh University and Clare College Cambridge. He served in France from 1914 to 1918, initially as a sapper and then in the Royal Flying Corp, when he was awarded the DFC. In 1922 he was elected MP for Warrington and was briefly PPS to Sir John Baird when First Commissioner of Works. He lost his seat in 1923, but regained it in 1924 and worked as PPS at the Ministry of Transport for the duration of that Parliament. He unsuccessfully contested Southampton in 1929 and was out of the House for three years until his return at St Marylebone.

MPs for Paddington

Paddington North

Sir William George Perring (Conservative), who was born in 1866 and educated at St Pancras Wesleyan School, went on to become the head of house furnishers William Perring and Company[10] and Managing Director of the Crossley Bedstead Company. He was President of the Paddington and Bayswater Chamber of Trade, the London and Suburban Retail Traders' Federation, and later of the National Chamber of Trade. He joined Paddington Council where he became mayor in 1911/12, and he was also a London magistrate. He retired in 1929 and died in 1937.

7 Douglas Hogg was elected as MP for Grantham (Lincolnshire) in 1979
8 The Marylebone Cricket Club, which is regarded as the 'spiritual' home of the sport, was founded in 1787.
9 Churchill's private papers list the three main objectives of the movement, as being to "stop the stream of inefficiency emerging from the Party Caucuses, to punish those in high places "as after Pearl Harbour, when they deserve it", and to encourage MPs and Parliamentary candidates who subscribe to the programme and fight those who do not".
10 Opened at 382 Harrow Road in 1892.

MPs for Paddington 1918-1945

From		To	Surname	First Names	Constituency	Party
1918	G	1929	Perring	Sir William George	Paddington North	Conservative
1929	G	1945	Bracken	Brendan		Conservative
1918	G	1922	Harris	Sir Henry Percy	Paddington South	Conservative
1922	G	1930	King	Henry Douglas (Commodore)		Conservative
1930	B	1945	Taylor	Ernest Augustus (Admiral)		Empire Crusade /Conservative

Notes: First returned at: B By-election, G General Election

Bracken House in Cannon Street was home to the Financial Times from the 1950s - 80s. The sundial above the door has the face of Winston Churchill at its centre. **John Nelson**

He was succeeded in 1929 by **Brendan Bracken** (Conservative), who was born in Sydney Australia in 1901 and educated there, but emigrated to Britain and became a journalist. He was a Director of the publishing company of Eyre and Spottiswoode, Chairman of the Union Corporation, and also of the *Financial Times*, editor of *The Economist,* and of a publication called *The Banker*. A prominent supporter of Winston Churchill's policies towards the threat of Hitler, he became the new Prime Minister's Principal Private Secretary in 1940, and the following year went into Government in succession to Duff Cooper as Minister of Information in the War Cabinet. When Churchill formed his provisional Government in 1945 Bracken was made First Lord of the Admiralty, but the Tories lost the General Election, and his seat with it. He was out of Parliament for five years, returning in 1950 for the new division of Bournemouth East and Christchurch, which seat he retained until his elevation to Viscount in 1952. From 1955 until his death in 1958 he was a Trustee of the National Gallery.

Paddington South

Sir Henry Percy Harris (Conservative), was first elected as MP for Paddington South in January 1910. He retired in 1922 and died in 1941. His main biographical details are included in Chapter 3.

He was succeeded at the 1922 election by **Commodore Henry Douglas King** (Conservative), born in 1877 and a man with a naval career behind him at the time of his election. He was, however, a man of many parts who had started out in the merchant Navy in 1891, became a farmer eight years later and then trained as a barrister being called to the bar at the Middle Temple in 1905. He first entered politics in 1910 when he was defeated in both elections that year when contesting the Liberal seat of Norfolk North. At the outbreak of the First World War he joined the Royal Navy organising the North Atlantic convoys and in 1918 was elected as the Independent MP for North Norfolk but rejoined the Tory Party the following year when he was briefly a Principal Private Secretary and actually became a Party Whip in 1921. In 1922 he was made a Junior Lord of the Treasury and after the election of the same year transferred to Paddington South when he was also appointed Aide de Camp to the King, George V, whom he served until 1925. From 1924 to 1928 he was Financial Secretary at the War Office and Secretary for Mines in 1928-9. Meanwhile in 1927 he had been made a Naval Commodore but sadly he was drowned in a shipwreck in 1930.

The 1930 by-election that followed King's demise was won by another Naval man, **Vice-Admiral Ernest Augustus Taylor** (Empire Crusade), who beat the official Conservative candidate, Sir Herbert Lidiard, by a margin of nearly 5% of the votes cast. The victory gave the Crusade campaign substantial momentum, and led to other by-election interest shortly afterwards at Islington East, and Westminster, St George's. After 1931, however, Taylor took the Conservative whip, and remained MP until 1945 when he retired. He was born in 1876, and educated at Stubbingham and HMS Britannia. During the Prince of Wales' Tour of Canada, Australia, and New Zealand in 1919-20, he commanded HMS Renown, but retired and sought an entry into Parliament. Initially he was unsuccessful, contesting Woolwich East in 1923 and Finsbury in 1924,and became a member of Finsbury Borough Council in 1925, serving until 1928.

West London

Chelsea, Kensington, Hammersmith, Fulham and West Middlesex (16 seats)

In West London there was a large increase from nine to sixteen seats. Three were unchanged, these being **Chelsea, Kensington North** and **Kensington South.** Details can be found in Chapter 3. However, in the wake of population expansion further west, the boroughs of Fulham and Hammersmith each gained a seat. **Fulham East** extended from Barons Court ward in the northeast of the borough, which included West Kensington, to the Sands End ward by the river Thames, and included the areas of Fulham around Lillie Road and Walham Green (Lillie and Walham wards). **Fulham West** extended south from Hammersmith Bridge to Putney Bridge and a little further downstream, incorporating Hurlingham ward, Fulham Palace Road and the district south of Hammersmith Broadway known as Margravine ward (Barons Court South). The Munster and Town wards, including Parsons Green, made up the rest of the constituency. **Hammersmith South** incorporated the area between Shepherds Bush and the Uxbridge Road in the north and Hammersmith Broadway in the south. Officially it comprised the three borough wards of River, Brook Green & St Matthews, and The Grove & Ravenscourt. Kensington Olympia fell within its borders. **Hammersmith North** extended south from Wormwood Scrubs to Shepherds Bush and incorporated five wards: St Stephen's, Starch Green, Wormholt, and College Park & Latimer.

Five of the seven new constituencies were in West Middlesex, which since 1885 had been represented by Brentford, Ealing, Uxbridge, and Harrow county seats.

Acton, based entirely on the new municipal borough, which had formerly been in the Ealing seat, was created a constituency in its own right, reflecting the industrial and suburban development that was fast moving outwards from London. It had become a centre for laundries and factory employment, especially after the London County Council started building council estates, there and in Hammersmith; both places became known as 'suburbs of production'. The Old Oak Estate is a good example of the LCC's 'cottage' ideal for the council home. This estate was planned around an extension of the Central Line of the Underground, and East Acton station was finally opened in 1920. The new constituency incorporated all parts of Acton south of Perivale, including Bedfont Park, Hanger Lane, Old Oak Common, Park Royal, and Pitshanger. The Acton place name dates from about 1181 AD, and is a common one deriving from the Old English 'Ac tun', meaning either, "farmstead or village by the oak trees", or "specialized farm where oak timber is worked." One of the main thoroughfares in the area today is Old Oak Common Lane.

The former **Ealing** county constituency was reduced in size, and became a borough seat that included the town and its immediate suburbs. Seven years later, in 1925, the Great West Road opened by King George V was dubbed 'the golden mile', as major factories quickly arrived to take advantage of a distribution system that also included the Western Avenue and North Circular Road. The Acton and Hammersmith council estates provided local labour for Ealing employers that included: Smith's Crisps, Curry's cycles and radios, Maclean's toothpaste, Firestone tyres, Gillette razor blades, and Hoover electrical machines, all of which opened factories on the Great West Road. The constituency included: Castle Bar, Drayton Green, Ealing Common, Little Ealing, Horsenden, Northfields, Northolt, and Perivale.

South and North of Ealing population changes also had their effect: Chiswick transferred from Ealing to the new constituency of **Brentford & Chiswick,** each now comprising an Urban District, and this subsequently created a unified borough in 1932. Brentford included Boston Manor, and Chiswick included Stamford Brook (West), Turnham Green, and Gunnersbury Park. Chiswick's name derives from the Saxon 'Ceswican' and means, "a place where cheese is made". Once a small riverside village on the Thames, it developed into a stylish London suburb after the railway opened there in 1849. By the late 19th Century, Underground stations had also opened at Turnham Green, and Brentford Road (Gunnersbury today). Bedford Park, first established in the mid-1870s, was England's first self contained garden suburb. Horse trams began between Hammersmith and Kew Bridge in 1882, and were succeeded in 1901 by electric traction, both developments opening up Chiswick and Brentford as popular residential suburbs.

To the south, two more constituencies were created from the former Brentford division. **Twickenham** comprised the Urban District (granted borough status in 1926), which included: Bushy Park, Hampton, St Margarets, Strawberry Hill, Teddington, and Whitton, together with Heston and Isleworth UD (which also included Cranford, Hounslow, Osterley Park, Syon Park and Spring Grove). "Tuicanhom" (AD 704) probably meant, "land in a river bend of a man called Twicca". Today Twickenham is internationally recognised as the home of English Rugby Union. However, well before that it had developed as a fashionable retreat from Court life, and was a place where elegant country houses were established. Twickenham was the 18th century equivalent of Beverley Hills, popular with the foremost artists, and many poets and artists visited their patrons in the town.

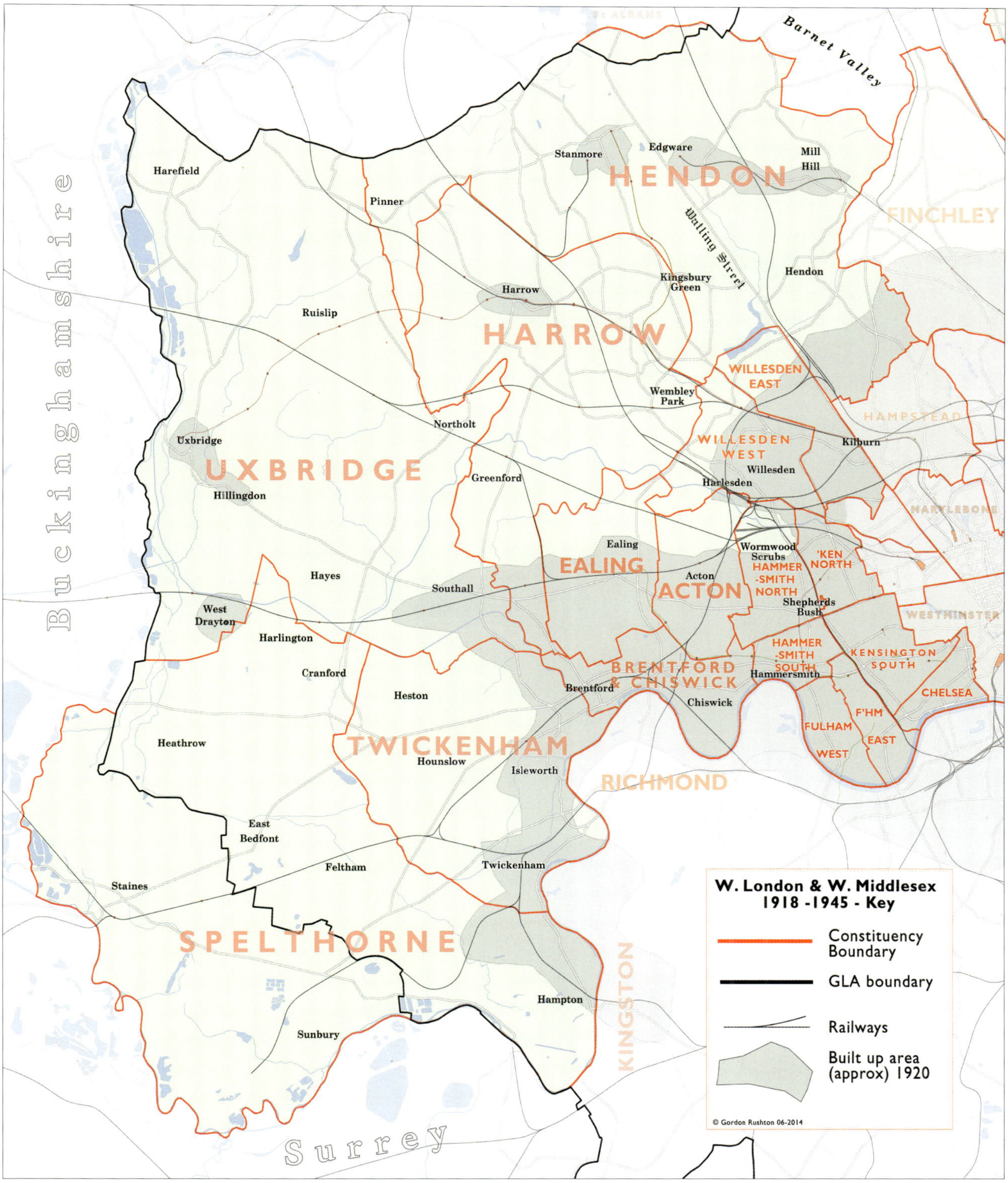

Meanwhile Sunbury, Hampton and Teddington UDCs were included with Feltham in a new **Spelthorne** constituency with both Staines urban and rural districts, which then included Harlington. Its communities included Bedfont, Halliford, Hanworth, Harmondsworth, Kempton Park, Laleham, and Shepperton.

Uxbridge acquired Southall-Norwood from Brentford, but lost the Staines area to Spelthorne. It was otherwise unaltered comprising Hayes. Ruislip, Norwood, Uxbridge and Yiewsley UDCs, and the Uxbridge RDC, which included Harefield, Ickenham, Hillingdon, and Cowley (which was dissolved in 1929 when it was combined with Uxbridge UDC). At the same time, West Drayton was transferred from Uxbridge RDC, and allied with Yiewsley to expand the UDC established in 1911. Other communities contained within the new Uxbridge seat were: Botwell, Dawley, Dormers Wells, Eastcoat, Hyde Green, Mount Pleasant, Northolt Park, Northwood, Ruislip, and Yeading.

Top Left: These Fulham Road shops, with flats above were built in 1906. In 1918 they were placed in the Fulham West Constituency. Still at the heart of this busy area today, the character change is exemplified by the use of the ground floor premises.

All pictures John Nelson

Top Right: *Fulham Town Hall was built in the 1890s. Election results for the East and West divisions were announced there. There are plans to transform the premises into a prestigious Fulham Road shopping Mall.*

Middle Left: *Church Road in the centre of Twickenham, is close to the River Thames. The expansion of this riverside suburb in the run up to the First World War justified the creation of a Constituency that has remained more or less intact ever since.*

Above: *The Hoover factory on Western Avenue was built in the late 1930s, after the creation of the new Ealing Constituency. It was one of several places of new employment, much of which was concentrated in the north of the Borough, made accessible by Western Avenue and the North Circular Road, both opened in the 1920s.*

Left: *Whitehall Road houses in Harrow-on-the-Hill typify the dwellings that sustained the substantial commuter expansion encouraged by the Metropolitan Railway which reached the town in 1880.*

All pictures John Nelson

Northwest of Ealing two new seats were created. **Harrow** was redrawn to become a geographically much smaller constituency, comprising five UDCs, including Wealdstone in the north, Wembley in the east, Harrow itself in the west, and Greenford, and Hanwell in the south. Communities included within its boundaries were: Alperton, Elthorne, Fryent, Greenford, Hanwell, Hatch End, Headstone, Kenton, Kingsbury, Pinner, Queensbury, Stanmore, and Sudbury.

Reflecting the fact that it was one of the four fastest growing towns in Britain, Willesden was established separately, with two new borough constituencies fashioned out of the former Harrow seat, other parts of which not placed in Harrow itself, were transferred to Hendon. (See North London later in this Chapter). **Willesden East** extended west of the Edgware Road from the ward of Cricklewood in the north via Mapesbury, Neasden, and Dollis Hill, to Kensal Rise ward in the south, and included Brondesbury Park ward and Kilburn's Mid, North, and South wards.

Willesden West embraced the Queens Park side of West Kilburn, and extended to Stonebridge Park ward in the north, Harlesden ward in the west, incorporating the Willesden Green, Church End and Roundwood wards of Willesden itself. "Willesdone" dated from 939 AD and the Normans knew it as "Wellesdone", meaning, "hill with a spring". Willesden comprised three parishes, all of which at the time of the Doomsday Survey came under the joint jurisdiction of the Canons of StPauls Cathedral, and the Monastery of St Arkenwold, to which King Athelstan had granted the Manors of Neasden-cum-Willesden. Willesden and Harlesden, together with Twyford, were the three parishes, though eventually the western part of the latter went into Ealing borough. Within them were ten manors: these included Willesden Green, Neasden, Oxgate (Dollis Hill), Harlesden, Twyford East, Chamberlain Wood (Kensal Rise), Kensal (Green), Brondesbury, and Mapesbury. West Twyford was the tenth but is now in Greenford, part of modern-day Ealing. Then, as now, the whole of the area that comprised the nine Willesden manors was bounded to the east by the Edgware Road (the Roman-built Watling Street), to the south by Kilburn Lane (leading to Kilburn Priory in neighbouring Hampstead), and the Harrow Road, which continue to divide Willesden from Hammersmith, Kensington, and Paddington today.

The area was entirely agricultural but with a great deal of uncultivated land. Wheat predominated up until the 17th Century when the growth of London's population meant that haymaking and animal husbandry became more prominent. Timber too was in demand, especially from the "Crekyll Woddes" (modern Cricklewood) on the estate belonging to All Souls College (which owned lands in the nearby Queens Park district of Paddington). In 1801 the population of the whole area was no higher than 750, but the Enclosure Act of 1805 changed the face of rural Willesden. By 1823 much of the common land had been sold to the Deans and Chapters of St Paul's and Westminster, the Duke of Buckingham and to All Souls College, Oxford. The population began to increase slightly but steadily. Then in 1846 the Church Commissioners sold land in the Chamberlain manor district in the southeast corner that resulted in the building of new houses between the Harrow Road and Kilburn Lane, where many workers at nearby Kensal Green cemetery lived. The London to Birmingham (later the London and North Western Railway) cut through the southern edge of the area, opening Kilburn High Road station in 1852. By the 1860s the development of South Kilburn was in progress and Willesden Lane began to acquire new villas. The Hampstead Junction Railway opened from Camden Road on the North London Railway to Old Oak Common near Willesden, with stations at Brondesbury, Kensal Green, and Harlesden, and as a result, by 1865 most of the area between South Kilburn and Brondesbury had become built up along the Edgware Road. In the 1870s the Church Commisioners and All Souls College sold land further west, leading directly to housing developments in Kensal Rise and Brondesbury Park.

Industry began, much of it associated with the railways, including signalling equipment manufacture, and housing spread in the area towards Willesden Green. Despite these developments, Willesden parish beyond Kilburn was still largely agricultural in the 1870s, turning to dairy farming to provide milk for London's growing population. Willesden Junction station was bounded on its southern side by housing and continuous development towards Kensington but to the north there were still open fields.

In 1874 the boundaries between Paddington, Hammersmith and Willesden were agreed, facilitating the provision of sewers and roads. So when the Willesden Local Government Board was formed in 1875 its wards were North and South Kilburn, and East and West Willesden. Development continued into the 1880s by which time most of Harlesden and Willesden Green became built up. By then the Metropolitan Railway had been extended beyond Swiss Cottage (where the building of a tunnel had been the reason why it had not arrived earlier), and new stations were opened at Kilburn and Willesden Green in 1879. The Kingsbury and Harrow Joint Committee was already in place to extend the railway towards Aylesbury, and this stimulated housing development along the line of route as it was constructed. Further industrial development was also encouraged, and in the early 1880s a huge engineering works was established at Neasden, with workers housing provided between the site and Neasden Lane.

Following the Local Government Act of 1888 Willesden became an Urban District Council but did not become part

Top Left: *After 1918 the Underground reached Acton. The Rolling Stock Works employed voters in the new Constituency created in 1918. It grew to become one of London's most industrial. This photograph is of workers in the Works canteen in 1923. Most, would have been unionised.* **©TfL from the London Transport Museum Collection**

Top Right: *128 Clifford Gardens was where the author's mother was born. This modest Kensal Green district of Willesden was in the West Constituency in 1918.*

John Nelson

Middle Left: *This station was opened by the Metropolitan Railway in 1879 and stimulated suburban development in the whole area up to WW1. The railway was the divide between Willesden East and West constituencies.*

Above: *Normanby Road, close to Dollis Hill station in the Willesden East constituency. These were homes for professional middle class families with live-in maids of all work. The author's grandparents lived here, and his father was born here in 1918, the year the constituency was created."*

Left: *The Piccadilly and District Lines diverge at Acton Town station. The latter formed the Constituency boundary between Ealing and Acton.*

Middle Left &, Above - John Nelson

of the London County Council when that body was formed in 1889 because the boundary chosen for inclusion was the one that had applied in 1855 for the Metropolitan Board of Works. Willesden was then included in the Middlesex Parliamentary constituency of Harrow. Willesden's electors numbered 16,815 as compared with 665 for Wembley and a mere 140 in Kingsbury. By 1901 Willesden's population had reached 115,000 living in over 16,000 houses and its expansion south of the Metropolitan Railway was almost complete. Yet it continued to expand and reached 154,212 in 1911, most of the development occurring between the Metropolitan and Midland Railway Lines in Cricklewood and Dollis Hill, north and east of Gladstone Park. By 1931 Willesden was the most populous district council in Middlesex and became a county borough in 1933. In its first elections on 11th November a majority of the councillors returned were from the Labour Party which never lost control for the time that the authority remained in being until superseded by the London Borough of Brent in 1965. At the end of the Second World War there were 38,000 houses in Willesden but less than half of all families living in them had a bathroom of their own. One quarter shared a lavatory. Population densities were least in Brondesbury (30 per acre) and highest in South Kilburn (over 150).

The Politics of West London

The political complexion of the older established Parliamentary Boroughs of west London did not change much after the First World War, but such changes that did occur saw the emergence of the Labour Party as the principal opponent of the Conservatives, who still held sway. There was only one Liberal success in the whole period, and that was with a majority of merely 0.4% at Willesden East in 1923. The franchise extensions that took place in 1918 and 1928 (when women got the vote) meant that, as voting became primarily class-based, constituencies with large concentrations of working class housing tended to favour Labour when the national "mood" was opposed to the Conservative Party. This did not occur much in the inter-War years and, given that the Tories themselves held about 30% of the working class vote, the Party survived the social and boundary changes quite well. Furthermore the Conservatives continued to benefit from the increasing spread of suburban middle class housing, except in areas such as Willesden that had become centres for new industries with large working class populations. There the Labour Party did much better.

As the table above shows, Conservative domination of politics in this part of Middlesex was almost total in the Inter-

Election Results in the Inter-war Period by % majority

Constituency	Pre 1918	1918	1922	1923	1924	1929	1931	1935
Chelsea	C	C58	C50	C30	C39	C33	C66	C50
Kensington North	C	C57	C26	C2	C6	Lab10	C27	C10
Kensington South	C	C34	C52	C100	C100	C49	C100	C78
Fulham East	C	C50	C37	C9	C23	C5	C43	C3
Fulham West		C41	C29	C5	C19	Lab6	C33	C10
Hammersmith North		C26	C17	Lab4	C8	Lab12	C22	Lab6
Hammersmith South	C	C46	C26	C7	C17	Lab1	C43	C25
Brentford & Chiswick	C	C50	C13	C27	C29	C11	C50	C31
Twickenham		C66	C100	C32	C41	C14	C48	C24
Spelthorne		C63	C29	C33	C39	C19	C57	C37
Acton		C47	C24	C14	C31	Lab2	C34	C17
Ealing	C	C58	C39	C26	C47	C30	C65	C48
Uxbridge	C	C22	C22	C8	C20	C3	C49	C17
Harrow	C	C65	Ind32	Ind20	C23	C13	C50	C25
Willesden East		C36	C6	L0.4	C25	C7	C41	C23
Willesden West		C17	C3	Lab21	Lab4	Lab20	C21	Lab8
C	9	16	16	13	15	10	16	14
L	0	0	0	1	0	0	0	0
Lab	0	0	0	2	1	6	0	2

Key: C = Conservative; L = Liberal; Lab = Labour; + = Party that won seat at General Election held by-election in same Parliament; - = Party that won seat at General Election lost by-election to main opposition Party in same Parliament. 100 = unopposed.

War years although there were some signs in 1929 of the emergence of a new pattern of two-party politics, one that was to predominate after the end of the Second World War. If anything Tory majorities after 1918 were even larger than they had been before. In Chelsea the majority never fell below 30% and on four occasions was at least 50%, whereas before the War their biggest majority was 21%, and the Liberals even took the seat once. Chelsea seems to have become far more exclusive and less cosmopolitan during this period and election results reflected this. Kensington South Tories recorded big majorities either side of the War, and in 1935 the largest Conservative majority ever recorded in a contested General Election in London was registered when the Party's candidate was returned with a majority of 78% of the votes cast. Kensington North also exhibited a post-War pattern that was similar to that before it. Tory victories were recorded in most Elections but radical parties also enjoyed a little success. Before the War the Liberals had taken the seat in 1892 and 1906, and after it Labour was victorious in 1929, by which time the Party had supplanted the Liberals as the radical alternative to the Conservatives.

MPs for Kensington and Chelsea

From	at	To	Surname	First Names	Constituency	Party
1918	G	1944	Hoare	Sir Samuel J.G.	Chelsea	Conservative Unionist
1944	B	1945	Noble	Allan Herbert Percy (Commander)		Conservative
1918	G	1922	Burgoyne	Sir Alan Hughes (Lt-Colonel)	Kensington North	Conservative
1922	G	1929	Gates	Percy George		Conservative
1929	G	1931	West	Fielding Reginald		Labour
1931	G	1945	Duncan	Sir James Alexander (Captain)		Conservative
1918	G	1945	Davison	Sir William Henry	Kensington South	Conservative

Notes: First returned at: B By-election, G General Election

Chelsea

Sir Samuel Hoare (Conservative), whose biographical details are contained in Chapter 3, was MP for Chelsea from January 1910 until 1944 when he died.

He was succeeded at the by-election that followed his death by **Commander Allan Herbert Percy Noble** (Conservative), the son of an Admiral. Born in 1908 he too entered the Navy, in 1926, following his education at Radley College. Between 1936 and 1938 he was Aide de Camp to the Viceroy of India, and during the Second World War he commanded destroyers. He witnessed the first Atom Bomb Test at Bikini in 1946 on behalf of the British Government, and remained Chelsea's MP until 1959, but he did not enjoy a significant political career. Fiercely anti-Labour, he was Parliamentary Secretary to the Admiralty from 1951 to 1955 and a sometime Joint Secretary of the 1922 Committee of Tory backbenchers.

Kensington North

Lieutenant-Colonel Sir Alan Hughes Burgoyne (Conservative), was MP from January 1910 until he retired in 1922. His principal biographical details are to be found in Chapter 3.

He was succeeded at the 1922 General Election by **Percy George Gates** (Conservative), the son of a Judge. Born in London in 1863, he was educated at Wellington College in Berkshire, and worked from 1886 to 1908 as a solicitor and Parliamentary Agent. He served on Kensington Borough Council where he was mayor in 1904/5, and became a member of the LCC in 1911, serving until 1919. He was also a Director of Hoare and Company, a Wapping brewery formed in 1894, and acquired in 1938 by Charrington's. He represented them on the Brewers Society of which he became Chairman in 1920/1. He lost his seat in 1929 and died in 1940.

Fielding Reginald West (Labour), was the first Socialist to represent the Royal Borough, although he only did so for two years between 1929 and 1931. Born at Huddersfield in 1892 and educated at the Regent Street Polytechnic, West became a teacher. He sat on Hammersmith Borough Council between 1923 and 1925 and meanwhile contested Kensington North for the first time in 1924 when Gates defeated him. During his brief tenure he was PPS to Mr. Lees-Smith who was initially Post Master General and then Minister of Education in the Labour Government between 1929 and 1931. Following his defeat in 1931, West succeeded in being elected again in 1934 when he won a by-election at Hammersmith North, but he died in October the following year.

Captain Sir James Alexander Duncan (Conservative), held the seat from 1931 until 1945, when he too was defeated. Born in 1899, the son of a Perthshire man, he was educated at Marlborogh School and served in the Scots Guards in both World Wars. Politically he liked to describe himself as a Conservative and Liberal Unionist, perhaps betraying his Scottish roots, and indeed his first attempt to enter the Commons came with his defeat at Caithness in 1929. He was for a number of years Chairman of the London Conservative Union, and served on the LCC between 1925 and 1928. He was a fairly obscure but loyal backbencher who during the 1930s was three times the PPS to Leslie Burgin when a Minister at the Board of Trade, the Department for Transport and at Supply. He was defeated at Kensington in 1945 but returned to the Commons in 1950 as MP for South Angus, which constituency he served until 1964. The year after he was given the freedom of Arbroath, one of the principal towns in his constituency.

Kensington South

Sir William Henry Davison (Conservative), served continuously as MP for Kensington South from 1918 to 1945, except that in the latter year he was elevated to the peerage as Baron Broughshane, three months after the Tories' defeat in the General Election. This was to accommodate Richard Law, who had been the Wartime Education Minister defeated at South West Hull in the General Election. Born in 1872, Davison was a lawyer who had been educated at Shrewsbury School and Keble College Oxford, before being called to the bar at the Inner Temple in 1895. He first entered politics as a councillor in Kensington where he was Mayor between 1913 and 1919. A Vice President of the Royal Society of Arts he was also Chairman of the Income Tax Payers Association, and served as Chairman of the National Association of Conservative Associations. In business he was Chairman of the East Surrey Water Company.

MPs for Fulham and Hammersmith

Although both Fulham seats followed the voting pattern of the former single-member borough division, there was a solitary Labour success in the more working class West constituency in 1929, but generally the Tories won both seats, and in the East division this was by substantial majorities for the best part of the Inter-War years. Nevertheless by 1935 the majorities in both seats fell to levels that looked capable of being overturned, as indeed they would be after the Second World War. Of the two Hammersmith seats, the South constituency was much more middle class than the North, and the election results of the period reflected the difference. Labour won the latter on three occasions and the former only once, and in 1929 Labour held both constituencies, as well as three of the four in the combined boroughs.

Fulham East

Sir Henry George Norris (Conservative), was MP from 1918 to 1922. Born in 1865 and educated privately he became an estate agent and was an active Freemason. Heavily involved in land and property he became Chairman of Kinnaird Park Estates, and of the Municipal Freehold Land Company, being also a Director of the Municipal House Property Trust. He was ten times Mayor of Fulham, an area where there was considerable housing development during that period, and was also a member of the LCC from 1916 to 1919. He was Chairman of Fulham Football Club, which entered the Football League in 1907 and of the then Woolwich Arsenal Club before it moved to Highbury, North London in 1913. He was closely involved with the 3rd Middlesex Artillery Volunteers, and with the 2nd Tower Hamlets Volunteers. A magistrate and Deputy Lieutenant for London County, Norris was a Conservative Unionist who sat for only one term. He died in 1934.

Norris was succeeded in 1922 by **Sir Kenyon Vaughan-Morgan** (Conservative), Chairman of the Morgan Crucible Company. Born in 1873, he was educated at Charterhouse School, and in France and Germany, and after he entered politics, became Chairman of the London Municipal Society, and of the Greater London Playing Fields Association, a branch of the national body set up in 1925 to ensure that everyone had access to quality recreation space close to where they lived. Additionally, he was a Governor of St Thomas's Hospital, and a General Commissioner for Income Tax. From 1915 to 1919 Morgan was with the Royal Artillery S.C., becoming a Lieutenant Colonel in 1917. He remained MP for Fulham East, and five years before his death in 1933, he was made a Deputy Lieutenant of London.

The by-election created by his death led to a change of political control, although **John Wilmot** (Labour), only kept the seat until the 1935 General Election, and was the sole Labour MP for the constituency in the whole Inter-War period. Born in 1895, and educated at Elementary School, Wilmot secured a place at Chelsea Polytechnic but from 1914 to 1919 served in the Royal Naval Air Squadron. After the Great War he went into banking, and London local government as a councillor, then an Alderman on the LCC until 1945, serving between 1939 and 1942 as Chairman of the Fire Brigade during the time of the Blitz. His first experience of a Parliamentary contest was in 1924 when he unsuccessfully sought election at Lewisham East, an experience he was to repeat in 1929 and again in 1931. Although he served as Fulham

MPs for Fulham and Hammersmith						
From	**at**	**To**	**Surname**	**First Names**	**Constituency**	**Party**
1918	G	1922	Norris	Sir Henry George	Fulham East	Conservative Unionist
1922	G	1933	Vaughan-Morgan	Sir Kenyon (Col)		Conservative
1933	B	1935	Wilmot	John		Labour
1935	G	1945	Astor	William Waldorf		Conservative
1918	G	1929	Cobb	Sir Cyril Stephen	Fulham West	Conservative
1929	G	1930	Spero	Dr.George Ernest		Labour
1930	B	1938	Cobb	Sir Cyril		Conservative
1938	B	1945	Summerskill	Dr. Edith		Labour
1918	G	1923	Foreman	Sir Henry George	Hammersmith North	Conservative
1923	G	1924	Gardner	James Patrick		Labour
1924	G	1926	Ashmead-Bartlett	Ellis		Conservative
1926	B	1931	Gardner	James Patrick		Labour
1931	G	1934	Pickford	Mary		Conservative
1934	B	1935	West	Fielding Reginald		Labour
1935	G	1945	Pritt	Denis Nowell		Independent Labour
1918	G	1929	Bull	Sir William James	Hammersmith South	Conservative
1929	G	1931	Chater	Daniel		Labour
1931	G	1945	Cooke	James Douglas		Conservative

Notes: First returned at: B By-election, G General Election

Bright and to the point, this election communication from 1945 has come down to us.
People's History Museum, Manchester

East's MP for only two years, he did resume his Parliamentary career in 1939 when he was elected for Kennington at a by-election. During this period he was a member of the National Executive Committee of the Labour Party, in 1939 and between 1940/1. He held the seat until 1945, when he transferred to Deptford but retired from the Commons in 1950, moving to the Lords as Baron Wilmot of Selmeston. Meanwhile following his return at Kennington he became a PPS to Hugh Dalton who until 1942 was Minister of Economic Warfare and from 1942 to 1944 President of the Board of Trade. In 1944 Wilmot himself was made Parliamentary Secretary at the Ministry of Supply and, with the return of Labour Government in 1945, he was made Minster, a post he held until 1947. From 1945 to 1946 he was also Minister of Aircraft Production. He died in 1964.

William Waldorf Astor (Conservative), the eldest son of Viscount and Lady Astor, who was the first woman MP, held Fulham East between 1935 and 1945. Educated at Eton and New College, Oxford, he was, at the age of 27, amongst the youngest Parliamentary candidates, and his mother was still an MP, for the Sutton division of Plymouth, where she was first returned at a 1919 by-election that followed the death of her husband. Prior to his election William had travelled extensively in the Far East, for the Institute of Pacific Relations, and was private secretary to Lord Lytton when he was Chairman of a League of Nations Commission which went to China in 1932 to resolve the conflict that followed the Japanese invasion of Manchuria. He worked for the Pilgrim Trust[11] and in the unemployment department of the National Council of Social Service, and accompanied the Duke of Kent on several tours of industrial areas badly affected by unemployment. Whilst at Oxford University he was a "half-blue" for polo and steeple chasing. In 1938 he joined the Royal Naval Voluntary Reserve and served in the Middle East during the War. He also had a keen interest in the farm at Cliveden, the family home in Buckinghamshire. He was defeated in 1945, and re-emerged as the Conservative candidate for his home constituency of Wycombe in 1950 when he lost narrowly to the Labour MP, John Hare. He won there in 1951 by a margin of nearly 2,000 votes, but served as MP for only a year before he died in 1952.

---

11 EDWARD STEPHEN HARKNESS of New York founded the Pilgrim Trust in 1930 with an endowment of about two million pounds. This was prompted by his admiration for what Great Britain had done in the 1914-18 war, and by his ties of affection for the land from which he drew his descent. He desired that the gift should be used to give grants for some of the country's more urgent needs and in promoting its future well-being.

Fulham West

Sir Cyril Stephen Cobb (Conservative) held the seat twice, initially from 1918 until 1929 and then between 1930 and 1938. Born at Margate (Kent) in 1861 and, following an education at Newton Abbott College and Merton College Oxford, he became a lawyer being called to the bar in 1887. He first embarked on a political career in 1905 when he became a member of the LCC on which he served until 1921. He took a particular interest in Education and chaired that Committee twice, between 1911 and 1913 and again from 1917 to 1921. He gave up the chairmanship in 1913 to become Chairman of the Council for the year 1913/14. From 1916 to 1917 he was a member of the Public Works Re-organisation Committee for India. After his defeat in 1929 he was re-elected at a by-election there a year later and remained the MP until his death in 1938.

The man who briefly displaced him in 1929 was **Dr.George Ernest Spero** (Labour), a medical practitioner who was Secretary to the Parliamentary Medical Committee in 1923/4 when coincidentally he was also MP for Stoke Newington. At that time he was a Liberal but after his defeat in 1924 he joined Labour. Born in 1894, the son of a dentist and educated privately, then at London University and the London Hospital, he became a physician and surgeon. During the First World War he was a Surgeon-Lieutenant between 1915 and 1917, serving on Destroyers and Minesweepers. After being wounded he was invalided out in 1917, and first entered politics in 1922 when he contested the Leicester West division at a by-election in the Liberal cause. He was also the author of several books and plays. Spero resigned in 1930 citing illness, but it soon emerged that he was involved in dubious and probably criminal business dealings in connection with the sale of his business. He apparently fled Britain for the USA leaving substantial debts behind, and as far as can be ascertained never returned to these shores.

Dr Edith Summerskill MP
Political Yearbook 1947

Dr. Edith Summerskill (Labour), took Fulham West at the by-election that followed Cobb's death in 1938. Born in 1901 she, like Spero, was a doctor of medicine, having been educated at Kings College and the Charing Cross Hospital. She was in general practice from 1924 until 1945, whilst also active in politics, and was Vice-President of the Socialist Medical Association. She became a Middlesex County councillor in 1931 and served for ten years. In the Churchill Wartime Government she was appointed Parliamentary Secretary to the Ministry of Food, a post she retained after the War in Attlee's 1945-50 Government. She was then made Minister of National Insurance in the short-lived 1950-1 Labour Government. Prior to her election in 1938 she had stood unsuccessfully for Putney and in Bury, but eventually remained MP for Fulham West until 1955 when the seat was merged with the East division. She was then selected as the candidate for Warrington, where she sat as MP from 1955 until 1961 when she was made a peer. She died in 1980.

Hammersmith North

Sir Henry George Foreman (Conservative), was MP from 1918 to 1923. Born in 1852, he was Mayor of Hammersmith from 1913 to 1920 and an Alderman between 1919 and 1924. Founder of the 20th London Cadet Corps, and Commander of the Hammersmith Red Cross; he retired from the Commons in 1923 and died a year later.

He was succeeded in 1923 by **James Patrick Gardner** (Labour), who was the first Socialist to be elected anywhere in West London. He lost in 1924 but was returned at a by-election in 1926, and retained the seat until Labour's heavy defeat in 1931. He was born in 1883 in Belfast where he was educated at the Christian Brothers School, and pursued an artistic career as an architectural sculptor. He sat as a councillor in Hammersmith from 1919-22, and again in 1928. Also a London magistrate, Gardner first contested Hammersmith North in 1922 when Foreman was re-elected.

Ellis Ashmead-Bartlett (Conservative), was a lawyer turned journalist who sat briefly as MP from 1924 to 1926. Born in 1881 and educated at Marlborough College, he was called to the Bar at the Inner Temple in 1902, having earlier served in the South Africa War from 1899 to 1902. He was a War Correspondent during the Russo-Japan War of 1904, and pursued the same role in later conflicts: in French Morocco (1908); Spanish Morocco (1909); Tripoli (1911); the Balkans (1912-13), and during the Great War (1914-15). He was a representative of the Newspaper Proprietors Association during the Dardanelles Campaign, and then at the French Headquarters. He was the author of several books about War, and first entered politics when he unsuccessfully contested the Normanton Division of the West Riding of Yorkshire in January 1910. He failed again in December 1910, this time at Poplar (Tower Hamlets). He also contested Hammersmith before finally succeeding in 1924. He died in 1931.

Mary Pickford (Conservative), was elected in 1931. Born in 1893 the daughter of Lord Sterndale, she was educated at Wycombe Abbey School and Lady Margaret Hall Oxford, after which she enjoyed an early career between 1917 and 1921 assisting with compiling a naval history of the First World War. She initially unsuccessfully contested Farnworth in Lancashire at the 1929 General Election, which was the first to follow universal women suffrage, and she was one of the first women to be elected to the House of Commons. Unfortunately she died in 1934 so her career was short.

She was succeeded at a by-election in 1934 by **Fielding Reginald West** (Labour), formerly the MP for Kensington North between 1929 and 1931, but he too died soon afterwards and the seat was vacant at the dissolution in 1935. His principal biographical details are contained in the section above relating to Kensington.

Denis Nowell Pritt MP
Bundesarchiv

Denis Nowell Pritt (Independent Labour), was elected in 1935. Born at Harlesden in 1887 and educated at Winchester School, London University and abroad in Germany, Switzerland and Spain, he became a barrister at the Middle Temple in 1909. He was for a while Chairman of the Howard League for Penal Reform and of the Bentham Committee for poor litigants, becoming a KC in 1927, and chairing the Bar's Reconstitution Committee. He was a left wing Socialist and admirer of the Soviet Union on which he wrote several authoritative books. He was Chairman of the Society for Cultural Relations with the USSR, and when he was elected for Hammersmith in 1935, it was initially as an Independent Labour candidate. He was a sometime member of the National Executive Committee of the Labour Party, and unsuccessfully contested Sunderland as an official candidate in 1931. After the outbreak of War he was expelled from the Party in 1940 when he continued to support the Soviet position following their pact with Hitler and the invasion of Finland. He was never readmitted to the Party but pushed its official candidate into third place in 1945, continuing to sit as Independent Labour MP until 1950. Then the official Labour candidate, Frank Tomney, won the seat, pushing Pritt into third place. From 1945 to 1950 he was Chairman of the Group of five Independent Labour MPs who sat in that Parliament. He was also Chairman of the Student Labour Federation. In some eyes Pritt would have been regarded as a Communist 'fellow-traveller' and he certainly acquired a number of honours from a variety of Soviet bloc countries during a period when the Iron Curtain was at its strongest. For example he was awarded the Lenin Peace Prize in 1954; the Freedom of the city of Leipzig in 1957, and LLD degrees: at Charles University, Prague (1957); Sofia University (1960); Humboldt University, Berlin (1960), and Moscow University (1961). Other honours from Communist countries included: the Order of Georgi Dimitrov, 1964; the Star of International Friendship, 1965, and the Gold Medal of the Czechoslovak Society for International Relations in 1968, the year in which there was a Soviet invasion of that country to protect its hard line interests. He died in 1972.

Hammersmith South

Sir William James Bull (Conservative, had been MP for Hammersmith since 1900, when he was adopted as the candidate for Hammersmith South in 1918. His biographical details are contained in Chapter 2. He remained the MP until his retirement in 1929.

Daniel Chater MP
Peoples History Museum, Manchester

Daniel Chater (Labour Co-operative), was the successful candidate at the 1929 election, though he lost the seat two years later. Born in 1870, he was an activist in both the National Union of General and Municipal Workers[12] and the Co-operative Movement, of which Society's Political Committee he was Chairman. He was active in Essex politics, sitting as a county councillor for the Seven Kings ward, and he first contested Parliamentary elections in nearby Ilford in 1923 and 1924, on both occasions unsuccessfully. After his defeat at Hammersmith South in 1931, he went in search of another seat, and was adopted at Bethnal Green North East, which he won in 1935, and where he remained as MP until his retirement in 1950, when the borough's two divisions were amalgamated.

James Douglas Cooke (Conservative), was MP from 1931 to 1945 when he was defeated in the post-War Labour landslide. He was born a New Zealander in 1879 and educated first at Melbourne University in Australia, and then at the London Hospital where he was awarded his BS in 1901, and became FRCS four years later. During the

12 The National Union of General and Municipal Workers was formed in 1924 by the amalgamation of the National Amalgamated Union of Labour, the National Union of General Workers and the Municipal Employees' Association.

First World War he was a Major in the Royal Army Medical Corps in France from 1916 to 1919. He contested Peckham unsuccessfully in May 1929, and died in 1949.

MPs for West Middlesex

The vast majority of MPs elected for West Middlesex constituencies during the inter-War years were Conservatives. Labour made a few incursions at Acton and Willesden West; a solitary Liberal MP was elected once at Willesden East and an Independent at Harrow; but all other constituencies were solidly Tory.

MPs for West Middlesex

From	at	To	Surname	First Names	Constituency	Party
1918	G	1929	Brittain	Sir Harry Ernest	Acton	Conservative
1929	G	1931	Shillaker	James Frederick		Labour
1931	G	1943	Duggan	Hubert John		Conservative
1943	B	1945	Longhurst	Henry Carpenter		Conservative
1918	G	1931	Morden	Walter Grant Peterson (Lt-Col)	Brentford and Chiswick	Conservative
1931	G	1945	Mitchell	Harold Paton		Conservative
1918	G	1931	Nield	Sir Herbert	Ealing	Conservative
1931	G	1945	Sanderson	Sir Frank Bernard		Conservative
1918	G	1922	Mosley	Sir Oswald Ernald	Harrow	Conservative
1922	G	1924	Mosley	Sir Oswald Ernald		Independent
1924	G	1941	Salmon	Isadore (Major)		Conservative
1941	B	1945	Bower	Norman Adolph Henry		Conservative
1918	G	1931	Pilditch	Sir Philip Edward	Spelthorne	Conservative
1931	G	1945	Blaker	Sir Reginald		Conservative
1918	G	1929	Joynson-Hicks	Sir (Lancelot) William	Twickenham	Conservative
1929	B	1932	Ferguson	Sir John		Conservative
1932	B	1934	Murray-Philipson	Hylton Ralph		Conservative
1934	B	1935	Critchley	Alfred Cecil		Conservative
1935	G	1945	Keeling	Edward Herbert		Conservative
1918	G	1922	Peel	Sidney Cornwallis	Uxbridge	Conservative
1922	G	1929	Burney	Charles Dennistoun (Cmdr)		Conservative
1929	G	1945	Llewellin	John Jestyn (Major)		Conservative
1918	G	1922	Mallaby-Deeley	Sir Harry	Willesden East	Conservative
1923	B	1924	Johnstone	Harcourt		Liberal
1924	G	1929	Stanley	George Frederick (Lt-Col)		Conservative
1929	G	1938	Somerville	Daniel Gerald		Conservative
1938	B	1945	Hammersley	Samuel Schofield		Conservative
1918	G	1922	Pinkham	Charles (Colonel)	Willesden West	Conservative
1922	G	1923	Furness	George James		Conservative
1923	G	1931	Viant	Samuel Philip		Labour
1931	G	1935	Tate	Mrs. Mavis Constance		Conservative
1935	G	1945	Viant	Samuel Philip		Labour

Notes: First returned at: B By-election, G General Election

Acton

Sir Harry Ernest Brittain (Conservative), was the son of Sheffield parents and was born in 1873. Educated at Repton and Worcester College Oxford, he took a Law Degree and was called to the Bar at the Inner Temple in 1897. However, he never practised, and instead became engaged in journalism and commerce. In time he became a director of numerous daily and weekly newspapers, including the *Illustrated London News*. He organised the first Imperial Press Conference in 1909, and soon afterwards established the Empire Press Union, which later became the Commonwealth Press Union, of which he became an Honorary Life Member. Its membership grew to include over 1,500 newspapers and news agencies throughout the Commonwealth and his name was perpetuated in the form of the annual Harry Brittain

Sir Harry Ernest Brittain MP, and Lady Brittain
US Library of Congress

Fellowship. He had close ties with the USA and was a member of the original Committee of Sulgrave Manor Board, which was set up in 1914 to commemorate 100 years of peace between Great Britain and the United States. He was engaged in several delegations as a member of the Executive of the Empire Parliamentary Association and in 1920 was made an Honorary Doctor of Letters at McGill University in Canada. Earlier, during the First World War, he had been employed on a mission to the USA and in 1917 founded the American Officers' Club. He was appointed Director of Intelligence at the National Service Department and from 1920-22 was also Chairman of the British International Association of Journalists. He was briefly Chairman of the Middlesex Conservative Associations in 1925/6. He died in 1974 six months after celebrating his centenary.

Sir Harry Brittain, the first Acton MP meeting Sir George Young, his successor 40 years later
Website: Sir George Young MP

James Frederick Shillaker (Labour), was elected in 1929 when he beat Brittain by nearly 500 votes and served as Acton's MP until 1931 when he too was defeated. Educated at Taplow Grammar School and at City of London College, he became a journalist but served as a Rifleman in the War between 1915 and 1917. After the ending of hostilities he was appointed Deputy Director for the Northern Division of the Ministry of Pensions in 1919, where he remained until 1923 when he went to work in the newly formed Labour Party Research Department, until his election as an MP in 1929. He died in 1949.

Hubert John Duggan (Conservative), took the seat in 1931 and remained its MP until his death in 1943. He was the stepson of the Tory grandee, Lord Curzon, his mother's second husband.[13] Born in 1904, he was educated at Eton and joined the Life Guards, in which he served from 1924 to 1928, and again during the Second World War from 1939 to 1943, being made Captain in 1940. He unsuccessfully contested East Ham South in 1929 before being elected at Acton in 1931, and from then until 1935 he was PPS to Euan Wallace, Civil Lord of the Admiralty.

Duggan was succeeded at the 1943 by-election by **Henry Carpenter Longhurst** (Conservative), who was born in 1909. Educated at Charterhouse School and at Clare College Cambridge, he was an author and journalist who was best known as a writer of books and newspaper articles about golf, notably a weekly column for *The Sunday Times*. He was only Acton's MP for a short while being defeated in 1945. He died in 1978.

Brentford & Chiswick

The first MP in 1918 was **Lieutenant-Colonel Walter Grant Peterson Morden** (Conservative), who served until 1931 when he retired. Born in 1880 and educated at the Collegiate Institute, Toronto, he lived his early life in Canada becoming an Honorary Lieutenant-Colonel in the Canadian Military Forces in 1914. He was a sometime Honorary Colonel of the 6th Duke of Connaught's Royal Canadian Hussars, and of the 4th Middlesex Cadet Battalion. He stayed closely associated with all things Canadian when he remained in Britain after the War, including being a founder and member of all Committees of the British Commonwealth Union, and a Life Governor of the Montreal General Hospital. In Britain he was made a Freeman of the City of London, was a Liveryman of the Shipwrights' Company[14], and a Buckinghamshire magistrate.

Harold Paton Mitchell (Conservative), was elected in 1931. Born in 1900 he was educated at Eton, the Royal Military College at Sandhurst, and University College Oxford. After his election he was made PPS to David Colville (Minister of Overseas Trade), serving in that role until 1935 when he performed a similar function for Ralph Assheton, the Minister of Labour and National Service from 1939 to 1942. During this period he was also the British Liaison Officer with the Polish forces from 1940-1. A landed Scot whose family seat was at Tulliallan Castle, Kincardine-on-Forth,

13 George Curzon (1859-1925) was a former Secretary of State for and Viceroy of India, Foreign Secretary and Leader of the House of Lords.The preferment of Stanley Baldwin over Curzon as Leader of the Conservative Party when Bonar Law died in 1923 was considered a surprise. A far right-winger, Curzon helped found the Anti Suffrage League in 1908, and refused to support the Qualification of Women Act introduced by the Coalition Government of which he was a member.
14 The Shipwrights Company is 59th in the order of seniority (fixed in 1515) of the 102 livery companies of the City of London, not having been granted livery itself until 1782. It is however incorporated 'by prescription', a legal acknowledgement that it existed before 1199. It is one of the larger companies, with over 400 liverymen and 250 freemen, whose qualification for admission is a professional maritime background.

Mitchell initially contested the local Scottish constituency of Clackmannan and East Stirlingshire in 1929 but was not successful. He remained MP for Brentford and Chiswick until his defeat in 1945. The author of books on skinning and on the Caribbean he entered academic life as Resident Professor of Latin-American Studies at Rollins College, Florida and was also a Lecturer at Stanford University (California) between 1959 and 1965, when he died.

Ealing

Sir Herbert Nield (Conservative), who had been the MP for the former County division of Ealing since 1906 was elected for the new borough seat in 1918, retiring in 1931. His principal biographical details are contained in Chapter 3

Sir Frank Bernard Sanderson (Conservative), who was born in 1880 and educated at Stowe School and Pembroke College, Oxford went into business in Hull and in 1904 founded Wray, Sanderson and Company, which specialised in crushing seeds for animal feed. He became chairman of the Hull based United Premier Oil and Cake Company, and of the Humber Fishing Company. During the First World War he was Controller of Trench Warfare, National Filling Factories and Stores at the Ministry of Munitions between 1916 and 1919, and afterwards advised on demobilisation. Created a baronet in 1920, he first entered the House at Darwen in 1922, representing the Lancashire division until 1923 when he was defeated, returning from 1924 to 1929 when he lost again. During this period he was a member of Parliamentary delegations to Poland and Canada. In 1945 Ealing was divided into East and West divisions and he became MP for the former, which he represented until 1950. He died in 1965.

Harrow

Sir Oswald Ernald Mosley MP
People's History Museum, Manchester

The infamous **Sir Oswald Ernald Mosley** (Conservative) was a strange and restless politician. His family were Anglo-Irish but his branch were prosperous landowners in Staffordshire. He was wounded during the War serving as Lieutenant in the Lancers between 1915 and 1919, and he married Lady Cynthia, the daughter of the 1st Marquis of Curzon in 1920. He was the youngest to take his seat in the Parliament of 1918 when he was only 21. He sat until 1924, but became an Independent in 1922 in opposition to the Coalition Government's oppression of Irish republicanism, and moved to Labour in 1923. He contested the Ladywood Division of Birmingham in 1924 where he opposed Neville Chamberlain in an energetic campaign with a knife-edge result in which Mosley was defeated by 77 votes. However, he was subsequently returned at a by-election in 1926 as Labour MP for the nearby West Midlands constituency of Smethwick, which he represented until 1931, serving in Ramsey MacDonald's Government as Chancellor of the Duchy of Lancaster for a year between 1929 and 1930, when he resigned over unemployment policy. He established the New Party in 1931 but after a tour of Germany and Italy became an admirer of fascist movements. In 1932 he founded the British Union of Fascists, popularly known as the Blackshirts, as a corps of black uniformed paramilitary stewards prevented disruption at his meetings. In 1933 his wife died of peritonitis leaving him free to marry his mistress, Diana Guinness in 1936, the ceremony taking place in the home of Joseph Goebels the Nazi propagandist who was in attendance. During the Second World War he was interned in Holloway prison, and afterwards re-formed the Fascist movement in various guises, seeking election to Parliament himself on a number of occasions, though never successfully, and usually recording derisory votes. Son of the 5th Baronet, also Sir Oswald, he was born in 1896 and educated at Winchester and at Sandhurst. He died in 1980

Major Isadore Salmon (Conservative), was a businessman who became the Managing Director of J. Lyons and Co., the High Street caterers[15]. He also sat on the LCC and was its Vice Chairman during his first year as an MP, in 1924/5.

15 From modest beginnings as a tea shop at 213 Piccadilly in 1894 and as a supplier of catering to the Newcastle Exhibition (UK), in 1887, J. Lyons and Co rapidly expanded to become the very first food empire, which, at its height, was the largest in Europe. In the process Lyons became a household name and the 'Joe Lyons' Corner Houses and teashops, with their 'Nippy' waitresses, caught the public imagination

He died in 1941 precipitating a Wartime by-election in December which was won by **Norman Adolph Henry Bower** (Conservative) when Labour declined to contest the seat due to the Party truce that was then in force. Born in 1907, educated at Rugby School and Wadham College Oxford, Bower was a lawyer who was called to the bar at the Inner Temple in 1935. His interest in politics started early when he contested West Bermondsey in 1931 and he followed this up with another failed attempt at Hammersmith North in 1935. His first successful election was as a Westminster City councillor in 1937 before finally moving into national politics at Harrow four years later. He retained his council seat until 1945 but during the Second World War served as a private in the Intelligence Corps and later joined the Foreign Office. After the War Bower was selected to fight the new Harrow West constituency where he was successful and which he held until 1951 when he died a few months before the General Election was called.

Spelthorne

Sir Philip Edward Pilditch (Conservative), was elected as the first Spelthorne MP in 1918. Born in 1861, he was educated at Cheveley Hall School, Mannamead and Kings College London. He was a man of many parts; an architect in the firm of Pilditch, Chadwick and Company, he also wrote about economics, publishing a book called 'Retrenchment' in 1923, and a history, including a 1929 publication entitled 'Elizabethan Plymouth', of his home town. His interest in politics first saw him contest, albeit unsuccessfully, the St Ives Division of Cornwall in 1906 but the following year he went onto the LCC. In December 1910 he failed to secure election at Islington East but remained an LCC councillor until 1917 and was Vice Chairman in 1912/13. During the War he was Founder and Treasurer of the Battalion Funds for the London, Middlesex and Surrey Regiments for which services he was knighted in 1918. He was made a Baron in 1929 remaining an MP until 1931. He died in 1948.

He was succeeded by **Sir Reginald Blaker** (Conservative), who remained MP until the end of the War when Labour took the seat for the only time. Born in 1900, Blaker was educated at Charterhouse School, and became a barrister at the Inner Temple in 1921. He also entered the Coldstream Guards (TA), rising to the rank of Major. He died in 1976.

Twickenham

Sir William Joynson-Hicks (Conservative), was Twickenham's first MP in 1918, although he had sat since 1911 for the Brentford constituency of which the new one was previously a part. His principal biographical details are contained in Chapter 3. Hicks was made Viscount Brentford in 1929 when he retired from the Commons, and this triggered a period in the representation of Twickenham that resulted in the election of no less than four new MPs within the space of six years.

He was initially succeeded by **Sir John Ferguson** (Conservative). He first entered politics as an unsuccessful Tory candidate at Hammersmith South in the General Election of May 1929. Born in 1870, Ferguson was a Scot who became a banker as well as being Chairman of the India Rubber, Gutta, Percha and Telegraph Works Company[16]. He was a Director of the Scottish Union and National Insurance Company[17], and of the British Shareholders' Trust. From 1925-7 he was President of the Institute of Bankers and a sometime Joint General Manager of Lloyds Bank. During the First War he was Assistant to the Surveyor-General of Supply at the War Office from 1917-18, and from 1918-19 was Chairman of Committee at the Ministry of Munitions. After the War he became Financial Adviser to the Ministry of Health and Housing, serving later as Chairman of the Russian Accounts Committee in 1920, and as a Member of the Unemployment Grants Committee. He died in 1932 shortly after his re-election the year before, and a by-election was called.

Following Ferguson's death in 1932, the by-election was won by **Hylton Ralph Murray-Philipson** (Conservative), a grandson of the 10th Baron Elibank. The Eton educated Scot was born in 1902, and went into business becoming Chairman of the North East Marine Engineering Company at Wallsend. He was also a County Councillor in Peebles from 1925-33, and as a member of the Royal Company of Archers he was part of the Kings Body Guard in Scotland. He assumed the name Murray in 1926, maintaining always his Scottish roots. He was Squadron Leader of the City of Edinburgh AAF and first contested a Parliamentary constituency at Peebles and South Midlothian in 1929. He was finally elected MP for Twickenham in 1932 but died two years later.

The 1934 by-election was won by **Brigadier-General Alfred Cecil Critchley CMG CBE DSO** (Conservative), who was born in 1890 near Calgary in Canada. He was educated in that country at St Bees and the Royal Military College, Kingston, and during the First World War joined the 7th Canadian Infantry receiving the DSO in 1916. A

16 In 1845 Charles Goodyear and Henry Bewley founded the Gutta Percha rubber Company in Silvertown and it was later a producer of telegraph wire insulant.
17 The Scottish Union and National Insurance Company was established in 1878 and acquired by the Norwich Union in 1959.

Brigadier Alfred Cecil Critchley MP
Wilkipedia

National Conservative he contested Gorton (Manchester) in 1929 and Islington East in 1931 before being elected at Twickenham in 1934. Remarkably he retired at the 1935 General Election, and went on to pursue a business career becoming Director-General of the British Overseas Airways Company[18] from 1943 to 1946, and Chairman of Skyways Limited from 1946 to 1954. He died in 1963.

Sir Edward Herbert Keeling MC (Conservative), whose first experience as a Parliamentary candidate came in 1931 when he unsuccessfully contested Southwark Central, succeeded Critchley in 1935 going on to represent the constituency for 15 years. The son of a clergyman, he was educated in Bradford and at University College, Oxford, after which he became a lawyer. During the First War he served in the Army in India and Mesopotamia, later escaping from capture whilst fighting as a Lieutenant Colonel in Turkey for which he was awarded the Military Cross. Although he qualified as a barrister he also went into business being a member of Lloyd's and Chairman of the Turkish Petroleum Company[19]. As Honorary Secretary-General of the Royal Academy International Exhibition of Persian Art, he consolidated his knowledge of the Middle East on which he became an authority. Amongst other interests he was a Vice-President of the Geographical Society, and Honorary Secretary of the British School of Archeology in Iraq. At home he was a member of the Westminster City Council (where he was Mayor in 1945/6), Chairman of the London Advisory Council on Smoke Abatement[20]; and an Executive Member of the National Trust[21]. He joined the RAF in 1939, and after his re-election at Twickenham in 1945 was a member of a Parliamentary delegation at the Conference of Dominion and US Parliamentarians held in Bermuda in 1946. He wrote about his escapades in Turkey and also of the Bolshevik Revolution in Russia. He died in 1954.

Uxbridge

The first MP after the War was **Sidney Cornwallis Peel** (Conservative Unionist), who was born in 1870, the son of the First Viscount Peel, a Liberal MP and former Speaker of the House of Commons whose grandfather was Sir Robert Peel, the Tory Prime Minister. Eton educated, he attended New College as well as Trinity Hall Oxford, and became a barrister at Lincolns Inn in 1898. He was Secretary to the Licensing Commission, and President of the Trust and Loan Company of Canada, as well as a Director of the National Bank of Egypt. He was also a Lieutenant in the Bedfordshire Yeomanry, being awarded the DSO during the Great War. He retired from politics in 1922, and for the whole of the period 1919 to 1938 was Chairman of the Export Credit Advisory Committee. He died in 1938.

Commander Charles Dennistoun Burney (Conservative), succeeded Peel in 1922. The oldest son of Admiral of the Fleet Sir Cecil Burney, Charles was born in 1888, and following a private education entered the Royal Navy in 1903 becoming a Midshipman in 1905. The inventor of the Patravane Explosive and Protector, he retired in 1917 and entered the world of politics. He died in 1968.

Maj. John Jestyn Llewellin MP
Wikipedia

Major John Jestyn Llewellin (Conservative), was MP from 1929 until 1945 when Labour took the seat for the first time. Born in 1893 he was Eton and Oxford (University College) educated, and went initially into the Army serving in France from 1915 to 1919. Returning from the War he trained to be a barrister, practising from 1921 and throughout his period in Parliament. He contested Southwark North in 1924 ,but was not elected until 1929 two years before he was appointed PPS to William Ormsby-Gore (Postmaster-General). From 1931-35 he served as PPS to the First Commissioner for Works. From 1935 to 1937 he was an Assistant Whip, and then until 1939 Civil Lord of the Admiralty. In the period 1931 to 1938 he maintained a significant interest in the military as TA Commander of the Dorset Heavy Brigade. During the Second World War Governments of Chamberlain and Churchill he held a number of posts that were key to the war effort including Parliamentary Secretary to the Ministry of Supply (1939-40) and Minister of Aircraft Production under Lord Beaverbrook (1940/1), which, given a significant RAF presence in Uxbridge, was perhaps a happy coincidence. He was War Transport Minister (1941/2), President of the Board of Trade (February 1942), Minister of Food Supply in Washington (1942/3) and Minister of Food (1943-5), a position he also held in the Caretaker

18 BOAC was founded in 1939 by Neville Chamberlain's Conservative government and incorporated in January 1944.
19 The Iraq Petroleum Company Limited was incorporated in 1911 as the African and Eastern Concessions Limited. Its name was changed to Turkish Petroleum Company Limited in 1912 and to Iraq Petroleum Company Limited in 1929.
20 Established in 1912
21 The National Trust was founded in 1895 to act as a guardian for the nation in the acquisition and protection of threatened coastline, countryside and buildings.

Government that preceded the 1945 General Election. Despite these ministerial appointments he was never a member of the Cabinet, and lost his seat after the War. From 1945 to 1953 Llewellin was President of the Royal Society for the Prevention of Accidents, and after the Tories were returned to Government he was appointed Governor-General of Rhodesia and Nyasaland where he remained from 1951 to his death in 1957.

Willesden East

Sir Harry Mallaby-Deeley MP

Sir Harry Mallaby-Deeley (Conservative), who had been the MP for Harrow since January 1910 was selected to fight the newly created Willesden East constituency in 1918 and remained its MP until 1922 when he resigned his seat. His principal biographical details are contained in Chapter 3.

A by-election was held in March 1923 resulting in victory by a substantial margin for **Harcourt 'Crinks' Johnstone** (Liberal), who secured 60% of the vote in a straight fight with the Conservative. Johnstone was born in 1895 and educated at Eton and Balliol College, Oxford. During the First World War he served on the General Staff of the Rifle Brigade from 1914 to 1919 and went into politics afterwards. He had also contested Willesden East in 1922, and was only briefly its MP from 1923 to 1924 when he lost following the decision of the Labour Party to field a candidate who polled almost as many votes as Johnstone. He contested Eastbourne unsuccessfully in 1925, followed by Westbury in 1927 and 1929. He was finally elected in 1931 as MP for South Shields, but was defeated by Labour in 1935. In 1940, when there was a pact amongst the main parties not to contest wartime by-elections, he was returned unopposed for the then marginal Liberal seat of Middlesbrough West. He died in March 1945.

In 1924 the seat was won by **Lieutenant-Colonel George Frederick Stanley** (Conservative), the sixth son of the 16th Earl of Derby, a Tory grandee. Born in 1872 and Winchester-educated, he attended the Royal Military Academy before entering the Royal Artillery. He served in the South Africa War and in the First World War was awarded the Legion of Honour and the Belgian Order of the Crown. He was first elected an MP for Preston in January 1910, and the following year was appointed PPS to Andrew Bonar Law, Leader of the Opposition, and became a Tory Whip in 1913. When Lloyd-George became Prime Minister at the head of the Wartime Coalition in 1916, he was appointed PPS to his brother, the 17th Earl of Derby who was the Secretary of State for War. In 1919 he was made Head of His Majesty's Household, and two years' later Financial Secretary to the War Office. In 1922 he was made Under-Secretary of State at the Home Department, but lost his seat at the General Election in 1923. He fought the 1923 Willesden by-election won by Johnstone, but recaptured the seat in 1924, after which he was made Parliamentary Secretary to the Minister of Pensions. He was knighted and appointed Governor of Madras in 1929 when he retired from the Commons. He served in India until 1934 and died four years later.

Lt Col. Sir George Frederick Stanley MP
Painting by Oswald Birley
Gov. Museum Chennai, India - Wilkipedia

The seat was still vacant when the 1929 General Election was called. It was won then by **Daniel Gerald Somerville** (Conservative), an Edinburgh man born in 1879. Educated at Watson's School and Heriot Watt College, he became a Civil Engineer who owned his own construction company. He was previously MP for Barrow (Lancashire) between 1922 and 1924 when he lost the seat and was out of the Commons for five years. He died in 1938, causing a by-election.

The by-election was won by **Samuel Schofield Hammersley** (Conservative), who defeated a Labour nominee, the only other candidate to contest the seat. No Liberal candidate was put up, and the comparison with the 1923 by-election is very instructive of the political trends of the time. In 1923 the Liberal share of the vote had been over 60% whilst at the 1935 General election it was a mere 7%, indicative of the massive decline in the Party's support that took place in the Inter-War period. Hammersley, the son of an Oldham cotton spinner, was born in 1892 and enjoyed the benefits of a University education at Kings College Cambridge. Soon afterwards, however, he was drawn into the Great War serving in Gallipoli with the East Lancashire Regiment, and then in France between 1915 and 1918 with the Royal Tank Corps. After the War he became Managing Director of S. Noton Ltd, and contested his first Parliamentary Election in 1923 when he was defeated at Stockport. However, at the following year's General Election he was returned for the Cheshire borough seat, retaining it until 1935 when he temporarily retired. After his 1945 defeat at Willesden East he tried in 1950, again without success, and never resumed his Parliamentary career. He became Chairman of the Anglo-Israel Association in 1951 holding that position for twelve years. He died in 1965.

Willesden West

Colonel Charles Pinkham (Conservative), was MP for Willesden West from 1918 until 1922 when he retired. He was born in 1853 at nearby Brondesbury and joined the County Volunteers in that district. He was Chairman of Willesden District Council and a Middlesex Alderman, chairing the County Council between 1927 and 1930. He was also a Middlesex JP and Deputy Lieutenant and, from 1920 to 1931, was High Sheriff of the County. He died in 1938.

George James Furness (Conservative) held the seat for his Party in 1922 but lost it a year later. Like his predecessor he was also a contractor but in railway construction, a business established by his father. Born in 1868, George was educated at King Williams College on the Isle of Man, became a qualified Civil Engineer at the Crystal Palace School, and joined the family business, which mainly involved the construction of foreign railways. For 18 years he was a Middlesex County councillor, but he made it to Westminster in 1922 when he became MP for part of his home borough. After the 1923 defeat he resumed his business career, though in 1936 he was appointed High Sheriff of the County. Unfortunately his tenure was brief because he died the same year.

Samuel Philip Viant MP
Peoples History Museum Manchester

Samuel Philip Viant (Labour) who sat on Willesden District Council was the first Socialist to be returned for a West Middlesex constituency. He was MP for Willesden West, initially from 1923 to 1929, and then again from 1935 until 1959 when he retired. Viant was born in 1882 at Plymouth where he was educated at the Devonport High Grade School. He later attended Ruskin College but from school became a joiner and a foreman in that trade. He was an active trade unionist and became Vice Chairman of the National Conciliation Board for the Building Industry, which considered issues of pay. In the Labour Government from 1929 to 1931 he was Assistant Postmaster- General. He died in 1964.

Between 1931 and 1935 Willesden West was represented by **Mrs Mavis Constance Tate** (National Conservative), a grand-niece of Quintin Hogg (founder of the Regent Street Polytechnic) and a cousin of the then Lord Hailsham, a recently ennobled MP for St Marylebone - see earlier part of this chapter). Born in 1893 she was Christened Maybird, a name she changed to Mavis in 1930, the year before she stood for Parliament. She was educated privately and at St Pauls Girls School, and though twice married was also twice divorced at a time when such things were generally frowned upon. She stood down in 1935. She died in 1947.

"What's that disturbance in the market place?"
"It's a mass demonstration of the women who've changed their minds since the morning and want to alter their voting -papers."

A cartoon from the 1918 General Election that makes fun of the general male attitude towards the franchise for women. Representation of the People Acts in 1918 and 1928 eventually granted a vote to all women over the age of 21.
People's History Museum, Manchester

Top Left: Bedford Square's splendid Georgian architecture was host to some influential people. It was in Holborn, a wealthy and steadfastly Conservative seat through the inter-war years. **John Nelson**

Top Right: Praed Street divided the Paddington Constituencies and gave on to St Marylebone at the junction with Edgware Road. The famous Station and the St Mary's Hospital are in this street. **Gordon Rushton**

Left: Birkenhead Street was transferred from the abolished St Pancras South Constituency to the extended South East constituency in 1918. **Gordon Rushton**

Above: Hendon Town Hall was built in 1901 from designs by T H Watson following the pre-Renaissance manner. This handsome building did the Borough great service until the formation of the Greater London Council in 1965. It is listed Grade II and is used as the Council Chamber for the London Borough of Barnet. **John Nelson**

Left: Grafton Road, Kentish Town provided neat homes for the middle classes in this part of the politically 'marginal' St Pancras North constituency. **John Nelson**

North London and North Middlesex

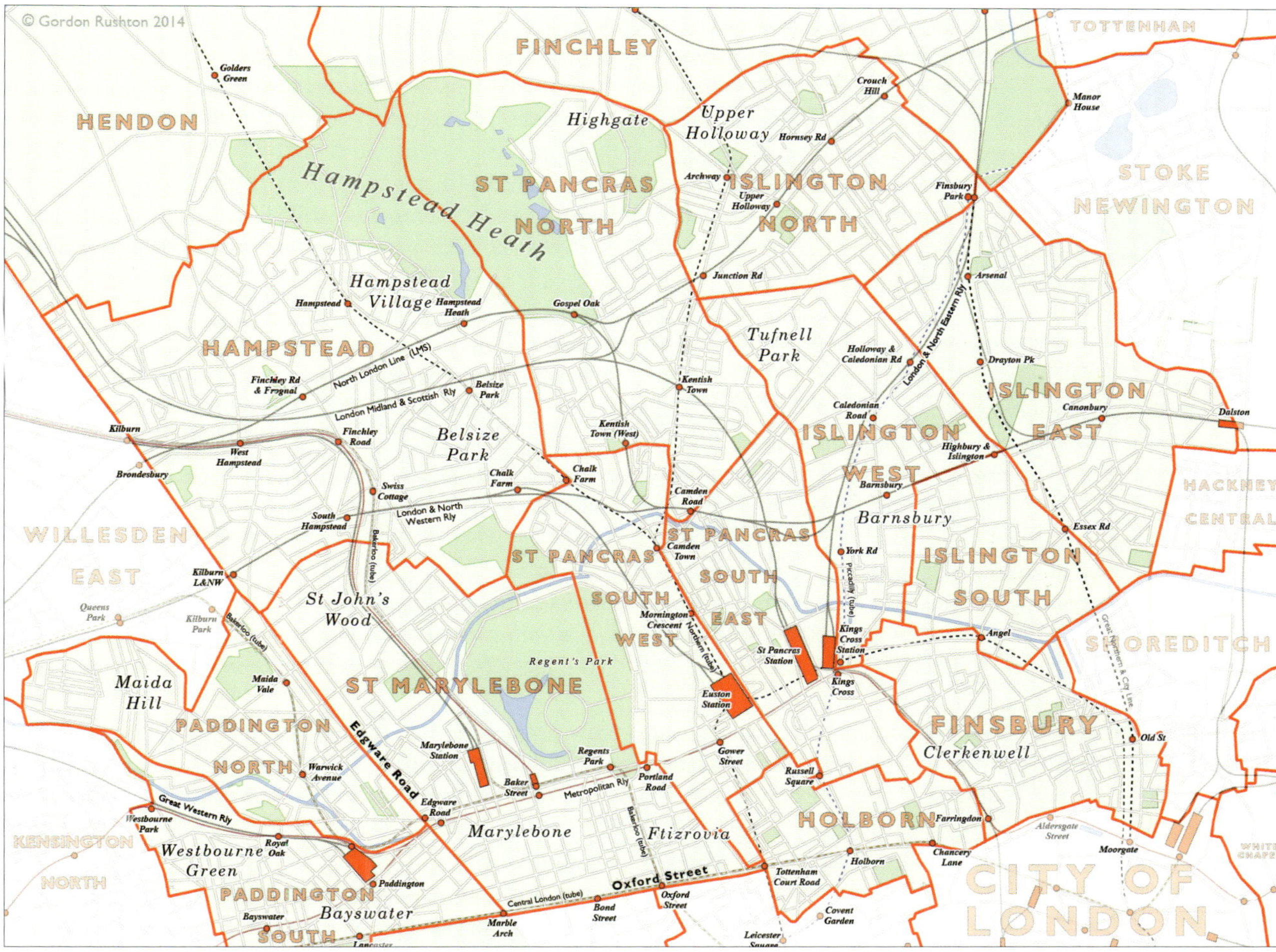

The effect of the redistribution of population can be seen in the changes of constituency boundary. The outer boroughs gained constituencies and Hendon and Finchley are added to this map. Their extent can better been seen on the NE London map on Page 254. To answer the rise in population in the outer areas, the Northern, Piccadilly and Bakerloo tube lines were all extended, and the London and North Western Railway, later LMS, electrified.

In this chapter North London includes Holborn, St Pancras, Finsbury, Islington, Hampstead, Finchley, and Hendon, where after the 1918 boundary review the total number of seats remained at 12. However, the balance changed as the outer suburbs increased at the expense of those closer to central London. Although **Holborn** and **Islington** boroughs remained unchanged, with one and four seat respectively, **Finsbury** was reduced from two to single-member status, and St Pancras from 4 to 3. Further out, **Hampstead** was unaltered, but the area beyond it, formerly in Harrow and classified in previous chapters as West Middlesex, spawned two extra North London seats.

St Pancras North combined with the northern parts it already held (Dartmouth Park, Kentish Town and Gospel Oak) with southern parts of Camden Town newly acquired from St Pancras East . The former South constituency was abolished and this resulted in even larger scale changes to the two remaining constituencies. **St Pancras South East** comprised Kings Cross and Corum Fields from the former St Pancras South, which were combined with St Pancras and Somers Town from the former East division. Further down the Euston Road, the district embracing London University from South division was combined with the whole of the former West division, to include Euston and eastern parts of Regents Park, Primrose Hill, Mornington Crescent, and Chalk Farm in a new **St Pancras South West.**

Whilst all four Islington seats and Hampstead remained unchanged, beyond them two new seats were created from the former West and North Middlesex seats of Harrow and Hornsey. **Finchley** comprised the Urban Districts of Finchley and Friern Barnet (both established in 1895), extending from Friern Barnet in the north to Childs Hill and Hampstead Garden Suburb in the south. Other communities included in the district were: Church End, Coppetts Wood (South Friern), Hampstead Garden Suburb (established in 1907), Oakley Park, and Woodside Park. Finchley became a municipal borough in 1933, but Friern Barnet UDC remained. **Hendon** was taken from Harrow and incorporated a large constituency that included: Pinner, Stanmore, Edgware, Kingsbury, and Golders Green. It was officially described as comprising Kingsbury UDC, and the Hendon UDC and RDC. Other communities included: Burnt Oak, Childs Hill,

Colindale, and Mill Hill. Hendon was made an Urban District in 1895, and after Edgware was added in 1931 it became a municipal borough the following year heralding bigger electoral changes that would occur at the next re-distribution.

'Finchelee' was first recorded in 1208 and meant, "woodland clearing frequented by finches". 'Heandun', on the other hand meant, "place at the high hill" and dated from around AD 975. From the Middle Ages onwards, successful City people wanted to live in pleasant countryside within range of London. Finchley Manor House had a long succession of such owners, and Hendon School occupies the site where the famous 16th century map maker John Norden lived. In 1807 Mill Hill School opened in a house on the Ridgeway, but the area remained agricultural until the late 19th century, with production geared to London's needs. Cattle were brought in by long-distance drovers to Barnet's markets and fairs and sold on to London dealers. Edgware too had a fair in the 18th and 19th centuries, while East Finchley had a major pig market. Most of the fields became devoted to hay for London's ever-expanding horse population and the hay harvest witnessed huge influxes of itinerant harvesters. As suburbs came closer some farms turned to milk production.

In the 1820s a new trunk road was built to link the Great North Road at Finchley with London's West End. The Finchley Road opened about a decade before the coming of railways ended the coaching era, but created two locally important junctions at Golders Green Crossroads and Tally Ho Corner, Finchley. The Welsh Harp reservoir was begun in the 1830s by damming the Silk Stream and Brent River, and in 1850 the first railway arrived in the shape of the Great Northern main line, running up through Friern (and New) Barnet. Next, in the 1860s, came the Midland mainline through Hendon and Mill Hill, and the Great Northern suburban lines through Finchley to Barnet, and to Edgware via Mill Hill. London had always expanded in rings, and since areas further in were not yet developed, these lines stimulated change only slowly at first. Later when a new Underground line to Golders Green opened in 1907, a new suburb developed simultaneously. During the First World War such development stopped, but in the 1920s the Northern Line line was extended onwards, through Hendon to Edgware; again housing spread concurrently. Hampstead Garden Suburb, straddling Hendon and Finchley constituencies, was started in 1907 and grew in the interwar years.

The North Circular Road (A406) was completed through New Southgate in 1933, and at the same time plans were laid and works were begun for extensions of the Northern and Piccadilly tube lines. The Northern Line's 'Northern Heights' extensions were ambitious and were much altered by the onset of the second World War and its aftermath. The Piccadilly Line, although lying just east of the borough, speeded the urbanisation of East Barnet. The extension came about in an interesting way, which is described in Chapter 19. Trams gave way to trolleybuses and then to motor buses, but the outbreak of the war in 1939 halted further tube extensions, and the imposition of the Green Belt immediately after the War halted all further major suburban development in this outer fringe area of London.

General Election Results in the Inter-War Years by % majority

Constituency	Pre 1918*	1918	1922	1923	1924	1929	1931	1935
Holborn	*C*	*C73*	*C41*	*C34*	*C51 +*	*C31*	*C69*	*C46 +*
Finsbury	*1xC 1xL*	*C28*	*C14*	*Lab9*	*Lab3*	*Lab28*	*Nlab28*	*Lab12*
St. Pancras South East	*1xLU 1xC 1xL*	*C10*	*C17*	*Lab4*	*C9*	*Lab10*	*C35*	*C7*
St. Pancras South West	*1xLU 1xC 1xL*	*C20*	*C16*	*C11*	*C16*	*Lab20*	*C43*	*C10*
St. Pancras North	*L*	*C9*	*C4*	*Lab11*	*C3*	*Lab9*	*C29*	*C11*
Islington East	*Shared C/L*	*C18*	*C15*	*L6*	*C12*	*Lab4 +*	*C35*	*C13*
Islington North	*C*	*C49*	*C19*	*C2*	*C9*	*Lab7*	*C32*	*C9 -*
Islington South	*Shared C/L*	*C8*	*C3*	*Lab1*	*Lab7*	*Lab15*	*C25*	*Lab5*
Islington West	*L*	*C22*	*C4*	*Lab11*	*Lab*	*Lab28*	*C18*	*Lab10*
Hampstead	*C*	*C51*	*C37*	*C17*	*C58*	*C37*	*C74*	*C55 +*
Finchley		*C51*	*C6*	*L9*	*C17*	*C13*	*C68*	*C43*
Hendon		*C57*	*C42*	*C23*	*C45*	*C27*	*C62*	*C39*
C/NLab	*7*	*12*	*12*	*5*	*9 +*	*4*	*12*	*9 - ++*
L	*5*	*0*	*0*	*2*	*0*	*0*	*0*	*0*
Lab	*0*	*0*	*0*	*5*	*3*	*8 +*	*0*	*3*

Key: C = Conservative; L = Liberal; N = NationaL; Lab = Labour; + = Party that won seat at General Election held by-election in same Parliament; - = Party that won seat at General Election lost by-election to main opposition Party in same Parliament. *These numbers are averages for all General Elections between 1885 and 1910 inclusive.

The Politics of North London

During the Inter-War period North London constituencies reflected the same Conservative dominance as the nation as a whole, and the table shows in particular the decline of the Liberal Party, which, before 1918 had won, on average, 5 seats at each General Election but which, thereafter, won only 2 in all General Elections combined. Labour won 19 MPs but the Conservatives strengthened their pre-War position, when on average they won 7 seats in the area, winning an average of 10 each time afterwards, or 69 in total.

Because the total number of seats in North London did not increase after 1918, it can be seen that the Tories did very well. How much this was due to changes in the political mood, and how much to boundary changes is difficult to assess, but the loss of inner-London seats and the creation of new ones in the middle class suburbs had an important impact on all three political parties. The Liberals lost out because seats that they had held were merged, whilst the Conservatives did well in the new, largely middle class seats that were created in suburbs like Hendon and Finchley. At the same time Labour benefited from the increasingly working class composition of the resident populations left behind in the central boroughs with declining electorates. The middle class sections of the population in Islington and StPancras also began to reduce, and Labour started to make significant inroads in these constituencies.

Holborn and Hampstead retained their total Tory dominance, neither showing any signs of an erosion of support in the Inter-War years. In Holborn's case this may have been partly due to a business vote (mainly lawyers) that even by 1945 represented an eighth of the electorate. However, Finsbury and the adjoining, socially similar constituencies of Islington South and West, all began to move away from the Conservatives who had enjoyed reasonable success there before 1918. Labour took all three as early as 1923, and won them at every subsequent election except 1931. Elsewhere the three St Pancras seats, together with Islington East and North, remained generally Tory, probably because they retained an important residential middle class, although Labour did manage to win each of them at least once, indicating that the underlying base of Conservative support was not especially solid. The Tories did find strong support in the new suburbs, although the Liberals briefly held Finchley from 1923-4 in a period when Labour did not contest the seat.

MPs for Holborn and St Pancras

From	*at*	*To*	*Surname*	*First Names*	*Constituency*	*Party*
1918	*G*	*1928*	*Remnant*	*Sir James Farquharson*	*Holborn*	*Conservative*
1928	*B*	*1935*	*Bevan*	*Stuart James*		*Conservative*
1935	*G*	*1945*	*Tasker*	*Sir Robert Inigo (Major)*		*Conservative*
1918	*G*	*1923*	*Lorden*	*Sir John William*	*St Pancras North*	*Conservative*
1923	*G*	*1924*	*Marley*	*James*		*Labour*
1924	*G*	*1929*	*Fraser*	*William Jocelyn Ian (Captain)*		*Conservative*
1929	*G*	*1931*	*Marley*	*James*		*Labour*
1931	*G*	*1936*	*Fraser*	*Ian (Captain)*		*Conservative*
1937	*B*	*1945*	*Grant-Ferris*	*Sir Robert G (Wing Cmdr)*		*Conservative*
1918	*G*	*1923*	*Hopkins*	*John Wells Wainwright*	*St Pancras South East*	*Conservative*
1923	*G*	*1924*	*Romeril*	*Herbert George*		*Labour*
1924	*G*	*1929*	*Hopkins*	*John Wells Wainwright*		*Conservative*
1929	*G*	*1931*	*Romeril*	*Herbert George*		*Labour*
1931	*G*	*1945*	*Beit*	*Sir Alfred Lane*		*Conservative*
1918	*G*	*1929*	*Barnett*	*Sir Richard Whieldon (Major)*	*St Pancras South West*	*Conservative*
1929	*G*	*1931*	*Carter*	*William*		*Labour*
1931	*G*	*1945*	*Mitcheson*	*Sir George Gibson*		*Conservative*

Notes: First returned at: B By-election, G General Election

Holborn

Sir James Farquharson Remnant (Conservative), sat for Holborn from 1900 until 1928 when he was elevated to the peerage. His main biographical details are included in Chapter 3.

He was succeeded at the 1928 by-election by **Stuart James Bevan** (Conservative), who was educated at St Pauls

School and later became a barrister. He was called to the bar of the Middle Temple in 1895 and in 1919 became a Kings Councillor, joining the Western Circuit.

He died in 1935 and was succeeded at the General Election by **Major Sir Robert Tasker** (Conservative) who was formerly the MP for Islington East from 1924 to 1929. His full biographical details can be found later in this chapter.

St Pancras North

Sir John William Lorden (Conservative), was MP from 1918 until 1923. Born at Colchester in 1862 and educated privately, he joined his father's building construction business[22], which he subsequently inherited. He was a member of Wandsworth Borough Council from 1900 to 1921, and from 1910 to 1913 represented the area on the LCC. He was twice Mayor of the Borough, first in 1903/4 and then in 1907/8, the year after, he was made an Alderman. He was a member of the Metropolitan Water Board, the Wandsworth Board of Guardians and sat as a magistrate. He lost his seat in 1923 and died in 1944.

He was succeeded in 1923 by **James Marley** (Labour), a Scot from Shotts, Lanarkshire, who became a teacher. When a Master at Haverstock Hill School, he was also the Joint Secretary and Founder of the Teachers' Labour League, a Trade Union for socialist teachers. He was defeated in 1924, re-elected in 1929 and beaten again in 1931.

Captain (William Jocelyn) Ian Fraser (Conservative), was Marley's opponent on three occasions. Firstly he defeated him by a majority of less than 800 votes in 1924. In 1929 he lost to Marley by a margin of over 3,000, but was returned with a comfortable victory in 1931, and remained the MP until 1936 when he was appointed a governor of the BBC. Born in 1897, the son of a South African man from Johannesburg, Fraser was educated at Marlborough School, and at the Royal Military College. During the Great War he served as Captain in the 1st Battalion of the King's Shropshire Light Infantry, and was subsequently attached to the 1st/4th Gloucestershire Regiment. He lost his sight in action and in 1921 became Chairman of St Dunstan's School for the Blind, founded in 1915 to help servicemen blinded during the First World War. The following year he was elected as a County Councillor for the St Pancras North Division, which ward he represented until 1925 when he stood down after his election as the area's MP in 1924.

Wing Commander Robert Grant-Ferris (Conservative), who was from the manor house of Cotteridge, near Kings Norton, Birmingham, was MP from February 1937, when he won a by-election, until 1945 when he was defeated. Born in 1907 and educated at Douai School Woolhampton[23], he joined the family business of estate agents and surveyors. Between 1933 and 1936 he was a member of Birmingham City Council, but meanwhile he studied law and was called to the Bar in 1936, the year after he had first dipped his toe into national politics at a by-election at Wigan, where he was defeated. During the Second World War he served in the Air Force (with which he had had a connection since 1933) in Malta (where he organised the air defence of the island) and in Egypt. He was demobilised in 1943, and returned to the House as PPS to Mr. W.S. Morrison, Minister of Town and Country Planning. During this period he was also the vice Chairman of the London Conservative Union. After his defeat in 1945 he contested Wandsworth Central unsuccessfully, in both 1950 and 1951 before returning to the Commons as MP for Nantwich, a constituency created in 1955. By then he described himself as a barrister, farmer, and land and property owner. He was elected Vice-President of the Inland Waterways Association in 1966, and was chairman of the original All-party Waterways Committee. He retired in February 1974 having served four years as Chairman of Ways and Means (Deputy Speaker), and was created a life peer as Lord Harvington of Nantwich in Cheshire. He died in 1997.

St Pancras South East

John Wells Wainwright Hopkins (Conservative), sat initially between 1918 and 1923, when he was defeated, and then again between 1924 and 1929 when he retired. He was born in 1863 and became a Civil Engineer. He first entered politics in December 1910, when he unsuccessfully contested the St Pancras East constituency and during the 1914-18 War was Chairman of the Welfare Committee for South American Volunteers.

Herbert George Romeril (Labour), was also MP for St Pancras South East on two occasion: firstly in 1923 /1924, and secondly from 1929 to 1931. Born in 1881, he was a clerk in the Railway Clearing House offices at Eversholt Street, Euston, (picture opposite) and an active trade unionist[24]. He became President of the Railway Clerks' Association[25] and

22 The firm of WH Lorden still exists at 107 Trinity Road, Tooting.
23 A Roman Catholic Benedictine school expelled from Douai, France in 1903 and re-established near Reading.
24 The Railway Clearing House was established in the 1880s to facilitate inter-company payments and relationships.
25 The Railway Clerks Association was established in London in 1865 and was the first white-collar trade union. It became the

Eversholt House, in Eversholt Street, the 1849 built HQ of the Railway Clearing House (RCH), where Romeril worked, that arranged inter-railway cash settlements, and thus it was a considerable employer of clerical labour for many years. The RCH issued detailed maps of junctions, showing railway ownership, thus permitting the accurate calculation of revenues for allocation purposes. Life became easier when the railways were grouped into four big conglomerates, but upon Nationalisation in 1947 the RCH's role diminished and it was closed in 1954 and used for railway offices. **Gordon Rushton**

entered politics through that route, the office in which he worked being located in the constituency for which he became the MP. He was also Chairman of the Metropolitan Branch of the Independent Labour Party. He died in 1963.

Sir Alfred Lane Beit MP
The Irish Museum

Sir Alfred Lane Beit (Conservative) was MP from 1931 until 1945. Born in 1903 and educated at Eton and Christ Church Oxford, in 1939 he married Clementine Mitford. In 1928 / 1929 he was Private Secretary to Sir Arthur Steel-Maitland (Minister of Labour during the General Strike) and became a baronet in 1930 a year after he had first contested the constituency unsuccessfully. He held the seat until he was defeated in 1945. During the War he was a Squadron Leader in the RAF Voluntary Reserve and served briefly as PPS to Sir Oliver Stanley when the latter was Secretary of the Colonies in 1944. He died in 1994 at the age of 101; the longest living of all the London MPs to have been elected in the whole period covered by this book.

St Pancras South West

Major Sir Richard Whieldon Barnet (Conservative) was MP from 1918 to 1929. The son of a Doctor from County Down and great grandson of the eminent potter, Thomas Whieldon, who was a partner of Josiah Wedgwood and High Sheriff of Staffordshire in 1787, Barnet was initially MP for Islington West between 1916 and 1918 and his main biographical details may be found in Chapter 3.

William Carter (Labour) won the seat in 1929. He was born in 1867 and became a railway worker having initially been employed as a coal miner. He was a Railway Trade Union official and from 1919 to 1920 was Mayor of St Pancras. A Member of the Metropolitan Water Board, he only sat for one term as an MP and was defeated in 1931. He died in 1940.

Sir George Gibson Mitcheson (Conservative) was born in 1883, the son of a solicitor from Heckmondwike in Yorkshire's West Riding. Educated privately he too became a solicitor but became prominent as Joint Managing Director

---

Transport Salaried Staffs Association in 1951.

of the Standard Industrial Trust Limited and the Vice President of the National Association of Building Societies. In addition he was Chairman of the Hosa Research Laboratories, a member of the Worshipful Company of Gardeners, Vice Chairman of the National Temperance Hospital[26] and of the Constitutional Club. A National Conservative he contested

MPs for Finsbury, and Islington

From	at	To	Surname	First Names	Constituency	Party
1918	G	1923	Archer-Shee	Sir Martin (Major)	Finsbury	Conservative Unionist
1923	G	1931	Gillett	Sir George Masterman		Labour
1931	G	1935	Gillett	Sir George Masterman		National Labour
1935	G	1945	Woods	Reverend George Saville		Labour
1918	G	1922	Smallwood	Edward	Islington East	Liberal
1922	G	1923	Hudson	Sir Austin Uvedale M (Capt)		Conservative
1923	G	1924	Carr	Arthur Strettell Comyns		Liberal
1924	G	1929	Tasker	Robert Inigo		Conservative Unionist
1929	G	1931	Bentham	Dr Ethel		Labour
1931	B	1931	Manning	Dame Elizabeth Leah		Labour
1931	G	1945	Cazalet-Keir	Miss Thelma		Conservative
1918	G	1923	Moore	Sir Newton James	Islington North	Conservative
1923	G	1929	Cowan	Sir (William) Henry		Conservative
1929	G	1931	Young	Robert Stanley		Labour
1931	G	1937	Goodman	Albert William (Col)		Conservative
1937	B	1945	Haden-Guest	Dr Leslie Haden		Labour
1918	G	1922	Higham	Sir Charles Frederick	Islington South	Conservative
1922	G	1923	Garland	Charles Samuel		Conservative
1923	G	1931	Cluse	William Sampson		Labour
1931	G	1935	Howard	Tom Forest		Conservative
1935	G	1945	Cluse	William Sampson		Labour
1918	G	1922	Elliott	Sir George Samuel	Islington West	Conservative
1922	G	1923	Despencer-Robertson	James St. George (Major)		Conservative
1923	G	1931	Montague	William		Labour
1931	G	1935	Donner	Patrick William (Squadron Leader)		Conservative
1935	G	1945	Montague	William		Labour

Notes: First returned at: B By-election, G General Election

Bradford South in 1923 and 1924 and was MP for St Pancras North from 1931 until 1945 when he retired from politics. He died ten years later.

MPs for Finsbury, and Islington

Finsbury

Finsbury was a seat that moved from Tory to Labour during the Inter-War years but was also one in which National Labour saw success in 1931. **Major Sir Martin Archer-Shee** (Conservative) was its MP until 1923. He was previously MP for Finsbury Central from 1910 to 1918 and his biographical details are contained in Chapter 3.

He was succeeded by **Sir George Masterman Gillett** (Labour), a Quaker who defected to National Labour in 1931 beating off a challenge from his former Party to remain Finsbury's MP until defeated in 1935. He first contested the seat unsuccessfully in 1922. Born in 1870, Gillett was the son of a banker who was educated by the Society of Friends in Scarborough and then in Paris. He too became a banker joining the family Discount Bank in Lombard Street in 1894. He was elected a Finsbury Borough councillor in 1900 and served until 1906. He was a London County Councillor from 1910 to 1922 and then an Alderman. In MacDonald's Labour Government of 1929 he was Secretary of the Overseas

26 The temperance movement believed that the then prevalent practice of using and providing alcohol in hospitals was impairing staff efficiency and patients' treatment. The London Temperance Hospital opened at 112 Gower Street in 1873 and changed its name to the National Temperance Hospital in 1932.

Trade Department and in the National Government was briefly Parliamentary Secretary of the Ministry of Transport between September and November 1931. He died in 1939.

The Reverend George Saville Woods (Labour) defeated Gillett in 1935. Born in 1886, the son of Thomas Woods, he was educated at Handsworth College Birmingham and Manchester College, Oxford after which he became a Presbyterian Minister. From 1932 to 1934 he was President of the Yorkshire Unitarian Union and also became active in the Co-operative Movement being a member of its Central Board and a Director of the Co-operative Press. He became President of the Society and was active in the Labour Party, initially in Taunton when he was a minister, then in York where he was Chairman of the City Party and a local councillor. He contested Taunton in 1918 and 1924, later trying for the Yorkshire constituency of Barkston Ash where he was unsuccessful in 1929 and 1931. He served as Finsbury's MP from 1935 to 1945 when he sought nomination at Mossley, Lancashire, a seat closer to the Cooperative Society's Manchester Head Quarters. He remained MP there until 1950 when the constituency was renamed Droylesden, which he represented until his retirement in 1951. He died soon afterwards.

Islington East

This constituency was unusual for the period in that three out of its seven MPs were women. Starting out as a seat that changed hands between Tory and Liberal Parties it moved to Labour in 1929 but the split in the party returned the seat to the Tory fold in 1931.

Edward Smallwood (Liberal) was MP from 1918 until 1922, having been first returned at a by-election in 1917. His biographical details are to be found in Chapter 3.

He was succeeded by **Sir Austin Uvedale Morgan Hudson** (Conservative) who was MP for less than a year. Born in 1897, the son of Leopold Hudson, he was an Eton-educated, Sandhurst-trained man who became a newspaper proprietor and Director of Morgan Brothers, a publishing company. After his election in 1922 he was briefly PPS to the Minister of Transport, Sir J. Baird. In 1924 he was returned for the neighbouring seat of Hackney North, which he represented until 1945 and was successively PPS at the Ministry of Labour (1925); assistant Whip (1931); Lord Commissioner of the Treasury (1931-5); Parliamentary Secretary at the Ministry of Transport (1935-9); Civil Lord of the Admiralty (1939-42); and lastly Parliamentary Secretary at the Ministry of Fuel and Power in the short-lived pre-1945 Election Conservative Government. He lost his seat but returned in 1950 as MP for Lewisham North, which he represented until 1956 when he died.

Arthur Stretell Comyns Carr (Liberal) was MP briefly in 1923 when he rose to the top of the pile in a three-horse race. Such was the volatility of three party politics that he came third in 1924, which election saw the Labour candidate take second place and his own vote slump to around half the level of the winner.

That was **Robert Inigo Tasker** (Conservative Unionist) who had failed in Bethnal Green North East the previous year. Born the son of a Dorset man in 1866 and educated at Ardingly College, he became a Quantity Surveyor. From 1885 until 1920 he was in the Volunteer and Territorial Army Forces. He was a magistrate for the County of London and a member of the Paviors', Fanmakers' and Gardeners' Companies[27], being a Master of the latter in1908/9. He became a councillor on the LCC in 1910. Born in 1882, he died in 1965.

Dr Ethel Bentham MP
Spartacus Educational

He was MP until 1929 when he was defeated by **Dr. Ethel Bentham** (Labour) who was MP until 1931. Miss Bentham was a Dubliner, born in 1861 and educated at the City's Alexandra School and College. She attended the Royal Free Hospital School of Medicine for Women and Brussels University, becoming a Doctor of medicine in 1895 and was a General Practitioner in Newcastle for 13 years before moving to London where she was politically active. She was a member of Kensington Borough Council from 1913 to 1926 and became one of the first women magistrates. She was elected to the National Executive Committee of the Labour Party in 1918 and was intermittently a member for most of the next 13 years. She contested Islington East unsuccessfully in the three General Elections that preceded 1929 but died in 1931.

Her successor was briefly **Dame Elizabeth Leah Manning** (Labour) who won a February 1931 by-election with a comfortable 11% majority but within months her majority was blown away following the economic collapse that precipitated the fall of the Labour Government in the October General Election. The Tories won the seat by a margin

27 The Paviors were established in 1276 to construct, repair and clean London's streets and pavements. The Fanmakers were incorporated in 1709. In 1345 gardeners successfully petitioned to sell produce publicly and the first Charter was granted in 1605. The Company was the sanitary cleansing authority for the City of London.

of over 35%. She was born in 1886 the daughter of Charles Perett of Illinois (USA) and was educated at St Johns School Bridgwater and then at Homerton College, Cambridge. She married William Henry Manning in 1914 and became a teacher. In 1929/30 she was President of the National Union of Teachers. Following her defeat at Islington in 1931 she became a member of the National Executive Committee of the Labour Party (1931-2) and contested Sunderland unsuccessfully in 1935. She was, however, returned at Epping in 1945 and served until 1950 when she lost again. Attempts at re-election there failed in 1951 and 1955. She was made a Dame in 1966 and died in 1977.

The book written by Thelma Cazalet-Keir about her experiences in broadcasting and film

Mrs Thelma Cazalet-Kier (Conservative) was MP from 1931 to 1945. Daughter of William Cazalet, she was also the granddaughter of Sir John Heron, 7th baronet and the sister of Victor Cazalet MP for Chippenham from 1924-43. Born in 1899, she entered local politics in 1925 when she was elected to the LCC where she was a councillor until 1931 and then an alderman. She married David Kier in 1935 and from 1937 to 1940 was PPS to the Parliamentary Secretary for Education, K. Lindsay. In 1940 she became a Governor of the British Film Institute[28] and of the Cinematograph Films Company, serving on both until 1944. In Churchill's provisional 1945 Conservative Government she became Parliamentary Secretary at the Ministry of Education but lost her seat at the Election. She was a Governor of the BBC from 1956 to 1961 and in 1964 President of the Fawcett Society, an organisation for the furtherance of equality between the sexes. She wrote a book called 'From the Wings' about her experiences in the broadcasting and film media. She died in 1989.

Islington North

Sir Newton James Moore (Conservative) was previously MP for Westminster (St Georges-Hanover Square) for a few months in 1918 before transferring to Islington North at the General Election of the same year when his former seat disappeared following boundary changes. His principal biographical details are contained in Chapter 3.

Sir (William) Henry Cowan (Conservative) succeeded Moore in 1923 and sat until 1929. Born in 1862 to Edinburgh parents he was a wealthy businessman and Chairman of the firm Parkinson and Cowan, manufacturers of gas and electric cookers. He sat initially as a Liberal for the Guildford division of Surrey between 1906 and January 1910, for Eastern Aberdeenshire until 1918 but thereafter as a Coalition Liberal until his defeat in 1922 at the redrawn constituency of Aberdeenshire East and Kincardineshire. He became a Unionist in 1922 but was first elected as a Conservative at Islington North.

He retired in 1929, three years before his death, to be succeeded by **Robert Stanley Young** (Labour), born in 1891 the son of a North Walean from Rhos on Sea. He was educated at Manchester Grammar School, becoming a Dramatic Critic and Theatrical Producer, but during the First World War served with the Maori Regiment of the New Zealand Forces in Gallipoli and France.

Albert William Goodman (Conservative) defeated Young in 1931. Born in Melbourne, Australia, in 1880 he was educated there before becoming an Honorary Colonel in the Royal Engineers in London. He went to India in 1904 and remained resident there for 20 years earning his living as an Estate developer. He contested Bow and Bromley in May 1929 before his election at Islington. He died in 1937.

Dr. Leslie Haden Haden-Guest MC (Labour) was elected at the by-election caused by Goodman's death. Born in 1877 at Oldham in Lancashire, he was educated at William Hulme's Grammar School and Owens College in Manchester before transferring to the London Hospital where he qualified as a Doctor of Medicine and Surgeon. He served in the Red Cross in South Africa in 1902 and in the Royal Army Medical Corps during the Great War, working in France, Palestine and Egypt. He was awarded the Military Cross and established the Anglo-French Committee of the Red Cross. After the War he went into politics. He unsuccessfully contested Southwark Central in 1918 and was a councillor on the LCC for East Woolwich between 1919 and 1922. In that year he sought election to the Commons at Southwark

28 Organisation founded in 1933 to promote the cinema as a 'means of entertainment and instruction'. It includes the National Film Archive (founded in 1935) and the National Film Theatre (founded in 1951).

North and, though defeated on that occasion, was returned in 1923. Re-elected in 1924, he resigned from the Labour Party in 1927 over the Party's policy towards China, contesting the by-election as an Independent Constitutionalist with Tory support. He came third behind the Liberal and Labour candidates and resumed his medical practice. He contested Southwark North as a Conservative in 1929 but was again defeated and, somewhat bizarrely given the nature of politics at the time, rejoined the Labour Party in the cause of which he contested Wycombe (South Buckinghamshire) in 1931 and Brecon and Radnor in 1935. He founded the Labour Party Commonwealth Group and was widely travelled, writing about imperial and foreign affairs. He served as MP for Islington North until 1950 although during the Second World War he once again joined the RAMC between 1940 and 1943. Following his retirement in 1950 he was made Baron and elevated to the House of Lords becoming Government Whip in 1951. After the defeat of the Labour Government in 1951 he continued to serve as Opposition Whip in the Lords until his death in 1960.

Islington South

Sir Charles Frederick Higham (Conservative) was MP for Islington South from 1918 to 1922 when he retired. Born at Walthamstow, Essex, in 1876, he was married four times and twice divorced. He was an advertising executive who assisted in wartime propaganda between 1914 and 1918, notably in the campaign for 'Men and Money'. He was also Assistant Organiser of the Victory War Loan Campaign and was subsequently an adviser to the Treasury, Admiralty, Navy and Army Canteen Board. He died in 1938.

Charles Samuel Garland (Conservative) succeeded Higham in 1923 but was defeated a year later. Born in 1887, he was educated at Camberwell Grammar School and the Royal College of Science, becoming a chemical engineer and rising to be Chairman of the Joint Council of the Gas Mantle Industry, then an important sector of the economy. After his defeat in 1923 he concentrated on his industrial activities but remained politically active in Dulwich. He was President of the British Association of Chemists (1925/6) founded in 1918, originally with a membership of graduate scientists in the UK chemical industry. He was also Treasurer of the National Union of Manufacturers (1925-51) and its President from 1957-8. Founded in 1915 as the British Manufacturers' Association, it became the National Union of Manufacturers in 1917 and finally, in 1961, The National Association of British Manufacturers. It came to resemble, and even to rival, the Federation of British Industry in providing services and national representation for its members, but was particularly strong among small and middle-sized firms. The National Association of British Manufacturers merged with the Federation of British Industries and the British Employers' Confederation in 1965 to form the Confederation of British Industry. Garland was also a member of the Clean Air Council from 1957 to 1960, when he died.

Will Cluse

People's History Museum, Manchester

William Sampson Cluse (Labour) was MP for Islington South for two fairly lengthy periods. First elected in 1923, he remained undefeated until the 1931 Labour rout. However, he won there again in 1935 and remained MP until 1950. He was born in Islington in 1875 but orphaned at the age of five and was educated at the orphanage and at an elementary school in Islington. He became a baker's boy at the age of eleven; by thirteen was a printer and by fifteen a compositor. He became interested in radical politics and in 1900 joined the Social Democratic Federation. At the outbreak of the Great War he served in the Royal Artillery Machine Corps, which he left in 1919, the year he first became an elected politician, as a councillor in Islington. He retained his position until 1925 but was elected meanwhile as MP for the Borough's South division. Most of his time in Parliament was spent in Opposition but in 1940, in Churchill's Wartime coalition, he served as Parliamentary Secretary at the Ministry of Transport transferring to the same position at the Ministry of Aircraft Production in 1941. After 1942 he returned to back bench obscurity and retired following boundary changes in 1950. He died in 1955.

Tom Forest (Conservative) won the seat from Cluse in 1931 but lost it back again four years later. Born in 1888 and educated at Higher Grade School in Bounds Green he became an account bookmaker. A strong supporter of Imperial protection he founded the Tariff Reform Scouts in 1909. During the First World War he served in France in the Machine Gun Corps from 1917 and went into local politics in 1922, serving initially on Finsbury Borough Council until 1925 when he was elected to the LCC where he was a councillor until 1928 and again from 1931 to 1934. His first Parliamentary contest was at Islington South in 1924, which he fought for a second time in 1929, being unsuccessful on both occasions. He succeeded in 1931 but served only for a single term and despite a further attempt in 1945 and two more in the reconstituted South West division in 1950 and 1951, he never returned to the Commons. He died in 1953.

Islington West

Sir George Samuel Elliott (Conservative) was MP from 1918 to 1922 when he retired. Born in 1847, in Islington, he was a member of the Old Vestry and thirteen times Mayor of the new Borough. He was also a Poor Law Guardian, a member of the Metropolitan Asylum Board and of the LCC. During the First World War he raised two battalions and entered the House as a Coalition Unionist in 1918. He died in 1925.

The commemorative shield in The Chamber of the House
House of Commons

He was succeeded by **Major James St George Despencer Robertson** (Conservative) who was born the son of Sir Helenus Robertson in 1886 and assumed the name Despencer in 1916. He was born in 1886 and educated at Eton and New College Oxford. In 1914 he joined the Royal Welsh Fusiliers in which he served until 1919. On entering Parliament for the first time in 1922 he was briefly PPS at the Ministry of Pensions but was defeated in 1923 and at the two subsequent elections. He was out of the House until 1931 when he was elected at Salisbury (Wiltshire). At the outbreak of the Second World War he became a Second Lieutenant and was soon made up to Acting Lieutenant Colonel. He died suddenly on active service in 1942. A shield commemorating his death, as a major, is in The Chamber of the House of Commons.

Frederick Montague (Labour), who won the seat from Robertson in 1923, was born at nearby Clerkenwell in 1876 and, following an elementary education became first a newsboy, then a shop assistant and finally a journalist and copywriter. He was an organiser for the Independent Labour Party in London and the Home Counties and in 1906 the editor of a political journal called *The Social Democrat*. He served in the Great War from 1915 to 1919 and gained a commission, a significant achievement for someone with his social background. From 1919 to 1925 he was an Alderman on Islington Borough Council and, following his return as an MP, he served on a Royal Transport Commission, set up in 1928 "to consider problems arising from the growth of road transport"[29]. In the 1929-31 Labour Government he was Under-Secretary for Air. He was defeated in 1931 but re-elected four years later and remained MP for Islington West until 1947 when he was created Lord Amwell. During the Second War he was PPS at the Ministry of Transport from 1940-1 and from 1941-2 at the Ministry of Aircraft Production. He died in 1966 at the aged of ninety.

Patrick William Donner (Conservative) was MP between 1931 and 1935 when he stood down and transferred to the Hampshire county division of Basingstoke, which he represented until 1955 when he retired. His political interests were in Imperial development, especially India. The son of the first Finnish Minister to Britain, he was born in 1904 and educated at Exeter College, Oxford. He became a Company Director and during the Second World War fought as a Squadron Leader in the RAF Voluntary Reserve. He died in 1988.

MPs for Finchley, Hampstead, and Hendon

From	at	To	Surname	First Names	Constituency	Party
1918	G	1923	Newman	Sir John Robert Pretyman (Lt Col)	Finchley	Conservative
1923	G	1924	Robertson	Thomas Atholl		Liberal
1924	G	1935	Cadogan	Sir Edward (Major)		Conservative
1935	G	1945	Crowder	Sir John Ellenborough		Conservative
1918	G	1941	Balfour	George	Hampstead	Conservative
1941	B	1945	Challen	Charles		Conservative
1918	G	1935	Cunliffe-Lister	Sir Philip	Hendon	Conservative
1935	G	1945	Blair	Sir Reginald		Conservative

Notes: First returned at: B By-election, G General Election

Finchley

Lieutenant-Colonel Sir John Robert Pretyman Newman (Conservative) was MP for Enfield from 1910 to 1918 and was elected for the newly created Finchley constituency in 1918. His principal biographical details may be found in Chapter 3 .

In 1923 Newman was defeated by **Thomas Atholl Robertson** (Liberal), a Glaswegian born in 1874 and educated

29 The Commission reported in 1931 and one of its recommendations was that trams be phased out as soon as possible since they 'cause congestion'.

at Clunies School in Blairgowrie, Perthshire. As an expatriate Scot he was Chief of the Scottish Clans Association of London in 1920/1 and a Governor of the Royal Caledonian Schools, Bushey, in Hertfordshire. Despite his Scottishness, he was also President of the English League for Taxation and Land Values, an organisation set up to oppose the interests of landowners who they perceived to be exploiting the poor. He contested Hammersmith South in 1918 and Finchley in 1922, on both occasions unsuccessfully, and although he was elected in 1923 he survived only until 1924 when he was defeated. He tried again in 1929 but lost once more and went on to fight two further elections (Kinross & West Perthshire in1931 and Aylesbury at a 1938 by-election) before retiring from politics. He died in 1955.

Major Sir Edward Cadogan (Conservative), son of the fifth Earl, took the seat in 1924. He was born in 1880 and attended Balliol College, Oxford, where he graduated in law becoming a barrister at the Inner Temple in 1905. He was also a Major in the Suffolk Yeomanry and served overseas during the First World War. By then he had already tried his hand at politics being defeated at Kings Lynn in January 1910. Soon afterwards he obtained a post as Secretary to the Speaker of the House of Commons, Sir James Lowther, whom he served until 1921 and was successful in obtaining a seat at Reading in 1922, though he lost it within one year and transferred to Finchley in 1924. He represented the division until retiring for the first time in 1935 and meanwhile, from 1927 to 1930, was a member of the Indian Statutory Commissions. He made no real progress in his political career but outside the House became Deputy Chairman of the Great Western Railway Company. After a five-year absence he decided to return to politics and was elected unopposed at a 1940 by-election at Bolton in Lancashire, serving until 1945 when he finally retired. After the War he was a London magistrate and Deputy Lieutenant, serving as Vice Lieutenant until 1958. He died four years later.

Sir John Ellenborough Crowder (Conservative) was MP from 1935 to 1959. Born in 1890 and educated at Eton and Christ Church Oxford, he became an underwriter at Lloyds of London. He served in both World Wars; in the Lincolnshire Yeomanry and Horse Guards (1914-19); and as a Staff Captain in 1939/40. As a resident of Hampshire, where he was a magistrate, he first entered local politics on the County Council in 1931 and Fleet Urban District Council two years later. He served on both until 1946. His Parliamentary career failed to take off because despite being appointed a PPS to the Minister of Labour in 1938/9 he never progressed beyond that rank, serving in similar capacities in a string of Ministries between 1938 and 1945 - at Home Security, Food, the Exchequer, and Aircraft Production. After the War he sat on the Opposition backbenches until 1951 when, following the return of a Conservative Government, he was made second Parliamentary Estates Commissioner, a post he held until 1957. He retired in 1959 and died two years later.

Hampstead

George Balfour MP
© **National Portrait Gallery**
Lafayette 1928

George Balfour (Conservative) was MP from 1918 until his death in 1941. Prior to 1918 he had contested the Scottish seat of Govan (Lanarkshire) in 1910 and at a by-election held there in 1911. Son of a Dundonian, he was born in 1872 but educated at Portsmouth before returning to Scotland as an undergraduate at the Technical and University Colleges in Dundee. George founded the famous construction company of Balfour Beatty when in 1909 he teamed up with Andrew Beatty, a chartered accountant. The company described itself as 'general and electrical engineers, contractors, operating managers for tramways, railways and lighting properties and for the promoting of new enterprises.' The company's first contract was for a new tramway system in Dunfermline in Fife. George was the Company Chairman, a role he also held in the Power Securities Corporation.

Charles Challen (Conservative) succeed at the 1941 by-election following Balfour's death and served until 1950 when the local Party Association failed to readopt him. Born in 1894, he was educated at the Merchant Taylors School (then in the City of London) and Jesus College Cambridge following which he became a barrister at Grays Inn where he was an Arden Prize winner in 1922. He joined Hampstead Borough Council in 1931 and remained a member until 1945. At the outbreak of the Second World War he was made Chairman of the Council's General Emergency Committee but a year later joined the Royal Air Force as a Flight Lieutenant and served until 1946. He died in 1960.

Hendon

Sir Philip Cuncliffe-Lister MC (Conservative) was Hendon's MP from 1918 until 1935. He was born a Yorkshireman, the son of Yarburgh Lloyd-Graeme in 1884 and his family home was Sewerby Hall near Bridlington,

Sir Philip Cunliffe-Lister MP
© National Portrait Gallery
Bassano Ltd 1920

overlooking Flamborough Head, one of Britain's most famous coastal features. After an education that embraced Winchester School and University College Oxford he trained as a barrister and practised at the Inner Temple from 1908. During the first years of the Great War he served as a Major in France but in 1917, after he had been awarded the Military Cross, was in 1918 appointed Joint Secretary to the Ministry of National Service and Chairman of the Cabinet's Permanent Labour Committe which oversaw the recruitment and provision of civilian labour to essential tasks during the War. In 1920 he was appointed PPS at the Board of Trade, in which capacity he was the principal British representative to the International Commission on Russian Famine and Relief set up following the failure of the grain harvests in Ukraine and Kazakstan. Thereafter he advanced quickly through the ministerial ranks. He was made Minister of Overseas Trade in 1921 and President of the Board of Trade a year later, a post he resumed in 1924 following his Party's return to Government after a year in Opposition. This was also the year in which he changed his name to Cunliffe-Lister, assuming by Royal Licence that family's arms and name in lieu of his own. He held the Trade post throughout the 1924-9 Parliament but was out of office until 1935 when he was made Viscount Swinton, the name of the place in North Yorkshire where he had his country mansion. He was appointed Secretary of State for Air but resigned in 1938 over the appeasement policies of the Chamberlain administration and it was not until the fall of that Government in 1940 that he was made Chairman of the Home Defence Security Committee and later from 1942 served as Minister Resident in West Africa. From 1944-5 he was Minister of Civil Aviation and after the 1945 election defeat devoted his political energies to the rehabilitation of the Conservative Party, establishing Swinton College in North Yorkshire for the purpose of training Party agents. When in 1951 Churchill became Prime Minister for the second time, Swinton returned to Government, initially as Chancellor of the Duchy of Lancaster (1951-2), then as Commonwealth Secretary (1952-5), serving throughout as Deputy Leader of the House of Lords. After the 1955 General Election he was made an Earl and retired from Government. He died in 1972.

Sir Reginald Blair (Conservative) was MP for Hendon from 1935 until 1945 but was previously MP for Bow and Bromley between 1912 and 1922. His principal biographical details are included in Chapter 3.

The 1923 General Election was hard fought on the question of tariff reform. Stanley Baldwin (MP for Bewdley) held office during the Lloyd George Lib-Con coalition that ended with the 1922 General Election which the Conservatives won. Prime Minister Andrew Bonar Law resigned through ill health, and Baldwin succeeded him as Prime Minister. Baldwin felt it advisable to seek another general election - despite the comfortable Conservative majority - but the judgement was ill-conceived. Fighting with concerns of unemployment and protectionism, the 1923 election battle delivered 258 Conservative, 191 Labour and 158 Liberal seats in Parliament. In North London Conservatives lost 7 seats, of which 2 went to the Liberals and 5 went to Labour. In the East End Labour won 6 seats to add to the 6 seats they had won in 1922. The first Labour Government was formed under Ramsay MacDonald with tacit support from the Liberals. MacDonald's minority government lasted 10 months. There was yet another General Election in 1924, and this time Baldwin gained a good majority, Labour lost 40 seats, but the Liberals lost 118 seats.
'Yes! We have no bananas' *was a popular song taken from the 1922 Broadway revue 'Make it Snappy'. The song became a No.1 hit in Britain in 1923, and is being used here in a Labour election communication to criticise Conservative policies - perhaps it was an effective ploy as the first Labour Government was the result.*
If we think we have turbulent political times today, then hark back to post-WW1, when there was fundamental change over such a short period of time.
People's History Museum, Manchester

Top Left: Shoreditch Town Hall, in the Shoreditch Constituency, was built in 1865 with a grand vestry hall to match the wealth of the neighbourhood; it was rebuilt in 1901. **Gordon Rushton**

Top Right: Limehouse Basin in the Limehouse Constituency. Here the Regents Canal and the Limehouse Cut enter the Thames. It was an extremely busy place, but was heavily bombed in WW2. **Gordon Rushton**

Left: Within walking distance of Bruce Grove Station, these comfortable Victorian villas in Broadwater Rd, Tottenham transferred to the Tottenham North Constituency in 1918. **John Nelson**

Above: In Fore St, Edmonton, the row of shops just off the North Circular Road offer roomy and convenient accommodation with the Edmonton Green station nearby and buses below. Won only twice by the Conservatives between the wars, Edmonton was mainly a Labour held constituency **John Nelson**

Left: Stoke Newington was a Borough at its peak between the two wars. Church Street was at the centre of the village-like community. Apart from a single Liberal victory in 1923 this was a staunchly Tory seat in the inter-War years. **Gordon Rushton**

The East End and North East Middlesex

In this chapter Bethnal Green, Hackney, Shoreditch and Tower Hamlets are defined as the East End with the Tottenham, Edmonton and Enfield districts comprising North East Middlesex. The maps on pages 253 and 254 illustrate the changes that took place.

The 1918 boundary changes meant that although the East End lost seats there was an overall increase of one seat to 18 in the area as a whole.

Tower Hamlets emerged from the review with 7 seats, a reduction of 2. Those remaining were contained within one or other of the new London boroughs of Bethnal Green, Poplar and Stepney, which together replaced Tower Hamlets. Two seats were lost through the creation of **Whitechapel, Stepney & St Georges** which combined former seats of those three names within the borough of Stepney. This enlarged constituency covered ten wards – officially Whitechapel (Middle South and Tower), Spitalfields (East and West), Wapping (St Georges-in-the-East, North West, North East, and South), Shadwell and Mile End New Town. It also included Aldgate, Stepney Green, St Katherine Docks and the Tower of London. The adjacent **Mile End** constituency of Stepney borough comprised the East Whitechapel ward and four Old Town wards (Centre, North, South, and West) covering the rest of Stepney and western parts of Mile End, including areas between Mile End Road and Bethnal Green. The Globe Town area of Mile End ward North East together with Mile End Old Town's south eastern ward (Stepney East) were allocated to **Limehouse** which also included Radcliffe.

Poplar was renamed **Poplar South** but acquired the South East ward of Bromley-by-Bow (between Limehouse Cut and the East India Dock Road). It retained Poplar (East, North West and West), Cubitt Town and Millwall. Blackwall, East India Dock, the Isle of Dogs, West India Dock and West Ferry were all included. Apart from the loss of the southeast ward, **Bow & Bromley** was unchanged covering the whole of Bow (Central, North, South and West) including Old Ford together with the North East, North West and South West wards of Bromley. Development in this area had been encouraged by the opening of an extension to the District Line beyond Whitechapel to Bow in 1902.

Bethnal Green North East and **Bethnal Green South West** constituencies remained unchanged (Details in Chapter 3).

Elswhere the two former **Shoreditch** divisions were merged and given the borough name to include Haggerston, Hoxton and Moorfields. However, changes affecting neighbouring Hackney saw an additional seat emerge at **Stoke Newington.** This had been created a municipal borough in 1900 following considerable local resistance to a proposal to unite it with Hackney. The formerly detached element of South Hornsey parish was made part of the new council area, which also included Clissold Park, Finsbury Park and Lordship Park Manor.

The new seat was mainly carved out of **Hackney North**, which was retained in what was still a growing suburb to cover Stamford Hill, Upper Clapton, Clapton Park, Rectory Road and Shacklewell. **Hackney Central** contained the western and central districts of the borough in West ward together with the Downs and Kingsland wards, including Dalson, De Beauvoir Town, London Fields and Lower Clapton, whilst **Hackney South** covered Homerton and South Hackney wards and the southern parts of Clapton Park ward around Lea Bridge Road. It included Victoria Park, Hackney Wick and Hackney Marsh.

Beyond Hackney rapid growth of affordable housing in the Haringey area led to Wood Green being separated from the Tottenham constituency, which at the same time was split into two parts. **Tottenham North** comprised five wards of the Urban District Council area – (Downlands) Park and Coleraine (Turnpike Lane), West Green (North Haringay), Bruce Grove, Stoneleigh Park (Bruce Grove east) and White Hart Lane (including Northumberland Park).

Tottenham South combined four wards - Green Lanes (South Haringay), Town Hall (Seven Sisters), Chestnuts (Tottenham Hale) and Stamford Hill (South Tottenham). The UDC (created in 1894) became a borough in 1934.

Wood Green , like its neighbour an UDC since 1894, was a new constituency where housing estates were developing fast in an area that included Southgate and Palmers Green (in Enfield today but from 1894 in Southgate UDC), Alexandra Palace, Arnos Grove, Bounds Green, Bowes Park, Cockfosters, Noel Park, Oakwood, Winchmore Hill and Wood Green. The place name dates from 1502 when it was known as 'Wodegrene' meaning, "green place near woodland". It received borough status in 1933.

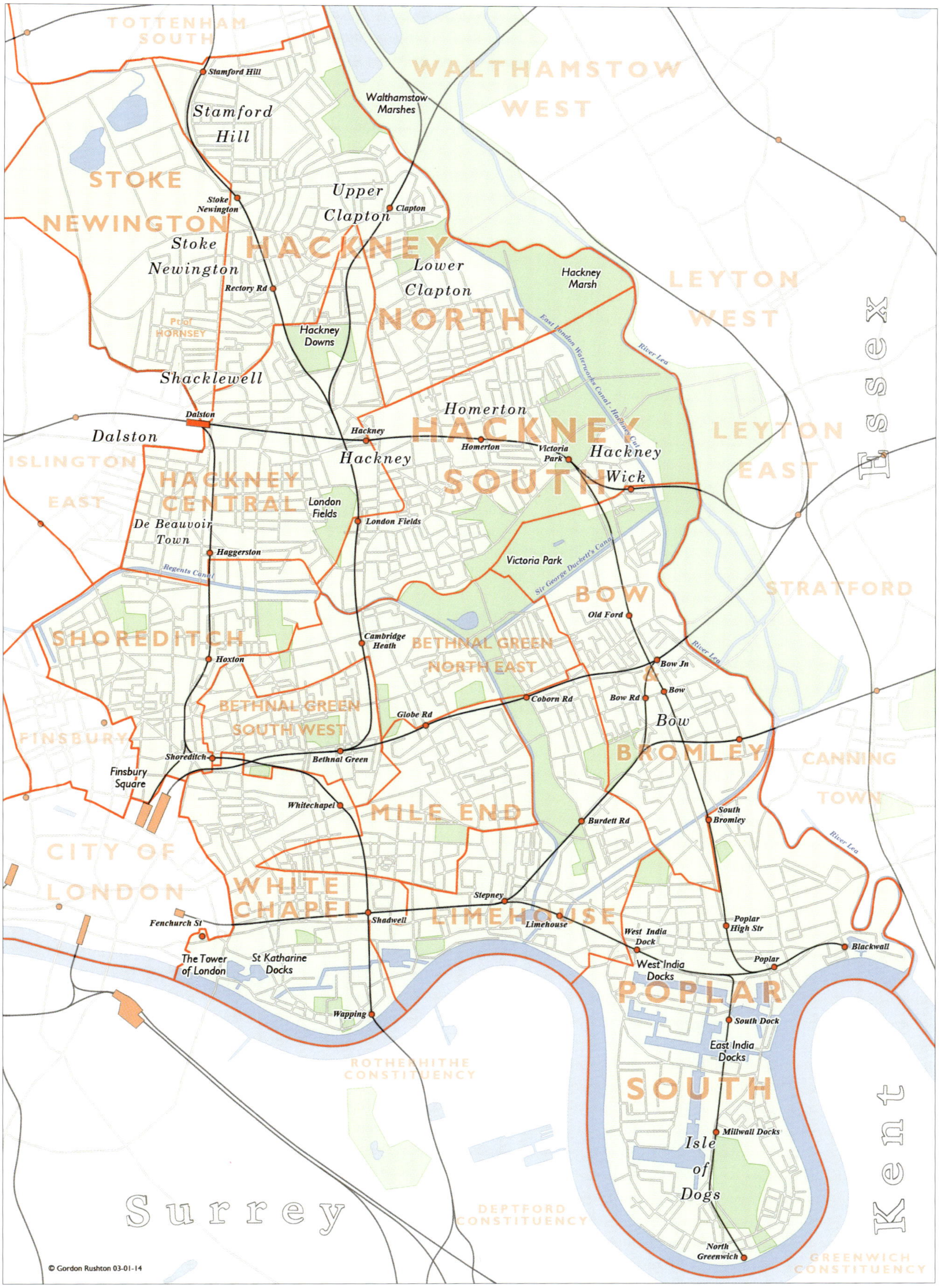

The East End map 1918-1945 showing constituency changes - by 1920 almost the whole map area was built up except for the green spaces and marshlands bordering the river Lea.

Hornsey lost Finchley (see North London above) and was reduced in size to cover the municipal borough established in 1903; in its new form it extended west to east between Highgate (inclusive) and Haringey (exclusive), north to Muswell Hill (inclusive) and south to Archway (exclusive) on the borders with Islington North. It included Crouch End, Fortis Green and Stroud Green.

In North East Middlesex population growth spurred by local industrialisation led to the creation of another new constituency. **Enfield** was re-drawn to exclude Edmonton, and extended from Trent Park in the west to Enfield village in the east. Officially it comprised the Urban District of Enfield together with the South Mimms Rural District. The constituency included Brimsdown, Bulls Cross, Clay Hill, Durants Park, Enfield Chase, Enfield Highway, Enfield Wash, Forty Hill, Grange Park, Hadley Wood, Potters Bar, South Mimms and Trent Park. Hadley Wood and Potters Bar had been created as an Urban District in 1896.

Edmonton, which had become an Urban District in 1894, emerged as a new borough seat between Enfield and Tottenham. The Enfield end was described as Lower Edmonton; Upper Edmonton was nearest Tottenham. It was bounded on its east side by the River Lea in the vicinity of Pickets Lock and to the West by the New River. In between

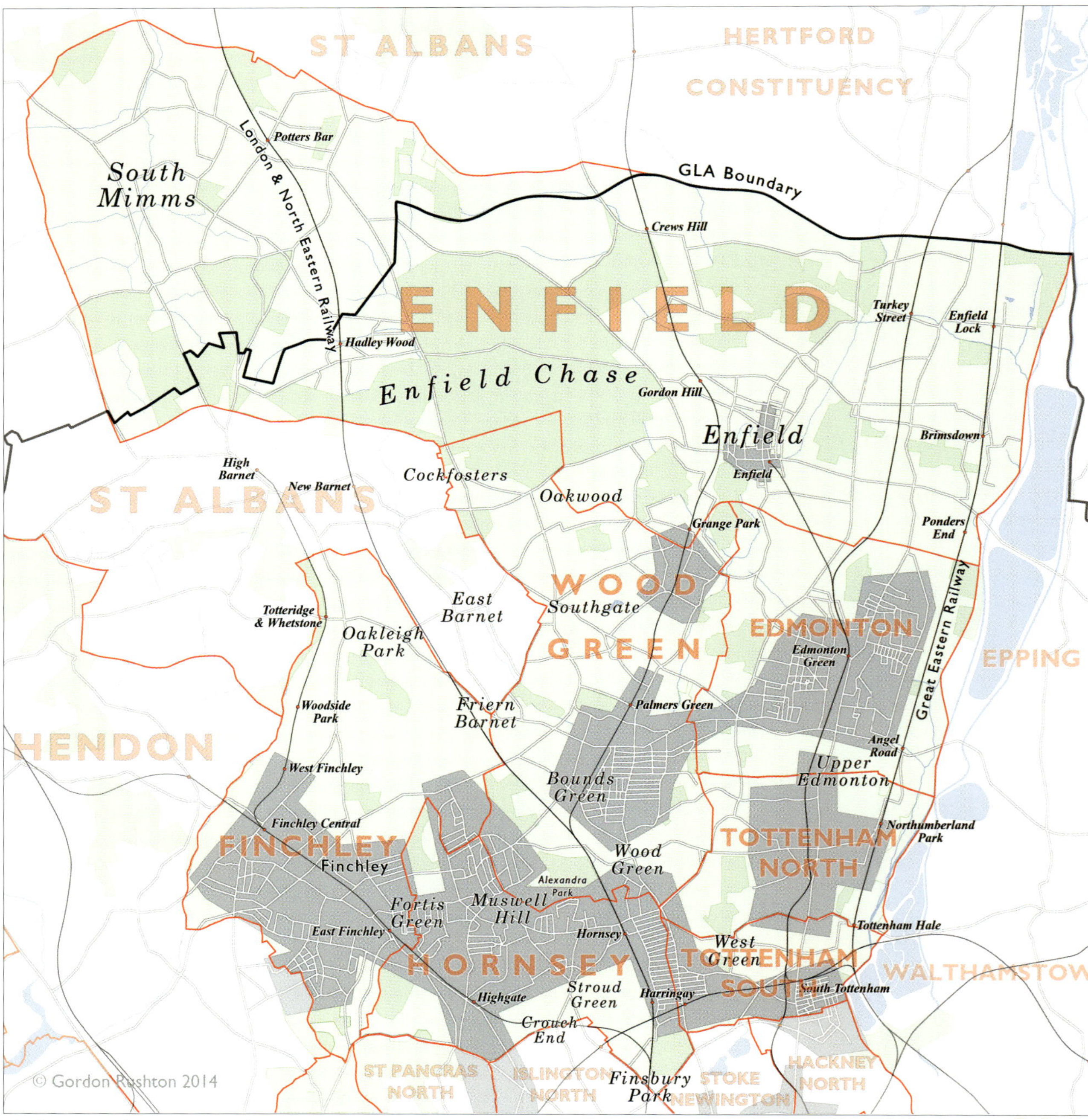

North East London: Steady population growth meant that constituencies needed to multiply to remain within bounds. The built up area, shown here in 1920 continued to spread as house building accelerated in the 1920s and 1930s.

were Bury Street, Bush Hill Park and Silver Street. Edmonton's name derived from 'Adelmetone' meaning, "farmstead of a man called Eeadhelm" and is recorded in the Domesday Book. The area had been a centre of market gardening for London but the coming of the Great Eastern Railway brought 'more the aspect of a suburban village' to Edmonton. As recently as 1871 the parish had a population of only 13,860 including Southgate and Winchmore Hill. Edmonton became a county borough in 1937.

Politics in the East End and North East Middlesex

Significant changes occurred in the political complexion of East London during the Inter-War period, which witnessed the rise of Labour to become the main Party. Despite the Tories' massive national majorities at certain General elections in the period – most notably in the first two following the Great War and then again in the crisis election of 1931 – the Labour Party emerged from nowhere before the War to secure most seats in four of the seven contests after it. Overall during the period Labour won 54 seats, the Tories and their allies 51 and the Liberals only 20 of which 7were in Bethnal Green South West at consecutive Elections from 1923. 1935 was the last time that a Liberal was sent to Parliament from an East End constituency.

Election Results in the Inter-War Years by % majority

Constituency	Pre 1918*	1918	1922	1923	1924	1929	1931	1935
Whitechapel	1xL 1 C/L	L6	Lab3 +	Lab4 +	Lab17	Lab42 +	L5	Lab9 +
Mile End	2xC	C38	C6	Lab10	Lab20	Lab17	C12	Lab14
Limehouse	1 C/L	L35	Lab11	Lab37	Lab30	Lab29	Lab2	Lab33
Poplar South	L	L24	Lab18	Lab30	Lab25	Lab41	Lab15	Lab46 +
Bow & Bromley	1 C/L	C5	Lab28	Lab38	Lab23	Lab39	Lab17	Lab54 +
Bethnal Green North East	L	L27	L1	Lab4	Lab0.4	L3	IL12	Lab27
Bethnal Green South West	L	C28	L9	L4	L1	L7	L37	L6
Shoreditch	2xL	L6	NL1	Lab13	Lab6	Lab19	NL13	Lab23
Hackney South	L	Ind15	C20	Lab13	L7	Lab24	C11	Lab19
Hackney Central	C	L100	NL14	L6	C6	Lab5	C24	Lab3
Hackney North	C	C41	C22	L8	C19	C3	C39	C4
Stoke Newington		C28	C26	L7	C32	C4	C47	C18
Tottenham South	C	C5	C7	Lab12	C6	Lab15	Nlab17	Lab17
Tottenham North		C24	Lab8	Lab17	Lab2	Lab25	C11	Lab22
Wood Green		C55	C40	C10	C35	C19	C57	C37
Hornsey	C	C100 +	C6	C5	C20	C19	C69	C43 +
Edmonton		C24	Lab9	Lab29	Lab6	Lab19	C14	Lab10
Enfield	C	C13	C9	Lab6	C8	Lab0.8	C29	C13
C, NLab and NL	7/10	11+	10	2	7	4	12	5 +
L	7/10	6	2	4	2	2	3	1
Lab	0	0	6 +	12 +	9	12 +	3	12+++
Ind	0	1	0	0	0	0	0	0

Key: C = Conservative; L = Liberal; N = NationaL; Lab = Labour; + = Party that won seat at General Election held by-election in same Parliament; - = Party that won seat at General Election lost by-election to main opposition Party in same Parliament. * These numbers are averages for all General Elections between 1885 and 1910 inclusive.

The source of Labour's greatest strength was undoubtedly the heavily unionised dock area of Stepney and Poplar in which they won all 5seats in 1923, 1924, 1929 and 1935. They even took 3 in 1931 winning Limehouse, Poplar South and Bow & Bromley at 6 consecutive elections from 1923. Shoreditch, Hackney South, Edmonton and Tottenham North (which they won at 5 General Elections) also emerged as Labour strongholds but there was far less certainty in the voting patterns in these more suburban areas than in docklands. The Lea Valley's new light industrial constituencies had become centres of employment providing many workers' jobs and they were also areas in which both private and council housing had been built in significant numbers. The Conservatives gradually lost their hold on constituencies in the East End and became more confined to the middle class outer suburbs such as Hackney North, Wood Green, Hornsey and Enfield; though Labour even won that in 1923 and 1929 going on to form a minority Government each time.

MPs for Bethnal Green, Stepney, and Poplar

From	at	To	Surname	First Names	Constituency	Party
1918	G	1922	Cornwall	Sir Edwin Andrew	Bethnal Green North East	Liberal
1922	G	1923	Edmonds	Garnham		Liberal
1923	G	1929	Windsor	Walter		Labour
1929	G	1935	Nathan	Harry Louis (Major)		Liberal
1935	G	1945	Chater	Daniel		Labour
1918	G	1922	Wilson	Sir Mathew Richard H	Bethnal Green South West	Conservative
1922	G	1945	Harris	Sir Percy Alfred		Liberal
1918	G	1922	Blair	Sir Reginald	Poplar, Bow and Bromley	Conservative
1922	G	1940	Lansbury	George		Labour
1940	B	1945	Key	Charles William		Labour
1918	G	1922	Yeo	Sir Alfred William	Poplar South	Liberal
1922	G	1931	March	Samuel		Labour
1931	G	1942	Adams	David Morgan		Labour
1942	B	1945	Guy	William Henry		Labour
1918	G	1922	Pearce	Sir William	Stepney, Limehouse	Liberal
1922	G	1945	Attlee	(Major) Clement Richard		Labour
1918	G	1923	Preston	Sir Walter Reuben	Stepney, Mile End	Conservative
1923	G	1931	Scurr	John		Labour
1931	G	1935	O' Donovan	William Joseph (Dr.)		Conservative
1935	G	1945	Frankel	Daniel		Labour
1918	G	1922	Kiley	James Daniel	Stepney, Whitechapel	Liberal
1922	G	1923	Mathew	Charles James		Labour
1923	B	1930	Gosling	Harry		Labour
1930	B	1931	Hall	James H		Labour
1931	G	1935	Janner	(Sir) Barnett		Liberal
1935	G	1942	Hall	James H		Labour
1942	B	1945	Edwards	Walter James		Labour

Notes: First returned at: B By-election, G General Election

Bethnal Green North East

Sir Edwin Cornwall (Liberal) was first elected at Bethnal Green North East in 1906 and retained the seat until he retired in 1922. His main biographical details can be found in Chapter 3 (Bethnal Green).

He was succeeded in 1922 by **Garnham Edmonds JP** (Liberal) but he only held the seat for a year. Born in 1866, he was a member of Bethnal Green Borough Council of which he was Mayor in 1908, and of the LCC from 1910 until 1922. He died in 1946.

He was defeated in 1923 by **Walter Windsor** (Labour) who held it until 1929 when the Liberals took it back again. Born in 1886, he was Secretary of the Bethnal Green branch of the General and Municipal Workers' Union and a sometime member of the local borough Council. Backed by the Communist Party, he first fought the North East Division in 1922 but was unsuccessful. Windsor was out of Parliament for six years, returning as the Labour MP for Hull Central, a seat which he held until 1945 when he died during the course of the general election campaign. A by-election was held a month after the General election.

Despite 1929 being the year Labour became the largest Party in the House, Walter Windsor lost to **Major Harry Louis Nathan** (Liberal) who sat until 1935 when he unsuccessfully fought Cardiff South for the Labour Party, which he had joined the previous year. He was born in 1889 and educated at St Paul's School and became a solicitor in 1913. He entered the War in 1914 serving until 1917 when he was severely wounded in France having fought earlier in Gallipoli and Egypt. After the War he was solicitor to the Land and Nation League and active in a number of Liberal organisations. He was in addition a Director of D. Gestetner Ltd., a company specialising in the provision of office equipment including early methods of copying, and author of *Free Trade Today*. Prior to being elected at Bethnal Green he had contested the Stepney division of Whitechapel and St Georges unsuccessfully in 1924. In 1937 he contested a by-election at Wandsworth Central, which seat he won and held until he was made a baron in 1940, making way for Ernest Bevin, General Secretary of the Transport and General Workers Union. He sat in the House of Lords until his death in 1963.

Daniel Chater (Labour) won the seat in 1935 and held it until 1950. He was formerly MP for Hammersmith South between 1929 and 1931 and his biographical details can be found earlier in this chapter.

Bethnal Green South West

Sir Mathew Richard Wilson (Conservative), who had first been elected at a by-election in 1914 held the seat after the War until 1922. His main biographical details may be found in Chapter 3 (Bethnal Green).

He was succeeded by **Sir Percy Alfred Harris** (Liberal), who won the seat in 1922 and held it until 1945 when Labour took it in a landslide. Born in 1876, Harris was Harrow and Trinity Hall educated, achieving a BA in 1897, and was called to the bar at the Middle Temple two years later. He entered politics in 1906 when he unsuccessfully contested the Ashford division of Kent but the following year became a member of the LCC. At the January 1910 General Election he was defeated again, this time at Harrow, but was eventually elected at a 1916 by-election for Harborough (Leicestershire). For the next two years he was Assistant Director Voluntary Services at the War Office. Defeated in 1918 he was out of the House until his return at Bethnal Green in 1922. From 1935 until 1945 he was Liberal Party Chief Whip in the Commons but was eventually defeated by Labour. He died in 1952.

Sir Percy Harris MP
People's History Museum, Manchester

Bow and Bromley

Sir Reginald Blair (Conservative) was first returned as MP for Bow and Bromley at a by-election in 1912. His biographical details are to be found in Chapter 3 (Tower Hamlets). He originally won the seat from George Lansbury only to lose it to the same man ten years later at the 1922 General Election.

George Lansbury (Labour) held the seat until his death in 1940. His biographical details may also be found in Chapter 3 (Tower Hamlets).

Charles Key MP
People's History Museum, Manchester

The by-election following Lansbury's death was won by **Charles William Key** (Labour) who, like his predecessor, was a Socialist pioneer. The son of a labourer who received Poor Law Relief and a mother who took in laundry in order to make ends meet, he was born locally at Mile End in 1883 and educated at an elementary school where he subsequently became a pupil-teacher. On leaving school he was awarded a King's Scholarship and attended the Borough Road Teacher Training College[30]. In 1905 he joined the teaching staff of Dempsey Street Elementary School in Mile End, joined the Independent Labour Party and became a Socialist orator. In 1920 he was elected to Poplar Borough Council and went on to be its Mayor three times; in 1923, 1926 and 1932. After his return at Bromley and Bow in 1940 he remained the constituency's MP until 1950 when it became part of the new Poplar division, which he represented until his retirement in 1964. From 1945 until 1947 he was a Private Secretary under Aneurin Bevan at the Ministry of Health when the legislation to create the National Health Service was being drafted and from 1947 to 1950 was Minister of Works, a non-Cabinet post. He died in December 1964, two months after stepping down at the October General Election.

Poplar South

Sir Alfred William Yeo (Liberal) was elected at a 1914 by-election in Poplar. He was returned at Poplar South in 1918 and remained MP until 1922. His biographical details may be found in Chapter 3 (Tower Hamlets).

30 Borough Road College originated in 1798 as Joseph Lancaster's School in Southwark and evolved through Lancaster's monitorial teaching system into the oldest teacher training college in the British Commonwealth. The College moved to Borough Road, Southwark in 1804, where it was first known as Borough Road College, and then to Isleworth in 1889.

The banner of the National Union of Vehicle Workers, Aldgate Branch, of which Samuel March MP was secretary.

In 1922 the seat was taken by **Samuel March** (Labour), a resident of East Ham, who was born in 1861 and prior to being elected to Parliament was Secretary of the National Union of Vehicle Workers, formed in 1919 by the amalgamation of the London and Provincial Coachmakers' Society, the Operative Coachmakers and Wheelwrights' Federal Labour Union, the London Coachsmiths and Vicemen's Trade Society and the United Kingdom Society of Coachmakers (founded in 1830)[31]. He was also a member of Poplar Borough Council on which he became an Alderman and Mayor (in 1920-1). He was a London county councillor from 1921 to 1925 and unsuccessfully contested Poplar South in 1918. He held the seat for nine years from 1922 to 1931 when he retired.

In 1931 the seat was won by **David Morgan Adams** (Labour), a former miner, sailor, soldier, docker and trade union official. Like his predecessor he had a long municipal service and was Mayor of Poplar in 1934-5 as well as being a member of the LCC.

He died in 1942 when **William Henry Guy** (Labour) was returned at a by-election remaining the MP until 1950 when the seat was abolished. Born in London in 1890 he was a Royal Navy Inspector of Armaments during the Great War and afterwards became a Director of the Amalgamated Tobacco Corporation. He was elected to the LCC in 1934 and subsequently to Poplar Borough Council in 1945 serving on both until 1965 when they were abolished. He served as Mayor of Poplar between 1953 and 1955.

Limehouse

Sir William Pearce (Liberal) was first elected at Limehouse in 1906 and was the constituency's MP throughout the period to 1922. His principal biographical details may be found in Chapter 3 (Tower Hamlets).

In 1922 **Clement Richard Attlee** (Labour), a future Leader of his Party and Prime Minister, was elected at Limehouse and remained its MP until 1950 when the constituency was abolished. He was then elected at Walthamstow West, a seat he held until he retired from the Commons in 1956 to become Earl Attlee. He was born in 1883 and educated at Hailyebury School and University College Oxford, after which he became a lawyer. He was called to the Bar

Below Left: *Attlee won the 1945 General Election with a Labour landslide. He is seen here in London as Prime Minister after his accession, with His Majesty King George VI.* **Crown Copyright**
Below Right: *Prime Minister Clement Attlee is seen conferring with his Chancellor of the Exchequer Hugh Dalton MP (Bishop Auckland) .* **People's History Museum, Manchester**

31 In 1925 the National Union of Vehicle Builders absorbed the Amalgamated Wheelwrights, Smiths and Kindred Trades Union and in 1948 the Wheelwrights and Coachmakers' Operative Union. The union transferred engagements to the Transport and General Workers' Union in 1972.

at the Inner Temple in 1905, but five years later became Secretary of Toynbee Hall, Britain's first university settlement, and named in memory of the social reformer, Arnold Toynbee. It was established in 1884 in Commercial Street, Whitechapel, as a place where students from Oxford and Cambridge Universities could work among and improve the lives of the poor during their holidays.

From 1913 to 1923 Attlee was also a lecturer in Social Sciences at the London School of Economics. From 1919-20 he was Mayor of Stepney and became an Alderman there in 1927. He fought throughout the Great War during which he was commissioned Major.

Attlee was appointed Under Secretary for War in the first Labour Government in 1923/4 and in the second attained Cabinet rank as Chancellor of the Duchy of Lancaster and Postmaster-General from 1929 to 1931. After Labour went into Opposition in 1931 he successfully contested the Leadership of the Party when George Lansbury, a neighbouring MP, resigned in 1935 and became Leader of the Opposition. When Chamberlain resigned as Prime Minister in 1940, he agreed to lead the Labour Party into a wartime coalition under Churchill joining the Cabinet as Lord Privy Seal and Secretary of State for the Dominions. In 1942 he was appointed Deputy Prime Minister and Lord President of the Council in which capacity he served until the coalition was disbanded shortly before the 1945 Election. After Labour's landslide victory he was appointed Prime Minister and remained head of the first ever majority Labour Government until its 1951defeat. He remained Leader of the Party and of the Opposition until 1956 when he was made Earl Attlee. He died in 1967.

His first duty as Prime Minister was to attend the Potsdam Conference, which brought about an end to the War against Nazi Germany and he lent British support to the dropping of two atomic bombs on Japanese cities by the Americans in ending the War in the Far East. However, five years later he successfully opposed similar action in the Korean War. His Government was amongst the most radical in British history and laid the legislative foundation of what came to be called the 'Welfare State', the central element of which was the National Health Service. During his tenure of office several other significant events occurred, notably the nationalization of the Bank of England, the coalmines, the iron and steel manufacturing companies and the railways. Tory Governments later returned all of these to the private sector, mostly in the 1980s and 1990s. However, other changes remained more permanent, including the granting of Independence to India and Pakistan, though this was not accomplished without considerable violence and a dispute over the territory of Kashmir has been the source of ongoing trouble ever since. The most lasting memorial to his Government is the National Health Service.

Mile End

Sir Walter Reuben Preston (Conservative) was elected in 1918 and defeated in1923. Born in 1875, Preston's father was from Hayes in Kent and he first stood for Parliament in January 1910 when he unsuccessfully contested St Pancras East. He remained outside the House until 1928 when he was returned at a by-election for the Gloucestershire constituency of Cheltenham, which he held until 1937, when he resigned. He was a Director of Stone and Company; marine and railway engineers based in Deptford, South East London and became a Director of the Midland Bank[32]. He was also Chairman of Platt Brothers and Company and of Textile Machinery Makers Ltd, a company that subsequently grew to acquire many businesses involved in the same trade and which in 1946 was subject to a Ministry of Supply investigation into price fixing. In 1914 when it was at its zenith, Platts, which was based in Oldham, was the largest manufacturer of cotton textile equipment in Britain employing fifteen thousand people on a site covering eighty five acres[33]. He died in 1946.

The John Scurr Primary School, Stepney Green as a polling station. Named after John Scurr MP (Labour) for Mile End, 1923-31. **Wikipedia**

John Scurr (Labour), who was probably best known as the founder of the Home Rule for India League, won Mile End in 1923 and held it until 1931 when he was defeated. Born in 1876 and of Irish descent he was a Member of the Executive of the United Irish League from 1900 to 1906 and a sometime member of the English

32 Midland Bank began trading as the Birmingham and Midland Bank in 1836. In 1891 it merged with the Bank of London to become the London and Midland Bank but after a period of expansion it became Midland again in 1923. By 1934 it had established itself as the largest deposit bank in the world. It lost its independence in 1992 when the Hong Kong and Shanghai Banking Corporation acquired a controlling interest in the company's affairs. It is now HSBC.

33 Henry Platt, a blacksmith started the company in 1770 and it closed in 1982. (Source: Manchester Forum, Winter 2003)

Land Restoration League, a mainly socialist organisation that favoured the nationalization of land. A member of Poplar Borough Council on which he was an Alderman and Mayor (1922-3), he was also an Alderman for London from 1915 and a member of the Poplar Board of Guardians. He fought several Parliamentary constituencies unsuccessfully, his first contest coming in 1913 at Chesterfield, with others following at Bethnal Green South West (1914), Ipswich (1914), Buckingham (1918) and Mile End (1922). He died in 1932.

Dr. William Joseph O'Donovan (Conservative), a skin specialist at the London Hospital in Whitechapel, took the seat in 1931. He was Chairman of the University of London Conservative Association and became politicised in 1926 when local socialists cut off electricity supplies to operating theatres and wards. During the First World War he served as Chief Medical Officer to the Ministry of Munitions. He died in 1955.

He was defeated by **Daniel Frankel** (Labour), who was elected in 1935. Frankel was born in Mile End in 1900 and took an active part in local Government in Stepney where he was Mayor in 1929, the Leader of the Council and Chairman of the Finance Committee. He became a member of the LCC in 1931. He remained MP for the constituency until 1945 when he had the unusual distinction of being defeated by a Communist. He died in 1988.

Whitechapel & St Georges

James Daniel Kiley (Liberal) was MP for Whitechapel & St Georges from 1918 to 1922 having been previously the MP for Whitechapel since 1916. His main biographical details may be found in Chapter 3 (Tower Hamlets).

Charles James Mathew (Labour) won the seat in 1922 but died within a matter of weeks of the General Election. Born in 1872, he was educated at the Oratory School in Birmingham and at Trinity Hall Cambridge where he graduated as a BA. He was called to the bar in 1897 and in 1913 became a KC, then a bencher in 1918. He was elected a LCC councillor for St George in the East in 1910 and served until 1919 when he was made an Alderman.

Harry Gosling MP
Wikipedia

The 1923 by-election that followed his death was won by **Harry Gosling** (Labour). Born in 1861 in Lambeth, Gosling lost his mother at the age of 7 and left his Blackfriars school aged 13 to become an office boy. However, in 1875 he got work on the river Thames getting involved with trade unionism at an early stage. In 1890 he became president of the Lambeth branch of the Amalgamated Society of Watermen and Lightermen and its General Secretary three years later. He was made an alderman on the LCC in 1898 and six years later was elected a councillor at Wapping serving until 1929. When the Transport Workers Federation was founded in 1910 he became its first President and was also the first President of the Transport and General Workers Union when it was formed from a further amalgamation of smaller unions in 1922. In 1908 he joined the TUC's Parliamentary Committee and was President of the TUC in 1916. He was later appointed a member of the Civil Service Arbitration Board, of the Port of London Authority and of the Imperial War Graves Commission. He first contested a Parliamentary seat in 1910 when he was defeated at Lambeth; then suffered the same fate at Uxbridge in 1918 and at Lambeth again four years later. After his election at Whitechapel in 1923 he was Minister of Transport and Paymaster-General in the first Labour Government.

Golsing died in 1930 and the by-election was won by **James Hall** (Labour) who, like his predecessor, was on the executive of the Transport and General Workers Union and had been an active Trade Unionist for forty years. Though he lost his seat at the 1931 general election he was reselected as the Labour candidate in 1935 and was once more elected serving until 1942 when he died.

Sir Barnett Janner (Liberal), who was born in 1892 and educated at Barry County School and Cardiff University, took the seat from Hall in 1931 but held it for only one Parliament. During the Great War he served in the Royal Garrison Artillery in France and Belgium but was best known as a solicitor who was chairman of the Jewish Board of Guardians in Cardiff, where he was also on the Royal Infirmary's Board of Management. This was his third attempt to become an MP having previously stood at Cardiff Central in 1929 and for Whitechapel at the by-election, which saw the return of James Hall. Janner joined the Labour Party in 1936 and was returned again as an MP in 1945 when he won Leicester West. In 1950 he was selected for the new seat of North West Leicester and remained an MP until 1970 when he retired and was succeeded by his son, Greville, who retired in 1997 and became a Lord. Sir Barnett became President of the Zionist Federation of Great Britain and Ireland[34] and was honorary rents adviser to the Labour Party.

34 The Zionist Federation of Great Britain and Ireland was established in 1899 to campaign for a permanent homeland for the

The 1942 by-election that followed Hall's death was won by **Walter James Edwards** (Labour), who was born in Limehouse in 1900 and educated at elementary school in the same neighbourhood. He became a docker and car man but in 1918 joined the Royal Navy. In 1923 he returned to the docks working as a casual labourer until 1937and was an active trade unionist in the Transport and General Workers Union. He became a local councillor in Stepney in 1934 and at the start of the Second World War re-joined the Navy serving on a minesweeper at Dunkirk and taking part in commando raids in Norway. He sailed in Artic convoys to Murmansk and served in a Russian arctic port but was released from the Navy to fight the 1942 by-election. He was made Mayor of Stepney in 1944 and the following year, after his re-election, a Civil Lord of the Admiralty in which post he remained until 1951. In 1950, following boundary changes, he became MP for Stepney which he held until his retirement in 1964. He died on election day of the same year.

MPs for Hackney, Stoke Newington, and Shoreditch

From	at	To	Surname	First Names	Constituency	Party
1918	G	1922	Woolcock	William James Uglow	Hackney Central	Coalition Liberal
1922	G	1923	Levy	Sir Arthur		National Liberal
1923	G	1924	Franklin	Sir Leonard Benjamin		Liberal
1924	G	1929	Gower	Sir Robert Vaughan		Conservative
1929	G	1931	Watkins	Frederick Charles		Labour
1931	G	1935	Lockwood	John Cutts TD (Lt-Col)		Conservative
1935	G	1945	Watkins	Frederick Charles		Labour
1918	G	1923	Greene	Sir Walter Raymond	Hackney North	Conservative
1923	G	1924	Harris	Sir John Hobbis		Liberal
1924	G	1945	Hudson	Sir Austin Uvedale (Capt)		Conservative
1918	G	1922	Bottomley	Horatio	Hackney South	Independent
1922	B	1923	Erskine-Bolst	Clifford Charles Alan Lawrence (Capt)		Conservative
1923	G	1924	Morrison	Herbert		Labour
1924	G	1929	Garro-Jones	George Morgan		Liberal
1929	G	1931	Morrison	Herbert		Labour
1931	G	1935	Graves	Miss F. Marjorie		Conservative
1935	G	1945	Morrison	Herbert		Labour
1918	G	1922	Addison	Dr. Christopher L.	Shoreditch	Liberal
1922	G	1923	Price	Ernest Griffith		National Liberal
1923	G	1931	Thurtle	Ernest		Labour
1931	G	1935	Summersby	Charles Harold		National Liberal
1935	G	1945	Thurtle	Ernest		Labour
1918	G	1923	Jones	Sir George William Henry	Stoke Newington	Conservative
1923	G	1924	Spero	Dr.George Ernest		Liberal
1924	G	1945	Jones	Sir George		Conservative

Notes: First returned at: B By-election, G General Election

Hackney Central

William James Uglow Woolcock (Coalition Liberal) was the son of a clergyman from Plymouth; he was born in 1878 and educated privately. He sat between 1918 and 1922 and for five years prior to his election was Secretary of the Pharmaceutical Society, the primary aim of which became the regulation of pharmacists in Britain [35]. For the last year of the First World War he was also Assistant Director of Army Contracts in which role he chaired the Medical Supplies Committee and was also in that year briefly Secretary-General of the War Office Supplies Department. After his election he was made PPS at the Ministry of Supply (1919-20) and to the Postmaster General in 1921/2 but from 1918 and during his period as an MP he was also General Manager of the Association of British Chemical Manufacturers, a role he held until 1928. He was President of the Society of the Chemical Industry from 1924 to 1926 and died in 1947.

Jewish people.

35 The society was formed on April 15 1841, at the Crown and Anchor Tavern in the Strand to unite the profession into one body, to protect its members' interests and advance scientific knowledge.

Sir Arthur Levy (National Liberal) was the MP for only one year (1922-3). Born in 1860 and educated privately; then at London University College and abroad, he was an Essex JP and initially Liberal MP for Harwich between 1906 and 1910 when he was defeated at the January Election, suffering the same fate in December at Wolverhampton South. He became a Baronet in 1912 and during the Great War was a member of the London War Pensions Committee and Deputy Director of Recruiting for the South East Region of England. He served briefly in 1917 with the Royal Fusiliers in France. He died in the year after his 1923 defeat at the polls.

Sir Leonard Benjamin Franklin (Liberal) took the seat in 1923 but lost it after a year. Son of Ellis Franklin, a banker, he was born in London in 1862 and educated at Kings College and the Athenee Royale in Brussels after which he became a barrister, practising at both Lincolns Inn and the Inner Temple. He too went into banking and became Senior Partner at the firm of A. Keyser and Company. His first attempt to get into the Commons at St Pancras North failed in December 1910 as did his next attempt in1918. He failed too at St Pancras South East in 1922 and, following his brief success at Hackney Central, he lost the three subsequent general elections there. His political career coincided with the decline of the Liberal Party and he died in 1944.

Sir Robert Vaughan Gower (Conservative) was the division's MP between 1924 and 1929. Born in 1880 he was a landowner, who lived in Tunbridge Wells where he was an alderman from 1914 to 1934. He was Mayor from 1917-19 and was made an Honorary Freeman in 1924. He also served on Kent County Council from 1910/25. He was President of the Property Owners' Protection Association and served on the RSPCA from 1928 until 1951, being elected its President in 1931. He was also an Honorary Colonel in the Territorial Army and President of 129 Squadron Air Training Corps. During the First War he gained several military honours from European Governments. In1929 he changed seats to become MP for Rochester & Chatham in his native Kent and remained in the House until 1945. He died in 1953.

Frederick Charles Watkins (Labour) was the MP from 1929 to 1931 and again from 1935 to 1945. Born in 1883 he joined the railways after leaving elementary school and became a Trade Unionist rising to become President of the Railway Clerks Association. He lived in Buckinghamshire, where he was a magistrate, and contested Aylesbury twice, in 1923 and 1924, both times unsuccessfully. Although he lost Hackney Central in the Labour debacle of 1931 he was re-elected in 1935 and served until he retired in 1945. During the War he was PPS to Herbert Morrison, himself a former Hackney MP, when he was Home Secretary from 1942-45. He died in 1954.

Lieutenant- Colonel John Cutts Lockwood TD (Conservative) took the seat from Watkins in 1931 and held it for one term. He was born at Romford, Essex in 1889 and educated at Chigwell School. He became a lawyer and in 1921 was called to the Bar at the Middle Temple after serving in the Great War in the Essex Regiment and the Coldstream Guards. Although Essex based, where he was also a magistrate, his first experience of Parliamentary elections came with his victory at Hackney and, though defeated in 1935, he re-emerged after the War to contest Bexley (Kent) in 1945 and again at a by-election in 1946. In 1949 he was elected to Essex County Council and remained a councillor or alderman until 1970, apart from a three year period between 1952 and 1955 which covered part of the time he was MP for his home Parliamentary seat of Romford, which he represented between 1950 and 1955 when it fell to Labour. Once again he became a County Councillor and retired in 1970. He was for a while Chairman of the RSPCA. He died in 1983.

Hackney North

Sir Walter Raymond Greene (Conservative) was MP for Hackney North from 1910 until 1923. His principal biographical details may be found in Chapter 3 (Hackney).

He was succeeded by **Sir John Hobbis Harris** (Liberal) who was MP from 1923 to 1924. He was born in Wantage in 1874 and spent 7 years as a missionary in Central Africa. He became Secretary of the Anti Slavery and Aborigine Protection Society and published several papers on the subject. He was also a member of the Executive Committee of the League of Nations Union, a citizen support group for international peace set up in 1918, and first contested a Parliamentary seat in 1922 when he was defeated at Camberwell North West. Following his short-lived period as an MP for Hackney North he unsuccessfully contested the Westbury division of Wiltshire in 1931. He died in 1940.

Captain Sir Austen Uvedale Hudson (Conservative Unionist) represented the seat between 1924 and 1945 but his main biographical details are contained earlier in this chapter under Islington East where he was MP in 1922/3.

Hackney South

Horatio Bottomley (Independent) represented Hackney South from 1918 to 1922. His main biographical details are contained in Chapter 3.

He was succeeded by **Captain Clifford Charles Alan Lawrence Erskine-Bolst** (Conservative) who was MP in 1922/3. Born at Kelso in the Scottish Borders in 1878, he was educated at Blair Lodge, Polmont in Perthshire. His mother was the daughter of an American Senator and he was a promoter of relationships between the UK and USA. He was a magistrate and freeman of the City of London, a fellow of the Royal Geographical Society and served in the first Battalion of the Black Watch. In 1918 he was appointed Agricultural Adviser for the Principality of Wales. Following his defeat in 1923 he was out of the House for some years but won Blackpool in 1931 and held it until his retirement in 1935. He died in 1946.

Herbert Morrison MP
© National Portrait Gallery
Bassano Ltd 1924

Herbert Morrison (Labour), the son of a London policeman, was the MP three times (1923-4, 1929-31 and 1935-45). He was born in 1888 in Lambeth and attended elementary schools in Stockwell Road and Lingham Street before he became an errand boy, then shop assistant and telephonist. As a child he lost the sight of one eye. He became interested in politics as a teenager and joined the Independent Labour Party in 1906 but decided it was insufficiently radical and joined the Social Democratic Federation[36]. He opposed the First World War, an unpopular position to take at the time, and joined the Labour Party. In 1915 he was a founder member of the London Labour Party of which he was elected Secretary remaining in that post until 1940 when he entered the War Cabinet under Winston Churchill.

From 1920-1 he was mayor of Hackney and in 1922 was elected to the London County Council where he became leader of the Labour Group. From 1934 to 1940 he was Council Leader. Elected as MP in 1923, he was defeated in 1924 but regained the seat in 1929 when Labour formed a Government in which he was appointed Minister of Transport and given Cabinet rank in 1931 shortly before the Party lost power. He broke furiously with Ramsey MacDonald, and publicly attacked King George V, whom he accused of seeking to split the Labour Party. Defeated at the 1931 election he was returned again in 1935 and five years later was made Minister of Supply in the Churchill Coalition Government; and Home Secretary later the same year serving until 1945, the last three years of which were in the War Cabinet.

In the 1945 Election he transferred to Lewisham East, and in 1950 to Lewisham South following boundary changes. During the whole of the period 1945 to 1951 he remained in the Cabinet and was also Deputy Leader of his Party. He served mainly as Lord President of the Council (effectively Deputy Prime Minister) from 1945 to March 1951 when, following the death of Ernest Bevin, he became Foreign Secretary, which post he held only until October when the Tories returned to Government. He remained Deputy Party Leader and retired from the Commons in 1959 when he went to the Lords as a Viscount. He was appointed president of the British Board of Film Censors and remained active in politics until his death in 1965[37]. He presided over a period of liberalisation at the Film Board following a test case in which the publishers of the novel 'Lady Chatterley's Lover' successfully defended a 1960 prosecution brought against them under the Obscene Publications Act (1959).

An 'old' Herbert Morrison, the Leader of the House of Commons makes a point to Hugh Gaitskell (Leeds South), Chancellor of the Exchequer.
People's History Museum, Manchester

George Morgan Garro-Jones (Liberal) was MP between 1924 and 1929. Son of the Reverend David Garro-Jones of Renfys, Milford Haven, he was born in 1894 and educated at Caterham, Surrey. Called to the Bar in 1922, after entering the House in 1924 he was made Private Secretary to Sir Hamar Greenwood, who was successively a Minister at the Home Office, the Board of Trade, and Ireland. An Honorary Captain in the RAF, Garro-Jones fought in the Great War in France with the 10th Battalion of the South Wales Borderers and Number 1 Squadron of the Royal Flying Corps. He also served in the USA as an adviser to their Air Service. A journalist, he became Editor of the *Daily Despatch*, and first fought Hackney South in 1923 when he was defeated. He retired in 1929 but subsequently joined the Labour Party, in whose name he served as MP for Aberdeen North between 1935 and 1945. He died in 1960.

36 The SDF was a Marxist socialist society, founded as the Democratic Federation in 1881 and renamed in 1884. In 1911 it became the British Socialist Party.
37 The Board, which is now The British Board of Film Classification, was established in 1912 to standardise the ratings for films.

Miss Marjorie Graves (Conservative) defeated Herbert Morrison in the 1931 National Government landslide but lost to him four years later. A member of Holborn Borough Council since 1928, she was a representative for London on the National Union of Conservative and Unionist Associations. During the First World War she served in the Foreign Office and in 1919/20 was secretary of the Intelligence Department at the Home Office. Born in 1884, she died in 1961.

Shoreditch

Christopher Addison (Liberal) was MP for Shoreditch from 1918 to 1922 but prior to that represented the Hoxton division of the same borough. His biographical details can be found in Chapter 3 (Shoreditch, Hoxton).

He was succeeded by **Ernest Griffith Price** (National Liberal) who was born in 1870 and died in 1962.

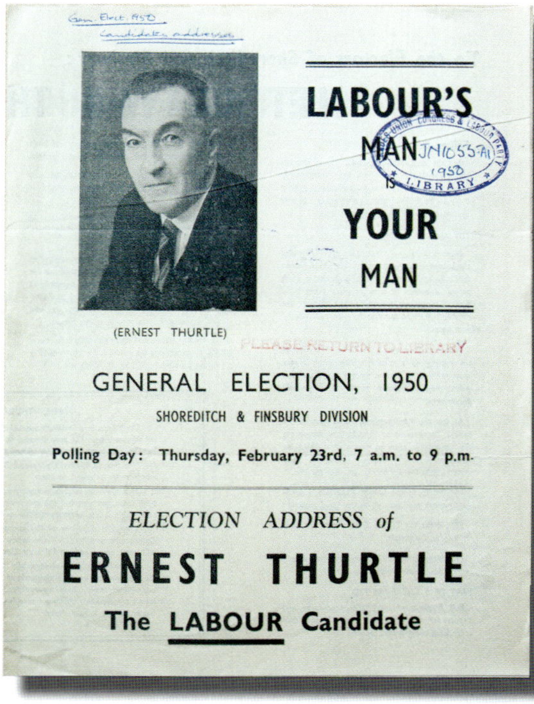

An election communication in favour of Ernest Thurtle, issued at the 1950 General Election, where Thurtle was again re-elected as an MP. Such ephemera are normally lost to us, but this one has been carefully preserved.
People's History Museum, Manchester

He was only briefly an MP, in 1922/3 being defeated then by **Ernest Thurtle** (Labour) who represented Shoreditch from 1923 to 1931 and again between 1935 and 1950 when the seat was merged with Finsbury. He held the combined seat of Shoreditch & Finsbury until his death in1954. Born in New York State in 1884, he was a son-in-law of the onetime Labour Party leader, George Lansbury. He received only an elementary school education but became an accountant, salesman, secretary and journalist. During the Great War he was severely wounded at Cambrai and as an MP campaigned for the rights of ex-servicemen. In 1930 he succeeded in persuading Parliament to abolish the death penalty for desertion from the Armed Services. He fought Bethnal Green South West in 1918 but was defeated and also failed at his next attempt, which was at Shoreditch in 1922. Elected a year later he was PPS at the Ministry of Pensions in 1924, then a Labour whip for a while and in 1929 became First Commissioner of Works. Between 1941 and 1945 he was Parliamentary Secretary at the Ministry of Information.

Between 1931 and 1935 Shoreditch was represented by **Charles Harold Summersby** (National Liberal), the son of a Congregational Minister. Born in Oxfordshire in 1884, he left school at 14 and moved to London where he served an apprenticeship as a draper, later becoming a Buyer for Derry and Toms, a London department store in Kensington High Street. In 1912 he set up in business himself and became the owner of a large store at Muswell Hill, where in 1919 he was elected to Hornsey Borough Council becoming Mayor in 1927. Thurtle defeated him in 1935. He died in 1961.

Stoke Newington

Sir George William Henry Jones (Conservative) was the first MP between 1918 to 1923 and sat again from 1924 until 1945. A barrister, he was also a member of the London County Council as well as Hackney Borough Council and was knighted in 1928.

Dr George Ernest Spero (Liberal) took the seat in 1923 but was defeated a year later. He subsequently joined the Labour Party and was MP for Fulham West between 1929 and 1931. His biographical details can be found in Chapter 3 (Fulham).

MPs for North East Middlesex						
From	**at**	**To**	**Surname**	**First Names**	**Constituency**	**Party**
1918	G	1922	Warren	Sir Alfred Haman	Edmonton	Conservative
1922	G	1931	Broad	Francis Alfred		Labour (Co-op)
1931	G	1935	Rutherford	John		Conservative
1935	G	1945	Broad	Francis Alfred		Labour (Co-op)
1945	G	1948	Durbin	Evan Frank Mottram		Labour
1918	G	1922	Bowles	Henry	Enfield	Conservative
1922	G	1923	Fermor-Hesketh	Sir Thomas George		Conservative
1923	G	1924	Henderson	William Watson		Labour
1924	G	1929	Applin	RVK (Lt Col)		Conservative
1929	G	1931	Henderson	William Watson		Labour
1931	G	1935	Applin	Reginald Vincent Kempenfeldt		Conservative
1935	G	1945	Bull	Bartle B.		Conservative
1918	G	1921	Jones	William Kennedy	Hornsey	Conservative
1921	B	1924	Ednam	Viscount		Conservative
1924	G	1941	Wallace	Euan (Captain)		Conservative
1941	B	1945	Gammans	Sir Leonard David (Captain)		Conservative
1918	G	1922	Prescott	Sir William Henry	Tottenham North	Conservative
1922	G	1931	Morrison	Robert Craigmyle		Labour
1931	G	1935	Doran	Edward		Conservative
1935	G	1945	Morrison	Robert Craigmyle		Labour
1918	G	1923	Malone	Patrick Bernard (Major)	Tottenham South	Conservative
1923	G	1924	Alden	Sir Percy		Labour
1924	G	1929	Malone	Patrick Bernard (Major)		Conservative
1929	G	1931	Messer	Sir Frederick		Labour
1931	G	1935	Palmer	Francis Noel		National Labour
1935	G	1945	Messer	Sir Frederick		Labour
1918	G	1935	Locker-Lampson	Godfrey	Wood Green	Conservative
1935	G	1945	Baxter	Sir Arthur Beverley		Conservative

Notes: First returned at: B By-election, G General Election

Edmonton

Sir Alfred Haman Warren (Conservative) was Edmonton's first MP between 1918 and 1922. Born in 1856 at Poplar, he was educated at the local Wesleyan School and made a career in insurance. He was a sometime Grandmaster of Manchester Unity of Oddfellows, a union of friendly societies established in 1810, and became President of the National Conference of Friendly Societies and a Parliamentary Agent. In the years prior to the modern Welfare State, Friendly Societies were often very important in providing benefits to people who encountered difficult circumstances[38]. He was Poplar's Mayor from 1913 to 1918 when he was awarded the OBE, Knighted and elected MP, all in the same year. He died in 1927.

He was succeeded by **Francis Alfred Broad** (Labour and Co-operative) who had been his opponent in 1918 and who, after 1922, remained Edmonton's MP until 1931 when he was defeated though he regained the seat in 1935 and retired in 1945. A scientific instrument maker and trade unionist, Broad was a President of the Instrument Makers Society who became a National Trustee of the Amalgamated Engineering Union[39]. Born in 1874, he died in 1956.

38 To counter the worst social effects of the industrialisation of Britain, friendly societies of all kinds were created. Self-help insurance schemes, they embraced a wide range of activity including building societies, retail and wholesale co-operatives, savings banks, trade unions, and welfare clubs. From 1910 to 1947, friendly societies administered the state sickness benefit scheme and, at their peak in 1945 also catered for the further needs of 8.75 million private subscribers through over 18,000 branches or societies. (Source: The Association of Friendly Societies)

39 Formed in 1887 as the Scientific Instrument Makers' Trade Society, the society was later renamed the Amalgamated Instrument Makers' Society. It amalgamated with the Amalgamated Society of Engineers and eight other unions to form the Amalgamated Engineering Union in 1920.

John Rutherford (Conservative) was elected Unionist MP in 1931 serving until Broad's re-election. Called to the Bar in 1928 he contested Deptford at the 1931 LCC elections but in the same year was elected to serve on Paddington Council. Born in 1904, he died in 1957.

Enfield

Henry Bowles (Conservative), who won the seat in 1918, had been Enfield's MP on and off since 1889 when he first took it at a by-election. He was defeated in 1906 but returned in 1918 when the defending MP opted for the new Finchley seat. Bowles held it until 1922 when he retired. His principal biographical details can be found in Chapter3.

He was succeeded by **Sir Thomas George Fermor - Hesketh** (Conservative), the 7th baronet, who was born in 1881 and owned over fifteen thousand acres at Towcester, Northamptonshire. He was honorary colonel of the 5th and 6th Battalions of the Liverpool Regiment but was MP for only a year, from 1922 to 1923. He died in 1944.

The seat was taken by **William Watson Henderson** (Labour) who was born in 1891 - the second son of Arthur Henderson, Foreign Secretary in the First Labour Government. William was MP for Enfield on two brief occasions, the first between 1923 and 1924 and secondly from 1929 to 1931. Educated at Darlington Grammar School, he was a journalist who became head of the press and publicity department of the Labour Party.

Lieutenant Colonel Reginald Vincent Kempenfeldt Applin DSO (Conservative) was twice MP for Enfield; once between 1924 and 1929 and then again from 1931 to 1935. He was born in 1869 and was educated at Sherborne School. A career soldier, he served in Northern Borneo, South Africa (where he was awarded the DSO) and in Europe during the Great War. He became a captain in the Hussars in 1905 and a Corps Machine Gun Commander from 1914-19 with the rank of Lieutenant Colonel. He was decorated again and given the OBE. In March 1920 he unsuccessfully contested Dartford (Kent) for the National Party and the Abbey Division of Westminster for the Anti Waste League in August 1921. He died in 1957.

Bartle Bull (Conservative) who succeeded him was MP between 1935 and 1945 when he was defeated. Born in Toronto in 1902, he came to England when he was 9 and following his school education at Eton, went to Oxford University where he became a well-known Rugby player. He was called to the bar and then spent a great deal of time visiting Canada, the USA, Cuba and travelling round the world before he became an MP. He was PPS to Euan Wallace, the MP for the adjacent Hornsey constituency who was Financial Secretary to the Ministry of Transport from1938 to 1940 and fulfilled the same role for Gwylim Lloyd-George when he was Minister of Fuel and Power between 1944 and 1945. He died in 1950.

Hornsey

William Kennedy Jones (Conservative) was elected at a by-election in 1916 and re-elected in 1918, serving as Hornsey's MP until 1921. His principal biographical details can be found in Chapter 3.

He was succeeded at a by-election in 1921 by **Viscount Ednam** (Conservative), son of the second Earl of Dudley who was Lord Lieutenant of Ireland between 1902 and 1905 and then Governor-General of Australia between 1908 and 1911 where he acquired a reputation as 'anti-Labour,' making him unpopular with half the Australian electorate. His son was a close friend of the royal family, in particular the Prince of Wales, and became the Third Earl in 1932. He was born in 1894, William Humble, the son of William Ward and Georgina Elizabeth Monfreiffe. He stood down in 1924 but re-emerged as MP for Wednesbury in 1931, serving until 1932 when he became the Third Earl Dudley. He died in 1969.

Captain Euan Wallace MP
Wikipedia

The MP from 1924 to 1941 was **Captain Euan Wallace** (Conservative) who was born at Dunblane, Perthshire in 1892. He attended Harrow School and went to the Royal Military College pursuing a military career in the Life Guards. He was wounded during the Great War but was mentioned in despatches four times and awarded the Military Cross. In 1919, the year of his divorce from his first wife, he was appointed Military Attaché at the British Embassy in Washington DC and the following year went to Canada as ADC to the Governor-General. The same year he married the daughter of Sir Edward Lutyens, the famous architect, who at the time was laying out the Government and Public Buildings in New Delhi, India, a project that made him famous. Wallace returned to Britain where he entered politics, initially as MP for the Rugby Division of Warwickshire between 1922 and 1923, when he was defeated. During that period he was appointed PPS to the First Lord of the Admiralty and after his election at Hornsey in 1924, PPS to the Secretary of State for the Colonies. In 1928 he was made an assistant Government whip (unpaid Junior Lord of the Treasury), from which post he resigned in 1929 but after the return of the National Government in 1931 he was appointed once again as a Junior Lord, but later the same year was made Civil Lord at the Admiralty, in which post he served until 1935. After the election of that year he was briefly Under-Secretary at the Home Office, but within five months transferred to Overseas Trade where he served until May 1937. He then became Parliamentary Secretary to the President of the Board of Trade, Oliver Stanley, and a year later was made First Secretary at the Treasury serving under Sir John Simon, the Chancellor of the Exchequer. Promotion came again when in April 1939 he became Minister of Transport, a non-Cabinet post. He died in 1941.

Leonard David Gammans MP
People's History Museum, Manchester

Captain Sir Leonard David Gammans (Conservative) succeeded him at a by-election in 1941 and served until his death in 1957, when his wife succeeded him. He was born in 1895 and educated at Portsmouth Grammar School, then at London University. He joined the Royal Field Artillery in 1914 at the age of nineteen and after the War continued his education at the Canadian Military College which was founded in Kingston, Ontario in 1876. In 1920 he entered the Malayan Civil Service and commenced a brief career in the diplomatic corps, which because of his ability to speak Japanese, took him to the British Embassy in Tokyo in 1925. He returned to Malaya where he studied the functioning of co-operative enterprises and after being taken ill in 1934 returned to Britain where he continued his interest becoming Director of the Land Settlement Association when it was set up in 1935 to promote the co-operative ownership of smallholdings for people blighted by unemployment. At the outbreak of the Second World War he joined the Ministry of Information serving there throughout the War. Following the election of the Conservatives in 1951 he was appointed Assistant Postmaster – General and shared the piloting of the Television Bill, establishing Commercial Television, through the Commons. He occupied this post until 1955 and died two years later.

Tottenham North

Sir William Henry Prescott (Conservative) was MP from 1918 until 1922. Born in 1874 and educated privately, he was a barrister at Grays Inn who in 1914-15 during the War commanded the 222nd Field Company of the Royal Engineers but was invalided out and became a consulting civil engineer. Awarded the CBE in 1920 he was active on several fronts. From 1928-40 he was Chairman of the Metropolitan Water Board and also served on the Lee Conservancy Board[40]. A Mason, he was Grand Deacon of the United Lodge of England, which administers Lodges of Freemasons in England and Wales and in many places overseas. He was also a Master of the Worshipful Company of Pavoirs, a Liveryman of the Glaziers Company[41] and a Freeman of the City of London. In 1929 he was High Sheriff of Middlesex and also of Cambridgeshire/Huntingdonshire. From 1936-42 he was chairman of the Edmonton Petty Sessions and was also a governor of Tottenham Grammar School and of the Prince of Wales hospital in the town. He died in 1945.

Robert Craigmyle Morrison (Labour) represented the seat from 1922 to 1931. Born in 1881, the son of an Aberdonian father, he became a teacher. A County Councillor for Middlesex from 1919 to 1925 and an active member of the London Co-operative Movement until 1923, he was PPS to Harry Gosling, the Minister of Transport during the First Labour Government, and in 1925 was appointed Parliamentary Secretary to Ramsey MacDonald, leader of the Opposition but Prime Minister after 1929. He parted company with MacDonald in August 1931 and did not follow him into the National Government but forfeited his seat as a result and became Managing Director of Film Industries Limited. He regained the constituency in 1935 and retired in 1945 when he was ennobled as the 1st Lord Morrison. From 1947 to 1948 he was a Lord in Waiting to the King and from 1948 to 1951 the Parliamentary Secretary at the Ministry of Works. He died in 1953.

Between 1931 and 1935 the seat was represented by **Edward Doran** (Conservative), a film producer. Born in Manchester in 1892 he was educated at Failsworth and Manchester Grammar Schools after which he became a lecturer in the political, social and industrial life of the USA. He was an authority on the history of the Western United States and, whilst in the States, developed an interest in railways going on to invent an automatic level crossing control system that was used in both the USA and Canada. He made little mark in the House and with hindsight at least appears to have held some unfortunate and possibly anti-Semitic views. In a Commons debate on Jewish immigration in March 1933 he

40 The River Lee (or Lea) and Stort Navigation is a canalised river, not an entirely new canal. The Lea Conservancy Act 1868 placed the navigation in the hands of a new conservancy board.
41 The Glaziers Company dates from 1328 but its modern focus is on the art and craft of historic and contemporary stained and decorative glass for buildings.

asked the Prime Minister if he would be taking any extra measures to prevent alien Jews from Germany entering Britain claiming that 'hundreds of thousands of Jews are now leaving Germany and scurrying from there to this country when other countries are closed to them... May I ask whether it is the declared policy of this country to allow aliens to come in from every country in the world while we have 3 million unemployed? If you are asking for a Hitler in this country you will soon get him.' Prior to his election he unsuccessfully contested the Silvertown division of West Ham in 1924. He died in 1945.

Tottenham South

The MP from 1918 to 1923 and again from 1924-29 was **Major Patrick Bernard Malone** (Conservative), born in 1857 the son of an Irishman from County Galway. He qualified as an accountant and became a JP and County Alderman for Middlesex, sitting as a member of the Metropolitan Water Board, and the War Pensions and Finance Committees.

He was involved in Tottenham's local government affairs for nearly 40 years. In 1918 Malone had defeated the former MP for Tottenham, **Sir Percy Alden** (Labour), but in 1923 the roles were reversed and it was Alden who was the successful candidate. His principal biographical details can be found in Chapter 3 .

In 1929 Malone was defeated for a second time. The victor, **(Sir) Frederick Messer** (Labour) was, like his predecessor, MP for two periods, the first from 1929 to 1931 and the second from 1935 to 1950 when, after boundary changes, he was elected MP for Tottenham, a seat he occupied until 1959 when he retired. Messer was born in 1886 and after an elementary education became a French polisher. This led him into trade unionism and in 1916 he became Treasurer of the French Polishers' Union, then Chairman of the London Area Industrial Orthopaedic Society of which he was formerly acting General Secretary and Organizer. He was a Middlesex County Councillor, Alderman and JP and from 1947 to 1948 was County Council Chairman. He was chairman of the North West Metropolitan Hospital Board and a member of the Nuffield Trust. His Parliamentary career never took off, although he was PPS to Ernest Bevin when he was Minister of Labour in 1944-5. He died in 1971.

Messer's 'reign' as MP was interrupted between 1931 and 1935 by the election of **Francis Noel Palmer** (National Labour), a supporter of Ramsey MacDonald. Palmer had joined the Labour Party in 1906 and was an active member of the movement in favour of Women's suffrage. He contested the Farnham division of Surrey for Labour in 1919 and was still the Party's candidate there when the Labour Government split over the national financial crisis in 1931. At that stage he abandoned his candidacy at Farnham and stood instead at Tottenham South, winning the seat comfortably in a two-man contest. He died in 1961.

Wood Green

Godfrey Locker-Lampson MP
Wikipedia

Godfrey Locker-Lampson (Conservative) was the first MP from 1918 until 1935. Born in 1875, he was educated at Eton and Trinity College, Cambridge after which he entered the Foreign and Diplomatic service and in 1906 made his first attempt to become an MP, going down to defeat at Chesterfield. He was called to the Bar at Lincoln's Inn in 1908 but two years later was successful in securing election to the Commons at Salisbury, which he represented from January 1910 until 1918. He served in the War from 1914 to 1916 but in 1917 was appointed a PPS, first at the Home Office then, a year later, at the Foreign Office. In the Bonar Law Government he was a Parliamentary Under-Secretary at the Home Office in 1923 and again in 1924/5 after the fall of the first Labour Government. From 1925-29 he performed the same role in the Foreign Office. In 1931 he formed the populist Blue Shirt movement, with his brother Oliver, the Tory MP for Handsworth Birmingham, to combat what they perceived as the spread of communism. He retired in 1935 and died in 1946.

Sir Arthur Beverley Baxter (Conservative) was MP from 1935 until 1950. Born in Toronto (Canada) in 1891, he was educated there and became a journalist. During the Great War he fought in the Canadian Expeditionary Force and became a Lieutenant in the Royal Engineers. After the War he continued as a journalist and in 1922 joined the *Sunday Express* as a leader writer. He was closely associated with Lord Beaverbrook (another Canadian) who in 1929 appointed him to be Managing Editor and Editor-in-Chief of the *Daily Express* of which company he was also made a Director. Following his election as a Tory MP his relationship with Beaverbrook took another turn when the latter was appointed Minister of Aircraft Production. From 1939 to 1945 Baxter was the Controller of Aircraft Factory Co-operation, a vital role in winning the War in the Air. Baxter's seat was redrawn in 1950 when he opted for the nearby and then safe Conservative seat of Southgate, which he represented until his retirement in 1964, also the year of his death.

Chapter 8
Metropolitan Essex 1918-1945

Parliamentary Representation in the Inter-war Years 1918 - 1945

In 1918 there was another major redistribution of seats in metropolitan Essex as Parliamentary representation was adjusted to reflect the massive population expansion that had been taking place. A more equitable balance was struck and the number of seats increased from four to thirteen. West Ham was expanded to four and East Ham emerged from the former Romford constituency as a two-seat borough. Both developments reflected the move downstream of the London Docks promoting a population expansion at the expense of the neighbouring Tower Hamlets where Poplar and Whitechapel lost one seat each. Suburban and industrial developments generated several more seats. Romford spawned three more, one based on the town itself, another on Ilford, and a third contributing to Epping whilst the single Walthamstow constituency fragmented four ways. Leyton was split from Walthamstow and each borough was divided in two.

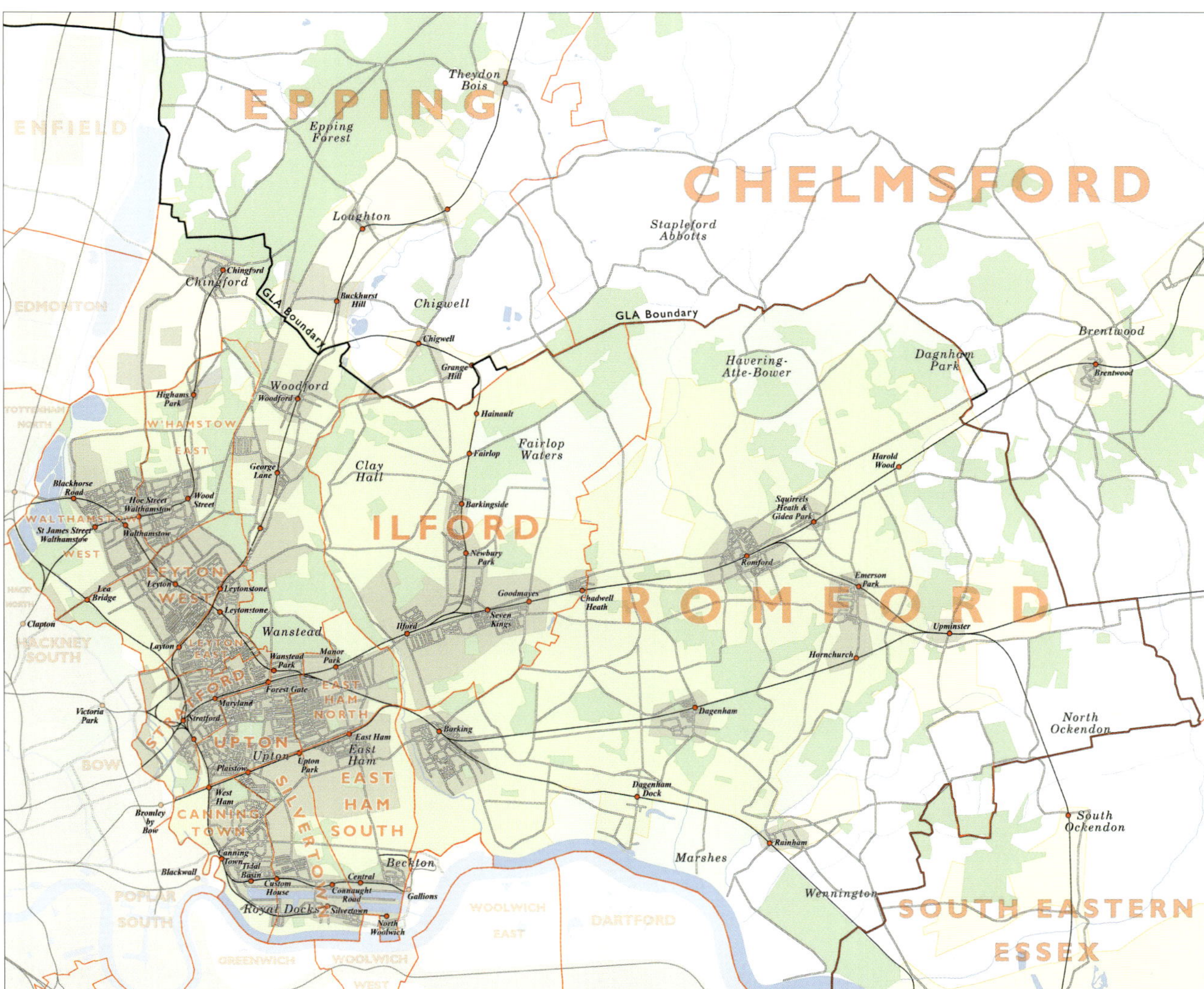

Contemporary postcard - London Borough of Newham

Gordon Rushton

Top Left: *The Green Man in Plashet Grove (East Ham North), with the corporation tramway, and nearby Upton Park and East Ham Stations was a well connected area.*

Top Right: *Church Lane Ell, outside Leytonstone Station (Leyton East Constituency). Independent Buildings was part of the 1930s building boom that developed the area.*

Left: *Beckton Gas Works on the Thames was one of the two biggest domestic gas producers in London. Many of it's large workforce lived in East Ham South.* **Wikipedia**

Above: *Tate & Lyle merged their sugar refining businesses on the north bank of the Thames at Plaistow/Silvertown in 1921. They grew to refine around 50% of Britain's sugar, such that the Thames refinery at Woolwich Reach became the largest cane sugar refinery in the world, producing around 14,000 tonnes per week, and employing over 1000 people. Much investment was placed in the plant, which was soon to become target for the German Luftwaffe. Sir Charles Lyle was the MP for nearby Stratford between 1918 and 1922.* **Gordon Rushton**

Left: *The area round Leyton High Street (Leyton West) had developed to be densely populated, but had excellent transport links to the labour intensive industries around the River Lea, and more widely in the local area.* **Gordon Rushton**

Top Left: *Ilford's magnificent Edwardian Town Hall, designed by B. Woolard in ornate Renaissance style, was enlarged in 1927 and 1933.*

Top Right: *There was a competition to design the Town Hall for Leyton, won by John Johnson. It was constructed in 1894-96 as an exuberant expression of civic pride*
Gordon Rushton

Left: *The rather sombre Havering (Romford) Town Hall opened in 1937. It was designed as part of a national competition in the 'International Modern' style, popular in those times.* **All images Wikipedia, except Top Right**

Queen of them all is undoubtedly Walthamstow Town Hall, designed by Philip Dalton Hepworth in a stripped classical 20th century style, with Art Deco details. Again, the design was the outcome of a competition begun in 1932. Construction began in 1937, but it was not finished until 1942. It was built in Portland stone, and it is a roomy building, much loved and much in use today.

The new **Stratford** constituency was essentially West Ham North West and covered the Broadway, Stratford New Town and Forest Gate districts. The name 'Stratford' meant 'ford on a Roman Road' and was where the London to Colchester highway crossed the river Lea. Originally 'Straetford' in old English, it became Stratford in 1177, nearly 10 years before its then neighbour, 'Westhamma' emerged. The North East constituency was **Upton** covering most of West Ham proper and Upton Park. 'Upton' meant simply, 'higher farmstead or village'. South of both constituencies was **Plaistow** which included part of Canning Town. The old English name of 'Plegstow' meant, 'Place for play or sport'. Lastly, **Silvertown** housed the main dock area around the Tidal Basin, Custom House and the rest of Canning Town. The name may derive from the Norman 'Sulfretone', meaning 'farmstead near the gully ford'.

East Ham North combined Manor Park with Little Ilford whilst **East Ham South** covered most of the town and the dockland communities between Beckton and North Woolwich. However, North Woolwich remained in Kent and was attached to a new Woolwich West constituency, details of which are in Chapter 9. It was at Beckton in 1867 that the Gas-Light & Coke Company bought a site by the Thames, allowing coal to be landed straight from barges. The plant was called Beckton after the governor of the company, Simon Adams Beck. East Ham's place name was originally 'Esthamma' but was not separately recorded until 1250, 64 years after its neighbour.

In addition to these mainly working class seats **Ilford** was established as a new much more middle class seat. The town got its name from 'Ilefort' which meant, 'ford over the river called Hyle' and was recorded in the Domesday Book. The Hyle was an early name for the River Roding below Ilford. By 1901 the Urban District had a recorded population of over 41,000 and the 1918 constituency covered a wide area that included Redbridge, Valentine's Park, Seven Kings, Goodmayes, Gants Hill and Hainault.

Woodford, Wanstead and Chingford remained in the **Epping** constituency. Barking and Dagenham populations meanwhile were growing to sustain **Romford** as a much more socially mixed constituency than it had been prior to the First World War. Barking, Dagenham, Romford and Hornchurch were its principal centres of population to which were also transferred Upminster and Rainham, formerly in Chelmsford and Essex South Eastern respectively.

Leyton East covered Leytonstone including Cann Hall and Cathall. **Leyton West** extended from Lea Bridge eastwards to the (Epping) Forest ward and south to include Leyton town centre itself. Leyton derives its name from its position on the river Lea. A Roman settlement called Leintuna on the eastern bank of the River became known as 'Lugetune' in 1050 during the Anglo-Saxon period. The river's name may come from the Celtic 'luge' meaning 'light'. Luton in Bedfordshire has the same derivation.The name was changed to the Norman 'Leintune' in 1086 and Leyton subsequently became a Manor owned by the Abbey of Stratford Langthorne from about 1200 until its dissolution in 1545.

The town's growth around the turn of the century was phenomenal. Three years after the Second Reform Act in 1871 the population of the parish of Leyton was only 10,394 of whom 5,480 souls lived in the town itself, the remainder living mainly in Leytonstone and surrounding hamlets. By 1901 Leyton had a recorded population of nearly 99,000 so it was somewhat surprising that representation had not been granted in 1885 and that the constituency name had been given to Walthamstow instead. Nevertheless it too developed massively during this period, after the construction of railway lines through the area. **Walthamstow East** covered Chapel End, Hoe Street, Wood Street and Hale End districts whilst **Walthamstow West** incorporated Lloyd Park, the High Street, Higham Hill and St James Street districts of the borough.

This all goes to show that there is nothing new in politics. This cartoon by Horrabin comes from a 1935 General Election communication from the Labour Party. This was in response to the 1931 National Government coalition that came to power in the wake of a financial crisis and slump. In fact the cartoon had been used in 1929, and it is poignant, and significant with a message that is echoed today. It might have done something for Labour's electoral fortunes, as these recovered in '35. In 1931 the Labour vote had collapsed - that Election was a disaster. Now they were on the 'up' again.

People's History Museum Manchester

Politics Between the Wars

The impact of these changes was to increase Labour's representation. West Ham South was already established as a Labour seat and the creation of Silvertown and Plaistow doubled the Party's strength immediately. Despite the national swings that occurred between 1918 and 1935 these two heavily unionised and radical docklands seats remained loyal to Labour throughout the period, including a by-election at Silvertown on 22nd February 1940 when, at the darkest hour of the Second World War, the Party secured a majority of 86% over an Independent. In accordance with the spirit of the times neither Conservatives nor Liberals contested the by-election. Labour had won the previous General Election in Silvertown by a margin of 62% and won again in 1945, when the seat was contested, by the even larger margin of 87%.

West Ham North, on the other hand, which had always been more marginal as a single constituency, became split both politically aand geographically after the redistribution. Stratford was Labour in every Election except the very first in 1918 whilst Upton, which was less working class, returned slightly more Conservatives. Even there Labour won three General Elections, including 1935 as well as the two following which it formed minority Governments, in 1923 and 1929. Labour also enjoyed by-election success there on 14th May 1934 when it regained the seat having lost to the Tories in 1931. Its majority of 16% compared with 17% for the Conservatives previously; in 1935 the majority slipped to 6%.

The creation of middle class seats based on Ilford and Epping gifted two MPs to the Conservatives. However, after the post War political shifts involving the Liberal Party had largely resolved themselves in Labour's favour the heavily working class East Ham South seat moved in their favour whilst the more socially mixed East Ham North became marginal, initially between Liberal and Tory but subsequently between Labour and Conservative. Labour first won there in 1923 but the Tories regained it in 1924. However, on 29th April 1926 Labour won a by-election by the margin of 6% over the Tories who had enjoyed a majority of slightly less than 4% at the General Election. Labour retained the seat in 1929 by a margin of 7%.

Metropolitan Essex - General Election Results - 1918-1935 by % majority

Constituency	pre-1918	1918	1922	1923	1924	1929	1931	1935
West Ham North	*L*							
W.Ham Stratford		*C28*	*Lab6*	*Lab 29*	*Lab12*	*Lab30*	*Lab0.8**	*Lab26*
W.Ham Upton		*C39*	*C13*	*Lab5*	*C8*	*Lab17*	*C17 -*	*Lab6*
W.Ham South	*Lab*							
W.Ham Plaistow		*Lab90*	*Lab27*	*Lab49*	*Lab34*	*Lab55*	*Lab100*	*Lab47*
W.Ham Silverton		*Lab20*	*Lab46*	*Lab63*	*Lab62*	*Lab71*	*Lab56*	*Lab62+*
Romford	*C/L*	*L29*	*NL17*	*C23*	*C6*	*Lab12*	*C23*	*Lab8*
E. Ham North		*L17*	*C2*	*Lab2*	*C4 -*	*Lab7*	*C32*	*C2*
E. Ham South		*NDP13*	*Lab18*	*Lab11*	*Lab4*	*Lab 29*	*C8*	*Lab19*
Ilford		*C41+*	*C20*	*C7*	*C32+*	*C6*	*C49*	*C26+*
Epping		*C52*	*C20*	*C6*	*C29*	*C10*	*C36*	*C35*
Walthamstow	*C/L*							
Leyton East		*L2*	*C8*	*Lab7*	*C7*	*Lab9*	*C25*	*C8*
Leyton West		*C35 -*	*C17*	*C0.2**	*C12*	*Lab6*	*C27*	*C8*
Walthamstow E.		*C27*	*C14*	*C1*	*C13*	*Lab5*	*C28*	*C8*
Walthamstow W.		*NDP22*	*Lab12*	*Lab9*	*L2*	*Lab22*	*Lab3*	*Lab24*
Party Totals	***Averages***							
C/NL/NLab	*1*	6+	8	5	8-+ ‡	2	9-	5+
L	2	3+	0	0	*1*	0	0	0
Lab/NDP	*1*	4	5	8	4+	*11*	4+	8+
Total	4	*13*	*13*	*13*	*13*	*13*	*13*	*13*

Key: C - Conservative; NL - National Liberal (allied with Con); L - Liberal; NLab - National Labour (allied with Con); Lab - Labour ; NDP - National Democratic Party: + by-election won by defending party; - lost by defending party. 100 = Unopposed ‡ two by-elections, one won, one lost

Despite the massive boundary changes affecting the Romford constituency itself, the 'swing 'nature of the seat was maintained after the First War. The growing middle class communities around Romford and Hornchurch were counter-balanced by working class communities in Barking and Dagenham so that the constituency was won by the Conservatives four times (including a National Liberal in 1922), once by the Liberals (in 1918) and twice by Labour (in 1929 and 1935). The winning of this seat by Labour in 1935 in a year when the Tories won comfortably on a national scale offers evidence that by then the expansion of Barking and Dagenham was having a disproportionate influence on the election outcome in the constituency. The 1918 changes also provided the Conservatives with two relatively safe seats in the shape of the adjoining Leyton West and Walthamstow East whilst Walthamstow West, a more working class suburb, was predominantly Labour. Leyton East, on the other hand, was marginal.

Despite the radical nature of the re-distribution the results cannot be said to have rested primarily on the way the boundaries were drawn as each of the seats changed hands at least once during the period. The national mood clearly played a significant part in determining the outcome of elections. Only Walthamstow West remained much stronger for one Party than any other and that was Labour, who even held the seat in the debacle of 1931. However, the Labour whitewash of 1929 when the Party took all four seats in the area clearly signalled that, with the public mood in their favour, socially mixed constituencies such as these could be expected to return Labour as well as Conservative MPs.

There were seven by-elections in the period. Conservatives won three, Labour three and Liberals one. Overall Labour won forty-five and the working class anti-socialist NDP two seats, whilst the Tories also secured forty-five plus one National Liberal. The Liberal Party, however, fared badly securing the return of only five. Three of these were won in the 1918 Election and another at a 1919 By-election. Only Walthamstow West fell to the Party at any other time and that was in 1924 when three-way politics reached its zenith, well illustrated in certain of the by-elections that occurred in the period.On 1st March 1919 a large swing took place at Leyton West where the Liberal candidate was returned by a margin of 15% over the Tories who in 1918 had recorded a 35% majority. At the 1922 General Election, however, the Tories were returned by a majority of 17% by which time Labour as well as the Liberals were splitting the non-Tory vote. By 1929 Labour was making the running and took the seat.

Three by-elections took place at Ilford and the Tories won each of them comfortably. However, Labour and Liberal jockeyed for second place. On 25th September 1920 there was a 24% majority over Labour compared with 41% over a Liberal in 1918. On 23rd February 1928 the Tories won by a margin of 11% over the Liberals having won the same seat at the 1924 General Election with a 37% majority over Labour. In 1929 their majority fell to 9%, again over Labour. On 29th June 1937 the Tories recorded a winning margin of 22% as against 27% in 1935 by which time Labour was firmly established as the main opposition.

MPs for West Ham

From	at	To	Surname	First Names	Constituency	Party Affiliation
1918	G	1945	Thorne	William James (Will)	Plaistow	Labour
1918	G	1940	Jones	John Joseph (Jack)	Silvertown	National Socialist Party/ Labour
1940	B	1945	Comyns	Dr. Louis		Labour
1918	G	1922	Lyle	Sir Charles Ernest Leonard	Stratford	Conservative
1922	G	1945	Groves	Thomas Edward		Labour
1918	G	1922	Wild	Sir Ernest Edward	Upton	Conservative
1922	G	1923	Margesson	Henry David Reginald (Capt)		Conservative
1923	G	1924	Gardner	Benjamin Walter		Labour
1924	G	1929	Holt	Herbert Paton (Major)		Conservative
1929	G	1931	Gardner	Benjamin Walter		Labour
1931	G	1934	Chotzner	Alfred James		Conservative

NOTE First returned at a B = By-election; G = General Election

MPs for West Ham during this period were very typical of the politics of the time. The Labour MPs were all from a local government background in the borough and most were active trade unionists whilst Conservatives were either the products of the British Empire or of local businesses.

Plaistow

William James (Will) Thorne (Labour) was MP for the entire period. His principal biographical details are in Chapter 4

Silvertown

John Joseph (Jack) Jones (Labour) was born at Nenagh in the Southern Irish County Tipperary in 1873 and educated there at Schools of the Christian Brothers. A building labourer he became a trade union organiser for the National Union of General and Municipal Workers in 1911 and got involved with politics. In 1906 he contested the Cornish borough constituency of Camborne for the Social Democratic Federation and in 1914 contested a by-election at nearby Poplar for the British Socialist Party. He was first elected to West Ham Borough Council in 1904 and was a member of the local Board of Guardians between 1908 and 1911. When he was elected Silvertown's first MP in 1918 it was as a candidate for the British Socialist Party but, although he had contested that election against an official Labour candidate, he nevertheless took that Party's whip in the Commons and remained a Labour MP until his death shortly after the outbreak of the Second World War.

Dr. Louis Comyns (Labour), who succeeded Jack Jones in 1940, had been a local general practitioner in West Ham since 1932, and was also a member of the Borough Council. He was born in Glasgow in 1904 and qualified as a Doctor at Edinburgh University before moving to West Ham. Most of his activities were involved with the health service. He was Chairman of the Management Committee of a West Ham Hospital and a board member of others in the London area including Hammersmith, West London and St. Mark's Hospitals and also sat on the North East Metropolitan Health Board. He resigned from the British Medical Association due to its opposition to the Labour Government's proposals for the National Health Service. Following re-distribution of seats in 1950 he did not continue in the Commons but renewed his involvement with the Borough Council in 1954. He died in 1962.

Stratford

Sir Charles Ernest Leonard Lyle (Conservative) was the first MP for Stratford and sat until 1922 when he was defeated. Born in 1882 and educated at Harrow and Trinity Hall Cambridge, he was a member of the Lyle family who, together with Tates, owned the largest sugar refining and canning business in Britain at that time. Canning Town was so named after the family business. Charles was the Company's President and a Director of Lloyds Bank but lived mainly in Canford Cliffs near Bournemouth and was Chairman of the East Dorset Conservative Association, although he was chairman of the Queen Mary Hospital in the East End from 1916-23 and was also a West Ham magistrate. From 1920-21 he was briefly PPS to the Food Controller in the Coalition Government led by Lloyd-George and after his defeat in 1922 transferred to the Epping division in 1923. After only a year he resigned to concentrate on his business interests, although in his later years he did resume a Parliamentary career when he was elected unopposed in his home town of Bournemouth at a 1940 by-election. He held the seat until 1945 when he retired and was made Baron Lyle of Westbourne. He died in 1954.

Thomas Edward Groves (Labour) was elected in 1922 and served continuously until he retired in 1945. Originally a lecturer in local government and economics, he was also a member of West Ham Council from 1919 and a local JP. He was born locally at Stratford in 1885 and educated at elementary school, the Carpenter's Company Institute and at Ruskin College, Oxford. He was initially a barrister at Grays Inn but also acquired business interests as Chairman of three companies; the British Bank of Commerce, Aero Holdings Limited and Box and Co. He also claimed to be a fruit farmer. He was a Labour whip from 1931 to 1944 but failed to secure adoption as the Party's candidate for the 1945 General Election at which point he decided to sponsor his son as an Independent. However, when his son withdrew, Groves decided to stand as an Independent himself and was defeated. He died in 1958.

Upton

Sir Ernest Edward Wild (Conservative) was Upton's MP from 1918 to 1922. He was born in Norwich in 1869 where he was educated at Norwich School before attending Jesus College, Cambridge and becoming a barrister. He was called to the Bar (Middle Temple) in 1893 and took silk in 1912. From 1897 to 1922 he was a Judge at the Norwich Guildhall Court of Record and prior to his election as MP for Upton contested Norwich twice, in 1904 and 1906, both unsuccessfully. He was also defeated at West Ham North on two occasions; once in December 1910 and again at a by-election in 1911. He was a member of the LCC from 1907 to 1910 and after his election at Upton, retired from politics in 1922 when he was appointed Recorder of the City of London and High Steward of Southwark. He served in both posts until 1934. Outside the Law and politics he maintained an interest in poetry on which he delivered a number of lectures.

Capt. Margesson MP who went on to great things, but not from a London seat. **Wikipedia**

Captain Henry David Reginald Margesson MC (Conservative) succeeded Wild in 1922 but was defeated the following year. Born in 1890 he was educated at Harrow School and Magdalene College Cambridge before becoming a Captain in the 11th Hussars. He entered politics in 1922 and was appointed PPS to Sir Montague Barlow, the Minister of Labour but both he and the Government lost in 1923. He sought another seat and in 1924 he was returned at Rugby, Warwickshire which seat he retained until 1942 when he was elevated to the House of Lords as Viscount Margesson. From 1924 he was an Assistant Government Whip, and a Junior Lord of the Treasury between 1926 and 1929 when his Party went into Opposition once more. On the creation of the National Government in 1931 he was re-instated as Junior Lord but after the General Election of the same year became Chief Government Whip (Parliamentary Secretary to the Treasury), a post he retained until May 1940 when he held it jointly after the Wartime Coalition was established. In December 1940 Churchill appointed him Secretary of State for War, a post he held until his elevation. In business he was a Director of the International Nickel Company and of Martins Bank. He died in 1965.

Benjamin Walter Gardner (Labour) was born in 1865, educated at elementary school and became a waterside labourer in the docks. He worked with Keir Hardie, the father of the Labour Party, on the staff of a publication called 'The Labour Leader' and was a founder of the Independent Labour Party in West Ham. He was three times MP for Upton and contested the seat in every election between 1918 and 1935. He was first elected in 1923 only to be defeated a year later and, although returned again in 1929, was defeated in 1931. He was returned again at a by-election in 1934 following the resignation through ill health of the Tory MP, A.J. Chotzner. He held the seat until he retired in 1945. He was also a local JP and alderman on West Ham Council and died in 1948.

Major Herbert Paton Holt MC (Conservative) was a Canadian born in Montreal in 1890 and educated at the St. Albans School and Canadian Royal Military Academy. In 1910 he entered the 3rd Dragoon Guards in which he became a Captain, retiring in 1920 to become a Director of Andrew Holt and Company, based in Montreal and the City of London. During the Great War he became a major and was awarded the Military Cross. He sat for Upton between 1924 and 1929 when he retired. He lived in Wiltshire where he became High Sheriff in 1935-6 and during the Second World War served as a Major in the Pioneer Corps in France in 1939-40. He died in 1971.

Alfred James Chotzner (Conservative) won the seat from Gardner in 1931 but retired through ill health in 1934. Born in 1873, he was educated at Harrow and St. Johns Cambridge where he obtained a BA in 1895 and joined the Indian Civil Service rising to become a District Sessions Judge for East Bengal and Assam in 1909 and subsequently a High Court Judge in Calcutta between 1924 and 1928. Despite his health problems whilst briefly an MP, Chotzner lived another twenty four years and died in 1958.

MPs for East Ham

From	at	To	Surname	First Names	Constituency	Party Affiliation
1918	G	1922	Bethell	Sir John Henry	East Ham North	Liberal
1922	G	1923	Crook	Charles Williamson		Unionist
1923	G	1924	Lawrence	Arabella Susan (Miss)		Labour
1924	G	1926	Crook	Charles Williamson		Unionist
1926	B	1931	Lawrence	(Arabella) Susan (Miss)		Labour
1931	G	1945	Mayhew	Sir John (Lieut-Col)		Unionist
1918	G	1922	Edwards	Allen Clement	East Ham South	NDP
1922	G	1931	Barnes	Alfred John		Labour
1931	G	1935	Campbell-Johnston	Malcolm		Unionist
1935	G	1945	Barnes	Alfred John		Labour

NOTE First returned at a B = By-election; G = General Election

East Ham North

Sir John Henry Bethell (Liberal) was the first MP for East Ham North but had previously sat for Romford since 1906. His principal biographical details are in Chapter 4.

Charles Williamson Crook (Conservative) was born in 1862 and educated in Lancashire at the St. James' National School (Barrow-in-Furness) and Alston College (Preston). He moved to London where he continued his education at St. John's College, Battersea and attended London University where he was awarded BSc in 1886 and BA six years later. He was additionally a member of the University Senate. He was a teacher who became headmaster of Wood Green secondary school. He was also a member of the Burnham Committee and President of the National Union of Teachers in 1916-17. He represented the constituency between 1922 and 1923 and again from 1924 until his death in 1926.

(Arabella) Susan Lawrence (Labour) first won East Ham North in 1923 but held the seat for only one year. However, she won the 1926 by-election brought about by Crook's death and held the seat until she was defeated in the 1931 landslide. Arabella was born in 1871, the daughter of a solicitor. She was educated at Newnham College, Cambridge, and joined the Labour Party when it was formed. From 1912-26 she was a London County Councillor and in her last year was its Deputy Chairman. She was also an alderman in Poplar borough and a member of the National Executive Committee of the Labour Party and its sometime Chairman. She unsuccessfully contested Camberwell North West at a by-election in 1920 and East Ham North in 1922. She was very active in promoting the rights of women, amongst other things as Organiser for the National Federation of Women Workers before it amalgamated with the National Union of General Workers. During the Great War she was a member of the Special Arbitration Tribunal on Women's Wages and of several Reconstruction Committees. She was a PPS to the President of the Board of Education in 1924. During the second Labour Government she was Parliamentary Secretary at the Ministry of Health. After her defeat in 1931 she sought re-election in 1935 at Stockton-on-Tees where she stood unsuccessfully against the Tory MP and future Prime Minister (1957-1963), Harold Macmillan. She died in 1947.

Lieutenant-Colonel (Sir) John Mayhew (Conservative) took East Ham in the 1931 landslide and retained the seat until he was defeated in 1945, suffering a similar fate in 1950. Born in 1884 and educated at King William College, the Isle of Man, he was from an Essex family with agricultural roots since the Seventeenth Century but embarked initially on a military career joining the 2nd Denbighshire Hussars Yeomanry in 1902. During the First World War he served between 1916-17 in the Infantry in France. An Essex Deputy – Lieutenant, he contested the Harwich division in 1929 but lost to a Liberal. He acquired land holdings in Sussex and studied agriculture. He died in 1954.

East Ham South

Allen Clement Edwards (National Democratic Party) was elected the first MP for East Ham South in 1918. Born in Shropshire in 1869 he was educated at Knighton's national school and went on to become a barrister being called to the bar at the Middle Temple in 1899. He had a particular interest in trade union cases and entered politics initially as a Liberal at the 1895 general election when he contested Tottenham. He fought Denbigh (North Wales) in 1900 and lost but gained the seat in the 1906 landslide and was its Liberal MP until defeated at the January election of 1910. In the December 1910 contest he won East Glamorgan (a coal mining area) and sat as the Liberal MP until 1918 at which point he became a founding member of the NDP and was elected at East Ham, though his task was made easier as he had the unofficial support of the Conservatives. He chaired the NDP in 1919-20 but Labour took his seat in 1922 and he left politics. He died in 1938. The National Democratic Party was formed in 1918 following a split in the Labour Party based on attitudes to nationalism during the Great War. It was essentially a right wing anti Socialist Party and fought and won a number of seats at the 1918 election with the support of the Coalition parties. It disbanded in 1923 when most of its leadership joined the National Liberal Party.

Alfred Barnes MP
© National Portrait Gallery
Bassano Ltd 1923

Alfred John Barnes (Labour & Co-operative) was born in 1887, the son of a North Woolwich docker. He received an elementary school education but studied design in metal work at the Northampton Institute and became a skilled worker in gold and silver. He was attracted to the Co-operative movement and in 1914 was elected to the Board of the Stratford Society of which he became President in 1915. He was active in bringing about the amalgamation of several Societies and was elected the first president of the London Combined Society. He actively campaigned for the Movement to put candidates forward for Parliamentary election and was himself elected at East Ham South in 1922 and became Chairman of the Co-operative Party from 1924 to 1945. He represented the seat, apart from a break between 1931 and 1935, until 1955. His first appointment as an MP was as PPS to the Financial Secretary to the

Treasury in 1924 and from 1925 to 1930 he was a Labour whip. Thereafter he held various ministerial offices including: Government Whip (1929-31); Minister of War Transport (1945); and Minister of Transport from 1946 until 1951. He died in 1974.

Between 1931 and 1935 East Ham South was represented by **Malcolm Campbell-Johnstone** (Conservative), a barrister who practised for five years at the South African Bar in Johannesburg. Born in 1871 he was educated at Marlborough School and abroad and became a barrister in 1893, being admitted to the Transvaal Bar (South Africa) in 1902. He had first contested a Parliamentary seat, unsuccessfully, at Osgoldcross (Castleford -West Yorkshire) in 1910. He was a member of the LCC for twelve years from 1922 to 1934 and again from 1937 but he died the following year.

MPs for Ilford

From	at	To	Surname	First Names	Constituency	Party Affiliation
1918	*G*	*1920*	*Griggs*	*Sir William Peter*	*Ilford*	*Conservative*
1920	*B*	*1928*	*Wise*	*Sir Frederic*		*Conservative*
1928	*B*	*1937*	*Hamilton*	*Sir (Collingwood) George Clements (Major)*		*Conservative*
1937	*B*	*1945*	*Hutchinson*	*Geoffrey Clegg*		*Conservative*

NOTE First returned at a B = By-election; G = General Election

Sir William Peter Griggs (Conservative) was elected Ilford's first MP in 1918 but died in 1920. Griggs lived at the Drive, Ilford but had been born at South Hackney in 1853 and educated privately. He became a Governing Director of the South Essex Recorders Ltd (a newspaper and magazine publishing group based in Romford) and of WP Griggs, his own company. He was elected to Ilford District Council in 1899 and became chairman in 1910 whilst also serving as a magistrate and Essex County Councillor (from 1901). He had earlier contested Romford unsuccessfully at the December 1910 election.

Sir Frederic Wise (Conservative), who won the by-election caused by Grigg's death, was the son of a Waterford JP though his mother was from Benton Hall, Newcastle-upon-Tyne. Born in 1871 and educated at Marlborough College, he married the daughter of Sir Thomas Wrightson of Neasham Hall, Darlington. He was a JP in Northumberland, a Director of 'Express' Newspapers and of the Sudan Plantations Syndicate as well as founder in 1903 of the stock broking firm of Wise, Speke and Company of Newcastle. In the Great War he worked in the Ministry of National Service, the Ministry of Food and the Treasury and went to Germany in 1919 to report to the National Peace Conference on the financial position of the defeated power, contributing something therefore to the vengeful terms imposed on Germany that are now seen to have been a major contributory factor to the rise of Hitler. He was Charter Mayor of Ilford in 1926 and died in 1928.

Major Sir (Collingwood) George Clements Hamilton (Conservative) was elected to succeed Wise at a 1928 by-election held in February. He was born in 1877, the son of Lady Louise Fraser, the sister of the Earl of Leitrim and the Venerable George Hans Hamilton, Archdeacon of Northumberland and Canon of Durham. He was educated at Charterhouse School and became an electrical engineer, a Director of several companies and a JP in Suffolk where he lived at Saxmundham. He was a Major in the Territorial Army Reserve and MP for Altrincham (Cheshire) from 1913 to 1923 when he was defeated. In 1916 he was appointed Director of Enrolment for National Service and two years later was made Controller of Contract Claims at the Ministry of Munitions, and from 1919-21 PPS to Sir Laming Worthington-Evans, Minister of Pensions. In 1921 he chaired the Officers' Warrant Committee which drew up the officers' warrant for pensions. After his defeat at Altrincham in 1923 he suffered a similar fate at Lincoln in 1924 before returning to the House at the 1928 by-election in Ilford. He resigned in 1937 and died ten years later.

Sir Geoffrey Clegg Hutchinson KC MC (Conservative) was born in 1893 and educated at Cheltenham and Clare College, Cambridge, where he qualified as MA in 1919. However, his University education was interrupted by the First World War in which he served throughout as a Captain in the Lancashire Fusiliers, being awarded the Military Cross. After his graduation he became a lawyer and was called to the bar at the Inner Temple in 1920. He first entered politics locally as a councillor in Hampstead (1931-5) and then unsuccessfully contested the Welsh constituency of Gower in 1935 before he was elected to succeed Hamilton at the 1937 Ilford by-election. Two years later he took silk but during the first three years of the Second World War resumed a military role as Major in his old regiment and between 1941 and 1942 was Deputy Assistant Military Secretary at the War Office. He remained Ilford's MP until 1945 when two seats were created and he was defeated at Ilford North. Between 1944 and 1952 he was a member of the LCC, a vice president of the Association of Municipal Corporations and from 1944 onwards, chairman of the local government advisory committee of the Conservative Party. In 1946 he became a master of the bench and two years later was also appointed an Honorary Colonel in the Lancashire Fusiliers, a post he held until 1954. Meanwhile in 1950 he had been returned as Ilford North's MP but he resigned in 1954 when he was appointed Chairman of the National Assistance Board, a role he maintained for ten years until the Wilson Government was returned. In 1962 he was made Baron Ilford and died in 1974.

MPs for Romford

From	at	To	Surname	First Names	Constituency	Party Affiliation
1918	*G*	*1923*	*Martin*	*Albert Edward*	*Romford*	*Liberal*
1923	*G*	*1929*	*Rhys*	*Charles Arthur Uryan*		*Conservative*
1929	*G*	*1931*	*Muggeridge*	*Henry Thomas Benjamin*		*Labour*
1931	*G*	*1935*	*Hutchison*	*William Gordon Douglas*		*Conservative*
1935	*G*	*1945*	*Parker*	*Herbert John Harry*		*Labour*

NOTE First returned at a B = By-election; G = General Election

Albert Edward Martin (Liberal) was Romford's first post war MP. Born in 1875 he was for twenty years a member of Barking Town Council (being Mayor in 1931-2). He was also a Captain in the Essex RASC, a local magistrate and a member of Essex County Council. Professionally he was managing director of his own Cinematograph Film Company. He retired in 1923 and died in 1936.

Charles Arthur Uryan Rhys MC (Conservative) was the eldest son of the Seventh Baron Dynevor of Dynevor Castle, Llandeilo, Carmarthenshire. His mother was daughter of the Seventh Earl of Jersey. Born in 1899 he was educated at Eton and the Royal Military College at Sandhurst becoming a Lieutenant in the Grenadier Guards Reserve of Officers. He was made a Deputy Lieutenant of Carmarthenshire where he was also a magistrate and a member of the Essex Territorial Army Association. In the invasion of Russia following the Bolshevik revolution he was awarded the Military Cross and the Order of St. Anne of Russia. He was elected for Romford in 1923 and between 1924-5 was PPS to the Financial Secretary to the War Office and from 1927-29 to Stanley Baldwin, the Prime Minister. He was defeated in 1929 but two years later was elected unopposed as MP for Guildford at a by-election in August, serving until 1935 when he retired from the Commons, a year after his marriage. In 1945 he made a failed attempt to gain re-election to the Commons at Islington North. He succeeded as Baron in 1956 and four years later was made President of the University College of South Wales but died in 1962.

Henry Thomas Benjamin Muggeridge (Labour) was the father of a famous son, Malcolm, a journalist and broadcaster in the pre and post Second World War periods. Henry was born at Penge in 1864 and attended the St. John's School there and in 1907 became a company secretary. A member of the Croydon Borough Council between 1911 and 1930, he was Chairman of the municipal electricity company in 1927 and contested his first Parliamentary election in the South Division there in 1918 but was defeated as he was when he tried again in 1922, 1923 and 1924. He was eventually elected at Romford in 1929 but was defeated in 1931 and did not resume a Commons career. He wrote a book entitiled 'A Labour Pilgrim's Progress' and died in 1942.

William Gordon Douglas Hutchison (Conservative) defeated Muggeridge in 1931 but was himself defeated four years later. Born in 1904 the son of an Edinburgh Colonel, he was educated at King's College on the Isle of Man and became an estate agent. With an interest in the economic problems of the British Empire he favoured strong tariff controls. However, he was also an actor whose business interests included being chairman of a film company and during the Second World War he served in the Royal Navy between 1941 and 1944. He was promoted to the rank of Lieutenant in 1943. He died in 1975.

Herbert John Harry Parker MP
The People's History Museum Manchester

Herbert John Harry Parker (Labour) was very left wing in his politics and went on to hold a metropolitan Essex seat for nearly fifty years. He sat for Romford from 1935 to 1945 when he transferred to the newly created Dagenham constituency which he retained until he retired. His first Parliamentary contest had been in 1931 at Holland-with-Boston, in Lincolnshire. Born in 1906, the son of a schoolmaster, he was educated at Marlborough College and Oxford University (St. John's College) where he was Chairman of the Labour Club in 1928 though he actually joined the Party in 1922. He was a member of staff of the Social Survey of Merseyside undertaken between 1929 and 1932 and joined the clerical section of the Transport and General Worker's Union. He was always a political activist and was general secretary of the Fabian Research Bureau when it was established in 1933 until 1939 and a lecturer on economics and statistics for the Workers Educational Association. He was General Secretary of the Society from 1939 to 1945. Between 1940-2 he was PPS to Ellen Wilkinson at the Ministry of Home Security, a member of the Labour Party Executive from 1943-4 and of the Speaker's Conference on Parliamentary Reform in 1944. In 1945 he was a member of a Parliamentary delegation to the Soviet Union. From 1945-6 he was Under Secretary at the Dominions Office but held no further office. He became father of the House in 1979 and retired in 1983, forty eight years after entering it.

MPs for Epping

From	*at*	*To*	*Surname*	*First Names*	*Constituency*	*Party Affiliation*
1918	*G*	*1923*	*Colvin*	*Richard Beale (Brig-General)*	*Epping*	*Conservative*
1923	*G*	*1924*	*Lyle*	*Sir Charles Ernest Leonard*		*Conservative*
1924	*B*	*1945*	*Spencer-Churchill*	*Sir Winston Leonard*		*Conservative*

NOTE First returned at a B = By-election; G = General Election

Brigadier-General Richard Beale Colvin (Conservative) was Epping's first MP in 1918 and had a background steeped in Essex pursuits and interests although he was actually born in 1856 at Sawbridgeworth, a small town just over the border in Hertfordshire. He was educated at Eton and Trinity College Cambridge. In 1900 he raised and commanded the 20th Battalion Infantry Yeomen and between 1902 and 1911 fulfilled the same commission for the Essex Yeomanry. From 1915 to 1916 he commanded the Second London Mounted Brigade and was County Commandant of the Essex Volunteers from 1916 to 1917 when he was made an Honorary Brigadier – General. From 1908 he was Chairman of the Essex Territorial Association and was also a Deputy Lieutenant of the County. Away from his military exploits he was immersed in country sports. Between 1885 and 1890 he was Master of the Essex Foxhounds and between 1891 and 1894 the combined Essex and Suffolk Foxhounds. In 1890 he was High Sheriff of Essex and after his retirement from politics in 1923 was Lord Lieutenant between 1929 and 1936 when he died.

Sir Charles Ernest Leonard Lyle (Conservative) was elected in 1923 but retired a year later. He was formerly MP for the Stratford division of West Ham between 1918 and 1922 and his principal biographical details may be found earlier in this chapter.

Sir Winston Churchill MP

Wikipedia

(Sir) Winston Leonard Spencer-Churchill (Constitutionalist), the formidable War time leader, is generally regarded as Britain's greatest Prime Minister, if only because of the enormity of the challenge that the country faced when he assumed that role in 1940 and the victory that ensued after Britain stood alone against Hitler's Germany. Churchill came from a family that was itself steeped in British history. The battle triumphs of his soldier forebear, the Duke of Marlborough, were themselves the stuff of legends and there was a tradition of public service going back through his lineage. Born in 1874, his father was Lord Randolph Churchill, a former Tory Cabinet Minister, though his mother was American. Winston's career was to combine the military and political traditions of his distinguished family. He was educated at Brighton Preparatory School, Harrow School and the Royal Military College at Sandhurst and became initially a Lieutenant in the 4th Hussars serving in a number of battle zones. As early as 1895 he was present with Spanish forces in Cuba including acting as a War correspondent. Next he was attached to the 31st Punjab Infantry being mentioned in despatches in 1897 when he was fighting with the Malakand Field Force. He was with the Tirah and Nile Expeditions in 1898 and was present at the battle of Khartoum and at the charge of the Lancers at Omdurman. During the South Africa War between 1899 and 1900 he was with the Light Horse, suffering imprisonment at the hands of the Boers, though he escaped, once again reporting the War, this time for the 'Morning Post' newspaper.

Before going to South Africa, he entered politics as a Conservative at Oldham in a 1899 by-election but was defeated. He stood again in 1900 and was elected but during the course of the Parliament crossed the House to join the Liberal Party, partly because of his commitment to Free Trade. In the 1906 Election he was elected as a Liberal at North West Manchester and appointed Under Secretary of State for the Colonies in Campbell-Bannerman's Government. In 1908 he was made President of the Board of Trade and, as was then the tradition, resigned his seat to fight a by-election, which he lost and was briefly out of Parliament until he was elected for the Scottish two-member burgh constituency of Dundee at a by-election later that year. As President of the Board of Trade he formed a significant Cabinet alliance with Lloyd George and there is no doubt that at the time he was on the radical wing of the Liberal Party. Asquith appointed him to one of the top three Cabinet posts, as Secretary of State for the Home Department, in February 1910 following the Party's January Election victory but in 1911 he was made First Lord of the Admiralty, a key post at a time when the German Kaiser was seeking to rival the British Navy, then regarded as the most powerful in the world. He held the post until 1915 when he was appointed Chancellor of the Duchy of Lancaster, a move that in his view substantially diminished his influence in the conduct of the First World War which by then had been under way for a little over a year. He took the blame for a serious failure of Naval tactics at the Dardanelles, in Turkey, resulting in severe loss of life to Imperial forces. He went instead to the front line, believing that, if he could not influence the conduct of the War in Government, he would seek to do so on active service instead. He was made a Lieutenant – Colonel Commanding of the 6th Royal Scots Fusiliers in France in 1916.

After Lloyd George became Prime Minister, it was not long before he recalled Churchill from the front and in 1917 he became Minister of Munitions, a post the new Prime Minister had himself held in the early years of the War. In the Coalition Government set up in 1918 Churchill became Secretary of State for War and Air, and two years later was made Secretary of State for the Colonies, though he retained the Air portfolio for a little longer. He resigned in 1922 in the aftermath of the fall of Lloyd-George's Coalition Government and was defeated at Dundee in the General Election of that year. He sought re-election at Leicester West in 1923 but was unsuccessful, and then began a series of transitional moves which saw Churchill move back to the Conservatives. Concerned at the prospect of Socialism and unsupportive of Lloyd-George's tacit support of the first Labour Government, he initially adopted the stance of an anti-Socialist standing at a by-election at the Abbey division of Westminster. He was only narrowly defeated but events – not least his opposition to any form of Dominion status for India - were now moving him closer to the Conservative cause and in 1924 he was adopted to fight the safe Epping seat. (He was to remain its MP until 1945 when he was elected for the successor seat of Woodford, which he held until he died.)

Churchill returned to the Cabinet in Baldwin's 1924-9 Government serving as Chancellor of the Exchequer. He was then out of Government for ten years, partly due to the return of a Labour Government in 1929 but also because his view of the emerging foreign crisis in Europe was opposed to the appeasement policies of successive Prime Ministers. When War finally broke out with Germany in 1939 he was recalled to the Cabinet by Neville Chamberlain and served once again as First Lord of the Admiralty. When the Government fell in the light of a backbench rebellion triggered by alarming setbacks in the conduct of the War, Churchill was the candidate around whom all parties could unite as the war leader. He became Prime Minister in 1940 and conducted the war effort in defiant, stoical and brilliant fashion. Through alliances at home with the other parties which he brought into Government and abroad with the United States and the Soviet Union, in the end victory was secured.

Winston Churchill gives the famous 'V' sign as Britain's wartime Prime Minister in 1940.

Wikipedia

As the end of the War approached normal peacetime politics were resumed and the Wartime Coalition came to an end. At the May 1945 Election the Conservatives were defeated and although this was considered surprising at the time, with hindsight it can be seen that the peace agenda favoured Labour more than it did the Conservatives. Churchill became Leader of the Opposition under whom the Party regrouped after its massive defeat, and by 1950 had begun to make a comeback. In 1951 Churchill returned as Prime Minister and he remained in power until overtaken by old age and illness. He finally gave way in 1954 to his long time protégée, Anthony Eden but remained in the House, a Commoner always, until he retired in 1964. He died on 24th January 1965 and his State funeral was held six days later.

MPs for Walthamstow						
From	at	To	Surname	First Names	Constituency	Party Affiliation
1918	G	1924	Johnson	Sir Louis Stanley	Walthamstow East	Conservative
1924	G	1929	Greenwood	Sir Hamar		Conservative
1929	G	1931	Wallace	Harry Wright		Labour
1931	G	1945	Beauchamp	Sir Bograve-Campbell		Conservative
1918	G	1922	Jesson	Charles	Walthamstow West	National Democratic & Labour
1922	G	1924	McEntee	Valentine la Touche		Labour
1924	G	1929	Crawfurd	Horace Evelyn (Major)		Liberal
1929	G	1945	McEntee	Valentine la Touche		Labour
NOTE First returned at a B = By-election; G = General Election						

Walthamstow East

Sir Louis Stanley Johnson (Conservative), who was Walthamstow East's first MP, was born at Hackney in 1869 and educated privately. He became a solicitor in the company of Downer and Johnson of London Wall and from 1914 to 1919 was mayor of Hackney. He was also a magistrate for London County and an Honorary Lieutenant-Colonel in the 9th Battalion, the county of London Volunteer Regiment. He raised the 189th Brigade of the RFA and the 152nd Battery RFA in 1915 and first contested a Parliamentary seat in 1910 when he was defeated at both elections in Walthamstow. He retired as MP for the East constituency in 1924 and died in 1937.

Lieutenant-Colonel Sir Hamar Greenwood (Conservative) was elected in 1924 having sat previously for York (1906-January 1910) and Sunderland (December 1910 –1922), both times as a Liberal. He also experienced defeat at Sunderland in 1923 before securing the Tory nomination at Walthamstow East. Born in Canada in 1870 he was educated in the town of Whitby and at the University of Toronto where he graduated as BA in 1895. He joined the Canadian army in 1888 and worked for a while in the Department of Agriculture, Ontario. He became a Lieutenant in the 1st King Edward's Horse in 1902 being a Captain in the reserve from 1905 until 1912 and as a Liberal MP was PPS to Winston Churchill between 1906 and 1910. He became a barrister in three countries – Grays Inn London, New Brunswick Canada and in Australia – but at the outbreak of war in 1914 was seconded to the British War Office at the Department of Recruitment. He raised and then commanded at the front the 10th Battalion of the South Wales Borderers in 1915 but returned to work again at the War Office in 1916. In January 1919 he was appointed Under Secretary at the Home Office moving in a similar capacity to the Department of Overseas Trade in July the same year. In April 1920 he was appointed to Lloyd-George's Cabinet as Chief Secretary for Ireland, at a time when the Irish question was especially dominant in British politics. He introduced the Government of Ireland Act which established the Irish Free State but which also created the six counties of Ulster as a remaining part of the United Kingdom. After the fall of the Lloyd-George Coalition he joined the Conservative Party in the re-alignment of Liberal politics that took place at the time and was elected as MP for Walthamstow East but remained a backbencher. He retired from politics in 1929. In 1937 he was made the 1st Viscount Greenwood and died in 1948.

Harry Wallace MP
The People's History Museum Manchester

Harry Wright Wallace (Labour), sat as MP from 1929 to 1931. He was born in 1885 and educated at a Council School in the Manchester area before joining the Post Office. He was Assistant Secretary of the Post Office Workers' Union for 27 years and served as a vice-chairman of the staff side of the Whitley Council, the pay negotiating body. He was also chairman of the joint industry councils for Government industrial workers. He first contested a Parliamentary seat at Bury in 1918, when he was unsuccessful, and experienced defeat there again in 1922, 1923 and 1924. Re-elected in 1945, he was defeated in 1955 and retired. He was a member of the LCC and of Lambeth Council (from 1937) being the borough's mayor in 1952-3.

Sir Brograve Campbell Beauchamp (Conservative) took the seat in 1931 and held it until he retired in 1945. In 1922 he had unsuccessfully contested Lowestoft in Sufolk. An old Etonian and Company Director, he had an undistinguished Parliamentary career. Born in 1897 he was the grandson of the 5th Earl Carnarvon and after Eton became a Lieutenant in the Life Guards. In 1940 he was made PPS to the Minister of Transport, John Reith and between 1942-3 fulfilled the same role for Richard Law when he was Under-Secretary for Foreign Affairs. He died in 1976.

Walthamstow West

Charles Jesson (National Democratic and Labour Party) was the first MP for Walthamstow West, a seat he held from 1918 until 1922 when he was defeated standing with Conservative support. He was born in 1862 and educated at Leicester County School, afterwards becoming a professional musician. He joined an Army Band in 1879 but later became Organizer of the Musician's Union. From 1906 to 1919 he was a member of the LCC. He died in 1926.

Valentine la Touche McEntee (Labour) who was born in 1871 the son of a Dubliner received an elementary education and became a woodworker in which trade he was an active trade unionist in the Amalgamated Society of Woodworkers. He became a member of Walthamstow Urban District Council in 1919 and when it became a Borough was its first mayor in 1929-30. However, he worked for his living on the staff of the London Council for which he bought timber. He first contested Walthamstow West in 1918 but won in 1922, 1923 and 1929. He lost to the Liberals in 1924 but following his re-election in 1929 remained the MP until he retired in 1950. From 1942-5 he was PPS to George Hicks, Parliamentary Secretary to the Minister of Works and Planning.

Horace Evelyn Crawfurd (Liberal) took the seat from Labour in 1924. He was born in 1881 and following an education at the Merchant Taylors' School and St. John's College, Oxford, he became a lecturer at Liverpool University and a merchant. He was involved in a number of tenant organisations including Hampstead, Ealing and Garden Cities, all limited companies. During the Great War he served with the Royal Naval Air Squadron and finally became a major in the RAF and was awarded the A.F.C. He entered politics initially at Walthamstow West in 1922 and fought it again in 1923 but was unsuccessful, losing to Labour on both occasions.

MPs for Leyton

From	*at*	*To*	*Surname*	*First Names*	*Constituency*	*Party Affiliation*
1918	*G*	*1922*	*Malone*	*Cecil John L'Estrange*	*Leyton East*	*Liberal/British Socialist Party*
1922	*G*	*1923*	*Alexander*	*Ernest Edward*		*Conservative*
1923	*G*	*1924*	*Church*	*Archibald George (Major)*		*Labour*
1924	*G*	*1929*	*Alexander*	*Ernest Edward*		*Conservative*
1929	*G*	*1931*	*Brockway*	*(Archibald) Fenner*		*Labour*
1931	*G*	*1945*	*Mills*	*Sir Frederick*		*Conservative*
1918	*G*	*1919*	*Wrightson*	*Harry (Lt.Colonel)*	*Leyton West*	*Conservative*
1919	*B*	*1922*	*Newbould*	*Alfred Ernest*		*Independent Liberal*
1922	*G*	*1929*	*Cassels*	*James Dale*		*Conservative*
1929	*G*	*1931*	*Sorenson*	*Reverend William Reginald*		*Labour*
1931	*G*	*1935*	*Sugden*	*Sir Wilfrid Hart*		*Conservative*
1935	*G*	*1945*	*Sorenson*	*Reverend William Reginald*		*Labour*

NOTE First returned at a B = By-election; G = General Election

MPs for Leyton East

Cecil Malone MP
Wikipedia

Cecil John L'Estrange Malone (Liberal) was a colourful and interesting character. Born in 1890 the son of a Rector, he was educated at Ludgrove School, New Barnet, at Corwalles, Maidenhead and at the Royal Naval College, Dartmouth where he was admitted RN in 1905. In 1912 he was appointed Assistant to the Director of the Air Department at the Admiralty and two years later was made Air Attaché at the British Embassy in Paris but at the outbreak of War served in the Royal Naval Air Squadron and in 1915 commanded HMS Benmy-Chree, serving in the ill fated Dardanelles expedition. In 1916 he commanded the seaplane squadron in the East Indies and Egypt where he was awarded the Order of the Nile and was subsequently awarded the OBE in 1919. Although he was elected as a Liberal in 1918 he attended the Labour Party Conference in 1920 claiming never to have been one and joined the British Socialist and Communist Parties. After a speech at the Albert Hall opposing British intervention in Russia he was arrested and charged with an offence against the Defence of the Realm Regulations. He was convicted at Bow Street Magistrates Court and sentenced to six months imprisonment also being deprived of his OBE. In 1924 he unsuccessfully contested Ashton-under-Lyne for the Labour Party but was elected at a by-election held at Northampton in 1928 and was one of the town's MPs until 1931, during his last year serving as PPS to the Pensions Minister, F.O.Roberts. During the Second World War he served on the City of Westminster Civil Defence Committee from 1942-3 and in the small vessels section of the Admiralty from 1943-5. He died in 1965.

Ernest Edward Alexander (Conservative) sat for Leyton East from 1922-23 and 1924-1929 and contested it unsuccessfully in 1918 and 1923. Born in 1872 and educated at the Stationers' Company's Foundation School he became a Master Printer. He was a councillor in Leyton from 1901-04 and also served on Essex County Council after 1918. He moved to live in Walton-on-Naze where he was a member of the Urban District Council from 1926. He died in 1946.

Major Archibald George Church MC (Labour) was MP between 1923 and 1924. Born in 1886 he was educated at Elementary and Secondary Schools and at University College, London where he obtained a BSc and became a schoolmaster (1909-1914). From 1914-19 he served in the Siege Artillery and was awarded the Military Cross in 1918 and the Order of Vladimir. From 1920 to 1931 he was the Secretary of the Association of Scientific Workers, a trade union and first embarked on a career in politics when he contested Spelthorne unsuccessfully in 1922. Whilst briefly a Leyton MP he was PPS to Sidney Webb in 1924 and subsequently held the post of Joint Secretary of the Co-ordinating Committee for Government Joint Industrial Councils. In 1929 he was elected MP for Wandsworth Central and served as PPS to the Secretary of State for War until 1931 when he was one of only a handful of Labour MPs to support Ramsey MacDonald's National Government. At the 1931 election he unsuccessfully contested London University as a National Labour candidate and suffered the same fate at Bristol East in the 1935 election and again at Derby in a 1936 by-election. From 1931 to 1933 he was Secretary of the Science Guide and from 1937 to 1951 Chairman of the Raven Oil Company. In 1945 he contested South Tottenham unsuccessfully as Independent National and died in 1954.

Fenner Brockway MP
Wikipedia

(Archibald) Fenner Brockway (Labour) was born the son of a minister of the church in Calcutta, India in 1888 and was educated at Eltham College. A pacifist, he became a journalist in left wing publications like the 'New Leader' and was an Honorary Director of the Blackfriars Press, the National Labour Press and the New Leader, which he edited from 1911 until 1945. He joined the Independent Labour Party in 1907 of which he was the Organising, General and Political Secretary between 1923 and 1929 and during the First World War was imprisoned as a conscientious objector. During the post war period he tried twice to become an MP but was unsuccessful at Lancaster (1922) and in the Abbey Division of Westminster (1924) where he stood against Winston Churchill, before his first success at Leyton East. He was defeated in 1931 and his leftward politics then led him to stand for the Independent Labour Party against Labour initially at a West Ham by-election at Upton in 1934 and then at Norwich in 1935, Lancaster in 1941 and Cardiff East in 1942. He was unsuccessful on each occasion but was the ILP's General Secretary again between 1933 and 1939 and in 1946 rejoined the Labour Party. He was selected to fight the new borough seat of Eton & Slough in 1950 and remained its MP until 1964 when he was one of only two Labour MPs to lose a seat at the General Election when the Tories lost power. The other was also a Leyton MP (see Sorenson biography, Leyton West later in this chapter, and also Gordon-Walker, Leyton in Chapter 12). His progressive attitude towards Commonwealth immigration was generally seen as the reason for his defeat, though he only lost by a handful of votes. He was Chairman of the Movement for Colonial Freedom for many years. After his defeat he accepted a peerage and died in his Nineties.

This statue of Fenner Brockway MP is in Red Lion square, Holborn. It was erected in his memory by the British Humanist Association. **John Nelson**

Sir Frederick Mills MP
Wikipedia

Sir Frederick Mills (Conservative) defeated Brockway in 1931 and remained Leyton East's MP until 1945 when he retired. Born in 1865, he was educated privately and at Durham University where he qualified as an engineer. He became Chairman of the Ebbw Vale Steel, Iron and Coal Company and became active in public life in Monmouthshire where he was a Deputy-Lieutenant, a magistrate and, in 1912, High Sheriff. He died in 1953.

MPs for Leyton West

Lieutenant-Colonel Harry Wrightson (Conservative) was elected MP for Leyton West in 1918 but died the following month before the first meeting of Parliament. The son of a vicar, he was born at Bromley in 1874 and was a Lloyd's Underwriter. He also served in the Essex Royal Army Service Corps.

Alfred Ernest Newbould (Liberal) was elected at the 1919 by-election and served for only three years, being defeated in 1922 and subsequently in 1923 and 1924. Born at Walsall in 1873, he was educated at Burton-on-Trent Grammar School and spent five years as a Private in the 1st Royal Dragoons, serving in South Africa where he was awarded two Africa medals and eight clasps. He had contested Leyton West in 1918 as an Independent Liberal but did so as a National Liberal at the by-election when he defeated a Tory opponent.

James Dale Cassels KC (Conservative) was elected in 1922 and defeated in 1929. Born in 1877 he was educated at Westminster School and was called to the Middle Temple Bar in 1908, although until 1911 he was a journalist working as sub editor on the 'Morning Post'. During the First World War he served as a Captain in the Royal Army Service Corps between 1916 and 1919 and afterwards returned to law practice becoming a KC in 1923. He was elected a member of the Bar Council in 1925 and appointed Recorder of Guildford in 1927, then two years later to the same role in Brighton which post he held until 1939 when he was appointed a Judge of the King's (later Queen's) Bench, from which he retired in 1961. For a brief period between 1931 and 1935 he was also MP for Camberwell North West. He was three times married and twice widowed, his first wife dying in 1904 and his second in 1957. He remarried in 1958 and died himself in 1976.

Rev Reginald William Sorenson MP
The People's History Museum
Manchester

Reverend Reginald William Sorenson (Labour) was MP for Leyton West between 1929 and 1931 and again from 1935 to 1950. Thereafter he served as MP for Leyton until 1964 when he was given a Life Peerage to enable the Foreign Secretary (Sir Patrick Gordon-Walker) to fight a seat after he had been defeated at the October General Election. He was born the son of a silversmith at Highbury in 1891 and attended an elementary school. He worked in a factory, an office and a shop but became a minister of religion in the Free Christian Church at Walthamstow, having initially joined the Order of Pioneer Preachers. He was also a tutor for the Workers Education Association in Essex where he became a member of the County Council. He was chairman of the Walthamstow Labour Party and also an Urban District Councillor being Chairman of the Education Committee. He was a co-founder of the Society of Socialist Christians and author of a play about the Tolpuddle Martyrs. He contested Southampton in 1923 and 1924 before his first successful election at Leyton West in 1929. Defeated in 1931, he sought a return to the Commons at the Lowestoft by-election in 1934 but succeeded again at Leyton in 1935. He was a passionate advocate of Indian Independence and was Parliamentary Secretary to the India League and a Vice President of the National Peace Council.

Sir William Hart Sugden (Conservative) briefly wrested the seat from Sorenson in 1931. Born in 1889 Sugden was educated at Waterloo School in Oldham and at London University before becoming a steel and constructional engineer. During the First World War, in which he was wounded on three occasions and mentioned in despatches, he rose to the rank of temporary Captain in a Special Brigade of the Royal Engineers. His early working life was spent in Oldham where he was a town councillor between 1913 and 1918 serving on the electricity, education, special schools and higher education committees. He first entered the House as MP for Royton (Lancashire) in 1918 and after his defeat there in 1923 stood successfully at the 1924 contest and was MP for The Hartlepools (County Durham) until 1929 when he transferred to Rossendale (Lancashire) and was defeated, moving two years later to Leyton West. Meanwhile he qualified as a barrister, being called to the bar in 1928, at both the Middle Temple and Grays Inn. From 1921-22 he was PPS to Sir Hamar Greenwood (see Walthamstow East) when Chief Secretary for Ireland. Following his defeat at Leyton West in 1935 he continued to seek re-election to the House but was unsuccessful on all subsequent occasions: at Islington North in 1937; Manchester, Platting in 1945; and Barrow-in-Furness in 1950. He died in 1960.

CUTTY SARK

Chapter 9
Metropolitan Kent 1918 - 1945

The Impact of the Boundary Review of 1917-18

At the 1918 General Election there was an increase in Kent seats from six to nine, reflecting the massive population growth that had been taking place in the southeast suburbs of London, prompted by the railway boom of the late 19th Century. Although the **Greenwich** and **Deptford** constituency boundaries remained unchanged, in Woolwich and Lewisham the 1885 single member seats were each divided East and West creating two more in total. Further out Dartford and Sevenoaks constituencies remained (the latter becoming a non metropolitan county seat) but two new county seats were also created within what we now recognise as the Greater London area.

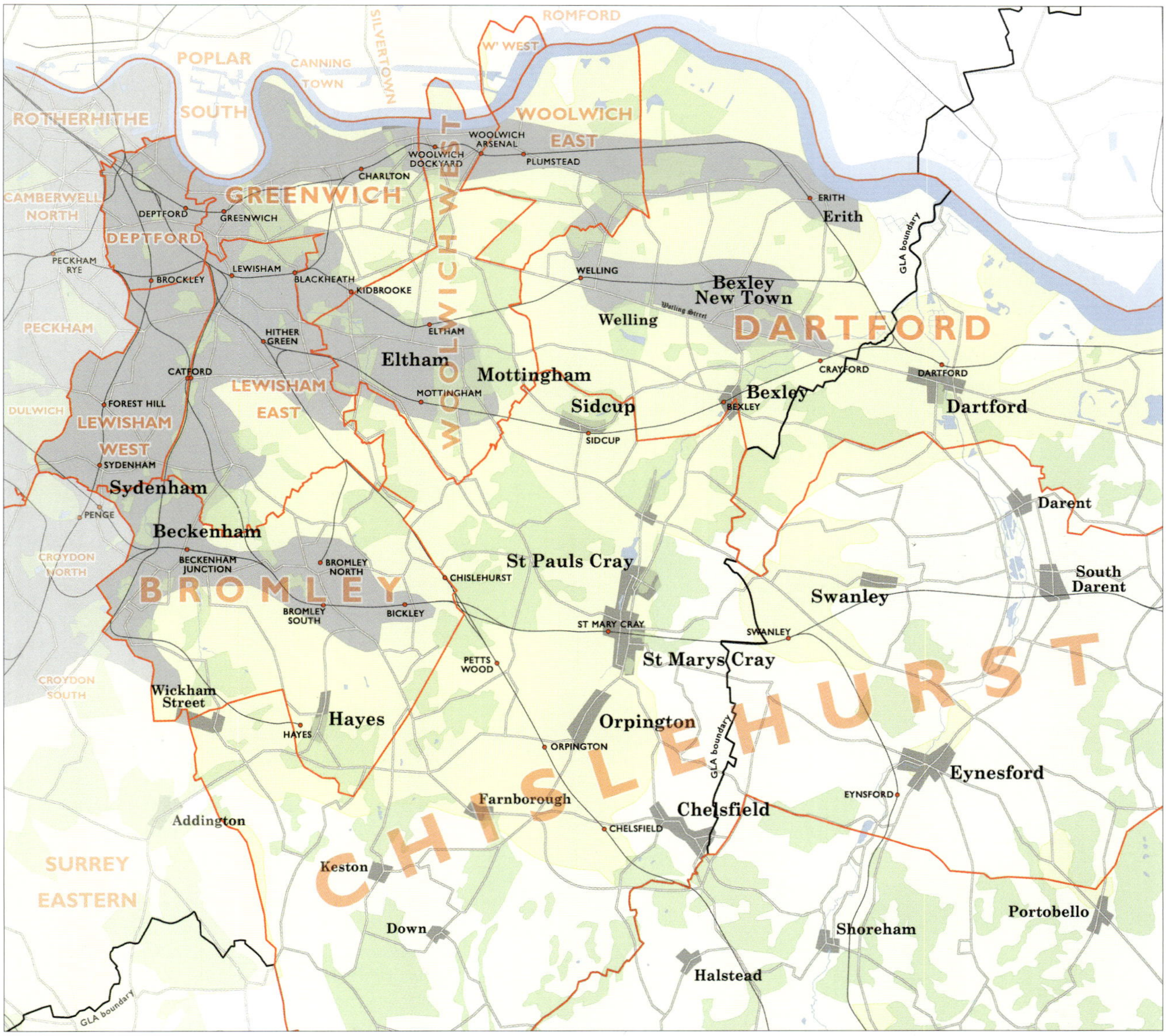

A huge expansion of population took place between the wars, and that can be seen by the grey shading showing the built up area in 1920. The yellow shading shows the extend of the built up area today. Further major growth took place in the housing boom during the period of this chapter.

Left: *A view south, in the East Constituency, looking down on to Lewisham High Street in 1939, showing the busy streets - free of car traffic - with tramcar and motor bus along with heavy goods vehicles on what is the A21 Hastings Road. An electric train cruises towards the station in the background.*

Courtesy Greenwich University

Below: *Catford Tram stand with customers waiting for the next service. The stop offered journeys to Lewisham, Forest Hill, the centre of London, Southend and Grove Park. Transport was frequent and cheap. Almost on the western border of the East Constituency the whole area was densely populated.*

©TfL from the London Transport Museum Collection

Below: *Catford Bridge Station, on the Mid-Kent Line to Hayes divided the Lewisham East and West Constituencies. The line was electrified early in 1926; unlike lines in Middlesex, there was such brisk competition for traffic here with the tramways, that tube lines were kept at arms length by the intensive service.*

John Nelson

Above: *This is a view from Westmoreland Road of houses for the new generation of home owners built in Sandford Road, in Bromley, after the Bromley Constituency was created in 1918. Before the First War 90% of people had rented their houses. Sandford Road is a very short walk from Bromley South station, and apart from some replacement building, remains the same today.*

Both: **©TfL from the London Transport Museum Collection**

Left: *Sevenoaks Road in Orpington, shown here in the 1920s, after it was transferred from Sevenoaks to the Chislehurst Constituency in 1918. The rather rural nature of the scene conceals the rapid change that the whole area was undergoing to be 'Commuterland', a process that continued throughout the Interwar years and after, transforming Orpington away from any suggestion of a rural idyll.*

Above Left & Above: *The Labour Party made play of their manifesto commitment to good housing in election communications. In fact what was built didn't quite conform to the idealised cartoon carried in the publicity, but the message was there. Above left is a 1930s 'semi' in Southwood Rd New Eltham (Woolwich West Constituency); a house in one of the large estates privately built by speculative builders. Mortgages were easy to obtain, and rates were low.*

Cartoon Peoples' History Museum; photos John Nelson

Left: *During the 1920s a large council house estate was built at Bellingham, within the Lewisham East Constituency. It was conveniently sited for Bellingham Station, and complemented the private housing developments that were also being built nearby. Between 1919 and 1939 central government provided subsidies for council house building totalling £208m.*

Woolwich East covered the area from the town centre to Erith Marshes including Abbey Wood, Plumstead, Shooters Hill and Woolwich Arsenal whilst **Woolwich West** stretched south from the Thames dockyard area to New Eltham incorporating the town centre and its massively expanded suburbs surrounding Eltham Palace and Well Hall. It also included North Woolwich, a detached part of the parish on the Essex shore. Of the two constituencies the East Division was generally heavily working class while the West was more middle class in its social and demographic composition. These factors were to shape the political affiliations of the two seats.

Lewisham East extended from Blackheath in the north via Lewisham town centre to Bellingham in the south and incorporated eastern districts of Catford (Rushey Green), together with Lee Green, Hither Green, Downham and Grove Park. After the constituency was established the LCC sponsored the construction of a new council estate at Downham, in Bellingham near Catford. This estate, begun in 1920, was eventually to provide homes for 35,000 people, mostly re-housed from inner London slums. It would in time bring about a change in the political complexion of Lewisham and a further increase in the number of seats. The Mid Kent Railway Line (between Lewisham and Hayes) formed the boundary that separated the East constituency from **Lewisham West** which extended from Ladywell in the north to Upper Sydenham in the southwest and incorporated the rest of Catford, Crofton Park, Forest Hill, Honour Oak and Lower Sydenham.

Before 1918 both Lewisham and Woolwich adjoined respectively the Sevenoaks and Dartford county constituencies but the rapidly expanding London suburbs within these latter two divisions brought about the creation of two additional seats, one based on Bromley and the other on neighbouring Chislehurst. Despite its relatively late inclusion as a constituency in its own right, **Bromley** was an ancient town with a long history. The first positive mention came in a charter of 862AD in which King Ethelbert of Wessex, the Saxon King who controlled Kent at the time, granted the manor of Bromleag ("woodland clearing where broom grows") to Dryhtwald, his minister. For centuries Bromley was first and foremost a market town but its importance was always greater than other places in the surrounding district, so much so that when the Western Kent Division was established as a constituency in 1832, Bromley was the polling place for voters across a wide area. The nearest alternative polling places were at Blackheath (between Lewisham and Greenwich) and Tonbridge. Bromley began to mushroom with the coming of the railways in 1858. In 1911 the locally born novelist H.G.Wells wrote of their impact on the town: "The roads came...the houses followed. People moved into them as soon as the roofs were on."

The new 1918 constituency covered the suburban area of Penge, which included Crystal Palace and Anerley, all transferred from the former Surrey county division of Wimbledon, together with Beckenham, and Bromley itself. It also included Bickley, Bromley Park, Coney Hall, Eden Park, Elmers End, Kelsey Park, and Shortlands.

The adjacent and new **Chislehurst** constituency abutted Lewisham borough at Mottingham and circled Bromley from southeast to southwest. It included Bexley, Bexley Woods, Biggin Hill, Black Fen, Chelsfield, East Wickham, Elmstead Woods, Falconwood, Farnborough, Foots Cray, Green Street Green, Hayes, West Wickham, Keston, Lamorbey, Longlands, Mottingham, North Cray, Orpington, Petts Wood, Plaistow, Pratts Bottom, Sidcup, St. Mary Cray, St. Pauls Cray, Sundridge Park, Welling and Widmore. Chislehurst derives its name from its natural characteristics; "ceosil" meaning, "pebble", and "hurst" meaning "a wood", that is "a wood on a stony hill".

As a result of these changes the former Sevenoaks constituency became a Kent county seat covering no part of the London metropolitan area but, despite losing much of its suburban hinterland to the Chislehurst division, neighbouring **Dartford** remained a substantial constituency in its own right because the population was growing there too. The seat still incorporated Erith, Crayford and Bexleyheath but lost Northfleet to neighbouring Gravesend. It also included Barnehurst, Belvedere, Danson Park, Northumberland Heath, Slade Green, Thamesmead and West Heath.

Politics between the Wars

General Election Results 1918-1935 by % majority

Constituency	Pre1918	1918	1922	1923	1924	1929	1931	1935
Deptford	C	Lab17	Lab5	Lab26	Lab9	Lab25	C9	Lab15
Greenwich	C	C39	C22	Lab6	C3	Lab18	C35	C5
Woolwich	C							
Woolwich East		Lab100 -	Lab14	Lab23	Lab17	Lab22	Lab6+	Lab16
Woolwich West		C26	C20	C4	C15	C0.8	C29	C17
Lewisham	C							
Lewisham East		C100	C29	C13	C27	C0.7	C34	C11
Lewisham West		C100+	C31	C2	C40	C23	C55	C29+
Bromley		C26+	C12	C3	C23	C13+	C67	C48
Chislehurst		C54	C31	C11	C49	C25	C70	C47
Dartford	C	L43-	C6	Lab8	C2	Lab19	C11	C4-
C/NL/NLab	6	6+++	7	5	7	5+	8	7+
L	0	1	0	0	0	0	0	0
Lab/NDP	0	2-+	2	4	2	4	1+	2+
Total	6	9++++	9	9	9	9+	9+	9++

Key: 100 = unopposed; C = Conservative; L = Liberal; Lab = Labour. + indicates seat retained at a by-election; - indicates seat lost at a by-election

The politics of Deptford changed little after 1918 with Labour's pre-eminence re-asserted in that General Election with a majority of 17%. In the two years in which Labour managed to form a minority Government (1923 and 1929), Deptford recorded its two largest Labour majorities before the Second World War: 26% and 25% respectively. However, the tidal wave of opposition to Labour in the aftermath of the World recession that came in the wake of the Wall Street Crash in 1931 meant that the Party actually lost the seat to the Conservatives in the election of that year. The Tories won for the first time since 1900 and by a margin of 9%. The Party has not won there since.

Greenwich had been a mainly Tory seat for the best part of the previous 50 years and the Party's 1918 majority of 39% did little to suggest that by 1923 this would become a Labour seat for the first time. The decline of the working class Liberal vote was in all probability the main factor in this change but the Tories remained in strong contention, regaining the seat in 1924 before losing to Labour again in 1929, and then finally re-capturing the constituency in 1931 and going on to hold it until the end of the Second World War.

In Woolwich the story was pretty much a "tale of two cities" but as so often in the case of politics, there was the occasional upset. The working class East division returned a Labour MP at General Elections throughout the period, even in the darkest days of 1931 when the Party also won a by-election. However, earlier, on 2nd March 1921, the Tory candidate did win a by-election taking the seat for a brief period. The 2.6% Conservative majority was overturned at the 1922 General Election when Labour re-took the seat by a margin of 14%. Meanwhile the Conservative Party was pretty firmly established in the West constituency, although in Labour's best year (1929) the Tories only just hung on by 0.8% of the votes cast.

Both Lewisham seats remained faithful to the Conservative Party throughout the period and in fact their candidates were returned unopposed in 1918. All subsequent elections were contested but a pattern began to emerge after 1924 that suggested the East constituency was less strongly held than the West. The growing population of the Bellingham council estates began to have an impact on the balance of the electorate, which became less middle class. From an initial position of parity in terms of the Conservative Party's standing in each constituency, a differential in the Tory majority between the two seats of about 20% became apparent over time. In 1929, the year in which Labour became the biggest Party nationally for the first time, the Tories only just managed to hang on at Lewisham East, winning by 0.7% of the votes cast. In neighbouring West Lewisham their majority was a healthy 23%. In the Tory landslide year of 1931 their 55% majority in Lewisham West was 21% higher than in the East division.

The conservative credentials of the electorate were very much in evidence in a by-election at West Lewisham on 13th September 1921 when an Anti-Waste Party candidate campaigning for a reduction in public spending ran the Tories very close. The Conservative candidate held the seat but with a small 3.6% majority. Labour did not contest it but the Liberals did and won just over a quarter of the votes cast. At the 1922 General Election and following a budget in which public spending was reduced (by the so-called "Geddes Axe") the Tory was returned with a much more comfortable vote and a majority of 31%. In the last General Election before the Second World War in 1935 the Conservatives won Lewisham West with a comfortable 29% majority but on 24th November 1938 their majority was halved in a by-election. There were signs in that result of a fundamental change in the mood of the electorate and in fact Labour went on to win the seat by a margin of 7% when another General Election finally took place in 1945.

The political complexion of the two new outer suburban constituencies was decidedly Tory. In fact since their inception they have been predominantly so throughout, although Chislehurst did turn Labour just twice, in 1945 and 1966. Bromley and its successors, on the other hand, have always been Conservative strongholds although Dartford's more socially mixed electorate returned both radical and Conservative MPs at various times.

Between the Wars Chislehurst returned massive Conservative majorities. In 1931 the margin reached a phenomenal 70% and only once did it fall below 25%. Bromley majorities were more modest, but nonetheless comfortable; yet in the early years following the establishment of the new seat it was not always plain sailing. In December 1919 the Tories had to fight a by-election at Bromley where Labour was their soul opponent. A majority of 59% over the Liberals at the 1918 General Election was dramatically reduced to only 5% over Labour. It rose back to 12% in 1922 but fell again to 3% in the 1923 Election, the smallest it has ever been in the Bromley constituency. Thereafter the Conservatives managed to consolidate their position and were helped from time to time by the fluidity of opposition support as between Labour and the Liberals. At the 1929 Election the Tory majority had been 13% over the Liberal but on 2nd September 1930 in a by-election the Liberal candidate came within 4% of capturing the seat. Labour trailed in fourth place behind an Independent. In the 1931 Election the Tory majority climbed to 67%.

At Dartford, despite their successes at four of the eight national contests, the Tories never managed to win by a margin greater than 11%, and that was in their landslide year of 1931. If anything the boundary changes in 1918 worked to the Tories' disadvantage. Labour won in the two elections when it went on to form a minority Government (1923 and 1929), whilst the solitary Liberal success came in the flush of patriotism in 1918 when a Coalition candidate seeking re-election recorded a majority of 43%, only to lose by 6% to the Tories in 1922. However, this masked an intriguing sequence of events indicative of the three party nature of politics at that time. On March 27th 1920 Labour had gained Dartford from the Liberals with a by-election majority of 34%. Then at the 1922 General Election Labour lost it to a Tory before winning it back again in 1923 by a margin of 8%. Fifteen years later on 7th November 1938 a much more significant by-election occurred at Dartford that saw a repeat of the 1920 result. This time Labour gained the seat by a 5% margin over the Tories who had won by a similar margin themselves in 1935. When the seat was contested again it was after the War when Labour retained it in 1945 with a majority of 37%, proof of the dramatic decline in Liberal support and the switch to Labour that took place between the ends of the two World Wars.

Overall the Conservatives won 50 seats at Parliamentary elections including by-elections in northwest Kent between 1918 and the 1945 General Election (exclusive). The Liberals won only once, at Dartford, a seat they soon lost at a by-election in 1920. They did not win another seat in the area for 40 years. Labour did rather better. They won 17 General Election seats and another 3 at by-elections, including two at Dartford, where their gaining of the seat on the second occasion was a harbinger of the Party's improving electoral prospects.

MPs for Metropolitan Kent, 1918 - 1945

From	at	To	Surname	First Names	Constituency	Party
1918	G	1919	Forster	Henry William (Lord)	Bromley	Conservative
1919	B	1930	James	Cuthbert (Lt – Col)		Conservative
1930	B	1945	Campbell	Sir Edward Taswell		Conservative
1918	G	1922	Smithers	Sir Alfred Waldron	Chislehurst	Conservative
1922	G	1924	Nesbitt	Robert Chancellor		Conservative
1924	G	1945	Smithers	Sir Waldron		Conservative
1918	G	1920	Rowlands	James	Dartford	Liberal
1920	B	1922	Mills	John Edmund		Labour
1922	G	1923	Jarrett	George William Symonds		Conservative
1923	G	1924	Mills	John Edmund		Labour
1924	G	1929	McDonnell	Angus		Conservative
1929	G	1931	Mills	John Edmund		Labour
1931	G	1938	Clarke	Frank Edward		Conservative
1938	B	1945	Adamson	Mrs Janet (Jennie) Laurel		Labour
1918	G	1931	Bowerman	Charles William	Deptford	Labour
1931	G	1935	Hanley	Denis Augustine		Conservative
1935	G	1945	Green	Walter Henry		Labour
1918	G	1922	Benn	Sir Ion Hamilton (Capt)	Greenwich	Conservative
1922	G	1923	Hume	Sir George Hopwood		Conservative
1923	G	1924	Palmer	Edward Timothy		Labour
1924	G	1931	Hume	Sir George Hopwood		Conservative
1929	G	1847	Palmer	Edward Timothy		Labour
1931	G	1945	Hume	Sir George Hopwood		Conservative
1918	G	1945	Pownall	Sir Assheton	Lewisham East	Conservative
1918	G	1921	Coates	Sir Edward Feetham (Maj)	Lewisham West	Conservative
1921	B	1938	Dawson	Sir Philip		Conservative
1938	B	1945	Brooke	Sir Henry		Conservative
1918	G	1921	Crooks	William	Woolwich East	Labour
1921	B	1922	Gee	Robert (Capt)		Conservative
1922	G	1931	Snell	Henry		Labour
1931	B	1945	Hicks	(Ernest) George		Labour
1918	G	1943	Wood	Sir (Howard) Kingsley	Woolwich West	Conservative
1943	B	1945	Beech	Francis William (Maj)		Conservative

Notes: First returned at a: B By-election, G General Election

Bromley

Lord Henry William Forster (Conservative) was formerly the MP for Sevenoaks, which he had represented since 1892, and he remained Bromley's MP until 1919. His principal biographical details are in Chapter 5.

He was succeeded at a by-election by **Lieutenant-Colonel Cuthbert James** (Conservative) who remained the MP until his death in 1930. Born in 1872 as the second son of the second Baron Northbourne, James was educated at Harrow School and Magdalen College, Oxford and entered the 2nd East Surrey Regiment in 1894 serving in Egypt where he was Financial Secretary to the Army. He joined the Sudan and then the Egyptian Civil Service (Ministry of Interior) but retired from his tour of duty in 1909 to join the Seventh Battalion of the East Surrey Regiment. Between 1915 and his entry into the House in 1919 he was Inspector for motor transport at the Admiralty.

Sir Edward Taswell Campbell Conservative) who won the 1930 by-election following James' death and who held it throughout the remaining period, had been MP for Camberwell North West between 1924 and1929. Full biographical details can be found in Chapter 10 (Surrey).

Chislehurst

Sir Alfred Waldron Smithers (Conservative), who lived at Knockholt, was elected in 1918 and retired in 1922.

Born at Buxton in 1850, his father worked for the Bank of England. He attended Lewisham Grammar School and went on to be Deputy Chairman of the English Association of American Bond and Shareholders (1905) and of the South Eastern and Chatham Railway Company (1911). He died in 1924.

He was succeeded as MP in 1922 by **Robert Chancellor Nesbitt** (Conservative), a solicitor, who was born in 1868 and became senior partner in the firm Markby Stewart and Wadesons. He was a member of the Law Society Council between 1909 and 1926 and was a director of several companies including the National Mutual Life Association of Australasia (of which he was Chairman), the Union Bank of Australia and the British Law Insurance Company. He sat on various committees set up by the Lord Chancellor including one that investigated Supreme Court Fees (1920) and another that reported on Circuit arrangements (1922). In between he was chairman of a Special Training Grants Committee at the Ministry of Labour (1921). A member of the Church Assembly, he died in 1944. He retired in 1924.

Sir Waldron Smithers (Conservative) was elected in 1924, two years after his father, Sir Alfred had retired. Born in 1880 he was educated at Arlington School, Brighton, at Charterhouse, and in France at the Lycee d'Angers before becoming a stockbroker. During the First World War he served as an unattached Captain in the cavalry. Knighted in 1934, he was a magistrate in Kent where he lived near Knockholt and was resident organist at the parish church there from 1900. He was also a Governor of St. Bartholomew's Hospital and a member of the Board of Reedham Orphanage. In 1945 he transferred to the new, more local and safer Orpington constituency which he continued to represent until he died in 1954.

Dartford

James Rowlands (Liberal) was re-elected in 1918 having held the seat, apart from the period from January to December 1910, since 1906. He died in 1920. Also a former MP for Finsbury East between 1886 and 1895, his principal biographical details may be found in Chapter 3 (Middlesex – North London).

The by-election that followed his death was won by **John Edmund Mills** (Labour) who held the seat for three periods but who was out of the House for two. He was MP initially from 1920 to 1922, again from 1923 to 1924, and finally from 1929 to 1931. Mills was born in 1882 and by the time of his election to Parliament was living in Eltham near his former work place, the Woolwich Arsenal ,where as a member of the Amalgamated Society of Engineers, he was a sometime Chairman and Secretary of the Shop Stewards Committee. He was also President of the National Housing Association in 1921 and when Labour formed a government in 1929 he was Parliamentary Secretary to the Chancellor of the Duchy of Lancaster.

He was defeated in 1922 by **George William Symonds Jarrett** (Conservative Constitutionalist) but the Tory was himself defeated by Mills in 1923. Jarrett was, however, briefly significant having helped found the National Democratic Party during the First World War as a vehicle for working class, essentially Labour voters who supported the war effort and imperialism generally. After the War he supported the Coalition Government as as a National Liberal when the NDP was disbanded and subsequently joined the Conservatives. After his defeat at Dartford he made several further attempts to secure election but failed in all of them.

In 1924 Mills lost again, this time to **Angus McDonnell** (Conservative), a younger son of the 6th Earl of Antrim, who went on to hold it until 1931 when Mills succeeded again. Educated at Eton he was a Colonel in the Canadian Railway Troops and was invested a Companion of the Order of St.Michael and St. George and given the Order of the Bath "for conspicuous services to the Crown" in 1918. The Antrim family motto was "Toujours Pret" (ever ready).

Janet Adamson MP
People's History Museum, Manchester

Following Mills' 1931 defeat the seat fell to **Frank Edward Clarke** (Conservative) who held it until his death in 1938. Born in 1886, Clarke was managing director of the family firm, Herbert Clarke and Sons of Erith where they were described as "road and river transport and general wharfingers". He was a Freeman of the Port of London, a Kent County Councillor and local magistrate.

The by-election victor following Clarke's death in 1938 was **Mrs Janet (Jennie) Adamson** (Labour) who represented the seat until 1945 when she was elected for the newly created constituency of Bexley from which she resigned in 1946 after she was appointed as Deputy Chairman of the National Assistance Board. Her appointment to this important role came at a historically significant moment as the Labour Government set about establishing the basis of the modern Welfare

State. The wife of William Murdoch Adamson, a national officer of the Transport & General Workers Union and MP for Cannock (Staffordshire), Jennie was only the second woman to be elected Chairman of the Labour Party (1935/6) and was also a member of the Royal Arsenal Cooperative and Political Purposes Committee. She was chairman of the South Metropolitan District Committee and in the Attlee Government was Parliamentary Secretary to the Ministry of Pensions. She was born in 1882 and died in 1962.

Deptford

Charles William Bowerman (Labour), whose principal biographical details can be found in Chapter 5, had first been elected in 1906 and was re-elected in 1918, retaining the seat until the Labour debacle of 1931.

He was finally defeated by **Denis Augustine Hanley** (Conservative), who retired after only one term in 1935. Born in 1903, he was educated at Downside School and Trinity College Cambridge and after leaving the Commons he worked in the Royal Naval Scientific Service from 1938 to 1954. He was the last Conservative to sit as a Deptford MP.

The Tories lost Deptford in 1935 to **Walter Henry Green** (Labour) who held the seat until his retirement in 1945. Born locally in 1878 he was educated at an LCC Elementary School and became an engineer. He was elected to the Borough Council in 1909 and remained a member until 1956, being mayor in 1920-1. Additionally he was a LCC Alderman between 1928 and 1936, being chairman of the Parliamentary Committee from 1934. He sat on the National Executive Committee of the Labour Party for many years and was its Chairman in 1941-2. A magistrate for London County and a member of the Metropolitan Water Board (1946-53), he was awarded the CBE in 1949 and died in 1958.

Greenwich

Sir Ion Hamilton Benn (Conservative) who had first been elected in January 1910 was returned in 1918 but retired in 1922. His principal biographical details can be found in Chapter 5.

He was succeeded in 1922 by **Sir George Hopwood Hume** (Conservative) who served initially until defeated in 1923, then secondly from 1924 to 1929, and lastly from 1931 to 1945. Born in 1866, he was educated at College Galliard in Lausanne, Switzerland and at Finsbury Technical College and was called to the Bar at the Middle Temple in 1900, the year he was elected to Greenwich Borough Council. He was elected to the LCC in 1910 and remained a councillor until 1922 when he became an alderman, a position he held until 1946. During a long career with the LCC he was Chairman of its Highways Committee (1913 and 1919), Leader of the Moderate Party (1918-25) and Council Chairman (1926-7) having chaired the London Electricity Company a year earlier. He served on the Thames Conservancy Board from 1916, was Chairman of the London Municipal Society, a magistrate and member of the Advisory Committee on Traffic at the Ministry of Transport in 1924-5. He was a member of several charities including the Mildmay Mission, the Trinitarian Bible Society and the Rachel Macmillan Training College. He died in 1946. He was the last Conservative to represent the Greenwich constituency.

In the periods that Hume was not its MP, Greenwich elected **Edward Timothy Palmer** (Labour), which occurred first in 1923 and again in 1929. Son of a fruiterer, he was born in1878 and educated at a local board school in Holloway (Islington) before becoming a grocer's assistant. He progressed to be an agent and supervisor with the Prudential Insurance Company where he became an active trade unionist, becoming General Secretary of the Prudential Staff Union in 1910, serving in that role until 1923, the year he was first elected at Greenwich, though he had also contested it unsuccessfully in 1918 and 1922. Defeated in 1924 he was re-elected in 1929 but lost his seat in 1931. He lived at Westcliffe on Sea near Southend and was a member of the Essex County Council between 1946 and 1947 when he died.

Lewisham East

Lieutenant - Colonel Sir Assheton Pownall (Conservative) held the seat for the entire period from 1918 to 1945. He was born in 1877 and educated at Rugby School and in 1897 became a second Lieutenant in the West Kensington volunteers rising to become a Lieutenant – Colonel in the 20th Battalion of the London Regiment in 1915. He first contested a Parliamentary seat at Rotherhithe in January 1910 but was unsuccessful. He repeated the experience in December 1910 and in 1911 was appointed the prospective candidate in Tottenham but transferred to Lewisham in time for the 1918 election. He was PPS to the Post Master General in 1923 and to the Minister of Labour between 1924 and 1929. Towards the end of his Parliamentary career he was chairman of the important Public Accounts Committee from 1943 to 1945. From 1942-7 he was Master of the Vintners' Company and died in 1953.

Lewisham West,

Sir Edward Feetham Coates (Conservative) had been MP for Lewisham since winning a by-election in 1903 and was re-elected in 1918. He died in 1921 and his principal biographical details may be found in Chapter 5.

Coates was succeeded at a by-election held in 1921 by **Sir Philip Dawson** (Conservative) who served until his death in Berlin in 1938. Born in 1866, Dawson was educated privately and at the Belgian Universities of Ghent and Liege. He married the daughter of a Rector and pursued a career as a consulting engineer, a role which saw him become a member of the Ministry of Transport's Electrification of Railways Advisory Committee and the Water Power Resources Committee. A member of both the Institution of Mechanical and of the Civil Engineers he first entered politics on the LCC, representing West Lewisham. He was Chairman of the Anglo – Italian Parliamentary Committee and President of the Institute of Fuel from 1937 to 1938.

Sir Henry Brooke MP
People's History Museum, Manchester

(Sir) Henry Brooke (Conservative) succeeded Dawson at the 1938 by-election occasioned by the latter's death and held the seat until 1945 when he was defeated. Brooke went on to become MP for Hampstead from 1950 to 1966 and a Cabinet Minister. Born in 1903, he was educated at Marlborough School and Balliol College, Oxford. He entered local politics on Hampstead Borough Council in 1936 and two years later was returned at a by-election as MP for Lewisham West. From 1944 to 1955 he was also a member of the LCC and in 1949 played a large part in producing a "dead heat" outcome at the polls, then a remarkable achievement for the Conservatives. Prior to the nationalization of the railways in 1948 he was a Deputy Chairman of the Southern Railway [1] and was active in support of private schools. He was on the governing bodies of two of them, namely Marlborough and Charterhouse, and was also a member of the Court of London University. From 1954 to 1958 he served as Financial Secretary to the Treasury under Butler and then Macmillan (Chancellors of the Exchequer), and when the latter was appointed Prime Minister in 1957 he joined the Cabinet as Minister of Housing, Local Government and Welsh Affairs, a post he retained until October 1961 when he was made Paymaster-General. A year later, after a major Cabinet re-shuffle, dubbed "the night of the long knives", he was made Home Secretary, a post he retained under Sir Alec Douglas-Home when Macmillan resigned in 1963 until his Party's defeat at the polls in 1964. He remained MP for Hampstead until he lost at the following election in 1966. He was made a Life Peer, Lord Cumnor in 1966 and died in 1984. His son, Peter Brooke was MP for the Cities of London & Westminster between 1977 and 2001, (See Chapter 15).

Woolwich East

William Crooks (Labour) had been elected at Woolwich in 1903 and apart from a short interval between January and December 1910, remained its MP until 1918. After the War he was returned for Woolwich East and remained its MP until he resigned in 1921 shortly before his death. His principal biographical details can be found in Chapter 5.

The 1921 by-election caused by Crooks' resignation was won by **Captain Robert Gee** (Conservative), who held the seat only until the 1922 general election. Nonetheless he enjoys the unique distinction of having been the only Conservative ever to have been elected for an East Woolwich constituency. He was born in 1876 and educated at Countesthorpe Cottage Homes before joining the Royal Fusiliers in 1892. He was commissioned in 1915 and placed on the staff of the 29th Division on active service in France. However, after the War he became a law student at Grays Inn and also entered politics for the first time. He contested Cardiff in 1918 for the National Democratic Party but moved to the Conservatives and was elected at the Woolwich East by-election in 1921. He lost his seat in 1922 and in the next general election, held in 1923, he contested Newcastle-upon-Tyne East followed by another North East England seat, Bishop Auckland at a by-election also in 1923. He was elected MP for Bosworth (Leicestershire) in 1924 but resigned in 1927 when he emigrated to Australia where he lived a long life until his death in 1960.

Henry Snell MP
© National Portrait Gallery
Walter Stoneman 1931

Henry Snell (Labour) took the seat in 1922 and held it until 1931. He was born in 1865 at Sutton-on-Trent (Nottinghamshire) where he was the son of an agricultural labourer. Educated at the village school he gained entrance to Nottingham University but also took degrees at the London School of Economics and Heidelberg University. In 1890 he became an agent for the Charity Organisation Society, a Fabian

1 Established in January 1923 by an Act of Parliament that grouped several former companies together.

Election communication on an important issue of the day.
The People's History Museum Manchester

Society Lecturer and Chairman of the British Ethical Union. He contested Huddersfield unsuccessfully in 1910 and 1918 but in 1919 was elected to the LCC, a body he was later to chair between 1934 and 1938. He was created Baron Snell in 1931 before the general election held later that year and was made Under – Secretary of State for India. In 1935 he was made Leader of the Labour peers and President of the National Council of Social Service in 1938. When Churchill became Prime Minister at the head of the Wartime Coalition Government in 1940, Snell was made Deputy Leader of the House of Lords. He was also the Vice President of the Royal Empire Society and, between 1940 and 1943, of the Royal Institute of International Affairs. He was vice chairman of the British Council and died in 1944.

George Ernest Hicks
© National Portrait Gallery
Lafayette

George Ernest Hicks (Labour) won the seat in 1931 and held it until 1950 when he retired. He was born the son of a builder in 1879 and at the age of 11, after attending an elementary school, became a bricklayer. He was an active trade unionist who became General Secretary of the Amalgamated Union of Building Trade Workers, a post he held for 20 years. In 1919 he was elected President of the National Federation of Building Trade Operatives, a role he relinquished in 1937. Meanwhile he was an active member of the TUC and was its President in 1927. From 1940 to 1945 he was Parliamentary Secretary at the Ministry of Works and when a liveryman of the Companies of Glaziers and Pavoirs he was made a Freeman of the City of London. He retired in 1950.

Woolwich West

Howard Kingsley Wood MP
© National Portrait Gallery
Bassano Ltd 1920

Sir (Howard) Kingsley Wood (Conservative) was the first MP for Woolwich West in 1918 and served until his death in 1943. Born in 1881 he was the son of a Wesleyan Minister who became a solicitor in 1903, being the senior partner in his own company. However, he joined the Woolwich Council in 1911 and embarked on a long and successful political career. From 1918 to 1922 he was: PPS to the Minister of Health; Secretary of the Parliamentary Allotments Committee in 1923; Parliamentary Secretary to the Ministry of Health between 1924 and 1929, and Minister of Education in 1931. In the National Government he served as Post Master General from 1931 to 1935 but was admitted to the Cabinet in 1933 and then served as Minister of Health from 1935 to 1938 when he was appointed Secretary of State for Air by Neville Chamberlain. When Churchill took over as Prime Minister in 1940 he was successively Lord Privy Seal (1940) and Chancellor of the Exchequer, being appointed to this post in 1940 and serving until his death in 1943. He was a member of the War Cabinet between 1940 and 1942. Amongst other things he was also a Brighton magistrate, Chairman of the National Union of Conservative and Unionist Organisations (between 1930 and 1932) and Grand Master of the Primrose League in 1938.

Sir Howard Kingsley Wood MP as Secretary of State for Air, during World War 2
Wikipedia - Imperial War Museum

Major Francis William Beech (Conservative) was returned at the 1943 by-election that followed Wood's death. Born in 1885 he was educated at Long Ashton in Bristol and at Lewis School, Pengam, near Cardiff and afterwards became a solicitor, being admitted in 1911. He joined the Army in 1915 as a Major and Staff Paymaster in the RAPC. He entered politics as an alderman on Woolwich Borough council and after his defeat at the 1945 general election was mayor of Woolwich in 1955-6. He was Deputy Chairman of the LCC in 1952-3, a magistrate in the county of London and a Freeman of the City of London. He died in 1969.

Chapter 10
Metropolitan Surrey 1918 - 1945

The Impact of the Boundary Review of 1917-18

In 1918 there was another major redistribution of seats in Surrey; no part of the metropolitan area was completely unaffected by the changes. Nine additional constituencies were created, five in the LCC area and four in the Surrey county area of the metropolis where representation doubled. Roundly two seats were created for each one of the former single seat constituencies.

The LCC Area in Surrey

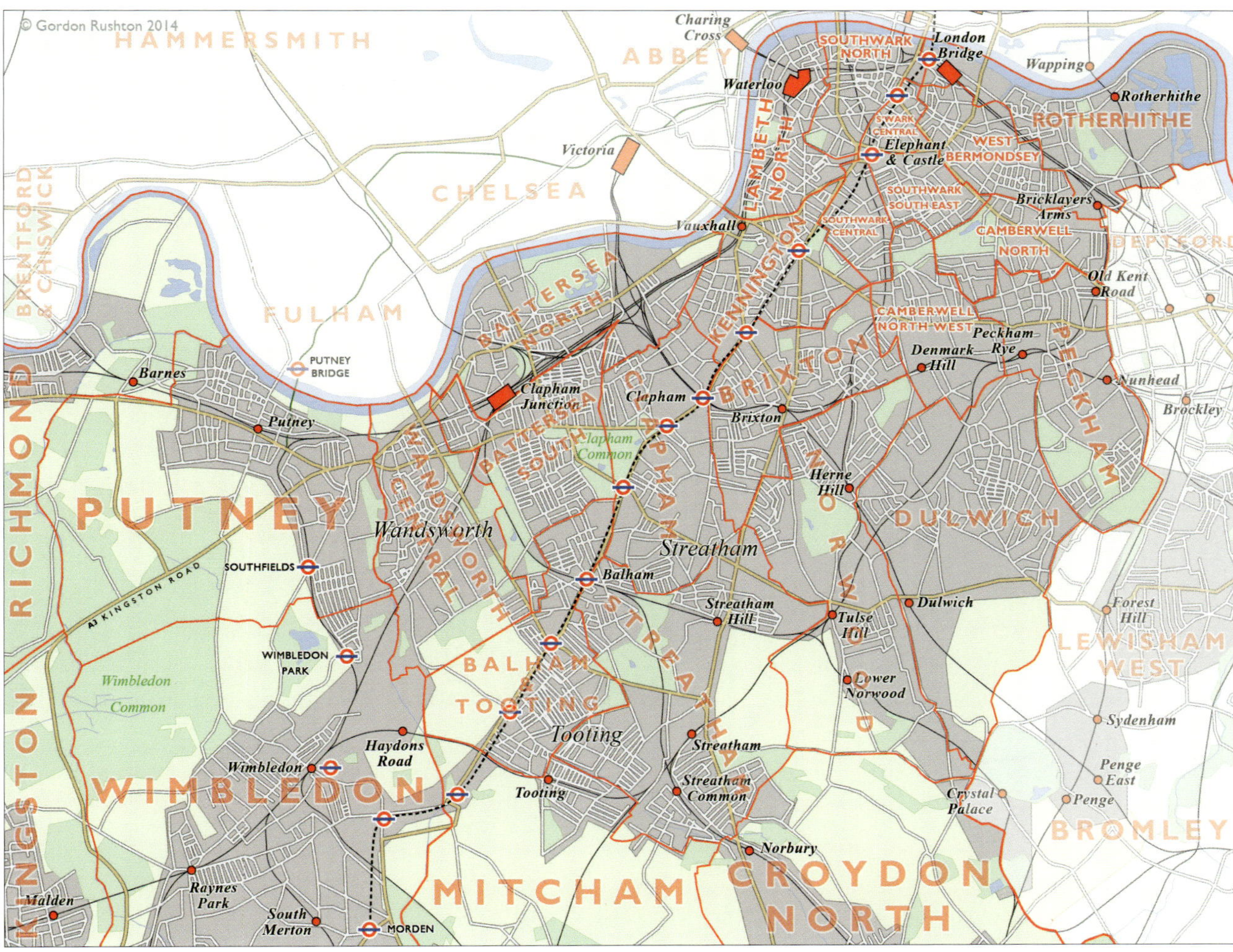

The boroughs of Bermondsey, Southwark, Camberwell, and Lambeth returned twelve MPs in 1885 and in 1918 this number was increased by one. The **Rotherhithe** constituency was unchanged whilst Bermondsey itself was renamed **West Bermondsey**. The former Newington Parliamentary Borough was absorbed by Southwark but the combined number of constituencies remained five. **North Southwark,** comprising the St Saviour's District, Christchurch, St Michael's and St Jude's wards, replaced the former West division of the borough, and covered the area closest to the

Left: The Northern Line tube was extended south in 1926 to serve the Kennington, Clapham, Balham & Tooting, Mitcham, and Wimbledon constituencies. It was a major undertaking that allowed continued expansion of housing in the areas served. Architect Holden of the London Passenger Transport Board designed suitably impressive yet practical stations to provide access - this view is of Clapham South, just before opening.

Below: The terminus of the Northern Line extension was at Morden (Wimbledon Constituency). This aerial view was taken in 1925, before the completion. It shows the open fields of the area, with roads placed ready for housing. The first houses have been completed, and in the lower part of the picture Morden tube station can be seen (in a cutting - the line was underground otherwise), leading to the new car sheds.

Below: Norwood was a bastion of what in the Inter-War years was termed 'Villa Conservatism'. The Party tailored its approach to the middle class electorate in habiting homes such as these in Bloom Grove, West Norwood. **Gordon Rushton**

Above: On Tooting Corner, (Balham & Tooting constituency) just after the end of WW1, the busy street scene shows a predominance of horse-drawn vehicles, something that will soon change - see neighbouring Croydon on P300. Note that the tramcar draws power from a central buried conduit, thus avoiding the complex net of defacing overhead wires.

Left: The Dover House Estate (Putney Constituency), was built by LCC in 1919, and became a show place in its day. Completed in 1927, it comprised 1212 homes, ranging from five-room houses to two-room flats, housing a population of 4400. It was laid out in 'garden city style' complete with a school. Barnes Station is 15 mins walk away in the Richmond Constituency.

cathedral, between the Blackfriars and London Bridges. **Central Southwark** replaced the former Newington West to include the St Mary's, Trinity and St Paul's wards (Elephant and Castle), and parts of the St George's ward south of the New Kent Road. **South East Southwark** replaced Newington, Walworth, comprising the St John's and St Peter's wards, together with the southern part of St George's ward between Elephant and Walworth.

Camberwell gained the additional seat. The Local Government Act of 1888 had encouraged the building of the first council homes, and these appeared initially at Grove Vale, and Newlands, expanding the borough's population. North Peckham was transferred from Peckham to join the Coburg, Marlborough, and St George's wards to form a restructured **Camberwell North**, whilst a new **Camberwell North West** appeared. This comprised the Addington, Lyndhurst, St Giles, Town Hall, and West wards of the borough (effectively Camberwell itself), extending east of Denmark Hill (transferred from Dulwich), and half way towards Peckham, but lying north of **Dulwich.** This itself comprised five wards:- St John's (Denmark Hill); Ruskin (Herne Hill and North Dulwich); Alleyn (East Dulwich); College (West Dulwich), and Hamlet (Sydenham Hill). **Peckham** extended south from the Old Kent Road via Queens Road and Nunhead to Peckham Rye, and comprised six wards: Clifton, Goldsmith and St Mary's (Queens Road area); Rye Lane and The Rye (Peckham Rye), and Nunhead. Peckham's 1911 population had fallen a little since 1901, but by 1921 the figure of 107,682 was higher. In fact this represented the peak, and although a council estate was built at South Nunhead in 1923, with others following in the 1930s, by 1931 its population had fallen to 99,604, as people moved away to the new suburbs.

Lambeth borough retained four seats in 1918, although there were some ward changes between them. **Lambeth North** retained the Marsh and Bishop's wards, and the whole of Prince's ward from Kennington. It included Waterloo, Lambeth Palace, the river frontage, and the cramped streets around the South Western railway viaduct. **Kennington** lost the part of the Prince's ward it had previously held, but added the adjacent new South Lambeth ward of Vassal to Vauxhall and The Oval. **Brixton** comprised the new Town Hall ward as well as Stockwell and Angel. The constituency extended from Stockwell in the west to Herne Hill in the east, and included a part of Tulse Hill. Expansion of this area had been further stimulated by the opening in 1890 of the world's first deep tube railway, connecting Stockwell with the City of London. This subsequently became part of the Northern Line. The rest of the Tulse Hill ward was in the **Norwood** constituency, together with Herne Hill and Knights Hill, which included Thurlow Park and West Norwood.

In Wandsworth three additional seats were created after the War. In addition, Clapham was transferred fully to Wandsworth Borough, and the two 1885 Battersea & Clapham constituencies became three making seven in total in the two neighbouring Thames-side boroughs. Battersea was divided two ways, **Battersea North** retained the Church, Latchmere, and Park wards of the former Battersea's six wards, and acquired Nine Elms from Clapham. It thus extended from Latchmere (Clapham Junction) in the west to Nine Elms in the east, where it adjoined the Kennington constituency. In between were Queenstown and Battersea Park.

Battersea South comprised three wards of the former Battersea seat together with two from Clapham. The three were: St John; Winstanley (West of Clapham Junction), and Shaftesbury (Clapham Common North Side). The other two were Bolingbroke, and Broomwood (covering the streets between Wandsworth and Clapham Commons).

Within Wandsworth borough there were now five seats. After the growth of Clapham as a residential suburb, house building started to take hold further afield, and the former villages of Balham, and Tooting grew substantially, along the railway, bus, and tramway routes that emanated ever outwards at that time. Tooting Junction (Tooting, Merton & Wimbledon Railway) was completed in 1868, offering service to Central London, and growth occurred thereafter, reaching such proportions that by 1918 a new Parliamentary constituency was justified.

Clapham constituency covered an area that today straddles two Boroughs (Wandsworth and Lambeth) but was mostly in the latter. It comprised the wards of Clapham North (Clapham High Street area), and South (Clapham Park), together with the Thornton Road area of Balham that lies beyond Clapham South station, north east of Balham, and north west of Streatham Hill. However, most of Balham ward was incorporated in a new **Balham & Tooting** division. 'Baelgenham' dated from 957 AD and may have meant, 'smooth or rounded enclosure' whilst 'Totinge' dates from as early as 675 AD and was a settlement belonging to a man called Tota.

A new **Putney** constituency extended from Southfields to Putney Bridge and Roehampton, the latter being distinguished as the location of the first LCC built overspill council estate, where building began in 1920. The constituency was established after the whole area had developed as a railway-commuting suburb for London. The London to Richmond/ Windsor railway was opened in 1846 but other stations were built in the latter part of the 19th Century prompting further growth. The West Brompton to Putney Bridge extension of the District line opened in 1880 and to Wimbledon in 1889, when Southfields station became operational. Horse drawn trams came to the area in the period between 1903

Right: *Purley Tram terminus, Brighton Road, the 1918 boundary between Croydon South and East Surrey constituencies. Motor vehicles now predominate.*

Below: *A 1925 poster by Frank Newbould, part of the LCC policy for bold, decorative art to promote transport.*

Above, right: *Children paddle in the pond at Mitcham, a new constituency from 1918. Behind, Mr Breach's steam fair waits setting up.*
Below: *The Elite Cinema stood on the corner of London and Richmond Roads in Central Kingston - Gracie Fields has star billing. This was the first place where the London Passenger Transport Board replaced trams with trolleybuses - a 'Diddler' glides north on the left of the street. In this 1934 view., a Ford Model 'A' de-luxe Tudor rolls along the traffic-free road, and a child's 'box-cart' is being pushed past an Edward V11 postbox that signals the rapid expansion of the Borough over the previous 20 years, all of it within the Kingston Constituency.*

and 1911 and helped to make Putney an even more accessible and attractive place in which to live. Putney itself was the site of a Roman settlement and was subsequently an Anglo Saxon settlement named 'Puttas Landing', Putta presumed to be a Saxon chief who arrived here during the invasions of the dark ages. Putney can claim to be one of London's first suburbs. Ever since the first bridge was built here in 1729 - replacing an ancient ferry - Putney has been an important route out of London, but away from the busy High Street is a tranquil part of London. Nevertheless, duels were fought on Putney Heath, with celebrated combatants including William Pitt and Lord Castlereagh - lined up against George Canning.

Streatham (since 1965 mainly in Lambeth borough) was also created a constituency in its own right in 1918. "Estreham" meant, "village on a Roman Road" and dated from Norman times. In 1918 it constituted a classic middle class suburb, comprising villas and flats of substantial construction. These communities were very well served by a multiplicity of railway stations on lines that cut swathes through South London. Further west was **Wandsworth Central**, shorn of its ties with Putney, Balham, Tooting, and Streatham, and covering the remaining Fairfield, and Springfield wards including Earlsfield, and Summerstown.

Outer Metropolitan Suburban Surrey

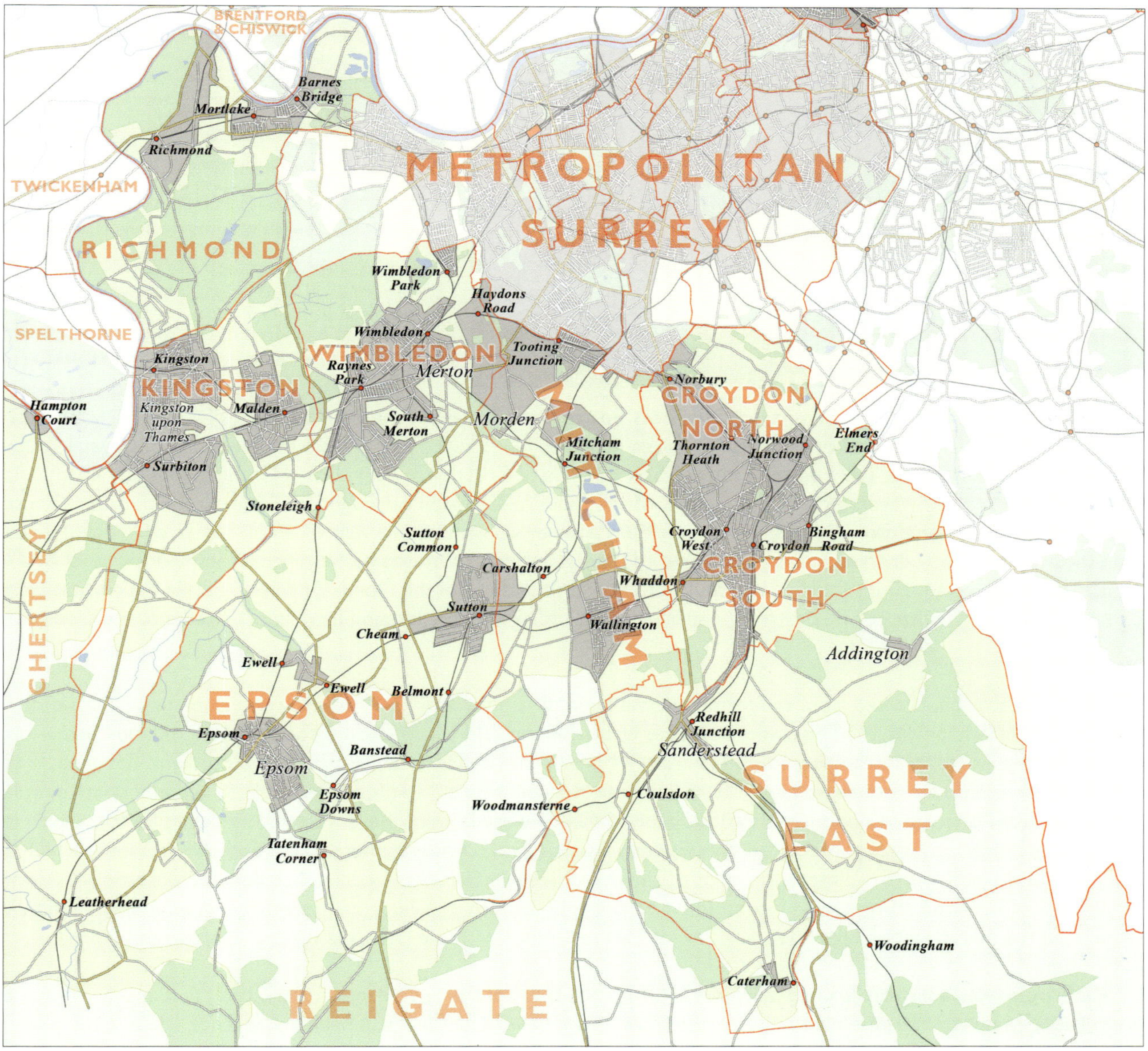

Croydon North officially comprised the seven borough wards of: South, and Upper Norwood; Norbury; West Thornton; Thornton Heath, Bensham Manor (all Thornton Heath), and Woodside. Confusingly, the separate Norwood seat in Lambeth borough was based on West Norwood. Incorporated in the new Croydon constituency was a large LCC overspill council estate built just outside the London boundary at Norbury, Surrey, and one half-mile from the

Above Left : *Mitcham was well served by public transport. Trams ran through to Central London, with no interruption from heavy traffic and the Tube came to nearby Morden in the 1920s to supplement many surface railways. The houses constructed in streets like these were highly desirable and well-built.* **John Nelson**

Above: *The Labour Party play in their manifesto of good housing included this stylised impression of what the interior of the 'ideal' house should look like. Such a view from the 1920s and 30s contrasts with what is expected today.* **People's History Museum, Manchester**

Left: *Richmond-upon-Thames saw its riverside built up and made accessible for pleasure right through the Victorian period and on into the Inter-War years. People would flock there at weekends in good weather to enjoy time on the River.* **Wikipedia**

tram terminus that was in London proper. **Croydon South** was the rest of the then borough of Croydon, which also comprised seven wards: Whitehorse Manor (the area round Selhurst Park football stadium, the home of Crystal Palace football club); Addiscombe; the Central, East, and South wards of Croydon proper; Broad Green (Waddon Marsh), and Waddon. It did not, however, include those parts of the modern Croydon borough like Purley and Coulsdon. These districts were transferred from Reigate to the new **East Surrey** constituency, a very much more narrowly defined seat than the original county division first established in 1832. Also including Caterham, Woldingham and Godstone, the new constituency served a growing middle class south of Croydon that lived in the North Downs. Officially the constituency comprised the Rural District of Godstone (which included Addington), the Urban Districts of Caterham, and Coulsdon & Purley.

West of Croydon, created from the former Wimbledon division, was a new **Mitcham** constituency ("Michelham" meaning, "large farm or village"). This comprised three Urban Districts (Mitcham, Beddington & Wallington, and Carshalton, which included St Helier) stretching south from the Wandsworth borders near Tooting and Streatham. Between 1919 and 1938 the LCC built cottage homes at St Helier near Morden tube station (opened 1926) to accommodate people from slum areas of central London, and by 1938 around 40,000 were housed there. The seat excluded Sutton, which in 1918 was the most populous part of a redrawn **Epsom** division. This officially comprised the Epsom RDC and the UDCs of Epsom and Leatherhead. Chessington, east of the Southwestern Railway was also included, although neighbouring Hook was in Kingston **Wimbledon** contracted to become a much smaller constituency geographically. It officially comprised the municipal borough (including Raynes Park) together with the Urban District of Merton and Morden.

Richmond-on-Thames (named by Henry VIII after the town of the same name in Yorkshire) first appeared on the constituency map in 1918 when it was separated from Kingston with which it had been linked since 1885. It comprised the municipal borough itself and the two Urban Districts on either side. Stretching from Barnes (UDC) in the northeast to Ham (UDC) in the southwest, the division also included Richmond Park, Kew, and Mortlake. Some expansion of the area had occurred after the opening of the railways in the area, the most recent of which had been the District Line of the London Underground to Richmond itself in 1877. The **Kingston-upon-Thames** constituency remained, covering the expanding suburbs around the Thameside town. It officially comprised the municipal borough together with two Urban Districts; Surbiton and The Maldens & Coombe including Hook and New Malden.

Politics between the Wars

Overall in the Inter-War period it was the Conservatives who had most to celebrate. They and their allies comprised 72% of all MPs during this period, securing the return of 134 MPs standing on their Party's platform and another 7 Coalitionists. Labour scored 37, Liberals 17, and the Communists just one. In the LCC area the Party won 78 seats and in addition secured the support of 7 National MPs, including one Labour. Labour itself became the main opposition Party during the period. None of the minority parties won any seats outside the LCC area, the Tories winning all eight constituencies at every single election, although one of these (Richmond in 1922) was an Independent Conservative. In all the Tories won 56 times at General Elections in these seats.

Inter-War by-election results presented a different picture. Labour won 12, the Tories 9, and Liberal Unionists one, whilst the Liberals proper could manage only a solitary victory. Despite the massive Tory dominance at General Elections, Labour's disproportionate successes at by-elections told the story of underlying political tensions within the electorate that were not finally to work through until the era ushered in by the ending of the Second World War in 1945. (See table overleaf.)

In Southwark and Bermondsey the end of the First World War marked a watershed. The pre-War preference for Liberalism began to be replaced by the much more working class Labour Party. This was not altogether surprising given the nature of the mainly dockland and railway employment in these boroughs especially at a time when Trade Unionism was becoming extremely powerful as a protection for the workers' wages and conditions. Certain of the franchise changes made in 1918 also favoured such groups in society, especially the reduction in the residence qualification from one year to six months. Initially the impact of the social and electoral changes was not obvious although Labour did secure its first MP in the area at Southwark Central, by a large majority of 44% but elsewhere the mix was much as before with the Liberals winning comfortably in the other two Southwark constituencies and in Bermondsey West. The Conservatives even managed to win Rotherhithe for the first time since 1900. However at a by-election on 14th December 1921 the Labour candidate captured South East Southwark from the National Liberals who had won the seat by a margin of 45% in 1918. This result displayed something of the volatility of politics during the Inter-War years but by the time of the next General Election in 1922 the Government had recovered sufficiently for the National Liberals to win the seat back with a majority of 13%.

The 1922 Election was the last in which the old allegiances were displayed. Lloyd-George was Prime Minister but since 1918 had governed in Coalition with the Conservatives on a wave of patriotism that followed the War. However, this split the Party and in 1922 some Liberals fought the election as Coalition Liberals, in which case they were unopposed by the Conservatives, whilst other Liberals went into opposition. This had unique political effects. It meant that the opposition vote to the Conservatives continued to be split between Liberal and Labour but it also meant that those Liberal voters who supported the Coalition voted for the Conservatives in certain seats. In others, where two Liberal candidates stood it was Labour who benefited. By then also the post-war euphoria had subsided and a period of economic depression, unemployment and social unrest had begun. The outcome of the Election in 1922 was that Coalition Liberals took all three seats in Southwark but in Bermondsey West Labour took the seat from the Liberals. Only Rotherhithe remained unchanged but the Conservatives saw their majority reduced to a mere 0.2%. The stage was set for fundamental changes and these occurred in 1923 when Labour took three seats and the Liberals (by now out of Coalition) took two. Labour won in Southwark North, Southwark South East and Rotherhithe, whilst Liberals took the other two seats at Central Southwark and West Bermondsey.

General Election results in the Inter-War Period

The Liberal vote declined nationally by 12% between the 1923 and 1924 General Elections whilst Labour's and the Tories' both increased. Nationally these trends favoured the Conservatives but in Southwark and Bermondsey Labour was the beneficiary, winning all five seats. Despite this there was a battle going on between Liberal and Labour Parties at constituency level and on 28th March 1927 the Liberals gained North Southwark at a by-election with a majority of 7% as compared with 6% for Labour in 1924. (See table overleaf)

However, Labour recovered from a result that may have been influenced by opinion in the aftermath of the General Strike and re-took the seat at the 1929 General Election. In fact Labour won all five seats again in 1929 increasing its majorities in four of them (the exception being North Southwark where the by-election result dented their campaign). The results in Southwark and Bermondsey helped Labour to form a Government as the largest single Party for the first time.

This state of affairs proved to be only fleeting, however, when a global economic catastrophe struck Britain in

General Election Results 1918-1935 by % majority

Constituency	Pre1918	1918	1922	1923	1924	1929	1931	1935
Rotherhithe	C	C18	C0.2	Lab18	Lab21	Lab42	C0.6	Lab19
West Bermondsey	L	L12	Lab14	L5	Lab14	Lab38	Lab0.4	Lab24
Southwark Central	L	Lab44	NL31	L10	Lab6	Lab28	Nlab31	Lab7+
Southwark North	L	L23	NL8	Lab2	Lab6 -	Lab2	NL30	NL0.4 -
Southwark South East	C/L	L45 -	NL13	Lab9	Lab20	Lab39	C7	Lab26
Camberwell North		C37 -	Lab2	Lab28	Lab18	Lab35	C4	Lab32+
Camberwell North West	L	L28	NL19	L0.4	C0.8	Lab9	C34	C3
Peckham	C	L27	C18	C0.7	Lab3	Lab17	C25	C3-
Dulwich	C	C58	C35	C7	C32	C19	C56+	C35
Lambeth North	C	L25	L4	L19	L0.1	Lab2	L30	Lab11
Kennington	C/L	L10	C11	Lab2	C13	Lab11	C29	C2 -
Brixton	C	C39	C10	L7	C31+	C13	C54	C22
Norwood	C	C32	C37	C18	C43	C22	C62	C34
Streatham		C58	C38	C20	C51	C32	C70	C52+
Battersea North	L	L33	Lab9	L1	Comm2	Lab7	C20	Lab17+
Battersea South		C54	C23	C4	C15 -	Lab1	C36	C15
Clapham	C	C41	C37	C18	C28	C11	C45	C21
Wandsworth Central	C	C31	C39	C19	C23	Lab1	C43	C17 - +
Balham & Tooting		C43	C36	C20	C36	C12	C49	C26+
Putney		C27	C20	C100	C45	C28+	C63	C33+
Richmond		C27	IndC25	C26	C54	C35+	C69+	C47
Kingston	C	C60	C33	C23	C50	C31	C65	C47+
Wimbledon	C	C63	C43	C40	C48	C29	C61	C36
Mitcham		C21	C30 -	C5	C24	C17	C53	C15+
Croydon North	C	C40	C100	C26	C41	C24	C62	C34+
Croydon South		C44+	C20	C14	C29	C20	C61+	C33
Surrey East		C66	C55	C100	C66	C38	C78	C58
Epsom	C	C48	C42	C42	C59+	C34	C71	C44
C/NL/NLab	12/14	19+	24 -	17	19+ - +	15++	26+++	21 - - + - +++++
L	5/7	8-	1	6	1	0+	1	0
Lab/Comm	0	1++	3+	5	8+	13-	1	7++++ ++++
Total	19	28	28	28	28	28	28	28

Key: 100 = unopposed; C = Conservative; Comm = Communist; Ind = Independent; L = Liberal; N = National (in alliance with the Conservatives) + indicates seat retained at By-elections; - = seat lost

1931 leading to a split within the Labour Party over the measures necessary to manage the situation. Most Labour candidates opposed the National Government led by the Labour Prime Minister Ramsey McDonald but a few did not. The impacts of this falling out within the Labour Party were in strong evidence at the 1931 General Election. Voters rallied to the cause of the National Government, including many Liberals, whose national vote fell to less than 7%, a fall of three quarters since 1918. Labour's vote fell less but despite receiving nearly one third of the votes cast, there were massive swings to the Conservatives throughout the country. Southwark was no exception and Labour was left with only one MP who hung on by just 0.4% of the votes cast at Bermondsey West. Conservatives took both Rotherhithe and Southwark South East whilst National candidates took the other two; Labour in the case of Southwark Central and Liberal in Southwark North. The 1930s became a period of further recession and international uncertainty and there was something of a return to two-Party politics although Tory-Labour by now instead of Tory-Liberal as before. In 1935 Labour's vote nationally was its highest up to that point, but the Tories were still by far the most popular Party and won the contest with a large majority. In Southwark and Bermondsey, however, Labour won four of the five seats, with a National Liberal holding on by his fingertips in North Southwark by just 0.4% of the vote.

In the run up to the Second World War a by-election was held at Southwark North on 17th May 1939. In a sign of what was to come after the War Labour took the seat from the National Liberals (by then effectively Tories) by a margin of 15%. After the outbreak of War a by-election was held at Central Southwark on 10th February 1940. There was by then an agreement between the main parties not to contest by-elections against one another. However, an Independent opposed Labour. Despite this Labour's increasing support was again evident, the Party's 1935 majority of 7% over the National Liberal increasing to 29%.

Election results in the four Camberwell borough constituencies were far more favourable to the Conservatives. They continued to take middle class Dulwich at every Election and the swings and vicissitudes that damaged the Labour and Liberal Parties seem to have benefited the Conservatives significantly during the Inter-War period in certain of the other, more socially mixed constituencies. Having won in Camberwell North West and in Peckham in the 1918 "Homes fit for Heroes" General Election, the Liberal Party began to lose votes in the light of the Post-War Coalition politics of Lloyd-George. After 1918 the Party only won again at Camberwell North West where a Coalition candidate was successful in 1922 and an Opposition Liberal took the seat by 0.4% in 1923. Apart from these results Labour emerged as the main opponents to the Tories, winning Camberwell North in all elections except 1918 and 1931, Peckham in 1924 and 1929, and Camberwell North in 1929. Tories won on every other occasion.

By-elections during the period saw National Liberals retain North West Camberwell on 31st March 1920 but two years later on 25th February 1922 Labour captured Camberwell North. The Conservatives had won this seat in 1918 with a large majority of 37% over Labour and Liberals who had tied with 21% of the poll each. The Liberals did not contest the seat at the by-election, which Labour won by a margin of 8%. Labour retained the seat at the 1923 General Election. On 8th June 1932 the Tories retained Dulwich with a majority of 41% over the Liberals as compared with 56% over Labour in 1931but their majority fell to 35% over Labour at the 1935 contest. These results, though insignificant in terms of the ebb and flow of power, did nevertheless show how Labour was damaged, especially perhaps in the eyes of the middle class electorates, by the events of 1931, although the signs of recovery were already in evidence. This was demonstrated at the Peckham by-election on 6th May 1936 when Labour captured the seat from the Conservatives with a tiny majority of 0.4% as compared with 2.6% for the Tories in 1935. The by-election result was significant as an indication of the way the political tide began to change after 1935. In fact Labour has not lost in any Peckham contest since then. A by-election at Camberwell North on 30th March 1944 offered further evidence of Labour's growing strength. Their majority rose from 32% in 1935 to 60%. However, the by-election was perhaps most significant for the very low Wartime turnout of only 11.2%.

In Lambeth based constituencies the pre-War political pattern of mainly Tory successes with occasional Liberal breakthroughs was replaced by one in which Labour became the second Party. As in neighbouring Battersea and Southwark there were also strong indications that the social composition of electorates was beginning to affect the voting allegiances of certain constituencies. The outer suburbs were solidly Tory whilst the inner core was Labour. The tussle for supremacy between the Labour and Liberal parties was in evidence in Lambeth North where the electorate had become rather more working class in its composition due to the changes in voter qualification that had taken place, not least the virtual elimination of plural voting and the reduction in the period of residency. Both factors seem likely to have had an impact in Lambeth given its proximity to Westminster and as the location of a number of second homes. The seat had been mainly Tory before the First World War but swung to the Liberals in 1918 before being gained by Labour in 1929. Although Liberals won it back at the height of Labour's unpopularity in 1931 a significant by-election occurred there on 23rd October 1934 that indicated a major shift in public opinion away from the Liberals and towards Labour. The Liberal winning margin in 1931 was a comfortable 31% over Labour but at the by-election Labour captured the seat with a majority of more than 32%. The Conservatives did not contest the seat on either occasion. Labour retained the seat in 1935 with a majority of 11% and has won the seat at every subsequent Election. The seat was re-named Vauxhall in 1950.

Kennington shared many of the characteristics of Lambeth North but after a solitary Liberal victory (in 1918) it was the Tories who shared the spoils with Labour at the other General Elections. Tories won in 1922, 1924, 1931 and 1935 (all General Elections following which they formed the Government) whilst Labour won it in 1923 and 1929, the only years in which they went on to do so. However, on 24th May 1939 Labour gained Kennington from the Conservatives in a by-election just a week after they had also captured Southwark North. Labour's majority of 20% compared with the Tory's 2.2% in 1935 and was a sign of even bigger things to come. The Brixton and Norwood seat were altogether much more predictably Tory, the latter invariably so at every election in the period, including a 1935 by-election. Brixton, on the other hand, returned a Liberal – perhaps rather unexpectedly –for one election only in 1923. Otherwise it returned Tories every time, including at a by-election in June 1927.

The boundary changes in Wandsworth generally helped the Conservatives as they began to envelop suburban electorates that had expanded into the area. Streatham proved to be one of the most strongly Tory seats in Britain at this time. Majorities in excess of 50% were recorded at four General Elections out of seven and only once was the margin of victory less than 30%.Battersea North represented the most working class part of the borough and the Lib-Lab tradition of the former single-member borough prior to the War was maintained after it. In fact the seat developed something of an unusual Left-Wing tradition. Although the Liberal candidate took the seat in 1918, Labour overturned his majority in 1922 but the seat reverted to the Liberals one year later. However, there was a sensational outcome to the election in 1924 when one of the very few Communist candidates ever to be elected in a British election was returned. The seat went back to Labour in 1929 but the Tories took it in their 1931 landslide national victory. The constituency did revert to Labour in 1935 and then on 17th April 1940 Labour held it at a by-election with a majority of 85% over an Independent. The other major parties did not contest the seat it being Wartime. Labour's majority over the Tories in 1935 had been 17%. At the next General Election in 1945 this increased to 48%. The pattern of politics there was nothing if it was not erratic.

By contrast with its northern neighbour Battersea South was a much more middle class Tory seat. The Conservatives won it in every election except 1929, when Labour sneaked in with a majority of 1%, so overall the boundary changes in Battersea had the effect of nullifying the former radical nature of the old borough's politics. Both the Clapham and Balham & Tooting seats were also essentially middle class suburbs and, true to the form shown at that time, the Conservatives were dominant. The Party won both at every General Election. In fact the two seats were remarkable for the similarity in the size of the majority at each election, a strong indication that the social composition of the electorate in each seat was broadly the same. The majorities, which ranged from lows in 1929 of 11% in Clapham and 12% in Balham & Tooting to highs of 45% and 49% respectively in 1931, were generally within one or two percentage points of each other, with Balham the slightly more Tory other than in 1922 when Clapham's majority was 1% higher. However, a change in the trend was indicated when, on 23rd July 1936 at a by-election, the Tories retained Balham and Tooting with a majority of only 7% compared with 26% at the 1935 Election. This heralded a bigger change that helped Labour take the seat by a margin of 15% at the 1945 Election.

Putney too was an overwhelmingly safe Conservative seat. Party majorities ranged from a General Election low of 20% in 1922 to a peak of 63% in 1931. However, in a by-election on 28th November 1934 the Tory majority dipped to only 9% over Labour. This was a very large swing since the 1931 Election when the Tory majority had been 63%, though it rose to 33% at the 1935 General Election. Seven years later there was another by-election held in Putney when, during the War on 8th May 1942, the Tories retained the seat with a majority over an Independent of 50% compared with 33% over Labour in 1935. Labour did not contest the by-election. In 1945 the Tory majority fell to 12%.

Wandsworth Central had a large working class element within the electorate, but in the years that Labour and Liberals were vying for the non-Tory votes, the Conservatives took the seat at every General Election except one when Labour won by 1% in 1929 and became the largest Party in the Commons for the first time. However, on 29th April 1937 Labour captured the constituency at a by-election by a margin of 2% compared with 17% for the Conservatives in 1935. At the 1945 General Election Labour's majority climbed to 22%.

Politically the Croydon area remained staunchly Conservative throughout the inter-War period. In fact the two borough constituencies each returned Tories at every General Election with large majorities. Those in the North division were usually well in excess of 20%, sometimes got above 40%, and in 1931 topped 60%. On 19th June 1940 in a Wartime by-election that Labour did not contest, the Tories actually retained North Croydon with a majority of 81% over an Independent as compared with 34% over Labour in 1935. Intriguingly, at the 1945 Election the Tories clung on by a mere 1% over Labour. Croydon South was only slightly less Tory. Majorities were mostly in double figures (including a by-election on 9th February 1932), only once dropping below 20% and, as in the neighbouring division, topped 60% in 1931. Surrey East also established itself as a Tory redoubt. Indeed it became one of the safest seats in the whole of Britain. The smallest majority for the Tories came in 1929 when their candidate led the poll by a margin of 38%. Generally in the period majorities were in excess of 55% and in 1931 actually reached an amazing 78%, recording a swing of 20% in two years.

Mitcham was also a fairly solid Conservative seat during the Inter-War period though there were indications that it could have other leanings. Although the Party won the seat at every General Election it did not show the same signs of impregnability as its neighbours. Indeed, at a by-election on 3rd March 1923 Labour actually captured Mitcham from the Tories with a majority of 3%. This was Labour's only outer London Surrey MP before the Second World War and its success was of short duration. At the 1922 Election the Tory majority had been 30% over the Liberals. Despite this the Tories recaptured the seat in the December General Election (later in 1923) by a margin of 5%.Otherwise its lowest majority in the constituency was 15% in 1935. Generally the majorities were in excess of 20% and reached 53% in 1931.

Wimbledon's majorities were very substantial in the Tories' favour and more consistent than other Surrey outer suburban seats. Unusually, though, the Party's largest win came, not in 1931 but in 1918, when it reached 63%. It never fell lower than the 29% recorded in 1929 although in the other three elections of the '20s it had exceeded 40% on each occasion.

Epsom repeated the pattern of Surrey seats that returned Tories with landslide majorities. Between 1918 and 1935 the majority fell below 40% only once (1929 when it was 34%) and in 1931 it peaked at 71%. On July 15th 1928 the Conservatives also won a by-election at Epsom with a comfortable 37% majority over the Liberals who had not contested the previous 1924 General Election when the majority was 59% over Labour.

Richmond too was a banker Tory seat in the Inter-War years although a dispute within the local Party brought about the victory of a renegade Independent Conservative there in 1922. Otherwise Conservative majorities ranged from a low of 26% in 1923 to a high of 69% in 1931. On 25th February 1937 the Tories held it at a by-election with a 45% majority over Labour, only 2% less than in the 1935 Election. Neighbouring Kingston-Upon-Thames also proved to be a seat where the Tories vastly outpolled their opponents at every election. Majorities reached a low in 1923 when the Conservative candidate's margin of victory was 23% and it peaked in 1931 at 65%.

The remarkable characteristic of all of these Conservative seats was the uniformity of the landslide majorities in an area that was overwhelmingly middle class. It was clear that this was a group amongst which the Tories had become extremely popular and the rapidity with which the suburbs that housed them spread across a plethora of new constituencies contributed greatly to the Party's overwhelming superiority during this particular period. What was also significant, though, was the extent to which Tory support during these years enabled the Party to capture seats in the more socially mixed areas of metropolitan London. Again they were helped by the population expansion that brought about a slight increase in such seats.

MPs for Bermondsey, Southwark and Camberwell

MPs for Bermondsey, Rotherhithe

John Rolleston Lort-Williams (Conservative) was born plain Williams at Walsall (Staffordshire) in 1881 and was the son of a solicitor. He adopted the additional name, Lort, later in life when he was a successful barrister. Educated at Merchant Taylors School and London University he was called to the bar in 1904 having been a Tancred[1] Law Student two years earlier. He was a barrister of three Inns of Court – Lincoln's Inn, the Inner and Middle Temples. In 1922 he took silk and practised on the Oxford Circuit but this was some years after he had also embarked on a political career. From 1907-10 he represented Limehouse on the London County Council, serving as Vice Chairman of Housing and first contested a Parliamentary election at Pembrokeshire in 1908, though he was defeated. He contested Stockport unsuccessfully at the December 1910 general election before becoming President of the Hardwicke Society in 1911. During the First World War he served in the Middlesex Yeomanry and afterwards was elected at Rotherhithe in 1918. However, he was defeated in 1923 and resumed his career as a Judge. He was first Recorder of West Bromwich (1923-4); then for neighbouring Walsall (1924-8); but in 1927 he was appointed Puisne Judge of the High Court of Bengal, a post he relinquished in 1941 when he reached the age of sixty. He died in 1966.

Sir Ben Smith MP, Disembarking from the liner RMS Queen Elizabeth
Wikipedia

(Sir) Ben Smith (Labour) won the seat in 1923. He was born in 1879 and married a local girl from Peckham in 1899. He became a cab driver and an activist in the Transport and General Workers Union, sitting as a member of the London Traffic Advisory Committee between 1919 and 1925. He was made a Labour Whip in 1925 and a Government whip after the 1929 election. A resident of Acton and later Chiswick, he was a Middlesex County Councillor as well as being an alderman of Bermondsey Borough Council. He was defeated in 1931 by the narrow margin of 131 votes but re-elected in 1935 with a majority of 4,665. By this time he was vice chairman of the Safety First Committee and an executive member of the Roads Improvement Association. During the Second World War he entered the Coalition Government in 1943 as the Minister for Supply Resident in Washington and following the election of the Attlee Government became Minister for Food. However, he retired in 1946 and died in 1964.

Mrs Norah Runge (Conservative) held the seat between 1931 and 1935 though she

1 **A Charity that funded law scholarships at Lincolns Inn**

MPs for Bermondsey, Southwark, and Camberwell

From	at	To	Surname	First Names	Constituency	Party
1918	G	1923	Lort-Williams	John Rolleston	Rotherhithe	Conservative
1923	G	1931	Smith	(Sir) Ben		Labour
1931	G	1935	Runge	Mrs Norah		Conservative
1935	G	1945	Smith	(Sir) Ben		Labour
1918	G	1922	Granville	Harold James	West Bermondsey	Liberal
1922	G	1923	Salter	Dr. Alfred		Labour
1923	G	1924	Kedward	Reverend Roderick Morris		Liberal
1924	G	1945	Salter	Dr. Alfred		Labour
1918	G	1923	Strauss	Edward Anthony	Southwark North	Liberal
1923	G	1927	Haden-Guest	Leslie		Labour
1927	B	1929	Strauss	Edward Anthony		Liberal
1929	G	1931	Isaacs	George Alfred		Labour
1931	G	1939	Strauss	Edward Anthony		National Liberal
1939	B	1945	Isaacs	George Alfred		Labour
1918	G	1924	Gilbert	James Daniel	Southwark Central	National Liberal
1924	G	1931	Day	Harry (Colonel)		Labour
1931	G	1935	Horobin	Sir Iain Macdonald		National Labour
1935	G	1939	Day	Harry (Colonel)		Labour
1940	B	1945	Martin	John Hanbury		Labour
1918	G	1921	Dawes	James Arthur	Southwark South East	Liberal
1921	B	1922	Naylor	Thomas Ellis		Labour
1922	G	1923	Alexander	Maurice (Lieu-Colonel)		National Liberal
1923	G	1931	Naylor	Thomas Ellis		Labour
1931	G	1935	Powell	Evelyn George Harcourt (Lt-Colonel)		Conservative
1935	G	1945	Naylor	Thomas Ellis		Labour
1918	G	1922	Knights	Henry Newton (Captain)	Camberwell North	Conservative
1922	B	1944	Ammon	Charles George		Labour
1944	B	1945	Manning	Cecil Aubrey Gwynne		Labour
1918	G	1924	Macnamara	Thomas	Camberwell North West	Liberal
1924	G	1929	Campbell	Sir Edward Taswell		Conservative
1929	G	1931	Morgan	Hyacinth Bernard Wenceslaus (Dr)		Labour
1931	G	1935	Cassels	James Dale		Conservative
1935	G	1945	Guest	Oscar Montague (Major)		Conservative
1918	G	1922	Richardson	Sir Albion Henry Herbert	Peckham	Liberal
1922	G	1924	Hughes	Collingwood James		Conservative
1924	G	1929	Dalton	(Edward) Hugh (John Neale)		Labour
1929	G	1931	Beckett	John		Labour
1931	G	1936	Borodale	Viscount		Conservative
1936	B	1945	Silkin	Lewis		Labour
1918	G	1932	Hall	Sir Frederick	Dulwich	Conservative
1932	B	1945	Smith	Sir Bracewell		Conservative

NOTE First returned at a B = By-election; G =General Election

had been active in the constituency since 1925 being appointed chairman of the women's branch of the local Unionist Association in 1927. She was born Norah Hasluck in 1884 and was educated privately before getting married in 1906. She had two children but was widowed and remarried in 1939. During the First World War she was superintendent of a free buffet for soldiers and sailors at Paddington Station between 1915 and 1919; for which she was awarded the OBE in 1918. She was President of Rotherhithe Conservative and Unionist Association from 1932 to 1946; a member of the LCC from 1937 to 1961; and its Deputy Chairman in1951/52. A Vice Chairman of the London Conservative Unionist Council, she was also vice chairman of the Central Women's Advisory Committee of Conservative & Unionist Associations in 1941/2. She contested the seat again in 1945, though unsuccessfully, and died in 1978 at the age of 94.

MPs for West Bermondsey

Harold James Glanville (Liberal) was previously the MP for Bermondsey from January 1910 and for Bermondsey West from 1918 to 1922 when he retired. His principal biographical details can be found in Chapter 6.

Dr. Alfred Salter MD, BS, DPH, MRCS, LRCP (Labour), was MP for West Bermondsey twice; from 1922 until his defeat in 1923; and again from 1924 until 1945 when he retired. He was born in 1873 and educated at the Roan School before becoming the youngest student ever to be accepted by Guy's Hospital as a medical student at the age of only sixteen. He graduated from London University in 1895, becoming a doctor of medicine the following year. Having come to the area to study he became struck by its poverty and social problems and decided to dedicate himself to its improvement. He established a surgery there in 1900 on the site of what is today the Bermondsey Underground Station, often caring for patients free of charge if they could not pay. At the turn of the century living conditions in the locality were very poor with multi occupation of single room and limited running water supplies serving perhaps 25 houses and with no sanitation. Salter determined to become involved in politics and in 1903 was elected to Bermondsey Council, serving as a Whip of the Liberal Group, the "Progressives". Three years later, feeling frustrated by the limited powers of the borough council, the doctor was selected as Progressive candidate for the London County Council. However, in 1908 he resigned from the Liberal Party and formed, with fourteen others, the local branch of the Independent Labour Party thus starting the Socialist movement in Bermondsey. He was elected to the LCC in 1907, serving for three years, but unsuccessfully contested Bermondsey at a Parliamentary by-election in 1909. The following year his wife Ada became the first woman councillor in London. A sometime member of the Bermondsey Board of Guardians, Alfred became a Labour Party activist fighting West Bermondsey unsuccessfully at the 1918 general election but serving on the Borough Council from 1919. He was the mayor in 1922-3 and the Salters led a campaign to turn the borough into a garden city. They planned to demolish two thirds of its land area and rebuild it with wide avenues, detached and semi-detached houses. Open spaces were turned into recreational grounds available to all the residents. A public health centre, The Grange Road Solarium Centre, was built that pre-dates the NHS by 20 years. A solarium was built in 1926 to help TB sufferers, the first such municipal facility in Britain. In 1927 public baths were opened, which included a swimming pool and public laundry, after research showed only 150 out of 19,000 dwellings in Bermondsey had a bath. President of the local Labour Party and Secretary of the Bermondsey Co-operative Bakery, he was also a Treasurer of the London Labour Party for many years. He retired in 1945 and died the same year.

From 1923 to 1924 the **Reverend Roderick Morris Kedward** (Liberal) was briefly the MP. Born in 1881, he was educated at Richmond College and in 1903 became a Wesleyan Minister going on to be the superintendent of the South London Mission in Bermondsey Street, London Bridge from 1918 until his death in 1937. During the First World War he fought in Egypt and France between 1914 and 1918 and first contested a Parliamentary election at Hull Central in the latter year. He was unsuccessful on that occasion as he was four years later when he contested Bermondsey West for the first time. However, he persisted and, with a position as Chairman of the Finance Committee of the Bermondsey Borough Council to add to his church activities, he was a well-known figure in the area. He won the seat in 1923 but the three Party nature of politics in the constituency during this period deprived him of it very quickly. Defeated in 1923 he did not seek a return in Bermondsey but was instead selected to fight Ashford, the Kent town from which he originally haled, and sat as the MP there for two year from 1929 to 1931 when he was once again defeated, this time not by Labour as in Bermondsey but by a Conservative. He tried again at a by-election held in Ashford in 1933 but lost a second time and did not seek a return to the House before his death. He was incidentally the President of the National Tithe payers' Association.

Edward Strauss MP
Wikipedia

MPs for Southwark North

Edward Anthony Strauss (Liberal) won Southwark Central in December 1910 and held it until 1918 when he transferred to Southwark North, which he represented until 1923 when he lost to Labour. He regained it at a by-election in 1927 but was defeated in 1929 only to emerge victorious once more in 1931 standing as a National Liberal in support of Ramsey McDonald. He was re-elected in 1935 but died four years later. His principal biographical details are in Chapter 6.

Leslie Haden-Guest MC (Labour) won the seat in 1923 and again in 1924 but resigned from the Party in 1927 and contested a by-election as an Independent Constitutionalist. He lost the seat to Strauss and fought it again in 1929 as a Conservative. He soon rejoined the Labour Party and fought elections at Wycombe and Brecon & Radnor before he was elected at a by-election as MP for Islington North in 1937. His principal biographical details are in Chapter 7.

George Isaacs MP
People's History Museum Manchester

George Alfred Isaacs (Labour) succeeded Strauss at the 1929 General Election, holding the seat for only two years, but took the seat back at the by-election triggered by Strauss's death in 1939. He went on to represent the same seat until it was redistributed in 1950 when he became the MP for Southwark, which he represented until he retired in 1959. Born in 1883 to working class parents, he was the eldest of ten children and first went to work at the age of ten as a newspaper boy and employee of a tea company whilst he attended a Wesleyan elementary school. He entered the printing trade at the age of twelve and became an active trade unionist. His great grandfather, A. Isaacs, also a printer, had been an activist who had supported the Tolpuddle Martyrs. At the age of twenty-five he became general secretary of the National Society of Operative Printers and Assistants (NATSOPA). In 1945 he was chairman of the Trade Union Congress General Council and of the World Trade Union Conference. He entered politics locally in Southwark and was its first Labour Mayor in 1919-21, then becoming an alderman. He became an MP in 1923 when he was returned at Gravesend (Kent) but was defeated the following year. In 1929 he was appointed PPS to the Secretary of State for the Dominions (initially Lord Passfield and in 1930 James Thomas) but lost his seat in 1931. Following his return in 1939 he sat on the Opposition benches until the creation of the Wartime Coalition and in 1942 was made PPS to the First Lord of the Admiralty, the Labour MP Arthur Alexander. He served in this position until 1944 and a year later became Minister of Labour. In 1951, shortly before the defeat of the Attlee Government he was made Minister of Pensions. He was a Surrey magistrate and one time chairman of the Kingston County bench in which area he later lived at East Molesey.

MPs for Southwark Central

James Daniel Gilbert (National Liberal) was elected at a 1916 by-election for the predecessor seat of Newington West. In 1918 he transferred to Southwark Central as a National Liberal but was defeated in 1924. His principal biographical details are in Chapter 6.

Colonel Harry Day (Labour) won Southwark Central in 1924 and held it until his defeat in 1931. Born in 1880, he was educated at Hanway Street School then at Stepney School and Tivoli House College, Gravesend. He was a colourful character who was active in the field of entertainment but who also pursued an interest in the military. He was a director of his own Amusements Company and of the Empire Theatre in Bristol; chairman of the Mutual Property Insurance Company; a sometime staff officer with the City of London Brigade; a Colonel of the 14th County of London Regiment and of the 3rd Battalion of the Essex Regiment. He contested Kingston-upon-Thames as an Independent in 1922 but joined the Labour Party in the cause of which he fought Southwark Central unsuccessfully in 1923 before becoming its MP the following year. Also a London County councillor, he was defeated in 1931 but elected again at the 1935 contest. He served until he died, precipitating a by-election in February 1940.

Sir Iain Macdonald Horobin (National Labour) was elected in a two horse race in 1931 but stood down four years later when Day was re-elected, again in a straight fight with a National Labour candidate. Horobin was a social worker and was for many years the Warden of Mansfield House Settlement, a University linked charity established in 1890 to promote social improvement in Canning Town. Born in 1899 the son of the Principal of Homerton College, Cambridge, he was educated at Highgate School and Sidney Sussex College, Cambridge and during the First World War in 1918 served in the RNVR. After standing down in 1935 he continued his social work but returned to the military at the outbreak of War in 1939, serving in the RAF until 1945 although he was captured by the Japanese and held prisoner. He resumed a career as an MP in 1950 when he was elected a Conservative at Oldham East which seat he held until 1959 when he once again retired. Three years later it was announced that he was to be made a Life Peer but he was forced by a scandal to withdraw when he was arrested for indecency at about the same time. He served a four-year prison sentence and died ten years later in Tangier in 1976.

The by-election triggered by Day's death was won by **John Hanbury Martin** (Labour) who was an author and journalist. Educated at Brasenose College Oxford he served during the First World War as a Captain in the Queen's Westminster Rifles. He died in 1948.

MPs for Southwark South East

James Arthur Dawes (Liberal) had been MP for Newington, Walworth since 1910 and transferred to its replacement seat in 1918. He died in 1921 precipitating a by-election. His principal biographical details can be found in Chapter 6.

Dawes was succeeded in 1921 by **Thomas Ellis Naylor** (Labour) who went on to represent the same constituency on and off until 1950 when he retired by which time he was in his early eighties. He lost the seat on two occasions;

firstly in 1922 to a National Liberal; and then in 1931 to a Conservative. Born in 1868, he had a rudimentary education at a London Board school and at a Working Men's club. He became a compositor but went on to be a journalist as the editor of a trade union publication, the *London Typographical Journal.* He was General Secretary of the London Society of Compositors for thirty two years from 1906 and a Vice chairman of the Joint Industrial Council for the Printing Industry in 1933-4. He was chairman the following year. From 1918 to 1933 he was Chairman of the London Labour Party.

Lieutenant-Colonel Maurice Alexander KC (National Liberal) won the seat in 1922 but held it only until 1923 when Naylor replaced him again. Born in 1899, Alexander was educated at McGill University, Canada and in 1910 became a barrister in Quebec where the following year he also joined the First Regiment of the Grenadier Guards (Canada). At the outbreak of war in 1914 he was part of the Expeditionary Force and was awarded the CMG medal in 1917. After the armistice he was appointed Secretary to the British Embassy in Washington but resumed a political career in 1925 when he contested a by-election unsuccessfully at Norfolk North. By 1931, when he contested Newcastle – upon-Tyne East unsuccessfully, he had joined the Labour Party but never regained a Commons seat. He died in 1945.

Lieutenant-Colonel Evelyn George Harcourt Powell (Conservative) was the MP from 1931 until 1935 when Naylor was re-elected. Powell was a soldier who served in the Grenadier Guards from 1901 and was a member of the original expeditionary force in 1914. He commanded the first battalion of his regiment from 1923 to 1927 and contested Southwark South East unsuccessfully in 1929 when he was in third place behind a Liberal.

MPs for Camberwell North

Captain Henry Newton Knights (Conservative) held the seat from 1918 to 1922. He was born locally in 1872 and became an engineer in the City of London where he was Sheriff in 1920-21. He raised the Camberwell Volunteers Battalion during the First World War and became the North division's MP after the conflict. However, he resigned in 1922 and never resumed a political career. He died in 1959.

People's History Museum, Manchester

Charles George Ammon (Labour) represented Camberwell North from a by-election held on February 22nd 1922 until his death in 1944. He won the by-election by taking Labour's vote from 21% to 54% when the Liberals decided not to contest the seat. Ammon was born in 1873, educated at public elementary schools and privately before becoming a postal worker. From 1919 to 1928 he was the Organising Secretary of the Union of Post Office Workers. He was a Labour Whip from 1922 until the election of the first Labour Government in which he served as Financial Secretary to the Admiralty in 1924. He was re-appointed to the same post when Labour returned to Government in 1929 but went into Opposition when the Party split in 1931. He was one of a minority of Labour MPs to hold his seat in the election held that year and he went on to hold it until his death. He remained a member of the borough council and was at one time President of the Brotherhood Movement,[2] an organization in the Socialist tradition of the Free Churches, aimed at the reform of society on Christian lines.

Cecil Aubrey Gwynne Manning (Labour) won the 1944 by-election precipitated by his predecessor's death. He was born in 1892 and educated at Board and LCC elementary schools. He was elected to Wandsworth Borough Council in 1919 and also served on the LCC for ten years, being its Deputy Chairman in 1930/1. He retired in 1950 when the seat was abolished.

MPs for Camberwell North West

Thomas Macnamara (Liberal) won Camberwell North in 1900 and went on to hold the seat until 1918 and then sat for Camberwell North West until 1924 when he was beaten into third place. His principal biographical details are in Chapter 6.

He was succeeded by **Sir Edward Taswell Campbell** (Conservative) who won a narrow majority over Labour.

2 The basic premise of the Brotherhood was that "... Christianity is chiefly concerned with man's brotherly relation to man, and with the redemption through human effort of every sphere of man's activity on earth"

He was elected MP for Camberwell North West in 1924 but was defeated in 1929 before returning at a by-election in Bromley in 1930. He was Chairman of the Anglo-Netherlands Society –presumably because of links he had with the Dutch colony in Java – and was also chairman of the Governors of James Allen Grammar School, Dulwich. From 1931 to 1943 he was PPS to Kingsley Wood and in 1943 to H. Willink Mott. He was a staff commissioner for the Special Constabulary and a Kent JP. He died in 1945 after polling day but before the result of the general election was declared. Campbell was born in 1879 and attended Dulwich College becoming a merchant in the East India company where his father –in-law had been active in Java. He was a county councillor for West Lewisham between 1922 and 1925 and a sometime British Consul in Java.

The somewhat quaintly and confusingly named **Dr. Hyacinth Bernard Wenceslaus Morgan** (Labour) was born in Grenada, West Indies in 1885, educated at the local Grammar School and then at Glasgow University where he studied medicine, qualifying in 1914. During the First World War he served as a Captain in the RAMC and in civil life held a number of medical practices in London. He was quite prominent in the Irish Nationalist Movement as a student. He was narrowly defeated by Campbell in 1924 but was successful in 1929, although he stood down in 1931. He was subsequently elected unopposed as MP for Rochdale at a by-election in 1940, a seat he retained until 1950 when he transferred to Warrington, serving there until he retired in 1955.

James Dale Cassels KC (Conservative) was Camberwell North West's MP from 1931 to 1935 having previously represented Leyton West from 1922 to 1929. His principal biographical details can be found in Chapter 8.

Cassels stood down in 1935 when the seat was taken by **Major Oscar Montague Guest** (Conservative), who served until 1945 when he retired and instead contested the Welsh constituency of Brecon and Radnor where he was defeated. Prior to 1922 Guest was a National Liberal MP, sitting for the Leicestershire town of Loughborough from 1918 for four years. At the beginning of the Great War, Major Guest joined the Lothian and Border Horse Regiment but later transferred to the Royal Flying Corps. He subsequently became a member of staff at the Air Ministry. He died in 1958. His older brother was also an MP who had started out with the Liberals but who ended up a Tory. FE (Freddie) Guest had been Liberal MP for East Dorset (1910-22); for Stroud (1923-4); and for Bristol North (1924-29) before joining the Conservatives in 1930. He represented Plymouth Drake from 1931 to 1937.

MPs for Peckham

Sir Albion Henry Herbert Richardson (Liberal) who took Peckham in December 1910 was re-elected in 1918 as a Coupon Liberal and Independent Conservative and held it until 1922. His principal biographical details are in Chapter 6.

He was succeeded in 1922 by **Collingwood James Hughes** (Conservative) who held the seat until 1924. Born in 1872 at Chatham, where his father was in the Royal Navy, he was educated at Plymouth Grammar School and at Kings College, London. He became Principal of the Civil Service College, Cape Town South Africa in 1900 and held the position until 1909. From 1915 to 1919 he served as Paymaster Lieutenant- Commander in the RNVR and was an official Admiralty lecturer between 1917 and 1919. He contested Peckham against Richardson in 1918. From 1943-45 Hughes was General Secretary of the Retail Distributors having served a year earlier as Manager of the Daily Express Centre of Public Opinion. He died in 1963.

Hugh Dalton MP
People's History Museum, Manchester

(Edward) Hugh (John Neale) Dalton (Labour) took the seat in 1924 but transferred to the Durham mining seat of Bishop Auckland in 1929. He lost this in 1931 but regained it in 1935 and went on to represent it until he retired in 1959. Dalton was born in 1887, the son of a former Canon of Windsor. He was educated at nearby Eton College going on to receive a higher education initially at Kings College, Cambridge and then at the London School of Economics where he became a lecturer. He was a prominent figure on the Labour benches under Attlee's leadership and during the War served as Minister for Economic Warfare (1940-42) and then as President of the Board of Trade (1942-45). By the end of the War he had become a key figure and was appointed Chancellor of the Exchequer in 1945. However, in a celebrated and unique case, he was compelled to resign when details of his Budget became known to the media before he had made his speech to Parliament. He was not out of office for long, however, returning as Chancellor of the Duchy of Lancaster (1948-50) and during the 1950-51 Government served as Under Secretary for Foreign Affairs. However, when Labour then also lost the 1955 election it became clear that Dalton's career was over and he retired in 1959.

John Beckett MP
National Portrait Gallery

When Dalton moved to the North East in 1929 his successor, **John Beckett** (Labour), moved in the opposite direction. From 1924 to 1929 he had been MP for Gateshead and prior to that in 1923 unsuccessfully contested Newcastle-upon-Tyne North. However, he was a Londoner, born in 1894 and educated at council school, the Latymer Secondary School and Polytechnic. He became a shop assistant but joined the army in 1914 serving until he was disabled in 1917. From 1918 to 1920 he was Chairman of the National Union of Ex-Servicemen. He was also an active trade unionist as National Organiser for the Retail Book, Stationery and Allied Trades Employees' Association. From 1919 to 1922 he was a member of Hackney Borough Council. He was defeated at Peckham in 1931 and following a visit to Italy soon afterwards became active in the British Fascist movement, joining it in 1934 and becoming director of Publications, until he was sacked by Sir Oswald Mosley in 1937. Thereafter he formed the National Socialist League, another Fascist organisation, with William Joyce, who gained notoriety during the War for his radio propaganda on behalf of Hitler. Beckett himself was interned during the War after which he formed yet another Right Wing party which failed to gain traction. He died in 1970.

In 1931 the seat was taken by **Viscount Borodale**,(Conservative) the eldest son of the Earl Beatty, Admiral of the Fleet from 1919. Borodale was then 26 and held the seat until 1936 when he succeeded to the Earldom. He too joined the Navy entering Osborne as a cadet in 1919 and, after serving as a midshipman, was posted to HMS Revenge in 1925 and promoted to sub-lieutenant the following year. In 1927 he joined his father's old flagship, Queen Elizabeth but the following year was appointed to the Royal Yacht Victoria and Albert where he was promoted to the rank of lieutenant. However, he was gazetted out of the Navy later that year when he was adopted as the candidate for Peckham.

Lewis Silkin MP
People's History Museum Manchester

The 1936 by-election that followed his elevation to the House of Lords was won by a prominent lawyer, **Lewis Silkin** (Labour) who went on to represent the seat until 1950 when he retired from politics. Two of his sons (Sam and John) followed him onto the Labour benches. Born in 1889 he received an elementary and secondary school education before attending London University. He was admitted as a solicitor in 1920 and contested his first Parliamentary seat in 1922 when he was unsuccessful at Wandsworth Central. He also lost at Stoke Newington in 1924. He was a member of the LCC chairing its Housing and Public Health Committee from 1934-40. He was also chairman of the Town Planning Committee and went on to develop an interest in the subject, studying amongst other things slum clearance policies in some European countries. When Labour was returned to Government in 1945, Silkin was made Minister of Town and Country Planning, a key role in the reconstruction of post-war Britain. He essentially pioneered the legislation that implemented Green Belt policies and instigated the development of New Towns. A chess expert in his spare time, he retired from the House in 1950 and accepted a peerage as Lord Silkin of Dulwich. He died in 1972.

MPs for Dulwich

Lieutenant-Colonel Sir Frederick Hall (Conservative) was elected in December 1910 and remained as the MP until his death in 1932. His principal biographical details are in Chapter 6.

He was succeeded at a by-election by **(Sir) Bracewell Smith** (Conservative), a Yorkshireman, who went on to hold Dulwich until he was defeated in 1945. A former member of the Holborn Borough Council since 1922, he was its Mayor in 1931-2 and also sat on the LCC from 1925-28. A Sheriff of the City of London in 1943-4, in the Commons he was Chairman of the Kitchen Committee of the House until his defeat. Amongst other things he was Honorary President of the Sport Turf Research Institute, established in 1929 by two Yorkshire golfers who persuaded the Royal and Ancient Golf Club of St Andrews and the British Golf Unions that scientific research was an essential pre-requisite to the upgrading of golf courses. Experimental fields were established at Bingley, near Keighley, Smith's hometown. He died in January 1966.

MPs for Lambeth, and Wandsworth

MPs for Lambeth North

Frank Briant (Liberal) was returned in 1918 and remained the MP until 1929 when he was defeated. He was re-elected at the 1931 election but retired in 1935. Born in 1863, the son of a Kennington man, he was a civil servant for 14 years and a member of the Lambeth Board of Guardians for 26, half of them as Chairman. From 1885 he was honorary superintendent of the Alford House Institute for Working Men and Lads, a youth club in the Oval district of Kennington. A county councillor, in 1914-15 he was Chairman of the Old Age Pension Committee for London.

MPs for Lambeth and Wandsworth

From	at	To	Surname	First Names	Constituency	Party
1918	G	1929	Briant	Frank	Lambeth North	Liberal
1929	G	1931	Strauss	George Russell		Labour
1931	G	1934	Briant	Frank		Liberal
1934	G	1945	Strauss	George Russell		Labour
1931	G	1934	Briant	Frank		Liberal
1934	G	1945	Strauss	George Russell		Labour
1918	G	1922	Purchase	Henry George	Kennington	Liberal
1922	G	1923	Harrison	Francis Capel		Conservative
1923	G	1924	Williams	Thomas Samuel Beachamp (L-Col)		Labour
1924	G	1929	Harvey	George		Conservative
1929	G	1931	Matters	Leonard Warburton		Labour
1931	G	1939	Harvey	George		Conservative
1939	B	1945	Wilmot	John Charles		Labour
1918	G	1923	Dalziel	Sir Davison	Brixton	Conservative
1923	G	1924	Laverack	Frederick Joseph		Liberal
1924	G	1927	Dalziel	Sir Davison		Conservative
1927	B	1945	Colman	Nigel Claudian Dalziel		Conservative
1918	G	1922	Samuel	Sir Harry Simon	Norwood	Conservative
1922	G	1935	Greaves-Lord	Sir Walter		Conservative
1935	B	1945	Sandys	Sir Edwin Duncan		Conservative
1918	G	1939	Lane-Mitchell	Sir William	Streatham	Conservative
1939	B	1945	Robertson	Sir David		Conservative
1918	G	1922	Morris	Richard	Battersea North	Liberal
1922	G	1923	Saklatvala	Shapurji		Ind Labour
1923	G	1924	Hogbin	Henry Cairn		Constitutionalist
1924	G	1929	Saklatvala	Shapurji		Communist
1929	G	1931	Sanders	William Stephen (Captain)		Labour
1931	G	1935	Marsden	Arthur (Commander RN)		Conservative
1935	G	1940	Sanders	William Stephen (Captain)		Labour
1940	B	1945	Douglas	Sir Francis Campbell Ross		Labour
1918	G	1929	Curzon	Francis Richard Henry Penn (Visc)	Battersea South	Conservative
1929	B	1931	Bennett	William		Labour
1931	G	1945	Selley	Harry Ralph		Conservative
1918	G	1922	Du Cros	Sir Arthur Philip	Clapham	Conservative
1922	G	1945	Leigh	Sir John		Conservative
1918	G	1924	Norton-Griffiths	Sir John Norton	Wandsworth Central	Conservative
1924	G	1929	Jackson	Sir Henry		Conservative
1929	G	1931	Church	Archibald George (Major)		Labour/Nat La
1931	G	1937	Jackson	Sir Henry		Conservative
1937	B	1940	Nathan	Harry Louis (Colonel)		Labour
1940	B	1945	Bevin	Ernest		Labour
1918	G	1922	Dennison-Pender	John Cuthbert Dennison	Balham & Tooting	Conservative
1922	G	1936	Butt	Sir Alfred		Conservative
1936	B	1945	Doland	George Frederick (Lt-Colonel)		Conservative
1918	G	1934	Samuel	Samuel	Putney	Conservative
1934	B	1942	Samuel	Marcus Reginald Anthony		Conservative
1942	B	1945	Linstead	Hugh Nicholas		Conservative

NOTE First returned at a B = By-election; G =General Election

Briant died in 1934 precipitating a by-election in October when the seat was taken by **George Russell Strauss** (Labour), the son of the former Unionist MP for Paddington North (1910-18) Arthur Strauss, who subsequently joined the Labour Party (See Chapter 3). George first contested the Lambeth North seat in 1924 when he lost to Briant by only 29 votes but won it in 1929 and, although temporarily out of Parliament between 1931 and 1934 following his second defeat by Briant, went on to represent the area for so many years that he became Father of the House as the longest

George Strauss MP
People's History Museum Manchester

serving MP between February 1974 and 1979 when he retired. He represented Lambeth North until 1959 when the seat was abolished and merged to become Vauxhall.

Despite his many years in the House he never really established a successful career. In 1942 he was made PPS to his friend Stafford Cripps (then Lord Privy Seal in Churchill's Coalition Government) and Minister of Aircraft Production until the end of the War. From 1945 to 1947 he was Parliamentary Secretary at the Ministry of Transport and Minister of Supply from then until 1951. Born in 1901 (and educated at Rugby School), he was well into his Sixties by the time a Labour Government was returned again and by then his chance had gone. He was a member of the LCC between 1925 and 1945, chairing the Highways Committee from 1934-37 and sitting successively for Lambeth North (until 1931) and then for South East Southwark. He was a member of the family metal merchant business in the City of London and a supporter of the Co-operative Movement. His private means allowed him to indulge his political interests and it was he who, with Stafford Cripps, put up most of the £20,000 capital necessary to launch the *Tribune* Newspaper. He became involved with many Left wing causes and was a principal advocate of the creation of a Popular Front of Left wing Governments to defeat fascism. He toured Spain during the Civil War in that country but in early 1939 his radicalism brought him into conflict with Attlee and he was expelled from the Labour Party. However, in return for a "vow of silence" he was re-admitted in November of the same year. In 1940 he was awarded substantial damages in a libel case in which it was said his cowardice stopped him from fighting in the First World War. In fact he was too young to do so. In 1979 he went to the Lords as Baron Strauss and died in 1993.

Kennington

Henry George Purchase (Liberal), a Surrey County cricketer, was the MP from 1918 until 1922. Born in London in 1873, he was educated at St Mark's College, University Tutorial College and Kings College London where he graduated with a degree in Law. In 1899 he was the Hon. Secretary of the Tercentenary Celebrations of the birth of Oliver Cromwell and in 1913 Assistant Secretary of the New Reform Club. Called to the bar at the Middle Temple in 1913, he worked on the Northern Circuit. At the end of the War in 1918 he assisted in setting up the Enforcement branch of the Ministry of Food of which he subsequently became Assistant Director and Parliamentary Secretary (unpaid). In 1919 he was Chairman of the National Insurance Joint Committee and also the Hon. Secretary of the London group of Liberal MPs. After his defeat in 1922 he contested Kidderminster in 1923 and 1924, South Leicester in 1929, Gainsborough in 1931 and Blackpool in 1935, but never regained a seat in the House. During the Second World War he was Senior Legal Assistant at the Ministry of Food between 1942 and 1943 and he died in 1945.

Francis Capel Harrison (Conservative) was MP for only one year between 1922 and 1923. He was born in Calcutta in 1863 and was educated at Rugby School and Balliol College, Oxford before joining the Indian Civil Service of which he became Comptroller and Auditor-General in 1911. However, he also entered local politics and in 1909 became chairman of the Finance Committee of the LCC. He retired from the House after one year and did not stand at the 1923 election. He died in 1938.

The somewhat grandly named **Lieutenant-Colonel Thomas Samuel Beauchamp Williams** (Labour) took Kennington in 1923 but lost it in 1924. A medical doctor, educated in the Punjab, he first entered politics as a candidate at Bridgwater (Somerset) where he was defeated, repeating the experience at Eastbourne (East Sussex) in a 1925 by-election. Born in 1877, he died fifty years later.

George Harvey (Conservative) took the seat in 1924 and, apart from 1929-31, remained MP until 1939. Born in 1870, Harvey was the son of a Scarborough man and became an hotelier. He was chairman of the Burlington Hotels Company, which included the Café Royal in Regent Street, and of the Connaught Rooms, the latter being in the Holborn area of London where he was a member of the Borough Council and Mayor (1920-4). He also sat on the County Council between 1922 and 1925.

Leonard Warburton Matters (Labour) defeated Harvey in 1929 but was in turn beaten in 1931. An Australian, born in 1881, he was educated at a State School in South Australia and became a journalist. He was subsequently managing editor of the *Review of South and Central America* based in Buenos Aires, Argentina, and was a director of British and Overseas Publications Limited. He was author of a book entitled, *Mystery of Jack the Ripper*. Following Labour's election in 1929 he joined an expedition to the Arctic but was recalled to fight the 1931 contest in which he was defeated. He contested the seat again, unsuccessfully, in 1935.

John Charles Wilmot (Labour) was elected at the 1939 by-election and remained the constituency's MP until 1945. Prior to this, from 1933 to '35 he had been MP for Fulham East and his principal biographical details are in Chapter 7.

Brixton

Sir Davison Octavius Dalziel (Conservative) was elected in 1910 and remained the MP until 1923 when he was defeated. However, he was re-elected in 1924 and stayed until he was elevated to the peerage as Baron Dalziel of Wooler in 1927. His principal biographical details are in Chapter 6.

Frederick Joseph Leverack (Liberal) was only briefly an MP, winning the seat in 1923 but losing it at the election held the following year. Born in Leeds in 1871, Laverack was a minister of the Congregational Church who promoted charitable works to help the children of servicemen blinded in combat. In 1921 and somewhat unusually for a Liberal he joined the Anti-Waste League; unsuccessfully contesting Brixton with the League's backing at the 1922 General Election. He died in 1928 a year after a failed attempt to be re-elected at the by-election precipitated by Dalziels' elevation to the peerage a year earlier.

Instead Dalziel was followed at the by-election by his grandson, **Nigel Claudian Dalziel Colman** (Conservative), a former London County councillor (1925-8) and a past President of the Hackney Horse Society[3] who was born in 1886. He was the son of the Chairman of J and J Colman Limited and served as a Lieutenant in the RNVR, then as a Captain in the RAF. He was defeated in 1945.

Norwood

Sir Harry Simon Samuel (Conservative) won the Norwood seat in January 1910 having previously sat for the Limehouse division of Stepney between 1895 and 1906. He represented Norwood until 1922. His principal biographical details can be found in Chapter 3.

Sir Walter Greaves-Lord (Conservative) succeeded Samuel and represented the seat until 1935 when, before the general election of that year, he became a High Court Judge and resigned his seat. He had taken silk in 1919 fully 19 years after being called to the bar and in 1925 was made Recorder of Manchester. Born in 1878, he was the son of Simeon Lord, a Lancastrian from Ince and was educated at Wigan Grammar School, Southport College and University College, Liverpool. He assumed the additional name of Greaves by deed poll in 1910 the year he contested the Ince division of Lancashire, where he was defeated. Appointed a bencher in 1920, he was a Freeman of the City of London, a member of the Feltmakers' Company and a member of the Bar Council. From1926 to 1927 he was Chancellor of the Primrose League.

Duncan Sandys MP in 1944, announcing the end of the V1 bombing campaign. **Wikipedia**

Sir Duncan Edwin Sandys (Conservative), who resigned from the Foreign Office in 1933 to enter politics, won a March 1935 by-election to become Norwood's MP and continued to represent the area until 1945 when he was defeated. He was subsequently adopted to fight the Streatham constituency, which he won in 1950 and went on to hold until he retired in February 1974. He came from a political family and married into another. His father was MP for Wells (Somerset) between 1910 and 1918 and he became a son-in-law- of Winston Churchill when he married Diana, though that marriage was later dissolved in 1960.

He was born in 1908 and educated at Eton and Oxford before he entered the diplomatic corps. In 1940 he was one of the Expeditionary Force sent to Norway where he was disabled the following year going on to become Finance Member of the Army Council and later the Chairman of the Inter-governmental Council for Empire Prisoners of War. In 1947 he was a founder of the European Movement and, following his return at Streatham, it was not long before he was made a minister serving in his father-in-law's Government as Minister of Supply between 1951 and 1954; then in Eden's as Minister of Housing and Local Government. When

3 The word 'Hackney' comes from the French "haquenee", and describes a riding horse with a particularly comfortable trot or amble.The Society was founded in 1883 to promote the breed in the UK and throughout the world.

Macmillan came to power in 1957, Sandys became Minister of Defence and after the 1959 general election was made Minister of Aviation which post he held until 1960. From 1960 to 1962 he was Secretary of State for Commonwealth Relations to which role the Colonies were added until 1964 when Labour returned to power. He was an Opposition spokesman for two years and then returned to the backbenches. In 1970 he was leader of the British delegation to the Assembly of the Council of Europe, a post he held until he was made Chairman of Lonrho[4] two years later. Following his retirement from the Commons he became a Life Peer in 1974 when he also assumed the surname of Duncan-Sandys (of the City of Westminster). He died in 1987.

Streatham

Sir William Lane – Mitchell (Conservative) was Streatham's MP from 1918 until 1939. He was born Mitchell in 1861 and later adopted the additional name of Lane. He was mayor of Camberwell between 1906 and 1908 but was principally a businessman. He was manager of R and W Davidson, frozen food importers and later Chairman of his own company, Lane Mitchell Limited, Produce Brokers. From 1907 until 1940 he was a member of the Cold Storage and Ice Association· the trade body for his industry. He stood down from the House in 1939 and died the following year.

He was succeeded by accountant **Sir David Robertson** (Conservative) who represented the seat until he made way for Duncan-Sandys in 1950. Robertson was the son of a Chief Inspector of the General Post Office in Glasgow where he was born in 1890 and educated at the Woodside and Allan Glens Schools before attending the City's University. He had connections with his predecessor as MP because he too was the Managing Director of cold storage companies. In addition he was a Captain in the Argyll and Sutherland Highlanders, which probably (if not, coincidentally) helped him secure the Tory candidacy at Caithness and Sutherland when he left Streatham. He was elected there in 1950 and remained its Tory MP until 1959 but resigned the Government whip in January of that year standing successfully as an Independent Conservative at the October general election. He stood down in 1964 and died in 1970.

Battersea North

Richard Morris (Liberal) was the MP from 1918 until 1922. Born in 1869 he trained as a schoolmaster but moved to London and entered the field of commerce. Before 1918 he had been a prominent supporter of the socialistic radical MP for Battersea, John Burns. He died in 1956.

Sharpurji Saklatvala MP
People's History Museum Manchester

The seat was captured in 1922 by **Shapurji Saklatvala** [5](Independent Labour) who had been born into a Parsee family at Bombay in 1874 and was educated there at St Xavier College. He was brought up during a period when the bubonic plague devastated the Bombay population but he survived through inoculation and started working in the (Tata[6]) family businesses in 1901when it was the policy of the British Government to encourage Indians to invest in their own industries. Having established an Iron works, Saklatvala, who was the great nephew of the founder of the company, Nusserwanji Tata, was sent to England to be deputy-managing director ofTata Ltd, London but in 1907 went to work for the Westinghouse Company. By then he was actively engaged in politics. Initially he was a member of the Liberal Party but, always a socialist, he resigned in 1910 by which time he had parted company with Westinghouse who it is suggested were only really interested in striking up a relationship with the Tata Group. He moved to Ashton-on-Mersey and became a consulting engineer in nearby Manchester.

Once in the North West he became very involved with the Labour movement, associating with key figures such as J.R Clynes (then the MP for Manchester North East) and Ramsey MacDonald who became Labour Party Leader in 1911. He joined the Independent Labour Party in 1909.He returned to India for a year in 1912 but returned to London and became the private secretary to Sir Ratan Tata, who lived in London (at York House, now Twickenham Town Hall) and who was an early devotee of Mahatma Ghandi. During the First World War he was a conscientious objector though he was never put to the test and called up. He saw similarities with India during the Russian revolution and gradually moved towards a communist ideology. He was a prolific orator for the ILP and delegate from the City of London to its 1918

4 Lonrho (originally the London and Rhodesia Mining and Land Company) was transformed by its Chief Executive, Tiny Rowland, between 1961 and 1994 from a small mining company into a huge international conglomerate. Rowland's approach to running Lonrho was famously referred to as the 'unpleasant and unacceptable face of capitalism' by Sandy's Party Leader and Prime Minister at the time, Edward Heath.
5 Source of biographical detail is a family website.
6 The Tata group exists today as the largest in India where its turnover is equivalent to 2.5% of the whole country's gross domestic product (Source: company website).

Conference. By 1921 he was living in Clapham and at the following year's general election was adopted as a candidate, winning the contest in adjoining Battersea North. He visited the Soviet Union for the first time in 1923 but was defeated at Battersea North at the general election that year standing as an official Labour candidate. However, he was returned in 1924, this time as a Communist, as in 1922 with Labour Party support, and can claim to be the third Indian MP and one of only four men ever to represent the Communist Party in the House of Commons. He was defeated in 1929 when Labour fielded its own candidate and although he contested the seat again twice more (in 1930 and 1931) he was never re-elected. He died in 1936.

Henry Cairn Hogbin (Constitutionalist) displaced Saklatvala briefly between 1923 and 1924. A National Liberal, he was supported by the Conservatives with the specific aim of defeating a man whom both parties regarded as being a non-constitutionalist; hence his standing as a "Constitutionalist". Born in 1880 he was a member of the firm of Lawe's Chemicals and during the First World War served at the Ministry of Food organising agricultural production. He first contested Battersea North when he lost to Saklatvala in 1922 but won in 1923 standing on an anti-socialist platform with the support of both the Conservative and Liberal parties. He joined the Conservative Party, fighting a by-election unsuccessfully at Stourbridge in 1927and became a Middlesex JP in 1928. He died in 1966.

Captain William Stephen Sanders (Labour) took the seat in 1929 pushing Saklatvala into third place. The son of a saddler, he was born in 1871 and attended elementary schools before attending Polytechnics and Universities in Berlin and Jena. He became a lecturer in English Working Class history at Ruskin College, Oxford, then an official of the International Labour Office of the League of Nations between 1920 and 1929, prior to which he had also been Secretary of the Fabian Society for 6 years and an alderman on the LCC from 1904 to 1910. From 1930-31, when the Government fell, he was Financial Secretary at the War Office. Out of Parliament until 1935 when he was re-elected, he retired in 1940 and died the following year.

From 1931 to 1935 Battersea North fell to the Conservatives. **Commander Arthur Marsden RN** (Conservative) had first contested the seat in 1929 following a distinguished career in the Royal Navy. He commanded HMS Ardent at the Battle of Jutland during the First World War but retired from the Navy in 1921. He played Rugby for the United Services, Cheltenham and Gloucestershire.

Following Sanders retirement in 1940 the by-election held on 17th April was won by **Sir Francis Campbell Ross Douglas** (Labour) who secured 92.6% of the votes cast in a contest where he was unopposed by the main parties who observed a wartime by-election "truce". He had previously contested Yeovil unsuccessfully in 1929. A Canadian, he was born in Manitoba in 1889 but was educated at Glasgow University where he obtained an MA after which he became a solicitor. From 1940 to 1946 he was the PPS to Chuter Ede when the latter was Education Minister during the War and Home Secretary afterwards. He was also a member of the LCC chairing its Finance Committee during the same period. From 1936 to 1946 he was a member of the Public Works Loan Board and of the Railway Assessment Authority[7] from 1938 to 1946. He retired from the Commons in 1946 to become Governor of Malta, which office he held until 1949. A year later he was made Baron Douglas of Barloch and between 1950 and 1962 was Chairman of the Corby Development Corporation. In 1962 he was elected Deputy Speaker of the House of Lords. He died in 1980. He first entered local politics in 1919 when he was elected to Battersea Borough Council on which he continued to serve until 1945. He was on the LCC from 1936 to 1946. He was also Battersea's mayor in 1922/3.

Battersea South

Francis Richard Henry Penn Curzon (Conservative) was elected in 1918. Son of the 4th Earl Howe, he was born in 1884 and educated at Eton and Christ Church, Oxford. From 1900 until 1929 he was styled Viscount Curzon. He joined the RNVR in which he was commissioned as a Lieutenant in 1906 and after the start of the First World War commanded the Howe Battalion 2nd RN Brigade in Belgium in 1914 serving also on board HMS Queen Elizabeth. Unusually for those days he was married three times and divorced twice, his first wife being Mary, the daughter of a Colonel Montagu Curzon. Bizarrely he also lived in Curzon Street. He was appointed a Government Whip (Junior Lord of the Treasury) in 1924 when he was responsible for the London group of Tory MPs and a year later was appointed an aide de camp to the King. His father died in 1929 (before the general election of that year) and he went to the Lords as the 5th Earl Howe. From 1928 when it was founded and until his death in 1964 he was Chairman of the British Racing Drivers' Club[8] set up to promote the interests of motor sport.

7 The Railway Assessment Authority existed from 1930 to 1948. Its role was to assess the rateable values of railway owned property and allocate these between local authorities.

8 The Club became a major force in international motor racing, taking over the lease of Silverstone from the RAC in 1952, subsequently purchasing the site's freehold from the Ministry of Defence and setting in motion a major redevelopment of what had been a wartime bomber training base to produce one of the world's foremost circuits.

The by-election that followed Curzon's elevation was held on 7th February 1929 and heralded the result of the subsequent general election. The seat was taken by **William Bennett** (Labour), a Somerset man born in 1873 and educated at Bath Grammar School then at the Metropolitan College of Pharmacy after which he practised as a chemist. He contested Guildford in three successive elections from 1918 to 1923 before he was elected at Battersea in 1929. Defeated in 1931 he sought re-election at by-elections at Hitchin (Hertfordshire) and Harborough (Leicestershire), both held in 1933, and at Cardiff East in the 1935 general election but lost on all three occasions.

Harry Ralph Selley (Conservative) represented Battersea South from 1931 until 1945 when he retired. Following an apprenticeship and born at Topsham near Exeter in 1871, he became a London house builder, and estate manager. Selley entered local politics on the LCC in 1925 and became chairman of the Housing Committee. He was a governor of Battersea Grammar School and of Sir Walter St John's School. A member of the borough council, prior to his election in 1931 he had come close to defeating his predecessor, Bennett, at the two 1929 elections. He was national president of the Federation of Master Builders from 1945. He died in 1960.

Clapham

Sir Arthur Philip Du Cros (Conservative) was MP from 1918 until 1922 when he resigned shortly before being divorced the following year. Son of a former MP for Hastings (East Sussex), he was born in 1871 and was educated for the Civil Service which he joined in 1886. His first wife was a Coventry woman and he established several family and business links in the area. He was President and life Director of the Dunlop Rubber Company[9] and also Chairman of the Patent Tyre Company. A Middlesex magistrate, he was also Honorary Colonel of the 8th Battalion of the Royal Warwickshire Regiment. He first entered politics in 1906 when he was unsuccessful at Bow and Bromley but won a 1908 by-election at Hastings, retaining the seat until 1918 when he transferred to Clapham. He died in 1955.

Du Cros was succeeded by **Sir John Leigh** (Conservative) who held the seat until 1945 when he retired. Born into a wealthy family in 1884 and brought up in the Brooklands district of Sale in Cheshire, he was educated at Manchester Grammar School. During the First World War he equipped a hospital for wounded officers at nearby Altrincham, maintaining it until 1919 when he dedicated it to the use of officers suffering from neurasthenia (shell shock). He gave a mansion and the eight acre estate at Brooklands as a hospital for soldiers and sailors suffering from the condition and also founded, maintained and chaired the Canadian Officers' Club in London's Chesterfield Gardens. He provided ambulances for the Lancashire and Cheshire Red Cross Society. A major philanthropist he also presented a public park to the town of Altrincham and gave £50,000 to the King's Fund for Disabled Sailors and Soldiers, of which he was also a trustee. He had a country seat at Witley Park near Godalming, Surrey and lived in London at 6, Carlton House Terrace.

Wandsworth Central

Sir John Norton Norton-Griffiths (Conservative) was the MP from 1918 until 1924 when he retired. Born in 1871 he was a Director of Norton-Griffiths and Company, an engineering and public works contractor. During the Colonial war in Southern Africa he commanded the Scouts against the Matabele and Mashona armies in 1896/7 subsequently becoming Captain Adjutant to General Lord Roberts' bodyguard when he commanded the British troops in South Africa. During the First World War he raised the 2nd King Edward's Horse and later in the conflict was awarded various foreign honours on account of his actions in Eastern Europe. These included Commander of the Grand Star of Romania, the Russian Order of Vladimir and the Croix D'Officier of the French Legion of Honour. Between January 1910 and 1918 he was MP for the Wednesbury constituency in Staffordshire. According to a review of a book of his life [10]Sir John Norton-Griffiths was "one of a breed of adventurer, pioneer, entrepreneur and soldier whose like is very seldom seen. Having learnt his trade and made his fortune mining the rich seams of South Africa, he turned his expertise to more deadly use in the Great War. He led the gallant miners who burrowed deep under enemy lines with devastating effect. He went on to wreak havoc on the Danube. Always a controversial figure, he died (or was he murdered?) in mysterious circumstances. This is the story of a true maverick who was a formidable force and legend wherever he went". Known also as "Empire Jack", the official records suggest that he committed suicide in Alexandria, Egypt in 1930.

He was succeeded by **Sir Henry Jackson** (Conservative) who represented the seat twice, from 1924 to 1929 and then from 1931 until 1937. A physician, Jackson, who was born in 1875, was formerly a Fellow and tutor at Downing College, Cambridge. Knighted in 1924, the year he became an MP, he was chairman of the London and Home Counties Advisory Committee on Traffic, a trustee of the London Passenger Transport Board[11] and chairman of the Standing

9 The Company was set up in 1889 and by 1954 owned 135 companies worldwide.
10 "Tunnelmaster and Arsonist of the Great War" by Tony Bridgland
11 The London Transport Passenger Board existed from 1933 to 1948 and was the predecessor of London Transport and Transport for London, bodies responsible for the planning and operation of public transport systems in the capital.

Committee on Mineral Transport. He was Honorary Treasurer of a local hospital, Bolingbroke near Wandsworth Common. He died in 1937.

Colonel Harry Louis Nathan (Labour) won the 1937 by-election that followed Jackson's death but only represented the seat for three years until 1940 when he vacated the seat to enable Ernest Bevin to enter Parliament. He was previously a Liberal MP for Bethnal Green North East, which he represented until 1935. His principal biographical details are in Chapter 7.

Ernest Bevin MP
© National Portrait Gallery
Pictorial Press

Ernest Bevin (Labour) was elected unopposed at a by-election in 1940 when he was brought into the Wartime Government at the behest of Winston Churchill who had a high regard for the man. Born at Winford, Somerset in 1881 "Ernie" was one of the most indomitable and significant figures in the history of the Labour movement. He was orphaned by the age of 6 and began work as a farm boy at 10 before moving to nearby Bristol aged 18 where he became a van driver. There he found an interest in religion and was for a while a Baptist lay preacher thereby developing skills as a speaker that would stand him in good stead in his future career. He joined the Dockers' Union and by the age of 30 was one of its leading figures. When Ben Tillet (also a Bristol man but by then active in the London Docks) and Harry Gosling (a London docker) set up the National Transport Workers Federation in 1921, Bevin was elected to the executive and a year later became General Secretary of the Transport and General Workers Union, a post he held until 1940 when he joined the Government. He sat on the TUC General Council from 1925 to 1940 and played an important role in negotiating an end to the General Strike in 1926. He served as Minister of Labour and National Service from 1940 to 1945 when he was one of the Cabinet's most important figures, amongst other things initiating a scheme for young men to be conscripted to the coal mines to assist with the war effort on the home front. They became known as "Bevin Boys". At the end of WW2 when Labour won the general election Bevin, an ardent anti-Communist, was appointed Foreign Secretary and represented Britain through a tumultuous post war period that saw the rise of the Soviet Bloc, the dropping of the Atom Bomb, the negotiation of the Marshall Aid plan, the establishment of the United Nations and the beginnings of the Korean War. Bevin was always regarded as a right-winger in his Party and it was he who took the decision for Britain to become a nuclear power, an issue that was to split the Labour Party over the period of the next forty years. Ill health forced his resignation from the Government in March 1951 and he died a month later. Meanwhile he had transferred from Wandsworth Central to Woolwich East following redistribution of seats in 1950.

Balham and Tooting

John Cuthbert Dennison Dennison-Pender (Conservative) sat from 1918 until his retirement in 1922. Born in 1882 and Eton- educated, he became a Director of two telecommunications businesses, the Eastern Telegraph and West African Companies, both of which had been established by his grandfather, Sir John Pender, who was elected Liberal MP for Totnes (Devon) in 1865 and who was famous as a co-founder of the Anglo-American Telegraph Company which laid the new Atlantic cable. John Cuthbert was also a Director of the Northern Assurance Company between 1910 and 1919. He served in France during the First World War and in 1918 worked at the War Office in the Red Cross division. He was elected MP for Newmarket (Suffolk) in 1913 and after his retirement from the House became Managing Director of the Cable and Wireless Company[12] in 1929, standing down in 1945. He was made Baron Pender in 1937 and died in 1949.

Sir Alfred Butt MP
Wikipedia

Sir Alfred Butt (Conservative) held the seat from 1922 until 1936. He was a theatrical manager and producer, knighted in 1918 for services to entertainment, and was involved with many theatres including the Theatre Royal Drury Lane, the Victoria Palace, the Glasgow Alhambra and the Dominion Theatre, Tottenham Court Road. From 1917 to 1918 he served at the Ministry of Food. He resigned his seat in 1936 when it was established by a Tribunal of Inquiry that Jimmy Thomas, a National Labour Cabinet Minister, had leaked details of the Budget to him and to a wealthy friend and businessman known as Alfred "Cosher" Bates, for personal gain. The issue brought about Thomas's resignation from the Government and, shortly afterwards, from the House.

12 In 1928 the Eastern Telegraph Company's telegraph network merged with that of Marconi to form Imperial and International Communications Limited. In 1934 the name was changed to Cable & Wireless Limited. In 1947 the company was nationalised by the Labour Government and most of its assets transferred to the Post Office.

Lieutenant-Colonel George Frederick Doland (Conservative) won the July 1936 by-election and held the seat until 1945 when he retired. Born in 1872, he was educated privately and during the First World War was Officer Commanding of the County of London Royal Army Services Corps, a transport supply operation. Between 1928 and 1929 and again from 1933-4, he was Mayor of Wandsworth, joining the LCC in 1933. A magistrate and Deputy-Lieutenant for London, he died in 1946.

Putney

Samuel Samuel (Conservative) was Putney's MP from 1918 until his death in 1934. Prior to 1918 he had been MP for Wandsworth since 1913. His principal biographical details are in Chapter 6.

He was succeeded at a by-election in 1934 by **Marcus Reginald Anthony Samuel** (Conservative), his nephew. A man described as having an intimate knowledge of world trade, he was an East Indies merchant and an executive member of the Spanish Chamber of Commerce. He died in 1942.

Hugh Nicholas Linstead (Conservative) was elected at the 1942 by-election and held the seat until he was defeated in 1964. Born in 1901, he was educated at the City of London School and the School of Pharmacy at the University of London. In 1929 he took a change of direction becoming a barrister being called to the bar of the Middle Temple but was also Secretary of the Pharmaceutical Society and a member of the Medical Research Council. He was a backbencher throughout his stay in the House but was for a while chairman of the Franco-British Parliamentary Relations Group and a member of the Wolfenden Committee on Homosexual Offences and Prostitution. He was a Parliamentary Charity Commissioner from 1956 to 1960. He died in 1987.

MPs for Outer Metropolitan Surrey

Richmond

Clifford Blackburn Edgar (Conservative) was Richmond's MP from 1918 until his defeat in 1922. Born in 1857, he was a graduate of the Universities of Manchester and London where he was awarded a Music Baccalaureate before becoming a Founder Director of the Niger Company[13] of which he was made vice chairman in 1910. With interests in the same region he was also a Director of the Bank of British West Africa. In politics he served as an alderman and Deputy Leader of Surrey County Council between 1917 and 1922 and was also active in Richmond borough where he was three times Mayor. From 1905 he sat as a Senator of London University where he chaired the Finance Committee between 1910 and 1920. A Surrey magistrate, Edgar was also Vice Chairman of the County's Territorial Force. He died in 1931.

Henry (Harry) Thomas Alfred Becker (Independent Conservative) defeated Edgar, the official candidate and sitting MP, in 1922 when he stood with the support of the Anti-Waste League. Born in Wandsworth in 1892 he was educated at Colet Court, the St Pauls preparatory school, Uppingham[14] and first entered politics as an ex-soldier Independent when he contested West Bermondsey in 1918, polling nearly one eighth of the votes, though finishing fourth. Following his victory at Richmond in 1922 he was adopted as the Tory candidate and retained the seat under his new colours in 1923. However, he retired from politics in 1924.

Sir Newton James Moore (Conservative) who had previously been MP for Westminster, St George's Hanover Square in 1918 and then for Islington North until 1923, was returned for Richmond in 1924 sitting until 1932 when he resigned. His principal biographical details are in Chapter 3 (Middlesex, Westminster).

Moore was succeeded by **Sir William Ray** (Conservative) who was born in 1876 and educated at St Thomas's School, Lancaster before attending St John's College, Battersea. During the First World War he was in the Remount Service (a cavalry division) between 1916 and 1918 and from 1913 to 1934 he sat on the LCC where he was leader of the Municipal Reform Party (the Conservatives) from 1925 until 1934 when he retired. From 1933 to 1936 he was chairman of the Electrical Development Association, a body which promoted the use of electricity. He first contested a Parliamentary seat in 1929 when he was defeated at Finsbury. He resigned as an MP in 1937 and died later the same year.

13 The Royal Niger Company was awarded a charter in 1886 to respect free trade in the Niger Basin, but its officials worked to obstruct French and German traders. It helped arrange a number of important trade treaties and its constabulary became involved in the Yoruba Wars which contributed to the establishment of British Nigeria by 1914.

14 A public school established in Rutland in 1584.

MPs for Outer Metropolitan Surrey						
From	**at**	**To**	**Surname**	**First Names**	**Constituency**	**Party**
1918	G	1922	Edgar	Clifford Blackburn	Richmond	Conservative
1922	G	1923	Becker	Henry (Harry) Thomas Alfred		Ind. Conservative
1923	G	1924	Becker	Henry (Harry) Thomas Alfred		Conservative
1924	G	1932	Moore	Sir Newton James		Conservative
1932	B	1937	Ray	Sir William		Conservative
1937	B	1945	Harvie-Watt	Sir George Steven		Conservative
1918	G	1922	Campbell	John Gordon Drummond	Kingston-Upon-Thames	Conservative
1922	G	1937	Penny	Sir (Frederick) George		Conservative
1937	B	1945	Royds	Percy Molyneaux Rawson (Ad)		Conservative
1918	G	1924	Hood	Sir Joseph	Wimbledon	Conservative
1924	G	1945	Power	Sir John Cecil		Conservative
1918	G	1923	Worsfold	Dr. Thomas Cato	Mitcham	Conservative
1923	B	1923	Ede	James Chuter		Labour
1923	G	1940	Meller	Sir Richard James		Conservative
1940	B	1945	Robertson	Sir Malcolm Arnold		Conservative
1918	G	1922	Borwick	George Oldroyd (Major)	Croydon North	Conservative
1922	G	1940	Mason	Glyn Keith Murray (Lt-Colonel)		Conservative
1940	B	1945	Willink	Henry Urmston		Conservative
1918	G	1919	Malcolm	Ian Zachary	Croydon South	Conservative
1919	B	1923	Smith	Sir Allan Macgregor		Conservative
1923	G	1932	Mitchell - Thomson	Sir William Lowson		Conservative
1932	B	1945	Williams	Sir Herbert Geraint		Conservative
1918	B	1922	Coats	Sir Stuart Auchinloss	Surrey East	Conservative
1922	G	1935	Galbraith	James Francis Wallace		Conservative
1935	G	1945	Emmott	Charles Ernest George Campbell		Conservative
1918	G	1928	Blades	Sir (George) Rowland	Epsom	Conservative
1928	B	1945	Southby	Sir Archibald Richard James		Conservative
Notes: First returned at: **B** By-election, **G** General Election						

Sir George Steven Harvie Watt (Conservative) was elected in 1937 at a by-election and remained Richmond's MP until 1954. Previously he was MP for Keighley (Yorkshire West Riding) between 1931 and 1935. Born in 1903, he was educated at George Watson's College, Edinburgh and at both Glasgow and Edinburgh Universities. He was called to the bar of the Inner Temple in 1930 and became a Kings Councillor in 1945. From 1938 to 1940 he was an Assistant Government Whip and during the Wartime Coalition he was Parliamentary Private Secretary to Winston Churchill from 1941 to 1945. He served on Kensington Borough Council for eleven years between 1934 and 1945 and from 1942 as a Deputy Lieutenant of Surrey. In 1948 he was appointed an aide de camp to the King, George VI and then fulfilled a similar role for Queen Elizabeth II between 1952 and 1958. He resigned his seat in 1954 to become Chief Executive and Deputy Chairman of Consolidated Goldfields Limited succeeding as chairman from 1960 to 1969 and as President between 1973 and 1981. He served on the Boards of several other companies at various times including the Monoytpe Corporation, Eagle Star Insurance, the Standard, Midland and Clydesdale Banks, the Great Western Railway, and British Steel. From 1966-78 he was a Deputy-Lieutenant of Greater London and was made a Freeman of the City of London in 1976. In 1980 he published papers on his wartime experiences with Churchill and died in 1989.

Kingston-Upon-Thames

John Gordon Drummond Campbell (Conservative) was Kingston's MP from 1918 to 1922 when he retired. In January 1910 he had contested Mansfield (Nottinghamshire) and in December of the same year the Eccles division of Lancashire, both times unsuccessfully. After leaving Charterhouse, where he was head boy, and Oxford, where he was a rowing Blue and achieved two first class degrees, he studied law and was called to the bar. However, he gave up law to join the Board of Education, and from 1899 to 1901 worked for the Siamese government organising an education system for that country. In Britain he lived on Kingston Hill, was a member of the Kingston Education Committee, chairman of the Kingston and District branch of the Tariff Reform League and from 1913 served on the committee of Kingston Conservative Association.

He was succeeded in 1922 by **Sir (Frederick) George Penny** (Conservative) who retained the seat until 1937. He was born in 1876, one of seven children and was educated at King Edward VI's Grammar School at Southampton which he left aged 14 and went to sea. After 9 years on a wool clipper he achieved his Master Mariner's certificate at the age of 23 and embarked on a business career, working mainly in the Far East where he was active in a number of trading enterprises. He was a Senior Partner in the firm of Fraser and Company, government brokers of Singapore, and managing director of the Eastern Smelting Company of Penang where he also served on the Chamber of Commerce. He was a joint representative of the Malay States Government in negotiations with the Dutch Indies Government in Java over the disposal of accumulated War Tin Stocks. From 1923-4 he served in Bonar Law's Government as PPS to the Financial Secretary at the War Office and became a Government whip in 1927, serving until 1929 in an unpaid capacity. In the National Government he served as a Conservative whip from 1931 to 1935. He continued in the same role in Baldwin's Tory-led National Government from 1935 to 1937 when he was elevated to the House of Lords. He sat there as the First Lord Marchwood until 1945 when he was made a Viscount. From 1938 to 1945 he was Treasurer of the Conservative Party and until 1953 Chairman of the Kingston wine company, Vine Products, which at the time was believed to be the largest winery in Europe. He died in 1955.

Admiral Sir Percy Molyneaux Rawson Royds (Conservative) won the 1937 by-election created by Penny's elevation. He was born in 1874 and his father, Sir Charles, was also a Vice-Admiral in the Royal Navy. Percy enjoyed a distinguished naval career including action during the First World War when he captained HMS Canterbury in the Battle of Jutland (1916), regarded as a defining moment in cementing British naval supremacy. He lived on Kingston Hill, close to Twickenham where he was an assiduous attendee and (in 1927-8) President of the Rugby Football Union. After his retirement from the House he wrote a definitive work on his favourite sport that was published in 1949 and entitled "The History of the Laws of Rugby Football". He died in 1955.

Wimbledon

Sir Joseph Hood (Conservative) was Wimbledon's MP from 1918 to 1924 when he retired. Born in 1863 in Ashby De la Zouch, Leicestershire, where he was educated at the local Grammar School, he became a solicitor, being admitted in 1890. He was Deputy Chairman of British American Tobacco until 1921 and after his retirement from the House sat on Wimbledon Borough Council where he was mayor from 1930 to 1931, the year he died.

Sir John Cecil Power (Conservative) succeeded him in 1924 and continued to serve until 1945 when he retired. Born in Ulster in 1870, Power went into business exporting iron and steel and other commodities to the Far East. He was a director of the Royal Insurance Company[15] from 1934 to 1949 and a member of the executive council of the Empire Industries Association[16], a pressure group set up by Joseph Chamberlain in 1925 to continue the work of the Tariff Reform League, which had ceased to function just after World War I, in promoting a trade system of Protection and Imperial Preference. He was a founder and treasurer until 1943 of the Royal Institute of International Affairs, established by Royal Charter in 1926 to "advance the sciences of international politics, economics and jurisprudence, and the study, classification and development of the literature of these subjects"[17]. He also served on the executive committee of the League of Nations Union, established in 1918 to promote better global understanding between nations[18]. He died in 1950.

Mitcham

Dr.Thomas Cato Worsfield FRCS (Conservative) was Mitcham's MP from 1918 until 1923 when he resigned. He was born in London in 1861and lived in the family home at The Hall Place, Mitcham before receiving further education at Trinity College, Dublin where he obtained his MA and Dr. of Laws degrees. In 1883 he was admitted as a solicitor and was also a Surrey magistrate. He was a Commissioner in Great Britain for the Supreme Courts of the British Colonies and Empire of India and fulfilled the same role for the High Courts of the USA. A keen archaeologist, he wrote several books on a variety of subjects including "A Concise Text Book on the Law of Repairs and Dilapidations", "The French Stone - henge", "Staple Inn and its Story" and "The Serpent Column of the Delphic Oracle". He was Chairman of Eastwoods Limited. He died in 1936.

The 1923 by-election occasioned by his resignation was won by **James Chuter Ede** (Labour) who, although he

15 Royal Insurance was established in 1845. In 1996 it merged with Sun Alliance to become Royal and Sun Alliance

16 The Association wound up in 1976 following confirmation by referendum of British membership of the European Common Market.

17 Description of its Aims on its own website.

18 The League terminated in 1971.

held the seat for a matter of only a few months until the general election that same year, went on to have a distinguished ministerial career in the Attlee Government and a long parliamentary tenure. He was elected for South Shields (County Durham) in 1929 and, although he was defeated in 1931, won again in 1935 retaining the seat until his retirement in 1964. Born in 1882 he received only an elementary and secondary school education but went on to attend Christ's College, Cambridge afterwards becoming a Surrey school teacher. In 1914 he joined the Army resuming teaching after the War. He lived in Epsom where he served for many years on the Urban District Council and was charter mayor of Epsom and Ewell in 1937[19]. In the Wartime Coalition Government led by Churchill he was Parliamentary Secretary to the Minister of Education from 1940 to 1945 and Home Secretary in Attlee's Cabinet from 1945 to 1951 when, in the reshuffle necessitated by the death of Ernest Bevin, he became briefly Leader of the House. In 1964 he was created Baron Chuter-Ede of Epsom and died the following year. In the last year of his life, Ede, who owned a small boat on the Thames called "Brown Duck", was appointed Chairman of the Inland Waterways Board, established to protect the heritage of Britain's canals and navigations.

Chuter Ede MP
© National Portrait Gallery

Sir Richard James Meller (Conservative), who was born in 1872 represented the seat from 1923 until 1940 when he died. A barrister called to the Bar at the Middle Temple in 1904, he was Secretary of the Prudential Approved Societies. He was a Surrey County Councillor (from 1919) and Alderman (from 1928) where he chaired the General Purposes Committee and also chaired the Croydon magistrates' bench. He chaired the Surrey Territorial Army and was a member of the Thames Conservancy. He unsuccessfully contested Parliamentary seats on two earlier occasions, at Dartford in a 1920 by-election; and at Camberwell North in 1922. He was Vice chairman of the County Council from 1937 and its chairman in 1940.

Sir Malcolm Arnold Robertson (Conservative) won the 1940 by-election but lost the seat in 1945. He was born in 1877 and educated at Marlborough College before becoming a diplomat. He entered the Foreign Office as a Clerk in 1898, serving as the 3rd Secretary Diplomatic Service, Berlin, 1903-4; 2nd Secretary Peking, 1905; Madrid, 1907; Chargé d'Affaires, Bucharest, 1910-11; 1st Secretary, 1912; Chargé d'Affaires, Montevideo, 1912-13; Rio de Janeiro, 1913-15; 1st Secretary, Washington, 1915-18; Hague, 1918-19; Counsellor of Embassy and Deputy British High Commissioner on Inter-Allied Rhineland High Commission, 1919; British High Commissioner on the same High Commission, 1920-21; Minister Plenipotentiary, 1921; HM Agent and Consul-General at Tangier, 1921-25; Envoy Extraordinary and Minister Plenipotentiary, Buenos Aires, 1925-27; and Ambassador, 1927-29. He retired in 1930. From 1942 to 1945 he was Chairman of the British Council[20] and latterly of the Spillers Company, specialists in animal feeds. He died in 1951.

Croydon North

Major George Oldroyd Borwick (Conservative) represented Croydon North from 1918 until 1922 when he retired. He was born in Leytonstone in 1879, taking his mother's maiden name as his second. He was educated at Harrow and Trinity College, Oxford and joined the family baking powder manufacturing company. He contested Poplar unsuccessfully at the 1906 election and suffered a similar fate at Limehouse in January 1910. During the Great War he served as a major in the Surrey Yeomanry being mentioned in dispatches three times and was awarded the DSO as well as the Legion 'D'Honeur by France. He retired from politics in 1922 and died many years later in 1964.

Lieutenant-Colonel Glyn Keith Murray Mason DSO (Conservative) succeeded Borwick in 1922 and continued to represent the seat until 1940. He was born in 1887, son of Sir William James Peake Mason, later Lord Blackford of Compton Pauncefoot, Somerset. Educated at Eton and the Royal Military College, Sandhurst, he embarked on an Army career in the 14th Hussars. During the First World War he served in Europe, Salonica and Palestine being awarded the DSO and bar and was mentioned in despatches several times. He was also wounded three times. A Director of the Guardian Assurance Company, the Midland Bank and several investment trusts he resigned from the House in 1940 and pursued a business career. Although he remained a backbencher for his entire Commons career, when he entered the Lords after his father, Lord Blackford died in 1947, he was elected Deputy Speaker, a post he occupied until 1966. From 1950-67 he chaired the Guardian Assurance Company, a role he also occupied at the Midland Bank between 1960 and 1967. He died in 1972.

19 A Charter Mayor is the first mayor of an authority following the granting of its charter.
20 The 'British Committee for Relations with Other Countries' was set up by the Foreign Office in 1934 to promote British values in the world. The name was shortened to the 'British Council' in 1936.

Sir Henry Urmston Willink as Vice-Chancellor of Cambridge University in 1953
National Portrait Gallery
©Gonville and Caius College
Antony Barrington Brown

Sir Henry Urmston Willink (Conservative) was elected at the 1940 by-election and went on to hold the seat for 8 years until 1948. Born in 1894 in Liverpool, he was educated at Eton where he was a Kings Scholar[21] and then at Trinity College, Cambridge where he was both an Entrance and a Senior Scholar. He volunteered in 1914 before completing his degree and served in the RFA until 1918 earning several mentions in despatches as well as being awarded the Military Cross and Croix de Guerre with Palm, commanding a Battery on the Somme at the age of only twenty two. In 1920 he was called to the bar at the Inner Temple and was appointed a Kings Councillor in 1935. He contested a by-election unsuccessfully at Ipswich (Suffolk) in 1938 and during the Second World War was a Special Commissioner responsible for re-housing families bombed out of London properties. He held this post from 1940-43 and from 1942 to 1943 was also Chancellor of the Diocese of Rochester (Kent). He was appointed a bencher in 1942 and then served as Minister of Health from 1943-45. Re-elected in 1945 and after suffering from a period of ill health he was appointed Master of Magdalene College, Cambridge, with effect from January 1949, and resigned his parliamentary seat at the end of 1948. On his retirement as Master of Magdalene in 1966 he was awarded an Honorary Fellowship of the College. During his time as Master he had served as Vice-Chancellor of Cambridge University (1953-5). Willink chaired the Royal Commission on Betting, Lotteries, and Gaming (1949-51), which recommended the legalisation of High Street Betting Offices, and two years later headed a Committee on Medical Manpower; then from 1961/1962 a Royal Commission on the Police. He died in January 1973.

Croydon South

Ian Zachary Malcolm (Conservative) sat for Croydon from December 1910 until 1918 and for Croydon South until 1919. His principal biographical details are in Chapter 6.

He was succeeded at a by-election by **Sir Allan Macgregor Smith** (Conservative) who was only the MP for four years, retiring in 1923. Born around 1871 he attended Glasgow University where he obtained his MA and LL.B going on to become a solicitor. He was Chairman of the National Employers' Federations and of the Employers' Section of the Joint Committee of the Industrial Conference. He stood down at Croydon in 1923 to fight the Partick division of Glasgow but was defeated and did not resume a political career. He died in 1941.

Sir William Lowson Mitchell – Thomson (Conservative) was MP for Croydon South between 1923 and 1932 but before that had represented North West Lanarkshire (1906-10); North Down (April 1910 by-election-1918); and Glasgow Maryhill (1918-1922). He was born in 1877 and educated at Winchester School and Balliol College, Oxford where he took a BA in 1900; then at Edinburgh where he graduated LL.B in 1902. He was the only son of Sir Mitchell Mitchell-Thomson, first Baronet of Polmood (Peeblesshire). His mother may have died giving birth to him as her death is also recorded in 1877. He became an advocate in Scotland in 1903 but enlisted as a Lieutenant in the RNVR[22] in 1914. A member of the Royal Company of Archers (the Royal body guards in Scotland) he was Director of Restriction of Enemy Supplies from 1916 to 1919. He was a representative of the Government on the Supreme Economic Council held as part of the armistice negotiations in Paris in 1919 when one of the Treasury civil servants advising the politicians was the famous economist John Maynard Keynes. In 1920 Thomson was appointed Parliamentary Secretary to the Ministry of Food. He fulfilled a similar role at the Board of Trade between 1921 and 1922 and served as Postmaster-General under Baldwin between 1924 and 1929. He was created Lord Selsdon (a suburb in his constituency) in 1932 and died in 1938.

Sir Herbert Geraint Williams (Conservative) was first elected at a 1932 by-election transferring in 1945 to the new East division of the borough which he retained until 1954. Born in 1884 and educated at Liverpool University, Williams was an electrical engineer who first contested the Combined Universities constituency unsuccessfully in 1918 and replicated the failure at Wednesbury (Staffordshire) in 1922 and 1923. In 1924 he was elected a MP for the two member borough constituency of Reading (Berkshire), which he represented until 1929. In the last year of the Parliament he was Parliamentary Secretary to the Board of Trade from 1928. Defeated in 1929 he sought re-election

21 Scholarships have been a central part of Eton ever since King Henry VI founded the College for the 70 King's Scholars in 1440. These are bursaries that still part pay the school fees for 70 scholars each year.
22 The Royal Navy Volunteer Reserve was established in 1903 and was affectionately known as the "Wavy Navy," during the war of 1914 - 18

at the Combined Universities[23] in 1931 but was again unsuccessful although the following year he was elected at the Croydon South by-election. He was a member of Wimbledon Borough and London County Councils, the latter from 1940-45. He died in 1954.

Surrey East

Sir Stuart Auchinloss Coats (Conservative) was elected MP for East Surrey in 1918 and retired in 1922. Formerly the MP for Wimbledon from 1916, his principal biographical details are in Chapter 6.

He was succeeded by **James Francis Wallace Galbraith** (Conservative) who represented the constituency until 1935 when he became a High Court Judge. Born in 1872, he was educated at Blackheath Preparatory School and at Oriel College Oxford before being called to the bar at Lincoln's Inn in 1895. He became a Kings Councillor in 1919 and a bencher three years later. He was Honorary Treasurer of the Bar Council for many years. He contested Halifax unsuccessfully at the general elections held in 1910 and after serving as a Judge for ten years died in 1945.

Charles Ernest George Emmott (Conservative) sat from 1935 until 1945 when he retired. A maternal grandson of the 8th Duke of Argyll, he was born in 1898 and educated at Lancing College before attending Christ Church Oxford where he was awarded a MA in Classics. In 1924 he was called to the bar of the Middle Temple and five years later contested his first Parliamentary election, at Preston (Lancashire) where he was defeated. At the 1931 contest he was, however, elected as Unionist MP for the somewhat unlikely constituency of Glasgow, Springburn, overturning a majority of 31% and winning by a margin of 0.2% of the votes cast, a result that would have been virtually out of the question at any other contest in such an industrial constituency. He transferred to the extremely contrasting seat of Surrey East in 1935, wisely, as he had no chance of retaining his Scottish seat which returned to Labour with a majority of 26% and has been held by the Party ever since. Chairman of the British-Italian Society[24], he died in 1953.

Epsom

Sir (George) Rowland Blades (Conservative) was Epsom's MP from 1918 to 1928. Born in 1868 he was educated at King's College School (Wimbledon) and joined the family business, Blades East and Blades Ltd (publishers and City of London printers of cheques) later becoming its Chairman. In 1902 he became President of the Institute of Printers and in 1917 of the Printers' Pension Corporation. He sold the company in 1927. He was active in the West Surrey Regiment as a volunteer where he was a sometime Captain and was Honorary Colonel of the 54th (City of London) Anti-Aircraft Brigade in the Royal Artillery (Territorial Army). An alderman and Sheriff (1917-18) of the City of London, he was also a magistrate there and in Surrey, serving in addition as a committee member of the City of London Savings Association. He lived at Leatherhead and in 1928 was elevated as Lord Ebbisham of Cobham in the County of Surrey. He died in 1953.

Archibald Southby MP
© National Portrait Gallery
Bassano Ltd 1928

Commander Sir Archibald Richard James Southby RN (Conservative) was elected at the 1928 by-election. He was born in 1886 and following a Preparatory School education at Brandon House, Cheltenham, went to the naval college, HMS "Britannia", Dartmouth, entering the Royal Navy in 1902. From 1912-13 he was Flag Lieutenant to Admiral Sir Alexander Bethell on the East Indies station, transferring to a similar role in support of Sir Montagu Browning with the Home and Grand Fleets on the North America and West Indies station until 1918. By now a lieutenant commander, he served on the allied Naval Armistice Commission and the Inter Allied Commission of Control until he retired in 1920. He was awarded the French Chevalier of the Legion D'Honeur. A Director of Garton & Sons, (manufacturers of starch, glucose and modified starches) of Southampton Wharf, Battersea, he was an assistant Government whip in 1931 and again between 1935 and 1937as Commissioner of the Treasury. He was a Deputy Lieutenant of Surrey and an Oxford magistrate where he lived at Burford Priory. He resigned in 1947, continuing as a Deputy-Lieutenant of Surrey where he was a magistrate, as he was also in Oxfordshire. He died in 1969.

23 The Combined English Universities constituency included Durham, Victoria (Manchester), Liverpool, Leeds, Sheffield, Birmingham and Bristol. It returned two MPs elected by "proportional representation".
24 The British-Italian Society (BIS) was established in 1941 as "Friends of Free Italy" at a time when the two countries were at War. It had the aim of increasing knowledge and understanding of Italian culture in the United Kingdom in terms of history, institutions, way of life, language and contribution to civilisation. It still exists today.

Chapter 11
Middlesex 1945 - 1974

In Middlesex eight new constituencies were formed in 1945 as part of a special post war review involving mainly those constituencies where populations had grown so much since 1918 that the electoral balance had become heavily distorted. No changes were made within the area of the LCC but in the outer suburbs new constituencies were created to accommodate vastly increased electorates in Hendon, Wembley, Harrow, Ealing and Hounslow. In addition the Hertfordshire Urban Districts of Barnet and East Barnet were created a new constituency covering suburbs that were later to be included in Greater London. These were stopgap measures and the Boundary Commission's major post war review was not enacted until 1948 so that further changes were applied in 1950 at the second Election after the War when the increase that had occurred in 1945 was reversed.

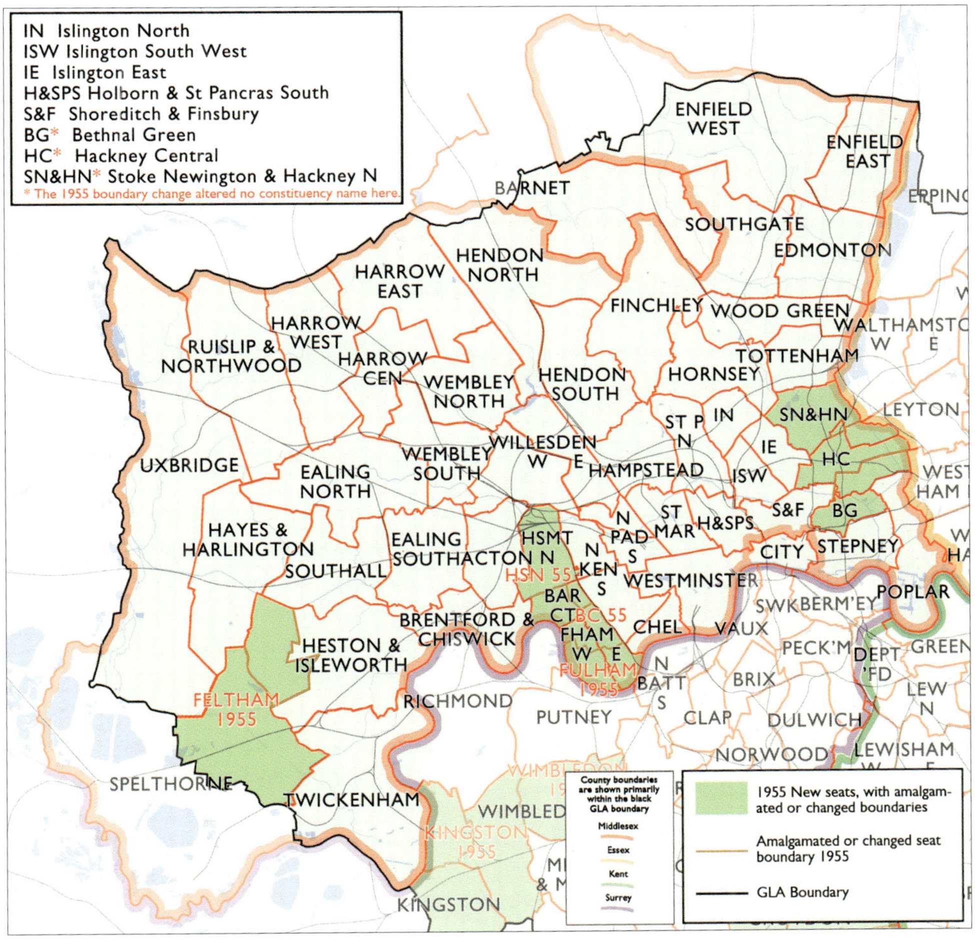

The map depicts Middlesex constituencies created in 1945, 1950 and 1955, though not those eliminated by these changes. The number of seats in the LCC was reduced compared with 1945. New seats were created in Enfield, Barnet, Hendon, Harrow, Wembley, Ealing, and Heston, and in 1955 Feltham emerged. Comparison with 1945 may be made by reference to the map on page 18 and with 1918 on page 16.

There was an overall reduction from 60 to 51 seats in 1950 reflecting the declining population of the inner areas, brought about by several factors, not least the Wartime bombing and general drift of both industrial and residential development to new suburbs. Docklands and inner areas of North London were particularly affected. Nevertheless the combined effect of the two boundary post War reviews was a reduction of only one in the number of MPs representing Middlesex constituencies comparing 1918 with 1950, although their distribution was markedly different. After a further review in 1954 minor revisions occurred affecting west London although most other parts of Middlesex were fundamentally unaltered and the impact was neutral in terms of the total number of seats. However, the changes made meant that the Spelthorne constituency no longer covered metropolitan areas included in today's Greater London Council area. Proportionately Middlesex was better represented in the 1950s than it was in 1918 with roundly 17% of all MPs compared with 14%.

Central London

Post War General Election Results 1945 to 1970 by % majority

Constituency	Pre 1945	1945	1950	1951	1955	1959	1964	1966	1970
Cities of London & Westminster (Abbey) (St Georges)	*4xC*	*1xNat29 1xC29 C28 C40*	*C34*	*C34*	*C40*	*C41*	*C28+*	*C20*	*C28*
St Marylebone	*C*	*C16*	*C31*	*C35*	*C41*	*C41+*	*C27*	*C26*	*C33+*
Paddington North	*C*	*Lab24+*	*Lab11*	*Lab11+*	*Lab7*	*Lab3*	*Lab16*	*Lab26+*	*Lab14*
Paddington South	*C*	*C16*	*C19*	*C20*	*C24*	*C29*	*C17*	*C7*	*C13*
C	*7*	*6*	*3*	*3*	*3*	*3+*	*3+*	*3*	*3+*
Lab	*0*	*1+*	*1*	*1+*	*1*	*1*	*1*	*1+*	*1*
Total	*7*	*7+*	*4*	*4+*	*4*	*4+*	*4+*	*4+*	*4+*

Key: Numbers indicate percentage majority of the votes cast in the election. 100 = Unopposed Key: C = Conservative; Lab = Labour; Nat = National Party (allies of the Conservatives); + = Party that won seat at General Election held by-election in same Parliament; - = Party that won seat at General Election lost by-election to main opposition Party in same Parliament.

City of London, Westminster, St Marylebone, and Paddington: (4 seats after 1950)

There was a reduction of three seats between the elections of 1935 and 1950, all of them in Westminster and the City. Although there were no changes in 1945 the opportunity was taken to give these areas the representation to which their resident populations entitled them at the 1950 Election. 1945 constituency boundaries are therefore the same as in Chapter 7.

The 1950 changes eliminated the anachronism of the business vote, which distorted electorates in two central London divisions, The City, where there were 6,608 such registered voters in 1945 (61% of the total electorate), and Westminster, Abbey where one voter in twelve was on the business list. So in 1950 the St George's and Abbey seats were not only eliminated but also merged with the former two-member City of London and re-named **The Cities of London & Westminster,** a single member constituency which covered Aldwych, Bank of England, St Pauls, Belgravia, Blackfriars, Charing Cross, Covent Garden, Hyde Park, Kensington Gore, Knightsbridge, Mayfair, Millbank, Pimlico, Smithfield, Soho, St James', Temple, Victoria, the West End and Whitehall. The new seat was, if anything, under-represented. At over 73,000 its electorate was 26% above the London average and, even though it fell by one fifth in the next twenty years, its 1970 electorate of fewer than 59,000 was still 7% above the average.

St Marylebone, Paddington North, and **Paddington South** boundaries were unaltered in 1945 and 1950 due in part to a requirement then to contain constituencies within London borough boundaries. On this criterion Paddington retained two seats but both were small. Paddington North had only 44,500 voters and South just above 48,000. Over the next 20 years all three constituencies experienced further large falls in their electorates. In 1950 St Marylebone's 57,680 voter list was only 1% below average yet by 1970 it had fallen by over 17% to little more than 47,500, which was 13% below the average at that time. There was a 20% decline in Paddington North and nearly 26% in Paddington South such that by 1970 their combined electorates were less than 68,000 compared with nearly 93,000 in 1950. North was 24% below the average for London in 1950 and by 1970 it was 38% below. Over the same period South moved from 17% to 37% below average. Despite this, boundary changes did not occur until 1974.

Politics in Central London

The 1950 changes did not benefit the Conservatives who held all 7 seats pre-War although the swing to Labour in 1945 had shifted Paddington North away from them. The Tories, therefore, suffered an even bigger loss at the hands of the Boundary Commission than from the swing to Labour. The relative position of the two Parties in terms of the number of seats they held remained the same from 1945 until after 1970 when the Paddington seats were merged. The table shows the position compared with that which obtained, on average, before the War.

By-election outcomes reflected the relative stability of two party politics in the 40s and 50s, results always favouring the Party defending the seat though they were sometimes indicative of deeper trends taking place within the wider electorate. Thus on 20th November 1946, whilst Labour retained Paddington North it did so with a majority halved compared with its 24% margin at the General Election and in 1950 it fell a little further to 11%. On 3rd December 1953, two years after the Tories had been returned to power, another by-election occurred in the same seat, which Labour won with a majority further reduced to 8%. In retrospect this may be seen as part of the trend that led to the Tories increasing their national majority in 1955. Despite this Labour hung on at Paddington North throughout the period of Tory Government that lasted from 1951 to 1964. Even in one of its darkest periods in office, Labour retained the seat with a majority of 3% at a by-election held on 30th October 1969.

MPs for the City of London and Westminster

From		To	Surname	First Names	Constituency	Party Affiliation
1945	G	1950	Duncan	Sir Andrew Rae	City of London	National
1945	G	1945	Broadridge	Sir George Thomas		Conservative
1945	B	1950	Assheton	Ralph		Conservative
1945	G	1950	Cooper	Alfred Duff	Westminster St.Georges	Conservative
1945	G	1950	Webbe	Sir Harold CBE	Westminster , Abbey	Conservative
1950	G	1959	Webbe	Sir Harold CBE	The Cities of London & Westminster	Conservative
1959	G	1965	Hylton-Foster	Sir Harry Braustyn		Conservative/Speaker
1965	B	1970	Smith	John Lindsay Eric		Conservative
1970	G	1974	Tugendhat	Sir Chistopher Samuel		Conservative
1945	G	1963	Wakefield	Sir Wavell	St. Marylebone	Conservative
1963	G	1970	Hogg	Quintin McGarrel		Conservative
1970	B	1974	Baker	Kenneth Wilfred		Conservative
1945	G	1946	Mason-MacFarlane	Sir Frank Noel Lt-Gen	Paddington North	Labour
1946	B	1953	Field	William James		Labour
1953	B	1969	Parkin	Ben(jamin) Theaker		Labour
1969	B	1974	Latham	Arthur Charles		Labour
1945	G	1950	Taylor	Sir Ernest Augustus (Admiral)	Paddington South	Conservative
1950	G	1951	De Chair	Somerset		Conservative
1951	G	1966	Allan	Robert Alexander		Conservative
1966	G	1974	Scott	Sir Nicholas Paul		Conservative
1906	B	1918	Banbury	Sir Frederick George		Conservative Unionist

NOTE First returned at a B = By-election; G =General Election

A famous by-election occurred at St Marylebone on 5th December 1963 after Lord Hailsham renounced his peerage to fight for the leadership of the Conservative Party in a bid to become Prime Minister. As Quintin Hogg he fought and retained the seat with a majority of 23% compared with 41% at the 1959 Election, heralding the Tories' defeat nationally in 1964. In the event Hogg was unsuccessful in his leadership bid and later returned to the House of Lords to serve as Lord Chancellor in the Thatcher Government after 1979. The by-election following his elevation occurred on 22nd October 1970. His biographical details are on page 331.

City of London

Sir Andrew Rae Duncan (National) and **Sir George Thomas Broadridge** (Conservative) had both been returned as MPs for the City of London prior to the 1945 General Election. Duncan remained until 1950 when he retired before the merger with Westminster but Broadridge was made a Lord after his election in 1945. Their biographical details may be found in Chapter 7.

Broadridge's place was taken by **Ralph Assheton** (Conservative) who was then the Chairman of his Party and who had previously been the MP for Rushcliffe (Nottinghamshire) after a by-election win there in July 1934 but who was defeated in 1945. He was born in 1901 and came from a north of England landowning family steeped in politics. Over twenty of its members had been in the Commons since his ancestor, Sir John de Assheton, was summoned to Parliament in 1324. Educated at Eton and Christ Church, Oxford, where he obtained his MA, Ralph was called to the Bar at the Inner Temple in 1925 but two years later joined the Stock Exchange Company of Shaw and Loebel of which he was a member until 1939. He was appointed PPS to Ormsby-Gore as First Commissioner of Works in 1935 and Secretary of State for the Colonies from 1936. He achieved his first ministerial post in 1939 as Parliamentary Secretary to the Ministry of Labour and National Service and went to the Ministry of Supply in 1942. A magistrate in Lancashire he represented Blackburn on the National Assembly of the Church of England. He was also a Board member of the London and North Eastern Railway Company and of Town Investments. When the City of London lost its unique Commons' status in 1950 he was elected MP for Blackburn West (Lancashire), which he represented until it too was merged in 1955. He was made Lord Clitheroe of Downham in the County Palatine of Lancaster and died in 1984.

Westminster Abbey, Westminster St Georges and The Cities of London and Westminster

Like their City of London colleagues the two MPs returned for Westminster constituencies in 1945 were also incumbents at that General Election. **Alfred Duff Cooper** (Conservative) had been MP for the St George's division since 1931 whilst **Sir Harold Webbe** (Conservative) was first elected at a by-election in the Abbey constituency in 1939. In 1950 Duff Cooper retired and Webb was elected MP for The Cities of London and Westminster and held the seat until his retirement in 1959. The biographical details of both men can be found in Chapter 7.

Sir Harry Braustyn Hylton-Foster MP
by Edward irvine Halliday
© Palace of Westminster Collection
www.parliament.uk/art

In 1959 the seat was won by **Sir Harry Braustyn Hylton-Foster QC** (Conservative) who had previously been MP for York since 1950. Born in 1905, he was educated at Eton and Magdalen College, Oxford. During the War he served in RAF Intelligence in 1940 and was Deputy Judge Advocate in North Africa and Italy from 1941-45. He first contested Shipley unsuccessfully for the Tories in 1945 and was later Recorder of Richmond and Huddersfield, then from 1950 to 1954 Recorder of Hull. For several years whilst MP for York he was also Chancellor of the diocese of Durham and Ripon. He was Solicitor-General in successive Conservative Governments from 1954 to 1959 when, following the General Election of that year, he was elected Speaker of the House of Commons. His death in office in 1965 created a minor crisis for the Labour Government which had a tiny majority at the time and which had been helped by the fact that Hylton-Foster had been a Tory and thus removed from the voting. He was replaced as Speaker by a Labour member, Horace King.

John Lindsay Eric Smith (Conservative) was elected at a by-election on 4th November 1965 following Hylton-Foster's death. He held the seat with a majority of 27%, only 1% down on the performance at the 1964 General Election. Born in 1923 and educated at Eton and New College, Oxford, Smith became a director of Rolls Royce, the *Financial Times* and other companies. He was a member of the executive of the National Trust and sat as a member of the Inland Waterways Redevelopment Committee (the latter from 1959-62), an advisory body established by the Ministry of Transport. Between 1957 and 1965, Smith was a member of the Standing Committee on Museums and Galleries and retired from politics in 1970. He died in 2007.

Sir Christopher Samuel Tugendhat (Conservative) replaced Smith at the 1970 General Election. Born in 1937, he was educated at Ampleforth College and Gonville and Caius Colleges Cambridge where he was President

Sir Christopher Tugendhat MP
University of Bath

of the University Union in 1960. A Director of Sunningdale Oils Ltd and Phillips Petroleum, both companies involved in the exploitation of oil and gas fields in the North Sea during this period, he was also an author and journalist. He served as MP until 1974 when the seat was recast as the City of London and Westminster South. He held it in both Elections of that year but resigned in 1977 when he was appointed a Conservative Commissioner of the European Community where he served simultaneously with Labour's Roy Jenkins, who became President of the Commission in that year. Tugendhat never resumed a Commons political career when he finished his spell in Brussels but returned to business instead being made Chairman of the Civil Aviation Authority then as a Lord becoming Chairman of the Abbey National until its takeover by the Spanish Banco de Santander in 2004. He was also a director of Blue Circle, British Oxygen and the Rio Tinto Corporation. He was Chancellor of Bath University 1998-2013.

St Marylebone

Sir Wavell Wakefield (Conservative) was elected MP in 1945 having sat for Swindon since 1935. Born in 1898 at Beckenham he was educated at Sedburgh School and Pembroke College, Cambridge, where he excelled at Rugby Union and went on to captain various teams including the University, Middlesex, the RAF, Harlequins and England. During the First World War he served in the Royal Flying Corp. He made his Rugby debut for his country against Wales in 1920 and captained England on 13 of the 31 occasions he turned out for them. A President of the Rugby Football Union to which post he was elected in 1950, he was an engineer turned director who sat on the executive of the National Union of Manufacturers. He was given a peerage as Baron Wakefield of Kendal in Harold Macmillan's 1963 resignation honours list and thereby a by-election was called. He died in 1983.

Quintin McGarrel Hogg (Conservative), formerly Lord Hailsham and son of the 1920s St Marylebone MP, Sir Douglas Hogg, announced his intention to renounce his peerage at the Conservative Party Conference held at the time of Macmillan's resignation. It was clear that his intention was to put his hat in the ring to become Prime Minister. Ironically, Lord Home, also a peer, was selected instead but Hailsham, by then Hogg once again, still contested and won the by-election on 5th December. He was re-elected at the subsequent general elections of 1964 and 1966 and remained in the Shadow Cabinet until the Party's victory in June 1970 when he resigned his seat to become Lord Hailsham once again, this time a Life Peer created by the Prime Minister, Edward Heath. Hailsham served in the 1970-4 Government as Lord Chancellor and again in Thatcher's Cabinet in the same role from 1979 until 1987, when he retired from front line politics. Born in 1907, he was educated at Eton and Oxford, where he was President of the University Union in 1929. He was later called to the bar and entered politics through a controversial by-election at Oxford where he was elected in 1938 on a pro-Chamberlain manifesto in the aftermath of the Munich agreement with Hitler. During the War he was commissioned in the Rifle Brigade in 1939, serving in the Middle East, and was wounded in the Western Desert in 1941. During the last weeks of the Wartime Coalition he was appointed joint Under-Secretary for Air, a post he retained in Churchill's caretaker Government until the Tories were defeated at the 1945 Election. In 1950, shortly after his re-election at Oxford, he succeeded as Viscount Hailsham. Sir Anthony Eden succeeded Churchill as Prime Minister and made Hailsham First Lord of the Admiralty in September 1956, and when Macmillan became Prime Minister a year later he entered the Cabinet for the first time, as Education Minister. Later in 1957 he was made Lord President of the Council, serving in that role until 1959 when he became Lord Privy Seal and Minister of Science. He reverted to Lord President in July 1960 but retained his Science portfolio, serving in both roles after his return to the Commons in 1963 until the Government's defeat in October 1964. He died in 2001.

Quintin Hogg (Viscount Hailsham)
© **National Portrait Gallery**
'Bern' Schwartz 1977

He was succeeded in 1970 by **Kenneth Wilfred Baker** (Conservative) who was born in 1934 and attended grammar schools in Southport and Hampton, St Paul's School and Magdalen College Oxford. From 1961 to 1963 he was a member of Twickenham Borough Council and first contested a Parliamentary election in 1964, at Poplar. He was defeated then and again in 1966 at Acton but following the death of its Labour MP won a by-election there two years later. He served on the Public Accounts Committee for a year from 1969 but was defeated at Acton in 1970. Hogg's elevation to the peerage after an unexpected Heath victory that year brought him quickly back as St Marylebone's MP a few weeks later. Baker won with a majority of 37%, which was 4% higher than Hogg's at the 1970 Election and two years later gained his first taste of Government as Parliamentary Secretary, at the Civil Service Department.

A 1970 by-election communication for Ken Baker MP in the St Marylebone Constituency, after Quintin Hogg MP had gone back to the Lords. **People's History Museum, Manchester**

Following Heath's General Election defeat in February 1974, Baker became his PPS for a year until 1975 and, perhaps because of his identification with the former PM, when Margaret Thatcher became Leader and later Prime Minister, it took him some time to resurrect his career. However, in 1981 he was made Minister of State for Industry and Information Technology and Local Government Minister in 1984 with specific responsibilities for the controversial proposal to abolish the Greater London Council. In the meantime, at the 1983 General Election, he had become MP for Mole Valley (centred on Dorking in Surrey), following boundary changes affecting Marylebone. In 1985 he was made Under Secretary at the Department of the Environment and joined the Cabinet as Secretary of State for Education and Science in 1986 becoming something of a Thatcher loyalist. He later served as Chancellor of the Duchy of Lancaster (and Tory Party Chairman) from 1989 to 1990 during which period Margaret Thatcher was compelled to resign. He served as Home Secretary in John Major's Government from 1990 to 1992 but when the Tories were re-elected in that year's General Election he refused the post of Welsh Secretary in John Major's Cabinet and retired in 1997 when he was made Lord Baker of Dorking.

Paddington North

Lt Gen Mason Macfarlane MP
Wikipedia

The first MP after the War was **Lieutenant - General Sir Frank Noel Mason – Macfarlane KCB, CB, DSO, MC** (Labour), who was born in 1889 and educated at Rugby School from where he entered the Royal Military Academy at Woolwich. He served in South Africa and India and in France, Belgium and Mesopotamia during the Great War. In 1919 he fought in the Afghan War joining the staff college at Quetta in 1920. Between 1931 and 1934 he was Military Attaché at Budapest, Vienna and Berne, joining the Imperial Defence College in 1935[1]. He was then successively the attaché at Berlin and Copenhagen between 1937 and 1939. He joined the British Expeditionary Force in 1939-40, was head of the British Military Mission to Moscow in 1941 and Governor-General of Gibraltar from 1942-44 when he became a member of the Allied Control Commission in Italy. In addition to his British War decorations he also held French and Russian orders. He took Paddington North from the Tory Minister, Brendan Bracken but only held the seat for a brief period, resigning in October 1946 to become Lieutenant-General Governor of Malta. He died in 1953.

The by-election following his resignation was won by **William James Field** (Labour), a department manager in a firm of food manufacturers, who held the seat until his resignation in 1953 following a criminal conviction for 'importuning for immoral purposes' in a West End public lavatory. Born in 1910, he was educated at Richmond County School and London University, entering active politics in 1945 when he was elected to Hammersmith Borough Council. In the same year he unsuccessfully contested Hampstead at the General Election but did reduce the Conservative majority from over 20,000 to 1,368. He served as Leader of Hammersmith Council from 1946 to 1949. He died in 2002.

Ben Parkin MP at a rally for CND
Stephen Theaker

Ben(jamin) Theaker Parkin (Labour) succeeded Field, winning the by-election caused by his resignation in 1953. Born in 1906, he was educated at Wycliffe College (Gloucestershire), Lincoln College Oxford and at Strasbourg University following which he became a schoolmaster, holding the post of headmaster of Stonehouse Council School, near Stroud (Gloucestershire), for some years. He served as a Flight Lieutenant in the RAF during the War and was afterwards elected MP for Stroud in 1945. In 1949 Parkin, with 64 other Labour MPs, received a formal warning from the Chairman of the Parliamentary Labour Party (PLP) and the Government Chief Whip regarding his conduct following the expulsion of two MPs and the dismissal of four parliamentary private secretaries for having voted against the Government on the Ireland Bill. After boundary changes

1 The College was founded in 1927 and was located at 9 Buckingham Gate until 1939. Its work was chiefly concerned with defence of the Empire, with 25 Members drawn from UK, Australia, Canada and New Zealand. The experience of the Second World War proved its benefits for training senior Service officers and after the War in 1946 the College reopened at Seaford House, Belgrave Square. The College was renamed The Royal College of Defence Studies in 1970.

he was defeated by just 28 votes in 1950 in the Stroud and Thornbury seat and lost again the following year. He briefly became a furniture manufacturer but served as a Paddington MP from 1953 until his death in 1969 and was an active campaigner against unscrupulous landlords who abused, exploited and evicted vulnerable tenants, many of who lived in his constituency. He coined the phrase 'Rachmanism' when exposing the activities of a particularly unscrupulous landlord, Peter Rachman, who operated in Paddington. Parkin believed the poverty and deprivation he witnessed there were partly caused by the series of 99-year leases which had been produced upon completion of the railway station in 1854 and were, therefore, due for renewal at that time. He sought redress for his constituents who were often tenants in poorly maintained, expensive, multiple occupancy dwellings. In 1968 he advocated the introduction of a licensing system for landlords that switched the onus of responsibility for ensuring that improvements were carried out from the local authority to the owner. He also called for measures to remove young prostitutes from the streets of Paddington. He died in 1969.

An election communication for Arthur Latham MP
People's History Museum, Manchester

Arthur Charles Latham (Labour) was elected at the December 1969 by-election that followed Parkin's death and served until 1974 when he became MP for the new, merged Paddington division of Westminster. Born in 1930, he was educated at Romford Royal Liberty School and the Garnett College of Education, a training centre for technical teachers opened in 1946 in North London as part of an emergency programme to train more teachers. He became a lecturer in further education at Southgate Technical College and was elected to Romford Borough Council in 1952 becoming an alderman in 1962. He was elected to Havering Council when it was created in 1964 and to the leadership of the Labour group. He contested the Woodford Parliamentary seat in 1959 and then the Rushcliffe division of Nottinghamshire in 1964. After his election at Paddington North he became leader of the Greater London Labour Party in 1977. He was defeated at the 1979 General Election and sought a return at Westminster North in 1983 but lost again.

Paddington South

Admiral Sir Ernest Augustus Taylor (Conservative), whose main biographical details are in Chapter 7, had been Conservative MP for Paddington South since 1930 and was re-elected in 1945 serving until his retirement in 1950.

He was succeeded by **Somerset de Chair** (Conservative), himself the son of an Admiral, who from 1935 to 1945 had been MP for South West Norfolk where he was elected at the early age of 24 but lost the seat in 1945. Educated at Kings School, New South Wales Australia, where his father was State Governor, and at Balliol College, Oxford, he served from 1942 as Parliamentary Private Secretary to Oliver Lyttleton, the Minister of Production during the War but prior to that had been wounded fighting in the 4th Cavalry Brigade. He was Vice Chairman of the Imperial Affairs Committee between 1950 and 1951 and active in the United Nations Association. He retired from politics in 1951. Born in 1911, he died in 1995.

Robert Alexander Allan (Conservative) sat from 1951 to 1964 when he retired. Born in 1914, he was educated at Harrow School (where he was a Rothschild Scholar), at Clare College Cambridge (where he was a Mellon Fellow), and at Yale University in the USA. During the War he served with the RNVR from 1939 until 1946 and was awarded several military honours, including the DSO, Croix de Guerre, Legion d'Honeur and the American Legion of Merit. He first contested a Parliamentary seat in 1945 at Dunbartonshire and was again unsuccessful at a by-election and in the General Election at West Dunbartonshire in 1950. Following his return at Paddington South he served as PPS to the Minister of State at the Colonial Office in 1952 and as an assistant Government whip after 1953. In 1958 he was appointed a Junior Minister at the Admiralty, then from 1959 to 1960 Under-Secretary at the Foreign Office when Selwyn Lloyd was Foreign Secretary. He retired from politics in 1966 and nine years later was made a life peer, Lord Allan of Kilmahew. He died in 1979.

Allan was succeeded in 1966 by **Sir Nicholas Paul Scott** (Conservative), a policeman's son who in 1963 became Chairman of the Young Conservatives. Born in 1933 he was educated at Clapham College and the City of London College following which he worked initially in marketing for Shell before becoming a director in a number of public relations companies. He served as a Holborn Borough councillor from 1956 to 1959 and contested Islington South West unsuccessfully twice, once in 1959 and then again in 1964. He was appointed Under-Secretary for Employment in the Heath Government just a few weeks before the February 1974 Election which the Tories lost. He also lost fighting the new combined Paddington constituency at the same election but at the October contest held later in the same year was elected MP for Chelsea. He was dropped by Margaret Thatcher when she became Tory leader in 1975 but in 1981 she appointed him an Under-Secretary to James Prior, the Northern Ireland Secretary, with whom he shared moderate

Left: *Barons Court Station, District Line (Underground) opened surrounded by fields in 1874, but the area developed rapidly, to be joined by the Piccadilly Line (tube) in 1906. Thus armed with such excellent connections local housing became well developed. When Hammersmith and Fulham seats were adjusted in 1955, it became a seat in its own right, sandwich between its two neighbours.*

Below: *Hesa Rd in Hayes shows the council housing in the northern part of the Hayes and Harlington Constituency, created in 1950. The tower block in the background was added later. Hesa Road is close to the Uxbridge Road, and within walking distance of a railway station; it was therefore a convenient location for building council houses.*

Below: *Murray Road in Northwood offers an example of mock Tudor in a rather splendid and well-to-do area of the Ruislip-Northwood Constituency, conveniently situated near to the Northwood Underground Station. The presence of such an Underground service so close made this a favoured area, with lots of green recreation space nearby.*

Above: *Harlington High St is a more tranquil setting in what was rapidly changing from a rural into an urban setting. This changed during the period of this chapter, as first the M4 Motorway was built through the Hayes and Harlington Constituency and second London's Heathrow Airport developed continuously, providing jobs for many in the area.*

Left: *South Drive in Ruislip has more mock Tudor, but this time in semi-detached form. These more affordable houses were sought after by the middle classes, and were a feature of the 1930s house building boom. These houses in the Ruislip-Northwood Constituency that was created in 1950 were popular from being so close to the Central Line Tube, extended to serve Ruislip in 1947.*

All images by John Nelson

views. He held this post until 1986 when he was promoted to Minister of State. After the 1987 Election victory he was made Minister of State for Social Security, in which post he succeeded John Major. When Major became Prime Minister in 1990 Scott retained the post including specific responsibilities for the disabled but his reputation as a progressive suffered in 1994 when he misled the House whilst seeking to undermine an all-party bill barring aspects of discrimination against disabled access and employment. His daughter publicly turned against him. Subsequently, in the run up to the 1997 General Election, he was involved in a driving incident in which his car struck a pram. Amid media speculation that he was drunk he announced his resignation paving the way for the return of Alan Clarke (Conservative). He died in 2005.

West London – Kensington, Chelsea, Hammersmith, Fulham, West Middlesex: (22 seats in 1945 and 25 seats after 1950)

In the Inter-War years a further huge expansion of the suburbs west of Ealing followed the extensions of the Central Line to Ealing Broadway in the 1920s and West Ruislip in the 30s. The building of several new trunk roads sponsored by the Ministry of Transport in the early 1920s, partly as a public works response to rising unemployment, also had a significant impact. The Great West Road between Gunnersbury towards Hanwell and Hounslow, the Western Avenue from East Acton to Greenford, and the North Circular from Park Royal to the North, all had the effect of stimulating both industrial and residential development. These developments brought about substantial changes to the shape of outer suburban constituencies in both 1945 and 1950. In the last pre-War General Election there had been 16 MPs in this area but the number was increased to 22 in 1945 and to 25 in 1950.

The alterations made in 1945 were especially substantial, though not in the area immediately west of Westminster and Paddington, which retained its seven former constituencies in 1945 and 1950 but lost one of these in 1955. **Chelsea, Fulham East, Fulham West, Hammersmith North, Hammersmith South, Kensington North** and **Kensington South** were unaltered in 1945 (see Chapter 7 for details) and in 1950 boundaries were little changed there being one minor switch involving Chelsea, which acquired the Brompton ward from Kensington South. However, in 1955 the four Hammersmith and Fulham constituencies were merged and divided three ways involving the loss of one seat and the creation of an intermediate constituency called **Barons Court,** which extended from Ravenscourt on both sides of Hammersmith Broadway and south to Lillie Road in Fulham. Officially it comprised the Fulham wards of Baron's Court, Margravine and Lillie together with the Hammersmith wards of Broadway, Brook Green, Grove and Ravenscourt. Within its boundaries were West Kensington and Olympia. A new **Fulham** constituency covered the area southwards to the Thames incorporating five borough wards – Hurlingham, Munster, Sands End, Town and Walham which also embraced Eel Brook Common and Parsons Green.

Hammersmith North incorporated the areas north of the Broadway to Old Oak Common including Shepherds Bush, White City and Wormwood Scrubs. Its nine wards were Addison, College Park & Latimer, Conigham, Old Oak, Olympia, St Stephen's, Starch Green, White City and Wormholt.

In 1945 Ealing was divided into two new constituencies, **Ealing East** and **Ealing West** but five years later was split differently. The 1945 boundaries placed Ealing, Ealing Common, Little Ealing and Perivale in Ealing East, with Ealing West comprising Castle Bar, Drayton Park, North Ealing, Greenford, Greenford Park, Horsenden, Northfields and Northolt. However, the re-allocation brought about significant changes five years later. In 1950 **Ealing North** extended from Northolt to Hanger Hill including North Ealing, Greenford, Greenford Park, Horsenden and Perivale whilst **Ealing South** covered all central districts of the town, including the Broadway and Common, plus Castle Bar, Drayton Green, Little Ealing and Northfields. **Acton** was untouched in both reviews..

Another seat added in 1945 was **Heston & Isleworth**, a new municipal borough that had been created in 1932. Carved out of the former Twickenham constituency, the new seat covered Cranford near Heathrow Airport, the fast developing town of Hounslow, which lay between the two places from which the constituency got its name, together with Osterley Park, Spring Grove and Syon Park. Heston was by then unrecognisable as the small agricultural village, famous for the high quality of its wheat in centuries past. The earliest form of the name, noted in 1125, was 'Hestone', meaning 'a farm among brushwood'. Neighbouring Isleworth, a riverside settlement from prehistoric times, was well established by the time of the Norman Conquest in the 11th century. The earliest form of the name was 'Gislhaesuuyrth' (AD 677) meaning, 'Gilhere's settlement'. This idyllic landscape was unrecognisable by the early 20th Century. On the borders between Heston and Cranford was Heston Airport, operational between 1929 and 1946. It was there in 1938 that the then Prime Minister, Neville Chamberlain, landed after signing the Munich Agreement with Adolf Hitler.

Twickenham remained to cover the whole of the former UDC granted borough status in 1926 and **Brentford & Chiswick** too was unaltered.

Uxbridge was changed in both 1945 and 1950. In all no less than three constituencies were created from the former county division. First **Southall** was created in 1945 based on the municipal borough of that name created in 1936 from the former Southall-Norwood District Council that had existed since 1894. The new constituency embraced Dormers Wells, Hyde Green, Mount Pleasant and Norwood Park from the Urban District together with the Hanwell wards of Ealing borough which included Elthorne Heights. Southall derives its modern name from the Old English 'Suhaull' meaning 'southern nook of land', as distinct from nearby Northolt, which, as 'Northealum' in 960 AD, meant the 'northern nook of land'. **Uxbridge** was thus reduced in size in 1945 but was still geographically large incorporating Botwell, Cowley, Dawley, Eastcote, Harefield, Hayes, Hillingdon, Ickenham, Northolt Park, Northwood, Northwood Hills, all districts of Ruislip, West Drayton, Wood End, Yeading and Yiewsley.

Two more new seats were extracted from Uxbridge in 1950, with the addition of some elements coming from Spelthorne. **Hayes & Harlington** comprised the unified Urban District created in 1934. This extended west of next-door Ealing and Southall, ran south to the boundary with Heston and included Heathrow, which was only then starting to develop as the UK's major Airport replacing the Heston and Northolt airfields nearby. Harlington and Heathrow were transferred from Spelthorne and combined with Botwell, Dawley, Hayes, Wood End and Yeading from Uxbridge. The name 'Hayes' is derived from 'Hesa', which in Saxon times was a brushwood enclosure used as a trap for deer and in 790 King Offa granted lands there to the Archbishop of Canterbury, and for more than seven centuries the place was closely associated with the See. Hayes itself had been created an Urban District in 1904 and Harlington had been a parish within the Staines Rural District until 1934.

North of Hayes and between Uxbridge and Harrow West was the new, wealthy, outer suburban constituency of **Ruislip & Northwood,** comprising the UDC (established in 1904) that included Eastcote. Other communities included were Northolt Park and Northwood Hills. The Abbey of Bec Herlewin in Normandy, originally held the Manor of Ruislip, where there was a cell of the Order, but the Manor was later seized by Henry V and granted as part of the endowment of King's College, Cambridge. Sale of the lands enabled modern housing developments to take place. Population had grown between the Wars from less than 10,000 in 1921 to nearly 50,000 in 1938, enabled by the extension of the tube lines to Uxbridge.

In 1950 **Uxbridge** was therefore further reduced to comprise the then Uxbridge and Yiewsley & West Drayton UDCs that included Cowley, Harefield, Harmondsworth (transferred from Spelthorne), Hillingdon, Ickenham and West Drayton. Five years later Uxbridge was designated a borough. The transfers from **Spelthorne** to Uxbridge and Hayes & Harlington meant that this constituency was also reduced in size in 1950 and comprised Ashford, Bedfont, Feltham, Halliford, Hanworth, Hatton Cross, Kempton Park, Laleham, Shepperton, Staines and Sunbury-on-Thames.

Spelthorne was altered again in 1955. As Heathrow Airport developed in the immediate vicinity and housing estates were built away from the old London suburbs, this part of outer London began to develop rapidly. Carved out of Spelthorne, a new **Feltham** seat based on the UDC also incorporated the Cranford and Hounslow Heath wards transferred from **Heston & Isleworth,** which was modified accordingly. Feltham incorporated Bedfont, Hanworth and Hatton Cross, transferred from **Spelthorne** which itself covered the Staines and Sunbury UDC's that included several wealthy Thames-side communities. Overall it embraced Ashford, Halliford, Kempton Park, Laleham, Shepperton, Staines and Sunbury-on-Thames, outside Greater London today.

Major expansion of North West Middlesex brought about big changes there in 1945. Harrow, which was created an Urban District in 1934, had gained 134,480 new residents since the Great War, the largest influx of any local authority in Greater London. The building by the Metropolitan Railway of two new electric lines, one towards Uxbridge/Watford and Amersham in 1925 and the other to Stanmore in 1932, brought about substantial property development in the years that followed. The Metropolitan Country Estates Company Limited acted as a housing developer in places around Pinner and Harrow. Population growth followed and in 1945 the former constituency was split into two divisions. **Harrow East** comprised Harrow Weald, Kenton, Queensbury, Stanmore and Wealdstone whilst **Harrow West** took in Greenhill, Harrow-on-the-Hill, Harrow, West Harrow, Hatch End, Headstone, Pinner, Rayners Lane and Roxeth.

Despite these alterations, Harrow was still under-represented and in 1950 further changes were made. **Harrow Central,** a new third seat, extended from Harrow-on-the Hill northwards to Wealdstone. Officially it comprised five wards of the Harrow UDC – Harrow-on-the Hill & Greenhill, Headstone, Wealdstone North and South, and West Harrow. Consequential changes affected the other two seats. **Harrow East** covered the area north and east of Wealdstone from Harrow Weald to Stanmore and south to Queensbury. Officially it comprised three and a half wards – Kenton, Stanmore North and South and part of Harrow Weald. **Harrow West** covered two Pinner wards (North and South), Roxeth and the rest of Harrow Weald. It included Hatch End, South Harrow and Rayners Lane. In 1955 a

Right: *These comfortable, mixed, semi-detached and terraced properites were originally built as council houses. In Syon Lane they are very well situated, near to the Great West Road and commuter railway station on the Hounslow Loop. The area was placed in the Heston & Isleworth Constituency created in 1945.*

Below: *These desirable semi-rural style bungalows in Slough Lane, Kingsbury, were placed in the Wembley North constituency in 1945. The area is predominated by post-War semi detached housing but in a leafy suburb. The houses back on to a large green recreational space, all near to the M1, several Underground and main railway lines, as well as not being far from Brent Reservoir.*

Below: *Valencia Road Stanmore is populated with affluent, detached houses of varied designs, in the Harrow East Consituency. It is bordered by the Stanmore Country Park in one direction, and a short walk away is the terminus of the Jubilee Line Tube at Stanmore. By any standard this is a desirable area in which to live.*

Above: *The white brick Southall Town Hall designed by Thomas Newall, was built in 1897 as the centre of local government in the area. It was the place where election results were announced for the new Borough's constituency, created in 1945. Its function as a town hall ceased in 1965. From 1950 Southall gradually established one of the largest settlements of South Asians outside India.*

Right: *Rayners Lane Station in the Harrow West Constituency has since 1933 offered a rapid and frequent service of Metropolitan and Piccadilly Line Underground services into London. The station has been instrumental in stimulating substantial residential development in the area.* **Wikipedia**

Photos John Nelson, except where marked

minor alteration was made with the transfer of Headstone from Harrow Central to **Harrow West** and of Kenton from **Harrow East** to **Harrow Central**.

The development of Wembley between the Wars brought about an increase in the local population of 552% leading to the creation of two more new constituencies formed out of Harrow in 1945 with no further alterations made until 1974. West of the Edgware Road and south of Harrow, **Wembley North** extended from South Kenton on the Harrow border, north to Kingsbury and south to Preston Road including Fryent, Northwick Park and Roe Green. **Wembley South** extended south from Kenton and west of Preston Road to include Wembley Central, Wembley Park, Sudbury and Alperton. The two **Willesden** seats (**East** and **West**) were unchanged.

Electorates

The difficulties faced by the Boundary Commission in maintaining a proper balance of electorates in the face of major population changes are well illustrated by the situation in West Middlesex during the period from 1950 to 1970. In the 1950s constituencies varied considerably in the size of their electorates. Throughout the period only Ealing and Southall had electorates that were close to the average for London[2]. In Acton, Brentford & Chiswick, Hayes & Harlington, Ruislip - Northwood and Uxbridge electorates were relatively small whilst in Heston & Isleworth, Spelthorne and Twickenham they were larger, although Spelthorne's was substantially reduced after Feltham was established in 1955. Between 1950 and 1970 Acton and Brentford & Chiswick got even smaller. The latter, which began in 1950 as the West London constituency with the smallest electorate (43,854) lost 14% of voters by 1970 when there were fewer than 38,000 on the register. It started the period with an electorate that was 25% below the average and ended it 31% below. Meanwhile Acton, which began with an electorate of nearly 50,000 lost 13% and by 1970 had an electorate of less than 44,000. Starting the period 13% below average it finished 21% below.

Ealing North and South had similar sized electorates in 1950. With just under 58,000 voters Ealing North was barely 1% below the London average whilst at just under 59,000 Ealing North was 1% above it. However, over the 20 years that followed Ealing North increased its electorate by 11% while Ealing South lost 9%. By 1970 Ealing North had over 10,000 more voters on its register than Ealing South, which fell below 54,000 at that election. In 1970 North had an electorate that was 16% above average whilst South's was 2% below. Southall's electorate in 1950 was nearly 61,000, about 4% above average and although over the next 20 years the total fell by 8%, in 1970 it was still above average, though by only 2%. Neighbouring Hayes & Harlington had an electorate of less than 44,000 in 1950 but in 1970 it was close to 50,000, an increase of 13%. Despite this it still 10% below the average London constituency, although this was substantially better than the 25% variation that had existed when it was first established in 1950.

Spelthorne had an electorate of over 70,000 in 1950, 20% higher than the average but after the separation from Feltham in 1955 it fell to 46,000. It ceased to be a constituency covering the Greater London area as it is defined for the purposes of this book, and consequently Spelthorne is not included for comparative purposes after 1955. Heston & Isleworth's 1950 electorate was over 77,000 and about one third above the average but the creation of Feltham reduced it to below 57,000 in 1955, which was only 1% higher than the average for that election. The electorate did fall very slightly thereafter but the 1970 total of 54,000 was still only 3% below the average. By contrast Feltham grew 19% after it was established with an electorate of nearly 51,000 in 1955. Although this was 10% lower than the average London constituency by 1970 it had grown to 60,000, or 10% higher.

Twickenham maintained a remarkable consistency throughout the period in question. Its electorate in 1950 was nearly 77,000 and at no election in the next 20 years did the number fall below 70,000. Indeed in relation to the average size of electorate in London constituencies as a whole Twickenham always had about one third more voters on its register. Between 1950 and 1970 the register at each election contained between 32% and 34% more electors than the average constituency.

Just like nearby Spelthorne, Uxbridge and Ruislip-Northwood both grew strongly between 1950 and 1970. The greater growth occurred in Uxbridge where the 1950 electorate of 49,000 (15% below average) expanded by 28% to reach 63,000 (15% above). In Ruislip-Northwood the electorate expanded by 20% from 45,500 (22% below the average) to 55,000 (1% below) over the same period.

In North West Middlesex the electorates established in 1950 declined in most of the constituencies over the next 20 years, the exception being Harrow West where residential development continued. The two Willesden constituencies had a combined electorate of 129,000 in 1950, the larger being the West division, which had 67,000 voters, about

2 The averages were 58,500 in 1950, 56,300 in 1955 and 55,000 in 1970.

Post War General Election Results 1945 to 1970 by % majority

Constituency	Pre 1945	1945	1950	1951	1955	1959	1964	1966	1970
Chelsea	C	C33	C37	C40	C47	C47	C36	C32	C42
Kensington North	C	Lab21	Lab8	Lab10	Lab8	Lab3	Lab8	Lab18	Lab14
Kensington South	C	C51+	C55	C59	C65	C61	C51	C45+	C52
Fulham East	C	Lab19	Lab7	Lab6					
Fulham West	C	Lab24	Lab7	Lab7					
Fulham					Lab10	Lab7	Lab14	Lab20	Lab12
Hammersmith North	C/Lab	ILP38	Lab9	Lab32	Lab22	Lab19	Lab26	Lab38	Lab25
Hammersmith South	C	Lab16+	Lab7	Lab9					
Barons Court					Lab0.4	C2	Lab4	Lab11	Lab4
Acton	C	Lab21	Lab6	Lab4	Lab1	C2	Lab18	Lab15-	Lab2
Ealing East	C	C9							
Ealing West		C34							
Ealing North			Lab5	Lab0.2	C0.4	C8	Lab0.1	Lab5	Lab0.7
Ealing South			C23	C25	C29+	C31	C22	C14	C21
Southall		Lab41	Lab17	Lab16	Lab14	Lab5	Lab5	Lab14	Lab12
Brentford & Chiswick	C	Lab15	C2	C4	C6	C9	C2	Lab2	Lab2
Twickenham	C	C6	C21	C24+	C28	C29	C22	C14	C22
Heston & Isleworth		Lab12	C7	C8	C15	C20	C9	C2	C12
Spelthorne	C	Lab16	C0.0	C2					
Feltham					Lab8	Lab5	Lab14	Lab20	Lab14
Hayes & Harlington			Lab30	Lab30+	Lab18	Lab11	Lab20	Lab27	Lab16+
Uxbridge	C	Lab2	Lab6	Lab4	Lab2	C2	C1	Lab2	C8+
Ruislip & Northwood			C24	C27	C30	C32	C24	C18	C32
Harrow Central			C15	C19	C20	C26	C13	C5	C12
Harrow (East)	C	Lab11	C3	C6	C9+	C14	C6	Lab1	C11
Harrow West		C17	C29+	C35	C40	C42+	C29	C24	C32
Wembley North		Lab1	C17	C20	C25	C28	C17	C12	C18
Wembley South		Lab10	C9	C12	C17	C20	C13	C4	C16
Willesden East	C	Lab21	Lab6	Lab4	Lab1	C5	Lab5	Lab18	Lab13
Willesden West	Lab	Lab44	Lab29	Lab29	Lab24	Lab17	Lab29	Lab40	Lab36
C	14/15	6+	13+	13+	13++	17+	13	10+	12+
ILP/ Lab	1/2	16+	12	12+	11	7	11	14-	12+
Total	16	22++	25+	25++	24++	24+	24	24+-	24++

Key: C = Conservative; Lab = Labour; ILP = Independent Labour; + = Party that won seat at General Election held by-election in same Parliament; - = Party that won seat at General Election lost by-election to main opposition Party in same Parliament.

5,000 more than East. Both were larger than the London average, East by 7% and West by 15%. However, there was a progressive decline in the two electorates and, even counting the under 21s who were enfranchised latterly, 1970 saw the lowest numbers in both constituencies. East dropped to 57,000 (4% above the average) and West to 55,000 (exactly on the average).The two Wembley constituencies also lost voters. Each had been allocated virtually identical electoral numbers in 1950 with 193 voters being the difference between the two totals. However, each was 13% below the London area average containing a couple of hundred electors fewer than 49,000. Both constituencies lost electors over the next 20 years, although the 8% drop in the roll in Wembley South was greater than the 2% experienced in Wembley North. By 1970 Wembley North's electorate of 48,000 was 13% below the London average whilst in Wembley South slightly fewer than 45,000 meant that the constituency was about 19% below.

The Harrow constituencies also contained relatively small electorates in 1950. Harrow West was smallest with fewer than 47,000 voters (20% below average) whilst Harrow East was the largest with close to 61,000 (4% above). Harrow Central lived up to its designation by having 51,000, a figure between the sizes of the other two (13% below average). The ward exchanges that occurred in 1955 were intended to balance the electorates more evenly and at the General Election in that year this was achieved. Central, East and West constituencies each had respectively 50,000, 50,000 and 55,000 electors compared with the average for London, which was 56,300 in 1955. Thereafter disparities began to occur once again as Central lost 9% of its electoral total between 1955 and 1970 compared with growth rates of 2% and 5% in East and West respectively. In 1970 Harrow West had grown to become the largest constituency and with 57,000 was almost exactly the size of the average London constituency. Harrow East had 50,000, which was 11% below average and Central had only 46,000, which was 17% below average.

Politics in West London between 1945 and 1970

Labour improved its position significantly in this part of Middlesex after the War. From an average of less than two seats won in General Elections between 1918 and 1935, they improved their position to average just less than twelve in all General Elections between 1945 and 1970. Whilst the Tories only seriously under performed in one post War election (in 1945) they won on average just under 13 seats, which compared with an average of near 15 in the Inter-War years. In fact only in 1959 did they secure more seats than they had averaged before the War. Whilst it might appear that Labour was the principal beneficiary of the post war boundary changes, in fact the socio-economic profile of West London was changing to produce a mix of industrial and residential developments, some of which favoured the Conservatives, others Labour. Overall it is probable that the shifting mood of the electorate, rather more than the boundary changes influenced the outcome of elections in the period.

The continuing movement of middle class voters away from the less fashionable suburbs meant that places like Fulham, North Kensington and Hammersmith became rather more working class and Labour-voting in character than they had been before the War, although the wealthy districts of Chelsea and South Kensington preserved their overwhelmingly middle and upper class, Conservative supporting electorates. Outer Middlesex remained largely suburban and middle class but significant pockets of industry, the growth of Heathrow Airport and the building of council houses meant that there were several constituencies in which Labour could expect to do well. This latter group included established seats at Acton and Willesden and new ones in Southall, Feltham and Hayes & Harlington (all close to Heathrow), whilst the Tories could rely on suburban constituencies like Twickenham, Ealing South and Harrow West.

Some of the social and economic changes affected certain constituencies in ways that made them very interesting politically. Ealing North and Brentford & Chiswick became marginal seats and were joined by Barons Court in 1955. Elsewhere a combination of boundary and demographic changes brought about safe seats, mostly Tory. These included Spelthorne, Harrow Central and West, Wembley North and South, Heston & Isleworth and Ruislip & Northwood, the creation of which also transformed Uxbridge into a very marginal seat during this period.

At all Parliamentary General Elections held between 1945 and 1970 the Tories won 97 seats and Labour 95, itself illustrative of the closeness of the contest in this part of Middlesex. Having said that Labour only came out on top in two of the eight General Elections held in the period. Both were landslides, in 1945 and 1966. Tories beat Labour in 6 contests, 2 of them being occasions when Labour formed Governments, in 1950 and 1964. In addition there were 12 by-elections held during the period of which 9 were won by the Conservatives and 3 by Labour. Only one seat changed hands, namely Acton at a 1968 by-election when the Tories took the seat only to lose it again at the 1970 General Election.

MPs for Kensington and Chelsea

Chelsea

Commander Allan Noble (Conservative) was elected at a by-election in 1944 and continued to serve as Chelsea's MP until he retired in 1959. His principal biographical details can be found in Chapter 7.

He was succeeded by another military man, **Captain John Shirley Sandys Litchfield RN** (Conservative). Born in 1903, he was educated at the Royal Naval Colleges at Osborne (Isle of Wight) and Dartmouth after which he became a regular naval officer, serving continuously in the senior service from 1917 until his retirement in 1955. From 1951 to 1953 he was captain of the battleship *HMS Vanguard* and Director, Naval operations in 1953-4. A member of Lloyds, when he entered civilian life in 1955 he was elected to Kent County Council (1955-8) and was chairman of the Maidstone

MPs for Kensington and Chelsea						
From	**at**	**To**	**Surname**	**First Names**	**Constituency**	**Party**
1945	*G*	*1959*	*Noble*	*Allan Herbert Percy (Commander)*	*Chelsea*	*Conservative*
1959	*G*	*1966*	*Litchfield*	*John Shirley Sandys (Captain RN)*		*Conservative*
1966	*G*	*1974*	*Worsley*	*Sir (William) Marcus John*		*Conservative*
1945	*G*	*1970*	*Rogers*	*George Henry Roland*	*Kensington North*	*Labour*
1970	*G*	*1974*	*Douglas-Mann*	*Bruce Leslie Home*		*Labour*
1945	*G*	*1945*	*Davison*	*Sir William Henry*	*Kensington South*	*Conservative*
1945	*B*	*1950*	*Law*	*Richard Kidston*		*Conservative*
1950	*G*	*1959*	*Spens*	*Sir (William) Patrick*		*Conservative*
1959	*G*	*1968*	*Roots*	*William Lloyd*		*Conservative*
1968	*B*	*1974*	*Rhys-Williams*	*Sir Brandon*		*Conservative*
NOTE First returned at a B = By-election; G =General Election						

Division Conservative Party for a year before his election to Parliament. He retired in 1966. He died in 1993.

Sir (William) Marcus John Worsley (Conservative), brother of the Duchess of Kent, was elected in 1966. He had contested Keighley (West Riding of Yorkshire) at the 1955 Election and in addition to being a farmer / landowner was director of an investment trust. He did win Keighley in 1959 but was defeated again in 1964. Born in 1925 he was educated at Eton and New College Oxford and from 1950-53 was a programme assistant for the BBC European Service. As an MP he was Chairman of the Conservative Health and Social Security Committee (1972) and of the Greater London Committee of his Party's MPs. He was additionally a Second Church Estates Commissioner. He retired from politics in October 1974 and became the Lord Lieutenant of North Yorkshire where he lived at Hovingham Hall. He died in 2012.

Kensington North

George Henry Roland Rogers (Labour) took the seat from the Conservatives in 1945 and held it until 1970 when he retired. He was born in Princes Risborough, Buckinghamshire in 1906 but his family moved to Willesden where he was educated at Elementary and Middlesex County Council Schools. He joined the railways as a clerk and in 1937 became a member of Wembley Borough Council, retiring in 1941 and joining the Royal Corps of Signals in 1942, becoming a Corporal. Once an MP he became Vice Chairman of the Labour Party's Parliamentary Transport Group and also took an interest in Defence matters. From 1947 to 1949 he was PPS to George Strauss, Minister of Supply, but resigned after voting against the Government's Ireland Bill. However, the following year he resumed a PPS role, this time to the Minister of State in the same department. Following Labour's 1951 defeat he became a Whip, a post he retained as a Junior Lord of the Treasury after the Party resumed office in 1964 but he was replaced in January 1966 and retired in 1970. He died in 1983.

People's History Museum, Manchester

Bruce Leslie Home Douglas-Mann (Labour) was elected as Rogers' successor. Born in June 1927, he was educated in Canada and at Jesus College, Oxford before embarking on a career as a solicitor working for trade unions as a specialist in industrial accident legislation and case law. He contested St Albans in 1964 and Maldon (Essex) two years later, but was unsuccessful. His North seat was merged with Kensington South in 1974 the year he was made Minister of State for Housing. He transferred to Mitcham & Morden, which he retained until 3rd June 1982 when he lost it at a by-election precipitated by his own decision (alone amongst Labour defectors to the Social Democratic Party) to resign his seat and fight under his new Party colours. His decision split the Left wing vote and saw the return of a Conservative who went on to hold the seat for 15 years. He died in 2000.

Kensington South

Sir William Davison (Conservative), who's biographical details are contained in Chapter 7, was first elected in 1918, retained the seat in 1945, but three months after the General Election resigned to make way at a November by-election for **Richard Kidston Law** (Conservative) who had been defeated in the General Election at South West Hull, which he had represented since 1931. Born in 1901 and the son of the former Tory Prime Minister Bonar Law, he was educated at Shrewsbury School and St John's College Oxford before becoming a journalist with *The Morning Post, The New York Herald Tribune* and other newspapers. During the War he was Financial Secretary at the War Office from May 1940 to July 1941 when he was appointed Under-Secretary of State at the Foreign Office under Anthony Eden, a post he occupied until 1943 when he was made Minister of State for European relief. He was made a Privy Councillor in the same year and, following the resumption of normal Party politics in the run up to the 1945 election, he was appointed Minister of Education in Churchill's Caretaker Cabinet but held the post for only a matter of weeks. He sat for South Kensington in only one Parliament, transferring back to his former constituency, renamed Haltemprice but reconstituted as a safe Tory seat, which he held until 1954 when he was made the 1st Lord Coleraine, reflecting his family's Ulster affiliations.

Law was succeeded at Kensington South in 1950 by **Sir (William) Patrick Spens** (Conservative), who was formerly the MP for Ashford (Kent) from 1933 to 1943 when he stood down to become Chief Justice of India, a post he held until that country's independence in1947. Born in 1885, Sir Patrick was educated at Rugby School and New College Oxford prior to being called to the Bar of the Inner Temple in 1910. Following his judicial role in India he was appointed Chairman of the arbitration tribunal that investigated partition disputes between India and Pakistan but in 1948 returned to England and took up a number of Company Directorships, including Prudential Assurance and the Bank of Scotland. He was also a director of the Southern Railway for a while before it was nationalized. He retired from the Commons in 1959, was elevated to the peerage and died in 1973

William Lloyd Roots QC (Conservative) who succeeded Spens and who had unsuccessfully contested Brixton in 1955, was born in 1911 and served as the MP until 1968 when he resigned. He was educated at Tonbridge School and Brasenose College, Oxford, then was called to the bar at the Middle Temple in 1933 and later took silk, specialising in local government and administrative law. During the War he served as a major in the Surrey and Sussex Yeomanry in Tobruk and the Western Desert Campaigns. He was an alderman of Kensington Borough Council and a sometime leader of his Party there. He was also the director of a brewery.

Sir Brandon Rhys-Williams MP
The town of Llantrisant

Roots was succeeded by **Sir Brandon Rhys-Williams** (Conservative), who was born in 1927 and educated at Eton College. He worked originally for the ICI Company and from 1962-3 was Assistant Director (Appeals) for what was then known as the Spastics Society but which today goes under the name of 'Scope'. He then became a management consultant. A Welshman, he contested Pontypridd in 1959 and Ebbw Vale (Monmouthshire) in the 1960 by-election that followed the death of Aneurin Bevan and which was won by the future Labour leader, Michael Foot. He contested the same seat in 1964 but his reward for fighting seemingly hopeless constituencies was his adoption as the Tory candidate in the safe South Kensington division, which he represented from 1968 until 1974 when he was adopted as the Party's candidate to fight the newly merged Kensington seat, which he won. In the same year he became a Tory member of the European Parliament and in 1979 was directly elected to the same body as the MEP for South East London, which he represented until 1984. He died in 1988 whilst still an MP.

MPs for Fulham, and Hammersmith

Fulham East, Fulham

Michael Stewart MP
© National Portrait Gallery
Bassano Ltd 1959

(Robert) Michael Stewart (Labour) was new to Fulham East in 1945, defeating the Conservative incumbent. Born in 1906 and educated at Elementary School, Christ's Hospital School and St John's College Oxford, where he was President of the Union in 1929, he obtained a First Class Honours Degree (BA). As an undergraduate he joined the Labour Party and was chairman of the University Labour Club. He obtained his MA in1934 and became a WEA[3] lecturer and schoolteacher, first at Merchant Taylors' and then at the Cooper's Company School. He entered front line politics in 1931 when he unsuccessfully contested Lewisham West, a performance he repeated in 1935. During the War he served in the Army Intelligence Corps and was commissioned as a Captain. After the War he entered Parliament and soon embarked upon a successful Ministerial career. His first post was as Vice-Chamberlain and Comptroller of His Majesty's Household (1946-7), then Under-Secretary for War (1947-51) during which period Britain was engaged in the Korean hostilities. Meanwhile, he was adopted for the single Fulham seat in 1950 and

3 The Workers' Educational Association, founded in 1903 to support the educational needs of working men and women is still the UK's largest voluntary provider of adult education.

MPs for Fulham, and Hammersmith						
From	*at*	*To*	*Surname*	*First Names*	*Constituency*	*Party*
1945	*G*	*1950*	*Stewart*	*(Robert) Michael*	*Fulham East*	*Labour*
1945	*G*	*1950*	*Summerskill*	*Dr. Edith*	*Fulham West*	*Labour*
1950	*G*	*1974*	*Stewart*	*(Robert) Michael*	*Fulham*	*Labour*
1945	*G*	*1950*	*Pritt*	*Denis Nowell*	*Hammersmith North*	*Independent Labour*
1950	*G*	*1974*	*Tomney*	*Frank*		*Labour*
1945	*G*	*1948*	*Adams*	*William Thomas*	*Hammersmith South*	*Labour*
1949	*B*	*1955*	*Williams*	*(Sir) (William) Thomas*		*Labour*
1955	*G*	*1959*	*Williams*	*(Sir) (William) Thomas*	*Barons Court*	*Labour*
1959	*G*	*1964*	*Carr*	*(William) Compton*		*Conservative*
1964	*G*	*1974*	*Richard*	*Ivor Seward*		*Labour*
NOTE First returned at a B = By-election; G =General Election						

continued to serve as its MP until his retirement in 1979. Stewart served on the Labour front bench during the Party's 13 years in Opposition from 1951 to 1964 and when Wilson's government was formed he entered the Cabinet for the first time, as Secretary of State for Education and Science. However, within a matter of only four months he was appointed Foreign Secretary when Wilson's preferred selection, Patrick Gordon-Walker, failed twice to secure election to the Commons. In August 1966 Stewart was switched with George Brown, Deputy Party Leader, to the role of First Secretary of State (Economic Affairs) but two years later, when Brown resigned from the Government, Stewart returned to the Foreign Office which by then also included Commonwealth Affairs and remained there until Labour's 1970 defeat. When Wilson returned to Government in February 1974 he did not find a place in it for Stewart who remained a backbencher until he retired in 1979 and was made a Life Peer, Lord Stewart of Fulham. He died in 1989.

Fulham West

Dr. Edith Summerskill (Labour) was MP from 1938 until the abolition of the seat in 1950. Her principal biographical details are contained in Chapter 7 (Fulham). She retired from the Commons as MP for Warrington in 1961 and was succeeded as the MP there by another former West London MP, Thomas Williams (see Hammersmith South below).

Hammersmith North

Denis Nowell Pritt (Independent Labour) was first elected as a Labour MP in 1935 and he remained in the Commons until his defeat in 1950. His principal biographical details may be found in Chapter 7 (Hammersmith).

An election leaflet for Frank Tomney
People's History Museum Manchester

He lost his seat in 1950, coming fourth to **Frank Tomney** (Labour) who went on to hold it until he retired in 1979. Born in 1910, Tomney had an elementary and technical school education after which he became a glass blower. It was through this trade that he entered active trade unionism as branch secretary of the Municipal and General Workers in Watford. He came into politics via the union route, joined the Labour Party in 1925 and became a member of both Watford Borough and Hertfordshire County Councils. He was an active member of both the Co-operative and (latterly) European Movements. He was a delegate to the Western European Union twice, from 1960-4 and again in 1973-4. This was established in 1955 as a consultative forum for military issues among the Western European governments.

Hammersmith South and Barons Court

William Thomas Adams (Labour) took the seat from the Conservatives in 1945 but held it for only three years until his death in 1948. Born in 1884 he had a London School Board education, became a clerk and joined the Clerical and Administrative Workers Union. He was elected to Hammersmith Borough Council and became leader of its Labour Group before being elected a local MP.

Adams was succeeded at a February 1949 by-election by **(Sir) (William)Thomas Williams** (Labour), a barrister, who was born in 1915, the son of a coal miner, and educated at Aberdare Grammar School, at Cardiff and Oxford (St Catherine's) Universities, and subsequently at Lincoln's Inn. He was a Baptist Minister and chaplain as well as welfare officer with the RAF during the Second World War. From 1946 to 1949 he was a tutor at Manchester College, Oxford and after becoming an MP was PPS to the Minister of Pensions in 1950 and to the Minister of Health, 1950-1. In 1955 he was adopted to fight Barons Court when his seat was abolished. Although returned for the new constituency he was defeated there in 1959 and was out of Parliament for two years, returning in 1961 at a by-election held at Warrington following the ennoblement of Edith Summerskill. He represented Warrington for twenty years, was Recorder of Birkenhead from 1969-71 and, during the same period, Chairman of the Labour Group of Co-operative MPs. A member of the National Union of Teachers, he was also President of the World Council of the International Parliamentary Union. He died in 1981 when still an MP.

(William) Compton Carr (Conservative) sat in just one Parliament for Barons Court, from 1959 to 1964, when he was defeated. Born in 1918, he was educated at The Leys, Cambridge and became a solicitor and company director. Co-opted to the LCC Education Committee in 1955, he was elected an alderman the following year, serving until 1958. He was elected an alderman once again in 1961.

Ivor Richard MP
The town of Ammanford

Compton was defeated by **Ivor Seward Richard** (Labour) who was born in 1932, the son of a mining and electrical engineer and educated initially at St Michael's School in Llanelli, then at Cheltenham College and Pembroke College Cambridge University where he was a Wightwick Scholar graduating with a BA in Jurisprudence in 1953. Two years later he was called to the Bar at the Inner Temple and practised until 1974. He first entered politics in 1959 when he contested South Kensington unsuccessfully but sat for Barons Court for ten years until 1974 when the seat was abolished. From 1965 to 1968 he was a delegate to the Western European Union and Vice Chairman of the Legal Committee of the Assembly Council of Europe. He was PPS to the Secretary of State for Defence between 1966 and 1969 and attained Government rank at the latter end of the Wilson Government in October 1969, as Army Minister under Dennis Healey, the Defence Secretary. He took his MA in Law in 1970 and during the Heath Government was Opposition Spokesman on Broadcasting, Posts and Telecommunications between 1970 and 1971 when he became a Foreign Affairs spokesman and also a QC. At the February 1974 General Election he was parachuted into the hitherto 'safe' Labour seat of Blyth (Northumberland) but this involved the de-selection of the sitting MP, Eddie Milne, who stood as an Independent against him winning by a comfortable margin. A fierce pro-European, Richard was perceived as too right wing to supplant a popular local left-winger and his career was seemingly in ruins. However, after his defeat he was appointed the UK's Permanent Representative at the United Nations in New York, a post he held until 1979.

During this period he also chaired the 1976 Rhodesia Conference at Geneva that tried and failed to resolve the white supremacists' rule in the British Colony. In 1981, a year that saw him made a Fellow of his former Cambridge College, he was also appointed as a Labour Party Commissioner to the Europe Economic Community serving in that role until 1984. The following year he became a bencher at the Inner Temple and was also appointed Chairman of the World Trade Centre, Wales, Ltd, based in Cardiff, a post he held until 1997. In the meantime, in 1990, he had been made a Life Peer, Baron Richards of Ammanford and was appointed Leader of the Opposition in the House of Lords following Labour's defeat at the 1992 Election. He held this post until the return of the Labour Government in 1997 when he was made Lord Privy Seal and Leader of the House of Lords. However, he did not stay long in the Cabinet as Tony Blair replaced him with Baroness Jay in 1998.

MPs for Acton, Ealing, and Southall

Acton

Joseph Alfred Sparkes (Labour) represented Acton from 1945 until 1959 when he was defeated. Born at Collumpton, Devon in 1901 he was educated locally at Ufculm village school and attended the Central Labour College, which had been formed by disaffected students at Ruskin College, Oxford in 1909, its principal trade union supporters being the National Union of Railwaymen and the South Wales Miners' Federation[4]. He joined the Great Western Railway as a porter, became a signalman and then progressed to become a parcels clerk at Paddington station in London. At the 1929 General Election he contested Taunton for the Labour Party but finished a poor third. He also unsuccessfully contested Chelmsford (1931) and Buckingham (1935) but did serve as a councillor and alderman on Acton Borough Council after 1932. He was a junior Government Whip between 1950 and 1951. He died in 1981.

(Sir) Philip Welsby Holland (Conservative) took Acton by under a thousand votes in 1959 and served for only one Parliament, the seat reverting to Labour in 1964. An industrial consultant born in 1917, he was educated at Sir John Deane's Grammar School in Northwich, and contested his first Parliamentary election at Yardley (Birmingham) in 1955,

4 In 1911 it moved to London and acquired an extension in Kew in 1920. The college closed in 1929.

MPs for Acton, Ealing, and Southall

From	at	To	Surname	First Names	Constituency	Party
1945	G	1959	Sparkes	Joseph Alfred	Acton	Labour
1959	G	1964	Holland	(Sir) Philip Welsby		Conservative
1964	G	1968	Floud	Bernard Francis Castle		Labour
1968	B	1970	Baker	Kenneth		Conservative
1964	G	1974	Spearing	Nigel John		Labour
1945	G	1950	Sanderson	Sir Frank Bernard	Ealing East	Conservative
1945	G	1950	Hudson	James Hindle	Ealing West	Labour
1950	G	1955	Hudson	James Hindle	Ealing North	Labour
1955	G	1964	Barter	John Wilfred		Conservative
1964	G	1974	Molloy	William John		Labour
1950	G	1958	Maude	Angus Edmund Upton	Ealing South	Conservative
1958	B	1974	Batsford	Brian Caldwell Cook		Conservative
1945	G	1950	Ayles	Arthur Walter	Southall	Labour
1950	G	1966	Pargiter	George Albert		Labour
1966	G	1974	Bidwell	Sydney James		Labour

NOTE First returned at a B = By-election; G =General Election

when he was unsuccessful. He sat as a councillor in Kensington from 1955 until 1959 when he won Acton. Following his defeat there in 1964 he went in search of another seat, finding one at Carlton (Nottinghamshire) where he was elected in 1966. Following his election he was Joint Secretary of the Conservative Parliamentary Employment and Productivity Committee and a member of the Public Accounts Committee. Outside the House he was President of the Conservative Trade Union National Advisory Committee and remained MP for Carlton until 1983, when the seat was renamed Gedling. He retired from the House in 1987. He died in 2011.

Bernard Floud MP
People's History Museum Manchester

Holland was defeated in 1964 by **Bernard Francis Castle Floud** (Labour) who held the seat until his suicide in 1968. It is rumoured (probably falsely) that he was a Soviet spy but he died at home after being interviewed by M15 at Prime Minister Wilson's request prior to a ministerial appointment. It has been written that he was 'bullied' under interrogation at a time when he had just lost his wife by the M15 operative Peter Wright. Born in 1915, he was educated at Gresham's School, Holt (Norfolk) and at Wadham College, Oxford, but also studied at Universities in Berlin, Grenoble and Toronto in Canada where his father was the High Commissioner. He joined the civil service but served in the Army from 1939 to 1942 and after the War was a National Executive member of the Society of Civil Servants from 1945-9. He reached a senior position in the civil service where he was an assistant secretary at the Board of Trade but left to become a Television company executive and unsuccessfully contested two seats (Chelmsford in 1955 and Hemel Hempstead in 1959) before being elected at Acton. He was also an Essex farmer and between 1952-5, an Ongar Rural District Councillor.

Nigel Spearing MP
People's History Museum Manchester

Kenneth Baker (Conservative) took Acton at the 1968 by-election that followed Floud's death but lost the seat at the 1970 General Election. His biographical details are to be found earlier in this Chapter (St Marylebone).

Nigel John Spearing (Labour), a teacher at Wandsworth School from 1956-68, won Acton in 1970 and held it until February 1974 when its boundaries changed. Born in 1930 and educated at Latymer Upper School as well as St Catherine's College, Cambridge, he was a member of the NUT who entered politics initially by way of an unsuccessful attempt to win Warwick and Leamington in 1964. Following his defeat he went in search of a new seat, which he found at Newham South in a May 1974 by-election. He remained its MP until he retired in 1997. From 1977 to 1986 he was Chairman of the British Anti-Common Market Campaign.

Ealing East

Sir Frank Bernard Sanderson (Conservative) was MP for Ealing from 1931 to 1945 when he was returned at Ealing East. His principal biographical details may be found in Chapter 7. He stood down in 1950 and died in 1965.

Ealing West, and Ealing North

James Hindle Hudson (Labour) was born in 1881 and educated at Davyhulme Wesleyan elementary school and then at Manchester University where he graduated as a BA and took an MA. From 1903 to 1907 he was a teacher in an elementary school and then at a Salford Municipal Boys School until 1916. He was the Directing Secretary of the National Council for Prevention of War, a pacifist organisation, for which he served a three-year prison term during the First World War. He first contested Huddersfield in 1922 and sat as the West Riding town's MP from 1923 to 1931. He served as PPS to the Chancellor of the Exchequer, Philip Snowden, who was MP for the neighbouring Colne Valley constituency, in 1924 and again from 1929 to 1931 but did not join Snowden in the National Government and lost his seat in 1931. He lived at Cheadle Hulme and subsequently contested nearby Altrincham (1933) and Stockport (1935) and was for many years Secretary of the National Temperance Federation, an organisation formed in 1884 to campaign against the consumption of alcohol. He was MP for Ealing West from 1945 until 1950 and then for Ealing North until 1955 when he was defeated by 246 votes. He died in 1962.

John Wilfred Barter (Conservative) was MP from 1955 until 1964 when he was defeated by the even smaller margin of 27 votes. Born in 1917, he was educated at the Royal Commercial Traveller's School, Hatch End, and went on to become a Secretary and accountant to a number of companies. He was elected to Middlesex County Council in 1949 and was area chairman and National Vice Chairman of the Association for Parents of Backward Children. From 1950-53 he was also a branch chairman of the Clerical and Administrative Workers' Union. He died in 1983.

William John Molloy MP
People's History Museum Manchester

William John Molloy (Labour) was MP for Ealing North for 15 years from 1964 to 1979 when he lost his seat and was made a Baron. Born in 1918, the son of a coal miner, he was educated at St Thomas Council School, Swansea and then at the University of Wales. He became a civil servant and was for a while chairman of the staff side of the Whitley Council of the Germany and Austria Sections at the Foreign Office[5]. As an MP he pursued his interest in European politics and from 1976-7 was a Member of the European Parliament whilst also being a member of the 'Get Britain Out' campaign. He was on the council of the Royal Geographical Society. From 1969-70 he was PPS to John Stonehouse, Minister of Posts & Telecommunications. He died in 2001.

Ealing South

Angus Edmund Upton Maude (Conservative) was born in 1912 and educated at Rugby School and Oriel College, Oxford. An author and journalist he was Director of the Conservative Political Centre from 1951-55 whilst the MP for Ealing South, where he was elected in 1950. However, he resigned his seat in 1958 to go to Australia as Editor of the *Sydney Morning Herald*, a post he held until 1961 when he returned to England and once again entered political life. He was unsuccessful at the 1962 Dorset South by-election, when the Tory vote was split by an anti-Common Market candidate, but was returned in 1963 at a Stratford-on-Avon by-election triggered by the resignation of John Profumo, the disgraced Cabinet Minister who got publicly involved with a prostitute, a scandal that hastened the demise of Macmillan's Government. Margaret Thatcher appointed Maude Chairman of the Conservative Party when she became Leader in 1975 and 4 years later he entered her Cabinet as Paymaster General. A heavy smoker, he retired through ill health in 1983 and died soon afterwards. His son Francis also became a prominent Tory MP and Minister in the Coalition Government formed in 2010.

Angus Maude MP
Dorset Life

Brian Caldwell Cook Batsford (Conservative) won the 1958 by-election created by Maude's resignation. Born in 1910, he was educated at Repton and the Central School of Arts and Crafts[6], joining the family publishing firm at the age of 18, later becoming chairman. He first contested a Parliamentary election in 1945 when he was defeated as the National Government candidate at a Chelmsford by-election but thereafter did not seek election until his successful attempt in 1958. From 1962-4 he was an Assistant Government Whip and Opposition Chief Whip from 1964-6. In 1967 Ted Heath appointed him the Parliamentary representative to the majority party on the Greater London Council. He retired at the February 1974 election when Ealing was subject to a major redistribution of seats.

5 The Whitley council is a formally constituted meeting of senior civil servants and trade union representatives and has been constituted since 1919 to discuss pay and conditions.
6 The Central School of Arts and Crafts was established in 1896 by London County Council to provide specialist art teaching for workers in craft industries.

Southall

Arthur Walter Ayles (Labour) was elected in 1945. Born in South Lambeth in 1879, the son of a railway porter, he was educated at elementary school and became an engineer and career trade unionist. He was a District Secretary in Birmingham from 1905-8 but moved around the country as his career developed and at various times served as a local councillor in Acton (where he was on the Board of Guardians in 1906), Bristol and Orpington. He joined the Labour Party in 1903 and was a sometime Secretary of the ILP in Bristol, where he sat as a councillor from 1911 to 1925. He contested Bristol North in the Party's cause at a number of General Elections, notably 1922, 1923, 1924,1931 and 1935 when he was unsuccessful but also at a December 1923 by-election and at the1929 General Election when he was returned as MP. During this period he was Chairman of the Bristol Labour Party. He was a Quaker and peace campaigner, being organizer and financial secretary of the 'No More War' movement in the mid Thirties and, in the run up to the Second World War, was General Secretary of the British Commonwealth Peace Federation. In 1950 he opted to be the Labour candidate in the newly created Hayes and Harlington constituency and held the seat until his death in 1953.

Arthur Ayles MP
© National Portrait Gallery
Lafayette 1927

George Albert Pargiter (Labour), who had been MP for Spelthorne since 1945, was elected for the Southall borough constituency in 1950. Born in 1897 and educated at Towcester Grammar School (Northamptonshire) he was an engineer who held many offices in the Amalgamated Engineering Union. From 1934 to 1945 he was a member of Southall Borough Council and was mayor from 1938-40. Even after his election as an MP he maintained his interest in local Government and served on Middlesex County Council as an alderman from 1946 to 1949. In 1954 he was made a Deputy Lieutenant of the County and retired from Parliament in 1966.

George Pargiter MP
People's Museum History
Manchester

Sydney James Bidwell (Labour) took over the Southall seat in 1966. Born in January 1917 he was educated at elementary schools, evening classes and through the trade union movement. A railway worker who became a lecturer for the National Council of Labour Colleges, he was a member of Southall Borough Council from 1951-55 who originally belonged to the National Union of Railwaymen but later transferred to the Transport and General Workers Union, which sponsored his candidacy. He contested Hertfordshire East, though unsuccessfully, in 1959, then South West Hertfordshire in 1964. Once elected at Southall he remained its MP after a wider distribution that took place in 1974 in which his seat was renamed Ealing, Southall. The character of the population changed enormously during the period that Bidwell was the town's MP. By the time of the 1991 census over half of the residents classified themselves in ethnic groups other than white, mostly defining themselves as of Indian origin. In fact Bidwell's most important act as an MP came in 1976 when he successfully sponsored the Motor Cycle Crash Helmets (Religious Exemption) Act that enabled Sikhs to legally ride wearing their turbans. Over time the mixed ethnicity of the constituency created some tensions within the local Labour Party, which selected a candidate of Asian origin to fight the seat in 1992, although Bidwell, even at the age of 75, sought to be re-nominated. He stood as 'True Labour' at the 1992 contest but secured only 10% of thevotes and retired from politics.

MPs for Brentford & Chiswick, Twickenham, Heston & Isleworth, Spelthorne, and Feltham

MPs for Brentford & Chiswick

Francis Edward Noel-Baker (Labour), whose father Philip was a Minister in the Attlee Government, took Brentford & Chiswick in 1945 at the age of 25, which made him the youngest Labour MP at the time. During the War, he had joined the Tank Corps as a private in 1940 and became an intelligence officer in the Middle East with the temporary rank of Major. Educated at Westminster School and Cambridge, he joined the Fabian Society and was chairman of the University Labour Club. He was a journalist and author of books on Spain and Greece, where the family owned estates. From 1955 to 1969, when he resigned from the Labour Party, he was MP for Swindon.

Francis Noel-BakerMP
Wikipedia

In 1950, Noel - Baker was succeeded by **Percy Belgrave 'Laddie' Lucas** (Conservative), a Wartime RAF fighter pilot who commanded the top-scoring squadron

MPs for Brentford & Chiswick, Twickenham, Heston & Isleworth, Spelthorne, and Feltham						
From	**at**	**To**	**Surname**	**First Names**	**Constituency**	**Party**
1945	G	1950	Noel-Baker	Francis Edward.	Brentford and Chiswick	Labour
1950	G	1959	Lucas	Percy Belgrave "Laddie" (Wing Commander)		Conservative
1959	G	1966	Smith	Sir Dudley		Conservative
1966	G	1974	Barnes	Michael		Labour
1945	G	1954	Keeling	Edward Herbert	Twickenham	Conservative
1955	B	1970	Cooke	Roger Gresham		Conservative
1970	G	1974	Jessel	Sir Toby Henry Francis		Conservative
1950	G	1970	Harris	(Richard) Reader	Heston and Isleworth	Conservative
1970	G	1974	Heyhoe	(Bernard) "Barney" John		Conservative
1945	G	1950	Pargiter	George Albert	Spelthorne	Labour
1950	G	1970	Craddock	Sir (George) Beresford		Conservative
1955	G	1966	Hunter	Albert Edward	Feltham	Labour
1966	G	1974	Kerr	Russell Whiston		Labour
NOTE First returned at a B = By-election; G =General Election						

WCdr Percy Lucas MP
Wikipedia

in the Battle for Malta. Later he helped at Air Defence HQ to develop counter measures against the bouncing bomb. An excellent left-handed golfer nicknamed 'Laddie', he was playing captain of the British Walker Cup team that went to the USA in 1949. Born in 1915, he was educated at Stowe School and Pembroke College, Cambridge, and at the 1945 Election he unsuccessfully contested Fulham West against Edith Summerskill. He retired in 1959 and died in 1998.

Sir Dudley Smith (Conservative) succeeded him and held the seat until 1966 when he was defeated. He was elected at Warwick and Leamington at a 1968 by-election, holding the seat until he retired in 1987. His first Parliamentary contest was at Peckham in 1955. Born in 1926 and educated at Chichester School, he became a management consultant and journalist before assuming a political career although from 1958 until 1963 he was a Middlesex County Councillor. From 1964-6 he was a Tory Whip and Under-Secretary for Employment in the Heath Government from 1970 until 1974 when he was for a brief period Under-Secretary for the Army at the Ministry of Defence. Pro-Europe and a delegate to both the Council of Europe and the Western Economic Union from 1979, he never resumed a ministerial career after Margaret Thatcher assumed the Premiership and was aptly chairman of the Wilderness Foundation from 1981.

Michael Barnes MP, an election communication
People's History Museum Manchester

In 1966 Smith was defeated by **Michael Barnes** (Labour) who held the seat until it was redrawn in February 1974. Born in 1932, he was educated at Malvern College and Corpus Christi College, Oxford and afterwards became a marketing consultant. In 1964 he contested Wycombe (Buckinghamshire). He was chairman of the Parliamentary Party's Social Security Group in 1969/70 and joint secretary of the Labour Committee for Europe. He belonged to the ASTMS Union. In the 1990s he served as the Ombudsman for Legal Services and subsequently for Financial Services.

MPs for Twickenham

Edward Herbert Keeling (Conservative) was first elected MP in 1935 and was re-elected after the War. He died in 1954. His principal biographical details may be found in Chapter 7.

He was succeeded by **Roger Gresham Cooke** (Conservative) who won the January 1955 by-election that followed his death. Born in 1907 and educated at Winchester and then New College Oxford, Cooke became a barrister at the Middle Temple in 1930. From 1935-8 he was joint secretary of the National Advisory Council, the Motor Manufacturing

Industry and Director of the Society of Motor Manufacturers and Traders from 1946 to 55[7]. He was also a former secretary of the United Steel Companies Limited and Chairman of the British Road Federation, a lobbying organisation for the building of more roads, from 1948. He retired in 1970 and subsequently died in the same year.

He was succeeded by **(Sir) Toby Henry Francis Jessel** (Conservative) who was born in 1934 and educated at the Royal Naval College Dartmouth and at Balliol College, Oxford. He fought Peckham unsuccessfully in 1964 whilst he was a member of Southwark Borough Council (1964-66) and a by-election at Hull North in 1966, which he also lost but the result of which, it is said, persuaded Harold Wilson to call the General Election two months later that brought about a Labour landslide after a period when they had governed with a wafer thin majority. Jessel became a member of the Richmond-on-Thames Borough Council in 1967, serving until 1973. He sat as the MP until a Liberal Democrat defeated him at the 1997 General Election. He could claim a family pedigree in politics. Sir George Jessel was elected a Liberal MP for Dover in 1868 and was appointed Solicitor-General by Gladstone three years later and was the first Jew to become a minister. In 1873 he became Master of the Rolls. Marcus Samuel was another of Toby's forebears who was an MP, sitting for Putney from 1934-42. His great grandfather Lord Berstead founded Shell Transport and Trading.

MPs for Heston & Isleworth

(Richard) Reader Harris (Conservative) was elected the first MP in 1950. Born in 1913 he was educated at Ramsgate's St Lawrence College and became a barrister. He joined the National Fire Service[8] in 1939, serving throughout the Second World War, and was negotiating secretary of the National Fire Officers' Association. He fought Hackney Central unsuccessfully in 1945 and entered a career in business becoming managing director of an export firm and secretary of the National Tyre Distributors Association. He retired from politics in 1970. He died in 2009.

Barney Heyhoe MP
People's History Museum Manchester

(Bernard) 'Barney' John Heyhoe (Conservative) won in 1970 and retained the seat until redistribution in February 1974 when he was adopted at Brentford and Isleworth, a seat he held until 1992. Born in August 1925, he was educated at elementary school and the Stanley Technical College, South Norwood. An interest in politics took him into the Young Conservatives and he was their Vice Chairman from 1951 to 53. From 1962-4 he was area Chairman of the Conservative Political Centre and contested Lewisham South in 1964. He was head of the Party's Research section from 1965-70 and was made Head of its International Office in1973. From 1972-4 he was Parliamentary Secretary to the Lord President and Leader of the Commons (James Prior) and an Opposition spokesman on employment between 1974 and 1979. After Margaret Thatcher's election victory in 1979 he became an Under Secretary for the Army at the Ministry of Defence and two years later was made Minister of State, Civil Service Department, transferring to the Treasury later that year but with the same remit. From 1985 to 1986 he served as Health Minister again with the rank of Minister of State. He retired in 1992 and became a life peer.

MPs for Spelthorne

George Albert Pargiter (Labour) was MP from 1945 to 1950, but transferred to Southall following 1950 boundary revisions that saw the incumbent MP there move to the new Hayes & Harlington seat. He remained an MP until 1966 and his principal details can be found above under Southall (above).

He was succeeded by **(Sir) (George) Beresford Craddock** (Conservative) who was Spelthorne's MP from 1950 to 1970. A barrister, born in 1898, he was educated at the Harris Academy, Dundee, and St Andrews University. During the First World War he served with the Royal Garrison Artillery and on the chemical welfare staff but afterwards went into industry before being called to the Bar. He contested Lichfield as a Tory at a 1938 by-election but as a National Government candidate at the 1945 General Election. He died in 1976.

MPs for Feltham

The first MP was **Albert Edward Hunter** (Labour) who was born in April 1900 and served with the Armed Forces during the Great War after which he became a sales representative and trade unionist rising to be President of

7 The SMMT was set up in 1902 to provide a focus for the promotion and representation of the industry.
8 The incendiary bomb attacks of the winter of 1940/41 demonstrated the inadequacy of the fire prevention services, which were still under a multiplicity of local authorities, though co-ordinated by the Home Office and supported by the Auxiliary Fire Service. Under the National Fire Service (Emergency Provisions) Act 1941, the Home Office set about creating a national service and until 1947 administered and controlled a national force of 350 000 men and women.

the National Union of Shop Assistants in 1938/9 and then its Treasurer until 1944[9]. From 1928 to 1934 he was a member of the Holborn Borough Council and a St Pancras councillor from 1949. He unsuccessfully contested Spelthorne in 1951 but was elected at Feltham when it was carved out of that constituency in 1955. He remained its MP until 1966, when he retired. He died three years later.

Russell Kerr MP
People's History Museum Manchester

He was succeeded by **Russell Whiston Kerr** (Labour) who was born in Australia in 1921 and educated at the Shore School and University in Sidney. During the Second World War he was a member of the RAF pathfinders and afterwards went into the airline business becoming a charter executive. A Left-winger, he first contested a seat for Parliament at Horsham, in 1951, then at Merton and Morden (1959) and Preston North (1964). On all three occasions he was unsuccessful but following his election at Feltham in 1955 he remained MP until defeated in 1983 in what 9 years earlier had become the Feltham & Heston constituency. He was Chairman of the Tribune Group[10] of Labour MPs in 1969-70 and a member of the National Executive Committee of the Labour Party from 1964-78. He died in 1983. His wife whom he married in 1960 was Ann Kerr, Labour MP for Rochester & Chatham from 1964-70. She died of cancer in 1973.

MPs for Hayes & Harlington, Uxbridge and Ruislip & Northwood

From	at	To	Surname	First Names	Constituency	Party
1950	G	1953	Ayles	Arthur Walter	Hayes and Harlington	Labour
1953	B	1971	Skeffington	Arthur Massey		Labour
1971	B	1974	Sandelson	Neville Devonshire		Labour
1945	G	1959	Beswick	Frank	Uxbridge	Labour
1959	G	1966	Curran	(Leslie) Charles		Conservative
1966	G	1970	Ryan	John		Labour
1970	G	1972	Curran	Charles		Conservative
1972	B	1974	Shersby	Michael		Conservative
1950	G	1974	Crowder	(Frederick) Petre	Ruislip and Northwood	Conservative

NOTE First returned at a B = By-election; G =General Election

Hayes & Harlington

Following the death of **Arthur Ayles** (Labour) – see Southall 1945-50 above - he was succeeded at the 1953 by-election by **Arthur Massey Skeffington** (Labour) who had previously been Lewisham West's MP from 1945 to 1950. His principal biographical details may be found in Chapter 13 (Kent 1945-74).

He died in 1971 and was succeeded at a by-election that year by **Neville Devonshire Sandelson** (Labour) who held the seat until 1983 two years after he had switched parties. Born in 1923, he was educated at Westminster School and at Trinity College, Cambridge after which he became a barrister and parliamentary and legal consultant. He was a member of the LCC from 1952-8 but contested seven Parliamentary elections before he was elected. His first contest was at Ashford (Kent), which he fought in 1950, 1951 and 1955. Then he lost at Beckenham (in a 1957 by-election), at Rushcliffe, Nottinghamshire (1959), at Leicester South West (in a 1967 by-election), and at Chichester (1970). He was on the right of his Party and when the Social Democratic Party was formed he resigned from Labour in 1981. He chose not to resign his seat, however, and remained as SDP spokesman on Northern Ireland and then the Arts but at the 1983 Election standing for his new Party he split the Labour vote enabling the Tories to win the seat. Sandelson just failed to take second place from Labour. He died in 2002.

Neville Sandelson MP
People's History Museum Manchester

Uxbridge

Frank Beswick (Labour) took the seat from the Conservatives after the War and represented it until 1959. The son of a Nottinghamshire coal miner, Beswick was born in 1912 and became a

9 The Union was formed in 1891 and became part of the Union of Shop, Distributive and Allied Trades in 1947.
10 The success of the Left Book Club in 1936 encouraged socialists to believe there was a market for a left wing weekly and it was agreed to start publishing a journal they decided to call Tribune. It became the focus for a well-organised group of Left Wing Labour MPs who met weekly to debate issues of the day and act as a pressure group on the Parliamentary Party.

Frank Beswick MP
People's History Museum Manchester

journalist. He fought his first local government election aged 22 and travelled extensively in Europe, including Spain during the Civil War. He joined the RAF in 1940 and became a pilot in Air Transport Command and in 1945 was an acting Captain in the British Overseas Air Corporation fighting the local Uxbridge seat in the General Election held the same year. In 1946 he was one of only two MPs who witnessed the exploding of the atom bomb at Bikini. In 1950-51 he was Parliamentary Secretary at the Ministry of Aviation but a ministerial career was ended by 13 years of Conservative Government, which involved the loss of his seat. He was made Baron Beswick and died in 1987.

In 1959 Beswick was defeated by **(Leslie) Charles Curran** (Conservative) whom he had beaten in the same constituency twice before. Born in 1903 and educated at Cardiff High School and Stonyhurst, Curran was called to the Bar at Gray's Inn in 1934. He was also a journalist and at the time of his selection to fight Uxbridge was assistant editor of the *Daily Mirror*. In earlier General Elections he lost at Walthamstow West (1945) and Uxbridge (1951 and 1955). He also lost Uxbridge in 1966 but retook the seat four years later. However, following his re-election in 1970, he died in 1972.

John Ryan (Labour) held the seat from 1966 to 1970. Born in 1940, he was educated at Lanark Grammar School and Glasgow University, afterwards becoming a market researcher and publishing executive. He contested the adjacent seat of South Buckinghamshire for Labour in 1964 prior to being returned at Uxbridge.

People's History Museum Manchester

Michael Shersby MP
Wikipedia

Michael Shersby (Conservative) was elected at the 1972 by-election created by Curran's death. Born in 1933 he was educated at John Lyon School, Harrow-on-the-Hill and spent 30 years working for the British sugar industry. He entered politics in 1959 as a councillor in Paddington and continued in that role until 1971 when it was merged with Westminster, of which Council he was Deputy Lord Mayor in 1967/8. Whilst still an MP he became secretary and then Director of the British Sugar Bureau, a trade association largely funded by Tate and Lyle and set up in 1966. He was a Parliamentary spokesman for the Police Federation from 1989 to 1997. He held Uxbridge for 25 years but, after winning it again in 1997, he died before he could take his seat.

Ruislip & Northwood

(Frederick) Petre Crowder (Conservative) was the seat's first MP and sat from 1950 when it was created until he retired in 1979. Born in 1919, he was educated at Eton and Christ Church Oxford and was the son of the MP for Finchley (1935-45), Captain JFE Crowder (see Chapter 7). A barrister at the Middle Temple from 1948, Crowder had joined the Coldstream Guards during the Second World War serving in North Africa and Italy. From 1951 to 1955 he was PPS to Sir Reginald Manningham-Buller, both as Solicitor-General and Attorney-General. Crowder continued to pursue a legal career and in 1959-63 was Deputy Chairman of the Hertfordshire Quarter Sessions and in 1960 was appointed Recorder of Gravesend. He became a QC in 1964 and Recorder of Colchester three years later. He fought his first Parliamentary contest unsuccessfully at a by-election in North Tottenham in 1945. He died in 1999.

MPs for Harrow, Wembley, and Willesden

Harrow Central

Sir (Frank) Patrick Bishop (Conservative) was elected the first Harrow Central MP in 1950. Born in 1900 and educated at Tottenham Grammar School he went on to Kings College, London University and was called to the Bar at Grays Inn in 1923. During the Great War he served in the RNAS and RAF from 1917-18 and during the 1939-45 War was second-in- command of the 5th City of London (Press Battalion) Home Guard. He was at one time chairman of the advertising committee of the Newspaper Proprietors' Association and subsequently general manager of the Newsprint Supply Company and of the Newsprint Rationing Committee, established in 1940 as a wartime measure but not finally eliminated until 1957. He retired as an MP in 1964 and died in 1972.

(Sir) (John) Anthony Grant (Conservative) succeeded him in 1964 and remained MP until 1983 when the seat was abolished. Born in 1925, he was educated at St Pauls School and Brasenose College, Oxford, became a solicitor and Liveryman of the Worshipful Company of City Solicitors, and a Freeman of the City of London. He contested Hayes and Harlington in 1959 but was not elected to the House until he fought Harrow. He was an Opposition Whip between 1966 and 1970 and after Heath's election victory in 1970, was appointed initially as Parliamentary Secretary at the Board

MPs for Harrow, Wembley, and Willesden

From	at	To	Surname	First Names	Constituency	Party
1950	G	1964	Bishop	(Sir) (Frank)Patrick	Harrow Central	Conservative
1964	G	1974	Grant	(Sir) John Anthony		Conservative
1945	G	1950	Skinnard	Frederick William	Harrow East	Labour
1950	G	1958	Harvey	Ian Douglas		Conservative
1959	B	1966	Courtney	Commander Anthony Tosswill		Conservative
1966	G	1970	Roebuck	Roy Delville		Labour
1970	G	1974	Dykes	Hugh John Maxwell		Conservative
1945	G	1951	Bower	Norman Adolph Henry	Harrow West	Conservative
1951	B	1959	Braithewaite	Sir Albert Newby		Conservative
1960	B	1974	Page	Sir (Anthony) John		Conservative
1945	G	1959	Orbach	Maurice	Willesden East	Labour
1959	G	1964	Skeet	(Sir) Trevor Herbert Harry		Conservative
1964	G	1974	Freeson	Reginald		Labour
1945	G	1959	Viant	Samuel Philip	Willesden West	Labour
1959	G	1974	Pavitt	(Lawrence)"Lawrie" Anstice		Labour Co-Op
1950	G	1974	Bullus	Wing Commander (Sir) Eric Edward	Wembley North	Conservative
1950	G	1974	Russell	(Sir) Ronald Stanley	Wembley South	Conservative

NOTE First returned at a B = By-election; G =General Election

of Trade and then, in October the same year, Under-Secretary for Trade and Industry, which post he retained until the Tories' election defeat in February 1974. He remained on the backbenches but in 1983, after the abolition of his Harrow constituency, transferred to Cambridgeshire South West and retired in 1997.

Harrow East

Frederick William Skinnard (Labour) was born in 1902, the son of a Plymouth engraver, and was elected as an MP in 1945. He was educated at Devonport High School and the Borough Road Teacher Training College and was a schoolmaster from 1922 until he was elected to Parliament. He joined the Labour Party in 1924 having previously belonged to the Union of Democratic Control, which was established during the first days of the First World War to work for parliamentary control of foreign policy and a moderate peace settlement.[11]

He retired from politics in 1950 after he was defeated and was succeeded by **Ian Douglas Harvey** (Conservative) who was born in 1914 and educated at Fettes College, Edinburgh and Christ Church Oxford where he was President of the Union and secretary of the Graduates' Conservative Association. During the War he saw service as a brigade major in the Royal Artillery and afterwards commanded the City of London Rifles Regiment of the Territorial Army. He became a business and advertising agent and entered politics in 1945 as an unsuccessful candidate at Spelthorne but in 1947 was elected to Kensington Borough council on which he served until 1951 and from 1949 to 1952 was also a LCC Councillor. In 1956 he was made a Parliamentary Secretary at the Ministry of Supply in Eden's Government and in 1957 an Under Secretary at the Foreign Office (to RA Butler) in Macmillan's. He remained MP until November 1958 when he resigned following a sex scandal. He resumed a career in advertising and subsequently became active in campaign organisations promoting equality for homosexuals. He died in 1987.

Ian Harvey MP
Fecund & Gay/Bi

Commander Anthony Tosswill Courtney (Conservative) was elected at the March 1959 by-election that followed Harvey's resignation. Born in 1908, he was educated at Edinburgh House, Lee on Solent, and at the Royal Naval Colleges, Dartmouth and Greenwich. He served with the Royal Navy for 31 years and was the heavyweight-boxing champion for the Senior Service for several years. During the Second World War he was deputy head of the Naval Mission in Russia and after it Head of the Russian section of the Naval Intelligence Division. He

11 The UDC also played a part in the terminal decline of the Liberal Party, especially after the formation of the Lloyd George coalition government in December 1916. Joining the UDC became a sort of half-way house between leaving the Liberals and joining the rising Labour Party. By July 1921 organisations affiliated to the UDC contained over one million members. Thirty members of the UDC were elected as Labour MPs in 1922. It disbanded in 1966.

then served as Chief Staff Officer (Intelligence) in Germany. He first entered politics in 1955 when he unsuccessfully contested Hayes and Harlington and was MP for Harrow East until defeated in the Labour landslide of 1966. He died in 1988.

He was succeeded by **Roy Delville Roebuck** (Labour) who held the seat for 4 years. Born in 1929, he was educated at State schools and Manchester College of Commerce after which he became a journalist. He contested Altrincham & Sale in 1964 and after his 1970 defeat fought unsuccessfully at Leek (Staffordshire) in 1974.

In 1970 Roebuck was defeated by **Hugh John Maxwell Dykes** (Conservative), a stockbroker, director and consultant. He became Chairman of ADA Video Systems Limited and was a director of Dixon's Stores Far East Limited. Born in 1939, he was educated at Weston-Super-Mare Grammar School and at Pembroke College, Cambridge. He contested Tottenham in 1966 and after entering the House, became a devoted pro-European serving also as an MEP between 1974 and 1977. From 1978-81 he was Chairman of the Conservatives for Europe Group and from 1982-7 was joint secretary of the European Movement, causes which over the ensuing years placed him increasingly at odds with his Party's thinking. As a 'One Nation Tory' he was a constant rebel against the Thatcher and Major Governments and in 1993 survived a local attempt to unseat him for 'being too close to Brussels'. In 1994 he led a successful backbench revolt against the privatisation of the Post Office. However, his opposition to his own Party's policies did not prevent him from going down to a heavy defeat at the 1997 General Election when he lost by over 9,000 votes to his Labour opponent. As the Conservative Party moved further to the right after 1997 he resigned following the defeat of Kenneth Clarke in the Party's leadership election and joined the Liberal Democrats. He became a peer and active member of the party's defence, foreign and European affairs team including acting as Vice-President of the British-German Association

Harrow West

Norman Adolph Henry Bower (Conservative) had been elected MP for Harrow at a 1941 by-election and after the War was selected to fight Harrow West, which he won in 1945. He retained the seat in 1950 but died in 1951 before the next General Election. His main biographical details may be found in Chapter 7(West London).

He was succeeded at a by-election in April 1951 by **Sir Albert Newby Braithwaite** (Conservative), MP for the East Riding of Yorkshire division of Buckrose (based on Bridlington and Driffield) from 1926 until 1945 when a Liberal defeated him. Born in 1883, he was educated at Leeds Grammar School and Leeds University after which he became an engineer and director of several companies and hotels. He interrupted his career to enlist as a private in 1914 and was commissioned the following year in the Yorkshire Hussars and after overseas service, joined a British Military Mission to the USA. He was awarded both the DSO and Military Cross. He was Chairman of Leeds United Football Club from 1924 to 1931. He died in 1959 after his return at the General Election of that year.

The by-election following his death was held in March 1960 and was won comfortably by **(Sir Anthony) John Page** (Conservative) who was born in 1919 and educated at Harrow School and at Magdalen College, Cambridge. He was a director of several companies and first entered politics when he unsuccessfully contested Eton and Slough in 1959. Despite a business background he was President of the Conservative Trade Unionists National Advisory Council between 1967-9. From 1971-78 he was President of the Independent Schools Association and from 1974-80 Chairman of the Council for Independent Education. He retired in 1987.

Willesden East

Maurice Orbach (Labour) took the seat from the Conservatives in 1945 and held it until the Tories' landslide national victory in 1959. He was subsequently elected for Stockport South (Cheshire) in 1964 and remained an MP until he died a few weeks before the1979 general election. Born in 1902, Orbach was educated at the Preparatory Technical College High School in Cardiff, and New York University where he graduated as an engineer and was himself a lecturer. He returned to England and contested the Huntingdonshire constituency for Labour in 1931, then Willesden East in the general election of1935 and at a 1938 by-election. A member of two Unions – ASTMS (Scientific, Technical and Managerial Staffs) and USDAW (Shop workers) – he was also Chairman of the Atlantic and Pacific Manufacturing Company and a former Director General of the Trades Advisory Council. This was sponsored by the Board of Deputies of British Jews, which in 1936 created a Committee that concerned itself with social, political and economic matters in which anti-Semitism played a part. Its work included investigating periodic complaints about economic discrimination and the Trades Advisory Council started in 1938.It met infrequently until the outbreak of war and in1940 was reconstituted and a Secretariat appointed under Orbach's leadership. He was also an executive member of the World Jewish Congress, an international organization founded in Geneva in 1936 to mobilize support throughout the world against the Nazis.

In 1959 Orbach lost to **(Sir) Trevor Herbert Harry Skeet** (Conservative) who was born in 1918 and educated at Kings College, Auckland and at the University of New Zealand. He became a barrister and industrial consultant who first contested a Parliamentary constituency in 1951, at Hackney North & Stoke Newington, where he was unsuccessful. He also lost in 1955 at Llanelli (Carmarthenshire). He only held Willesden until 1964 but was returned to Parliament again in 1970 when he took Bedford from Labour. He held the seat until 1983 when it was redrawn as Bedfordshire North, a safe seat, which he retained until further redistribution recreated a Bedford borough constituency in time for the 1997 election. Despite attempts to oust him on the grounds of his old age (he was by then the second oldest MP in the House next to Ted Heath) he fought Bedford but was defeated. He was a member of many different Parliamentary Committees but was never more than a long serving backbencher who in his last Parliament was a constant rebel against the Major Government on matters relating to Europe. He died in 2004.

Skeet's successor at Willesden East was **Reginald Freeson** (Labour) who was born in 1926 and educated at a Jewish Orphanage in West Norwood. He entered politics at a young age and was a councillor in Willesden Borough 1952-65, then from 1964-8 he was a member of Brent Council and its Chairman from 1964-5, the year of his election to the Commons. In 1967 he was appointed Parliamentary Secretary at the Ministry of Power, moving in1969to a similar post in Housing and Local Government. When Labour went into opposition in 1970 he was made spokesman on housing and construction, a post he then held as a Minister from 1974 to 1979 after he was returned for the newly redrawn seat of Brent East, which he continued to represent until 1987 when a locally organised coup saw him deselected in favour of Ken Livingston, Leader of the Greater London Council which had been abolished the previous year. He was elected a councillor for Brent once again in 2002 serving until defeated in May 2006, which was also the year he died.

Willesden West

Samuel Philip Viant (Labour) had been MP for Willesden West since 1935 and was re-elected in 1945, retaining the seat until his retirement in 1959. His principal biographical details can be found in Chapter 7 (West London).

He was succeeded by **(Laurence) 'Laurie' Anstice Pavitt** (Labour & Co-operative), who was born in 1914, educated at elementary schools and who was a member of Ilford Borough Council from 1949-52 and national organizer of the Medical Practitioners' Union between 1956-9[12]. He was Chairman of the Parliamentary Labour Party's health group from 1964 to 1974 when he was appointed an Assistant Government whip following Wilson's minority election victory. He retired in 1987 having transferred to the Brent South constituency in February 1974 following boundary changes. He died in 1989.

Wembley North

Wing Commander (Sir) Eric Edward Bullus (Conservative), who held the seat throughout its period of existence between 1950 and 1974, was born in 1906 at Peterborough but brought up and educated in Leeds, at the Modern School and the University there. He became a journalist and was elected to Leeds City Council in 1930 serving as a member for 10 years. He was in the RAF Voluntary Reserve during the Second World War, at the Air Ministry and in South East Asia, where he was a member of Lord Mountbatten's staff. From 1946-50 he was Secretary to the London Municipal Society and between 1947 and 1950 was a member of the Harrow District Council. Parliamentary Secretary to the Minister of State, Board of Trade from 1953-55, Bullus was also a Church of England diocesan lay reader. He retired in 1974. He died in 2001 at the age of 94.

Wembley South

(Sir) Ronald Stanley Russell (Conservative), like Bullus in the neighbouring constituency, was also MP throughout the period of the seat's existence from 1950 until 1974. An author and journalist, he was born in 1904 and educated at Haileybury School, then Gonville and Caius Colleges, Cambridge. He first contested a Parliamentary seat in 1935, at Glasgow Shettleston, followed in 1945 by a failed attempt in another safe Labour Scottish citadel, Coatbridge. During the War he served in the Royal Artillery. He was a member of the LCC between 1946 and 1952 and after the return of a Conservative Government in 1951, was PPS to Duncan Sandys, firstly when he was Minister of Supply, then at Housing and Local Government. He retired in at the February 1974 general election and died two months later.

People's History Museum Manchester

12 Founded as the Medico-Political Union in 1914, it became the Medical Practitioners' Union in 1922. It amalgamated with the Association of Scientific, Technical and Managerial Staffs in 1970.

North London – Finsbury, Shoreditch, Islington, St Pancras, Hampstead, Finchley, Hendon and Barnet (15 seats in 1945 and 11 after 1950)

In 1945 there was an increase of two seats in North London to a total of 15, though the number fell to 11 in 1950 as an increase in the suburbs was more than offset by reductions in the LCC area. One of the new seats was derived from the Hertfordshire constituency of St Albans which was divided to spawn a new constituency of **Barnet** comprising the Hatfield and Elstree Rural Districts and the Urban Districts of Barnet and East Barnet Valley. It was thus even more centred on its Greater London electorates than before and included Arkley, Brunswick Park, East Barnet, High Barnet, New Barnet, Hadley Wood, Monken Hadley, Potters Bar South Mimms and Totteridge, thus straddling present day Hertfordshire and Greater London.

In Middlesex only one constituency was affected in 1945. Hendon, which by then had the largest electorate in the country, was divided in two parts in the wake of suburban expansion engendered by an extension to the Northern Line of the Underground, opened beyond Hampstead to Hendon in 1923, and then to Edgware. **Hendon North** covered the Edgware, Mill Hill, Burnt Oak, and West Hendon wards of the borough including Colindale on the east side of the Edgware Road.

Hendon South ran south of Mill Hill to the border with Hampstead and included the central Hendon, Golders Green, Park, and Childs Hill wards including Mill East. The effect was to create two constituencies that were around the average size of electorate for London. Hendon North had 54,000 and the South constituency 57,000 registered voters, 7% and 2% respectively below the then average. **Finchley,** which included neighbouring Friern Barnet, had unaltered boundaries but an electorate that at nearly 72,000 was 23% larger than average. Over the next 20 years the Finchley electorate remained the same (though of course it included new electors over the new voting age of eighteen in 1970) whilst Hendon North fell to 52,000 and South to 56,000, by 4% and 3% respectively. The relative decline of London electorates generally meant that by 1970 Finchley was fully 31% larger than the average constituency whilst Hendon North was 6% below it and Hendon South 1% above.

More fundamental changes were made in 1950 when there was a loss of 4 seats overall in North London compared with 1945 and 2 since 1935. The boroughs of St Pancras and Holborn lost 2 of their 5 seats. Holborn was merged with St Pancras South, which in turn absorbed most of the former South East and South West constituencies. Islington borough also lost one seat being redrawn as North, East and South whilst, as population densities thinned in the formerly congested central areas of London, the borough of Finsbury was coupled with Shoreditch from the East End.

Holborn & St Pancras South comprised wards 5-8 of St Pancras together with the borough of Holborn covering the area between Camden Town and the boundary with the City of London and Westminster north of the Strand and Covent Garden. It included Bloomsbury, Corum Fields, Euston, Hatton Garden, Holborn, Kings Cross, London University, Mornington Crescent, Somers Town and St Pancras. **St Pancras North** comprised wards 1-4 extending north as far as Parliament Hill near Highgate including Camden Town, Chalk Farm, Dartmouth Park, Gospel Oak, Kentish Town and Primrose Hill. **Hampstead** remained unaltered but with 71,000 voters the constituency was 22% larger than the average for Greater London in 1950 and by 1970 was 31% larger than the average, a similar profile to Finchley. By contrast the two St Pancras seats lost voters. North started in 1950 with 66,000 electors (13% higher than the average) but by 1970 had only 50,000 (9% below the average), a decline of 24%. Holborn & St Pancras South was the smallest of the three at every stage. In 1950 it had 55,000 electors (6% below the average) but by 1970 it had less than 42,000 (24% below average), like North St Pancras a fall of 24%.

Comprising two London boroughs, **Shoreditch & Finsbury** extended from Clerkenwell, Bunhill Fields and Moorfields on the boundary with the City of London to Haggerston and Hoxton. It included Farringdon, Golden Lane, Old Street/St Lukes and Pentonville Road. Its electorate in 1950 was 57,000, which in that year was only 2% below the average size of constituency electorate in London and in 1951 was almost exactly representative of London electorates. However, over the next 20 years the electorate fell by 22% and by 1970 was 19% below the average for London.

Although **Islington North** and **Islington East** remained unaltered the borough lost one seat, **Islington South West** being an amalgamation of the former South and West divisions covering Barnsbury, Caldedonian Road, Lower Holloway, the area round Upper Street, the Angel and Pentonville contained in the St Mary and St Peter wards, and the Thornhill ward between the Liverpool and Caledonian Roads. In 1950 the combined electorates of the three constituencies was 173,000, the largest being Islington South West which contained nearly 63,000 voters, 7% higher than the average for London. Islington North had 59,000 electors (1% above average) and Islington East had 51,000 (13% below). However, over the next 20years there was a massive reduction in the electorates of all three. Between 1950 and

Left: *Chipping Barnet nestles in the former South Hertfordshire Hills. The Barnet area of Hertfordshire developed strongly as a suburb of London in the Inter War period. A new Constituency was created there in 1945. Chipping Barnet lay at its centre and gives its name to the equivalent Constituency today.*

Below: *Not all suburban expansion came in the form of the semi detached house. These more modest 1950s terraced houses in Silkstream Road Burnt Oak were council built and in the Hendon North Constituency. Once again the housing development was well supported by public transport, with the Burnt Oak tube station adjacent.*

Below: *Hendon Central Station is on the Edgware Branch of the Northern Tube Line. It offers direct services into Central London for the large areas of housing that surround it. The A41 trunk road nearby runs in to the North Circular Road.*

Above: *In 1950 the inner London seats were reduced in number as those to the North increased. The rather austere 1883 built Peadbody Trust estate off Whitecross Street in the Bunhill ward of Finsbury was placed in a new combined Shoreditch & Finsbury Constituency. This is an example of model housing provided for the working classes.* **Gordon Rushton**

Left: In complete contrast, t*he Heathview stylish flats opposite Lissenden Gardens, where John Betjeman was born, are in Gordon House Road. Gospel Oak was in the North division of the Constituency of St. Pancras, the southern part of which was combined with Holborn. Very close nearby is Gospel Oak station, and not far away are four tube stations - so the area is exceptionally well-served by public transport.*

All images John Nelson except where marked

1970 Islington South West lost 32% of its numbers whilst Islington East lost 14% and Islington North 24%. In total 40,000 electors were lost, even after the increase that occurred in 1970 when the franchise was extended to the over 18s. By that time Islington East and South West were both 21% below the average for London and North was 18% below. It was inevitable in the face of falling rolls that there would be significant changes after the next Boundary Commission Review.

Politics in North London

Post-War General Election Results 1945 to 1970 by % majority

Constituency	*Pre 1945*	*1945*	*1950*	*1951*	*1955*	*1959*	*1964*	*1966*	*1970*
Finsbury (&) Shoreditch	*La La*	*Lab42 Lab48*	*Lab35*	*Lab45+*	*Lab47+*	*Lab34*	*Lab37*	*Lab47*	*Lab34*
Holborn & St. Pancras South (South East) (South West)	*C C C*	*C8 Lab28 Lab24*	*Lab3*	*Lab4+*	*Lab3*	*C2*	*Lab9*	*Lab19*	*Lab10*
St. Pancras North	*C*	*Lab29+*	*Lab19*	*Lab21*	*Lab16*	*Lab15*	*Lab26*	*Lab32*	*Lab21*
Hampstead	*C*	*C4*	*C22*	*C21*	*C24*	*C25*	*C4*	*Lab5*	*C1*
Islington South West	*1xC 1xLa*	*Lab42 Lab48+*	*Lab37*	*Lab36*	*Lab36*	*Lab30*	*Lab35*	*Lab41*	*Lab30*
Islington East	*C*	*Lab31*	*Lab20*	*Lab30*	*Lab21*	*Lab15*	*Lab24*	*Lab29*	*Lab23*
Islington North	*C*	*Lab35*	*Lab21*	*Lab19*	*Lab21+*	*Lab12*	*Lab24*	*Lab29+*	*Lab23*
Finchley	*C*	*C11*	*C21*	*C21*	*C23*	*C29*	*C17*	*C18*	*C24*
Hendon North		*Lab12*	*C5*	*C5*	*C9*	*C12*	*C3*	*C2*	*C9*
Hendon /South	*C*	*C5*	*C20*	*C21*	*C26*	*C29*	*C18*	*C11*	*C17*
*Barnet**	*C*	*Lab2*	*C17*	*C21*	*C22*	*C25*	*C16*	*C10*	*C17*
C	*11*	*4*	*5*	*5*	*5*	*6*	*5*	*4*	*5*
Lab	*2*	*11++*	*6*	*6++*	*6++*	*5*	*6*	*7+*	*6*
Total	*13*	*15*	*11*	*11*	*11*	*11*	*11*	*11*	*11*

Key: C = Conservative; Lab = Labour; + = Party that won seat at General Election held by-election in same Parliament; - = Party that won seat at General Election lost by-election to main opposition Party in same Parliament. * St. Albans before 1935.

The results of General Elections between 1945 and 1970 are shown in the table immediately above. They reflect the fundamental change in politics that occurred after the Second World War, with Labour assuming major significance as the largest Party in the elections of 1945, 1950, 1964 and 1966. It is equally clear that they established themselves as the most popular Party in this part of London, even in years when they failed to impress the electorate nationally. On the other hand, the impact of boundary changes, especially the rationalisation of seats in Islington and St Pancras coupled with the expansion in Hendon, on balance worked to the disadvantage of Labour.

Although one of the Hendon seats fell to Labour in 1945, this proved to be exceptional and at other times the division of the then Middlesex County Borough provided the Tories with two rather than the single seat the Party had held before the War. The merging of the two southern St Pancras seats with Holborn effectively removed two Labour seats and one Tory, replacing them with one marginal, whilst the merging of South with West Islington was a straight loss of one Labour MP. Had the 1945 seat structure remained unaltered this would have provided Labour with majorities in all general elections in the period as they were probably safe enough to survive Tory challenge, even in 1959.On the other hand it can be argued that the social composition of the older established areas of North London changed during the period with the wealthier residents moving out to the new suburbs and being replaced by more working class and increasingly ethnically diverse populations. The extent to which these favoured Labour was a factor that offered some compensation for the loss of safe seats through boundary changes.

During the period in question there were 7 by-elections in North London, all of them in Labour-held seats and, reflecting the relative political stability of the times, every one was retained. Two were in Shoreditch & Finsbury which

Labour retained on 21st October 1954 with a majority of 56% over the Tory as compared with 45% in 1951. On November 27th 1958 Labour won with a majority of 52% as compared with 47% in 1955. Holborn and St Pancras South experienced a by-election on 19th November 1953, when Labour held on with a majority of 7% compared with 4% at the 1951 Election. It retained the seat in 1955 Election by another slender margin, 3%.

On 25th September 1947 Labour retained Islington West with a majority of 31%. Though healthy, this did represent a substantial drop in support since 1945 when their majority was 48%. In the same Parliament Labour retained St Pancras North on 10th March 1949 by a margin of 18% compared with 29% at the 1945 contest. Both heralded a changing national mood that was to manifest itself in much closer general elections in 1950 and 1951. In Islington North there were two by-elections in the period. The first was on 15th May 1958 when Labour won by a margin of 38% compared with 21% at the 1955 Election and on 30th October 1969 when Labour's majority fell to 10% compared with that of 29% at the 1966 General Election.

Holborn

MPs for Holborn, St Pancras, and Hampstead

From	at	To	Surname	First Names	Constituency	Party
1945	G	1950	Aitken	Sir (John William Maxwell) 'Max'	Holborn	Conservative
1945	G	1950	Davies	Haydn	St. Pancras South West	Labour
1945	G	1950	Jeger	Dr. Santo Weyburn	St Pancras South East	Labour
1950	G	1953	Jeger	Dr. Santo Weyburn	Holborn & St. Pancras South	Labour
1953	B	1959	Jeger	Lena		Labour
1959	G	1964	Johnson Smith	Sir Geoffrey		Conservative
1964	G	1974	Jeger	Lena		Labour
1945	G	1949	House	George	St. Pancras North	Labour
1949	B	1970	Robinson	Kenneth		Labour
1970	G	1974	Stallard	Albert William		Labour
1945	G	1950	Challen	Charles	Hampstead	Conservative
1950	G	1966	Brooke	Sir Henry		Conservative
1966	G	1970	Whitaker	Ben(jamin) Charles George		Labour
1970	G	1974	Finsberg	Sir Geoffrey		Conservative

NOTE First returned at a B = By-election; G =General Election

Gp Cap. Max Aitken MP
St Pancras story

Group Captain Sir (John William Maxwell) 'Max' Aitken DSO, DFC, was born in Montreal in 1910, the son and heir of Lord Beaverbrook, the newspaper magnate and owner of the Express Group who had served under Churchill during the War. Educated at Westminster School and Pembroke College, Cambridge, where he was a soccer 'blue', he too entered the trade of journalism. During the War he served in the RAF and fought in the Battle of Britain. A night fighter pilot, he destroyed 16 German planes in 147 sorties and was Group-Captain of No. 601 County of London Squadron. He followed his father as the owner of the Express Group and succeeded as Lord Beaverbrook in 1964. Jonathan Aitken, a subsequently disgraced Tory MP and Cabinet Minister, was his son. Sir Max left politics in 1950 when Holborn was abolished as a stand-alone constituency. He died in 1980.

St Pancras South West

Haydn Davies (Labour) was elected in 1945. Son of a Welsh miner, he was born in 1905 and attended elementary school gaining a scholarship to the University of Wales where he took an Honours degree in English Literature. Originally a miner he subsequently became a teacher in London and President of the Schoolmasters' Association, a professional trade union formed in 1919. In 1929 he fought St Pancras South West unsuccessfully as a Liberal and two years later joined the Labour Party. In 1931 he led a march on County Hall in protest against the salary and education cuts made by the National Government. He entered journalism as education correspondent of the *News Chronicle*, a Liberal newspaper started in 1930, and then became Labour and industrial correspondent of *The Star*, one of London's evening papers between 1915 and 1960. He studied at the London School of Economics under Hugh Dalton, later Chancellor of the Exchequer under Attlee, and during the War was employed at the Ministry of Economic Welfare and the Board of Trade. Following his failure to be adopted for a St Pancras seat after re-distribution, he fought York in 1950 but lost by the slender margin of 77 votes and retired from politics. He died in 1976.

St Pancras South East, Holborn & St Pancras South

Dr Santo Jeger MP
People's History Museum Manchester

Dr Santo Weyburn Jeger (Labour) was born in 1898 and educated at elementary and secondary schools, then at University College, Cardiff. He trained and practised as a doctor at London and St Mary's Hospitals. In 1925 he was elected to Shoreditch Borough Council and was its mayor in 1930, the same year that he and others founded the Socialist Medical Association which campaigned for a free national health service. He was a member of the LCC from 1931 to 1946 during which period he also helped as a doctor working for the Republicans in the Spanish Civil War. In 1945 he was elected MP for St Pancras South East, moving in 1950 to the new seat of Holborn and St Pancras South, which he represented until his death in 1953.

Lena Jeger (Labour) won the Party nomination following the death of the husband she had married five years earlier and was elected at a November 1953 by-election. Born Lena May at Yorkley, Gloucestershire in 1915, she was educated at Southgate County School and London University and during the War was employed at the Ministry of Information and the Foreign Office. A fluent Russian speaker, she was assistant editor of *British Ally*, a newspaper published by the British Government for distribution in the Soviet Union but also worked in the British Embassy, Moscow. She lost her seat in 1959 and became a staff reporter on the *Guardian*, a moderate left wing national newspaper established in Manchester in 1825. She regained the constituency in 1964 and remained MP until 1979 when she was made a Baroness and elevated to the House of Lords. She was for many years after 1968 a member of the Labour Party's National Executive Committee and a Member of the Consultative Assembly of the Council of Europe and of Western European Union, between 1969-71. She was a councillor in St Pancras between 1945 and 1959 and on the LCC from 1952-55. She died in 2007.

Lena Jeger MP
Life in Legacy

Geoffrey Johnson-Smith MP
Public Record

(Sir) Geoffrey Johnson-Smith (Conservative) took the seat in 1959. Born in 1924, he went to Charterhouse School and Lincoln College, Oxford, before spending six years as a television interviewer with the BBC on the early evening 'Tonight' programme that made his name. Following his defeat in 1964 he entered Parliament again through a by-election at East Grinstead (East Sussex) a year later. From 1965-71 he was a Vice Chairman of the Tory Party under Ted Heath and a junior minister (at Defence) between 1971-2 and the Civil Service Department (1972-4). Following the Party's defeat and Margaret Thatcher's election as Leader, his career declined into that of a kindly backbencher and 1922 Committee member. His seat was renamed Wealden in 1983 and he retired in 2001. He died in 2010.

St Pancras North

George House (Labour) won the seat in 1945 but died precipitating a by-election in 1949. Born in 1892, he was educated at Avondale Road School in Bristol and at the Queen Elizabeth's hospital in that city. He became a steel erector in the construction industry and an active trade unionist. Prior to being elected an MP he was late Secretary of the Constructional Engineering Union. He became a London County Councillor in 1937.

Kenneth Robinson (Labour) won the 1949 by-election and retained the seat until 1970. Robinson was born in 1911 and educated at Oundle Public School. During the Second World War he became a lieutenant commander in the RNVR. A member of St Pancras Borough Council from 1945-9, he was also a member of the Metropolitan Regional Hospital Board and of the executive committee of the National Trust. After his election to Parliament he was made a Government Whip in 1950 and held the post until Labour's defeat at the 1951 General Election. In 1964 he was appointed Minister of Health in Harold Wilson's first Government, although this was not a Cabinet post at the time, and when the new post of Health and Social Services Secretary was established in 1968, Robinson moved to become Minister for Planning and Land under Anthony Greenwood. However, just under a year later this post was also abolished and he retired from politics in 1970 and was subsequently appointed Chairman of the English National Opera in 1972, holding the post until 1977. Part way through this term he was also made Chairman of London Transport, a post he held from 1975 to 1978. He also served on the Arts Council.

Albert William Stallard (Labour) was elected in 1970. Born in 1921, he was educated at Low Waters School in Hamilton and at the Lanarkshire town's Academy. A technical training officer, he was elected to St Pancras Borough Council in 1953 and to the successor Camden Council in 1963. Chairman of the Camden Town Disablement Committee and Mental Health Association, he was sponsored by the Amalgamated Union of Engineering Workers. When the Labour Government of February 1974 was returned he became a Whip and was also Chairman of the all-party committee for homeless and rootless people. In the elections of 1974 his Conservative opponent was John Major, the future Prime Minister. Stallard's seat was subsequently abolished and he ceased to be an MP at the 1983 election. He died in 2008 having been made a life peer in the year of his retirement from the Commons.

Hampstead

Charles Challen (Conservative) had been elected at a 1941 by-election and served until 1950 when the local Party Association failed to readopt him. His main biographical details may be found in Chapter 7.

(Sir) Henry Brooke (Conservative) was elected in 1950 and held the seat until defeated in the Labour landslide of 1966. His full biographical details can be found in Chapter 9 (Kent, Lewisham West).

When **Ben(jamin) Charles George Whitaker** (Labour) took the seat from Brooke in 1966 the result was regarded as a sensation as it was the first time in the constituency's history that it had not returned a Conservative. Despite this the seat reverted to its former loyalties in 1970 and remained in Tory hands until 1983 when it was redrawn as Hampstead and Highgate. Whitaker was born in 1934, educated at Eton and New College Oxford, and became a barrister at the Middle Temple in 1959. Also an author and journalist, he was a member of the executive committees of Justice and the Society of Labour Lawyers. He was an extra-mural lecturer at London University between 1963-4 and vice chairman of the Danilo Dolci Trust, an organisation established in support of the social improvement and anti-Mafia Italian campaigner of that name. After his election at Hampstead he became a Vice Chairman of the Parliamentary Labour Party's Home Affairs Committee and from 1969-70 was Parliamentary Secretary at the Ministry of Overseas Development. He died in June 2014

Hampstead, 1964: fragments of recorded history offer a window on the concerns of the moment. For Tories the 'Socialist threat' to Hampstead was very real, and this rather emotional appeal to Conservative voters indicates this. From 1966 to 1970 the seat was held by Labour, so the voters did not heed the advice!

Sir Geoffrey Finsberg (Conservative) was MP from 1970 until 1983, then for the new combined seat of Hampstead & Highgate, which he lost to Labour in 1992. Born in 1926 and educated at the City of London School for boys, he served as a councillor on Hampstead Borough and then Camden Council from 1949 to 1974. He was Council Leader of Camden from 1968 to 1970, when he became an MP, although his first incursion into Parliamentary politics came in 1955 when he stood unsuccessfully at Islington East. From 1968 to 1979 he was chairman of the Post Office Panel and of its Users National Committee from 1970-77 and was Opposition spokesman on the Greater London Council from 1974-9. He was also a vice chairman of the Conservative Party between 1975 and 1979 and attained ministerial rank as Under-Secretary of State for the Environment in 1979, then at Health and Social Security in 1981, a post he held until 1983 when he once again became a vice chairman of the party. He was a Director of Great Universal Stores[13] Transport Ltd and of Asda Property Holdings as well as

13 GUS was originally a mail order business known as Great Universal Stores. It was founded in Manchester by Abraham and George Rose in 1900. In 1930, the company became known as The Great Universal Stores Limited and, in the following year, was listed on the London Stock Exchange. By this stage, the company had grown to be the leading mail order business in the UK.

being a consultant to the OCS Group of Companies (Overseas Containers)[14]. In 1984 he was made a vice-chairman of the South East Regional Board of the Trustee Savings Bank. He died in 1996.

MPs for Finsbury, Shoreditch, Shoreditch & Finsbury, and Islington

From	at	To	Surname	First Names	Constituency	Party
1945	G	1950	Platts-Mills	John FaithfulFortescue	Finsbury	Labour/Ind
1945	G	1950	Thurtle	Ernest	Shoreditch	Labour
1950	G	1954	Thurtle	Ernest	Shoreditch & Finsbury	Labour
1954	B	1958	Collins	Victor John		Labour
1958	B	1964	Cliffe	Michael		Labour
1964	G	1974	Brown	Ronald William		Labour
1945	G	1970	Fletcher	Sir Eric George Molyneaux	Islington East	Labour
1970	G	1974	Grant	John		Labour
1945	B	1950	Haden-Guest	Leslie Haden	Islington North	Labour
1950	G	1951	Hughes	(Ronw) Moelwyn		Labour
1951	G	1958	Fienburgh	Wilfred		Labour
1958	B	1969	Reynolds	(Gerald) 'Gerry' William		Labour
1969	B	1974	O'Halloran	Michael Joseph		Labour
1945	G	1950	Cluse	William Sampson	Islington South	Labour
1945	G	1947	Montague	Frederick	Islington West	Labour
1947	B	1950	Evans	Albert		Labour
1950	G	1970	Evans	Albert	Islington South West	Labour
1970	G	1974	Cunningham	George		Labour

NOTE First returned at a B = By-election; G =General Election

Finsbury

John Faithful Fortescue Platts-Mills (Labour) was elected MP for Finsbury in 1945. Born in 1906 and raised in Wellington, New Zealand, he lived an outdoor life there until he was 21, working in the 'bush' and as a deck hand on the Pacific marine routes. He won a series of scholarships and studied under the Secretary of the country's Labour Party, Walter Nash. He represented the Victoria University at rowing, boxing, rugby and athletics, became a New Zealand Barrister, and then was sent as a Rhodes Scholar to Balliol College, Oxford where he obtained a BA and BCL with First Class Honours. He was there for three years from 1928 and would have rowed in the 1931 Boat Race had it not been for a last minute injury. He toured the US with the British Universities Debating Team and in 1932 became a London Barrister. He chaired the Lawyers' Labour Party Organisation and the Haldane Society[15] and was also a member of the National Council of Civil Liberties Executive. For a period he was also Treasurer of the Czechoslovakia-British Friendship Club and Secretary to the National Enquiry into Conditions of Youth in Industry. During the War he joined the RAF as he had previously qualified as a pilot in the RAF Auxiliary Unit when an undergraduate. He was subsequently also a Bevin Boy and worked down a coal mine in Yorkshire[16]. He was extremely left wing and in 1946, a year after being elected at Finsbury, visited both Yugoslavia and the Soviet Union. He fell out with the Labour Party over several issues, in particular international policy, and from 1947 he described himself as Independent Labour. He was expelled from the Party in 1948 and in 1950 went down to defeat, running fourth behind his erstwhile colleague and former Labour MP for Shoreditch,

John Platts-Mills MP, as he appeared on the cover of his book, 'Muck, Silk and Socialism'

14 In 1965, Overseas Containers Limited was formed by four major UK shipping companies to pioneer the development and use of containerisation and through transport. In 1986, it became wholly owned by P&O and was renamed P&O Containers.

15 The Haldane Society was founded in 1930. It is an organisation that provides a forum for the discussion and analysis of law and the legal system both nationally and internationally, from a socialist perspective.

16 The inception of the Bevin Boy scheme (named after the Minister of Labour, Ernest Bevin) was brought about by a shortfall of 50,000 coal miners due to men leaving the industry, either to join the armed forces or to work in other industries with better pay or more congenial working conditions. From December 1943 to May 1945 some 48,000 Bevin Boys were conscripted into the mining industry with around 26,000 being volunteers or men who had opted out of certain branches of the armed forces to return to the mining industry, the remaining 22,000 shortfall being made up of ballotees. During the period 1 in 10 men who became eligible for national service were directed to the mining industry.

Ernest Thurtle, in the newly merged constituency of Shoreditch & Finsbury. He resumed his career as a barrister in the early 1960s defending several notorious criminals including the 'Great Train Robbers' and the Kray twins. He died in 2001. He had been re-admitted to the Labour Party in 1969.

Shoreditch, Shoreditch & Finsbury

Ernest Thurtle (Labour) represented Shoreditch from 1923 to 1931 and from 1935 to 1945 when he was once again adopted for the seat, which he held until 1950 when it was merged with Finsbury. He remained MP for Shoreditch and Finsbury until his death in 1954. His principal biographical details are contained in Chapter 7 (Hackney and Shoreditch).

Victor Collins MP
UK Parliament

Victor John Collins (Labour) was returned at the by-election held in October 1954 following Thurtle's death. He had formerly been the MP for Taunton, which he represented from 1945-50, the only time in its history that the Somerset constituency was held by his Party. Born in London in 1903, Collins was educated at the Regent Street Polytechnic and the London School of Economics. A Somerset farmer and basket manufacturer, he was awarded the OBE for his wartime services to the basket trade in which he served as Chairman of the National Basket and Willow Trades Advisory Committee. He was also the President of the National Willow Growers' Association. He was made a life peer in 1958 and sat in the Upper House as Lord Stonham. From 1964-7 he was an Under-Secretary at the Home Office and a Minister of State from then until 1969. He died in 1971.

Michael Cliffe (Labour) took the seat at the by-election held in November 1958 when Collins became a life peer. Born in 1904, he was a clothing worker who rose through his industry's trade union, the Tailor and Garment Workers (UTWG), to join its National Executive. Although this was a Leeds based Union many of its members worked in the garment shops around Shoreditch, Finsbury and Whitechapel and there was therefore a strong presence in the constituency. A tailor's union had existed in London as early as 1417 but the UTGW was a late Victorian amalgamation of several smaller societies including the London Clothiers Cutters and the Amalgamated Jewish Tailors, Pressers and Machinists' Trade Union. He was a member of Finsbury Borough Council from 1949 to 1964, being mayor in 1956/7 and an alderman for the last 11 years. He died in 1964 and his seat was vacant at the dissolution.

People's History Museum Manchester

Ron(ald) William Brown (Labour) was born in 1921 and following an education at elementary school and the Borough Polytechnic, became a Lecturer[17]. He was a Senior Lecturer in Engineering and Principal of the Industrial Training School. Born in Camberwell, he was a member of the Borough Council there from 1956-65 when he was elected to the new Southwark Council on which he served until 1971. A strong pro-European, he was the younger brother of George Brown the Deputy Labour Leader and Cabinet Minister under Harold Wilson. Ron was a Parliamentary member of the Council of Europe Association and of the Western European Union from 1965-8, a member of the Council of Europe from 1974 and a Member of the European Parliament from 1977-9. A member of the British Institute of Management, he was also Chairman of the Energy Commission and 'rapporteur' on science, technology and aerospace at the European Parliament. He was Parliamentary Adviser to the Trade Union representing Furniture, Timber and Allied Trades, then a large part of the local Shoreditch economy[18]. When Brown's seat was redrawn he became MP for one that partly replaced it, namely Hackney South & Shoreditch, which he represented until 1983. However, he changed parties in 1981 to join the Social Democratic Party. Standing for the SDP/Liberal Alliance in 1983 he came third to Labour and was heavily defeated. He died in 2002.

Islington East

(Sir) Eric George Molyneaux Fletcher (Labour) was elected in 1945 and went on to serve as the MP until 1970 when he retired. Born in 1903 and educated at Radley School and the University of London, Fletcher was the son of a former Islington Town Clerk. A DDL (1932) he became a solicitor and author of various legal textbooks. For a while he was deputy chairman of the Associated British Picture Corporation, which was set up in the 1930s when talking movies began. During the 1950s the Corporation was split about whether to enter independent television. Pathe Pictures were

17 The Polytechnic was founded in 1892 and amalgamated with four other colleges in 1970 to become South Bank Polytechnic. Located in the Borough Road near the Elephant and Castle, it now has University status.
18 The union came into existence in 1871 with an amalgamation of the National Union of Furniture Trade Operatives and The Amalgamated Society of Woodcutting Machinists. It amalgamated with the GMB in 1994.

very keen, using the reasoning that television would reduce cinema audiences and therefore reduce ABPC profits, but Eric Fletcher, who represented Warner Brothers, was opposed. Fletcher's view was a minority and ATV was born in the Midlands in 1955. His political career had started in 1934 when he was elected a councillor on the LCC representing South Islington and was Chairman of its Finance Committee. Following Labour's election victory he was appointed a Minister without Portfolio in the 1964-6 Wilson Administration but did not return to Government after the General Election of 1966 and retired in 1970 when he was elevated as a life peer (Fletcher of Islington) and died in 1990.

John Grant (Labour) was MP for East Islington from 1970 to 1974 when he was adopted and elected for the newly drawn Central division, which he went on to represent until 1983. He joined the Social Democratic Party in 1981 and stood unsuccessfully for the SDP/Liberal Alliance in Islington North at the 1983 election coming in third behind Labour and the Conservative. Born in 1932, Grant was educated at grammar school and the Stationers' Company's School, Hornsey, after which he became a journalist working initially on regional papers and then for the Daily Express from 1955 to 1970 (from 1967 as its chief industrial correspondent). He contested Beckenham (South East London) in 1966 and after his election in 1970 became an Opposition spokesman on broadcasting and other media. After Labour's victory in February 1974, Grant was made Parliamentary Secretary at the Civil Service Department and following the victory in the October election became Under-Secretary of State, Overseas Development, which post he held until 1976 when he was moved to Employment. He later became Chairman of the SDP's Trade Unionists Association and fought Carshalton, where he lost in 1987. Out of the House he worked as public relations chief for the Electricians and Plumbers Union from 1984 to 1989 (then under the firm control of moderates) and after 1990 was also a member of the Radio Authority, and became chairman of Radio South-East. He died of cancer in 2000.

John Grant MP
People's History Museum Manchester

Islington North

Dr. Leslie Haden Haden-Guest (Labour) was elected at a 1937 by-election and remained MP until 1950 when he was made a life peer. His principal biographical details may be found in Chapter 7.

He was succeeded in 1950 by **(Ronw) Moelwyn Hughes KC** (Labour), who was born in 1897, the son of a former Moderator of the Welsh Presbyterian Church. He was educated at the University of Wales and at Cambridge after which he pursued a career as a barrister and judge, becoming Recorder of Bolton in 1946 and serving until 1953. In 1941 he was elected MP for Carmarthen at a by-election but unusually lost the seat at the 1945 General Election and was out of the House for the whole of the 1945 Parliament. During this period he was asked by the Government to report into an appalling accident at Bolton Wanderers' Burnden Park Football Ground, where serious overcrowding and lack of effective crowd control gave rise to 33 deaths and injuries to hundreds on the occasion of a Cup-Tie with Stoke City. The turnstile count was approximately 65,000 with some 2,000 gaining illegal entry and an estimated 15,000 were turned away when the gates were closed. The problems were exacerbated because the Ministry of Supply had requisitioned the Burnden Stand as storage space during the War and the facility had not yet been returned to its normal usage and the turnstiles at the east end of the Railway Embankment which adjoined that stand had been closed since 1940. His proposals did not lead to much stricter safety standards at grounds or to licensing but to self regulation that was not superseded by changes to the law until the Ibrox (Glasgow) disaster in 1971[19]. He retired in 1951 after only a very brief spell as an Islington MP and died in 1955.

Wilfred Fienburgh (Labour) was elected in 1951. Born in 1919 he was educated at the Belle Vue School in Bradford (West Riding of Yorkshire). During the War he served with the Rifle Brigade and became a Major in the General Staff. He joined the civil service and became Assistant Secretary of the Civil Service Clerical Association[20], 1946-7, and worked for the Labour Party Research Department from 1947-51, being the secretary for the final year. From 1950-1 he was also the Labour Party representative on the economic committee of the TUC. He died in 1958.

Gerald (Gerry) William Reynolds (Labour) was MP from 1958 until his death in 1969. Born in 1927 and educated at Acton County Grammar School he went on to become Treasurer of the London Federation of Trade Councils (1952-64). He entered local politics as a councillor in his native Acton in 1949 and served until it became part of the new London Borough of Ealing, which he chaired in its inaugural year, 1964-5. He first contested a Parliamentary election

19 Source: 'Have They Forgotten Bolton?' (The British Society of Sports History).
20 The Civil Service Clerical Association was formed in 1921 after the amalgamation of the Civil Service Clerical Union and the Clerical Officers Association. It was first formed to promote the interests of both permanent and temporary Civil Service staff. The union then had a membership of over 16,000 and was affiliated with the TUC and the Labour Party until 1927, when under the terms of the Trade Disputes Act, government employees were forced to disaffiliate. It re-affiliated with the TUC in 1946. In 1969 it adopted its current title, the Civil and Public Services Association (CPSA).

at Worthing (West Sussex) where he was unsuccessful in 1951 but won the by-election at Islington North in May 1958. From 1964-5 he was Under Secretary at the Ministry of Defence under Dennis Healey and was made Minister of Defence for the Army in 1965. He died in 1969.

Michael Joseph O'Halloran (Labour) was returned at the by-election in October 1969, following Reynolds' death. Born in 1928 in the Republic of Ireland and educated at Clohane's National School in Skibbereen, County Cork, he came to England as a building worker before becoming a railwayman and later, office manager. A member of Islington Council from 1967 to 1971, this provided a power base for him to launch a surprise but successful bid to become the party's candidate at the by-election. He joined the Social Democratic Party in 1981 but subsequently resigned from that as well, sitting as Independent Labour. He remained an MP until 1983 but came fourth at the General Election behind the official Labour candidate, a Conservative and Grant, the Alliance candidate and former Labour MP for East and Central Islington. This election was unique in that three of the candidates contesting the seat were effectively all sometime members of the Labour Party. This is not as peculiar as might at first appear because at the time the Labour Party in Islington was in the grip of particularly militant left wingers and erstwhile moderates were under threat of de-selection prompting them to seek new political allies. He died in 1999.

Islington South

William Sampson Cluse (Labour) was MP for two fairly lengthy periods. First elected in 1923, he remained the constituency's MP until he was defeated in Labour's 1931 rout. However, he won there again in 1935, was re-elected in 1945 and remained MP until 1950. His principal biographical details are in Chapter 7.

Islington West, Islington South West

Frederick Montague (Labour) won Islington West in 1923, was defeated in 1931 and re-elected four years later. He remained its MP until 1947 when he retired. His main biographical details are contained in Chapter 7.

He was succeeded by **Albert Evans** (Labour), who was born in 1903, won the by-election in 1947 and was re-elected in 1950 for the newly created South West Islington division. He was a master engraver and had been a member of the Goldsmiths' Jewellers and Allied Trades Society since 1925. A member of Islington Borough council from 1937, he was also an LCC councillor from 1946-9. He retired in 1970. He died in 1988.

George Cunningham (Labour) was born in Scotland in 1931 and educated at Dunfermline High School. His family then moved to Blackpool and he continued his education at the Lancashire town's Grammar School before completing it at the Universities of Manchester and London. He became the Commonwealth Officer of the Labour Party and contested Henley (Oxfordshire) in 1966. Returned at Islington South in 1970, he was re-elected for the newly drawn Islington South & Finsbury in February 1974, retaining the seat until 1983. In the run up to the 1979 election when Scottish devolution was a major issue, the Callaghan Government introduced legislation to allow a referendum. With the House largely divided on Party lines but with a few Labour MPs opposed to devolution, Cunnigham introduced an amendment to the Bill that proved decisive in ensuring that the electorate would be unlikely to approve the measure. With the support of five Labour MPs (including Robin Cook and Tam Dalyell) he managed to insert into the Bill the reservation that unless 40% of the total electorate voted 'yes', then the measure would fall. In the event this is what occurred and devolution had to wait over 20 years for the political tide to turn. The measure also prompted the wrath of the Scottish Nationalists so that when the Tory Opposition called a 'no confidence' motion in the Government, Labour was defeated precipitating a general election and the rise of Margaret Thatcher. Cunningham was for a brief period between 1979 and 1981 an Opposition spokesman on home affairs but he resigned from the Party in November of that year to become an Independent Labour member. In June 1982 he joined the Social Democratic Party and fought the 1983 General Election for the SDP/Liberal Alliance, polling just 1% fewer votes than the Labour winner, Chris Smith. Several years later he re-joined the Labour Party but never resumed his career.

MPs for Finchley, and Hendon

MPs for Finchley

Sir John Ellenborough Crowder (Conservative) was MP from 1935 to 1945 when he was re-elected and remained until 1959. His principal biographical details are contained in Chapter 7.

Mrs Margaret Hilda Thatcher (Conservative) was returned in 1959 and retained the seat until 1992, when she was elevated to the House of Lords as a Baroness. One of the most important figures of modern political, indeed of

MPs for Finchley, and Hendon						
From	**at**	**To**	**Surname**	**First Names**	**Constituency**	**Party**
1945	*G*	*1959*	*Crowder*	*Sir John Ellenborough*	*Finchley*	*Conservative*
1959	*G*	*1974*	*Thatcher*	*Mrs. Margaret Hilda*		*Conservative*
1945	*G*	*1950*	*Gould*	*Mrs. Barbara Bodichon Ayrton*	*Hendon North*	*Labour*
1950	*G*	*1970*	*Orr-Ewing*	*Sir Charles Ian*		*Conservative*
1970	*G*	*1974*	*Gorst*	*Sir John*		*Conservative*
1945	*G*	*1950*	*Munro-Lucas-Tooth*	*Sir Hugh Vere*	*Hendon South*	*Conservative*
1970	*G*	*1974*	*Thomas*	*Peter John Mitchell*		*Conservative*
NOTE First returned at a B = By-election; G =General Election						

British history, she was the first and so far the only woman to become Leader of a major political party at Westminster, and to attain the rank of Prime Minister. She is also historically important as the only serving Prime Minister to have been overthrown entirely by the actions of her own Party, when she stood down in 1991 after the first ballot of a leadership election that had been forced on her by a disaffected Parliamentary Party. The same could be argued about Tony Blair, who was the Labour Prime Minister from 1997 to 2007 when he was succeeded by Gordon Brown, but in this case Blair stood down and did not therefore face an election for the leadership of his Party.

Wikipedia

Born at Grantham (Lincolnshire) in 1926, she was the daughter of a local grocer and town mayor, Albert Roberts. She attended the Kesteven and Grantham High School for Girls in the town and won a bursary to Somerville College Oxford where she took a BSc (Research) in Chemistry. Whilst at the University she became only the third woman to become President of the University Conservative Association. Afterwards she became a research chemist, working in the Colchester area, and in 1950 contested her first Parliamentary election at Dartford in Kent where she lost to Labour by nearly 14,000 votes. She also became a law student and in 1951 was personal assistant to the director of the Joint Iron Council. She fought Dartford again in 1951, though unsuccessfully, and afterwards married Denis Thatcher, a businessman who was also a member of her local Conservative Association. She became a barrister in 1954 being called to the bar at Lincoln's Inn. She had twin babies, a boy and a girl, and spent the first few years of her life as a housewife and mother. However, in 1959 she returned to the hustings on being selected as the Tory candidate for the then safe seat of Finchley, which she won with a comfortable majority. In 1961 she was made Parliamentary Secretary at the Ministry of Pensions, a post she held until the Tory Government was defeated at the 1964 Election at which point she returned to the backbenches but this time in Opposition. From 1969-70 she was Shadow Education Minister and, when Edward Heath unexpectedly took the Conservatives back to power in 1970, she was appointed Secretary of State for Education and Science. She acquired an unwanted reputation as something of a 'Scrooge' character when she implemented a proposal to eliminate the provision of school milk and earned the title, 'Margaret Thatcher, Milk Snatcher' in Labour supporting newspapers. The Tories were defeated in February 1974 and she returned to Opposition, this time as spokesperson on the environment in Heath's Shadow Cabinet.

In 1975 Thatcher challenged Heath and William Whitelaw for the leadership of the Party and was unexpectedly elected, going on to become Prime Minister after winning the 1979 General Election. Her early years of power were controversial as she followed a monetarist policy that created huge unemployment in the heavy industry sector of the economy. She looked as though she would be a one term Premier but, following the invasion by Argentina of the British Falkland Islands in 1982, she prosecuted a War with great determination and ruthlessness, the success of which provided a strong basis for another election victory in 1983, aided by a split in the Labour Party which led to the creation of the Social Democratic Party and the loss of a number of its prominent MPs. Confronting a split opposition, she remained Prime Minister throughout the 1980s and pursued a radical agenda of economic liberalisation, tax cuts and privatisation. However, with an increasing confidence she came to be perceived as increasingly shrill and strident in her tone and lost much of her former public support. This led to an erosion of support within her own Parliamentary Party. Her decision

With Ronald Regan at the White House in 1988
White House

to proceed with the Community Charge (or 'Poll Tax' as it was popularly known at the time) caused enormous social upheaval and unrest as well as dissension within her own Party. She gradually lost the support of an increasing number of Tory MPs and in late 1991 she was challenged for the Party leadership by a so called 'stalking horse' (Sir Anthony Meyer MP), a relatively obscure back bencher whose role was to test the water for a stronger candidate. He attracted a fairly large number of votes triggering an official challenge from Michael Heseltine, her main opponent from the more moderate wing of the party and a former Cabinet Minister who had resigned from her Government a few years earlier. She just failed to secure the requisite number of votes in the first ballot but, following the advice of most of her Cabinet that she should resign, she did so and quit Number Ten. So ended a premiership that had lasted 12 years, the longest of the Twentieth Century. She retired in 1992 and was made a Baroness but remained a powerful and vocal critic of the Party in Government under her successor, John Major, arguably contributing to an unwanted image of divisiveness that led to its biggest election defeats in 1997 and 2001. She died in 2013 and was accorded the privilege of a funeral with full military honours in St Paul's Cathedral.

Hendon North

B Ayrton-Gould MP
Wikipedia

Mrs. Barbara Bodichon Ayrton Gould (Labour) was educated at Notting Hill High School between 1919 and 1921 and entered left wing politics at an early stage in her life. She was Publicity Manager of the *Daily Herald* and helped organise the Miners' Wives and Children's Fund during a lockout by employers. The *Herald* had been launched in 1911 as a strike sheet for the newspaper unions who were conducting a dispute for better pay and conditions. It was so successful that it was continued as a socialist daily though it was so beset by financial problems that the TUC subsidised it until 1929 when it was acquired by Odhams Press. By 1933 the paper had increased its circulation to two million daily copies making it the world's best selling newspaper at that time[21]. From 1926 to 1934 Gould was a Trade Union member of the Labour Exchange Committees and Courts of Referees (early forms of industrial arbitration and conciliation) and from 1936-7 sat on the Labour Party Distressed Areas Commission[22]. She was a member of the National Executive of the Party for sixteen years, then Vice Chairman and Chairman between 1939 and 1940. She led a delegation to Spain in 1937 and was a member for the Standing Joint Committee Working Women's Organisation from 1929 onwards, becoming Chairman in 1931-2. She was the widow of Gerald Gould, a poet and writer, and the daughter of parents, both of who were physicists. Her mother was active in a militant arm of the women's suffragette movement, a campaign which Barbara joined in 1906 at the age of twenty. She was elected for Hendon North in 1945 but was defeated at the next contest in 1950 and died later that year.

She was succeeded by **Charles Ian Orr-Ewing** (Conservative), born in 1912, who was educated at Harrow School and Trinity College, Oxford. He served an apprenticeship in the radio industry and joined the BBC television service in 1937, a year after Baird's thirty line system was replaced by the world's first regular high-resolution (405 lines per picture) system. Throughout the Second World War he worked on radar systems for the RAF, serving in North Africa, Italy, France and Germany. He was adopted as Tory candidate for Hendon North in 1946 and from 1947-8 was a member of the executive of the Conservative Party. He was a Member of the Institute of Electrical Engineers and a Governor of Imperial College. In Macmillan's Government he was under-Secretary at the Air Ministry from 1957-59 (January) and a First Secretary at the Admiralty in early 1959, then Civil Lord from October 1959 until the end of the Macmillan Government in 1963. He retired in 1970 and was made a life Peer (Lord Berkhamstead) the following year. He died in 1999.

(Sir) John Gorst (Conservative) succeeded him in 1970. Born in 1928, he was the great grandson of Sir Eldon Gorst, who was the first Conservative Party chairman under Benjamin Disraeli[23]. Educated at Branksome-Hilders School, Haslemere, Surrey, at Ardingly School in Sussex, and at Corpus Christi College Cambridge, and after a two year spell as a teacher in 1951-53, and a short period working at a Bognor Regis Holiday Camp, he went to work for the Pye

21 The Herald's fortunes gradually declined and in 1964 was re-launched as the Sun which went on to become Britain's largest circulation newspaper though when it came under the ownership of Rupert Murdoch in 1969 it moved from being a left wing to a right wing newspaper and was a staunch supporter of the Tory Governments of the 1980s and early 1990s though it reverted to supporting Labour under Tony Blair's leadership.

22 In its 1935 manifesto Labour promised to 'attack the problem of the distressed areas by special steps designed to deal with the root causes of their troubles, as part of a vigorous policy of national planning'.

23 Sir Eldon was the first chairman of the National Union of Conservative and Constitution Associations in 1867 and established what became the Party's Central Office. He was a strong advocate of working class Toryism but towards the end of his career stood as a Liberal candidate in 1910 and saw Asquith's Government introduce many of the social reforms that he had advocated as a Conservative.

Conservative

Sir John Gorst MP
People's |History Museum

Corporation and from 1953-63 was its advertising and public relations manager.[24] He set up his own public relations consultancy before entering the House in 1970. He held the seat for many years but was defeated at the 1997 General Election. He died in 2010 at the age of 82.

Hendon South

Sir Hugh Vere Munro-Lucas-Tooth of Teaninich (Conservative) was born in 1903, the son of Major Hugh Munro Warrand of the Queen's Own Cameron Highlanders. Eton and Balliol College Oxford – educated, he assumed the name Lucas-Tooth in 1920 when the baronetcy was recreated in favour of the eldest grandson of the first baronet, who died after losing three sons in France during the War. In 1965 he added the Scottish lairdship, Munro of Teaninich, and changed his name by deed poll. From 1924-9 he was Tory MP for the Isle of Ely (Cambridgeshire) and in 1933 was called to the bar at Lincoln's Inn. During the Second World War he served as a Lieutenant Colonel, like his father in the Queen's Own Cameron Highlanders, and was at one time an assistant to the Adjutant-General at the War Office. From 1952-55 he was Under-Secretary at the Home Office. He retired in 1970. He died in 1985.

Peter John Mitchell Thomas (Conservative) was elected in 1970. Born in 1920, he was educated at Epworth College, Rhyl and Jesus College, Oxford and became a barrister at the Middle Temple in 1947 and a QC in 1965. From 1951 to 1966 he was MP for Conway in his native North Wales. He served under Macmillan in junior ministerial roles, initially as Parliamentary Secretary, Ministry of Labour from 1959-61, then as Under-Secretary of State at the Foreign Office until 1963. When Alec Douglas-Home became Prime Minister in that year he was made a Minister of State at the Foreign Office and after the Party's defeat at the 1964 Election he became an Opposition spokesman on law and foreign affairs. He lost his seat to Labour in 1966 and was appointed Deputy Chairman of the Cheshire Quarter Sessions, then of Denbighshire Quarter Sessions from 1968. From 1965-70 he was also a member of the Historic Buildings council for Wales. After his election at Hendon South in 1970 he was appointed Secretary of State for Wales in Edward Heath's new Government. Following the return of a Labour Government in 1974, Thomas was President of the National Union of Conservative and Unionist Associations from 1974-6. He retired in 1987 and was made a life peer. He died in 2008.

MPs for Barnet

From	*at*	*To*	*Surname*	*First Names*	*Constituency*	*Party*
1945	*G*	*1950*	*Taylor*	*Dr Stephen James Lake*	*Barnet*	*Labour*
1950	*G*	*1974*	*Maudling*	*Reginald*	*Barnet*	*Conservative*

NOTE First returned at a B = By-election; G =General Election

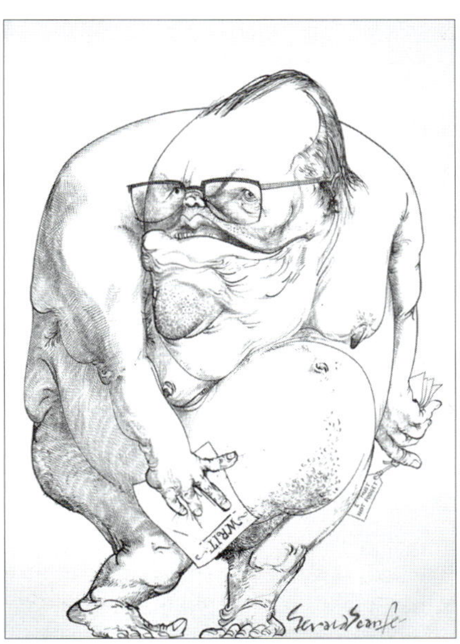

Gerald Scarfe's cartoon of Maudling in 1967
© National Portrait Gallery

Dr. Stephen James Lake Taylor (Labour) was elected in 1945. Born in 1910, he was educated at Stowe School and St Thomas's Hospital after which he became a neuro-psychiatric specialist. During the Second World War he served in the RNVR as a Lieutenant-Commander. In 1940 he was Director of the Ministry of Information Home Intelligence Division and of the Wartime Social Survey. During the 1945-50 Parliament he was PPS to Herbert Morrison and a policy adviser on the setting up of the National Health Service. Created a Baron in 1958, Taylor served in the first Wilson Government as an Under Secretary (Commonwealth Relations and the Colonies) but subsequently left the Labour Party in the period it suffered major conflicts of ideology and became a cross bencher in the House of Lords. He died seven years later in 1988

In 1950 Taylor was defeated by **Reginald Maudling** (Conservative) **who** was MP for the Hertfordshire constituency of Barnet from 1950 until 1974 and for the London seat of Chipping Barnet from 1974 until 1979 when he retired. Born in 1917, he was educated at Merchant Taylors' School and Merton College, Oxford, became a barrister at the Middle Temple in 1940, and a company director. He first contested a Parliamentary seat in 1945

24 In 1896 William George Pye started a part time business making scientific instruments while he was employed at the Cavendish Laboratory in Cambridge. It grew to manufacture radios, televisions and gramophones. About the time Gorst joined the Company it launched the famous Pye Record Label.

when he lost at Heston & Isleworth but was elected in 1950 at Barnet. His ministerial progress was rapid, marking him out as a possible leader of his Party. In 1952 he was made Parliamentary Secretary at the Ministry of Civil Aviation followed a year later by promotion to be Economic Secretary at the Treasury. He was Minister of Supply in Eden's Government from 1955 to 1957 and then successively Paymaster-General (1957-9), President of the Board of Trade (1959-61), Secretary of State for the Colonies (1961-3) and Chancellor of the Exchequer (1962-4), serving also in that capacity under Sir Alec Douglas-Home after Macmillan resigned. Following his Party's defeat in 1964 he was a candidate for the Party Leadership in 1965 but lost to Edward Heath and instead became his Deputy. When Heath became Prime Minister in 1970 Maudling was made Home Secretary but stepped down two years later amidst the whiff of financial scandal and concentrated on defending his business activities[25]. He was re-elected in 1974 but retired from politics in 1979 and died the same year.

The East End and North East Middlesex – Stepney, Poplar, Bethnal Green, Hackney, Stoke Newington, Tottenham, Wood Green, Hornsey, Edmonton, and Enfield (17 seats in 1945 and 12 after 1950)

In 1945 there were no boundary changes affecting East London which retained the 17 seats created in 1918, namely **Whitechapel & St George's, Mile End, Poplar South, Bow & Bromley, Limehouse, Bethnal Green North East, Bethnal Green South West, Hackney South, Hackney North, Hackney Central, Stoke Newington, Tottenham North, Tottenham South, Wood Green, Hornsey, Edmonton** and **Enfield.** Full details are in Chapter 7.

However, in 1950 several changes of significance occurred resulting in a net loss of five seats. In docklands, where wartime bombing had wiped out so much housing, the boroughs of Stepney and Poplar lost four seats and were reduced to three. **Stepney** became a single member borough in what was essentially a merger of the former Whitchapel & St Georges, Limehouse and Mile End divisions, comprising Aldgate, Globe Town, Limehouse, Mile End, Ratcliffe, St Katherine Docks, Shadwell, Spitalfields, Stepney Green, Stepney, the Tower of London, Whitechapel and Wapping. **Poplar** was a similar merger of the former Bow & Bromley and Poplar South constituencies. It extended south from Victoria Park to Millwall Docks and incorporated Blackwall, Bow, Bow Common, Bromley by Bow, Cubitt Town, East India Dock, the Isle of Dogs, Millwall, Old Ford, Poplar, West India Dock and Westferry. **Bethnal Green** too became a single-member borough constituency as a result of the merger of the two former North East and South West divisions and extended from beyond Spitalfields and Liverpool Street station to Cambridge Heath and London Fields incorporating Roman Road and Weavers.

Stoke Newington & Hackney North also became one seat instead of two. Officially it comprised the borough of Stoke Newington (including Clissold Park, Finsbury Park, Lordship Park Manor and Stamford Hill) and five Hackney wards embracing all districts of Clapton – Upper (Springfield ward), Lower with Clapton Park (Leaside ward), Upper Clapton/ Stamford Hill(Stamford and Springfield wards), and Clapton proper (Maury and Southwold wards). **Hackney South** covered all the remaining districts in the borough of Hackney, that is everywhere except Clapton. These were Dalston, De Beavoir Town, Homerton, Hackney Downs, Hackney Wick, Hackney Marsh, London Fields, Shacklewell, South Hackney and Victoria Park. Hackney Central was abolished so the area's representation was reduced from four to two. However, in 1955 further changes affected the three boroughs of Stoke Newington, Hackney and Bethnal Green, which were amalgamated for the purposes of creating more equitable boundaries, though the number of seats remained the same in total. Hackney South disappeared this time with four wards re-allocated to **Bethnal Green.** As a result this constituency incorporated Bethnal Green, Cambridge Heath, Hackney Wick, Homerton, London Fields (Triangle ward), Roman Road, South Hackney, Victoria Park and Weavers. **Hackney Central** re-appeared acquiring South Hackney's remaining wards together with parts of Clapton. These were now represented by nine newly designated wards – Albion (Dalston), Kingsland (De Beavoir Town), Pembury (Hackney Downs), Town Hall (Central Hackney), Kenninghall (Clapton), Rushmore (Clapton) Leabridge (Lower Clapton), Kingsmead (Clapham Park), and Chatham (Homerton/ Clapton). **Stoke Newington & Hackney North** gained the West Downs area of Shacklewell from the former South division. It comprised all of Stoke Newington borough (including Clissold Park, Finsbury Park, Lordship Park Manor and Stamford Hill) and four Hackney wards – Rectory (Shacklewell), Northfield (Stamford Hill), Northwold (Clapton), and

25 Lewis Baston's biography 'Reggie' reveals that several weeks after he had become Home Secretary in 1970 Maudling sought money from the former Poulson organisation writing a letter saying that '£3,000 will meet my cash requirements for the foreseeable future'. This was under the letterhead of International Technical and Constructional Services, even though he had already resigned from its board on becoming a minister. The money was paid and Baston concludes: 'It was grossly improper conduct, involving abuse of office, an unacceptable private interest, and quite probably fraud and theft.' (The Times December 11th 2004)

Left: *Following war time bombing and slum clearances, the Victorian character of the East End changed. Many down at heel terraces were replaced by forbidding looking but modern council blocks, like these in Rich St on the boundary between the Stepney and Poplar Constituencies, created in 1950.* **Gordon Rushton**

Below: *The affluent Cotswold Way houses are part way between Oakwood tube and Enfield Chase railway stations in a leafy suburb of the Enfield West Constituency. It was when built, and still is now, on the edge of the 'permitted' development of London that was intensively built in the 1930s. Further urban sprawl ceased after the Green Belt restrictions came into operation with the Town and Country Planning Act in 1947.*

Below: *Just down the road from Manor House Piccadilly Line tube station is the Amwell Council Estate in Green Lanes. It backs onto the New River path, that leads to the West and East reservoirs. In 1950 the then new flats in the Amwell Estate were placed in the Hackney North & Stoke Newington Constituency.*

Above: *WW2 left massive damage in the East End of London, so much so that the decision was made to clear the area and set some of it aside as recreation area. This is Mile End Park, a 79 acre stretch of land from Cambridge Heath almost as far as Limehouse. It forms the boundary between the 1950 Stepney and Poplar Constituencies.*

Left: *Palmers Green Railway Station in the Southgate Constituency. The line between London and Enfield opened in 1871, but serious development had to wait until the turn of the Century. Then the area became built up, with an excellent service of trains facilitating travel into the City. In 1960 the line was electrified to Enfield, and eventually the whole Hertford Loop was done .* **Wikipedia**

All images John Nelson except where marked

Springfield (Upper Clapton).

Further afield **Tottenham** reverted to a single seat in 1950 based on the entire borough less three wards. The constituency comprised Bruce Grove, Downhills Park, Harringay, Seven Sisters, South Tottenham, Tottenham proper, and Tottenham Hale. **Wood Green** was extended eastwards to include the White Hart Lane (including Northumberland Park), Park and Coleraine wards (Turnpike Lane) that had been in Tottenham North since 1918. These joined Alexandra Palace, Bounds Green, Noel Park and Wood Green itself. At the same time certain residential areas to the north were transferred to a new Southgate constituency (see below). **Hornsey**, was unaltered compared with 1918. The electorates of these three new seats were similar but all larger than the London average at the time. Hornsey had 74,000 electors, Tottenham 67,000 and Wood Green 66,000. The total electorates of these three seats, one less than in 1945, was only 14,000 fewer than Enfield, Edmonton and Southgate combined, which were allocated four seats, two more than 1945. Even if they were not intended to do so, the 1950 changes anticipated the population trends of the next twenty years.

Enfield's expansion resumed after the War with many green acres lost. In 1950 it was divided into two constituencies and a third was created centred on Southgate in the increasingly affluent outer suburban area. **Enfield East** covered the town closest to the River Lea and was officially embraced within three UDC wards – Central, South East and North East including Brimsdown, Bulls Cross, Durants Park, Enfield proper, Enfield Highway, Enfield Lock, Enfield Wash, Ponders End and Turkey Street. **Enfield West** covered the rather wealthy, middle class communities around and including Enfield Chase. Potters Bar (now in Hertsmere) was included, as were Gordon Hill, Forty Hill and west Bullsmoor in the South West and West wards of Enfield UDC. Other communities within its boundaries were Clay Hill, Forty Hill, Grange Park, Hadley Wood and Trent Park. South of Enfield, the **Edmonton** constituency remained unaltered covering the then county borough. **Southgate** sat due west of Edmonton and was of a similar geographical size taking all of its electors from parts of the former Wood Green constituency. In 1950 it incorporated Arnos Grove, Bowes, Bowes Park, Cockfosters, Oakwood, Palmers Green, Southgate itself and Winchmore Hill.

Despite these attempts to balance electorates there were still major variations. Enfield East had less than 48,000 voters and West barely more than 41,000, both well below the average, whereas Edmonton had grown to 75,000 and the new Southgate seat had over 57,000. Although there was some room for expansion, by 1970 Enfield East was more or less unchanged and Enfield East had grown to 53,000 including new 18-year-old voters. Edmonton's electorate fell to 63,000, whilst Southgate fell only slightly to 56,000, all trends making for a generally better balance than had existed in 1950. By 1970 the combined electorates of the four Enfield based seats was about the same (220,000) but the three around Tottenham had fallen to 171,000 (Hornsey 65,000, Tottenham 51,000 and Wood Green 55,000)

Politics in the East End and North East Middlesex

The 1945 Election (Results shown in the table opposite) marked a major change in the political map of the East End and north East London with Labour becoming entrenched as the Party of preferred choice in most constituencies. However, the reduction in seats that after 1950 worked mainly to Labour's disadvantage as this occurred, with the exception of Wood Green, in what would otherwise have been Labour-held seats in good times as well as bad. The creation of additional seats in the Enfield area on the other hand worked mainly to the advantage of the Conservatives.

What is most striking is the lack of marginal seats, each one being relatively safe, probably due to the polarised social composition of the seats in question during this period. Another notable outcome was the return of a Communist at Mile End in 1945. Philip Piratin had been the first Communist member of Stepney Borough Council on which he became a 'one man opposition', though he lost his council seat in 1949. He also lost his status as an MP when the Mile End constituency was merged with Whitechapel in 1950, and the new Stepney constituency returned Labour with over five times the number of votes received by Philip Piratin.

There were only 3 by-elections in the East End during this period. On 13th December 1945 Labour retained North Tottenham but its majority fell from 44% to 27%. On 13th November 1948 a by-election at Edmonton showed further evidence of a swing towards the Tories. Labour held the seat that it had won at the 1945 General Election by a commanding 39% margin with a new majority of only 13%. On 30th May 1957 a by-election was held at Hornsey. The Tories retained the seat with a majority of 7% compared with 23% at the 1955 General Election. The majority remained at 7% in the 1959 Election and failed to record the swing back to the Tories seen nationally.

Post War General Election Results 1945 to 1970 by % majority									
Constituency	**Pre 1945**	**1945**	**1950**	**1951**	**1955**	**1959**	**1964**	**1966**	**1970**
Bethnal Green (North East) (South West)	*L 1L/La*	*La29 La21*	*Lab33*	*Lab49*	*Lab53*	*Lab44*	*Lab47*	*Lab53*	*Lab41*
Stepney (Limehouse) (Mile End) (Whitechapel)	*La C/La Lab/L*	*La68 Com11 Lab75*	*Lab57*	*Lab50*	*Lab58*	*Lab48*	*Lab51*	*Lab60*	*Lab55*
Poplar (Bow & Bromley) (Poplar South)	*La La*	*La68 La78*	*Lab63*	*Lab64*	*Lab63*	*Lab54*	*Lab55*	*Lab69*	*Lab61*
Hackney Central/ South (Central) (South)	*L/La C/L*	*Lab45 Lab27*	*Lab35*	*Lab36*	*Lab27*	*Lab23*	*Lab33*	*Lab42*	*Lab30*
Hackney North & Stoke Newington (North) (Stoke Newington)	*C C*	*Lab43 Lab23*	*Lab23*	*Lab25*	*Lab23*	*Lab20*	*Lab29*	*Lab39*	*Lab28*
Tottenham (North) (South)	*La 1C/La*	*Lab44+ Lab55*	*Lab26*	*Lab25*	*Lab20*	*Lab16*	*Lab22*	*Lab31*	*Lab23*
Wood Green	*C*	*C9*	*Lab16*	*Lab12*	*Lab8*	*Lab3*	*Lab13*	*Lab22*	*Lab14*
Hornsey	*C*	*C27*	*C18*	*C17*	*C23+*	*C7*	*C8*	*C1*	*C9*
Edmonton	*Lab*	*Lab39+*	*Lab18*	*Lab17*	*Lab13*	*Lab0.8*	*Lab10*	*Lab15*	*Lab5*
Southgate			*C39*	*C40*	*C42*	*C40*	*C31*	*C29*	*C36*
Enfield/ East	*C*	*Lab19*	*Lab27*	*Lab27*	*Lab22*	*Lab10*	*Lab19*	*Lab22*	*Lab13*
Enfield West			*C26*	*C30*	*C35*	*C38*	*C28*	*C27*	*C32*
Conservative	*5-8*	*2*	*3*	*3*	*3+*	*3*	*3*	*3*	*3*
Labour	*6-10*	*14++*	*9*	*9*	*9*	*9*	*9*	*9*	*9*
Liberal	*1-5*	*0*	*0*	*0*	*0*	*0*	*0*	*0*	*0*
Communist	*0*	*1*	*0*	*0*	*0*	*0*	*0*	*0*	*0*
Total	*17*	*17++*	*12*	*12*	*12+*	*12*	*12*	*12*	*12*

Key: C = Conservative; Lab = Labour; + = Party that won seat at General Election held by-election in same Parliament; - = Party that won seat at General Election lost by-election to main opposition Party in same Parliament.

MPs for the East End

Bethnal Green North East

Daniel Chater (Labour) was first elected MP for in 1935. Re-elected in 1945, he retired in 1950 when the seat was merged with the South West division of the Borough. Formerly an MP elsewhere in London, his biographical details are contained in Chapter 7 (Hammersmith).

Bethnal Green South West, Bethnal Green

Percy Holman (Labour) took Bethnal Green South West from the Liberals in 1945 and retained the seat until 1950 when he was returned for the new single borough constituency. Born in 1891 and educated at Mill Hill School and the London School of Economics, Holman was a paper merchant. During the First World War he served in the Red Cross in France and was active in both the Co-operative Movement and the Labour Party, contesting Twickenham at four consecutive Parliamentary General and By-elections in 1931, 1932, 1934 and 1935, all unsuccessfully. From 1928 to 1931 he was a member of Middlesex County Council and served on Twickenham UDC between 1928 and 1934. He was a sometime lecturer for the Workers' Educational Association. He died in 1978.

MPs for the East End

From	at	To	Surname	First Names	Constituency	Party
1945	G	1950	Chater	Daniel	Bethnal Green North East	Labour
1945	G	1950	Holman	Percy	Bethnal Green South West	Labour
1950	G	1966	Holman	Percy	Bethnal Green	Labour
1966	G	1974	Hilton	William Samuel		Labour
1945	G	1950	Attlee	(Major) Clement Richard	Stepney, Limehouse	Labour
1945	G	1950	Piratin	Philip	Stepney, Mile End	Communist
1945	G	1950	Edwards	Walter James	Stepney, Whitechapel & St. Georges	Labour
1950	G	1964	Edwards	Walter James	Stepney	Labour
1964	B	1974	Shore	Peter David		Labour
1945	G	1950	Key	Charles William	Poplar, Bow & Bromley	Labour
1945	G	1950	Guy	William Henry	Poplar South	Labour
1950	G	1964	Key	Charles William	Poplar	Labour
1964	G	1974	Mikardo	Ian		Labour
1945	G	1950	Hynd	Henry	Hackney Central	Labour
1950	G	1955	Seat abolished			Nil
1955	G	1970	Butler	Herbert William		Labour
1970	G	1974	Davis	Stanley Clinton		Labour
1945	G	1955	Butler	Herbert William	Hackney South	Labour
1945	G	1950	Goodrich	Henry Edwin	Hackney North	Labour
1945	G	1950	Weitzman	David	Stoke Newington	Labour
1950	G	1974	Weitzman	David	Hackney North & Stoke Newington	Labour

NOTE First returned at a B = By-election; G =General Election

Holman retired at the 1966 General Election when his seat was taken by **William Samuel Hilton** (Labour), a Scotsman born at Saltcoats, Ayrshire in 1926. Educated at Ardrossan Academy and the Co-operative College, Stanford Hall, near Loughborough, and a sometime railway fireman, he became a Trade Union Research Officer working for the National Federation of Building Trade Operatives from 1952 until his election at Bethnal Green in 1966. He was also a Director of the Master Builders' Federation established after the War as a trade association to protect the interests of small and medium-sized building firms. However, his main interest was politics. He contested East Hertfordshire in 1955 and Ealing North four years later, both times unsuccessfully. He retired in 1974 and died in 1999.

Stepney - Limehouse

Clement Richard Attlee (Labour), the Labour Leader, Wartime Deputy Prime Minister and Prime Minister from 1945-51, was re-elected in 1945 and remained the MP until the constituency was merged into Stepney in 1950. He had been MP there since 1922. His principal biographical details are in Chapter 7 (Bethnal Green, Stepney and Poplar).

Stepney - Mile End

Philip Piratin (Communist) was elected as the MP in 1945 and served one term. The son of a tradesman he was born locally in 1907 and obtained a scholarship to a secondary school where he aimed to become an architect, but had to discontinue his studies after matriculation in order to earn a living. In 1932 Mosley established the British Union of Fascists (BUF) which by 1934 was expressing strong anti-Semitic views and organising provocative marches through Jewish districts of East London. Piratin played a leading role in protecting Jewish people living in these areas. In 1936 a quarter of a million people stopped Mosley's party marching through the East End. He joined the Communist Party in 1934 and played an active part in the Stepney campaign for lower rents by, amongst other things, leading a demonstration of 70 East London Communists at the Savoy Hotel. He was elected as the first Communist councillor in London on

Stepney council in1937 and was re-elected in 1945. He was a member of a delegation to Poland in 1946. Only the second Communist MP to be elected, he was strongly opposed to the formation of the NATO Alliance against Soviet Russia and he failed to gain re-election when he stood for the new Stepney Borough seat in 1950. He came third, 27,000 votes behind Labour.

Stepney - Whitechapel & St George's, Stepney

Walter James Edwards (Labour) was elected at a by-election in 1942 and remained MP until 1950 when he was elected as the new Stepney borough MP defeating Piratin. He retained the seat until he died on the day of the 1964 General Election. His principal biographical details are in Chapter 7.

People's History Museum Manchester

Peter David Shore (Labour) was elected in a 1964 by-election and served as the local MP until 1974 when he was returned for Bethnal Green & Stepney, which he represented until his retirement at the 1997 General Election. He then became a Life Peer and died in 2001.Born in 1924, he was educated at Quarry Bank High School, Liverpool and at Kings College Cambridge where he became a political economist. A journalist and lecturer for the WEA and United Nations Association, he contested St Ives (Cornwall) in 1950 and Halifax (Yorkshire, West Riding) in 1959.From 1959-64 he was Head of the Labour Party's Research Department and was Parliamentary Private Secretary to the Prime Minister, Harold Wilson between 1965-6 when, after the Party's election victory, he was made Parliamentary Secretary to the Minister of Technology. He served for a year when he moved in a similar capacity to the Ministry of Economic Affairs, serving there until 1969 when he was made a minister without Portfolio and Deputy Leader of the House of Commons.

After Labour's defeat nationally in 1970 he was made opposition spokesman on Europe and when the Party returned to power four years later he joined the Cabinet for the first time as Secretary of State for Trade. He held this office until 1976 when Wilson unexpectedly resigned as Prime Minister and James Callaghan made Shore Secretary of State for the Environment. He held the post until 1979 when the Party once more went into Opposition. Thereafter he remained a front bench spokesman for many years and was prominent throughout for his Euro-sceptical views. He died on September 24th, 2001.

Not the best photograph but showing principals of the Wilson Administration in the House. Reading R-L: Barbara Castle, Roy Mason, Tony Benn, **Peter Shore,** *Dennis Healey, Harold Wilson, Jim Callaghan,* **Roy Jenkins** *and* **Bob Mellish**

People's History Museum Manchester

Those in red were all London MPs at one time or another

Poplar South

William Henry Guy (Labour), who continued to represent Poplar South after 1945, was elected initially at a Wartime by-election in 1942. He retired in 1950 and his principal biographical details are in Chapter 7.

Poplar - Bow & Bromley, Poplar

Charles William Key (Labour) was also elected at a wartime by-election (in 1940) and was re-elected to serve as MP for Poplar, Bow and Bromley in 1945. He remained the area's MP until 1950 when he went on to serve as MP for Poplar until 1964 when he retired. His principal biographical details are also in Chapter 7.

Ian Mikardo (Labour) was elected for Poplar in 1964 and remained its MP until 1974 when he was returned at Bethnal Green & Bow, which he represented until 1983 when he transferred to Bow & Poplar. He retired in 1987. Born in 1908, he was educated at the Portsmouth Southern Secondary School and later at the town's Municipal College. He became an industrial consultant after a period in which he taught journalism and undertook translation work. He was

Ian Mikardo MP
People's History Museum Manchester

a member of the Association of Supervisory Staffs and Engineering Technicians of which he was President from 1968-73, having much earlier in his life been an executive member from 1945-7[26]. A member of the Jewish Labour Party, he was first elected an MP for the then two-member borough constituency of Reading in 1945, transferring in 1950 to Reading South. In 1955 he was returned for the then newly formed single borough seat at Reading but was defeated there in 1959. He was a member of the Labour Party's National Executive for much of his career and was noted for his 'hard' Left opinions. He served on the NEC from 1950-9 being a Vice Chairman from 1958-9. He was elected to the same body in 1960 and remained a member until 1978. He was Vice Chairman again in 1969-70 and Chairman from 1970-1. In 1974 he was elected Chairman of the Parliamentary Labour Party. Despite the strength of his views he was an amiable politician with an infectious sense of humour and was notable as the House of Commons 'bookmaker', accepting bets on many different political and parliamentary events and personalities. He died in 1993.

Hackney Central

Henry Hynd (Labour) was MP between 1945 and 1950 when the seat was abolished. He then transferred to a Lancashire constituency where he remained MP for Accrington until 1966 when he retired. Born in 1900 and educated at Perth Academy in Scotland, Hynd was a railway clerk from 1915 to 1920 when he became an official of the Railway Clerks Association (the forerunner of the Transport Salaried Staffs Association), the country's oldest white-collar union. In 1946 he was made Parliamentary Private Secretary to AV Alexander from 1946-50. He was a member of Hornsey Borough Council from 1939-52 and was Chairman of the Parliamentary Branch of the Scouts. He died in 1985.

Hackney South & Hackney Central

Herbert Bulter MP
People's History Museum Manchester

Herbert William Butler (Labour) was MP from 1945-55 when he was elected for Hackney Central, which he served until his retirement in 1970. Born in 1897, he was educated at elementary school in Hackney and was a member of the Borough Council between 1928 and 1961, being the Borough's mayor in 1936/7. From 1916 to 1919 he served in the Royal Navy and was briefly a PPS at the Admiralty from 1950-51. He was a member of various local Hospital Committees in his home area and was made a freeman of the Borough. He died in 1971.

Stanley Clinton Davis (Labour) was born in 1928 and attended Hackney Downs School, the Mercer's School and Kings College, London, where he became involved in Labour politics through the National Association of Socialist Students. He became a solicitor in 1953 and was senior partner in his own firm until 1974 when he became a Minister. He was elected a member of Hackney Borough Council in 1959, serving as Mayor in 1968-9. He contested the Langstone division of Portsmouth in 1955 and Great Yarmouth twice, in 1959 and 1964, unsuccessfully on all occasions. He was MP for Hackney Central from 1970 until 1983 during which period from 1974-79 he served as Parliamentary Under Secretary of State for Trade with special responsibility for companies, aviation and shipping. He retired from the Commons but two years later in 1985 was made a European Commissioner for Environment and Transport. He returned from Brussels in 1989 and was made a Life Peer the following year having been awarded the Grand Cross of the Order of Leopold II by the King of Belgium for services to the European Community. He served as Chairman to the Refugee Council from 1990-1995 and amongst several other commitments was President of the British Airline Pilots Association (BALPA) and Joint President of the Society of Labour Lawyers. When Labour returned to Government in 1997 he was for the first year a Minister of State at the Department of Trade and Industry until July 1998.

Henry Edwin Goodrich (Labour) was elected in 1945. Born in 1887, he attended Balham Grammar School. He served in the Royal Navy during the First World War and was in the Metropolitan Police before becoming a solicitor's clerk. He was a member of Hackney Borough Council from 1925-50 and Mayor in 1935-6. In 1919 he was General Secretary of the Police Strikers Union in circumstances that were historically important. Due to wartime inflation the wages of the police were seriously eroded leading to discontent and concerns amongst senior officers that policemen might become susceptible to bribes. A strike of Metropolitan Police led to improved pay but the fledgling police trade union, the National Union of Police & Prison Officers, believed it had the Government on the back foot and struck for union recognition in 1919. It was relatively well supported in London and on Merseyside but there was serious rioting and robbery in Liverpool and the Army found it hard to cope. The strike collapsed within 24 hours, all the strikers were dismissed and never re-engaged. The subsequent Desborough Report led to the 1919 Police Act, which further improved police pay and conditions and set up

26 Formed in 1918 as the National Foremen's Association, it changed its name in 1942. It became part of the Association of Scientific, Technical and Managerial Staffs when it was formed in 1968 and MSF through a further amalgamation in 1988.

the Police Federation and other representative machinery to prevent a recurrence. He retired in 1950 and died in 1961.

David Weitzman MP
People's History Museum Manchester

Stoke Newington & Hackney North, Hackney North & Stoke Newington

David Weitzman (Labour) was elected for Stoke Newington in 1945 having previously contested the seat unsuccessfully in 1935. Born in 1898, he was educated in Glasgow at the City's Hutchesons School, then at the Central School in Manchester, where his father, Chaim, was a prominent Jew who is reputed to have persuaded Arthur Balfour, then MP for Manchester East, of the case for a Jewish State in Israel. David attended Manchester University and became a barrister, being called to the bar at Grays Inn in 1922. During the First World War he served in the Manchester Regiment from 1916. He took silk in 1951 and retired from the House in 1979. From 1950 he was MP for Stoke Newington & Hackney North and from 1974-9 when the place names were reversed, for Hackney North & Stoke Newington. He died in 1987.

MPs for North East Middlesex

From	at	To	Surname	First Names	Constituency	Party
1945	G	1945	Morrison	Robert Craigmyle	Tottenham North	Labour
1945	B	1950	Irving	William John		Labour
1945	G	1950	Messer	Sir Frederick	Tottenham South	Labour/SDP
1950	G	1959	Messer	Sir Frederick	Tottenham	Labour
1959	G	1964	Brown	Alan Grahame		Labour/Ind/Cons
1964	G	1974	Atkinson	Norman		Labour
1945	G	1950	Baxter	Arthur Beverley	Wood Green	Conservative
1950	G	1955	Irving	William John		Labour
1955	G	1974	Butler	Joyce Shore(Mrs)		Labour
1945	G	1957	Gammans	Sir Leonard David (Captain)	Hornsey	Conservative
1957	B	1966	Gammans	Lady Ann Muriel		Conservative
1966	G	1974	Rossi	Sir Hugh Alexis Louis		Conservative
1945	G	1948	Durbin	Evan Frank Mottram	Edmonton	Labour
1948	B	1974	Albu	Austen Harry		Labour
1945	G	1950	Davies	Ernest Albert John	Enfield	Labour
1950	G	1959	Davies	Ernest Albert John	Enfield East	Labour
1959	G	1974	(John-)Mackie	John		Labour
1950	G	1970	Macleod	Ian Norman	Enfield West	Conservative
1970	B	1974	Parkinson	Cecil		Conservative
1950	B	1964	Baxter	Arthur Beverley	Southgate	Conservative
1964	G	1974	Berry	Sir Anthony George		Conservative

NOTE First returned at a B = By-election; G =General Election

Tottenham North

Robert Craigmyle Morrison (Labour) was re-elected in 1945 having represented the seat since 1935. His biographical details are in chapter 7.

Shortly after the 1945 general election he was elevated to the Lords and a by-election was held in December at which **William John Irving** (Labour) was elected serving until the seat was abolished in 1950. He had previously been Morrison's election agent. Born in 1892, Irving was educated at Workington Secondary School, Ruskin College and at WEA classes. A transport worker and member of the Dock, Wharf and General Workers' Union, he was a stevedore at Workington Docks and an active trade unionist who later served on the National Executive Committee of the Transport and General Workers' Union when it was created from the merger of thirteen smaller unions[27]. He was a member of Workington Borough Council from 1921-27and in 1936 was elected a County councillor for Tottenham where he also became a magistrate three years later. He was a member of the Lea Conservancy Catchment Board in 1946-7. Following the abolition of his seat he was adopted and elected for Wood Green in 1950, retiring in 1955. He died in 1967.

27 Founded after the great docks strike in 1889 the Dock, Wharf and General Workers' Union initiated the amalgamation that resulted in the formation of the Transport and General Workers' Union in 1922.

Tottenham South, Tottenham

Sir Frederick Messer (Labour) was MP for South Tottenham intermittently from 1929 to 1950 when he was elected for Tottenham, retiring in 1959. His biographical details are in Chapter 7.

He was succeeded by **Alan Grahame Brown** (Labour) who fell out with his Party in 1961 and sat as an Independent until 1962 when he crossed the floor of the House to take the Tory Whip. Born in 1913, Brown was educated at Bedford School and the College of the Pharmaceutical Society, the University of London, after which he became a chemist. He was elected to Middlesex County Council in 1956 and as MP for Tottenham in 1959. He was defeated standing as a Conservative in 1964. He died in 1972.

Norman Atkinson (Labour) sat as MP from 1964 until 1987 when he was de-selected by his local Party in favour of Bernie Grant, Britain's first Afro-Caribbean MP. Atkinson was born in 1923 and educated in elementary and technical schools in the Manchester area before attending Manchester University as a mature student between 1957 and 1964. There he qualified as a mechanical engineer. From 1945-9 he was a member of Manchester City Council and contested its Wythenshawe Parliamentary division unsuccessfully in 1955 followed by Altrincham & Sale (Cheshire) four years later. A Governor of Imperial College, he was sponsored as an MP by the left-wing Amalgamated Engineering Union and was Treasurer of the Labour Party with a seat on the National Executive Committee from 1976-81.

Wood Green

Arthur Beverley Baxter (Conservative) was re-elected MP for Wood Green in 1945. First elected in 1935, he remained the MP until 1950 when the seat was redrawn and transferred to Southgate remaining its MP until 1964. His biographical details are contained in Chapter 7.

He was succeeded by **William Irving** (Labour) - see Tottenham North above.

Mrs. Joyce Shore Butler (Labour) succeeded Irving in 1955 and sat until 1979 when she retired from politics. Born Joyce Wells in 1910, she was educated at King Edward's High School in Birmingham and at Woodbrooke College in the Selly Oak district of that city. Following her marriage she moved to Wood Green where she became a member of the borough council in 1947, serving until 1964 when she was made an Alderman of the new Haringey Borough Council, serving as its first Chairman, and then as Mayoress in 1965-6. From 1965-70 she was a vice Chairman of the Parliamentary Labour Party and of the Co-operative Group of MPs and PPS to the Minister of Land and Natural Resources between 1965 and 1967. She was President of the Spurs Ladies' Football team and died in 1992.

Hornsey

Captain Sir Leonard David Gammans (Conservative) was re-elected in 1945 following his by-election victory there in 1941. He remained MP until his death in 1957. His main biographical details are in Chapter 7.

He was succeeded by his wife, **Lady Ann Muriel Gammans** (Conservative) who continued to serve until she retired at the 1966 General Election. Born Ann Paul in March 1898, she was educated at High School in the town of Portsmouth where her husband had attended the Grammar School and whom she married in 1917. She travelled widely in the Far East, Europe and North America and was a holder of the Japanese Order of the Sacred Treasure (second class), one of the highest honours bestowed by the Japanese Government on foreigners[28]. She died in 1989.

Sir Hugh Rossi MP
People's History Museum Manchester

(Sir) Hugh Alexis Louis Rossi (Conservative), born in 1927, first won in 1966. Educated at Finchley Grammar School and Kings College, London University, he was a solicitor in a West End partnership, which he joined in 1956. He was a member of Hornsey Borough Council from 1956-65, being deputy mayor in the last year of its existence. He was then a member of Haringey Council. Between 1959 and 1965 he served on the housing committee of the Association of Municipal Corporations and between 1961-5 was also a County Councillor for Middlesex. A Non Executive Director of the Bolton Building Society, he was made an assistant Government Whip in 1970 and a full whip (Lord Commissioner of the Treasury) in 1972, serving in this role until shortly before the 1974 election defeat of the Heath administration when he was briefly Under Secretary of State for the Environment. In Opposition he was a spokesman on housing

28 The reason for this award has not been established.

and land issues but following Thatcher's victory in 1979 was appointed Minister of State for Northern Ireland, in which post he served until being made Minister for Social Security and the Disabled in 1981. He remained in post until 1983 when his seat was redrawn as Hornsey & Wood Green but after that General Election he lost his Ministerial rank and became Chairman of the Select Committee on the Environment. He retired in 1992.

Edmonton

Evan Frank Mottram Durbin (Labour) who was MP from 1945 to 1948 was an outstanding academic economist from the London School of Economics where he, like his Party Leader Clement Attlee, was a lecturer. Born in 1906 he was the son of a Baptist Minister and secured an Open Scholarship from elementary and secondary schools in Taunton to New College Oxford where he gained a first class Honours degree in PPE. He was a brilliant scholar who won both Junior and Senior Medly Scholarships at Oxford and secured the Ricards Fellowship at London University where he became a foremost economist and author of many books. He contested East Grinstead in 1931 and Gillingham four years later, both unsuccessfully. From 1940-42 he was a member of the Secretariat of the War Cabinet and between 1942 and 1944 was Deputy Prime Minister Clement Attlee's Personal Assistant. Following Labour's election victory he was appointed as Parliamentary Secretary to the Minister of Works in March 1947 but died in September the following year just as a promising career appeared likely.

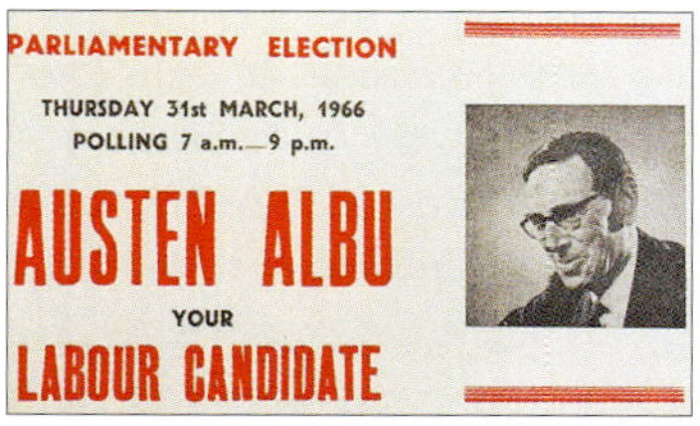

People's History Museum Manchester

Austen Harry Albu (Labour) won the 1948 by-election. Born in 1903, he was educated at Tonbridge School, the City and Guilds College and the Imperial College of Science and Technology, where he was later a Governor, as he was also at Battersea College of Technology. At the time of his election he was Deputy Director of the British Institute of Management and later became Chairman of Harvester Press, publishers of radical articles and books. From 1962-5 he was Chairman of the Parliamentary and Scientific Committee and from 1965-7, Minister of State for Economic Affairs. He retired in 1974 and died 20 years later.

Enfield, Enfield East

Ernest Albert John Davies (Labour) took Enfield from the Tories in 1945 and became MP for Enfield East in 1950 when the borough was divided. He remained that constituency's MP until he retired in 1959. Born in 1902, he was educated at Wycliffe School and London University and became engaged in journalism in Canada. He was editor of a publication called the *Clarion*, a socialist journal established in Manchester in 1890. He was also associated with Arthur Henderson, an early leader of the Labour Party, in the formation of the University Labour Federation, a body established to foster support amongst students, becoming its first Treasurer. He first contested a Parliamentary seat in 1935 when he was beaten at Peterborough. He died in 1991.

John John-Mackie (Labour) represented Enfield East from 1959 to 1974 when he retired. Born in 1909, he was educated at Aberdeen Grammar School and the North of Scotland College of Agriculture, of which he later became Vice-chairman. He came from a farming family and was a Director of a company that farmed over 2,000 acres. In 1951 he contested the rural Scottish consistency of Angus North & Mearns, where he was defeated by a Conservative, and he was also unsuccessful four years later at Lanark. When the Wilson Government was elected in 1964 Mackie became a junior minister, occupying the post of Parliamentary Secretary, Ministry of Agriculture and Fisheries throughout the period until 1970. After his retirement from the Commons he was Chairman of the Forestry Commission between 1976 and 1979. Two years later he was given a life peerage and was made while he was opposition spokesman on agriculture and fisheries until 1988. He died in 1994.

Ian Mcleod MP
© National Portrait Gallery
Walter Bird

Enfield West

Ian Norman Macleod (Conservative) was elected as the first MP for Enfield West when the seat was created in 1950. Born in 1913 at Skipton (West Riding of Yorkshire), he was educated at Fettes College, Edinburgh and at Gonville and Ciaus College, Cambridge. From 1948-50 he was head of the home affairs department of the Conservative Party. He contested his first Parliamentary election in 1945 in the constituency from which his parents hailed, The Western Isles (The Outer Hebrides). Labour defeated him, but after his election at Enfield in 1950 he made

Ian Mcleod MP sitting next to Prime Minister and fellow London MP Edward Heath in the Chamber of the House of Commons.
People's History Museum Manchester

an early impression as a politician with good career prospects. He was appointed Minister of Health in 1952 and from 1955 to 1959 was Minister of Labour. Then from 1959-61 he was Secretary for the Colonies at a time when the Macmillan Government had embarked on a major decolonisation policy. From 1961-3 he was Chancellor of the Duchy of Lancaster as well as chairman of the Conservative Party. When Macmillan resigned in 1963 and was replaced by Lord Home (Sir Alec Douglas-Home), Macleod was one of two former Ministers who declined to serve under him. Instead he became editor of the *Spectator* but, in Opposition from 1964-5, he did agree to take the role of spokesman on the steel industry and led the Tories' attack on the re-nationalization proposals of the Wilson Government. When Ted Heath became Leader of the Party in 1965, Macleod served as Opposition chief spokesman on the Treasury and after the 1970 election was promoted to the Cabinet as Chancellor of the Exchequer. Tragically he died suddenly in July within five weeks of his appointment.

Cecil Parkinson (Conservative) was born in 1931, the son of a Carnforth railway worker, and was educated at Lancaster Grammar School from where he went to Emmanuel College, Cambridge. He became a Chartered Accountant and was the founder Chairman of Hart Securities Limited. He entered politics initially when he contested Northampton unsuccessfully at the June 1970 General Election. However, Macleod's death created an opportunity for him to launch a successful political career, although this was tarnished latterly when he fathered a baby by his secretary, Sarah Keys. He was appointed an assistant Government Whip in early 1974 but the Party was defeated at the polls in February and went into Opposition. Following a further redistribution of seats in 1974 Parkinson became MP for neighbouring Hertfordshire South (which contained parts of his former Enfield constituency) and remained its representative until 1983 when it was once again reorganised to become Hertsmere, which he held until his retirement in 1992. From 1974 to 1976 he was an Opposition Whip and then until 1979 was spokesman on Trade and Industry. During this period he also built up his business career becoming a director of several companies, including Sears Holdings, Babcock International, The Save and Prosper Group, Tarmac plc, and several others. When the Thatcher Government was returned he was made Minister of Trade serving until 1981 when he was promoted to the Cabinet as Paymaster General and Chairman of the Conservative Party acquiring the additional title of Chancellor of the Duchy of Lancaster in 1982. After the 1983 election he was appointed Secretary of State for Trade and Industry but resigned as a result of the sex scandal in October the same year. Following the 1987 General Election he returned to high office as Secretary of State for Energy, in which role he oversaw the privatisation of the electricity supply industry and in 1989 was made Secretary of State for Transport. However, he resigned in 1990 when Mrs Thatcher was deposed as Leader and he left the Commons in 1992. He was made a life peer, Lord Parkinson of Carnforth, but took little part in politics until 1997 when William Hague made him Party Chairman once again, after Hague was elected Leader following the Party's massive defeat at the general election. He held the post for one year.

Southgate

Arthur Beverley Baxter (Conservative) was MP from 1950 until 1964 (see Wood Green above and in Chapter 7).

He was succeeded by **Sir Anthony George Berry** (Conservative) who was the MP from 1964 to 1984 when he was murdered. The IRA killed him when they bombed the Imperial Hotel, Brighton whilst he was attending the Conservative Party Conference. Born in 1925, he was Eton educated before going to Christ Church, Oxford. The sixth and youngest son of Viscount Kemsley, he was a director of the family firm of Kemsley Newspapers[29] from 1954-9, he was an assistant editor of the *'Sunday Times'*. In 1962 he was appointed High Sheriff of Glamorgan a county from which his grandfather originated. From 1970-4 he was Parliamentary Private Secretary to Peter Walker and an Opposition whip between 1975 and 1979. He held various minor Ministerial offices in the household between 1979 and 1983 including that of Deputy Government Chief Whip at the time of his murder.

29 At the time the group included the Sunday Times, the Daily Graphic, the Sunday Chronicle, the Daily Dispatch and a number of provincial newspapers. The group was owned by Viscount Kemsley and all publications supported the Conservative Party.

Chapter 12
Metropolitan Essex 1945 - 1974

Prior to the post-War General Election in 1945, the Boundaries Commission's review of twenty exceptionally large constituencies in England affected suburban areas of Essex that had grown massively since 1918. Five new seats were created giving a 1945 total of eighteen, a figure that was reduced to fifteen in 1950 when a more thorough review had been undertaken.

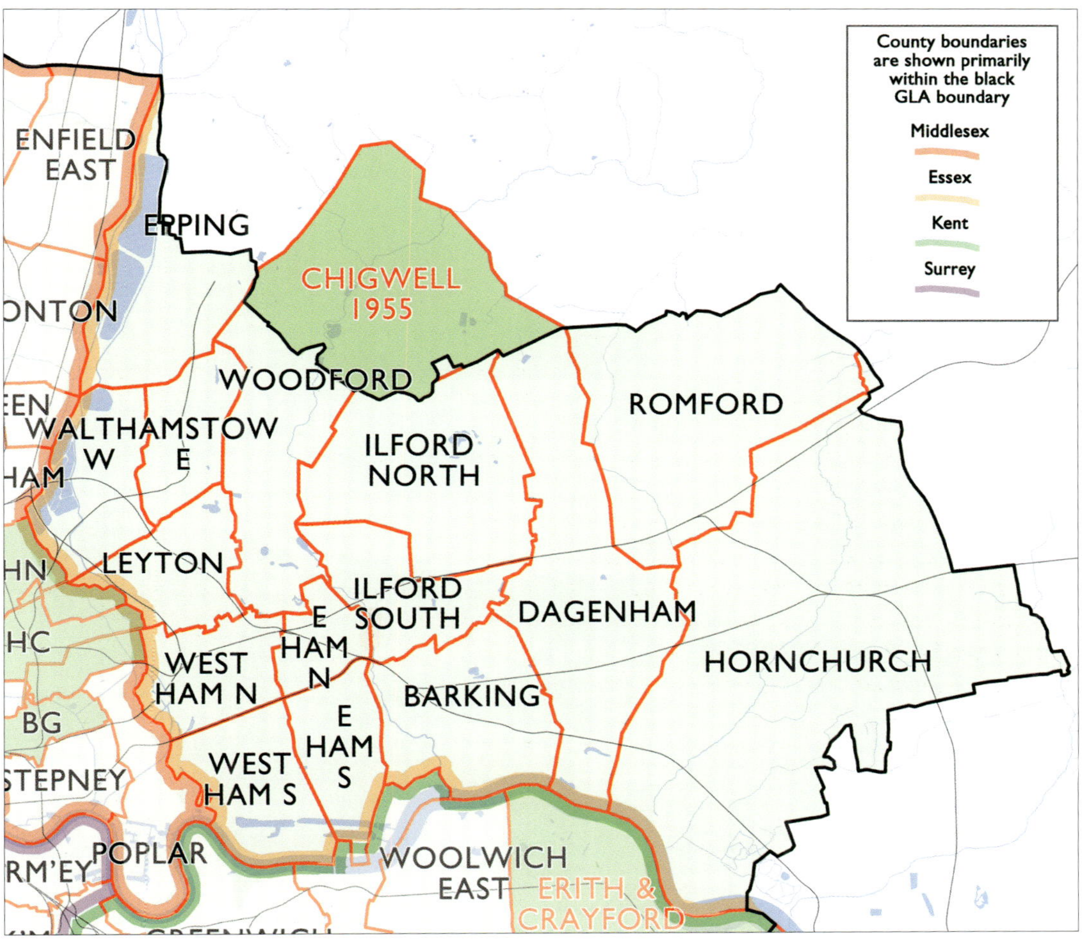

The map depicts Essex constituencies created in 1950 and those that were modified in 1955. The number of seats in West Ham was halved compared with 1945, whilst new seats in the outer suburbs emerged at Barking, Dagenham, Hornchurch, and Woodford. Comparison with 1945 may be made by reference to the map on page 18 and with 1918 on page 16.

Once again Romford was at the centre of this expansion spawning three new seats. Between 1921 and 1938 the population of **Hornchurch** had increased by 335% and a new constituency of that name was created, based on the Urban District covering communities between Romford and the Thames, including Ardleigh Green, Corbets Tey, Cranham, Elm Park, Emerson Park, Hacton, Harold Wood, North Ockenden, Rainham, Squirrell's Heath, Upminster and Wennington. Hornchurch had been a Parish Council in the Romford Rural District prior to 1926 when it became an Urban District in its own right. This was extended twice (in 1934 and 1936) to include the surrounding villages of Upminster, Rainham, Cranham and North Ockendon and became the largest Urban District in the country with a population estimated at

Left: 1950s terraced council houses along Parsloes Avenue (in the new Dagenham constituency) were within a short walk of the District Line, Dagenham Heathway station, and within easy communication for the Ford factory at Dagenham. The buildings were not originally designed for car ownership, and there has been improvisation. Only 50% of cars here are by Ford.

Below: The affluent Gidea Park area in the Romford constituency sprang from a 1910 experiment to create the Romford Garden Suburb, an exhibition of town planning. The houses shown here built in the 1930s in Crossway, offer a pattern of quality making this an affluent and desirable area from the start. The close proximity of Gidea Park Station added to this.

Below: Barking gained municipal status in 1931. The Town Hall was completed in 1958, as the culmination of plans laid down in 1931. Construction was halted by WW2 but finished off for active use, which continues to this day. The area has been refurbished with an attractive pedestrian area in front of the building.

Above: Lodge Close houses (Hornchurch constituency) were built in the 1920s and 1930s, following the familiar pattern of urban expansion and sufficient to warrant the creation of the new constituency. This is an area just off the High Street and within walking distance of Hornchurch and Upminster Bridge, District Line stations.

Left: The eastern arm of the Central Line and the Eastern Avenue towards Chelmsford both generated suburban development north of Ilford in the inter-war years. The South Constituency was and still is characterised by long streets of terraced suburban housing in the Seven Kings district. This is Elgin Road, close to the Great Eastern Railway line to Liverpool Street and the City.

All images John Nelson except where marked

134,140. The town's name originated in 1233 and meant "church with horn-like gables".

Seats at Barking and Dagenham also appeared for the first time. The development of new council estates in response to slum clearance and bomb damage in the East End, coupled with the building of the huge car factory by Fords, meant that populations had increased rapidly. The **Barking** constituency extended south of Ilford to the Thames at Barking Reach and from Beckton on the western side of Barking Creek to the Dagenham Dock. It included Beckton, Becontree, Mayesbrook, Parsloes Park, Rippleside and Valence Park. The town's name derives from the Anglo-Saxon "Berecingum" which meant "settlement of the family or followers of a man called Berica". Barking Abbey was founded around 670 and stood for nearly nine hundred years until its dissolution in 1539. The parishes of Barking and Dagenham were part of the manor belonging to the Abbey. By 1086 the town's name was "Berchinges". It was a fishing village for many centuries giving its name in the early Eighteenth Century to the Barking Well Smack, a vessel that fished the Dogger Bank. Eventually it became a market gardening area and barges stacked with produce regularly travelled between the Town Quay and London during the 19th century taking vegetables to the markets. In return they carried night soil from London, slaughterhouse waste and dust from the dust yards as fertilizers. In early Victorian times new laws on pollution in Middlesex forced many factory owners to move to sites in nearby counties including Essex. In 1857 an artificial fertilizer and sulphuric acid factory was built at Creeksmouth in Barking, on the shores of the Thames. As its fishing industry collapsed new industries moved in. In 1866 the largest jute works in the world opened, making mail sacks. River transport by barges along the River Roding was unusually good and by 1900 Barking was attracting small factories to its riverside sites. Heavy industry and chemical plants opened and later oil refineries and storage buildings for hazardous waste.

"Daeccanaam" was the AD 690 Saxon name of the place that is now known as Dagenham. It meant "homestead or village of a man called Deacca". In 1945 the new **Dagenham** constituency extended from Markgate in the north via Chadwell Heath to the Thames between Dagenham Dock and Hornchurch Marshes. In between were Becontree Heath, Eastbrook, Goresbrook and Dagenham Heathway. In 1887 a barge builder called Samuel Williams built a new deep-water dock on the Thames but it failed to attract new business until 1929 when the Ford Motor Company began to build the largest motorcar factory in the world. Local labour was in plentiful supply as in 1921 the Becontree Estate, one of several major council estates, was built by the London County Council to provide improved housing for slum dwellers from central London. It took 18 years to complete but when finished it was bigger than many provincial towns. Between 1921 and 1931 alone the population of Dagenham grew from 9,127 to 89,362.

The consequence of these changes was that the revised **Romford** constituency extended west to east from the boundary with Dagenham to Brentwood. Within today's London boundary it included Collier Row, Gidea Park, Harold Hill, Havering Attebower, Noak Hill, Oldchurch and Rush Green. However, in 1955 the Brentwood Urban District was transferred to the new Billericay constituency so Romford contracted to an even more urban core.

Elsewhere **Epping** retained Chingford but disgorged Wanstead and Woodford, which emerged as a new seat whilst Ilford was split in two. These developments reflected the growth of commuting populations living in affordable housing built around the Central Line of the London Underground and the Eastern Avenue built between Wanstead and Romford via Gants Hill. **Woodford** officially incorporated the Wanstead and Woodford UDC including Snaresbrook (all within Greater London today), Hainault and, until 1955, Chigwell (outside it).

In that year Chigwell was taken into the Chelmsford constituency and North Hainault was transferred to **Ilford North**, which also embraced Aldborough, Barkingside, Clayhall, Fairlop, Gants Hill, Newbury Park, Redbridge and Seven Kings. **Ilford South** covered Clementswood (around the High Road), Cranbrook, Loxford, Mayfield, [Valentine's] Park and Goodmayes. Chingford remained in **Epping**, most of which constituency lay outside the metropolitan area, however.

In constituencies west of Woodford, as the population drifted outwards **Leyton** reverted to single representation in 1950. It included Cann Hall, Cathall, Lea Bridge, Leytonstone and Whipps Cross. **Walthamstow East** and **West** remained. The first included Hoe Street, Wood Street and Hale End (including Chapel End and Highams Park) whilst the latter incorporated three wards - High Street (including Lloyd Park), Higham Hill and St.James Street (including Blackhorse Road),

A similar fall in population was experienced in West Ham. Industrial and port developments were moving further down the Thames Estuary and in 1950 West Ham reverted to two seats. **West Ham North** embraced the area north of the London to Tilbury Railway and was in effect a merger of the Stratford and Upton seats. It included Maryland, Forest Gate, Stratford including the Marsh, Upton Park and West Ham proper, whilst **West Ham South**, which replaced the former Plaistow and Silvertown constituencies comprised Canning Town, Custom House, Plaistow, Silvertown and the Victoria Docks. The neighbouring **East Ham North** and **East Ham South** constituencies were unaltered. Details are in Chapter 8.

Thus in metropolitan Essex there was a total of fifteen constituencies at the 1950 General Election, two more than had existed pre-War, though three less than in 1945. With only minor adjustments taking place in 1955 this was the pattern of representation that lasted up to and including the February 1974 General Election when further changes occurred.

Post War General Election Results 1945 to 1970 by % majority

Constituency	pre-1945	1945	1950	1951	1955	1959	1964	1966	1970
West Ham North			Lab43	Lab41	Lab40	Lab36	Lab41	Lab48	Lab38
Stratford	Lab	Lab54							
Upton	C/Lab	Lab49							
West Ham South			Lab70	Lab70	Lab66	Lab61	Lab61	Lab66	Lab55
Plaistow	Lab	Lab75							
Silvertown	Lab	Lab87							
East Ham North	C	Lab40	Lab24	Lab21	Lab18+	Lab14	Lab21	Lab32	Lab20
East Ham South	Lab	Lab48	Lab33	Lab30	Lab28	Lab23	Lab32	Lab40	Lab24
Barking		Lab54	Lab44	Lab42	Lab38	Lab30	Lab40	Lab44	Lab39
Dagenham		Lab67	Lab53	Lab52	Lab48	Lab38	Lab46	Lab52	Lab44
Hornchurch		Lab24	Lab3	Lab2	C2	C10	C0.3	Lab4	C8
Romford	C	Lab18	C2	C2	Lab5	Lab1	Lab11	Lab15	Lab5
Ilford	C								
Ilford North		Lab6	C15	C18+	C20	C26	C15	C7	C16
Ilford South		Lab12	C8	C10	C13	C16	C3	Lab6	C3
Woodford		C45	C30	C29	C46	C42	C30	C30	C35
Epping	C	Lab3	C8	C10	C6	C6	Lab4	Lab9	C3
Walthamstow East	C	Lab21	Lab8	Lab3	C3	C8	C1	Lab6-	C2
Walthamstow West	Lab	Lab47	Lab35	Lab34	Lab31+	Lab28	Lab30	Lab36-	Lab22
Leyton			Lab18	Lab16	Lab15	Lab7	Lab17-	Lab18	Lab13
Leyton East	C	Lab31							
Leyton West	C	Lab30							
Party Totals	Ave								
Conservative	7.5	1	5	5+	6	6	5+	2++	6
Labour	5.5	17	10	10	9++	9	10-	13–	9
Liberal	0	0	0	0	0	0	0	0	0
Total	13	18	15	15+	15++	15	15+	15++	15

Key: C = Conservative; Lab = Labour; + = Party that won seat at General Election held by-election in same Parliament; - = Party that won seat at General Election lost by-election to main opposition Party in same Parliament.

Politics in Metropolitan Essex

The immediate impact of the 1945 changes was beneficial to Labour. The creation of Barking, Dagenham and Hornchurch handed the Party three additional seats whilst the swing against the Tories meant that they were able to secure another five – both Ilford seats, Romford, Epping and Walthamstow East – to add to the number of safe seats that they already held. Their tally rose to seventeen and Woodford, where the Wartime Prime Minister Winston Churchill was the incumbent, was the only constituency won by the Conservatives. However, the reductions in Leyton and West Ham in1950 meant that Labour's representation fell. On the basis of pre-War results it could be argued that Leyton represented a marginal rather than a Labour seat but there was no denying that the loss of seats in West Ham only damaged Labour. A swing o the Conservatives that also occurred in1950 switched four more seats from Labour to Tory in addition to the three that Labour lost through the reduction in the total number of seats. Romford, both Ilford seats and Epping all returned to the Conservatives but in 1955 the boundary changes that transferred Brentwood to Billericay returned Romford to Labour despite a national swing to the Conservatives. However, the same swing meant that the Tories gained Hornchurch and Walthamstow East from Labour. Thereafter the same seats tended to change hands when there was a change of Government and in Labour's 1966 landslide the Tories only won two seats, Ilford North and Woodford.

Overall Labour outperformed the Tories in Metropolitan Essex in every General Election between 1945 and 1970. The only seat that remained solidly Conservative was Woodford. The Tories won forty contests compared with eighty-nine for Labour. During the period there were only six by-elections in the area but three of them were significant. The three that weren't took place in the 1950s. On 3rd February 1954 a by-election at Ilford North resulted in an easy win for the Conservatives who recorded a 28% majority, 10% higher than in 1951. In 1955 the Party's majority was 20%. On 1st March 1956 Labour won a convincing majority of 45% at Walthamstow West compared with 31% in 1955. However, by 1959 their support had waned and they recorded a 28% majority. On 30th May 1957 Labour won East Ham North with a majority of 27% compared with 18% in 1955. Again their popularity faltered and in1959 the majority fell to 14%.

The three significant by-elections took place in the 1960s. On 21st January 1965 a landmark by-election took place at Leyton. The MP who had won the seat for Labour in 1964 with a majority of 17% was persuaded to stand down to enable Harold Wilson's choice as Foreign Secretary, Patrick Gordon-Walker to win a seat in the Commons following his defeat at Smethwick where he had lost a relatively safe seat to a Tory who fought the election mainly on the issue of Commonwealth immigration. Walker lost the by-election by a margin of 0.5% to the Conservative candidate and had to wait until 1966 to re-take the seat, which he did with a majority of 18%, one percent higher than the 1964 general election result. Labour was re-elected nationally in 1966 with a much increased majority but shortly after the devaluation of sterling the Party began to lose support. On 21st September 1967 Labour lost a safe seat at Walthamstow West in a by-election. The Conservatives may have won by the slender margin of 0.4% but they overturned a 1966 majority of 36%. Labour recovered to win the seat in 1970 by a majority of 22% but still lost nationally, unable to pull back enough of the support they had lost in their last four years of Government. Less dramatic and more typical of the way the mood of the country was changing, was the loss of Walthamstow East in a by-election on 27th March 1969. Labour's 1966 majority of 6% was overturned by the Conservatives who won by a margin of 27% going on to retain the seat in 1970 by a small but crucial margin of 2%.

MPs for West Ham

From	at	To	Surname	First Names	Constituency	Party
1945	*G*	*1950*	*Comyns*	*Dr. Louis*	*Silvertown*	*Labour*
1945	*G*	*1950*	*Jones*	*(Sir) Frederick Elwyn (Major)*	*Plaistow*	*Labour*
1950	*G*	*1974*	*Jones*	*(Sir) Frederick Elwyn (Major)*	*West Ham South*	*Labour*
1945	*G*	*1950*	*Nicholls*	*Henry Richard*	*Stratford*	*Labour*
1945	*G*	*1950*	*Lewis*	*Arthur William John*	*Upton*	*Labour*
1950	*G*	*1974*	*Lewis*	*Arthur William John*	*West Ham North*	*Labour*

Notes: First returned at: **B** By-election, **G** General Election

West Ham's two MPs for most of the period between 1945 and 1974 could not have been more different, one being a highly educated and eminent lawyer; the other man a boxer with an elementary education and a trade union background. Both men came from humble origins.

Silvertown

Dr. Louis Comyns (Labour), who had been the MP since 1940 remained in the Commons until the 1950 re-distribution when he retired. His principal biographical details are in Chapter 8.

Plaistow, West Ham South

Sir (Frederick) Elwyn Jones (Labour) succeeded Will Thorne in 1945. Born on 24th October 1909 in Llanelli, Jones was educated at the local Grammar School in the Carmarthenshire town and then at Gonville and Caius College, Cambridge, where he was President of the Union. He became a barrister at Grays Inn in 1935 and was a major in the Royal Artillery during the Second World War. At the end of the War in 1945-6 he joined the British War Crimes Executive

Lord Elwyn Jones
© National Portrait Gallery
Lucinda Douglas-Menzies 1988

and was a Deputy Judge Advocate in the prosecuting team at the Nuremberg trials when senior Nazis were tried for their atrocities. During the term of the 1945-51 Labour Government he was PPS to the Attorney General whilst also occupying a judicial role as the Recorder of Merthyr Tydfil (1949). In 1950 he was elected as MP for West Ham South into which his Plaistow constituency was absorbed by the boundary changes. In 1953 he became a QC and Recorder of Swansea and from 1956-59 was a member of the Bar Council. From 1960-64 he was Recorder of Cardiff and for a time treasurer and a trustee of Amnesty but when Labour was returned to Government in 1964 he became Attorney – General, a post he held until 1970 when the Party went into Opposition once again. Meanwhile, in 1966 he had also been appointed Recorder of Kingston-on-Thames. When Harold Wilson became Prime Minister after the February 1974 election, Elwyn Jones, who had been returned as MP for the redrawn constituency of Newham South, was ennobled to become Lord Chancellor in the new Government, a post he held throughout the Wilson and Callaghan Governments until 1979. He died ten years later.

Stratford

Henry Richard Nicholls (Labour) won Stratford in 1945 but when the seat was absorbed in 1950 he left Parliament. Born in 1893, he received an elementary school education and initially emigrated to Australia but returned to become a coach painter with the London North Eastern Railway and a union official at the company's Stratford Works. From 1929-32 and then from 1942-62 he was a West Ham councillor. He died in 1962.

Upton, West Ham North

Arthur Lewis MP
Peoples History Museum Manchester

Arthur William John Lewis (Labour) who was born in 1917 and was educated at elementary school and the Borough Polytechnic, became an official of the General and Municipal Workers Union in 1938 before entering the Army in 1940, though two years later he was appointed a member of the Ministry of Labour Appeal Board, a post he held until the end of the War. He was elected MP for Upton in 1945; for West Ham North in 1950; and for Newham North West in February 1974; and retired from politics in 1983 after being de-selected by his local Labour Party for allegedly Trotskyite views and support for the IRA. He was an amateur boxer with a rumbustuous political style who remained a backbencher throughout his time in the Commons. He was a member of the Council of Europe after 1976 and a sometime chairman of the Eastern Regional Group of Labour MPs and of the London Party Executive Committee. Although he fought the 1983 election as an Independent Labour candidate, he lost. He died in 1998.

MPs for East Ham

From	at	To	Surname	First Names	Constituency	Party
1945	G	1957	Daines	Percy	East Ham North	Labour Co-operative
1957	B	1974	Prentice	(Sir) Reg(inald) Ernest		Labour
1945	G	1955	Barnes	Alfred John	East Ham South	Labour Co-operative
1955	G	1974	Oram	Albert Edward		Labour Co-operative

Notes: First returned at: **B** By-election, **G** General Election

Percy Daines MP
Peoples History Museum Manchester

East Ham North

Percy Daines (Labour & Co-operative) took the seat from Sir John Mayhew, the Tory incumbent in 1945 and held the seat until his death in 1957. He was born in 1902 and received an elementary school education before joining the railways becoming a locomotive fireman. During the War he served with the Royal Engineers from 1940 but was invalided out. Daines was a member of Enfield council for a number of years and an active member of the Co-operative movement serving on its national executive committee. He was employed by the Co-operative Insurance Company and specialised in Social Insurance. He died in 1957.

Reg Prentice MP
Peoples History Museum Manchester

(Sir) Reg(inald) Ernest Prentice (Labour) was returned at the 1957 by-election having previously unsuccessfully contested Croydon North (in 1950 and 1951) and Streatham (in 1955). He was born in 1923 and attended the Whitgift School in Croydon. In 1940 he became a temporary civil servant but in 1942 joined the Royal Artillery, being commissioned a year later. He saw war service in Italy and Austria and was discharged in 1946 when he attended the London School of Economics. After the LSE he joined the staff of the Transport and General Workers Union where he worked from 1950 to 1957 as assistant to the legal secretary and also started a political career serving as a councillor in Croydon between 1949 and 1955. He was appointed Minister of State for Education and Science in 1964 and, after the 1966 election, Minister of Public Building and Works, which post he held until 1967 when he was appointed Minister of Overseas Development. Two years later he was made Minister of State, Technology and Power but resigned after only four days in office. In 1970-1 he served as an alderman of the Greater London Council and between 1971 and 1974 was Opposition spokesman on Employment. When Harold Wilson became Prime Minister again in 1974 Prentice, having been returned this time for Newham North East, became Secretary for Education and Science in the Cabinet. However, he was subject to much constituency opposition to what were perceived as his increasingly rightwing politics and faced de-selection in his Newham seat. He stood down as Cabinet minister in 1975 to fight his de-selection but in 1977 resigned from the Labour Party and joined the Conservatives, to some extent justifying the view that his more left wing critics held of him. He continued to represent Newham North East as a Conservative but in 1979 was adopted for the safe Tory seat of Daventry (Northamptonshire), which he held until 1987 when he retired from the Commons. In the intervening period he held the post of Minister of State for Social Security in Margaret Thatcher's Government from 1979 to 1981. From 1988-90 he was an executive member of the National Union of Conservative Associations, a far cry from his younger days as a Trade Union worker. He was made a life peer in 1992 and died in 2001.

East Ham South

Alfred John Barnes (Labour & Co-operative) held the seat from 1929-31 and 1935 -1945 before he was re-elected in 1945 going on to hold it until he retired in 1955. His principal biographical details are in Chapter 8.

He was succeeded by **Albert Edward Oram** (Labour & Co-operative) who was born in 1913, the son of a blacksmith, and was educated at Brighton Grammar School before attending the London School of Economics, becoming a teacher and a member of the National Union of Teachers. He entered politics at the end of the War, in which he served for three years in the Royal Artillery. He unsuccessfully contested Lewes (East Sussex) in 1945 and the following year was appointed research officer for the Co-operative Party, a post he held when he embarked on his political career, losing at Billericay in 1950 before winning East Ham South in 1955. He was President of the Management Committee of Brighton Co-operative Society between 1959 and 1964 and then PPS to the Minister of Overseas Development until 1969. After Labour lost power in 1970 he became Co-ordinator of Development Programmes for the International Co-operative Alliance, a position he held until 1973. When the number of seats in the area was reduced from four to three in 1974 Oram retired from the Commons but the following year was created a Baron and became a member of the Commonwealth Development Corporation. From 1976-8 he was a Government Whip in the House of Lords and in 1978 was appointed Chairman of the Commonwealth Development Association. He died in 1999.

MPs for Ilford

Ilford North

Mabel Ridealgh MP
Peoples History Museum Manchester

Mrs Mabel Ridealgh (Labour) won the newly constituted North division in 1945, though she lost it in 1950. The daughter of a butcher, she was born in 1898 and married in 1919. She was active in the Enfield Labour Party and in 1941-42 was National President of the Women's Cooperative Guild when she was made an Honorary Regional Organiser for the Board of Trade, serving in that role until 1944. She was defeated in 1950 and again in 1951. From 1953 to 1963 she was a member of the Women's Advisory Committee of the British Standards Institute and also General Secretary of the Women's Co-operative Guild. She died in 1989.

Sir Geoffrey Clegg Hutchinson KC (Conservative) was first elected for Ilford in 1937 but lost the new North division to Mrs Ridealgh in 1945. Returned in 1950, he served until 1954 when he resigned to become chairman of the National Assistance Board. His principal biographical details are in Chapter 8.

MPs for Ilford						
From	**at**	**To**	**Surname**	**First Names**	**Constituency**	**Party**
1945	*G*	*1950*	*Ridealgh*	*Mabel (Mrs)*	*Ilford*	*Labour*
1950	*G*	*1954*	*Hutchinson*	*Sir Geoffrey Clegg*	*Ilford North*	*Conservative*
1954	*B*	*1974*	*Iremonger*	*Thomas Lascelles Isa Shandon Valiant (Tom)*		*Conservative*
1945	*G*	*1950*	*Ranger*	*James*	*Ilford South*	*Labour*
1950	*G*	*1966*	*Cooper*	*Albert Edward*		*Conservative*
1966	*G*	*1970*	*Shaw*	*Arnold John*		*Labour*
1970	*G*	*1974*	*Cooper*	*Albert Edward*		*Conservative*
Notes: First returned at: **B** By-election, **G** General Election						

Tom (Thomas Lascelles Isa Shandon Valiant) Iremonger (Conservative) succeeded him. Iremonger, a cousin of Sir Anthony Eden, the newly appointed Prime Minister, was born in 1916 and educated at Oriel College, Oxford (where he was a sailing blue in 1938) and served as a District Officer in the Colonial Service in the Western Pacific from 1938 to 1946. In 1942 he joined the Royal New Zealand Navy and was commissioned the following year, serving until 1946. He became a journalist and public relations officer but was also a Lloyd's Underwriter and entered politics initially in 1950 when he was defeated at Birmingham, Northfield. He was a member of Chelsea Borough Council between 1952 and 1955 but was meanwhile elected for Ilford North, a seat he retained until beaten by Labour in October 1974, this being one of the few seats that changed hands after the February election of that year and thus helped to give Labour a small overall majority in the House. In 1979 Iremonger stood as an Independent Conservative against the official Party candidate but secured only 1.6% of the votes. His political career never took off despite a promising start as PPS to Sir Fitzroy Maclean, when he was Under Secretary for War between 1954 and 1957. It is possible that he was too closely identified with Eden's policies during the Suez Crisis, which led to his replacement as Prime Minister by Macmillan.

Ilford South

James Ranger (Labour) was elected in 1945 and served one Parliament though he sought re-election in 1951 and 1955. He was born in 1889, the son of a bookbinder and was educated at Plaistow Council School.He became a company secretary and advised on welfare problems. He entered politics as a member of the West Ham Independent Labour Party in 1908 and joined the Co-operative Movement in 1915. He first contested a seat in 1931 when he was the Labour candidate at Epping, Winston Churchill's seat. He also contested that seat in 1935. He died in 1975.

Albert Edward Cooper (Conservative) was born in 1910 and educated at the London Choristers School; in Australia and in New Zealand. He was an Ilford Borough councillor from 1935 to 1952 and a navigator in a Mosquito Aircrew. At the outbreak of war he joined the RAF in which he became a squadron leader. Managing Director of Dispersions Ltd., Ault & Wiborg (International) Ltd, McIntyre & Sons Ltd. and S.Vollier & Co. Ltd, he unsuccessfully contested Dagenham in 1945 but after his return at Ilford South remained its MP until he was defeated in 1966, though he regained it in 1970, losing again in February 1974. He was briefly PPS to Peter Thorneycroft when he was President of the Board of Trade in 1953. He died in 1986.

Arnold Shaw MP
Peoples History Museum Manchester

Arnold John Shaw (Labour) was born in 1909 and educated at the Coopers' Company School and at the Universities of Southampton and London. A teacher between 1932 and 1966; and member of the NUT, he was a member of Stepney Council from 1938 to 1948 and of Ilford between 1952 and 1965. When the new London Boroughs were created he was elected to Redbridge Council in 1965 but lost his seat in 1968, though he was re-elected in 1971, serving until 1974. He was MP twice, initially from 1966 to 1970 and subsequently from February 1974 to 1979 when he was defeated and retired from politics. Between 1977 and 1979 he was PPS to Reginald Freeson, Minister of Housing and Construction. He died in 1984.

The massive Ford motor plant at Dagenham, in the Dagenham Constituency, taken from the river in 1950. This was a decade of expansion for Ford with factory size increased by 50% and output doubling and with up to 40,000 people employed there. By the end of the period covered in this chapter the Dagenham plant was one of the oldest in Europe. Unfortunately in 1971 a lengthy strike damaged Dagenham's long term prospects, making it vulnerable to migration of work to other Euopean plants operating concurrently. **Wikipedia - Ben Brooksbank**

MPs for Barking, and Dagenham

From	at	To	Surname	First Names	Constituency	Party
1945	G	1959	Hastings	Dr. Somerville	Barking	Labour
1959	G	1974	Driberg	Thomas Edward Neil		Labour
1945	B	1974	Parker	Herbert John Harvey	Dagenham	Labour

Notes: First returned at: **B** By-election, **G** General Election

Barking

Dr. Somerville Hastings (Labour) was elected for Barking in 1945 but had been an MP on two previous occasions. He sat for Reading (Berkshire) in 1923-4 and again from 1929-31 and also contested Epsom (Surrey) in 1922 and Reading again in 1935, though unsuccessfully. In 1924 he was PPS to CP Trevelyan, then the President of the Board of Education. Born at Warminster, Wiltshire in 1878, he was educated at Wycliffe College and the University of London and Middlesex Hospital where he later became the foremost Ear and Throat Surgeon. During the First World War he served in the Royal Army Medical Corps as a Captain. He was President of the Octological Section of the Royal Society of Medicine and between 1934 and 1944 was Chairman of the London County Council Hospitals and Medical Services Committee. He served on the LCC from 1932 to 1964 being its chairman in 1944-5 and was the first President of the Socialist Medical Association in 1930. He died in 1967.

Tom Driberg MP
© National Portrait Gallery
Ronald Franks 1966

Thomas Edward Neil 'Tom' Driberg (Labour) succeeded Hastings in 1959 and remained the MP until he retired in 1974. Born in 1905, he was educated at Lancing College and Christ Church, Oxford and became a lecturer, broadcaster and journalist, writing the William Hickey Column for the "*Daily Express*" from 1933 to 1943. He had started with the "*Express*" in 1928 and also contributed to "*Reynolds News*". During the World and Korean Wars he was a war correspondent but entered politics in 1942 when as an Independent he contested a by-election in the Conservative-held seat of Maldon, it being the convention that major parties did not contest by-elections in wartime. He was elected and then re-elected in 1945,

1950 and 1951 as a Labour candidate, finally going down to defeat in 1955. He was a left-wing member of the Labour Party National Executive Committee from 1949 until 1974 and its Chairman in 1957-8 but was also a lay preacher in the Church of England. After his death his autobiography, "Ruling Passions" was published posthumously which showed him to have been an active homosexual. Had this been more widely known in his lifetime, it could have adversely affected his political career. He was made Baron Bradwell in 1975, but died the following year.

MPs for Hornchurch and Romford

From		To	Surname	First Names	Constituency	Party
1945	G	1955	Bing	Geoffrey Henry Cecil (Major)	Hornchurch	Labour
1955	G	1966	Lagden	Godfrey William		Conservative
1966	G	1970	Williams	Alan Lee		Labour
1970	G	1974	Loveridge	John Warren		Conservative
1945	G	1950	Macpherson	Thomas	Romford	Labour
1950	G	1955	Lockwood	Lt-Colonel John Cutts		Conservative
1955	G	1970	Ledger	Ronald Joseph		Labour
1970	G	1974	Leonard	Richard Lawrence		Labour

Notes: First returned at: **B** By-election, **G** General Election

Dagenham

Herbert John Harvey Parker (Labour) who sat for Romford from 1935 to 1945 was elected at Dagenham in 1945 and served until his retirement in 1983. His principal biographical details are in Chapter 8.

Hornchurch

Geoffrey Bing MP in the 1940s
Peoples History Museum Manchester

Major Geoffrey Henry Cecil Bing QC (Labour) was born in 1909, the son of a schoolmaster and educated at Tonbridge School and Lincoln College, Oxford, and in 1934, the year he became a barrister in England, founded the National Council for Civil Liberties. He subsequently qualified as a barrister in Gibraltar, Nigeria and the Gold Coast, the latter in 1950 when he also took silk. During the Second World War he was wounded serving as a signals officer with the rank of Major in North Africa and Europe and was mentioned in despatches. He was briefly until 1946 an assistant Whip in the 1945 Labour Government but his very left wing politics inhibited his political career and after his defeat in 1955 he moved to the British colony of Ghana where he worked as the Constitutional Adviser for the soon to be President of that country, Dr. Kwame Nkrumah, working as Attorney General there from 1957 to 1961. He died in 1977.

Godfrey William Lagden (Conservative) was born in 1906, educated at Richmond Hill School and became a sales representative. During the Second World War he was a bomb reconnaissance officer attached to the Essex Police and served on the Hornchurch Urban District Council between 1948 and 1954 and on the Essex County Council from 1949-55 when he became an alderman. He contested Thurrock (Essex) unsuccessfully in 1951 and sat for Hornchurch from 1959 to 1966 when he was defeated. In 1958 he became a director of a local company, Elm Park Petrol and Oil Supplies Limited. He died in 1989.

Alan Lee Williams (Labour) won the seat in 1966. Born in 1930, he was educated at the Roan School, Greenwich and at Ruskin College, Oxford and from 1956 to 1962 was national youth officer of the Labour Party; then fulfilled the same role for the United Nations Association between 1962 and 1966. He was also chairman of the British Committee of the World Assembly of Youth. He was a member of Greenwich Borough Council from 1952-55 and contested the Epsom Parliamentary seat unsuccessfully in 1964. After his return at Hornchurch he was a delegate to the Council of Europe between 1967 and 1970 and in 1969-70 was PPS to Denis Healey when the latter was Minster of Defence. He was made a Freeman of the City of London in 1969, the year in which he became a delegate to the United Nations. He was defeated in 1970 and became Deputy Director of the European Movement; then in 1972 Director of the British Atlantic Movement but regained Hornchurch in February 1974 and held it until defeated once again in 1979. From 1975 until the end of the Parliament he was PPS to Roy Mason, firstly when he was Defence Secretary and then when he had responsibility for Northern Ireland. In 1976 he was appointed a Governor of the Greenwich Hospital School and in 1986 was made Warden and Chief Executive of Toynbee Hall, the East End based charity established to support individuals from disadvantaged communities.

(Sir) John Warren Loveridge (Conservative) was born in 1925 and educated privately; and at St. John's College, Cambridge. A farmer- landowner who became Principal of St. Godric's College, London in 1954, he was a member of Hampstead Council from 1953 to 1959 and a Treasurer of the Hampstead Conservative Association between 1959 and 1974. He contested the safe Labour seat of Aberavon in 1951 and was Hornchurch's MP from 1970 to February 1974 when he transferred to the new and somewhat safer Upminster constituency which he held until he retired in 1983. He was vice - chairman of the Conservative Small Businesses Committee after 1974 but had an undistinguished political career. He was a Freeman of the City of London and a magistrate for the West Central area of London. He died in 2007.

Romford

Thomas Macpherson MP
Peoples History Museum Manchester

Thomas Macpherson (Labour) was born in Glasgow in 1888 and educated at St. George's Road School in the city. During the First World War he served in the Highland Light Infantry. He was a successful businessman and chaired his own foreign and colonial merchants company of Macpherson & Train and was also Chairman of the Ethiopian Produce & Trading Company. A chairman of the London Provision Exchange from 1941, he bred Ayrshire cattle at his Essex farm at Great Warley, near Brentwood, which was then in the Romford constituency. Between 1924 and 1927 he was a member of Romford Urban District Council. During the Second World War he was Regional Port Director for Scotland from 1942-45 and was awarded the Medal of Freedom by the United States of America and in 1948 was appointed an Officer of the Order of Orange Nassau in the Netherlands. Elected at Romford in 1945, he was defeated in 1950 but the following year was elevated to the House of Lords as Baron Macpherson of Drumochter. He had diverse public and private interests including Board membership of the Port of London Authority (1949-62); the Essex River Board (1956); and chairmanship of the Scottish Clan Society (1952-56). He died in 1965.

Lieutenant-Colonel John Cutts Lockwood (Conservative) was elected in 1950 though he had been an MP before, representing Hackney Central from 1931-35. His principal biographical details are in Chapter 7.

Election leaflet showing Leonard and Williams, Hornchurch and Romford respectively.
Peoples History Museum Manchester

Ron(ald) Joseph Ledger (Labour) was born in 1920 and educated locally at Skinners' Grammar School in Tunbridge Wells and at the University of Nottingham where he founded the Labour Club and was its first Chairman in 1948. However, the Second World War interrupted his education and he served in the RAF from 1942, leaving active service in 1947. He was an engineer and staff training officer who joined the Co-operative Movement and became Director of the London Society in 1961. He contested Rushcliffe in Nottinghamshire in 1951 and from 1952 to 1954 was a councillor in Hertfordshire before he was elected at Romford in 1955. He also had some unusual aspects to his c.v, being for a period the proprietor of a casino and from 1966 the Chairman of the Hairdressing Council. He died in 2004.

Richard 'Dick' Lawrence Leonard (Labour) was born in 1930 and was educated at Ealing Grammar School, London University Institute of Education and Essex University where he was a research fellow in politics. Between 1953 and 1955 he was a schoolteacher then was appointed Deputy General Secretary of the Fabian Society, a post he held until 1960 when he became a political journalist and broadcaster. He was an unsuccessful Parliamentary candidate at Harrow West in 1955 at the age of twenty-four and in 1964 published a guide to the General Election of that year. He was appointed a Senior Research Fellow at the University of Essex in 1968 but two years later was elected Romford's MP which he was for one term only between 1970 and February 1974. During this period he was PPS to Anthony Crosland but retired from politics to return to journalism as the Assistant Editor of "*The Economist*". Between 1977 and 1978 he was Chairman of the Fabian Society and from 1978 was Chairman of the Library Advisory Council for England.

MPs for Epping, and Woodford						
From		**To**	**Surname**	**First Names**	**Constituency**	**Party**
1945	*G*	*1950*	*Manning*	*Dame Elizabeth Leah*	*Epping*	*Labour*
1950	*G*	*1951*	*Davies*	*Dr Claude Nigel Brian*		*Conservative*
1951	*G*	*1964*	*Finlay*	*Sir Graeme Bell*		*Conservative*
1964	*G*	*1970*	*Newens*	*Arthur Stanley*		*Labour*
1970	*G*	*1974*	*Tebbit*	*Norman Beresford*		*Conservative*
1945	*G*	*1964*	*Spencer-Churchill*	*Sir Winston Leonard*	*Woodford*	*Conservative*
1964	*G*	*1974*	*Jenkin*	*Sir Charles Patrick Fleeming*		*Conservative*
Notes: First returned at: **B** By-election, **G** General Election						

Epping

Mrs. (later Dame) Elizabeth Leah Manning (Labour), who had briefly been MP for Islington East in 1931, took the redrawn Epping constituency in 1945 and retained it until her defeat in 1950. Her principal biographical details are in Chapter 7.

She was succeeded by **Dr. Claude Nigel Brian Davies** (Conservative) who was born in 1920 and educated at Eton; in France and Germany and then at Sandhurst Military College. During the War he served in the Grenadier Guards in the Near East and in Italy and had been Managing Director of an Essex company (Windolite) for three years at the time of his election in 1950. However, he only remained in the House for one term and stood down in 1951. Later he took a PhD in archaeology at London University in 1970 writing several works on South American civilisations. He died in 2004.

He was succeeded by **Sir Graeme Bell Finlay** (Conservative) who was born in 1917 and educated at Marlborough College and University College London. During the Second World War he attained the rank of acting Major having served initially in the South Wales Borderers and then the 5th Royal Ghurkha Rifles, which he left in 1946. He was called to the bar at Gray's Inn in 1950, the same year that he contested Aneurin Bevan's safe Labour seat at Ebbw Vale. As President of the Hardwicke Society he presided over the first joint debate involving both the Oxford and Cambridge Union Societies. After his election at Epping in 1951 he became Vice-chairman of the Conservative members' housing committee and embarked on a career as a government whip. He was appointed an assistant whip in 1957 and a senior whip (Lord Commissioner of the Treasury) in 1959, serving until 1960 when he became a Vice-Chamberlain of the Household, remaining in that role until 1964. He retired from politics after his defeat and resumed his law career. In 1972 he was appointed a Deputy Judge of the County Court and five years later became a Circuit Judge and until 1977 served in the States of Jersey as Sous Judge D'Instruction. He died in 1987.

Arthur Stan(ley) Newens (Labour) took the seat in 1964 but lost in 1970. Born in 1930 he was educated at Buckhurst Hill County High School; at University College; and at London & Westminster Teacher Training College after which he became a coal miner and local NUM trade unionist between 1952 and 1956; and then a teacher. He joined the Labour Party in 1949 and was also a member of the NUT, who sponsored his candidacy at Epping and was President of the union's Hackney Branch. He was Chairman of the London Co-operative Society and of the Movement for Colonial Freedom. After his defeat at Epping he was out of the House for four years but returned in February 1974 as the MP for the new constituency of Harlow, which did not include any part of the London metropolitan area but which replaced much of the Epping seat after boundary changes. He was chairman of the left wing Tribune Group of Labour MPs in 1982-3 but lost the seat to the Conservatives in 1983 and was defeated there again in 1987, though he was meanwhile elected as a Member of the European Parliament (for Central London) in 1984 becoming the chairman of the British Labour Group.

Stan Newens MP
Peoples History Museum Manchester

Norman Beresford Tebbit (Conservative) was born at Enfield in 1931 and educated at Edmonton Grammar School before becoming a journalist on the staff of the *Financial Times* in 1947. In 1949 he did his National Service as a pilot and remained with the RAF for four years; then trained as an airline pilot, which he was from 1953-1970; and became a trade union official for the British Airline Pilots' Association. His politics were right wing and he became an area officer for the Young Conservatives and Chairman of the Conservative Political Centre at Hemel Hempstead before he was elected at Epping in 1970, though he had been the prospective candidate in Islington South West as recently as 1969. The seat was redrawn in 1974 and the southern part of it formed the new constituency seat of Chingford, which

Alfie, it's that man again! (With ackowledgments to the Daily Mirror, 19.5.45)

The shock at the outcome of the 1945 General Election has now faded away, but it was confidently predicted that the Tories under Winston Churchill would be sure to win, bearing in mind their leader's superlative record of power and leadership during the second World War. However, the mild-mannered Major Attlee, the Labour Party Leader, was rewarded with a landslide for Labour. This cartoon from the Daily Mirror in May 1945 was employed in election communications, and it happened to attune perfectly with the electors' feelings in the matter of who should govern. It was evident that, as the cartoon highlights, the last thing the majority wanted was 'more of the same', which was the general perception of what the Tories were offering. What the country got was a radical agenda, that though it seems it was unaffordable in its full glory, much of it still resounds today, if only in the NHS. From 1945 British politics was in flux. The end of this chapter, in 1974, sees the start of another Labour Government under Wilson.
The People's Museum, Manchester

Baron Tebbit of Chingford
© National Portrait Gallery
Nick Sinclair 1992

he represented until he retired from the Commons in 1992 when he was ennobled. In the intervening years Norman Tebbit was not often out of the headlines. Named a "semi house-trained polecat" by Labour's Michael Foot, he was subsequently also known as the "Chingford skinhead" for his forthright views, though these did nothing to slow his progress as a high flying Cabinet minister under Margaret Thatcher, of whom he was a devoted follower. Nevertheless his early career started during Edward Heath's ill fated 1970-4 Government when he was PPS to the Minister of State for Employment, but when Thatcher was returned in 1979 he was immediately appointed Under Secretary for Trade; then Minister of State for Industry in 1981, and in the same year he entered the Cabinet as Secretary of State for Employment, pushing through what at the time was highly contentious legislation limiting the powers of trade unions. From 1983-85 he was moved to the post of Secretary of State for Trade and Industry, and in 1985 became Chancellor of the Duchy of Lancaster, a post he combined with that of Chairman of the Conservative Party, which he held until 1987. However, he was a victim of an IRA bombing of the Imperial Hotel in Brighton, where the Tories held their Party conference and he left government to look after his wife who was seriously disabled by the atrocity. He remained a vocal supporter of Margaret Thatcher and was especially dismissive of those elements in the Party that later ousted her from the leadership. He decided to retire from the Commons in 1992 and was ennobled as Baron Tebbit of Chingford.

Woodford

(Sir) Winston Leonard Spencer-Churchill (Conservative), the Prime Minister and former MP for Epping, opted for the Woodford constituency at the 1945 election. He retained the seat until his retirement from politics in 1964. His principal biographical details are in chapter 8.

Wanstead & Woodford

In 1964 Churchill was succeeded by **Sir Charles Patrick Fleeming Jenkin** (Conservative) in the newly named Wanstead & Woodford seat. He was born in 1926 and educated at Clifton College and Jesus College, Cambridge before becoming a barrister, company secretary, industrial adviser and a Director of various companies including Distillers (1957-70), the Tilbury Contracting Group, Royal Worcester and the Continental and Industrial Trust Ltd. Initially he was called to the bar (Middle Temple) as a Harmsworth scholar in 1952 and entered politics in Hornsey where he was a member of the Borough Council from 1960-63. A member of the Bow Group, after his election in 1964 he was made an Opposition spokesman on finance, economic and trade affairs in 1965 and in the Heath Government served as Financial Secretary to the Treasury (1970-2); Chief Secretary to the Treasury (1972-4); and briefly in 1974 as Energy Minister during the miners' strike and three day week that provoked Heath to call the February General Election, which the Party lost. He remained a Front Bench spokesman (on Energy 1974-6 and Social Services after 1976) and with the return of the Thatcher Government in 1979 was appointed Secretary of State for Social Services. Other Cabinet posts followed – Industry (1981-3) and Environment (1983-5), when he was dropped from the Government. He retired from the Commons in 1987 and was made Lord Jenkin of Roding.

MPs for Leyton, and Walthamstow

From		To	Surname	First Names	Constituency	Party
1945	*G*	*1950*	*Bechervaise*	*Albert Eric*	*Leyton East*	*Labour*
1945	*G*	*1950*	*Sorenson*	*Reverend William Reginald*	*Leyton West*	*Labour*
1950	*G*	*1964*	*Sorenson*	*Reverend William Reginald*	*Leyton*	*Labour*
1965	*B*	*1966*	*Buxton*	*Ronald Carlile*		*Conservative*
1966	*G*	*1974*	*Gordon - Walker*	*Sir Patrick Chrestien*		*Labour*
1945	*G*	*1955*	*Wallace*	*Harry Wright*	*Walthamstow East*	*Labour*
1955	*G*	*1966*	*Harvey*	*John Edgar*		*Conservative*
1966	*G*	*1969*	*Robinson*	*William Oscar James*		*Labour*
1969	*B*	*1974*	*McNair-Wilson*	*Sir Robert Michael Conal*		*Conservative*
1945	*G*	*1950*	*McEntee*	*Valentine la Touche*	*Walthamstow West*	*Labour*
1950	*G*	*1956*	*Attlee*	*Clement Richard*		*Labour*
1956	*B*	*1967*	*Redhead*	*Edward Charles*		*Labour*
1967	*B*	*1970*	*Silvester*	*Frederick John*		*Conservative*
1970	*G*	*1974*	*Deakins*	*Eric Petro*		*Labour*

Notes: First returned at: **B** By-election, **G** General Election

Leyton East

Albert Eric Bechervaise (Labour) was born in 1884 and was educated locally at Mayville Road School Leytonstone after which he became a piano worker (1900), a Co-operative agent and a lecturer (1927). He was elected to Leyton council in 1922 and was its Mayor in 1930 continuing on the council until 1965. He contested Southend-on-Sea in 1931, where he was heavily defeated, but only failed at Leyton East in 1935 by a little over three hundred votes. He was an MP from 1945 to 1950 when the seat was merged with Leyton West and he retired. Between 1954 and 1960 he was a member of the Metropolitan Water Board. He died in 1966.

Leyton West, Leyton

Reverend Reginald William Sorenson (Labour) who was MP for Leyton West between 1929 and 1931 and again from 1935 was re-elected in 1945 and became MP for Leyton in 1950 retaining the seat until he retired after the 1964 election when he was made a Life Peer. His principal biographical details are in Chapter 8.

The by-election created by Sorenson's departure was unexpectedly won by **Ronald Carlile Buxton MC** (Conservative) who defeated Patrick Gordon – Walker, whom Harold Wilson had appointed Foreign Secretary despite his defeat at Smethwick at the 1964 General Election. Buxton, a chartered structural civil engineer, won the January 1965 by-election at Leyton, largely because of a perception that Walker had been foisted on the constituency. Born in 1923, the son of a naval officer and educated at Eton and Trinity College, Cambridge, during the Second World War he served as a Captain in the Royal Electrical Mechanical Engineers and was awarded the Military Cross. He was an unlikely MP for the 1960s Leyton and was soundly defeated at the 1966 General Election. He tried again in 1970 but was defeated for a second time and retired from politics.

Sir Patrick Chrestien Gordon - Walker (Labour) was born in 1907, the son of a Judge, and educated at Wellington College and Christ Church College, Oxford, where he became a history tutor for nine years. He was subsequently employed by the BBC's European Service broadcasting to German workers between 1940 and 1944 when he was made chief editor, Radio Luxembourg and then assistant director of the BBC German Service in 1945. He was active in the National Union of Journalists, becoming Chairman of the BBC branch in 1946. He entered politics initially in 1935 when he contested Oxford City but was not elected to the House until 1945 when he was returned for the

PARLIAMENTARY GENERAL ELECTION 1970

PUBLIC MEETING

TUESDAY JUNE 2nd

at 8 p.m.

at the MUNICIPAL OFFICES, HIGH ROAD, (OLD TOWN HALL) LEYTON, E.10.

GORDON WALKER

LABOUR CANDIDATE FOR LEYTON

and SUPPORTING SPEAKER

This fragment from an election communication in 1970 promotes Gordon-Walker's re-election and would normally be thrown away after the event. Fortunately it has been preserved. A photo of the venue appears on Page 271.
Peoples History Museum Manchester

Black Country seat of Smethwick, which he represented until 1964 when he was defeated in the very year that Labour returned to Government after a lapse of thirteen years. The influx of Commonwealth immigration was held to be the factor that swung the seat away from Labour. One of the covert campaign themes in the constituency was, "if you want a nigger for a neighbour, vote Labour". Following his defeat, Gordon-Walker, who was Harold Wilson's choice as Foreign Secretary, was adopted as the candidate for the 1965 by-election when Sorenson became a Life Peer. Defeated, Gordon-Walker was successful in 1966 but while he was out of Parliament he lost his Cabinet post to Michael Stewart (see Fulham, Middlesex, Chapter 11). Following the election of the Attlee Government in 1945, Gordon-Walker was appointed as PPS to Herbert Morrison in 1946, then Under Secretary of State for Commonwealth Relations in 1947, moving to become Secretary of State in the same department in 1950. Following his return in 1966 he was first made a Minister without Portfolio by Harold Wilson in 1967 and then from 1967 to 1968 was Secretary of State for Education but by then the momentum of his career had essentially been lost. He was re-elected in 1970 but retired in 1974 when he was made a Baron; briefly became a member of the European Parliament, and died in 1980.

Walthamstow East

Harry Wright Wallace (Labour), sat from 1929 to 1931 and again from 1945 to 1955. His biographical details are in Chapter 8.

John Edgar Harvey (Conservative) won the seat in 1955 and held it until 1966. Born in 1920, he was educated at the Xaverian College, Bruges (Belgium) and at Lyme Regis Grammar School after which he secured a clerical post, joining the National Union of Clerks in 1938. During the war he was a wireless operator in the Merchant Navy, afterwards becoming an export sales representative and in 1953 General Manager of a firm of lubricating oil distributors. He joined the Young Conservatives and from 1948-9 was Chairman of the Woodford Division, Winston Churchill's seat. He was Middlesex Chairman of the Y.C's from 1949-51 and first contested a Parliamentary seat at St. Pancras North in 1950, though unsuccessfully. From 1953 he was Chairman of the Association of Prospective Conservative Parliamentary Candidates prior to his election in 1955 and was also a member of the Party's National Executive Committee between 1950 and 1955. He contested Walthamstow East in 1951 and served as its MP from 1955 to 1966 when he was defeated. Between 1963 and 1968 he was a member of the NSPCC's Central Executive and in 1970 was appointed a Verderer of Epping Forest. In the same year he was made a Director of Burmah Castrol (Europe) and in 1974 of Burmah Oil Trading. He died in 1980.

In the Tories' landslide defeat of 1966 the seat was taken by **William Oscar James Robinson** (Labour) but he sadly died two years later. Born in 1909 and educated locally at schools in Leyton and at London University, he became a solicitor. From 1945-52 he was a member of the Leyton Borough Council and then from 1952-65 of Wanstead & Woodford of which Borough he was Mayor in 1962/3. Prior to winning the seat he had previously but unsuccessfully contested Windsor (Berkshire) in 1955 and Harwich (Essex) in 1959.

The by-electon that followed Robinson's death was contested on 27th March 1969 when it was won by **Sir Robert Michael Conal McNair-Wilson** (Conservative), who held the seat until February 1974 when, following boundary changes, he transferred to the safer seat of Newbury (Berkshire).Born in 1930 and educated at Eton College, he undertook his national service in the Royal Irish Fusiliers and was commissioned. Afterwards he went into local journalism in Northern Ireland having decided that farming was not for him. He first entered politics with an unsuccessful attempt to win Lincoln in 1964 but after his success at Walthamstow was in the House until 1992 when he retired. Meanwhile in 1984 he was unfortunate to suffer kidney disease and was the first MP to to use a dialysis machine and receive a kidney transplant. Between 1979 and 1983 he was PPS to the Minister of Agriculture and was joint secretary to the Greater London Group of Conservative MPs in 1969-70. He died in 1993.

Walthamstow West

Valentine la Touche McEntee (Labour) first won the seat in 1922 then again in 1923 and 1929 and remained the MP until he retired in 1950. His biographical details are in Chapter 8.

He made way for the Prime Minister, **Clement Richard Attlee** (Labour) who's Stepney, Limehouse seat disappeared with re-distribution. Attlee's principal biographical details are in Chapter 7. Attlee represented the seat until 1956 when he was made an Earl.

Edward Redhead MP
Peoples History Museum Manchester

Edward Charles Redhead (Labour) was selected to fight the by-election that arose from Attlee's ennoblement. He represented the seat from 1956 to 1967 when he died. Born in 1902 he was educated locally at the Walthamstow higher elementary school and then privately. A boy clerk with the Post Office in 1917, he entered the Customs and Excise in 1919 finishing as a Higher Executive Officer in 1948 when he was elected General Secretary of the Society of Civil Servants, a post he held until 1956. He first entered politics in 1929 as a member of the Walthamstow borough council becoming mayor in 1949-50 and again in 1961-2, serving as an alderman from 1945 to 1965. He contested Gillingham (Kent) unsuccessfully in 1951. From 1959-64 he was an Opposition Whip in the Commons and in 1964 joined the Government as a Minister of State at the Board of Trade and in 1965 took on a similar role at the Department of Education and Science but his career was cut short by his death in 1967.

Frederick John Silvester (Conservative) was the only Conservative ever elected for the Walthamstow West constituency. Having previously lost heavily when contesting a seat for the first time in 1966 he won the by-election in 1967 when the popularity of the Labour Government was at its lowest ebb but lost the seat in 1970. Born in 1933 and educated at Sir George Monoux Grammar School, Walthamstow and at Sidney Sussex College, Cambridge, he was initially a teacher (1955) who became a barrister (at Gray's Inn, 1957) and an advertising executive including an associate directorship with J.Walter Thompson. He was active in Conservative politics locally and was his constituency party's political education officer between 1957 and 1960 and its chairman from 1961-64. He was also a member of the Borough Council, between 1961 and 1965. In February 1974 he was elected in the Withington division of Manchester and from 1974 to 1976 was an Opposition Whip; and from 1976-79 Vice chairman of the Conservative employment committee. After the election of the Thatcher Government he was PPS to James Prior when he was the Secretary of State for Employment (1979-81) and Northern Ireland Secretary (1981-3). Unfavourable demographic changes eventually eroded his majority at Withington and he was defeated there in 1987. He retired from politics.

An election communication in favour of Eric Deakins, for Labour.
Peoples History Museum Manchester

Eric Petro Deakins (Labour) won the seat in 1970. Born in 1932 and educated at Tottenham Grammar School and the London School of Economics, he embarked on a career in management with the FMC meat company in 1956 becoming its general manager but leaving in 1971 after his election to the Commons. He entered politics in 1958 as a member of Tottenham Borough Council, serving until 1961 and again in 1962-3. He contested the Finchley constituency in 1959 (against Margaret Thatcher) and the Essex seat of Chigwell in 1966 before also being defeated at the Walthamstow West by-election in 1967. He held the seat from 1970 to 1974 when he was returned for the single Walthamstow constituency, which he held until 1987 when the Conservatives won it in a strong swing from Labour in the London area. From 1974-6 he was Under Secretary for Trade in the Wilson Government and then fulfilled a similar role at the Department of Health and Social Security in the Callaghan Government from 1976-9 when the Party lost power.

Chapter 13
Metropolitan Kent 1945 - 1974

The immediate post war review of boundaries in 1945 created two additional constituencies in Kent, both of them in the outer suburban area where population growth had been greatest. **Orpington** was formed mainly from parts of the former Chislehurst constituency but also contained elements of Dartford and Sevenoaks. Including Biggin Hill, Chelsfield, Farnborough, Green Street Green, Petts Wood, Pratts Bottom and St. Mary Cray, the new constituency also incorporated Swanley (a Kent town to this day) near Dartford. In 1950 Orpington's electorate of 50,704 was 13% below the London average, though within a year the number had grown by nearly 2,500 as housing development in the area continued. The town's name is corrupted from the original 'Dorpentune', partly British and partly Saxon, signifying 'the village where the spring of water rises'; in this case the river Cray.

Chislehurst was consequently reduced in size to extend from the border with Lewisham, southeast-wards to St. Pauls Cray. It included Blackfen, Elmstead Woods, Foots Cray, Lamorbey, Longlands, Mottingham, North Cray, Sidcup and St. Pauls Cray. Sidcup was its most populous district. Despite its reduced geography the constituency's electorate was still 12% higher than the average for London so much so that between the General Elections of 1950 and 1951 alone, the number of people on the register increased by over 5,500 to reach a total of 70,906.

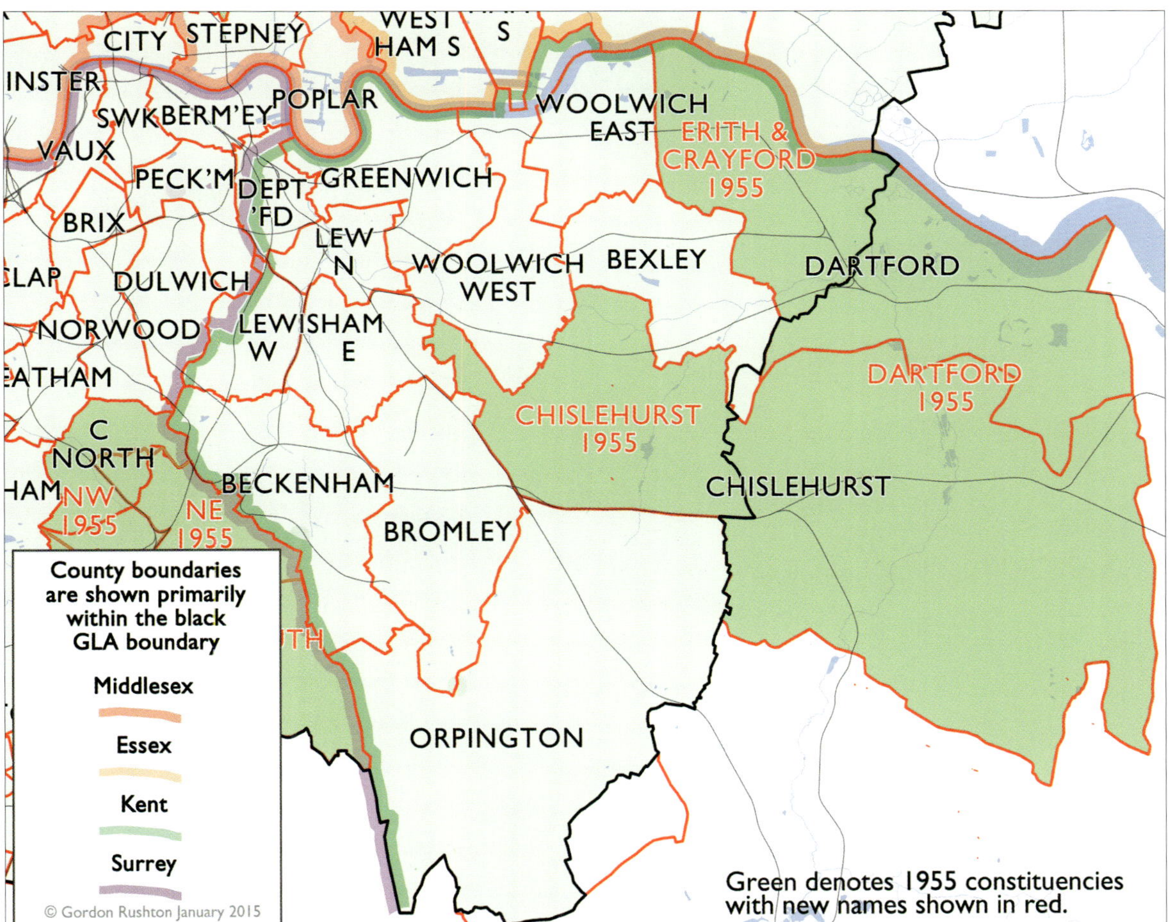

The map depicts Kent constituencies created in 1945, 1950 and 1955, including modifications in areas beyond today's Greater London boundary. Beckenham, Orpington and Bexley were created in 1945, whilst Lewisham expanded from two to three seats in 1950. Erith & Crayford emerged in 1955, leaving Dartford outside Greater London. Comparison with 1945 may be made by reference to the map on page 18 and with 1918 on page 16.

Left: *Willett Way in well-to-do Petts Wood continues today, with an array of sumptuous automobiles and splendid houses, to demonstrate the affluent nature of this part of the 1945 Orpington Constituency. Petts Wood was created in the 1920s and building started from the station. It is in an ideal place for affluent commuters.*

Below: *Bexley was created a new constituency in 1945 but was altered in 1955 with the creation of Erith & Crayford when it lost much of its Labour voting electorate. The water meadows of the River Cray divided the seat from the Chislehurst Constituency and are viewed here from the London bound platform of Bexley Station, familiar to its many, generally Conservative voting commuters.*

Below: *Beckenham was created a constituency in 1950 when it was carved out of Bromley. This sign stands proudly on the commuter town's High Street, a stone's throw from Beckenham Junction Station. The municipal borough had been created 15 years earlier.*

Above: *Equitable House in General Gordon Place, central Woolwich, in the Woolwich East constituency, was for many years the HQ of the famous Woolwich Building Society. Built in 1935 in the Art Deco style it lasted as HQ until 2002, when it was bought by Barclays. During the period of this chapter, job totals ran down in Woolwich, with the reduction of activity at the Arsenal.* **Gordon Rushton**

Left: *Although Erith & Crayford was a Labour seat following its creation in 1955, it too was home to the commuting middle classes. Grasmere Road, Barnehurst is typical of the period and was close to Erith Road, a boundary with Bexley.*

All pictures John Nelson, unless otherwise attributed.

A new seat was also created from the former **Dartford** constituency, which remained in its smaller format and included Belvedere, Crayford, Erith, Northumberland Heath, Slade Green and Thamesmead. The new **Bexley** constituency was geographically small covering the neighbourhoods of Bexleyheath and Bexley only, which included Barnehurst, Bexley Woods, Danson Park, East Wickham, Falconwood and Welling. By 1950 Bexley's electorate was 63,429, some 9% higher than the London average. The name Bexley, which means the 'clearing in the box wood', first turned up in records in 814 when King Kenulph, the King of the Mercians, granted lands at Bexley to Wulfred, Archbishop of Canterbury.

The review of constituencies undertaken in advance of the 1950 General Election brought further alterations. This time changes also affected the LCC boroughs of Deptford, Greenwich, Woolwich and Lewisham but the outer suburban constituencies were altered again, reflecting the substantial population changes taking place in the post War period. The changes brought about a further increase in the representation of the area when two additional seats were created; one in Lewisham and another in neighbouring Beckenham.

There were no boundary changes in **Greenwich,** which retained its borough identity containing an electorate of 61,198 that was 5% larger than the average and which remained pretty stable until the mid 1960s when it began to fall. Despite reducing by about 7% between 1950 and 1970, Greenwich nevertheless retained a slightly above average London electorate throughout the period. **Deptford** too remained unaltered and with an electorate of around 55,000 was only 6% below the average for London at that time. However, the area suffered a gradual decline in its population throughout the 1950s and 1960s such that by 1970 the electorate had fallen by over 22%, even after the voting age had been reduced to 18.

In neighbouring Woolwich there were some ward transfers from Woolwich West to East. **Woolwich West** (the more middle class constituency) was then in its heyday as a London suburb and lost the more industrial riverside area between the docks and Woolwich Common to working class **Woolwich East.** The West constituency comprised Eltham, New Eltham, Well Hall and the Woolwich Dockyard whilst East was made up of Abbeywood, Plumstead, Plumstead Marshes, Shooters Hill, Woolwich Arsenal, Woolwich Town centre and North Woolwich on the north bank of the Thames. After these transfers the two electorates were very similar in size at around 52,000 each but were approximately 10% smaller than the London average. Both constituencies were to remain unaltered until 1974 by which time one had declined whilst the other had continued to grow. Woolwich East experienced a fall of nearly 6% in its electorate between 1950 and 1970 but Woolwich West grew by nearly 10%. The diverging trends were in part related as people in the older parts of the borough sought the better housing on offer in the newer suburbs.

Lewisham's two seats increased to three as the population of the former East division increased. **Lewisham North** acquired the Blackheath, Ladywell, Park, Village and Lee wards from the former East constituency whereas Hither Green, Downham and Grove Park were placed in **Lewisham South**, which also gained Bellingham, Rushey Green and western parts of Catford from **Lewisham West.** In turn this seat retained Crofton Park, Forest Hill, Honour Oak Park, Beckenham Hill, Lower and Upper and Sydenham. The changes reflected a large increase in population that had occurred within the Lewisham borough during the 1920s and 30s; in particular the growth of council estates in Bellingham and Downham.

Electorates between the three divisions were pretty evenly matched and remained so throughout the period from 1950 to1974. Lewisham South and West contained electorates of about 56,000 whilst Lewisham East was a couple of thousand fewer. Throughout the entire period no constituency electorate in Lewisham ever varied by more than 8% from the London average and in most cases the variation was within 5%. Lewisham West was almost exactly the same size as the overall London average in both 1964 and 1966.

The new **Beckenham** constituency (literally the 'ham' or homestead on the 'bec', the river Ravensbourne) was created in 1950 out of the former Bromley division and extended from Penge, south-eastwards to Beckenham, Elmers End, Eden Park, Kelsey Park, Shortlands, West Wickham, Hayes and Coney Hall. With an electorate of nearly 74,000 it was, even then, 26% larger than the average London constituency, a position that actually worsened over the next couple of decades as Beckenham registered an increase in voters whilst other seats were in relative decline. By 1970 Beckenham's electorate was over 77,000 and even allowing for the lowering of the age at which adults could vote, the constituency was by then 41% larger than the average.

The neighbouring **Bromley** constituency remained but, following the creation of Beckenham, was smaller geographically extending south from Plaistow and Sundridge Park to Keston including also Bromley Town, Bromley Hill, Bromley Common, Widmore and Bickley. At that time Bromley's electorate was not much greater than 47,000 (some

19% smaller than the London average) and the numbers remained pretty stable throughout the 1950s and '60s. Before the granting of the vote to 18 year-olds its electorate never quite reached 50,000 and although it increased slightly the constituency was smaller than the average throughout the period in question. The electorate topped 54,000 in 1970, following the extension of the franchise, and in the Election of that year Bromley was only 1% smaller than the average for Greater London as a whole. Given the stability in its own population and electorate over a twenty year period, this change was relative and demonstrates how the London average fell throughout the post-war period until the franchise was extended in time for the 1970 Election.

After the General Election of 1951 another boundary revision took place in Kent and this resulted in yet further alteration to the London area constituencies, these being implemented in 1955. Although the **Bexley** constituency, established in 1945, remained unchanged a new **Erith and Crayford** seat was separated from Dartford as London overspill continued down the south side of the Thames estuary, a mirror image of what was taking place on the north side in Essex. Included within this seat were Belvedere, Northumberland Heath, Slade Green, Thamesmead and West Heath. Erith derives its name from the Saxon 'Earhyth' (960 AD) meaning, 'muddy or gravely landing place' and it was a fishing village for much of its history, although in the early sixteenth century ships were also built there. Crayford means 'ford of the river Cray' and was recorded as 'Creiford' in 1199. Erith was always a significant centre having a population of nearly 10,000 in 1881, only a few hundred fewer than neighbouring Dartford in which constituency it was placed in 1885.

The 1955 changes meant that the Dartford division itself ceased to be a constituency covering Metropolitan Kent. **Chislehurst** comprised Blackfen, Elmstead Woods, Foots Cray, Lamorbey, Longlands, Mottingham, North Cray, Sidcup and St. Pauls Cray. **Orpington** included Biggin Hill, Chelsfield, Farnborough, Green Street Green, Petts Wood, Pratts Bottom and St. Mary Cray, while Swanley was returned to Dartford.

The number of seats in metropolitan Kent was unchanged as a result of these changes and the immediate impact was to reduce the size of the electorates in Orpington and Chislehurst. There were about 6,500 fewer voters in Orpington in 1955 than there were in 1951 and at the time the new boundaries were established the seat contained an electorate that was 17% smaller than the average for London. However, this was a short-term phenomenon as the electorate grew by nearly 40% over the next 15 years. Even allowing for the expansion of the electorate to include everyone over the age of 18 this was a remarkable growth, so much so that by 1970 the boundaries contained an electorate that was 18% greater than the London average. The Chislehurst constituency, which had been 12% larger than the average in 1950, was only 3% higher in 1955 after boundary changes with a total of 58,063 electors. Expansion continued in the years that followed so that by 1970 the electorate had grown by another 14.5% to reach a total of 66,483, which was 21% above the then London average. Erith & Crayford constituency itself contained over 52,000 electors in 1955 and this number increased by a little under 2,000 until 1970 when it rose by another 4,000 as a result of the extension of the franchise to 18 year-olds. Throughout the period the size of its electorate was never outside the range of 5% greater or 7% below the average for the Greater London area. In fact in 1964 the electorate was within about 70 voters of the average.

Politics in Metropolitan Kent

These constituency changes lasted until 1974 and there were political impacts arising from them. The obvious change was that between the General Elections of 1935 and 1955 the number of MPs returned from Metropolitan Kent increased from 10 to 13, or 30%. Dartford was effectively a London area seat until 1955 and therefore the creation of Erith & Crayford in that year did not significantly affect the comparison. A summary of the results between 1945 and 1970, together with a comparison with the position in the period before the War, is shown top, opposite.

Between 1945 and 1974 (the latter exclusive) there was a very even pattern of success between the major Parties. 52 Conservative MPs were returned at Parliamentary Elections including by-elections and 50 for Labour whilst the Liberal Party won on only three occasions, all at Orpington, including a famous by-election there. Overall, apart from that by-election, the main political interest was in Lewisham and Woolwich where three marginal seats held the attention.

The distribution of seats between the Parties was influenced by the boundary changes. All three constituencies that had been included in Bromley before the War were staunchly Conservative. Beckenham (including a March 1957 by-election), Bromley (including a November 1945 by-election) and Orpington (including a by-election in January 1955) all returned Conservative MPs with large majorities in successive elections with the exception of Orpington which returned a Liberal in 1964 and 1966 following a sensational by-election win there on 14th March 1962. This massive reverse for the Conservatives occurred when the Liberals secured a majority of 18% in a seat the Tories held in 1959 by a margin of 34% over Labour, who dropped to third place, heralding a trend in largely middle class seats in much of England that was to gather strength throughout the latter part of the 20th Century . Eric Lubbock retained the seat at the

Post War General Election Results 1945 -1970 by % majority

Constituency	pre-1945	1945	1950	1951	1955	1959	1964	1966	1970
Deptford	Lab	Lab47	Lab33	Lab30	Lab31	Lab24+	Lab33	Lab41	Lab31
Greenwich	C	Lab31	Lab22	Lab21	Lab18	Lab12	Lab25	Lab30	Lab20+
Woolwich East	Lab	Lab44	Lab29+	Lab21	Lab27	Lab29	Lab47	Lab43	Lab31
Woolwich West	C	Lab23	C0.2	C3	C4	C8	Lab4	Lab9	Lab1
Lewisham East	C	Lab25							
Lewisham North			C5	C7	C8-	C11	C1	Lab6	Lab3
Lewisham South (East)	C	Lab25	Lab16	Lab14	Lab15	Lab7	Lab20	Lab26	Lab26
Lewisham West	C	Lab7	C5	C5	C10	C14	C2	Lab5	C2
Beckenham			C31	C35	C38+	C39	C30	C25	C33
Bromley	C	C11+	C27	C31	C36	C40	C29	C26	C35
Chislehurst	C	Lab12	C0.3	C2	C8	C13	C3	Lab2	C7
Orpington		C11	C24	C25	C32+	C34-	L7	L3	C3
Bexley		Lab27+	C0.3	C3	C9	C17	C9	C4	C16
Erith & Crayford					Lab21	Lab13	Lab21	Lab21	Lab12
Dartford	C	Lab37	Lab20	Lab18					
Conservative	8	2+	8	8	8++	8-	6	3	6
Labour	2	10+	5	5	5+	5	6	9	7
Liberal	0	0	0	0	0	0+	1	1	0
Total	10	12++	13	13	13+	13+	13	13	13+

Key: C = Conservative; Lab = Labour; + = Party that won seat at General Election held by-election in same Parliament; - = Party that won seat at General Election lost by-election to main opposition. Party in same Parliament.

1964 General Election with a majority of 7%. However, in 1970 Orpington returned to the Tory fold and has remained there ever since. Bromley and Beckenham continued to return Conservatives throughout the period.

The other newly formed constituencies were more mixed. In 1945 (the year of Labour's first landslide victory) both Bexley and Chislehurst returned Labour MPs. However, in 1950 they reverted to the Conservatives, albeit by the tiny margin of 0.3% in each case. There had been early signs of disaffection with Labour in a by-election in July 1946. Although Labour held Bexley with a 5% majority over the Tories as compared with 27% at the 1945 Election this represented a substantial swing against the Party (partly brought about by the continued building of homes for the middle classes) and it was less surprising that it lost the seat in 1950. Thereafter, apart from another Labour landslide in 1966 when the Tories lost Chislehurst again, four of the five outer suburban seats were more or less solid for the Conservatives until 1974. The exception was Erith & Crayford, which retained the former Dartford constituency's more radical traditions, and with a mainly working class electorate was a safe Labour seat throughout the period.

The 1945 General Election in the L.C.C. area of southeast London was a whitewash for the Labour Party. The national swing to the Party since 1935 was sufficient to wipe out the Conservatives in seats that they had held comfortably before the War at Lewisham East, Lewisham West, Greenwich and Woolwich West. The swing in Lewisham and Greenwich was 18% and in Woolwich West reached 20%. Interestingly, the two Labour held seats recorded lower swings; 16% in Deptford and 14% in Woolwich East, suggesting that the Labour landslide resulted from a slightly greater swing in middle class as opposed to working class seats. Perhaps this also explained the results in neighbouring Bexley and Chislehurst in 1945.

The swing of the political pendulum back to the Conservatives in the subsequent four General Elections changed the picture significantly. In Lewisham Labour only retained a single seat in elections between 1950 and 1959 and that was the South division, which contained big council estates. Lewisham North and West both became Conservative seats between 1950 and 1966 when once again a national landslide swept them out of Tory hands. Labour did celebrate a gain in a North Lewisham by-election on 14th February 1957 when they won by a margin of 3% compared with the Tories' 8% in 1955 but by the time of the 1959 General Election the Tories had more than recovered the ground and won a majority of 11%. Even the 1964 Election, which saw a national swing sufficient to bring about a change of Government, did not shift either of the two Tory seats in Lewisham to Labour.

Labour held on comfortably, though with diminishing majorities between 1950 and 1959, to Deptford (including a by-election in July 1963), Greenwich and Woolwich East (including a by-election shortly before the 1951 Election) but Woolwich West was lost to the Conservatives in 1950 on a swing of nearly 12%, much larger than any other in the area, suggesting it was the boundary changes before 1950 that made the difference. In that Election the Tory majority was 0.2% though it rose successively to reach 8% in 1959. If the swing between 1945 and 1959 had been the same in Woolwich West on its 1945 boundaries as in neighbouring Greenwich, it is unlikely that Woolwich West would have become a Conservative seat at all during that period. The movement of population from East to West Woolwich probably also helped the Conservative position.

The period between 1964 and 1970 was one in which the two major Parties vied for supremacy in the southeast London seats that by then had become notoriously marginal. A combination of boundary changes, political swing, and the slowly changing social demography of the area with middle class families moving to the outer suburbs and new working class populations, often from ethnic minority backgrounds, moving in, slowly changed the area's political face. Woolwich West was regained in 1964 and in 1966 Labour once again secured every seat in the LCC area of south east London. Interestingly when the Tories won power back in 1970 Labour still clung on in Woolwich West and Lewisham North. The swing in the increasingly working class seats of Lewisham North and South was significantly lower than in the more middle class West division. It seems likely that this was due as much to the changing social demography as to other factors. Certainly boundary changes were not a factor in these elections as there were none.

There were occasional by-elections in safe Labour seats during the period including 8thJuly 1971 when the Party increased its majority at Greenwich from 21% to 39% compared with June 1970. The majority fell back to 23% at the February 1974 General Election, repeating a familiar pattern of swings to and from Governments who lost popularity in mid-term only to win much of it back again at the subsequent General Election.

MPs for Metropolitan Kent

Beckenham

Patrick George Thomas Buchan-Hepburn (Conservative) was elected in 1950 for the new Beckenham constituency and had previously been MP for the East Toxteth division of Liverpool from 1931 to 1950, having also contested Wolverhampton East, though unsuccessfully, in 1929. Between 1930 and 1931 he served on the London County Council. He was born in 1901, the son of the 4th baronet, Sir Archibald, and educated at Harrow School and Trinity College, Cambridge where he gained an MA. He joined the diplomatic corps and was appointed attaché at the British Embassy in Constantinople serving in that capacity from 1925 to 1927. He was made an assistant whip in 1939 and later a Lord Commissioner of the Treasury, a grand title for a similar role. During the War he joined the 11th City of London Yeomanry and became a brigade major. When Labour was in power after 1945 he was the Conservative Deputy Chief Whip and with the return of Churchill's peacetime Government in 1951 he was appointed Chief Whip, serving until 1955. In 1957 he was elevated to the House of Lords as the first Lord Hailes and died in 1974.

Sir Philip Carter Goodhart (Conservative) won the 1957 by-election created by his predecessor's ennoblement. Born in 1923, Goodhart came from a wealthy Kent family from nearby Langley Court, the centre of what became a 20th century housing development known as Langley Park. Born in 1925 he was educated at Hotchkiss School in the United States and at Trinity College, Cambridge after which he became a journalist with the *'Daily Telegraph'* and *'Sunday Times'*. At the 1950 election he unsuccessfully contested Consett (County Durham) and after his election at Beckenham failed to make a substantial mark. He sat on the council of the Consumer Association from 1959 to 1968 and again from 1970 to 1979 and was a member of a British delegation to the United Nations from 1963 to 1979 and an executive member of the British Council between 1974 and 1979. Despite entering the House for a safe seat and at a young age he never attained ministerial rank of any kind. From 1960 to 1979 he was a joint secretary of the 1922 Committee. He was ennobled after his retirement at the 1992 election.

Bexley

Mrs Jeannie Laurel Adamson (Labour) was previously MP for Dartford between 1938 and 1945. Her biographical details are in Chapter 9 (Dartford).

She was succeeded at a July 1946 by-election by **Sir Ernest Ashley Bramall** (Labour), who was born in 1916 and became a barrister in 1945 when he was able to complete his studies after war service. He was educated at Westminster and Canfield Schools and attended Magdalen College, Oxford where he took a degree in Philosophy,

MPs for Metropolitan Kent

From	at	To	Surname	First Names	Constituency	Party
1950	G	1957	Buchan-Hepburn	Patrick George Thomas	Beckenham	Conservative
1957	B	1974	Goodhart	Sir Philip Carter		Conservative
1945	G	1946	Adamson	Mrs Jeannie Laurel	Bexley	Labour
1946	G	1950	Bramall	Sir Ernest Ashley		Labour
1950	G	1974	Heath	Sir Edward Richard George		Conservative
1945	G	1945	Campbell	Sir Edward Taswell (deceased)	Bromley	Conservative
1945	B	1964	Macmillan	Sir Maurice Harold		Conservative
1964	G	1974	Hunt	Sir John Leonard		Conservative
1945	G	1950	Wallace	George Douglas	Chislehurst	Labour
1950	G	1966	Hornsby-Smith	Dame Patricia		Conservative
1966	G	1970	Macdonald	Alistair Huistean		Labour
1970	G	1974	Hornsby-Smith	Dame Patricia		Conservative
1945	G	1955	Dodds	Norman Noel	Dartford	Labour
1955	G	1965	Dodds	Norman Noel	Erith & Crayford	Labour
1965	B	1974	Wellbeloved	Alfred James		Labour
1945	G	1950	Wilmot	John	Deptford	Labour
1950	G	1951	Cooper	John		Labour
1951	G	1963	Plummer	Sir Leslie Arthur		Labour
1963	B	1974	Silkin	John Ernest		Labour
1945	G	1959	Reeves	Joseph	Greenwich	Labour
1959	G	1971	Marsh	Sir Richard William		Labour
1971	B	1974	Barnett	Nicolas Guy		Labour
1945	G	1950	Morrison	Herbert Stanley	Lewisham East	Labour
1950	G	1959	Morrison	Herbert Stanley	Lewisham South	Labour
1959	G	1974	Johnson	Carol Alfred		Labour
1950	G	1957	Hudson	Sir Austen Uvedale Morgan	Lewisham North	Conservative
1957	B	1959	MacDermot	Niall		Labour
1959	G	1966	Chataway	Sir Christopher John		Conservative
1966	G	1974	Moyle	Roland Dunstan		Labour
1945	G	1950	Skeffington	Arthur Massey	Lewisham West	Labour
1950	G	1964	Price	Henry Alfred		Conservative
1964	G	1966	McNair-Wilson	Sir Patrick Michael Ernest David		Conservative
1966	G	1970	Dickens	James McCulloch York		Labour
1970	G	1974	Gummer	John Selwyn		Conservative
1945	G	1954	Smithers	Sir Waldron	Orpington	Conservative
1955	B	1962	Sumner	William Donald Massey		Conservative
1962	B	1970	Lubbock	Eric Reginald		Liberal
1970	G	1974	Stanbrook	Ivor Robert		Conservative
1945	G	1950	Hicks	Ernest George	Woolwich East	Labour
1950	G	1951	Bevin	Ernest		Labour
1951	B	1974	Mayhew	Christopher Paget		Labour
1945	G	1950	Berry	Henry	Woolwich West	Labour
1950	G	1959	Steward	Sir William Arthur		Conservative
1959	G	1964	Turner	Sir Colin William Carstairs		Conservative
1964	G	1974	Hamling	William		Labour

Notes: First returned at: **B** By-election, **G** General Election

Politics and Economics and was Treasurer of the Union and Chairman of the Labour Club in 1938. In 1938-9 he was the private secretary to an MP and Treasurer of his local Labour Party in Chelsea. In 1939 he was for a year Assistant to the secretary of the Food Manufacturers' Federation but joined the Army as a trooper in 1940 and reached the rank of

Major in the Reconnaissance Corps. He married and moved to Teddington where he was a councillor in Twickenham. He was defeated in 1950. He died in 1999.

Sir Edward Richard George 'Ted' Heath (Conservative) took Bexley at the 1950 General Election and held it for over 50 years. He finally retired at the 2001 election by which time he was father of the House (that is its longest serving member). Heath was born the son of a builder at Broadstairs, Kent in 1916 and educated at Oxford, where he was elected President of the University Conservative Association in 1937. In 1938, as Chairman of the Federation of University Conservative Associations and President of the Oxford Union, he opposed the policy of appeasement toward Nazi Germany pursued by Prime Minister Neville Chamberlain and, following a visit to Spain to observe the Civil War, also became a strong opponent of Franco and fascism. During the Second World he was commissioned as a second lieutenant in the Royal Artillery in March 1941 serving in the 107 Heavy Anti-Aircraft Regiment which was involved in heavy fighting in Belgium, the Netherlands and Germany taking part in Operation Veritable to capture territory between the rivers Rhine and Maas. He remained in Germany after the war and attended the Nuremburg Trials. He worked in the Ministry of Civil Aviation in 1946-47, was editor of the Church Times from January 1948 to October 1949, and then became a member of a merchant banking firm. In 1950 Heath worked for the Conservative Central Office before being elected at Bexley in the same year.

Edward Heath MP
Wikipedia

His maiden speech evoked a strong commitment to a United Europe, no doubt influenced by his earlier experiences, and this became his principal political mission. In 1951 he became an assistant whip and was made chief government whip under Prime Minister Anthony Eden in 1955. Between 1959 and 1960 he served as Minister of Labour in the Government of Harold Macmillan, a neighbouring Kent MP; then he became Lord Privy Seal with Foreign Office responsibilities representing Britain in negotiations for entry into the European Economic Community. In October 1963 he became Secretary of State for Industry, Trade, and Regional Development and President of the Board of Trade. After the Conservative defeat in October 1964, Heath became a major opposition figure and was elected Leader of his Party in July 1965. Although his party suffered a heavy defeat in the March 1966 general election he won a surprise victory in June 1970. As prime minister, Heath had to deal with some of the worst aspects of the troubles in Northern Ireland, over which he imposed direct British rule in 1972. He eventually achieved British entry into the European Economic Community in 1972-73, an event of historic significance for the country but one which was subsequently to create huge divisions within the Conservative Party. At home his government wrestled with a number of problems including high inflation and a series of crippling labour strikes that brought significant social unrest. Hoping to win a new mandate in the wake of a miners' strike, which led him to impose a three-day week through the rationing of electricity, Heath called for a General Election on Feb. 28th 1974. Despite having a slight majority of votes, the Conservatives lost seats in the Commons to Labour. Heath failed to form a coalition government with the Liberals and Harold Wilson succeeded him on March 4th. After the Conservatives were defeated in another General Election in October, Margaret Thatcher replaced Heath as party leader in February 1975 following a contest that he was not expected to lose but in which he was defeated by just 11 votes. He never regained office and he reacted badly to his leadership defeat becoming critical of Thatcher throughout her premiership. A talented musician and world beating yachtsman, he died in 2005.

An extract from an election communication in favour of Ted Heath MP in the General Election campaign of 1966. The Conservatives lost the election.
Peoples History Museum Manchester

Bromley

Sir Edward Taswell Campbell (Conservative) who had represented Bromley since 1930 was re-elected in 1945 but died before the result was declared, necessitating a by-election that took place in November. His principal biographical details may be found in Chapter 9 (Bromley).

Campbell was succeeded by **Sir (Maurice) Harold Macmillan** (Conservative), in many ways an archetypal Conservative figure in the genre of the 'landed gentry' but one in fact whose life experiences in the war and as a northern MP during the Depression moulded him into a more radical Tory politician. Born in 1894, the son of an American-born mother and the grandson of Daniel, a founder of the London publishing house of Macmillan & Co., he was educated at Eton and Balliol College, Oxford after which he joined the Grenadier Guards in 1914 and married the daughter of the Duke of Devonshire. During World War I he served with distinction on the Western Front and was wounded on three occasions. After the Armistice he joined the family business in 1920 but soon entered politics as the MP for the

Harold Macmillan MP
Wikipedia

borough of Stockton-on-Tees (County Durham) which he represented from 1924 until 1929, when he was defeated, and then again between 1931 and 1945, when he lost it for the second time. Macmillan was a strong believer in social reform and his left-wing Tory views were so unpopular with the Party leadership that the whip was withdrawn from him between 1936 and 1937 after he had been critical on the subject of unemployment. Macmillan also opposed the appeasement policies of Baldwin and Chamberlain and remained a backbencher until Churchill appointed him Parliamentary Secretary to the Ministry of Supply in 1940. After 10 months as Colonial Under Secretary in 1942, he was sent in December of that year to northwest Africa as British minister resident at Allied Forces Headquarters, Mediterranean Command where he worked closely with high ranking Allied officers including Dwight D. Eisenhower and Charles de Gaulle, with whom he was to engage in his subsequent roles in government after the War.

At the end of the war in Europe, Macmillan was made Secretary of State for Air in Churchill's short-lived 'caretaker' government (May-July 1945). At the 1945 Election he lost his seat at Stockton but was returned a few months later at the Bromley by-election and after the Conservatives regained power in 1951, he was successively appointed Minister of Housing and Local Government (October 1951) and Minister of Defence (October 1954) by Churchill; and then served as Foreign Secretary (April-December 1955) and Chancellor of the Exchequer (1955-57) under Eden. In this latter role he avoided any personal criticism arising from the Government's controversial involvement in the Suez invasion of Egypt and, following Eden's resignation he emerged as Prime Minister on Jan. 10th 1957.

After they had taken a knock during the Suez crisis, Macmillan worked to improve British-U.S. relations, and his wartime partnership with now President Eisenhower was helpful in this regard. He visited the Soviet leader, Khrushchev in Moscow in February 1959. At home, he promoted social programs and led his Party to a landslide victory in 1959 campaigning under the slogan 'You've never had it so good.' His tradition as a reformer was also evident in his 'wind of change' speech at Cape Town in 1960 where he acknowledged the inevitability of African independence. In Europe his policies were less successful. The Nassau agreement (December 1962) between Macmillan and President Kennedy, under which the United States provided nuclear missiles for British submarines, did little to win over the anti-US President Charles de Gaulle of France to Macmillan's objective of securing British membership of the European Economic Community, which he vetoed the following year..

His Government's response to Britain's worsening balance of payments was a wage freeze and other deflationary measures which, from 1961 on, caused the Tories to lose popularity but the major setback that brought about the eventual demise of his government was an apparent Soviet espionage attempt involving John Profumo, the Secretary of State for War, in an affair with a prostitute who was apparently also sharing the bed of a Soviet military attaché. After undergoing prostate surgery Macmillan resigned on Oct. 18th 1963. He initially refused a peerage and retired from the Commons in September 1964 but did eventually accept one and was created an Earl in 1984. He subsequently made a devastating attack on the privatisation policies of the Thatcher Government, which he compared to 'selling the family

Prime Minister Harold Macmillan with 35th US President, John F. Kennedy, on the occasion of their meeting at the naval air station at Boca Chica Key on Sunday March 26th, 1961, soon after Kennedy's inauguration in January 1961. Macmillan was on a mission as one of the 'Big Two' world powers, to send an important message to the Russians over the recent peace settlement in Laos. The two men 'hit it off' when Harold Macmillan and John F. Kennedy stood side by side outside the White House in April 1961. Macmillan was the 67-year-old son-in-law of the Duke of Devonshire, and Kennedy was the 43-year-old son of a self-made millionaire. The relationship was helpful when Macmillan courted support from Kennedy in Britain's bid to join the European Common Market. The French President Charles de Gaulle was against this to the pont of blocking it, fearing a lessening of French influence in his good relationship with Germany. Kennedy was prepared to help because he thought that the British were more understanding in world affairs than France or Germany. Such were the affairs of the MP for Bromley. **Wikipedia**

silver'. He died in 1986.

Sir John Leonard Hunt (Conservative) succeeded Macmillan at the 1964 Election and went on to represent Bromley and its successor seat, Ravenbourne, until his retirement in 1997. Unlike his predecessor he had an undistinguished though relatively long career as a Tory backbencher. Born in 1929 he was educated at Dulwich College and became a stockbroker. He was a member of Bromley Council between 1953 and 1965 and mayor in 1963-4, the year he became the local MP. He had previously contested Lewisham South unsuccessfully at the 1959 Election. He was President of the Institute of Administrative Accountants, later Financial Accountants, from 1970 to 1988; chairman of the Indo-British Parliamentary Group from 1979-91; and a member of the British-Caribbean Association from 1968. He was a Freeman of the Haberdasher's Company and of the City of London, a member of the Council of Europe and of the BBC advisory council.

Chislehurst

George Douglas Wallace (Labour) was elected the first Labour MP for Chislehurst in 1945. Born in 1906 in Cheltenham where he attended the Central School he was a onetime cashier who joined the local Chislehurst and Sidcup UDC in 1939 and remained a councillor there until 1946. During the War he was a Sergeant in RAF Fighter Command from 1941 to 1945. In 1947 he became an Assistant Government whip but was defeated in 1950 and his short Parliamentary career came to an end. He became a stock clerk in the wholesale meat trade. He continued to contest Chislehurst unsuccessfully being the candidate in all elections between 1945 and 1955. He was made a life peer in 1975 and died in 2003.

Dame Patricia Hornsby-Smith MP
© National Porttrait Gallery

His opponent at all elections from 1950 was **Dame Patricia Hornsby-Smith** (Conservative) who defeated him then and served until defeated herself in 1966; then was again the MP from 1970 to 1974 when she retired. Born in 1914 at East Sheen, she was educated at Richmond Grammar School and was a member of Barnes Borough Council between 1945 and 1950. A director of Andre Bernard Ltd and of Sutton Harbour Improvement Company, Plymouth, she was PPS at the Ministry of Health between 1951 and 1957 and then an Under-Secretary at the Home Office from 1957 to 1959. She was Parliamentary Secretary at the Ministry of Pensions and National Insurance from 1959 to 1961 after which she held no further offices. She died in 1985.

Alistair Macdonald MP
Peoples History Museum Manchester

Alistair Huistean Macdonald (Labour), who contested Beckenham in 1964, defeated Hornsby-Smith in 1966 but was himself defeated by her four years later. Born in 1925 he was educated at Dulwich College, Enfield Technical College and Corpus Christi College, Cambridge, and was a bank clerk. A member of Chislehurst and Sidcup UDC from 1958-62 and an alderman on Bromley Council between 1964 and 1968 and after 1971, he had a brief and undistinguished Parliamentary career losing at Chislehurst again in 1974. He died in 1999.

Dartford, Erith and Crayford

Norman Noel Dodds (Labour) won Dartford for the first time in 1945 and when the new Erith & Crayford constituency was created in 1955 transferred, remaining MP there until his death in 1965. Born in 1903 he was educated at Dunston-on-Tyne Council School in Gateshead and got a job with the Newcastle Co-operative Wholesale Society in 1918 where he worked until 1929, transferring then to London as the Society's Publicity Manager in charge of exhibitions. During the War he served with the RAF between 1943 and 1945 and following his election as an MP sat as a backbencher until 1951 when he was briefly PPS to the Minister of Labour. He was honorary secretary of the Home Workers Products Society, an organisation that provided work for disabled people. He died in 1965.

Alfred Wellbeloved MP
Peoples History Museum Manchester

Alfred James Wellbeloved (Labour) won the by-election in November 1965 occasioned by Dodds' death and held the seat until 1983, two years after he defected to the Social Democratic Party. He contested the seat in his new colours and although he came second, split the anti-Tory vote so that a Conservative was returned. Born in 1926 he was educated at Elementary School and South

Norman Dodds MP
Peoples History Museum Manchester

Thamesmead was a new town, planned and executed from the 1960s in the Erith and Crayford Constituency. It was intended to be a futuristic, modern and exciting place to live with leisure space, walkways and waterways. During the time of Norman Dodds it must have seemed a wonderful social project. Alas for a number of significant reasons, one was communications, Thamesmead has not lived up to original expectations.

Gordon Rushton

East London Technical College after which he described himself as a Commercial and industrial consultant. He was a councillor on the Erith Borough Council between 1956 and 1965 when he became leader of the newly created Bexley Borough Council. From 1972-3 he was an Opposition whip and a sometime joint vice-chairman of the Manifesto Group of moderate Labour MPs. In the Callaghan Government he served from 1976-79 as Under Secretary for Defence for the RAF. He died in 2012.

Deptford

John Wilmot (Labour) won Deptford in 1945 having previously represented Fulham East (1933-5) and Kennington (1935-45). He retired in 1950 and his principal biographical details may be found in Chapter 7 (Fulham East).

He was succeeded by **John 'Jack' Cooper** (Labour), born in 1919 into a working class Lancashire family. Originally an office worker he was later an official of the Municipal and General Workers' Union. Whilst in Lancashire he was a councillor in Manchester and on moving to London was an alderman on the LCC and a member of the Metropolitan Water Board. Cooper served only one term as Deptford's MP and stood down at the 1951 Election and resumed his trade union career, becoming General Secretary of the National Union of General and Municipal Workers Union in 1961, a post he held for twelve years. Ennobled in 1966, he died in 1988.

He was succeeded by **Sir Leslie Arthur Plummer** (Labour), a journalist with the *'Daily Herald'* and then business manager of the *'New Leader'*, who went on to become assistant general manager and a Board director of *'Express'* Newspapers. From 1947 to 1950 he was chairman of the Queensland British Food Corporation and was knighted in 1949. Born in 1901 he was educated at Tottenham Grammar School. He died in 1963.

John Ernest Silkin (Labour) won the July 1963 by-election that followed Plummer's death and went on to hold the seat until 1974 when he was returned for the revised constituency of Lewisham, Deptford. Silkin came from a family steeped in the Labour Party in South East London. He was the third son of Lewis Silkin (MP for Peckham between 1936 and 1950 and later 'Baron Silkin of Dulwich) who had been a key figure in Britain's post-war reconstruction being responsible for the 1947 Planning Act, when Minister of Town and Country Planning, which led to the development of new towns. His elder brother Sam (later Lord) Silkin was also a prominent MP (for Camberwell in 1964 and later for Southwark until 1983) and who was also a minister in Wilson's Governments serving as Attorney General. Born in 1923 John was educated at Dulwich College and the University of Wales but after a short time was called up serving as an Intelligence Officer in the Royal Navy from 1941to 1946 when he resumed his education at Trinity Hall, Cambridge. After qualifying as a solicitor in 1950 he entered politics initially unsuccessfully as the candidate for Marylebone in 1950. He was subsequently defeated at Woolwich West in 1951 and Nottingham South in 1959 before his return at Deptford in 1963. He gained an early promotion as a Government whip in 1964 and was made initially Deputy and

John Silkin MP
Peoples History Museum Manchester

then Chief Whip in July following Labour's March 1966 General Election victory. He also served as Deputy Leader of the House during this period until 1969 when he became Minister of Public Buildings and Works. During the period of Opposition from 1970-74 he was a front bench spokesman on local government and then on social services but when Wilson formed another Government in March 1974 Silkin became Minister for Planning and Local Government. In Callaghan's Government he was Minister of Agriculture, Fisheries and Food from 1976 until Labour's defeat in 1979 when he once again became a front bench opposition spokesman for his Party, including industry and defence. He announced his retirement from politics shortly before the 1987 Election but died beforehand.

Greenwich

Joseph Reeves (Labour) who had previously contested Woolwich West in 1931 was elected for Greenwich in 1945 and remained the MP until he retired at the 1959 Election. Born in 1888 and educated at Elementary school and Morley College he had a long association with the Co-operative movement of which he was a pioneer in London, sending parties to the Soviet Union after the Revolution. He was education secretary of the Royal Arsenal Co-operative Society for 20 years and was also a Deptford Borough Council alderman from 1926. He became a film producer, specialising in social commentary documentaries, being the manager of the Workers Film Association between 1938 and 1945. He sat on several Labour Party committees and was the author of a book on the Co-operative movement, 'A Century of Rochdale'. He was a member of the Labour Party's National Executive Committee from 1946-1953.

Joseph Reeves MP
Peoples History Museum Manchester

Sir Richard William Marsh (Labour) was elected in 1959 and remained until 1971 when he was appointed Chairman of the British Railways Board. Born in 1928 at Belvedere, Kent, the son of a foundry worker, he was educated at elementary school, Woolwich Polytechnic and Ruskin College, Oxford after which he became an officer with the National Union of Public Employees for which he worked from 1951 until his election as an MP. A member of the national executive of the Fabian Society, he first contested a seat at Hertford in 1951. After the return of the Wilson Government, Marsh received a ministerial appointment straight away as Parliamentary Secretary at the Ministry of Labour but was moved to a similar role at the Ministry of Technology in 1965.

A faded, 50 year old election leaflet from 1966, demonstrates the criteria thought necessary to achieve re-election. Apparently it worked.
Peoples History Museum Manchester

He entered the Cabinet in 1966 as Minister of Power and two years later became Minister of Transport, serving until 1969 when he left the Government over its policies to promote greater democratic accountability in the trades unions. Following Labour's election defeat in 1970 he remained a backbencher but in 1971 was appointed by the new Conservative Government to be Chairman of the British Railways Board. Thus he embarked on a journey that took him from trade unionist to industrialist and from the Labour benches in the Commons to the cross benches in the House of Lords. He died in 2011.

Nicolas Guy Barnett (Labour) was elected at a July 1971 by-election and remained the MP for Greenwich until 1986. Born in 1928, he was educated at Highgate School and St. Edmund Hall, Oxford where he was Chairman of the University Labour Party Group in 1951, becoming Secretary of the Oxford Union two years later. He became a schoolteacher but later moved to become chief education officer of the Commonwealth Institute. He contested Scarborough & Whitby (North Riding of Yorkshire) unsuccessfully in 1959 but in 1962 was sensationally returned at a by-election in South Dorset, largely through the intervention of an anti-Common Market candidate who split the Tory vote. He lost that seat in 1964 and remained out of the House until 1971. He too was anti-Europe and sat on the Council of the Get Britain Out campaign. Between 1976 and 1979 he was a junior minister in Callaghan's Government – Under Secretary for the Environment. In Opposition he was a spokesman on overseas development and European affairs during a period when his Party was opposed to the Common Market. He died in 1986.

Lewisham East, Lewisham South

Herbert Stanley Morrison (Labour), who had previously been MP for Hackney South was elected at Lewisham East in 1945 and at Lewisham South in 1950, serving until he retired in 1959. His principal biographical details may be found in Chapter 7(Hackney South).

Morrison's successor was **Carol Alfred Johnson** (Labour) who held the seat from 1959 until its abolition in 1979 when he retired from the House. Born in 1903 he was educated at council schools, the Law Society's School of Law and at the London School of Economics after which he became a solicitor. He was elected to Lambeth Borough Council in 1937 and sat until 1949 but from 1943 to 1959 he was also secretary to the Parliamentary Labour Party. His Party and Lambeth connections both meant that he would have had many dealings with his predecessor, Morrison, and this may have helped him when it came to looking for a seat. Once elected he remained a back bencher until his retirement. His principal interest appears to have been the British Council of the European Movement of which he was secretary. Born in 1903, he died at the age of 97 in 2000.

Lewisham North

Captain Sir Austin Uvedale Morgan Hudson (Conservative) was MP for Lewisham North from 1950 until 1956 when he died. Previously he had been MP for Islington East (1922-3) and Hackney North (1924-45). His principal biographical details are in Chapter 7 (Islington East).

Niall MacDermot (Labour) won the February 1957 by-election caused by Hudson's death. Born in 1916 he was educated at Rugby School, Corpus Christi College, Cambridge and at Balliol College, Oxford following which he became a barrister at the Inner Temple in 1946. He was a Deputy Chairman of the Bedfordshire Quarter Sessions and a Recorder of Newark. After losing Lewisham North at the 1959 General Election he was returned at Derby North in a 1962 by-election and held the seat until his retirement in 1970. He was Financial Secretary to the Treasury from 1964 to 1967 and a Minister of State at the Ministry of Housing and Local Government between 1967 and 1968. He died in 1996.

A famous athlete, **Sir Christopher John Chataway** (Conservative), who is remembered as the World record holder for the 5,000 metres in 1954, recaptured the seat for the Conservatives in 1959. Born in 1931 he was educated at Sherbourne and Magdalen College, Oxford after which in 1952 he joined the Guinness Company in an executive capacity. Following his world record run he was voted the BBC Sports Personality in 1954 but after the 1956 Olympics he retired from athletics to enter journalism as a television reporter and commentator, becoming the first person to read a news broadcast on ITN. Embarking on a career in politics, in 1958 he was elected to the LCC representing Lewisham North.

Prime Minister Harold Macmillan electioneering with fellow Kent MP Christopher Chataway in 1959
© National Porttrait Gallery

In 1959 he was elected to the Commons for the same area and made a mark in his maiden speech in which he urged the MCC not to tour South Africa as a protest against the apartheid policies there. This and his efforts to raise money for displaced African refugees marked him out as a progressive Tory at a time when many in his Party were supporters of the South African regime. He was appointed Parliamentary Secretary at the Ministry of Education in 1959 being promoted to Joint Secretary at the Ministry of Education and Science in a re-shuffle that took place in 1964. Unfortunately his political career was stopped in its tracks by the advent of the Wilson Labour Government in 1964 which, in Chataway's case, was marred further when he lost his seat in 1966 at which point he threw in his lot with the Inner London Education Authority of which he was appointed alderman chairman in 1967. This unusual move was ordered by the Party leader, Ted Heath, who sought to block the appointment of a right-winger, Seton Forbes – Cockell. Chataway stood down from this post when he won a by-election at Chichester (West Sussex) in 1969 and when the Heath Government was elected in 1970 he was appointed Minister of Posts and Telecommunications in which role he introduced commercial radio broadcasting for the first time ending the monopoly of the BBC; then in 1972, Minister of Industrial Development. The Government was defeated at the February 1974 Election and Chataway determined on a career outside of politics. He went into business, becoming Managing Director of Orion Bank and a Director of British Electrical Traction Ltd. He was given some public appointments including the Chairmanship of the Civil Aviation Authority and also remained active in support of African charities. He was appointed President of the Commonwealth Games Council for England in 1990 and was knighted five years later. He died in 2014.

Roland Dunstan Moyle (Labour) won Lewisham North in 1966 and held it until 1974 when he was retuned for the new constituency of Lewisham East which he held until 1983 when he was defeated. Born in 1928 he was educated at elementary schools in Bexleyheath and at county school in Llanidloes, Montgomeryshire after which he attended the University College of Wales at Aberystwyth and Trinity College, Cambridge. He became an industrial relations executive in the gas and electricity industries but entered the law at Grays Inn and became a barrister before he went into politics. Successful at his first attempt he did not achieve a ministerial position until 1974 when he was appointed first of all as Parliamentary Secretary at the Ministry of Agriculture; then from 1974-76 was a Minister of State for Northern Ireland; and from 1976-9 was a Minister of State for Health in Callaghan's Government. He was an Opposition spokesman on health and latterly on Commonwealth affairs but lost his seat in 1983 bringing an end to his Commons career.

It took hard work in committee rooms such as these in Lewisham North to get the voters out to the Polling Stations.
Peoples History Museum Manchester

Lewisham West

Arthur Massey Skeffington (Labour) won the seat in 1945 having fought it first at a by-election in 1938 when he reduced the Tory majority by 7,500 votes but, following his election in 1945, served only until he was defeated in1950. Born in 1909 he was an economist who was educated at Streatham Grammar School and London University where he took an early interest in left wing politics and became a specialist in industrial organisation. He was a lecturer in Economics and tutor for the Workers' Educational Association and the National Council of Labour Colleges. He was adopted as Labour's candidate at Streatham in 1933 and subsequently fought that seat in 1935; then Lewisham West at the 1938 by election. From 1943-45 he was Assistant Director of Medical Supplies at the Ministry of Supply and after 1950 when he was out of the House, he became a barrister being called to the Bar at the Middle Temple in 1951, though he did contest Lewisham West again at the Election held in that year. However, he soon returned to the House at a by-election in the Middlesex seat of Hayes and Harlington in 1953 and when the Wilson Government was returned in 1964, Skeffington was appointed Parliamentary Secretary to Fred Willey, Minister of Land and Natural Resources. When that Ministry was wound up in 1967 he was made Parliamentary Secretary to Anthony Greenwood, Minister of Housing and Local Government but he lost office after the General Election in 1970 and died the following year.

Henry Alfred Price (Conservative) took the seat in 1950 and held it until he retired in 1964. Born in 1911 he was educated at elementary and county schools; then trained as a baritone singer and undertook a great deal of concert work. He was also a businessman and was Managing Director of a firm of paper merchants. He was a London County councillor from 1946-52 and a Lewisham Borough councillor from 1945-49. He died in 1982.

In 1964 Price was succeeded by **Patrick Michael Ernest David McNair – Wilson** (Conservative), who only held the seat for 18 months, going down to defeat at the 1966 General Election. Born in 1929, he was educated at the Hall School Hampstead, at Eton College and entered the Coldstream Guards in which he held a regular commission from 1947 to 1952, serving in Palestine and North Africa. He became a television and radio broadcaster but joined the Conservative Party's Central Office team in 1955 serving on the staff of the Party's Political Centre. After his brief tenure at Lewisham he was elected at a 1968 by-election in the safe seat of New Forest (Hampshire), which he represented until 1997 when he retired. Despite his long parliamentary career he held no ministerial office of any kind, though from 1974-6 he was an Opposition spokesman on energy. He held a few non-executive directorships towards the end of his Commons career. His younger brother, Michael, was an MP for Walthamstow East and Newbury and sat in the House with him for a number of years. (See Chapter 12).

James McCulloch York Dickens (Labour) won the seat in 1966 but went down to defeat in 1970. Born in 1931 he was educated at Newcastle Abbey College, Midlothian; at Ruskin College, Oxford; and at St. Catherine's College, Oxford; after which he became a management consultant. He had been elected previously to Westminster Council in 1962 and had unsuccessfully contested the Chelsea Parliamentary seat in 1964. He did not resume his Commons career after his defeat in 1970 and became Personnel Director of Thames Water.

John Selwyn Gummer (Conservative) beat Dickens in 1970 but was himself defeated at the next Election in February 1974. He was born at Stockport in 1939 and as the son of an Anglican parson was educated at Kings School, Rochester; then at Selwyn College, Cambridge where he was President of the Union in 1962. He was a publisher and journalist but entered politics early as a candidate in Greenwich at the 1964 and 1966 Elections. A vice-chairman of the Tory Party, after his defeat in 1974 he was selected to fight the safe seat of Eye in Suffolk in 1979 which he retained following its re-designation as Suffolk Coastal in 1983 which he held until standing down in 2010.

He was appointed as a Government whip in 1981; then minister of Employment in 1983; Agriculture from 1985-8; and Local Government 1988-9. In the meantime he was chairman of the Party in 1983-5 and again from 1984-5 when he was also designated Paymaster – General. He was appointed to the Cabinet in 1989 to be Minister of Agriculture, famously feeding his daughter a hamburger to demonstrate his faith in British beef when the link between BSE and the human form of the disease (CJD) was being denied by the Government. In 1994 he was appointed Secretary of State for the Environment by John Major and remained in that post until 1997 when the Tories were defeated. He was for many years a prominent member of the Synod of the Anglican Church but left it to become a Roman Catholic when it voted to ordain women priests. He was made Baron Deben in 2010.

Orpington

Sir Waldron Smithers (Conservative) was previously the MP for Chislehurst and wisely opted for the new Orpington constituency after the 1945 boundary changes. Whilst Chislehurst was lost to Labour, Smithers secured re-election and remained in the House until he died in 1954. His principal biographical details are in Chapter 9 (Chislehurst).

William Donald Massey Sumner (Conservative) succeeded Smithers at a January 1955 by-election and held the seat until 1962 when he resigned on being appointed a Judge. Born in 1913 he was, like his predecessor, educated at Charterhouse School but attended Cambridge University at Sidney Sussex College, after which he qualified as a barrister. During the War he served in the Royal Artillery as a Lieutenant Colonel and later as Assistant Adjutant – General in the 21st Army Group. He was variously decorated for his wartime activities, receiving the Belgian Order of the Crown, the Croix de Guerre and the American Bronze Star. He became a councillor on the Orpington District Council in 1950, serving until 1953, and the following year was appointed Recorder of Plymouth. He died in 1990.

Eric Reginald Lubbock (Liberal) won one of the most sensational by-elections of modern political history in March 1962. The election was held at a time when the Government of Harold Macmillan (then the MP for the adjoining seat of Bromley) was particularly unpopular due to the impact of its stringent economic policies. Lubbock was born in 1928 and educated at Upper Canada College, Ontario and then at Balliol College, Oxford. A liberal thinking patrician from a wealthy background who converted to Buddhism, Lubbock adopted several progressive causes including the Fluoridation Society and the Air Safety Group, both of which he chaired. In addition his business interests included being a Director of two family concerns, C.L. Projects Ltd. and Cook, Lubbock and Company. He was elected to Orpington UDC in 1961 and after his return as the town's MP he was the Chief Whip and also chaired the Liberal Party's Candidates Committee. He was a member of the Party's executive and council. A year after he lost his seat in 1970 his cousin died and he succeeded to the peerage as Lord Avebury. He sat on the Royal Commission on Standards of Conduct in Public Life (1974-6), and was Liberal Spokesman on Immigration and Race Relations (1971-83). In 1976 he founded the Parliamentary Human Rights Group, and chaired it for the next 21 years.

Eric Lubbock MP
by Godfrey Argent © National Porttrait Gallery

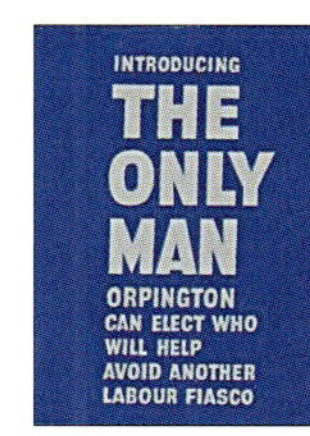

Stanbrook's 1970 election pitch was dramatic; he was elected, defeating the Liberal, Lubbock - not Labour!.
Peoples History Museum Manchester

Ivor Robert Stanbrook (Conservative) re-captured the seat in 1970 and held it until 1992. Born in 1924 he was educated at Willesden Central School, Birkbeck and University Colleges, London and Pembroke College, Oxford becoming a barrister but emigrated to Nigeria as a Colonial District Officer in 1950 serving there for ten years. He founded the Britain – Nigeria Association in 1961 and contested his first Parliamentary seat at East Ham South in 1966, unsuccessfully. He chaired several backbench committees during his membership of the House but never attained ministerial office and retired in 1992. He died in 2004.

Woolwich East

George Ernest Hicks (Labour) won Woolwich East in 1931 and retained the seat in 1945. He retired in 1950 and his principal biographical details are in Chapter 9.

He was succeeded by **Ernest Bevin** (Labour), who formerly sat for Wandsworth Central and whose principal biographical details are in Chapter 10.

Unfortunately by the time he won this seat to which he transferred following boundary changes in Wandsworth, which he had represented since 1940, he was approaching the end of his life and **Christopher Paget Mayhew** (Labour) was elected at the by-election that followed his death in 1951. Mayhew was previously MP for South Norfolk between 1945 and 1950 when he lost his seat. He retained Woolwich East until he retired from the Commons at the October

1974 Election by which time he had become disillusioned with the Wilson Government's approach to Europe, of which he was a passionate advocate. After he was re-elected at the February 1974 General Election he resigned the Labour Whip in July of that year and crossed the House to join the Liberals who by then had come to be more representative of his views and in the October Election contested the Tory seat at Bath, which he came close to winning, though when he tried again in 1979 he was quite heavily defeated. He unsuccessfully contested Surrey for election to the European Parliament in 1979 and London South West in a by-election for the same body in September of the same year but was nominated for a life peerage in 1981 and sat on the Liberal benches as Lord Mayhew of Wimbledon until his death in 1997. From 1980-1997 he was the Party's spokesman on defence.

Born in 1915, Mayhew was educated at Haileybury School and Christ Church, Oxford where he was President of the Union in 1937. He was employed by the Fabian Bureau and during the War served in the Surrey Yeomanry and Royal Artillery being part of the British Expeditionary Force, serving in North Africa, the Central Mediterranean, the Special Operations Executive (in which he attained the rank of major) and with the British Liberation Army in 1944. A television broadcaster and writer he was Herbert Morrison's PPS from 1945-6 and then Bevin's Under-Secretary of State for Foreign Affairs from 1946 to 1950 and it was perhaps unsurprising that he succeeded his boss as Labour MP for the same seat. He chaired a company called Middle East International (Publications) Limited and was a strong advocate of the Palestinian cause being President of the Parliamentary Association for Euro-Arab Co-operation between 1980 and 1987 and President of the Arab Non-Arab Friendship Foundation, in 1992. He was also chairman of the National Association for Mental Health. In the Wilson Government he was Minister of Defence for the Royal Navy, a post with plenty of connections with his own constituency, but he resigned in 1966 in protest at cuts in the aircraft carrier programme.

Woolwich West

Henry Berry (Labour) won the seat in 1945. Born locally in 1883, he was educated at Woolwich Polytechnic and Goldsmiths' College and became a consulting engineer, qualifying as M.I.Mech.E. and A.I.Struct.E. A Director of the Investment Corporation of Canada, he was a member of Woolwich Borough Council from 1922 to 1945 and of the London County Council in 1940-41. He was a member of the Metropolitan Water Board for 23 years and was its chairman from 1940 to 1946. Other involvements were the Allotments Society Ltd, of which he was Treasurer for 24 years and in which he was active in promoting the Grow More Food Campaign during the War. He was a member of the Thames Conservancy Board from 1940 and chaired the War Emergency Water Committee of the London Civil Defence Region. A Vice-President of the Royal Society of Arts, he lived locally at Eltham and was defeated at the 1950 Election which brought an end to his political career.

Sir William Arthur Steward (Conservative), replaced Berry in 1950 and held the seat until he retired in 1959. Born in 1901 and educated at Norwich Model School as well as privately, Steward became a restaurateur and farmer. A liveryman of the Worshipful Company of Distillers, he contested Southwark in 1945 and was elected chairman of the London Conservative Union in 1953. He died in 1987.

Sir Colin William Carstairs Turner (Conservative), succeeded Steward in 1959 and remained the MP until he was defeated in 1964. Born in 1922 and educated at Highgate School he went into publishing and became a company director having seen wartime service in the Desert Air Force throughout the North African campaign and for which he was awarded the DFC in 1944. He entered politics in Enfield where he unsuccessfully contested the East division at the 1950 and 1951 Elections before joining the council in 1956, though he only served for two years. He was a member of the first Young Conservatives national committee and sat on the Party's national executive from 1946 to 1953. He became a marketing and media consultant.

William 'Bill' Hamling (Labour) won Woolwich West at the 1964 General Election and held it until his death in 1975. He had previously contested the same seat in 1955 and 1959 and was also unsuccessful in other earlier contests in Southport (1945), Liverpool Wavertree (1950 and 1951); and at Torquay (Devon) in a 1956 by-election. He was born in 1912 and educated at elementary school in his native Liverpool where he also attended the Institute and University going on to become a lecturer though during the Second World War he served in the Royal Marines. In 1966 he was PPS to Kenneth Robinson, Minister of Health; then Minister of Planning and Land; but in1969 he was made a Government whip, a role he continued in opposition between 1970 and 1973 when he was appointed a defence spokesman. When Labour returned to power in 1974 Hamling was made PPS to Harold Wilson, the Prime Minister but unfortunately a more promising career was cut short when he died in 1975. Outside of Parliament, he was a Trustee of the National Maritime Museum, and a Justice of the Peace (Blackheath Division).

Chapter 14
Metropolitan Surrey 1945 - 1974

Between 1921 and the outbreak of the Second World War there were significant movements in populations throughout metropolitan Surrey. All of the boroughs nearest the Thames declined with Bermondsey, Southwark and Camberwell experiencing the biggest losses of between 16% and 30%. Battersea and Lambeth suffered less but still declined by 6% and 15% respectively. Wartime bombings only made matters worse and of the inner boroughs only Wandsworth increased its population. In contrast there was remarkable growth in the suburbs. The biggest occurred in Carshalton, Sutton, Cheam and Surbiton where rates of increase varied between 150% and 300%.

The Boundary Commission's immediate post War Review created two additional constituencies - Sutton & Cheam and Carshalton. Other alterations were reserved until 1950.

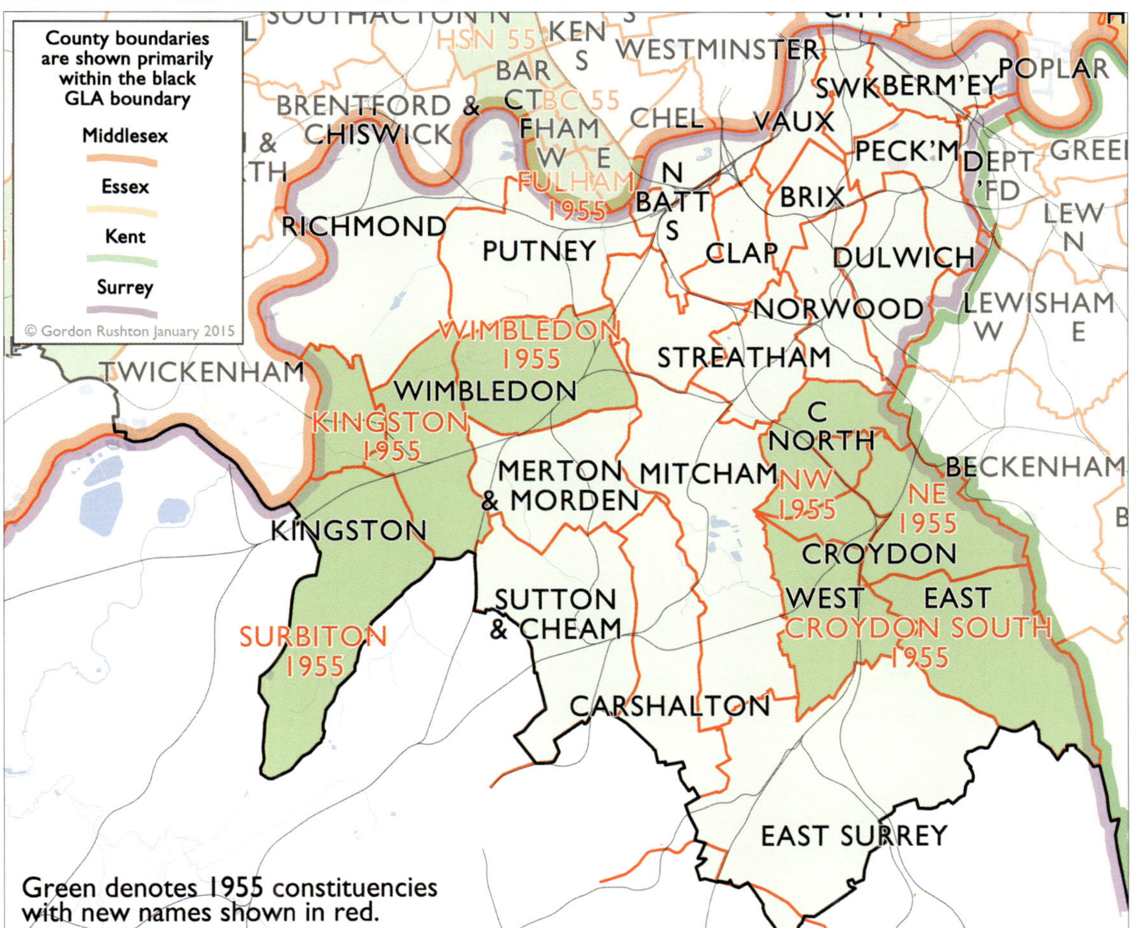

The map depicts Surrey constituencies created in 1950 and those that were modified in 1955. The number of seats in Southwark and Lambeth was reduced compared with 1945. In Croydon a third seat was added in 1950 and the boundaries were changed in 1955. Surbiton was created from Kingston, leading to changes in the boundaries of Kingston and Wimbledon. Comparison with 1945 may be made by reference to the map on page 18 and with 1918 on page 16.

Sutton & Cheam was carved out of the former Epsom constituency of which it had formed the northern part since 1918. Sutton (meaning, "south farmstead or village") originally belonged to the Benedictine Abbey of Chertsey, founded around the year 666, but after its dissolution the manor passed into the hands of absentee landowners. Although only

Left: *Waverley Way in leafy Carshalton Beeches typifies the middle class composition of the Carshalton constituency following its separation from neighbouring Mitcham in 1945.*

Below: *Although designated "The Beeches", this 1960s council estate in London Road, Mitcham, comprised mostly Labour voters, fewer of whom were to be found in next door Carshalton. Although somewhat stark, for the time these flats were considered modern with all contemporary conveniences. Siting was excellent, next to the Wandle Valley, and only yards from a railway station that was eventually to transform into the successful Tramlink service 50 years on.*

Below: *These 1960s office blocks in Brighton Road, central Croydon, bear testament to the suburb's success in working to becoming a business centre that hosted a major centre of clerical and technical employment in the post war period.*

Above: *Despite its mainly middle class electorates, Croydon was also home to industry and working class voters as evidenced here in Martin Crescent, Waddon Marsh, in the Croydon South constituency,*

Left: *Every day commuters 'do their stuff', walking from their homes down to the station to catch the train to work. The process began 150 years ago and is still going strong, from dormitory suburbs, into London, and back in the evening, with leisure time at their domicile at weekends. Here commuters in the Streatham Constituency, line up on the platform edge of their local station waiting for the train.* **Wikipedia**

All pictures John Nelson, unless otherwise attributed.

a village on the 18th Century coach route between London and Brighton, and the building of a railway from Croydon to Epsom in 1847 led to its expansion. A line to Epsom Downs opened in 1865 and its importance increased with the opening of a line to Mitcham Junction in 1868. Property development started in 1852 and by 1901 Sutton had a population of 17,223. Housing development continued into the Edwardian period to the east of Brighton Road, along the south side of Cheam Road and to the west of the High Street. When the First World War ended more housing was built in the north of the Borough and on the Downland to the south in the 1920s and 1930s.

Parts of Cheam are also thought to have belonged to Chertsey Abbey, the name deriving from "Cegham" dating from about AD967 and meaning,"homestead by the tree stumps". Its development was later than Sutton's but by 1913 housing was advancing towards it from its neighbour. By 1939 most of Cheam was built up and the place had assumed its modern form. By 1950 Sutton & Cheam had an electorate of 59,141, which made it within 2% of the average size for London constituencies as a whole. The electorate remained pretty stable throughout the next twenty years during which period it increased by about 2% (including the addition of eighteen year-olds in time for the 1970 contest). The constituency remained slightly above the average for London electorates, increasing from 2% to 11% over two decades.

Carshalton had previously formed the southern part of the **Mitcham** constituency, which remained in 1945 but was split in two. Mitcham covered the northern districts of the former constituency while Carshalton, then a Surrey county division and not a borough, included the neighbouring towns of Wallington and Beddington, both of which lay on the Croydon side of the town. In 1950 the size of Carshalton's electorate was 9% above the London area average with over 63,000 voters, but numbers gradually increased at each succeeding Election. The 1970 electorate (inflated by the extension of the franchise to 18 year olds) topped 71,000 and exceeded the average size of greater London divisions by 29%.

Carshalton was known for its springs which gave the place its name "Cres - Aul – ton". "Aul" means well. A "ton" is a farm, which was in some way enclosed. The meaning of the "Car" element is uncertain but may derive from water"cress". The village first began to develop in the 17th Century when water mills were built along the river Wandle. These brought about some industrial activity in leather, copper, gunpowder, snuff, paper and linseed oil. During the 17th and 18th Centuries there was also building development with large country houses erected for wealthy London merchants and financiers. Nevertheless, the population remained small at around 2,400 in mid 19th Century and when the railway line between Croydon and Epsom was built in 1847, the owner of the Carshalton Park estate objected to having a station on his property so this was built south of Wallington instead. The station made Wallington ripe for property development and in the early 1860s the local Lord of the manor laid out a housing estate on the east side of Manor Road. Beddington and Wallington became an Urban District Council in 1915 by which time Wallington was by far the largest settlement in the area and the local authority's headquarters was there. A town hall was built in 1935. The suburban development of Carshalton itself began in the early 1890s when the Carshalton Park Estate was sold for development. Most of its development took place in the 1920s and 1930s. The biggest single development was the St Helier Estate, which was built for the LCC between 1928 and 1936.

Mitcham remained a substantial constituency in its own right and actually had a greater number of voters on the register than Carshalton, which had previously formed a part of the division. Its electorate in 1950 was over 73,000 and in 1951 rose above 73,500, the largest in the post War period for that constituency. Numbers dropped below 67,000 in 1966 but rose again in 1970 to 72,600 following the extension of the franchise to include 18 year olds. For most of the two decades after 1950 the Mitcham electorate was about one quarter larger than the average for London as a whole but in 1970 it rose as high as 32% larger.

The review of constituencies undertaken in advance of the 1950 General Election brought further alterations. The LCC 'Surrey' boroughs lost seven seats whilst the outer suburban area gained two. Although this was mainly in response to a population expansion fed by commuting to central London by train, there were other factors at play. Croydon town centre had become congested by the 1930s and after World War Two the Council decided to introduce a major redevelopment scheme. The Croydon Corporation Act of 1956 led to the building of new offices at precisely the time that the Government was beginning to encourage businesses to move out of central London. Croydon, with its excellent rail links, was an ideal site for relocation, and the town boomed as an important business centre in the 1950s and 1960s, with an increasing number of office blocks being built employing around 20,000 workers.

Three seats were created: in **Croydon North** (comprising Thornton Heath, Norbury and Upper Norwood): **East** (comprising Addiscombe, Addington, East Croydon, South Norwood and Woodside), and **West** (comprising Selhurst, Central and South Croydon and Waddon).

Left: *Rutlish Road, Merton Park, near Wimbledon, was on the boundary between the Wimbledon and Merton & Morden constituencies. Conservative Prime Minister, John Major, was brought up in the area and attended nearby Rutlish School. The area became built up in the last quarter of the 19th century. Well served by public transport as well as green spaces, it is a middle class suburb.*

Below: *Richmond on Thames was and remains one of the most affluent districts of London, epitomised here by these palatial houses in Portland Terrace, overlooking Richmond Green. In nearby Little Green, Labour Prime Minister Harold Wilson who first came to power in 1964, lived in retirement and declining health in a modest flat in Fitzwilliam House*

Below: *This Cock pub sign in Sutton Town Centre at the junction of two historic turnpikes, also acts as a milestone indicating the proximity of Cheam (with which it was twinned as a Constituency) and neighbouring Carshalton, to the East. The pub was demolished in 1961 as Sutton developed a modern character.*

Above: *Putney developed as a marginal seat in the post War period following the development of new LCC council estates. The Alton estate, pictured here, was built in the 1950s and provided a Labour vote to counteract the generally more Conservative middle class electorate of the Putney constituency*

Left: *Surbiton Station was rebuilt in 1937 in the Art Deco style. It is a busy station with a frequency of service as high as an Underground line, and commuter patronage of several millions of journeys. It served the 1955 created Surbiton Constituency, and is surrounded by a densely populated middle class area.* **Wikipedia**

All pictures John Nelson, unless otherwise attributed.

The three Croydon constituencies had combined electorates of over 181,000 in 1950. However, these were not evenly distributed with Croydon West containing only 54,000 voters compared with over 63,000 each in the other two seats. These were reconfigured once again in 1955. **Croydon North West** took Norbury, Upper Norwood, Thornton Heath West and Selhurst whilst **Croydon North East** comprised South Norwood, the rest of Thornton Heath, Addiscombe, Woodside and East Croydon. **Croydon South** took Addington, South Croydon, Central Croydon, West Croydon (Broad Green), Shirley and Waddon. Following the adjustment, each had an electorate of close to 60,000 voters. The smallest was North East which had 58,663 and this fell to around 55,000 in 1966 before rising again to the 1955 level in 1970 after the extension of the franchise to 18 year olds. Croydon North West followed a similar downward trend but, even after the inclusion of younger voters, its 1970 electorate of 57,000 was below the level it had been in 1955. This was because the older residential areas were in the north of the borough and these began to decline in population during the 1960s whereas the outer suburbs, particularly south of the town centre, were still expanding. The Croydon South constituency's electorate rose from slightly over 62,000 in 1955 to over 73,000, a substantial increase.

Surrey East remained covering the Coulsdon and Purley districts of the county south of Croydon but a new constituency comprising the Urban District of **Merton & Morden** was established further west. Suburban development south of Wimbledon had been stimulated by the extension of the Northern Line of the Underground to Morden via Merton in 1926. In 1921 the combined population of Merton ("farmstead by a pool", dating from AD 967) and Morden ("hill in marshland" dating from AD 969) had been 17,532 but by 1938 it was 68,980, an increase of 223% in less than 20 years. The Boundaries Commission caught up with these developments in time for the 1950 General Election.

Wimbledon remained covering the northern parts of the former constituency comprising Wimbledon borough to which was added the Urban District of Malden and Coombe, which included New Malden, Kingston Vale and Norbiton. **Kingston** lost Malden and Coombe communities and **Richmond** was unaffected by changes.

When it was established in 1950 the electorate in Merton & Morden was nearly 56,000, about 4% lower than the average for London but Wimbledon retained a very much larger electorate of around 77,000, about 32% higher than average. The Merton electorate remained fairly stable over the next twenty years and although it fell by 9% it was still only 8% lower than average in 1970. Wimbledon, on the other hand, was affected by the creation of a new **Surbiton** constituency in 1955 and reduced considerably in size as a result. The Malden and Coombe Urban District was once again transferred back to Kingston-on-Thames. "Suberton" meant "southern grange" and dated from 1179.

Kingston's 1950 electorate was over 73,000, some 26% higher than the average for London and it too fell following the creation of Surbiton in 1955. Richmond also had an electorate above the London average but well below those of neighbouring Kingston and Wimbledon. In 1950 it was 62,367 and fell over the next twenty years. In 1970 it was 57,000 but still 4% above the average for London compared with 7% in 1950. When Surbiton was created in 1955 it was based on the Borough of that name, previously attached to the Kingston seat. However, it did have a small electorate. Its 44,261 electors in 1955 were 21% fewer than the average for London although Wimbledon's total of 43,099 was 24% below. Kingston's, however, remained higher at 61,762, which was 10% above the London average. Over the next fifteen years the area of southwest London embraced by these three suburban constituencies remained very stable. Surbiton's electorate increased by 8% between 1955 and 1970 whilst Kingston's fell by 3% and Wimbledon's hardly changed. By 1970 Wimbledon, which had lost Malden and Coombe, was 22% below the London average, Surbiton 13% below and Kingston 9% above.

In the older established boroughs of the LCC it was a different story. Several had been badly affected by bomb damage leading to evacuation of the population and loss of employment. Altogether seven seats were eliminated in 1950, the main losses coming from the working class Thames - side inner London boroughs. Southwark and Bermondsey suffered the major losses and were reduced from five to only two seats. In the Second World War Bermondsey had been one of the most heavily bombed parts of Britain with 709 civilians killed and thousands injured. The former West Bermondsey and Rotherhithe constituencies were combined to form simply **Bermondsey,** a seat based wholly on the then borough's boundaries including the Surrey Docks and Bricklayers Arms. At the same time Southwark Central, Southwest and Southeast were all merged to form **Southwark**, which included Walworth, the Borough, Newington and the Elephant & Castle.

The combined electorates of Bermondsey and Southwark in 1950 amounted to 111,000, which gave an average number of voters per constituency of 55,000. Such a figure would have compared reasonably well with the London average of 58,000 had the electorates been equally divided between the two seats but they were not. Instead the constituencies comprised the wards within the two boroughs' discrete boundaries, which meant that Southwark's electorate of over 69,000 was 27,000 greater than neighbouring Bermondsey's. Over the next 20 years both constituencies lost population in similar proportions so that by 1970 Bermondsey's electorate had fallen by 27% and Southwark's by 25%. So severe was the decline in population that the electorates in 1970 were both below the 1966 levels even though there had been an extension of the franchise to 18 year olds between the two General Elections.

In 1950 Camberwell Borough was reduced from four seats to two. World War Two hit the area particularly badly with 937 people killed and nearly all its buildings were damaged. Bomb impact also damaged 90% of all houses in Peckham. The new borough seat of **Camberwell, Peckham** resulted from a merger of the former division of that name and the two other Camberwell based constituencies. It extended from North Peckham to Denmark Hill. Between 1945 and the end of the Twentieth Century council flats were built in Peckham to replace the bomb-damaged pre-War housing stock, especially during the 1950s and 60s. Whereas before the War most tenants had been private, afterwards they were mainly public and this also had an impact on the political complexion of Peckham's electorate. However, there were also consequential impacts on **Camberwell, Dulwich** to the south, which acquired south Peckham, including the Rye, and Nunhead. During this period Dulwich also became much more socially mixed as the LCC and Camberwell Borough Council built substantial local authority housing estates and flats in the area in the 1950s and 60s, although there were still plenty of private housing developments as well, especially near the Common. Generally though, the mix of the electorate became more working class than it had been in the past.

The two constituencies had a combined electorate of nearly 128,000, with the difference between them numbering only about 2,000, Dulwich being slightly the larger in 1950. However, over the next 20 years there was a marked decline in the electorate in Peckham which by 1970 had fallen by 20% to just over 50,000, even after the over 18s had been enfranchised after the 1966 General Election. Dulwich by contrast retained a pretty stable electorate. A trend comparison shows that Peckham went from having an electorate that was 9% larger than the Greater London constituency average in 1950 to one that was 8% smaller by 1970. Dulwich by contrast went from 13% larger in 1950 to 20% larger in 1970.

In Lambeth Borough the Kennington and North constituencies were merged in 1950 to be renamed simply **Lambeth, Vauxhall,** a loss of one seat in the previously four-member authority. Vauxhall ("Fox Hall" deriving from "Faukeshale") means "manor of a man called Falkes" and dates from around 1279. Some districts were transferred to **Brixton**, which also covered Stockwell and the central Lambeth districts round the Town Hall. **Norwood** though, remained largely unaltered covering Herne Hill, Knights Hill and Tulse Hill wards.

Brixton's electorate of 56,000 placed the constituency within 4% of the average sized London constituency electorate in 1950. However, by 1970 the disparity was 21% below average due principally to a decline in the local population. Vauxhall also lost voters at a rapid rate after it was established. Between 1950 and 1970 its electorate fell by 26%, some 3% more than Brixton. In absolute terms the numbers fell from just below 51,000 to fewer than 38,000. Norwood, which was more middle class and further from central London, fared rather better but its electorate still fell by a little over 12%, about half the rate of the rest of Lambeth. In 1950 the electorate of 61,000 was 5% larger than the London average but by 1970 had fallen to 53,000, which was 3% below it.

In previously five - member Wandsworth and two - member Battersea boroughs, the number of seats fell by one with the merging of Balham & Tooting and the adjacent Wandsworth Central and Clapham constituencies. **Streatham** remained a separate borough constituency in 1950, which straddled the southern districts on both sides of the current boundary between the London Boroughs of Wandsworth and Lambeth. Its 1950 electorate of 57,000 placed the constituency only 2% light compared with other London seats, but its numbers fell over the next 20 years so that, even with the injection of new voters when the franchise was extended to 18 year olds, the 1970 electorate was only a little over 53,000. Despite this the relative decline was no worse than the London average because in 1966 (the last election before the franchise extension) the variation remained 2% light and was still only 3% below average in 1970. **Clapham** straddled the northern districts across the same divide being sandwiched between Brixton and **Battersea South**, which covered the area south of Clapham Junction around Wandsworth Common. Tooting was attached to **Wandsworth Central** and Balham was split between it and Clapham. The Fairfield ward by the Thames in Wandsworth town centre was transferred from Wandsworth Central to **Putney**, which was otherwise unchanged. **Battersea North** remained covering the more working class districts of Queenstown and Battersea proper south of the River Thames.

Clapham's electorate in 1950 was nearly 61,000, almost identical to the nearby Lambeth Norwood seat, and with a similar population mix. In 1950 its electorate was about 5% larger than the London average but its population fell over the next twenty years and by 1970 its electorate was 13% fewer, even after the franchise had been extended to include adults over the age of 18. Despite this it remained a viable constituency in its own right being only 4% below the size of the average London electorate.

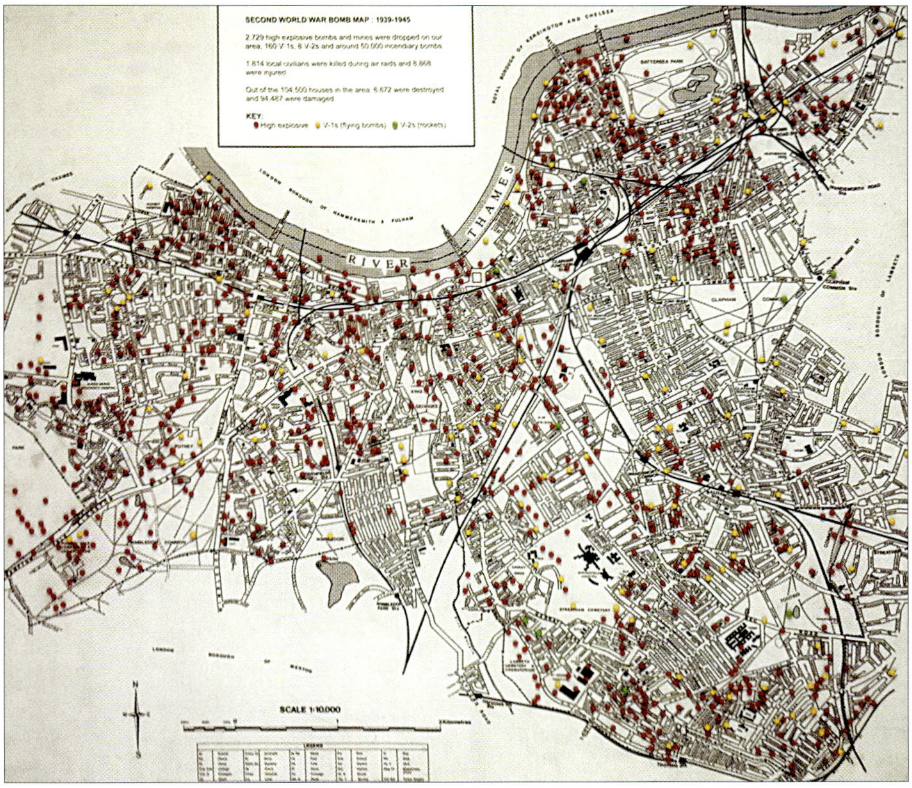

This map of the 1965 Borough of Wandsworth depicts the recorded bombs that fell during the Second World War. The red marks record the fall of a high explosive bomb - these varied in size from 500 - 2500kg, and the latter was capable of taking out buildings in a wide area. Not recorded are the hundreds of incendiary weapons also dropped to set fires. The yellow marks denote the fall of the Buzzbombs, or doodlebugs, the V1 flying bombs that carried an 850kg warhead, and could strike without warning anywhere. The far fewer green marks, denote the fall of one of the V2 rocket bombs that flew supersonically and delivered a 1000kg warhead, with no warning, and to which there was no answer, except by the Allies eliminating their launch sites. These sites are not 'the Docks', they represent the concept of 'totaller krieg' (total war), where civilians and industry alike suffered. The results post-war meant large areas of demolished buildings that were used as a fund of rebuilding sites, gradually being used up even into the 1970s, such was the scope of the damage done. There was no post-war rehabilitation 'fund' for Britain!
John Nelson

Battersea South was already a small constituency in 1950 when it was decided by the Boundaries Commission, constrained by the need to match seats as far as possible to London boroughs, to leave the borough with two divisions. South was the smaller of the two and had an electorate of less than 41,000, some 3,400 fewer than Battersea North. The electorate of Battersea fell by 24% over the next twenty years with the area of worst housing in the North falling by 32%. The more middle class Battersea South also lost population but its electorate fell by 12%, similar to neighbouring suburbs such as Clapham and Norwood. By 1970 Battersea South's electorate was 37% below the London average, making it the smallest not only in Surrey but in the whole Metropolitan area.

Wandsworth Central also lost population. However, when it was established in 1950 its electorate of 69,200 was 19% higher than the London average and even after its population had fallen by 15% its electorate in 1970 still remained 6% above average. Putney, on the other hand, was a constituency where the electorate grew. Even in 1950 its electorate of 66,000 was large by local and London comparisons being 14% greater than the average size. Yet by 1970 its electorate had grown to nearly 77,000, an increase of 14%, in part a result of population movements from Battersea and Wandsworth. By 1970 Putney constituency was 39% larger than the average London electorate.

Politics in Metropolitan Surrey

The impact of these boundary changes on Party representation in the Surrey metropolitan area was fairly significant. Generally speaking they worked in favour of the Conservative Party at the expense of Labour. Overall the Tories won 115 seats and Labour 90 in the eight General Elections held during the Post War period. In by-elections the Tories won 5, Labour 4 and the Liberals just 1.

Post War General Election Results 1945 to 1970

Overall the 1945 result in Metropolitan Surrey was that Labour took twenty-one seats and Tories were returned in seven. However, fought on 1950 boundaries, it is quite likely that the outcome would have been much closer, possibly as few as fourteen for Labour and nine for the Conservatives, a margin of five instead of fourteen, a substantial difference for such a small geographical area. Despite this there is no doubt that the convincing nature of Labour's victory in 1945 was due to the Party's newfound popularity. Its majorities in inner London seats were large but the swings in the hitherto Tory suburbs were even greater.

Post War General Election Results 1945 -1970 by % majority									
Constituency	**pre-1945**	**1945**	**1950**	**1951**	**1955**	**1959**	**1964**	**1966**	**1970**
Bermondsey Rotherhithe West	2 Lab	Lab58+ Lab52	Lab59	Lab63	Lab62	Lab54	Lab59	Lab61	Lab54
Southwark Central North South East	2 Lab 1L	Lab44+ Lab38 Lab54	Lab59	Lab63	Lab62	Lab54	Lab59	Lab61	Lab54+
Peckham Camberwell North Camberwell NW	1C 1L 1Lab	Lab37 Lab62 Lab39	Lab39	Lab40	Lab35	Lab30	Lab28	Lab44	Lab35
Dulwich	C	Lab1	Lab2	C1	C4	C4	Lab6	Lab13	Lab2
Vauxhall Kennington Lambeth North	1L 1C/L	Lab40 Lab47	Lab35	Lab32	Lab29	Lab24	Lab28	Lab33	Lab27
Brixton	C	Lab27	Lab11	Lab12	Lab14	Lab6	Lab16	Lab23	Lab15
Norwood	C	Lab6	C4	C6	C11	C16	C1	Lab6	Lab2
Streatham	C	C18	C24	C27	C31	C32	C20	C9	C34
Clapham	C	Lab18	Lab2	Lab3	Lab1	C4	Lab2	Lab11	C9
Battersea North	Lab	Lab48+	Lab44	Lab45	Lab44	Lab36	Lab39	Lab47	Lab38
Battersea South	C	Lab23	Lab1	C1	C2	C6	Lab6	Lab15	Lab8
Wandsworth Central Balham & Tooting	C C	Lab22 Lab15	Lab4	Lab2	C2	C4	Lab5	Lab14	Lab8
Putney	C	C12	C11	C12	C14	C9	Lab2	Lab6	Lab3
Wimbledon	C	Lab2	C30	C33	C31	C34	C23	C19	C24
Merton & Morden			C6	C9	C14	C19	C7	C1	C9
Richmond	C	C18	C25	C27	C27	C30	C19	C14	C20
Kingston	C	C13	C25	C27	C32	C35	C23	C18	C25+
Surbiton					C30	C35	C21	C16	C21
Croydon East			C16	C18+					
Croydon North	C	C1+	C17	C19					
Croydon North East					C19	C20	C9	C1	C10
Croydon North West					C23	C23	C13	C7	C12
Croydon West			C2	C4					
Croydon South	C	Lab7			C14	C16	C6	Lab0.2	C7
Mitcham	C	Lab15	C8	C9	C13	C17	C7	C1	C10
Carshalton		C2	C14	C7	C21	C24+	C19	C11	C21
Sutton & Cheam (formerly Epsom)	C	C5	C22	C26+	C32	C33	C26	C21	C31-
Surrey East	C	C23	C38	C46	C50	C46	C28	C26	C42
Conservative	18/19	8+	14	16++	18	19+	14	12	14+-
Labour	6	21+++	10	8	7	6	11	13	11+
Liberal	3/4	0	0	0	0	0	0	0	0+
Total	28	29++++	24	24++	25	25+	25	25	25+++

Key: C = Conservative; Lab = Labour; + = Party that won seat at General Election held by-election in same Parliament; - = Party that won seat at General Election lost by-election to main opposition Party in same Parliament.

Brixton, which had been Tory in every election except two since 1885 and had never previously returned a Labour candidate, recorded a swing of nearly 25% yielding a Labour majority of 27%. Brixton was never Tory again. The smallest swings took place in Labour's safest seats in Southwark and Bermondsey where there were fewer middle class voters available to "swing". Interestingly swings of a similar order also occurred in very middle class constituencies where the working class had yet to penetrate on any significant scale in 1945. These included Streatham and Putney, where the swings were 3% to 5% lower than in constituencies with more mixed electorates.

The swing to Labour amongst the middle classes also meant that the Party picked up seats in the outer suburban area for the first time. Labour won in Mitcham, Wimbledon and Croydon South whilst the Tories won Sutton & Cheam, Carshalton, Croydon North, Kingston-upon-Thames and Richmond. However, had the election been fought on the 1950 boundaries it is probable that the Tories would have won at least one extra seat and possibly two. The Wimbledon constituency might have stayed with the Tories (instead of falling to Labour) although it is more likely that the new constituency of Merton & Morden would have opted for Labour in 1945 had the seat been created in time for that Election. In Croydon it is possible that two of the three seats would have been Tory.

Following the redistribution of seats in 1950, the majority of seats in the area went to the Government Party except in 1950, when the redistribution of seats seemed to favour the Tories, and in 1970, when it favoured Labour. The 1950 Election marked a big reversal of Labour's advance. Not only were there fewer seats left to occupy but the Conservative Party also staged a recovery after five years of post-war austerity and in Metropolitan Surrey these changes brought about a transformation in the representation of the two Parties. By-election results since 1945 had also generally shown less enthusiasm for Labour although, despite this, the Party did not lose a single seat nationally during that Parliament. There were straws in the wind, though, in respect of Labour's future prospects. On 25th July 1946 there was a by-election in Battersea North, which Labour retained with a majority of 39% compared with 48% at the 1945 General Election. At the 1950 contest Labour claimed a majority of 44%, a swing of two percent to the Tories since 1945. A by-election at Rotherhithe on 19th November 1946 saw a Labour majority of 52% over the Tories reduced to 43% over a Liberal and two and a half years later at Southwark Central on 29th April 1948 a similar fall in Labour support was evident with a majority reduced from 44% to 31% since 1945. A month earlier, on 11th March 1948, Croydon North was the scene of a by-election that saw the Tories increase their majority from only 1% in 1945 to 17%. In 1950 their majority was unchanged compared with the by-election, indicating that the middle class were swinging back to the Tories in large numbers.

When the 1950 General Election was called these trends were reflected in the national results. In the outer suburban area Labour lost all its seats and the Tories picked up the new ones that had been created, winning a total of 10. Even in the L.C.C. area the Tories did a lot better. Deprived of seven seats, the residue of thirteen constituencies split, ten Labour and three Tory (the additional one being Norwood which they regained from Labour), meaning that in Metropolitan Surrey as a whole Conservative MPs outnumbered Labour 13 to 10. The difference in seats between the two Parties in the House of Commons as a whole changed by seventeen, compared with 1945, a figure large enough to be of significance in terms of the outcome nationally.

When the General Election of 1951 came around there was a further movement of public opinion away from Labour and towards the Tories, which this time resulted in a change of Government. The swing was small (only about 1%, and indeed nationally Labour outpolled the Conservatives in votes cast) but it was decisive. Labour lost two seats to the Conservatives in Metropolitan Surrey, Battersea South and Dulwich both falling to swings of between one and one and a half percent. The Conservatives were returned nationally and in this part of Surrey outnumbered Labour by fifteen seats to eight, a majority of seven. Given that the Tories' overall majority in the House of Commons was only seventeen, this was a significant contribution to their overall position.

In the third year of the new Tory Government there were two by-elections in outer London, both of which indicated that the Party was, if anything, strengthening its position. On 30th September 1954 they retained Croydon East with a majority of 31% compared with 18% in 1951 whilst on 4th November 1954 they held Sutton and Cheam with a 33% majority as compared with 26% in 1951. The 1955 General Election saw these results confirmed, marking a further national swing to the Conservatives but they were assisted in Surrey by the creation of the additional seat at Surbiton, a middle class area. Wandsworth Central fell on a 2% swing and the Tories' advantage increased from a majority of 7 seats in the area to ten. There were seventeen Tory and only seven Labour MPs. Further crumbling of the Labour vote at the 1959 Election saw Clapham regained by the Conservatives who by then had an advantage of eighteen seats to six, the latter total being one less than Labour had achieved in 1935 when it was only in the initial stages of a political recovery after the Wall Street Crash in 1931.

Despite this, the margin of Conservative victory in several seats was quite small and some were poised to swing back to Labour in the event of a recovery in their national political fortunes. This occurred in the early 1960s and was first in evidence at by-elections although at one such at Carshalton on 16th November 1960 the Tories actually registered the same 24% majority over the Liberals as they had over Labour at the 1959 Election. This was one of the earliest signals that in suburban in south west London constituencies Tory voters were prepared to consider voting Liberal, rather than Labour, as a protest when their Party was in power. Years later the Liberals were to take this seat and hold it at four consecutive elections between 1997 and 2010.

At the 1964 General Election the Labour Party regained four seats, three of which were in Battersea and Wandsworth where in addition they secured Putney for the first time in their history. The character of this constituency had been changed somewhat over the preceding years by the building of a large council estate at Roehampton. Dulwich was the other seat regained.

Although Labour failed to make inroads into the Tory seats elsewhere in the metropolitan area the Party's five gains in the L.C.C. boroughs were highly significant because its national majority was only four seats over all other parties. With a further swing nationally in Labour's favour taking place in 1966, two more Tory seats were lost, namely Norwood and Croydon South, whilst the taking of Putney compensated for not regaining neighbouring Wimbledon. Labour's position in 1966 was not equivalent to that which the Party had enjoyed in 1945. The redistribution of seats in the intervening years had witnessed an expansion in the number of middle class suburban constituencies at the expense of the working class inner London boroughs. Thus in 1966 Labour won thirteen seats in metropolitan Surrey compared with twenty-one in 1945. The Conservatives, on the other hand, won eleven compared with seven.

Labour lost nationally again in 1970 with the Tories overturning a large majority to win. Despite this, of the six seats they had lost to Labour in 1964 and 1966, the Party only regained Clapham and Croydon South. This may be taken as some indication of the changing social composition of some seats, many of which had changed significantly since the War, not least experiencing an increase in ethnic minority immigration from certain Commonwealth Countries. These trends probably helped Labour, who won as many seats in the area as they had done in 1964 when they formed a Government.

After 1970, however, the Tories did enter something of a decline in by-elections, three of which held in 1972 indicated a swing away from them. On 4th May 1972 at Southwark Labour increased its majority from 39% to 61% whilst on the same day the Tories retained Kingston- upon -Thames with a 21% majority as compared with 25% in 1970. Seven months later, on 7th December 1972, there was a sensational by-election defeat for the Conservatives at Sutton & Cheam, which the Liberal Graham Tope gained with a majority of 22%. At the 1970 Election the Liberal had been third and the Tories had then secured a majority over Labour of 31%. Although the Tories were to win the seat back at the 1974 General Election, there were nevertheless the seeds of an impending national defeat in these Surrey by-election results.

MPs for Bermondsey, Southwark, and Camberwell

From	at	To	Surname	First Names	Constituency	Party
1945	G	1950	Sargood	Richard	Bermondsey West	Labour
1945	G	1946	Smith	Sir Ben	Rotherhithe	Labour
1946	B	1950	Mellish	Robert Joseph		Labour
1950	G	1974	Mellish	Robert Joseph	Bemondsey	Labour
1945	G	1948	Martin	John Hanbury	Southwark Central	Labour
1948	B	1950	Jenkins	Roy Harris		Labour
1945	G	1950	Naylor	Thomas Ellis	Southwark South East	Labour
1945	G	1950	Isaacs	George Alfred	Southwark North	Labour
1950	G	1959	Isaacs	George Alfred	Southwark	Labour
1959	G	1972	Gunter	Ray Jones		Labour
1972	B	1974	Lamborn	Harry George		Labour
1945	G	1950	Manning	Cecil Aubrey Gwynne	Camberwell North	Labour
1945	G	1950	Corbet	(Mrs) Freda Kunzlen	Camberwell North West	Labour
1945	G	1950	Silkin	Lewis	Peckham	Labour
1950	G	1974	Corbet	(Mrs) Freda Kunzlen	Camberwell, Peckham	Labour
1945	G	1951	Vernon	Wifred Foulston (Major)	Camberwell, Dulwich	Labour
1951	G	1964	Jenkins	Robert Christmas Dewar		Conservative
1964	G	1974	Silkin	Samuel Charles		Labour

Notes: First returned at: **B** By-election, **G** General Election

Bermondsey West

Richard Sargood (Labour) was elected in 1945 in succession to the long-serving, retiring MP, Dr. Alfred Salter. Sargood only sat for one term as his seat was abolished in 1950 and he did not secure a replacement seat. He was born in Lambeth in 1888 and educated in Kennington at an elementary school followed by the Workers Education

Association. He became a District Officer of the TGWU and chaired the Peckham Labour Party for 15 years. He became a London magistrate in 1930 and four years later was elected to the LCC. He died in 1979.

Bermondsey, Rotherhithe, Bermondsey

Sir Ben Smith (Labour) who was re-elected in 1945 had been MP for the area for most of the period since 1923, with the exception of 1931-5 when he was out of the House following the landslide defeat of his Party. However, he retired in1946 and died in 1964. His principal biographical details are in Chapter 10.

Bob Mellish MP
Peoples History Museum Manchester

Smith was succeeded by **Robert 'Bob' Joseph Mellish** (Labour) who was born in 1913 and educated at St. Joseph's, Deptford before becoming a docker and an official of the TGWU. He held a number of ministerial posts in the Governments of Harold Wilson including Parliamentary Secretary at the Ministry of Housing and Local Government (1964-7), Minister of Public Buildings and Works (1967-9), and Government Chief Whip (1969-70 and 1974-6). He was Opposition Chief Whip between 1970 and 1974 and when Labour was returned to Government in that year he joined the Cabinet for the first time. However, when Wilson resigned and Callaghan became Prime Minister in 1976, Mellish was not a member of his Government. He was a heavyweight right wing politician within the Party and eventually fell out with its leadership during its militant phase in the early 1980s, facing de-selection. He briefly sat as an Independent in 1982 when he was appointed Deputy Chairman of the Docklands Development Corporation[1] and resigned his seat to take up the post. He died in 1998.

Southwark Central

John Hanbury Martin (Labour), who had been returned at a by-election in 1940, was re-elected in 1945 but died in 1948. His biographical details are in Chapter 10.

Roy Jenkins MP
Bassano Ltd © National Portrait Gallery

He was succeeded by a man who was to have a major influence on the political life of Britain for the next sixty years. **Roy Harris Jenkins** (Labour) only held the Southwark Central seat for two years, referring to it in his memoirs as a 'rotten borough'. He went on to represent constituencies in two of Britain's other great cities, Birmingham and Glasgow. Jenkins came from a political family, his father having been a Vice-President of the Welsh Miners Federation and MP for Pontypool, Monmouthshire, where Roy was born at Abersychan in 1920. In fact father and son were both in the House during the time Roy represented Southwark since his father was MP from 1935 until 1950. Jenkins attended the local Grammar School at Abersychan and then Oriel College, Oxford, where he achieved a 1st Class Honours degree in PPE in 1941. Whilst at Oxford he joined the Labour Party and was secretary and librarian of the Oxford Union Society, the famous debating forum set up in 1823. During the War he served in the Royal Artillery and for a while was a code breaker at Bletchley Park. An economist by qualification he first contested a Parliamentary seat at Solihull (Warwickshire) in 1945, when he was defeated. He became Secretary of the Fabian Society and wrote a biography of Clement Attlee, Labour's leader and Prime Minister after 1945, this one of the first of many political biographies he was to write during the course of his life. Others included a book about Chancellors of the Exchequer and Prime Ministers Asquith, Gladstone and Churchill, this his last completed shortly before his own death in 2003.

In 1950 Jenkins was elected MP for the Stechford division of Birmingham but it was not until the return of a Labour Government in 1964 that his career took off, almost literally as his first ministerial post was that of Aviation Minister. In 1965 he received rapid promotion, becoming Home Secretary with a reputation for reforming liberalism. During his period of office legislation was passed to legalise homosexuality and abortion. When Sterling was devalued in 1967, the then Chancellor of the Exchequer, Jim Callaghan, tendered his resignation and in the ensuing changes he switched places

1 THE LDDC was an urban development corporation set up under the Local Government, Planning and Land Act 1980. Mellish was appointed by the Conservative Environment Secretary of the day, Michael Heseltine. It led to the transformation of London's docklands into vibrant commercial and residential areas.

with Jenkins who moved to the Treasury. Pursuing a policy to improve the Balance of Payments, the economy began to improve and amid signs of an improvement in Labour's poll ratings, a General Election was called in 1970, which nevertheless the Party lost. During the four-year period that Labour was out of office the major issue of the day was whether or not Britain should join the European Common Market. The Party was split down the middle on the issue with Jenkins the most prominent advocate of the case for joining. The Party adopted a policy of seeking to re-negotiate the terms of entry that had been secured by the Conservative Prime Minister, Ted Heath (See Chapter 13 Kent, Bexley) and putting new terms to a referendum of the British people. Jenkins was elected Deputy Leader of the Party in 1970 and somehow the Party managed to hold together during a very difficult period so much so that when Labour returned to Government in March 1974, Jenkins went back to the Home Office and in the ensuing 1975 referendum led the campaign for accepting the terms that Wilson had negotiated. The referendum was a vindication of his position. When Wilson unexpectedly resigned in 1976, Jenkins stood for the leadership but lost to Callaghan. By now the focus of much vilification from the Party's militant left wing, when an opportunity arose to remove Jenkins from the domestic scene, Callaghan seized it with both hands. In 1977 he resigned his Stechford seat to become President of the European Commission in Brussels and with the continuing drift of the Labour Party leftwards under the new leadership of Michael Foot, he re-emerged in 1981 as one of the so-called "Gang of Four", a group which left the Party to form the new Social Democratic Party (SDP). Jenkins became leader of the new Party and after fighting a by-election unsuccessfully at Warrington(Cheshire) in July 1981 he was returned to the Commons at a March 1982 by-election in the Hillhead division of Glasgow, formerly a Conservative seat. He was re-elected there in 1983, a general election in which the SDP achieved 25% of the votes cast nationally in conjunction with the Liberals, with whom they were allied. Until the 2010 election this was the largest share of the vote for a third party in a national election since 1923. The result also brought Labour to its lowest percentage of the vote since 1918.

The result had dramatic consequences for British politics. In the short term the split in anti-Tory votes helped Mrs Thatcher secure re-election in 1983 and 1987 and, with Labour's fourth consecutive defeat in 1992, the move rightwards of the Party culminated in the election of Tony Blair as its leader in 1994 with the invention of "New" Labour. In turn this move to the centre ground of politics served to marginalize the Conservative Party in three consecutive general elections – 1997, 2001 and 2005. Much of this can be traced back to Jenkins' decision to leave the Labour Party. However, Jenkins can claim an even more devastating impact on the fortunes of the Tory Party. The demise of the Major Government can be traced back to the enforced withdrawal of the UK from the European Exchange Rate mechanism, an event that caused enormous damage to the Party's reputation for economic competence. Ironically the EMS was one of Jenkins' initiatives whilst European Commission President. Despite these consequences, results for the SDP meanwhile only got worse. After the 1983 election, Jenkins resigned as leader in favour of David Owen under whom the Party failed to make further ground. The SDP formed an alliance with the Liberals in 1987 but Jenkins lost his seat to Labour's George Galloway[2] (See Chapter 15 – Middlesex, Bethnal Green and Bow) showing that splits in votes can cut more than one way, as Glasgow Hillhead had previously always been a safe Tory seat. In fact when Jenkins took it in 1982 it was the last remaining Conservative seat in Glasgow. No Tory has been elected for the City since then.

After the 1987 election the majority of SDP members voted to join the newly formed Liberal Democrats. Jenkins became leader of the new party in the House of Lords where he was created Lord Jenkins of Hillhead. From his position there and especially after the 1997 election, he gave a certain amount of support and encouragement to Tony Blair who by now had taken the Labour Party back to power on a platform that was not unrecognisable from the policies of the former SDP. The difference was that Labour was back with a landslide and the Liberal Democrats were still a third force, arguably vindicating those in the Labour Party who had said that the way to reform it in the 1980s was from within. Critics of Jenkins continue to maintain that his split from the Labour Party kept it from power throughout the 1980s. In his final years Jenkins was elected Chancellor of the University of Oxford in 1987, wrote his autobiography (1991), and headed a commission established by Tony Blair in 1997 to review alternative voting systems to "first past the post", though no action was ever taken on its findings[3]. Jenkins remained a vocal force to the end of his life, which came on 5th January 2003.

Southwark South East

Thomas Ellis Naylor (Labour), was re-elected in 1945 having served as the constituency's MP for most of the period since 1921. He retired in 1950 when his seat was abolished and his biographical details are in Chapter 10.

2 Galloway was subsequently expelled from the Labour Party and formed a new one called Respect. He was elected as its only MP at the 2005 general election in Bethnal Green and Bow.

3 The Independent Commission on the Voting System, headed by Lord Jenkins, recommended a new system of voting, the alternative vote "plus" to replace the traditional system of first-past-the-post. Although the Government did not pursue these proposals a partial system of proportional representation was introduced for elections to the Scottish Parliament, the Welsh Assembly and the Greater London Authority.

Southwark North, Southwark

George Alfred Isaacs (Labour), who was first elected at Southwark North in 1929 and again in 1935, was re-elected in 1945 and held the seat until 1950 when he became the new MP for Southwark, going on to represent the area until he retired in 1959. His principal biographical details are in Chapter 10.

Ray Gunter MP
Ida Kar © National Portrait Gallery

In 1959 he was succeeded by **Raymond 'Ray' Jones Gunter** (Labour), who held the seat until 1972 when he resigned the Labour whip. Born in 1907 at Abertillery and with an elementary school education at Newbridge, Pontypool, South Wales, Gunter joined the railways and became an active trade unionist in the Railway Clerks Union, later the Transport Salaried Staffs Association. However, during the Second World War he rose to become a Captain at Movement Control Headquarters in Iraq. In 1945 he successfully contested South East Essex but transferred to Doncaster (Yorkshire West Riding) in 1950, representing the railway and mining town until he was defeated at the 1951 election. He contested the same seat again in 1955 and, following a second defeat, was elected President of the TSSA, a post he held until 1964 when the first Wilson Government was returned. During the period 1956-66 he was also a member of the National Executive of the Labour Party. As MP for Southwark he was Vice Chairman of the Party in 1963-4 and then its Chairman in the following year. Having been the Opposition spokesman on Power (1960-1) and then on industrial affairs, he was Minister of Labour from 1964-8 and Minister of Power from April to June 1968 when he resigned from the Cabinet, complaining about the number of intellectuals in the government who he claimed were too far removed from ordinary people. It is probable, however, that he was bitter that his previous role as Labour Minister had been taken over by Barbara Castle, a prominent left winger, and that he resented not being able to put forward his ideas for the reform of industrial relations. Michael Foot and others sought to discipline him for bringing the Party into disrepute but failed, his local constituency party supporting him in a vote by 33 to 1. He retired in 1972 after resigning the Labour whip and died five years later.

He was succeeded at a June 1972 by-election by **Harry George Lamborn** (Labour), who held the seat until 1974 when the seat was redrawn and he transferred to Southwark, Peckham, which he represented until his death in 1982. Born in 1915, he was educated at a LCC Secondary school and became a shop worker. He joined the shop workers union in 1933 and by 1965 had risen to become a Director of the London Co-operative Society. He was a member of Camberwell Borough Council from 1953-65 and was its mayor in 1963-4. A governor of the King's College Hospital from 1965, he also sat on the Greater London Council between 1964 and 973 having been previously a councillor on the LCC from 1958. He was Deputy Chairman of the GLC in 1971-2. From 1974-79 he was PPS to Denis Healey as Chancellor of the Exchequer.

Camberwell North

Cecil Aubrey Gwynne Manning (Labour), who had won a 1944 by-election was re-elected in 1945 but retired five years later when the constituency was abolished. His principal biographical details are in Chapter 10.

Peckham

Lewis Silkin (Labour), won the seat at a by-election in 1936 but retired in 1950 when the seats in the area were reduced. His principal biographical details are in Chapter 10.

Camberwell North West, Camberwell, Peckham

Mrs Freda Kunzlen Corbet (Labour), was elected in 1945 and, following boundary changes in 1950, represented the new constituency of Camberwell, Peckham (later Southwark, Peckham) until February 1974 when she retired. Born Freda Mansell in 1900 and educated at Wimbledon County School and University College, London, she was variously a farmer, teacher, lecturer and barrister, having been called to the bar at the Inner Temple in 1932. She was a member of the LCC from 1934-65 and of the London Tourist Board. She died in 1993.

Camberwell, Dulwich

Major Wilfrid Foulston Vernon (Labour), won the seat in 1945 and held it for six years being defeated in 1951. Born in 1882, he was educated at the Stationer's Company's School[4] and the City and Guilds Technical College[5]. He was refused for Submarine service in 1914 but volunteered as an Air Observer and was trained as an aero-engine officer becoming technical assistant to Colonel Forte, a pioneer in marine aviation. He was appointed a Senior Technical Officer at Felixstowe Air Station in the R.A.A.S. where he designed flying boats. He remained in the service of the Air Ministry until 1937 when he was required to leave, possibly because his socialist politics were seen as a risk to national security by the powers that be at the time. However, during the Second World War he served in the Naval Reserve, the RNAS and RAF and was on the staff at the War Office Guard School at Dorking, Surrey, with the rank of Major. A governor of Dulwich School, he was an executive member of the Association of Scientific Workers, a trade union. He died in 1975.

Vernon was defeated in 1955 by **Robert Christmas Dewar Jenkins** (Conservative) who held the seat until he retired in 1964. Born in 1900 he was educated at Latymer School and went into business locally in Kensington where he joined the borough council in 1927. He was the borough's mayor throughout the Second World War. He also represented Kensington on the LCC, from 1934-46. He first contested Dulwich in 1950. He died in 1978.

This election leaflet from 1966, though degraded, evokes the period.
Peoples History Museum Manchester

Samuel Charles Silkin (Labour) was elected in 1964. Attorney-General in the Wilson and Callaghan Governments between 1974 and 1979, he was the son of Lewis Silkin (MP for the adjacent Peckham constituency from 1936 to 1950 and also a former Minister in the Attlee Government), and the elder brother of John (MP for nearby Deptford), who was contemporaneously a Minister in the same Governments. Born in 1918, he was educated at Dulwich College and at Trinity Hall, Cambridge before becoming a barrister. He was called to the bar at the Middle Temple in 1941 but served as a Lieutenant Colonel during the Second World War. From 1965-6 he was a member of the Royal Commission on the Penal System for England and Wales and in the following year was Chairman of the Select Committee on Parliamentary Privilege. He chaired the Parliamentary Labour Party's Group on Common Market and European Affairs (1966-70), led the UK Delegation to the Assembly of the Council of Europe (1968-70), and was Chairman of the Council of Europe Legal Committee (1966-70). Outside the House he was President of the Alcohol Education Centre and a Governor of the Maudsley, a psychiatric Hospital in Camberwell. He retired from the Commons in 1983 and two years later was created Baron Silkin of Dulwich. He died in 1988.

MPs for Lambeth

From	at	To	Surname	First Names	Constituency	Party
1945	G	1950	Gibson	Charles William	Kennington	Labour
1945	G	1950	Strauss	George Russell	Lambeth North	Labour
1950	G	1974	Strauss	George Russell	Vauxhall	Labour
1945	G	1974	Lipton	Marcus (Lt-Colonel)	Brixton	Labour
1945	G	1950	Chamberlain	Ronald Arthur	Norwood	Labour
1950	G	1966	Smyth	Sir John George (Brigadier)		Conservative
1966	G	1974	Fraser	John Denis		Labour

Notes: First returned at: **B** By-election, **G** General Election

Lambeth, Kennington

Charles William Gibson (Labour) won the seat in 1945 and held it until 1950 when it was lost in redistribution. He was then adopted to fight the Clapham division of Wandsworth, which he represented until he was defeated in 1959.

4 In 1403 the Mayor and Aldermen of the City of London approved the formation of a fraternity or Guild of stationers (booksellers who copied and sold manuscript books and writing materials and limners who decorated and illustrated them). The Stationers' Company's School opened in Bolt Court, Fleet Street in 1858, but outgrew its premises, moving to Hornsey in 1894. It was a grammar school until 1967 when it joined the Comprehensive system but closed in 1984.

5 The former City & Guilds College owes its origins to the City Livery Companies, sixteen of whom, with the Corporation of London, formed the 'City & Guilds of London Institute for the Advancement of Technical Education' in 1878. The Institute almost immediately set up the Finsbury Technical College for the provision of technical education, and shortly afterwards the 'Central Institution', at South Kensington, as a place of advanced technical education. It was the latter which became firstly the Central Technical College, and then in 1907 the City & Guilds College, a 'constituent college' forming part of the new Imperial College of Science & Technology.

Born in 1889, he was educated at St. Peter's School Lambeth and then studied at Morley Working Men's College (South Bank), Ruskin College and at the London School of Economics. He became an official of the Transport and General Workers Union. A member of the LCC (1928-31 and from 1934), he chaired its Housing Committee from 1943. He died in 1977.

Lambeth North, Lambeth Vauxhall

George Russell Strauss (Labour) first won Lambeth North in 1929, lost it in 1931 and held it again from 1935 until 1950 when it was abolished. He was selected to fight the new Vauxhall constituency in 1950 and held it until he retired in 1979. His principal biographical details are in Chapter 10.

Brixton

Marcus Lipton MP
Peoples History Museum Manchester

Lieutenant-Colonel Marcus Lipton (Labour) was Brixton's MP from 1945 until 1974 and was subsequently returned for Lambeth Central which he held until his death in 1978. Born in 1900, he was educated at the Bede Grammar School, Sunderland before attending Merton College, Oxford. He became a barrister being called to the bar at Grays Inn in 1926. During the Second World War he served in the Army Education Corps and was demobilised with the rank of Lieutenant- Colonel.

From 1934-7 he was a Stepney Borough councillor, then a member of the Lambeth Borough Council from 1937 to 1956 having first contested the Brixton Parliamentary seat in 1935. He was Chairman of the Anglo-Nepalese and Anglo-Bulgarian Parliamentary Groups. Lipton famously exposed the Soviet spy Kim Philby as the so-called "third man" in an espionage scandal that came to light after publication of his name in the *New York Times*. The Foreign Secretary, Harold Macmillan (See Chapter 13 Kent – Bromley), issued a flat denial in response to a Parliamentary question from Lipton and Philby himself issued a public denial, challenging Lipton to make the same allegation without the privilege of the House of Commons. Lipton was forced to retract but Philby fled to the Soviet Union in 1963 and in a book published five years later admitted he was indeed a spy. He died in 1978.

Norwood

Ronald Arthur Chamberlain (Labour) won Norwood in 1945 but was defeated five years later. Born in 1901 he was educated at (Dame Alice) Owens School, Islington and at Gonville and Cauis Colleges, Cambridge, where he graduated as a MA. A lecturer and teacher, from 1936 to 1940 he was Secretary of the National Federation of Housing, set up in 1935 to promote better housing for working people, then Chief Executive Officer of the Miners' Welfare Commission until 1943. In 1944-5 he was Assistant Administration Officer of the National (Service) Hostels Corporation[6] and a year later worked as Housing Consultant to the Co-operative Movement. After the 1945 election he became PPS to Lewis Silkin, the Minister of Town and Country Planning, a role he fulfilled until 1948. A member of Middlesex County Council, he was defeated at Norwood in 1950 and again when seeking a return in 1951. He died in 1987.

An unsuccessful election leaflet from 1987
Peoples History Museum Manchester

Brigadier Sir John George Smyth (Conservative) held Dulwich from 1950 to 1966. Born in 1893 and educated at Repton School, he passed out at Sandhurst serving a long career in the Army from 1912 until 1942. At the time of the Japanese invasion of Burma he commanded the 17th Division attaining the rank of Acting Major-General.

An author and journalist, after his election he was appointed Parliamentary Secretary at the Ministry of Pensions in 1951, a role that was extended two years later to include National Insurance. However, he held no further post after 1955. He died in 1983

Smyth retired in 1966 when the man whom he had defeated in 1964 won the seat. **John Denis Fraser** (Labour), a solicitor, went on to hold the seat until he failed to win the seat for Labour for Dulwich & West Norwood in 1987. Born in 1934 and educated at the Sloane Grammar School, Chelsea, he attended the Co-operative College, Loughborough before going on to the Law Society's School of Law. He was a member of Lambeth Borough Council

6 Set up by Ernest Bevin in 1941

from 1962-8 and after the return of the 1974 Wilson Government became a minister, initially as under Secretary for Employment until 1976 and then Minister of State for Prices and Consumer Protection until the Government lost power in 1979. He remained an Opposition spokesman until his retirement.

MPs for Wandsworth, and Battersea

From	at	To	Surname	First Names	Constituency	Party
1945	G	1950	Robertson	Sir David	Streatham	Conservative
1950	G	1974	Sandys	Sir Edwin Duncan		Conservative
1945	G	1946	Douglas	Sir Francis Campbell Ross	Battersea North	Labour
1946	B	1974	Jay	Douglas Patrick Thomas		Labour
1945	G	1951	Ganley	(Mrs) Caroline Selina	Battersea South	Labour
1951	G	1964	Partridge	Ernest		Conservative
1964	G	1974	Perry	Ernest George		Labour
1945	G	1950	Battley	John Rose	Clapham	Labour
1950	G	1959	Gibson	Charles William		Labour
1959	G	1964	Glyn	Dr. Alan		Conservative
1964	G	1970	McKay	(Mrs) Margaret		Labour
1970	G	1974	Shelton	Sir William Jeremy Masefield		Conservative
1945	G	1950	Adams	Harold Richard (Captain)	Balham & Tooting	Labour
1945	G	1950	Bevin	Ernest	Wandsworth Central	Labour
1950	G	1955	Adams	Harold Richard (Captain)		Labour
1955	G	1964	Hughes-Young	Michael Henry Colin		Conservative
1964	G	1970	Kerr	Dr. David Leigh		Labour
1970	G	1974	Cox	Thomas (Tom) Michael		Labour
1945	G	1964	Linstead	Hugh Nicholas	Putney	Conservative
1964	G	1974	Jenkins	Hugh Gater		Labour

Notes: First returned at: **B** By-election, **G** General Election

Streatham

Sir David Robertson (Conservative) who had won the seat at a 1939 by-election was re-elected in 1945 but retired five years later. His principal biographical details are in Chapter 10.

The vacancy permitted the return to the Commons of **Sir Duncan Edwin Sandys** (Conservative) who had been defeated at Norwood in 1945. His principal biographical details are also in Chapter 10 (Surrey – Norwood). He went on to hold the seat until he retired in February 1974.

Battersea North

Sir Francis Campbell Ross Douglas (Labour) won the seat at a 1940 by-election and retained it in 1945 but he died in 1946. His principal biographical details are in Chapter 10.

Douglas Jay MP
Peoples History Museum Manchester

He was succeeded by **Douglas Patrick Thomas Jay** (Labour) who held the seat until its abolition in 1983. Born in 1907, he was educated at Winchester School and New College, Oxford becoming a Fellow of All Souls from 1930 to 1937 and then again much later in his life from 1968 until 1996. In 1937 he wrote a book entitled "The Socialist Case" and two years later made a statement that typified the classical left - leaning intellectual position of the period. He said "the gentleman in Whitehall really does know better what is good for the people than the people know themselves". Between 1929 and 1941 he was a financial journalist successively with the *Times*, the *Economist* and the *Daily Herald* and an exponent of central economic planning advocated by the Labour Party. After the Second World War in 1945-6 he served as Clement Attlee's Personal Assistant when he was Prime Minister and following his return at the 1946 by-election was Economic Secretary to the Treasury from 1947-50, then Financial Secretary in 1950-51. When Harold Wilson became Prime Minister in 1964, Jay returned to the Cabinet as

President of the Board of Trade, a post he held until 1967. A fierce opponent of the European Common Market he was dropped from the Government and in 1970 was appointed Chairman of the Common Market Safeguards Campaign. He died in 1996 having been ennobled as Lord Jay of Battersea in 1987.

Battersea South

Selina Ganley MP
Peoples History Museum Manchester

Mrs Caroline Selina Ganley (Labour) won the seat in 1945 and held it until 1951 when she was defeated. Born in 1879 and with only an elementary education behind her, she became a school manager and entered politics following the 1918 extension of the suffrage to older women and was amongst the first to be elected a local councillor. She was a member of Battersea Borough Council from 1919 until 1925 when she was elected to the LCC on which she served twice, from 1925-28 and 1934-7. In the meantime she contested Paddington North unsuccessfully at the 1935 General Election. She was President of the London Co-operative Society from 1942-46. Following her defeat in 1951 she returned to local politics in Battersea and was a member of the Council there again from 1953 to 1965. She died the following year.

Ernest Partridge (Conservative) who had lost to Mrs Ganley in 1945 and 1950 defeated her in 1951 and went on to represent the area for thirteen years. Born in 1895, he was educated at Wilson's Grammar School, Camberwell. He went on to a business career that included the chairmanship of a Building Society and directorships of engineering companies. He was a Holborn Borough councillor from 1928-34. He died in 1974.

Ernest Perry MP
Peoples History Museum Manchester

He was defeated in 1964 by **Ernest George Perry** (Labour) who held the seat until he retired in 1979. Born in 1910 and educated at London elementary schools he was an insurance contractor. He entered local politics in Battersea in 1934 and served continuously until 1965. He was Mayor in 1955-6. A member of the General and Municipal Workers Union he sat on the local Trades Council. He was an assistant whip in the Labour Government between 1968 and 1970, then an Opposition whip, returning to fulfil the same role in Government again following the 1974 February election. He was not re-appointed after the October election. He died in 1998.

Clapham

John Battley MP
Peoples History Museum Manchester

John Rose Battley (Labour), a printer and trade unionist, was elected in 1945 but retired at the end of that Parliament in 1950. He was born in 1880 and received an elementary education at Basnett Road School in Battersea where his parents ran a grocer's shop. In 1894 he was apprenticed as a printer working for the London, Chatham & Dover Railway Company at its nearby Victoria offices. He was a member of the Baptist Church in Clapham where he undertook charitable work including teaching on Saturdays at the Shaftesbury Ragged School. His religious beliefs meant that he became a pacifist during both the Boer and First World Wars when he became a conscientious objector in 1916. He had meanwhile started his own printing business in Queen's Road Battersea and after the Great War became active in the Independent Labour Party which he had first joined in 1913. He entered politics late in life having experienced a series of mental health problems during the 1930s which included a stay at the Maudsley Hospital. He became a councillor on the LCC in 1938, was made a London magistrate in 1940, and lived in Clapham Park Road. He died in 1952.

He was succeeded in 1950 by **Charles William Gibson** (Labour) who was previously the MP for Kennington (see Lambeth MPs above for fuller biographical details).

Gibson was defeated at the 1959 general election by **Dr. Alan Glyn** (Conservative), a member of Chelsea Borough Council between 1958 and 1962, who was born in 1918 and educated at Westminster School before graduating from Cauis College, Cambridge, and also from St. Bartholomew's and St. George's Hospitals as a medical practitioner. He was called to the bar of the Middle Temple in 1955 and had the unusual experience of being in Hungary the following year at the time that the uprising against the Communist regime was suppressed by an invasion of Soviet tanks. Following his defeat at Clapham in 1964 he sought a successful return in 1970 for the safe Berkshire constituency of Windsor, later re-named Windsor and Maidenhead, which he represented continuously until he retired in 1992. Although a long serving MP, he never progressed beyond the backbenches and contented himself with a series of outside interests including

Margaret McKay MP
Peoples History Museum Manchester

membership of the Board of Governors of national heart and chest hospitals (from 1982) and the Kensington, Chelsea and Westminster Medical Committee from 1974. He was a freeman of the Worshipful Company of the Art of Mystery of Apothecaries of the City of London. He died in 1998.

Glyn was beaten by **Mrs Margaret McKay** (Labour) in 1964. Born Margaret McCarthy in 1911, she received an elementary education and initially became an administrative worker for various trade unions, including the Transport and General Workers and the Civil Service Clerical Association. She became the chief woman officer of the Trades Union Congress and later a public relations consultant. In 1965 she was the UK representative on the United Nations Commission on the status of women. She contested Walthamstow East unsuccessfully in 1959 but after her election at Clapham in 1964 sought re-election only once and retired in 1970. She died in 1996.

Sir William Jeremy Masefield Shelton (Conservative) won the seat in 1970 and held it for four years. Born in 1929, he was educated at Radley College, Tabor Academy Massachusetts, Texas University and at Worcester College, Oxford before moving into the world of advertising to become Managing Director of Colman, Prentis and Varley (International). A member of Lloyds and a Governor of Chelsea School of Art, he was elected to the GLC in 1967 and the following year was appointed chief whip for his Party on the Inner London Education Authority. In 1974 he transferred to the adjacent but safer seat of Streatham and from 1975-79 was PPS to Margaret Thatcher, Leader of the Opposition. From 1981-83 he was Under Secretary of State for Education and Science but never resumed a ministerial career. From 1987 to 1992 he was a member of the British delegation to the Council of Europe. He was defeated at the 1992 election. He died in 2003.

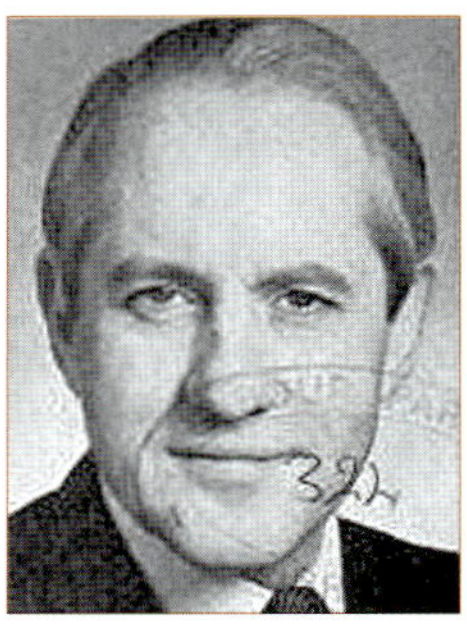

William Shelton MP
Peoples History Museum Manchester

Balham and Tooting

Harold Adams MP
Peoples History Museum Manchester

Captain Harold Richard Adams (Labour) was elected in 1945 and held the seat until 1950 when he transferred to Wandsworth Central (see below). Born in 1912, after a Public School education he attended the London School of Economics and during the Second World War was an officer in the 25th Tank Brigade serving in Tunisia and Italy. Before the War he was an advertising and sales executive and was a member of the council of the Association of Incorporated Statistics. His first Parliamentary contest was at Canterbury (Kent) in 1935 when he was defeated, and he was a member of Wandsworth Borough Council being its youngest member at the time of his call up in 1940. He was a Government whip from 1947 to 1951. He retired in 1955. He died in 1978.

Wandsworth Central

Ernest Bevin (Labour) was elected unopposed at a by-election in 1940 when he was brought into the Wartime Government at the behest of Winston Churchill. His principal biographical details are in Chapter 9 (Kent, Woolwich East).

He held the Wandsworth Central seat until boundary changes in 1950 when he was succeeded by **Captain Harold Richard Adams (**Labour), formerly the MP for Balham and Tooting (see above for fuller biographical details) who held the seat until 1955.

Lieutenant-Colonel Michael Henry Colin Hughes – Young (Conservative) sat between 1955 and 1964 when he was defeated. At the 1951 election he had contested St.Helens (Lancashire) unsuccessfully. Born in 1912 and after an education that took him to Sandhurst via Harrow School, he joined the Black Watch in 1932. He was attached to the French Army in 1934 and the following year was seconded to the King's African Rifles. He fought in the Abyssinian War and after service in the Second World War in Europe retired in 1947 having reached the rank of Lieutenant Colonel. From 1948 to 1955 he worked at Conservative Central Office and after his election that year was made an assistant Government whip in 1956. He remained a whip after the 1959 election when he was made Deputy Chief Whip and from 1962 until defeated in 1964 held the title, Treasurer of the Household. He died in 1980.

Dr. David Leigh Kerr (Labour) who won the seat in 1964 was born in 1923 and educated at the Whitgift School,

Croydon and Middlesex Hospital going on to be a Machoglen Scholar at the Royal College of Surgeons He was born in 1923 and from 1958 until 1965 was a member of the LCC. From 1957 to 1963 he was Secretary of the Socialist Medical Association and also a founder member of the College of General Practitioners. He retired in 1970 when he returned to medicine and was active in the reform of several areas of psychiatric practice at that time, notably in the Sexual Reform Society and the Albany Trust, two organisations that advocated a change in the laws relating to homosexuality[7]. In 1983 he was appointed Chief Executive of the Manor House Hospital. He died in 2009.

Tom Michael Cox (Labour), who was an electrician, took over the seat in 1970. In 1974 he was returned for Tooting, which seat he retained until retiring from the House in 2005. Born in 1930, he was educated at state schools and at the London School of Economics and was an alderman on Fulham Borough Council until its abolition. Between 1945 and 1948 he was a "Bevin boy", working in the South Wales coalfield and from 1949 to 1970 was a power station worker. As a Parliamentarian he spent most of his time as a backbencher although between 1974 and 1979 he was a Government whip.

Putney

Hugh Nicholas Linstead (Conservative) was Putney's MP from 1942 until 1964. His principal biographical details are in Chapter 10.

Hugh Jenkins MP
Peoples History Museum Manchester

He was defeated in 1964 by **Hugh Gater Jenkins** (Labour) who went on to hold the seat until 1979. Born in 1908, the son of a dairyman and a butcher's daughter, and educated at Enfield Grammar School, Jenkins worked for ten years for the Prudential Assurance Company. In 1941 he joined the RAF, becoming an air traffic controller and flight lieutenant and after the War, but still in uniform, he was seconded to the government of Burma and put in charge of English language programmes on Rangoon Radio. Returning to London in 1947 he became organiser of the National Union of Bank Employees and then in 1951 moved to become assistant general secretary of the actors' union, Equity. He fought Enfield West unsuccessfully in 1950 and repeated the experience at Mitcham in 1955. He became an activist in the anti-nuclear movement and was elected chairman of the Victory for Socialism group, a body that played a crucial role in 1956 opposing the Suez invasion. Thinking himself too left wing to be selected for a winnable seat he went into local politics representing Stoke Newington and Hackney North on the LCC from 1961. Meanwhile he moved to Putney and despite a local party split about his fitness as a candidate, he was adopted in 1963 and elected the following year. After losing his seat in 1979 he became chairman of CND and, from 1981, its vice president. In the same year he was also back at Westminster as a life peer, becoming chairman of the Lords CND group and advocating the return of the Elgin Marbles to Greece. A Governor of the National Theatre, chairman of the Theatres Advisory Council and from 1977-8 Chairman of the Parliamentary Labour Party's Arts and Amenities Group, he was Opposition spokesman on the arts between 1973 and 1974 and in 1974-8 Under Secretary of State at the Ministry of Education and Science, where he was essentially the Minister for Arts. While in office he abolished museum charges and sought to shift the emphasis of subsidy away from minority interests, like opera and ballet, in favour of improving majority pursuits such as film and television, and tackled the issue of authors' public lending rights. He died in 2004 at the age of 95.

Arthur Palmer MP
Peoples History Museum Manchester

MPs for Wimbledon, Kingston, and Richmond

Wimbledon

Arthur Montague Frank Palmer (Labour) was the victor in this seat in 1945, holding it for only one term being defeated in 1950 after which he contested the new constituency of Merton and Morden, formed from the old seat. Although he lost again in 1951 he was soon

7 The Homosexuality Law Reform Society was founded in June 1958 following the recommendation of the Wolfenden Report that homosexual behaviour between consenting adults in private should no longer be a criminal offence. The Society was reconstituted in 1970 as the Sexual Law Reform Society in order to campaign for further legal changes, particularly relating to the age of consent. The Albany Trust was founded as a registered charity in May 1958 as a complimentary organisation to the HLRS with a remit 'to promote psychological health in men by collecting data and conducting research: to publish the results thereof by writing, films, lectures and other media: to take suitable steps based thereon for the public benefit to improve the social and general conditions necessary for such healthy psychological development'. The Trust developed into a pioneering counselling and investigating organisation for gay men, lesbians and sexual minorities. Following the Sexual Offences Act of 1967, which decriminalised adult homosexual relationships, the Albany Trust became primarily an educational and counselling organisation.

MPs for Wimbledon, Kingston, and Richmond

From	at	To	Surname	First Names	Constituency	Party
1945	G	1950	Palmer	Arthur Montague Frank	Wimbledon	Labour
1950	G	1970	Black	Sir Cyril Wilson		Conservative
1970	G	1974	Havers	Sir Robert Michael Oldfield		Conservative
1950	G	1955	Ryder VC	Robert Ellis Dudley (Captain)	Merton & Morden	Conservative
1955	G	1970	Atkins	Sir Humphrey Edward Gregory		Conservative
1970	G	1974	Fookes	(Miss later Dame) Janet Evelyn		Conservative
1945	G	1959	Harvie-Watt	Sir George Steven	Richmond	Conservative
1959	G	1974	Royle	Sir Anthony		Conservative
1945	G	1972	Boyd-Carpenter	John Archibald (Major)	Kingston-Upon-Thames	Conservative
1972	B	1974	Lamont	Norman Stewart Hughson		Conservative
1955	G	1974	Fisher	Sir Nigel Thomas Loveridge	Surbiton	Conservative

Notes: First returned at: **B** By-election, **G** General Election

returned at a by-election held in 1952 at Cleveland (North Riding of Yorkshire) but lost there in 1959. Out of the House for five years he was elected for the safe seat of Bristol Central in 1964 holding it until 1974. Born in 1912 and educated at Ashford Technical Grammar School (Middlesex), then at Brunel Technical College (Acton), he qualified as a chartered electrical engineer going on to become a national official of the Electrical Power Engineers' Association in 1945 and editor of its magazine. In 1974 he transferred to Bristol North East in the face of a reduced electorate in his former constituency and sat in the House until further redistribution abolished his seat in 1983. He died in 1994.

Sir Cyril Black MP
Elliot & Fry © National Portrait Gallery

Palmer was succeeded by **Sir Cyril Wilson Black** (Conservative), who sat for 20 years, retiring in 1970. Born in 1902, he was educated locally at the King's College School and became a chartered surveyor and chairman of his own and other property and investment companies. A strong Baptist by faith he was chairman of the Temperance Building Society. From 1942 he was a member of Wimbledon Borough Council, being mayor in 1945-7 and an alderman in 1948. From 1956-9 he was also an alderman and chairman of Surrey County Council. During the 1960s Black was a prominent campaigner against increasingly liberal attitudes towards sexual expression being involved, amongst other campaigns, in attempts to prevent the publication of *Lady Chatterly's Lover*. He was a member of the Clean Up Television Campaign and in 1966 brought a successful prosecution against the publishers of a book for containing allegedly "pornographic" content. He died in 1991.

Sir Robert Michael Oldfield Havers (Conservative) represented Wimbledon from 1970 until 1987 when he was ennobled and became Lord Chancellor. Born in 1923, he was educated at Westminster School and Corpus Christi College, Cambridge following which he became a barrister. He was Recorder of Dover from 1962-68 when he transferred to the same position in Norwich. A Chairman of the Conservative Legal Committee, after the Party returned to power in 1970 he was appointed Solicitor-General in 1972 and when it returned to Opposition was its front bench spokesman on Law for the duration of the 1974-9 Parliament. He was Margaret Thatcher's Attorney General from 1979 to 1987. He fulfilled the role of Lord Chancellor only for a matter of months being replaced the same year by Lord Mackay of Clashfern. It has been alleged[8] that she knew Lord Havers' health was failing at the time and only made the appointment to give him a lucrative settlement on retirement. He lasted 126 days in the post but died in 1992. His son, Nigel is a well-known actor.

Merton and Morden

Captain Robert Ellis Dudley Ryder VC (Conservative) represented this new seat from 1950 until 1955, defeating the former Wimbledon Labour MP Arthur Palmer (see above). He was born in 1908 in India and educated at Hazelhurst School, Frant and Cheltenham College before serving in the Royal Navy between 1926 and 1950. He was a Midshipman

8 See Scotsman Newspaper, 24th December 2002.

in the battleship *HMS Ramillies*, 1927-9, and a Lieutenant in the submarine *HMS Olympus* in China, 1930-3. He was also an explorer, captaining the ketch *Tai-Mo-Shan* on a 16,217 mile voyage from Hong Kong to Dartmouth via the Panama Canal, 1933-4, and took part in the British Graham Land Expedition to the Antarctic, commanding the three-masted schooner *Penola*, 1934-7. As a Lieutenant Commander in the battleship *HMS Warspite* he served with the force of decoy or Q-ships in1940, later that year becoming Commander of the frigate *HMS Fleetwood*. He then captained the *Prince Philippe*, which sank after a collision in the Firth of Clyde in 1941 and was appointed Naval Liaison Officer on the staff of GOC Southern Command at Wilton House, near Salisbury, 1941-2. He led the naval forces in Operation Chariot, the raid on the dry dock at St Nazaire, 27-28 March 1942, destroying the only dock on the French western seaboard capable of taking the German battleship *Bismarck*. He also took part in Operation Jubilee, the attack on Dieppe, 19 August 1942, which was commanded by Hughes-Hallett, who was later to become a fellow Tory MP (for Croydon North East from 1954-64, see below). He was awarded the Victoria Cross. He was promoted to the rank of Captain in 1949, and served as Naval Attaché in Oslo, 1948-50. He retired from politics in 1955 and died many years later in 1986 when on a sailing trip to France.

Sir Humphrey Edward Gregory Atkins (Conservative) won the seat in 1955 and held it until 1970 when he transferred to the Surrey (formerly Middlesex) constituency of Spelthorne. His first electoral contest was at East Lothian (Scotland) where he was defeated in 1951. Born in 1922, he was educated at Wellington College and went on to become a director of an advertising agency. He was Secretary of the Conservative Party Parliamentary Defence Committee from 1965 to 1967 when he was made an Opposition Whip and after the return of the Heath Government served as Deputy Chief Whip until 1973 when he was promoted to the Cabinet as Parliamentary Secretary to the Treasury and Chief Whip. He remained Chief Whip in Opposition until 1979 and was Secretary of State for Northern Ireland between 1979 and 1981. He remained in the Cabinet as Lord Privy Seal and the Government's principal spokesman in the House of Commons on Foreign Affairs when Lord Carrington held the senior post. However, he resigned along with Carrington following the invasion by Argentina of the Falkland Islands in April 1982. He retired from the Commons in 1987 and was made a life peer. As Lord Colnbrook he was Chairman of the Association of Conservative peers and died in 1996.

Atkins was succeeded in 1970 by **Miss (later Dame) Janet Evelyn Fookes** (Conservative) who represented the seat until the boundaries were re-drawn in 1974 when she transferred to the Drake division of Plymouth, where she continued in the House until her retirement in 1997. Born in 1936, she was educated at Hastings and St. Leonards Ladies' College, Hastings High School, Royal Holloway College and the University of London. From 1958 until 1970 she was a teacher in Hastings (East Sussex) and for much of the period was a councillor in her home town (1960-1 and 1963-70). Although a long standing MP she never once held ministerial office despite the fact that her Party was in power for most of the time she was in Parliament. However, in her last term, from 1992 to her retirement in 1997, she was a Deputy Speaker of the Commons. She was created Baroness Fookes of Plymouth in the County of Devon in September 1997.

Richmond

Sir George Steven Harvie Watt (Conservative) was elected in 1937 at a by-election and remained Richmond's MP until 1959. His principal biographical details are in Chapter 10.

His successor was **Sir Anthony Henry Fanshawe Royle** (Conservative) who held the seat until his retirement in 1983. Born in 1927 and educated at Harrow and Sandhurst, Royle was a member of Lloyds and a director of several companies. He first contested an election at St. Pancras North, where he was defeated in 1955, and suffered a similar fate at Torrington (Devon) in a 1958 by-election when a Liberal gained the previously Tory seat. Following his 1959 victory he enjoyed only minor ministerial success, being appointed first in 1970 when he served for the duration of that Government as Under Secretary of State for Foreign and Commonwealth Affairs. Thereafter he held no office although in 1979 he was appointed Vice- Chairman of the Conservative Party in which role he was responsible for candidate selection. In September 1983 he was created Lord Fanshawe of Richmond of South Cerney in the County of Gloucestershire and died in 2001.

J. Boyd-Carpenter MP
Walter Stoneman © National Portrait Gallery

Kingston upon Thames

Sir John Archibald Boyd - Carpenter (Conservative) represented the seat from 1945 until 1972 when elevated to the House of Lords and he went to chair the Civil Aviation Authority. Born in 1908 he was educated at Stowe School and at Balliol College, Oxford where he was President of the Union in 1930. Called to the bar of the Middle Temple in 1934, he joined the Churchill peacetime Government in 1951 as Financial Secretary to the Treasury, moving to become Minister of Transport and Civil Aviation in 1954. In the 1955 Government he was Minister of Pensions and National Insurance, a post he held in the Eden and Macmillan Cabinets, though he was moved to become Chief Secretary to the Treasury and Paymaster General in 1962. He was Chairman of the Conservative Greater London area local government advisory committee and in business chaired the Orion Insurance Company. He was High Steward of Kingston [9] from 1973 until his death in 1998.

Norman Stewart Hughson Lamont (Conservative), a Scot from Lerwick in Shetland, was born in 1942 and educated at Loretto School, Musselburgh, then at Fitzwilliam College, Cambridge where he was President of the Union in 1964. A merchant banker, he worked for N M Rothschild from 1968-79 but embarked on a Parliamentary career in 1970 when he was defeated contesting John Prescott's seat of Kingston upon Hull East. Following his return at the other Kingston (on-Thames) in 1972 he retained the seat until its abolition in 1997 when it was merged with neighbouring Surbiton. However, he failed to secure the nomination for this new seat and was eventually adopted to fight the supposed Tory stronghold of Harrogate and Knaresborough, which he lost in the anti-Tory landslide which saw him defeated by a Liberal Democrat, as incidentally he would have been had he fought Kingston and Surbiton. From 1979-81 he was Under Secretary of State for Energy and then Minister of State for Industry until 1985 when he became Minister of State for Defence Procurement. From 1986-89 he served as Financial Secretary to the Treasury and then joined the Cabinet for the first time as Chief Secretary to the Treasury. When Margaret Thatcher was forced to resign in 1990, Lamont was John Major's campaign manager in his successful leadership bid and it was no great surprise that he was appointed Chancellor of the Exchequer when the new Cabinet was formed. In effect the two men continued the relationship they had forged when Major was Chancellor and Lamont his deputy.

As Chancellor Major had persuaded Mrs Thatcher to take Britain into the European Exchange Rate Mechanism but when the arrangement proved too difficult to sustain, it was Lamont who was forced to take the country out of it on September 16th 1992, a day that became known as "Black Wednesday". It was the day that Conservative hegemony in British politics in the latter quarter of the 20th Century ended. Lamont was made the scapegoat for what had happened, though he maintained that it was Major who had panicked, but his ministerial and political careers both came to an end as a result. Major tried to move him to another post in 1993 but Lamont refused, preferring to resign. He was the only person ever to have held all three senior ministerial posts in the Treasury. In 1998 he was made Lord Lamont of Lerwick in the Shetland Islands.

Surbiton

Sir Nigel Thomas Loveridge Fisher (Conservative) was elected as the first MP for Surbiton in 1955 and held the seat until 1983. Born in 1913, he was educated at Eton and Trinity College, Cambridge going from there into business, becoming a director of a group of pharmaceutical companies. He contested Chislehurst unsuccessfully at the 1945 election but represented Hitchin (Hertfordshire) from 1950-55 when he transferred to Surbiton. From 1962-3 he was Under Secretary for the Colonies, adding Commonwealth Relations to his brief a year later. Although he remained Party spokesman on the same subject in Opposition from 1964-66, he never resumed a front bench role after that, though he was a member of the 1922 Committee's Executive. He died in 1996.

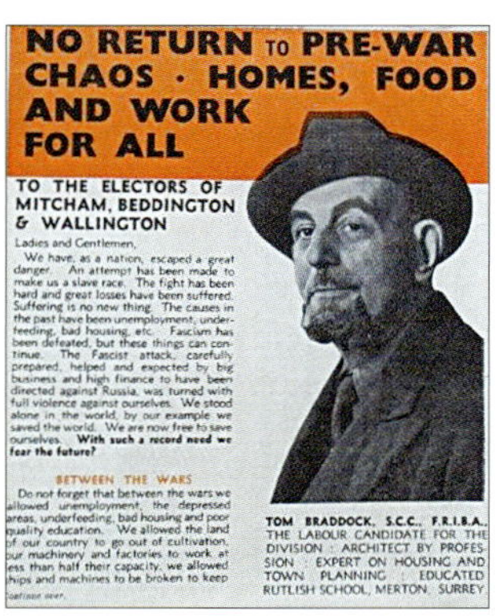

Tom Braddock MP
Peoples History Museum Manchester

MPs for Mitcham, Carshalton, Sutton and Cheam, and Croydon

Mitcham

Thomas 'Tom' Braddock (Labour) won the seat in 1945 and held it for five years. Born in 1887, he was a local man educated at Rutlish School Merton, the same one attended by future Tory Prime Minister, John Major. Braddock was an early Socialist and founder member of the Labour Party, a member of Wimbledon Borough (from 1938), and (from 1934) Surrey County Councils. He was accomplished in his professional life as an architect. A Fellow of the Royal Institute of British Architects, of which he was a Grissell Gold Medallist (for constructive architecture), he was also a holder of the

9 The Royal Borough of Kingston upon Thames has the privilege of appointing its own High Steward and Recorder. Generally a person of high rank held the position of High Steward. The most famous High Steward was Lord Howard of Effingham, who was Lord High Admiral and Commander in Chief of the forces which defeated the Spanish Armada in 1588.

MPs for Mitcham, Carshalton, Sutton and Cheam, and Croydon						
From	**at**	**To**	**Surname**	**First Names**	**Constituency**	**Party**
1945	G	1950	Braddock	Thomas	Mitcham	Labour
1950	G	1974	Carr	Leonard Robert		Conservative
1945	G	1960	Head	Anthony Henry (Brigadier)	Carshalton	Conservative
1960	B	1974	Elliot	Walter Elliot (Captain)		Conservative
1945	G	1954	Marshall	Sidney Horatio	Sutton & Cheam	Conservative
1954	B	1972	Sharples	Sir Richard Christopher		Conservative
1972	B	1974	Tope	Graham Norman		Liberal
1945	G	1948	Willink	Henry Urmston	Croydon North	Conservative
1948	B	1955	Harris	Frederic Walter		Conservative
1955	G	1970	Harris	Frederic Walter	Croydon North West	Conservative
1970	G	1974	Taylor	Robert George		Conservative
1945	G	1950	Rees-Williams	David Rees (Lt-Colonel)	Croydon South	Labour
1950	G	1955	Thompson	Sir Richard Hilton Marler	Croydon West	Conservative
1955	G	1966	Thompson	Sir Richard Hilton Marler	Croydon South	Conservative
1966	G	1970	Winnick	David Julian		Labour
1970	G	1974	Thompson	Sir Richard Hilton Marler		Conservative
1950	G	1954	Williams	Sir Herbert Geraint	Croydon East	Conservative
1954	B	1955	Hughes-Hallett	John (Vice Admiral)		Conservative
1955	G	1964	Hughes-Hallett	John (Vice Admiral)	Croydon North East	Conservative
1964	G	1974	Weatherill	Sir Bruce Bernard		Conservative
1945	G	1951	Astor	Michael Langhorne (Captain)	Surrey East	Conservative
1951	G	1970	Doughty	Charles John Addison		Conservative
1970	G	1974	Clarke	Sir William Gibson Haigue (Major)		Conservative

Notes: First returned at: **B** By-election, **G** General Election

silver and bronze medals of the London Architectural Association. He contested Wimbledon in 1929, 1931 and 1935. Belonging to the "hard left", he collaborated with others in 1948 to produce the paper, "Socialist Outlook"[10], and in 1949 was instrumental in setting up the Socialist Fellowship, a grass-roots socialist organisation within the Labour Party. He died in 1976.

Robert Carr MP, giving his all at an election rally with Conservative Party Leader Edward Heath at his side
Peoples History Museum Manchester

Braddock was defeated in 1950 by **Leonard Robert Carr** (Conservative) who went on to hold the seat until it was redistributed in 1974. He then became MP for Carshalton, which he represented until 1976 when he was elevated to the House of Lords as Baron Carr of Monken Hadley in Greater London. Born in 1916, Carr was educated at Westminster School and Gonville and Caius College, Cambridge, where he took a degree in metallurgy going on to become an industrialist and company director. He was PPS to Sir Anthony Eden (Foreign Secretary) from 1951-55 and occupied his first ministerial position from 1955-58 when he was Parliamentary Under Secretary at the Ministry of Labour. His ministerial career went into suspension at that time – preferring to concentrate on his business activities – and it was not until 1970 that he regained office, going straight into Ted Heath's Cabinet as Secretary of State for Employment, a controversial role in which he introduced legislation that had the effect of putting trade union organisers who contravened the new laws into prison. He was then appointed Lord President of the Council in 1972 but after a period of only a few months was promoted to Home Secretary in the light of the resignation of Reginald Maudling (See Chapter 11 – Barnet). He held the post until 1974 when the Tories were defeated again. He died in 2012.

Anthony Head MP
Peoples History Museum

Carshalton

Brigadier Antony Henry Head MC (Conservative) represented the seat from 1945 to 1960.

10 The Marxist publication continues to exist. It espouses revolutionary politics based on the theories of Leon Trotsky. The International Socialist Group, which now publishes the paper, is the British Section of the Fourth International, which Trotsky founded in 1938.

Born in 1906, he was educated at Eton and Sandhurst Royal Military College before joining the Life Guards in 1937 and becoming a brigade major of the 20th Guards Division three years later. He served on the staff of the Chief of Combined Operations during the Second World War and worked with the Director of Plans for Amphibious Operations, a crucial element of the invasion of Normandy in 1944. A holder of the Military Cross, Head was appointed Secretary of State for War by Churchill in 1951, a position he held until October 1956 when he stood down following the abortive Suez War conducted by Sir Anthony Eden. He never regained ministerial office and in 1960 went to the House of Lords as Viscount Head of Throope in the County of Wiltshire. He died in 1983.

Captain Walter Elliot (Conservative) succeeded Head at a 1960 by-election and represented the seat until 1974 when he retired. Born in 1910, he was educated at the Royal Naval College HMS Conway, and London University where he studied economics before joining the Navy in 1929 where he specialised in naval aviation. An accomplished sportsman, he was a boxing champion in the Navy and played Rugby Union for England. He died in 1988.

Sutton and Cheam

Sidney Horatio Marshall (Conservative) represented the seat from 1945 until 1954. Born in 1883 and (unusually for a Conservative) educated only at elementary schools, Marshall made a business career for himself as a manufacturing chemist and became active in politics locally. He was Chairman of Sutton and Cheam UDC in 1933, its Charter Mayor the following year, and Mayor again from 1936 to 1937. He was also Vice Chairman of Surrey County Council, chairing its Education Committee and in 1938 was appointed chairman of the Sutton and District Juvenile Advisory Committee as well as of the County's Assistance Board, established by the 1934 Unemployment Assistance Act to administer financial support. After its creation as a borough he was an alderman in Sutton and Cheam. He was additionally a member of the London Tribunal for Conscientious Objectors, a body set up after the 1916 Military Service Act introduced conscription to the Armed Forces during Wartime. Such tribunals considered the basis for conscientious objectors to avoid military call-up. Marshall resigned his seat in 1954 and died in 1973.

Sharples 1966 Election Leaflet
Peoples History Museum Manchester

Following Marshall's resignation **Sir Richard Christopher Sharples** (Conservative) won the by-election, remaining the local MP until 1972 when he retired shortly before he died the following year. He was born in 1916 and was subsequently educated at Eton and Sandhurst Military College. Commissioned into the Welsh Guards in 1936, he was military assistant to Field Marshal Montgomery[11] between 1951 and 1953 going on to work in the economic section of the Conservative Party Central Office research department until his election in 1954. He was an assistant Government whip between 1959 and 1961 when he was appointed Parliamentary Secretary at the Ministry of Pensions and National Insurance. In the reshuffle of 1962 he moved in a similar capacity to the Ministry of Public Buildings and Works remaining in post until the 1964 General Election. In Opposition he was a Vice chairman of the Party from 1967, responsible for organisation, and when the Tories returned to power in 1970 he was appointed Minister of State for Home Affairs. He died in 1973.

The 1972 by-election that followed Sharples' retirement was sensationally won by **Graham Norman Tope** (Liberal), the first person from that Party to represent a Surrey based London constituency since 1939. Born in 1943, Tope was educated at the Whitgift School in Croydon. He joined the Young Liberals (then a very radical grouping) and became Chairman of the South East of their England Region in 1971 going on two years later to be National Vice-Chairman. He was employed as an insurance officer. He lost the seat in 1974 but was elected to the Sutton Borough Council going on to become its leader in 1986, serving in that role until 1999. In 1994 he was appointed a Life Peer, Lord Tope of Sutton, and ten years later was elected under the proportional representation system as a London-wide member of the Greater London Authority.

Croydon North, Croydon North West

Sir Henry Urmston Willink (Conservative) was elected at a 1940 by-election and held the seat for eight years until 1948. His principal biographical details are in Chapter 10.

11 As commander of British troops in northern Europe from 1944, Montgomery received the German surrender in 1945. From 1951–58 he was deputy Supreme Commander, Europe.

He was succeeded by **Frederic Walter Harris** (Conservative) who from 1950 until 1970 represented the successor constituency of Croydon North West. Born in 1915, he was educated at Belmont College, Streatham. A farm owner in Kenya and chairman of several companies he was previously a member of the Croydon Borough Council. Harris retired in 1970 and died in 1979.

Robert Taylor MP
Peoples History Museum

He was succeeded in 1970 by **Robert George Taylor** (Conservative), a former Sussex County Rugby player who was educated at Cranleigh, founded in 1865 as a boys' boarding school, and went into business as an architectural ironmonger becoming a director of Glasgow based G and S Allgood Ltd, and chairman of its property and South African subsidiaries. Though privately educated himself and a Deputy Chairman of the Public Schools Club after 1966, he was a governor of a Battersea Comprehensive school between 1961 and 1970 during which period he was also politically active in that area. He unsuccessfully contested Battersea North in 1959 and 1964 but after his return at Croydon North West in 1970 remained its MP until October 1981 when he died.

Croydon South/Croydon West

Lieutenant-Colonel David Rees Rees-Williams (Labour) won the Croydon South seat in 1945 and held it for a single Parliament. Born in 1903 and a native of Bridgend, Glamorgan, he was educated at Mill Hill School and the University of Wales in Cardiff after which he qualified as a solicitor. From 1930 to 1935 he was a member of the Straits Settlements Bar[12] and from 1935 to 1945 Clerk to the Cardiff Assessment Committee. He married the daughter of a Lord Mayor of Cardiff. During the Second World War he was a Staff Officer, First Grade in the Royal Artillery, including a period as Chief Legal Adviser to the Berlin Military Government. In 1946 he was appointed Under Secretary for the Colonies, a post he held until his defeat in 1950 when he fought the successor West Croydon constituency. He retired from politics and died in 1976.

He was defeated in 1950 by **Sir Richard Hilton MarlerThompson** (Conservative) who represented the successor Croydon West constituency until 1955 when he transferred to the restored Croydon South which he represented until 1966, and then again from 1970 until 1974. Born in 1912 and educated at Malvern College, in India, Burma and Ceylon, after leaving school he worked in Calcutta but in 1940 enlisted as an ordinary seaman in the Royal Navy rising to the rank of Lieutenant-Commander, serving on HMS Hermione when the ship was sunk on a convoy mission to Malta. After the War he became a director of two publishing companies and subsequently joined the Boards of bus companies, Rediffusion Television and the Capital and Counties Property Company of which he was made Deputy Chairman in 1966, following his defeat at Croydon by the slim margin of 81 votes. He won it back in 1970 with a majority of 3,703 votes. From 1956-7 he was Vice Chamberlain of the Household and then Parliamentary Secretary at the Ministry of Health until 1959 when, after the election of that year, he was made Under-Secretary at the Commonwealth Relations Office, transferring to a similar role at the Ministry of Works from 1960 to 1962. He died in 1999.

David Julian Winnick (Labour) served as Croydon South's MP only from 1966 to 1970 when he was defeated but was subsequently elected for Walsall North in 1979 being re-elected at subsequent elections. He previously contested Harwich (Essex) unsuccessfully in 1964. Born in 1933 in Brighton, he was a wartime evacuee who subsequently obtained a diploma in Social Administration at the London School of Economics and became an advertising manager for the Tribune newspaper from 1963-66. He was a Croydon councillor from 1959-66. In March 2013 he announced his intention to seek re-election for Walsall North at the next general election, presumed to be held in 2015 at which point in time he would be aged 82.

Croydon East, Croydon North East

Sir Herbert Geraint Williams (Conservative) was first elected at a 1932 by-election in the former Croydon South and then in 1945 for the new East division, which he retained until he died in 1954. His principal biographical details are in Chapter 10.

He was succeeded at the 1954 by-election that followed his death by **Vice-Admiral John Hughes-Hallett** (Conservative) who held the seat until he retired in 1964. He was born in 1901 and educated at Bedford Grammar School, at Osborne and Dartmouth Naval Colleges, then at Cauis College, Cambridge before going on to the Royal Naval College at Greenwich. He commanded the raid on Dieppe in the Second World War (in which his fellow MP, Robert Ryder – Merton and Morden – also took part) and was the Naval Chief of Staff for the planning of the invasion of Normandy in 1944. In 1953 he undertook his last active naval command as Flag Officer of the Heavy Squadron operating

12 The Straights Settlements refers to British Territories around the Malacca Straights in Malaysia and Singapore.

mostly from HMS Eagle, an aircraft carrier. Hughes-Hallett retired in 1964 and died eight years later.

Bernard Weatherill MP Speaker of the House
Wikipedia

Sir (Bruce) Bernard Weatherill (Conservative) took over in 1964 and remained the constituency's MP until 1992 when he went to the Lords. Born in Guildford in 1920, he was educated at Malvern College before entering the family sports tailoring business as an apprentice at the age of 17, going on to be its managing director in 1958 and Chairman in 1967. He served in the Army for 7 years during the War, mostly as a Captain in the Far East, in India and Burma. He became a Freeman of the City of London in 1948 being a member of three Livery Companies – the Merchant Taylors, Blacksmiths and Gold and Silver Wyre Drawers. Chairman of the Guildford Conservative Association from 1959-64 and a member of the Party's National Union from 1963-4, he sat on the Opposition benches until 1970 when he was appointed a Government whip initially as Lord Commissioner of the Treasury, then in 1972 Comptroller of the Household, and was appointed Deputy Chief Whip in 1973. He remained in that position also in Opposition throughout the Labour Government from 1974 to 1979 when he was elected Deputy Speaker and Chairman of Ways and Means. Following the 1983 general election he was elected the 154th Speaker of the House of Commons, a post he held for two Parliaments. In 1992 he was made Lord Weatherill of North East Croydon in the Borough of Croydon and became a crossbencher, as befits a former Speaker, going on to become a convenor of the crossbench group of peers. In 1999 he played a crucial facilitation role in successfully seeking to achieve a compromise with the Labour Government on retaining a limited number of hereditary peers in a reformed Upper House. He was made a Deputy Lieutenant of Kent in 1994. He died in 2007.

Surrey East

Captain Michael Langhorne Astor (Conservative) was elected in 1945 and sat until 1951 when he stood down. The third son of the Second Viscount and Nancy Astor, the first woman MP, he was born in 1916 then educated at Eton and New College, Oxford where he read Agriculture and Political Economy. He joined the Territorial Army in 1938 and during the Second World War served in Europe, partly in the "Phantom" Regiment as a Captain attached to Field Marshal Montgomery's HQ. In 1946 he was made a director of Westminster Airways. Married in 1942, many years later in 1969 he adopted Joshua, the birth son of Joe Kagan, an industrialist who was on friendly terms with Harold Wilson, the Labour Prime Minister at the time, and there ensued a custody dispute that left the boy a ward of court throughout his childhood. Michael Astor died in 1980.

Clark 1983 Election Leaflet for Croydon South
Peoples History Museum Manchester

He was succeeded in 1951 by **Charles John Addison Doughty** (Conservative), who retired in 1970. Doughty was born in 1902 and following an Eton education attended Magdalen College, Oxford after which he was called to the bar by the Inner Temple in 1926. A Queens Councillor in 1954, he was appointed Recorder of Brighton. In 1950 he had unsuccessfully contested the Aston division of Birmingham. He died in 1973.

From 1966 to 1974 **Major Sir William Gibson Haigue Clarke** (Conservative) represented Surrey East but then transferred to Croydon South when parts of his former seat were transferred to Greater London. He remained the MP until his retirement in 1992. Born in 1917 and educated at a London Secondary School, he qualified as a certified accountant. During the War he rose from the rank of private in 1941 to that of Major at the time of his demobilisation in 1946. He sat on Wandsworth Borough Council between 1949 and 1953 and was vice-chairman of its Finance Committee. In 1955 he unsuccessfully contested Northampton but was returned at Nottingham South in 1959, a seat he held until 1966 when Labour took it back. Although a loyal backbencher he never attained any kind of ministerial office, concentrating on cultivating his links with business. He was a consultant to the Commercial Union Assurance Company, the Life Assurance Association, Texaco and Tate and Lyle. Following his retirement from the Commons he was ennobled. He died in 2004.

Chapter 15
Middlesex since 1974

1974 - 1983: Greater London Authority Boundaries Fully Reflected in the Second Periodic Review

Although the London Government Act of 1963 had established a new local government structure, it was not until the General Election of February 1974 that Parliamentary constituencies took these changes into account. These were proposed following the Second Periodic Review, undertaken by the Boundary Commission for England which made its recommendations to Parliament in 1969. As far as Middlesex was concerned this meant that it had ceased to exist as a local government entity, and its former councils were replaced by fifteen new London Boroughs and part of one other. The following table summarises the changes that occurred.

Old Council Areas in Middlesex	New Boroughs	Remarks
City of London (Corporation)	*City of London*	*No change*
Marylebone, Paddington, Westminster (Boroughs)	*City of Westminster*	*3-way amalgamation*
Chelsea, Kensington (Boroughs)	*Kensington & Chelsea*	*2-way amalgamation*
Fulham, Hammersmith (Boroughs)	*Hammersmith & Fulham*	*2-way amalgamation*
Acton, Ealing, Southall (Boroughs)	*Ealing*	*3-way amalgamation*
Brentwood & Chiswick, Heston & Isleworth (Boroughs), Feltham (UDC)	*Hounslow*	*3-way amalgamation*
Twickenham (UDC)	*Richmond*	*3-way amalgamation also involving Surrey (see Ch18)*
Staines UDC and Sunbury UDC	*Spelthorne (Surrey)*	*Not in London*
Uxbridge, Hayes & Harlington, Ruislip-Northwood, Yiewsley & West Drayton (UDCs)	*Hillingdon*	*4-way amalgamation*
Harrow (Borough)	*Harrow*	*No change*
Wembley, Willesden (Boroughs)	*Brent*	*2-way amalgamation*
Finsbury, Islington (Boroughs)	*Islington*	*2-way amalgamation*
Holborn, St. Pancras, Hampstead	*Camden*	*3-way amalgamation*
Barnet , East Barnet, Friern Barnet (UDCs), Finchley, Hendon (Boroughs)	*Barnet*	*5-way amalgamation also involving Hertfordshire*
Bethnal Green, Poplar, Stepney (Boroughs)	*Tower Hamlets*	*3-way amalgamation*
Hackney, Shoreditch, Stoke Newington (Boroughs)	*Hackney*	*3-way amalgamation*
Enfield, Edmonton, Southgate (Boroughs)	*Enfield*	*3-way amalgamation*
Hornsey, Tottenham, Wood Green (Boroughs)	*Haringey*	*3-way amalgamation*

As a result of the Review a big reduction in the inner London, former LCC Middlesex boroughs occurred. East and West Central London were affected the most, but seats were lost in the outer suburban areas as well. The new total of 43 Middlesex constituencies was 8 fewer than in 1955 and the lowest since before 1885.

Left: *Much of Kensington is still characterised by splendid Victorian Mansions, such as this one on the corner of Stanley Crescent and Kensington Park Gardens in Notting Hill. Solid Tory territory.*

Below: Arthur Henderson House (named after one of the Labour Party's founding fathers) was council built in the Fulham Rd to provide accommodation for what at the time was a working class population. Margaret Thatcher's Government introduced a "right to buy" scheme for such homes, and today these sell to middle class residents at high prices. The changing composition of the electorate has also changed the politics of Fulham which in 2010 was paired with the even more affluent Chelsea when it was the 6th safest Tory seat in the country.

Below: *Built in the 'brutalist' style on London's last bomb site in the 1960s and 70s, the massive Barbican Estate houses over 4,500 residents, with 'all-mod cons', and superb amenities. Its voters share their MP with neighbouring Westminster, and also gained the right to buy their flats from the City of London Corporation.*

Above: *This Food Store in South Street, Southall offers provisions to cater for the tastes of a large population of ethnic Asian residents who comprise over two thirds of the population in this area of West London. Since 1992 the constituency's MPs have been of Asian ethnicity.*

Left: *Much development in London since the 1960s has come in the form of flats. Those depicted here surround the shopping precinct in Feltham Town Centre which has been in the Feltham & Heston constituency since 1974.*

All pictures John Nelson, unless otherwise attributed.

Central London - City of London and Westminster (3 seats 1974-83)

Overall one seat was lost compared with 1950 and four since 1945. Within the new borough the **St Marylebone** constituency was unaltered but the two former North and South divisions of **Paddington** were amalgamated and even though its boundaries did not change, the former City of London & Westminster constituency was re-named **The City of London & Westminster South**, a designation that more accurately described it in the geographical context of the new borough. The communities contained within these constituencies are described in Chapter 11.

West London - Kensington, Chelsea, Hammersmith, Fulham; West Middlesex (19 seats 1974-83)

The combined impact of the 1974 changes was to reduce the number of seats by five since 1950, although the comparison with 1945 was only two fewer. Two seats were lost in the two boroughs closest to Central London. **Chelsea** gained five wards south of Kensington High Street, covering Earls Court and West Brompton from Kensington South, but was otherwise unaltered. The remainder of Kensington South was amalgamated with the former North division to form **Kensington**, which contained Holland Park, Kensal Green, Ladbroke Grove, Latimer Road, Notting Hill Gate, and West Kilburn.

Hammersmith, Fulham acquired Barons Court, West Kensington, Margravine, and Lillie Road from the former Barons Court constituency, which was abolished. It covered the area between Hammersmith Bridge, the Broadway, Talgarth Road, and the Thames. Four districts were covered by thirteen wards: West Kensington (Avonmore); Barons Court (Gibbs Green, Normand, Margravine, and Crabtree); Walham Green (Walham, Sands End, Eel Brook); Hurlingham (Sulivan, Palace), and Parsons Green (Colehill, Sherbrooke and Town). The new **Hammersmith North** was an amalgamation of all the former constituency's wards, plus the remaining districts of the former Barons Court division lying north of Hammersmith Broadway. North to south the districts covered by ten wards were: Wormwood Scrubs (College Park and Old Oak); Shepherds Bush (Wormholt, Conigham, White City, and Shepherds Bush); Brook Green (Addison and Brook Green); Ravenscourt (Starch Green and Ravenscourt), and Hammersmith (Grove, Broadway and Olympia).

Significant changes were made to electoral boundaries within the new London Borough of Ealing. Population decline relative to electoral quotas brought about a reduction of one seat, effectively Ealing South. **Ealing, Acton** acquired most of Perivale, and Hanger Hill north of the Uxbridge Road from Ealing North, Ealing Common from Ealing South, together with all Acton wards. Its seven new wards were Pitshanger, Hanger Lane, Ealing Common, Victoria (North Acton), Vale (East Acton), Springfield (Acton Town), Southfield (Bedfont Park) and Heathfield (South Acton). **Ealing North** extended from the Uxbridge Road between Ealing Broadway and Hanwell stations, north to Perivale, Greenford, Northolt and Horsenden. Its nine wards were Argyle (Drayton Green), Hobbayne (Castle Bar), Perivale, Costons (Greenford), Horsenden, Ravenor, West End (Yeading Lane), Mandeville (Northolt) and Wood Green (Northolt Park). Of **Ealing, Southall**'s eight wards, two (Northfield and Walpole) covering Little Ealing, Northfields and Ealing were acquired from Ealing South, and the remaining six, with minor adjustments, comprised the whole of the former Southall constituency. These were: Elthorne (also covering Hanwell and Elthorne Heights); Dormers Wells (including Norwood Green); Waxlowe (Greenford Park); Northcote, Mount Pleasant, and Glebe (Southall proper including Hyde Green).

Within Hounslow two constituencies were created, neither taking any part of their designations from the new borough's name. **Brentford & Isleworth** still incorporated Chiswick and most of Hounslow. The constituency embraced eleven new wards which, east to west, were: Turnham Green (including Stamford Brook West); Homefields and Riverside (Chiswick); Gunnersbury (including Kew Bridge); Clifden (Brentford Central and Boston Manor Park); Isleworth North (Syon Park), Isleworth South (Isleworth village); Spring Grove (Osterley Park); Hounslow Central, and South. **Feltham & Heston,** the latter having formerly been paired with Isleworth, lay west of the other Hounslow constituency, and comprised: Hounslow West (including Lampton Park), and Heath; Heston (East, Central and West wards); Cranford, East Bedfont (including Hatton Cross), Feltham (North, Central, and South wards), and Hanworth.

Twickenham remained unaltered but was transferred to a new Borough of Richmond-on-Thames, the east bank of which had formerly been in Surrey.

In the newly established Hillingdon Borough, **Uxbridge** passed all of Heathrow Airport to **Hayes & Harlington** and **Ruislip-Northwood** was unaltered . As with Hounslow none of them acquired any part of their designation from the new borough's name. Harrow borough boundaries and seats were basically unchanged; namely **Harrow Central, Harrow East,** and **Harrow West.** Details are in Chapter 11.

The creation of Brent, combining the former Wembley and Willesden boroughs, once separated by the river whose name came to unite them, meant that when redistribution occurred the new seats did bear the new name and were designated geographically. However, in the process there was a reduction of one seat overall. **Brent North** was the wealthiest of the three constituencies and combined the former Wembley North with most of Sudbury and Wembley Park from Wembley South. The seat covered ten wards in all - the parts of Kenton (Northwick Park) and Queensbury that were not part of Harrow borough; Roe Green; Kingsbury, Fryent (including Kingsbury Green); St Andrew's and Barnhill (Wembley Park); Preston (South Kenton and North Wembley); Sudbury Court and Sudbury.

Brent East was extended from Dollis Hill and Neasden to Kilburn and Kensal Rise. Of its eleven new wards most were formerly in Willesden East except parts of Neasden, Willesden Green and Queens Park, which had all formerly been in Willesden West. The new wards were Brentwater and Gladstone (Dollis Hill); Church End (Neasden); Cricklewood; Willesden Green; Mapesbury (Brondesbury); Brondesbury Park; Chamberlayne (Kensal Rise East); Kilburn; Carlton (Kilburn Park); and Queens Park. **Brent South** covered the rest of the borough fanning out west from Kensal Rise to Wembley Central and Alperton on the borders of neighbouring Ealing near Park Royal. Its eleven wards were Kensal Rise (mainly comprising Kensal Green); Manor (Kensal Rise west); Harlesden; Roundwood (Willesden); Stonebridge (Park Royal); St Raphael's (Stonebridge); Alperton; Tokyngton (Wembley Hill); Wembley Central and Barham (Sudbury Town). The last four wards were allocated from Wembley South and the remainder from Willesden West.

North London (10 seats 1974-83)

The new Boroughs comprising North London were Islington, Camden, and Barnet, but the amalgamations brought about no change in the number of seats, which remained ten.

In Camden all three constituencies (**Hampstead, St Pancras North** and **Holborn & St Pancras South**) were unchanged, but Islington was altered to take account of the abolition of the Shoreditch & Finsbury constituency, the retention of which would have contravened the new rule about seats not straddling different boroughs. As before **Islington North** covered the Tuffnell Park and Upper Holloway areas including Archway but acquired Hillmartin (part of Lower Holloway around the Caledonian Road) additionally from the South West division. A new **Islington Central** comprised most of the former East constituency (Arsenal, Drayton Park, Highbury, Mildmay, Essex Road and Canonbury) and gained (Lower) Holloway ward from the former South West division. **Islington South & Finsbury** comprised Barnsbury and Upper Street from Southwest together with Clerkenwell and Bunhill from the former Shoreditch & Finsbury seat. It also included the south end of Caledonian Road near Kings Cross station, Clerkenwell, Farringdon, the Golden Lane estate, Pentonville including the Pentonville Road and the Angel, Islington.

The new London borough of Barnet comprised five former council areas. Finchley and Hendon boroughs with the Friern Barnet Urban District from Middlesex were joined by the Hertfordshire Urban Districts of East Barnet and Barnet. Four new constituencies were formed, each comprising five of the new borough's wards. **Chipping Barnet** incorporated Arkley (including the South Barnet Underhill district and Chipping Barnet itself); Hadley (including Hadley Green, North, High and New Barnet); East Barnet; Brunswick Park (also in East Barnet); and Totteridge (including Woodside Park), which was mostly acquired from the former Finchley seat. Of these all but Hadley Green, New Barnet and Woodside Park had formerly been in Hertfordshire, but were transferred to London in 1965. Communities that remained within Hertfordshire, and that had formerly been part of the Barnet constituency, were transferred to new South Hertfordshire or Welwyn-Hatfield divisions. These included Borehamwood, Elstree, and South Mimms.

Finchley incorporated Friern Barnet (Oakleigh Park and Whetstone); Woodhouse (Colney Hatch and Coppetts Wood); East Finchley; Finchley (Central) and Church End (West Finchley). The eastern part of the [Hampstead] Garden Suburb ward was transferred to Hendon South, which also acquired West Hendon from Hendon North in exchange for Mill Hill East. **Hendon North** also comprised five new wards –Edgware; Hale (Watling Street and Mill Hill Broadway); Mill Hill; Burnt Oak and Colindale. **Hendon South** comprised Garden Suburb; Childs Hill; Golders Green; Hendon; and West Hendon.

The East End and North East London (11 seats 1974-83)

The overall impact in East and North East London was the loss of one seat; reductions in docklands and Enfield being partially offset by the creation of a new Hackney based seat with the transfer of Shoreditch into that borough.

In the new London borough of Tower Hamlets the three former constituencies were reduced to two in 1974, then

Left: *Late Twentieth Century blocks of flats around Cricklewood Broadway mark the three way boundary between Hendon (South), Hampstead, and Brent (East). Southern parts of Brent in Kilburn were combined with Hampstead in 2010 and Cricklewood was transferred to Brent Central.*

Below: These flats on The Burroughs housed voters of the Hendon South constituency until 1997 when it was combined with Hendon North.

Below: *Close to the Barbican estate, but just outside the City is cosmopolitan Whitecross Street. Central to an area of dense local authority and housing trust flats, it has been in the Islington South & Finsbury Constituency since 1974.*

Above: *Islington Town Hall in Upper Street, in the centre of the borough, is the point where election results for the borough's two constituencies are announced. Islington has the highest population density of all local authorities in England and Wales. From a low-point of 157k residents in 1981, the population has risen steadily to 216k in 2013.*

Left: *These private flats overlooking Kingsbury Green were transferred from Wembley North to Brent North and have remained in that constituency since 1974.*

All pictures John Nelson, unless otherwise attributed.

the area's lowest representation since before 1868. **Bethnal Green & Bow** retained the former Bethnal Green constituency wards, but lost the Victoria Park and Wick areas of Hackney that had been acquired in 1955, and which were returned to Hackney Central. Bethnal Green & Bow also acquired the northern portion of the former Poplar constituency, and extended overall from the City of London boundary at Aldgate, northeast to Victoria Park, comprising eight wards north of the Whitechapel Road, and Bromley ward to the south. The other wards were: Spitalfields; Weavers and St Peter's (Roman Road and North East Bethnal Green); St James' (Cambridge Heath); Holy Trinity (Globe Town); Park (Old Ford), and Bow. **Stepney & Poplar** was an amalgamation of the southern portion of Poplar with the former Stepney constituency. The new division extended south of the Whitechapel Road to the Thames and incorporated ten wards – St Katherine's (Wapping); St Mary (Whitechapel); Shadwell; Redcoat and St Dunstan's (Stepney and Mile End); Blackwall, Lansbury and East India (Poplar); Limehouse; and Millwall (The Isle of Dogs). These also included Ratcliffe and Shadwell, the West India Docks and West Ferry.

Hackney incorporated the former borough of that name together with Stoke Newington and Shoreditch; the inclusion of the latter enabling three constituencies to be created. **Hackney South & Shoreditch** covered seven wards, five based on the former Shoreditch borough - Moorfields; Wenlock (Hoxton); De Beavoir Town; Haggerston; and Queensbridge (also Haggerston) – and two drawn from Hackney – Dalston and (Victoria)Park (South Hackney). Homerton and central districts including Hackney Downs were transferred to **Hackney Central** which comprised eight wards – West Down, Rectory and East Down (Hackney Downs); Leabridge (Lower Clapton); Homerton and Chatham (also Homerton); Kings Park (Clapton and the Marshes) and Hackney Wick. **Hackney North & Stoke Newington** covered the remainder of the borough and also incorporated eight wards – Brownswood; New River; Northfield; North and South Defoe; and Clissold (all districts of Stoke Newington) together with Northwold (Upper Clapton) and Springfield (Stamford Hill).

In North East London Enfield Borough was affected by boundary changes whilst neighbouring Haringey was not. There the three constituencies remained unchanged – **Hornsey, Wood Green** and **Tottenham,** none taking the new borough's designation. However, significant adjustments were made in Enfield Borough, which lost one of its four constituencies. This was in part due to the transfer of Potters Bar (formerly in Enfield West) to South Hertfordshire.

Enfield North acquired ten wards, incorporating the area from Enfield Chase to the River Lea as far south as Ponders End. It included from the former Enfield East, Green Street (Brimsdown), Worcesters (Bulls Cross), Durants Park, Town, and Willow wards (Enfield Central); Enfield Wash and Enfield Lock, including Enfield Highway and Turkey Street, Ponders End and Southbury, together with Enfield Chase ward (Gordon Hill and Clay Hill); Bullsmore (between Bulls Cross and Southbury), and Willow (Forty Hill), acquired from the former Enfield West.

Enfield, Southgate acquired some of the south-western parts of the former West division, including Cockfosters and Hadley Wood in the Trent [Park] ward. Ten other wards comprised the former Southgate borough: Oakwood and Merryhills (Oakwood); Grange Park [Hill]; Highfield, Grovelands, and Winchmore Hill; Palmers Green; Southgate Green; Arnos (New Southgate); and Bowes (Park). **Edmonton** extended south of Ponders End and diagonally from Bush Hill Park to Angel Road on the Tottenham border. It included all wards of the former borough seat. There were eleven wards in total: Raglan, Village, St Mark's and Jubilee (Bush Hill Park); St Alphege and St Peter's (Picket's Lock); Latymer, Huxley and Craig Park (Lower Edmonton); Weir Hall (Sliver Street), and Angel [Road].

1983-97: The Third Periodic Review

The third review of the Boundary Commission reported on 1st February 1983, and further seat reductions in Middlesex followed at the June Election, in the same year. The overall impact was significant. A further reduction of six seats (nearly 14%) gave a new total of 37.

Central London – City of London and Westminster (Reduced from 3 to 2 seats)

Marylebone's famous constituency name disappeared for the first time since 1832 and was merged with parts of Westminster, including Paddington, the name of which also disappeared for the first time since 1885. Five wards of the former Paddington seat were allocated to **Westminster North:** Queen's Park; Harrow Road including Kensal Town ; Latimer Road; Maida Vale including Maida Hill; Little Venice and Westbourne [Park] - together with four former Marylebone wards north of the Euston Road: Church Street (Lisson Grove), Hamilton Terrace, Lords, and Regents Park (St John's Wood).

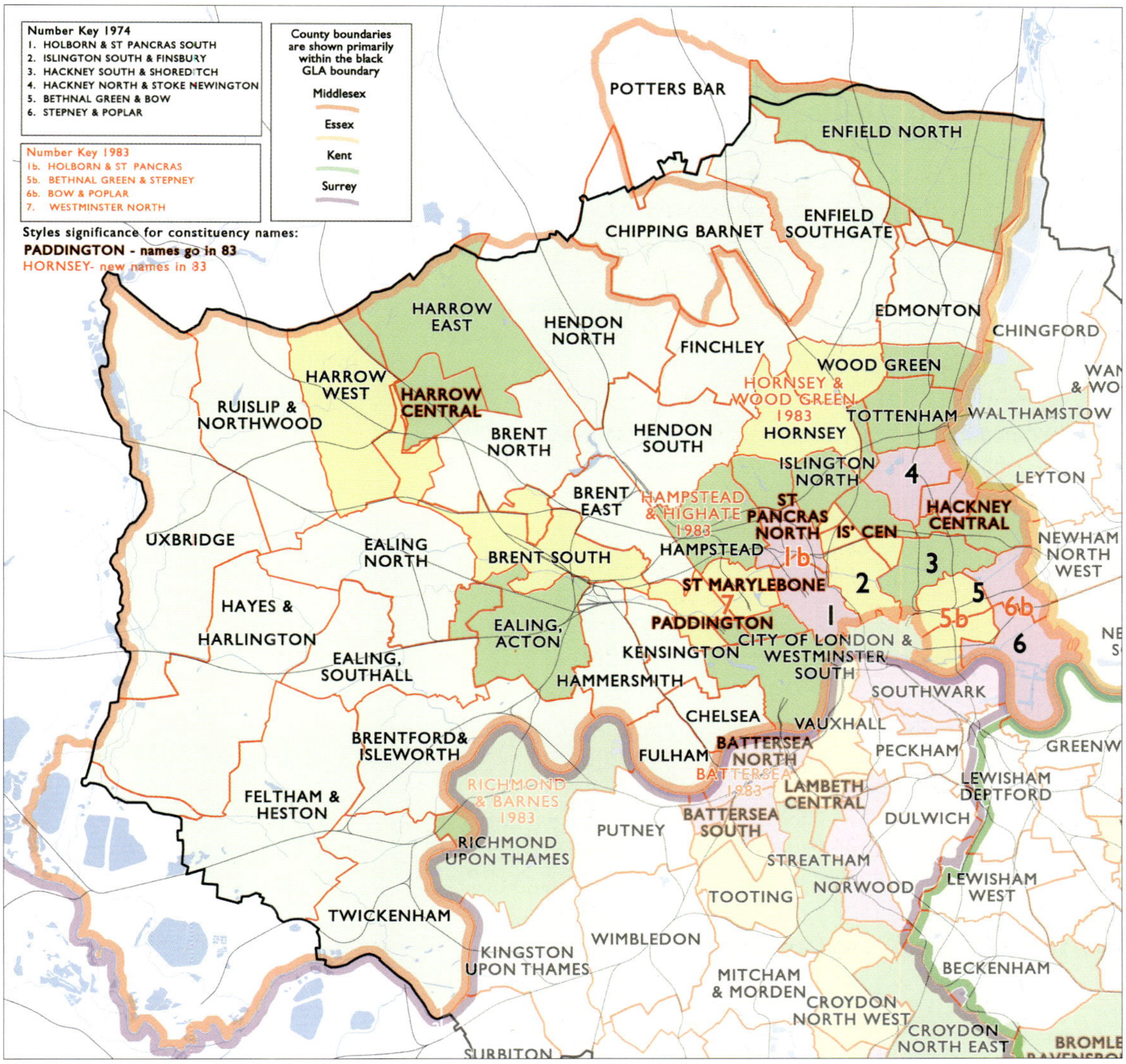

The map depicts Middlesex constituencies created in 1974, and those that were modified in 1983. The number of seats in Inner London was again reduced, compared with 1974. Seats were eliminated in Camden, Haringey, Hackney, Islington, and Westminster. In the suburbs Harrow (Cen) was lost, and there were minor ward transfers in Brent and Ealing. St Margarets in Twickenham was paired with Richmond in Surrey.

The area between Lancaster Gate and Langham Place north of the Bayswater Road and Oxford Street, and south of the Euston Road was transferred from St Marylebone to the **City of London & Westminster South** constituency. It combined three former Paddington wards: Bayswater, Hyde Park, and Lancaster Gate, with three from Marylebone: Baker Street (Marylebone proper), Bryanston (Square), and Cavendish (Square) including Fitzrovia and Harley Street, and nine from the former Cities of London and Westminster: the City itself (extending from the boundary with Tower Hamlets at Aldgate as far west as the Temple); St James's (Strand and Westminster including Whitehall); West End (including Soho and Mayfair); Knightsbridge; Belgrave; Churchill and St George's (Pimlico); Millbank, and Victoria (including the Houses of Parliament).

West London - Kensington, Chelsea, Hammersmith, Fulham; West Middlesex (Reduced from 19 to 18 seats)

Harrow's constituencies were the only ones in the entire area to be affected. Harrow Central was abolished, the borough reverting to its 1945 status of two constituencies. **Harrow East** acquired three wards from Central. These were Greenhill (formerly coupled with Harrow-on- the Hill); Wealdstone (formerly Wealdstone North), and Marlborough (Wealdstone South). The rest of the constituency was unchanged, comprising seven more wards: Canons (Brockley Hill and Canons Park, Stanmore); Stanmore Park (Stanmore proper); Wemborough (Stanmore South/Canons Park West); Stanmore South (Queensbury/Little Stanmore); Harrow Weald; Kenton East, and West. **Harrow West** incorporated the Ridgeway ward (Harrow West) from the former Central seat and retained other districts represented by Headstone North and South; Hatch End; Pinner West; Pinner (Harrow Garden Village); Rayners Lane; Roxbourne, and Roxeth (South Harrow). The only other alteration was a name change. Hammersmith North lost its orientation description and was renamed simply **Hammersmith**. Its boundaries were unaltered.

Left: This is a view of the busy Broadway at Wood Green. It was a constituency in its own right until 1983 when it was combined with Hornsey. With the Piccadilly Line Wood Green station at one end, it has Turnpike Lane at the other, as well as the electrified line into Kings Cross down the road. Wood Green is a bustling suburb.

Below: The flats seen here overlook the reservoirs at Stoke Newington. They are in the Hackney North & Stoke Newington constituency created in 1974 but are very close to the boundary with Tottenham

Below: *Much of Edmonton's terraced housing was replaced with flats in the 1970s, such as these at Edmonton Green*

Above: *Hoxton was in the borough of Shoreditch but when this was transferred to Hackney it found itself in the new Hackney South & Shoreditch constituency in which it has remained since 1974. These local authority built flats are typical of the area and are sandwiched between Hoxton Street and Kingsland Road.*

Left: These council flats in the Old Ford district of Tower Hamlets are close to the boundary at Hackney Wick and were placed in the Bethnal Green & Bow Constituency in 1974. Old Ford transferred to Bow and Poplar between 1983 and 1997 when it was restored to its original home. The houseboats also accommodate electors.

All pictures John Nelson, unless otherwise attributed.

North London (Reduced from 10 to 8 seats)

In North London Camden and Islington Boroughs each lost a seat. Islington Central was merged with parts of the former North and South & Finsbury divisions. **Islington North** gained four wards southeast of Finsbury Park: Gillespie (Arsenal and Drayton Park); Highbury; Quadrant, and Mildmay (including the Canonbury Station area) from the former Central division. These were combined with existing electorates in Archway (Hillrise); Crouch Hill (Highview ward); Upper Holloway (Junction, St, George's and Sussex wards); and Tollington ward, covering the area between Finsbury Park and Upper Hollway north of Seven Sisters Road. **Islington South & Finsbury** acquired the two Canonbury wards either side of Essex Road, and Hillmarton covering Lower Holloway. It retained all other former electorates in Lower Hollway around the Caldeonian Road (Holloway ward);Thornhill ward (Caledonian Road south); Barnsbury (including Pentonville); Upper Street (St Mary); Angel (St Peter); Bunhill Fields (including Golden Lane), and Clerkenwell (Farringdon, Finsbury, and the Pentonville Road).

In Camden the St Pancras North, South & Holborn and Hampstead constituencies were recast and renamed; three seats were reduced to two. The Highgate ward (Dartmouth Park) of the North division was transferred to Hampstead, which was renamed **Hampstead & Highgate.** This also comprised its existing wards of Belsize (Park): Kilburn (Finchley Road); Town, Frognal, and South End (Hampstead Village wards); Highgate (Kenwood with Waterlow Park); Priory (Kilburn Grange Park); Adelaide (South Hampstead); Swiss Cottage; and West End (West Hampstead).The remainder of both former St Pancras constituencies formed a new **Holborn & St Pancras** division that extended south from Gospel Oak to the City border. It incorporated Bloomsbury including London University and St Giles Circus; Camden Town's Caversham and Camden wards; Chalk Farm with Primrose Hill; Corum Fields (Kings Cross ward): Euston (Somers Town ward); Gospel Oak; Hatton Garden (Holborn ward); Kentish Town (Castlehaven, Grafton and St John's wards); Mornington Crescent (Regents Park ward); and St Pancras itself.

The East End and North East London (Reduced from 11 to 9 seats)

Within Tower Hamlets there was no reduction, but the two seats were re-aligned on a north to south axis instead of east to west. Bethnal Green was paired with Stepney and Bow and with Poplar. **Bethnal Green & Stepney** acquired five wards from the former Bethnal Green & Bow constituency north of the Whitechapel Road - Spitalfields; Weavers and St Peter's (Bethnal Green North East); St James' (Cambridge Heath); and Holy Trinity (Globe Town). These were joined with four former Stepney & Poplar wards - St Katherine's (including Wapping, the Tower of London and Aldgate); St Mary (Whitechapel); and Redcoat and St Dunstan's (Stepney). The new **Bow & Poplar** constituency covered the remaining Tower Hamlets wards of Grove (Mile End); Park (Old Ford); Bow; Bromley and East India (Bromley by Bow); Blackwall (including Poplar, East and West India Docks); Lansbury (Bow Common); Millwall (The Isle of Dogs, Canary Wharf and Westferry); Limehouse and Shadwell including Ratcliffe. Lansbury ward was named after the former Labour Party Leader and MP for Bow & Bromley, George Lansbury, whose biographical details are in Chapter 3.

In North East London, Hackney and Haringey each lost a seat. As had occurred in Harrow and Islington, the Central seat was abolished in Hackney. Five wards were transferred to the South seat and three to the North. **Hackney South & Shoreditch** acquired Schacklewell (Westdown ward); Homerton and Chatham (also Homerton); Kings Park (Clapton and the Marshes); and Hackney Wick from Central; which were placed with existing electorates in Dalston; De Beavoir (Town and Kingsland); Victoria (Park); Queensbridge; Haggerston; Moorfields; and Wenlock (Hoxton). **Hackney North & Stoke Newington** acquired the remaining wards of the former Central constituency – Rectory (Road) and East Down (Hackney Downs); and Leabridge (Lower Clapton). These were added to the existing electorates in Springfield (Upper Clapton/Stamford Hill East): incorporating Northfield (Stamford Hill West); Northwold; North Defoe; South Defoe (Stoke Newington); Clissold (Park); Brownswood (Finsbury Park), and New River (Lordship Park Manor).

In Haringey Borough, Hornsey, Wood Green and Tottenham were merged and the number of MPs reduced by one. The new two-member status of the Borough saw it divided into western and eastern constituencies. The former was **Hornsey & Wood Green** which comprised twelve wards , incorporated four from Wood Green - Alexandra (Park); Bowes Park; Woodside (Park); and Noel Park – together with nine Hornsey wards - Central; Vale; and South (Hornsey proper); Muswell Hill; Fortis Green; Highgate and Archway (also Highgate); and Crouch End. The eastern Haringey constituency of **Tottenham** gained Harringay from Hornsea and three wards from Wood Green – Park and Coleraine (Northumberland Park); and White Hart Lane together with seven former Tottenham wards – West Green and Bruce Grove (both covering Bruce Grove); High Cross (Tottenham Hale); Green Lanes (Haringay); Tottenham Central; South Tottenham and Seven Sisters.

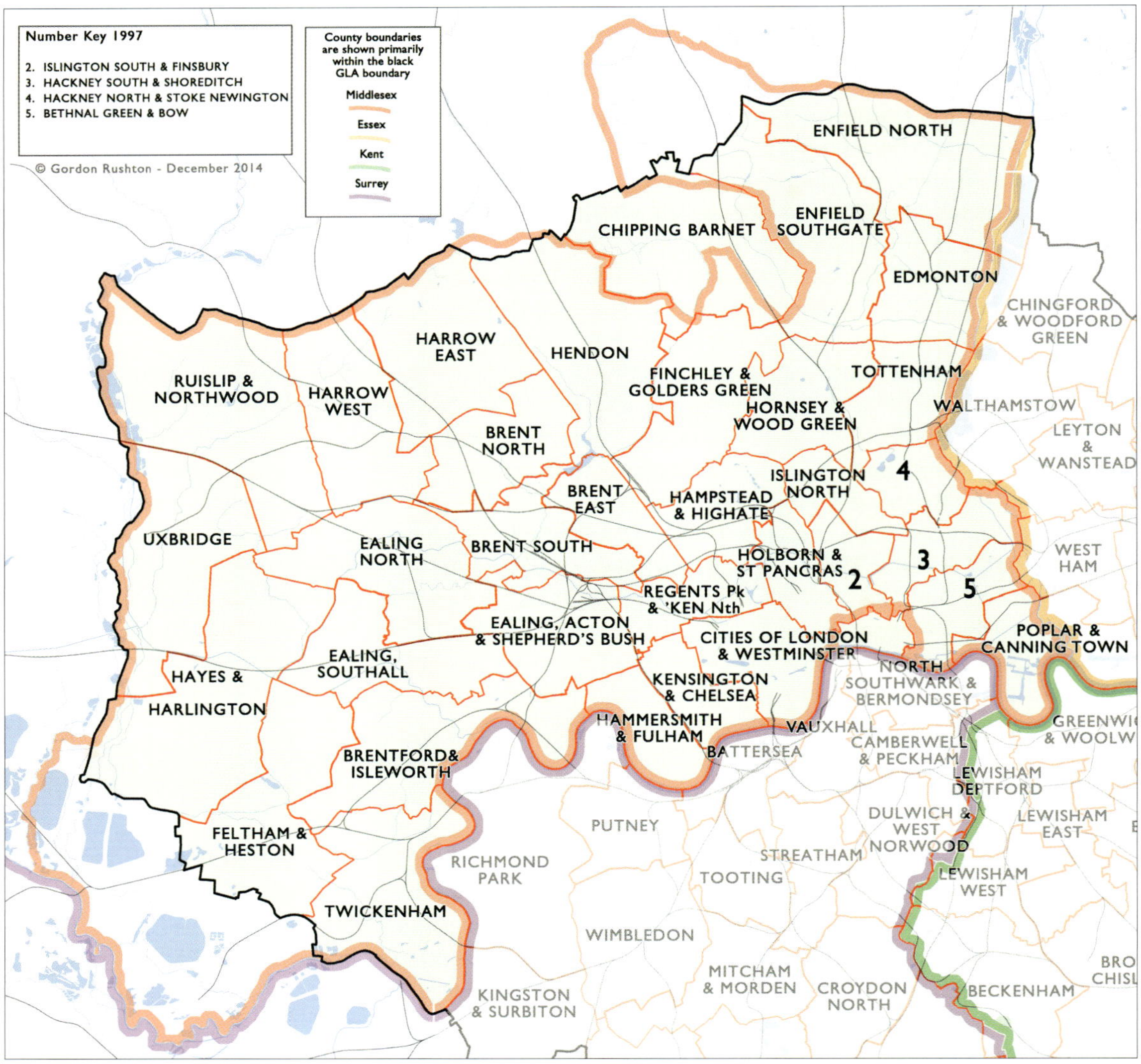

The map depicts Middlesex constituencies created in 1997. The number of seats in Inner London was again reduced compared with 1983. Seats were eliminated in Barnet Borough, and through the merging of others in Ealing, Hammersmith, Kensington & Chelsea, Westminster, and Tower Hamlets. In this latter case, Poplar was merged with adjoining Canning Town in Newham (Essex). Elsewhere there were boundary changes only.

1997-2010: The Fourth Periodic Review

The Boundary Commission next reported in February 1995 and its recommendations were implemented at the 1997 General Election. The impact was to reduce by three the number of MPs representing Middlesex constituencies. This time the rule that constituencies could not straddle more than one borough was changed which meant that a much broader review of boundaries was possible. Most constituencies were affected and the total number remaining was 34.

Central and West London - City of London, Westminster, Kensington, Chelsea, Hammersmith, Fulham; West Middlesex (Reduced from 20 to 18 seats)

Several Central and West London constituencies were considered together. **Kensington & Chelsea** involved the amalgamation of some South Kensington wards with Chelsea, which lost its single place name designation for the first time since it was established in 1867. The new constituency comprised sixteen wards altogether. Holland and Norland (Holland Park); Pembridge (Notting Hill Gate); Campden and Queens Gate (Kensington proper) from Kensington were combined with the former Chelsea wards of Abingdon (Cromwell Road); Earls Court; Courtfield; Brompton; Church and Hans Town (South Kensington); Royal Hospital; Cheyne and South Stanley (Chelsea riverside); and North Stanley and Redcliffe (Kings Road). The remaining five North Kensington wards were amalgamated with eleven from the former Westminster North division. The resulting constituency was called **Regents Park & Kensington North**. Its Kensington wards were Avondale (Latimer Road); Colville; Golborne; Kelfield (Ladbroke Grove); and St Charles (Kensal Town) to which were added the Westminster wards of Queen's Park; Harrow Road (Maida Hill); Maida Vale; Little Venice; and Westbourne [Park]. These wards embraced districts that included Latimer Road, Church Street (Lisson

Grove), Hamilton Terrace, Lords, and Regents Park (St John's Wood).

These changes enabled a third constituency to be styled **The City of London & Westminster**, comprising fourteen wards and the City from the former Cities of London & Westminster South seat plus Bayswater and Lancaster Gate acquired from Westminster North. The names of the wards taken from the former Cities seat were City of London; St James' (including Aldwych, Charing Cross, Covent Garden, St James' and Whitehall); West End (including Hyde Park, Mayfair and Soho); Knightsbridge (including Kensington Gardens); Belgrave (including Buckingham Palace); Victoria (Westminster itself including the Houses of Parliament); Millbank; Churchill and St George's (both Pimlico). From Westminster North six wards were added, namely Baker Street (including Harley Street); Bayswater; Bryanstone (including Marylebone proper); Cavendish (including Fitzrovia); Hyde Park (Mayfair); and Lancaster Gate.

The southern part of Hammersmith was joined with Fulham and called **Hammersmith & Fulham**. All thirteen wards in the former Fulham seat were joined with five between Goldhawk Road and Hamersmith Broadway – Addison (Brook Green); Brook Green (Olympia); Broadway and Grove (Hammersmith); and Ravenscourt (Park). The Fulham wards were Avonmore (West Kensington); Margravine; Gibbs Green and Normand (Barons Court); Crabtree; Palace and Colehill (Fulham Palace Road); Sulivan (Hurlingham); Eelbrook; Sherbrooke and Town (Parsons Green); Sands End and Walham (Green). Five northern Hammersmith wards - College Park and Old Oak (Wormwood Scrubs); Wormholt; White City & Shepherds Bush; and Conigham (Shepherds Bush) were paired with all but two of the wards in Ealing, Acton. These were Pitshanger and Ealing Common. The new seat straddling Hammersmith and Ealing was called **Ealing, Acton & Shepherds Bush**, comprising all districts of Acton, Bedfont Park, Hanger Lane, Old Oak Common, Park Royal, Shepherds Bush, Starch Green, White City and Wormwood Scrubs.

The creation of this constituency caused boundary changes to the other Ealing seats, which gained the western areas of the former Acton division. Pitshanger (incorporating Ealing Common and North Ealing) was transferred to **Ealing North** which retained all of its previous wards, namely Argyle (Drayton Green); Costons and Ravenor (Greenford); Hobbayne (Elthorne Heights); Horsenden; Mandeville and West End (Northolt). Ealing Common ward, which incorporated Ealing south of the Broadway, was transferred to **Ealing, Southall** which was otherwise unaltered incorporating Dormers Wells ward (including Hyde Green and Norwood Green, south of the Great West Main Line railway); Glebe and Northcote (Southall west); Mount Pleasant; Waxlow (Greenford Park); Elthorne (including Hanwell); Northfield (including Little Ealing); and Walpole (between the Uxbridge Road and Northfields station.

Other West Middlesex seats were little affected. In Brent, Neasden Lane (St Andrew's ward) was transferred from the North to the South division leaving **Brent North** comprising nine wards, namely Queensbury (Northern Kingsbury west of the Edgware Road); Roe Green; Kingsbury; Preston (Road including South Kenton); Kenton; Fryent (Kingsbury Green); Barnhill (Wembley Park); Sudbury Court (including Northwick Park); and Sudbury (including Sudbury Hill). **Brent South** comprised St Andrews (Neasden Lane); Tokyngton (Wembley Park); Wembley Central; Stonebridge (Park); Alperton; Barham (including Sudbury Town); Roundwood and Manor (Willesden); Harlesden and Kensal Rise (including Kensal Green). **Brent East, Harrow East** and **Harrow West** were unaltered.

In Hillingdon Borough the **Hayes & Harlington** constituency was unchanged while the Harefield ward was transferred from Uxbridge to Ruislip & Northwood. **Uxbridge** thus incorporated the wards of Ickenham; Uxbridge North; Uxbridge South; Hillingdon North; Hillingdon East; Hillingdon West; Cowley; Colham (a district between Uxbridge and Yiewsley); Yiewsley; and West Drayton. **Ruislip-Northwood** comprised the ten wards of Harefield; Northwood; Northwood Hills; Eastcote; Ruislip; St Martins (Ruislip Gardens); (Ruislip) Manor; Bourne (the districts surrounding Northolt aerodrome); Cavendish (East Ruislip); and Deansfield (South Ruislip).

In Hounslow borough the Hounslow Heath ward transferred from Feltham & Heston to Brentford & Isleworth and northern parts of Hatton Cross were shifted from Feltham to Hayes & Harlington. **Feltham & Heston** thus comprised three Heston wards (Central, East and West); three from Feltham (Central, North and South); together with Hounslow Heath (including Hounslow West and Lampton Park); Cranford; East Bedfont and Hanworth. **Brentford & Isleworth** comprised ten wards. These were Chiswick Homefields (Stamford Brook West); Turnham Green; Chiswick Riverside; Brentford and Clifden (including Boston Manor); Isleworth North (including Syon Park); and Isleworth (South). **Twickenham** lost the east ward[1] of the town linking it via the Twickenham and Richmond river bridges to the Surrey constituency opposite. Those remaining were 4 Twickenham town wards (Central, East, South, including Strawberry Hill, and West); Whitton with Heathfield, Teddington, Hampton Hill, Hampton including Bushy Park, Hampton Nursery (Marling Park) and Hampton Wick.

1 A small part of St Margarets north of Twickenham Bridge and opposite Old Deer Park, formerly in Brentford and Isleworth, was transferred to the Twickenham East ward at the same time.

North London (Reduced from 8 to 7 seats)

The biggest changes were in Barnet, which lost a seat. **Hendon** was formed out of the whole of the former Hendon North (Burnt Oak, Colindale, Edgware Mill Hill and Mill Hill East) plus the central and western wards of Hendon itself from the former South constituency; the other wards of which – covering Childs Hill, Golders Green and Hampstead Garden Suburb – were combined with the whole of the former Finchley seat except Friern Barnet ward. It retained Church End, Colney Hatch and all districts of Finchley. The constituency was renamed **Finchley & Golders Green. Chipping Barnet** gained Friern Barnet (Oakleigh Park and Whetstone) and retained all its former wards.

Camden Borough saw only minor change, with the transfer of one ward (Gospel Oak) from **Holborn & St Pancras** to **Hampstead & Highgate** whilst in Islington there were no changes: so **Islington North** and **Islington South & Finsbury** remained unaltered compared with 1983.

The East End and North East London (Retained 9 seats)

Hackney North & Stoke Newington, Hackney South & Shoreditch, Tottenham, Hornsey & Wood Green, Enfield North, Enfield Southgate and **Edmonton** all remained unaltered by the Review.

However, the East End lost some representation in docklands as a result of a combined review of seats in Tower Hamlets and neighbouring Newham. Tower Hamlets was left with only one seat wholly within its boundaries, bringing about its lowest level of representation since before 1832. A second seat included districts of Newham, a former Essex borough. **Bethnal Green & Bow** retained all the wards of the 1983 Bethnal Green & Stepney constituency and gained Grove (Mile End); Park (Old Ford); and Bow from Bow & Poplar. **Poplar & Canning Town** retained the remaining wards of the former Bow & Poplar constituency - Bromley; Blackwall, Lansbury and East India (Poplar); Millwall (The Isle of Dogs); Limehouse; and Shadwell; which were joined by Beckton with Ordnance; Canning Town & Grange (all covering Canning Town); together with Custom House & Silvertown from Newham South. Poplar & Canning Town thus became the first London seat to straddle the old Essex-Middlesex border. Since 65.4% of the 64,385 electorate were within Tower Hamlets, this constituency has been included as a Middlesex seat and the reduction is therefore accounted for in Essex (Chapter 16).

2010: The Fifth Periodic Review

The Boundary Commission published its recommendations about future London constituencies during the course of 2001 but the final changes were not implemented until the 2010 general election held on May 6th. Barnet, Ealing, Enfield, Hackney, Haringey, Hounslow, Islington and Tower Hamlets Boroughs were assessed separately. The number and names of constituencies in these boroughs were mostly unchanged except in Ealing and Tower Hamlets. Ealing was again awarded three constituencies; in effect an increase since the borough had been previously paired with Hammersmith & Fulham. Tower Hamlets was once again awarded two, restoring the representation it lost in 1997. Overall the number of Middlesex MPs remained 34.

Central and West London - City of London, Westminster, Kensington, Chelsea, Hammersmith, Fulham; West Middlesex (Reduced from 18 to 17 seats)

Westminster Borough and the City of London were once again returned to single borough status and two seats were allocated. **Westminster North** reappeared taking eight wards from Regents Park & North Kensington; and these were combined with two (Bayswater and Lancaster Gate) from the former City of London & Westminster seat. The others were Queens Park; Harrow Road (Maida Hill); Westbourne; Little Venice (including Warwick Avenue); Maida Vale; Abbey Road and Regents Park (St John's Wood including Lords Cricket Ground); and Church Street (Lisson Grove). However, the ward boundaries were changed somewhat from the former configuration so that the area in the vicinity of Marylebone station was placed in Bryanston & Dorset Square ward which was allocated along with all remaining Westminster borough wards to **The Cities of London & Westminster**. Apart from the loss of Bayswater and Lancaster Gate, this was broadly the same as the former equivalent seat comprising nine more Westminster wards plus the City of London. These are described in the section above relating to the 1997 changes.

In the review Kensington & Chelsea and Hammersmith & Fulham Boroughs were paired. The northern districts of Hammersmith that had been in the Ealing, Acton & Shepherds Bush constituency since 1997 were transferred to **Hammersmith** whilst northern parts of the former Hammersmith & Fulham were also vested in the new seat,

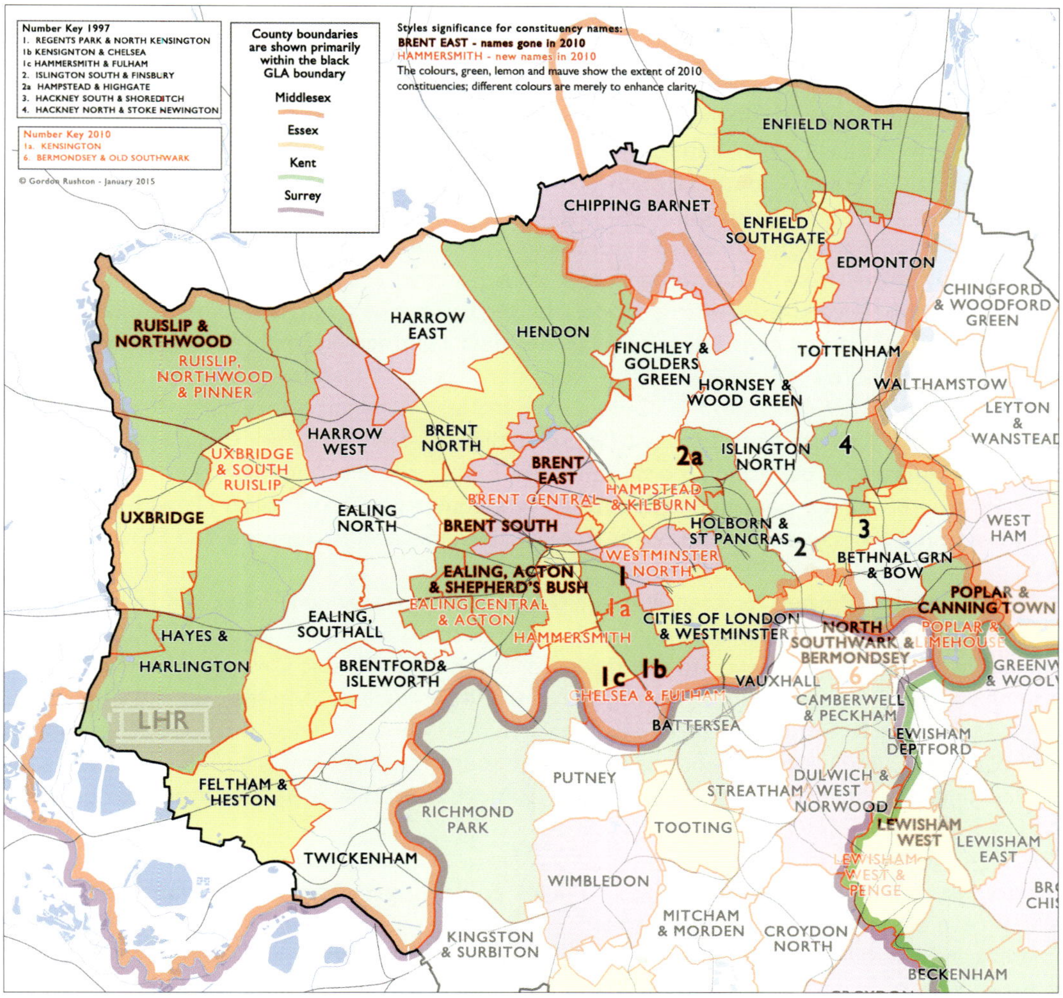

The map depicts Middlesex constituencies created in 2010, when the number of seats was unchanged. Changes against 1997 are highlighted. As before, some boroughs were paired for review, which resulted in seats merging in: Pinner (Harrow) with Ruislip & Northwood (Hillingdon); Kilburn (Brent) with Hampstead (Camden), and Fulham with Chelsea. Ealing and Tower Hamlets Boroughs returned to having seats that were self-contained.

which extended North to South from College Park & Old Oak ward (including Wormwood Scrubs) to Fulham Reach (Margravine) and North End (West Kensington); via Wormholt and White City, Askew (Wendell Park west of Shepherds Bush), Shepherds Bush Green, Ravenscourt Park, Hammersmith Broadway, Addison, Avonmore and Brook Green (including Olympia and Barons Court); the latter five wards coming mainly from Hammersmith & Fulham. Southern districts of Hammersmith & Fulham – essentially Fulham proper – were for the first time since the period 1867- 1885 allied with Chelsea, which was in turn once again largely, though not completely, detached from Kensington. **Chelsea & Fulham** comprised the former Kensington & Chelsea wards of Stanley and Cremone; Redcliffe (Chelsea); Royal Hospital (including Sloane Square); Hans Town and Redcliffe (West Brompton); to which were added the former Hammersmith & Fulham wards of Palace Riverside (Fulham Palace Road, Fulham Palace, Putney Bridge and Hurlingham); Sands End; Parsons Green and Walham (Green); Fulham Broadway (Walham Green); Town and Munster (Parsons Green).

Coupling most of Chelsea with Fulham meant that Kensington was once again detached from its neighbouring Westminster wards with which it had been associated since 1997 in the Regents Park & North Kensington constituency. The new **Kensington** seat comprised north and south parts of Kensington plus three wards in Chelsea, namely Brompton; Courtfield (sandwiched between Gloucester Road and the Fulham Road near Brompton Hospital); and Earls Court. Its other wards were all in Kensington, namely Queens Gate (between Gloucester Road and Kensington Gardens); Abingdon (Kensington High Street); Holland (Park); Campden (including Kensington Palace); Pembridge (Notting Hill Gate); Norland (Notting Hill including Latimer Road); Notting Barns; Colville; Golborne; and St Charles (Ladbroke Grove); the latter ward extending as far north as Kensal Green cemetery.

Ealing Central & Acton was established to comprise all districts of Acton (East, including Old Oak Common; Central and South Acton wards) together with Bedfont Park (Southfield ward); Hanger Lane; and Park Royal (Hanger Hill); all taken from Ealing, Acton & Shepherds Bush. To these were added Ealing (Walpole) and Ealing Common, taken from Ealing, Southall; and North Ealing (Broadway) taken from Ealing North. The 2010 **Ealing North** constituency gained Pitshanger (Cleveland ward) from Ealing, Acton & Shepherds Bush, but retained all its previous districts covering Castle Bar and Elthorne Heights (Hobbayne); Drayton Green (also in Cleveland ward), Greenford (Greenford Broadway and Greenford Green wards); Horsenden (North Greenford); Northolt (Mandeville and West End wards); and Perivale. **Ealing, Southall** lost Ealing Common ward but retained all its other areas of Dormers Wells with Mount Pleasant; Little Ealing and Northfields (Northfield ward); Elthorne and Hanwell (Elthorne ward); Hyde Green and Norwood Green; and Southall proper (Southall Green and Southall Broadway wards).

Harrow and Hillingdon boroughs, reviewed separately in 1995, were paired this time. The two returned a total of five MPs after 1997, three from Hillingdon and two from Harrow; and the same number of constituencies was proposed again but with boundary changes to provide a better balance of electorates. The resultant mix retained the names of only three of the existing constituencies. **Harrow East** contracted slightly to lose Greenhill, Harrow Town (Marlborough ward) and Harrow-on-the Hill, which were transferred to Harrow West. The other electorates were unchanged, namely Canons ward (Brockley Hill, Canons Park and Stanmore station area); Edgware (west of Burnt Oak); Queensbury; Kenton East; Kenton West; Belmont (South Stanmore); Stanmore Park (Stanmore proper); Wealdstone and Harrow Weald. **Harrow West** gained the three former East wards but shed the Pinner area and Hatch End to a new Ruislip, Northwood & Pinner constituency. Harrow West comprised Marlborough (Town); Greenhill; Headstone North; Headstone South; Harrow-on-the-Hill; West Harrow; Rayners Lane; Roxbourne; and Roxeth.

Ruislip, Northwood & Pinner replaced Ruislip - Northwood which gained Pinner and Hatch End from Harrow West and Ickenham from Uxbridge. Its remaining wards were Eastcote and East Ruislip; West Ruislip; Northwood and Northwood Hills. In turn the former seat also lost three wards. (Ruislip) Manor; Cavendish (a residential area south of Eastcote station); and South Ruislip (including Ruislip Gardens and Northolt aerodrome); were transferred to Uxbridge to form a new **Uxbridge & South Ruislip** constituency. Other wards included were Uxbridge North and South (including part of Cowley); Hillingdon East; Brunel (Hillingdon South, most of Cowley and the University); and Yiewsley. This was the first time since its creation in 1885 that the Uxbridge constituency had acquired an additional place name in its designation.

West Drayton was transferred from Uxbridge to **Hayes & Harlington** which was otherwise unaltered retaining the geographical coverage it had first acquired when it was set up in 1955. It comprised Yeading; the two north Hayes wards of Charville and Barnhill; the south Hayes Botwell, Townfield and Pinkwell wards; together with the optimistically named Heathrow Villages ward (including the Airport, Harlington and Harmondsworth). Meanwhile on the south side of Heathrow airport the boundary changes in Hounslow borough were relatively minor. There were none at all in **Twickenham** and **Feltham & Heston** gained parts of Heston East, Heston West and Hounslow Central from **Brentford & Isleworth.** They were otherwise as described earlier in this Chapter under 1997 changes.

Significant changes affected Brent, which was reviewed alongside Camden. The map below illustrates how the Brent wards were reallocated in 2010. The borough effectively lost much of what had formerly been Brent South. A new **Brent Central** comprised the remaining five wards from the former Brent South which were newly constituted as Welsh Harp (Neasden); Tokyngton (Wembley Park); Stonebridge (Park); Harlesden and Kensal Green; to which were added four former Brent East wards, namely Dollis Hill; Mapesbury (including Cricklewood); Willesden Green; and Dudden Hill (including Willesden proper). **Brent North** comprised Queensbury (Northern Kingsbury west of the Edgware Road and Roe Green); Fryent (Kingsbury Green and Kingsbury); Preston (Road including South Kenton); Kenton; Barnhill (Wembley Park); Northwick Park (including Sudbury Court); Sudbury (including Sudbury Hill); Wembley Central and Alperton; the latter two from Brent South. The Barnhill ward was also enlarged compared with previous boundaries and extended further south to take in Brent Town Hall, an area also formerly in Brent South. However, ward boundary changes in the area of Brentwater saw a transfer the other way with a residential area south of Kingsbury Green being transferred from Brent South to Brent North.

North London (Retained 7 seats)

In adjoining Camden, the former Hampstead & Highgate lost Dudden Hill, Highgate and Gospel Oak and was renamed **Hampstead & Kilburn,** acquiring the three Brent East wards, namely Queens Park (including Kensal Rise); Kilburn; and Brondesbury Park which were amalgamated with seven wards from the former seat, which were now renamed Kilburn (Kilburn Grange and Finchley Road); Swiss Cottage; West Hampstead; Fortune Green; Frognal & Fitzjohn; Hampstead Town; and Belsize. The new constituency is depicted in the map above.

Holborn & St Pancras retained all of its previous electorates but gained Gospel Oak and Highgate (Waterlow Park, Dartmouth Park and Parliament Hill) wards from Hampstead & Highgate. Its other wards were Kentish Town,

Haverstock (Chalk Farm), Camden Town with Primrose Hill, Cantelowes (Camden Town East), St Pancras & Somers Town, Regents Park (including Mornington Crescent and Euston), Kings Cross (including Corum Fields), Bloomsbury (including London University) and Holborn & Covent Garden (including St Giles Circus).

Adjoining **Islington South & Finsbury** and **Islington North** were unaltered whilst further north in Barnet borough there were minor changes associated with revisions to local ward boundaries which resulted in a misalignment with the existing constituencies. There were only two of significance. The first involved the inclusion of the whole of North Finchley in the Woodside ward, which was allocated to Finchley & Golders Green as before, except that formerly the northernmost parts had been in Chipping Barnet. The second transfer was that of Coppetts Wood / South Friern, which was joined with Friern Barnet in a new Coppetts ward, the whole of which was allocated to **Chipping Barnet.** This seat incorporated Underhill and High Barnet (including Arkley and Monken Hadley); Oakleigh Park (including New Barnet); Brunswick Park; East Barnet; Totteridge (including Whetstone and Woodside Park); and Coppetts Wood (including Friern Barnet). **Hendon** was little altered whilst **Finchley & Golders Green** consisted of Woodhouse (including North Finchley); West Finchley; Finchley Church End; (Hampstead) Garden Suburb; Childs Hill; and Golders Green (including Brent Cross).

The East End and North East London (Retained 9 seats)

Adjustments to council ward boundaries in Enfield meant some changes occurred there but they were relatively minor. The areas affected were Grange Park ward in the **Enfield, Southgate** constituency which was expanded eastward to take in the Bush Hill area of Edmonton and the Town Park between Enfield Town and Enfield Chase stations, which it acquired from Enfield North. However, it lost Highlands to Enfield North as a result of the ward having been expanded so that it would otherwise have straddled both seats. The area around Highlands Hospital went to Enfield North. Remaining electorates were contained within six wards, namely Cockfosters (including Hadley Wood and Trent Park); Southgate (including Oakwood Park); Winchmore Hill; Palmers Green; Southgate Green (including New Southgate and Arnos Grove); and Bowes. **Enfield North** comprised Enfield Chase (including Crews Hill, Clay Hill and Bulls Cross); Highlands (including Gordon Hill); Town; Turkey Street; Enfield Lock (Wash); and Enfield Highway (including Durants Park and Brimsdown). **Edmonton** comprised Upper Edmonton, Edmonton Green, Haselbury, Bush Hill Park, Jubilee, Ponders End and Southbury wards.

In Haringey borough there were no changes affecting either **Tottenham** or **Hornsey & Wood Green** while Hackney borough had only minor changes brought about by alterations to ward boundaries; notably Dalston, which was extended marginally northwards towards Shacklewell; Hackney Downs, which lost a small area at the south end to Hackney Central; and Leabridge, which acquired a small district of Lower Clapton from Kings Park ward. The new distribution saw the whole of Dalston ward transferred from the South to the North division. **Hackney North & Stoke Newington** was made up of ten wards, namely New River (Stamford Hill); Brownswood (Finsbury Park); Lordship (Lordship Park Manor and Clissold Park); Clissold (Stoke Newington West); Stoke Newington Central; Hackney Downs (including Shacklewell); Cazenove and Springfield (Upper Clapton); Leabridge (Lower Clapton); and Dalston. **Hackney South & Shoreditch** included Kings Park (Clapton Park and Hackney Marsh); (Hackney) Wick; Chatham (Homerton); Victoria (Park including South Hackney); Hackney Central; Queensbridge (Haggerston and Moorfields); De Beavoir (Town including Kingsland); and Hoxton.

Finally, the increase in the population of docklands coupled with the economic success of the Canary Wharf development on the Isle of Dogs led to an increase in seats covering Tower Hamlets, which was decoupled from Newham and restored to the two seats that had existed between 1974 and 1997. Bethnal Green & Bow was reduced slightly in size with two wards transferred to a new Poplar & Limehouse seat. **Bethnal Green & Bow** thus covered nine wards, namely Spitalfields and Banglatown (including Brick Lane); Weavers; Bethnal Green North (including Cambridge Heath);

Contrasting housing is evident in many parts of the Borough of Tower Hamlets. The high quality of the flats (see left) at Limehouse, sponsored by the Docklands Development Corporation, is in stark contrast to the low grade tenements depicted in nearby Cable Street. (see right). The population of the area is becoming more socially and ethnically mixed. Political outcomes have reflected these changes. Riverside wards now represent high incomes, but not yet across the main elected Council. **Gordon Rushton**

General Election Results 1974 - 2010 by % majority

Constituency	1950 to 1970	Feb 1974	Oct 1974	1979	1983	1987	1992	1997	2001	2005	2010
Marylebone	C	C30	C26	C33							
Paddington	1C 1Lab	Lab2	Lab6	C0.3							
Cities of London & Westminster South	C	C26	C21+	C35	C38	C36	C37	C12	C13	C22	
Cities of London & Westminster											C30
Westminster North					C4	C8	C8				Lab5
Chelsea (& South Kensington)	C	C40	C41	C48	C50	C47	C48	C26+	C31	C40	
Chelsea & Fulham											C42
Kensington	C Lab	C13	C6	C16	C17+	C14	C11				C25
Regents Park & North Kensington								Lab32	Lab28	Lab15	
Fulham	Lab	Lab8	Lab13	C4	C12-	C15	C16				
Hammersmith & Fulham								Lab7	Lab5	Con10	
Hammersmith (North)	1Lab 1C/La	Lab18	Lab24	Lab10	Lab6	Lab7	Lab14				
Hammersmith											Lab8
Ealing, Acton	Lab	C3	C2	C14	C23	C28	C16				
Ealing Central & Acton											C8
Ealing, Acton & Shepherds Bush								Lab33	Lab29	Lab14	
Ealing North	Lab	Lab4	Lab5	C2	C12	C27	C12	Lab12	Lab26	Lab14	Lab20
Ealing, Southall	Lab	Lab17	Lab22	Lab22	Lab22	Lab15	Lab14	Lab39	Lab29	Lab24+	Lab22
Ealing South	C										
C	6-7	5	5	8	7+	7	7	2	2	2	4
Lab	7-8	5	5	2	2	2	2	5+	5	5+	4
L	0	0	0	0	0	0	0	0	0	0	0
Total	14	10	10	10	9+	9	9	7+	7	7+	8

Key: C = Conservative; Lab = Labour; + = Party that won seat at General Election held by-election in same Parliament - = Party that won seat at General Election lost by-election to main opposition Party in same Parliament.

Bethnal Green South; Bow West (including Roman Road); Bow East (including Old Ford); Mile End and Globe Town; St Dunstans & Stepney Green; and Whitechapel. **Poplar & Limehouse** covered eight wards which were St Katherine's and Wapping (including the Tower of London); Shadwell (including Ratcliffe); Limehouse (including Poplar); Millwall (including West India Dock, Canary Wharf and Westferry); Blackwall and Cubitt Town (including East India Dock); East India and Lansbury (South east Bromley); Bromley by Bow; and Mile End East.

Politics in Central and West London: The City, Westminster, Kensington & Chelsea, Hammersmith & Fulham and Ealing (table above)

The 1974 changes were fairly well balanced in their impact. Labour's loss of a seat in Kensington was effectively balanced by the loss of a Tory seat in Paddington, whilst the abolition of the safe Tory seat of Ealing South was counteracted somewhat by the creation of the Ealing, Acton seat which Labour would probably have won in 1974 on the basis of its previous boundaries. The Tory gains from Labour in the 1979 election were the result of a mood swing in the electorate, and it is unlikely that Labour would have fared any better under the previous boundaries. The 1983 changes, on the other hand, do seem to have been to the disbenefit of the Tories, the reduction in Westminster meaning the loss of a safe seat. The swing from Labour to Tory that took place in the 1983 and 1987 elections were insufficient to shift any further seats away from Labour, who clung on to their boltholes in Hammersmith and Southall throughout this period. However, in 1997 when Labour was returned on the back of a landslide victory, the Party only secured five of the reduced total of seven seats available. Had the 1992 boundaries been in place, it is probable that the Labour Party would have secured two more, Westminster North, and Kensington. The Tories' performance between 1997 and 2005 had some echoes of Labour's "wilderness years", with Labour holding onto its bolthole seats in Westminster and Chelsea throughout. 2010 bore some resemblance to the two 1974 elections in this part of London, an equality of representation between the two main Parties reflecting the closeness of the national outcome on all three occasions.

The effect of restoring three seats to Ealing borough whilst at the same time pairing Hammersmith & Fulham with Chelsea was to make one of the seats (Ealing Central & Acton) Conservative in place of the former Labour seat of Ealing, Acton & Shepherds Bush. Although Hammersmith was notionally a Labour seat it was significantly more marginal than the seat that disappeared, and was vulnerable to only a moderate swing to the Tories. At the same time the amalgamation of Fulham with Chelsea created a very safe Tory seat in place of the formerly marginal (but by then Tory held) seat of Hammersmith & Fulham. The abolition of the Regents Park, seat coupled with the separation of South Kensington from Chelsea, and the restoration of a Kensington constituency, also favoured the Conservatives, effectively making this a Tory seat. The approximate replacement for Regents Park, Westminster North, became a slender Labour marginal.

Results in Fulham are of interest in that the gradual erosion of Labour's position there can be seen in the election results. Although the swing from Labour to Conservative was clearly a factor, the demographic changes in that area were also very significant. The increasingly middle class nature of the population was to the benefit of the Conservatives and although there was a Labour by-election gain there in on 10th April 1986 this was reversed at the 1987 general election. During the period that Fulham was attached to parts of Hammersmith Labour was able to win the seat but with its new association with Chelsea, created in 2010, the certainty of the outcome was clear.

On 19th July 2007 there was a by-election in the safe Labour seat of Ealing, Southall, which took place shortly after Gordon Brown had succeeded Tony Blair as Prime Minister. David Cameron, the Tory Leader, targeted the seat for a by-election upset but the outcome saw the Tory candidate take third place. The Liberal Democrat came second and Labour held onto the seat with a majority of 14% (19% over the Tory). In some ways this was a harbinger of what was to happen in the 2010 general election when contrary to many expectations, the Conservatives failed to secure an overall majority in the Commons. The lower than average swing in London seats was in part responsible for the Tories' failure to win the election outright.

Other by-elections that took place during the period were at Kensington on 14th July 1988 when Labour came within 3.5% of taking the seat (though after the fall of Margaret Thatcher, the Tories took it more comfortably in 1987); and at Chelsea & South Kensington in September 1999 which saw the return of Michael Portillo after his surprise defeat at Enfield, Southgate in the 1997 general election. His majority of 34% was 7% higher than at the general election. His biographical details are later in this chapter (North East London).

Politics in West Middlesex: Hounslow, Hillingdon, Harrow, and Brent (table p454)

The abolition of Heston & Isleworth and the merging of Wembley with Willesden in the borough of Brent in 1974 clearly disadvantaged the Conservatives though other boundary changes compensated them so that Uxbridge (a Labour seat for much of the period before 1974) swung in their favour, even in times when Labour did well nationally. The redistribution probably also tipped Brentford & Isleworth their way in 1974. However, the changes in 1983 brought about a further Tory loss with the abolition of Harrow Central. Despite this, the swing to the Conservatives that occurred in the 1980s meant that they actually took as many seats as they had done before 1974 despite there being three fewer in total. Even with a swing back towards Labour in 1992 they only lost Feltham & Heston, whilst hanging on at Hayes & Harlington by the skin of their teeth. In the Blair years it was the national mood that affected election outcomes more than boundary changes, the Liberal Democrats also benefiting from the anti-Tory swing by taking the previously rock solid safe Twickenham seat. Some of the biggest swings away from the Conservatives were recorded in this area, the largest of all occurring at Brent North. Latterly, and when the national swing was away from the Party, Labour benefited from the allocation of Pinner to Ruislip-Northwood which had the effect of strengthening its position in Harrow. Had it not been for these changes it is probable that Labour would have lost Harrow West in 2010. On the other hand Labour's position in Harrow had improved partly as a result of changes in the ethnic mix of the electorate. Though still middle class, a significant Asian electorate with a higher preponderance of Labour voters helped the Party. However, the loss of one seat in Brent (essentially Brent South) and the redistribution that it entailed, did not particularly favour Labour. Although its majority in Brent North was notionally strengthened, Brent Central was significantly less favourable to the Party than the former South constituency (albeit against the Liberal Democrats rather than the Tories) and the new seat

General Election Results 1974 - 2010 by % majority

Constituency	1950 to 1970	Feb 1974	Oct 1974	1979	1983	1987	1992	1997	2001	2005	2010
Brentford & Chiswick (& Isleworth)	C	C1	C0.5	C9	C18	C15	C4	Lab26	Lab23	Lab10	C4
Twickenham	C	C19	C18	C22	C10	C14	C11	L7	L15	L19	L20
Heston & Isleworth	C										
Feltham (& Heston)	Lab	Lab13	Lab17	Lab7	C4	C9	Lab3	Lab33	Lab35	Lab18	Lab10+
Hayes & Harlington	Lab	Lab24	Lab24	Lab8	C10	C14	C0.1	Lab35	Lab42	Lab34	Lab25
Uxbridge	Lab	C5	C5	C17	C29	C33	C27	C2+	C6	C18	
Uxbridge & South Ruislip											C25
Ruislip, Northwood & Pinner	C	C26	C26	C39	C32	C39	C45	C17	C20	C22	C38
Harrow Central	C	C8	C6	C13							
Harrow East	C	C11	C9	C21	C22	C31	C19	Lab17	Lab23	Lab9	C7
Harrow West	C	C26	C28	C34	C21	C28	C33	Lab2	Lab13	Lab4	Lab7
Brent Central											L3
Brent East	Lab	Lab18	Lab24	Lab17	Lab12	Lab4	Lab16	Lab45	Lab45-	L9	
Brent North	2xC	C14	C14	C20	C33	C35	C24	Lab11	Lab30	Lab16	Lab15
Brent South	Lab	Lab25	Lab30	Lab29	Lab26	Lab20	Lab27	Lab57	Lab61	Lab38	
C	9	8	8	8	9	9	8	2	2	2	4
Lab	5	4	4	4	2	2	3	8	8-	7	4+
L	0	0	0	0	0	0	0	1	1+	2	2
Total	14	12	12	12	11	11	11	11	11+	11	10+

Key: C = Conservative; Lab = Labour; + = Party that won seat at General Election; + = Party that won seat at General Election held by-election in same Parliament; - = Party that won seat at General Election lost by-election to main opposition Party in same Parliament.

that was created to take in parts of south Brent, namely Hampstead & Kilburn (see North London overleaf), effectively created a wafer thin Labour marginal, with the Liberal Democrats and Tories both in hot pursuit.

There was also a significant by-election in the period. This took place at Brent East on 18th September 2003 and resulted in the first defeat at a by-election in a Labour held seat since the Party had come to power in 1997. The seat was won by the Liberal Democrats who secured a majority of 5% compared with 45% for Labour at the 2001 general election. The Liberal Democrats increased their majority in 2005. The significance of the by-election was that it took place during the Iraq War and that the constituency itself had a sizeable Asian ethnic population, many of them Muslims; and it is thought that this combination of factors brought about what was a major shift of voters between the Labour and Liberal Democrat Parties; one reflected in several similar constituencies at the 2005 general election.

A by-election in Feltham & Heston on 15th December 2011 recorded a substantial swing of 8.5% to Labour from the Conservatives. The by-election majority of nearly 27% represented an increase of 17% since 2010.

Politics in North London: Camden, Islington and Barnet (table p455)

The initial impact of the 1974 changes reduced Labour's tally by one seat, brought about by the abolition of one of Islington's four safe Labour seats. Subsequent changes in 1983 and 1997 also reduced the number of seats winnable by Labour. In 1983 the loss of another Islington seat and one in Camden had the effect of halving the Party's seats total compared with the position before 1974. Having said that Labour's performance in 1983 and 1987 was mainly the result of swings against the Party which, in the case of Islington South & Finsbury, involved a battle with the SDP. Also the reduction in the number of seats that affected the inner London communities also started to have an impact in the more middle class constituencies beyond them. In 1983 and 1987 these changes in Hampstead & Highgate were masked by the swing to the Conservatives that occurred, though in 1992 this was one seat that the Labour Party did manage to wrest from the Conservatives. The 1997 changes, on the other hand, effectively reduced the Conservative total through the merging of seats affecting Barnet as a whole and Hendon in particular. Coupled with a significant swing to Labour the effect was to deliver to Labour the same number of seats it had won on average before 1974. Indeed a slightly larger swing in 1997 would have resulted in a clean sweep for Labour.

General Election Results 1974 - 2010 by % majority											
Constituency	**1950 to 1970**	**Feb 1974**	**Oct 1974**	**1979**	**1983**	**1987**	**1992**	**1997**	**2001**	**2005**	**2010**
Holborn & St. Pancras (South)	Lab	Lab17	Lab26	Lab10	Lab17	Lab20	Lab27	Lab47	Lab36	Lab14	Lab18
St. Pancras (North)	Lab	Lab24	Lab31	Lab20							
Hampstead (& Highgate)	C	C5	C4	C9	C8	C5	Lab3	Lab32	Lab22	Lab10	
Hampstead & Kilburn											Lab0.1
Islington South & Finsbury	2xLab	Lab31	Lab41	Lab18	Lab1	Lab2	Lab26	Lab50	Lab26	Lab2	Lab8
Islington Central	Lab	Lab30	Lab37	Lab16							
Islington North	Lab	Lab26	Lab30	Lab19	Lab15	Lab25	Lab34	Lab56	Lab43	Lab21	Lab28
Finchley (& Golders Green)	C	C14	C10	C20	C24	C22	C16	Lab6	Lab9	Lab2	C12
Hendon (North)	C	C6	C5	C16	C24	C30	C18	Lab5	Lab18	Lab6	C0.2
Hendon South	C	C16	C14	C23	C18	C32	C34				
Chipping Barnet	C	C22	C19	C32	C30	C35	C31	C2	C6	C14	C24
C	5	5	5	5	5	5	4	1	1	1	3
Lab	6	5	5	5	3	3	4	6	6	6	4
L	0	0	0	0	0	0	0	0	0	0	0
Total	11	10	10	10	8	8	8	7	7	7	7

Key: C = Conservative; Lab = Labour; + = Party that won seat at General Election; + = Party that won seat at General Election held by-election in same Parliament; - = Party that won seat at General Election lost by-election to main opposition Party in same Parliament.

The 2010 changes in general had little impact on election outcomes except that merging with parts of Kilburn meant that at the time there was a strong Liberal Democrat vote imported into the Hampstead based constituency which served to make this the closest three-way marginal seats in the country. The Labour share of the vote was 32.8% compared with 32.7% for the Conservatives and 31.2% for the Liberal Democrats.

Politics in The East End and NE London: Hackney, Tower Hamlets, Haringey and Enfield (table p456)

In 1974 the Labour Party lost one seat through re-distribution in Tower Hamlets. The Tories also initially lost a seat, in Enfield, when the former East and West divisions were reformed as Enfield North but this proved to be a marginal seat and the longer-term impact was less favourable to Labour when the political mood was against the Party. So when the Conservatives returned to Government in 1979 it was this particular seat that Labour lost.

In 1983 the loss of two more seats seems to have been to Labour's immediate disadvantage. These resulted from a reduction in Hackney, a Labour stronghold; whilst Wood Green was also lost following a merger with Tory-held Hornsey. However, had the Tories not won a landslide victory in the 1983 Election it is possible that Hornsey & Wood Green would have been a Labour seat. The only loss Labour seems to have suffered purely as a result of a change in the electorate's mood was Edmonton in 1983. In 1992 Labour staged a partial revival, the Tories losing only Hornsey & Wood Green, whilst holding Edmonton by a margin of 1%.

The 2005 election produced some remarkable results in this part of London. The most stunning was the loss of Bethnal Green & Bow by Labour to the Respect candidate, George Galloway. This – and a massively reduced majority in the adjacent constituency of Poplar and Canning Town – appears to have been principally due to the Iraq War which was hugely unpopular amongst Muslim voters who, in Bethnal Green, represented over 50% of the electorate. The War was probably also the explanation for the loss of Hornsey & Wood Green to the Liberal Democrats, although there it was the radical middle class that had lost faith in Tony Blair citing lack of trust arising from his decision to take Britain to War. Labour also suffered big swings against it to the Liberal Democrats in Hackney. Labour's vote held up much better

General Election Results 1974 - 2010 by % majority

Constituency	1950 to 1970	Feb 1974	Oct 1974	1979	1983	1987	1992	1997	2001	2005	2010
Hackney South & Shoreditch	Lab	Lab39	Lab49	Lab26	Lab20	Lab19	Lab24	Lab46	Lab50	Lab32	Lab33
Hackney Central	Lab	Lab41	Lab50	Lab31							
Hackney North & Stoke Newington	Lab	Lab29	Lab38	Lab18	Lab23	Lab20	Lab31	Lab48	Lab46	Lab25	Lab31
Bethnal Green & Bow	Lab	Lab46	Lab56	Lab23				Lab25	Lab26	Res2	Lab23
Bethnal Green & Stepney					Lab21	Lab17	Lab34				
Stepney (& Poplar)	Lab	Lab65	Lab67	Lab42							
(Bow &) Poplar	Lab				Lab18	Lab14	Lab23				
Poplar & Canning Town								Lab48	Lab41	Lab19	
Poplar & Limehouse											Lab13
Tottenham	Lab	Lab29	Lab35	Lab25	Lab22	Lab8	Lab27	Lab54+	Lab54	Lab41	Lab42
Wood Green	Lab	Lab21	Lab25	Lab7							
Hornsey (& Wood Green)	C	C5	C2	C10	C7	C3	Lab9	Lab40	Lab24	L5	L13
Edmonton	Lab	Lab12	Lab17	Lab5	C3	C15	C1	Lab30	Lab28	Lab23	Lab24
Enfield, Southgate	C	C27	C31	C39	C35+	C40	C32	Lab3	Lab13	C4	C17
Enfield North	C/Lab	Lab6	Lab10	C7	C24	C27	C18	Lab14	Lab6	Lab5	C4
C	3	2	2	3	4+	4	3	0	0	1	2
Lab	10	9	9	8	5	5	6	9+	9	6	6
L	0	0	0	0	0	0	0	0	0	1	1
Respect	0	0	0	0	0	0	0	0	0	1	0
Total	13	11	11	11	9+	9	9	9+	9	9	9

Key: C = Conservative; Lab = Labour; Res = Respect, a Party established as a direct result of the War in Iraq and which appealed especially to Muslims; + = Party that won seat at General Election held by-election in same Parliament; - = Party that won seat at General Election lost by-election to main opposition Party in same Parliament.

in the outer constituencies and although they lost Enfield Southgate to the Conservatives they retained Enfield North and Edmonton.

At the 2010 election, changes in Enfield borough effectively switched Enfield North from Labour to Tory and although Enfield Southgate saw the notional Tory majority reduced this would only have been of benefit to Labour in circumstances where the national mood favoured the Party which in 2010 it did not. Nevertheless their majority in Edmonton was strengthened in a seat that in the Thatcher and Major years had been Tory. In the East End, there were no significant changes in Hackney but in Tower Hamlets the re-creation of two seats meant that notionally the Respect Party's majority in Bethnal Green & Bow was increased from wafer thin to ultra marginal whilst the new seat of Poplar & Limehouse created a notional Labour seat but with a small enough majority to be vulnerable either to the Tories or to the Respect Party. This compared with a much more significant Labour majority in the former seat of Poplar & Canning Town (shared with Newham).

There were two by-elections in the period. The first came at Southgate on the 13th December 1984 and followed the assassination of the local MP. The Tories won with a reduced majority of 14% over the Liberal compared with 35% in 1983. Then on 22nd June 2000 Labour retained Tottenham with a majority of 34% compared with 54% in 1997.

MPs for The City of London, Westminster, Kensington and Chelsea

St Marylebone

Kenneth Wilfred Baker (Conservative) was first elected for Marylebone in 1970. He remained MP until 1983

MPs for The City of London, Westminster, Kensington and Chelsea						
From	at	To	Surname	First Names	Constituency	Party
1974	G	1983	Baker	Kenneth Wilfred	St. Marylebone	Conservative
1974	G	1979	Latham	Arthur Charles	Paddington	Labour
1979	G	1983	Wheeler	Sir John		Conservative
1983	G	1997	Wheeler	Sir John	Westminster North	Conservative
2010	G	Date	Buck	Karen		Labour
1974	G	1977	Tugendhat	Christopher Samuel	City of London & Westminster South	Conservative
1977	B	1997	Brooke	Peter Leonard		Conservative
1997	G	2001	Brooke	Peter Leonard	Cities of London & Westminster	Conservative
2001	G	Date	Field	Mark		Conservative
1974	G	1974	Worsley	Sir Marcus	Chelsea	Conservative
1974	G	1997	Scott	Nicholas Paul		Conservative
1974	G	1988	Rhys Williams	Sir Brandon	Kensington	Conservative
1988	B	1997	Fishburn	John Dudley		Conservative
2010	G	Date	Rifkind	(Sir) Malcolm		Conservative
1997	G	1999	Clarke	Sir Alan Kenneth Mackenzie	Kensington & Chelsea	Conservative
1999	B	2005	Portillo	Michael Denzil Xavier		Conservative
2005	G	2010	Rifkind	(Sir) Malcolm		Conservative
2010	G	Date	Hands	Greg	Chelsea & Fulham	Conservative
1997	G	2010	Buck	Karen	Regents Park & North Kensington	Labour

Notes: First returned at: **B** By-election, **G** General Election

when a redistribution of seats occurred. He then became MP for Mole Valley in Surrey. His principal biographical details are in Chapter 11.

Paddington, Westminster North

Arthur Charles Latham (Labour) was MP for Paddington North from 1969 to 1974 when he was elected for Paddington. He was defeated in 1979. His principal biographical details may be found in Chapter 11.

He was succeeded by **Sir John Wheeler** (Conservative) who also became MP for Westminster North in 1983 remaining there until 1997 when he retired. Born in1940, he was educated at a County School in Suffolk and joined the prison service. He attended the Staff College at Wakefield and was, from 1968-72 an Assistant Governor of Wandsworth prison, transferring to Brixton in 1972. From 1977 to 1988 he was Director of the National Supervisory Council for intruder alarms, a body created in 1971 to deal with the problem of poor quality equipment and workmanship in the market. From 1976-88 he was also the Director-General of the British Security Industry Association Limited, the professional trade association for the security industry in the UK. He became a member of Lloyds and a Director of Hunterprint Ltd (which in the 1990s had several printing contracts associated with the flotation of the privatised utilities). A member of the Council of the Order of St John for London, he was an active backbencher but never attained ministerial office.

Karen Buck (Labour) won the reconstituted seat in 2010. Her details are below under Regents Park & North Kensington.

City of London & Westminster South, Cities of London & Westminster

Christopher Samuel Tugendhat (Conservative) was MP for the Cities of London and Westminster from 1970 until 1974 when he transferred to the newly drawn seat of London and Westminster South. He was appointed a European Commissioner in 1977. His main biographical details are contained in Chapter 11.

His seat was taken at the February 1977 by-election by **Peter Leonard Brooke** (Conservative), the son of the former Tory Home Secretary and MP for Hampstead, Henry Brooke (See Chapter 9, Lewisham West). Peter won handsomely with a majority of 39% compared with 21% at the October 1974 Election. Born in 1934, he was educated at

Peter Brooke MP
Peoples History Museum Manchester

Marlborough School and Balliol College Oxford, where he was President of the University Union in 1957. He attended Harvard Business School as a Commonwealth Fund Fellow[2] and much later in life was made a Presentation Fellow of Kings College, London, in 1989. He was also a Senior Fellow of the Royal College of Art, a member of Lloyds and a Lay adviser to St Pauls Cathedral. He first contested a Parliamentary seat in October 1974 at Bedwellty (Gwent), a safe Labour mining seat held by Neil Kinnock who was to become Leader of the Opposition during a period when Brooke attained Cabinet rank as Paymaster-General (whilst Chairman of the Tory Party between 1987-9); and Northern Ireland Secretary (1989-92). During this latter period, Brooke led clandestine Tory Government attempts to establish a dialogue with the IRA. After his election at Westminster in 1977 he made rapid ministerial progress. He was an assistant Government whip from 1979-81 and Chief Whip from 1981-3 when he was appointed Under Secretary of State for Education and Science. He served as a Treasury minister from 1985-7 when he became Party Chairman. Following the 1992 General Election he resigned from the Government to contest the Speakership of the Commons but was defeated by the first woman to hold that post, Betty Boothroyd. After a sex scandal, which forced the resignation of David Mellor[3], Secretary of State for National Heritage, Brooke rejoined John Major's Cabinet in September 1992 and held that post until he stood down in 1994. He remained an MP until he retired in 2001 when he was made Lord Brooke of Sutton Mandeville. He is also Pro-Chancellor and Chairman of Council at the University of London.

Mark Field (Conservative) was elected in 2001. Then aged 36, he was educated at Reading School and St Edmund College, Oxford where he read Law and was Secretary of the University Conservative Association. He went on to practise as a solicitor with the international law firm Freshfields, and in the mid 1990s set up a successful publishing and law recruitment business in the City. He was elected a councillor on Kensington and Chelsea Borough Council in 1994 and contested his first Parliamentary seat, unsuccessfully at Enfield North in 1997. After the 2005 election he was appointed Shadow Financial Secretary to the Treasury and under David Cameron served as spokesman on culture, media and sport. He was born in Germany where his father was a serving officer in the British Army.

Mark Field MP
UK Parliament

Chelsea

Sir Marcus Worsley (Conservative) was elected MP for Chelsea in 1966 and remained until October 1974 when he retired. His principal biographical details are in Chapter 11.

Nicholas Paul Scott (Conservative) succeeded him in October 1974 having previously been MP for Paddington South since 1966. His principal biographical details are also in Chapter 11.

Chelsea & Fulham

Greg Hands (Conservative) formerly the MP for Hammersmith & Fulham was elected in 2010. His biographical details are to be found below.

Kensington

Sir Brandon Rhys Williams (Conservative) had been elected MP for Kensington South in 1968 and was MP for Kensington from February 1974 until his death in 1988. His main biographical details are in Chapter 11.

He was succeeded at a by-election in July 1988 by **John Dudley Fishburn** (Conservative), an Eton and Harvard educated economist and journalist who held off a strong Labour challenge winning by a margin of only 3.5% compared with 14% in 1987. He was a consultant to several companies including JP Morgan (one of the world's leading investment banks) and Pepper Hamilton & Sheetz, a US law firm; the director of a bank; and of the English National Ballet, a school that promotes classical ballet dancing. From 1969-88 he was a free-lance journalist with the *Economist* of which he became executive editor in 1979, resigning to fight the by-election. He had previously contested the Isle of Wight in October 1974 and again in 1979, both times unsuccessfully being beaten by a Liberal. He became PPS to Timothy Sainsbury, the Minister for Trade in 1990. In 1995 he advised businessmen to prepare for a Labour Government; declared that there were too many MPs with too little to do; and announced that he would not contest the 1997 General Election when he

2 The Commonwealth Fund is a private foundation based in New York City that supports independent research on health and social issues and makes grants to improve health care practice and policy.
3 Mellor was MP for Putney – see Chapter 18

retired aged 50. He became a Director of the Tobacco Company, Philip Morris International.

At the 2010 election the newly reinstated Kensington seat was represented by **Malcolm Rifkind** (see Kensington & Chelsea below).

Kensington & Chelsea

In 1997 there was intense competition for the Kensington & Chelsea nomination as this was the safest Tory seat in the country. The former Minister, **Alan Kenneth Mackenzie Clarke**, son of the historian Arthur C. Clarke, was adopted and comfortably took the seat. He was a former MP for Plymouth, Sutton (Devon) who had gained notoriety as an indiscrete politician with a sensational private life of self-confessed, constant infidelity. He had retired at the 1992 election but missed political life and society. Despite the public exposure of several of his dalliances, and the publication of an autobiography that was open about his private life, he remained married to his wife Jane and gained a popular reputation. A man of great personal wealth, he was apparently beholden to no one but unfortunately did not remain long an MP after his return to the House as he died of cancer in 1999. Born in 1928, Clarke had been educated at Eton and Christ Church, Oxford after which he became a barrister and historian. He was first elected an MP at Plymouth in February 1974 and in 1983 was made Under Secretary of State for Employment, then Minister of State at the Department of Trade and Industry in 1986. He served as a Defence Minister after 1987.

Alan Clarke MP
Wikipedia

Clarke was succeeded at a by-election in 1999 by another controversial character, **Michael Denzil Xavier Portillo** (Conservative), a former Secretary of State for Defence in John Major's Government, who had been sensationally defeated at Enfield, Southgate at the 1997 General Election. He was the son of a Spanish University lecturer who had been a Republican fighting against Franco during the Civil War, and who had fled to England, where Michael was born in 1953. He attended Harrow County School and Porterhouse College, Cambridge, after which he entered politics, initially as a political researcher for Television, and then as a special adviser to the Secretary of State for Trade and Industry in 1983; and to the Chancellor of the Exchequer in 1984. Then he was adopted as the Tory candidate for Southgate at the 1984 by-election following the death of Sir Anthony Berry, killed in the IRA bombing of the Imperial Hotel, Brighton during the Conservative Party Conference. He became PPS to the Minister of Transport in 1986 and served as an assistant Government Whip from 1986-7; Under Secretary of State for Health & Social Security (1987-8); Minister for Public Transport (1988-90); then as Minister for Local Government (1990-2). He was promoted to the Cabinet in 1992, as Chief Secretary to the Treasury; became Employment Secretary in 1994 and Defence Secretary in 1995. On the libertarian Right of the Tory Party he became a noted Eurosceptic and was generally believed to have been included in John Major's definition of "bastards" in the Cabinet who were plotting to undermine his position. Unable to contain an outwardly ambitious persona, he came to epitomise everything that the electorate disliked about that Government and his defeat at Southgate in 1997 was one of the most celebrated moments of Election night, so much so that a book was published, entitled, "Were you up for Portillo?"

Michael Portillo MP
Wikipedia

After his defeat he appeared to soften his image, even to the point of admitting publicly to homosexual liaisons as a University student, not something that historically would be expected to enhance a career in the Conservative Party. Nevertheless it was always assumed he would seek a return to politics and when he did so at Kensington & Chelsea it was not long before he re-appeared as Shadow Chancellor under William Hague, the new Tory leader. Following a further landslide defeat, in 2001, Hague resigned and Portillo put his name forward to succeed him. Initially the front-runner, he failed to secure the votes of sufficient Tory MPs to allow his name to go forward to the Party membership in the final election run-off and he was once again marginalised. Following the election of Iain Duncan-Smith he announced his retirement from Front Bench politics and in 2003, after Duncan-Smith was compelled to stand down as leader, he confirmed his intention to retire from the Commons at the subsequent General Election. Following his retirement from the House he pursued a career in broadcasting.

Sir Malcolm Rifkind (Conservative), who was elected in 2005, was born the son of a draper of Lithuanian Jewish origins, in Edinburgh in 1946 where he attended George Watson's School and the University where he took a Law degree and a post graduate degree in political economy. In 1967-9 he lived in Southern Rhodesia (now Zimbabwe) and taught as a University politics lecturer. Returning to Scotland he practised as an advocate until 1979 and six years later was appointed a Queens Council. He entered politics initially in 1970 when he unsuccessfully contested Edinburgh Central and was an Edinburgh City councillor until 1974 when he was returned as MP for the Pentlands division of his

Sir Malcolm Rifkind MP
© Sir Malcolm Rifkind

home city, a constituency he represented until he was defeated in 1997, an election that saw the historic defeat of every Conservative standing in Scotland. A Scottish Tory who was in favour of devolved government, he resigned from a front bench position in 1977 as his Party was opposed but when the Tories returned to power in 1979 he was appointed a Parliamentary Under Secretary of State at the Scottish Office. He was transferred in a similar role to the Foreign and Commonwealth Office in the wake of resignations at the time of the Falklands War and was promoted to Minister of State in 1983. He entered the Cabinet as Secretary of State for Scotland in 1986 but four years later became Secretary of State for Transport; and in 1992 Secretary of State for Defence. He was Foreign Secretary between 1995 and 1997. In defeat he turned his attentions to consultancy and his other interests as a member of the Court of Edinburgh University; the Queen's Bodyguard in Scotland (The Archers); and his role of colonel in the Territorial Army. He stood again at Edinburgh Pentlands in 2001 but was defeated. Following his election in 2005 he was appointed Shadow Work and Pensions Minister. After the leadership election in which David Cameron became Tory leader, Rifkind stepped down from the Shadow Cabinet, having failed to be selected as Shadow Foreign Secretary. In 2010 he was appointed Chairman of the Intelligence and Security Committee.

Regent's Park & Kensington North

Part of an election leaflet for Karen Buck MP
Peoples History Museum Manchester

Karen Buck (Labour) was born in 1958 at Castle Derg, Tyrone, Northern Ireland but was educated at Chelmsford High School followed by the London School of Economics where she obtained three degrees; BSc (Econ), MSc (Econ), and MA. She became a local government and charity worker with the unemployed but from 1989-97 worked at Labour Party Headquarters at Walworth Road in London, latterly in the campaigns team. She was a Westminster City Councillor between 1990 and 1997.

One of the first candidates to be adopted from an all-female shortlist of candidates, she faced a Court challenge from an excluded male aspirant but was subsequently elected for Regents Park & Kensington North in 1997, after which she was elected Chairman of the London Group of Labour MPs. After the 2005 election she was appointed a Parliamentary Secretary at the Ministry of Transport, a post she held until 2007. At the 2010 election she defended Westminster North and against most expectations retained her seat.

MPs for Hammersmith, Fulham, and Ealing

From	at	To	Surname	First Names	Constituency	Party
1974	G	1979	Tomney	Frank	Hammersmith North	Labour
1979	G	1983	Soley	Clive Stafford		Labour
1983	G	1997	Soley	Clive Stafford	Hammersmith	Labour
2010	G	Date	Slaughter	Andrew		Labour
1974	G	1979	Stewart	Michael	Fulham	Labour
1979	G	1986	Stevens	Martin		Conservative
1986	B	1987	Raynsford	Wyvill Richard Nicolls		Labour
1987	G	1997	Carrington	Matthew Hadrian Marshall		Conservative
1997	G	2005	Coleman	Iain	Hammersmith & Fulham	Labour
2005	G	2010	Hands	Greg		Conservative
1974	G	1997	Young	Sir George	Ealing, Acton	Conservative
1997	G	2005	Soley	Clive Stafford	Ealing, Acton & Shepherds Bush	Labour
2005	G	2010	Slaughter	Andrew		Labour
2010	G	Date	Bray	Angie	Ealing Central & Acton	Conservative
1974	G	1979	Malloy	William John	Ealing North	Labour
1979	G	1997	Greenway	Harry		Conservative
1997	G	Date	Pound	Stephen Pelham		Labour
1974	G	1992	Bidwell	Sydney James	Ealing, Southall	Labour
1992	G	2007	Khabra	Piara		Labour
2007	B	Date	Sharma	Virendra		Labour

Notes: First returned at: B By-election, G General Election

MPs for Hammersmith North and Hammersmith

Frank Tomney (Labour) was MP for Hammersmith North from 1950 until he was deselected in 1979 in favour of a more left wing candidate. His main biographical details are in Chapter 11.

Clive Soley MP
Peoples History Museum Manchester

Clive Stafford Soley (Labour) succeeded him and continued to represent the area as MP for Hammersmith from 1983 and for Ealing, Acton and Shepherds Bush after 1997. Born in 1939, Soley attended Downshall Secondary Modern School, Ilford and later, as a mature student, Strathclyde and Southampton Universities. He became a probation officer and was sponsored by the General and Municipal Workers Union. A Tribunite "soft" left winger, he became a Party spokesman on Northern Ireland (1982-4), home affairs (1984-7) and housing (1987-92) but was dropped from the front bench after the 1992 General Election. He supported the "Blair-Prescott" combination as Leader and Deputy Leader in 1994 and in 1997, after the Party returned to power, was elected Chairman of the Parliamentary Labour Party[4]. He retired in 2005 and was ennobled as Lord Soley of Hammersmith.

He was succeeded by **Andrew Slaughter** (Labour) who was born in 1960 and educated at Exeter University where he attained his BA. He attended a Law College going on to practise as a barrister at the Middle Temple in 1993. A specialist in criminal, housing and personal injury law, he entered politics as a councillor for the North End ward of Hammersmith & Fulham borough in 1986 rising to become deputy leader in 1991 and council leader in 1996. He contested a by-election unsuccessfully at Uxbridge in 1997. Between 2005 and 2008 he was successively appointed PPS to three Ministers. When his seat was redistributed in 2010 he opted to fight the notional Labour seat of Hammersmith rather than Ealing Central & Acton, which was notionally Conservative; and won. He was appointed Shadow Justice Minister in 2010. Unlike his predecessor, he opposed the expansion of Heathrow Airport.

Fulham

Michael Stewart (Labour) was a Fulham MP from 1945 until he retired in 1979. His main biographical details are in Chapter 11.

At the 1979 election the constituency was won by **Martin Stevens** (Conservative), who continued to represent the area until his death in 1986. Stevens was born in 1929 and educated at Bradfield School and Trinity College, Oxford. He went into business and became a partner in a marketing consultancy group. He lived in Dulwich where he was a member of the LCC from 1955-8 and also sat on Camberwell Borough Council, from 1959-65. He contested Dulwich unsuccessfully at the 1964 and 1966 General elections and opposed Michael Stewart in both 1974 contests. From 1956 he was active as a member of the Cancer Research Campaign's Appeals Committee and was its chairman in 1968. Once elected to the House in 1979 he became a Parliamentary "consultant" for several organisations including British Gas, FW Woolworth, the Society of Company and Commercial Accountants, and the National Association of Probation Officers. In 1981 he was elected joint secretary of the Greater London Conservative MPs.

Wyvill Richard Nicolls ("Nick") Raynsford (Labour) took Fulham at the April by-election following Stevens' death in 1986 with a majority of 10% compared with 12% for the Conservative in 1983. Born in 1945 at Northampton, Raynsford was educated at Repton School; at Sidney Sussex College, Cambridge (where he graduated as MA); and at Chelsea Art College, where he obtained a Diploma. He worked in market research for AC Nielsen, a market research company, between 1966 and 1968 and then for various housing charities including the Society for Co-operative Dwellings, a national organisation that supported the establishment of new housing cooperatives and of which he was General Secretary. He was a member of Hammersmith & Fulham Council from 1971-5 and also worked for the London Aid Housing Centre (SHAC) of which he became Director from 1976-86, when he stood down to fight the by-election. Following his election he was appointed Parliamentary Private Secretary to Roy Hattersley, Deputy Leader of the Opposition but was defeated by a margin of 15% at the 1987 General Election and set up a company of housing consultants, Raynsford & Morris. In 1992 he was elected MP for Greenwich; then for Greenwich & Woolwich in 1997. He was appointed a Parliamentary Under-Secretary of State at the Department of the Environment in 1997, then Minister of State, Housing and Planning, London in 1999, transferring in 2001 to work in a similar capacity as Minister for Local Government for John Prescott at the Office of the Deputy Prime Minister. After Labour's 2005 election victory he was not re-appointed a Minister.

4 The Chairman of the PLP chairs meetings of the Parliamentary faction and is elected by Labour MPs at the start of each annual session of Parliament. Between 1906 and 1922 the Chairman of the PLP was usually the Party Leader.

Matthew Carrington MP
Peoples History Museum Manchester

Matthew Hadrian Marshall Carrington (Conservative) took Fulham back for the Tories in 1987 having failed to take it at the by-election won by Raynsford but held it for ten years until 1997 when he was defeated in the newly redrawn Hammersmith & Fulham constituency. Born in 1947 and educated at the Lycee Francais, Imperial College London and the London Graduate School of Business Studies, Carrington worked for the Saudi International Bank before going into politics. He served as John Patten's PPS whilst the latter was Secretary of State for Education but when he lost office Carrington's political ambitions were unrealised. He was defeated again fighting Hammersmith & Fulham in 2001. He subsequently became Chief Executive of the Retail Motor Industry (2002-06) and in 2007 was made a deputy chairman of Gatehouse Bank plc.

Hammersmith & Fulham

Iain Coleman MP
Peoples History Museum Manchester

Iain Coleman (Labour) was elected MP for Hammersmith & Fulham in 1997 at the age of 39. Born in London in 1958, he was educated at Tonbridge School after which he became a local government officer in Islington. He was elected a councillor in Fulham & Hammersmith in 1991 when he became Leader and was also elected Mayor on one occasion. From 1992 to 1997 he was vice chairman of the Association of London Authorities and after that Hon Secretary of the London Group of Labour MPs. He stood down through illness in 2005. In May 2010 he was re-elected as a councillor in his local borough.

Greg Hands (Conservative) was elected in 2005. Born in New York in 1965, his parents moved to Britain when he was seven and he was educated at Dr. Challoner's Grammar School, Amersham, and then at Cambridge University where he took a first class modern history degree. Whilst there he joined the University Conservative Party and became its chairman. After graduation he went into banking and got involved in local politics in 1998 when he was elected a councillor for the Eel Brook ward, then the Town ward, in Hammersmith & Fulham. He was elected Tory leader of the council the following year. In January 2009 he was appointed a spokesman on Treasury affairs. In 2010 he was selected to fight and won Chelsea & Fulham rather than the notionally Labour-held marginal of Hammersmith; a wise decision as it turned out. After the formation of the Coalition Government in 2010 Mr Hands was made PPS to the Chancellor of the Exchequer, George Osborne and from 2011, Deputy Chief Whip.

Hammersmith

At the 2010 General Election **Andrew Slaughter** (Labour), formerly the MP for Ealing, Acton & Shepherds Bush, was elected. His biographical details are described above.

Ealing, Acton

George Young MP, as an opposition whip, with Margaret Thatcher
Sir George Young

Sir George Young (Conservative) was elected MP for Ealing, Acton in 1974 and retained the seat until its impending redistribution in 1997 when he transferred to the safer seat of North West Hampshire (Andover). Born in 1941, Young came from a wealthy family and attended Eton College and Christ Church, Oxford. He started his career as a merchant banker with Hill Samuel but moved into the public sector, initially at the National Economic Development Office, where he was a researcher at Surrey University, then to the Post Office as an economist from 1969-74. He was a councillor on the London Borough of Lambeth from 1968 to 1971, and a GLC member for the London Borough of Ealing between 1970 and 1973. Two years after his election as Acton's MP he became an assistant opposition whip under Margaret Thatcher in 1976, and when the Party returned to Government in 1979 he was appointed Under Secretary for Health. This was a position which he held until 1981 when he moved to the Environment in a similar post, which he then left in 1986 when he seemed to be out of tune with her policies. His career resumed in 1990 when in July she reinstated him as a Government whip. After her downfall he was appointed Minister of State for the Environment under Michael Heseltine, whom he had backed for the leadership against John Major, but kept his post until 1994 when he was made Financial Secretary to the Treasury. In 1995 he made it to the Cabinet as Transport Secretary in which capacity he saw through the completion of the controversial proposals to privatise the railways before the Party's defeat at the 1997 Election. He transferred to the safe seat of Hampshire North West and remained on the Tory front bench as shadow Defence Secretary moving to become shadow Leader of the House in 1999. He resigned to stand for Speaker in 2000 but was unsuccessful. He was subsequently elected Chairman of the Standards and Privileges Committee. He stood again for the post of Speaker following the resignation of Michael Martin in 2009 but was again defeated, this time coming second to JohnBercow. However, a year later following the 2010 general election he once again entered government as Leader of the Commons and Lord Privy Seal, in which posts he attended the new Conservative-Liberal Democrat Coalition Cabinet until September 2012 when he was not re-appointed. However, following the resignation of the Chief Whip, Andrew Mitchell for allegedly maligning police officers, George Young was once again appointed to the Cabinet in his place, a post he held until July 2014.

Ealing North

In 1974 the constituency was held by **William John Malloy** (Labour) who had first taken it in 1964. His principal biographical details are in Chapter 11.

He held the seat until 1979 when he was defeated by **Harry Greenway** (Conservative) who held it until he was defeated in 1997. Born in 1934, he was educated at Warwick School and the College of Mark and St John, London before working as a teacher from 1957 to 1979, spending the last two years of this period as deputy head teacher of a comprehensive school in Catford, South London. A populist right-winger, he was one of 40 MPs who voted against the Government over the Maastricht Treaty. Prior to his success at Ealing North he had unsuccessfully contested three previous general elections; in 1970 at Stepney; and in the two 1974 elections at Stepney & Poplar.

Stephen Pound MP
Wikipedia

Stephen 'Steve' Pelham Pound (Labour), a Roman Catholic Church lay reader, took the seat in 1997. Born in 1948 in Hammersmith, he worked variously as a seaman, bus conductor and hospital porter before going as a mature student to the London School of Economics where he took a BSc (Economics) and a Diploma in Industrial Relations. He spent a year there as Student Union President. He also undertook a TUC Postal Studies Course and before entering Parliament was Area Manager of Paddington Churches Housing Association. He was also a member of Ealing council between 1982 and 1997, being Mayor of the borough in 1995/6. In opposition after 2010 he was appointed Shadow Minister for Northern Ireland.

Ealing, Southall

Sydney James Bidwell (Labour) was MP for Southall from 1966 to 1992. His biographical details are in Chapter 11.

After he was de-selected he was succeeded in 1992 by an ethnic Indian, **Piara Khabra** (Labour), a Punjabi Sikh born in 1924 who came to Britain in 1959. He obtained two degrees at the University of the Punjab (BA and BEd), but when he came to England initially got work as a labourer before becoming a social worker for the Inner London Education Authority. From 1978-82 he was an Ealing Borough councillor. He was also Chairman of the Indian Workers Association[5], a onetime Chairman of the Ealing Law Centre and founder member of the Ealing Race Equality Council. He became a JP in1977. He was selected by the local Labour Party amidst allegations of vote rigging, not just by the incumbent MP Syd Bidwell, who stood as an independent against him, but also by a fellow Asian aspirant, Valerie Vaz, the sister of Keith, the MP for Leicester East. Aged 67 at the time of his election in 1992, Khabra was the oldest person to reach the House for the first time and only the fifth of Asian or Afro-Caribbean origin to become a Labour MP. He died in June 2007 aged 82.

Khabra was succeeded by India born **Virendra Sharma** (Labour) in one of a pair of by-elections held on July 19th 2007 three weeks after the succession of Gordon Brown as Prime Minister. The other by-election was held in his predecessor, Tony Blair's seat of Sedgefield in Durham. The Tory candidate, Tony Lit, who only a month earlier had been photographed with Tony Blair at a fund raising dinner for the Labour Party and who joined the Tories only just in time to fight the by-election, came third standing for "David Cameron's Conservatives" in a bad result for the Party in the light of the changed Labour leadership. Sharma served on Ealing council for twenty five years before his election to the Commons. On arrival in England in 1968 he was a bus conductor and studied at the LSE on a Trade Union scholarship prior to becoming a day services manager for people with disabilities, in the neighbouring borough of Hillingdon.

Virendra Shara MP
Virendra's Sharma website

5 The Indian Workers Association was founded in Coventry shortly before the outbreak of the Second World War by a handful of students, professional men, and Sikhs. It sought to prepare Indian workers to take part in the struggle for Indian independence upon their return to India; promote social and cultural activities between the Indian and British people and provide for the general welfare of Indian workers.

MPs for Brentford & Isleworth, Feltham & Heston, Twickenham, Hayes & Harlington, Uxbridge & South Ruislip, & Ruislip- Northwood

From	at	To	Surname	First Names	Constituency	Party
1974	G	1992	Hayhoe	Sir Bernard 'Barney' John	Brentford & Isleworth	Conservative
1992	G	1997	Diva-Aditya	Niranjan Joseph 'Nirj' De Silva		Conservative
1997	G	2010	Keen	Ann		Labour
2010	G	Date	Macleod	Mary		Conservative
1974	G	1983	Kerr	Russell Whiston	Feltham & Heston	Labour
1983	G	1992	Ground	Reginald Patrick		Conservative
1992	G	2011	Keen	Alan		Labour Co-op
2011	B	Date	Molhotra	Seema		Labour Co-op
1974	G	1997	Jessel	Sir Toby Henry Francis	Twickenham	Conservative
1997	G	Date	Cable	Dr Vince (Vincent)		Liberal Democrat
1974	G	1983	Sandelson	Neville Devonshire	Hayes & Harlington	Labour/SDP
1983	G	1997	Dicks	Terence 'Terry' Patrick		Conservative
1997	G	Date	McDonnell	John		Labour
1974	G	1997	Shersby	Michael	Uxbridge	Conservative
1997	B	2010	Randall	John		Conservative
2010	G	Date	Randall	Alexander John	Uxbridge & South Ruislip	Conservative
1974	G	1979	Crowder	Frederick Petre	Ruislip-Northwood	Conservative
1979	G	2005	Wilkinson	John Arbuthnot Du Cane.		Conservative
2005	G	2010	Hurd	Nicholas 'Nick' Richard		Conservative
2010	G	Date	Hurd	Nick	Ruislip, Northwood & Pinner	Conservative

Notes: First returned at: B By-election, G General Election

Brentford & Isleworth

(Sir) Bernard "Barney" John Hayhoe (Conservative) was first elected MP for Heston & Isleworth in 1970 and in 1974 contested the new seat against the former Labour MP for Brentford & Chiswick following a redistribution that affected both constituencies . Heyhoe came out the winner in the February 1974 election by 726 votes, or 1.3% of the number cast and remained MP until 1992 when he retired. His main biographical details are in Chapter 11.

Nirj Diva MP with Margaret Thatcher (from an election leaflet)
Peoples History Museum Manchester

He was succeeded by **Niranjan Joseph De Silva Diva-Aditya 'Nirj Deva'** (Conservative), only the second ever Tory MP with an Asian background. The previous one was Sir Mancherjee Bhownagri who sat for Bethnal Green North East between 1895 and 1905 (See Chapter 3). Diva was born in Sri Lanka (Ceylon) in 1948 where he was educated at the St Joseph's Roman Catholic College in Colombo but came to England at the age of 17 and attended Loughborough University where he obtained a Bachelor of Technology Honours Degree in Aeronautical Engineering. He was also a Research Fellow and graduated from the Royal Aeronautical Society and the Institute of Mechanical Engineers. An integrationist emphasising his Britishness, he contested Hammersmith unsuccessfully in 1987, and was Brentford and Isleworth's MP from 1992 to 1997. A Deputy Lieutenant for London he was at one time editor of the Conservative magazine, *Crossbow*. He was elected a Member of the European Parliament representing South East England in 1999. He was made a Deputy Lieutenant for the City of London in 1985 and awarded a Knighthood with Merit of the Sacred Constantinian Military Order of St George for global work on poverty eradication.

Anne Keen MP
Wikipedia

He was defeated in 1997 by **Ann Keen** (Labour) who was born in 1948, educated at Elfed Secondary School in Clwyd, North Wales; and attended Surrey University. She became a Registered Nurse; was at one time Head of the Faculty of

Advanced Nursing at Queen Charlotte's College, Hammersmith Hospital and, before entering Parliament, was General Secretary of the Community and District Nursing Association. Working in the NHS she amalgamated five hospitals' nursing schools, bringing their courses into higher education at Thames Valley University. She was married to Alan Keen the MP for neighbouring Feltham & Heston between 1997 and 2011. She was private secretary to Gordon Brown, Chancellor of the Exchequer between 2001 and 2007, when he became Prime Minister. She was then appointed an Under Secretary of State at the Department of Health. During 2009 she and her husband (see Feltham & Heston below) became embroiled in the MPs' Expenses Scandal and were reprimanded by the Commons Standards and Privileges committee which ruled that they should repay £1,500 which they had wrongly claimed in respect of second home expenses given that their main home was empty and uninhabitable at the time.

Mary Macleod MP
Mary Macleod

Ann Keen was defeated in 2010 by **Mary Macleod** (Conservative), who was appointed a PPS to the Minister of State for Policing and Justice shortly after the General Election. She subsequently served in a similar capacity to the Secretary of State for Culture. Born in London and living in Chiswick she was an Ambassador for the Charity Action Aid and for twenty years was a management consultant with Andersens and Accenture. During the ill fated 2007 takeover of AMRO by the Royal Bank of Scotland which led to the collapse of Britain's largest banking corporation, she was Group Communications Head of Transition at RBS.

Feltham & Heston

Russell Whiston Kerr (Labour) had been elected MP for Feltham in 1955 and retained the seat when it was redrawn in 1974 but was defeated in 1983. His principal biographical details are in Chapter 11.

He was succeeded by **(Reginald) Patrick Ground QC** (Conservative) who had contested the same seat unsuccessfully at three preceding General Elections. Born in 1932, Ground was educated at Beckenham & Penge County Grammar School; the Lycee Guy Lussac, Limoges (France); Selwyn College, Cambridge; and Magdalen College, Oxford, where he was President of the University Conservative Association in 1958. He was a member of the Hammersmith Borough council from 1968-71 representing the Parsons Green ward and, following his election at Feltham & Heston, was made PPS to Sir Nicholas Lylle, Solicitor-General from 1987 until 1992, when he lost his seat. A Barrister specialising in Judicial Review, administrative and public law, property litigation, planning and local government, he was unsuccessful in seeking nomination as the Tory candidate for the new post of London Mayor in 1999.

Alan Keen (Labour Co-operative), who won the seat in 1992, was married to Ann Keen, (MP for the neighbouring seat of Brentford & Isleworth 1997-2010). Born in 1937 in Lewisham, he was brought up near the Grangetown steelworks in Middlesbrough; and was educated at Sir William Turners School, Redcar. He left Teesside at the age of 22 to join the army and did three years military service mostly at Wellington Barracks, Westminster. He did not sever his Teesside links completely, however, and worked for 18 years on a part-time basis as tactical scout for Middlesbrough Football Club assessing future opponents' tactics for several of the club's managers. A fire protection consultant, systems analyst, accountant and manager, he was a member of Hounslow Borough Council from 1986-90. Between 1999 and 2001 he was PPS to Stephen Timms MP. During the 2005 Parliament he was chairman of a House of Commons Committee that investigated Football. In 2009 Alan Keen was censured together with his wife due to an ineligible claim for second home allowance. (See Ann Keen above). Re-elected in 2010 he died of cancer in November 2011.

Seema Molhotra (Labour Co-operative) was returned at the by-election following Alan Keen's death which was held on 16th December 2011. She was born in Feltham in 1972 and was educated locally and at Warwick University going on to take her MA at Aston University. From 1995, in common with her neighbouring MP Mary Macleod, she worked as a management consultant with Accenture; and for Price Waterhouse Coopers. She was a co-founder of the Fabian Womens Network and the 2006 Chair of the Fabian Society.

Twickenham

Sir Toby Henry Francis Jessel (Conservative) was returned for Twickenham in 1970 and sat until defeated in 1997. His main biographical details are in Chapter 11.

He was beaten by **Dr Vince(nt) Cable** (Liberal Democrat) who was born in 1943 and educated at Nunthorpe Grammar School, York and Fitzwilliam College, Cambridge where he read Natural Science and Economics; and was President of the Union. He then went to Glasgow University where he gained his PhD. He worked as Treasury Finance Officer for

Dr Vince Cable MP from an election leaflet
Peoples History Museum Manchester

the Kenya Government between 1966 and 1968 when he returned to Scotland as a lecturer in economics at Glasgow University. Cable served as a Labour Councillor in Glasgow between 1971 and 1974, and contested the Glasgow Hillhead Division for the Party unsuccessfully at the 1970 General Election. He became a civil servant and worked as a first Secretary in the Diplomatic Service in the Foreign and Commonwealth Office (1974-1976). He was then Deputy Director of the Overseas Development Institute, including a period working as a Special Advisor to the then Labour Secretary of State for Trade and Industry, John Smith MP. Smith later became Leader of his Party but by then Cable had joined the Social Democrat Party after its formation in 1981 and contested York unsuccessfully for the SDP/Liberal Alliance in both the 1983 and 1987 General Elections. Between 1983 and1990 he worked as Special Advisor on Economic Affairs for the Commonwealth Secretary General, Sir Sonny Ramphal and from 1990 worked for Shell International: after 1995 as the company's Chief Economist. He was head of the economic programme at Chatham House[6] and on becoming an MP was appointed a fellow of Nuffield College, Oxford. He first contested Twickenham for the Liberal Democrats in 1992, squeezing the Conservative majority to make it the most marginal Conservative/Liberal Democrats seat in the capital. After becoming its MP in 1997 he was a member of the Treasury Select Committee; chairman of the all party Police Group, and treasurer of the all party Internet Group. He was the Party's 'shadow' Chancellor of the Exchequer during the period of global financial collapse in 2008/9 and was often cited in the media as the most convincing of the three Parties' spokesmen on the subject. Following the formation of a Conservative-Liberal Democrat Coalition Government after the 2010 election, Dr. Cable was appointed Business Secretary in the new Cabinet. This was despite reports that he was personally more favourable towards the idea of a coalition with the Labour Party. He remained an outspoken member of the Government and often appeared to be at odds with the overall thrust of economic policy pursued by the Chancellor, George Osborne.

Hayes & Harlington

Neville Devonshire Sandelson (Labour) was MP from 1971 until 1983, for the last two years sitting as a Social Democrat. He was defeated in 1983. His main biographical details are in Chapter 11.

(Terence) "Terry" Patrick Dicks (Conservative) was elected to succeed him and somewhat surprisingly held the seat that had been Labour since its inception in 1955, for 14 years. Born with cerebral palsy in 1937, he was University educated at Oxford and the London School of Economics after which he went to work for the Imperial Tobacco Company (1952-9) followed by the Ministry of Labour (1959-66). Between1971 and 1986 the Greater London Council employed him as an administrative officer and in 1974 he was himself elected a Hillingdon Borough councillor, becoming its deputy leader and chairman of housing from 1982-4. Earlier, from 1981-3, he had been personal assistant to the former leader of the opposition on the GLC. His first Parliamentary contest was at Bristol South in 1979 in which contest he was unsuccessful. A right winger, one equally forthright left wing opponent, Tony Banks MP, once said of him "His speeches are made additionally entertaining by the looks of horror on the faces of so many of his colleagues on the Conservative benches." Following his defeat he became a councillor in the Runnymede District of Surrey.

John McDonnell (Labour) took the seat in 1997 having

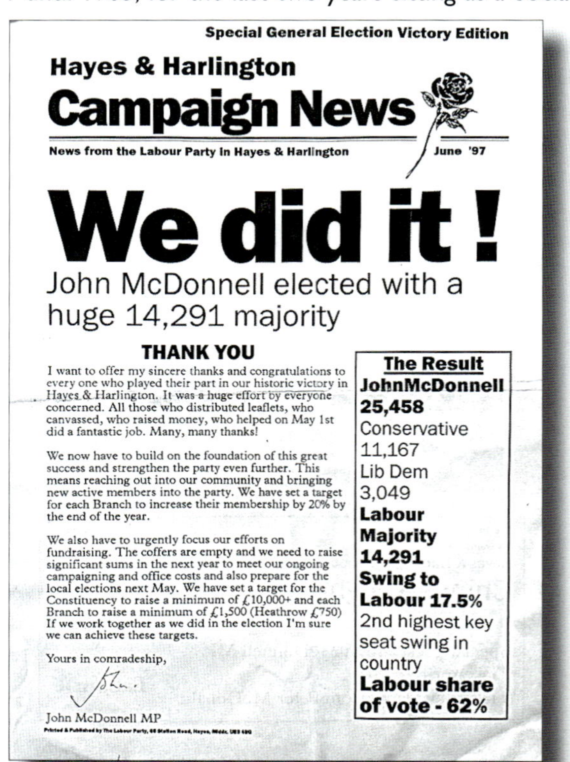
Special General Election Victory Edition

Hayes & Harlington
Campaign News
News from the Labour Party in Hayes & Harlington — June '97

We did it !
John McDonnell elected with a huge 14,291 majority

THANK YOU

I want to offer my sincere thanks and congratulations to every one who played their part in our historic victory in Hayes & Harlington. It was a huge effort by everyone concerned. All those who distributed leaflets, who canvassed, who raised money, who helped on May 1st did a fantastic job. Many, many thanks!

We now have to build on the foundation of this great success and strengthen the party even further. This means reaching out into our community and bringing new active members into the party. We have set a target for each Branch to increase their membership by 20% by the end of the year.

We also have to urgently focus our efforts on fundraising. The coffers are empty and we need to raise significant sums in the next year to meet our ongoing campaigning and office costs and also prepare for the local elections next May. We have set a target for the Constituency to raise a minimum of £10,000+ and each Branch to raise a minimum of £1,500 (Heathrow £750) If we work together as we did in the election I'm sure we can achieve these targets.

Yours in comradeship,

John McDonnell MP

The Result
JohnMcDonnell 25,458
Conservative 11,167
Lib Dem 3,049
Labour Majority 14,291
Swing to Labour 17.5%
2nd highest key seat swing in country
Labour share of vote - 62%

Peoples History Museum Manchester

6 Founded in 1920, and based at Chatham House in London, the Royal Institute of International Affairs which is based there, works to stimulate debate and research on political, business, security and other key issues in the international arena.

been defeated there by Dicks in 1992. Born in 1951 at Liverpool, McDonnell was educated in Great Yarmouth, at Burnley Technical College, Brunel University and Birkbeck College, London. A former local government officer and Secretary of the Association of London Government, his political interests included Membership of the Labour Party Irish Society; the League Against Cruel Sports; and Action for South Africa and Liberty. Chairman of the Socialist Campaign Group of Labour MPs, McDonnell was a leading advocate of traditional socialist principles in the 2001-05 Parliament. In one article entitled "Labour Awakes" he urged "socialists who have left the party in recent years in disgust at New Labour's policies to rejoin the party, and throw their weight behind this campaign for a [socialist] Labour future". His politics could not have been more different from those of his predecessor Terry Dicks of whom he said in his maiden speech, "I shall not perjure myself by praising my immediate predecessor". Following the 2010 election defeat of Labour, he announced that he would be standing as a candidate for the leadership in the wake of Gordon Brown's resignation. However, he subsequently withdrew in favour of Diane Abbot MP (Hackney North & Stoke Newington, see below).

Uxbridge, Uxbridge & South Ruislip

(Sir) Michael Shersby (Conservative) was first returned at a by-election in 1972 and held the seat until 1997 when he died days before he could take his seat in the House. His main biographical details are in Chapter 11.

(Alexander) John Randall (Conservative), who had been Shersby's election agent, was returned in the first by-election of the 1997 Parliament. Born in 1955, he was educated at Rutland House School, Hillingdon and at the Merchant Taylors School, Hertfordshire prior to graduating from London University with a degree in Languages (Serbo Croat). He went to work in the family retail business, Randalls of Uxbridge, of which he became Managing Director in 1988. He was also chairman of the Uxbridge Retailers Association. A keen ornithologist he was appointed an Opposition Whip in 1999 and served as such until 2010 apart from a period between 2003 and 2005 coinciding with the Iraq War which he opposed. Following the creation of the Conservative-Liberal Democrat Coalition in 2010 he was appointed Deputy Government Chief Whip. In the press (Guardian 18th December 2012) he was reported to have had a "strained relationship" with the Chief Whip, Andrew Mitchell MP, who was forced to resign following an incident in which he was alleged to have sworn at a police officer guarding the entrance gates at Downing Street. It was further suggested that Randall was responsible for reporting the police version of events to the Prime Minister's Office.

Ruislip-Northwood, Ruislip, Northwood & Pinner

Frederick Petre Crowder (Conservative) was the constituency's first MP and held the seat from 1950 until he retired in 1979. His principal biographical details are in Chapter 11.

He was succeeded by **John Arbuthnot Du Cane Wilkinson** (Conservative) who was born in 1940 and educated at Eton where his father was a teacher. He attended the RAF College at Cranwell and then Churchill College, Cambridge becoming an aviation specialist and RAF officer. Wilkinson worked at Conservative Central Office between 1967 and 1969; first as Head of the Universities Department and then from 1968 in the Research Department. In 1970 he contested and won Bradford West (West Yorkshire) and, though defeated in February 1974, remained to fight the October 1974 election in which he lost again. During the Major Government he was one of the leading Maastricht opponents and had the Whip temporarily withdrawn. He never held Ministerial rank but was a PPS from 1979-82. He retired in 2005.

Peoples History Museum Manchester

Nick Hurd MP
Wikipedia

(Nicholas) "Nick" Richard Hurd (Conservative), the son of the former Conservative Foreign Secretary Douglas Hurd and the fourth generation of his family to serve as a MP; was born in 1962 and brought up in Oxfordshire (in his father's constituency of Witney) and in London. He graduated from Oxford University and embarked on a business career; and from 1995 to 1999 represented a British bank in Brazil. From 2007 to 2009 he was an Opposition whip before being made Shadow Minister for Charities, Enterprise and Volunteering in July of that year. Following his re-election he was appointed to the post of Parliamentary Under Secretary of State for Charities, Social Enterprise & Volunteering (or Minister for Civil Society) at the Cabinet Office in the Conservative-Liberal Democrat coalition government promoting the Big Society concept advanced by David Cameron.

MPs for Brent, and Harow						
From	**at**	**To**	**Surname**	**First Names**	**Constituency**	**Party**
2010	G	Date	Teather	Sarah	Brent Central	Liberal Democrat
1974	G	1987	Freeson	Reginald	Brent East	Labour
1987	G	2001	Livingstone	Ken		Labour/Independent
2001	G	2003	Daisley	Paul		Labour
2003	B	2010	Teather	Sarah		Liberal Democrat
1974	G	1997	Boyson	Sir Rhodes	Brent North	Conservative
1997	G	Date	Gardiner	Barry		Labour
1974	G	1987	Pavitt	Lawrie Anstice	Brent South	Labour
1987	G	2005	Boeteng	Paul Yaw		Labour
2005	G	2010	Butler	Dawn Petula		Labour
1974	G	1997	Dykes	Hugh John Maxwell	Harrow East	Conservative
1997	G	2010	McNulty	Tony		Labour
2010	G	Date	Blackman	Bob		Conservative
1974	G	1987	Page	Sir (Anthony) John	Harrow West	Conservative
1987	B	1997	Hughes	Robert Gurth		Conservative
1997	G	Date	Thomas	Gareth		Labour
Notes: First returned at: B By-election, G General Election						

Brent East, Brent Central

Reg(inald) Freeson (Labour) held Brent East from 1974-1987 but had formerly been the MP for Willesden East since 1964. His principal biographical details are in Chapter 11.

Ken Livingstone MP
© Andrew Tift: National Portrait Gallery

He was succeeded by **Ken Livingstone** (Labour), who was born in 1945 and educated at Tulse Hill Comprehensive School and the Philippa Fawcett College of Education. He became a laboratory technician but quickly went into full time local politics. From 1971-8 he was a member of Lambeth Borough Council transferring to Camden between 1978 and 1982. He was also a member of the Greater London Council between 1973 and 1986. Until 1981 he represented Hackney North on the council and then from 1981-6 he sat for Paddington. He led a coup against the leadership after the Party won the 1981 elections and became Leader himself gaining a high profile for often controversial policies but generally endearing himself to most Londoners who were opposed to the abolition of the GLC promoted by Mrs Thatcher's Government. During this period he also found time to be joint editor of the "Labour Herald", the Party's official newspaper.

When the authority was abolished in 1986, Livingstone embarked on a career in national politics and gained the Labour nomination at Brent East leading another "putsch", this time locally against Reg Freeson. He also sat on the Labour Party's National Executive Committee from 1987-9. Despite retaining his seat at two subsequent General Elections he never made a mark on Parliamentary politics and with the advent of New Labour his left wing credentials made it unlikely that he would progress much further than the back benches. When the Blair Government brought in legislation to create a new Greater London Authority and a Citywide Mayor, Livingstone put his name forward to be the Labour candidate. The Blair leadership tried everything to defeat him for the Party's nomination and were in the end successful. However, despite previous indications to the contrary, Livingstone declared himself a candidate anyway and ran as an Independent against the official Labour candidate, Frank Dobson (See Holborn & St Pancras later in this chapter). As was required by its rules, Livingstone was expelled from the Labour Party but nevertheless won the Mayoralty and commenced the first term in the year 2000. He thus had the distinction of being not only the first holder of this office but also the first nominally independent holder of any major elected office in British political history. Despite this he sought to be readmitted to the Labour Party and was eventually successful in early 2004 in the months ahead of the next Mayoral Election when Tony Blair said that he had been wrong about the consequences of Livingstone's leadership of the metropolis. This time he was adopted as Labour's candidate by the overwhelming vote of members and affiliated organizations. He was re-elected with only a slightly reduced majority. The most notable achievement of his tenure was the introduction of a congestion-charging scheme, the first of its kind in the world to impose a tariff on motorists crossing a defined cordon in central London. Defeated for the mayoralty in 2008 he was once more adopted by his Party to fight the incumbent Boris Johnson in 2012 but lost that election too, though by a narrower margin.

Livingstone's successor as MP for Brent East in 2001 was **Paul Daisley** (Labour) who was born in 1957 in Acton and was educated at Littlemoor School in Oxford and Abingdon College. He became an accounting officer with Texaco, an oil company, for which he worked between 1976 and 1984 after which he established his own business. In 1990 he was elected a councillor in Brent and by 1996 was the Council Leader, serving until his election to the Commons. Sadly he had already been diagnosed with cancer and used his maiden speech, which he did not make until early 2002, to thank medical staff for his treatment. Already terminally ill, he died in 2003, less than two years after his election..

His death precipitated a by-election in September 2003 that was sensationally won by **Sarah Teather** (Liberal Democrat) who, with a swing of 29%, came from third place to take the seat with a majority over Labour of 5%. It was Labour's first by-election defeat in a seat it was defending for 15 years and the Tory candidate was pushed into third place winning only 16% of the votes cast. At 28 Sarah Teather also became the youngest MP in the House. Born in 1974, she joined the Liberal Democrats whilst a University student in 1993. A scientist by training, she worked for the Macmillan Cancer Relief charity at the time of her election and previously worked in science policy, first at the Royal Society advising the UK government on controversial aspects of science; and later as a science policy consultancy, evaluating public policies on science and innovation for Governments across Europe. She was elected to Islington Borough Council and at the 2001 General Election unsuccessfully contested Finchley & Golders Green. Following her success in the new Brent Central seat at the 2010 election, Miss Teather was appointed to the new Conservative-Liberal Democrat Coalition government in the role of Minister of State at the Department of Education. However, in September 2012 she lost her job in a Government re-shuffle.

Sarah Teather MP, speaking at Harrogate
Wikipedia

Brent North

Dr Rhodes Boyson MP
Peoples History Museum Manchester

Dr (Sir) Rhodes Boyson (Conservative) who was the first MP for Brent North was born in Lancashire in 1925 and educated at Haslingden Grammar School in Rossendale. He attended four Universities; Cardiff, Manchester, London (where he attained his PhD) and Cambridge. He became a teacher and, at the time of his election at Brent North, was the headmaster of one of the country's largest Comprehensive Schools; Highbury Grove in Islington. Although from a Labour voting family of cotton textile workers he became a Conservative and in 1968 was elected to Waltham Forest Borough Council. In 1970 he stood unsuccessfully as the Tory candidate for Eccles in Lancashire at the General Election and after his return at Brent in February 1974 embarked on a moderately successful ministerial career. From 1979-83 he was Under-Secretary for Education and successively a Minister of State, initially for Social Security in 1983-4, then in Northern Ireland until 1986; and finally for Local Government from 1986-7. He was dropped after the 1987 General Election and knighted, joining the backbench 1922 Committee. He was well to the right of the Party and in the 1990s was notably Euro sceptical, voting against some parts of the Maastricht Treaty legislation in 1992-3. His defeat at the 1997 Election on a huge constituency swing of nearly 19% was one of the notable events of election night. He died in 2012.

Barry Gardiner (Labour) defeated Boyson in 1997. Born on the 10th March 1956, Gardiner was educated at Glasgow High School, St Andrews University, Corpus Christi, Cambridge, and Harvard winning a John F Kennedy scholarship to do research there in 1983. Before becoming an MP he worked for 10 years as the Senior Partner for the Mediterranean Average Adjusting Company (Maritime Arbitrators). His political interests included Leasehold Reform and he also founded as well as chaired the Labour Friends of India; unsurprisingly perhaps given a large ethnic minority population from the sub continent in his constituency. He was a Cambridge City Councillor (1988 - 1994); and held the offices of Chair of Finance and Mayor. He was made Parliamentary Under-Secretary of State for Northern Ireland in April 2004. After the 2005 election he was appointed Parliamentary Secretary at the Department of Trade and Industry but in the run up to the 2010 election he was one of several MPs who received adverse publicity for the amounts of expenses claimed, not least the fact that he claimed a second home allowance despite living only 8 miles from Westminster. He also employed his wife as his office manager/secretary. In the end he successfully defended his seat in 2010.

Brent South

Lawrie Anstice Pavitt (Labour) was first elected at Willesden West in 1959 and for Brent South in 1974. He retired in 1987. His principal biographical details are in Chapter 11.

Paul Boateng MP: A portrait: oil on canvas by Jonathan Yeo 2003.
© Palace of Westminster Collection WOA 6483 www.parliament.uk/art

He was succeeded by **Paul Yaw Boeteng** (Labour), who was born in Hackney in 1951, the son of Ghanian and British parents, who lived in Ghana until his politician father was forced to leave the country. He was educated at the Ghana International School and Accra Academy prior to moving to England and the town of Hemel Hempstead. He attended Apsley Grammar School, Bristol University and College of Law; becoming a solicitor and later a barrister. He married a West Indian and rose through Labour's ranks as a black activist and radical GLC councillor from 1981-85. His other activities included membership of the World Council of Churches' Commission to combat racism; the board of the charity Christian Aid; and director of the English National Opera Company. He was appointed a minister in Tony Blair's first Government serving as Under Secretary for Health from 1997-8; then as Minister of State at the Home Office from 1998-9 and Deputy Home Secretary until 2001. After the 2001 General Election he was made Chief Secretary to the Treasury to become the first person of Afro-Caribbean ethnicity to reach the Cabinet. Prior to the 2005 election it was announced that he would stand down and, in the event of a Labour victory, would be appointed as British High Commissioner to South Africa, a post he held until 2009 when he returned to London. He was ennobled in 2010.

Paul Boeteng was succeeded by **Dawn Petula Butler** (Labour), then aged thirty-five, her Party's third black woman MP. She was formerly a national trade union officer of the GMB. In November 2005 she was appointed PPS to the Health Minister, Jane Kennedy and the following year was elected Chair of the All Party Group on Youth Affairs. She was also honorary president of the British Youth Council In 2008 she was appointed an assistant Government whip becoming the first black woman to attain ministerial office in the UK and in 2009 was named MP of the Year in the Women in Public Life Awards. However, in the same year she was reported in the Mirror newspaper as having claimed expenses for the fitting of a Jacuzzi at her North London home whilst also claiming for a house in the East End. In 2010 she contested the new Brent Central seat but lost narrowly to Sarah Teather (see Brent East/Central). She was the first black woman MP to speak for the government; as a junior minister in 2009.

Harrow East

Hugh John Maxwell Dykes (Conservative) sat as MP for Harrow East from 1970 until 1997. His principal biographical details may be found in Chapter 11.

He was succeeded by **Tony McNulty** (Labour) who took the seat at the age of 38. Born in London in 1958 he was educated at Salvatorian College, Harrow; Stanmore Sixth Form College and Liverpool University, where he gained a BA (Hons) degree in Political Theory and Institutions. McNulty later took an MA in Political Science at Virginia Polytechnic Institute & State University in the USA. Returning to England he was appointed a lecturer in organisational behaviour at the University of North London. He was a Councillor in the London Borough of Harrow from 1986-1997 where he became Deputy Leader of the Labour Group in 1990 and was Labour Leader from 1995. After Labour's 1997 victory he was appointed PPS to David Blunkett, Secretary of State for Education; served as a Government Whip between 2001-2; and then as a Transport Minister in 2003 until he was appointed as Parliamentary Under Secretary of State, Office of the Deputy Prime Minister in May 2004. After the 2005 election he was appointed a Minister of State at the Home Office in which role he had the controversial responsibility of promoting the introduction of Identity Cards. He was a founding member of the Labour Friends of India with his neighbouring colleague from Brent North, Barry Gardiner. Between 2005 and 2008 he held a succession of posts as a minister of State in the Home Office (Immigration, Security,

Tony Mc Nulty MP, from an election leaflet
Peoples History Museum Manchester

Counter Terrorism, Crime and Policing) until in October of that year he was transferred to the Ministry of Work and Pensions where he held successive posts responsible for welfare reform and employment; and was also Minister for London. However, in 2009 he became a central figure in the Commons expenses scandal for claiming a second home allowance on a house inhabited by his elderly parents. His constituency was also only eight miles from Westminster. He resigned from the Government in June 2009 and was subsequently heavily censored and forced to apologise to the House of Commons.

McNulty was defeated by **Bob Blackman** (Conservative) in 2010, a former compliance manager for BT (British Telecom). Born in 1956 and educated at Preston Manor High School in Brent and at Liverpool University where he gained a BSc in Physics and Mathematics, Blackman's first employment was with the Unysis Corporation in 1979. In 1991 he took a job with British Telecommunictions as a "Sales Tutor", which post he held until 1995. He entered into a career in local government in the London Borough of Brent to which council he was first elected in 1986 representing the Preston ward. From 19991-96 he was Leader of that Council following the decision of a number of Labour councillors to cross the council chamber. In 2003 he was unsuccessful in getting the Tory nomination for Mayor of London but was elected to the Greater London Authority in 2004. He was unsuccessful in securing election to the House on three earlier occasions – at Brent South (1992), Bedford (1997) and Brent North (2005). A fierce opponent of "gay marriage" and an advocate of a "one man one woman marriage", he was reported in the Daily Mirror on December 15th 2012 as having had an eleven year affair with a former councillor in Brent.

Harrow West

Sir (Anthony) John Page (Conservative) was first returned at Harrow West at a by-election in 1960 and remained its MP until he retired in 1987. His principal biographical details are in Chapter 11.

He was succeeded by **Robert Gurth Hughes** (Conservative), who represented the seat until 1997. Hughes was born in 1951 and attended Spring Grove Grammar School in Hounslow before going on to Harrow College of Technology after which he worked as a picture editor at BBC Television News. He entered local politics in 1974 as a councillor in Hounslow (1974-8) and sat on the GLC for Croydon Central between 1980 and 1986 when the council on which he was deputy Tory Whip was abolished. He contested Bermondsey at a by-election in 1983; and again at the General Election held in the same year. From 1989-90 he was PPS to the former Tory Prime Minister, Sir Edward Heath and from 1990-2 to Nicholas Scott, another reputedly left leaning Conservative. He helped run John Major's election campaign for leadership of the Party in 1990 and in 1992 was made a whip, being promoted two years later to be Under-Secretary for Public Service in which role he was responsible for the launch of the "Citizen's Charter" initiative aimed at improving standards in the public sector. He resigned in February 1995 admitting to an extra marital relationship. He was defeated at the 1997 General Election.

Gareth Thomas MP out on morning postal delivery with Royal Mail postie Sam out of Harrow's Elmgrove Road office
Gareth Thomas Twitter Feed

Gareth Thomas (Labour) was only 29 when he won Harrow West, the first time his Party had won the seat. Born in 1967 and educated at Hatch End School in Harrow, he graduated in 1988 from the University of Wales, Aberystwyth, with a degree in Political Science and became a schoolteacher after qualifying at Greenwich University. He was a local councillor in Harrow from 1990-7 and Labour's chief whip in 1996. After his election as an MP in 1997 he became PPS to Charles Clarke, who was then Minister of State at the Home Office; and in 2003 Thomas was appointed International Development Minister with regional responsibility for Asia, Eastern Europe, Latin America and the Caribbean. He too was a founding member of the Labour Friends of India with his neighbouring colleagues from Brent North and Harrow East. After the 2005 General Election he was appointed Parliamentary Secretary for International Development serving in that role until 2007 when in June he was transferred to the Department for Business, Enterprise & Regulatory Reform. He held a couple more Junior Ministerial roles until in October 2008 he became a Minister of State in the same department. In June 2009 he was appointed Minister of State at the Department of International Development. In 2001 he was elected Chairman of the Co-operative Party. In opposition after 2010 he was made Shadow Charities Minister.

MPs for the Boroughs of Camden, Islington, and Barnet

From	at	To	Surname	First Names	Constituency	Party
1974	G	1979	Jeger	Lena	Holborn & St. Pancras South	Labour
1979	G	1983	Dobson	Frank		Labour
1974	G	1983	Stallard	Albert William	St. Pancras North	Labour
1983	G	Date	Dobson	Frank	Holborn & St. Pancras	Labour
1974	G	1983	Finsburg	Sir Geoffrey	Hampstead	Conservative
1983	G	1992	Finsburg	Sir Geoffrey	Hampstead & Highgate	Conservative
1992	G	2010	Jackson	Glenda		Labour
2010	G	Date	Jackson	Glenda	Hampstead & Kilburn	Labour
1974	G	1983	Cunningham	George	Islington South & Finsbury	Labour/SDP
1983	G	2005	Smith	Dr Chris		Labour
2005	G	Date	Thornberry	Emily		Labour
1974	G	1983	Grant	John	Islington Central	Labour/SDP
1974	G	1983	O'Halloran	Michael Joseph	Islington North	Labour/SDP/Ind
1983	G	Date	Corbyn	Jeremy		Labour
1974	G	1992	Thatcher	Mrs Margaret Hilda	Finchley	Conservative
1992	G	1997	Booth	Hartley		Conservative
1997	G	2010	Vis	Dr. Rudi Jan	Finchley & Golders Green	Labour
2010	G	Date	Freer	Michael Whitney		Conservative
1974	G	1997	Gorst	Sir John	Hendon North	Conservative
1974	G	1987	Thomas	Peter John Mitchell	Hendon South	Conservative
1987	G	1997	Marshall	John Leslie		Conservative
1997	G	2010	Dismore	Andrew	Hendon	Labour
2010	G	Date	Offord	Dr Matthew James		Conservative
1974	G	1979	Maudling	Reginald	Chipping Barnet	Conservative
1979	G	2005	Chapman	Sir Sydney		Conservative
2005	G	Date	Villiers	Theresa		Conservative

Notes: G = First returned at General Election

Holborn & St Pancras South
Holborn & St Pancras

Lena Jeger (Labour) was MP from 1964-1979 when she retired. Her principal biographical details are in Chapter 11.

Frank Dobson MP
Wikipedia

Frank Dobson (Labour) took the seat in 1979 and won the newly combined Holborn & St Pancras constituency in 1983. Born in 1940, the son of a railway worker in York, he attended Archbishop Holgate's Grammar School in the City and graduated with a degree in Economics from the L.S.E. He was subsequently employed as a manager in the electricity industry before becoming assistant secretary to the office of the Ombudsman between 1976 and 1979. He was a local councillor in Camden for five years and its leader from 1973 to 1975. An Opposition spokesman for most of Labour's period out of power in the 1980s and 90s, when his Party won the 1997 election he was promoted to the Cabinet in one its most high-profile roles; Secretary of State for Health. His tenure coincided with the half centenary of the founding of the NHS which Dobson marked with some key innovations. He set up NHS Direct, a telephone and web based advice and information service in 1998, and the National Institute for Clinical Excellence, a body providing guidance, advice and quality standards for effective of medical treatments and procedures. He launched a massive hospital building programme whilst taking steps to increase the number of medical and nursing students. In 1999 he was persuaded by Tony Blair to stand down in order to contest the official Labour Party nomination for the new post of Mayor of London but lost the subsequent election when Ken Livingstone, who had lost the nomination, stood as an Independent and won, splitting the Labour vote. Dobson became a critic of several

Frank Dobson MP
Peoples History Museum Manchester

government policies. He was particularly trenchant in his opposition to the Iraq War, to invasions of civil liberties and to privatisation of parts of the NHS.

St Pancras North

Albert William Stallard (Labour) was MP for St Pancras North from 1970 until 1983 when the seat was abolished. His principal biographical details are in Chapter 11.

Hampstead, Hampstead & Kilburn

Sir Geoffrey Finsburg (Conservative) was MP from 1970 to 1983 and then for the successor seat of Hampstead and Highgate until 1997. His principal biographical details are in Chapter 11.

Glenda Jackson MP
as Gudrun Branwen in 'Women in Love'
© **David James: National Portrait Gallery**

He was succeeded by the world famous actress and film star, **Glenda Jackson** (Labour). She was born in 1936 in Birkenhead, the daughter of a bricklayer, going to the West Kirby Grammar School in the Wirral and then on to the Royal Academy of Dramatic Art after which she became a professional actress giving Oscar - winning performances in the film adaptation of DH Lawrence's *"Women in Love"* (1969); and in *A Touch of Class (1972)*. Some critics considered her the screen's greatest Elizabeth I, both in *Mary, Queen of Scots* (1971) and TV's *Elizabeth R* (BBC, 1971) but she played many starring screen roles over three decades until her last in 1991 just before she was elected to the Commons. She was always a political radical and left acting to concentrate on politics. She had been adopted in 1987 to fight the Greenwich by-election but lost the previously Labour seat in the face of a strong showing by the winning Social Democrat candidate Rosie Barnes (see Chapter 17). Nevertheless Jackson's personality was deemed an asset and the Hampstead & Highgate Party adopted her in 1990. Returned in 1992, she became a front bench spokesperson, opposing the latter stages of the privatisation of the railways by the Tory Government. Following Labour's victory in 1997 she was made the Under Secretary for Environment and Transport but, like Frank Dobson (see Holborn and St Pancras above), was encouraged to contest the Labour nomination for the Mayor of London but lost out and found herself in the wilderness in 1999 after which she too became a thorn in the side of the Government, being pointedly hostile to Tony Blair over the War in Iraq in 2003. She narrowly, and against most predictions, retained the new seat, twinned with Kilburn, at the 2010 general election.

Islington South, Islington South & Finsbury

George Cunnigham (Labour) was MP for Islington South and its successor seat including Finsbury from 1970 until 1983 when he was defeated standing for the Social Democratic Party. His principal biographical details are in Chapter 11.

He was succeeded by **Dr Chris Smith** (Labour), the first openly "gay" MP, who announced his homosexuality in 1984. Born the son of a Scottish civil servant in Edinburgh in 1951, he was educated at George Watson's School and Pembroke College, Cambridge, where he obtained a PhD in English Literature and was President of the University Union in 1972; he subsequently continued his education at Harvard. He was appointed a Whip in 1986 and was Shadow Treasury spokesman from 1987-92. He was elected to the Shadow Cabinet in 1992 and led on the Environment post but when Tony Blair became leader, he was appointed Shadow Heritage Secretary, to which Cabinet post he was also appointed when Labour won the 1997 General Election. When Blair won his second term in 2003, Smith was surprisingly dropped from the Government and returned to the backbenches where he too opposed the 2003 Iraq War. He was also a leading critic of the decision to levy University Top-Up fees. He was Chairman of the Environment Agency from 2008-14.

Emily Thornberry (Labour) succeeded Chris Smith in 2005 when he retired. Born in 1960 and aged forty-four at the time of her election, she was brought up by a single mother on a council estate and joined the Labour Party when she was seventeen. Educated at a Secondary Modern School and at Kent University, where she obtained a BA (Law) and LL.B, she worked at the Chambers of Michael Mansfield QC, a well-know radical civil liberties campaigner. A member of the Society of Labour Lawyers and of the Haldane Society of Socialist Lawyers, she contested Canterbury unsuccessfully at the 2001 election. A junior ministerial aide in the Department of Energy & Climate Change, she attended the Copenhagen Climate Change Summit in 2009 and after Labour's election defeat in 2010 was initially a Shadow Health Minister. In October 2011 she was made Shadow Attorney General by Ed Miliband in whose department she had worked in government. However, she was forced to resign in November 2014 over comments she made in a Twitterfeed during the bi-election at Rochester and Strood (Kent). These were widely reportedas disrespecting some voters.

Islington East

John Grant (Labour) was MP for Islington East (1970-4) then for Islington Central from 1974 to 1983 when he was defeated standing as a Social Democrat in Islington North. His principal biographical details are in Chapter 11(Islington).

Islington North

Michael Joseph O'Halloran (Labour) was MP from 1969 until 1983 when he was defeated standing as an independent, having left the Labour Party for a brief dalliance with the SDP in 1982. His principal biographical details are in Chapter 11.

Jeremy Corbyn MP
Peoples History Museum Manchester

He was succeeded by **Jeremy Corbyn** (Labour) who was born at Chippenham, Wiltshire in 1949 and educated at Adams Grammar School in Newport, Shropshire; subsequently attending the North London Polytechnic. He was for ten years a full time officer of the National Union of Public Employees which later sponsored him in his bid to become an MP, which he did representing the hard left in 1983 seeing off no less than two defecting former MPs in that contest, namely Grant and O'Halloran. An unreconstituted Marxist Socialist, close to Sinn Fein, which given the heavily Irish nature of his constituency in North London was perhaps unsurprising, he remained an oppositionist type of MP even after his Party was returned to power in 1997.

Finchley

Mrs MargaretThatcher (Conservative) represented Finchley from 1959 until 1992 when she was made a Baroness. Her principal biographical details are in Chapter 11.

Hartley Booth (Conservative) succeeded her but served only one term. Born in 1946 and educated at Queen's College, Taunton, Bristol University and Downing College, Cambridge; he became a barrister and Lloyds' under-writer. From 1981-3 he was a political adviser to the Home Office and to the Number Ten Policy Unit from 1984-7. Then in 1988, as a protégé of the Prime Minister, he was appointed Chief Executive of the British Urban Development Corporation, which office he held for two years. Following his election in 1992 he was made PPS to Douglas Hogg until in 1994 he resigned over a tabloid newspaper exposé of an affair with his researcher, an unfortunate and career stopping disclosure for someone with a strong Methodist upbringing. He failed to secure nomination for the new Finchley & Golders Green constituency in 1997 and became chairman of the charity Resources for Autism, established in 1997.

Finchley & Golders Green

Dr. Rudi Jan Vis (Labour), a strong pro-European and leading member of the Council of Europe who was elected in 1997, was born in 1941 in Alkmaar, The Netherlands. Following his school education in Holland he attended the University of Maryland where he obtained a BsC in Economics, moving to London to take his MsC (Econ) at the LSE and a PhD at Brunel University. He also received an Honorary PhD from Schiller International University. Before entering Parliament he was a Principal Lecturer at the University of East London and a Councillor in the London Borough of Barnet from 1986, continuing to serve until 1998. Politically his interests included CND, Friends of the Earth, Friends of Cyprus and Labour Friends of Israel, the latter reflecting to some extent the composition of the constituency's electorate. He died in 2010.

Vis was defeated in 2010 by **(Michael) Whitney "Mike" Freer** (Conservative) who was born in Manchester in 1960 where he was educated at Chadderton Grammar School (Oldham) and then at St Aiden's College, Carlisle. A relationship manager with Barclays Bank, Freer initially moved into local politics in Barnet in 1900 and subsequently became council leader in 2002. He unsuccessfully contested the nearby Harrow West constituency at the 2005 general election.

Hendon North

Sir John Gorst (Conservative) was first elected in 1970 and retained the seat until he was defeated at Hendon in 1997. His principal biographical details are in Chapter 11.

Hendon South

Peter John Mitchell Thomas (Conservative) was MP for Hendon South from 1970 until he retired in 1987. His biographical details are in Chapter 11.

He was followed by **John Leslie Marshall** (Conservative) who sat until 1997, when following the redistribution of seats in Barnet, he secured the Party nomination for Finchley & Golders Green, but was defeated. Before his election he had been a Member of the European Parliament, representing London North since 1979 but stood down from this role in 1989. Born in 1940 and educated at Harris Academy, Dundee; at Glasgow Academy and St Andrew's University, Marshall became a lecturer in Economics at Glasgow and Aberdeen before becoming a stockbroker in 1970, retiring in 1999. He was appointed PPS to Nicholas Scott in 1989 and then to Tony Newton in 1990 but progressed no further than that. He sought re-election at Finchley and Golders Green in 2001 but failed and entered local government as a councillor for the Garden Suburb ward of Barnet council becoming a member of the "cabinet". He was Mayor of Barnet in 2008/9.

Hendon

Andrew Dinsmore, campaigning for Labour for the Hendon seat.
www.dismore4hendon.co.uk

Andrew Dismore (Labour) was returned for Hendon in 1997. Born in 1954 in Bridlington, East Yorkshire, where his family were well known in local politics, he went to the local Grammar School going on to obtain two law degrees; firstly LLB at the University of Warwick, then LLM at the London School of Economics. Before entering Parliament he was a solicitor specialising in helping victims of accidents and crime, working on cases that included the Zeebrugge ferry disaster and the Kings Cross fire. In 1982, he was elected to Westminster City Council and from 1990 to 1997 was leader of the Labour Group on the Council in which role he did much to expose the activities of the Tory leadership of Dame Shirley Porter in the "homes for votes" scandal. Following his election to Parliament he was elected Hon Treasurer of the London Group of Labour MPs adding this to other interests, including Action for Southern Africa, the Co-operative Party, the Fabian Society and the Society of Labour Lawyers. After his defeat in the 2010 General Election he re-entered politics in 2012, when he was elected as a member of the Greater London Authority, representing Barnet and Camden.

Dismore was defeated in 2010 by **Dr Matthew James Offord** (Conservative) who was born at Alton in Hampshire in 1969. He took a first degree at Trent University in Nottingham going on to take a Masters at Lancaster; and in 2010 a PhD at King's College, London. He became a political analyst with the BBC and first contested a general election at Barnsley East & Penistone (South Yorkshire) in 2001 where he was defeated. The following year he was elected for Hendon and sat on Barnet Council of which he was Deputy Chairman. A member of the Royal Geographical Society, he trekked across the Libyan Desert in 2005.

Barnet, Chipping Barnet

Sir Sydney Chapman (Conservative) followed Reginald Maudling as MP in 1979. Born in 1935, he was educated at Rugby School and Manchester University and became an architect, town planner and consultant to a construction company. From 1964 to 1970 he also lectured at Wigan Technical College and between 1976 and 1979 was Director (Information) at the British Property Federation. In the 1964 General Election he unsuccessfully fought Stalybridge & Hyde (Greater Manchester) but was elected MP for the Handsworth division of Birmingham (1970-4) and was Parliamentary Private Secretary at the Department of Health and Social Security (1973-74). Despite being an MP for over a quarter of a century he only attained minor office. From 1979 to 1983 he was PPS to Norman Fowler both as Secretary of State for Transport and for Social Services and five years later he became a Government whip, a post he held until 1995. He retired in 2005.

Theresa Villiers MP
theresavilliers.co.uk

Theresa Villiers (Conservative) was elected in 2005. Born in 1968, she was brought up in North London and educated at the Francis Holland School before obtaining a first class Law degree at the University of Bristol; then her BCL from Jesus College, Oxford. She became a law lecturer at Kings College, London. In 1999 she was elected to the European Parliament to represent North London and in 2001-2 was Deputy Leader of the Tory Group. She was also a member of the governing board of the Conservative Party and Vice President of its youth wing, Conservative Future. Under David Cameron when Leader of the Opposition she occupied the post of Shadow Secretary of State for Transport but when the Conservative-Liberal Democrat Coalition Government was formed in 2010 she failed to secure a Cabinet role and was instead appointed Minister of State, effectively number two, at the Department for Transport. However, in a subsequent re-shuffle she was appointed to the Cabinet post of Secretary of State for Northern Ireland in 2012.

MPs for the Boroughs of Tower Hamlets, Hackney, Haringey, and Enfield

From	at	To	Surname	First Names	Constituency	Party
1974	G	1983	Shore	Peter David	Stepney & Poplar	Labour
1983	G	1997	Shore	Peter David	Bethnal Green & Stepney	Labour
1974	B	1983	Mikardo	Ian	Bethnal Green & Bow	Labour
1997	G	2005	King	Dr Oona		Labour
2005	G	2010	Galloway	George		Respect
2010	G	Date	Ali	Rushanara		Labour
1983	G	1987	Mikardo	Ian	Bow & Poplar	Labour
1987	G	1997	Gordon	Mrs Mildred		Labour
1997	G	2010	Fitzpatrick	Jim	Poplar & Canning Town	Labour
2010	G	Date	Fitzpatrick	Jim	Poplar & Limehouse	Labour
1974	G	1983	Brown	Ronald William	Hackney South & Shoreditch	Labour/SDP
1983	G	2005	Sedgemore	Brian		Labour
2005	G	Date	Hillier	Meg		Labour
1974	G	1983	Davis	Stanley Clinton	Hackney Central	Labour
1974	G	1979	Weitzman	David	Hackney North & Stoke Newington	Labour
1979	G	1987	Roberts	Ernest		Labour
1987	G	Date	Abbott	Diane Julie		Labour
1974	G	1987	Atkinson	Norman	Tottenham	Labour
1987	G	2000	Grant	Bernie		Labour
2000	B	Date	Lammy	David		Labour
1974	G	1979	Butler	Joyce	Wood Green	Labour
1979	G	1983	Race	Dr Reginald		Labour
1974	G	1983	Rossie	Sir Hugh	Hornsey	Conservative
1983	G	1992	Rossie	Sir Hugh	Hornsey & Wood Green	Conservative
1992	G	2005	Roche	Barbara Maureen.		Labour
2005	G	Date	Featherstone	Lynne		Liberal
1974	G	1983	Graham	Thomas Edward	Edmonton	Labour
1983	G	1997	Twinn	Dr Ian David		Conservative
1997	G	Date	Love	Andy		Labour
1974	G	1984	Berry	Sir Anthony	Enfield, Southgate	Conservative
1984	B	1997	Portillo	Michael Denzil Xavier		Conservative
1997	G	2005	Twigg	Stephen		Labour
2005	G	Date	Burrowes	David		Conservative
1974	G	1979	Davies	Bryan	Enfield North	Labour
1979	G	1997	Eggar	Timothy		Conservative
1997	G	2010	Ryan	Joan		Labour
2010	G	Date	De Bois	Nick		Conservative

Notes: First returned at: B By-election, G General Election

Stepney & Poplar, Bethnal Green & Stepney

Peter David Shore (Labour) was MP for Stepney and Poplar from 1974 to 1983 and then for Bethnal Green and Stepney, which he represented until his retirement at the 1997 General Election. Prior to 1974 he was MP for Stepney for ten years. His principal biographical details are in Chapter 11 (East London).

Bethnal Green & Bow, Bow & Poplar, Bethnal Green & Bow

Ian Mikardo (Labour) was elected for Poplar in 1964 and remained its MP until 1974 when he was returned at Bethnal Green & Bow, which he represented until 1983 when he transferred to Bow and Poplar. He retired in 1987. His principal biographical details may be found in Chapter 11(East London).

Mrs. Mildred Gordon (Labour) succeeded him in 1987 holding the seat until she retired in 1997 following boundary changes. Born in 1923 she was educated initially at Raines Foundation School and then attended the Forest Teacher training college Walthamstow, leaving in 1945 to teach English, History, then later English as a second language in the multi-ethnic London borough of Brent. She also taught typing to female inmates of Holloway Prison. In 1979 she unsuccessfully contested London North West in the European elections and was subsequently active in Greater London Labour Party activities as a member of the London executive from 1983-5 and as Joint Chair of the Party's policy committee.

Baroness King of Bow
www.oonaking.com/

Dr Oona King (Labour), only the second black woman MP (the first was Diane Abbott – see Hackney North and Stoke Newington below) was elected at Bethnal Green & Bow in 1997. She was born in Sheffield in 1967 and educated at Haverstock Hill School London, then at York University gaining a 1st class BA Politics (1990). She was also awarded a scholarship to spend a year studying at Berkeley-University of California. Graduating as a PhD she worked initially as a Researcher for the Socialist Group of the European Parliament and then as assistant to Glyn Ford MEP and Glenys Kinnock MEP and as researcher to the Socialist Group in the European Parliament. From 1995 to 1997 she worked as Regional Organiser for the GMB Union's Southern Region. During her time in the Commons she was PPS to the Minister for e-Commerce, and then PPS to the Secretary of State for Trade & Industry. She was defeated at the 2005 election. She sought the Labour nomination to be Mayor of London in 2012 but was defeated in the Party ballot by Ken Livingstone. She was appointed as Baroness King of Bow in January 2011.

George Galloway MP
© Steve Schofield: National Portrait Gallery

George Galloway (Respect), defeated King by just under 2% of the votes cast in 2005. Born in 1954 in Dundee, where he attended the Harris Academy, he worked for a garden centre and then for the Michelin Tyre Company. In 1977 he became a Labour Party organiser in Dundee (1977-83) and in 1980 was elected Chairman of the Scottish Labour Party. He moved to London in 1983 as General Secretary of the charity War on Want, a post he relinquished in 1987 when he was selected to fight Glasgow Hillhead, where he defeated the SDP leader, Roy Jenkins (see Chapter 14 –Southwark). A left-winger, he opposed attempts to drive out militants from the Party in the early 1980s and developed a close interest in Middle East affairs, amongst other things negotiating a twinning agreement between the City of Dundee and the Palestinian town of Nablus.

In 1994 he visited Baghdad and secured an audience with the Iraqi dictator, Saddam Hussein. He was recorded saying "Sir, I salute you, your strength, your indefatigability…" and was reprimanded by Party whips. In the tabloid press he was often described as being the 'MP for Baghdad Central' but he maintained that his aim was to ameliorate the suffering of Iraqi children caught up in the economic sanctions imposed on exports to the country. In 1998, he brought a young girl, Mariam Hamza to Glasgow for leukaemia treatment claiming that sanctions prevented her from receiving treatment at home.

He was totally opposed to the second Iraq War that took place in 2003, and after he suggested that Prime Minister Tony Blair was a war criminal he was expelled from the Labour Party. Following the fall of Saddam the Daily Telegraph published documents which they claimed were found in the Iraqi foreign ministry, and which made allegations of his receiving direct rights to acquire Iraqi oil. He won a libel case against the newspaper in December 2004 and was awarded £150,000 in damages.

In 2004 he was instrumental in setting up the new Respect Party, many of whose members were drawn from the Muslim communities disaffected by the Iraq War. He took Bethnal Green & Bow largely on the back of his opposition to the War. In 2005 the Telegraph's earlier allegations were made again, this time in the United States, and he demanded to appear before a Congressional Committee that was considering the issue. In so doing he took the opportunity to ridicule the Committee Chairman and enhanced his reputation as an orator.

George Galloway had promised to stand down from the constituency at the following election and instead fought the neighbouring constituency of Poplar & Limehouse where he was defeated, coming third. Despite this experience he bounced back at a by-election held in the West Yorkshire constituency of Bradford West in 2012, where he defeated Labour. This seat was another with a large Muslim electorate. During the Scottish Independence Referendum he was a tireless speaker on many platforms, opposing the "Yes" campaign, and was also one of only 43 MPs who voted against British air strikes on the positions of terrorist insurgents in Iraq which commenced in September 2014.

George Galloway's former seat of Bethnal Green and Bow was won in 2010 by **Rushanara Ali** (Labour). Born in Bangladesh, she came to Tower Hamlets as a seven year old child and following a local education attended Oxford University, and at the time of her election was an Associate Director of the Young Foundation. She formerly worked in the Home Office and as an assistant to Oona King, the MP defeated by George Galloway in 2005.

Poplar & Canning Town, Poplar & Limehouse

Jim Fitzpatrick (Labour) was elected in 1997. A Scot, born in 1952, he attended Holyrood Senior Secondary School in Glasgow where he worked until 1973 moving then to London where after a year working as a driver for a company called Mintex he joined the London Fire Brigade and was a fire fighter for 22 years. On the National Executive Council of the Fire Brigades Union from 1988 to 1997, after his election to the Commons he was made Parliamentary Secretary to Alan Milburn when he was appointed Health Secretary in 1999. After the 2001 General Election Fitzpatrick was an Assistant Government Whip (2001-02) and in 2002 was made a Lords commissioner. After the 2005 election he was appointed Minister (Parliamentary Secretary) for Local e-Government in the Office of the Deputy Prime Minister with the remit of exploiting the benefits of internet technology in local authorities.

Hackney Central

Stanley Clinton Davis (Labour) was MP from 1970 until 1983 when he retired from the Commons. His principal biographical details may be found in Chapter 11 (Hackney).

Hackney North & Stoke Newington

David Weitzman (Labour) was MP for Hackney North & Stoke Newington from 1974-9 but was first elected in 1945 for Stoke Newington. His principal biographical details may be found in Chapter 11 (Hackney).

He was succeeded by **Ernie Roberts** (Labour) who was MP until 1987 when he was deselected. Born in 1912 he was educated at St Chad's Boys elementary School in Shrewsbury and became an engineering worker. He became Coventry's youngest ever district union president in 1944, a Labour councillor a few years later, and assistant general secretary of the in the Amalgamated Union of Engineering Workers (AEU) in 1957 and was assistant General Secretary from 1957. From 1945-57 he was a member of Coventry City Council and in 1955 fought his first Parliamentary election, being defeated at Stockport. He was a founder member of the Institute of Workers' Control, the Anti Nazi League and the Campaign for Nuclear Disarmament. In 1982 he moved the writ for the by-election in Fermanagh and South Tyrone after the death of the sitting MP Bobby Sands while on hunger strike. He died in 1994.

Diane Abbott MP: A portrait: oil on canvas by Stuart Pearson Wright 2004.
© Palace of Westminster Collection WOA 6270 www.parliament.uk/art

Diane Julie Abbott (Labour) was first elected in 1987 after she beat Roberts in a selection contest. The first woman black MP, Abbott made a reputation as a "hard" left-winger, often opposed to the actions of her own Government after 1997. However, she fell from grace in 2003 when it emerged that she had sent her son to a Public School in preference to one in the State system. She was born in 1953, the daughter of Jamaican-born parents and attended Harrow County Grammar School for Girls and Newham College Cambridge, working afterwards successively as a Home Office Civil servant (from 1975-8), a Television reporter (1980-4) and as a GLC press officer, a role she also fulfilled for Lambeth Borough Council. Following Labour's 2010 general election defeat, she stood unsuccessfully to be Party Leader but was subsequently appointed to the opposition front bench.

Hackney South & Shoreditch, and Tottenham

Ron(ald) William Brown (Labour) was MP from 1974 until 1983. However, he changed parties in 1981 when he joined the Social Democratic Party but, standing for the SDP/Liberal Alliance in 1983, came third to Labour and was heavily defeated. His principal biographical details are in Chapter 11 (Hackney).

He was beaten by **Brian Sedgemore** (Labour) who was born at Exmouth, Devon in 1937. He attended Hele's School Exeter and Corpus Christi College, Oxford and was an administrative grade civil servant at the Ministry of Housing and Local Government between 1962 and 1966 when he became a barrister, practising until he was elected Labour MP for Luton West in 1974. When he lost the seat in 1979 he became a researcher for Granada Television. A left-winger opposed to Europe he voted with Tory rebels against the Maastricht Treaty in 1993. When he retired in 2005 he announced his defection to the Liberal Democrats during the election campaign and made a vitriolic speech against Tony Blair.

Meg Hillier (Labour) was elected in 2005. She was born in 1969 and educated in Oxford and at City University in London before she became a journalist. She was a member of Islington Borough Council for 8 years and in 1998/9 was its youngest ever mayor. In 2000 she was elected to the Greater London Assembly to represent Hackney, Islington and Waltham Forest going on to chair the London Assembly's Culture, Sport and Tourism committee. A trustee of the charity War Memorials Trust, she stood down from the GLA when she was adopted as Labour's candidate at Hackney South in 2004.

Tottenham

Norman Atkinson (Labour) represented Tottenham for 23 years between 1964 and 1987 when he was deselected. His principal biographical details are in Chapter 11 (Tottenham).

Bernie Grant MP
© **Geoff Wilson: National Portrait Gallery**

He was followed by **Bernie Grant** (Labour), the first fully black, Afro-Caribbean MP in British Parliamentary history. An insulin-dependent diabetic since the 1970s, he represented Tottenham from 1987, when he was selected in preference to Atkinson, until his death in 2000 when a black MP of a very different kind succeeded him. Grant was born in British Guyana, the son of teacher parents and educated at St Joseph's RC, Sacred Heart and Ituni Government Schools, and later at St Stanislaus College, Georgetown and then worked as an analyst in the Demerara Bauxite Company, Guyana. He came to England in 1963 at the age of 19 and worked as a railway clerk for two years before studying at Tottenham Technical College and Herriot-Watt University in Edinburgh, though he did not graduate, leaving in 1969 in protest at discrimination against black students. From 1969 to 1977 he worked as a telephonist, becoming a trade union officer for NUPE, then a race relations adviser in the housing department of Newham Council. He joined the Labour Party in 1973 and became a vocal activist in favour of Black sections and helped form the Black Trade Unionists Solidarity Movement for which he worked from 1981 to 1984. In 1978 he was elected to Haringey Borough Council of which he became leader in 1985, the first ever-black person to hold such a role anywhere in Europe. After rioting on the Broadwater Farm estate in 1985 when a policeman was horrendously murdered he is quoted as saying, "*The youths around here believe the police were to blame for what happened on Sunday and what they got was a bloody good hiding* ". Although his position as a Parliamentary candidate hung in the balance following this incident which attracted wide spread criticism from the right wing press, he was elected to Parliament in 1987. Famously, he entered his first State Opening of Parliament in African dress, attracting outrage in some quarters - but huge respect in others. After his election as MP for Tottenham in 1987 Grant remained prominent in promoting the cause of black people in Britain and famously said, "just because there are a few black MPs black people think we're part of society but we're not." He founded the Parliamentary Black Caucus, and took a leading role in establishing contacts with black people and politicians throughout the world. He travelled widely and in 1990 accompanied the Reverend Jesse Jackson (a famous American Democrat equal rights campaigner) to South Africa, greeting Nelson Mandela on the day of his release. He died in April 2000 from a heart attack at the age of 56.

David Lammy (Labour) was elected at the by-election in 2000 following Grant's death. Black like Grant, Lammy was born in London in July 1972 and at the time of his election was the youngest MP in the House. A highly intelligent and

David Lammy MP
davidlammy.co.ukvv

articulate man, he was educated at the University of London and Harvard University and became a lawyer, initially as an attorney for Howard Rice in California between 1992 and 1998, working also as a barrister at Serjeant's Inn in London from 1994-98 and for DJ Freeman until his election as an MP in the year 2000. A Member of Young Labour, Society of Labour Lawyers he also became a Trustee of Action Aid, a charity working in under developed countries, in December 2000; a member of the Archbishops Council and a Director of the Church of England's Board of Finance[7]. In 1991 he put his name on the list of lawyers as part of the Free Representation Unit a charity established in 1972 and dedicated to the provision of free representation to those who cannot afford legal representation in cases where legal aid does not apply. In 2000 he was elected a Labour member of the new Greater London Authority and once an MP was appointed PPS to Estelle Morris, the Education Secretary between 2001 and 2002. In a reshuffle that was precipitated by her resignation, Lammy was promoted to Health Minister and in 2003 was made a Minister in the Department of Constitutional Affairs. After the 2005 election he was appointed Minister for Culture in the Department of Culture, Media and Sport.

Wood Green

Mrs Joyce Butler (Labour) was MP from 1955 to 1979 when she retired from politics. Her principal biographical details are in Chapter 11 (Wood Green).

Reginald Race (Labour) succeeded her but only served one term. Born in 1947, he was educated at Sale Grammar School and the Universities of Kent and Essex where he studied Politics & Sociology, Political Behaviour and took a PhD in Bureacracy back at Kent. As a student he was chairman of Kent University Labour Club. He became secretary of the Kent Committee for the Defence of Trade Unions and was later employed as a trade union research officer with the National Union of Public Employees and was sponsored by them. He contested Ruislip - Northwood in the two elections of 1974. Following his defeat at Wood Green in 1983 he was appointed Head of the Programme Office at the Greater London Council and after its abolition went into business consultancy working in the Health Service, the trade unions and local government. He made a brief return to the political stage in 2001 when he was adopted to succeed Tony Benn, his mentor, as the Labour candidate for Chesterfield, Derbyshire, but lost the seat to a Liberal.

Hornsey, Hornsey & Wood Green

(Sir) Hugh Rossi (Conservative) was MP for Hornsey from 1966 until 1983 when he transferred to Hornsey & Wood Green, which he represented until 1992 when he retired. His principal biographical details are in Chapter 11 (Hornsey).

Mrs Barbara Maureen Roche (Labour) was elected in 1992. Born in 1954 in Hackney, she was educated at the Jewish Free comprehensive school in Camden and gained a BA (Hons) degree in Philosophy, Politics and Economics at Lady Margaret Hall, Oxford University. She trained as a barrister and prior to entering Parliament worked in a south London law centre. She was also a one-time executive committee member of the National Council for Civil Liberties. From 1981-5 she was chairman of the Battersea Labour Party and in 1984 contested Surrey South West in a by-election. She first contested Hornsey and Wood Green in 1987 and following Labour's election victory in 1997 was appointed Parliamentary Under-Secretary of State in the DTI and then briefly in 1999 was a Financial Secretary to the Treasury. From 1999-2001 she was Home Office Minister of State and counted amongst her responsibilities the issue of asylum, a political hot potato, not least for someone with her civil liberties background. After the 2001 Election she was appointed Minister of State in the Cabinet Office but resigned in 2003 over the invasion of Iraq. Despite her opposition to the War she was defeated at the 2005 election in which this proved to be the dominant issue.

Lynne Featherstone MP
lynnefeatherstone.org

Lynne Featherstone (Liberal Democrat) was elected in 2005. Born in 1951, she was educated at primary school near Archway, South Hampstead High School and Oxford Brookes University after which she became a designer, running her own company and then working for a national transport company. She was also a director of an electrical business in London. She was Leader of the Opposition on Haringey Borough Council between 1998 and 2003, representing the Muswell Hill ward. Also a member of the Greater London Authority from 2000 as a London-wide member elected on the proportional representation "top-up"

7 The Council was set up following the 1994 Turnbull Report to provide strategic guidance to the management of the Church of England.

principle, she was appointed the chair of the Assembly's Transport Committee between 2003 and 2005. Following the 2010 election and the formation of a Conservative-Liberal Democrat Coalition, Ms Featherstone was appointed to the role of Parliamentary Under Secretary of State at the Home Office as Minister for Equalities.

Edmonton

Thomas (Edward) "Ted" Graham (Labour) was MP from 1974 until 1983 when he was defeated. Born in 1925, he was educated at the Workers Education Association Co-operative College and the Open University. He contested Enfield West in 1966 and was finally elected at nearby Edmonton in February 1974. He was a Government Whip from 1976-79 and an Opposition spokesman on the environment until his defeat four years later in 1983 when he became a Lord.

Dr. Ian David Twinn (Conservative), who beat Graham, was born in 1950 and educated at Netherhall Secondary Modern and at the Boys Grammar Schools in Cambridge before attending the University College of Wales in Aberystwyth; and then the University of Reading. From 1975-83, when he was elected, he was a senior lecturer in planning at the South Bank Polytechnic and Chairman of the Dulwich Conservative Association. From 1985 to 1990 he was PPS to Sir Peter Morrison and then to David Trippier, Minister of State for Employment from 1990-92. After being defeated in 1997 Twinn became Director of Public Affairs at the ISBA, a lobby group for 400 UK advertising companies but in 2003 went part time after his election as a Member of the European Parliament following the resignation of another MEP, Lord Bethel. However, he lost out in 2004 when his Party won fewer seats and resumed his full time role at the ISBA.

Andy Love (Labour) who succeeded Twinn in 1997 was born at Greenock in 1949. He was educated at State schools and at Strathclyde University where he gained a BSc in Physics, afterwards moved to London where he managed a small import-export company, joined the Labour Party in Hornsey & Wood Green and became active in the Co-operative movement.. From 1980 to 1988 he was a Councillor in the London Borough of Haringey where he was Chair of Finance and Chair of Housing. Before entering Parliament he worked as a Parliamentary Officer for the Co-operative Retail Society and the Co-operative Party. In 2001 he became Parliamentary Private Secretary to Jacqui Smith MP, Minister of State for Health.

Andy Love MP
andylovemp.com

Enfield, Southgate

Sir Anthony Berry (Conservative) was MP from 1974 to 1984 when the IRA murdered him. Prior to that he was MP for the Southgate division of Middlesex for ten years. His principal biographical details are in Chapter 11.

He was succeeded at a by-election in 1984 by **Michael Denzil Xavier Portillo** (Conservative) whose principal biographical details may be found earlier in this Chapter (see Kensington and Chelsea)

Stephen Twigg (Labour) defeated Portillo in the most sensational result in the 1997 election. Born locally in Enfield on Christmas Day 1966, he was educated at Southgate Comprehensive School and Balliol College, Oxford; and from 1990-92 was President of the National Union of Students. He became the General Secretary of the Fabian Society and remained in post until his election to the Commons. From 1992 to 1997 he was also a councillor in the London Borough of Islington. An openly "gay" MP he was made PPS at the Privy Council Office but, following Labour's election victory in 2001, served as Deputy Leader of the House of Commons until 2002 when he was appointed Parliamentary Under-Secretary of State (Schools) with a particular focus on London schools and Primary schools. In December 2004 he was appointed Minister for School Standards in a re-shuffle that followed the resignation of the Home Secretary, David Blunkett. However, at the May 2005 general election he was defeated and whilst out of Parliament he worked for the Foreign Policy Centre, the Holocaust Centre and the Aegis Trust, an organisation that campaigns against crimes against humanity and genocide. At the 2010 election Twigg was returned for the safe Labour seat of Liverpool, West Derby. In 2011 he was appointed Shadow Secretary of State for Education but was demoted in 2013.

Stephen Twigg MP
Wikipedia

David Burrowes MP
Being a postman for the day
© David Burrowes

David Burrowes (Conservative) won the seat in 2005. He was born in 1969 and graduated from the University of Exeter where he was Vice chairman of the Conservative Association and, having been born and brought up in Enfield, also of the Eastern Area Tory Students. In 1994 he was elected for the Trent ward on Enfield Borough Council transferring to Winchmore Hill in 2002. He held various minor offices and in 2001 fought Edmonton unsuccessfully at the general election. Prior to his election he worked as a solicitor for a local company in Enfield serving as an advocate in police stations and courts in Enfield, Haringey and Hertfordshire. After his election he became a PPS working sequentially for Francis Maude, Cabinet Office Minister; Oliver Letwin, Minister responsible for Government Policy; and Owen Patterson, Environment Secretary.

Enfield North

Baron Davies of Oldham
Wikipedia

Bryan Davies (Labour) was MP from 1974 to 1979 when he was defeated. Born in 1939 he was educated at Redditch High School and at University College, London; at the Institute of Education in London; and at the London School of Economics. He became a teacher and lecturer and entered politics initially as the unsuccessful Labour candidate for Norfolk Central in 1966. Shortly before his defeat at the 1979 general election in Enfield he was made a Lord Commissioner to the Treasury (a Government Whip). In 1983 he contested Newport West (Gwent), which would ordinarily have been a Labour seat, but was defeated in the Tory landslide by a small margin of the votes cast. However, he did eventually make a return to the Commons, representing Oldham Central & Royton (Greater Manchester) between 1992 and 1997 when he was ennobled. From 2003 to 2010 he was Deputy Government Whip in the House of Lords bearing the title, "Captain of the Queen's Bodyguard of the Yeomen of the Guard".

Tim(othy) Eggar (Conservative) won the seat from Davies in 1979 and held it until he retired in 1997. Born in 1951, he was educated at Winchester School and Magdalen College, Cambridge where he took a Law degree; then at the Inner Temple. He never practised as a barrister but became a merchant banker and director of an oil company. He began his career with Hambros Bank and spent eight years with the European Banking Company. He entered Government in 1985 as Under-Secretary at the Foreign and Commonwealth Office in which post he served until 1989 when he was briefly Minister of State at the Department of Employment until 1990. From 1990 until 1992 he was Minister of State at the Department of Education and from 1992-1997 at the Department of Trade and Industry, where his principal achievement was the privatisation of the coal industry. However, he took a keen interest in the oil industry and after leaving Parliament became Chief Executive of Monument Oil which was acquired in 1999 by Lasmo, then an oil exploration company, for over half a billion pounds. This company was in turn acquired in the year 2000 by the Italian company Eni. Eggar was appointed vice-chairman of corporate finance at ABN AMRO, a global banking group with responsibility for the integrated energy sector and in 2004 his appointment as a non-executive director of Expro International Group PLC, another oil and gas company, was also announced. He became President of the Russo-British Chamber of Commerce in 2003.

Joan Ryan (Labour) won the seat in 1997. Born in Warrington in 1955, she obtained a BA (Hons) in Sociology and History at the City of Liverpool College of Higher Education before obtaining an MSc at the South Bank Polytechnic in London. She then worked as a teacher with the 16-19 age group at a 6th form college in Hammersmith. A former Barnet Councillor for the East Finchley ward elected in 1990, she became Deputy Leader of the Council in 1994 when a combination of Labour and Liberal Democrat Councillors overturned the Conservative Party's control for the first time in the council's history. After her election as MP for neighbouring Enfield North, she was PPS to Andrew Smith from 1998 at the Department of Education and Employment, moving with him when he became Chief Secretary to the Treasury in 2003 when she was made an Assistant Government Whip. After the 2005 election she was promoted to the role of Lord Commissioner of the Treasury, one of five Government whips but the following year became Parliamentary Secretary at the Home Office where she was responsible for immigration. A Vice Chair of the Parliamentary Party and Special Envoy to Cyprus, she was sacked from both positions in 2008 when she attempted to encourage fellow Labour MPs to seek a leadership election against Prime Minister Gordon Brown. She was defeated in 2010.

Nick de Bois MP
Wikipedia

Nick de Bois (Conservative) took the seat in 2010. He was born in 1959 in Ely Cambridgeshire and following his private education at Culford School Bury St Edmunds, took a HND in Business Studies at Anglia Ruskin University in Cambridge. A former public relations manager and managing director of an exhibition, conference and event company, he first entered politics in 1997 as the unsuccessful Tory candidate in Stalybridge & Hyde (Greater Manchester) and was also defeated in the Enfield North constituency in both 2001 and 2005.

Chapter 16
Metropolitan Essex since 1974

1974 - 1983: Greater London Authority Boundaries Fully Reflected in the Second Periodic Review

Although the Boundary Commission started its Second Periodic Review on 16th February 1965 it was not until February 1974 that a General Election was fought on its recommendations. These not only took account of population changes that had occurred but also of the new local authority boundaries that had been implemented in 1965. It was a requirement for London constituencies to be established wholly within the boundaries of the new Boroughs which in Metropolitan Essex were Newham, Barking & Dagenham, Waltham Forest, Redbridge and Havering. These were newly constituted as shown below:

Old Council Areas in Metropolitan Essex	New Boroughs	Remarks
West Ham, East Ham (Boroughs); North Woolwich parish of Woolwich (Kent Borough); small part of Beckton west of the River Roding and Barking Creek from Barking (Borough)	*Newham*	*4-way amalgamation*
Barking (not Beckton), Dagenham (not the area between Chadwell Heath and Hainault) (Boroughs)	*Barking & Dagenham*	*2-way amalgamation*
Leyton, Walthamstow Chingford (Boroughs)	*Waltham Forest*	*3-way amalgamation*
Wanstead & Woodford, Ilford (Boroughs); small part of southern Chigwell UDC known as the Manford estate in Hainault; the area between Chadwell Heath and Hainault from Dagenham (Borough).	*Redbridge*	*4-way amalgamation*
Romford, Hornchurch (Boroughs)	*Havering*	*2-way amalgamation*

Overall the impact was to reduce the total number of constituencies by one to fourteen. One seat was lost from East and West Ham whilst Walthamstow was also effectively reduced by one seat once boundary adjustments with Epping were taken into account. In Havering an additional seat was created based on Upminster.

Newham (3 seats)

In Newham the constituencies all took the Borough's name, though this had no historical significance being invented solely to describe the new local authority area. **Newham North West** covered the whole area of the former West Ham North (including Stratford Marsh, Stratford Town, Maryland, Forest Gate, West Ham and Upton) plus the northern parts of Plaistow taken from the former West Ham South. **Newham North East** covered the whole of the former East Ham North (namely Manor Park, Plashet, Woodgrange and Woodgrange Park); but acquired central East Ham and Little Ilford from East Ham South. Other parts of East Ham South and West Ham South were combined as **Newham South** including southern parts of Plaistow, Custom House, Canning Town, Silvertown, North Woolwich (transferred from Woolwich West in Kent) and Beckton, including the small part mainly comprising a massive sewage works transferred from Barking. It included the whole of the Royal Victoria and Albert Docks.

Waltham Forest (3 seats)

There were wholesale changes to boundaries. A new **Chingford** constituency (formerly part of Epping), extended

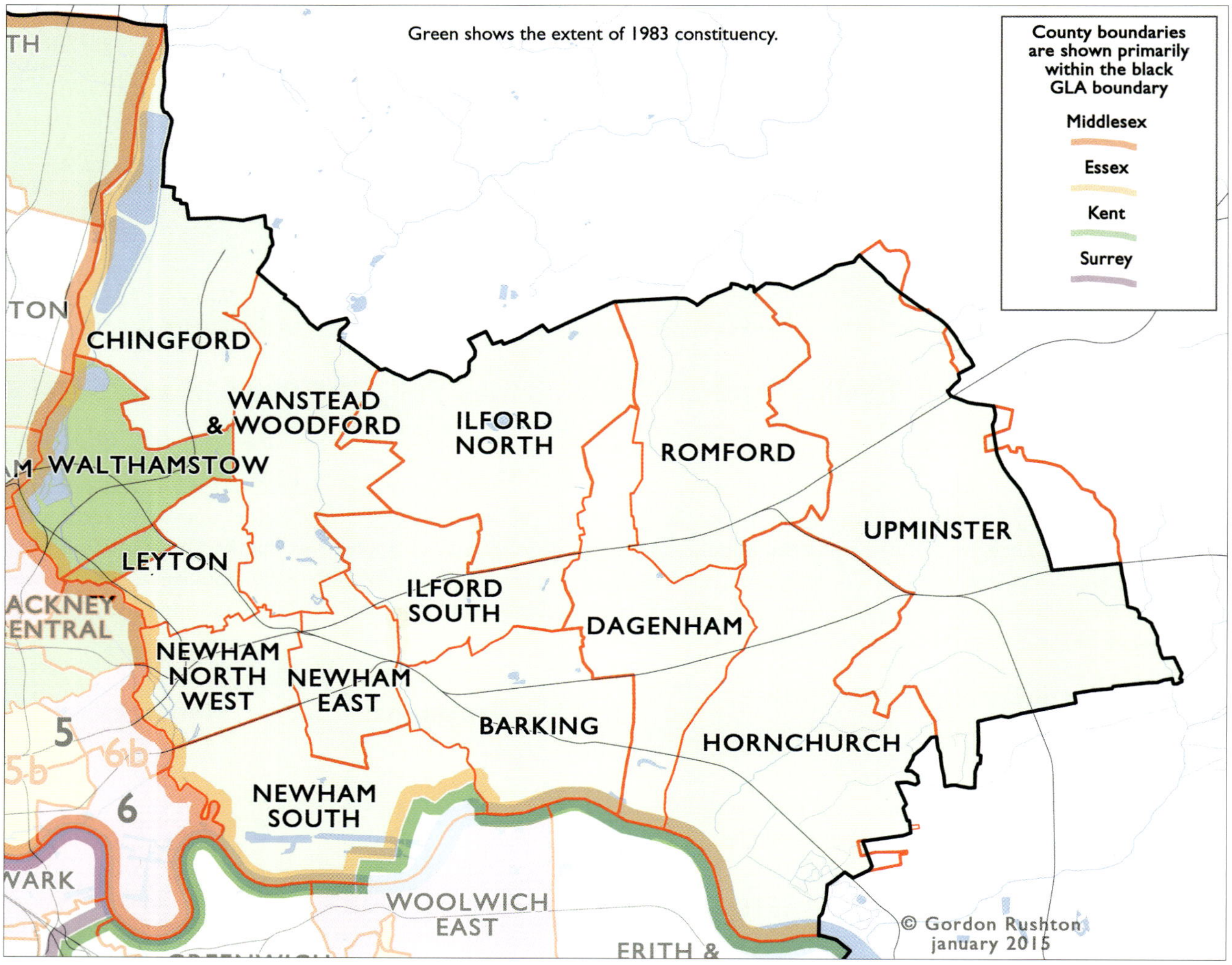

The map depicts Essex constituencies created in 1974. There was only one minor change in 1983 when the Lea Bridge Ward of Leyton was transferred to neighbouring Walthamstow.

from the new border between Greater London and Essex close to Epping Forest and Loughton as far south as Walthamstow's Church End ward. The place gets its name from the Norman "Cyngefort" which meant, "shingle ford" and which was altered to "Chingelford" in around 1243 AD. The Lea Valley bounded the new seat on the west side and the border with Woodford (in Redbridge Borough) formed the eastern boundary. It incorporated Chingford and Chingford Hatch (formerly in Epping) with Hale End and Highams Park (formerly in Walthamstow East).

Walthamstow ran west to east from the River Lea via Hoe Street to Wood Street; north to Highams Hill on the River Lea side of the constituency; and south to St. James Street. It comprised all of the former Walthamstow West together with those parts of Walthamstow East not placed in Chingford. Its principal districts were, therefore, Blackhorse Road, Higham Hill, Hoe Street, Lloyd Park, St. James Street and Wood Street. **Leyton** was also bounded by the River Lea and was altered so that it included Lea Bridge, Leyton Town, Cann Hall, Cathall, Leytonstone and Whipps Cross at the boundary facing Wanstead which was in Redbridge Borough.

Redbridge (3 seats)

Woodford constituency was renamed **Wanstead and Woodford** and extended southwards from the new Essex border near Buckhurst Hill and Chigwell via the Roding Valley to Wanstead flats adjacent to the Manor Park cemetery. It included Snaresbrook and all districts of Woodford (Bridge, Green and Wells); and Wanstead either side of the Epping branch of London Underground's Central Line; plus the Clayhall ward northwest of Ilford town centre including Redbridge itself. The Wanstead & Woodford constituency established in 1974 also covered wards that had previously been in Ilford North including Clayhall and Redbridge. Chigwell was outside London and so was not included.

Neighbouring **Ilford North** on the opposite side of the river Roding extended east as far as Hainault and south to the A12 dual carriageway; plus the Seven Kings and Chadwell districts east of Ilford town centre. It included Aldborough;

Barkingside; Chadwell (west of the Heath); Fairlop; the northern parts of Gants Hill and Newbury Park; and Seven Kings. **Ilford South** extended east from the River Roding opposite Wanstead and the south side of the A12 to Ilford town centre including wards to the south. It incorporated Cranbrook Park, Goodmayes, Loxford, Mayfield and Valentine's Park on the border with Barking.

Havering (3 seats)

East London housing had spread even further out since the previous review and the result was the creation of a third seat. The new **Upminster** constituency was to the east of both Romford and Hornchurch but did not extend as far south as the Thames, stopping short at the boundary with Essex north of Ockendon. The town got its name from "Upmunstra" which in 1086 meant "higher minster or church". Included in the constituency were Harold Hill (in the north transferred from Romford); Harold Wood, Ardleigh Green, Corbets Tey, Emerson Park, North Ockenden, Cranham and Upminster itself; all transferred from Hornchurch. **Hornchurch** extended from just south of Romford town centre as far as the river Thames at Rainham and included Squirrel's Heath, Elm Park, Hacton, Rainham and Wennington. To the north was **Romford** itself, which extended from Havering-Atte-Bower on the new Essex county border to the town centre and east to Gidea Park, including Collier Row, Noak Hill, Oldchurch and Rush Green.

Barking & Dagenham (2 seats)

Barking lost Beckton to Newham South but was otherwise unchanged including Creekmouth, Becontree, Mayesbrook, Parsloes Park, Rippleside and Valence Park. **Dagenham** was also little altered, although it lost a little populated area north of Billet Road to Ilford North. It incorporated Mark Gate, Chadwell Heath, Becontree Heath, Eastbrook, Goresbrook, Dagenham Heathway, Dagenham Dock and Hornchurch Marshes.

1983 - 2010: The Third and Fourth Periodic Reviews

Further reviews of constituencies took place in 1976 and 1995. The first of these had no real impact the only alteration being the transfer from **Leyton** of the Lea Bridge ward which was allocated to **Walthamstow** in 1983.

However, the Fourth Periodical Review resulted in changes to the shape of constituencies that were implemented at the 1997 General Election. For the first time the Commission was permitted to create constituencies that crossed Borough boundaries and the overall effect was to reduce the number of seats in the area from fourteen to twelve.

Newham (2 seats)

This Plaistow roadsign symbolises the cultural diversity of Newham Borough **John Nelson**

The boroughs of Tower Hamlets and Newham were considered together as were Redbridge and Waltham Forest. A new cross-borough constituency was created covering **Poplar & Canning Town**. This mainly Tower Hamlets based seat retained certain wards of the former Bow & Poplar constituency but gained Custom House, Silvertown and North Woolwich along with Canning Town from the former Newham South, including the whole of the Royal Docks. For the purposes of this book the new seat has been counted in Middlesex and details are in Chapter 15. Newham itself was reduced to two seats. **West Ham** comprised the whole of the former Newham North West together with the Plaistow area of the former Newham South. It included Forest Gate; Maryland; Plaistow; Stratford including the Marsh and Temple Mills; and Upton Park. **East Ham** covered the whole of former Newham North East with the addition of Beckton and the Royal Docks area of Newham South. It included Beckton; Little Ilford; Manor Park; Plashet; Woodgrange and Woodgrange Park. In effect by 1997 each constituency represented more or less the same areas of the former boroughs that after the First World War were covered by six constituencies.

Waltham Forest and Redbridge (5 seats)

Waltham Forest and Redbridge were considered together to create more evenly balanced electorates and one seat was lost. Wanstead & Woodford was abolished and merged with Ilford North to the east and with Chingford and Leyton to the west; the latter two being mainly in Waltham Forest. **Chingford & Woodford Green** comprised the former Chingford division, minus the Chapel End ward which was transferred back to Walthamstow; whilst those parts of Woodford that lay west of London Underground's Epping branch of the Central Line were added; namely the Church End and Monkhams wards of Redbridge. The new constituency comprised Chingford, Chingford Hatch, Hale End, Highams Park, South Woodford, Woodford Green and Woodford Wells. **Walthamstow** gained Chapel End but

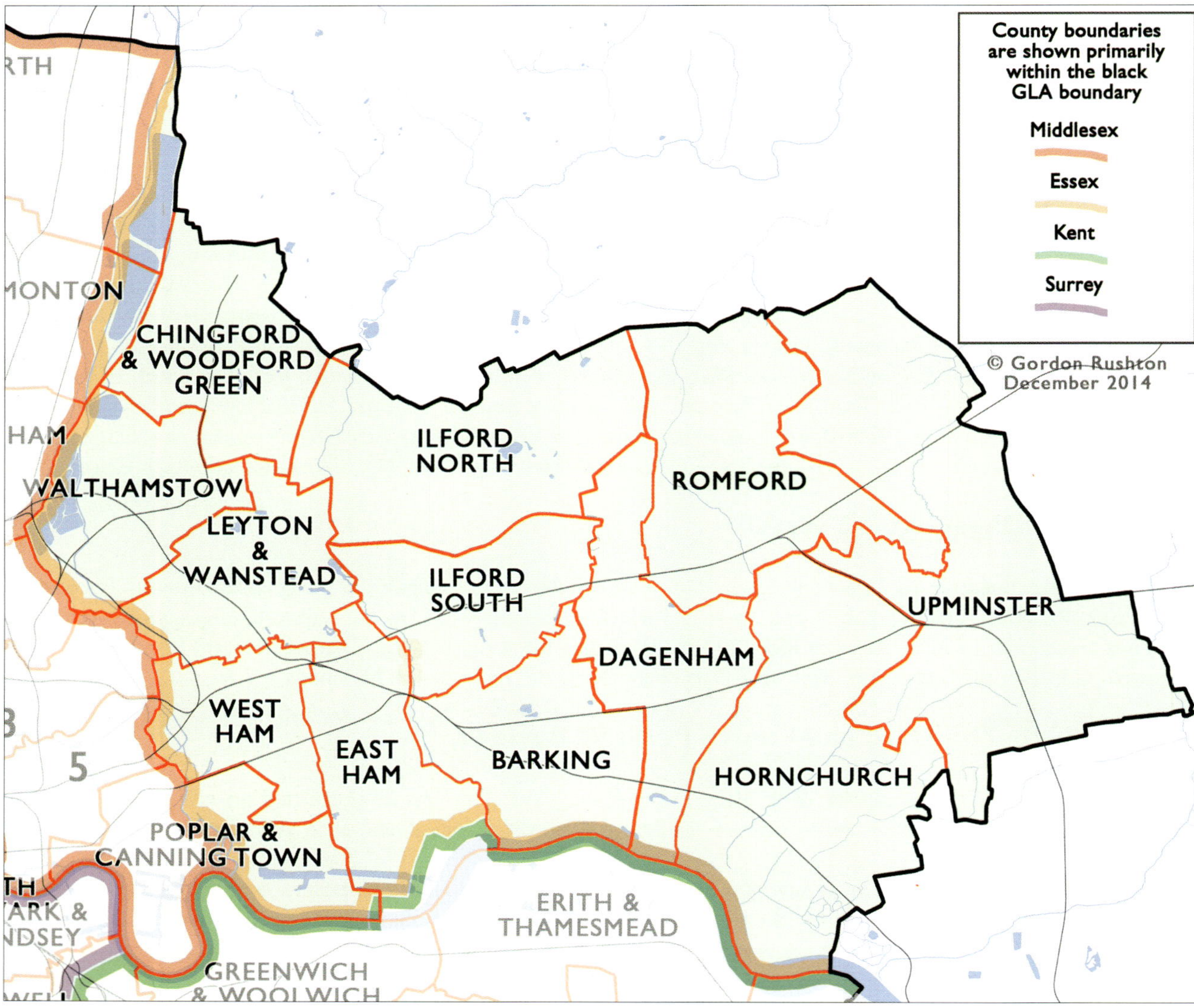

The map depicts Essex constituencies in 1997, when all were altered. The most significant change was the linking of Canning Town in Newham, with Poplar in Tower Hamlets, formerly Middlesex. The encroachments of Leyton into Wanstead, and Chingford into Woodford were also notable.

returned Lea Bridge to Leyton which in turn gained Snaresbrook and Wanstead wards from Redbridge (formerly in Wanstead & Woodford). Walthamstow thus incorporated Blackhorse Road, Chapel End, Higham Hill, Hoe Street, Lloyd Park, St. James Street and Wood Street. **Leyton & Wanstead** constituency included Cann Hall, Cathall, Lea Bridge, Leyton, Leytonstone, Snaresbrook, Wanstead and Whipps Cross. **Ilford North** gained the two wards of Woodford that were east of the Central Line of the London Underground and west of the River Roding. In turn the south-eastern wards of Chadwell and Seven Kings were lost to **Ilford South**, which experienced no other alterations. Ilford North comprised Aldborough, Barkingside, Clayhall, Fairlop, Gants Hill, Hainault, Newbury Park, Redbridge, Woodford and Woodford Bridge. Ilford South included Cranbrook Park, Goodmayes, Ilford Town, Loxford, Mayfield, Seven Kings and Valentine's Park.

Havering (3 seats)

In Havering only minor changes took place. Ardleigh Green transferred from **Upminster** to **Romford** and **Hornchurch** was unchanged.

Barking & Dagenham (2 seats)

The small Becontree ward that bordered Ilford South at Goodmayes was switched from **Dagenham** to **Barking** and was the only alteration to take place.

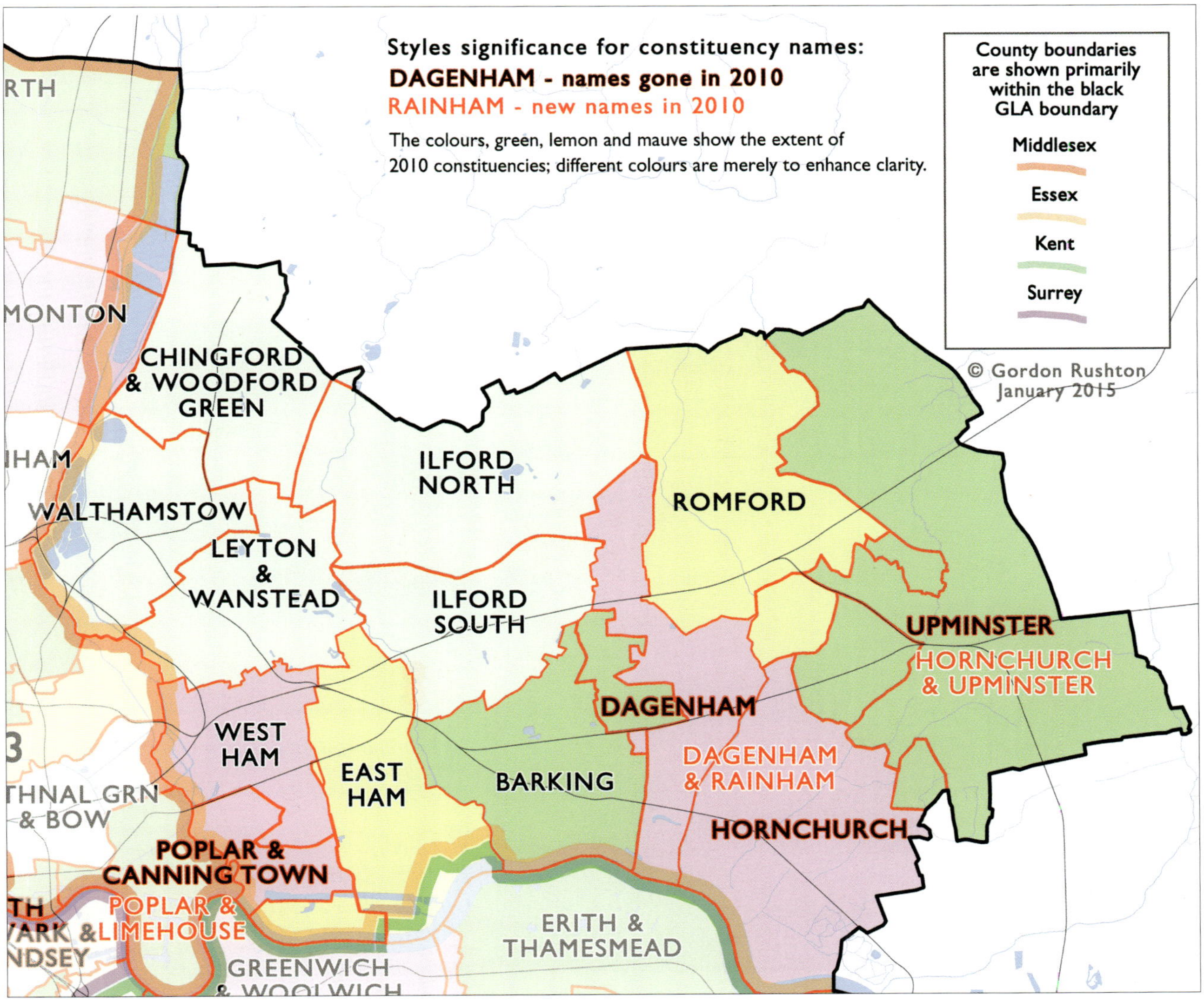

The map depicts Essex constituencies in 2010, when one seat was lost with the redrawing of boundaries around Hornchurch, parts of which were merged with Dagenham, Romford, and Upminster. Canning Town was restored to West Ham and Barking was affected; other constituencies were unaltered.

2010: The Fifth Periodical Review

In changes following (see map above) the most recent Boundary Commission review, Metropolitan Essex lost one more seat reducing the total to eleven, the lowest since before 1885. The previous pairings of Newham with Tower Hamlets and Redbridge with Waltham Forest were retained but this time no seats were lost or gained as a result, although boundary changes did occur in some cases and one seat was renamed. However, a new pairing of Barking & Dagenham with Havering resulted in a reduction from five to four seats there.

Newham (2 seats)

In Newham the former East and West Ham constituencies were returned to their historic borders as the Poplar & Canning Town seat was abolished and the burgeoning Dockland districts re-allocated so that Tower Hamlets regained two whole seats (see Chapter 15). **East Ham** gained North Woolwich, Silvertown and the Royal Albert Docks from Poplar & Canning Town and retained Beckton, Little Ilford, Manor Park, Plashet, Woodgrange and Woodgrange Park. **West Ham** gained Canning Town, Custom House and the Victoria Docks from Poplar & Canning Town; and retained Forest Gate, Maryland, Plaistow, Stratford, Stratford Marsh, Temple Mills, including the 2012 Olympics site, and Upton Park.

Waltham Forest and Redbridge (5 seats)

The boundaries of these seats were unaltered, apart from a tiny switch of electors in Snaresbrook, from **Ilford North** to **Leyton and Wanstead.**

Top Left: *This view shows Station Road Upminster, but the centre of town is less tranquil with many modern buildings and offices to sustain the 35.5k population.*

Top Right: *Romford Town Centre is a magnet for shoppers all over this part of London as it has been able to retain top rank retailers to make an enticing offer.*

Left: *The Olympic Village in Stratford (now providing local housing in the West Ham constituency) is seen across the River Lea, the boundary between Essex and Middlesex.*

Above: *This Aerial view of Beckton (East Ham Constituency since 1997) is taken from the Thames Cable Car, making connection from Expo to the Millennium Dome. The Essex terminal is in Custom House (West Ham). A trip in it illustrates clearly the new mix of housing that has developed around the Royal Docks where London City Airport has also been built."*

Left: *The area around Stratford has drawn benefit from connections with Eurostar (HS1) and the Docklands Light Railway, offering unrivalled connection across Europe and leading to unprecedented development of office and residential accommodation. Here in Stratford High Street a new tower block of apartments offers views across office blocks, with the legacy of the 2012 Olympic facilities nearby as 'cream on the cake'.*

All pictures John Nelson, unless otherwise attributed.

Havering and Barking & Dagenham (4 seats)

Northern parts of Dagenham were transferred to Barking which retained all of its former area. **Barking** thus comprised Becontree, Chadwell Heath, Dagenham Heathway, Marks Gate, Mayesbrook, Parsloes Park, Rippleside, Upney and Valence Park. Dagenham meanwhile acquired southern districts of the former Hornchurch constituency and was renamed **Dagenham & Rainham**. This comprised Becontree Heath, Dagenham Dock, Eastbrook, Elm Park, Goresbrook, South Hormchurch, Rainham and Wennington. **Hornchurch & Upminster** was an amalgamation of parts of the former two seats that bore those names. It comprised Corbet's Tey, Cranham, Emerson Park, Harold Wood, North Ockendon and Upminster (from Upminster); together with Hacton and Hornchurch from Hornchurch. Both former seats lost wards to **Romford**, which was otherwise unaltered. Harold Hill was added from Upminster together with Squirrel's Heath from Hornchurch. Other communities remained, namely Ardleigh Green, Gidea Park, Havering Attebower, Oldchurch and Rush Green.

General Election Results 1974 - 2010 by % majority

Constituency	1955 to 1970	Feb 1974	Oct 1974	1979	1983	1987	1992	1997	2001	2005	2010
Newham North West)		Lab40	Lab49	Lab35	Lab25	Lab30	Lab35				
Newham North East		Lab30	Lab35	Lab24	Lab22	Lab21	Lab28+				
Newham South		Lab51+	Lab58	Lab42	Lab27	Lab9	Lab8				
West Ham	2xLab							Lab58	Lab53	Lab32	Lab48
East Ham	2xLab							Lab49	Lab56	Lab33	Lab55
Leyton (& Wanstead)	Lab	Lab21	Lab29	Lab14	Lab12	Lab12	La30	Lab39	Lab38	Lab21	Lab16
Walthamstow	1xC 1xLab	Lab23	Lab31	Lab13	Lab4	C4	Lab8	Lab43	Lab44	Lab23	Lab12
Chingford (& Woodford Green)		C12	C11	C28	C30	C41	C34	C13	C15	C27	C30
(Wanstead &) Woodford	C	C27	C27	C42	C36	C39	C39				
Epping	C/Lab										
Ilford North	C	C0.5	Lab2-	C14	C26	C28	C20				
Ilford South	C	Lab3	Lab5	C4	C11	C11	Lab0.9	Lab28	Lab34	Lab22	Lab22
Ilford North								Lab7	Lab5	C4	C11
Barking	Lab	Lab39	Lab48	Lab20	Lab12	Lab10	Lab18+	Lab48	Lab38	Lab31	Lab36
Dagenham	Lab	Lab48	Lab48	Lab22	Lab8	Lab6	Lab16+	Lab47	Lab32	Lab25	
Dagenham & Rainham											Lab06
Hornchurch	C	Lab13	Lab15	C2	C20	C23	C19	Lab13	Lab4	C1	
Upminster		C2	C1	C17	C27	C34	C27	Lab7	C4	C17	
Hornchurch & Upminster											C31
Romford	Lab	C7	C7	C21	C27	C33	C27	Lab2	C17	C33	C36
C	5.5	5	4+	7	7	8	6	1	3	5	4
Lab	9.5	9+	10	7	7	6	8+++	11	9	7	7
Total	15	14	14	14	14	14	14	12	12	12	11

Key: C = Conservative; Lab = Labour; + = Party that won seat at General Election; + = Party that won seat at General Election held by-election in same Parliament; - = Party that won seat at General Election lost by-election to main opposition Party in same Parliament.

Politics in Metropolitan Essex: Newham, Waltham Forest, Redbridge, Havering; and Barking & Dagenham

The impact of the 1974 boundary changes on the political affiliation of constituencies was quite significant. The revisions reduced the total number of MPs by one. Labour lost one seat in Newham whilst the Tories picked up the added Upminster seat in Havering. Other changes in Havering probably secured Hornchurch for Labour but meant that they lost neighbouring Romford, which the Party had held since 1955. This is demonstrated by the 1974 results in which there was a swing away from the Tories. Revisions affecting Walthamstow, Chingford and Epping also seem to have favoured the Conservatives, who picked up the new Chingford seat comfortably in 1974 whereas on previous boundaries the swing to Labour would probably have delivered both Walthamstow East and Epping to the Party given the small majorities the Tories held there in 1970.

Overall it seems likely that had the 1974 Election been held on 1970 boundaries Labour might have won thirteen and the Tories only two seats; as it was Labour won only nine and the Tories five. However, it would be mistaken to view this necessarily as unfair because on the national scale Labour won more seats than the Conservatives but with fewer votes. They still went on to form a Government and strengthened their position in October 1974. Furthermore the new Havering seats were all fairly marginal and therefore capable of being won by either Party.

During the 1974 to 1992 period there were two by-elections in the area. On 23rd May 1974, only three months into the minority Labour Government, a by-election took place at South Newham. This was the one and only by-election of the short lived February 1974 Parliament. Labour retained this safe seat with a 50% majority over the Liberals, slightly below the 51% margin in February. In the October 1974 General Election Labour's majority increased to 58% However, substantial swings to the Conservatives occurred at Parliamentary elections throughout the late 1970s and the 1980s, driven by a change in the public mood. This was especially significant in Essex where working class loyalties to Labour began to break down during this period. The Callaghan Labour Government began to run into trouble and a by-election on 2nd March 1978 indicated that the Party would struggle to win the coming General Election. Ilford's fifth by-election of the 20th Century took place in the North constituency as it had in earlier by-elections in the borough. The Labour Party had won the seat in October 1974 by the small margin of 2% over the Conservatives. However, the Tories won the by-election by 12% and went on to record an even higher majority of 14% at the 1979 Election, which also saw the return of Conservative Government.

With the Thatcher administration encouraging council tenants to buy their own homes and with traditionally unionised industries reducing and losing their grip on the workforce, the Conservative Party succeeded in attracting support from Labour who were reduced to only six seats in the 1987 General Election, their lowest number of MPs elected in Metropolitan Essex since 1931. Ever since 1906 at least one seat in Walthamstow had elected a radical MP but in 1987 Walthamstow swung to the Conservatives; which would have been inconceivable in previous years. In retrospect it seems that the boundary changes that occurred in 1974 probably contributed to Labour's defeats during this period, although clearly the scale of its unpopularity at the time was the primary cause.

After the departure of Margaret Thatcher there was a change of mood and, although this was insufficient for Labour to win the 1992 general election, the Party did nonetheless manage to regain Walthamstow and Ilford South. During the 1992 Parliament there were further swings to Labour in by-elections. A sign of the Tories' impending defeat at the next general election came at a series of by-elections held on the same day (9th June 1994) in the adjacent Labour-held seats of Barking, Dagenham and Newham North East. The results in Barking and Dagenham recorded massive swings to Labour and away from the Conservatives of 27 and 27.9% respectively. The 1992 majority of 18% over the Tories at Barking was increased to 60% over the Liberal Democrats though this fell back to 48% at the 1997 Election. At Dagenham a 1992 majority of 16% over the Tories was increased to 62% although this too fell back; to 47% in 1997. In Newham North East a 1992 Labour majority of 28% over the Conservatives was translated into 60%. The constituency was re-drawn in 1997 but most of the area comprised the new seat of East Ham, which Labour retained with a majority of 49%.

When the 1997 Election was fought the political consequences of reducing the total number of seats by two were balanced. The loss of a seat in Newham and another based on Woodford would in normal circumstances have adversely affected both Labour and Tory Parties equally. As it turned out, however, the swing of opinion against the Conservatives in that Election was so decisive that they suffered their worst result in metropolitan Essex since 1945; winning only one seat based, as in that earlier General Election, on Woodford. Labour's tally of eleven seats at the 1997 contest, whilst stunningly convincing, was however nowhere near as good as it had been in its equivalent 1945 landslide when the Party secured the return of seventeen MPs in the area. The reduction was primarily the consequence of the relative decline in the populations of those working class areas just across the River Lea from the East End of London where Labour once did so well; although with the perspective we have now it may be seen that this was actually a very brief period indeed in electoral history.

A swing back to the Tories took place in 2001. They did better in nine out of the twelve constituencies and actually won back two seats from Labour; at Romford and Upminster. However, the real significance was that these were the only seats in the whole country that the Conservative Party won back from Labour in 2001. The so-called "Essex" effect that had benefited previous Tory administrations at Elections throughout the seventies, eighties and nineties appeared to have returned. Despite this Labour actually strengthened its position in Ilford South, recording a majority of 34% in a seat that they held as recently as 1992 with a majority of only 0.9% and which the Conservative Party would have hoped to win in order to form a Government. It seems probable that the ethnic mix of this constituency worked in Labour's favour.

At the 2005 election, however, a much larger swing back to the Conservatives was evident in this part of London. This resulted in the loss of two Labour seats (Ilford North and Hornchurch); and the strengthening of Tory majorities throughout the area. The relative position between the two main parties was very similar to 1992 when the Conervatives won a majority nationally; except that this time the national outcome favoured Labour, another indication that voting patterns in this part of London had become different. Party politics also remained something of a two-horse race, with the Liberal Democrats failing to win any seats. The anti-War vote in West Ham and East Ham, where there were large minority ethnic populations, including many Muslims, was also evident; with strong swings away from Labour.

The political impact of the 2010 changes meant that on the basis of the 2005 election outcomes both Barking and Dagenham & Rainham would probably have been Labour seats whilst Hornchurch & Upminster would have been Tory. Romford, though still Tory, would have been slightly more marginal on the basis of the new boundaries. In the event these outcomes were confirmed by the results in 2010 and the Conservatives were the net losers following the redistribution involving Hornchurch which effectively left them one seat short of their 2005 tally.

In all general elections held between February 174 and 2010 the Conservatives won 60 seats compared with Labour's 79. In addition the Tories won one by-election and Labour four.

MPs for Newham Borough

From	at	To	Surname	First Names	Constituency	Party
1974	*G*	*1979*	*Prentice*	*Reginald Ernest*	*Newham North East*	*Labour/Conservative*
1979	*G*	*1994*	*Leighton*	*Ron(ald)*		*Labour*
1994	*B*	*1997*	*Timms*	*Stephen*		*Labour*
1974	*G*	*1983*	*Lewis*	*Arthur William John*	*Newham North West*	*Labour*
1983	*G*	*1997*	*Banks*	*Tony*		*Labour*
1974	*G*	*1974*	*Jones*	*(Frederick) Elwyn*	*Newham South*	*Labour*
1974	*B*	*1997*	*Spearing*	*Nigel J.*		*Labour*
1997	*G*	*date*	*Timms*	*Stephen*	*East Ham*	*Labour*
1997	*G*	*2005*	*Banks*	*Tony*	*West Ham*	*Labour*
2005	*G*	*date*	*Brown*	*Lynn Carol*		*Labour*

Notes: First returned at: **B** By-election, **G** General Election

Newham North East, East Ham (from 1997)

Reginald Ernest Prentice (Labour) was returned at a 1957 by-election in East Ham and was elected for Newham North East in 1974 but in 1977 resigned from the Labour Party and served out the rest of his term until 1979 as a Conservative. His principal biographical details are in Chapter 12.

Prentice was succeeded by **Ron(ald) Leighton** (Labour) who held the seat from 1979 until his death in 1994. Leighton was born in 1930 and educated at Monteagle and Bifrons School, Barking; then at Ruskin College, Oxford. He was a printer by trade and within the Labour Party became an active campaigner against British membership of the European Community. From 1967-70 he was secretary of the Labour committee for safeguards on the Common Market and director of an all-party campaign from 1970-73. During the 1975 referendum campaign on British membership, he was national organiser of the national "No" campaign. In 1964 he contested Middleton & Prestwich (Lancashire) and in February 1974, Horsham & Crawley (West Sussex) but was finally elected at Newham in 1979. He was an Opposition Whip between 1981 and 1984.

The by-election following Leighton's death was won by **Stephen Timms** (Labour) who at the time had been Leader of the Council since 1990. Born in 1955 at Oldham, Lancashire, he was educated at Farnborough Grammar School (Hampshire) and subsequently gained an MA and MPhil at Cambridge University. Before entering Parliament he worked as a telecommunications analyst. In the Blair Government he was appointed Minister for Social Security (1998);

A 1997 election leaflet for Stephen Timms.
Peoples History Museum, Manchester

Financial Secretary (1999); Schools Minister (2001); and Trade and Industry Minister in 2002. A member of the Ramblers Association, the Plaistow Christian Fellowship and the Christian Socialist Movement, after the 2005 election, Timms was appointed Minister of State for Pensions. A year later he moved to be Chief Secretary at the Treasury under Gordon Brown who, when he became Prime Minister in May 2007, demoted him from the Cabinet and made him Minister of State for Competitiveness. A year later he made another move, this time to become Minister of State for Work and Pensions, where his remit was to reform the state pension system. Shortly before the General election of 2010 he became Parliamentary Under Secretary at the Department for Business, Innovation and Skills. Less than two weeks after his re-election in 2010 he was stabbed twice in the stomach by a woman at a constituency event. She was alleged to have been inspired by Al Qaeda, an Islamic fundamentalist terrorist movement. His injuries were not life threatening. In the trial at the Old Bailey following which she was sentenced to fifteen years imprisonment, militant Islamist protesters shouted from the public gallery, "God is great" and "British go to Hell".

Newham North West, West Ham (from 1997)

Arthur William John Lewis (Labour) was elected MP for Upton in 1945; for West Ham North in 1950 and for Newham North West in February 1974; and retired from politics in 1983. His principal biographical details are in Chapter 12.

A young Tony Banks campaigning unsuccessfully in Watford with the support of Tony Benn in 1979.
Peoples History Museum, Manchester

Lewis was succeeded by **Tony Banks** (Labour), who was born in Belfast in 1945 but educated at Archbishop Tenison's School, Kennington and later graduated from York University with a BA; and the London School of Economics with an MSc. Before entering Parliament in 1983 he was a researcher with the AUEW (1969-75) and an assistant General Secretary of the Association of Broadcasting Staffs (1975-83); and political adviser to Judith Hart, the Minister for Overseas Development in 1975. From 1970 to 1986, when it was abolished, he was a prominent member of the Greater London Council, being its chairman in its last year. He represented Hammersmith (1970-77) and Tooting (1981-6); and between 1971 and 1974 was also a councillor in Lambeth when his contemporaries included Ken Livingstone and future Tory Prime Minister John Major. A flamboyant and charismatic character, Banks resigned from the Labour front bench twice – once as a whip in 1987-88; and later when a social security spokesman in 1991 in opposition to the first Iraq War. An animal rights activist who introduced bills to ban fox hunting and to protect badgers, he was somewhat surprisingly chosen by Tony Blair to be the Sports Minister in 1997, though he was replaced in 1999 to become the Prime Minister's Envoy for the 2006 World Cup Campaign. Blessed with a great sense of humour he retired from the Commons at the 2005 general election and chose the title Lord Stratford of Stratford. He said that he would have preferred to have been known as Lord Banks of the Thames. He died in 2006.

Lyn Carol Brown (Labour) succeeded Banks in 2005. She was born in 1960 and was educated locally at Drew Road primary school in Silvertown and at Plashet Comprehensive School before graduating with a BA in English and Religion from London University (Roehampton College) where she was President of the Student Union. She worked initially as a Residential Social worker in Ealing. She was elected to Newham Borough Council in 1988 representing the Little Ilford ward and in 1992 stood unsuccessfully as the Parliamentary candidate in Wanstead and Woodford but was elected chair of Newham's Leisure Services Committee. A member of the London Region Sports Board; the London Arts Board and the Museums, Libraries and Archives Council, London; she established the London Library Development Agency. Whilst at Newham she played a leading role in promoting the idea of the Olympic Games coming to the area. In 2000 she was elected Chair of the Local Government Association's Cultural Services Committee. In 2006 she was appointed PPS to the Minister for Local Government and Communities and the following year went to a similar post working for the Secretary of State for Innovation, Universities and Skills. In 2009 she was made an assistant Government whip, a role she continued in opposition after Labour's 2010 defeat.

Newham South

(Frederick) Elwyn Jones (Labour) was elected as MP for West Ham South when the Plaistow constituency he had won in 1945 was absorbed by boundary changes. At the February 1974 election he was returned for Newham South but was immediately ennobled to become Lord Chancellor in the new Government and a by-election was held in May. His principal biographical details are in Chapter 12.

The by-election was won by **Nigel John Spearing** (Labour); a teacher at Wandsworth School from 1956-68, who had won Acton in 1970 and held it until February 1974 when its boundaries changed. His principal biographical details are in Chapter 11(Acton).

MPs for Waltham Forest Borough

From	at	To	Surname	First Names	Constituency	Party
1974	G	1992	Tebbit	Norman Beresford	Chingford	Conservative
1992	G	1997	Smith	(George) Iain Duncan		Conservative
1997	G	date	Smith	(George) Iain Duncan	Chingford & Woodford Green	Conservative
1974	G	1983	Magee	Bryan Edgar	Leyton	Labour
1983	G	1997	Cohen	Harry Michael		Labour
1997	G	2010	Cohen	Harry Michael	Leyton & Wanstead	Labour
2010	G	Date	Cryer	John Robert		Labour
1974	G	1987	Deakins	Eric Petro	Walthamstow	Labour
1987	G	1992	Summerson	Hugo Hawksley Fitzthomas		Conservative
1992	G	2010	Gerrard	Neil Francis		Labour
2010	G	Date	Creasy	Stella Judith		Labour

NOTE: First returned at a B = By-election; G =General Election

Chingford, Chingford and Woodford Green

Norman Beresford Tebbit (Conservative) was Epping's MP from 1970 to 1974 when the seat was redrawn and the southern part of it formed the new constituency seat of Chingford, which Tebbit represented until he retired from the Commons in 1992. His principal biographical details are in Chapter 12.

Iain Duncan Smith MP
© Palace of Westminster Collection
WOA 6383 www.parliament.uk/art

(George) Iain Duncan Smith (Conservative) was selected to succeed Norman Tebbit in 1992. Born in 1954 he claimed to have been educated at Dunchurch College of Management and at the *Universita di Perugia* in Italy, though it was subsequently disclosed that neither of these were what would be recognised as conventional study. The former was a management college of his employer at the time; the latter was a Summer language course. There was also some controversy about his name. He was christened with Duncan as a fore name but at some time in his life appears to have adopted it as part of his surname. He attended the Royal Military Academy at Sandhurst and entered the Scots Guards as an officer in 1975, serving until 1981 when he joined GEC-Marconi, where he remained until 1988 when his own C.V. shows him becoming a director of Bellwinch, a Property Company and a publisher of military information with Janes. He married a wealthy aristocratic heiress and entered Conservative politics when he contested Bradford West in 1987 and became vice chairman of his local Association in Fulham in 1991. He was adopted to fight Chingford which he won in 1992. In the House he proved to be a seriously Euro-sceptical opponent of the Major Government and rebelled against the whip several times on the Maastricht Treaty and was a supporter of John Redwood when he opposed Major for the leadership. Following the Tories' crushing electoral defeat in 1997 he joined the Front Bench team under the new leader, William Hague as Defence spokesman and after the further heavy defeat in 2001 put himself forward as a candidate for the leadership when Hague resigned. This was the first Tory leadership contest to be undertaken under new rules which enfranchised all Party members and, when Michael Portillo – up until that moment regarded as the front runner of the right wing – lost out in a qualifying ballot of Tory MPs, Duncan-Smith found himself in a run-off with the candidate of the moderate wing, Kenneth Clarke. Duncan-Smith was elected Party leader in 2002. However, his leadership is said to have proved both divisive; and in the perception of many of his Parliamentary colleagues incompetent. In the end sufficient MPs requested another ballot in which he was defeated in 2003. He was replaced by Michael Howard, who was elected by "acclamation". With his career apparently at its lowest ebb, Duncan-Smith was restored to the Shadow Cabinet in 2006 when David Cameron became leader and focused his attention on a detailed study of "broken families", a subject dear to his heart. One of the themes of the Tories in opposition under Cameron was "Broken Britain", implying a loss of social cohesion, largely arising from the breakdown of traditional family units. Following the formation of a Conservative-Liberal Democrat Coalition in 2010, Duncan-Smith was appointed to the Cabinet as Secretary of State for Work and Pensions in which role he was able to implement plans in his favoured area of policy, though by this time the seriousness of the national debt and the government's programme of public spending cuts placed his work in a new and more difficult context.

Leyton, Leyton & Wanstead

Bryan Edgar Magee (Labour) succeeded Patrick Gordon-Walker as MP for Leyton in 1974 and held the seat until 1983 when he defected to the Social Democrat Party but came bottom of the poll in a three-way contest at the general election of that year. Magee was born in1930 in Hoxton and educated at Christ's Hospital School; the Lycee Hoche in Versailles; Keble College, Oxford; and at Yale University. When at Oxford he was President of the Union in 1953 after which he initially became a teacher working in Sweden. He became a well-known journalist and television broadcaster in the field of current affairs, working on one of the early current affairs programmes on ITV called "This Week". As a Labour candidate he contested Mid Bedfordshire at the 1959 general election and again at a 1960 by-election. Out of the House he pursued a writing and literary career mostly in the field of political philosophy, and wrote an autobiography of his childhood in working class Hoxton.

Harry Michael Cohen (Labour) succeeded Magee in 1983 and remained MP for Leyton until 1997 when, after boundary changes, he was returned for Leyton & Wanstead. Born in Hackney in 1949, he was educated at George Gascoigne Secondary Modern School and attended East Ham Technical College where he qualified as an accountant (CIPFA). He worked as an auditor in local government and with trade unions and was a councillor in Waltham Forest where he was chairman of the Planning Committee and Labour Group Secretary. Later, as an MP, he attended Birkbeck College, London where he obtained a degree in Politics and Administration (MSc). Though a Jew, his views on the Palestine question placed him in opposition to the Israeli Government. Cohen came to prominent attention during the latter years of the 2005-10 Parliament as a result of the MPs' expenses scandal, exposed by a whistle blower at Westminster who leaked substantial information about what individuals were claiming. In the run-up to the 2010 election Cohen was under police investigation for claiming £70,000 in second home allowances for a house he was said to visit only rarely. Meanwhile he was renting out his own home. He stood down before the general election.

John Cryer MP
Peoples History Museum, Manchester

Cohen was succeeded in 2010 by **John Robert Cryer** (Labour). His father (Bob) was a former Labour MP for Keighley and his mother Anne sat in the House after her husband's death (also for Keighley). John was at that time MP for Hornchurch between 1997 and 2005, though he was defeated in that election. Born in Darwen, Lancashire, in 1964, he was educated at Oakbank School, Keighley going on to attend the London College of Printing and Hatfield Polytechnic after which he became a journalist with left wing papers – "*Tribune*" and "*The Morning Star*". He also worked for the trade unions UNITE and ASLEF.

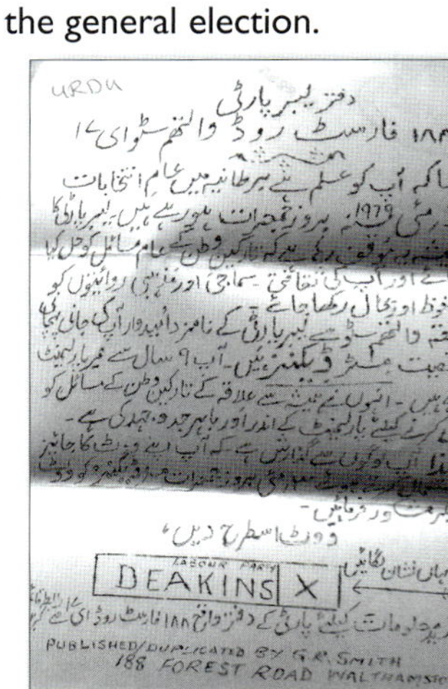

This Deakins 1979 handbill was aimed at Urdu speaking voters
Peoples History Museum, Manchester

Walthamstow

Eric Petro Deakins (Labour) won Walthamastow West in 1970 and in 1974 was returned for the single Walthamstow constituency, which he held until 1987. His principal biographical details are in Chapter 12.

Hugo Hawksley Fitzthomas Summerson (Conservative) was the surprise winner in 1987, a result that reflected a big swing to the Conservatives in the metropolitan Essex area. Born in 1950, he was a chartered surveyor and director of a company called Palatine Properties; who had been educated at Harrow School and the Royal Agricultural College. He contested Barking unsuccessfully in 1983. Following his defeat he established a company in 1993 to teach public speaking skills, including training for people appearing before Parliamentary Select Committees.

Walthamstow swung back in 1992 when **Neil Francis Gerrard** (Labour) was returned. Born at Farnworth, Lancashire, in 1942 and educated at Manchester Grammar School and Wadham College, Oxford, he obtained a BA and a Diploma in Education which he followed by obtaining a Masters degree in Education at Chelsea College. He became a lecturer and entered politics locally as a member of Waltham Forest Council where he was a councillor from 1973 to 1990. He was leader of the Labour Group from1983 and Council leader from 1986. He was a candidate at Chingford in 1979 when he lost to Norman Tebbitt. He served as PPS to Dawn Primorolo (A Treasury Minister at the time); but resigned in 1997over benefit cuts to single parents. He stood down in 2010.

Stella Judith Creasy (Labour and Co-operative) was elected in 2010 prior to which she was educated to PhD level obtaining this qualification in philosophy at the London School of Economics where she was awarded the Richard Titmus Prize in 2005. Before becoming an MP she was head of campaigns at the Scout Association. A Waltham Borough councillor for the Leabridge ward, she was Mayor and Deputy Leader during a relatively short spell on the council between 2002 and 2006. During this period she was also head of the think tank Involve, an organisation aiming to find innovative ways of securing greater involvement in the democratic process; she was a former aide to Douglas Alexander, a Cabinet minister (Former Transport Secretary and Secretary of State for Overseas Development). In 2011 she was appointed Shadow Minister for Crime Prevention.

MPs for Redbridge Borough

From	*at*	*To*	*Surname*	*First Names*	*Constituency*	*Party*
1974	*G*	*1974*	*Iremonger*	*"Tom" (Thomas) Lascelles*	*Ilford North*	*Conservative*
1974	*G*	*1978*	*Miller*	*Mrs. Millicent (Millie)*		*Labour*
1978	*B*	*1997*	*Bendall*	*Vivian Walter Hough*		*Conservative*
1997	*G*	*2005*	*Perham*	*Linda*		*Labour*
2005	*G*	*Date*	*Scott*	*Lee*		*Conservative*
1974	*G*	*1979*	*Shaw*	*Arnold John*	*Ilford South*	*Labour*
1979	*G*	*1992*	*Thorne*	*(Sir) Neil Gordon*		*Conservative*
1992	*G*	*date*	*Gapes*	*"Mike" (Michael) John*		*Labour*
1970	*G*	*1987*	*Jenkin*	*(Sir) Charles Patrick Fleeming*	*Wanstead & Woodford*	*Conservative*
1987	*G*	*1997*	*Arbuthnot*	*James Norwich*		*Conservative*

NOTE: First returned at a B = By-election; G =General Election

Peoples History Museum, Manchester

Ilford North

"Tom" (Thomas) Lascelles Isa Shandon Valiant Iremonger (Conservative) who had been the MP since a 1954 by-election held the seat until he was defeated at the October 1974 general election, this being one of the few seats to change hands since February. His principal biographical details are in chapter 12.

Mrs. Millicent (Millie) Miller (Labour) who succeeded him was born in 1923 and was educated at Dame Alice Owens' Girls' School in Islington. She became a social worker; a member of the General and Municipal Workers Union; and was briefly a councillor on the former Stoke Newington Borough Council in 1957/8. In 1967 she was elected to Camden Council where she was the leader from 1971 to 1973 when she resigned to contest Ilford North at the February election. Unsuccessful on that occasion, she was elected by a narrow majority in October but died in 1977.

Vivian Walter Hough Bendall (Conservative) won the 1978 by-election and went on to hold the seat until 1997. Born in 1938 and educated at Coombe Hill House Preparatory School and Broadgreen College, Croydon where he joined the family estate agents firm of Bendall and Featherby established by his grandfather becoming the Principal in 1963;

Bendall was a Croydon Borough Councillor from 1964-78 and sat on the GLC between 1970 and 1974. In 1967/8 he was Chairman of the Greater London Young Conservatives having previously been Vice Chairman of the South Croydon YCs in 1965.He contested Hertford & Stevenage unsuccessfully in both elections in 1974. His Parliamentary career was not especially noteworthy. For a while he was described as a"consultant" to the London Taxi Drivers' Association and he also remained in charge of the family firm. He attempted to regain the Ilford seat in 2001 but was unsuccessful.

A 1997 election leaflet for Linda Perham
Peoples History Museum, Manchester

Linda Perham (Labour), who took the seat in 1997, was born in London in 1947 and went to Mary Datchelor Grammar School, Camberwell, and then to the University of Leicester where she obtained an honours degree in Classics. She undertook a postgraduate diploma in librarianship at Ealing College and worked at the Fawcett Library in the City of London Polytechnic as an information officer; at the GLC research library; and then as a bibliographical librarian at Epping Forest College. She was a founder member of Redbridge Under Fives and a post-natal co-ordinator for the National Childbirth Trust and served as a local JP; and on the Community Health Council for her area before she was elected as an MP. She was a councillor between 1989 and 1997; and Mayor of Redbridge in 1994/5. She was defeated in 2005 but remained active in local affairs including as a trustee of the Women's Library, as vice chair of the London Voluntary Service Council (2005-8), the Consumer Council for Water (2005-11), and Chair of East Living: a civic and social organisation providing care and support for East London residents with a wide range of needs.

Lee Scott (Conservative) took the seat in 2005 at the age of forty-seven. Born and brought up in the area he was educated at Clarke's College, Ilford. His personal website stated that he had worked as a professional fund raiser for charities. He has a particular interest in promoting the interests of people with autism. More than that "he has worked with President George Bush in his role as a fundraiser for a large national charity"; as Campaign Director for the United Jewish Israel Appeal, which he was from 1988 to 1998. A member of Redbridge Borough Council, he was one of its Cabinet members from 2002 with responsibilities for regeneration. In 2001 he was unsuccessful in contesting the Waveney (Lowestoft) division of Suffolk. In 2010 he was appointed PPS to the Transport Secretary, a position he resigned when he failed to support the Government's Bill to introduce student loans. In 2012 he was appointed PPS to the Secretary of State for Justice.

Ilford South

Arnold John Shaw (Labour) who was MP initially from 1966 to 1970, also sat from February 1974 to 1979 when he was defeated and retired from politics. His principal biographical details are in chapter 12.

(Sir) Neil Gordon Thorne (Conservative) won the seat in 1979 and held it throughout the Thatcher period until he was defeated at the 1992 general election. He was born in 1932 and educated at the City of London School for Boys before going to London University after which he became a senior partner in Hull and Company, chartered surveyors, where he worked from 1962 to 1976. He was a councillor (1965-8) and alderman (1975-8) in Redbridge and was also active in the City of London where he was a Deputy Lieutenant, freeman and liveryman. He was also a Lloyds Underwriter. He was especially active in promoting aspects of policy affecting the armed forces and was the founder and chairman of the Armed Forces Party Scheme which was established in 1988 to engage MPs in various aspects of military life as a means of facilitating their understanding of forces issues.

Mike Gapes MP
© Mike Gapes' Website

(Michael) 'Mike' John Gapes (Labour) who won the seat in 1992 was born in 1952 in Wanstead and was educated at Buckhurst Hill High School and Fitzwilliam College, Cambridge (MA), where he was secretary of the Students Union in 1973. In 1976-7 he was chairman of the National Organisation of Labour Students. He joined the National Health Service as an Administrative Officer but before entering Parliament worked for the Labour Party as National Student Organiser, Research Officer and Senior International Officer. He was PPS to Lord Rooker in the 1992 Parliament and to Paul Murphy MP (1997 - 1999). A member of the Co-operative Party, the Fabian Society and the European Movement, Gapes was elected Chairman of the All-Party United Nations Group in 1997. From 2005 to 2010 he was Chairman of the Foreign Affairs Committee of the House of Commons.

Wanstead & Woodford

Sir Charles Patrick Fleeming Jenkin (Conservative) was the MP from 1964 to 1987. His principal biographical details are in Chapter 12.

James Arbuthnot MP
© Conservative Home

He was succeeded by Scottish landowner, **James Norwich Arbuthnot** (Conservative), who was born in 1952, the son of Sir John who was the MP for Dover between 1950 and 1964; and was educated at Wellesley House, Broadstairs; Eton and Trinity College, Cambridge. A member of Lloyd's, he became a chancery barrister at Lincoln's Inn in 1977specialising in tax, company law, landlord and tenant law, probate and trust law. In 1983 and at a by-election the following year he unsuccessfully contested Cynon Valley (Glamorgan), a Welsh mining seat; and was then selected to fight Wanstead & Woodford. He was PPS to Archie Hamilton from 1988-90 and to Peter Lilley until 1992 when he entered the Government as an assistant whip, a post he held until 1994. In 1994-5 he was Under Secretary for Social Security and Minister of State for Defence from 1995 until the Major Government was voted out in 1997. His seat was carved in two at the election and he went in search of an alternative seat, which he found at Hampshire North East, in which constituency he was re-elected at the subsequent three general elections. After the 2010 Election he was elected Chairman of the House of Commons Defence Select Committee.

MPs for Barking and Dagenham Borough

From	*at*	*To*	*Surname*	*First Names*	*Constituency*	*Party*
1974	*G*	*1994*	*Richardson*	*Miss Jo(sephine)*	*Barking*	*Labour*
1994	*B*	*date*	*Hodge*	*Mrs. Margaret*		*Labour*
1974	*B*	*1983*	*Parker*	*Herbert John Harvey*	*Dagenham*	*Labour*
1983	*G*	*1994*	*Gould*	*Bryan Charles*		*Labour*
1994	*B*	*2001*	*Church*	*Judith*		*Labour*
2001	*G*	*2010*	*Cruddas*	*Jon(athan)*		*Labour*
2010	*G*	*date*	*Cruddas*	*Jon(athan)*	*Dagenham & Rainham*	*Labour*

NOTE: First returned at a B = By-election; G =General Election

Barking

Jo(sephine) Richardson (Labour) was MP from 1974 until her death in 1994. Born in 1923, she was educated at Southend High School for Girls and was secretary of the Keep Left (later the Bevan Group) from 1948-1978 when, four years after her own election as an MP, she became chairman of its successor, the Tribune Group. She contested elections unsuccessfully on several occasions before being selected for a safe seat, a reflection perhaps of the difficulties women faced in trying to pursue a political career. She fought Monmouth in 1951 and 1955; Hornchurch in 1959; and Harrow East in 1964. From 1983 she was Chief Opposition spokesperson on women's rights joining the Front Bench in 1987. From 1979-91 she was a member of the Party's National Executive Committee and was especially active in promoting the rights of women, blacks and Asians within the movement.

Margaret Hodge MP
© Margaret Hodge Website

Mrs Margaret Hodge (Labour) was born in Egypt in 1944, the daughter of the steel-trading millionaire, Harry Oppenheimer, and was educated at Bromley High School for Girls, Oxford High School, and the London School of Economics. She became a teacher and market researcher but entered politics in the 1970s as an Islington councillor. For ten years between 1982 and 1992 she was the council's leader, when the authority had a reputation for 'politically correct' policies. Then began a slow conversion to a Blairite, New Labour persona which saw her become a consultant with Price Waterhouse between 1992 and 1994 and then stand for Parliament at Barking in the by-election following Jo Richardson's death. She was elected chairman of the group of London Labour MPs elected in 1997 and was subsequently appointed as a Parliamentary Under Secretary at the Ministry of Employment and Education. In 2001 she was appointed Minister for Higher Education; and then in 2003 came a much more controversial appointment as Minister for Children, a posting which gave rise to a major though unsuccessful campaign in sections of the media for her dismissal on the grounds that when she had been Leader of Islington Council there had been a number of cases of child abuse perpetrated by

Council employees. After the 2005 election she was appointed Minister for Work at the Ministry of Work and Pensions, working alongside Stephen Timms, MP for adjacent East Ham. In 2007 she was made a Minister for Culture, Media and Sport but took a year out to care for her terminally ill husband in 2008/9. At the 2010 general election her principal opponent was the leader of the British National Party, Nick Griffin, who had been previously elected as a member of the European Parliament and who had great expectations of winning the Barking constituency from Labour on the back of local election successes in the borough. However, Margaret Hodge secured a substantial victory, increasing her majority over the Conservatives, with Griffin coming in third with less than 15% of the vote, fewer than his party had secured in 2005. Following the 2010 election she was appointed Chair of the important Public Accounts Select Committee in which role she exposed tax avoidance on a large scale, especially amongst multi national companies.

Dagenham

Herbert John Harvey Parker (Labour) who sat for Romford from 1935 to 1945 was elected at Dagenham in 1945 and served until his retirement in 1983. His principal biographical details are in Chapter 12.

Bryan Gould MP's 1983 Election leaflet
Peoples History Museum Manchester

He was succeeded in 1983 by **Bryan Charles Gould** (Labour), New Zealand born in 1939 and educated there at Dannevirke High School; and at the Victoria and Auckland Universities before coming to Britain to study at Balliol College, Oxford. In 1964 he joined the Foreign Office moving in 1966 to Brussels in the diplomatic service but returned to Oxford in 1968 to become a Fellow and tutor in Law at Worcester College, a post he held until February 1974 when he was elected MP for Southampton Test, a seat he lost in 1979. After his defeat he joined Thames Television as a presenter and reporter of a current affairs programme called 'TV Eye', resigning in 1983 when he became Dagenham's MP. He was appointed to the Opposition Front bench in 1983 to speak on Trade and Industry matters and was elected to the Shadow Cabinet in 1986, becoming party campaigns co-ordinator and Shadow Chief Secretary. In 1987 he was elected to the Party's National Executive Committee and was chief spokesman on trade and industry until 1989 when he was given the environment portfolio. During this period he was with Neil Kinnock and John Smith, one of the main architects of Labour's modernisation. When Labour lost the 1992 election, Gould fought a hopeless contest with John Smith for the Party leadership following Kinnock's resignation and, disillusioned, resigned his seat in 1994 and returned to New Zealand to resume an academic life.

Judith Church (Labour) won the June 1994 by-election. Born in 1953, she was educated at St. Bernard's Convent, Slough and Leeds University; and became a factory inspector and a MSF union official. In 1992 she was the first woman to be elected to the trade union section of the Labour Party's National Executive Committee and in the same year stood unsuccessfully for Stevenage (Hertforshire) at the general election. She retired from the Commons in 2001.

Jon Cruddas MP
© Jon Cruddas' Website

Jon(athan) Cruddas (Labour) succeeded her in 2001. Born at Helston in Cornwall in 1962, he was educated at Oaklands RC Comprehensive School and at Warwick University where he became a well qualified academic with a PhD to add to an MA and BSc. In 1989 he became a policy adviser to the Labour Party and in 1994 was appointed Chief Assistant to the General Secretary and, following the election of the Blair Government in 1997; became Deputy Political Secretary to the Prime Minister, Tony Blair. Despite this he was critical of the Party for not keeping close enough to its traditional supporters and in 2007 when John Prescott resigned the Deputy leadership at the same time that Tony Blair resigned, Cruddas stood for the position, polling very well at the head of the count in the first round but ultimately losing to Harriet Harman. Following the resignation of Gordon Brown as leader of the Labour Party after the Party's 2010 election defeat, Cruddas, who had been expected to stand, announced that he did not consider himself to have the necessary qualities and ruled himself out of the leadership contest. He remained a close adviser on policy matters to Ed Miliband, the new Labour leader elected in 2010.

MPs for Havering Borough						
From	at	To	Surname	First Names	Constituency	Party
1974	G	1979	Williams	Alan Lee	Hornchurch	Labour
1979	G	1997	Squire	Robin Clifford		Conservative
1997	G	2005	Cryer	John Robert		Labour
2005	G	2010	Brokenshire	James Peter		Conservative
2010	G	Date	Watkinson	Angela	Hornchurch & Upminster	Conservative
1974	G	1997	Neubert	(Sir) Michael Jon	Romford	Conservative
1997	G	2001	Gordon	Eileen		Labour
2001	G	date	Rosindell	Andrew		Conservative
1974	G	1983	Loveridge	John W.	Upminster	Conservative
1983	G	1997	Bonsor	Sir Nicholas Cosmo		Conservative
1997	G	2001	Darvill	Keith Ernest		Labour
2001	G	2010	Watkinson	(Dame) Angela Eileen		Conservative

NOTE: First returned at a B = By-election; G =General Election

Hornchurch

Alan Lee Williams (Labour) won the seat in 1966; was defeated in 1970 but regained the seat in February 1974 and held it until defeated once again in 1979. His principal biographical details are in Chapter 12.

Squire Election sticker
Peoples History Museum Manchester

Robin Clifford Squire (Conservative) had unsuccessfully contested the seat in October 1974 but won it in 1979 and went on to hold it for the full eighteen years of the Thatcher and Major Governments. Born in 1944, he was educated at the Tiffin Boys School, Kingston upon Thames; and became a chartered accountant rising to be Deputy Chief Accountant of Lombard North Central plc. He rose through the ranks of the Young Conservatives; joined Sutton Council and became its leader. After his election in 1974 he was PPS to Robert Carr, the Carshalton MP. He joined the Board of the housing charity Shelter in 1982 and the same year became a programme presenter with Capital Radio, a post he relinquished in 1987. He also became a presenter for British Satellite Broadcasting in 1990 and the following year was appointed PPS to Chris Patten, then Conservative Party Chairman and Chancellor of the Duchy of Lancaster. In 1993 he was made Schools Minister at the Department of Education in which role he introduced the Ofsted inspection regime, performance tables, grant-maintained schools and nursery education vouchers. He lost his seat in 1997 and took some time to find another role. In 1999 he was appointed chief executive of a group of Essex environmental charities known as the Veolia ES Cleanaway Pitsea Marshes Trust.

John Robert Cryer (Labour) was MP from 1997 to 2005 when he was defeated. His biographical details are earlier in this chapter, under MPs for Waltham Forest.

James Brokenshire MP
© James Brokenshire's Website

James Peter Brokenshire (Conservative) won the seat in 2005. Born in Southend in 1968, he was educated at Davenant Foundation Grammar School, Loughton; and the Cambridge Centre for Sixth Form Studies before graduating with an honours degree in Law from the University of Exeter; after which he joined a large international law firm advising on business start-ups. He was National Vice Chairman of the Young Conservatives; Deputy Chairman of Epping Forest Conservatives; and a member of the Conservative Party's National Union Executive Committee. From 2006 he was appointed Shadow Minister for Crime Reduction. In 2010, following the merging if his seat with Upminster he sought nomination for the safe Conservative seat of Old Bexley & Sidcup where he was elected. (See Chapter 17). He was subsequently appointed a Minister at the Home Office where his responsibilities included counter terrorism.

Romford

(Sir) Michael Jon Neubert (Conservative) had unsuccessfully contested Romford in 1970 but following redistribution he won the seat in 1974 and held it until 1997. Born in 1933, he was educated at Queen Elizabeth's School, Barnet; Bromley Grammar School and Downing College, Cambridge. He went into business as a travel agent organising holiday air tours and into local government politics in his home borough of Bromley. He first joined the Council in 1960 and was its leader from 1967-70 and mayor in 1972-3. He unsuccessfully contested Hammersmith North in 1966. His Parliamentary career was long but undistinguished. He was a PPS from 1980-3 and an assistant whip from 1983-88 when he was appointed Under-Secretary for Defence but he was dropped in 1990 when John Major became Prime Minister and his career came to a final end when he was defeated in 1997. He died in January 2014.

Neubert Election poster
Peoples History Museum Manchester

He was beaten in 1997 by **Mrs Eileen Gordon** (Labour), who was, however, defeated at the 2001 election; one of only a handful of Labour MPs to lose a seat. A local teacher, she was beaten by a strident, rightwing Tory candidate in the Tebbit mould (see Epping, Chapter 12) who campaigned with a bulldog wrapped in a Union flag and Tory rosette.

Andrew Rosindell MP
© Andrew Rosindell's Website

Andrew Rosindell (Conservative), who was Chairman of the local Party Association, was thirty-five when he won the seat and had since 1997 been Director of the European Foundation (a Euro sceptic organisation). He was educated at Rise Park and Marshalls Park Schools in Romford and contested Glasgow Provan in 1992 and Thurrock (Essex) in 1997.

Upminster

(Sir) John Warren Loveridge (Conservative) was Hornchurch's MP from 1970 to February 1974 when he transferred to Upminster constituency which he held until he retired in 1983. His principal biographical details are in Chapter 12.

Loveridge Election leaflet 1979
Peoples History Museum Manchester

He was succeeded then by **Sir Nicholas Cosmo Bonsor** (Conservative) who held the seat until defeated in 1997. He was born in 1942, the grandson and great grandson of MPs, and was linked through his mother to the Hambro banking family. He was educated at Eton and Keble College, Oxford; and at the Inner Temple where he practised at the Bar for eight years before concentrating on his country estate in Buckinghamshire where he was chairman of the Wing Conservative Association. Having contested Newcastle-under-Lyme unsuccessfully in 1974, he was elected MP for Nantwich (Cheshire) in 1979; but failed to be selected for the re-drawn seat in 1983 and transferred to Upminster. Although right wing on the economy, law and order and defence, he was more liberal on other issues and in 1985 joined Francis Pym's "Centre Forward" Campaign which sought to moderate Thatcherite excesses. Later, in the Major years, he contested the Chairmanship of the backbench 1922 Committee in 1994, arguing against what he saw as a tendency to "air dirty linen in public". He was rewarded when Major appointed him Minister of State at the Foreign Office in 1995, two years before his political career was ended at the next election. A Deputy Lord Lieutenant of Buckinghamshire, in the 2010 general election he supported Nigel Farage, the Leader of the United Kingdom Independence Party who stood in the Buckingham constituency as the only candidate to oppose the sitting MP, John Bercow, who was the Speaker at the time, though previously he had been a Conservative MP.

Keith Darvill MP
Peoples History Museum Manchester

Keith Ernest Darvill (Labour), who was born at Forest Gate in 1948, was a one term MP, from 1997-2001. He was educated at Norlington Secondary Modern School at Leyton and then studied at various University rated colleges in the London area. He worked for the Port of London Authority before he became a solicitor. Following his defeat he was elected to Havering council.

(Dame) Angela Eileen Watkinson (Conservative) unseated Darvill in 2001. Then aged fifty-nine she was educated at Wanstead County High School and Anglia University; where she gained a Higher National Certificate. She worked for a bank and was also a charity worker raising a family of three children before becoming a local government officer for twelve years. She was Chairman of the Emerson Park Branch of her Party Association and was a governor of two local schools. She spent her whole family and working life in Metropolitan Essex having been born in Leytonstone and served as a councillor in Havering and on the Essex County council. Between 2010 and 2012, she was a government whip.

Chapter 17
Metropolitan Kent since 1974

1974 - 1983: Greater London Authority Boundaries Fully Reflected in the Second Periodic Review

Although the Boundary Commission started its Second Periodic Review on 16th February 1965 it was not until February 1974 that a General Election was fought on its recommendations. These not only took account of population changes that had occurred but also of the new local authority boundaries that had been implemented in 1965. It was a requirement for London constituencies to be established wholly within the boundaries of the new Boroughs which in Metropolitan Kent were Lewisham, Greenwich, Bromley and Bexley. These were newly constituted as shown below

Old Council Areas in Metropolitan Essex	New Boroughs	Remarks
Deptford, Lewisham (Boroughs)	*Lewisham*	*2-way amalgamation*
Greenwich, Woolwich (Boroughs)	*Greenwich*	*2-way amalgamation*
Beckenham, Bromley (Boroughs); Penge (UDC); Chislehurst (from Chislehurst & Sidcup UDC)	*Bromley*	*4-way amalgamation*
Bexley, Erith (Boroughs); Crayford UDC; Sidcup (from Chislehurst & Sidcup UDC)	*Bexley*	*4-way amalgamation*

Overall Southeast London's representation was unchanged as a result of the review except that it became more "suburban" in the distribution of seats.

The splitting of the Chislehurst and Sidcup urban district alone made boundary alterations inevitable due to the requirement to allocate constituencies to boroughs. Population increases also prompted changes. Sidcup became a new constituency occasioning redistribution of the existing two seats, namely Erith & Crayford and Bexley, which was renamed Bexleyheath in view of the alterations that were made to it.

Bexley and Bromley (7 seats)

Bexleyheath included Danson Park, East Wickham, Falconwood and Welling, all from the former Bexley seat; whilst Bexley itself and Bexley Woods were transferred to **Sidcup**, which also contained Blackfen, Foots Cray, Lamorbey, Longlands and North Cray, all formerly in **Chislehurst**. This latter seat retained its communities of Elmstead Woods, Mottingham and St. Pauls Cray to which were added the wards covering Bickley, Plaistow, Sundridge Park and Widmore, previously in the Bromley seat. **Erith & Crayford** was unchanged comprising the two Thames-side towns plus also Belvedere, Northumberland Heath, Slade Green, Thamesmead, Barnehurst, and West Heath.

The number of Parliamentary seats in the Bromley area remained four but there were boundary changes within them. **Beckenham** covered a much smaller area that included Elmers End, Eden Park, Kelsey Park and Shortlands whilst Hayes, West Wickham and Coney Hall were transferred to **Ravensbourne** (the renamed Bromley) along with Bromley, Bromley Common, Bromley Park and Keston from the former Bromley division, and Biggin Hill from Orpington. Apart from this, the new **Orpington** division retained all its former areas including Chelsfield, Farnborough, Green Street Green, Petts Wood, Pratts Bottom and St. Mary Cray.

Left: *Bexleyheath Town Centre, with its modernised, pedestrian area sits in a bustling hub of this South East London suburb which was created a named constituency for the first time in 1974 giving it a separate identity to nearby Bexley.*

Below: *Sidcup was also created a named constituency in its own right in 1974. A huge commuting suburb, Longlands Road shown here, typifies the character of the area. There is a 15 minute train service frequency to London (Charing Cross), 30 minutes away by train, and Sidcup is bordered by the A2 and M25 roads, making it a sought after place to live.*

Below: *Since it was established as a middle class suburb in the late Victorian era, Lewisham has developed into a diverse and pulsating inner London community. These flats are in the centre of the town, above its thriving shopping centre and next to its busy railway and bus stations.*

Above: *Originally a detached part of the Surrey parish of Battersea, Penge was created an urban district within Kent in 1900. Traditionally attached to either Bromley or Beckenham Constituency, it was joined with West Lewisham in 2010. It retains its late Victorian, turn of the century character.*

Left: *Greenwich retained its charm and history as a long established riverside destination as well as a suburb. Although its industrial features have been superseded, tourism has grown so strongly that the place burgeons with visitors all-year round. The superb transport connections to the Canary Wharf financial centre by the Docklands Light Railway, as well as river services and the first main line railway in London maintain excellent access for residents and visitors alike, to this suburban area so filled with visitor attractions.*

Photos John Nelson, except where marked

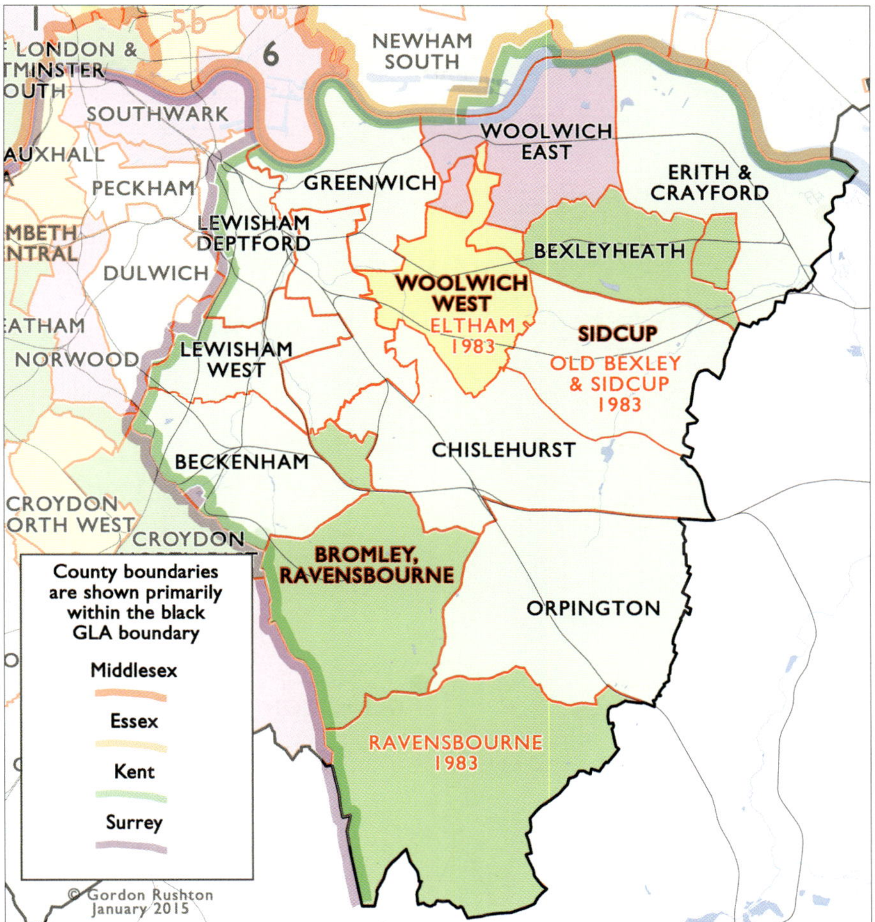

The colours, green, lemon and mauve show the extent of 1983 constituencies; different colours are merely to enhance clarity.

The map depicts Kent constituencies created in 1974, and those that were modified in 1983. The changes show: the transfer of Barnehurst from Erith & Crayford to Bexleyheath; the transfer of Biggin Hill from Orpington to Ravensbourne, and some minor alterations around Woolwich Common affecting Woolwich East and Eltham. Sidcup was renamed Old Bexley and Sidcup, and Woolwich West became Eltham.

Lewisham and Greenwich (6 seats)

Within the former L.C.C. area the enlarged boroughs meant that more widespread boundary revisions were now possible and the impact of re-distribution was that Lewisham and Deptford combined lost one seat. **Lewisham, Deptford** included all communities contained in the former Deptford borough seat (Brockley, New Cross, New Cross Gate and St. Johns); but was also extended southwards taking Crofton Park and Honour Oak from Lewisham West, and Ladywell from Lewisham North - which seat was abolished. **Lewisham East** was restored comprising Blackheath, Lee Green, Lewisham Park and Village from the former North constituency, and the south eastern districts of Hither Green, Downham and Grove Park from the former South seat. **Lewisham West** retained Beckenham Hill, Forest Hill and Sydenham but acquired Bellingham and Catford from the former South division. **Greenwich, Woolwich East** and **Woolwich West** were little altered, apart from the transfer of North Woolwich. to Newham South (Essex).

1983 - 2010: The Third and Fourth Periodic Reviews

At the next boundary review which came into effect at the 1983 general election there were few boundary changes but three seats were renamed. Woolwich East became **Woolwich**; whilst Woolwich West was re-designated **Eltham** and Sidcup was renamed **Old Bexley & Sidcup**. Other seats retained their names.

In 1995 the Boundaries Commission decided to pair the Boroughs of Greenwich and Bexley whilst Bromley and Lewisham remained separate for the purposes of allocating boundaries. In the changes that were implemented at the 1997 General Election Erith (Bexley borough) was combined with Thamesmead in the former Woolwich division of Greenwich Borough, necessitating alterations to Greenwich and Eltham constituencies as well. In Bromley borough the Ravensbourne and Chislehurst seats were merged with associated revisions to the boundaries of Beckenham and Orpington. Lewisham borough, on the other hand was unaltered.

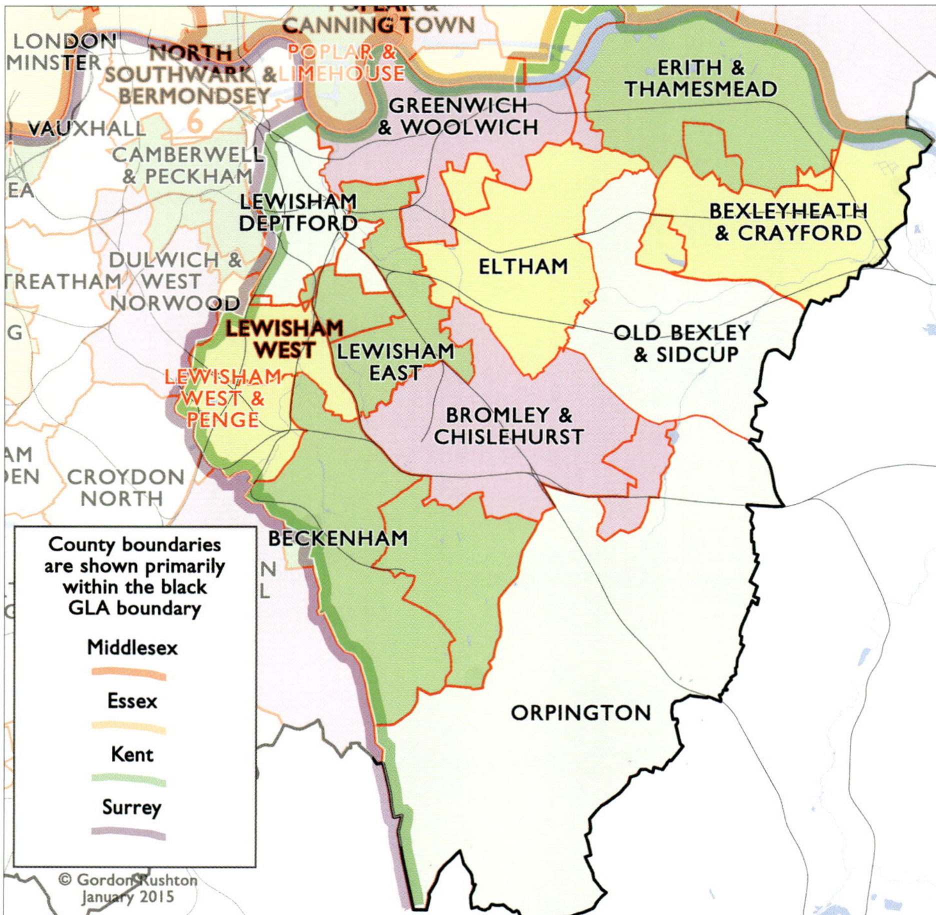

The colours, green, lemon and mauve show the extent of 2010 constituencies; different colours are merely to enhance clarity.

The map depicts Kent constituencies in 1997, and those that were modified in 2010. In 2010, the expansion of Lewisham West to include Penge, necessitated other alterations in Lewisham and Beckenham which expanded further south to embrace Bromley Common. Elsewhere the changes were minor to balance the electorates.

Bexley and Greenwich Boroughs (5 seats)

Erith, Belvedere, Northumberland Heath and eastern districts of Thamesmead were removed from their former link with Crayford and coupled instead with the north eastern parts of Woolwich including western districts of Thamesmead, Abbey Wood, the Abbey Wood Estate, Plumstead and Plumstead Marshes. The new constituency was named **Erith & Thamesmead**. The Bostall area, formerly also in Erith & Crayford, lost its association with the former but kept it with the latter in the new **Bexleyheath & Crayford** constituency. This retained all central and eastern parts of Bexleyheath including Barnehurst, West Heath and Slade Green but lost the western districts of Falconwood, Danson, Welling and East Wickham, which comprised the north western part of Bexley and were transferred to join Bexley Woods, Black Fen, Sidcup, Foots Cray, Lamorbey, Longlands, and North Cray in **Old Bexley & Sidcup**.

Greenwich & Woolwich became a merged constituency that saw the former Greenwich division expand beyond the original borough boundaries to embrace the whole of central Woolwich (most of which was transferred from the former Woolwich constituency), with the small Nightingale ward east of the Common brought in from Eltham. Greenwich & Woolwich thus incorporated: Charlton; Charlton Park; Greenwich Peninsular (including the site of the Millennium Dome/O2 Centre); Kidbrooke; Maze Hill; Westcombe Park; Woolwich Arsenal; Woolwich Common; Woolwich Dockyard, and Woolwich Town Centre. The new **Eltham** survived with its name unchanged and still included New Eltham and Well Hall, but its boundaries were extended to take in the areas of Shooters Hill fringing Plumstead Common, and formerly in the Woolwich division. Overall there was a loss of one seat in the two boroughs combined.

Bromley Borough (3 seats)

Neighbouring Bromley borough lost a seat to total three. The former Ravensbourne constituency, which had included the Martins Hill and Masons Hill districts of Bromley, Hayes, West Wickham, Keston and Biggin Hill, was abolished, and boundary changes occurred involving every other seat in the borough. **Beckenham** retained its core districts of Penge,

Anerley, Elmers End, Beckenham, Kelsey Park, Eden Park and Shortlands; but regained West Wickham and Coney Hall that had been lost in 1974 to Ravensbourne: the Biggin Hill wards of which were transferred to **Orpington**. This latter constituency also acquired St. Pauls Cray from the Chislehurst constituency. It continued to include: Chelsfield; Farnborough; Green Street Green; Pratts Bottom; Petts Wood, and St. Mary Cray. The remaining districts of Ravensbourne (Bromley, Bromley Park, Hayes and Keston) and Chislehurst (Elmstead Woods, Mottingham, Plaistow, Sundridge Park and Widmore), were merged to form a new **Bromley & Chislehurst** constituency. **Lewisham Borough (3 seats) - Lewisham, Deptford, Lewisham, East** and **Lewisham West** constituencies were unaltered.

2010: The Fifth Periodic Review

For the next boundary changes implemented at the 2010 general election as a result of the fifth review, it was decided to consider all the boroughs in paired combinations. These were Greenwich with Bexley (as before), and Bromley with Lewisham (new). The resulting total number of constituencies was the same as before, but the name of one of the Lewisham seats was changed to reflect the reallocation of wards.

Bexley and Greenwich (5 seats) – minor ward exchanges only.

Bromley and Lewisham (7 seats)

Beckenham lost Anerley, Crystal Palace, and Penge to Lewisham West, but gained Hayes and Keston from Bromley & Chislehurst. Its remaining wards, which it retained, were Beckenham, Eden Park, Elmers End, Kelsey Park, Shortlands, West Wickham and Coney Hall. **Bromley & Chislehurst** retained Bickley, Chislehurst, Elmstead Woods, Mottingham, Plaistow, Sundridge Park and Widmore, and gained St Mary Cray and St Pauls Cray from Orpington, but lost Hayes and Keston to Beckenham. Apart from the loss of the Cray Valley, **Orpington** remained the same, retaining Biggin Hill, Chelsfield, Farnborough, Green Street Green, Petts Wood, and Pratts Bottom.

The boundaries of **Lewisham, Deptford** remained unchanged but the remaining two Lewisham constituencies were altered. **Lewisham East** acquired Catford from Lewisham West to include Rushey Green and also acquired Beckenham Hill from the same constituency. It retained all of its former wards covering Blackheath, Downham, Grove Park, Hither Green and Lee Green. Lewisham West, however, was restructured with the loss of Catford, Rushey Green and Beckenham Hill to acquire Anerley, Crystal Palace, Penge, Kent House and Cator Park from Beckenham. The seat was renamed **Lewisham West & Penge** and continued to include the former Lewisham wards covering Bellingham, Forest Hill, Upper and Lower Sydenham.

Politics in Metropolitan Kent: Lewisham, Greenwich, Bromley and Bexley

General Election Results 1974 to 2010 (p506)

Overall during this period the Conservative Party secured victory in 65 seats at General Elections as against 54 for Labour and 3 for the Social Democratic Party. In addition the Conservatives won 2 by-elections, and the SDP 1.

The political impact of the changes that took place in 1974 in the inner boroughs was to marginally favour Labour in the sense that the merger of four seats into three in the new combined borough of Deptford and Lewisham did nothing to dent the Party's hold on Deptford whilst the two new Lewisham divisions of East and West, though still marginal, probably became slightly less promising for the Tories. Woolwich West (renamed Eltham in 1983) remained a marginal constituency and, though Labour-held in 1974, fell to the Conservatives in 1979 and was held by them until the next re-distribution in 1997.

Despite the boundary changes being of slight benefit to Labour, political factors undermined them considerably, especially in the new borough of Greenwich. The influence of the Militant Left within the Labour Party had given rise to the creation of a new Party, the Social Democrats, which initially comprised a number of Labour MPs who formed its Westminster core. One of these was John Cartwright, the MP for the previously very safe Labour seat of Woolwich East. His majority in 1979 (a bad year for Labour) was 28% but when he stood in 1983 for the SDP he had a majority of 7%. He retained the seat in 1987 when there was a further swing away from Labour in the London area.

On 26th February 1987 Labour suffered another humiliation in one of its bedrock seats. In 1983 Greenwich had returned a Labour MP with a majority of only 3%, the lowest in the constituency since the War, and it seemed unlikely that Labour support could fall further, but at the by-election it did. Tactical voting by Tories (who had come second in

General Election Results 1974 - 2101 by % majority

Constituency	1950 to 1970	Feb 1974	Oct 1974	1979	1983	1987	1992	1997	2001	2005	2010
Lewisham, Deptford	Lab	Lab28	Lab36	Lab22	Lab17	Lab18	Lab33	Lab56	Lab53	Lab39	Lab30
Lewisham North	C										
Lewisham East (South)	Lab	Lab12	Lab19	Lab3	C5	C11	Lab3	Lab32	Lab30	Lab22	Lab15
Lewisham West	C	Lab5	Lab13	Lab2	C6	C8	Lab4	Lab38	Lab39	Lab31	
Lewisham West & Penge											Lab13
Greenwich	Lab	Lab23	Lab29	Lab19	Lab3-	SDP6	Lab4				
Greenwich & Woolwich								Lab45	Lab41	Lab29	Lab25
Woolwich					SDP5	SDP5	Lab6				
Woolwich East	Lab	Lab32	Lab38	Lab28							
Woolwich West/ Eltham	C/Lab	Lab5	Lab9	C6	C19	C16	C4	Lab23	Lab21	Lab9	Lab4
Erith &Thamesmead								Lab42	Lab33	Lab31	Lab13
Erith & Crayford	Lab	Lab14	Lab19	Lab5	C2	C16	C5				
Bexleyheath & Crayford								Lab7	Lab4	C11	C24
Bexleyheath		C9	C5	C21	C23	C25	C30				
Bexley	C										
(Old Bexley &) Sidcup		C23	C20	C34	C34	C41	C39	C7	C8	C12	C35
Chislehurst	C	C12	C10	C23	C29	C35	C36				
Bromley & Chislehurst								C21	C21	C29+	C32
Ravensbourne (Bromley)	C	C22	C24	C42	C36	C38	C42				
Orpington	C	C3	C7	C10	C29	C23	C27	C27	C5	C9	C35
Beckenham	C	C22	C21	C32	C31	C30	C33	C9+	C11	C17	C37
C	7.5	6	6	7	10	10	8	4+	4	5+	5
Lab	5.5	7	7	6	2-	1	5	7+	7	6	6
SDP	0	0	0	0	1+	2	0	0	0	0	0
Total	13	13	13	13	13+	13	13	11+	11	11	11

Key: C = Conservative; Lab = Labour; + = Party that won seat at General Election held by-election in same Parliament - = Party that won seat at General Election lost by-election to main opposition Party in same Parliament.

1983) ensured the election of the Social Democrat MP Rosie Barnes with a majority over Labour of 19%. She retained the seat at the 1987 General Election by a majority of 6%.

In the outer boroughs changes benefited the Conservatives, notably the additional middle class commuting seat in Sidcup. Apart from Erith & Crayford, the Party won every seat at every General Election in the outer suburban area between 1974 and 1992. The Tories even won Erith & Crayford in 1983 and went on to hold it for the rest of the period until the 1997 election. Initially the Party was the beneficiary of the defection to the SDP of the Labour MP, James Wellbeloved, who had held the seat in 1979 with a majority of 5%. Because the Tories were so close, when he stood for the new Party it seems that he did not attract tactical votes so much as split the vote of "left" leaning electors. Additionally there were similarities in voting trends in this part of outer Thameside with those described in Chapter 16 in Metropolitan Essex on the opposite side of the river, both areas having similar demographic profiles.

Labour support in the area as a whole plumbed the depths during the 1980s. Both Lewisham seats were lost to the Conservatives at the 1983 and 1987 elections. In the second of these elections the Tory majorities actually increased despite 1983 having been Labour's worst national result since the General Election of 1918. The only seat to remain Labour throughout the period was Lewisham, Deptford. However, with the approach of the millennium the tide turned dramatically in Labour's favour. The scale of the Party's two landslide victories of 1997 and 2001 was such that discussion of the impacts of the boundary changes on the outcome of those elections is somewhat academic. Nevertheless, studies done at the time of the boundary changes in 1995 suggested that on the basis of the 1992 results and assuming no swing either way, there was no significant political impact in any constituency with the exception of Erith & Thamesmead which, it was estimated, would have had a Labour majority of over 11% had the 1992 Election been held on its revised boundaries. In net terms this meant that the number of Labour seats in the area would have remained the same but the Conservatives would have lost one. However, it should not be forgotten that the result of the 1992 General Election had been close in terms of seats and that any changes brought about by boundary alterations could have been significant. As it turned out the swing to Labour was so great in 1997 that the boundary changes were of only passing interest.

Labour won every seat in the inner London area including all three Lewisham seats; Greenwich & Woolwich; Eltham, and Erith & Thamesmead. In the outer boroughs Labour also won Bexleyheath & Crayford leaving the Conservatives holding only: Old Bexley & Sidcup; Bromley & Chislehurst; Orpington, and Beckenham where, following the resignation over a sex scandal of the Conservative MP Piers Merchant who had been returned at the 1997 General Election, Labour came remarkably close to taking this traditionally safe Tory seat at a by-election on 21st October 1997; but the Conservatives clung on with a majority of just 2.85%. The Tory had won in 1997 by 9%; up until the by-election - its worst performance in that seat since it was established in 1950.

The 1997 results in all constituencies were replicated at the 2001 General Election although the Liberal Democrats came within 0.5% of taking Orpington back from the Conservatives and Labour's majority of 4% at Bexleyheath & Crayford was arguably within the margins that favoured Labour when the new seat was established by the boundary review. In 1992 it would have been considered to be a safe Tory seat.

The results of the 2005 general election mirrored many others in the London area generally with the two main parties reverting to a position similar to that which had prevailed in 1974, that is with Labour maintaining only a slight advantage over the Conservatives. The Liberal Democrats made no progress even in their target seat of Orpington yet at a by-election at Bromley & Chislehurst early in the Parliament held on 29th June 2006 there was a substantial swing towards the Liberal Democrats who came within 2.2% of overturning the Tories' general election majority of 29%.

The 2010 results reflected the erratic swing to the Conservatives felt across London as a whole but Labour held its most marginal seat at Eltham and, although the transfer of the wards of Penge & Cator, Clock House and Crystal Palace from Beckenham to Lewisham West reduced its majority there by an estimated 9% it still remained a Labour seat after the election.

MPs for Lewisham

Lewisham, Deptford

John Ernest Silkin (Labour) won a July 1963 by-election in the former Deptford constituency and was re-elected for Lewisham, Deptford in 1974. He remained MP until he died shortly before the 1987 general election. His principal biographical details are in Chapter 13.

Joan Ruddock in 1983.
© Pam Isherwood National Portrait Gallery

Silkin was succeeded at the 1987 election by a well-known anti-nuclear campaigner, **(Dame) Joan Mary Ruddock** (Labour), who was born at Abergavenny in 1943 and attended Pontypool Grammar School, going on to Imperial College, London where she read and also taught physics. She abandoned lecturing in 1968 in favour of a job with "Shelter", the housing charity where she worked until 1973 as the director of research/publications. A significant figure in the Campaign for Nuclear Disarmament which she chaired in the early 1980s, she subsequently resigned from the Campaign Group, a left wing pressure group, when Tony Benn sought a leadership role in the Labour Party in 1988. Before entering Parliament, she managed the Reading Citizens' Advice Bureau from 1979 to 1986, and also worked as a special programmes officer for unemployed young people. After her election as an MP she was a front bench spokesperson on transport, home affairs and the environment, and remained a champion of women's rights as Vice-President of the Family Planning Association, Vice-President of SERA, Secretary of the All-Party Breast Cancer Group, Secretary of Parliamentary Labour Party Women's Group, and was a co-founder of 'Women Say No to GMOs' (Genetically Modified foods). She introduced the organic food and farming target's bill (1999) and a Ten Minute Rule Bill to amend the 1975 Sex Discrimination Act enabling political parties to take positive action in parliamentary selections. In 2007 she was appointed by Gordon

Brown to be Under Secretary of State at DEFRA, (the Department for the Environment, Farming and Rural Affairs), becoming Minister for Energy & Climate Change. She was the partner of the Labour MP for Aberdeen North, Frank Doran.

MPs for Lewisham Borough

From	at	To	Surname	First Names	Constituency	Party
1974	G	1987	Silkin	John Ernest	Lewisham, Deptford	Labour
1987	G	date	Ruddock	(Dame) Joan Mary		Labour
1974	G	1983	Moyle	Roland Dunstan	Lewisham East	Labour
1979	G	1992	Moynihan	Colin Berkeley		Conservative
1992	G	2010	Prentice	Mrs Bridget Theresa		Labour
2010	G	Date	Alexander	Heidi		Labour
1974	G	1983	Price	Christopher	Lewisham West	Labour
1983	G	1992	Maples	John Cradock		Conservative
1992	G	2010	Dowd	Jim Patrick		Labour
2010	G	Date	Dowd	Jim Patrick	Lewisham West & Penge	Labour

Notes: First returned at: B By-election, G General Election

Lewisham East

Roland Dunstan Moyle (Labour) won Lewisham North in 1966 and held it until 1974 when he was returned for the new constituency of Lewisham East. He held this until 1983 when he was defeated. His principal biographical details are in Chapter 13.

Election leaflet 1983
Peoples History Museum Manchester

Moyle lost his seat to **Colin Berkeley Moynihan** (Conservative), the second son of Lord Moynihan, who held the seat from 1983 until 1992 when he too was defeated. Born in 1955, he was educated at Monmouth School and University College, Oxford, where he excelled at rowing and boxing, being a lightweight in both sports. At the 1978 Olympics he won a gold medal for rowing (as a Cox) and subsequently gained silver medals in other international competitions. A member of the Sports Council from 1982 to 1985 he enjoyed a business as well as a sporting career, being an external adviser to Tate and Lyle from 1983 to 1987, chief executive (1982-3), and vice chairman (1983-6) of Ridgways, the tea and coffee merchants. He was PPS to Kenneth Clarke between 1983 and 1987 and joined the Government as Minister of Sport with the rank of Under Secretary of State for Environment, between 1987 and 1990. Between 1990 and 1992 in John Major's Government he was Under Secretary of State for Energy. On the death of his half brother in 1991 he took five years to prove his eligibility to the Baronetcy of Moynihan taking his seat in the Upper House in 1997, and afterwards was elected as one of the Hereditary peers to remain in the House of Lords after the passing of the House of Lords Act in 1999. He was Shadow Minister of Sport between 2003 and 2005 when he was elected Chairman of the British Olympic Committee for the 2012 London Games.

Mrs Bridget Theresa Prentice (Labour) won the seat in 1992. Born in Glasgow in 1952 she went to school at Our Lady and St. Francis in the city and then took an MA in English Literature and Modern History at Glasgow University. She obtained a teaching qualification at London University and a law degree at South Bank University, afterwards becoming a teacher. She was a magistrate and local councillor in Hammersmith and Fulham between 1988 and 1992, and after Labour's election victory was made an Assistant Government Whip (1997 – 1998), PPS to Brian Wilson, Minister of State at the DTI, PPS to the Lord Chancellor (1999 - 2001), and from 2003 Assistant Government Whip for a second time. After the 2005 election she was appointed Parliamentary Secretary at the Department of Constitutional Affairs, and from May 2007 held a similar post at the Ministry of Justice. She stood down in 2010.

Heidi Alexander (Labour) won the seat for Labour in 2010. Born in 1975 and the daughter of a Swindon electrician, she was politicised at University. She moved to Lewisham in 1999 where she worked for Joan Ruddock MP (Deptford), and in 2004 was elected to serve the Evelyn ward of Deptford on Lewisham Borough Council where she became the full time Deputy Mayor and council member for Regeneration. Between 2007 and 2009 she chaired the Board of Greater London Enterprise, an economic development company.

Lewisham West, Lewisham West & Penge (from 2010)

Christopher Price (Labour) won the seat in 1974 and held it until 1983 when he was defeated. Born in 1932, he was educated at Leeds Grammar School and Queen's College, Oxford, where he was secretary of the Labour Club in 1953. A teacher of the Classics and a freelance journalist, he was a member of Sheffield City Council from 1962 to 1966 and the following year was appointed Editor of '*New Education*', moving in 1968 to become education correspondent of the *"New Statesman"*, in which role he continued until his election as an MP in 1974. His first Parliamentary contest was at Shipley, (Yorkshire West Riding), in 1964, and he was MP for Birmingham, Perry Bar between 1966 and 1970. After his defeat he was appointed Director of the Leeds Polytechnic which became Leeds Metropolitan University in 1992, when he was its Vice-Chancellor.

John Cradock Maples (Conservative) took the seat in 1983 and held it until 1992 when he was defeated. Born in 1943, he was educated at Marlborough College, various foreign language schools in France and Spain, at Cambridge University and Harvard Business School, and initially qualified as a barrister in 1965. He was Parliamentary Private Secretary to the Chief Secretary to the Treasury between 1987 and 1990. From 1990 to 1992 he was Treasury Minister (Economic Secretary), responsible for monetary policy, banks and building societies, Treasury interest in the financial system, oil taxation, Civil Service pay, environmental and international issues. After his defeat in 1992 he was Chairman and Chief Executive of Saatchi & Saatchi between 1992 and 1996 when he was adopted as the Party's candidate at Stratford-upon-Avon. Elected there in 1997 he subsequently held a variety of shadow ministerial posts - Shadow Foreign Secretary, Shadow Secretary of State for Defence and Shadow Secretary of State for Health. David Cameron appointed him a Deputy Chairman of the Conservative Party in 2006. He was ennobled in 2010; he died two years later.

Jim Dowd MP
Peoples History Museum Manchester

Jim Patrick Dowd (Labour) was elected in 1992. Born in 1951 at Bad Eilsen, Germany, he studied at Sedgehill Comprehensive school in London and the London Nautical School. Before entering Parliament he worked as a telecommunications electronics engineer for Plessey/GPT and as a petrol station manager. He was a senior trade union negotiator for ASTMS and the Manufacturing, Science and Finance Union. From 1974 to 1994 he was a member of Lewisham council, chairman of its finance committee, deputy mayor in 1987, and mayor in 1992. He contested Beckenham unsuccessfully on two occasions, in 1983 and 1987. In Opposition from 1992 he was a whip (for London Labour MPs) and then from 1995 a spokesman on Northern Ireland. From 1997 to 2001 he was a Government whip. He continued to represent the area after boundary changes added Penge to the constituency, in 2010 becoming the first and so far only Labour politician to represent any part of Bromley Borough in the Commons. Previously Penge had always been represented by Conservative MPs.

MPs for Greenwich Borough

Greenwich, Greenwich and Woolwich (from 1997)

Nicolas Guy Barnett (Labour) who was elected at a July 1971 by-election remained the MP for Greenwich until 1986. His principal biographical details are in Chapter 13.

Barnett died in 1986 precipitating a February 1987 by-election that caused a sensation at the time because in the run up to a general election that was widely expected to be held within months, Labour's candidate (the actress Glenda Jackson – see Hampstead, Chapter 15) was defeated by **"Rosie" Susan Barnes** (Social Democratic Party). Born in 1946 and educated at Bilborough Grammar School and Birmingham University, she was a market researcher who came new to politics, attracted by the creation of the SDP. She succeeded in holding the seat at the 1987 election but was defeated in 1992 after which she returned to the voluntary sector, working as the organiser for the Birthright Charity. The SDP was short lived, but between 1987 and 1992 it had two MPs in the Borough of Greenwich, the other being John Cartwright (see next page).

Rosie Barnes MP
© Miriam Reik National Portrait Gallery

Wyvill Richard Nicolls "Nick" Raynsford (Labour) won the seat in 1992 and went on to retain the new Greenwich and Woolwich constituency in 1997, 2001 and 2005. He was formerly but briefly the MP for Fulham from 1986 to 1987, and his principal biographical details are in Chapter 15 (Fulham).

MPs for Greenwich Borough						
From	**at**	**To**	**Surname**	**First Names**	**Constituency**	**Party**
1974	G	1986	Barnett	Nicolas Guy	Greenwich	Labour
1987	B	1992	Barnes	Mrs Rosemary (Rosie)Susan		SDP
1992	G	1997	Raynsford	Wyvill Richard Nicolls		Labour
1997	G	date	Raynsford	Wyvill Richard Nicolls	Greenwich & Woolwich	Labour
1974(1)	G	1974(2)	Mayhew	Christopher Paget	Woolwich East	Labour
1974(2)	G	1983	Cartwright	John Cameron		Labour
1983	G	1992	Cartwright	John Cameron	Woolwich	SDP
1992	G	1997	Austin-Walker	John		Labour
1997	G	2010	Austin-Walker	John	Erith & Thamesmead	Labour
2010	G	Date	Pearce	Teresa		Labour
1974	G	1979	Hamling	Will(iam)	Woolwich West	Labour
1979	G	1983	Bottomley	(Sir) Peter		Conservative
1983	G	1997	Bottomley	(Sir) Peter	Eltham	Conservative
1997	G	Date	Efford	Clive		Labour
Notes: First returned at: B By-election, G General Election						

Woolwich East, Woolwich, Erith & Thamesmead (from 1997)

Christopher Paget Mayhew (Labour), who had been elected at a 1951 by-election was returned again at the February 1974 election but soon afterwards defected to the Liberal Party, standing down in October 1974 and seeking election at Bath. His principal biographical details are in Chapter 13.

John Cartwright MP
Peoples History Museum Manchester

He was succeeded in October 1974 by **John Cameron Cartwright** (Labour), who later joined the SDP and successfully sought re-election at the 1983 general election when the seat was re-designated "Woolwich". Cartwright was born in 1933 and educated at Woking County Grammar School and became a civil servant in 1952, but three years later he embarked on a full time career as a Labour Party organizer, a role he held until 1967 when he became the political secretary of the Royal Arsenal Co-operative Society, which was headquartered in Woolwich. In 1970 he unsuccessfully contested Bexley being defeated by the incoming Prime Minister, Ted Heath, but in 1971 was elected Leader of Greenwich Borough Council, a post he held until 1974, being for much of that period the chief whip of the London Boroughs Association (1971-5). Elected at Woolwich East in October 1974, he was also a member of the Labour Party's National Executive Committee (from 1971-5 and 1976-8) but he became increasingly disillusioned with the leftward drift of his Party and in 1981 resigned to join the Social Democrats, successfully standing in their colours at both the 1983 and 1987 general elections. In 1983 he was appointed SDP Chief Whip, was a Vice President of the Party and a defence and foreign affairs spokesman. Although happy with the Social Democrat – Liberal Alliance, he opposed the amalgamation of the two parties so that when the Liberal Democrats were formed in 1990 he sat as an Independent Social Democrat. Following the creation of "New" Labour he re-joined the Labour Party.

John Austin-Walker (Labour), who contested the seat unsuccessfully in 1987 won Woolwich in 1992, and was subsequently returned for Erith and Thamesmead in 1997 and 2001. Born in 1944 in Blaby, Leicestershire, he was educated at Epsom Grammar School and subsequently obtained a Certificate in Community and Youth Work at Goldsmiths College, New Cross, and a MSc in Policy Studies at Bristol University. Before entering Parliament he was Director of Bexley Council for Racial Equality, a Community Social Worker, Labour Party Organiser, and Medical Laboratory Technician. He was a Councillor in Greenwich from 1970-94, Leader of that Council between 1982 and 1987, and its Mayor from 1987 to 1989. A Vice-Chairman of the International Parliamentary Union, his other political interests included the Co-operative Party, Greenpeace and the Council for the Advancement of Arab British Understanding. During the 2001-5 Parliament he rebelled against the Government over amendments to the Prevention of Terrorism and Higher Education Funding Bills. He stood down in 2010.

Teresa Pearce (Labour) won the Erith & Thamesmead seat in 2010. Born in Southport (Lancashire) in 1955, her parents moved to Eltham when she was ten. She left school aged 17 and a year later found herself a single parent living in a council flat in Belvedere after her marriage break-up. She was formerly a borough councillor in Bexley and a senior manager at PricewaterhouseCoopers.

Woolwich West. Eltham (from 1997)

Will(iam) Hamling (Labour), who won Woolwich West at the 1964 general election, was re-elected at successive general elections until October 1974 but died in 1975. His principal biographical details are in Chapter 13.

Peter Bottomley MP Election Leaflet 1979
Peoples History Museum Manchester

Labour lost the 1975 by-election and the seat was taken by **(Sir) Peter Bottomley** (Conservative) who was born in 1944 and educated at a mixed comprehensive school in Washington DC, at Westminster (Public) School, and Trinity College, Cambridge. An industrial economist, his non-political career included industrial sales and industrial relations. Married to Virginia Bottomley, MP for South West Surrey (1984-2005), he was a sometime Chairman of the Church of England Children's Society and a trustee of Christian Aid and MIND, amongst other charities. He founded Family Forum and was a member of the Child Poverty Action Group. Bottomley was President of the Conservative Trade Unionists from 1978 to 1980 and described his special interests as including family policy and foreign relations. He contested Woolwich West unsuccessfully in the general elections of February and October 1974 and when he won the seat in June 1975, it was the first by-election win under Margaret Thatcher's leadership of the Conservative Party. He served as Secretary of the Conservative Parliamentary Committee on Health and Social Services (1977-1979), and Foreign and Commonwealth Affairs (1979-1981). He was PPS to Cranley Onslow MP, Minister of State in the Foreign and Commonwealth Office (1982-1983), and then PPS to Norman Fowler MP, Secretary of State for Social Services. In 1984 he was made Parliamentary Under-Secretary of State at Employment, Transport two years later, and at the Northern Ireland Office in 1989 where his responsibilities included agriculture and the environment. Approaching the 1997 election, Bottomley went in search of a safer seat and was elected at Worthing West where he was re-elected at successive elections in 2001, 2005 and 2010.

Clive Efford (Labour) who won Eltham in 1997 was born in 1958 and educated at Walworth Comprehensive School in nearby Southwark working in the family's jewellery shop, later becoming a taxi driver. A Greenwich councillor between 1986 and 1998, he was elected Vice Chairman of the London Group of Labour MPs. After the 2005 election he was one of the formerly loyal group of Labour MPs who called for Tony Blair to stand down. In Gordon Brown's Government he was appointed a PPS at the Housing Department in 2008. A supporter of Ed Miliband, he was appointed to the Opposition Front Bench in 2011, initially with a Home Office brief, and then as Shadow Minister for Sport.

MPs for Bexley Borough

Bexleyheath

Cyril Townsend MP Election Poster 1974
Peoples History Museum Manchester

Cyril Townsend (Conservative), is believed to have got this seat in 1974 by knowing the then leader, Ted Heath, the MP for the adjoining constituency, for whom he had worked between 1968 and 1970 before moving to the Conservative Party Research Department for three years. He was born in 1937 and educated at Bradfield and Sandhurst Military College after which he spent ten years in the Durham Light Infantry. He was not enamoured of Mrs Thatcher's politics holding left wing views for a Conservative. He was opposed to capital punishment and to fox hunting, supporting Michael Hesltine in 1990. When his seat was re-drawn he was de-selected in 1995 in advance of the 1997 election. He subsequently joined the Liberal Democrats. He died in 2013.

Erith and Crayford

Alfred James Wellbeloved (Labour) had first been returned at a November 1965 by-election and held the seat until 1983 when he was defeated standing for the SDP. His principal biographical details may be found in Chapter 13.

He was defeated by **David Evennett** (Conservative) who held the seat until 1997 when he was adopted as the candidate for Bexleyheath and Crayford, but was defeated as he was again in 2001. He was born in 1949 and attended Buckhurst Hill High School and the London School of Economics becoming a teacher after he

MPs for Bexley Borough						
From	**at**	**To**	**Surname**	**First Names**	**Constituency**	**Party**
1974	G	1997	Townsend	Cyril	Bexleyheath	Conservative
1974	G	1983	Wellbeloved	Alfred James	Erith & Crayford	Labour
1997	G	2005	Beard	Nigel	Bexleyheath & Crayford	Labour
2005	G	Date	Evennett	David		Conservative
1974	G	1997	Heath	(Sir) (Ted) Edward Richard George	Sidcup	Conservative
1997	G	2001	Heath	(Sir) (Ted) Edward Richard George	Old Bexley & Sidcup	Conservative
2001	G	2008	Conway	Derek		Conservative
2008		2010	Conway	Derek		Ind Conservative
2010	G	Date	Brokenshire	James		Conservative
Notes: First returned at: B By-election, G General Election						

graduated. He changed career direction working as a marine broker at Lloyds from 1974 to 1981 becoming a director of his father's underwriting agency in 1982. Elected in 1983 his first sniff of promotion came in 1992 when he was appointed PS to the Baroness Blatch whom he served when she was an Education Minister. Then in 1993 he fulfilled the same role for John Redwood when he was Secretary of State for Wales until his resignation in 1995 to fight John Major for the leadership of the Conservative Party. This seems to have put an end to Evennett's ministerial prospects. Selected to fight the new Bexleyheath and Crayford constituency in 1997 in preference to Cyril Townsend (see Bexleyheath above) and turning his back on the certainty of defeat in Erith and Thamesmead (see below), he was nevertheless still defeated in the Labour landslide. However, he fought the seat again in 2001 and four years later was successful in the 2005 contest after which he served as an Opposition whip. In 2010 he was elected for the redrawn seat of Bexleyheath & Crayford.

Bexleyheath & Crayford

Nigel Beard MP
Election leaflet 1997
Peoples History Museum
Manchester

Nigel Beard (Labour) won this new seat in 1997, defeating David Evennett, the former Tory MP for the old Erith & Crayford constituency (see above) who had been selected in preference to Cyril Townsend to contest the constituency. Born in Leeds in 1936, Beard was educated at Castleford Grammar School and obtained a BSc in Physics at University College, London, and later attended the London Business School. He worked for the Ministry of Defence, the Greater London Council and was at one time Head of Docklands Development. Between 1979 and 1983 he worked for ICI and from then until 1997 for Zeneca, a drugs company. At the 2005 election, Evennett, who had continued to contest the seat, was returned and Beard defeated. (See Erith and Crayford above for full biographical details). He was a Party whip in the 2005 Parliament.

Sidcup, Old Bexley & Sidcup

Sir Edward Richard George Heath (Conservative) was MP for Bexley from 1950 to 1974, for Sidcup from 1974 to 1983, and for Old Bexley & Sidcup from 1983 until he retired in 2001. His biographical details are in Chapter 13.

He was succeeded in 2001 by **Derek Conway** (Conservative) who had lost his former Shrewsbury & Atcham seat, which he had held since 1983, at the 1997 general election. Born at Newcastle-upon-Tyne in 1953, he attended Beacon Hill Boys' School and the Technical College in Gateshead, and then moved on to Newcastle Polytechnic. The owner of several holiday cottages he also worked for various charities including Action Research for the Crippled Child and the Cat Protection League of which he was Chief Executive. He was Parliamentary Private Secretary to the Minister of State for Wales from 1988-91 and to the Minister of State for Employment from 1992-93. He was subsequently Assistant government whip from 1993-94 and a Government whip from 1993-97. Conway's career was dramatically changed in 2008 when it emerged that he had been paying his family to undertake various allegedly fictitious roles. He was forced to resign the Tory whip and sat as an Independent until the general election.

James Brokenshire (Conservative) the former MP for Hornchurch was adopted as the Tory candidate after his seat was lost through boundary changes. Details of his biography are in Chapter 16.

MPs for Bromley Borough						
From	***at***	***To***	***Surname***	***First Names***	***Constituency***	***Party***
1974	*G*	*1992*	*Goodhart*	*(Sir) Philip Carter*	*Beckenham*	*Conservative*
1992	*G*	*1997*	*Merchant*	*Piers*		*Conservative*
1997	*B*	*2010*	*Lait*	*Jacqui*		*Conservative*
2010	*G*	*Date*	*Stewart*	*(Colonel) Bob*		*Conservative*
1974	*G*	*1997*	*Hunt*	*(Sir) John Leonard*	*Ravensbourne*	*Conservative*
1974	*G*	*1997*	*Sims*	*Roger*	*Chislehurst*	*Conservative*
1997	*G*	*2006*	*Forth*	*Eric*	*Bromley & Chislehurst*	*Conservative*
2006	*B*	*Date*	*Neill*	*Bob*		*Conservative*
1945	*G*	*1992*	*Stanbrook*	*Ivor Robert*	*Orpington*	*Labour*
1992	*G*	*date*	*Horam*	*John*		*Conservative*
2010	*G*	*Date*	*Johnson*	*Jo*		*Conservative*

Notes: First returned at: B By-election, G General Election

Beckenham

Sir Philip Carter Goodhart (Conservative) had represented Beckenham since 1957 and continued to do so until his retirement in 1992. His principal biographical details may be found in Chapter 13.

BECKENHAM CONSERVATIVE ASSOCIATION
31 BECKENHAM ROAD, BECKENHAM (650 1944)

CONSERVATIVE FIGHTING FUND

Dear Sir or Madam,

The expected General Election is now upon us—the Conservative Government has made much progress in restoring the greatness of our nation but needs another term to complete its programme.

General Elections cost a great deal of money and we look to our members and supporters to give generously to our Fighting Fund which will be used to:—

(1) Return Sir PHILIP GOODHART to the House of Commons as the member for Beckenham.

(2) Help marginal seats, **which must be won** if a Conservative Government is to be returned

(3) Help the Conservative Party generally.

Yours faithfully,

NIGEL KELSH, Divisional Chairman

GRAHAM PAULL, Divisional Treasurer

Name ....

Address ....

Please place your donation in this envelope. It will be collected in a few days by one of our voluntary collectors. Each collector has an official letter of authority issued from 31 Beckenham Road. If you require a receipt please tick in this space. ☐

Published by D. Hamon, 1a Palace View, Bromley, Kent and printed by Brewster Printing Co. Ltd., The Common, Rochester, Kent ME1 1PR

Evidence of how local funds were raised for the Goodhart re-election campaign.
Peoples History Museum Manchester

Goodhart was succeeded by **Piers Merchant** (Conservative) who had earlier sat as MP for Newcastle Central between 1983 and 1987. Born in 1951, he was educated at Nottingham High School and Durham University after which he became a journalist. In 1992 he was appointed PPS to Peter Lilley and in 1955 backed John Redwood's leadership bid against John Major. In the run-up to the 1997 election he became embroiled in a personal scandal involving an alleged affair with his secretary but survived the poll with a reduced majority. However, shortly afterwards more details emerged about his private life and he resigned his seat, triggering an early by-election in the 1997 Parliament. He died in 2009.

Piers Merchant MP
Derek Bennett Wikipedia

At the 1997 by-election Merchant was succeeded by **Mrs Jaqui Lait** (Conservative), who had lost Hastings and Rye at the General Election, having served there since 1992. A Glaswegian born in 1947, she was the goddaughter of the former Chislehurst MP, Dame Patricia Hornsby-Smith. She attended Paisley Grammar School and Strathclyde University and made a career as a lobbyist for the Chemical Industries Association later becoming a parliamentary consultant with her own company after 1985. From 1986 to 1989 she was a Lloyds Underwriter. In 1994 she was appointed PPS to the junior social services ministers and private secretary to William Hague when he was Welsh Secretary. In 1996 she became the first ever woman Tory whip.

Jaqui Lait retired at the 2010 election and was succeeded by a former military man, **Colonel Bob Stewart**, a well known media figure following his leadership of the United Nations forces sent to Bosnia in 1992/3.

Ravensbourne

Sir John Hunt (Conservative), previously MP for Bromley since 1964, was elected for the re-titled constituency in 1974 and held it until its abolition in 1997. His principal biographical details may be found in Chapter 18.

Chislehurst

Roger Sims (Conservative), inherited this seat from Dame Patricia Hornsby-Smith who retired in 1974. He held it until 1997 when it was redrawn and he retired. Born in 1930 and educated at Leicester Boys School and St. Olave's Grammar School, Southwark, he worked in various city trading companies before his election in 1974. For four years between 1979 and 1983 he was PPS to William Whitelaw.

Bromley & Chislehurst

Eric Forth (Conservative), a flamboyant and outspoken politician, was elected in 1997 having previously represented Mid Worcestershire since 1983. He was born in Glasgow in 1944, and educated at Jordanhill College School, and Glasgow University, where he gained an MA (Hons) in Politics and Economics, going on to pursue a mainly political career although he also worked as a management consultant in the computing industry. He was a councillor in Brentwood Urban District from 1968 to 1972 and in both elections of 1974 unsuccessfully contested the Barking constituency. He was Secretary of Llandeilo Conservative Association 1975 to 1977 and Chairman of Ross-on-Wye CPC from 1978 to 1979 and then served as a Member of the European Parliament for Birmingham North until 1984. He was Vice Chairman of the Conservative Parliamentary European Affairs Committee from July 1983 to 1986, and Chairman from 1987 until 1988 but embarked on a modest ministerial progression in 1986 when he was appointed PPS to the Minister of State in the Department of Education and Science. In 1990 he was appointed Parliamentary Under Secretary of State at the Department of Employment, and in 1992, to a similar role at the Department of Trade and Industry. He was a Minister of State at the Department for Education from July 1994 until July 1995, and Minister of State at the Department for Education and Employment from July 1995 until May 1997. From 2001 to 2003, he was Shadow Leader of the House of Commons. He died from cancer in May 2006, just over a year after his re-election in 2005.

Forth's successor was **Bob Neill** (Conservative), who was returned at a by-election on 29th June 2006 with a wafer thin majority of only 2.2% over the Liberal Democrat. Born in 1952 and educated at Abbs Cross Technical High School, Neill was a barrister who had cut his political teeth as a Havering Borough councillor and as the Conservative representative for Romford on the GLC. He unsuccessfully contested Dagenham in the 1983 general election and in 2000 was elected a member of the London Assembly for Bexley and Bromley.

Orpington

Sir Ivor Stanbrook (Conservative), held the seat between 1970 and 1992 when he retired. His principal biographical details may be found in Chapter 13.

He was succeeded by **John Horam** (Conservative), a man who changed parties twice. He was born in 1939 in Preston, Lancashire but was educated in Yorkshire at Silcoates School, Wakefield, and St Catherine's College, Cambridge (Exhibition in History, MA in Economics). He formed a business information company, Commodities Research Unit International Ltd, in 1968 having previously worked for the *Financial Times* and *The Economist*. In 1966 he contested Folkestone & Hythe for Labour and in 1970 was returned for Gateshead West when he was sponsored by the Transport and General Workers Union. From 1976 to 1979 he was Parliamentary Under Secretary at the Ministry of Transport under Bill Rodgers with whom he defected to the SDP, sitting until 1983 for Gateshead. He fought Newcastle Central in 1983 but lost to Piers Merchant (see Beckenham above), who was to become a fellow-Tory MP in Bromley Borough. In 1987 he joined the Conservative Party and was selected to succeed Ivor Stanbrook in 1992. Three years later he was appointed as Under Secretary of State for Public Service, in which role he was in charge of the Citizens' Charter Unit, but a few months later was shifted to become Parliamentary Secretary at the Ministry of Health, returning to the back benches in 1997 when the Tories were defeated. He stood down in 2010.

John Horam MP
© Horam website

Jo Johnson MP
© Jo Johnson website

Jo Johnson (Conservative), the younger brother of Boris Johnson, succeeded Horam. Like his brother, educated at Eton and Oxford University, where he was awarded a First Class Honours degree in modern history, he was a journalist who prior to entering the House was head of the Asia Bureau for the *Financial Times*.

Chapter 18
Metropolitan Surrey since 1974

1974 - 1983: Greater London Authority Boundaries Fully Reflected in the Second Periodic Review

In 1965 the outer suburban areas of London that were still in Surrey were finally transferred to Greater London. People living in various urban districts and boroughs of Surrey found themselves in one of Kingston, Sutton & Cheam, Croydon or Merton London Boroughs. Richmond was unique in that it also covered the former Middlesex districts of Twickenham and Teddington[1]. In the former LCC area boroughs were also amalgamated. It was a requirement for London constituencies to be established wholly within the boundaries of the new Boroughs which were newly constituted as shown below

Old Council Areas in Metropolitan Surrey	New Boroughs	Remarks
Bermondsey, Camberwell, Southwark (Boroughs)	*Southwark*	*3-way amalgamation*
Lambeth Borough; Streatham and eastern parts of Clapham from Wandsworth Borough	*Lambeth*	*2-way amalgamation*
Battersea, Wandsworth (Boroughs); except Streatham and parts of Clapham	*Wandsworth*	*2-way amalgamation*
Barnes, Richmond, Twickenham (Boroughs)	*Richmond upon Thames*	*3-way amalgamation*
Wimbledon, Mitcham (Boroughs); Merton & Morden UDC	*Merton*	*3-way amalgamation*
Kingston, Surbiton; Malden & Coombe (Boroughs)	*Kingston upon Thames*	*3-way amalgamation*
Sutton & Cheam, Beddington & Wallington (Boroughs); Carshalton UDC	*Sutton*	*3-way amalgamation*
Croydon Borough; Coulsdon & Purley UDC	*Croydon*	*2-way amalgamation*

These changes were eventually felt on the constituency map in 1974 when the immediate overall effect was that the number of constituencies in Metropolitan Surrey was reduced by 3 from 25 to 22 , two in inner-London and one in the outer suburbs. The rationalisation of seats in the LCC area was brought about by falling electoral rolls whilst in the outer suburban area although Croydon's representation was increased this was cancelled out by redistribution elsewhere, while Surrey East ceased to be a London constituency by giving up its metropolitan electorates altogether.

Southwark & Lambeth (7 seats)

Continuing economic decline affected Southwark. For example, a new breed of super tankers needed deeper docks than Bermondsey could offer and by 1970 they had closed. With their decline much of the food processing industry also moved away. The former Southwark and Bermondsey constituencies were mainly combined as **Southwark, Bermondsey** although the southern fringes of Newington were allocated to **Southwark Peckham**, which included the Elephant & Castle, Walworth, Denmark Hill, Camberwell and North Peckham. **Southwark Dulwich** included South Peckham, Nunhead, and all districts of Dulwich itself, as far south as the border with Crystal Palace.

Lambeth borough retained four seats despite some redistribution that saw Brixton replaced by the more aptly named Lambeth Central. However, the apparent stability was in part due to the transfer of Streatham from Wandsworth to

1 Twickenham (now in Richmond Borough) and Spelthorne (now in Surrey) are considered in preceding Chapters of this book relating to Middlesex.

Left: *Purley is a wealthy and very leafy suburb (note illustration) straddling the Brighton Road and Railway. It was transferred into Greater London in 1963 and ever since constituency boundaries were realigned in 1974 Purley has, with neighbouring Coulsdon, been a part of the safe Conservative constituency of Croydon South.*

Below: *Wallington has always been paired with Carshalton but was only included in the constituency name from 1983. The High Street is pictured here with modern flats surrounding the Southern Railway station, offering good commuting to Central London, Croydon and other south west London suburbs.*

Below: *Barnes has been part of the Richmond Constituency since it was founded in 1918. However, between 1983 and 1997 it was also included in the constituency name. Elm Bank Gardens pictured here, is an affluent enclave close to the Thames and to the station at Barnes Bridge*

Above: *This view of St John's Avenue Putney shows the replacement of Victorian dwellings in modern times with the high density housing so needed in London. The Putney constituency is well supplied with transport to be a dormitory suburb and in recent years has swung between Labour and Conservative.*

Left: Less affluent and much more socially diverse than neighbouring Putney, the atmosphere of Tooting is epitomised by this African grocery stall in its Indoor Market. The market is close to a Northern Line tube station, and that and main line stations nearby connect the Tooting constituency well to the rest of London.

Photos John Nelson, except where marked

Lambeth. **Lambeth, Vauxhall** was extended south to include Kennington, while **Lambeth, Central** included North Clapham, Stockwell, Brixton and the Town Hall area of Lambeth. **Lambeth, Streatham** combined parts of the former Clapham constituency on the southeast side of Clapham Common including Clapham Park, with Streatham Hill and Streatham proper. **Lambeth, Norwood** remained pretty much unaltered including Herne Hill, Brockwell Park, Tulse Hill, Knights Hill, West Norwood and the west side of Gipsy Hill.

Wandsworth (4 seats)

Battersea North was extended southwards to embrace the area north and west of Clapham Common, whilst **Battersea South** acquired Wandsworth town centre from Wandsworth Central, and the area south of Clapham Common including Balham from Clapham. It retained the districts in between including Wandsworth Common, and the area around Wandsworth Prison either side of the main South-western Railway line including Earlsfield. **Wandsworth, Tooting** acquired the eastern and southern districts of the former Wandsworth Central constituency including all districts of Tooting, Furzedown and north Balham, which it acquired from Clapham. **Wandsworth, Putney** remained more or less as before.

Richmond, Kingston and Merton (5 seats)

Richmond, Kingston-upon-Thames and **Surbiton** were unaltered. A new **Mitcham & Morden** comprised the former borough of Mitcham plus districts to the west, namely, Lower Morden, St. Helier, and Ravensbury, places that had previously formed the southern part of Merton and Morden. Merton itself, including Raynes Park and Cannon Hill, transferred to **Wimbledon**. Twickenham, though in Richmond Borough, is accounted for in Middlesex (Chapter 15)

Sutton & Croydon (6 seats)

Carshalton acquired Beddington and Wallington from the former Mitcham constituency and lost Banstead to Reigate, a non-metropolitan division of Surrey. **Sutton & Cheam** was unchanged whilst Croydon borough's expansion to include Purley and Coulsdon brought about a revision of all its seats. **Croydon Central** was the new additional seat, comprising most of the former South constituency. Addington, Shirley, Central, Heathfield and Waddon districts were acquired from Croydon South, together with Forestdale from Surrey East. **Croydon South** retained Croham and Selsdon but acquired Sanderstead, Purley, Coulsdon, Kenley and Woodcote from Surrey East. **Croydon North West** acquired Broad Green from the former South constituency whilst **Croydon North East** was little altered embracing Upper and South Norwood, Thornton Heath, Addiscombe and Woodside.

1983 - 1997: The Third Periodic Review

In 1983 two more seats were lost, one from each of the inner London boroughs of Wandsworth and Lambeth, reducing the Metropolitan Surrey total to 20. Once again all seats were contained within discrete borough boundaries

Southwark & Lambeth (6 seats)

Southwark kept three seats and the allocation of wards was little changed. An area south of Bricklayers Arms on the borders of North Peckham was transferred from Bermondsey to **Peckham**. As a consequence the Bermondsey constituency was renamed **Southwark & Bermondsey**. **Dulwich** was unchanged.

In Lambeth the Central seat was lost through merger with Vauxhall, Streatham and Norwood. The **Vauxhall** constituency acquired the northern districts of Stockwell and Clapham, whilst most of central Brixton was allocated to **Streatham.** Angell Town and the area between Brixton town centre and Herne Hill were transferred to **Norwood**.

Wandsworth (3 seats)

In Wandsworth both Battersea seats together with Tooting were merged into two new constituencies, called **Battersea** and **Tooting**. Basically Tooting expanded northwards to acquire Wandsworth Common and the area around the Prison from Battersea South, whilst Wandsworth town centre, also formerly in the South division, was transferred to Battersea. For most of the Twentieth century Battersea had remained a prominent working class suburb close to central London but during that period the bulk of the population began to disperse southwards as slum clearances progressed and the suburban railway network encouraged people to live further out. Its 1991 population was 67,560, a substantial

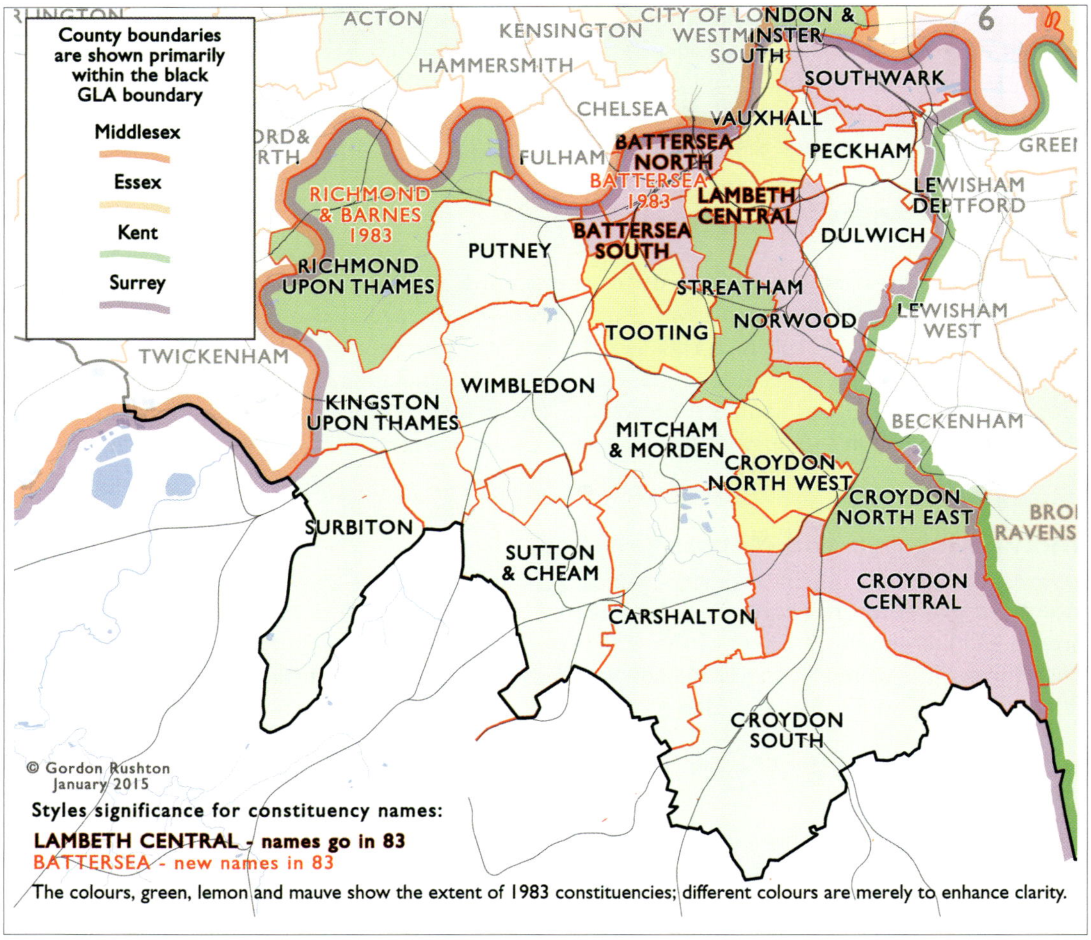

The map depicts Surrey constituencies created in 1974, and the modifications that occurred in 1983, when two seats were eliminated, one in Battersea, and the other in Lambeth. The St Margarets Ward of Twickenham (Middx) was transferred to Richmond & Barnes in 1974. Carshalton was renamed Carshalton & Wallington in 1983 without boundary alterations. Elsewhere the small ward switches are shown on the map.

drop from its Nineteenth Century peak. Meanwhile the social characteristics of the area were also altering, becoming more middle class, reflecting the demographic changes taking place on the opposite side of the river in nearby Fulham.

The Outer Suburban Boroughs (11 seats)

In the outer suburban area the number and ward composition of all but one of the seats remained unchanged. There were a couple of minor name changes. **Richmond & Barnes** was a new designation for the former Richmond seat although this failed to highlight the inclusion of the east Twickenham ward from the Middlesex side of the Thames, transferred in from Twickenham constituency (see Chapter 15). Barnes village had been home to the composer Gustav Holst and novelist Henry Fielding whilst nearby East Sheen was where Whig Prime Minister Earl Grey had lived. The place name meant simply 'place near the barns'. The Hanoverian Royal Family made nearby Kew their home in the eighteenth century and the national archive is also based there. The Public Record Office holds 900 years of historical records, including the Domesday Book.

Carshalton & Wallington was also a new designation, though it did not change in its composition. Despite suffering serious damage in the Second World War, Wallington, which was now added to the seat's designation, had been subject to much redevelopment since 1945. Many of its oldest large houses on the Bridges estate had been demolished and replaced by flats and there were other major developments in the area, all of which combined to give a boost to the Carshalton & Wallington district.

Minor changes occurred in **Croydon** with ward swaps affecting the **North East, North West,** and **Central** constituencies. All other constituencies were unaltered.

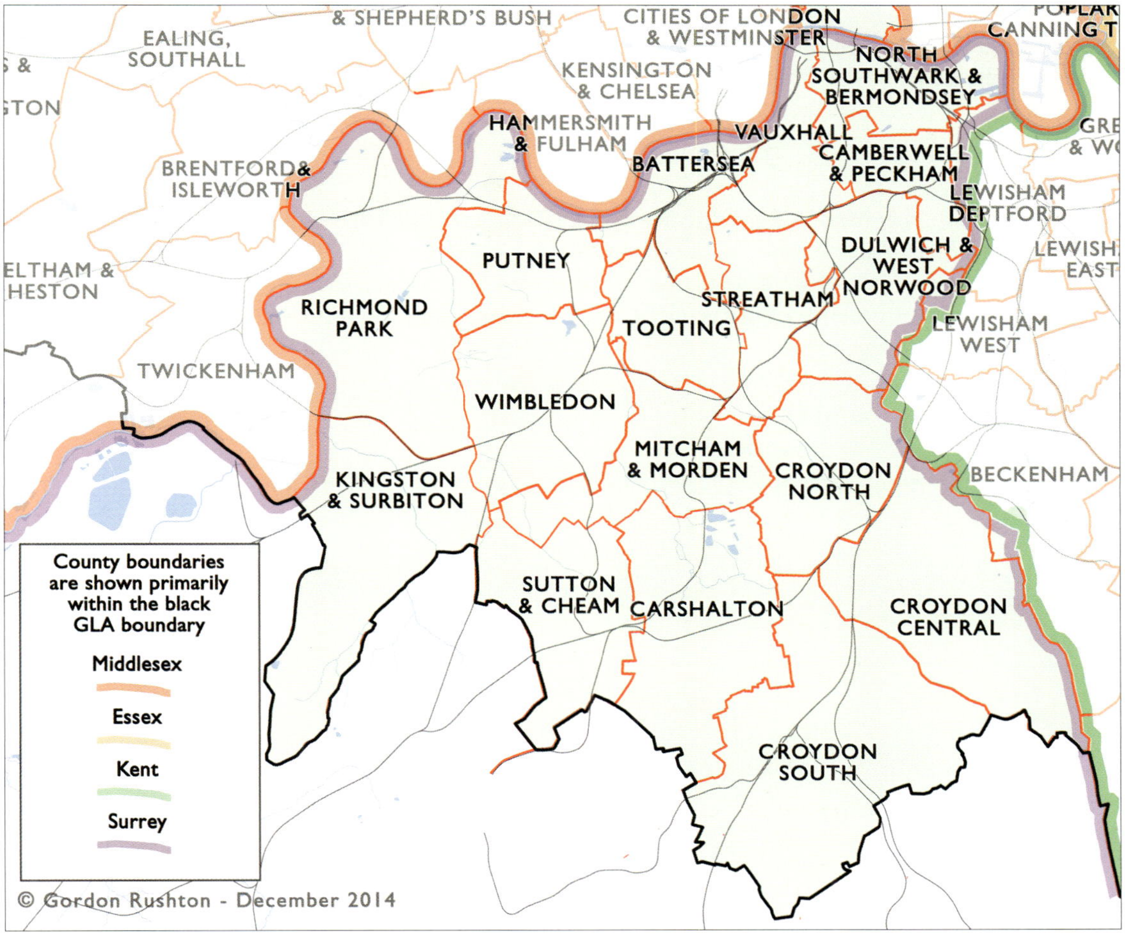

The map depicts Surrey constituencies created in 1997, when there was a reduction of three seats, one through the merger of Dulwich with Norwood, another through the merger of Kingston with Surbiton, and the other in Croydon. Richmond and Barnes was renamed Richmond Park, in consequence of acquiring northern parts of Kingston.

1997 – 2010: The Fourth Periodic Review

When the Boundaries Commission next reviewed London constituencies in 1995 the restriction on allocating constituencies to discrete boroughs was lifted. Lambeth Borough was paired with Southwark, and Richmond with Kingston. Wandsworth, Merton, Sutton and Croydon boroughs remained separate for the purposes of allocating boundaries, and Middlesex districts of Richmond borough also reverted to being kept discrete. Overall there was a loss of three seats when the General Election was fought in 1997 yielding a reduced total of 17.Taken together the boroughs of Southwark and Lambeth lost one seat, principally through the merger of Dulwich with West Norwood, whilst Camberwell and Peckham reappeared as a constituency name to go alongside the renamed Southwark North and Bermondsey.

Southwark and Lambeth (5 seats)

Dulwich & West Norwood was formed as a cross-borough constituency that comprised Gipsy Hill, Herne Hill, Knight's Hill and Thurlow Park (from Norwood), with all parts of the former Dulwich, apart from Peckham Rye, which was transferred to **Camberwell & Peckham**. This comprised mostly the former Peckham division apart from West Newington which was transferred to the renamed **North Southwark & Bermondsey**, which was otherwise unaltered comprising the whole of Southwark, Bermondsey and Rotherhithe. **Vauxhall** gained Angell Town (around Loughborough Junction) from Norwood, whilst **Streatham** extended further east to acquire the whole of Tulse Hill and Thurlow Park from Dulwich.

Kingston and Richmond (2 seats)

The merging of Kingston and Richmond boroughs for the purpose of allocating electorates brought about a reduction from three to two seats. Richmond & Barnes lost the East Twickenham ward it had absorbed in the Third Review on the opposite side of the river which was re-allocated to Twickenham (Middlesex), whilst it also acquired Coombe and the northern districts of Kingston-on-Thames. In consequence it was renamed **Richmond Park**. Southern districts of Kingston were combined with New Malden, Berrylands, Tolworth and Chessington, and re-titled **Kingston & Surbiton**.

Croydon (3 seats)

In Croydon borough the whole of the former North-West constituency was combined with Upper and South Norwood from the North-East division to become **Croydon North,** whilst the wards covering Addiscombe and Woodside (formerly in the North East division) were linked with New Addington, Shirley and Fairfield from **Croydon Central** to form a new constituency of that name. **Croydon South** was the least changed of the former seats gaining only the Waddon district, from Central.

Other Boroughs (7 seats)

Wandsworth, Merton and Sutton boroughs involved no changes at all.

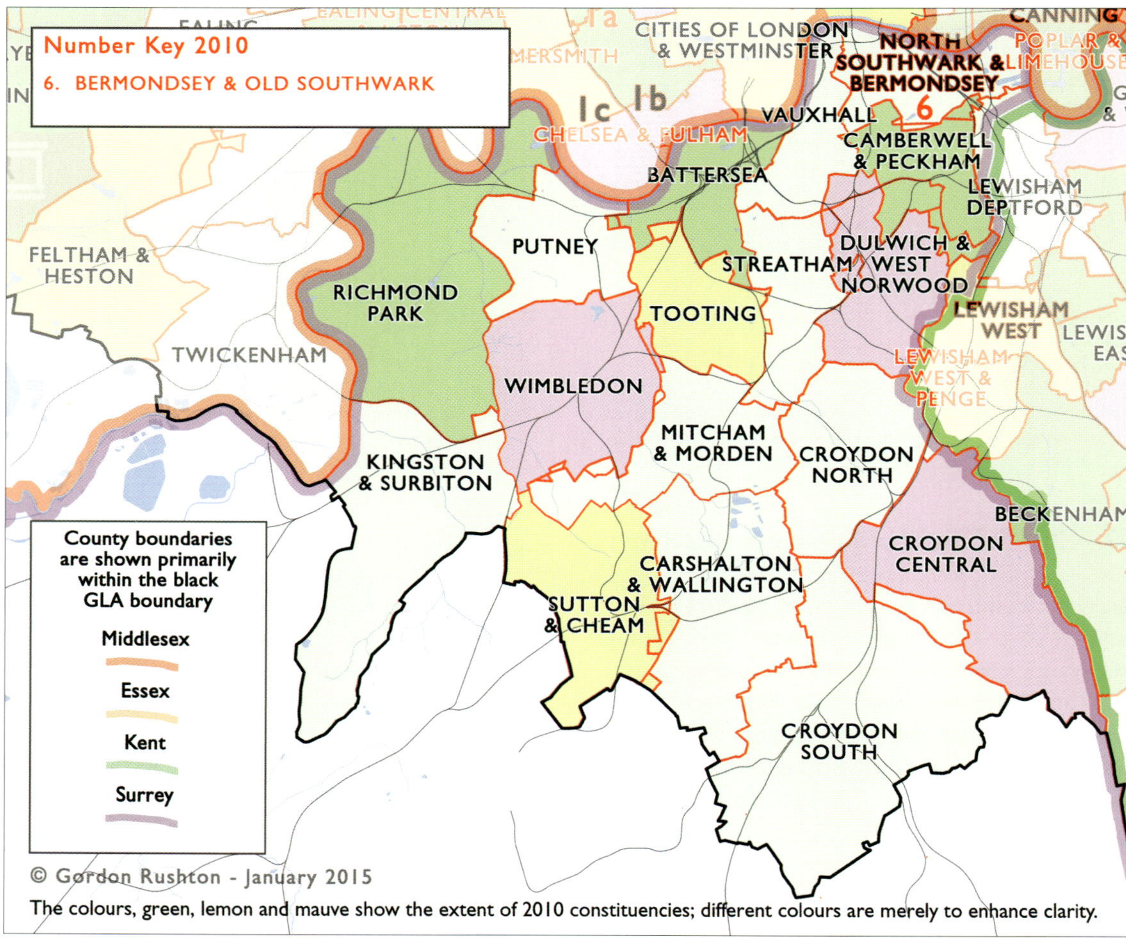

The map depicts Surrey constituencies created in 2010 and highlights the ward switches that took place compared with 1997. Of all the former Metropolitan Counties in London, Surrey was the least affected by boundary changes in 2010. There was one minor constituency name change affecting Bermondsey.

2010: The Fifth Period Review

The boundary changes implemented for the 2010 General Election affected every constituency, though in most cases to a very minor extent. These changes arose from a need to place newly drawn-up borough wards so that they were undivided between constituencies. Only in the case of the boroughs of Lambeth and Southwark were these changes anything other than purely marginal. The total number of seats remained 17 and were allocated between the boroughs in the same proportions as they had been previously.

All parts of Herne Hill and parts of Thurlow Park were transferred to the **Dulwich & West Norwood** constituency, mostly from **Streatham** but partly also partly from **Vauxhall,** whilst the South Camberwell elements of the Peckham Rye and The Lane wards were transferred from Dulwich and West Norwood to **Camberwell & Peckham,** along with parts of the Faraday and Livesey wards covering Walworth from North Southwark & Bermondsey, which was renamed **Bermondsey & Old Southwark** to more accurately describe the areas it covered. In Wandsworth borough there were only minor changes with a very small part of Wandsworth Common being transferred from **Battersea** to **Tooting,** and part of Fairfield ward moved from **Putney** to Battersea.

Minor changes also occurred in Merton borough to align new ward boundaries with constituencies, **Wimbledon** and **Mitcham & Morden**, which were largely unaltered, while in Sutton borough there were transfers of handfuls of electors between **Sutton & Cheam** and **Carshalton & Wallington**. Elsewhere approximately two thousand electors to the north of New Malden station in Beverley ward were transferred from **Richmond Park** to **Kingston & Surbiton. Croydon Central** lost parts of Selsdon and Ballards, and Roham and Wadham wards to **Croydon South** with parts of Broad Green and South Norwood being moved to **Croydon North**.

Politics in Metropolitan Surrey

General Elections - Overall Results 1974 - 2010 (detail table p522)

Constituency	*Feb 1974*	*Oct 1974*	*1979*	*1983*	*1987*	*1992*	*1997*	*2001*	*2005*	*2010*
Labour	*11*	*11*	*10*	*5*	*4*	*7*	*11*	*11*	*8*	*7*
Liberal	*0*	*0*	*0*	*1*	*1*	*1*	*5*	*5*	*5*	*4*
Tory	*11*	*11*	*12*	*14*	*15*	*12*	*1*	*1*	*4*	*6*
Total	*22*	*22*	*22*	*20*	*20*	*20*	*17*	*17*	*17*	*17*

Overall during this period the Conservative and Labour Parties each secured 85 wins at General Elections as against 22 for the Liberal Democrats, making this part of London one its most successful battlegrounds in recent electoral history, especially in the period from 1997 when they significantly out-polled the Tories. The Conservative, Bernard Weatherall was also elected twice standing as The Speaker, in 1983 and 1987. In addition the Tories and SDP/Liberals won 2 by-elections, and Labour 3.

The political impacts of the earlier changes made in 1974 and 1983 were on balance favourable to the Conservatives in as much as they involved the elimination of what, by the latter part of the Twentieth Century, had become deprived inner City constituencies with declining populations, including significant numbers of ethnic minority groups. Such seats had become solidly Labour since 1945 and the impact was the loss of safe seats in Southwark, Lambeth and Wandsworth.

In 1974 Labour lost a safe seat in Southwark through boundary changes and was probably also deprived of a gain from the Conservatives in Wandsworth that would have arisen at that election. There the Tories might have expected to lose the Clapham seat they had held in 1970 by 9% of the votes cast. At the 1974 General Election, however, this was the seat that disappeared and so the Tories lost it anyway. It might be argued that Labour would have been one seat to the better, and the Tories one worse off, had the election taken place on the basis of the former boundaries.

The outer borough changes in Croydon and Merton did not appear to have any marked impact on the political allegiances of the new constituencies, although the Conservative Party may have gained a marginal benefit. Both the former Merton and Mitcham seats had been Tory-held and were also fairly marginal. It would have been unsurprising had Labour won at least one of these seats at the 1974 election when there was a swing in their favour. The Labour Party did in fact win the new Mitcham & Morden seat, possibly aided by the boundary changes, but the Tories were compensated by the creation of an additional seat in nearby Croydon where they previously held all three of the former seats and won all four of the new ones after the boundary review was implemented.

The SDP was formed in 1981 and started to fight by-elections soon afterwards, three of which arose in this area. The first took place during a period of public disaffection with both the Tory Government and the Labour Party. On 22nd October 1981 the Social Democrat-Liberal Alliance won North West Croydon from the Conservatives. The Alliance's majority of 10% over the Tories compared with 9% for the Conservatives over Labour in 1979. Labour's vote slumped from 40% to 26% of the vote at the by-election. Next, on 3rd June 1982 the Tories captured Mitcham and Morden from Labour following the resignation of the MP to fight a by-election following his defection to the Social Democratic Party. Bruce Douglas-Mann was the only such MP to resign and fight a by-election at the time. Labour's share of the vote

General Election Results 1974 - 2010 by % majority

Constituency	Pre 1974	Feb 1974	Oct 1974	1979	1983	1987	1992	1997	2001	2005	2010
Bermondsey (and Old Southwark)	2Lab	Lab52	Lab60	Lab39-	L15	L8	L26	L8	L26	L14	L19
(Camberwell &) Peckham	1 Lab	Lab45	Lab59	Lab32+	Lab27	Lab27	Lab38	Lab57	Lab58	Lab47	Lab37
Dulwich (& West Norwood)	1Lab	Lab11	Lab17	Lab0.3	C5	C0.4	Lab5	Lab37	Lab32	Lab21	Lab19
Vauxhall	1 Lab	Lab30	Lab40	Lab19	Lab20	Lab21	Lab27	Lab50	Lab39	Lab27	Lab25
Lambeth Central	1 Lab	Lab24	Lab34+	Lab22	-	-	-	-	-	-	
Norwood	C	Lab11	Lab15	Lab19	Lab8	Lab12	Lab21	-	-	-	
Streatham	C	C11	C8	C14	C15	C7	Lab6	Lab41	Lab39	Lab18	Lab7
Tooting	1.5 Lab 0.5 C	Lab16	Lab23	Lab15	Lab6	Lab3	Lab8	Lab33	Lab28	Lab13	Lab5
Battersea (North)	1Lab	Lab33	Lab40	Lab23	Lab8	C2	C9	Lab11	Lab14	Lab0.4	C12
Battersea (South)	1Lab	Lab5	Lab10	Lab1	-	-	-	-	-	-	
Putney	C	Lab3	Lab6	C5	C11	C14	C16	Lab7	Lab8	C5	C25
Wimbledon	C	C22	C18	C27	C25	C23	C30	Lab6	Lab9	C5	C24
Mitcham & Morden	2 C	Lab6	Lab13	Lab1-	C14	C13	C3	Lab29	Lab36	Lab32	Lab31
Richmond (& Barnes) Park	C	C9	C10	C6	C0.1	C4	C9	L5	L10	L7	C7
Kingston (& Surbiton)	C	C22	C20	C32	C22	C26	C25	L0.1	L32	L18	L13
Surbiton	C	C17	C18	C31	C26	C27	C28	-	-	-	
Croydon Central		C3	C0.3	C16	C30	C32	C24	Lab7	Lab9	C0.2Ind	C6
Croydon North		-	-	-	-	-	-	Lab33	Lab40	Lab32	Lab32+
Croydon North East	C	C8	C5	C16	C27	C28	C16	-	-	-	
Croydon North West	C	C7	C4	C9-	C10	C10	Lab4	-	-	-	
Croydon South	2 C	C32	C32	C44	C38	C40	C41	C22	C19	C28	C28
Carshalton (& Wallington)	C	C10	C7+	C20	C22	C28	C19	L5	L11	L3	L11
Sutton & Cheam	C	C27	C11	C32	C22	C32	C21	L5	L11	L7	L3
Conservative	15.5	11	11+	12+	13	14	12	1	1	4	6
Labour	9.5	11	11+	10-+	5	4	7	11	11	8	7+
SDP/Liberal	0	0	0	0++	1	1	1	5	5	5	4
Speaker	0	0	0	0	1	1	0	0	0	0	0
Total	25	22	22++	22 ++++	20	20	20	17	17	17	17+

Key: C = Conservative; Lab = Labour; SDP = Social Democratic Party; L= Liberal Democrat; + = Party that won seat at General Election held by-election in same Parliament; - = Party that won seat at General Election lost by-election to main opposition Party in same Parliament.

dropped from 45.2% to 24.4%, the same as the Social Democrats, and the Tories took the seat with a majority of 19% even though their share of the vote also fell, by 0.5%. Labour's majority in 1979 had been 1%.

On 28th October 1982 at a by-election in Peckham, Labour saw a majority over the Tories of 32% reduced to one of 18% over the Social-Democrat/Liberal Party Alliance, an indicator of the impact that a split on the Left of politics would do to the Party at the forthcoming General Election in 1983. On 24th February 1983 - in the run up to the general election later that year - a particularly damaging by-election saw Labour lose Bermondsey to the Alliance by a majority of 32%. Labour had held a 1979 General Election majority over the Conservatives of 39% and had nearly 64% of the vote compared to only 6.8% for the Liberals. At the by-election much was made of the sexual orientation of the 'gay' Labour candidate who was also depicted as 'far left' in his politics, which led to another local candidate standing as 'true Labour'. The Tory vote and the Labour vote both collapsed and the Liberal took 57% of the votes cast. At the 1983 General Election the Alliance retained a 15% majority and the Liberal Democrats went on to hold the seat at every subsequent election until 2010 (inclusive).

1983 boundary changes also favoured the Conservatives. The loss of Lambeth Central and one of the two Battersea constituencies meant that Labour lost two seats before the General Election was contested. That said, it is highly likely that Labour would have lost Battersea South anyway (they held only a 1% advantage in 1979), so it can be argued that the boundary changes merely guaranteed their losing a seat as opposed to it being almost certain. In the longer term the loss of Lambeth Central did begin to change the social mix of the Streatham and Norwood constituencies which, when the political tide turned again in the 1990s, worked to the longer term advantage of Labour.

From 1997 it was not boundary changes that were the main factor in the transformation of the political map that took place in this part of London. The main factor was a massive haemorrhaging of traditional support from the Conservative Party. The Tories won only one seat, the ultra-middle class suburbs contained within the boundaries of Croydon South. Liberal Democrats added to their single seat of North Southwark & Bermondsey by taking four middle class suburban commuting constituencies from the Conservatives, Richmond Park, Kingston & Surbiton, Sutton & Cheam and Carshalton & Wallington. Labour scooped the rest of the pot winning not only all seats in Southwark, Lambeth and Wandsworth, but also both seats in Merton, and the other two Croydon seats. Labour's tally of eleven (all retained in 2001) comprised Camberwell & Peckham, Dulwich & West Norwood, Lambeth-Vauxhall, Lambeth-Streatham, Battersea, Tooting, Putney, Wimbledon, Mitcham & Morden, Croydon North and Croydon Central.

Such results in the outer suburban area were unprecedented, never before had Labour won more than a handful of seats there and hitherto Liberals had enjoyed only isolated successes at by-elections in the dark days of Tory middle terms in the 1970s and 1980s. What was even more remarkable was that the Labour Party actually increased its majorities in the outer suburban area in 2001, although interestingly, within the inner London area, its majorities were mostly slightly reduced. There is no escaping the conclusion that Labour's success – and that of the Liberal Democrats – reflected a major movement of opinion away from the Conservatives amongst their traditional supporters. In fact this was so dramatic that it may even be argued that had the reduction in seats not taken place, the Liberal Democrats would also have won Surbiton, whilst Labour would have picked up two more - Lambeth, Norwood, and Croydon North East. The scale of the Conservatives' rout in 2001 was such that, in the whole of Metropolitan Surrey, only three of the sixteen seats held by Labour and Liberal Democrat MPs had majorities of less than 10% of the votes cast.

On the other hand, the 1997 changes were quite favourable to Labour. The reduction in seats in Kingston and Richmond was entirely at the expense of the Tories, and the revisions in Croydon had the same effect because most of the Labour-held North West division formed the basis of the North constituency and all three of the previous seats were Conservative. Although in Dulwich & Norwood the immediate impact was to deprive Labour of one seat compared with 1992, Dulwich had previously been marginal and it would be fairer to describe it as a 'swing seat', rather than one that was allied to any particular party.

In 2005 there was the start of a swing back to the Conservatives, although this was at the expense of Labour rather than the Liberal Democrats who held all the seats they had won from the Tories in previous general elections. The Conservatives won Putney, Wimbledon and Croydon Central from Labour, though none of them with a majority of more than 5% of the votes cast and the number of Tory MPs still accounted for under a quarter of the total in Metropolitan Surrey. Even in 1945 the proportion of seats held by the Party was nearer 30%.

The 2010 boundary changes had very little impact on results although it is possible that on its revised boundaries Croydon Central would have changed from highly marginal Tory to highly marginal Labour in the event of there being no inter-party swing. As it was, the swing from Labour to Tory saw the Conservatives win Battersea whilst they also took Richmond Park from the Liberal Democrats who otherwise did relatively well to hang on to their other seats. A by-election at Croydon North on 29th November 2012 was the first test of opinion in metropolitan Surrey since the 2010 general election. Labour's majority increased from 32% to 48%.

The overall results in the period 1974-2005 were a loss of five seats altogether (though eight compared with 1970), but with the Conservatives holding around 50% of the seats available in the 1970s to between 60% and 75% in the 1980s. This proportion fell drastically after 1997. Whilst Labour's proportion of seats at the end of the period was about what it was at the beginning, the big winners were the Liberal Democrats who claimed 30% of the seats in three of the later general elections of the period, when they also won more in total than the Conservatives.

MPs for Southwark, and Lambeth Boroughs						
From	**at**	**To**	**Surname**	**First Names**	**Constituency**	**Party**
1974	*G*	*1983*	*Mellish*	*(Robert) 'Bob' Joseph*	*Southwark, Bermondsey*	*Labour*
1983	*B*	*1983*	*Hughes*	*Simon*		*Liberal*
1983	*G*	*1997*	*Hughes*	*Simon*	*Southwark & Bermondsey*	*Liberal*
1997	*G*	*2010*	*Hughes*	*Simon*	*North Southwark & Bermondsey*	*Liberal*
2010	*G*	*Date*	*Hughes*	*Simon*	*Bermondsey & Old Southwark*	*Liberal*
1974	*G*	*1982*	*Lamborn*	*Harry George*	*Southwark, Peckham*	*Labour*
1982	*B*	*1997*	*Harman*	*Harriet Ruth*		*Labour*
1997	*G*	*Date*	*Harman*	*Harriet Ruth*	*Camberwell & Peckham*	*Labour*
1974	*G*	*1983*	*Silkin*	*Samuel Charles*	*Southwark, Dulwich*	*Labour*
1983	*G*	*1992*	*Bowden*	*Gerald Francis*		*Conservative*
1992	*G*	*1997*	*Jowell*	*(Dame) Tessa Jane*		*Labour*
1974	*G*	*1997*	*Fraser*	*John Denis*	*Lambeth, Norwood*	
1997	*G*	*Date*	*Jowell*	*(Dame) Tessa Jane*	*Dulwich & West Norwood*	*Labour*
1974	*G*	*1978*	*Lipton*	*Marcus (Lt-Colonel)*	*Lambeth Central*	*Labour*
1978	*B*	*1983*	*Tilley*	*John*		*Labour*
1974	*G*	*1979*	*Strauss*	*George Russell*	*Lambeth, Vauxhall*	*Labour*
1979	*G*	*1989*	*Holland*	*Stuart Kingsley*		*Labour*
1989	*B*	*Date*	*Hoey*	*(Catharine) Letitia 'Kate'*		*Labour*
1974	*G*	*1992*	*Shelton*	*(William) 'Bill' Jeremy Mansfield*	*Streatham*	*Conservative*
1992	*G*	*Date*	*Hill*	*(Trevor) Keith*		*Labour*
2010	*G*	*Date*	*Umunna*	*Chuka*		*Labour*
Notes: First returned at: B By-election, G General Election						

Southwark, Bermondsey, Southwark & Bermondsey, North Southwark & Bermondsey Bermondsey & Old Southwark

(Robert) 'Bob' Joseph Mellish (Labour) was Southwark & Bermondsey's MP from 1974 to 1983 when he resigned on his appointment as Deputy Chairman of the Docklands Development Corporation. His principal biographical details are in Chapter 14. The by-election that followed Mellish's resignation was one of the most notorious of modern political times. The local Labour Party was split between its traditional right wing, dockworker membership and the militant groups who won the day in the selection process, choosing a gay rights campaigner, Australian Peter Tatchell, to fight the seat. As a result of the split a traditional Labour nominee also stood in the election and for a while it seemed that Michael Foot, Labour's leader might not endorse Tatchell's candidacy. However, he did so and the election was conducted in a poisonous atmosphere, which made it ripe for an upset. The Liberal candidate won the seat with a record swing between parties of over 50%.

Simon Hughes' Election poster in 1983
Peoples History Museum Manchester

The consequence was that **Simon Hughes** (Liberal) was elected. He was re-elected at successive general elections between 1983 and 2010, making him the longest serving Liberal Democrat during this period of electoral history. Hughes was born in Cheshire in 1951 and educated in Wales and Herefordshire, after which he attended Selwyn College, Cambridge where he obtained a law degree. He was called to the bar of the Middle Temple in 1974 and the following year undertook a course in European Studies at the College of Europe in Bruges. Working with the European Commission and Parliament he became a civil rights lawyer, returning to work in chambers in London, living in Southwark from 1980. Elected in 1983 he became a prominent spokesman for his Party and was a founder of the Liberal Democrats in 1988. He unsuccessfully contested the leadership of the Party in 1999 against Charles Kennedy and in 2004 came third in the contest to be Mayor of London. In the same year he was elected President of his Party. The seat was renamed Southwark & Bermondsey in 1983, North Southwark & Bermondsey in 1997 and Bermondsey & Old Southwark in 2010. During the 2005 Parliament Hughes was 'outed' as being gay by a national newspaper in something of an ironical turn of events given the circumstances of his election back in 1983. In 2006, Tatchell (by then a member of the Green Party) publicly stated that it was 'time to forgive the Liberal's dirty tricks in Bermondsey'. However, he did revive memories of the infamous by-election alleging that 'some of the (Liberal) male canvassers went around the constituency wearing lapel stickers emblazoned with the words 'I've kissed Peter Tatchell' in a blatant bid to win the homophobic vote'. He also said that 'Simon's election leaflets described him as 'the straight choice''.[2] Mr Hughes was appointed Justice Minister in December 2013.

Southwark, Peckham, Camberwell & Peckham

Harry George Lamborn (Labour) had initially been elected MP for Southwark at a by-election in 1972. He represented Southwark, Peckham until 1982 when he died. His principal biographical details are in Chapter 14.

Harriet Harman MP
Peoples History Museum Manchester

He was succeeded at a by-election by the civil rights activist **Harriet Ruth Harman** (Labour), who served continuously as the area's MP, and was re-elected in 2010. From 1997 she sat for Camberwell & Peckham. She was born in 1950 and attended St. Paul's Girls School and York University. Although from a privileged background (she was the daughter of a Harley Street consultant and niece of Lord Longford), she adopted a radical approach to politics and became a leading advocate of civil, including women's, rights. She trained as a solicitor going on to work at the Brent Law Centre and for the National Council for Civil Liberties as its Legal Officer from 1978-82. Married to a top official of the Transport & General Workers' Union (Jack Dromey)[3], she was promoted to the front bench in 1984 and elected to the Labour Party National Executive Committee in 1993. When Labour was elected in 1997 she was appointed to the Cabinet as Social Services Secretary and Minister for Women but remained for only a year when radical proposals for reforming the social security system were diluted. There was controversy that she had sent her children to a school in a nearby Conservative borough rather than to a school in her constituency. She was subsequently appointed as Solicitor-General in 2001. When John Prescott stood down as Deputy Prime Minister in 2007 Harman successfully contested the Deputy Leadership of the Labour Party and was appointed Leader of the House of Commons, Lord Privy Seal and Minister for Women in Gordon Brown's Cabinet. Following Labour's 2010 defeat she was Shadow to the Liberal Democrat Deputy Prime Minister, Nick Clegg.

Southwark, Dulwich, Dulwich & West Norwood

Samuel Charles Silkin (Labour) represented Dulwich from 1964 until 1983 when he retired. His principal biographical details are in Chapter 14.

Geral Bowden MP
Peoples History Museum Manchester

His seat was subsequently taken by **Gerald Francis Bowden** (Conservative), a barrister and chartered surveyor, who was born in 1935. Educated at Battersea Grammar School and Magdalen College, Oxford, he was called to the bar at Grays Inn but also attended the College of Estate Management in London. From 1972-83 he was the principal lecturer in Estate Management at the South Bank Polytechnic. He was GLC member for Dulwich from 1977-81, a co-opted member of the Inner London Education Authority (1981-5), and a Lieutenant Colonel in the Territorial Army. A member of Lloyd's, he held no ministerial office but from 1990-2 was PPS to the Arts Minister, Timothy Renton. He was defeated in 1992 and resumed a career with property management links. In 1994 he was appointed to the London Rent Assessment Panel and to the Leasehold Valuation Tribunal,also becoming President of the Appeals Tribunal on Building Regulations. In 1995 he became a member of the Council of the Royal Albert Hall.

(Dame)Tessa Jane Jowell (Labour) was elected in 1992 having previously and unsuccessfully contested Ilford North at a 1978 by-election, and again at the subsequent general election a year later. She was born in 1947, the daughter of a hospital consultant, and was educated in Scotland at St. Margaret's school Aberdeen, and at the Universities of Aberdeen and Edinburgh. She went to Goldsmith's College in London where she became politically active whilst being

2 Peter Tatchell Website 25th January 2006, 'Celebrating 60 Years'

3 MP for Birmingham, Erdington since 2010

Tessa Jowell's 1978 Election poster
Peoples History Museum Manchester

employed initially as a childcare officer between 1969 and 1971. From 1971 to 1986 she was a member of Camden Borough Council and from 1984-6 chaired the social services committee of the Association of Metropolitan Authorities. In the early part of this period she was also employed as a psychiatric social worker between 1971 and 1974, then from 1974 to 1986 was assistant director of MIND, the mental health charity. After her election in 1992 she was made a Labour whip in 1994 and the following year was selected in preference to the Norwood MP John Fraser to fight the newly merged Dulwich & West Norwood,which she represented from 1997. She joined the Government as Minister of State for Public Health in 1997 and from 1999-2001 served as Minister of State for Education and Employment in which role she was responsible for Welfare to Work and for Women (the latter in succession to Harriet Harman). She joined the Cabinet as Secretary of State for Culture, Media and Sport in 2001 and was re-appointed in 2005, leading Britain's bid for the 2012 Olympic Games. Although appointed as Paymaster-General in 2008 she remained Minister for the London Olympics, and following Labour's 2010 election defeat remained on its Board. She was made a Dame as a result of her contribution to this very successful event. In 2006 she separated from her husband, David Mills, after he was accused of accepting an illegal pay-off from the Italian Prime minister, Silvio Berlusconi. A subsequent conviction was overturned. She left the Labour front bench following the end of London 2012. It was reported in 2013 that she had been re-united with her husband. The Guardian reported that she would stand down as an MP at the 2015 Election.

Lambeth, Norwood

John Denis Fraser (Labour) represented Norwood from 1966 until the abolition of the seat in 1997 when he retired having failed to secure nomination for Dulwich & West Norwood. His principal biographical details are in Chapter 14.

Lambeth Central

Lieutenant-Colonel Marcus Lipton (Labour) represented Lambeth Central from 1974 until his death in 1978 having previously represented Brixton since 1945. His principal biographical details are in Chapter 14.

He was succeeded at a 1978 by-election by **John Tilley** (Labour) who represented the seat until 1983. Born in Derby in 1941 and from a local grammar school, he won a scholarship to study at Trinity College Cambridge, where he read History. He was initially a journalist with the *Newcastle Journal* in 1968 but two years later became the London based industrial correspondent of the *Scotsman*. He contested Kensington unsuccessfully at both 1974 elections but in the meantime was elected to Wandsworth Borough Council representing a Battersea ward in 1968 and in 1971 became Council Leader, a post he relinquished when he was elected an MP. He was an Opposition spokesman on home affairs between 1980 and 1982. Following the abolition of his seat, he was adopted to fight Southwark & Bermondsey in 1983 but was defeated by Simon Hughes and did not resume a political career although from 1983 to 1988 he was chief economic adviser to the London Borough of Hackney, and was active in the Co-operative Movement between 1998 and 2002. He died in 2005.

Lambeth, Vauxhall

George Russell Strauss (Labour) who had first won the equivalent seat in 1929, retired in 1979. His principal biographical details are in Chapter 10.

He was succeeded by **Stuart Kinsley Holland** (Labour) who represented the seat until 1989. Born in 1940, he was educated at Christ's Hospital School, the University of Missouri, and at Balliol and St. Antony's Colleges, Oxford. He earned his living as an academic working as a political economist at the University of Sussex. From 1966-7 he was an economist attached to the Cabinet Office and between 1967-8 personal assistant to Harold Wilson, the Prime Minister. Between 1971-2 he was a special adviser to the Commons Expenditure Committee when he was engaged as a consultant to the social affairs committee of the Council of Europe in 1973. He fulfilled a similar role at the Ministry of Overseas Development between 1974 and 1975. In 1977 he advised the OECD[4], and the United Nations University from 1977-82. From

Stuart Holland's 1979 Election leaflet
Peoples History Museum Manchester

4 The Organisation for Economic Co-operation and Development was set up in 1961 to stimulate economic progress and world trade in democratic countries.

1984 he was a member of the Socialist International's economic committee. He resigned in 1989 to pursue an academic and publishing career concentrating on trade issues. Amongst other activities he became visiting professor at the Faculty of Economics at the University of Coimbra, Portugal.

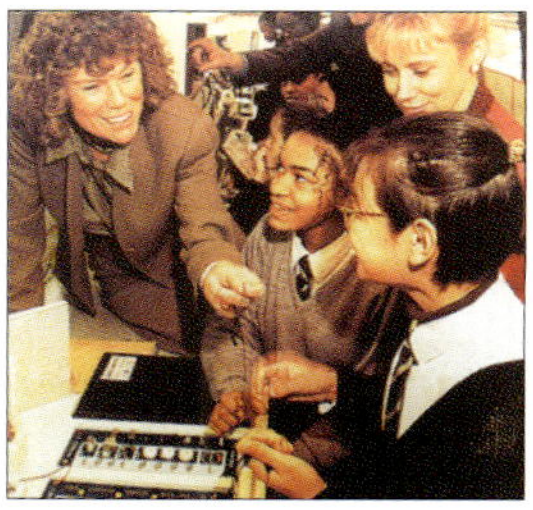

Kate Hoey MP
Peoples History Museum Manchester

He was succeeded at a 1989 by-election by **(Catharine) Letitia 'Kate' Hoey** (Labour), who had previously fought and lost at Dulwich in 1983 and 1987. She had earlier been a Councillor on Hackney Borough Council (1978 - 1982), and in Southwark (1988 - 1989). She was imposed upon the local Labour Party whose preferred choice was a Nigerian-born activist and Haringey councillor. She was born into a Protestant Unionist family in Belfast in 1946 and was educated at the city's Royal Academy, the Ulster College of Physical Education, and at the City of London College. She became a lecturer in physical education at Kingsway College from 1976-85 and took a particular interest in football. For a while she undertook a training role with the Arsenal football team as educational adviser (1985-9). After the 1997 election she was appointed PPS to Frank Field MP when he was Minister of State at the Department of Social Security. From 1999-2001 she was Minister of Sport. An outspoken politician she had views sometimes at variance with mainstream party thinking. She held no appointment after the 2001 election. In 2005 she was elected chairman of the Countryside Alliance, which opposed the ban on fox-hunting brought in by a private member's Bill. She also opposed London's Olympic bid on the basis that Paris was more deserving. She was fiercely critical of the Speaker Michael Martin, at the height of the MPs' expenses scandal, when she perceived him to be closing down open debate on the subject. She likened him to a football manager 'who, out of loyalty to his team, indignantly attacks a referee's decision. But Mr Speaker is not meant to be the manager. He's meant to be the referee'.[5]

Lambeth, Streatham

Sir (William) 'Bill' Jeremy Masefield Shelton (Conservative) was the MP from 1974 to 1992 when he was defeated. Before that he represented Clapham between 1970 and 1974. His biographical details are in Chapter 14.

Keith Hill MP
Peoples History Museum Manchester

His place was taken in 1992 by **(Trevor) Keith Hill** (Labour) who was the political officer of the National Union of Railwaymen (subsequently the Rail, Maritime and Transport Workers) from 1976. Born in Leicester in 1943, the son of a printer, he was educated at the City of Leicester Boys Grammar School and achieved a scholarship to Corpus Christi, Oxford. He completed a Diploma in Education at the University of Wales, and from 1966-74 taught politics at Leicester and Strathclyde Universities. Between 1974 and 1976 he was a research officer with the Labour Party's international department, and worked as a political officer for the NUR[6]. When Labour was returned to Government in 1997 he was PPS to Hilary Armstrong, then an assistant whip, and in 1999 was appointed a Parliamentary Under-Secretary as Minister for Transport and for London. He was Deputy Chief Government whip (Treasurer of Her Majesty's Household) from 2001-03, and Minister of State for Housing and Local Government between 2003 and 2005. After the 2005 election he was appointed PPS to the Prime Minister, Tony Blair. He stood down in 2010 and has since worked in social housing.

Chuka UmunnaMP
© Chuka Ummmuna Website

Chuka Umunna (Labour), a Londoner born of Nigerian parents in 1978 and educated at schools in Streatham and Catford (the latter an independent school), the Universities of Manchester and Burgundy, and at Nottingham Law School, he became a lawyer working mainly in the area of employment protection. He was also a journalist, editing the on-line publication TMP, a multi-cultural political magazine and forum. He was elected in 2010 and, following the election of Ed Miliband to succeed Gordon Brown as leader of the Party, he was appointed initially as his PPS and was subsequently promoted in 2011 to the role of Shadow Business Secretary, opposite Twickenham MP Vince Cable.

MPs for Wandsworth Borough

Battersea North

Douglas Patrick Thomas Jay (Labour) was MP for Battersea North from 1946 to 1983. His principal biographical details are in Chapter 14.

5 House of Commons proceedings reported in the Daily Telegraph: 12th May 2009
6 National Union of Railwaymen, later the RMT (Rail and Maritime Transport Workers)

MPs for Wandsworth Borough

From	at	To	Surname	First Names	Constituency	Party
1974	G	1983	Jay	Douglas Patrick Thomas	Battersea North	Labour
1974	G	1979	Perry	Ernest George	Battersea South	Labour
1979	G	1983	Dubs	Alf(red)		Labour
1983	G	1987	Dubs	Alf(red)	Battersea	Labour
1987	G	1997	Bowis	John Crocket		Conservative
1997	G	Date	Linton	(John) Martin		Labour
2010	G	Date	Ellison	Jane Elizabeth		Conservative
1974	G	2005	Cox	Thomas (Tom) Michael	Tooting	Labour
2005	G	Date	Khan	Sadiq Aman		Labour
1974	G	1979	Jenkins	Hugh Gater	Putney	Labour
1979	G	1997	Mellor	David		Conservative
1997	G	2005	Colman	Tony		Labour
2005	G	Date	Greening	Justine		Conservative

Notes: First returned at: B By-election, G General Election

Battersea South, Battersea

Ernest George Perry (Labour) represented the seat from 1964 until his retirement in 1979. His principal biographical details are in Chapter 14.

Alf Dubs MP
Peoples History Museum Manchester

He was succeeded by **Alf(red) Dubs** (Labour) who was first elected as MP for Battersea South in 1979, and after it was merged with Battersea South in 1983, represented the new combined seat until he was defeated in 1987. He was a member of Westminster City Council between 1971-8 and chaired the Westminster Community Relations Council from 1972-7. Born in 1932 in Prague, then the capital of Czechoslovakia, he came to Britain when his parents escaped the Nazis and was educated at the London School of Economics where he obtained a BSc. He became a local government worker. In 1970 he unsuccessfully contested the City of London and Westminster seat and also failed at both 1974 elections in Hertfordshire South. From 1985-7 he was joint vice-chairman of the London group of Labour MPs and a front bench spokesman on home affairs from 1983-7. In 1988 he was appointed director of the British Refugee Council and also of the Broadcasting Standards Council. He sought re-election at Battersea in 1992 but was again defeated, and two years later was made Lord Dubs of Battersea. From 1995 to 1997 he was Deputy Chairman of the Labour peers but when his Party won the general election he was appointed a junior Northern Ireland Minister in 1997, a post he vacated when the new Northern Ireland Assembly was initiated two years later as part of the Belfast Agreement. He was elected Chairman of the Labour group in the Lords in 2000. Four years later he was appointed chair of the Independent Code Panel of the Association of Energy Suppliers.

John Crocket Bowis (Conservative) who gained the seat in 1987 was born in Brighton in 1945. He was educated at Tonbridge School and Brasenose College, Oxford University where he obtained an MA in 1966. He was the public affairs director of the British Insurance Brokers' Association, and a local councillor in Kingston upon Thames from 1982 to 1986, where for the last two years he was Chairman of Education. After his election at Battersea he was PPS to the Secretary of State for Wales from 1989, and at the Department of Health between 1993 and 1996, and was briefly a transport minister responsible for Road Safety (1996-7). Following his defeat he was returned as a Member of the European Parliament for London in 1999 and held that position for ten years. He was subsequently elected chairman of the pro European Union Conservatives Europe Group.

(John) Martin Linton (Labour) was elected in 1997. The son of a Church of England clergyman, he was born in Stockholm, Sweden in 1944, but was educated at Limpsfield Primary School, Christ's Hospital School, Lille and Oxford Universities, attending Pembroke College. He became a journalist working for the *Daily Mail* (1966-71), the *Financial Times* (1971), the *Daily Star* (1980-81), and *The Guardian* (1981-97). He worked for *Labour Weekly*, the Party's newspaper between 1971 and 1979. He was appointed PPS to Baroness Blackstone, Minister for the Arts, in July 2001, and in June 2003 moved to become PPS to Peter Hain, Leader of the Commons. He was not re-appointed following Labour's third consecutive election victory in 2005.

Jane Elizabeth Ellison (Conservative) took the seat from Linton in 2010. She was born in Bradford in 1964 going on to read PPE at Oxford after which she joined the John Lewis Partnership. At the time of her adoption as the Tory candidate she was editor of the John Lewis House Magazine. A keen singer and season ticket holder at Tottenham Hotspur FC, she was twice a councillor in the London Borough of Barnet, and came a close second to Labour at Pendle (Lancashire) in the 2005 General Election. In 2013 she was appointed Under Secretary of State for Public Health.

Tooting

Tom Michael Cox (Labour) won Wandsworth Central in 1970 and Tooting in 1974. He was re-elected at every subsequent election until he retired in 2005. His principal biographical details are in Chapter 14.

He was succeeded by **Sadiq Aman Khan** (Labour) in 2005, who had been a Tooting ward councillor in Wandsworth since 1994 and Deputy Labour Leader until 2002. Khan was a civil liberties lawyer with Christian Khan, a practice that backed British detainees in Guantanamo Bay, a prison camp set up by the US Government on the Island of Cuba following the war in Afghanistan. He specialised in discrimination law and was an advisor to the National Black Police Association and the Metropolitan Black Police Association. He was born in St. George's hospital, Tooting in 1970, the year that his predecessor was first elected. His father was a bus driver and the family lived in a council house in Earlsfield. He attended local primary schools (Wandle and Fircroft), before a secondary education at the Ernest Bevin School, after which he went to University and Law School. His first government appointment came in 2007 when he was made PPS to Jack Straw, then the Lord Privy Seal/Leader of the House of Commons, a post he held for only a matter of weeks before being appointed a government whip on June 28th. He occupied that post until October 2008 when he was made a government minister as Parliamentary Under Secretary at the Department for Communities and Local Government. In June 2009 he was appointed Minister of State at the Department for Transport in which role he led for the government in the Commons as deputy to Lord Adonis, the Secretary of State. He then became the first British Muslim to attend the Cabinet. A member of the National Executive Committee of the Labour Party, he was the youngest member of Ed Miliband's Shadow Cabinet in 2010. He was appointed Shadow Justice Secretary and in January 2013 was given additional responsibilities for London.

Putney

Hugh Gater Jenkins (Labour) who was elected in 1964 held the seat until 1979 when he was defeated. His principal biographical details are in Chapter 14.

He was beaten by **David Mellor** (Conservative), who represented the seat until he was defeated in 1997. Born in 1949, the son of a teacher, he was educated at Swanage Grammar School (Dorset) and at Christ's College, Cambridge, after which he was called to the bar of the Middle Temple. He was appointed a Parliamentary Under-Secretary at the Energy Department in 1981, then at the Home Office two years later, moving to the Foreign and Commonwealth Office in 1987-8, to Health in 1988-9, and thence back to the Home Office in 1989-90, when he was appointed Arts Minister. Having worked for the election of John Major as Prime Minister, he was appointed to the Cabinet as Financial Secretary in 1990, and in 1992 became the first Secretary of State for National Heritage, a role that covered his own interests in activities as diverse as soccer, classical music and the national lottery, which he launched. He became embroiled in a scandal of a sexual nature involving an out-of-work actress and a Chelsea football kit, colourfully displayed by the tabloid press. He was forced out of the Government and embarked on a very successful alternative career as a broadcaster (including of Classical music), and a football pundit. He lost the seat in 1997.

Tony Colman MP
Peoples History Museum Manchester

Tony Colman (Labour) was the man who defeated Mellor in 1997 but who was himself defeated in 2005. Born in 1943 and educated at Paston Grammar School, North Walsham (Norfolk) from 1955 to 1961, and Magdalene College, Cambridge, from 1961 to 1964 when he embarked on a career in management. From 1964-69 he worked for Unilever (United Africa Company), and then until 1990 for The Burton (tailoring) Group where he was a Board Director and allegedly became a millionaire. From 1991 until 1997 he was Leader of the London Borough of Merton. He also chaired the London Research Centre (1994-97) and was a Director of the London Arts Board (1994-98). After Labour's 1997 victory he was PPS to Adam Ingram MP, Minister of State at the Northern Ireland Office from 1998 to 1999, taking responsibility for setting up the transitional programme for the new Northern Ireland Assembly in 1998. Following his defeat in 2005 he became a Director of Africa Practice Ltd[7] , and a member of the World Future Council, a charitable foundation with membership across all continents of the world providing 'a voice for the rights of future generations'. In 2009 he commenced PhD studies at the University of East Anglia writing a dissertation on water management practices in Botswana.

7 A company advising investors and public sector bodies including governments on identifying opportunities and managing risk in Africa.

Justine Greening (Conservative) won Putney in 2005. Born in Rotherham in 1969, she was educated at a local comprehensive school before studying economics at Southampton University. She obtained an MBA from the London Business School and before her election was a Finance Manager with Centrica plc established following the privatisation programme of the Tory Government, and with the parent company of British Gas, OneTel (a telecommunications company), and several energy supply companies. She unsuccessfully fought Ealing, Acton & Shepherds Bush in 2001, and was also a local councillor in Epping Forest (Essex). After the 2010 election she was appointed to serve in the new Conservative-Liberal Democrat Coalition Government as Economic Secretary at the Treasury and in 2011 she was appointed Secretary of State for Transport following a series of moves occasioned by the enforced resignation of the Defence Secretary, Liam Fox. However, in 2012 following a mishandling by her department of a the procurement process for letting the West Coast Main Line train franchise, which she had defended, but which coincided with a Cabinet reshuffle occasioned by the resignation of another Cabinet Minister (the Government Chief Whip), she was transferred to the role of Secretary of State for International Development.

MPs for Merton, Richmond, and Kingston Boroughs

From	*at*	*To*	*Surname*	*First Names*	*Constituency*	*Party*
1974	*G*	*1987*	*Havers*	*Sir Robert Michael Oldfield*	*Wimbledon*	*Conservative*
1987	*G*	*1997*	*Goodson-Wickes*	*Dr. Charles*		*Conservative*
1997	*G*	*2005*	*Casale*	*Roger*		*Labour*
2005	*G*	*Date*	*Hammond*	*Stephen*		*Conservative*
1974	*G*	*1982*	*Douglas - Mann*	*Bruce*	*Mitcham & Morden*	*Labour*
1982	*B*	*1997*	*Rumbold*	*(Dame) Angela*		*Conservative*
1997	*G*	*Date*	*McDonagh*	*Siobhain*		*Labour*
1974	*G*	*1983*	*Royle*	*Sir Anthony*	*Richmond*	*Conservative*
1983	*G*	*1997*	*Hanley*	*Jeremy James*	*Richmond & Barnes*	*Conservative*
1997	*G*	*2005*	*Tonge*	*Dr. (Jennifer) 'Jenny' Louise*	*Richmond Park*	*Liberal*
2005	*G*	*2010*	*Kramer*	*Susan Veronica*		*Liberal*
2010	*G*	*Date*	*Goldsmith*	*Zac*		*Conservative*
1974	*G*	*1997*	*Lamont*	*Norman Stewart Hughson*	*Kingston-Upon-Thames*	*Conservative*
1974	*G*	*1983*	*Fisher*	*Sir Nigel Thomas Loveridge*	*Surbiton*	*Conservative*
1983	*G*	*1997*	*Tracey*	*Richard*		*Conservative*
1997	*G*	*Date*	*Davey*	*Ed(ward) Jonathan*	*Kingston & Surbiton*	*Liberal*

Notes: First returned at: B By-election, G General Election

Wimbledon

Sir Robert Michael Oldfield Havers (Conservative) represented Wimbledon from 1970 until 1987. His principal biographical details are in Chapter 14.

He was succeeded by **Dr. Charles Goodson-Wickes** (Conservative) who retained the seat until he was defeated in 1997. He was born in 1945 and educated at Charterhouse School, and at the Inner-Temple. From 1972 he served successively as a house physician at Addenbrooke's Hospital, Cambridge, a Surgeon Captain in the Life Guards, a physician at St. Bartholomew's Hospital (City of London), and as a consulting doctor for BUPA, a private medical company, between 1977 and 1986. Between 1982 and 1987 he was chairman of the Asbestos Licensing Regulations Appeals Tribunal. In 1979 he stood unsuccessfully for Islington Central. During his period as the MP for Wimbledon he re-enlisted in 1991 to serve as a surgeon with the rank of Lieutenant-Colonel for the duration of the first Gulf War. He was also chairman of the British Field Sports Society, leading the opposition to a private members Bill aiming to ban fox hunting. That 1995 Bill was defeated, although subsequent to his leaving Parliament, legislation was passed. A company director of De La Rue (a printing company), and adviser to many property and construction companies, he was appointed PPS to Sir George Young, Environment Minister (1992-4), and then from 1994 worked in a similar role for Anthony Nelson at the Treasury. After his defeat he was initially chairman and then chief executive of the London Playing Fields Foundation, serving until 2007 and subsequently remained actively involved with several charities and businesses.

C Goodson-Wickes MP
Peoples History Museum Manchester

Roger Casale (Labour) won the seat in the 1997 landslide and retained it in 2001. He was born locally at the Nelson Hospital in 1960 and after his school education at Hurstpierpoint College, a private boarding school near Brighton, took a degree at Brasenose College, Oxford, attended Maximillian University, Munich, and then took a Masters in

International Affairs at the John Hopkins University in Baltimore, Maryland. A multi-linguist, he became a University lecturer in European Studies. Between 2003 and 2005 he was PPS to a group of ministers at the Foreign Office.

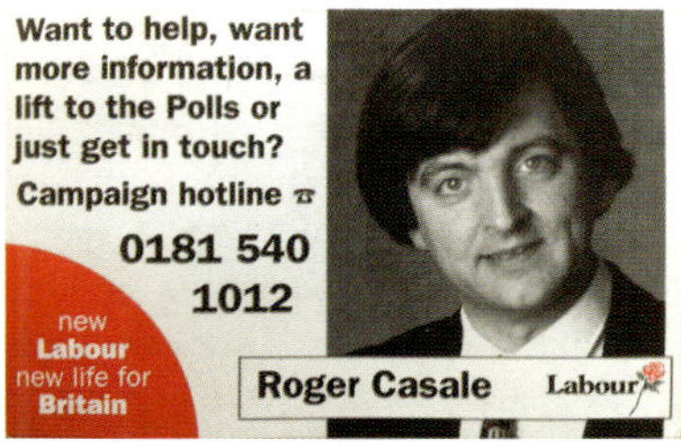

Roger Casale MP
Peoples History Museum Manchester

Stephen Hammond (Conservative) defeated Casale in 2005. Born in 1962 and educated in Southampton, where he attended King Edward VI School, after graduating in Economics from London University he embarked on a career in fund management and investment banking. His first major appointment was Director of the Equities division of Dresdner Kleinwort Benson, an investment bank in 1994, and in 1998 he joined Commerzbank Securities, Germany's third largest private bank, being promoted to Director, Pan European Research in 2000. He joined the Conservative Party after leaving university and was chairman of Stevenage Conservatives for three years. In 1997 he contested North Warwickshire unsuccessfully, an outcome he subsequently also experienced at Wimbledon in 2001. In 2010 he was appointed PPS to Eric Pickles, the Communities Secretary. He was also appointed by David Cameron as the Parliamentary link man with the Conservative Mayor of London, Boris Johnson. From 2012 to 2014 he was Parliamentary Under Secretary of State at the Department for Transport.

Mitcham and Morden

Bruce Douglas-Mann (Labour) represented the seat from 1974 to 1982 when he changed parties, resigned the seat to fight a by-election, and lost standing for the SDP. He was previously MP for Kensington North and his principal biographical details are in Chapter 15.

The 1982 by-election was won by **(Dame) Angela Rumbold** (Conservative), who retained the seat until her defeat in 1997. The Tories were to wait 26 years before they gained another seat at a by-election (Crewe & Nantwich 2008). Born Angela Jones in Bristol in 1932, she was the daughter of a famous physician. She attended the Perse School for Girls, Cambridge, and high schools in Notting Hill and Ealing, and subsequently obtained a degree from King's College, London. She married a solicitor and raised a family of three children. She was a councillor in Kingston from 1974-83 and also Chairman of the National Association for Children in Hospital. At the interviews prior to her adoption as the Tory candidate for the by-election she was confronted by a notice above the bar in the Conservative Club which apparently read, 'Ladies should not come to the bar unless accompanied by a man'.[8] From 1982-5 she was PPS to the Financial Secretary to the Treasury, then from 1985-6 to the Parliamentary Under-Secretary of State at Department of the Environment. In 1986 she was appointed Minister of State at the Department of Education & Science, and Minister of State, Home Office in 1990. From 1992-5 she was Joint Deputy Chairman of the Conservative Party and its vice chairman until the Party's defeat in 1997. She died in 2010.

Siobhan McDonagh MP
Peoples History Museum Manchester

Siobhain McDonagh (Labour) was elected in 1997. She was born in the constituency in 1960 of Irish parentage, attending school in Tooting and the Holy Cross Catholic Girls School in New Malden before taking a politics degree at Essex University. Her first job was as a Clerical Officer in the Benefits office in Balham. She was then a benefit adviser for the Homeless Families Unit of Wandsworth Council and later worked as a development manager for the Battersea Churches Housing Trust, and became active in the field of welfare advice. In 1982 she was elected to Merton Council for her home ward of Colliers Wood, being the youngest local councillor in London at that time. In 1990 she was elected Chair of the Housing Committee. She unsuccessfully contested the Parliamentary constituency twice, in 1987 and 1992. Between 2007 and 2008 she was a government whip but was the only minister who failed to nominate Gordon Brown for the Party's leadership election in September of that year and was sacked. In 2010 her mobile telephone was stolen from her car, and was 'hacked' by the Sun newspaper, from which she accepted damages in 2013.

Richmond, Richmond and Barnes, Richmond Park

Sir Anthony Henry Fanshawe Royle (Conservative) was first elected in 1959 and held the seat until his retirement in 1983. His principal biographical details are in Chapter 14.

Sir Jeremy James Hanley (Conservative) won Richmond & Barnes in 1983 and held it until 1997 when he was defeated defending the newly named Richmond Park constituency. He was born in 1945, the son of a comedian (Jimmy) and the actress Dinah Sheridan. He was educated at Rugby School and began an accounting career with Peat Marwick Mitchell & Company (KPMG) as an articled clerk in 1963. He qualified as a Chartered Accountant in 1969 and joined The Financial Training Company, which trained aspiring Chartered Accountants from 18 of the top 20 United Kingdom accountancy firms. Starting there as a Lecturer in Law and Accountancy he rose to become Deputy Chairman, helping

8 **Guardian Obituary, 21st June 2010**

the company achieve a stock market flotation. He also qualified as a Certified Accountant, and as a Chartered Secretary and Administrator in 1980. His other directorships before becoming a Government Minister included the Chairmanship of fund managers Nikko Fraser Green Ltd. After his election as an MP he was made PPS to the Minister for the Civil Service and the Arts, and then to the Secretary of State for the Environment (Chris Patten). In 1990 he was appointed Under Secretary of State at the Northern Ireland Office in John Major's Government and three years later became Minister of State for the Armed Forces. In 1994 he was made Chairman of the Conservative Party and Minister without Portfolio, a role with Cabinet rank. It was not a successful period for the Party and he lost his job within two years reverting to the role of a Minister of State (at the Foreign Office). He lost his seat in 1997 and returned to accountancy and to several non executive Board directorships including the Arab British Chamber of Commerce for which he led a number of trade delegations to the Middle East and Asia. He was a Freeman of the City of London.

Dr. (Jennifer) 'Jenny' Louise Tonge (Liberal Democrat) won the newly named Richmond Park in 1997 and held it until her retirement in 2005. She was born in Walsall in 1941 and attended Dudley Girls High School before going on to the University College Hospital, London where she qualified as a Doctor. From 1968 to 1978 she was in general practice also specialising in family planning, and from 1980-1985 was a senior medical officer responsible for women's services in the NHS. From 1992 to 1996 she was a manager of community health services, all in the Richmond area. She first contested the Richmond & Barnes constituency in 1992, though unsuccessfully on that occasion. One of her Party's most radical MPs, she was a front bench spokes person on a variety of topics until 2003 when she was dismissed from her International Development role following remarks she made from which it was construed that she condoned Palestinian suicide bombers. She retired in 2005 and was made a life peeress. Between 2009 and 2010 she was her Party's spokesperson on Health in the House of Lords.

Susan Veronica Kramer (Liberal Democrat) succeeded Jenny Tonge in 2005. Born in 1950 in Holborn, she was educated at St Paul's Girls' School and won a scholarship to Oxford where she was only the second woman President of the Oxford Union. She made her career in finance as a Vice-President of Citibank Chicago, a leading international bank, and later, with her husband, set up a firm working on transport projects in Central and Eastern Europe. In 1997 she unsuccessfully contested Dulwich & West Norwood but was elected to the regional executive, and in 2001 became chair of Twickenham and Richmond Liberal Democrats. She contested the European elections in 1999 and in 2000 she was adopted to contest the new London mayoralty but was defeated. She was defeated for the Presidency of her Party in November 2010 and in 2011 was made a Life Peeress. Two years later she was appointed a Minister of State at the Department for Transport.

Baroness Kramer
©Lib Dems Website

Zac Goldsmith MP
©Zac Goldsmith Website

(Frank Zacharias) 'Zac' Robin Goldsmith (Conservative), defeated Kramer in a closely contested election in 2010 prior to which he had been selected by an 'open primary' system of adoption whereby registered voters in the constituency were offered the choice of short listed candidates. Born in 1975, the Eton educated middle child of the billionaire Sir James Goldsmith, he was an environmentalist who placed himself on the 'green' wing of the Conservative Party. He edited *Ecologist* magazine between 1998 and 2007 a post to which he was appointed by his uncle, Edward Goldsmith, who had founded the publication.

Kingston – upon – Thames

Norman Stewart Hughson Lamont (Conservative) who was first elected in 1972 represented the seat until its abolition in 1997. His principal biographical details are in Chapter 14.

Surbiton

Sir Nigel Thomas Loveridge Fisher (Conservative) who was elected as the first MP for Surbiton in 1955 held the seat until 1983 when he retired. His principal biographical details are in Chapter 14.

He was succeeded by **Richard Tracey** (Conservative), who held the seat until he was defeated in 1997. Born in 1943 and educated at King Edward VI Grammar School, Stratford-on-Avon, he obtained a degree at Birmingham University before going to work for the BBC in 1966. In 1978 he set up his own public relations company. He was Sports Minister between 1985 and 1987. A Freeman of the City of London, Tracey was Chairman of the Wandsworth Conservative Party between 2003 and 2008. Locally he was President of The Kingston Amateur and of Kingston Rugby Club. In 2012 he was elected as an Assemblyman for Greater London representing Merton and Wandsworth.

Kingston and Surbiton

Ed(ward) Jonathan Davey (Liberal Democrat) was elected in 1997. Born in 1965 in Mandfield (Nottinghamshire), Davey was orphaned by the age of fifteen. He attended Nottingham High School and Jesus College, Oxford where he was awarded a First Class Honours Degree in Politics, Philosophy and Economics. He then went straight into politics working for the Party between 1989 and 1993 becoming a Senior Economic adviser. During this period he also took an MSc at Birkbeck College, London, after which he moved into management consulting with a firm called Omega Partners, prior to his election in 1997. In opposition he was appointed to a variety of Shadow ministerial roles culminating in Shadow Foreign Secretary when Nick Clegg was elected Party Leader in 2007. Following the creation of the Conservative-Liberal Democrat Coalition Government in 2010 he was appointed a Parliamentary Under Secretary at the Department for Business, Innovation and Skills, but following the February 2012 resignation of Chris Huhne the Secretary of State for Energy and Climate Change, arising from a criminal prosecution, he was promoted to that role in the Cabinet.

MPs for Sutton and Croydon Boroughs

From	at	To	Surname	First Names	Constituency	Party
1974	G	1976	Carr	(Leonard) Robert	Carshalton	Conservative
1976	B	1983	Forman	Francis Nigel		Conservative
1983	G	1997	Forman	Francis Nigel	Carshalton & Wallington	Conservative
1997	G	Date	Brake	(Thomas) 'Tom' Anthony		Liberal
1974	G	1992	Macfarlane	David Neil	Sutton & Cheam	Conservative
1992	B	1997	Maitland	LadyOlga		Conservative
1997	G	Date	Burstow	Paul		Liberal
1974	G	1983	Weatherill	Sir Bernard	Croydon North East	Conservative
1983	G	1992	Weatherill	Sir Bernard		Speaker
1992	G	1997	Congdon	David Leonard		Conservative
1974	G	1981	Taylor	Roger George	Croydon North West	Conservative
1981	B	1983	Pitt	(William) 'Bill' Henry		Liberal
1983	G	1992	Malins	Humfrey Jonathon		Conservative
1992	G	1997	Wicks	Malcolm		Labour
1997	G	2012	Wicks	Malcolm	Croydon North	Labour
2012	B	Date	Reed	Steve Mark Ward		Labour
1974	G	1992	Moore	John Edward Michael	Croydon Central	Conservative
1992	G	1997	Beresford	(Sir)(Alexander) Paul		Conservative
1997	G	2005	Davies	Geraint		Labour
2005	G	2010	Pelling	Andrew John		Conservative
2010	G	Date	Barwell	Gavin Laurence		Conservative
1974	G	1992	Clarke	(Major) (Sir) William Gibson Haigue	Croydon South	Conservative
1992	G	Date	Ottaway	Richard Geoffrey James		Conservative

NOTE First returned at a B = By-election; G =General Election

Carshalton, Carshalton and Wallington

Leonard Robert Carr (Conservative) who had previously represented Mitcham since 1950 was elected for Carshalton in 1974 which he represented until 1976 when he was elevated to the House of Lords. His principal biographical details are in Chapter 14.

Carr was succeeded in 1976 by **Francis Nigel Forman** (Conservative), a liberal Tory, who represented Carshalton until 1983, then the newly named Carshalton and Wallington until 1997 when he was defeated. He was born in the Indian town of Simla in 1943 and educated at Shrewsbury School, New College Oxford, and Harvard. He also obtained a doctorate at Sussex University and went to work for five years in the Conservative Research department. From 1979 – 83, he was PPS to Douglas Hurd at the Foreign and Colonial Office, and between 1979-83 to Nigel Lawson when he was Chancellor of the Exchequer. In 1992 he was briefly Under-Secretary for Higher Education in John Major's government but resigned after six months for personal reasons. Despite standing down from ministerial duties he remained a backbencher and contested the seat in 1997 when his defeat was amongst the most noteworthy in that landmark general election.

He lost the seat to **(Thomas) 'Tom' Anthony Brake** (Liberal Democrat), who was born in 1962 in Melton Mowbray, Leicestershire, but his family moved to France when he was eight and he was educated there at the Lycée International, Paris, returning to the UK and Imperial College, London where he gained a BSc (Hons) degree in Physics.

He joined Amnesty International and was chairman of the Imperial College students group from 1981 to 1982. When he graduated he joined Hoskyns (later taken over by Cap Gemini, a consulting business focussed on computer applications and management consulting). He remained there as a Principal Consultant until he entered the House in 1997. In 1988 he became a Liberal Democrat Councillor in the London Borough of Hackney, and then moved to Carshalton in 1990 where he was elected a Sutton Councillor in 1994. After the 2005 Election, he was appointed as the party's Shadow Secretary of State for Transport, and also chaired the National Council for Civil Protection, an all party Parliamentary group concerned with the protection of the citizens of this country against disasters, major incidents or acts of war. He had previously contested Carshalton & Wallington unsuccessfully in 1992. He was re-elected at subsequent general elections and in 2012 was appointed Deputy Leader of the House of Commons.

Sutton and Cheam

David Neil Macfarlane (Conservative) represented the constituency from 1974 until 1992 when he retired. Born in 1936, he was educated at St. Aubyns School, Woodford Green, and Bancrofts School, Woodford Wells. He pursued a business career as an oil company executive and as a Chairman of a Company that owned public schools before entering the House, when he was appointed Deputy Arts Minister in 1979 and Sports Minister two years later, a post he retained until 1985, the year in which two football stadia disasters brought about the deaths of many people, one following a surge of Liverpool supporters on the terrace at the Heysel Stadium (Brussels), and the second a catastrophic fire at Bradford City's Valley Parade. Chairman of the Sports Aid Foundation, he was also an adviser to the Professional Golfers' Association, a vice-President of the European Tournament Players Division, a member of the Royal and Ancient Golf club, the MCC, and Essex County Cricket Club.

Lady Olga Maitland MP
©Trevor Ray Hart
National Potrait Galery

Following his retirement in 1992 his seat was won by **Lady (Helen) Olga Maitland** (Conservative), who sat until 1997 when she was defeated. She also lost when she was selected to fight the seat in 2001. She was born in 1944 and educated at St Mary and St. Anne's School, Abbots Bromley, then at the Lycée Francais, London. She was the daughter of a Scottish aristocrat, Patrick Maitland, sometime 17th Earl of Lauderdale and himself a Tory MP for Lanark between 1951 and 1959. She became a journalist joining the *Blackheath & District Reporter*, and Fleet Street News Agency in 1964. A year later she became a reporter with the *Sunday Express* for which she was a gossip columnist between 1975 and 1991 when she became a freelance with the *Daily Mail*. She came to prominence politically with her opposition to the Greenham Common Women who demonstrated against the deployment of American Cruise Missiles to bases in the UK. She set up an alternative group entitled, Families for Defence. She was married to a barrister, Robin Hay, with whom she had three children. She was an unsuccessful candidate for Holborn and St. Pancras on the Inner London Education Authority in 1986 and suffered the same fate when she stood for the Labour Parliamentary seat of Bethnal Green & Stepney at the 1987 general election. She was PPS to Sir John Wheeler, PC MP, Minister of State, Northern Ireland, from 1996 to 1997. Following her defeat she became chief executive officer of Money Transfer International Associates Limited, a trade association[9].

Paul Burstow MP
© Paul Burstow Website

Lady Olga was defeated in 1997 by **Paul Burstow** (Liberal Democrat). Burstow was born in 1962 at the local St. Helier hospital, the son of a Savile Row tailor, and was educated locally at the Glastonbury High School, Carshalton, after which he attended the South Bank Polytechnic. He worked for a Chiswick Printing Company and then for Allied Shoe Repairs and in 1986, the same year he was elected to Sutton Council, he was appointed Organising Secretary for the Association of Social Democrat Councillors. He undertook a number of roles in Opposition and in 2006 became the Party's Chief Whip. Following the creation of the Conservative-Liberal Democrat Coalition Government in May 2010 he was for two years Minister of State at the Department of Health with responsibilities for care services.

Croydon North East

Sir (Bruce) Bernard Weatherill (Conservative/Speaker) took the seat in 1964 and remained the constituency's MP until 1992 when he went to the Lords. His principal biographical details are in Chapter 14.

9 Its website states that the association is dedicated to promoting the development and interests of the global remittance and money transfer industry.

He was succeeded in 1992 by **David Congdon** (Conservative), who was born in 1949 and educated at Alleyn's School, and at the Thames Polytechnic, after which he became a computer analyst working initially for ICL as a graduate trainee before moving to Phillips Electronics in Croydon where he worked from 1973 to 1992. The son of a policeman, he was a Croydon councillor for sixteen years before his election in 1992. He was defeated in 1997 defending the new Croydon North constituency. Later he was appointed Head of Campaigns for Mencap, a post he held from 1998 to 2012.

Croydon North West, Croydon North

Roger George Taylor (Conservative) was MP from 1970 until his death in 1981. His principal biographical details are in Chapter 14.

Window sticker
Peoples History Museum Manchester

He was succeeded at the 1981 by-election by **(William) 'Bill' Henry Pitt** (Liberal Democrat), a lighting engineer who was born in 1937 and educated at Heath Clark School, Croydon, the London Nautical School, and the South Bank Polytechnic. In 1959/60 he was Chairman of the South Norwood Young Conservatives but subsequently joined the Liberal Party. He contested the seat initially in 1974 and also 1979 - on all three occasions unsuccessfully. He was a former Chairman of the London Liberal Party. He lost the seat at the 1983 election, and in 1987 stood unsuccessfully at Thanet South. He left the Liberals in 1996 and joined the Labour Party. In 2004 he became Managing Director of a company called Perpetua Training, specialising in Health and Safety at Work.

Pitt was beaten in 1983 by **Humfrey Jonathon Malins** (Conservative), who held the seat until he was defeated in 1992. He was born in 1942 and educated at St. John's School, Leatherhead, then at Brasenose College, Oxford and the Guildford College of Law, following which he embarked on a career as a solicitor, becoming an assistant Recorder. In the House he was PPS to the Minister of State at the Home Office from 1987-89, and then fulfilled a similar role for Virginia Bottomley (Health Minister, 1989-92). Defeated in 1992, he transferred to Woking where he was elected in 1997. He retired in 2010. In 2012 he expressed an interest in standing for the Conservatives as their candidate for the new position of Police Commissioner in Surrey but withdrew from the short list.

Malcolm Wicks (Labour) was the man who defeated Malins in 1992. He was educated at Elizabeth College, Guernsey, North West London Polytechnic and the London School of Economics. From 1968 to 1974 he was a social policy analyst at the Home Office working in the urban deprivation unit and then from 1974 and 1977 a university lecturer. He was Director of the Family Policy Studies Centre before entering Parliament. His first ministerial appointment came in 1999 as Parliamentary Under Secretary of State for Lifelong Learning at the Department for Education and Employment, then he was successively Parliamentary Under Secretary of State for Work (June 2001 - June 2003) at the Department for Work and Pensions, Minister of State for Pensions (June 2003 - May 2005), and Minister of State for Energy at the Department of Trade and Industry (after the 2005 election). He first contested Croydon North West in 1987. He died in 2012.

Steve Mark Ward Reed (Labour) was returned at a November 2012 by-election. Born in 1963, he was brought up in St Albans Hertfordshire and studied English at Sheffield University. He pursued a work career in publishing but a political one in local government in Lambeth where he was a councillor from 1998 to the time of his election at Croydon. He was leader of the Council between 2006 and 2012.

Croydon Central

John Edward Michael Moore (Conservative) was elected in 1974 and retained the seat until 1992. Born in 1937, he was educated at the Licensed Victualler's School, Slough, from which he went to the London School of Economics where he was Chairman of the Conservative Association and Union President between 1959 and 1960. In 1961 he went to live in the USA where he continued his political involvement, with the Democratic Party which at that time was led by Jack Kennedy. Moore was Precinct Captain in 1962 and Ward Chairman two years later. He returned to Britain in 1965. An investment banker and stockbroker by profession, he was a member of Merton Borough Council from 1971-4, but even after his return to the House in 1974 he continued in business becoming chairman of a Witter International in 1975, a post he held until 1979 when the Tories returned to power. He was then appointed Under Secretary of State for Energy, until after the 1983 Election, he was made Financial Secretary to the Treasury. In 1986 Margaret Thatcher promoted him to Secretary of State for Transport, and after the 1987 election, to the senior post of Secretary of State for Social Services. However, he was replaced in 1989. He retired from politics at the next election and was made Lord Moore of Lower Marsh of Lambeth.

Moore was succeeded by **Sir (Alexander) Paul Beresford** (Conservative) who sat from 1992 until he failed to secure adoption in one of a reduced number of Croydon constituencies in 1997. He was, however, adopted at Mole Valley (Surrey), where he was successful and remained the MP at subsequent general elections. A New Zealander, born in 1946, he attended Richmond primary school and Waimea College, in Nelson, then the University of Otago, Dunedin, before training in dentistry at the Eastman Dental Hospital, London University. He settled in Wandsworth where he set up his dental practice and became active in local politics in the borough in 1978. He chaired various council committees, including policy and finance, and established a low council tax approach to managing public finances that did much to cement the Party's control of that council over subsequent years. He was leader of the council from 1983 to 1992 when he was elected to the House. From 1994 to 1997 he was Under Secretary of State at the Department of the Environment where he was responsible for housing.

Geraint Davies (Labour) won the Central seat in 1997, and survived until he was defeated by the slender margin of seventy-five votes in 2005. Born in Chester in 1960, he was educated at Llanishen Comprehensive School, Cardiff, and at Jesus College, Cambridge. He moved to Croydon to take up a post with Unilever, becoming a senior marketing manager there. He worked for Colgate Palmolive before setting up two travel related businesses on his own account, both specialising in air holidays to Crete. From 1986 to 1997 he served as a councillor for New Addington, and in 1994 he became Chairman of the Housing Committee when Labour won the council for the first time in its history, two years later he became Leader of the Council. He had previously unsuccessfully contested Croydon South in 1987, and Central in 1992. A member of the Co-operative Party, after 2001 he was appointed PPS in the Department for Constitutional Affairs, working with Lord Falconer. He was also a Vice-President of the Labour Finance & Industry Group, that advised the Government on economic policy relative to the private sector. In 2010 he was returned as MP for Swansea West.

Davies lost his seat in 2005 when he was beaten by **Andrew John Pelling** (Conservative), also Croydon and Sutton's assembly member on the Greater London Authority, and a member of Croydon Borough Council where he was leader of the opposition from 2002 until the time of his election to the House. Aged 45 at the time of his return, he attended Trinity School, Croydon, and New College, Oxford where he was Chairman of the University Conservative Association in 1980. He was a Vice-President of the Students Union but failed to secure election as President despite four attempts. After University he pursued a career in international investment banking, rising to become head of syndicate for Nat West markets, and head of organisation with UFJ International Plc. He was first elected to Croydon Council for the Broad Green ward in 1982 and subsequently transferred to Heathfield. He chaired the Education Committee from 1990 to 1994 when he became Deputy Leader of the Tories in Opposition. Almost immediately after the election it was alleged in the *Evening Standard* that he had left his wife for a twenty-four year old Conservative Party activist. In September 2007 he was arrested for assaulting his wife and in January 2008 had the Tory whip withdrawn. He subsequently sat as an Independent but it emerged locally in 2011 that he had joined the Labour Party.[10]

At the 2010 election Pelling stood as an Independent but the seat, which had been redrawn to slightly favour the Labour Party, was nevertheless won by **Gavin Laurence Barwell** (Conservative) who was born locally in 1972. A Trinity College Cambridge Natural Sciences graduate, he became Conservative Party operations director in 1990. He was responsible for the party's target seats campaign. Born in Cuckfield, Sussex, but brought up in Shirley near Croydon, he was educated at the local independent Whitgift School and Trinity College, Cambridge, where he was President of the Cambridge University Society. For a period he was a councillor in the Coulsdon West ward of Croydon borough council. In 2011 he was appointed PPS to the Minister for Cities and Decentralisation, then in 2012 PPS to the Secretary of State for Education. He was made a government whip in 2013.

Croydon South

Major Sir William Gibson Haigue Clarke (Conservative) represented Surrey East from 1966 before transferring to Croydon South in 1974 remaining the MP until his retirement in 1992. His biographical details are in Chapter 14.

His place was taken in 1992 by **Richard Geoffrey James Ottaway** (Conservative), born in 1945, the son of a Bristol academic. He was educated at Backwell secondary modern school from where he attended the Royal Naval College at Dartmouth, spending nine years in the Navy before taking a law degree at Bristol University, then practising as a solicitor in admiralty law from 1977. He was first elected to Parliament for the formerly safe Labour seat of Nottingham North in 1983 but lost it in the 1987 General Election. He was PPS at the Foreign Office between 1985 and 1987 and went to work in industry after his defeat at Nottingham. Following his return at Croydon South, he was PPS to Michael Heseltine from 1992-5 when the latter was Deputy Prime Minister, he then worked as a Government whip until 1997, during a period when the Party lost its majority in the Commons through a combination of by-election defeats, defections to other parties and expulsions. In 2012 he announced he would stand down at the next General Election.

10 'Inside Croydon' website February 21st 2011.

Chapter 19
The hidden engines of Evolution

The hidden process of change

As cities evolved in order for skills and effort to be freely available to further commerce, it was necessary to offer reward, and the results of this benefitted everyone. London was established and grew for geographic reasons. It assumed the title of the biggest city in the world for decades. The whole time is was subject to many fundamental forces of change - in technology, sanitation, transportation, as well as in housing, commerce and the economy, bringing about substantial and rapid change, which had a marked effect on franchise.

There are limits on city size, but the coming of the railways solved them. Between 1841 and 1911 the population grew by five million people. The spread of population to the suburbs together with the extension of the franchise drove massive changes in London's Parliamentary constituencies that have been described in the preceding chapters. Clean drinking water and proper sanitation, prerequisites for a functioning city of size were provided after the Metropolis Water Act 1852 with Bazalgette's sewerage works in Victorian times, and thus any constraints upon population growth were eliminated. The railways facilitated a steady outward movement of the more affluent. Better accommodations

Popular Science Monthly in 1925 presented this vision of the future of city living to its readers. At that time such periodicals were much given to exotic excursions such as these. Perhaps this is not surprising given the activity of architectural visionaries such as Le Corbusier, from whom this vision undoubtedly springs. Yet the principles of this and other visions were based on the valid notion that steel-framed buildings and reinforced concrete would dominate big buildings of the future, and that big buildings would form the basis for city construction - and in that instance, the visionaries were correct. Other predictions, assumed to flow from the form of the buildings, have not emerged as shown. However, if this vision is placed in the context of today's Canary Wharf, then the similarities are apparent. The aircraft landing field is present, but handling heavier than air machines requires a lot more space than was assumed 80 years ago, and it remains on the ground. Lighter than air machines disappeared after unfortunate experiences with R101 and LZ 129 Hindenburg *- their return has so far proved to be elusive. Electric trains are present in strength: Crossrail, Docklands Light Railway and the Jubilee Line inhabit galleries below City streets. The motor cars shown appear all to be three-wheelers - a technology that failed to gain a hold. Cars underground have problems with ventilation thus until the electric car they must inhabit city streets. Freight tubes did not appear, yet although the size of freight road vehicles earns them the title Juggernauts, well-ordered cities manage to make them almost invisible by regulating access. Spiral escalators never happened in the form intended, and simple considerations of the practicality of entry and exit show why. Mitsubishi has developed a practical spiral escalator, as a complex version of the simpler 'moving stairway', that revolutionised high buildings and underground railways. Elisha Otis had a handle on elevator/lift and escalator, both of which were 'old hat' and thus not shown.*

were established in desirable areas outside the populated area, at first to escape insanitary conditions, and later for space, the 'views' and the 'airs'. Speculative builders were on the scene early in the Victorian era to offer affordable house prices in the suburbs which established commuting, thus the city's working population could live in the outskirts, and later outside the area completely.

Before the Reform Act of 1832 Parliament consisted of a small land and business owning elite, whose priorities were their own power and prosperity. Despite the rapid population growth, universal suffrage took another century to arrive. As the right to vote extended, so changes brought about by it took place. Much of the change in where voters lived was driven by commercial matters: the siting of industry, of offices, the growth of finance and accountancy, management, and 'clerking', the availability of suitable, affordable housing. Some of the changes were driven by events: World War 2 (WW2) destroyed industry and housing in equal measure. Some of the biggest changes have been driven by the emergence of new technologies: the increase in the size of ships, air travel, computers, the growth in car ownership, the decline of heavy industry and the emergence of e-commerce. Sometimes counter-intuitive, often with unanticipated consequences, the changes have always been mirrored in the political landscape. This has not always been a calm process, as political change has sometimes rendered it disputatious, but change continues. Some examples follow to highlight the hidden processes behind London's political evolution.

Docklands

London's geographical advantage is its position on the River Thames with easy access to the sea, at the river's first practical bridging point. Docks were gradually built along the river, spurred by the expansion in British trade. This called for a steadily rising workforce to load and unload the ships, and for industries set up to serve them: repair, building, chandlery, lighterage, tugs, and so one. The docks encouraged riverside locations for industries requiring imported raw materials and those dependent upon export trading, like: sugar refining, edible oils, and vehicle manufacture. The expanding City was served by gas works and electricity generating stations that required coal. The Port of London became for a while the key importing point for England. As ships expanded in size, powered by steam, new docks were constructed to handle the increasing trade. The Pool of London, India Docks, Surrey Docks, Victoria Dock, Albert Dock spread down the River as far as Greenwich. The workforce lived in constituencies such as Poplar South, Limehouse, Whitechapel, Canning Town, Silvertown, East Ham, Rotherhithe and Deptford created for the purpose. The owners, managers and clerks meanwhile migrated initially from the City to new suburbs such as Hackney, Islington and Lewisham.

This typical Moor Line steamer is being manoeuvred in the Thames by tugs, just off the Surrey Docks in 1950. SS Avonmoor (7,268 grt) was built by Doxford Shipyard on the River Wear in 1943. The Newcastle based Moor Line was owned by Walter Runciman & Co, and later absorbed the Anchor Line. SS Avonmoor was sailing between London and Karachi. She lasted in service until 1959, was sold to China, and scrapped in 1968. Two Sun tugs are about to handle the vessel. Midships is Sun VI, built by Allsups in Preston in 1902; astern, is Sun II, built by Earles of Hull in 1909. Both tugs went for scrap in the 1960s as river traffic scaled back. In 1950 the Thames was very busy with shipping. The photographer took the photo from an excursion steamer sailing to Southend - something that could be done in 1950. It was an interesting trip, among such busy river traffic. Yet change was taking place right then.
Ben Brooksbank - Wikipedia

The growth of the Docks, from trade with foreign lands, brought with it a wave of immigration that has varied throughout the years, and led to the establishment of many ethnic communities that enriched the East End of London. Some 100k people were directly employed in the Docks (though the number varied), with many more engaged in dependent industries, and these people had homes nearby, leading to the increases in population, and constituencies described in the chapters of this book.

On the night of 7th September 1940, 348 German bombers, escorted by 617 fighters attacked London in the late afternoon. They dropped 1000 bombs; many of them were incendiary weapons that set fires that raged for a week, laying waste large areas of Dockland. Some 250 acres (100 hectares) were set on fire and during that bombing 448 people were killed. Major areas of employment were heavily damaged, and hundreds of dwellings were rendered uninhabitable. The

This well-known 'doctored' German propaganda photograph shows a Heinkel bomber cruising unmolested across the Surrey docks. The campaign wreaked havoc across the whole Dock estate, and across the large areas of housing adjacent. Britain got by via other ports, but London Docks were ruined. **Wikipedia**

extent of the damage was played down, as Prime Minster Churchill considered the Docks to be a tactical target, and preferable to the fierce destruction of RAF Fighter Command airfields (strategic targets) that had been taking place immediately beforehand. London was practically undefended during this air raid; subsequent raids were contested, and the RAF rose up to inflict heavy losses upon the Luftwaffe. However, the damage to the Docks, to the East End, and to London continued in subsequent raids. When the War ended in 1945 the biggest redistribution of Parliamentary seats in London since 1885 took place. Maps on Pages 18 and 20 show this well.

The damage was so extensive, that business transferred to ports elsewhere. Ships grew in size and cargoes became containerised - a process stimulated by poor industrial relations within the docks, where cargos were still handled manually. The investment in handling containers was not made in the Port of London; instead Tilbury was developed, because the economics of ships called for vessels of such a size that they could no longer negotiate the tidal river Thames. Gradually, one by one, the docks fell silent. The whole area declined from its immediate post-War bustle to a state of dereliction by the mid-1970s. The population reduced sharply, and parliamentary constituencies were merged again in response to the loss of electors.

The large area of derelict land next to the Capital was not to be permitted for long. In 1981 the Thatcher Administration set in motion the regeneration of the entire vacant Docklands area, creating a massive commercial centre at Canary Wharf, and linking it with transport to other parts of London. Added to the Docklands Railway, described below, there was a new tube railway built - the Jubilee Line, an airport - London City Airport, and a high-speed, direct rail link - the Eurostar to Paris and Brussels. The commercial development was augmented with housing, and after London won the 2012 Olympic bid, the Olympic Village was constructed at Stratford in the West Ham Constituency. The 2012 Olympics were held there, leaving the wonderful legacy of the sporting venues, as well as the housing of the Village. The jobs generated now equal those lost by the disappeared Docks. All has come full-circle. Such is the process of change.

Above: *In the course of a couple of decades the Docklands Light Railway has appeared to connect the old City of London with the massive new commercial centre at Canary Wharf. The railway has used old dock railway rights-of-way to link Stratford with Beckton, Silverton, Greenwich, and Lewisham with comprehensive connections that bring the whole estate together on both sides of the River Thames, no longer the social barrier of yesteryear.*

Left: *the buildings at Canary Wharf rise skyward, housing up to 105k people who work there. This development, together with a new airport, an Olympic Village, a massive exhibition arena, and numerous splendid leisure facilities has restored the jobs level to that pre-War. At the same time there has been a real attempt to create housing for those that want it: new build, and in refurbished warehouse buildings. In addition there is a regular, rapid service of catamaran ferries (Clippers) on the river. This is true regeneration that has begun to reflect an increase in East End constituencies taking place in 2010 for the first time since 1885. Comparison between this picture and that on Page 537 is interesting - the visionaries of the 1920s were not so far short of the mark!*

London's Roads

There were eight Roman roads serving London; well known are *Ermine Street* (The Old North Road): now the A10, Kingsland Road; *Watling Street*, now the A2 headed southeast, and the A5 headed north; *Stane Street*, heading southwest to Chichester; *Portway* from Farringdon Road towards Staines, and the A12 road to Colchester. Whilst the countryside was peaceful under *Pax Romana,* these roads also served those who wished to avoid *Londinium's* dirt and clangour. Roman Villas, large farms and estates outside London were centres of development through the ages that depended upon the roads. Some of the roads that endure today appear in this book as boundary points between constituencies.

As London gradually expanded a more local, linking, road network was necessary, and these roads served to encourage 'out of town' ribbon development. As the city became more densely populated towards the beginning of the Industrial Revolution, the demand for dwellings outside grew because city life was insanitary, and those who could afford to avoid it did so; only the rich and their servants were able to take advantage. However, with the coming of the railways, larger city size was facilitated, together with domiciles outside. When the sewerage system removed the insanitary constraint, the city grew commercially even more rapidly, and with it the suburbs, and the network of roads.

The draught horse developed into a large and numerous animal without which London could not have 'worked' as a large urban centre. Shown here is a Clydesdale, one of the most common of the draught horses. Two would pull a tramcar, but from four to six were needed to handle heavy loads on a freight waggon. Before the railways horses were essential everywhere - their problem was the constant need for food and water, and what they produced as waste products. With tens of thousands of horses in use, this was a most serious problem to cope with and had an economic effect.

Horses were used for passenger and freight transport on roads, and the problem was the requirement for at least 20lb of provender daily; and water to drink regularly. Horses produced almost as much waste as the food and drink they were fed; they were labour intensive: they needed to be kept, groomed and led. Their provender needed to be grown and transported too. Light horses were ridden; heavy horses singly or in multiples pulled cabs, carts and waggons. As London expanded, and the demand for transport increased, dependence upon the horse limited development. The railways depended on London's roads for distribution. Cabs, freight waggons, horse buses and carts caused transport chaos, and the new invention by George Train, the horse tram added to it, but it was a new idea.

The Tramway

London's horse trams began in 1860, and the steel rails permitted three horses to pull a 60-person car. Trams were cheaper, smoother and roomier than competing omnibuses, and the system spread to serve Blackheath, Vauxhall, Peckham, Camberwell, Brixton, Whitechapel, Bow, Kensington and Oxford Street. The cheapness of the trams, half the cost of train travel, encouraged their use. Such a spread of destinations supported the mobility of working people, and sustained the spread of the population to the suburbs, that proliferated new constituencies in 1885. There was a major boost from the introduction of electric trams in the early 20th century to the limits of London. The London County Council (LCC) saw trams as a fast service that encouraged people to move out of the crowded inner city. Croydon, West Ham, Leyton, and Bexley had tramways, although the City of London and the West End never had electric trams .

The electric tram ran across London, via the Kingsway Subway.
©TfL from the London Transport Museum Collection

When the systems north and south of the Thames were connected by the Kingsway Subway, and comfortable, modern, electric tramcars linked Croydon with Hampstead, Leyton and Barking, the railways faced severe competition from this convenience. The cheap and rapid electric tram held sway until the late 1930s, when motor traffic began to rise. Then the trams were slowed down and seen as a major obstruction as the middle classes were persuaded that possession of a motor car should be their aim. After WW2 even the electric trolley bus did not prevent the flexible the motor bus taking over. Despite tramway profitablity they were starved of investment as outmoded traffic blockers. Their prime patrons, the working classes, were disregarded.

In their day tram services were prodigious carriers. The LCC's first route sold 3.3 million tickets in one year, five-times more than the traffic carried by its horse trams. In 1935 the London Passenger Transport Board had decided to replace all tramways with trolleybuses. All tramways north of the Thames had been removed by 1940, and it was decided that diesel buses were cheaper to run and more flexible. By 1952 trams had been cleared from all of London's streets, and from 1954 the trolleybuses began to decline with final removal in 1962. Motor buses now ruled, yet there was little improvement to road traffic flow - the removal of trams had been prejudiced in favour of the motorist. In fact it soon became clear with the burgeoning traffic that trams were not the main factor causing congestion - it was cars.

Trams reappeared in Croydon in 2000, allowing the large housing estates in New Addington to be served. The system was extended to Wimbledon, Beckenham Junction and Elmers End. Four routes are operated, and the cars run mainly on reserved trackway, reaching speeds of 80kmh and linking 5 major railway stations. Some 31 million passenger

The tram came back to East Croydon partly because unrestricted road traffic was a hindrance to development, not a help. The new Tramlink of 2000 allowed large housing developments to be served at New Addington, as well as offering Croydon excellent communication links with main line and underground rail services at Wimbledon, West and East Croydon, Beckenham Junction and Elmers End. These unrivalled connections have allowed Croydon to further its development into a varied and large commercial and business centre .

journeys were generated annually in 2014, and Tramlink buttresses the ability of Croydon and the area it serves to act as a business and financial centre of employment, by doing the age-old job of connecting where people live with where they work. There is much talk of extension, but the high capital cost has so far muted its realisation. In 2015 the Green Belt is still defended strongly, but if housing spreads significantly, then the tramway may well be extended to serve it.

The Docklands Light Railway (see picture on page 539) has the effect of a tramway, even though it was determined that the whole system should be clear of the street, to take advantage of old railway rights of way, with new tunnels bored to make connection with the Underground system at Bank. In the 21st century it was considered essential that a major new development such as Docklands, and the 2012 Olympic Park, should be served by high capacity, reasonably priced, frequent, rail-based transport. The DLR is connected into the Underground system, the suburban rail system, and its stations are well served by buses. In return it carried some 101 million people in 2014, which makes it (like Croydon Tramlink) indispensable in linking places of employment with employees' domiciles, or routes to them. As a 'control' note that all of London Underground generated 1.3 billion journeys in 2013/14 (almost doubled in 10 years). The constituencies in the places the DLR serves were recombined after WW2 when population had collapsed. In 2010 the number of constituencies in Tower Hamlets increased whilst the adjacent borough of Newham is the fastest growing in London. It would be surprising if this repopulation were not reflected in future boundary reviews.

The Road Network Develops

The planning and construction of ring roads around London in the growing era of the mechanically propelled vehicle began in 1911, with a proposal for a planned North and South Circular Road, but it took time for the roads to be built. After WW1, the release of surplus road goods vehicles encouraged expansion of trade by replacement of horse drawn cartage. In addition, despite strict regulations in force, longer distance road transport was encouraged to grow by the flexibility of the lorry, its attraction as a means of direct service to customers, and costs that were under the promoters' control. The demand for better roads followed rapidly from this expansion. Goods transport was facilitated by the development of smooth and hardy tarmacadam and asphalt road surfaces that spread in response to the general call for better roads. The improvements made it clear that transport of freight by lorry was practical.

The first dual carriageway was introduced on the Great West Road (A4) in 1925 and concrete or tarmacadam roads spread rapidly. However trams, suburban railways, Underground and Tube lines still remained the principal means of public transport in the 1920s, although the trolleybus and motor bus emerged as contenders in the 1930s. The Ministry of Transport (formed in 1924) facilitated the start of construction of the North Circular Road (A406), with work going on between Hanger Lane (A40/A406) and Gants Hill (A406/A12). By 1936 its 19 mile length had 4 miles of dual carriageway. The South Circular Road was by comparison a hotch-potch linking of sub-standard suburban roads. Nevertheless, the new roads encouraged the growth of motor traffic.

This Austin 7 saloon car was a small and popular car built in Britain that was affordable to many and popularised motoring. Designed in the 1920s, it was in production during the 1930s and was seen everywhere. It is shown here in Amberley Museum as in a commercial garage, under maintenance.

The rather crude, handbuilt motor cars gave way after the WW1 as Ford's ideas of mass production were adopted by Austin[1] and Morris. The car became affordable, so the demand rose, as after the mid 1930s' economic recovery, the price of petrol had come down, and speed limits[2] were largely abolished for cars. By 1934, 2½ million road vehicles were circulating on Britain's roads, and just over half of these were private cars. The pressure for road improvements was strengthened, and the Trunk Road System was planned in 1937. At the same time the demand for housing was being met by speculative builders, backed by government encouraged mortgage lending. House building in the areas served by the North Circular Road was stimulated by a move from public to private transport - it was the 'smart' thing to do. The message about the 'freedom of the road' was already widespread in the 1930s

All development came to a halt at the start of the Second World War. Afterwards the expansion of car ownership accelerated, and journeys to work by private car were widespread. However, with green belt policies stopping further extensions to the 1930s Outer London estates, growth in population shifted beyond the suburbs. Commuting by car was the natural answer until, despite the provision of extra road space and a motorway system, traffic congestion could no longer be avoided.

More recently the regeneration of the war-damaged areas has led to the return of people into London's centre. It is recognised in the 21st century that it is impossible to accommodate the demand for private transport: thus the road building programme has been scaled back; a prohibitive Congestion Tax has been applied to roads in Central London; the London Bus has come back into its own, with special lanes for it from which other traffic is excluded; new tube lines have been built, and the rail network has been electrified and modernised.

Population continues to rise, and although the difference made by road transport's increase in the 1930s was marginal, it certainly was not post-War in the outer suburbs which were commutable to London by train, but had countryside accessible by car at weekends. This heightened the attractiveness of constituencies such as Orpington, Sidcup, Harrow, Ruislip, Surbiton, and Hendon. But although the steady growth of the outer suburbs was enabled by the motor car, and sustained by it until recent times, unanswerable traffic congestion has led to a renaissance in public transport.

---

1 An Austin 7 in 1930 cost £175, equivalent to £10k in 2015. Such a good price for a small family car led to 300k being made.
2 In 1934 built-up areas were limited to 30mph for cars; elsewhere there was no limit, but all goods vehicles were limited to 20mph everywhere.

London Heathrow Airport

London had an aerodrome at Beddington, Croydon, in the Croydon South constituency. At the end of WW2 it was clear that as aircraft grew in size, and post-War air traffic grew in volume, Croydon could not expand, as it was enclosed by housing. London Heathrow began as an airfield intended for long distance military flights in 1944. The area had no space constraints, although it was productive farmland, but it was available for development, and only 15 miles out of London, on the Great West Road (A4).

Heathrow Airport's expansion was steady, contained initially within the Spelthorne constituency but more recently in Hayes & Harlington. By the 1980s the number of passengers had risen to 30 million, and the Piccadilly Line was extended to the Airport. When in private ownership in the 1980s, the British Airports Authority (BAA) expanded the retail and catering offer, adding considerably to the large number of jobs that were generated. The number of terminals increased to five by 2008 and aircraft size grew steadily ultimately to the massive Airbus A380.

By 2011 Heathrow was handling 475k aircraft movements, with 70m passengers and nearly 1.5m tonnes of cargo annually. Third in the world, Heathrow is first in Europe for its volume. There are 76k people directly employed at the Airport, and 116k jobs are employed indirectly in the immediate area notably in constituencies like Uxbridge, Southall, Hayes & Harlington, Feltham & Heston, Brentford & Isleworth, Twickenham, and Kingston. The large number of offices close by, and the huge economic activity the Airport generates contributes nearly 3% of London's GVA.

The social impact of the Airport is considerable too. Heathrow as an entry point for immigrants remained a focus for jobs. Dispersal post 1945 was easier for the workforce, but in 2011, adjacent Hounslow had 32.9% of residents born outside the EU, and one in ten of the employed local residents worked at the Airport. One in fifteen living in the five local boroughs works at the Airport. It employs 30% of people from outside the EU, 2% from EU, and 57% as white British. So the social impact of Heathrow Airport has gradually risen to be as significant as Dockland - though different.

A third runway is considered operationally essential or Heathrow will surrender its European Hub status, as already long-haul airlines (notably to destinations in China) are unable to gain the flight 'slots' they require, and so will be forced to choose airports like Paris (Charles de Gaulle) or Amsterdam (Schipol) in preference - downgrading Britain. The extra runway is hotly contested, and the most recent contender for its positioning is north of the A4 to obliterate the small settlements of Sipson and Harmondsworth. The huge rise in jobs and prosperity is currently vying for position over the further degradation of environment from noise and air pollution and environmental considerations. The fuss is quite unlike that of Dockland, and the controversy of Britain's policy for air is typically short-term, though the commercial impact of Heathrow is significant. Many say that any development should be outside London.

Heathrow has five terminals and two runways currrently, and its runways spend much of their time operating at near maximum capacity. The new Terminal 5 was sited away from the other terminals, on the west side of the airport, close to the M25 motorway. It was opened in 2008 and has 60 aircraft stands, including those for the huge Airbus 380, seating over 500 people . Terminal 5 is used exclusively by British Airways and its partner Iberia. The fast rail link to London Paddington, the Heathrow Express, was extended to Terminal 5, and the Piccadilly Line also runs there. At least 1:10 of London's Parliamentary seats have substantial employment links with the Airport. **Wikipedia - Warren Rohner**

The railway the people got built

Above: *Arnos Grove Piccadilly Line tube station today bears the architectural style of the 1930s extension.*

Left and Right: *The London Passenger Transport Board took great pains to illustrate their forthcoming achievements by well designed posters, showing the opening to Arnos Grove in 1932, and the completion of the whole Piccadilly Line extension on 31st July 1933.*

both ©TfL from the London Transport Museum Collection

The big city was made possible by the coming of the railways. It was possible to travel in to work in the city, and as the population grew outside, the number of parliamentary constituencies increased, with increased geographical spread. Southgate's and neighbouring Barnet (St Albans Constituency), population rose steadily throughout the Inter War Years, but the main line railway companies did not have the spread to accommodate everyone. Tramways had reached Enfield and Barnet, but there was particular discontent in the 1920s about the slow access to reach the then Piccadilly Line terminus at Finsbury Park. A petition of 30,000 signatures to extend the tube north of Finsbury Park put pressure on the Minister of Transport in 1923. The difficulty in finding space at peak times on buses and trams from Finsbury Park was examined in an Inquiry in 1925. When the London and North Eastern Railway (LNER) did not proceed with its own suburban electrification in 1925, it was compelled to waive its veto on tube extensions. Their objections could not be sustained against the clean, electric tube trains. Now there was political demand for transport to serve the popular, affordable houses created. In 1929 the new Labour government passed an Act for schemes to relieve rising unemployment, and existing steam country branch lines became the electrified Northern Line, serving the West End and City direct. The Piccadilly Line was newly constructed for 7½ miles from Finsbury Park to Cockfosters, and opened throughout on 31st July 1933. In the housing boom that followed, 11 constituencies were created by 1950 compared with 5 that had existed up to the end of the First World War. Growth was stilled by WW2; after, the Green Belt saved the remaining countryside in Totteridge and northern Barnet, and the grand Northern Line extension scheme was dropped. (see p 546)

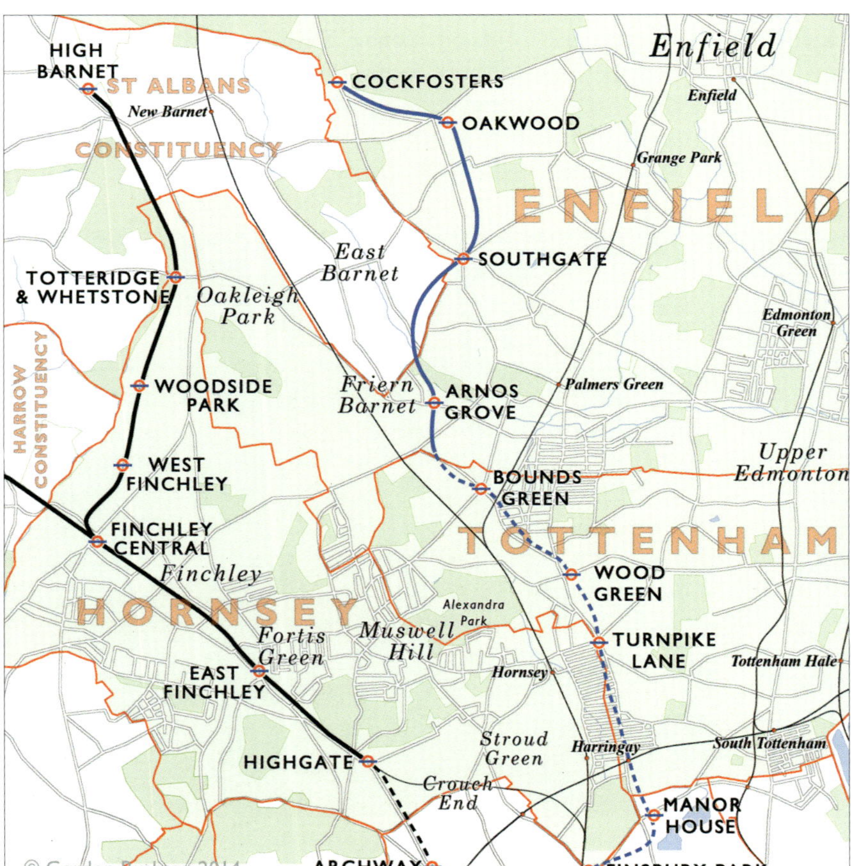

The Northern Line to High Barnet (in black) opened as a 'tube' in April 1940. It was already a steam railway, and was connected in to the underground, south of Highgate. The Piccadilly Line (blue) was all new construction, underground from Finsbury Park to Bounds Green, and surface thereafter.

Metro-land and the railways built for the people

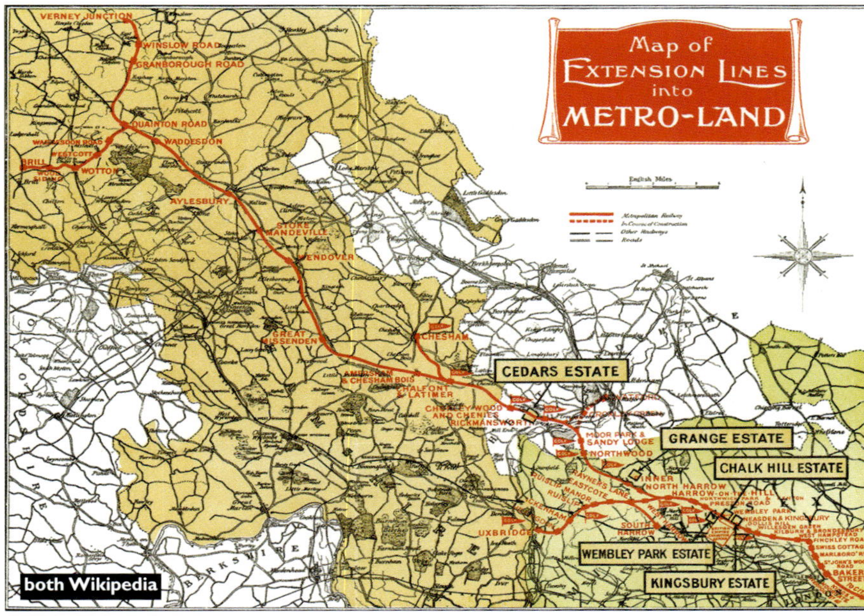

both Wikipedia

The Metropolitan Railway (1863) rapidly expanded from connecting main line termini in London (Paddington, Euston, Kings Cross) with the City, to serving rural northwest Middlesex. It had no intention of it remaining rural, as by 1892 Aylesbury was connected with Baker Street, and spurred on by dynamic Chairman Edward Watkin, the railway was looking for business. This railway was in a privileged position, with an Act allowing it to retain surplus land which in Willesden and Pinner was sold to builders for housing. After WW1, under the Metro-land name, the Railway created its own subsidiary company to build houses for sale at Neasden and Wembley Park. The idea was promoted further along the line with speculative builders, and after 1933, when the Metropolitan Railway was amalgamated with the Underground railways to form the London Passenger Transport Board, the Metro-land Guide, brain-child of the Metropolitan Railway Publicity Department, advertised land development and train travel to London at stations from Baker Street to Uxbridge, to Aylesbury (Bucks) and beyond. They did so in the Guide, from which the 1921 cover is shown top left. The London and South East area underwent a housing boom in the mid-1930s, partly from a rapid fall in interest rates and higher inflation. Mortgages were easier to come by for those who had a job, and unemployment was held back in the South East by the boom. Speculative builders found a ready sale for differing types of housing in Metro-land, as between the wars, few in Britain owned their own homes. The heady mix of a house in the leafy suburbs, or even in the country, with a station nearby offering affordable electric train services to take you to work, was as desirable then at it is today ninety years on. In 1929 the Metropolitan Railway railway estimated that 12,000 houses had been built within half a mile of a station, and a further 17,000 dwellings were planned. The effect on railway traffic was huge. Following electrification to Rickmansworth in 1925, Ruislip, and Ruislip Manor sales nearly doubled, and at Preston Road, Northwick Park, and Wembley Park, the rise was more than 700%. The most spectacular growth of all was at Ickenham, where only 59 monthly tickets were sold in 1921, compared to 1497 in 1928. New Parliamentary seats were created in response at Ruislip-Northwood, Wembley North & South, whilst Harrow's number increased from one to three.

It was not just to rural Middlesex that population was tempted to move; other migrations were in operation elsewhere. In Surrey and Kent, the Southern Railway worked hard to keep out the tube railways, as it had been facing severe competition for passengers from the tramways. It did this from the 1920s by an extensive programme of electrification of its suburban lines. These lines came together in a very dense network of previously competing company lines, and there was a good level of service to London that was able to handle the passenger load from expanding housing developments as they took place. Speculative house builders, together with local councils, were encouraged to build extensively, safe in the knowledge that the good railway service would make the houses attractive. In the 1930s the boom of housing expansion was spread across the London and South East area, and it did much to ensure that this area did not feel the full force of the recession, with 133k houses built in 1931 rising through 293k in 1933 to 279k in 1935-6, with a total positive GDP impact of £80m - mostly funded by increased personal lending. It was Orpington, Bromley, Surbiton, Kingston, New Malden, Mitcham, Croydon, Sutton, and many other similar places that gave land for new housing. New seats emerged at Bexley, Orpington, Sidcup, Erith & Crayford, Surbiton, Carshalton, and Croydon. These places had electrified rail services into London in the mid-1920s or just after, and thus was the great railway commuting boom to the south of London begun. Although the southern expansion brought about an increase of seats in these areas, the population of London as a whole remained static, so there was in effect a redistribution from the centre to the suburbs

Above Left: *Hainault Station on the Essex loop of the Central Line (then in the Ilford constituency) was designed in 1935 for the expected continuation of the housing boom. At the same time planning for Green Belt was gathering pace - but the Second World War intervened. The half-completed building plans were placed on hold during the conflict, with the newly constructed tunnel section used for war production and air raid shelters. After the War, all had changed. The 1930s designed structures were completed in the late 1940s and the massive spread of semi-detached houses at Fairlop was attenuated by the Green Belt building restrictions.*
Above Right: *The grand plans for the Northern Heights extension of the Northern Line also went into suspension during the War. The line from Highgate to East Finchley opened in 1939 , and to High Barnet in 1941 - but by this time there were no new houses being built; they were being bombed instead. The line to Mill Hill from Finchley Central opened in 1941 to serve a barracks, and there the matter remained until hostilities ceased. The plan, and with it the expended works for the Alexandra Palace line, the extension onward to Aldenham, Elstree and Bushey Heath (and talk of eventually reaching Watford) was dropped after the war, as the Metropolitan Green Belt prevented the anticipated residential development in the area.*

The demand for housing in London and the South East was so strong during the economic depression of the 1930s, such that economic hardship was greatly diminished in these areas. Rise in population grew the demand for transport but it was not immediately obvious to most that a second German war was coming, and provision for new transport services intended to facilitate house building around new stations needed several years of advance planning. Extensions to the Central Line in West Middlesex, to the Northern Line in North Middlesex, and to the Central Line in Essex were planned, and construction was well advanced before hostilities broke out. They were all tube lines[1], as the little trains had already proved they could offer adequate service on the surface. The western part of the Central Line was extended from East Acton (on the line to Ealing Broadway) in the direction of Denham, but it was not completed until after WW2 and was built only as far as West Ruislip. Likewise the new Central Line eastern extension into Essex, from Liverpool Street (to Epping, via Woodford, direct, and via Gants Hill and Hainault), due to open in 1940 was held up by the war until 1946. On the Northern Line, the Surrey extension to Morden had been made in 1926, and to Edgware in 1923-4, with an immediate surge in user. The steam line from Highgate was planned to extend by the 1935 plan via Mill Hill to join the Hampstead line to Edgware - with extension beyond to Elstree and Bushey Heath. Existing steam lines would be electrified to Alexandra Palace and to High Barnet, and a through service would be created from Moorgate and Finsbury Park to Highgate. It was a complex scheme indeed, and would have seen new houses spread all over Elstree, Aldenham and East Watford. The War halted construction, leaving the steam line to Edgware unelectrified and unextended, save to Mill Hill East and High Barnet post war. The uncompleted modernisation works were abandoned and the steam lines to Edgware and Alexandra Palace closed in the 1950s. The Northern Line extension became a 'dead letter', but the traffic continued to grow and the Central Line development helped to generate new constituencies in Ealing to the West and Woodford and Ilford to the East, whilst Hendon, Finchley and Barnet were stimulated by the Northern Line .

In 1935 the LCC had proposed a Metropolitan green belt to control the too rapid spread of urban growth. In 1947 the Town and Country Planning Act allowed local authority green belt proposals to go forward, and in 1955 the Minister of Housing encouraged the protection of land around towns and cities. The LCC halted the outward expansion of the urban sprawl within its domain. Although existing lines gradually became busier, no more railway extensions and new railways were built until the Victoria Line in 1967. Demand across the London and South East railway system continued to grow from the relentless rise in road congestion. More recently the introduction of new trains, extensions in electrification, and radical improvements in service frequency have led to a 125% increase in rail user and there is renewed pressure for suburban expansion into the green belt, whilst investment in rail services has led to a surge in long distance commuting. The rise in London house prices makes it an economic option for some to buy outside the (old) GLA area, whilst the very cost of commuting for others encourages higher density living in areas closer to the centre. Whatever the future holds the constituency boundaries will surely reflect the changes that occur.

1 They were surface steam lines converted (or with added tracks) to allow tube trains to run over them, direct from the centre of London - most convenient!

Chapter 20
Index & Afterword

Index of MPs

MPs are listed Alphabetically. Page Numbers refer to where they are tabulated in the Book.
Within the book biographies generally follow the tables of MPs. Some MPs are listed more than once either because they represented different constituencies at different times, or because they served across more than one time period covered by the chapters, or both. *Surname, first name/s, then first entry and second entry (if relevant).*

Index of Parliamentary Constituencies

Constituencies are listed Alphabetically. In some cases Constituencies have more than one entry for ease of reference. Eg: Camberwell & Peckham also appears as Peckham (including Camberwell).

Constituency name, then up to four page entries follow as relevant.

William A Kermode designed this poster in 1924 for The Underground Electric Railways Company that had just extended their tube railway to Edgware. They were attempting to attract users of the existing system to move to Edgware and use the new; when they did, the political map changed.
© TfL from the London Transport Museum Collection

Index of Parliamentary Constituencies within today's Boroughs

Constituencies are listed Alphabetically within today's London Boroughs. Where constituencies straddle two Boroughs they may be shown twice.

The modern Borough name is followed by the constituency name, and then entries follow as relevant.

Above: *After the London General Omnibus Co. was bought by the Underground, this 1913 poster by Spradberry was issued to popularise the 35 route.*
Right: *This 1926 poster promotes bus Route 92 from Barnes right through to countrified Romford, suggesting a day out on Sunday*

Afterword

The end of this book is reached with mixed feelings, partly of relief, partly of amazement that the objective has actually been achieved, but there is also immense satisfaction from bringing together neatly such a diverse collection of information to offer a focus not available elsewhere. It has been a joy to complete not least because of the voyage of discovery necessary to do so. Visiting places that I knew from a map or had hitherto glimpsed only from a train window heightened my appreciation of London, enriching my knowledge of the field of study at the same time. If I thought I knew London when I started out then I know and appreciate it so much more now. How lucky we are to have a capital city that so enriches our lives.

Though the journey of collection was an adventure, the sources of written information were so numerous and varied that it was a problem knowing where to start. Mentioning some of them runs the risk of not acknowledging the importance of all of them. Yet I must acknowledge the London Boroughs' history archives, on line and in the written form in libraries from Barnet to Bexley, Ealing to Enfield, Havering to Hillingdon, Kensington to Kingston, and Redbridge to Richmond. "British History on Line" was a valuable source too.

As Frank Dobson wrote in his foreword, constituencies are about place and a unique contribution to the book has been the painstaking compilation of maps; something that has not been done before to the extent portrayed here. There were many points of reference to help, amongst them the Ordnance Survey's Historical Maps and the Boundaries Commission for England. Older sources included Pigot's maps of 1840. A.D. Mills' *"Dictionary of English Place Names"* was simply a bonus.

I drew especial pleasure from illustrating the narrative and I hope the reader appreciates the images that were chosen to bring the subject matter to life. Many of them were taken on excursions I made and which gave me a pavement view of all parts of the capital; not quite the knowledge of the London cabbie but almost that of the Party canvasser at election time. From my interest in transport I suspected at an early stage that the London Transport Museum might prove a fruitful source of images but until I was introduced to its archive I had no idea how vast was its store. This source of images enabled me to illustrate places in London as they have looked in times past. I hope that the reader shares my excitement at how they help bring to life the places and times described in the book.

A particularly delightful find was the People's History Museum archive of election material going back to 1906. Ostensibly the archive of the Labour Party, in fact I found it to contain a cornucopia of material of all political parties. Access to this abundant supply in Manchester enabled me to illustrate the book with images that are redolent of the periods covered by the narrative. Some of the items - cartoons, photographs, leaflets and posters - are unique and bring a contemporaneous feel of elections as they used to be fought. The Reference Library staffs were unfailingly helpful and patient on the several visits I made to Manchester.

There were too many MPs in the book to include images of more than a minority. The most important politicians have mostly been portrayed but it was only practical to include a selection of the others whose images contribute greatly to bring the book to life. The National Portrait Gallery was helpful in providing access to many images and the Parliamentary Art Archive has enabled me to access unique paintings which I hope not only provide the book with interest but with colour. In other cases the magnificence and diligence of Wikipedia provided images and information that otherwise would have been tricky to source. I have tried to provide political balance in the process.

As to the biographies themselves, in the interests of protecting both the rainforests and my own budget I applied economy in the words used to describe London's MPs. I did not do justice to them all and had particular difficulty with contemporary MPs in weighing up what might be relevant in an historical context. Describing MPs who no longer grace the green leather benches was easier. I apologise if some feel they have given them less than fulsome recognition. In compiling the biographies I drew on many different sources, the prime ones being M. Stenton's *"Who's Who of British MP's"*, Keith Laybourn's *"British Political Leaders, A Biographical Dictionary"*, and several editions of Debrett's *"House of Commons and the Judicial Bench"*. Occasional forays on the internet were also helpful, notably to *"Spartacus Educational"*, *"Brittanica Biographies on Line"*, and *"Wikipedia"*. For biographies of central political figures I drew on published works such as Max Egremont's *"A Life of Balfour"*, Robert Blake's *" The Conservative Party from Peel to Thatcher"*, *"A short History of the Liberal Party"* by Chris Cook, *"Speak for Britain, A New History of the Labour Party"* by Martin Pugh, Rodgers & Donoughue's *"The People into Parliament"*, Frank Field's *" Attlee's Great Contemporaries"*, Roy Jenkins' *"Gladstone"* and *"Churchill"*, Alan Bullock's *"The Life & Times of Ernest Bevin"*, and autobiographies including those of Ted Heath and Margaret Thatcher.

Numbers have always fascinated me and at their most fundamental level elections are about the numbers. So exploration of election results recorded by F.H. McCalmont's *"Parliamentary Poll Books (1832-1918)"*, FW Craig's several volumes (1885-1972), including his ***"Chronology of British Parliamentary By-Elections"***, not to mention Chris Cook's *"Chronology of British Parliamentary By-Elections 1833-1987"*, David Boothroyd's *"United Kingdom Election Results"*, and the many *Times' "Guides to The House of Commons"*, engaged my interest from the start of this project. As my interest grew I found myself referring frequently to Charles R. Dod's *"Electoral Facts 1832-53 Impartially Stated"*, *"British Electoral Facts 1832-1999"* compiled and edited by Colin Rallings & Michael Thrasher, and *"British Political Facts"* by David Butler with Anne Sloman and Gareth Butler.

"The significance of variation" was a tool that I employed a great deal in my days of managing big organisations and I found that it had a place in the writing of this book. As I became immersed in London's history I found myself asking questions about electoral data in the context of the census information that I used to track the capital's development. The GLA's London Data Store was equally compelling. Several tabulations provide unique data derived from all these sources.

Finally I must acknowledge the singular efforts and skills of my publisher, Gordon Rushton, who, in addition to designing the book, produced the stunning maps that adorn its pages.

In ending, perhaps a little Betjeman to keep us human in among all those politics.

Middlesex (Ruislip-Northwood 1950)
Gaily into Ruislip Gardens
Runs the red electric train,
With a thousand Ta's and Pardon's
Daintily alights Elaine;
Hurries down the concrete station
With a frown of concentration,
Out into the outskirt's edges
Where a few surviving hedges
Keep alive our lost Elysium – rural Middlesex again.

Above: *The Underground is being sold on the old theme of moving out of town to country living in this 1925 evocative poster by Hembrow of the delights of the Piccadilly Line, after it had been extended into south west Middlesex. The house builders were at work, and soon the population burgeoned.*
Right: *The Underground Electric Railway is here seeking traffic for days out from the city on lines into the country. (Unknown artist)*

London's Parliament

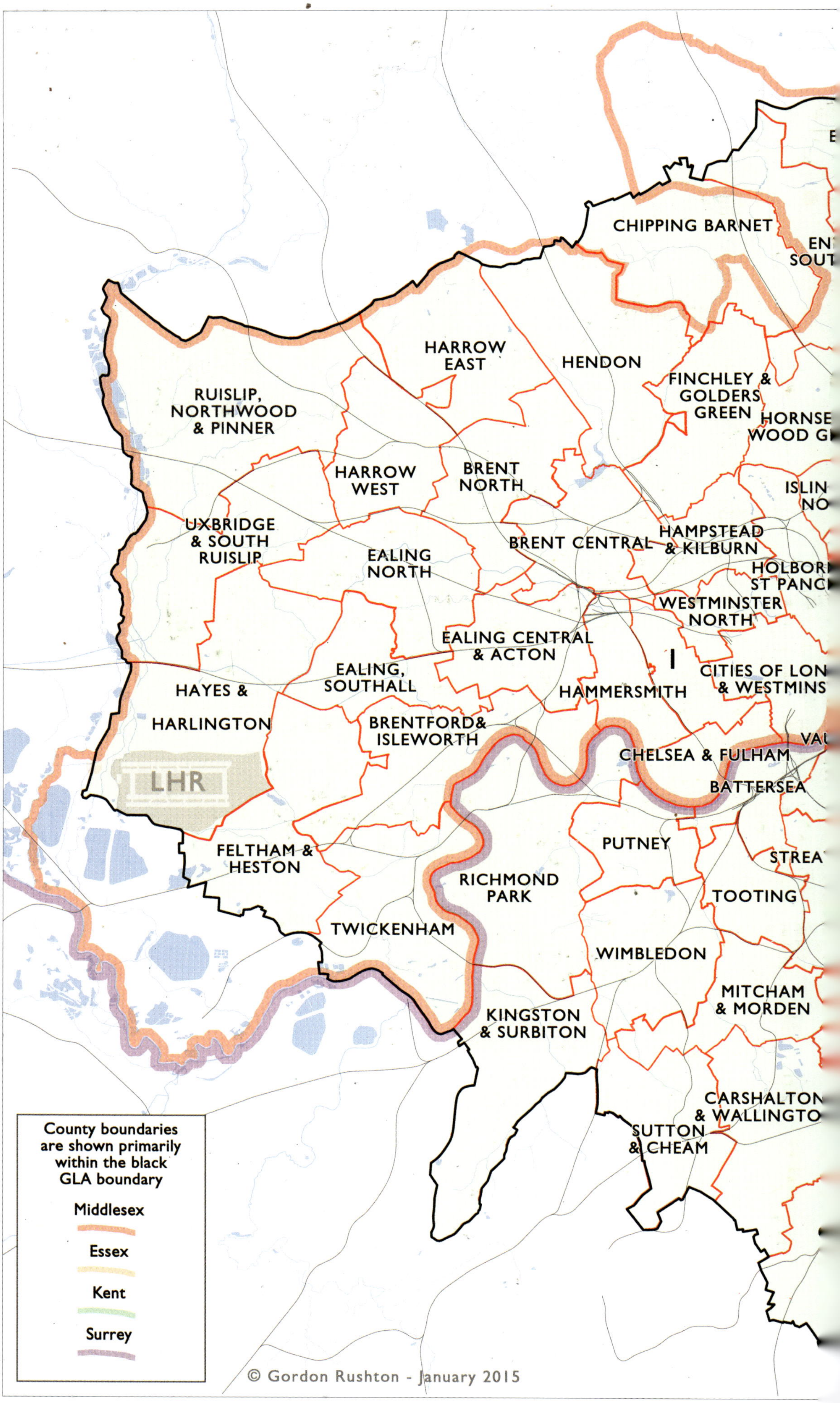